Twentieth-Century Literary Criticism

Guide to Gale Literary Criticism Series

When you need to review criticism of literary works, these are the Gale series to use:

If the author's death date is:	**You should turn to:**
After Dec. 31, 1959 (or author is still living)	***CONTEMPORARY LITERARY CRITICISM*** for example: Kōbō Abé, Anthony Burgess, William Faulkner, Mary Gordon, Ernest Hemingway, Iris Murdoch
1900 through 1959	***TWENTIETH-CENTURY LITERARY CRITICISM*** for example: Willa Cather, F. Scott Fitzgerald, Henry James, Mark Twain, Virginia Woolf
1800 through 1899	***NINETEENTH-CENTURY LITERATURE CRITICISM*** for example: Fedor Dostoevski, Emily Brontë, Gerard Manley Hopkins, Emily Dickinson
1400 through 1799	***LITERATURE CRITICISM FROM 1400 to 1800 (excluding Shakespeare)*** for example: Anne Bradstreet, Pierre Corneille, Daniel Defoe, Alexander Pope, Jonathan Swift, Phillis Wheatley ***SHAKESPEAREAN CRITICISM*** Shakespeare plays and poetry

---

Gale also publishes related criticism series:

CONTEMPORARY ISSUES CRITICISM

Presents criticism on contemporary authors writing on current issues. Topics covered include the social sciences, philosophy, economics, natural science, law, and related areas.

CHILDREN'S LITERATURE REVIEW

Covers authors of all eras. Presents criticism on authors and author/illustrators who write for the preschool to junior-high audience.

Twentieth-Century Literary Criticism

**Excerpts from Criticism of the
Works of Novelists, Poets, Playwrights,
Short Story Writers, and Other Creative Writers
Who Lived between 1900 and 1960,
from the First Published Critical Appraisals
to Current Evaluations**

**Dennis Poupard
Editor**

**Thomas Ligotti
James E. Person, Jr.
Associate Editors**

**Gale Research Company
Book Tower
Detroit, Michigan 48226**

STAFF

Dennis Poupard, *Editor*

Thomas Ligotti, James E. Person, Jr., *Associate Editors*

Mark W. Scott, *Senior Assistant Editor*

Earlene M. Alber, Sandra Giraud, Denise B. Grove,
Marie Lazzari, Sandra Liddell, Serita Lanette Lockard, *Assistant Editors*

Sharon K. Hall, *Contributing Editor*

Robert J. Elster, Jr., *Production Supervisor*
Lizbeth A. Purdy, *Production Coordinator*
Denise Michlewicz, *Assistant Production Coordinator*
Eric F. Berger, Michael S. Corey, Paula J. DiSante, Maureen Duffy, Amy T. Marcaccio,
Brenda Marshall, Janet S. Mullane, Gloria Anne Williams, *Editorial Assistants*

Karen Rae Forsyth, *Research Coordinator*
Jeannine Schiffman Davidson, *Assistant Research Coordinator*
Ann Marie Dadah, Barbara Hammond, Robert J. Hill, James A. MacEachern,
Mary Spirito, Margaret Stewart, Carol Angela Thomas, *Research Assistants*

Linda M. Pugliese, *Manuscript Coordinator*
Donna D. Craft, *Assistant Manuscript Coordinator*
Colleen M. Crane, Maureen A. Puhl, Rosetta Irene Simms, *Manuscript Assistants*

L. Elizabeth Hardin, *Permissions Supervisor*
Filomena Sgambati, *Permissions Coordinator, Text*
Janice M. Mach, *Assistant Permissions Coordinator*
Margaret Chamberlain, Susan Nobles, Anna Maria Pertner, Joan B. Weber, *Permissions Assistants*
Elizabeth Babini, Virgie T. Leavens, *Permissions Clerks*

Patricia A. Seefelt, *Assistant Permissions Coordinator, Photos and Illustrations*
Margaret Mary Missar, Audrey B. Wharton, *Photo Research*

Library of Congress Catalog Card Number 76-46132
ISBN 0-8103-0221-7
ISSN 0276-8178

CONTENTS

PREFACE

It is impossible to overvalue the importance of literature in the intellectual, emotional, and spiritual evolution of humanity. Literature is that which both lifts us out of everyday life and helps us to better understand it. Through the fictive lives of such characters as Anna Karenin, Lambert Strether, or Leopold Bloom, our perceptions of the human condition are enlarged, and we are enriched.

Literary criticism can also give us insight into the human condition, as well as into the specific moral and intellectual atmosphere of an era, for the criteria by which a work of art is judged reflects contemporary philosophical and social attitudes. Literary criticism takes many forms: the traditional essay, the book or play review, even the parodic poem. Criticism can also be of several kinds: normative, descriptive, interpretive, textual, appreciative, generic. Collectively, the range of critical response helps us to understand a work of art, an author, an era.

The Scope of the Book

The usefulness of Gale's *Contemporary Literary Criticism (CLC),* which excerpts criticism on current writing, suggested an equivalent need among literature students and teachers interested in authors of the period 1900 to 1960. The great poets, novelists, short story writers, and playwrights of this period are by far the most popular writers for study in high school and college literature courses. Moreover, since contemporary critics continue to analyze the work of this period—both in its own right and in relation to today's tastes and standards—a vast amount of relevant critical material confronts the student.

Thus, *Twentieth-Century Literary Criticism (TCLC)* presents significant passages from published criticism on authors who died between 1900 and 1960. Because of the difference in time span under consideration *(CLC* considers authors who were still living after 1959), there is no duplication between *CLC* and *TCLC.*

Each volume of *TCLC* is carefully designed to present a list of authors who represent a variety of genres and nationalities. The length of an author's section is intended to be representative of the amount of critical attention he or she has received from critics writing in English, or foreign criticism in translation. Critical articles and books that have not been translated into English are excluded. Every attempt has been made to identify and include excerpts from the seminal essays on each author's work. Additionally, as space permits, especially insightful essays of a more limited scope are included. Thus *TCLC* is designed to serve as an introduction for the student of twentieth-century literature to the authors of that period and to the most significant commentators on these authors.

Each *TCLC* author section represents the scope of critical response to that author's work: some early criticism is presented to indicate initial reactions, later criticism is selected to represent any rise or fall in an author's reputation, and current retrospective analyses provide students with a modern view. Since a *TCLC* author section is intended to be a definitive overview, the editors include between 20 and 30 authors in each 600-page volume (compared to approximately 75 authors in a *CLC* volume of similar size) in order to devote more attention to each author. An author may appear more than once because of the great quantity of critical material available, or because of a resurgence of criticism generated by events such as an author's centennial or anniversary celebration, the republication of an author's works, or publication of a newly translated work or volume of letters.

The Organization of the Book

An author section consists of the following elements: author heading, biocritical introduction, principal works, excerpts of criticism (each followed by a citation), and an annotated bibliography of additional reading.

- The *author heading* consists of the author's full name, followed by birth and death dates. The unbracketed portion of the name denotes the form under which the author most commonly wrote. If an author wrote consistently under a pseudonym, the pseudonym will be listed in the author heading and the real name given in parentheses on the first line of the biocritical introduction. Also located at the beginning of the biocritical introduction are any name variations under which an author wrote, including transliterated forms for authors whose languages use nonroman alphabets. Uncertainty as to a birth or death date is indicated by a question mark.

- The *biocritical introduction* contains biographical and other background information about an author that will elucidate his or her creative output. Parenthetical material following several of the biocritical introductions includes references to biographical and critical reference series published by the Gale Research Company. These include *Contemporary Authors, Dictionary of Literary Biography,* and past volumes of *TCLC.*

- The *list of principal works* is chronological by date of first book publication and identifies genres. In the case of foreign authors where there are both foreign language publications and English translations, the title and date of the first English-language edition are given in brackets. Unless otherwise indicated, dramas are dated by first performance, not first publication.

- *Criticism* is arranged chronologically in each author section to provide a perspective on any changes in critical evaluation over the years. In the text of each author entry, titles by the author are printed in boldface type. This allows the reader to ascertain without difficulty the works discussed. For purposes of easier identification, the critic's name and the publication date of the essay are given at the beginning of each piece of criticism. Unsigned criticism is preceded by the title of the journal in which it appeared. For an anonymous essay later attributed to a critic, the critic's name appears in brackets in the heading and in the citation.

  Important critical essays are prefaced by *explanatory notes* as an additional aid to students using *TCLC.* The explanatory notes will provide several types of useful information, including: the reputation of a critic; the reputation of a work of criticism; the specific type of criticism (biographical, psychoanalytic, structuralist, etc.); and the growth of critical controversy or changes in critical trends regarding an author's work. In many cases, these notes will cross-reference the work of critics who agree or disagree with each other.

- A complete *bibliographical citation* designed to facilitate location of the original essay or book by the interested reader accompanies each piece of criticism. An asterisk (*) at the end of a citation indicates the essay is on more than one author.

- The *annotated bibliography* appearing at the end of each author section suggests further reading on the author. In some cases it includes essays for which the editors could not obtain reprint rights. An asterisk (*) at the end of a citation indicates the essay is on more than one author.

Each volume of *TCLC* includes a cumulative index to critics. Under each critic's name is listed the authors on which the critic has written and the volume and page where the criticism may be found. *TCLC* also includes a cumulative index to authors with the volume numbers in which the author appears in boldface after his or her name. A cumulative nationality index is another useful feature in *TCLC.* Author names are arranged alphabetically under their respective nationalities and followed by the volume numbers in which they appear.

Acknowledgments

No work of this scope can be accomplished without the cooperation of many people. The editors especially wish to thank the copyright holders of the excerpts included in this volume, the permission managers of many book and magazine publishing companies for assisting us in locating copyright holders, and the staffs of the Detroit Public Library, University of Detroit Library, University of Michigan Library, and Wayne State University Library for making their resources available to us. We are also grateful to Jeri Yaryan for her assistance with copyright research.

Suggestions Are Welcome

Several features have been added to *TCLC* since its original publication in response to various suggestions:

- Since Volume 2—An *Appendix* which lists the sources from which material in the volume is reprinted.
- Since Volume 3—An *Annotated Bibliography* for additional reading.
- Since Volume 4—*Portraits* of the authors.
- Since Volume 6—A *Nationality Index* for easy access to authors by nationality.
- Since Volume 9—*Explanatory notes* to excerpted criticism which provide important information regarding critics and their work.

If readers wish to suggest authors they would like to have covered in future volumes, or if they have other suggestions, they are cordially invited to write the editor.

AUTHORS TO APPEAR
IN FUTURE VOLUMES

Adamic, Louis 1898-1951
Ady, Endre 1877-1919
Agate, James 1877-1947
Agustini, Delmira 1886-1914
Aldanov, Mark 1886-1957
Aldrich, Thomas Bailey 1836-1907
Annensky, Innokenty Fyodorovich
  1856-1909
Arlen, Michael 1895-1956
Austin, Mary 1868-1934
Bahr, Hermann 1863-1934
Balmont, Konstantin 1867-1943
Barea, Arturo 1897-1957
Barry, Philip 1896-1949
Bass, Eduard 1888-1946
Benet, William Rose 1886-1950
Benjamin, Walter 1892-1940
Benson, E(dward) F(rederic) 1867-1940
Benson, Stella 1892-1933
Bentley, E(dmund) C(lerihew) 1875-
  1956
Berdyaev, Nikolai Aleksandrovich
  1874-1948
Beresford, J(ohn) D(avys) 1873-1947
Bergman, Hjalmar 1883-1931
Bergson, Henri 1859-1941
Bethell, Mary Ursula 1874-1945
Binyon, Laurence 1869-1943
Bishop, John Peale 1892-1944
Blackmore, R(ichard) D(oddridge)
  1825-1900
Blasco-Ibanez, Vicente 1867-1928
Blum, Leon 1872-1950
Bodenheim, Maxwell 1892-1954
Bojer, Johan 1872-1959
Bosman, Herman Charles 1905-1951
Bottomley, Gordon 1874-1948
Bourget, Paul 1852-1935
Bourne, George 1863-1927
Brancati, Vitaliano 1907-1954
Broch, Herman 1886-1951
Bromfield, Louis 1896-1956
Byrne, Donn (Brian Oswald Donn-Byre)
  1889-1928
Caine, Hall 1853-1931
Campana, Dina 1885-1932
Cannan, Gilbert 1884-1955
Chand, Prem 1880-1936
Chatterji, Sarat Chandra 1876-1938
Churchill, Winston 1871 1947
Comstock, Anthony 1844-1915
Corelli, Marie 1855-1924
Corvo, Baron (Frederick William Rolfe)
  1860-1913
Crane, Stephen 1871-1900
Croce, Benedetto 1866-1952

Davidson, John 1857-1909
Day, Clarence 1874-1935
Dazai, Osamu 1909-1948
De Gourmont, Remy 1858-1915
Delafield, E.M. (Edme Elizabeth Monica
  de la Pasture) 1890-1943
Delisser, Herbert George 1878-1944
DeMille, Cecil B(lount) 1881-1959
DeMorgan, William 1839-1917
Dent, Lester 1904-1959
DeVoto, Bernard 1897-1955
Doblin, Alfred 1878-1957
Douglas, (George) Norman 1868-1952
Douglas, Lloyd C(assel) 1877-1951
Dovzhenko, Alexander 1894-1956
Drinkwater, John 1882-1937
Dujardin, Edouard 1861-1949
Durkheim, Emile 1858-1917
Duun, Olav 1876-1939
Eisenstein, Sergei 1898-1948
Ellis, Havelock 1859-1939
Erskine, John 1879-1951
Ewers, Hans Heinz 1871-1943
Fadeyev, Alexandr 1901-1956
Fargue, Leon-Paul 1876-1947
Feydeau, Georges 1862-1921
Field, Michael (Katherine Harris Brad-
  ley 1846-1914 and Edith Emma
  Cooper 1862-1913)
Field, Rachel 1894-1924
Fisher, Rudolph 1897-1934
· Flaherty, Robert 1884-1951
Flecker, James Elroy 1884-1915
Fletcher, John Gould 1886-1950
Frank, Bruno 1886-1945
Frazer, (Sir) George 1854-1941
Freeman, Douglas Southall 1886-1953
Freeman, John 1880-1929
Freud, Sigmund 1853-1939
Gladkov, Fydor Vasilyevich 1883-1958
Glyn, Elinor 1864-1943
Gogarty, Oliver St. John 1878-1957
Golding, Louis 1895-1958
Goldman, Emma 1869-1940
Gosse, Edmund 1849-1928
Gould, Gerald 1885-1936
Grahame, Kenneth 1859-1932
Gray, John 1866-1934
Griffith, D(avid) W(ark) 1875-1948
Guiraldes, Ricardo 1886-1927
Gumilyov, Nikolay 1886-1921
Gwynne, Stephen Lucius 1864-1950
Haggard, H(enry) Rider 1856-1925
Hale, Edward Everett 1822-1909
Hall, (Marguerite) Radclyffe 1886-1943
Harper, Frances Ellen Watkins
  1825-1911

Harris, Frank 1856-1931
Hergesheimer, Joseph 1880-1954
Hernandez, Miguel 1910-1942
Herrick, Robert 1868-1938
Hewlett, Maurice 1861-1923
Heyward, DuBose 1885-1940
Hichens, Robert 1864-1950
Hilton, James 1900-1954
Hodgson, William Hope 1875-1918
Hofmannsthal, Hugo Von 1874-1929
Holtby, Winifred 1898-1935
Hope, Anthony 1863-1933
Hudson, Stephen 1868-1944
Hudson, W(illiam) H(enry) 1841-1922
Hulme, Thomas Ernest 1883-1917
Ivanov, Vyacheslav Ivanovich 1866-
  1949
Jacobs, W(illiam) W(ymark) 1863-1943
James, Will 1892-1942
James, William 1842-1910
Jerome, Jerome K(lapka) 1859-1927
Jones, Henry Arthur 1851-1929
Khodasevich, Vladislav 1886-1939
King, Grace 1851-1932
Korolenko, Vladimir 1853-1921
Kuzmin, Mikhail Alexseyevich 1875-
  1936
Lampedusa, Giuseppeldi 1896-1957
Lang, Andrew 1844-1912
Lawson, Henry 1867-1922
Leverson, Ada 1862-1933
Lewisohn, Ludwig 1883-1955
Lindsay, (Nicholas) Vachel 1879-1931
Lonsdale, Frederick 1881-1954
Loti, Pierre 1850-1923
Louys, Pierre 1870-1925
Lowndes, Marie Belloc 1868-1947
Lubitsch, Ernst 1892-1947
Lucas, E(dward) V(errall) 1868-1938
Lumiere, Louis 1864-1948
Lynd, Robert 1879-1949
MacArthur, Charles 1895-1956
Manning, Frederic 1887-1935
Marriott, Charles 1869-1957
Martin du Gard, Roger 1881-1958
Masaryk, Tomas 1850-1939
McCoy, Horace 1897-1955
McCrae, John 1872-1918
Melies, Georges 1861-1938
Mencken, H(enry) L(ouis) 1880-1956
Meredith, George 1828-1909
Mirbeau, Octave 1850-1917
Mistral, Frederic 1830-1914
Mitchell, Margaret 1900-1949
Monro, Harold 1879-1932
Monroe, Harriet 1860-1936

Authors to Appear in Future Volumes

Moore, Thomas Sturge 1870-1944
Morgan, Charles 1894-1958
Mori Ogai 1862-1922
Morley, Christopher 1890-1957
Murnau, F(riedrich) W(ilhelm) 1888-1931
Murray, (George) Gilbert 1866-1957
Musil, Robert 1880-1939
Nervo, Amado 1870-1919
Nordhoff, Charles 1887-1947
Norris, Frank 1870-1902
Olbracht, Ivan (Kemil Zeman) 1882-1952
Ophuls, Max 1902-1957
Pickthall, Marjorie 1883-1922
Pinero, Arthur Wing 1855-1934
Platonov, Audrey 1899-1951
Pontoppidan, Henrik 1857-1943
Porter, Eleanor H(odgman) 1868-1920
Porter, Gene(va) Stratton 1886-1924
Prevost, Marcel 1862-1941
Quiller-Couch, Arthur 1863-1944
Rappoport, Solomon 1863-1944
Reid, Forrest 1876-1947
Riley, James Whitcomb 1849-1916
Rinehart, Mary Roberts 1876-1958
Roberts, Elizabeth Madox 1886-1941

Rohmer, Sax 1883-1959
Rolfe, Frederick 1860-1913
Rolland, Romain 1866-1944
Rolvaag, O(le) E(dvart) 1876-1931
Rosenberg, Isaac 1870-1918
Rourke, Constance 1885-1941
Roussel, Raymond 1877-1933
Ruskin, John 1819-1900
Sabatini, Rafael 1875-1950
Santayana, George 1863-1952
Sardou, Victorien 1831-1908
Seeger, Alan 1888-1916
Service, Robert 1874-1958
Seton, Ernest Thompson 1860-1946
Shestov, Lev 1866-1938
Slater, Francis Carey 1875-1958
Solovyov, Vladimir 1853-1900
Spitteler, Carl 1845-1924
Squire, J(ohn) C(ollings) 1884-1958
Steiner, Rudolph 1861-1925
Stockton, Frank R. 1834-1902
Strachey, Lytton 1880-1932
Stroheim, Erich von 1885-1957
Sturges, Preston 1898-1959
Sudermann, Hermann 1857-1938
Sully-Prudhomme, Rene 1839-1907

Symons, Arthur 1865-1945
Tabb, John Bannister 1845-1909
Tey, Josephine (Elizabeth Mackintosh) 1897-1952
Tolstoy, Alexei 1882-1945
Turner, W(alter) J(ames) R(edfern) 1889-1946
Vachell, Horace Annesley 1861-1955
Van Dine, S.S. (William H. Wright) 1888-1939
Van Doren, Carl 1885-1950
Vazov, Ivan 1850-1921
Veblen, Thorstein 1857-1929
Verhaeren, Emile 1855-1916
Wallace, Edgar 1874-1932
Wallace, Lewis 1827-1905
Walser, Robert 1878-1956
Webb, Mary 1881-1927
Webster, Jean 1876-1916
Welch, Denton 1917-1948
Wells, Carolyn 1869-1942
Wister, Owen 1860-1938
Wren, P(ercival) C(hristopher) 1885-1941
Wylie, Francis Brett 1844-1954
Zoshchenko, Milchail 1895-1958

Readers are cordially invited to suggest additional authors to the editors.

A.E.

1867-1935

(Pseudonym of George William Russell; also wrote under pseudonyms of Y.O., O.L.S., and Gab) Irish poet, essayist, editor, journalist, dramatist, autobiographer, and novelist.

A key figure in the Irish Literary Revival, A.E. contributed more to the movement through his personality than through his artistry. He was a gifted conversationalist, a popular lecturer, and a generous man who brought many of the members of the Revival together. Although A.E.'s interests were varied, he earned a modest literary reputation based on his mystical poems and his drama, *Deirdre*. He was central to the rise of the Irish National Theatre, and, with W. B. Yeats, J. M. Synge, and Lady Gregory, was one of the founders of the Abbey Theatre. Through his work and his charismatic personality, A.E. was an important influence on the writers of the Irish Revival, a generation which sought to reduce the influence of English culture and create an Irish national literature.

A.E. had a pious upbringing and from his youth was inclined toward mysticism. While studying painting at the Dublin Metropolitan School of Art, A.E. met Yeats, who became his lifelong friend. Through Yeats, A.E. became involved in the theosophical movement, in which he found a channel for his mystical interests. These interests were a mixture of belief in Buddhism, theosophy, magic, reincarnation, pantheism, and elements of Irish mythology that served as the inspiration for his early poems, collected in *Homeward: Songs by the Way*, *The Earth Breath*, and *The Divine Vision*. The poems of these early volumes are characterized by their colorful imagery, archaic language, and exaltation of the Earth as a life-sustaining mother, which is a recurring motif throughout A.E.'s work. It was during this period that A.E.'s unusual pseudonym was acquired. A typesetter was unable to decipher the scribbled pen name Æon, with which A.E. had signed an article, and so printed only the first two letters. A.E. was delighted with the result and used the pseudonym throughout his life.

By 1905, A.E. had become a guiding force behind the Agricultural Cooperative Movement and was appointed editor of its chief organ, *The Irish Homestead*, which later became *The Irish Statesman*. The political essays he published in the magazine and in his book *The National Being: Some Thoughts on an Irish Polity* propose plans for the development of a more practical Irish government. A.E. promoted Irish Home Rule, but unlike many of his fellow nationalists, he stressed the importance of political moderation and reconciliation with Great Britain. One of A.E.'s most widely read books of political essays, *The National Being*, definitively states the author's economic policies, calling for a cooperative commonwealth for the new Republic of Ireland. In addition to his political activities, A.E. was very involved in the cultural life of Ireland at this time. His only play, *Deirdre*, treats the ancient legend of the Red Branch, and was, with Yeats's *Cathleen ni Houlihan*, one of the earliest productions of the modern Irish theater. Together, the two dramas contributed to the period now known as the Celtic Twilight, a late nineteenth-century period when Irish artists attempted to give Irish art and culture a distinct

national and spiritual identity based on ancient Celtic legend. Always interested in encouraging and promoting other Irish authors, A.E. hosted a weekly gathering at his home, attracting such artists as Yeats, George Moore, Padraic Colum, and James Stephens. As editor of *The Irish Statesman*, he also provided a forum for these writers. In his last years, broken by the death of his wife, and saddened by the increasing factional hatred and violence in Ireland, A.E. retired to England, where he died.

A.E. was devoted to the work of Ralph Waldo Emerson, and shared with him an interest in pantheism and transcendentalism as well as a desire to wed spiritual beliefs with social action. A.E. also recognized his own vision in the life-affirming poetry of William Blake. In *The Candle of Vision*, a work often referred to as his spiritual autobiography, A.E. expressed a thorough and thoughtful elucidation of his development from childhood to adulthood. His discussion of visions and intuition led Leslie Shepard to claim that *The Candle of Vision* "is an essential key, not only to Russell, but also to the mystic life itself, which is the inheritance of everyone." The book won A.E. recognition and respect as a mystic both in Ireland and North America. The essay collection *Song and Its Fountains* is A.E.'s explanation for the creation of poetry. Stating that poetry originates from the divine inner being rather than from experience, A.E. relates his mystical revelations in an auto-biographical style similar to that of *The Candle of Vision*.

Although his poetry is generally characterized by monotonous repetitions of themes and images, critics praise the sincerity of A.E.'s thought and inspiration. Some critics, such as Ernest Boyd, suggest that the repetitiveness of his verse results "because words as fresh as the emotion prompting them are not always to be found." Yeats, whose poetry overshadows A.E.'s, referred to him as "the most subtle and spiritual poet of his generation." But other critics question the legitimacy of A.E.'s spiritual inclinations, and believe that his mystical ideals often outweigh his artistry, and that his poetry is highly derivative and facile. The critical consensus is that he survives not as a painter, poet, or politician, but as the embodiment of the beliefs and principles of the Irish Revival.

(See also *TCLC*, Vol. 3 and *Contemporary Authors*, Vol. 104.)

PRINCIPAL WORKS

Homeward: Songs by the Way (poetry) 1894
The Earth Breath, and Other Poems (poetry) 1897
Deirdre (drama) 1902
The Divine Vision, and Other Poems (poetry) 1904
*Co-operation and Nationality: A Guide for Rural Reformers
    from This to the Next Generation* (essays) 1912
Collected Poems (poetry) 1913
Gods of War (poetry) 1915
The National Being: Some Thoughts on an Irish Polity
    (essays) 1916
The Candle of Vision (autobiography) 1918
The Interpreters (novel) 1922
Enchantment and Other Poems (poetry) 1930
Vale and Other Poems (poetry) 1931
Song and Its Fountains (essays) 1932
The Avatars: A Futurist Fantasy (novel) 1933
The House of the Titans and Other Poems (poetry) 1934
Selected Poems (poetry) 1935
The Living Torch (essays) 1937
Letters from A.E. (letters) . 1961
Selections from the Contributions to the "Irish Homestead."
    2 vols. (essays) 1978

W. B. YEATS (essay date 1894)

[*Yeats offers an approving review of* Homeward: Songs by the Way.]

About twelve years ago seven youths began to study European magic and Oriental mysticism, and because, as the Gaelic proverb puts it, contention is better than loneliness, agreed to meet at times in a room in a dirty back street and to call their meetings "The Dublin Hermetic Society." . . . These periodical meetings started a movement, and the movement has begun to make literature. One of the group published last year a very interesting book of verse which he withdrew from circulation in a moment of caprice, and now "A.E.," its arch-visionary, has published '**Homeward: Songs by the Way,**' a pamphlet of exquisite verse. He introduces it with this quaint preface: "I moved among men and places and in living I learned the truth at last. I know I am a spirit, and that I went forth from the self-ancestral to labours yet unaccomplished; but, filled ever

and again with home-sickness, I made these songs by the way." The pamphlet is in no sense, however, the work of a preacher, but of one who utters, for the sake of beauty alone, the experience of a delicate and subtle temperament. He is a moralist, not because he desires, like the preacher, to coerce our will, but because good and evil are a part of what he splendidly calls "the multitudinous meditation" of the divine world in whose shadow he seeks to dwell. No one who has an ear for poetry at all can fail to find a new voice and a new music in [the lines of A.E.]. . .

There are everywhere such memorable lines as "Come earth's little children, pit pat from their burrows in the hill," "White for Thy whiteness all desires burn," . . . and "No image of the proud and morning stars looks at us from their faces."

The book has faults in plenty, certain rhymes are repeated too often, the longer lines stumble now and again, and here and there a stanza is needlessly obscure; but, taken all in all, it is the most haunting book I have seen these many days. (p. 148)

> W. B. Yeats, "A New Poet," in The Bookman, London, Vol. VI, No. 35, August, 1894, pp. 147-48.

[THE EARL OF] LYTTON (essay date 1899)

[*Lord Lytton examines A.E.'s philosophy as revealed in* The Earth Breath, and Other Poems.]

"A.E." is one of a group of Irish writers whose works have been much ridiculed where they have been but little read. These writers are united by a common bond, and their work is largely directed to a common end. The tie which binds them is a deep-rooted love for Ireland, and the aim which they have set themselves is the revival of a literature which shall be essentially Celtic in its character. . . . The word Celtic is chiefly associated in the mind of the average Englishman with strange dialects which he cannot understand, and long names which he cannot pronounce, and he therefore finds it hard to sympathize with this revival. But the writer who is the subject of this review, is not one of those whose genius lies concealed in a language of which few have knowledge. (p. 254)

["A.E.'s" *The Earth Breath and Other Poems*] reveals the mind of a true poet and an original thinker. His imagination is sometimes so fantastic, and the expression of his ideas so brief and sudden, that it is easy to reject his work for its obscurity, and to leave unnoticed its rare qualities of thought and feeling; but a patient and sympathetic reader will find something delightful in almost every verse.

The central idea of his poetry is the revelation of the divine in nature. Humanity is dwarfed and cramped and surrounded by a "vesture of pain," but in rare moments when nature speaks to us through cloud or sunshine, dawn or twilight, mountain or sea, we transcend the limits of mortal sense and feel thrillingly our divine birthright. Nature then ceases to be a mere effect of field and sky, a beautiful thing to be described, and becomes an actual being to be intimately known and loved. These poems show us how great a power she can exercise over the human mind when once a communion has been established. "The Mighty Mother" is constantly spoken of as an influence at once soothing and inspiring; she is the recipient of all the poet's secrets, she only knows "the wounds that quiver unconfessed." Thus through the medium of nature we get an insight into the character of the man himself, and become aware of that other great characteristic of the Celt, his "indomitable personality." In reading a poem, for instance, on **"Morning"** or "**Dusk**," we are at first chiefly occupied with the scene which has called it forth, but gradually we find our interest shifting to the human being through whose eyes we are looking at the picture, until at last the poet rather than the poem is uppermost in our thoughts. (p. 255)

Another most fascinating characteristic of these poems is their author's firm belief in the connection between our own world and a world of fairies. . . . In Ireland the spirits of earth and sky, of mountain and river, form part of the national life. "*They stand to reason,*" as another peasant said to Mr. Yeats. So it is with "A.E." His fairies are no mere visionary embodiments of ideas, but as real and familiar to him as the most common-place details of business life are to a London stockbroker. They appear in his poems in three forms. Sometimes they are the lost companions of a former life, now almost forgotten. . . . (pp. 257-58)

At other times they appear as playmates in his everyday existence. . . .

And lastly we see them as companions of his dreams. When the body becomes unconscious, the soul escapes from its prison, and wanders free "down the twilight stairs of sleep," to meet once more on equal terms the inhabitants of the spiritual world. At such times the visions become more glorious, and are described with delightful extravagance—opal fire kings who move on "pathways of rainbow wonder," or flaming stars that "swing along the sapphire zone"—visions that fade with the daylight, leaving only a lingering memory behind. . . .

There are [other poems in **The Earth Breath and Other Poems**] which treat of more palpable subjects and appeal more directly to human interests; and yet even in these he never loses that vagueness and yearning after the infinite which are the very essence of his nature. There are a few poems which deal with human love, though they cannot be called love poems in the accepted meaning of the phrase. It is the abstract more than the actual which appeals to him, and love is represented rather as a spiritual communion of souls than a definite intercourse of persons. . . . (p. 258)

His attitude towards human sorrow is the same. The sadness which is found in his poems is something quite different from morbidness, or from that despair which follows disillusionment and paralyses effort: it arises rather from the consciousness of an ever-fleeting ideal of a goal that is forever out of reach, or from the longing after a loved one that is lost. For this kind of sorrow there are many sources of consolation—nature herself offers a superficial comfort; but above all there is the great faith which opens to his spiritual insight wide domains of unceasing joy, and carries him far beyond the misery of earth. (p. 259)

If examined critically, his poetry, like everything else, has its faults. Many may find it unmusical. It is certainly lacking in the kind of beauty which belongs to the poetry of Tennyson. Its characteristic is not smoothness, but it has unquestionably a music of a wild and irregular kind, a natural open-air music like the sighing of the wind, or the yearning murmur of the waves on the seashore.

Others again may think him obscure and eccentric. Now and then, where he has given free play to his imagination, some effort is certainly required to follow him. But as a rule, if we accept his utterances as merely expressing the transitory moods of a highly imaginative nature, and do not press their meaning too closely, their very extravagance has a peculiar charm.

Those, however, who require great culture and study in a poet will be disappointed. For them "A.E.," the mystic, will have no charm. For while his mind has subtlety, delicacy and beauty, it yet lacks the distinction of a scholarly education, and something also of the great commonplace which humanity requires of its heroes and teachers. For this reason it is possible that he may never appeal to a wide public, but time alone will show whether his merits or his faults are the greater. (p. 260)

[*The Earl of*] Lytton, "*An Irish Poet*," *in* The Living Age *(copyright 1899, by the Living Age Co.), Vol. CCXXII, No. 2872, July 22, 1899, pp. 254-60.*

PADRAIC COLUM   (essay date 1918)

[*Colum, an Irish-born American poet and dramatist, was one of many young writers whom A.E. admired and encouraged in the early stages of their careers.*]

Before Nietzsche had made known to us his notion that the universe was creation designed by an artist for the aesthetic pleasure of artists, A.E. was speaking of it as the Adventure of the Spirit Errant. Men in his reveries are the strayed Heaven-dwellers; they are divine beings who have descended into chaos to win a new Empire for the Spirit; they are the angels "who willed in silence their own doom"; they are the gods who "forgot themselves to men"; they are kings in exile who await the hour of their restoration. This thought of man as the strayed Heaven-dweller runs through his poetry, his pictures and his economics. The claim in his economics is to make way for man who is divine in his soul and his imaginings.

Like all mystics A.E. is content to express in his poetry a single vision, a single intuition. We are eternal beings. Further, the earth we tread on is alive, the earth is a great being. Poetry of mystical vision seems empty when it is only a call to meditation. But A.E.'s vision, like the vision of Saint Theresa and William Blake and Michael Angelo, is heroic. Heroism is praised in his poetry. . . . As one reads his **Collected Poems** one has a sense of hearing a deep sound in nature, a sound that becomes more significant as one listens to it. How is it that these short poems, very many of them only of three stanzas, give one the sense of fullness and profundity? It is because they are all glimpses of the same river of vision.

One might speak too of a power he possesses, the power that is so effective when a real poet uses it, the power of rhetoric. When one reads his oration, **On behalf of some Irishmen not Followers of Tradition**, one has to acknowledge that eloquence in verse could hardly be more stirring. The oration is by way of reply to the ultra-Celtic party who would deny the Irish heritage to those who are not of Gaelic name and stock. And yet no Irish poet has had such reverence for the Celtic past of Ireland. He has dared to make the obscure deities of Celtic mythology as potent as the Olympians; when he speaks of Angus, Dana, or Lugh he makes them great and imposing figures. The heroic age for him is the heroic age in Ireland.

No poet of our civilization is as cosmic as A.E. Everything he knows, everything he feels, has a history that is before the stars and sun. His own face reflected in an actual river recalls the brooding of the Spirit over the Waters. The sorrow and helplessness that has entered his own heart is the shadow of the dark age that the world has entered into. (pp. 173-74)

It is from such spiritual spaces that A.E. now and again makes a social or political declaration—such a declaration was his eloquent letter to the Dublin employers during the strike of

1913, and such another was his recent letter to the Manchester Guardian on behalf of the Irish Nationalists. Few men can say with as much sincerity as he: "I see all this with grief. I have always believed in brotherhood between the peoples, and I think hatred corrupts the soul of a nation." (p. 174)

Padraic Colum, "'A.E.,' Poet, Painter and Economist," in The New Republic *(© 1918 The New Republic, Inc.), Vol. 15, No. 188, June 8, 1918, pp. 172-74.*

A. R. ORAGE (essay date 1918)

[*Psychologist, theosophist, and editor of the socialist weekly* The New Age, *Orage discusses various ideas presented by A.E. in* The Candle of Vision.]

"AE's" **Candle of Vision** is not a book for everybody, yet I wish that everybody might read it. . . . "AE's" narrative and criticism of his personal experiences may be said to take the form of intimate confessions made *pour encourager les autres.* For, happily for us, he is an artist who is also a philosopher, a visionary who is also an "intellectual"; and, being interested in both phases of his personality, he has had the impulse and the courage to express both. What the ordinary mind—the mind corrupted by false education—would say to "AE's" affirmations concerning his psychological experiences, it would not be difficult to forecast. What is not invention, it would be said, is moonshine, and what is neither is a pose to be explained on some alienist hypothesis. Only readers who can recall some experience similar to those described by "AE" will find themselves able to accept the work for what it is—a statement of uncommon fact; and only those who have developed their intuition to some degree will be able to appreciate the spirit of truth in which the **Candle of Vision** is written. A review of such work is not to be undertaken by me, but I have made a few notes on some passages.

Page 2. *"I could not so desire what was not my own, and what is our own we cannot lose . . . Desire is hidden identity."* This is a characteristic doctrine of mysticism, and recurs invariably in all the confessions. Such unanimity is an evidence of the truth of the doctrine, since it is scarcely to be supposed that the mystics borrow from one another. But the doctrine, nevertheless, is difficult for the mere mind to accept, for it involves the belief that nothing happens to us that is not ourselves. . . . The unforeseeable, the margin of what we call Chance, allows for events that belong to Fate rather than to Destiny. (pp. 93-4)

Page 16. *"I could prophesy from the uprising of new moods in myself that without search I should soon meet people of a certain character, and so I met them. . . . I accepted what befell with resignation. . . . What we are alone has power. . . . No destiny other than we make for ourselves."* I have already expressed my doubts whether this is the whole truth. It is, of course, the familiar doctrine of Karma; but I do not think it can be interpreted quite literally. There is what is called the Love of God, as well as the Justice of God, and I would venture to add, with Blake, the Wrath of God. Judgment is something more than simple justice; it implies the consent of the whole of the judging nature, and not of its sense of justice only. Love enters into it, and so, perhaps, do many other qualities not usually attributed to the Supreme Judge. In interpreting such doctrines we must allow for the personal equation even of the highest personality we can conceive.

Page 19. *"None needs special gifts of genius."* "AE's" **Candle of Vision** is confessedly propagandist. It aims deliberately at encouraging age to discover eternal youth, and to lay hold of everlasting life. It is to this end that "AE" describes his own experiences, and offers to his readers the means of their verification. He is quite explicit that no "special gifts" or "genius" are necessary. "This do and ye shall find even as I have found." The special gift of genius does not, I agree, lie in the nature of fact of the experience (though here, again, favour seems sometimes to be shown), but it does, I think, lie in the bent towards the effort involved. . . . [Desire], in the mystical sense, is the desire that is left when all the transient wishes or fancies have either vanished or been satisfied. Only such a desire leads the student to make the effort required by "AE," and the possession of such a desire is something like a "special gift" or "genius." (pp. 96-8)

Page 54. *"Is there a centre within us through which all the threads of the universe are drawn?"* An ingenious image for a re-current doctrine of mysticism, the doctrine, namely, that everything is everywhere. One of the earliest discoveries made in meditation is the magnitude of the infinitesimal. The tiniest point of space appears to have room enough for a world of images; and the mediaeval discussion concerning the number of angels that could dance on the point of a needle was by no means ridiculous. If I am not mistaken, "AE's" problem is identical with it.

Page 89. The Architecture of Dreams. In this chapter "AE" sets himself to casting some doubts (shall we say?) on the sufficiency of the Freudian theory of dreams. Dreams, according to Freud, are the dramatization of suppressed desires; but what, asks "AE," "is the means by which desires, suppressed or otherwise, dramatize themselves?" "A mood or desire may *attract* its affinities"; in other words, there may be a congruity between the desire and the dream which serves the Freudian purpose of interpretation; but desire can hardly be said "to *create* what it attracts." Between anger, for instance, and a definite vision of conflict, such as the dream may represent, there is a gulf which the theory of Freud does not enable us to cross. What, in fact, *are* dreams? *Who* or *what* carries out the dramatization? Assuming, with Freud, that their impulse is a desire, what power shapes this desire into the dream-cartoon? "AE" throws no light on the mystery, but, at any rate, he does not dismiss it as no mystery at all. Its philosophical discussion is to be found in the Indian philosophy known as the Sankhya. (pp. 101-02)

Page 90. "Have imaginations body?" In other words, are the figures seen in dream and vision three-dimensional? "AE" describes several incidents within his experience that certainly seem to suggest an objective reality in dream-figures, and the occasional projection of dream-figures into phantasms is a further evidence of it. But, once again, I would refer "AE" to the Sankhya aphorisms, and to Kapila's commentary on them. The question is really of the general order of the relation of form to thought.

Page 114. Here, and in the succeeding essay, "AE" develops his intuitional thesis that sound and thought have definite affinities. For every thought there is a sound, and every sound is at the same time a thought. The idea is, of course, familiar, and, like many more in the **Candle of Vision,** is found recurring like a decimal throughout mystical and occult literature in all ages. . . . "AE" has approached the problem . . . experimentally, with the aid of his intuition. If, he said to himself, there is really a definite correspondence between sound and idea, meditation on one or the other should be able to discover it. In other words, he has attempted to rediscover the lost language, and to find for himself the key whose fragments bestrew the ancient occult works. This again, however, is no novelty, but another of the recurrent ideas of mystics and would-be occultists. All of them have tried it, but, unfortunately, most of them come to different conclusions. "AE's" guesses must, therefore, be taken as guesses only, to be compared with the guesses with other students.

Page 132. One of the features of the *Candle of Vision* is the occasional ray cast by "AE" upon the obscure texts of the Bible. . . . "He made every flower before it was in the field, and every herb before it grew." This points, says "AE," to the probability that the Garden of Eden was the "Garden of the Divine Mind," in which flowers and herbs and all the rest of creation lived before they were made—visible! Such a conception is very illuminating. Moreover, it brings the story of Genesis into line with the genesis stories of both ancient India and the most recent psychology. For modern psycho-analysis, in the researches of Jung in particular, is undoubtedly trembling on the brink of the discovery of the divine mind which precedes visible creation. The process is indissolubly linked up with the psychology of imagination, phantasm, and vision.

Page 137. On Power. *"If we have not power we are nothing, and must remain outcasts of Heaven."* In this chapter "AE" shakes the fringes of the most dangerous subject in the world, that of the acquisition of "spiritual" power. I put the word under suspicion, because while in the comparative sense spiritual, the powers here spoken of may be anything but beneficent. . . . "AE," like his authorities, is full of warning against the quest of power. At the same time, like them, he realizes that without power the student can do nothing. Here is the paradox, the mightiest in psychology, that the weakest is the strongest and the strongest the weakest. I commend this chapter to Nietzscheans in particular. They have most to learn from it.

Page 153 et seq. "AE" makes an attempt to systematize "Celtic cosmogony." It appears to me to be altogether premature, and of as little value as the "interpretation" of Blake's cosmogony, which Messrs. Yeats and Ellis formerly attempted. Celtic cosmogony, as found in Irish legend and tradition, may be a cosmogony, and perhaps one of the oldest in the world (for Ireland is always with us!). But the fragmentary character of the records, the absence of any living tradition in them, coupled with the difficulty of re-interpretation in rational terms, make even "AE's" effort a little laborious. There is little illumination in the *Candle* when it becomes an Irish boglight. (pp. 103-07)

> *A. R. Orage, "'Candle of Vision'" (originally appeared in* The New Age, *1918), in his* Readers and Writers *(copyright 1922 by Alfred A. Knopf, Inc.), Knopf, 1922, pp. 93-107.*

ST. JOHN G. ERVINE (essay date 1922)

[*Ervine is critical of both A.E.'s visions and ideals relating to a democratic Ireland as presented in* The National Being.]

In a strange and, to me, incomprehensible book, called **"The Candle of Vision,"** ["A.E."] has wrought his mysticism to such a pitch of practicality that he is able to offer his readers an alphabet with which to interpret the language of the Gods! It manifests itself in some of his pictures, where strange, luminous and brightly-coloured creatures are seen shining in some ordinary landscape, creatures that seemed to me, when I first saw them, akin to Red Indians. . . . [While] I do not believe that "A.E." saw a fairy, otherwise than in his imagination, I am certain that he believes he saw one, not as a creature of the mind, but as one having flesh and blood. He claims no peculiar merit for himself in seeing visions. "There is no personal virtue in me," he writes in **"The Candle of Vision,"** "other than this that I followed a path all may travel but on which few do journey." He tells his readers how they, too, if they have the wish, may see the things which he has seen, and he gives descriptions of some of his visions. (pp. 35-6)

These visions form the foundation of his political and economic faith. (p. 38)

All ["A.E.'s"] political strivings have been directed towards making this "a society where people will be at harmony in their economic life," as he writes in **"The National Being,"** and "will readily listen to different opinions from their own, will not turn sour faces on those who do not think as they do, but will, by reason and sympathy, comprehend each other, and come at last, through sympathy and affection, to a balancing of their diversities, as in that multitudinous diversity which is the universe, powers and dominions and elements are balanced, and are guided harmoniously by the Shepherd of the Ages." Whether such a world, balanced in that way, can be rightly described as a democracy is not a matter on which I offer any opinion here, though it seems to me to be a very long way from what the common man considers a democracy to be.

It is when we come to connect his visions and the beliefs he derives from them with the actual circumstances in which we find ourselves that we begin to be most dubious. "National ideals," he says in **"The National Being,"** "are the possession of a few people only." That is an argument for aristocracy.

> Yet we must spread them in wide commonalty over Ireland if we are to create a civilisation worthy of our hopes and our ages of struggle and sacrifice to attain the power to build. We must spread them in wide commonalty because it is certain that democracy will prevail in Ireland. The aristocratic classes with traditions of government, the manufacturing classes with economic experience, will alike be secondary in Ireland to the small farmers and the wage-earners in the towns. We must rely on the ideas common among our people, and on their power to discern among their countrymen the aristocracy of character and intellect.

With the deletion of the word "Ireland" and the substitution of the word "America," that quotation might stand just as effective for the United States as for Ireland. Why is it certain that democracy will prevail in Ireland? Because the small farmers and the wage-earners in the towns will take precedence over the aristocracy and the manufacturing classes! I do not follow that argument. I have seen nothing in England or America or Ireland or France to convince me that if the small farmers and the wage-earners in the towns were authoritative they would be any more democratic than the aristocratic or the manufacturing classes. I have seen much to make me feel certain that they will use their authority as implacably in their own interests as any aristocrat or manufacturer ever used or ever will use his. (pp. 39-41)

Is not the world at this moment suffering to the point of distraction because the multitude cannot live up to its own ideals long enough to make them practical? "The gods departed," says "A.E.", "the half-gods also, hero and saint after that, and we [i.e. the Irish people] have dwindled down to a petty peasant nationality, rural and urban life alike mean in their externals.'' But he does not despair. ''Yet the cavalcade, for all its tattered habiliments, has not lost spiritual dignity.'' And he hopes ''the incorruptible atom'' in us will make us great again. Divine optimism, but what is there in peasant society to justify it? (pp. 43-4)

> *St. John G. Ervine, '' 'A.E.': George William Russell'' (originally published in a slightly different version in* The North American Review, *Vol. CCXII, No. 777, August, 1920), in his* Some Impressions of My Elders *(© 1922 by St. John G. Ervine), The Macmillan Company, 1922, pp. 25-60.*

EDWARD DAVISON   (essay date 1928)

> [*Davison compares A.E.'s poetry with that of Yeats, finding the former to be more ethereal and abstract than the latter.*]

The atmosphere in the poetry of A.E. superficially resembles that of Mr. Yeats, but it is essentially different in its cause and quality. Mr. George Russell's (that is, A.E.'s) sympathy with the aims of the Irish literary movement has been more theoretic than practical so far as concerns his poetry. The vital mood underlying his work actually has little in common with the moods of his fellow poets. Where Mr. Yeats and Mr. James Stephens have tended to see the world in terms of Ireland, he has seen Ireland relatively in terms of the world. He has been concerned primarily with the types of things while they delight to particularize, preferably with Irish examples. To put the matter crudely, Mr. Yeats sees his swans at Coole and tells us so. His lake-isle is pinned down to Innisfree. A.E. would have reduced them respectively to swans anywhere and a lake-isle nowhere. . . . There is something [in A.E.'s poetry] of the atmosphere that belongs notably to Shelley's poetry, a certain mistiness, an unreality; the poet is describing a world of his own which, though it may have some counterpart in this physical world, would not appear in the same way to any other eyes. In short, Mr. Yeats and Mr. Stephens see the landscape as it is, while A.E. sees it as it is not, bathed in something of ''The light that never was on sea or land.'' His stress is laid on the feeling, the colour, the atmosphere, never on the concrete form. The resemblance to Shelley appears throughout this poet's work more in the kind of imagery and simile employed than in the philosophic significance of the ideas which are essentially Wordsworthian. . . . A.E.'s poetry is none the worse because it springs from one of the oldest ''mystic''—I prefer to say philosophic, if not actually scientific—realizations of a certain type of mind. Most of his lyrics are in the nature of variations on the same theme. (pp. 181-84)

Thus A.E. appears as a poet whose work refers to a point of view, a point of view by no means original in its philosophic character, yet startlingly original by means of the poetic ways whereby it is presented. (pp. 186-87)

> *Edward Davison, ''Three Irish Poets,'' in his* Some Modern Poets and Other Critical Essays *(copyright 1928 by Harper & Row, Publishers, Inc.; reprinted by permission of Harper & Row, Publishers, Inc.), Harper & Brothers Publishers, 1928, pp. 173-96.**

W. B. YEATS   (essay date 1932)

> [*Yeats often quarrelled with A.E. for failing to question the validity of his mystical revelations as other visionaries had done. In* Song

and Its Fountains, *however, A.E. attempted an explanation of his mystical experiences and prompted the following critique by Yeats.*]

[In **Song and its Fountains**] A.E. attempts to describe and explain some part of his [mystical] experience. Swedenborg, metallurgical expert, scientific speculator, was a man of boundless curiosity, but the author of **Song and its Fountains**—landscape-painter and pastellist, when his visions were still a novelty—escapes with difficulty from mere pleasure and astonishment at the varied scene. I began by hating the book for its language. My friend, whose English at the close of the civil war was so vigorous and modern—I remember an article which found its way into the prisons and stopped a hunger strike—writes as though he were living in the 'nineties, seems convinced that spiritual truth requires a dead language. He writes 'dream' where other men write 'dreams,' a trick he and I once shared, picked up from William Sharp perhaps when the romantic movement was in its last contortions. Renaissance Platonism had ebbed out in poetic diction, isolating certain words and phrases as if they were Platonic Ideas. He has heaped up metaphors that seem to me like those wax flowers of a still older time I saw in childhood melted on the side towards the window. Yet I came to love the book for its thought.

It is almost wholly an illustration and commentary upon Plato's doctrine of pre-natal memory. It traces back A.E.'s dominating ideas to certain impressions, the colour of a wild flower, an image from a child's story, something somebody told him about a neighbour, a vision seen under closed eyelids; always, it seems, to single images, single events, which opened, as it were, sluice-gates into the will. A poet, he contends, does not transmute into song what he has learned in experience. He reverses the order and says that the poet first imagines and that later the imagination attracts its affinities. The more we study those affinities as distinct from the first impulse the more realistic is our art, which explains why a certain novelist of my acquaintance, who can describe with the most convincing detail the clothes, houses, tricks of speech of his characters, is yet the most unobservant of men. The author of **Song and its Fountains** shows the origin of certain of his poems and believes that we can all trace back our lives as a whole from event to event to those first acts of the mind, and those acts through vision to the pre-natal life. While so engaged he came upon a moral idea which seems to me both beautiful and terrible. He had an intuition that in some pre-natal life there had been 'downfall and tragic defeat'; he had begun a 'concentration upon that intuition' and almost at once became terrified. He seemed to be warned away from some knowledge he could not have endured, a warning which may have preserved his sanity while confining vision to a seemingly sensuous and external panorama, and substituting an emotional apprehension for analysis. He thinks that when a man is to attain great wisdom he first learns all the evil of his past, assumes responsibility for his share in that evil, follows out with a complete knowledge the consequence of every act, repents the sin of twenty thousand years, unified at last in thought, and only when this agony has been exhausted can he recall what was 'lovely and beloved.' We do not re-live the past, for our life is always our own, always novel, but dream back or think back to that first purity. Is not all spiritual knowledge perhaps a reversal, a return? (pp. 415-17)

I turn the pages once more and find that my friend has excused his lack of questioning curiosity better than I had thought. 'The Spirit,' as he calls the ultimate reality, gave to some 'the infinite vision,' but he had been content 'to know that it was there,' and through that knowledge was 'often happy'; had he stirred 'it would have vanished.' . . . (pp. 417-18)

W. B. Yeats, "My Friend's Book" (1932), in his Essays and Introductions *(reprinted with permission of Macmillan Publishing Company; in Canada by Michael and Anne Yeats; © by Mrs. W. B. Yeats 1961), Macmillan, 1961, pp. 412-18.*

J. PATRICK BYRNE (essay date 1941)

[In a general essay, Byrne outlines the characteristics of A.E.'s poetry.]

A E's poetry blows from the boundless mental and spiritual realm of the dreamer and mystic, mingled with national imagination and pride, the whole bathed in the evanescent glow of an Irish twilight or dawn. . . . (pp. 241-42)

He is the poet of ideas rather than of things. He changed little, developed little; to the last he never avoided either clichés or the most conventional of poetic diction. There is too much sameness of theme, imagery, metre, and rhythm in his verse—it would be instructive to know just how many times in **Collected Poems** occur such words as: twilight, dawn, crystal, diamond, blue, aery, ether, veil, mist, starry, high, and their derivatives. He was no lord of language.

A E's monotony of theme, of course, comes because most of his verse was written as a result of religious experience—for a moment he was lifted beyond himself, and after strove to put that experience into words. . . . (p. 242)

The fact that twilight and dawn are traditionally times most conducive to religious meditation, may perhaps account for their prevalence in his settings and imagery. (p. 243)

In A E's belief the dominant principle in a man's life is begotten at the first complete union in a single experience of the inner and outer selves, mind and spirit, when the individual first becomes conscious of self—that self which has lived a myriad lives before and carries in its consciousness the memory of those lives or, rather, is itself the product of all their innumerable actions and influences. He believed the impulse then born decides, though perhaps unconsciously, all after life; and that this bridal occurs in the turbulence of puberty. In **Vale** . . . , his second last and one of his better books of verse, **Germinal** . . . perhaps most perfectly expresses this—at the same time showing the unchanged texture of his verse from youth to age. . . . (pp. 245-46)

[The] philosophy of being is the theme of **Song and Its Fountains.** One of his most profound books—it might well be studied by every aspiring poet—it yet can be read and enjoyed by anyone, for its language is of the simplest. Much of his prose is good because of this very quality of simple clarity. This is true of his posthumous **The Living Torch.** . . . This is a good book—to read right through, or to pick up and dip into, as an anthology; pertinent in its comment on books old and new, with some particularly good criticism of current poetry; and upon those "politics of time and of eternity" which—with the quest for Beauty, in which he saw divinity manifest—mainly concerned A E. . . . (pp. 246-47)

He has said, "I have touched the lips of clay"; and that his poems were "all conceived and written in the open air." Despite this the roots of his poetry are not sufficiently in and of the clay of reality. He has also said in a letter to Seán O'Faoláin:

I really tried to write poetry as if I were on the slopes of death myself and was testing my thought by that consciousness.

But though many of his poems are externally effective—being ear-minded he made beautiful vowel patterns in much of his verse—others do not satisfy. He was not sufficiently Gaelic to make his work part of the main stream of Irish literature, though he could appreciate the true Gaelic genius—which is not, as many people believe, fiery, but rather akin to ice, which can also sear, or to the chill, polished steel of a surgical scalpel. (p. 247)

[**Vale**] fortunately belied its name, being followed in 1934 by **The House of the Titans.** The long title poem of this book is curious in that, embedded in it, is a fragment published years before as a separate poem under the title **Dana,** the Celtic Mother Goddess, symbolizing Earth. . . . [**Dana**] contains a line which is surely among his greatest:

My heart shall be in thine when thine forgives.

There is no incongruity: A E's style, the texture of his verse, changed little. It is true, though, that Chapter IX of **Song and Its Fountains** implies the first conception and draft of this poem, . . . belonged to his youth. But he is not at home in long poems such as this, **The Dark Lady of the Sonnets,** nor in the older **Michael.** However, many of the shorter lyrics in these two books are among his best in poetry—**Sibyl,** whose genesis is discussed on pp. 95-8 of **Song and Its Fountains,** and **Dark Rapture.** (pp. 248-49)

J. Patrick Byrne, "A E, Poet and Man," in Poet Lore *(copyright, 1941, by Poet Lore, Inc.; reprinted by permission of Heldref Publications), Vol. XLVII, No. 3, Autumn, 1941, pp. 240-49.*

JAMES STEPHENS (essay date 1942)

[Like Padraic Colum, the novelist and poet Stephens was one of A.E.'s protégés. In the following excerpt from his uncollected writings, Stephens praises A.E.'s work as that of a "wonderful amateur."]

[A.E.] was a miraculous critic, particularly of poetry. . . .

What was strange was that A.E. could not criticize immediately and subtly his own work in writing. He would not observe that fairly early in life he had evolved his own mannerisms, formulas, clichés, and would not cease from over-using them. In verse or prose or painting his status is really that of a wonderful amateur, not that of a great professional. Yet there are a certain dozen or so of his poems, and some dozens of his pictures, which only he could have composed and painted. . . . ["**The Voice of the Waters**" is] I think, the slowest measure in English verse. . . . (p. 114)

I would advise anybody interested in his literature to get his **Selected Poems,** which he read to me only about a fortnight before he died; of his prose, I would suggest **The Candle of Vision, Imagination and Reveries** and **The Interpreters.** A.E.'s poetry is singular because there is only one other poet in the English language who did the same thing—George Herbert and A.E. always wrote about God and the soul, and you might say that these two great artists had no other subject but the soul in relation to Deity.

"**Reconciliation**" I consider to be the finest prayer in the English language. . . . (p. 115)

James Stephens, "A.E.: I" (1942), in his James, Seumas and Jacques, *edited by Lloyd Frankenberg (reprinted with permission of The Society of Authors as the literary representative of the Estate of James Stephens and the copyright owner, Mrs. Iris Wise; © Iris Wise 1962, 1964), The Macmillan Company, 1964, pp. 110-15.*

JOHN EGLINTON   (essay date 1951)

[*A well-known Irish essayist, Eglinton shared A.E.'s friendship for many years and is the author of a comprehensive biography of A.E. (see bibliography). Here, he discusses various features of his friend's poetry.*]

[In] AE's own lifetime, Yeats, on an occasion which I remember, began some disparaging remarks on the man personally, by saying deliberately, "I think he is a great poet."

It would, I believe, be more accurate to say of Russell that he was a great poetic spirit. Certainly, of all the interests and activities of this many-sided man, poetry was nearest to his heart. (p. 5)

[Did] Russell ever write one perfect poem? Is there any one of his poems which leaps to the choice of an anthologist? Did he ever even, as Traherne did, record his exalted experiences in language which enables us to share it with him? Did he ever produce a poem which, as Matthew Arnold claimed to do even with Isaiah, we can "enjoy"? When we look down the long list of beautiful titles he has invented for his poems, and turn to one of them, are we ever fully satisfied? Take for instance, **"A Summer Night."** Here is certainly a poet sensible of the beauty and mystery of his theme; but a poet must never forget his craft: he must "keep his eye on the object," to use the phrase of the early nineteenth century poets. Think of Keats listening to the nightingale in the woods at Hampstead; he "cannot see what flowers are at his feet"; but how we are present with him when "the plaintive anthem fades up the hill side, and now 'tis buried deep in the next valley glades." In Russell's poem, on the other hand, there is neither time nor place. There are "jewels of glittering green"; "the little lives that lie deep-hid in grass"; the dews that "lift with grey fingers all the leaves"; lawns, lakes and stars—"far too many things," as the poet himself exclaims when he realizes that he is thinking of something quite different from the sounds and sights around him—how far apart we are from the "one single Being." (pp. 5-6)

Besides this lack in Russell of the literary artist's objectivity there is the further hindrance to the general acceptance of his poetry in the peculiar beliefs which he made the main subject-matter of his poems. There is nothing particularly wrong with poetry having a "message," provided that the message is a source of inspiration to the poet. Wordsworth, Shelley had messages; and Browning, though his message was often a heavy load for poetry to carry, could be objective enough, and he is always a man and a brother. This can hardly be said of AE, who seldom speaks to us with the voice of a brother man. The truth is that AE conceived himself to be more than a poet, as indeed he was; he would have amazed the Lamas of Tibet by his insight into their mysteries, and—what more concerns us here—he was the modern hierophant of the Celtic otherworld. Matthew Arnold, in his *Treatise on the Study of Celtic Literature,* detecting, as he thought, a unique element in English poetry which he called "natural magic," had asked whence it could have come if not from Celtic sources; and before him Emerson, in one of his poems, had written of "England's

genius" as "taught by Plinlimmon's Druid power." There is little or none of this "natural magic" in AE's poetry, but of the magical religion of the Celt he was the fervent apostle. Theosophy had been the main inspiration of his first little book **Homeward: Songs by the Way,** written before he had begun to think much about Ireland; but later on, reading with passionate interest Standish O'Grady's history of Ireland's *Heroic Period,* the scales fell from his eyes, and he beheld the country of "those heavenly adventurers the Gael, ere to a far-brought alien worship they inclined;" and no doubt, engendered by scholarship, withheld him from identifying the Druidic lore with the wisdom of the East. This new clairvoyance was extended to the so-called "animistic" beliefs of all primitive peoples—I think he excluded the Saxons and the Jews—to all those races which in their beginnings had recognized the great doctrine of the "divinity of Earth." Our earth, he firmly held, is a sacred Being, the Virgin Mother, "a goddess to whom men should pray." . . . In the air is its breath; in its memory the very presence of ancient gods and heroes. There are specially favoured centres, he held, for this magical clairvoyance, and in Ireland was one of these.

The reader of AE's poems, then, needs to be deeply imbued with the conviction that there are more things in heaven and earth than are dreamt of by the philosophers. It should be remembered, however, that Russell was a very clever man, a keen follower of the progress of science, who could talk understandingly with eminent biologists and astronomers. It may even be that his beliefs, which he proclaimed with the most courageous conviction, may accord better than they seem to do at present with some future view of the universe. . . . It must be confessed, however, that in AE's idealism a "patriotic bias" is evident. A vague influence proceeded from it to a small but not negligible circle: it affected, I think, the mystical politics of P. H. Pearse, and reached even Arthur Griffith.

To AE what is ancient is almost what is divine; the ignoble present is redeemed by its embodiment of the still-living past. This seems to be the theme of a beautiful poem, **"Inheritance,"** written before his "Celtic" period. . . . (pp. 6-7)

On more than one occasion AE addressed a wide audience in his verse. During the first world war he was listened to by many when he contributed to the London *Times* his strange series of poems, afterwards collected in the little volume **Gods of War,** written in a spirit of lofty detachment. But perhaps the best known of all his poems is that with the title **"On behalf of some Irishmen not followers of tradition,"** with its famous culminating line, "The golden heresy of truth." It brings to my mind an early poem called **"Truth"** (*one* "perfect poem," at any rate) which made me forever a believer in George Russell the poet. . . . (p. 8)

John Eglinton, "The Poetry of AE," in The Dublin Magazine, *n.s. Vol. 26, No. 3, July-September, 1951, pp. 5-9.*

THOMAS RICE HENN   (essay date 1964)

[*Henn's essay indicates several major differences between A.E. and the contemporary to whom he is often compared, Yeats. Henn agrees with most critics that Yeats was the greater talent, having concentrated on his profession as a poet, while A.E. chose varied paths in which to make his contributions.*]

Of A.E.'s poetry it is not easy to speak without seeming pompous or affected. . . .

I am left with the impression of a vast mass of competent, worthy, even 'noble' work, most of it irredeemably in the middle of the second rank; where, in the Nineteenth Century, we should put Coventry Patmore, Stephen Phillips, a little below Dowson, Lionel Johnson, Francis Thompson. Yet we should recall that Symons and Gosse admired the collection called *The Earth Breath,* and in 1898 Yeats praised his style as resembling that of a Jacobean writer of lyrics. (I cannot, I confess, see the resemblance.) Philosophically, in the broadest sense, it is 'worthy' and 'noble': I have chosen these two words, and I repeat them, deliberately. There are, I think, four 'centres' in A.E.'s mind.

First, there is a layer of Celtic legend, and you will be familiar with most of it through Yeats. (p. 147)

The second group, and by far the largest, is something that we might call, rather vaguely, 'mystical nature poetry'. These poems seem to be written to a kind of formula. There is a description of some kind of natural scene: written often with great skill, great sensitivity to light, colour, the moods of the countryside. They are clearly what we might call 'painter's pieces' in their first conception. After the description comes, almost uniformly, the gathering-up (as it were) of the description into an assertion of the unity of the natural elements of the scene with the Infinite, the earth-spirit, the Eternal. Typical of these are two [pieces], . . . called **'Winter'** and **'Answer'.** Sometimes the statement is pessimistic, the romantic's longing for the past: sometimes the reverse. Behind both, and in the Love Poems, there is a strong flavour of neo-Platonism, which A.E. shared with Yeats: both owing much, I think, to Stephen Mackenna's great translation: which still remains in its revised form the best, and certainly the most poetical, version that has yet been made. And in this, of course, his thought is in direct conflict to the ascetic Christian view: as in [the poem] called **'Dust'** . . . which has a Tennysonian flavour, and the eternal banality of the God-rhyme, which has bedevilled so many poets and hymn-writers. . . . [This poem illustrates,] I think, A.E.'s chief weakness. It is what Yeats, with detestation, called 'abstraction': generalized and vague. In the lines

> . . . Is thrilled with fire of hidden day,
> And haunted by all mystery

he cannot convince us of the connection between 'lips of clay' and 'rudest sod'. I think, indeed, that this obsession with the sacred character of a literal earth is responsible for much of A.E.'s weakest verse.

Then there is a group of Love Poems [exemplified by the poem] **'Pity'** (to the girl called Olive). Here there is a note of tenderness, of pity, of the *suffering* of love, of the coming of old age: that theme so often handled by Ronsard, Villon, Shakespeare, Yeats, Synge. It is not untypical that one of the poems should be called **'The Grey Eros'.** . . . We are now, I think, in a position to suggest comparisons and contrasts with Yeats: and to ask ourselves 'What is it that makes this poetry, in spite of its nobility, its tenderness, the essential and apparent *goodness* of the poet, so irredeemably of the second rank?'

As always, there is no one answer. The first, I think, is A.E.'s commitment to an extraordinarily narrow technical range. His favourite metre is the conventional four-foot iambic couplet, fully rhymed, a b a b. Quite often he varies this with a final three-stress line, also fully rhymed, to give the effect of a falling close. Sometimes there is a long rather dragging many-stressed metre, in the line of descent from Swinburne, Morris, not unlike parts of *The Wanderings of Oisin.* Yeats discarded those long metres, with their inevitable redundancy and padding, at a very early stage. But let us not be intolerant, many young poets are (or were) attracted to them, for the sake of the sonority, the sheer drive of the rhythm: and I think they are perhaps less pernicious for the young poet as initial models than the deceptive facile slackness of free verse.

One trouble with A.E. is the monotony of his rhymes. . . . That is one trouble; the monotony of the rhythms, the banality of the rhymes. But more important is the diffuseness, the lack of 'edge' or 'attack' in most of A.E.'s poems. One reason may well be that he never gave himself wholly to poetry; having (in his view) more important things to do to secure his world. There is little energy from the verbs: the adjectives (often chosen with the sensibility with which a painter chooses colour) seem over-prominent. This is because there is, as a rule, to be no genuine fusion, as it were, between image and idea. His natural scenery, the actual living world of his poems, seems continually to be subordinated to the *idea:* itself so vague, so diffuse, that it is seldom or never integrated with the image. (pp. 148-50)

Perhaps the failure is in sheer craftsmanship. Many of the poems are in the long dragging metres that Yeats abandoned after *Oisin.* The stanzaic forms quickly grew monotonous; and there is a certain sameness of subject, a re-handling of basic themes, which leave an impression of weakness. For all the invocation of the divine fire there does not appear to be sufficient power to over-ride the impression of a diction that is largely spent. (p. 150)

It may seem a strange opinion; but it is as a prose writer that I would chiefly praise A.E.: the more so, indeed, since his books have for long been inaccessible and little appreciated. The prose can afford to pass by those elements of poetic technique that seem to me lacking. It is a gracious and generous kind of writing. *Song and Its Fountains* contains his theory of poetry. It seems to me by far the most penetrating account— always excepting that of Coleridge—of the workings of the creative mind. (pp. 150-51)

The second book to which I invite your attention is called *The Interpreters.* . . . Its theme is of special interest to us today. The form is that of a discussion among a group of men condemned to death for their part in some Rising, talking freely to each other of their hopes and dreams in what one of them calls "the ante-chamber of death". Each man declares what is in his mind, and I do not doubt that we have A.E.'s political and poetic thinking (one of the characters recites a longish 'poem of pilgrimage') at its most mature. . . . (p. 152)

What, then, are we to say of A.E.? I think of him as a man of the utmost integrity, of genuine vision, of a moderate poetic gift; whose circumstances, a sense of duty, the perception of a significance in his own childhood experiences, combined to produce a body of work in which the prose is more significant than the poetry, and the life's work than either.

Unlike Yeats he was never a single-minded, dedicated professional poet. His gifts were diffused in the Civil Service, organization, theosophy, the agricultural cooperative movement, editorial work. (p. 153)

A.E. found and mined his own vein of poetry: traditional in its return to the innocence and ecstasy of childhood, traditional and certified by so many noble names. (We think of Herbert, Traherne, Vaughan, Smart, Wordsworth, Blake, de la Mare.) This perception of the glory, this sensitivity to the minute particulars of the sensuous world is, first, to be apprehended, then drawn into a unity of the whole poetic statement. Above and behind the world of the senses A.E. is conscious of the powers which offer to him the prospect of this unity. But those powers are many and diffuse; like the vague capitalizations which the early Yeats used and then abandoned. 'The Poet Speaks with the Elemental Powers', 'The Mystic Rose', and others. In A.E.'s pantheon there is not only the awareness of the praeter-natural world (he quotes Kant in support) but awareness of a multiplex world of the Irish countryside, both historical and actual, in which an unorthodox God, the Earth Mother, the Celtic heroes, together with some of the Vedic deities, move uneasily together. His intention is to communicate his sense of unity with the whole created world; and, through that unity, to reach towards the love of God.

But there are two difficulties for him and for us. Firstly, he is striving towards too many and too diffuse objects: so that we seem to move in a vague cloud of these concepts. I doubt very much whether this tissue of allusions to past mythologies, whether Hindu or Druid or Celtic, can have validity today. It is, as Yeats called it, 'a dusty dream'. The vocabulary of classical and Biblical mythology and allusions were poetic tools only for as long as an educational system, and life-long habits of reading, burnt them into the consciousness of Western Europe. Lir, Lugh, Dana, the Morrigu, Kali, Shiva, have to be re-evoked or recovered by sheer labour. They can never have the familiarity of the gods of Greek and Rome; whose names live at least in the stars. Yeats solved the problem by abandoning all the 'heroic' images except that of Cuchulain; and he established his validity by repeated and many-sided re-alignments and linkages with Irish history in the present. The Yeatsian synthesis works in a wholly different manner. It is ultimately concerned with the same problem of unity of being, the conveyance of the One and the Many, but with a concreteness of living imagery, a tautness of control, a rhythmical attack that is foreign to A.E. (pp. 153-54)

> *Thomas Rice Henn, "The Sainthood of A.E." (originally a lecture delivered at The Yeats International Summer School, Sligo, Ireland, in 1964), in his* Last Essays: Mainly on Anglo-Irish Literature *(copyright © 1976 The Estate of T. R. Henn; by permission of Barnes & Noble Books, a Division of Littlefield, Adams & Co., Inc.), Barnes & Noble, 1976, pp. 137-56.*

ROBERT BERNARD DAVIS (essay date 1977)

[*Davis's* George William Russell, *from which this excerpt is taken, provides a valuable critical study of A.E.'s major works. The following excerpt offers a thematic study of A.E's poetry and prose.*]

The excellence and the limitation of AE's poems lie in the fact that he emphasized the spiritual aspect of life and that he injected into them the painter's love of color. His poetry was the embodiment of his religious feeling, and Ernest Boyd has rightly attributed this characteristic to an unconscious drive in him toward the religious: "It is the apparent absence of deliberate intention in the form and setting of the poems. The dusky valleys and twilight fields, the pictures which captivate the eye, are incidental, it might almost be said accidental. They occur merely as the accompaniment of an idea, the prelude to a statement which constitutes the real reason of the poem's existence." For the most part, AE's poetry must be accepted and evaluated as religious poetry. (p. 51)

AE has been compared with Algernon Charles Swinburne for his poetical skill, and with Ralph Waldo Emerson and William

Blake for his thought. The comparison to Blake is quite apt since both were visionaries and since both were visual artists as well as poets. There is evidence that AE was very familiar with both Blake's writings and his drawings, but AE greatly resembles another poet-painter, Dante Gabriel Rossetti, in his love of color and in his willingness to sacrifice ideas or sense to the sounds and colors of poetry. But, of course, the poet with whom AE is most often compared is his friend Yeats. Eglinton, who has called the two poets the *Dichterpaar* of modern Irish poetry, has indicated that Yeats had the greater poetic endowment and the wider worldly experience but that his range of abilities and activity was narrower than that of AE. Diarmuid Russell has said that his father readily acknowledged Yeats to be the better poet. . . . They were also different in their reactions to mystical ideas; for, while AE accepted the mystical ideas that he encountered, and made them a part of his life, for Yeats they were only the material for his poetry. (p. 52)

The lack of variety in AE's poetry has been noted by his friends and his critics; his favorite verse form is the four-line ballad stanza, and most of his poems are about nature and the mystery behind it. Poem after poem describes the mighty being who stands mysteriously behind his creations. His poetry is full of color, not just violet and purple but with many others; and **"The Great Breath"** is an example of this profusion of color. . . . We also see here certain other characteristics of his early verse: the painter's eye for color and the vagueness of meaning where sense is sacrificed to music. Both of these characteristics identify him with Rossetti. The lines are not sharp but hazy and suggestive—a style which would be called "painterly" in the visual arts. The inverted sentence structure, as in "Sparkle the delicate dews," marks him as a nineteenth-century poet; Robert Browning reveals the same style in "Rabbi Ben Ezra," with the line "Irks care the cropful bird?" What thought emerges is also typical of AE and the tradition of Romanticism: the mystery of nature, its beauty, its divinity, and its fragility. The difficulty in this poem comes in the final line where AE seems to be saying that Beauty must die; yet Beauty is also identified with **"The Great Breath,"** which is a kind of divinity in Nature. If she is eternal, then why must she die? This kind of confusion is typical of the early AE, who did not sufficiently rework his material.

We see the same tendencies in **"The Divine Vision,"** plus certain other characteristics of AE's verse, including the use of such archaic diction as *thee, thy, thou, ope, seest.* The theme is the human soul in exile, another typical theme for AE. (pp. 53-4)

[The] majority of AE's poems in the *Collected Poems* volume of 1935 serve as vehicles for his mystic philosophy, and the first group of poems to be described is concerned with the nature of God. These poems include [**"Oversoul," "The Unknown God," "By the Margin of the Great Deep,"** and **"The Twilight of Earth"**]. . . . The supreme deity, as differentiated from the Divine Mother who appears in some of the poems, is always designated as a male god; but AE does not know much about him. Mysterious and ineffable, he is known chiefly through his creation, the world of nature. (p. 55)

Sometimes AE relates his typical themes to Indian mythology and religion, as in **"Krishna."** . . . In this poem, one of AE's best, he describes the human condition by pointing to the divinity in man and by contrasting that with his depravity.

In **"The Heroes"** . . . , another poem about the latent divinity in man, AE is walking in the city, dejected by all the corruption he sees. A man approaches who seems to be a Christ figure, and he shows AE the more lovely aspects of the city. In a long speech—a rather improbable one from a mere chance acquaintance in the street—the man says that the lost and fallen people we see in the street will pass into the divine world when they sleep tonight. They have divinity within them. . . . AE is constantly asking us to look with deeper eyes through the surfaces of life, penetrating to the divine within man and nature. (pp. 59-60)

"Germinal" . . . , one of AE's later poems, is in the same vein; for the title refers to the early stage of the development of man and his divine origin. This poem shows, however, greater firmness and has more intensity than the early poem because it is developed chiefly through allusions to other materials, has a sense of paradox, and contains freshness and intensity of thought. (p. 60)

Another group of poems describes the blessedness of children and childhood [**"Awakening," "Childhood," "The Dream of the Children,"** and **"Om"**]. . . . The basic idea in these poems is the usual primitivist concept that children, being closer to God, are more blessed than adults. In **"Childhood,"** the poet contrasts with the adult world of care, strife, and duty the divinely inspired life of the child. In this respect, AE is similar to Wordsworth in his belief about the unconscious divinity of children that is revealed in such poems as the sonnet, "It Is a Beauteous Evening" or the "Intimations" ode. To AE, men learn only from pain and sorrow, but an inner joy guides the child. . . . (p. 61)

AE's attitude toward the city is revealed in a group of poems including [**"Pity," "The City," "Michael," "New York,"** and **"In A Strange City"**]. . . . His distrust of the city is typically Romantic, and it is based on the primitivistic idea that man is good by nature but corrupted by civilization—an idea which goes back to Rousseau. But AE's attitude toward the city is ambivalent: in **"Pity,"** he sees it as evil; in **"The City,"** he sees possibilities of spiritual values. (p. 62)

When AE visited New York in the 1920's, he was impelled to write a quite different poem about the city; and St. John Ervine may have been right in thinking that a journey would be good for AE. The poem, entitled **"New York,"** shows a new, tighter style, and it also reveals AE's admiration of the architectural wonders of that city. Although the question at the end of the poem is difficult to understand, his poetry has a unity and a firmness of style that places it among AE's best verses. . . . (p. 63)

Two poems deal with the subject of pain and sorrow as aspects of the human condition, and AE was familiar with both. In the short poem **"Pain"** . . . , he writes that he has made a god of pain, just as others have made gods of love, the sun, the giver of rain, and the spirits of hill and grove. Although anguish exists in the touch of this god, "Yet his soul within is sweet." In **"The Man to the Angel"** . . . , the persona of the poem is speaking to an angel, and is contrasting the human with the angelic condition. The angel comes from the pure world, but the impure human condition is better because we learn from pain and sorrow. Not all pain comes from sin; sometimes it comes from aspiring to be great, and we are nearer to the fountain of life because of this pain. . . . (p. 65)

Turning from pain to love, AE wrote a group of poems concerned with both the physical and the spiritual aspects of this perennial subject. In *Collected Poems,* the earliest poem concerned with this subject is **"The Symbol Seduces"** . . . in which AE refers to physical love as being seductive and mis-

leading. The "her" of the poem is physical love, a "symbol of the world's desire," which binds the soul of fire to the earth. But, when "the robe of Beauty" falls away and reveals the universal, the spirit, he deserts physical love for Truth and spiritual love. (pp. 65-6)

AE is not at his best in his love poems: they are somewhat hackneyed and old-fashioned, reminiscent of the style, idea, and technique found in Rossetti's love poems. We find in both poets the same theme about a spiritual love that triumphs over physical love, but AE is more sincere about this change; and we also note in each of these poets the same vagueness and misty quality in the diction and imagery. It may be true that spiritual love is superior to physical love, but there is a limit to the number of ways it can be said, and AE has reached that limit. (p. 66)

A turning point in AE's poetry seems to be promised in a poem entitled **"A New Theme."** . . . Though the style and diction of the poem do not agree with its thought, AE suggests that his future poems will be different. . . . We certainly cannot expect much in the way of change from a poem that begins with "I fain would . . . .". The antique diction (*fain, oft-sung, untrodden*) does not indicate that a change in style is coming very fast or very soon. But a change did come with the volume entitled *Gods of War,* a group of poems inspired by World War I. . . . The first poem in the volume, **"Gods of War,"** compares World War I with the war between Carthage and Rome. Modern warships, airplanes, and submarines now add to the conflict; but, though the weapons are modern, the war is still the old battle between good and evil which no one wins but the Devil. Christ is defied again, and the gods of war are now fashionable.

This new subject seems to have brought about a development in AE's poetic style which was promised but not delivered in **"A New Theme."** Although he does not get completely away from the older style and although he still speaks of the ancestral self quite often, his style becomes firmer. This development is seen in **"Battle Ardour,"** a companion piece to Yeats's "An Irish Airman Foresees His Death," in which AE describes the ecstasy of an airman as he fights and dies in an aerial battle. He is free of the earth and finds triumph even in death; he is fighting not for the "right of kinds" but for the experience itself. . . . The syntax is more modern (with the exception of "tryst do keep"); the vocabulary is no longer antique (except for *tryst*); and the run-on lines help to break up the usual regular rhythms of the poem. A.E.'s poem lacks the originality and the singing quality of Yeats's poem, but for AE it is an achievement. (pp. 66-8)

Another class of AE's poems was inspired by the Irish Rebellion and by the Civil War which followed it. There are not too many of these poems, possibly because AE was too busy during these years working for a solution to the Home Rule problem. The most important of these poems is **"Salutation,"** a poem about the 1916 Easter Rising. . . . Though AE was a nationalist and though he felt that Irish myth and legend were important heritages of Ireland, he opposed revolution, bloodshed, and violence even in the cause of Irish independence. That he felt the future was more important than the past is made clear in a poem entitled **"On Behalf of Some Irishmen Not Followers of Tradition."** . . . As if to balance this poem, AE places immediately after it the poem **"An Irish Face"** in which he reflects about the sorrow in the face of a woman he has met. Such sorrow is not only from the unhappiness in her own life but from the sorrows of the race—those of Deirdre,

Cuchulain, and the Wild Geese. Contemplation of this face makes us realize the strength of our tradition, but how can these two seemingly opposing positions on tradition be reconciled? AE realizes the strength and power of tradition, but he also insists that tradition is of value only if it leads to a greater country and to a better race.

A number of AE's poems do not fit into any of the usual patterns, and one of the most interesting of these is **"The Dark Lady"** which appeared in *The House of the Titans and Other Poems*. The point of departure is Shakespeare's Sonnet 134, in which we read about someone, presumably a woman, who has enslaved both the poet and his friend, presumably a man. (pp. 69-70)

This poem, so unusual for AE, is so very fine that we wonder what would have happened had he been carried away more often from his accustomed themes. The constant reiteration of the old theme of the fall of man and of his ability to return to the divine, if only he would, weakens the force of AE's total poetic output. But, from time to time, his lines leap from the page, seize the imagination, and fall upon the ear with compelling accents. **"The Dark Lady"** shows clearly that he had the ability to write other than in a mystical vein and that he is at his best when he is least didactic—when he depends upon the worth of his poetic ideas to convey the true sense of his wisdom. (pp. 71-2)

Deirdre is taken from the Irish legend of the Red Branch, a part of the Ulster Cycle; the name of the story is *Longes Mac Nusnig* or *The Exile of the Sons of Usnech*. The play follows the story closely; and AE adds little that is new. The story concerns Deirdre, who, according to prophecy, is fated to cause the destruction of the Red Branch. (p. 73)

AE's career as a dramatist was based on this single play. The plot is slight and simple, depending purely on suffering for its tragic effect. The movement is slow, and it follows the theory of Yeats that drama should not be an excitement of the nerves but the establishment of a mood. The characters are not particularly moving, having been changed little from the legend. Though the work is in prose, the language is poetic in places. For example, at the beginning of Act I, Lavercam says: "The harp has but three notes; and after sleep and laughter, the last sound is of weeping." This statement sets the mood of the play, which moves relentlessly to the end, where Deirdre's fears are confirmed as all of the principal persons die. There is a sense of foreboding in the play, which is typical of much of Irish tragedy, including even the modern playwrights such as Synge and O'Casey. The chief interest in this play is its Irish legendary subject matter, for Yeats and Russell agreed as to the purpose of Irish drama at this time in the early days of the Abbey Theatre: Their aim was to awaken the heroic sense of the Irish people by acquainting them dramatically with their ancient heritage. (p. 74)

The Interpreters, which can hardly be truly classified as a novel, is more of a dialogue like those of Plato: It is a fictional account of a group of men in a given situation who develop philosophical ideas about human life as a Transcendental experience on earth. AE was capable of writing fiction, but he was too much interested in ideas to write a novel in the ordinary sense of the genre. *The Avatars* . . . is a little closer to being a novel, but its ideology is still more important than either plot or characters. He called it a "futuristic fantasy," and the center of the story consists of two avatars who visit the earth. An avatar in the Hindu religion is a god who comes to the earth in human form; the word is from Sanskrit, according to Eglin-

ton, and it means literally "he who goes down or passes beyond." This word AE uses often, and it derived from his interest in Theosophy.

The avatars in the narrative are never seen very clearly, but their presence is felt distinctly. The epigraph, taken from Claude Monet, the French Impressionist painter, reads, "The Light is the real person in the picture." This quotation suggests that the avatars are like the light in an Impressionist painting: spiritual and luminous, it is not fully realized nor made definite. AE's prefatory note makes this interpretation clear: "No more than an artist could paint the sun at noon could I imagine so great beings. But as a painter may suggest the light on hill or wood, so in this fantasy I tried to imagine the spiritual excitement created by two people who pass dimly through the narrative, spoken of by others but not speaking themselves." (p. 83)

As a novelist of the spirit, AE has created in *The Avatars* a new kind of book. Though the plot moves slowly and the transitions are clumsy, the characters are convincing, and their thoughts are sublime. As we have already observed, the idea is more important than the development of plot and character; and AE achieves his full effect in separate passages of luminous beauty. The reader is led into a beautiful world where fine people love each other not for their physical but for their spiritual qualities.

But, in another sense, we cannot call AE a novelist any more than we could consider him a dramatist. Like his poetry, his fiction and his drama have a specific motive—to advance his mystical theories and his spiritual concept of the destiny of mankind in general and of Ireland in particular. Once again, we note the narrow range of his thought and his art, for AE's dominant theme is about the spiritual origin of man and about the inherent powers which are his to use if only he can be made aware of them. This singleness of purpose defines AE's work; and, although he worked in many different areas, his central purpose was always the same: to improve the lot of mankind and to make men aware of their spiritual nature. AE certainly cannot be compared with Yeats in poetry, with O'Casey in drama, or with either E. M. Forster or Conrad in fiction; in artistic ability, they are by far his superior. In the realm of literature, he was more a philosopher than an artist. (p. 89)

In the years between 1912 and 1916, much happened in Ireland; and AE continued to write about the economic and political issues of the day, with such short works as [*The Rural Community, Oxford University and the Cooperative Movement, Ireland, Agriculture and the War,* and *Talks with an Irish Farmer*]. . . . But his greatest work in this area was *The National Being*, which appeared in 1916. After decades of fruitless attempts to secure freedom for Ireland, the Third Home Rule Bill had finally passed the British Parliament in 1914. Because of World War I, the bill was temporarily set aside since Great Britain did not want a hostile or even a neutral Ireland that was so close to her own shores to be available as a base for enemy agents. But, since AE was hopeful that the bill would finally be implemented, he anticipates in *The National Being* an Irish Free State which he hopes will develop in the years to come—one that looks back to its ancient origins in myth and legend and ahead to its future as a modern European state. (pp. 97-8)

Much of what AE says in *The National Being* repeats what he had said previously in *Co-operation and Nationality*. Although the need for agriculture, and for the cooperative movement had been covered, he develops some ideas such as the necessity for the organization of farm labor. But the main difference between the two books is that, in the time that had intervened, AE had seen the Dublin Strike of 1913, the beginning of World War I, and growing rebelliousness in Ireland. He was now more interested in the plight of the industrial worker than he had been in 1913, and this book reveals that change of attitude. (pp. 98-9)

Another aspect of *The National Being* not found in *Co-operation and Nationality* was concerned with the ideal form of government for Ireland. AE, who was opposed to the importation of English representative government, had definite ideas as to what the new government should be like. . . . The ideal government for Ireland, he felt, should have two representative assemblies. The first, the general assembly or parliament, "should be elected by counties or cities to deal with general interests, taxation, justice, education, the duties and rights of individual citizens as citizens." . . . The second assembly would consist of specific organized bodies or committees elected by the persons who were involved in specific occupations: farmers, laborers, professional men. These specialists would be responsible for their own areas of concern, and they would insure the consideration of expert knowledge in solving the problems of the nation. (p. 100)

The last part of *The National Being* deals with military affairs, conscription, and foreign relations. AE does not see Ireland as becoming a great power in terms of military strength; moreover, to become such a military power is not even desirable nor the best way to achieve national unity. Military strength not only makes the state harsh and cruel but creates the same condition in its enemies. AE is ready to admit, however, that society has not found a more efficient way of uniting a people. In wartime, under the influence of military discipline, men learn to be brave and endure hardships, wounds, and even death. The great problem is how to apply this lesson to peaceful purposes, and AE's faith was that the cooperative movement would do so. (p. 101)

The National Being concludes with an appeal to all of the spiritual leaders of Ireland—the clergy, the poets, the writers, and the thinkers—for help in changing the life of Ireland from the competitive to the cooperative model. AE once again reviews the ancient heritage of Ireland, rooted in the myths and legends of her past, and affirms the importance of national policy at this historical moment. . . .

Although Oliver St. John Gogarty called AE an "angelic anarchist," he was not entirely correct. AE was not an Anarchist, as we have seen, for he held firm beliefs about the necessity of the nation and its divine origin. What he objected to strongly was the tyrannical state which would deprive its members of the liberty to seek their own destiny. Other, more apt names for AE would be a "heavenly economist," a "metaphysical nationalist," or a "spiritual politician." But, in the end, all labels fail with AE; he was simply a man who was seeking the destiny and the true spiritual nature of man. (p. 104)

> *Robert Bernard Davis, in his* George William Russell ("AE") *(copyright © 1977 by Twayne Publishers, Inc.; reprinted with the permission of Twayne Publishers, a Division of G. K. Hall & Co., Boston), Twayne, 1977, 163 p.*

JOHN WILSON FOSTER (essay date 1980)

[*Foster examines* The Interpreters *as a symposium of the varied philosophies of A.E.'s contemporaries—who were key figures in the Irish Literary Revival and nationalist movement—as perceived by A.E.*]

AE calls [*The Interpreters*] a "symposium," and it has some affinity with that classical form and with such a modern version of it as Dryden's *Essay of Dramatic Poesy* (1668). There is, however, greater narrative and descriptive content in *The Interpreters* than in Dryden's work, and we may speak of it as something very close to a novel. It is set some centuries in the future, "so that," according to AE in the Preface, "ideals over which there is conflict today might be discussed divested of passion and apart from transient circumstance." This was a forlorn hope, deliberately so or otherwise. It is true that although the discussion takes place in a gaol cell in the aftermath of an abortive insurrection, there is little that is clear in the reader's mind in the way of material events. What is said early on about these events as they strike the chief character, the poet-rebel Lavelle, extends to the novel's welter of ideas as they at first strike the reader: "Of the physical conflict in the arsenal the poet remembered little. It was blurred to the eye by excess of light." . . . However, it could only have escaped the most sheltered of readers that AE had re-created in his own peculiar way the Easter Rebellion. . . . The times are reproduced in detail—despite the poetic blur of AE's prose—down to the theosophical adventuring in which AE himself had been involved: "It was an era of arcane speculation, for science and philosophy had become esoteric after the visible universe had been ransacked and the secret of its being had eluded the thinkers." . . . And, thinking no doubt of 1916 and subsequent events in Ireland that so angered Yeats, AE has one of his characters remark: "You will find . . . that every great conflict has been followed by an era of materialism in which the ideals for which the conflict ostensibly was waged were submerged. The gain if any was material. The loss was spiritual." . . . The spiritual is AE's professed concern: "Those who take part in the symposium," he tells us in the Preface, "suppose of the universe that it is a spiritual being and they inquire what relation the politics of Time may have to the politics of Eternity." . . . Equally might it be said that the symposiasts inquire into the role of the self in the spiritual and political systems of the universe.

Since the speakers as well as the setting can be fairly readily identified, *The Interpreters* can be called a *roman à clef*. However, it is the ideas associated with or suggested to AE by the historical figures, and not the figures themselves (more than one of whom can in the novel inhabit the same fictional body), that are important. The plot too is mere scaffolding for the discussion. Lavelle's band of rebels commandeer a city arsenal, only to find that the unguarded gates were a trap. The band is captured and gaoled. During the night, other rebel-leaders are ushered into the gaol cell. Over the city, air-ships, "winged shapes of dusk and glitter," manoeuvre to quell the insurrection, and we recognize in them not only futuristic aeroplanes but also the extra-terrestrial winged beings that swarmed through AE's visions and paintings. Meanwhile the captives argue, each speaker being given by AE and the others the opportunity of outlining without interruption his philosophy.

For most of the novel, Lavelle is recognizable as Patrick Pearse. He holds a spiritual theory of nationality which according to the sceptic rebel, Leroy, would lead to theocracy if implemented. This theory Lavelle has derived from the history of his nation "which began among the gods"; and from history (really mythology) he turned to literature and thence politics and insurrection. The "unity of character" and "national culture" of his country are traceable, almost uniquely among nations, back to the divine origin of things and today are vested especially in the peasant. Beside his country and his race he professes to account himself of little importance, except as a self-sacrificial helper in the national cause: "He was one of those who suffer on behalf of their nation that agony which others feel over personal misfortunes." . . . (pp. 70-2)

At times Lavelle would seem to shade into Yeats. Like Yeats Lavelle believes that his country is unusual in not having to turn to other ancient cultures, such as those of the Greek and Jew, for its cosmogony, mythology and culture. For the inhabitants of most countries "distant lands are made sacred, but not the air they breathe"; Milton's "Heaven-world," for example, "is rootless and unreal and not very noble phantasy," . . . remarks that echo Yeats's sentiments and AE's own conviction that Christianity had robbed Ireland of a pantheon of native divinities and removed the sacred realm to an exotic afterlife from the earth underfoot where it resided in pagan times. The Revivalists considered themselves to be engaged in the task of repatriating Irish culture and spirituality after centuries of 'exile' and of being displaced by foreign faiths and systems. And like Yeats Lavelle is sadly aware of "how little high traditions move the people." . . . Certainly AE had Yeats rather than Pearse in mind when it is told how the work of one of the captives, an imaginative historian, "had been followed by creative writers like Lavelle, in whom the submerged river of nationality again welled up shining and life-giving." . . . Brehon the imaginative historian is of course Standish James O'Grady. (Brehon, Irish *breathamh:* an ancient Irish judge; Brehon law is the code of law which prevailed in Ireland before its occupation by the English. The ancient Irish connection between judge and bard is also implied in the name.) Lavelle has come to believe that "The heroic is the deep reality in you and all of us," as he tells a fellow captive, and is implanted and reawakened through "the ennobling influence of heroic story" and of "the dream of the ancestors" that Brehon first made available to the poet's generation. Brehon is in gaol because the authorities consider it better he be out of the way while the trouble continues (putting all the rebel luminaries together in one cell would seem to be an odd way of going about quelling the revolution), but, in fact, like O'Grady, "after his history had appeared, the historian seemed to take no interest in the great movement he had inspired. He became absorbed in more abstruse studies, the nature of which was known to but few among his countrymen." . . . Brehon's participation in the symposium is not only AE's salute to O'Grady, but also AE's reminder to the aloof historian that he bears some considerable responsibility for the events of 1916 and after.

As he is meant to do, the figure of Leroy blows a breeze of scepticism and cynicism through the proceedings. He is perhaps in part Oliver St John Gogarty, but because he is a "fantastical humorist", he may also be in part James Stephens, as Henry Summerfield suggests, and because an individualist, perhaps too John Eglinton (W. K. Magee). And being the greatest shape-changer in the novel, despite or because of his theory of individualism, he might also be in part James Joyce. Leroy has Joyce's self-possession, believing his vision to be as valid as the next man's, whatever institutional weight or theory of divinity lies behind the next man's, and he shares Joyce's parallactic and relativistic perspective. "You, if you dreamed," he tells Lavelle, "would see a vision so beautiful that you would imagine it was a vision of Paradise, but it would be no less of yourself than my fantasy." . . . Leroy has taken part in the revolution despite himself, and this reminds us of the

surprising militancy of Gogarty and Stephens, as well perhaps as of that residual patriotism that made Joyce fiercely and proudly Irish. In the aftermath of insurrection Leroy prefers reason to heroic passion and, Stephen Dedalus-like, considers it absurd to exchange the shackles of colonialism for the shackles of socialism or theocratic nationalism offered him by his fellow captives. . . . His belief in freedom sustains his cynicism; in a prediction fulfilled by the fate of Yeats's poetry if not O'Grady's history, he tells Lavelle: "Your poetry and Brehon's History will be favourite studies in imperial circles in a few years." . . . It also sustains an arrogance reminiscent of Stephen Dedalus': "You may think of me as a rebel angel . . . I am in revolt against Heaven." . . . Leroy is the only interpreter who believes in the unadorned and free-standing self, and he entertains the notion of dying in the insurrection so that in the moments before death all his ideas and feelings would return to him "and I could be my entire self if but for a few seconds," . . . a fate enjoyed symbolically and under different circumstances by Gabriel Conroy in Joyce's long story, "The Dead."

Very much in contrast to this hope, the somewhat sentimental socialist impulses of another captive, Culain, came into being when an old woman in the tenement where he was raised "wept a quarter of an hour or so before she died being unable to rise and give help to another. That self-forgetfulness when the self was passing from life seemed to me to be wonderful." . . . He elaborates: "Whatever makes us clutch at the personal, whatever strengthens the illusion of separateness, whether it be the possession of wealth, or power over the weak, or fear of the strong, all delay the awakening from this pitiful dream of life by fostering a false egoism," . . . an illusion shared outside the novel by O'Grady in his homage to strong heroes as well as by Culain's more evident opponents within the novel. Like Lavelle, Culain—James Connolly and Jim Larkin in thin disguise—believes in an Ancestral Self, but it is that of humanity and not just that of the individual race or nation. Culain is opposed to nationalism . . . , but makes common cause with Lavelle as Connolly made common cause with Pearse at Easter 1916. His name has been chosen well. Culain is of course the smith whose watchdog young Cuchulain, then called Setanta, kills and replaces (hence Cuchulain, the Hound of Culain). 'Smith' is a common name that sits well with Culain's socialism; a smith is also a manual worker of the kind championed by Culain (Connolly). Connolly had sympathy with the Gaelic Revival, and AE had a social, even socialistic interest in the old sagas, both of which make felicitous AE's use of the Cuchulain saga as a source for his socialist's name.

If Leroy is unique in his advocacy of self, Heyt is unique in his military imperialism. Heyt is "president of the Air Federation", whose airships now beleaguer the rebels (Heyt = height?), and has been arrested in error, conveniently for the symposium. In his anti-labour views and lofty arrogance (another kind of height), he conjures up the figure of William Martin Murphy, the industrial magnate and leader of the Employers' Federation against whom Larkin's strike during the Dublin lockout of 1913 was directed. Beyond Irish commercialism, Heyt is enlarged into British imperial power and the bureaucracy and centralization AE railed against in his essay, **"Ideals of the New Rural Society."** And this is not all. Heyt's ideal society is the world state which "will absorb its romantics," like Lavelle, Culain and Brehon, "and transmute emotion into wisdom." . . . Whereas Leroy is for variety among individuals and Lavelle for variety among nations, Heyt is for total uniformity, and human evolution he sees as "the eternal revealing of the Self to the selves.'' . . . In what seems to be a contradiction, Heyt upbraids Leroy for nourishing ''a fantastic conception of freedom'' while, according to Heyt, every cell of the sceptic's body and every atom of nature stirs with impulses beyond Leroy's control, but then defines the will as power, as the self, ''the king principle in our being.'' But the paradox is resolved: ''The will,'' says Heyt, ''grows stronger by self-suppression than in self-assertion.'' That the figure of Heyt does not prove an anomaly or imbalance in AE's symposium is due to the fact that where power and self-denial are concerned, Heyt speaks language Culain and Lavelle can readily understand. Indeed, AE himself believed that we must cultivate power and an unshakeable will if we are to scale the Heavens, but that we must do so by purifying our being into selflessness so that the energy of the awakening power be not misdirected. Heyt, on the other hand, cultivates power and will for unspiritual ends and suppresses others rather than suppressing himself. He threatens to take Paradise by storm. Heyt, however, belongs philosophically and even spiritually in AE's world by being an object of that ''inverted love that is hate'' and a ''perverted hindrance that is truly helpful,'' an enemy who like many enemies can be ''dearer to you than ever your friend can be.'' These are notions attributed to AE by James Stephens in a reminiscence, and in a sequel reminiscence Stephens recalled a belief of AE's that would suggest that a vigorous symposium like *The Interpreters* was a literary form especially congenial to AE: ''It was his belief that we travel through life and time with our own company of friends and enemies. That there is a small clan of personages, and that this is the real family. The wives, husbands and children of such a person are almost unimportant, almost accidental.'' (pp. 72-6)

A virtual handbook of attitudes in Revival Ireland, *The Interpreters* is, just as absorbingly, AE's philosophical autobiography, and as such more interesting in form than most autobiographies. For in the independent theories we can trace to real holders, AE contrived to reflect the various facets of his own complexity. It is not merely that since AE creates (even while borrowing) the diverse characters in *The Interpreters* then he must *be* all those characters, as Shakespeare must in a sense be the veriest villain he portrays: it is that AE in a very sincere fashion shared many of the attitudes of the fictional symposiasts with their real-life models. There is a good deal of AE in Leroy's shifting viewpoints, as well as in Leroy's championing of ''the freedom of the local community,'' . . . and in Leroy's intellectual remove, a version of which enables AE to re-create, rather fairly, contradictory, occasionally distasteful ideas. Culain's socialism is a heightened and urban equivalent of AE's involvement with the rural co-operative movement, while Culain's contempt for separateness and egotism accords with AE's blueprint for the ideal rural society: ''The first thing to do,'' he asserted, ''is to create and realize the feeling for the community, and break up the evil and petty isolation of man from man.'' Too, AE supported the Dublin strike of 1913 and spoke on behalf of it at a rally in the Albert Hall, London. And in Rian the architect we see something of AE the painter. The relationship with Brehon and Lavelle is more complex. Towards the end of the symposium Brehon, perhaps in his judicial role, is given thirty pages in which to sum up his philosophy, and in so doing he ceases to be O'Grady and becomes AE. He labours to harmonize the divergent views he has listened to, and delivers himself of the judgment that only Leroy, the self-sufficing and anarchic man asserting absolute kingship over his own being, is on the true path since only anarchy correctly founded guarantees justice not only for the individual but for

congregations of men, including nations. . . . Yet Leroy will not attain his full stature until he comprehends ''the spiritual foundations on which other political theories rest, and can build on them as do the devotees of beauty or love or power.'' . . . Once the spiritual ideal was a widespread reality during a Golden Age (O'Grady's Heroic Period, presumably) before it gave way to ''the terrible and material powers ruling in the Iron Age,'' . . . by which Lavelle seems to mean the 'Anglo-Saxon' age of industry and the megalopolis. Now it is simply that, an ideal, but it must not on pain of loss be striven for or defended by material means such as those employed by the insurrectionists. The goal is psychic evolution towards self-fulfilment that sheds interest in the politics of time and awakens and attracts spiritual powers and elements akin to our expanding consciousness.

Although Lavelle earlier protested that ''all distinctions of nationality seem to dissipate in a haze in this transcendentalism,'' . . . he is finally converted to Brehon's position. Before the guards come to release Heyt whose side will be the probable winner of the material battle raging outside, Lavelle stands in Brehonic contemplation: ''Everything was understood. Everything was loved. Everything was forgiven. He knew after that exaltation he could never be the same again. Never could he be fierce or passionate.'' . . . The exaltation has caused him to add to a poem he had written before the rising and believed finished a final section in the light of Brehon's transcendentalism. What is interesting is that the poem, **''Michael''**, a curious piece of over four hundred lines in four-beat couplets with stylistic elements from Wordsworth, Yeats and Pearse and which has the same kind of importance for *The Interpreters* as has Stephen's villanelle for *A Portrait of the Artist as a Young Man*, is a verse *immram* (or voyage tale) and *fís* (or vision tale). It is, according to Lavelle, ''the last poem in a Book of Voyages wherein I, like the poets of our country before me, tell of journeyings to the Land of Immortal Youth.'' . . . He might well be thinking of that account of a journey to Tirna-nOg written centuries before: Yeats' *The Wanderings of Oisin* (1889), part of which was also cast in four-beat lines. Lavelle's title hero lives in the west of Ireland in a cabin where old tales and legends are told, and embarks on a visionary voyage that closely resembles the voyages in *Immram Brain (The Voyage of Bran)* and *Immram Maíle Dúin (The Voyage of Maelduin)*, both Medieval tales. The journey amidst glimmering isles and cloudy seas filled with mythic forms is a spiritual pilgrimage on which Michael is vouchsafed a momentary sight of paradise. Since phrases from the journey echo phrases from the beginning of *The Interpreters* describing Lavelle's journey to the city, 'Immram Michael' in a sense repeats Lavelle's own spiritual journey in the course of the symposium towards the momentary and exalting vision of the spiritual destination and ideal provided by Brehon. . . . The poem is a clever use of the ancient *immram* and *fís* as a mould into which the content of Pearse's career is poured. But now, having heard Brehon (AE), Lavelle adds a harmonic new ending in which the slayer and the slain are pictured united and the be-all and end-all of life are seen as one spirituality ''To which all life is journeying.'' In short, Lavelle becomes AE, that most myriad-minded and peacemaking of the Revivalists. Having shattered himself into the fragments of his diverse activities and beliefs, fleshed out as simulacra of real people, AE re-composes himself into a harmonic self-conception. It is as if in writing *The Interpreters* AE had kept in mind what Yeats wrote to him in 1898: ''You are face to face with the heterogeneous, and the test of one's harmony is our power to absorb it and make it harmonious.'' (pp. 76-80)

The Interpreters is not really a novel, as AE in his Preface admits. "I was not interested in the creation of characters but in tracking political moods back to spiritual origins." To do this he uses the symposium which seems an appropriate form for the democratic side of AE, but Northrop Frye might remind us of other appeals it made to AE the Revivalist writer when he remarks that "Most of the Renaissance humanists show a strong sense of the importance of symposium and dialogue, the social and educational aspects respectively of an elite culture." It is AE who comes closest of all the Revivalists to recalling for us, through an encyclopedic interest and refined concern for humanity, the ethos of Renaissance humanism. For the form to accommodate AE's other side, the transcendentalist, was not so difficult, given the association of the symposium with Plato, but it did require him to draw the characters into the unanimity of one dominant voice, AE's, which, though it might be autobiographically satisfying, sacrificed, especially in the case of Brehon who changes shamelessly from O'Grady into the author, any autonomy of character; it also sacrifices AE's humanism on the altar of AE's mysticism. *The Interpreters* at the end and upon a second reading becomes less a symposium than a transformation and imitation of the pre-humanist *immram*. It is a spiritual and philosophical journey in which, until Brehon's high nonsensical words and Lavelle's exaltation upon hearing them, various philosophical positions on the map of intellect take the role of place in the spiritual landscape of the Old Irish *immrama*. *The Interpreters* is a voyage-tale where ideas, not places are visited, but one that ends in a vision whose resemblance to the *físi* is more literal. In that vision, contraries are harmonized in "that multitudinous meditation which is the universe." (pp. 80-1)

> John Wilson Foster, "'The Interpreters': A Handbook to A.E. and the Irish Revival," in Ariel *(copyright © 1980 The Board of Governors The University of Calgary), Vol. 11, No. 3, July, 1980, pp. 69-82.*

WAYNE E. HALL   (essay date 1980)

[*Hall examines A.E.'s earliest poetry,* Homeward: Songs by the Way *and* The Earth Breath and Other Poems, *concluding that A.E.'s varied interests did not "allow him time to develop his poetry beyond its crude beginnings"; that instead he "gave his energies to others rather than to his work."*]

[In both *Homeward: Songs by the Way* and *The Earth Breath and Other Poems*] a general, inconsistent progression emerges within the separate volumes. The earlier collection, by example, begins with the **"Prelude,"** a caution against the visionary losing sight of the divine because of the attractions of the "sun-rich day"; by the final poem, however, real and ideal have merged into a stable union, the divine made manifest in common things. As in *The Earth Breath,* this movement from pure vision to inclusion of the real world passes through poems of pain in which the narrator is separated both from his vision and from other people. Yet the awareness of pain and suffering rarely becomes more explicit than as a loss of vision and a separation from the divine. In recording what he regarded as his most intense experiences, therefore, his ecstatic visions, Russell produced his most notable work.

The most successful poems of vision in *Homeward* are **"By the Margin of the Great Deep," "The Great Breath,"** . . . and the sequence **"Dusk," "Night," "Dawn,"** and **"Day".** . . . The first of these begins in sunset, the typical occasion for Russell's poetic visions, and the spirit of unity running through all of nature and humankind brings him feelings of "peace and sleep and dreams." Yet the vision, at this early part of the volume, also draws him apart from domestic life and even human contact in his longings for the "primeval being." Sunset likewise introduces **"The Great Breath,"** the fading sky suggesting both a cosmic flower and an awareness that the death of beauty occasions its most complete fulfillment. This unstable insight, like the paradox of spiritual union through physical separation in the above poem, becomes more nearly resolved in the four-poem sequence. Instead of sunset, the mingling of chimney fires from a village signifies the merging of humanity within "the vast of God." Night, for Russell, usually brings on despair and loss of vision, as in **"The Dawn of Darkness"** . . . ; in **"Waiting"** . . . he can only hope that dawn will shake off this sadness and reawaken humanity to its former joy. The above sequence reverses this process, however. **"Night"** brings on a rebirth of spirit and beauty, a complete union of "living souls," while **"Dawn"** begins to fragment the unity. In the light of common day, vision is lost but not entirely forgotten, for a dim awareness of "a thread divine" keeps humankind still yearning for the "dim heights" and recalling, in dream, the "Light of Lights." This last phrase, echoing *The Countess Cathleen,* or the "hair of the twilight" (**"Mystery"** . . .) that shields the visionary in ways similar to *The Wind Among the Reeds,* or the characteristic combination of "sad and gay" feelings (**"Inheritance"** . . .)—all these directly link Russell's work with Yeats's.

The range of vision that Russell sketches out in the above sequence and the unity of the four poems succeed far better than his attempts elsewhere to link mortal pain with immortal vision. **"Self-Discipline"** . . . argues the necessity of realizing "our lofty doom" through a combination of the world's pain with the beauty of the divine. The Christ figure of **"To One Consecrated"** . . . draws wisdom from the "Mighty Mother" along with a "crown of thorns." To have a human spirit is to know sorrow, Russell argues, and to be burdened by the world, for that is the path to wisdom. No one would argue the point; the difficulty lies in Russell's failure to integrate one into the other beyond the level of unconvincing abstraction. The intense feelings he brings to the poems of vision here disperse into assertion ("I have made a god of Pain" . . .) or hollow comfort ("[O]nly / Gods could feel such pain" . . .). (pp. 146-48)

More successful are the poems that simply present occasions of sorrow. **"Pity"** . . . oppresses the visionary with the sight of the "monstrous fabric of the town," its "cries of pain" drifting up from dimly lighted streets. A poem from *The Earth Breath,* **"The Dark Age,"** presents a similar scene with more precise details of the city as dirty, cold, metallic, and impersonal: "[T]he iron time / Manacles us in night." These two poems are separated in time by Russell's discovery of the Irish legends and his more historical awareness of the Irish present. At first a personal hell from which he longed to escape through vision, the city came to represent a historical period imprisoning all of humanity. He wrote of his own feelings of "despair in the Iron Age;" but believing it to be an Age and hence subject to time and change, he could envision a Golden Age as well, history transformed for an entire people. (p. 148)

Human love in the *Homeward* poems also fails to overcome the pain of the world or the loss of vision. Beauty, as with Yeats, is sometimes identified with the timeless woman of romance, a similarity of vision Russell makes more explicit in *The Candle of Vision:* "The beauty for which men perished is still shining; Helen is there in her Troy, and Deirdre wears the beauty which blasted the Red Branch." Yeats's poems, however, despair of winning Maud Gonne, whereas Russell here regards the entire principle of human love as a diversion from the divine. In **"Divided"** . . . , the two, as children, "were not apart" but united in their common awareness of the spirit of "ancient magic." Now adults, they have come to love and thus come to lose this spiritual unity: "We know no more of the superhuman: / I am a man and you are a woman." Their kisses, in **"Echoes"** . . . , seem but an "echo of a deeper being." The woman's palpable sexual presence in **"Parting"** . . . is apparent only after their vision has "died away"; she becomes a mere part of "the outer things," separating him from the "Mother's heart." As in **"Warning"** . . . , Russell sees no "middle way" for love to follow. If the two fail to unite their spirits in vision, then they face, as physical lovers, only "sadness and decay." One of the most striking poems on this theme, **"The Symbol Seduces"** . . . , creates the image of the poet rushing headlong from the lures of a prostitute, all the while exclaiming how "the great life calls." The "symbol of the world's desire" would seduce him with her wiles and bind his soul to earth. Suddenly, "The robe of Beauty falls away," a vision, Russell claims, although he doesn't hang around to watch. (pp. 148-49)

"The Veils of Maya" . . . deals with an idea similar to **"The Symbol Seduces"** but without the unintended humor. Maya represents the illusion of beauty, the "lesser glow" of life that, if accepted, separates the visionary from the divine. The poem immediately following, **"Symbolism"** . . . , abruptly reverses the poet's flight from earth. The imagery turns to rural, domestic scenes, the lighted cottage to which the laborer returns, the "loved earth things" that have a new symbolic function. No longer "delusion," they acquire a "seal celestial" and lead him to love in its complete, spiritual form. **"The Secret"** . . . , the final poem in the collection, makes a similar claim. He learns to see "the mystic vision" in all of nature and humanity, and the "dream of life" finally merges with his "own dreams." As an ending to *Homeward,* the sentiments are admirable but not entirely convincing, confined to but two poems, neither of them written out of the imaginary power Russell invests in the accounts of his visions. *The Earth Breath* will deal more fully with the belief that common things also manifest the divine; *Homeward* has not yet reached that goal. (p. 149)

[The] limitations of *Homeward* are immediately apparent. Russell's metrical effects are too mechanical, his rhymes too predictable, his diction too conventional and artificial, his ideas too vague, his range of themes too narrow, his voice either too breathless or too philosophically preachy. There are good poems here, but many are deeply flawed by a naivete of vocabulary. Clouds become ["veils of pearly fleece," the moon a "wizard glow" or a "pale primrose," the wind "tremulous lips of air," the stars "the tiny planet folk"]. . . . Even more serious is the paucity of clear images around which Russell's spiritual concepts might conceivably take shape. The village scene in **"Dusk,"** with the chimney smoke "like a thin grey rod, / Mounting aloft through miles of quietness," is a rare success, one the reader fastens onto with something akin to desperation. Another good effect: "O'er the waters creeping the pearl dust of the eve / Hides the silver of the long wave rippling through." . . . The opening phrase, its participle delayed, further delays the subject and the final movement of the water. The word order re-enacts the natural process, motion that is present but barely perceptible, becoming suspended in time. (pp. 149-50)

What *Homeward* lacks . . . is a consciousness sufficiently vivid and rich to communicate itself as clearly as impressions from without. The work remains too intent on serving the purposes of soul and neglects the purposes of poetry.

The Earth Breath, although it suffers from many of the same problems that dog *Homeward,* represents a significant advance in Russell's poetic range. The poems are generally longer, including several extended pieces, and they rely much more on a clearer imagery as Russell expands his earlier idea of the divine made manifest in the world around him. A new, more specifically Irish note also runs through many of the works, extending from an identification of personal vision with Irish legend to poems celebrating an awakening national spirit. One of the first of Russell's Irish poems, **"The Dream of the Children"** . . . , recounts a visionary journey into faeryland on a haunted hillside. The faeries offer the children the kind of world that is so alluring in works like Yeats's *The Land of Heart's Desire:* "And this was a cure for sadness, / And that the ease of desire." Identified with Ireland, the faeries differ from Yeats's in that nothing about them suggests evil or danger. As in **"Song,"** . . . their call promises a "land more fair" with none of the attendant threats to mortals.

Russell's best poems in *The Earth Breath* remain those like **"A Vision of Beauty,"** . . . a classic poem of vision in its broadest sense. Dawn again provides the cosmic backdrop to the ecstasy in which all of time and space unites within "the mystic heart of beauty." Russell's vision of the whole simultaneously allows him attention to the particulars of nature, as in the striking sense of winds being shaken loose from the forest leaves. The long, fifteen-foot lines with their heavy trochaic meter and the long sentences that blur subjects and verbs all combine in an appropriate obliteration of outlines. The **"Alter Ego",** . . . Russell explains, is the spiritual part of him that leads him into the timeless, joyous, visionary world of the faeries. **"The Fountain of Shadowy Beauty"** . . . reveals more about this spirit. He is a "Brother-Self," a "Dream Bird," godlike in his eternal youth, the Pilot who leads the poet on an elaborate boat journey suggesting Yeats's *The Shadowy Waters.* (pp. 150-51)

Russell is on somewhat firmer poetic ground in writing about the Mother, the spirit of the earth in contrast to the universal spirit represented by the Father. **"The Earth Breath"** . . . is a hymn to the force permeating all of nature, transforming the world and those who perceive that transformation into a visionary divinity. In poems like this one, [**"A New World,"** **"Brotherhood,"** **"The Seer,"** or **"In the Womb"**]. . . . Russell more effectively develops the ideas only beginning to take shape at the close of *Homeward.* Nature becomes "dense with revelation," . . . and divinity emerges beneath the surface of common humanity rather than in far-off worlds. The visionary suffers his inevitable return to "the human / Vestiture of pain," yet he retains the memory of what lies beyond the veil. The **"Star Teachers,"** . . . symbolizing the divine, inspire him to find the "God-root within men."

The inspiration did not always work for Russell. He wrote to Yeats that he thought "sadly" of *The Earth Breath;* "It is too melancholy." Poems like **"Tragedy"** . . . come to mind, with their ironic pain at humanity's separation from the gods. The human subject of the poem, not unlike a clerk at the end of a "long day's toil," draws from the stars only the knowledge of his exile from past glory: "He turned him homeward sick and slow." The speaker in **"Weariness"** . . . similarly mourns the absence of vision, the "petty tasks" that imprison him within time. **"Blindness"** . . . expands Russell's sense of suffering to include the inadequacy of human love, a theme that has changed little from its *Homeward* treatment. The lovers meet only in pain, their longing and loneliness unremedied because of their visionary need for a higher life that cannot be satisfied by human love.

The Earth Breath is dedicated to Yeats, and the opening **"Prelude"** . . . captures a distinctly Yeatsian style and diction. Instead of "quietness and ease and peace," the poet proposes to give to his "beloved" what he has learned from pain and sorrow. The growing internal conflict in Russell's feelings about Violet North here transforms the beloved in ways similar to *The Wind Among the Reeds.* As in [**"A Woman's Voice,"** **"Heroic Love,"** or **"Illusion,"**] . . . the realization of love can only come about through vision, through an obliteration of the actual beloved in a unity with the more attractive ideal. North, as deeply committed to theosophy as Russell, was not dismayed by these notions. He had written in **"Dream Love"** . . . : "I shall not on thy beauty rest, / But Beauty's ray in you." But he had also written **"Love"** . . . , which expresses the hope that he may not entirely lose himself in vision, that he may always return from his experience of the divine back to that of the human. This idea, only suggested in *Homeward,* becomes a much stronger integral part of *The Earth Breath.* **"Duality"** . . . asserts the need to unite pain with glory, peace with strife, the divine with the human. **"The Tide of Sorrow"** . . . likewise asks for acceptance of the passage of pain. Through that knowledge alone may life and death become as one and dark unite with light. The poem closes, however, by wondering what voice exists "for the world of men" before such universal harmony can be achieved.

Russell answers that question with his new theme of the messianic seer, a theme derived from his belief that Ireland was about to awaken into a new spiritual age, one free of the old confines of Church and England and inspired by the ancient Celtic past. [**"The Hour of the King"** and **"A Leader"**] . . . both suggest that a spiritual leader will arise, and **"The Message of John"** . . . explores this idea more fully. St. John, one of those seers who "arise as Gods from men," prepares the way for God's revelation to the world. Inspired by his vision, he knows the elemental unity of this world with the divine, its origins in a universal spirit that will again become manifest. The poem offers an interpretation of St. John, 1:1-33, but Russell's opening trinity of the Mother, the Father, and the Wise makes clear that the poem is far outside traditional Christianity. (pp. 151-53)

[Russell's poems, which] Yeats termed in 1898 "perhaps the most beautiful and delicate that any Irishman of our time has written," retreat finally from the conflict of matter with spirit. Relying too much on vision to do the work of intellect, on the spirit within to replace the world without, they fail adequately to communicate that spirit or to transform the world. Russell's deeply personal qualities resisted dramatic expression, and he gave his energies to others rather than to his work. His vision remains religious without ever becoming, as he wanted, a religion, one that could free the Irish to become as gods as it did free George Russell to become A.E. (p. 154)

> *Wayne E. Hall, "George Russell," in his* Shadowy Heroes: Irish Literature of the 1890s *(copyright © 1980 by Syracuse University Press), Syracuse University Press, 1980, pp. 141-54.*

ADDITIONAL BIBLIOGRAPHY

Bose, Abinash Chandra. "A.E. (George William Russell)." In his *Three Mystic Poets: A Study of W. B. Yeats, A.E. and Rabindranath Tagore,* pp. 47-102. Folcroft, Pa.: Folcroft Press, 1970.
    Examination of the mystical aspects of A.E. and his poetry. Bose refers to A.E. as "one of the greatest modern mystic poets."

Boyd, Ernest. "The Dublin Mystics: The Theosophical Movement, George W. Russell (A.E.), John Eglington." In his *Ireland's Literary Renaissance,* pp. 212-52. New York: Barnes & Noble, 1968.*
    Insightful account of the philosophical development of the Irish Literary Revival and a critical survey of A.E.'s early work.

Canby, Henry Seidel. "Deepness of Earth." In his *American Estimates,* pp. 29-31. 1929. Reprint. Port Washington, N.Y.: Kennikat Press, 1968.
    Relates the impression A.E. made on audiences during his lecture tour in America.

Denson, Alan. *Printed Writings by George W. Russell (AE): A Bibliography with Some Notes on His Pictures and Portraits.* Evanston, Ill.: Northwestern University Press, 1961, 255 p.
    Thorough bibliography with interesting notes on A.E.'s paintings.

Eglinton, John. *A Memoir of AE: George William Russell.* London: Macmillan, 1937, 290 p.
    A detailed biography.

Gogarty, Oliver St. John. "An Angelic Anarchist." *Colby Library Quarterly* IV, No. 2 (May 1955): 24-8.
    A tribute to A.E. and the varied facets of his personality. This issue of the *Colby Library Quarterly* is devoted entirely to A.E.

Kain, Richard M. and O'Brien, James H. *George Russell (A.E.).* Lewisburg, Pa.: Bucknell University Press, 1976, 93 p.
    Contains a short biography and consideration of A.E.'s poetry and theosophy.

McFate, Patricia Ann. "AE's Portraits of the Artists: A Study of *The Avatars.*" *Eire-Ireland* VI, No. 4 (Winter 1971): 38-48.
    An interpretation of *The Avatars* which delineates the models for A.E.'s characters.

Moore, George. "Ave." In his *Hail and Farewell: Ave, Salve, Vale,* annotated ed., edited by Richard Cave, pp. 128-44. Toronto: Macmillan, 1976.*
    Moore's impression of A.E. and other writers of the Irish Literary Revival. Incidents and thoughts of Moore's daily life are also retold.

Phelps, William Lyon. "AE." In his *Autobiography with Letters,* pp. 828-35. New York: Oxford University Press, 1939.
    Fond reminiscence of A.E. Phelps recounts his pleasure in presenting A.E. with an honorary degree in literature from Yale.

Russell, Diarmuid. "'AE' (George William Russell)." *The Atlantic Monthly* 171, No. 2 (February 1943): 51-7.
    A son's remembrance of his multi-talented father.

Shepard, Leslie. Introduction to *The Candle of Vision,* by A.E., pp. vi-xi. Wheaton, Ill.: The Theosophical Publishing House, 1974.
    Acclaims *The Candle of Vision* as a revealing book. Shepard states: "This book is an essential key, not only to Russell, but also to the mystic life itself, which is the inheritance of everyone."

Summerfield, Henry. *That Myriad-Minded Man: A Biography of George William Russell "A.E." 1867-1935.* Totowa, N.J.: Rowan and Littlefield, 1975, 354 p.
    Considered the definitive biography of A.E.

Sherwood Anderson

1876-1941

(Also wrote under pseudonym of Buck Fever) American short story writer, novelist, autobiographer, essayist, editor, poet, critic, and dramatist.

Anderson was one of the most original and influential early twentieth-century American writers. A writer of brooding, introspective works, he was among the first American authors to explore the effects of the unconscious upon human life. Anderson's ''hunger to see beneath the surface of lives'' was best expressed in the collection of bittersweet short stories which form the classic *Winesburg, Ohio: A Group of Tales of Ohio Small Town Life*. This, his most important book, exhibits the author's characteristically simple, unornamented prose style and his personal vision, which combined a sense of wonder at the potential beauty of life with despair over its tragic aspects. Anderson's style and outlook were influential in shaping the writings of Ernest Hemingway, William Faulkner, Thomas Wolfe, John Steinbeck, and many other American authors.

The post-Civil War Midwest of Anderson's childhood and youth was a land in the midst of transitions that deeply affected the author's life and works. Industrialization and the rise of organized labor made obsolete the work of many skilled artisans and brought into serious question the optimistic American work ethic. Born in the small town of Camden, Ohio, Anderson was the son of an out-of-work harnessmaker and a washerwoman. He was raised in Clyde, Ohio (which later served as the model for Winesburg), where he grew to hate the irresponsible loafing and drinking of his father and the self-sacrificing drudgery to which his mother was reduced. His father, a Civil War veteran and an adept yarn-spinner, greatly influenced Anderson's own storytelling abilities. Through his readings—notably Walt Whitman's verse—and through listening to his father's tales, Anderson came to believe that, due to the destructive effects of the Gilded Age, America was in the twilight of an era of independent, wise, and fulfilled agrarian folk. Attending school infrequently, Anderson took a number of temporary jobs to help his impoverished, migrant family; he worked as a newsboy, a housepainter, a field worker, and a stablehand, gaining experiences which later provided subject matter for his fiction. After a stint in the U.S. Army during the Spanish-American War, he married, became an advertising copywriter in Chicago, then managed his own paint factory: the Anderson Manufacturing Company of Elyria, Ohio. Despite his commercial success, Anderson considered himself ''a mere peddler of words'' who, by writing advertising copy, trivialized his literary skills for commercial gain. To satisfy himself, he spent his spare time writing fiction.

Overworked and beset by various worries, Anderson suffered a mental breakdown in late 1912; he suddenly walked out of his office, to be discovered four days later and many miles away, incoherent and amnesiac. Shortly thereafter, following the failure of his business and his marriage, Anderson returned to Chicago, where he met such writers of the ''Chicago Renaissance'' as Floyd Dell, Carl Sandburg, and Theodore Dreiser, who read his early fiction and encouraged him in his literary work. Anderson's first published short stories appeared in the pages of *The Little Review, The Seven Arts,* and other ''little''

magazines. His first novel, the partly autobiographical *Windy McPherson's Son,* was published in 1916 to moderate critical acclaim. Three years later, *Winesburg, Ohio* brought Anderson international recognition as an important new voice in American literature. ''Here is the goal that [Edgar Lee Masters's] *The Spoon River Anthology* aimed at, and missed by half a mile,'' wrote H. L. Mencken. The ''goal'' which Anderson achieved was a fusion of simply-stated fiction and complex psychological analysis that revealed the essential loneliness and beauty of Midwestern town life. The results, in the case of *Winesburg, Ohio* and many of Anderson's later works, were disturbingly insightful yet compassionate studies of human life.

Acknowledged as an authentic voice of the American Midwest, Anderson befriended many aspiring writers during the 1920s. He was largely responsible for arranging the publication of Faulkner's first novel, *Soldier's Pay,* and for influencing the simple style of Hemingway's early Nick Adams stories. Anderson's own thought was shaped during the 1920s by the works of D. H. Lawrence; in such novels as *Many Marriages* and *Dark Laughter,* he attempted to develop the English author's beliefs concerning the psychologically crippling effects of sexual repression. In *Dark Laughter,* Anderson's most popular novel, amoral sexual experience is presented as a means for the protagonists to escape the mores of modern society and return to a more natural existence. Continuing to explore the psychological undercurrents of life in industrial America, Anderson wrote some of his strongest works in the 1920s. In addition to *Dark Laughter,* he published what is considered his best novel, *Poor White,* which forms an attack on the dehumanizing effects of mass production; the acclaimed short stories collected in *The Triumph of the Egg* and *Horses and Men;* and two partly fictional autobiographies, *A Story Teller's Story* and *Tar: A Midwest Childhood.* In 1927, Anderson settled in the town of Marion, Virginia, where he bought, edited, and wrote for two weekly newspapers. He spent much of the rest of his life in rural southwestern Virginia, occasionally publishing collections of his newspaper columns and essays on American life. He leaned toward socialism during the Great Depression, but eventually concluded that the work of the artist and that of the reformer were incompatible. He wrote little during the late 1930s, declaring that writing was a dead art in America, and that the future for artistic achievement lay in motion pictures. While on a cruise to South America in 1941, Anderson died of peritonitis.

When asked by the editor of *The Bookman* to define his vision of life, Anderson referred to a story from *Winesburg, Ohio* titled "Paper Pills." The story tells of Doctor Reefy, who spent most of his life driving about the Ohio countryside in his horse-drawn buggy. "Hours of quiet as he drove through the country—long empty stretches of road passed over slowly. Thoughts came to him. He wrote the thoughts out on bits of paper and put them in his pocket." The truths he conceives overwhelm Doctor Reefy's mind for a short time after their discovery, but eventually they are consigned to paper and drift to the bottom of his pocket, where they form round, hard balls. Soon, the paper pills and the thoughts written therein are fit only to be dismissed with deprecating laughter and thrown away. "If you cannot find what philosophy of life I have in that story," concluded Anderson, "I am unable to give it to you." Anderson's folksy, poignant tone and sense of wonder at the beauties of rural life lend a compelling quality to his works, a quality which many critics feel tempers his nihilistic outlook. Critics agree that it was in his short stories that Anderson was most successful in conveying his impressions of life. In addition to "Hands," "The Untold Lie," and "Sophistication" from *Winesburg, Ohio,* the stories "The Egg," "Death in the Woods," "I'm a Fool," "The Man Who Became a Woman," and "I Want to Know Why" are considered to be among his best short tales and among the best works of American short fiction. Utilizing as they do Anderson's innovative form, which Mencken described as "half tale and half psychological anatomizing," these stories capture the essence of lives divided by insensitivity, convention, circumstance, and personal weakness, and which are joined but briefly by love, sympathy, and shared moments of spiritual epiphany. Anderson evoked a haunting, nearly mystical quality in the portraits of his characters, who lead their lives of "quiet desperation" and then disappear, forgotten, "into the darkness of the fields." "In Anderson, when all is said and done," wrote Henry Miller, "it is the strong human quality which draws one to him and leads one to prefer him sometimes to those who are undeniably superior to him as artists."

Scholars of Anderson's work have found the author to be a much more complex writer than his seemingly accessible stories reveal. He has long been called a leader in American literature's "revolt from the village." But although Anderson examined in his fiction the troubled, darker aspects of provincial life, he saw the small town as an admirable feature of American life, and attacked Sinclair Lewis for his satirical novels that exaggerated village vulgarity. Conservative reviewers of Anderson's works called the author "Sherwood Lawrence" and tended to portray him as a writer obsessed with sex, although the next generation of American writers made his treatment of the theme seem tame. Some critics and readers who had early enjoyed Anderson's books found them in later years to be stylistically and thematically juvenile and repetitive: after several years of friendship, Hemingway spoofed *Dark Laughter* in his Andersonesque parody *The Torrents of Spring,* Faulkner caricatured his former friend in the novel *Mosquitoes,* and Thomas Wolfe claimed that Anderson had written himself out early in his career and was "finished" as a writer. During the last decade of Anderson's life, T. S. Matthews spoke for many critics when he wrote that he was "so used to Anderson now, to his puzzled confidences, his groping repetitions, his occasional stumblings into real inspiration that perhaps we tend to underrate him as an American phenomenon. Or perhaps we no longer overrate him." For his simple, impressionistic style and his frequent acknowledgement that he was puzzled by life's basic questions—an unfashionable admission to make during the intellectually self-assured Jazz Age and the politically opinionated climate of the Great Depression—Anderson has often been dismissed as a primitive minor talent who was of more value as a literary catalyst than as an artist in his own right. But the continued popularity of his works has led critics to reexamine them more closely, and Anderson has regained recognition as an important American author. Perhaps Faulkner best summed up Anderson's current status when he said, "He was the father of my generation of American writers and the tradition of American writing which our successors will carry on. He has never received his proper evaluation."

(See also *TCLC,* Vol. 1; *Contemporary Authors,* Vol. 104; *Dictionary of Literary Biography,* Vol. 4: *American Writers in Paris, 1920-1939;* Vol. 9: *American Novelists, 1910-1945;* and *Dictionary of Literary Biography Documentary Series,* Vol. 1.)

PRINCIPAL WORKS

Windy McPherson's Son   (novel)   1916
Marching Men   (novel)   1917
Mid-American Chants   (poetry)   1918
*Winesburg, Ohio: A Group of Tales of Ohio Small Town
    Life*   (short stories)   1919
Poor White   (novel)   1920
*The Triumph of the Egg: A Book of Impressions from
    American Life in Tales and Poems*   (short stories and
    poetry)   1921
Horses and Men   (short stories)   1923
Many Marriages   (novel)   1923
*A Story Teller's Story: The Tale of an American Writer's
    Journey through His Own Imaginative World and
    through the World of Facts, with Many of His
    Experiences and Impressions among Other Writers*
    (autobiography)   1924
Dark Laughter   (novel)   1925
The Modern Writer   (essays)   1925
Sherwood Anderson's Notebook   (sketches)   1926
Tar: A Midwest Childhood   (autobiography)   1926
A New Testament   (poetry)   1927
Beyond Desire   (novel)   1932
Death in the Woods and Other Stories   (short stories)
    1933

WILLIAM LYON PHELPS   (essay date 1916)

[*Phelps reveals his mixed reaction to* Windy McPherson's Son *in this early review.*]

["**Windy McPherson's Son**"] has a certain raw vitality . . . , but its crudity jars. One longs for less matter, with more art. Not a single person in this book seems real to me, and the reason is just the opposite from the common one. Most characters in works of fiction are unreal because their outlines are faint, vague, confused; the author has never realized them himself. Here each person is stressed with such force, the color laid on with such daubing profusion, that each man and woman is to me a caricature. They represent the *reductio ad absurdum* of certain traits and tendencies. Nor is there any architectural skill displayed. Like so many "life" novels of the twentieth century, there is a plentiful supply of incidents without any plot. The hero is a little newsboy when we see him first, and well on in years, with a recrudescent paunch, when we see him last—the story progresses in time, but not in art. The last third of the book is picaresque. The hero takes to the road, and passes through a series of indiscriminate adventures, which might have taken twenty, or twenty thousand pages, instead of the hundred arbitrarily allotted by the author. Yet although I cannot admire this book as an achievement, I think its failure contains the seeds of success. It is more promising than many novels which surpass it in dignity. The conglomeration of incident and the exaggeration of human characteristics display an abundant vitality and a high aim. The author has done his level best to write the great American novel, to represent unsparingly what he believes to be the truth. Some day his decided natural gifts will ripen; he will not only see things in their proportion, he will be able to draw them according to scale; and he will read many pages of this work with a smile. (pp. 196-97)

> William Lyon Phelps, "*Three Not of a Kind,*" in The Dial *(copyright, 1916, by The Dial Publishing Company, Inc.), Vol. LXI, No. 725, September 21, 1916, pp. 196-97.**

SHERWOOD ANDERSON   (essay date 1917)

[*Anderson reveals his theory of style in the insightful essay* "An Apology for Crudity," *excerpted below.*]

For a long time I have believed that crudity is an inevitable quality in the production of a really significant present-day American literature. . . .

If you are in doubt as to the crudity of thought in America, try an experiment. Come out of your offices, where you sit writing and thinking, and try living with us. Get on a train at Pittsburg and go west to the mountains of Colorado. Stop for a time in our towns and cities. Stay for a week in some Iowa corn-shipping town and for another week in one of the Chicago clubs. As you loiter about read our newspapers and listen to our conversations, remembering, if you will, that as you see us in the towns and cities, so we are. We are not subtle enough to conceal ourselves and he who runs with open eyes through the Mississippi Valley may read the story of the Mississippi Valley.

It is a marvelous story and we have not yet begun to tell the half of it. . . .

As I walk alone, an old truth comes home to me and I know that we shall never have an American literature until we return to faith in ourselves and to the facing of our own limitations. We must, in some way, become in ourselves more like our fellows, more simple and real. (p. 437)

To me it seems that as writers we shall have to throw ourselves with greater daring into the life here. We shall have to begin to write out of the people and not for the people. We shall have to find within ourselves a little of that courage. To continue along the road we are travelling is unthinkable. To draw ourselves apart, to live in little groups and console ourselves with the thought that we are achieving intellectuality, is to get nowhere. By such a road we can hope only to go on producing a literature that has nothing to do with life as it is lived in these United States. . . .

The road is rough and the times are pitiless. Who, knowing our America and understanding the life in our towns and cities, can close his eyes to the fact that life here is for the most part an ugly affair? As a people we have given ourselves to industrialism, and industrialism is not lovely. If anyone can find beauty in an American factory town, I wish he would show me the way. For myself, I cannot find it. To me, and I am living in industrial life, the whole thing is as ugly as modern war. I have to accept that fact and I believe a great step forward will have been taken when it is more generally accepted. . . .

It is, I believe, self-evident that the work of the novelist must always lie somewhat outside the field of philosophic thought. Your true novelist is a man gone a little mad with the life of his times. As he goes through life he lives, not in himself, but in many people. Through his brain march figures and groups of figures. Out of the many figures, one emerges. If he be at all sensitive to the life about him and that life be crude, the figure that emerges will be crude and will crudely express itself.

I do not know how far a man may go on the road of subjective writing. The matter, I admit, puzzles me. There is something approaching insanity in the very idea of sinking yourself too deeply into modern American industrial life.

But it is my contention that there is no other road. If one would avoid neat, slick writing, he must at least attempt to be brother to his brothers and live as the men of his time live. He must share with them the crude expression of their lives. To our grandchildren the privilege of attempting to produce a school of American writing that has delicacy and color may come as a matter of course. One hopes that will be true, but it is not true now. And that is why, with so many of the younger Americans, I put my faith in the modern literary adventurers. We shall, I am sure, have much crude, blundering American writing before the gift of beauty and subtlety in prose shall honestly belong to us. (p. 438)

> Sherwood Anderson, "*An Apology for Crudity,*" in The Dial *(copyright, 1917, by The Dial Publishing Company, Inc.), Vol. LXIII, No. 753, November 8, 1917, pp. 437-38.*

M[AXWELL] A[NDERSON]   (essay date 1919)

[*Anderson praises* Winesburg, Ohio *in the following early review.*]

Every middle westerner will recognize Winesburg, Ohio, as the town in which he grew up. . . .

There is outward repose over Winesburg, a garment of respectable repose covering alike the infinite pain, the grief, the agony of futile groping, the momentary flare of beauty or passion of which the citizens are ashamed.

We are given our view of Winesburg through twenty-three sketches dealing with the crises in as many lives. The lives are inter-related, and a multitude of subsidiary figures drift through the incidents, appearing and disappearing, grouping and changing, in the manner of pedestrians along a by-street. The stories are homely and unemphatic. Crime and love and merry-making come casually into being; chance exalts and flatters, thwarts and subdues. The character that re-emerges oftenest is George Willard, reporter for the Winesburg Eagle. He is the ordinary, bumptious young man with dreams of getting "away from all this" and doing "something" huge and vague in distant cities. To him the town is dull and queer. . . .

The most satisfactory of the sketches is the one called **Paper Pills,** a bit from the lives of Doctor Reefy and the tall dark girl who became his wife. There are only five pages of it, and it is told effortlessly, almost carelessly, yet it suggests better than any of the more conscious attempts that engages Mr. Anderson throughout, the loneliness of human life, the baffled search of every personality for meanings and purposes deeper than anything that may be said or done, answers that will cut under the superficial axioms by which we are judged. (p. 257)

As a challenge to the snappy short story form, with its planned proportions of flippant philosophy, epigrammatic conversation, and sex danger, nothing better has come out of America than *Winesburg, Ohio.* Because we have so little in the field it is probably easy to over-estimate its excellence. In Chekhov's sketches simplicity is an artistic achievement. With Sherwood Anderson simplicity is both an art and a limitation. But the present book is well within his powers, and he has put into it the observation, the brooding "odds and ends of thoughts," of many years. It was set down by a patient and loving craftsman; it is in a new mood, and one not easily forgotten. (pp. 257, 260)

M[axwell] A[nderson], "A Country Town," in The New Republic (© 1919 The New Republic, Inc.), Vol. 19, No. 242, June 25, 1919, pp. 257, 260.

HART CRANE   (essay date 1921)

[*In this laudatory review of* Poor White, *Crane provides a general appraisal of Anderson's career.*]

We have come a long way from the pattern-making preoccupations of an Henry James when we can welcome a statement from an artist with as bold a contrasting simplicity as the answer that Sherwood Anderson once gave me to an analysis I had attempted of one of his short stories. "I am in truth mighty little interested in any discussion of art or life, or what a man's place in the scheme of things may be. It has to be done, I suppose, but after all there is the *fact* of life. Its story wants telling and singing. That's what I want,—the tale and the song of it." And it is that Anderson has so pre-eminently captured the "tale and the song of it" that I find his words so acceptable—at least in so far as they relate to his own work.

I spoke of an "attempted" analysis because of being since satisfied that beyond the possibility of a certain uneven surface penetration, Anderson's stories possess a too defiant and timeless solidity,—too much a share of life and clay itself,—to be tagged and listed with mechanical precisions. And what a satisfaction this is, to read stories over and again without a bundle of dry bones and cogwheels of "situations" and "plots" spilling out into one's lap. It must have been because of a surfeit of such disappointments that **"Winesburg, Ohio,"** when it first appeared, kept me up a whole night in a steady crescendo of emotions. Here was "stark realism," but a realism simplified and strangely sophisticated by the inscrutable soil. And by "soil" I mean something much more than a kind of local colour. There is plenty of that quite wonderfully applied, both in **"Winesburg"** and in **"Poor White,"** but there is also something more important and rare than this,—a contact with animal and earthy life so indefinably yet powerfully used as a very foundation to the stories that it might be compared to the sap that pervades the tree-trunk, branches, and twigs. (pp. 433-34)

It is his love for rows of corn on flat lands, fields bending over rolling Ohio hills, and the smell of barns under the warm hours of noon, that has given Anderson's descriptions of modern city life with its mechanical distortions of humanity, such thrust and bite.

In **"Poor White"** there is the "machine" of modern existence,—the monster that is upon us all. . . . One sees all through this book how character is bent, blunted, regulated, diverted, or lacerated by the "machine." There is the perfect episode of a harness-maker whose love for manual perfection of craft finally drives him to the murder of an upstart apprentice who had insisted in over-ruling him by adopting machine made saddles as substitutes for the carefully wrought saddles of the old man.

Looking back at two earlier books, **"Windy McPherson's Son"** and **"Marching Men,"** one can see a great advance in **"Poor White."** There has always been the propagandist threatening the artist in Anderson; and in these first two books the propagandist comes out too dangerously near a victory to satisfy us despite the much brilliant description these books contain. Since then he has freed himself from much of this. Not that he has chosen to ignore any fact or problems, but rather that he has succeeded in treating them more impersonally, incorporating them, less obviously, in character and action. To appreciate this advance from the seductive stagnations of sentimentality to a clear acceptance and description of our life today for what it be worth, is to realize how few other Americans have had the courage, let alone the vision, to do anything like it. Norris and Dreiser, and one or two others of native birth have been the only ones. In Anderson there has been some great sincerity, perhaps the element of the "soil" itself personified in him, that has made him refuse to turn aside to offer the crowds those profitable "lollypops" that have "made" and ruined so many other of our writers.

Of course it is patent that people do not like to be told the truth. Especially our Puritans! **"Winesburg"** was the first book to tell the truth about our small mid-western towns. And what a fury it threw some people into! It seemed to be so much easier for those people to fling back,—"Neuroticism!" "Obscenity!" and "Exaggeration!" than to recognize themselves and others there. I could understand it perfectly myself, having lived for a while in a small town of similar location and colour. But my real point for admiring it was not because it merely told the truth; it was that **"Winesburg"** represented a work of distinct aesthetic achievement, an example of synthetic form,—not merely a medley of a thousand exterior details such as Lewis's "Main Street." It takes more than the recognition of facts as facts to move us in fiction. There must be some beauty wrung from them to hold us long. We can recognize this quality without having it pointed out to us if our hearts are not too deadened, our sensibilities too dulled. In "**Winesburg,**" the windows, alleys and lanes of the place are opened to us to find what we may. There is an exalting pathos in the episode called "**Mother.**" The ironic humor and richness of "**An Awakening**" has the vivid and unbroken vitality of a silhouette. "**Paper Pills,**" to me the finest thing in the book, has an idyllic beauty that sets it beside the old legend of "Daphnis and Chloe," and there are other chapters and episodes unmatched anywhere. (pp. 435-37)

The time has already arrived when Anderson is beginning to be recognized as among the few first recorders of the life of a people coming to some state of self-consciousness. He is without sentimentality; and he makes no pretense of offering solutions. He has a humanity and simplicity that is quite baffling in depth and suggestiveness, and his steady and deliberate growth is proving right along the promise it gives of finer work. (p. 437)

> Hart Crane, "Sherwood Anderson (II)" (originally published as an essay in The Double Dealer, Vol. II, No. 7, July, 1921), in Twice a Year (copyright 1945 by Dorothy S. Norman, Twice a Year), Nos. 12 & 13, 1945, pp. 433-38.

JOHN PEALE BISHOP (essay date 1921)

[*Bishop provides a valuable overview and a comparison of Anderson's work with that of D. H. Lawrence in a review of the acclaimed short story collection* The Triumph of the Egg.]

Sherwood Anderson alone among the Americans seems to bear a resemblance to Lawrence. When I first read *Out of Nowhere Into Nothing,* as it appeared serially in the *Dial,* I thought to have detected the influence of Lawrence on Anderson's phrasing. But this is slight, if indeed it exists. They are alike rather in their mode of apprehending certain things. If Lawrence has influenced Anderson, it is by confirming the American in his own discoveries. Both are interested in searching out what men hide from the world, in probing under worm-riddled floors and ransacking blind attics. In *The Triumph of the Egg,* Anderson is more than ever concerned with those private struggles of the soul in which Lawrence's interest also lies; but where in Lawrence this struggle is almost always between the cruel aloofness of the male and the tender, devastating pervasiveness of the woman, in Anderson it is between some dream of impossible loveliness, which the dreamer wishes to attach to the body of the beloved, and the inane fecundity of life. Always in this new book of his, it is the blind insistent instinct of life for endless recreation which triumphs over the dreamer. This is, I take it, the meaning of the title.

Anderson, like Lawrence, understands the physical ecstasy and contentment that would come of belonging utterly to the dark rich life of the earth and moving with the ancient rhythms of light and dark, of green and sterile seasons, of dayrise and nightfall. "That would have been sweetest of all things," he says, "—to sway like the tops of young trees when a wind blew, to give himself as the grey weeds in a sunburned field gave themselves to the influence of passing shadows, changing color constantly, becoming every moment something new, to

live in life and in death too, always to live, to be unafraid of life, to let it flow through his body, to let the blood flow through his body, not to struggle, to offer no resistance, to dance."

He has, too, a sympathy with the simple unthinking life of the African Negro and is stirred strangely by the remembered songs their timid, degenerate descendants sing, songs of defiance and hate and relentless love. He shares with Lawrence a mythopoeic faculty, which peoples the darkness with forgotten devils and inhuman ghosts. But where the Englishman piles words upon words, approximating his meaning by a rich welter of words, Anderson is so sparing in statement as to be almost inarticulate. There is at times in his books an unbelievable and glamorous beauty, but it is the beauty of things seen with delight or known in an intensity of emotion, haltingly recovered and scarcely set down in words.

I have emphasized these qualities in Anderson, because, in casually grouping him with the newer American realists, the critics have largely ignored them. Even in those two earliest books of his, *Marching Men* and *Windy McPherson's Son,* there was no question of his powers of observation, his sincerity, his understanding of American types. He was one of the first to describe accurately and without sentimentality the dreary and monotonous towns of the Middle West and the dwellers in those towns—old grey-headed men, thwarted and disgruntled, bragging of fine deeds that had never been done; silent, pale, stoop-shouldered women, strutting young louts, awkward boys with unuttered longings. In *Winesburg, Ohio,* such a town is always in the background. In this series of short stories, loosely held together by the figure of the boyish reporter, Anderson seemed finally to have found his form. With *Poor White,* he returned to the novel to tell the story of another town, one of the tiny agricultural towns of Ohio, which between the boyhood of the protagonist and his middle age grows into a manufacturing city, another Dayton or Youngstown. Excellent in most respects as it is, the book does not achieve form. There is a constant confusion in the element of time, which always seems to give Anderson trouble; and in an attempt to carry a sense of multitude, he continually follows his minor characters into blind alleys from which there is a difficult return.

In *The Triumph of the Egg,* Anderson again reverts to the short story, and he has gained considerably in artistry since last touching the more restricted forms. He is here more nearly the subtle and facile craftsman than he has ever been before. He will always perhaps labor breathlessly with words; there is still a choppiness in movement, a confusion in the time element. His characters are, more than elsewhere, reduced to a few essential gestures. But there is here, and in clearer form, all that passionate imagination which from the first marked him apart from the other American realists. The first and last stories in this volume are as fine as anything which has come out of this movement.

I Want to Know Why is a tale told by a Kentucky boy of fifteen, a boy for whom all the glamor of life is concentrated on the racetracks, the paddocks and the thoroughbreds. . . . He aches with inexplicable longing and delight but to look at Sunstreak, a stallion that "is like a girl you think about sometimes, and never see," and, because the trainer shares the boy's understanding of the horse, he reaches out toward the trainer in warm, boyish adoration. Then, through a lighted window, leaning across a rosebush, he sees the trainer go into a ramshackle evil-smelling farmhouse, and brag among drunken men after the races, and kiss a tall red-headed woman, with a hard, ugly mouth. He sees the man's eyes shine, just as they had shone when the stallion was running. Suddenly he hates the man, and the glamor of the courses is lost and the goodly smell of the air is gone. The egg has triumphed.

In *Out of Nowhere into Nothing* there is a young woman who has seen in her girlhood, going down a marble stairway, bright youths and maidens and old men, noble and serene. Having fallen in love with her employer, a man with a wife and two children—she is a stenographer in Chicago—she returns to her native village to draw advice from her mother. She turns to her mother with her secret. . . . And her mother's answer is that there is no such thing as love. "Men only hurt women. They can't help wanting to hurt women. The thing they call love doesn't exist. It's a lie. Life is dirty."

In both these stories there is this conflict between the desire of the young for a seen or imagined beauty, and the cruel ugliness of life and the meaningless need for perpetuating it. Anderson hates the village, not so much for its dreariness, its repressions, its hideousness, but because it has the power to stop the longing stuttering cry of the villagers who dream of something that is not and "run through the night seeking some lost, some hidden and half forgotten loveliness." One suspects that Anderson's own mind is very like one of these grey towns, and that in it, as in these towns, there is a conflict, and that out of that conflict his books are made. (pp. 238-40)

> John Peale Bishop, "The Distrust of Ideas (D. H. Lawrence and Sherwood Anderson)," in Vanity Fair (copyright © 1921, by The Condé Nast Publications, Inc.), Vol. 17, No. 4, December, 1921 (and reprinted in The Collected Essays of John Peale Bishop by John Peale Bishop, edited by Edmund Wilson, Charles Scribner's Sons, 1948, pp. 233-40).*

F. SCOTT FITZGERALD   (essay date 1923)

[*Fitzgerald, a spokesman for the iconoclastic Jazz Age, enthusiastically reviews* Many Marriages, *which another critic deemed "the most clearly and completely immoral book that one can well imagine."*]

In the last five years we have seen solidify the reputations of two first class men—James Joyce and Sherwood Anderson.

"Many Marriages" seems to me the fullblown flower of Anderson's personality. . . . On the strength of "Many Marriages" you can decide whether Anderson is a neurotic or whether you are one and Anderson a man singularly free of all inhibitions. The noble fool who has dominated tragedy from Don Quixote to Lord Jim is not a character in "Many Marriages." If there is nobility in the book it is a nobility Anderson has created as surely as Rousseau created his own natural man. (p. 42)

I read in the paper every day that, without the slightest warning, some apparently solid and settled business man has eloped with his stenographer. This is the central event of "Many Marriages." But in the glow of an unexhaustible ecstasy and wonder what is known as a "vulgar intrigue" becomes a transaction of profound and mystical importance. . . .

The method is Anderson's accustomed transcendental naturalism. The writing is often tortuous. But then just as you begin to rail at the short steps of the truncated sentences (his prose walks with a rope around the ankle and a mischievous boy at the end of the rope) you reach an amazingly beautiful vista seen through a crack in the wall that long steps would have carried you hurriedly by. Again—Anderson feels too pro-

foundly to have read widely or even well. What he takes to be only an empty tomato can whose beauty he has himself discovered may turn out to be a Greek vase wrought on the Ægean twenty centuries before. (p. 43)

"Many Marriages" is not immoral—it is violently anti-social. But if its protagonist rested at a defiance of the fallible human institution of monogamy the book would be no more than propaganda. On the contrary, "Many Marriages" begins where "The New Machiavelli" left off. It does not so much justify the position of its protagonist as it casts a curious and startling light on the entire relation between man and woman. It is the reaction of a sensitive, highly civilized man to the phenomenon of lust—but it is distinguished from the work of Dreiser, Joyce and Wells (for example) by utter lack both of a concept of society as a whole and of the necessity of defying or denying such a concept. For the purpose of the book no such background as Dublin Catholicism, middle Western morality or London Fabianism could ever have existed. For all his washing machine factory the hero of "Many Marriages" comes closer than any character, not excepting Odysseus, Lucifer, Attila, Tarzan and, least of all, Conrad's Michaelis, to existing in an absolute vacuum. It seems to me a rather stupendous achievement.

I do not like the man in the book. The world in which I trust, on which I seem to set my feet, appears to me to exist through a series of illusions. These illusions need and occasionally get a thorough going over ten times or so during a century.

The man whose power of compression is great enough to review this book in a thousand words does not exist. If he does he is probably writing subtitles for the movies or working for a car company. (pp. 43-4)

> F. Scott Fitzgerald, "Sherwood Anderson on the Marriage Question" (reprinted by permission of Harold Ober Associates; copyright © 1923 by F. Scott Fitzgerald), in The New York Herald, March 4, 1923 (and reprinted in Critical Essays on Sherwood Anderson, edited by David D. Anderson, G. K. Hall & Company, 1981, pp. 42-4).

SINCLAIR LEWIS   (essay date 1924)

[*Famous as a leader in American literature's "revolt from the village"—a role long-associated with Anderson, as well—Lewis reviews* A Story Teller's Story *with praise.*]

Sherwood Anderson is of importance in American letters—in all of modern letters. Whether by reason of admiration or sharp dislike, all of us who desire fiction to be something more than a Ford manufactory of smart anecdotes must consider his stories of American peasant life, so rigorously simple in expression, so forthright in thought. We have damned or adored him or uncomfortably done both. Either way, there are few of us who have not been guilty of stating that, of course, whatever his merits, Mr. Anderson "lacks a sense of humor" and "is obsessed by sex."

Aside from the pleasure of viewing a human soul, it will be for the beneficial increase in our humility to read *A Story Teller's Story* and to discover that Sherwood Anderson is not obsessed by sex and that he has a shining sense of humor.

When he portrays his father, telling a farmer audience of Civil War heroisms, Mr. Anderson shows a humor equally free of the hysterical vulgarity of the Bill Nye school and the neat little jabs of contemporary New York wit. The father changes and enhances his tale to suit his auditors. He never exactly lies, but—wouldn't it be just as well, when in the story he returns to his old Southern home as a pro-Lincoln prisoner in the hands of stern Southern troops, to contrive to meet on the doorstep his non-existent but otherwise absolutely satisfactory former body-servant?

Another example of humor which the reviewer commends to the study of all anti-Andersonites is his explanation that there is reason for the frequent comparison of his stories to those of the Russians, since, like them, he was reared on cabbage soup. It is an admirable burlesque of the literary influence brand of criticism.

Humor—in plenty. And as to this matter of "sex"—the intense terrifying vision which intimidated or revolted so great a share of us in Mr. Anderson's *Many Marriages*—he honestly shows us in this volume how bewildered he has been that the critics should call him "unclean" for attributing to his characters the experiences and chaotic beautiful bewilderments which in real life do secretly besiege every man and woman.

Aside from the book's absolute worth and its special value as a revelation of an authentic craftsman, it has another value as an explanation of that emerging Middle West of whose recent literature so much has been written—so little understood.

Like Mr. Carl Sandburg, Mr. Anderson has the calmness to see that the most vulgar and seemingly inarticulate of his corn-belt villagers are not inarticulate or in any slightest way vulgar, but rich with all life—significant and beautiful as any Russian peasant, any naughty French countess, any English vicar, any tiresomely familiar dummy of standard fiction. A Negro race-track follower, a nail factory truckman, the daughter of a boarding-house keeper, a man who to the eye was but a small-town merchant forgetting his invalidism in a periodical drunk in Chicago, yet to the understanding a seer—such people come out, in *A Story Teller's Story*, in all their friendliness, their *importance*. (pp. 167-68)

Sinclair Lewis, "A Pilgrim's Progress," in New York Herald Tribune Books *(© I.H.T. Corporation; reprinted by permission), November 9, 1924 (and reprinted in* The Man from Main Street: A Sinclair Lewis Reader; Selected Essays and Other Writings, 1904-1950, *edited by Harry E. Maule and Melville H. Cane, Random House, 1953, pp. 165-68).*

ERNEST HEMINGWAY (essay date 1925)

[*Hemingway's glowing review of* A Story Teller's Story *was written but a year before his scathing parody of Anderson,* The Torrents of Spring.]

The reviewers have all compared ["**A Story Teller's Story**"] with the "**Education of Henry Adams**" and it was not hard for them to do so, for Sherwood Anderson twice refers to the Adams book and there is plenty in the "**Story Teller's Story**" about the cathedral at Chartres. Evidently the Education book made a deep impression on Sherwood for he quotes part of it. He also has a couple of other learned quotations in Latin and I can imagine him copying them on the typewriter verifying them carefully to get the spelling right. For Sherwood Anderson, unlike the English, does not quote you Latin in casual conversation. (p. 84)

"**A Story Teller's Story**" is a good book. It is such a good book that it doesn't need to be coupled in the reviewing with Henry Adams or anybody else.

This is the Life and Times of Sherwood Anderson and a great part of it runs along in a mildly kidding way as though Sherwood were afraid people would think he took himself and his life too seriously. But there is no joking about the way he writes of horses and women and bartenders and Judge Turner and the elder Berners and the half allegorical figure of the poor devil of a magazine writer who comes in at the end of the book. And if Sherwood jokes about the base-ball player beating him up at the warehouse where he worked, you get at the same time, a very definite sharp picture of the baseball player, drunk, sullen and amazed, knocking him down as soon and as often as he got up while the two teamsters watched and wondered why this fellow named Anderson had picked a fight when he couldn't fight.

There are very beautiful places in the book, as good writing as Sherwood Anderson has done and that means considerably better than any other American writer has done. It is a great mystery and an even greater tribute to Sherwood that so many people writing today think he cannot write. They believe that he has very strange and sometimes beautiful ideas and visions and that he expresses them very clumsily and unsuccessfully. While in reality he often takes a very banal idea of things and presents it with such craftsmanship that the person reading believes it beautiful and does not see the craftsmanship at all. When he calls himself "a poor scribbler" don't believe him.

He is not a poor scribbler even though he calls himself that or worse, again and again. He is a very great writer and if he has, at times, in other books been unsuccessful, it has been for two reasons. His talent and his development of it has been toward the short story or tale and not toward that highly artificial form the novel. The second reason is that he has been what the French say of all honest politicians *mal entouré*.

In "**A Story Teller's Story**," which is highly successful as a piece of work because it is written in his own particular form, a series of short tales jointed up sometimes and sometimes quite disconnected, he pays homage to his New York friends who have helped him. They nearly all took something from him, and tried to give him various things in return that he needed as much as a boxer needs diamond studded teeth. And because he gave them all something he is, after the manner of all great men, very grateful to them. They called him a "phallic Chekov" and other meaningless things and watched for the sparkle of his diamond studded teeth and Sherwood got a little worried and uncertain and wrote a poor book called "**Many Marriages**." Then all the people who hated him because he was an American who could write and did write and had been given a prize and was starting to have some success jumped on him with loud cries that he never had written and never would be able to write and if you didn't believe it read "**Many Marriages**." Now Sherwood has written a fine book and they are all busy comparing him to Henry Adams.

Anyway you ought to read "**A Story Teller's Story**." It is a wonderful comeback after "**Many Marriages**." (pp. 85-6)

Ernest Hemingway, in his extract from "Reviews of 'A Story-Teller's Story'" (originally published in Ex Libris, *Vol. 2, No. 6, March, 1925), in* Sherwood Anderson: A Collection of Critical Essays, *edited by Walter B. Rideout, Prentice-Hall, Inc., 1974, pp. 84-6.*

WILLIAM FAULKNER (essay date 1925)

[*Faulkner surveys Anderson's work. As becomes evident in the following essay, Faulkner's knowledge of the chronological order of Anderson's books is somewhat faulty.*]

For some reason people seem to be interested not in what Mr. Anderson has written, but from what source he derives. The greater number who speculate upon his origin say he derives from the Russians. If so, he has returned home, **"The Triumph of the Egg"** having been translated into Russian. A smaller number hold to the French theory. A cabinet-maker in New Orleans discovered that he resembles Zola, though how he arrived at this I can not see, unless it be that Zola also wrote books.

Like most speculation all this is interesting but bootless. Men grow from the soil, like corn and trees: I prefer to think of Mr. Anderson as a lusty corn field in his native Ohio. As he tells in his own story, his father not only seeded him physically, but planted also in him that belief, necessary to a writer, that his own emotions are important, and also planted in him the desire to tell them to someone. (p. 89)

"Winesburg, Ohio." The simplicity of this title! And the stories are as simply done: short, he tells the story and stops. His very inexperience, his urgent need not to waste time or paper taught him one of the first attributes of genius. As a rule first books show more bravado than anything else, unless it be tediousness. But there is neither of these qualities in **"Winesburg."** Mr. Anderson is tentative, self-effacing with his George Willards and Wash Williamses and banker White's daughters, as though he were thinking: "Who am I, to pry into the souls of these people who, like myself, sprang from this same soil to suffer the same sorrows as I?" The only indication of the writer's individuality which I find in **"Winesburg"** is his sympathy for them, a sympathy which, had the book been done as a full-length novel, would have become mawkish. Again the gods looked out for him. These people live and breathe: they are beautiful. There is the man who organized a baseball club, the man with the "speaking" hands, Elizabeth Willard, middle-aged, and the oldish doctor, between whom was a love that Cardinal Bembo might have dreamed. There is a Greek word for a love like theirs which Mr. Anderson probably had never heard. And behind all of them a ground of fecund earth and corn in the green spring and the slow, full hot summer and the rigorous masculine winter that hurts it not, but makes it stronger.

"Marching Men." Just as there are lesser ears and good ears among the corn, so are there lesser books and good books in Mr. Anderson's list. **"Marching Men"** is disappointing after **"Winesburg."** But then anything any other American was doing at that time would have been disappointing after **"Winesburg."**

"Windy McPherson's Son." After reading **"A Story Teller's Story,"** one can see where Windy McPherson came from. And a comparison, I think, gives a clear indication of how far Mr. Anderson has grown. There is in both **"Marching Men"** and **"Windy McPherson's Son"** a fundamental lack of humor. This lack of humor mitigates against him, but then growing corn has little time for humor.

"Poor White." The corn still grows. The crows of starvation can no longer bother it nor tear its roots up. In this book he seems to get his fingers and toes again into the soil, as he did in **"Winesburg."** Here again is the old refulgent earth and people who answer the compulsions of labor and food and sleep, whose passions are uncerebral. A young girl feeling the sweet frightening inevitability of adolescence, takes it as calmly as a tree takes its rising sap, and sees the spring that brought it become languorous and drowsy with summer, its work accomplished.

"Many Marriages." Here, I think, is a bad ear, because it is not Mr. Anderson. I don't know where it came from, but I do know that it is not a logical development from **"Winesburg"** and **"Poor White."** The man here is a factory owner, a bourgeois, a man who was "top dog" because he was naturally forced to run his factory with people who had no factories of their own. In his other books there are no "under dogs" because there are no "top dogs"—save circumstance, your true democracy being at the same time a monarchy. And he gets away from the land. When he does this he is lost. And again humor is completely lacking. A 40-year-old man who has led a sedentary life must look sort of funny naked, walking up and down a room and talking. What would he do with his hands? Did you ever see a man tramping back and forth and talking, without putting his hands in his pockets? However, this story won the Dial prize in its year, so I am possibly wrong.

This has been translated into Russian and has been dramatized and produced in New York.

"Horses and Men." A collection of short stories, reminiscent of **"Winesburg,"** but more sophisticated. After reading this book you inevitably want to reread **"Winesburg."** Which makes one wonder if after all the short story is not Mr. Anderson's medium. No sustained plot to bother you, nothing tedious; only the sharp episodic phases of people, the portraying of which Mr. Anderson's halting questioning manner is best at. **"I'm a Fool,"** the best short story in America, to my thinking, is the tale of a lad's adolescent pride in his profession (horse racing) and his body, of his belief in a world beautiful and passionate created for the chosen to race horses on, of his youthful pagan desire to preen in his lady's eyes that brings him low at last. Here is a personal emotion that does strike the elemental chord in mankind. (pp. 89-91)

In this book there are people, people that walk and live, and the ancient stout earth that takes his heartbreaking labor and gives grudgingly, mayhap, but gives an hundredfold.

"A Story-Teller's Story." Here Mr. Anderson, trying to do one thing, has really written two distinct books. The first half, which was evidently intended to portray his physical picture, is really a novel based upon one character—his father. I don't recall a character anywhere exactly like him—sort of a cross between the Baron Hulot and Gaudissart. The second half of the book in which he draws his mental portrait is quite different: it leaves me with a faint feeling that it should have been in a separate volume.

Here Mr. Anderson pries into his own mind, in the same tentative manner in which he did the factory owner's mind. Up to here he is never philosophical; he believes that he knows little about it all, and leaves the reader to draw his own conclusions. He does not even offer opinions.

But in this second half of the book he assumes at times an elephantine kind of humor about himself, not at all the keen humor with which he pictured his father's character. I think that this is due to the fact that Mr. Anderson is interested in his reactions to other people, and very little in himself. That is, he has not enough active ego to write successfully of himself. . . . But the corn is maturing: I think the first half of **"A Story-Teller's Story"** is the best character delineation he has done; but taking the book as a whole I agree with Mr. Llewellyn Powys in the Dial: it is not his best contribution to American literature.

I do not mean to imply that Mr. Anderson has no sense of humor. He has, he has always had. But only recently has he got any of it into his stories without deliberately writing a story with a humorous intent. (pp. 92-3)

No one . . . can accuse him of lacking in humor in the portrayal of the father in his last book. Which, I think, indicates that he has not matured yet, despite his accomplishments so far. He who conceived this man has yet something which will appear in its own good time. (p. 93)

American, and more than that, a middle westerner, of the soil: he is as typical of Ohio in his way as Harding was in his. A field of corn with a story to tell and a tongue to tell it with. (p. 94)

> *William Faulkner, "Sherwood Anderson," in* The Dallas Morning News, *Part III, April 26, 1925 (and reprinted in* The Princeton University Library Chronicle, *Vol. XVIII, No. 3, Spring, 1957, pp. 89-94).*

H. L. MENCKEN (essay date 1926)

[*Mencken praises* Dark Laughter *in this glowing review. Privately, as is revealed in his letters, Mencken believed Anderson was an artist of erratic talent, given to alternate phases of brilliance and "muddleheadedness."*]

The history of Sherwood Anderson is the history of a man groping painfully for an understanding of his own ideas. They flash before him out of the void, and he contemplates them with a sort of wonder, seeking to penetrate their significance, and sometimes not succeeding. Here I do not simply speculate grandly; I say only what the man has said himself, and in plain terms. *Mid-American Chants* represents his effort to turn this puzzlement into ecstasy; in *Many Marriages* he takes refuge in metaphysics; in such acrid and revelatory short stories as *Death in the Woods* he contents himself with stating his problem, and letting the answer go. But the man grows. He is still a wanderer in a wood, but he has begun to find paths and landmarks. In *Dark Laughter,* I believe, there are plain foreshadowings of the Anderson who is ahead—an Anderson still happily free from the ready formulae of the Bennetts and Wellses, and yet making contact with an ordered and plausible rationale of life. In *Dark Laughter,* the latest of his books, Anderson begins to be oriented. It is, I think, one of the most profound American novels of our time. It has all the cruel truthfulness of a snapshot, and it is at the same time a moving and beautiful poem. Sherwood Anderson is one of the most original novelists ever heard of. He seems to derive from no one, and to have no relation to any contemporary. An aloof, moody, often incoherent, mainly impenetrable man, he has made his own road. There is, at the top of his achievement, an almost startling brilliance; there is in him, even at his worst, every sign of a sound artist—sometimes baffled by his material perhaps, but never disingenuous, never smug, never cheap.

> *H. L. Mencken, "America's Most Distinctive Novelist—Sherwood Anderson," in* Vanity Fair *(courtesy The Condé Nast Publications, Inc.; copyright ©1926, renewed 1954, by The Condé Nast Publications, Inc.), Vol. 27, No. 4, December, 1926, p. 88.*

UPTON SINCLAIR (essay date 1927)

[*Sinclair, a socialist author-activist, demanded of writers a melding of social consciousness and artistry. Sensing Anderson's sympathetic concern for humanity, he attacks Anderson for not making clearer his vision of life.*]

Eleven years ago I came on a first novel by an unknown writer; a novel which gave me a thrill because it showed real knowledge of poverty and real tenderness for the poor. So few of our magnificent wealthy writers condescend to be aware of poverty—except when they need a contrast to heighten the charms of a plutocratic career. So I wrote a letter to the author of **"Windy McPherson's Son,"** seeking to make a Socialist out of him. He answered, on the letter-head of an advertising firm in Chicago, and we had a little correspondence, from which I quote a few sentences.

"To me there is no answer for the terrible confusion of life. I want to try to sympathize and to understand a little of the twisted and maimed life that industrialism has brought on us. But I can't solve things, Sinclair. I can't do it. Man, I don't know who is right and who wrong. . . . Really, I am tempted to go at you hard in this matter. There is something terrible to me in the thought of the art of writing being bent and twisted to serve the ends of propaganda . . . Damn it, you have made me go on like a propagandist. You should be ashamed of yourself."

And then came a second novel, **"Marching Men,"** to make clear to me that I need have no hope of social understanding from Sherwood Anderson. Here is the story of a labour leader who rouses the workers; and for what? To march! Where shall they march? He doesn't know. What shall they march for? He doesn't know that. What is their marching to be understood to symbolize? Nobody knows; but march, and keep on marching—"Out of Nowhere into Nothing," to quote the title of a Sherwood Anderson short story. (pp. 113-14)

Upon the basis of the data in the books, I venture to psychoanalyse Mr. Anderson, and tell him that he is the victim of a dissociated personality. From childhood he wanted to create beauty, and had to live in a dirty hovel, upon a supply of cabbages which rowdies had thrown at his mother's door one night. Then he had to go out into the world of hustle and graft, to fight for a living; he had to become manager of a paint factory, without the least interest in that kind of paint. And all the while the repressed artist in him sobbed and suffered, and lived its own subconscious life, and occasionally surged up to the surface, driving the respectable paint factory manager to actions which his stenographer and office force considered insane. It drove him to drop the paint job, all of a sudden, right in the middle of the dictating of a letter; it drove him to a nervous breakdown, and the life of a wanderer; it drove him to throw up a first-class advertising job in Chicago; and finally it made him a man of genius, the object of adoration of all those critics who have been fed on warmed-over cabbage soup, and whose test of great literature is that it shall be muddled. (p. 114)

And so came Sherwood Anderson, right in the Freudian swim; all his characters are victims of dissociation, and always they find the solution of their problem in following a sexual impulse. Civilization is repressed, says our novelist, and he writes a long novel, **"Dark Laughter,"** to show a man and a woman, mentally disordered, and therefore drawn to each other, as happens with all neurasthenics, and discovering in the free, happy laughter of negroes the state of naturalness they seek. Mr. Anderson finds about the negroes what Whitman found about the animals, they do not worry about their sins; and so his couple go off together, and we are left to assume that they will be happy. But I can tell him that they won't, because I have lived a good part of my life among neurasthenics—who has not, in modern civilization?—and I see his two people presently discovering that they have a complex, due to the fact that one is repressing the other's nature.

There is a cancer, eating out the heart of our civilization; but no one is permitted to diagnose that cancer, under penalty of losing his job and social standing. No one who understands economic inequality as a cause of social and individual degeneration is permitted to hold any responsible post in capitalist society; and so it comes about that muddlement is the ideal of our intellectuals. Suppose that Mr. Anderson had written in his letter to me, "Yes, of course, I see the class struggle. How could any clear-sighted man fail to see it? How could any honest man fail to report it?" Would he then have become the white hope of all the intelligentsia, as he is to-day? No indeed! The way to be a genius of the Freudian age is to write, "How are you going to understand anyone or anything?" When the intellectual reads that, he slaps his leg and cries, "Aha! Here is sincerity! Here is naturalism! Here is the real, elemental, primitive, naïve! Here is a true overflow, red-hot lava boiling up from the subconscious! Here is something Russian! Here is cabbage soup!"

You laugh, perhaps; people generally laugh when you state an obvious truth about this crazy world. But take the thirteen volumes of Sherwood Anderson and analyse the characters: men and women who cannot adjust themselves to any aspect of life, cannot live in marriage or out of it, cannot make love, cannot consummate love, cannot restrain love, cannot keep from being suspected of perversity; and always, everywhere, over and over again, the one repressed artist personality making agonized efforts to state himself in words, saying the same thing over and over, a dozen times on a single page. He tells us that artist's story in **"Windy McPherson's Son,"** and then he tells it, with variations, in **"Poor White"**; he tells it, full and complete, in **"A Story-Teller's Story"**; he tells the childhood over again in **"Tar,"** and the married part in **"Many Marriages,"** and again, with changed circumstances, in **"Dark Laughter"**; and then the philosophy of it in a **"Notebook"**; and then the short stories—this or that aspect of the same theme. Some of them are great short stories, but I have said to myself, long or short, I have read that story enough times! (pp. 115-17)

> *Upton Sinclair, "Muddlement," in his* Money Writes! *(copyright by Upton Sinclair), A. & C. Boni, 1927 (and reprinted by Scholarly Press, 1970, pp. 113-17).*

WYNDHAM LEWIS (essay date 1929)

[*Lewis found little to praise in Anderson's work, comparing it to that of D. H. Lawrence in the following essay on racial elements in Anglo-American literature.*]

Of all the children of Walt Whitman, Sherwood Anderson is perhaps the most celebrated: and he has exercised a very great influence upon all the young school of american fiction, and indeed throughout the intelligent life of America. (p. 143)

With Sherwood Anderson the pure romance of whitmanesque tradition remains. At a first reading he looks a little like a Strindberg softened in the prosperous optimistic air of America, and brought up in the shadow of Whitman. (p. 146)

[If you understand D. H. Lawrence's] *Mornings in Mexico*, you will be in a much better position to understand exactly what Mr. Anderson wants to say to you, at the same time that he spins you an excellent yarn. (p. 196)

The negresses in *Dark Laughter* (they are the black servants, and their mocking laughter usually rises from the scullery or kitchen) perpetually release their 'high shrill laughter of the negress,' as they observe with astonishment and derision the feebleness and absurdity of their White Overlords up in the parlour and out on the lawn. 'Up goes the wild, sliding Indian whistle in the morning' from the parrots (mocking the human beings in the court beneath, from which, owing to the overlordship of the human species, they are excluded, and forced to pass their time hanging upon the trees) in Mr. Lawrence's *Mornings in Mexico*: and up goes the 'high shrill laughter' of the negroes in Mr. Sherwood Anderson's *Dark Laughter*. The *negresses* in Mr. Anderson's book are in the rôle of the *parrots* in Mr. Lawrence's book: and the White Overlords in Mr. Anderson's book are in the rôle of Homo Sapiens in Mr. Lawrence's book. But in Mr. Lawrence's book, as in Mr. Anderson's, the *White Overlord*, rather than the more abstract and fundamental Human Being, is the true objective. And the Mexican Indian in *Mornings in Mexico* plays the part of the Negro in *Dark Laughter*. I think this parallel can be missed by no one. So there is a good deal of truth, it seems, in the 'moron' critic's gibe, 'Sherwood Lawrence,' in Mr. Mencken's *Americana*. (pp. 197-98)

The dread of sexual impotence, thoughts about impotence, taunts about impotence, anxious appeals to the 'chinook'—of such cheerful and 'manly' material as this are many of the pages of Mr. Lawrence and Mr. Sherwood Anderson composed. But there is a strain of frank and free modesty in Mr. Anderson, whenever he casts a glance in the direction of his own 'maleness.' It leaves much to be desired, in his eyes. Throughout his books Mr. Anderson indeed is comparing himself unfavourably, on the score of his 'manhood,' with other men (his brother, for instance, in the account of his childhood). In his *Story-Teller's Story*, and indeed everywhere when he appears in a more or less veiled form, these dark doubts beset him. The adulterous Bruce in *Dark Laughter* feels that a *real man* would behave quite differently from what he does in most things. He would make less fuss, *think* about things less, *act*. He is a bit of a poet, really, that is what it is, not a man of action he says to himself. Perhaps Mr. Anderson is over-modest. He is probably as 'manly' as most men: but, however that may be, he is very much puzzled and befuddled: he is a poor henpecked, beFreuded, bewildered White, with a brand-new 'inferiority complex.'

Mr. Lawrence is quite a different story. He is in full and exultant enjoyment of a full battery of 'complexes' of every possible shade and shape of sexiness. . . . Beside him Anderson strikes one as a rather muddle-headed, clumsy, in some ways very stupid sensationalist, doing his best for a group of 'dark' influences which he very imperfectly understands, and often misinterprets. (pp. 203-04)

Mr. Sherwood Anderson in *Dark Laughter* writes in a manner that is really distracting. What the manner is I don't know: it may be a supremely undeft imitation of Mr. Joyce. I will give you a specimen of it. (p. 204)

> Once he had read a book of Zola, *La Terre*, and later, but a short time before he left Chicago, Tom Wills had shewn him a new book by the Irishman Joyce, *Ulysses*. There were certain pages. A man named Bloom standing on a beach near some women. A woman, Bloom's wife, in her bedroom at home. The thoughts of the woman—her right of animal-

ism—all set down—minutely. Realism in writing lifted up sharp something burning and new like a raw sore. Others coming to look at the sores. . . .

Pick up any monthly magazine devoted to the most popular sort of fiction, and you will read 'He flung out bitterly, in short jagged sentences, as though it was painful for him to speak: "No good. All is over between us.—Things might have been different. If—Ah well. It's too late. Good-bye."' This is intended to represent a person labouring under an emotion too deep for words. In the above passage of Mr. Anderson's the effect aimed at is a sort of bitter brevity—stuff flung out carelessly by a man who in the opinion both of the author and of himself is rather a fine fellow. (p. 206)

Now, above, in the . . . passage by Mr. Anderson that I have quoted, Zola is mentioned first, and Joyce afterwards. Zola, standing for 'brutal realism,' or for 'animalism,' like Joyce (in Mr. Anderson's eyes) must have been always at the back of his mind, I suspect. *La Terre* is surely a recognizable forebear of **Dark Laughter.** All that is *suety,* and *stupid*—all the thick, fat *dummheit*—in this book, is the authentic zolaesque romance—Nature, sensuality, hot lowering sulphurous Summers—bursting, sappy Springs; cows mooing for bulls, bulls bellowing for cows, etc. etc. It all is there. But Freud has come in, too. So when the hero is thinking about his childhood, no one will be surprised to find that he first of all describes himself as a small boy, sitting beside his mother on a river-steamer, and 'sensing' that his mother was 'lusting' for a young man who stood near them with a dark moustache; and that then he half withdraws the young man with the dark moustache, and half-exonerates his mother from these fresh sensations, and takes the blame himself. It was *he*, the little boy, who in reality (the author's dutiful eye on Dr. Freud) was 'lusting' for his mother. (pp. 207-08)

So much for the usual incest. Next I will take the mystical communism. (Not that Freud's teaching is not an integral part of communism, too, for it is the psychology appropriate to a highly communized patriarchal society in which *the family* and its close relationship is an intense obsession, and the obscene familiarities of a closely packed communal sex-life a family-joke, as it were. It is a psychology foreign to the average European and his individualistic life. The incest-theme is inappropriate to the european communities, on whom no severe religious restrictions of race or of caste have been imposed.) So by 'communism' here I mean what currently we mean when we say communism. Mr. Anderson is describing happenings on the Mississippi before the coming of industrialism, and especially he is glorifying the negroes.

> —black mysticism—never expressed except in song or in the movements of bodies. The bodies of the black workers belonged to each other as the sky belonged to the river. . . .
>
> Brown bodies trotting, black bodies trotting. *The bodies of all the men running up and down the landing-stage were one body. One could not be distinguished from another. They were lost in each other.—Could the bodies of people be so lost, in each other,* etc.

He apostrophizes american painters, and calls them 'silly American painters!' He says that silly painters 'chase a Gauguin shadow to the South Seas.' Why don't they stay at home and paint the american Negro? he asks. If they want to find ro-

mance—mystical romance, or 'black mysticism,' here it is at their doors. (pp. 208-09)

The 'brown mysticism' of Gauguin's dusky mistresses he wishes to transport into the Mississippi, and create a *Noa-Noa* upon its flood. And Niggerland shall henceforth be their Pacific, for those inland populations that have never seen the sea, and each man be a Gauguin in his own back-yard.

There is an important feature of the teaching of Mr. Sherwood Anderson with which I am much in sympathy. This he inherits too from Walt Whitman. But it is flatly contradicted by the communism of the rest of his work. I refer to his eloquent opposition to the influences of industrial life—to the killing of life and natural beauty that that entails. (p. 212)

When we in Europe discuss America, we picture it only as this 'soulless' (to use Lawrence's word in another connection) desolation of the Machine Age. It typifies to the European the Robot, Machine-life, in excelsis. We forget, or we have no means of knowing, that the more intelligent American sees this, 'sees through it,' as well as we do; and happens to hate it with far more intensity, sometimes, than is found with us. (p. 215)

Nowhere in the Old World have I ever met such a thorough aversion for all the things that we regard as typically american, and which the American of the popular imagination is always supposed to be boasting about.

That Mr. Anderson realizes that in this attitude towards the staggering material achievements of his country, he, and the many Americans of his way of thinking, are rebels against an entire scheme of things—the whole of our 'americanized' civilization, in fact—is clear from what happens in his book, **Poor White.** That is the story of a child of Poor Whites on the Mississippi, who discovers a genius for engineering. His inventions are highly profitable to himself and those with whom he is associated, and the town where he is settled rapidly turns from a village into a big factory town. We have a picture of the struggle between the old order and the new—between the craftsman and handiworker, and the new industrialism.

But eventually Hugh the inventor begins turning against his own mechanical-toys, and even loses his power of inventing these. But by this reaction, Mr. Anderson says, he is still in advance of his fellows. He has become *conscious;* before he had been *unconscious* (that is certainly a step in advance: but does it tally with Mr. Anderson's teaching elsewhere?). (p. 216)

Mr. Anderson is (whatever the origin of those impulses may be with him) insurgent or reactionary where the great mailed fist of Big Business is concerned—rebellious to all that giant orthodoxy of mercantile collectivism which is pulverizing the life of the contemporary world, in herding people in enormous mechanized masses. (p. 219)

Mr. Anderson no doubt would be incapable of seizing the fundamental liaison of many of his favourite ideas with the materialist aspect of the communist doctrine. Where he bestows upon Clara, in **Poor White,** a lesbian chum, and makes her respond to her life experience *à la garçonne;* or, again, where he advertises in **Dark Laughter** a passion, as a child of six, for his mother (so conforming to the incest motif of Freud), he is far from realizing, I should say, where these ideologic borrowings would lead him, had he the curiosity to track them back to their true sources. All this is hidden from Mr. Anderson: but that is not for a moment to say that, had he the energy or intelligence to track the principal and most picturesque notions by which he has been influenced back where they most truly belong, he would not be even better pleased with himself than now he is. Nor do I say that, swiftly navigating the broad stream of influences (to which he, in common with everybody else to-day, has been subjected) up to its fountain head, and finding himself at last in the company of early Generals of the Society of Jesus, or Grand Inquisitors, closeted with the chiefs of the Templars or passing into the shadow of the Star Chamber. . . . (pp. 219-20)

I think that the emotional insurgence of Mr. Anderson against the conditions of Big Business is flatly contradicted by his communism. I will repeat the quotation where he is exclaiming about the peculiar solidarity of the negro workers.

> The bodies of all the men running up and down
> the landing-stage were one body. One could
> not be distinguished from another. They were
> lost in each other. Could the bodies of people
> be so lost in each other?

The answer of course to that last question (the exclamations of Mr. Anderson have usually the form of questions) is 'Yes, they can. It is quite easy for White Men, as well as Negroes, to become *Mass men*, "not to be distinguished from one another." Intensive Industrialism is able to achieve that for you whoever the bosses.' But Intensive Industrialism is what Mr. Anderson never ceases to fulminate against. And his reasons for hating it appear to be precisely that it *does* merge people in the way that he exultantly describes the Negro workers as being merged, in one featureless anonymous black organism, like a gigantic centipede. So in the same breath he is gloomy and joyful over the same phenomenon! (pp. 221-22)

[Elsewhere in this book], I have quoted Mr. D. H. Lawrence, where he says, 'It is almost impossible for the white people to approach the Indian without either sentimentality or dislike.'

And I remarked that Mr. Lawrence showed himself to be a *good White Man* in that respect: for there is a great deal of 'sentimentality' about the Hopi in the books of Mr. Lawrence.

Where the american Negro is concerned it is the same thing with Mr. Sherwood Anderson, although it is a different sort of 'sentimentality.' In any book of his you pick up you will find, wherever Negroes occur, that they are used to score off the White; or are compared, with considerable 'sentiment,' very favourably with the White 'Overlord.'

This invariable attitude on the part of Mr. Anderson is partly the effect of fashionable *primitivist* doctrine: and it is partly the revolutionary, 'radical,' impulse at work. The Negro is 'kept in his place,' is 'looked down on,' is used as a hireling, and laughed at, by the arrogant Lord of Creation, the White Man. Mr. Anderson has learnt his little 'radical' lesson. So, wherever the Negro occurs, and he occurs fairly often in his books, he is made to take the White down a peg or two. What blissful ignorance of really *dark* realities is displayed by these old-fashioned habits—old-fashioned because they came into existence amongst and were proper to conditions that have passed! (pp. 222-23)

In my analysis of the primitivism of Messrs. Lawrence and Anderson, especially with regard to their attitude to the Negro or Indian, I point out how in both cases they were careful to accuse all other people who had ever approached Blacks or Indians of being 'sentimental towards,' or else full of hatred for *those coloured aliens*. It seems plain to me that this was a step, merely, to protect themselves against an accusation that they realize they have deserved.

It will be useful, however, to get some meaning into the tag 'sentimental' before we leave it.

Any idea should be regarded as 'sentimental' that is not taken to its ultimate conclusion. I propose that as a working definition of 'sentimentality.' (p. 248)

Why I regard the spirit of the works of Mr. Anderson and of Mr. Lawrence as sentimental, is because it indulges in a series of emotions that, if persevered in by the Public they are intended to influence, would cancel themselves. I regard Mr. Anderson as more sentimental than Mr. Lawrence, because I do not think he suspects what the real issues are at all; whereas I daresay Mr. Lawrence knows to some extent, though just as he was in the first instance a little vague as to where the ideas he used came from, he probably is not over clear as to whither they are bound, or what their affiliations are. Alternatively, if both Mr. Anderson and Mr. Lawrence see these conclusions with extreme clearness, then they are deliberately employing, at least, the machinery of sentimentality. But I think they both use it too naturally for it not to be native to them. (p. 249)

> *Wyndham Lewis, "Paleface" (originally published in part in a somewhat different form in* The Enemy, *No. 2, September, 1928), in his* Paleface: The Philosophy of the "Melting Pot" *(reprinted by permission of the Literary Estate of Wyndham Lewis), Chatto & Windus, 1929 (and reprinted by Scholarly Press, Inc., 1971), pp. 97-288.**

GRANVILLE HICKS (essay date 1935)

[*Hicks, a Marxist when he wrote* The Great Tradition, *offers a general discussion of Anderson's art, particularly of* Beyond Desire, *Anderson's novel most influenced by Communist thought.*]

Like Dreiser, Sherwood Anderson came from a mid-western family with many children and little money. Like Dreiser, he at first worshipped the bitch goddess, achieving moderate prosperity as a business executive and as a writer of advertisements, and he too discovered the emptiness of material success. But if their early experiences are somewhat similar, their literary gifts are utterly different. Incapable of sustained, exact description, Anderson relies upon the lightning flash. Surfaces, deeds, even words scarcely concern him; everything is bent to the task of revelation. When he succeeds, there is the character of Elmer Cowley or Dr. Reefy or Louise Hardy, about whom we need to be told nothing more. If one were to judge Anderson only by his best work, one could scarcely avoid the conclusion that his talent was of the first order. Here, one would note, was a prose-writer with the courage to create his own idiom and his own rhythms. One would marvel at the man's penetration, his understanding of the strangeness and terror that life holds even for the humblest. And one would find, in such a book as *Winesburg, Ohio,* an authentic picture of the small town, and, in *Poor White,* the record of the small town's transformation. Except in *Poor White,* one would find little about industrialism, and yet one could never be unaware that the civilization portrayed was in travail. Others have described more fully how the common people live; no one has shown so authoritatively what they feel. (pp. 229-30)

The mystery of life, so distressing to Dreiser, has been scarcely less terrifying to Sherwood Anderson. Though *Winesburg, Ohio,* gave the impression that he was principally concerned with the blighting effects of small town life, it soon became apparent that he regarded industrialism as the real enemy. In *Poor White* he traced the transition in the Middle West from agriculture and the handicrafts to machine industry, and showed that Hugh McVey's inventions not only failed to bring happiness but destroyed values that had previously existed. The real hero of the story is Joe Wainsworth, the harness maker who takes pride in his work. "What has mankind, in America, not missed," Anderson asked in *A Story-Teller's Story,* "because men do not know, or are forgetting, what the old workman knew." . . . It is little wonder that in the later twenties, when he felt his creative powers flagging, Anderson went back to the small town. The small town newspaper, he said, might help in the struggle against industrialism and standardization, and he advised young men and women to use such papers to start a backfire in favor of individualism.

But Anderson can never be satisfied with an easy solution. He continued to worry about the machine, and to wonder if it could not somehow be made to serve the ideals in which he believed. He wondered if poets could not take a different attitude towards machines, and he wrote poems himself in which he made tentative affirmations. He went even farther: he began to realize that all the problems that troubled him were bound up in one problem, and like Dreiser he took his stand with the party of revolution. These two men, both of them intimately acquainted with poverty and hardship, both of them very close to the common people, have both discovered that their hopes are inextricably linked with the hopes of the working class. Since he made this discovery Anderson has written one book, *Beyond Desire.* It has most of the virtues of his earlier work, and most of the faults. It shows that his approach to communism is almost purely personal; it attracts him because it seems to answer some of the questions that have long troubled him. The economic and philosophical implications of communism mean little to him, and certainly he is not yet filled with the spirit of the fighting vanguard of the proletariat. Therefore he is still a long way from overcoming the effects of years of bewilderment and frustration, and *Beyond Desire* is as lacking in unity and as chaotic in its analyses as any of its predecessors. But the book is significant because a change in Anderson may signify a change in the American people, to whom he has always been extremely close. And when one compares the characterization of Red and the description of the mill girls with the work Anderson did in *Many Marriages* and *Dark Laughter,* there is reason to believe that he may have found a basis for further development. (pp. 232-34)

> Granville Hicks, "Two Roads," in his The Great Tradition: An Interpretation of American Literature since the Civil War *(copyright © 1933, 1935 by Macmillan Publishing Co., Inc.; copyright © 1969 by Granville Hicks; reprinted by permission of Russell & Volkening, Inc., as agent for the author), revised edition, Macmillan, 1935, pp. 207-56.**

THEODORE DREISER (essay date 1941)

[*Dreiser, one of Anderson's early influences and literary friends, pays homage to Anderson in this tribute written shortly after Anderson's death.*]

Anderson, his life and his writings, epitomize for me the pilgrimage of a poet and dreamer across this limited stage called Life, whose reactions to the mystery of our being and doings here (our will-less and so wholly automatic responses to our environing forces) involved tenderness, love and beauty, de-

light in the strangeness of our will-less reactions as well as pity, sympathy and love for all things both great and small. Whenever I think of him I think of that wondrous line out of "The Ancient Mariner"—"He prayeth best who loveth best all things both great and small." And so sometimes the things he wrote, as well as the not too many things he said to me personally, had the value of a poetic prayer for the happiness and the well being of everything and everybody—as well as the well-outcoming of everything guided as each thing plainly is by an enormous wisdom—if seemingly not always imbued with mercy—that none-the-less "passeth all understanding." He seemed to me to accept in humbleness, as well as in and of necessity in nature, Christ's dictums "The rain falleth on the just and unjust." Also that we are to "Take no thought for your life, what ye shall eat, or what ye shall drink: nor yet for your body, what ye shall put on. Is not the life more than meat, and the body than raiment?"

As I see him now there was something Biblical and prophetic about him. Through all his days he appears to have been wandering here and there, looking, thinking, wondering. And the things he brought back from the fields of life! **"Dark Laughter!" "Many Marriages!" "The Triumph of the Egg!" "Mid-American Chants!" "Winesburg!"**—in which is that beautiful commentary on the strain of life on some temperaments called **"Hands!"** It is to me so truly beautiful, understanding and loving, and weeping, almost, for the suffering of others.

> Theodore Dreiser, "Sherwood Anderson," in Story *(copyright, 1941, by Story Magazine, Inc.; copyright renewed © 1969 by Scholastic Magazines, Inc.; reprinted by permission of Scholastic Inc.), Vol. XIX, No. 91, September-October, 1941, p. 4.*

ALFRED KAZIN (essay date 1942)

[*Kazin masterfully examines Anderson's career and his place in American literary history.*]

If it was the first trombone blasts from Mencken's *Prejudices* in 1919 that sounded the worldliness and pride of the new emancipation, it was two stories of revolt against small-town life in the Middle West—Sherwood Anderson's *Winesburg, Ohio* in 1919 and Sinclair Lewis's *Main Street* in 1920—that now brought new life into the American novel by dramatizing that emancipation in terms of common experience. Signalizing "the revolt from the village," as Carl Van Doren described it at a moment when Edgar Lee Master's *Spoon River Anthology* had already set the tone of the new spiritual migration in the twenties, these two books signalized even more the coming of a fresh new realism into fiction. (p. 205)

Reveling in the commonplace, the new realists felt that with them the modern novel in America had at last come to grips with the essentials, and the vigor with which they described the mean narrowness and sterility of their world had in it a kind of exuberance. (pp. 209-10)

[Anderson's] great subject always was personal freedom, the yearning for freedom, the delight in freedom; and out of it he made a kind of left-handed mysticism, a groping for the unnamed and unrealized ecstasy immanent in human relations, that seemed the sudden revelation of the lives Americans led in secret. If Sinclair Lewis dramatized the new realism by making the novel an exact and mimetic transcription of American life, Anderson was fascinated by the undersurface of that life and became the voice of its terrors and exultations. Lewis turned the novel into a kind of higher journalism; Anderson turned fiction into a substitute for poetry and religion, and never ceased to wonder at what he had wrought. He had more intensity than a revival meeting and more tenderness than God; he wept, he chanted, he loved indescribably. There was freedom in the air, and he would summon all Americans to share in it; there was confusion and mystery on the earth, and he would summon all Americans to wonder at it. He was clumsy and sentimental; he could even write at times as if he were finger-painting; but at the moment it seemed as if he had sounded the depths of common American experience as no one else could.

There was always an image in Anderson's books—an image of life as a house of doors, of human beings knocking at them and stealing through one door only to be stopped short before another as if in a dream. Life was a dream to him, and he and his characters seemed always to be walking along its corridors. Who owned the house of life? How did one escape after all? No one in his books ever knew, Anderson least of all. Yet slowly and fumblingly he tried to make others believe, as he thought he had learned for himself, that it was possible to escape if only one laughed at necessity. That was his own story, as everything he wrote—the confession in his *Memoirs* was certainly superfluous—was a variation upon it; and it explained why, for all his fumbling and notorious lack of contemporary sophistication, he had so great an appeal for the restive postwar generation. For Anderson, growing up in small Ohio villages during the eighties and nineties at a time when men could still watch and wait for the new industrial world to come in, enjoyed from the first—at least in his own mind—the luxury of dreaming away on the last margin of the old prefactory freedom, of being suspended between two worlds. Unlike most modern American realists even of his own generation, in fact, Anderson always evoked in his books the world of the old handicraft artisans, the harness makers and Civil War veterans like his father, the small-town tailors and shoemakers, the buggy and wagon craftsmen of the old school. (pp. 210-11)

It was certainly on the basis of his experiences in this world that Anderson was able ever after to move through the world that Chicago now symbolized as if he, and all his characters with him, were moving in puzzled bliss through the interstices of the great new cities and factories. No other novelist of the time gave so vividly the sense of *not* having been brought up to the constraints, the easy fictions, the veritable rhythm, of modern commercial and industrial life. It was as if he had been brought up in a backwater, grown quaint and self-willed, a little "queer," a drowsing village mystic, amidst stagnant scenes; and the taste of that stagnance was always in his work. A certain sleepy inarticulation, a habit of staring at faces in wondering silence, a way of groping for words and people indistinguishably, also crept into his work; and what one felt in it was not only the haunting tenderness with which he came to his characters, but also the measureless distances that lay between these characters themselves. They spoke out of the depths, but in a sense they did not speak at all; they addressed themselves, they addressed the world around them, and the echoes of their perpetual confession were like sound-waves visible in the air.

"I would like to write a book of the life of the mind and of the imagination," Anderson wrote in his *Memoirs*. "Facts elude me. I cannot remember dates. When I deal in facts, at once I begin to lie. I can't help it." The conventional world for him was a snare, a cheat that fearful little men had agreed among themselves to perpetuate; the reality lay underground, in men and women themselves. It was as if the ageless dilemma of men caught by society found in him the first prophet naïve enough, and therefore bold enough, to deny that men need be caught at all. His heroes were forever rebelling against the material, yet they were all, like Anderson himself, sublimely unconscious of it. The proud sons who rebel against their drunkard fathers, like Windy McPherson's son, sicken of the riches they have gained, but they never convince one that they have lived with riches. The rebels against working-class squalor and poverty, like Beaut McGregor in *Marching Men,* finally do rise to wealth and greatness, but only to lead men—as Anderson, though a Socialist in those early years, hoped to lead them—out of the factory world itself into a vague solidarity of men marching forever together. The businessmen who have revolted against their families, like John Webster in *Many Marriages,* make an altar in their bedrooms to worship; the sophisticated artists, like Bruce Dudley in *Dark Laughter,* run away from home to hear the laughter of the triumphantly unrepressed Negroes; the ambitious entrepreneurs, like Hugh McVey in *Poor White,* weep in despair over the machines they have built. And when they do escape, they all walk out of the prison house of modern life, saying with inexpressible simplicity, as Anderson did on the day he suddenly walked out of his paint factory in Ohio: "What am I going to do? Well, now, that I don't know. I am going to wander about. I am going to sit with people, listen to words, tell tales of people, what they are thinking, what they are feeling. The devil! It may even be that I am going forth in search of myself."

"I have come to think," he wrote in *A Story-Teller's Story,* "that the true history of life is but a history of moments. It is only at rare moments that we live." In those early days it was as if a whole subterranean world of the spirit were speaking in and through Anderson, a spirit imploring men to live frankly and fully by their own need of liberation, and pointing the way to a tender and surpassing comradeship. . . . Out of his wandering experiences at soldiering and laboring jobs, at following the race horses he loved and the business career he hated, he had become "at last a writer, a writer whose sympathy went out most to the little frame houses, on often mean enough streets in American towns, to defeated people, often with thwarted lives." Were there not people, people everywhere, just people and their stories to tell? Were there not questions about them always to be asked—the endless wonderment, the groping out toward them, the special "moments" to be remembered? (pp. 212-14)

Between the people he saw and the books he read, Anderson saw the terrible chasm of fear in America—the fear of sex, the fear of telling the truth about the hypocrisy of those businessmen with whom he too had reached for "the bitch-goddess of success"; the fear, even, of making stories the exact tonal equivalent of their lives; the fear of restoring to books the slackness and the disturbed rhythms of life. For Anderson was not only reaching for the truth about people and "the terrible importance of the flesh in human relations"; he was reaching at the same time for a new kind of medium in fiction. As he confessed explicitly later on, he even felt that "the novel form does not fit an American writer, that it is a form which had been brought in. What is wanted is a new looseness; and in *Winesburg* I had made my own form." Significantly enough, even such warm friends of the new realism as Floyd Dell and H. L. Mencken did not think the *Winesburg* stories stories at all; but Anderson, who had revolted against what he now saw as the false heroic note in his first work, knew better, and he was to make the new readers see it his way.

For if "the true history of life was but a history of moments," it followed that the dream of life could be captured only in a fiction that broke with rules of structure literally to embody moments, to suggest the endless halts and starts, the dreamlike passiveness and groping of life. What Gertrude Stein had for fifteen years, working alone in Paris, learned out of her devotion to the independent vision of modern French painting, Anderson now realized by the simple stratagem of following the very instincts of his character, by groping through to the slow realization of his characters on the strength of his conviction that all life itself was only a process of groping. The difference between them (it was a difference that Gertrude Stein's pupil, Ernest Hemingway, felt so deeply that he had to write a parody of Anderson's style, *The Torrents of Spring,* to express his revulsion and contempt) was that where Miss Stein and Hemingway both had resolved their break with the "rules" into a formal iconoclastic technique, a conscious principle of design, Anderson had no sense of design at all save as life afforded him one. Although he later listened humbly enough to Gertrude Stein in Paris—she had proclaimed him one of the few Americans who could write acceptable sentences—he could never make one principle of craft, least of all those "perfect sentences" that she tried so hard to write, the foundation of his work. Anderson was, in fact, rather like an older kind of artisan in the American tradition—such as Whitman and Albert Pinkham Ryder—artisans who worked by sudden visions rather than by any sense of style, artisans whose work was the living grammar of their stubborn belief in their own visions. (pp. 214-15)

Anderson did not merely live for the special "moments" in experience; he wrote, by his own testimony, by sudden realizations, by the kind of apprehension of a mood, a place, a character, that brought everything to a moment's special illumination and stopped short there, content with the fumbling ecstasy it brought. It was this that gave him his interest in the "sex drive" as a force in human life (it had so long been left out), yet always touched that interest with a bold, awkward innocence. He was among the first American writers to bring the unconscious into the novel, yet when one thinks of how writers like Dorothy Richardson, Virginia Woolf, and James Joyce pursued the unconscious and tried to trace some pattern in the fathomless psychic history of men and women, it is clear that Anderson was not interested in contributing to the postwar epic of the unconscious at all. What did interest him was sex as a disturbance in consciousness, the kind of disturbance that drove so many of his heroes out of the world of constraint; but once he had got them out of their houses, freed them from convention and repression, their liberation was on a plane with their usually simultaneous liberation from the world of business. It was their loneliness that gave them significance in Anderson's mind, the lies that they told themselves and each other to keep the desperate fictions of conventionality; and it was inevitably the shattering of that loneliness, the emergence out of that uneasy twilit darkness in which his characters always lived, that made their triumph and, in his best moments, Anderson's own.

The triumph, yes; and the agony. It is a terrible thing for a visionary to remain a minor figure; where the other minor figures can at least work out a minor success, the visionary who has not the means equal to his vision crumbles into fragments. Anderson was a minor figure, as he himself knew so

well; and that was his tragedy. For the significance of his whole career is that though he could catch, as no one else could, the inexpressible grandeur of those special moments in experience, he was himself caught between them. Life was a succession of moments on which everything else was strung; but the moments never came together, and the world itself never came together for him. It was not his "mysticism" that was at fault, for without it he would have been nothing; nor was it his special way of groping for people, of reaching for the grotesques in life, the homely truths that seemed to him so beautiful, since that was what he had most to give—and did give so imperishably in *Winesburg,* in stories like **"I'm a Fool,"** in parts of *Poor White* and *Dark Laughter,* and in the autobiographical *Tar.* It was rather that Anderson had nothing else in him that was equal to his revelations, his tenderness, his groping. He was like a concentration of everything that had been missed before him in modern American writing, and once his impact was felt, the stammering exultation he brought became all. That was Anderson's real humiliation, the humiliation that perhaps only those who see so much more deeply than most men can feel; and he knew it best of all. (pp. 215-16)

"If you love in a loveless world," he wrote in *Many Marriages,* "you face others with the sin of not loving." He had that knowledge; he brought it in, and looked at it as his characters looked at each other; but he could only point to it and wonder. "There is something that separates people, curiously, persistently, in America," he wrote in his last novel, *Kit Brandon.* He ended on that note as he had begun on it twenty-five years before, when Windy McPherson's son wondered why he could never get what he wanted, and Beaut McGregor led the marching men marching, marching nowhere. The brooding was there, the aimless perpetual reaching, that indefinable note Anderson always struck; but though no writer had written so much of liberation, no writer seemed less free. He was a Prospero who had charmed himself to sleep and lost his wand; and as the years went on Anderson seemed more and more bereft, a minor visionary whose perpetual air of wonder became a trance and whose prose disintegrated helplessly from book to book. Yet knowing himself so well, he could smile over those who were so ready to tell him that it was his ignorance of "reality" and of "real people" that crippled his books. What was it but the reality that was almost too oppressively real, the reality beyond the visible surface world, the reality of all those lives that so many did lead in secret, that he had brought into American fiction? It was not his vision that was at fault, no; it was that poignant human situation embodied in him, that story he told over and again because it was his only story—of the groping that broke forth out of the prison house of life and . . . went on groping; of the search for freedom that made all its substance out of that search, and in the end left all the supplicators brooding, suffering, and overwhelmed. Yet if he had not sought so much, he could not have been humiliated so deeply. It was always the measure of his reach that gave others the measure of his failure. (p. 217)

Alfred Kazin, "The New Realism: Sherwood Anderson and Sinclair Lewis," in his On Native Grounds: An Interpretation of Modern American Prose Literature *(copyright 1942, 1970 by Alfred Kazin; reprinted by permission of Harcourt Brace Jovanovich, Inc.), Reynal & Hitchcock, 1942, pp. 205-26.**

HORACE GREGORY (essay date 1949)

[*Gregory critically surveys Anderson's work.*]

As one reads Anderson's stories and autobiographies, three

older writers come to mind: one is Herman Melville, another Mark Twain, and the third George Borrow. (p. 7)

Anderson's liking for Borrow has an instinctive rightness beyond anything he could have learned through a conventional education. Borrow showed what a writer could do while ignoring the conventional rules for writing autobiographies and novels. This was a valuable lesson that Anderson never forgot; he became, as Thomas Seccombe wrote of Borrow, not a "matter-of-fact," but a "matter-of-fiction" man. He did not allow Borrow to influence him directly, and in matters of style, in which Borrow was notoriously uneven, Anderson greatly improved upon him. The choice of Borrow as one of his models placed Anderson on the side of those who see and feel things from the ground up, from the pavement of a city street, from the grasses of a field, from the threshold of a house. This view is always an independent view that refuses to become housebroken.

Anderson's debt to Mark Twain is less veiled than that to Borrow, for Mark Twain's *Huckleberry Finn* is literally close to an American time and place that Anderson knew. . . . The people of Anderson's boyhood in the Middle West were but a single generation beyond Tom Sawyer and Huckleberry Finn, and there was an unbroken continuity between the two generations. Huckleberry Finn's skepticism concerning the virtues of church-going was of a piece with the world that Anderson knew, a world whose enjoyment was of the earth. Anderson's affinity to Mark Twain was as "natural," as unstudied as Anderson's memories of growing up and coming of age. Equally natural was the example of perspective taken from Borrow, choosing the life of the out-of-doors as the true center of worldly experience.

With Melville, Anderson's affinities are of a far less conscious order; they belong to the inward-looking, darkened "nocturnal" aspects of Anderson's heritage. The affinities to Twain and Borrow are of daylight character; they are clear and specific, and are sharply outlined within the lively scenes that Anderson created, but his kinship with Melville belongs to that diffused and shadowy area of his imagination which Paul Rosenfeld named as mysticism. . . . It was once fashionable to call such "mysticism" Freudian, because it touched upon the emotions of adolescent sexual experience. In Anderson those emotions are transcended in **"Death in the Woods,"** and whatever "mysticism" may be found within them, including the expression of mystery and awe, is of an older heritage than are the teachings of Freud in America. . . . The diffused affinity that Anderson has with Melville is not a facile one, for Anderson made it one of his few rules to stand aside from "literary precedent," to re-create scenes of action in terms of his own experience rather than to lean upon experiences gained from reading the works of others. The kinship of Anderson's writings with *Moby Dick* embraces that side of Anderson's imagination which is "non-realistic," and which converts what is outwardly the simple telling of a story into a series of symbolic actions. The fluttering, "talking" quality of Wing Biddlebaum's "slender expressive fingers, forever active," in **"Hands,"** is endowed with the mystery that Anderson makes his readers feel. (pp. 8-10)

If the "real Anderson" is seen more clearly in legendary episodes of the autobiographies than when he employs too consciously the pronoun "I," how vividly, how memorably he moves before the reader in his major novel, *Poor White.* (p. 15)

Poor White belongs among the few books that have restored with memorable vitality the life of an era, its hopes and desires,

its conflicts between material prosperity and ethics, and its disillusionments, in a manner that stimulates the historical imagination. The book belongs to the period, those years between the middle 1870's and the first ten years of the present century, that gave Thorstein Veblen's *The Theory of the Leisure Class* . . . its air of immediate reference. It was in *Poor White* that the ideas, the talk overheard in Anderson's boyhood, bore fruit. (pp. 16-17)

Anderson did not reach the accomplishment of *Poor White* without preparation; in writing *Winesburg, Ohio* he had begun to discover his style, and in the last chapters of the book he had really found it. He records the importance of that discovery in his *Memoirs,* how the book came to life in a series of stories while he was living in a Chicago rooming house. But *Poor White* also has behind it *Windy McPherson's Son* and more particularly, *Marching Men,* which, Anderson afterwards wrote, should have been a poem. The book was not a poem, but a novel that failed to accomplish its intentions, and yet foreshadowed the kind of novel *Poor White* became. In theory *Marching Men* is a good idea for a book; it embraces the problem of labor leadership in America and the spectacle of American workingmen marching together to redress industrial wrong. But the good idea in the novel remained too theoretical to take on the semblance of life; its hero "Beaut" McGregor, the tall, awkward, red-haired miner's son who becomes a lawyer, and afterwards a leader of workingmen, is too thinly drawn; he is an unindividualized type, whose eventual failure as a leader of men is not felt by the reader. And the entire book is punctuated by fictional clichés. . . . The only scene in *Marching Men* that comes to life is irrelevant to the historical and social themes of the book—and that is the passionate recital of the woman problem by a minor character, a barber. In the barber's speech on his unhappy marriage and his relationship to women the accents of the future Anderson are heard; the barber's theme is expanded in *Many Marriages,* and is heard with greater clarity in *Dark Laughter.* It is sounded fitfully in Anderson's first novel, *Windy McPherson's Son.*

A too broad, too loose fictional method of writing cultural (and industrial) history begins in *Windy McPherson's Son,* grows into a more clearly discerned view of Anderson's world in *Marching Men,* and then achieves a justly proportioned design in *Poor White.* (pp. 18-20)

Poor White, a tribute to a cultural past, does not, of course, resemble the costume historical novel in any of its features: it is as plotless as though Anderson had wisely taken to heart Mark Twain's warning to the readers of *Huckleberry Finn*— "persons attempting to find a plot in it will be shot." And he drew as much from the example of Mark Twain's kind of plotlessness (which never, however, permitted a story to lack action and incident) as from the examples provided by the stories in Gertrude Stein's *Three Lives.*

No novel of the American small town in the Middle West evokes in the minds of its readers so much of the cultural heritage of its milieu as does *Poor White;* nor does Anderson in his later novels ever recapture the same richness of association, the ability to make memorable each scene in the transition from an agrarian way of living to a twentieth-century spectacle of industrial conflict with its outward display of physical comfort and wealth.

One of Anderson's critics has remarked on his ability to write at his best only when the impulse to write urgently moved him, and that statement has an enlightening truth within it for anyone examining his short stories. In these he held to his position of being one whose concern for prose was like a poet's concern for verse: he was a story-teller who desired only to gratify his need to talk and to charm his listeners, with no thought of pecuniary reward. But if his standards seem often those of one who perpetuates the folk tale in its simplicity, he is also the artist, who with a limited number of brush strokes leaves his style, the impress of his personality, along with the image of an undraped figure, or a landscape, upon his canvas. And if one finds the impact of any style of plastic art in Anderson's stories, it is the style of Renoir and Pissaro, of late Impressionism. For often there seems to be light and air between his sentences, as in **"The American County Fair,"** for example, and the same loose Impressionistic strokes introduce the reader to scenes in **"The Egg"** and **"The Man Who Became a Woman."** It is in seeming at times to wander away from his story that Anderson so often relaxes and lures his readers, and within the details of an Impressionistic haze of light and color that he often creates an "artlessness" that conceals his art.

In Anderson's stories, from the early pieces which became parts of a series in *Winesburg, Ohio,* to his masterpiece **"Death in the Woods,"** one sees the particulars of people, rather than the types that one finds in his novels. The first edition of *The Triumph of the Egg: A Book of Impressions from American Life in Tales and Poems* (its subtitle is not to be ignored) is illustrated by photographs of grotesques in clay by Tennessee Mitchell. The grotesques, nearly burlesque portrait heads of the people in the book, are in spirit with the stories told about these people, for their individuality is carried upward, slightly off the earth, into a higher register of fancy. Since Anderson's view is always from the earth upward, in the story of **"The Egg"** the flight of fancy takes off from a child's-eye-view level, and we are warned early in the story that a grotesque humor will be released: we are told, "Grotesques are born out of eggs as out of people." . . . From the child's-eye-view through which Anderson presents it, the story has the authenticity of a fable, an air of candor which saves it from falling into bad taste, and the high spirit in which it is told rescues it from a mawkish concern over the spectacle of repeated failure, for the grotesque man is no more successful as a restaurant-keeper and panic-stricken salesman than he was as a chicken-farmer. It is the kind of story that having been told once cannot be told again; it is the story that makes the entire book, *The Triumph of the Egg,* memorable, and all the other stories and verses in the volume grow pale beside it; these others seem to have been written with less urgency of impulse, and though no less lyrical in tone, are thin and diffused. The book is in fact The Triumph of the Egg.

Anderson's ventures into the higher registers of fancy (which make it strange to think of him as a realist, as he was once classified) did not end with *The Triumph of the Egg*—the ventures had actually begun in **"Hands,"** the first of the *Winesburg* stories, and indeed the prelude to *Winesburg* was called **"The Book of the Grotesque."** As the image, the theme, and the fear of being grotesque matured in Anderson's imagination, some of the most clearly inspired of his stories were possessed by it. The fears of being strange and, similarly, the painful, half comic experiences of "growing up," pervade the stories and sketches of *Horses and Men.* The book is literally of horses and men, and no American writer of Anderson's generation or any other has caught the colors, the lights and shadows, the spirit of the race track as well as he; the race track is Anderson's milieu quite as the American county fair is, and among those who write of sports, he is in the company of Ring Lardner and

Ernest Hemingway. But here also his view of the scene is a characteristic upward glance, the view of country boys in **"I'm a Fool"** and **"The Man Who Became a Woman."** The boys are grooms' helpers, "swipes," and they follow the circuit of race-track activities with the same delight with which their younger brothers would try to enter the world of the traveling wild west show or circus. The influence of George Borrow's attraction to gypsy life is active here, but Anderson translates it wholly into American sights and scenes.

Yet all this is finally only the happy choice of a decor for what he really has to say, and in **"The Man Who Became a Woman"** what is said touches upon the fears, the mysteries of adolescence—the fear of the boy (now grown to a man) on discovering that he is "strange," is not wholly masculine, and underlying this, the fear of sterility and death. With a touch as sure as that of D. H. Lawrence, and with none of the mechanical features of overt psychological fiction, Anderson uses, with deceptive simplicity, the scenes in the bar-room and the hayloft, and the incident of the boy's fall, naked, into the shell of bones which was once the carcass of a horse, as the means to tell his story. None of Anderson's stories, with the exception of **"Death in the Woods,"** is a better example of his skill in giving the so-called common experiences of familiar, everyday life, an aura of internal meaning. In this story there is also the fear of Negro laughter, a fear which enters at extended length into two of his later novels, *Dark Laughter* and *Beyond Desire.* In **"The Man Who Became a Woman,"** that particular fear is made more convincing, more appropriate than in the novels; the boy's innocence, his lack of experience, do much to justify his fear, and the fear properly belongs to the immature, the unpoised, the ignorant.

"I'm a Fool" is done with the same turning of light upon common experience—the telling of an awkward, grotesque, foolish lie. Again it is part of the painful experience of growing up, a boyish shrewdness that failed of its desires; it is the image of the concealed, the fatal mistake made by the glib, the young, the unworldly, who parade their candor and innocence wherever they walk and breathe.

"Death in the Woods," Anderson's masterpiece among his shorter stories, is of a different temper and key than the colorful, high-spirited narratives of *Horses and Men.* It is a story which, as Anderson realized, demanded perfection of its kind: he rewrote it several times; it had originally been an episode in *Tar,* and had continued to haunt Anderson's imagination. The strong, initial impulse to write it was not enough, for the story, beyond any other story that Anderson wrote, was the summing up of a lifetime's experience, and in its final version it became Anderson's last look backward into the Middle West of his childhood. It was the last of his *Mid-American Chants,* the book of verses in prose, the last of the prose poems in *A New Testament,* and though its external form is plainly that of a story, its internal structure is that of poetry; it has the power of saying more than prose is required to say, and saying it in the fewest words. But of more importance than the phonetic art of the story is the interplay of those prose rhythms of which Anderson had become a master, and the control of its central theme. (pp. 22-7)

[**"Death in the Woods"**] contains the kind of poetry that we associated with Wordsworth—the recollection of youthful experience, the figures of common speech, the instinctive dignity and life of the poor, the moonlit rural scene—done with the simplicity that Wordsworth sought and attained. It is for this reason (among others) that the story transcends its regional atmosphere, and becomes the universal story that it is. One can think of it, and not inappropriately, as a story that applies to the years of cold and famine in postwar twentieth-century Europe; it has that kind of universality, one that makes possible analogies in life as well as literature. In writing it Anderson's transcendental note was clearly sounded. The note transcends, in more than one meaning of the verb, the writers from whom Anderson drew inspiration—his own contemporaries, Gertrude Stein, Dreiser, D. H. Lawrence, as well as the writers who came before him in revolt against the Puritan New England tradition—and places him not too far from the figures of Thoreau and Emerson.

To enter that dangerous ground which lies between prose and poetry, and to emerge at last, as Anderson does in **"Death in the Woods,"** unscarred by its pitfalls, is a considerable accomplishment, one that has been achieved by few writers in America, and of this small number most are writers whose books provide larger scenes of action than are witnessed in any of Anderson's short stories or novels. It was his contribution and perhaps his destiny, to limit the size of his canvas, to give those who read him a view whose depth, like that of a picture, is greater than the span of the frame around it, and that is one of the reasons why Anderson's best stories have the penetrating quality of Ishmael's gaze in the opening chapters of *Moby Dick*. (pp. 27-8)

> *Horace Gregory, in his introduction to* The Portable Sherwood Anderson *by Sherwood Anderson, edited by Horace Gregory (copyright 1949 by The Viking Press, Inc.; copyright renewed 1976 by Horace Gregory; reprinted by permission of Viking Penguin Inc.), Viking Penguin, 1949, pp. 1-31.*

JON S. LAWRY (essay date 1959)

[*Lawry discusses one of Anderson's best short stories,* "Death in the Woods."]

"Death in the Woods" contains an explicit interior statement of its own meaning. . . . Anderson's statement is, of course, that the life of the old woman of the story was given over to "feeding animal life."

The objective incidents of the story, which in themselves support Anderson's "moral," involve an "old" woman, Mrs. Grimes, who is bent and worn at forty. Abandoned by her unwed mother at birth, the girl had been bound to a German farmer. He later attempted to rape her, and fought over her with Jake Grimes, a sullen young scoundrel. She was then "bound" in marriage to Grimes, bore him a worthless son, and settled into a grinding service to the two men and the animals of the farm, all of whom—"horses, cows, pigs, dogs, men"—had to be fed. On the wintry day of her death, she had gone to town for meat. Feeling weak, she took a short cut through the woods, sank down to rest, and could not bring herself to rise. A pack of dogs circles her as she dies. Upon her death, they wolf the raw meat that she had carried and rip the clothing from her body. A hunter finds the body, thinks it to be that of a young girl, and leads a group of village men to the scene. "No one knew who she was," and each man finds her beautiful. The boyish narrator and his brother receive a partly prurient, partly mystical shock upon seeing her thin girlish body, frozen, like marble, in the snow. The town blacksmith carries her tenderly back into the village.

"She had spent all her life feeding animal life": that statement of the meaning of the story, unnecessary in itself, is wholly insufficient for all that follows the discovery of the body, and for the eerie death ritual that precedes it. The revelation of the woman to the boys, gathered into a context of idealization of woman and rejection of actual sexual experience, and the tender care of the village men for the dead woman they knew but did not know, has no relation to such a "moral." The statement is even more inadequate for the extremely important element in the story omitted in the sketch above: the narrator, who "creates" the meaning of the story. For him it becomes, after his own experience of life and fragmentary recollections of the woman and her death, "music," a revelation created upon memory by contemplation. For him the meaning is, moreover, a conscious, willed creation: "The notes had to be picked up slowly one at a time," if the music was to be heard. It is the narrator, then, who realizes the "meaning," yet for him the ascribed meaning is especially incomplete.

The narrator is a man, now, recalling the events. At first he scarcely remembers them. . . . Thereafter, gradually, [the old woman's] full personal sensations become his own. He feels with her the bondage to "horses, cows, pigs, dogs, men." Once this communion is effected, an arc swings from her life to his own: as he evokes her death, he recalls that he too once faced a circling pack of dogs on a freezing day. Finally, their lives converge directly as the narrator remembers that he, as a boy, saw the body of the "old" woman transformed by death into that of a young girl, wholly beautiful. The boy, it would seem, had even striven to continue the contact of their lives, for he had later been drawn to the abandoned farmhouse and had seen there two dogs still prowling, still waiting to be fed. From these recollections (or this created fiction), the man extracts the statement that the woman had fed animal life, and claims that her story is a beautiful "whole" which he heretofore had been unable to comprehend.

But his statement is flat, largely because he—the explicator or creator—is unaccounted for. Also, the transformation of the woman is absent, save in a merely pitiable application (only in death was she other than a drudge for animal hungers).

It therefore becomes clear that the story is really concerned not with the woman alone, but with the receiving (here, a creating) consciousness—the "I" of the story. His progress is revealing. Like the townspeople, the German family, and the Grimes men, he had at first seen only an anonymous thing (in the words later used to describe her corpse, "no one knew who she was"): one "old woman," no different from her kind in any other town. Some few historical details collect around her, but he still recalls her with indifference. As he nears his own experience through rendering hers, however, he fully enters into her life as an *old* woman, realizing now that she was blank only because life had been drained from her. Their lives converge, as we have seen, culminating in the sense of revelation the narrator feels in seeing the unknown woman's body, perfected in death, which permits him to see the *young* woman and, beyond her, the freed human being behind the anonymous thing called "Mrs. Grimes." This wholeness of realization had, however, to await the mature man's creation, for the boy had seen only two different women, both to some extent "unknown" and unrelated one to the other, and both senses of the woman had faded from his memory.

The narrator has progressed from blank observation of historical fragments, through pity, to whole knowledge. But that knowledge is not of the old woman, primarily; it is of himself.

The story is, in almost every sense, about him as well as by him. Not only had the old woman and her experience been insignificant, merely historical, but so as well had his own experience, heretofore. He had not known that his experience of the death ritual of the dogs had human relationship and meaning; he had not known that his seeing the dead woman in the snow was no mere event, but rather definition for him of the mystery and beauty of woman. The creation of the woman's story, the discovery (through sympathy and communion) of *her* self, leads him into whole recognition of *his* being. He is no longer ''I'' as a statistic, a recorder of isolated experiences. With her, because of her, he becomes complete; his own experiences now take on significant human relationship, symbolic fullness. In reaching to and beyond the unknown woman resident in the labeled thing, he finds or constructs the ''I'' which is not only part of what he has met but also the human center wherein experience achieves meaning.

It is important to note that this process of discovery existed, in stunted form, for the men of the town who were present at the death scene. . . . Only the one mature man recovers and absorbs the two aspects of the woman. Anderson has through him led us to a further emphasis upon this consciousness. The narrator is now revealed as an artist in the essential gesture of art: creation, minting from his own and others' objective experiences the personal expression of meaning, the personal ingathering to form. Such an act justifies the ascription of ''music'' to the story, and the feeling of the creator that he has given coherence and beauty to unrelated fragments.

In **''Death in the Woods,''** then, the discovery of ''I'' necessarily involves the artistic expression of that discovery. The process whereby human sympathy gives rise to self-discovery is presented as one creative act. There is no realized ''I'' until entry has been gained into general human meaning, just as experience remains mere history until the significant ''I'' emerges.

Anderson's interior explanation of ''meaning'' is revealed to be only a preliminary statement. It perhaps indicates an attempt on his part to give firmness and resolution to the story, conscious as he was of objections that his stories evaporated or collapsed. But the attempt was surely misguided. This story actually is uncharacteristically stable and dynamic, largely because of the narrator's progress from recorder to creator. Instead of clarifying the story, Anderson's explicit comment obscures its real concern, which is not the death of the old woman but the creation her history gives rise to. Only in that creation is she given her due.

The creative narrator of this story is not, as is usually the case with narrators in Anderson's stories, involved with his subject through personal concerns, familial relation, or friendship. The distance between them, however, serves to enhance their sympathetic contact; they have only disinterested humanity in common. Even their shared experiences, being so different in cause, are unrelated save in that most general, yet finally most immediate, of relationships. Such distance permits this narrator— one among Anderson's ''oral'' narrators who is ''deeply involved in the outcome of his own story''—to achieve a similarly paradoxical contact-through-distance with his audience. . . . The unacknowledged audience is asked, by such a style, to share directly not only the narrator's responses but his act of discovering and creating those responses. The very distance and privacy of the narrator's record become its insurance of personal reception from an audience. (pp. 306-08)

Jon S. Lawry, '' 'Death in the Woods' and the Artist's Self in Sherwood Anderson,'' in PMLA, 74 *(copyright © 1959 by the Modern Language Association of America; reprinted by permission of the Modern Language Association of America), Vol. LXXIV, No. 3, June, 1959, pp. 306-11.*

WALTER B. RIDEOUT　(essay date 1962)

[*A noted scholar of Anderson's works, Rideout is currently at work on the definitive biography. In the essay below, he discusses Anderson's poetry in* Mid-American Chants *and his artistic relationship to Walt Whitman.*]

Robert Frost once remarked in comparing Sherwood Anderson to Edgar Lee Masters that the former ''was more of a poet.'' What Frost seems to have been thinking of was Anderson's peculiar ability as a storyteller, in talk and print, suddenly to live within an imagined mood or human relationship and to speak from its heart with a quiet, lyric intensity. Anderson of course did write some actual poems. His third book, which appeared in the spring of 1918, was a verse collection entitled **Mid-American Chants,** and nine years later he published **A New Testament,** fragments of a poetic ''autobiography of the fanciful life.'' Neither volume has ever received much critical approval, and justly, for Anderson was a better poet in prose than in verse, despite his feeling that the poems were among the most intimate expressions of his inner life. It is the very fact of this intimateness, however, that justifies the biographer's attention to Anderson's poetry. An examination even of **Mid-American Chants** by itself provides insights into both man and writer, and demonstrates that his life and his work are reciprocally illuminating. (pp. 149-50)

Why should Anderson have been suddenly and overwhelmingly ''seized'' with ''song'' in the mid-winter and spring of 1917? The response presupposes a commensurate stimulus, and such a stimulus can in fact be found in the visit Anderson paid to the *Seven Arts* editors in New York during, as he wrote Waldo Frank in anticipation, ''the week beginning February 12th.'' Anderson's subsequent correspondence with Frank and Van Wyck Brooks reveals the very great impact the visit had on him. After several days crammed with conversations, impressions, and ideas, Anderson came home from New York, as he shortly thereafter wrote Frank, with gratitude for his willingness and that of Brooks and Oppenheim ''to listen to my provincial, Western point of view'' and ''with an odd feeling of reverence and humbleness.'' (p. 153)

Toward his ''dear brothers of the East'' Anderson felt himself in part to be the coarse-grained provincial, the unsophisticate, even the child ''suckled face downward in the black earth of my western cornland,'' as he wrote in **''Mid-American Prayer.''**

But in another part of himself Anderson did not feel reverent and humble at all. With an ambivalence that a biographer of Anderson comes to expect, he at the same time felt big-brotherly and even superior toward the Easterners. Strongly attracted to these intellectuals as he was and recognizing in them qualities that he admittedly lacked himself, he felt a correlative need to assert his independence and worth. (pp. 154-55)

If we assume, as I think we must, that the New York visit precipitated Anderson's sudden turn to verse as a means of self-expression, then the verse itself should record this double attitude on the part of its creator. As we shall shortly see, this is indeed what it does. Again and again, in statement, theme, image, and symbol, sometimes separately in different poems and sometimes together in the same poem, Anderson announces his twin attitude of humbleness and pride. Admitting the crudeness, the provinciality, the immaturity of himself and of "Mid-America," the terrible ugliness of the industrial cities, the lack in both poet and region of a sure art and a clear purpose, he constantly counterbalances his anger and despair with the joyous affirmation of his own and his region's contribution to American culture, a contribution which he asserts to be different in kind from that of the more learned, more sophisticated Easterners, yet potentially of even greater value.

When the *Chants* are looked at in this way, as expressions of Anderson's complicated, even paradoxical, response to a concrete confrontation of the East, the poet's bardic language and prophetic posture are not surprising. Quite evidently the poems were an attempt by Anderson to define a public image both of the poet and of the Midwest. But the suddenness and near uncontrollability of this rush of poetry still seem to require behind it a greater psychological pressure, a more intense necessity. What that pressure and necessity were will become clearer after an examination of the poems themselves. (pp. 156-57)

[One] of the obvious influences on *Mid-American Chants* is [Walt Whitman], whom Anderson had long considered as belonging "among the two or three really great American artists." The indebtedness to Whitman appears frequently and variously in the *Chants:* the long, unrhymed lines; the rhetorical rhythms with their balanced elements and repetitions; even brief catalogues of states, cities, rivers ("Keokuk, Tennessee, Michigan, Chicago, Kalamazoo—don't the names in this country make you fairly drunk?"). Like Whitman's, Anderson's diction mixes the declamatory, the colloquial, and the lyrical, though it is noteworthy that Anderson lacks Whitman's love of nouns and verbs that freshly and exactly describe sense impressions. Like Whitman's too, is Anderson's desire for honesty and "perfect personal candor," but his inclusiveness is admittedly not that of Whitman. He will sing the ugly and the common, but only the latter gladly, for he hates the ugliness of factories too much to see optimistically any ultimate good in hideous sound and black smoke. Most importantly, Anderson is a latter-day, lesser Whitman in concealing a multiple personality behind the pervasive pronoun "I," the actual personality of the poet fusing with that of a mystically representative American through whose voice other Americans may be heard. (pp. 158-59)

The second major influence on the *Chants,* besides Whitman, is the Bible. Anderson's quite nonsectarian love for the prose of the King James Version is well documented, and its rhythms often sound in his stories. Echoes of Genesis and the Song of Songs can be heard in the *Chants.* Thus the poet in **"Song of Stephen the Westerner"** says, "My children are as the dust of city streets for numbers," a statement that recalls God's promise to Jacob in Genesis 28:14 that "thy seed shall be as the dust of the earth"; and in at least eight of the Chants the poet addresses some unnamed, generalized person as "my beloved," while the abrupt transitions, the sensuous imagery, and the calculated ambiguousness in parts of the Song of Songs are often imitated in Anderson's poems. (p. 160)

[The] Bible's cadenced prose and Whitman's relatively loose line were both vehicles for certain religious or quasi-religious beliefs, to some of which, particularly Whitman's, he was much attracted. Here was a vital tradition of which he had been long aware, a prophetic idiom ready shaped for what he was feeling and what he wanted, needed, to say.

What did he have to say? A number of the *Chants* are slight in content, attempts to fix evanescent moods or to recall memories. But very many of them, so many that they reveal a basic preoccupation on Anderson's part, relate in some way to his conception of the development of American life, a development most fully and effectively to be embodied in *Poor White* and toward which he was already working when his poetic seizure interrupted his first attempts at the uncompleted *Immaturity.* It is a familiar conception that may here be pieced together from different poems. The farm and small-town society of the past was a golden age. "Our fathers in the village streets / Had flowing beards and they believed," Anderson writes in **"Industrialism."** In **"Song of Stephen the Westerner,"** he nostalgically recalls the time when, as in pre-industrial Bidwell in *Poor White,* everyone lived under an invisible roof of secure, unconscious community. "In the long house at evening the old things were sweet"; and "On the straw in the stables sat Enid the maker of harness," at whose side were old men who "talked of old gods" while "Long we lay listening and listening." (p. 161)

But this craftsman age with its patriarchal American heroes has vanished before the "terrible engine" of industrialism. . . .

The Machine Age has broken the old ties of community, herded people like animals into the great, grim cities, where, in the roar and smoke, they either starve or grow fat on lies and the telling of lies. As in *Poor White,* industrialism is the destroyer—of the land, of beauty, of the ancient simplicity and dignity, of human community, of all order. Significantly, in both **"Song of Industrial America"** and Hugh McVey's dream in Chapter II of *Poor White,* modern machine civilization is imaged in terms of storm and flood, of "disorder and darkness."

Just as Anderson's revulsion against his present time issues from him in extreme images, so he hints at the coming of a new age in highly charged but vague terms that show how remote the *Chants* are from the verse of programmatic social protest. In some of the "anti-industrial" poems the poet breaks his own bonds—or "bands," as Anderson prefers to call them—of emotional numbness and spiritual blindness; for to Anderson the worst enslavement produced by industrialism is psychological rather than economic. In other poems, as in **"Song of Industrial America,"** the poet metaphorically seeks community with his "brothers." . . . (p. 162)

A more positive, though no more specific, way of imaging the approach of the new age involves Anderson's conception of the "I" in the *Chants,* a conception that clearly is indebted to *Leaves of Grass.* Very much as in Whitman's poems, the multiple personalities of the "I" may at any one time include Anderson himself, Anderson as representative American, and Anderson the inspired bard and prophet who speaks to America and articulates its hidden dream. Thus **"Song of Cedric the Silent"** becomes a fragmentary "Song of Myself" in which, at first, literal biography is joined to figurative statement: "The Son of Irwin and Emma I am, here in America, come into a kingship." Cedric (Sherwood) prophesies that "Into the land of my fathers, from Huron to Keokuk, beauty shall come—out of the black ground, out of the deep black ground." He, the poet, will "hurl" his songs "into the mighty wheels of the engine." . . . (pp. 162-63)

Often directly linked with this many-personed "I" is a theme that recurs again and again through these poems, and is indeed one of the chief devices for intimating the coming of a new American age—the theme of death and rebirth. Sometimes, as in three of the poems on the war, this theme is asserted in terms of creation proceeding out of destruction. . . . More often death and rebirth are expressed in fertility images of human procreation and nurture or of the planting and growth of seeds in soil. **"Song of Stephen the Westerner"** illustrates Anderson's typical reliance on the death-rebirth pattern to suggest a cycle of eternal return, from the acknowledgment of which the poet and his listeners may derive hope that some ineffable future will come out of the wasteland of the industrial present.

> Deep in the corn I lay—ages and ages—folded
> and broken—old and benumbed. My mother
> the black ground suckled me. When I was strong
> I built a house facing the east. The hair on
> my arm was like the long grass by the edge of
> the forests.

This passage, with its Whitmanesque fusing of the poet and his Midwest land, reveals the very close connection between the death-rebirth theme and yet another element in the poems— the symbolic use of corn and cornfields. That corn symbolism is of peculiar importance in the *Chants* is implied even by so mechanical a piece of evidence as a count of the poems in which it significantly appears. Of the forty-nine poems in the book, twelve, or about a quarter of them, make central use of corn as symbol. In addition, corn or cornfields are specifically mentioned in fourteen more "songs," while in several others corn may presumably be referred to within the general class of growing crops. Considering Anderson's usual fondness for the symbolisms of both hands and doors, it is remarkable that neither of these appears more than occasionally in the poems; and no other symbols, not even those drawn from industrialism or war, occur anywhere nearly so frequently as that of corn. . . . Corn is the master symbol of the book.

This symbol was an appropriate one for use by the poet who could tell his Eastern friend, Van Wyck Brooks: "The place between mountain and mountain I call Mid-America is my land. Good or bad, it's all I'll ever have." At the simplest level, the cornfields, so much a part of the Midwest landscape, were for Anderson a means of distinguishing his own physical setting from that of his new friends in the East, but the corn theme could dramatically state a contrast in cultural background as well. The poem **"Manhattan,"** almost certainly written soon after Anderson's return from New York, records his visit in such terms of contrast. . . . Out of an emotional contact with the city crowds he achieved, the poet says, a sense of himself; and he proudly asserts his identity in one of the finest passages in the book, a passage directly recalling both Whitman and the Bible:

> I am of the West, the long West of the sunsets,
> I am of the deep fields where the corn grows.
> The sweat of apples is in me. I am the beginning
> of things and the end of things.

To the poet, thus represented as a kind of culture-hero, came the men of the city, old men full of pain. And the poem concludes:

> In the morning I arose from my bed and was
> healed. To the cornfields I went laughing and
> singing. The men who are old have entered into
> me. As I stood on the high place above the city

> they kissed me. The caress of those who are
> weary has come into the cornfields.

The full complexity of Anderson's emotional response to his New York visit is pointedly lacking here; for, while the poet admits to having been emotionally modified by his experience, Anderson's real though partial sense of inferiority has been minimized. Instead, we observe, through the insistence on the cornfields the worth of Anderson and of Mid-America have become symbolically enlarged.

As **"Manhattan"** further suggests, the symbol of corn is for Anderson much more than a geographical or even a cultural index; it assumes, in fact, a quasi-religious meaning, to which is closely joined the Whitmanesque conception of the poet as prophet and priest. . . . Dying into the ground, as the seed which is the soul in the New Testament parable, the poet is reborn in the cornfields and "will renew in my people the worship of gods," will "bring love" into their hearts. Where Whitman found both death and new life in his master symbols of the sea and the grass, Anderson finds them in the corn, which dies and is reborn in an endless circle of renewal. What Anderson calls for, of course, is not at all a simple, literal "return to the land" or "return to the village"; rather, he urges a change of heart. As **"The Cornfields"** makes clear despite the intentional vagueness of its prophetic utterance, the poet seeks to re-establish in each person, man or woman, the love of his fellows so that instead of living as now their fragmented, isolated, and emotionally impoverished lives, all may dwell once again, as in America's golden age, under the invisible roof of community, but now a roof extended to cover the world.

This sub-rational, highly intuitive "message" is reinforced by two other attributes of the corn, though it is useful first to observe the ways in which corn is *not* described. It is never referred to by any color word, such as "yellow" or "golden," or by any word suggesting shape. (It is said in one poem to be "fat" and in another to be "rich, milky," but these are generalized words mostly suggesting fullness of growth.) It is characterized by smell only once (again "rich, milky") and by movement only twice ("sways" and "nods"). Somewhat more frequently the sound of the corn ("rustling" or "whispering") is mentioned, but even this attribute seems to have little significance. Anderson simply is not interested in creating hard, clear, descriptive images.

What *is* significant is his tendency, as it appears in several *Chants,* to refer to corn within the context of sexuality, a sexuality far more diffuse than that of Whitman's songs but like it in transcending the merely physical. Not once in *Mid-American Chants* does Anderson make the obvious, even expected, link between corn ear or cornstalk and phallus. Instead, as in most of Anderson's writing in either prose or verse, sex and the sexual act are primarily metaphors for the intuitive union of one personality with another. So in **"Spring Song"** the poet begins by stating that the rhythm of death and rebirth manifests itself again in forest and field. "Now, America," he continues in Whitmanesque idiom, "you press your lips to mine, / Feel on your lips the throbbing of my blood." And the poem reaches its climax by asserting a union of the physical with the spiritual, of a people with its prophet. . . . The poem ends with men singing in unison, while "Everywhere in the fields now the orderly planting of corn."

Given Anderson's acquaintance with Whitman, it is not at all surprising that in **"Spring Song"** an explicit sexual context should be furnished for the dual planting, of corn seeds in the earth and of prophetic revelations in the consciousness of mankind; but the poem also assigns to the corn an unexpected final attribute, the extraordinary importance of which to Anderson is established by the frequency of its appearance in the **Chants.** Again and again it is the spatial arrangement of the corn in the field, not its color or odor or shape, but its "orderly planting" and growth that the poet emphasizes. In poem after poem the corn is described as standing in long, deep, or endless rows; and, as in **"Spring Song,"** the endless symmetry of the lines of corn is always to be understood as far more than an aesthetic matter. Again the meaning is quasi-religious. In **"Song of the Middle World"** the poet has "been to the Dakotas when the fields were plowed" and "stood by the Ohio when the dawn broke forth," and he has seen the "Promise of corn, / Long aisles running into the dawn and beyond / To the throne of gods." The physical order of the corn on the land, in short, symbolizes the metaphysical order of "the gods," who represent the essentially religious harmony of brotherhood toward which the poet hopes to guide Mid- and all America, indeed the whole of mankind.

The reiteration of the image of the cornfields and their symmetry suggests that order had an obsessive value for Anderson, and there is evidence external to the poems to confirm this suggestion into something more definite. Writing to Van Wyck Brooks only a few weeks after the publication of *Mid-American Chants,* in a letter that ambivalently mingles praise and censure, self-assertion and self-effacement, Anderson plaintively asks his Eastern friend why he does not "sympathize with me in such expressions as my essay **'An Apology for Crudity'** or my *Chants*"

> In the chants I reached into my own personal muttering, half insane and disordered, and tried to take out of them a little something ordered. You should see how I clutched at the ordered cornfield[s], insisted on them to myself, took them as about the only thing I could see.

Here is the missing final figure in the pattern of desire and need that lay behind Anderson's sudden outpouring of song in the late winter and early spring of 1917. Through the poems Anderson hoped to define not only a public image but a private one as well. For him they would be new steps in an old journey toward self-discovery, toward self-identification. They would be attempts to find order, not only within the confusion of a particular time, but also within the confusion of the poet still seeking his way from businessman to artist.

The need to find an order was a compelling one for Anderson, who in the spring of 1917 had already written and was soon to publish his novel, *Marching Men,* which told of Beaut McGregor's revolt against the disorder of contemporary society and his vision of achieving order through the striding of men in wordless unison. Like the symbol of the marching men, the symbol of the corn rows in *Mid-American Chants* was another in a series of efforts by Anderson to integrate his world, both external and internal. What made him return from his excursion into prophetic verse almost as abruptly as he set off on it must ultimately have been his realization that he could express his meaning and his need more fully and exactly in the "other harmony" of prose. *Poor White,* his best novel, exists to show that he was right. (pp. 163-70)

Walter B. Rideout, "Sherwood Anderson's 'Mid-American Chants'" (copyright © 1962 by the Ohio State University Press; reprinted by permission of the author), in Aspects of American Poetry, *edited by Richard M. Ludwig, Ohio State University Press, 1962, pp. 149-70 [the excerpts of Sherwood Anderson's poetry used here were originally published in his* Mid-American Chants *(copyright, 1918, by John Lane Company; reprinted by permission of Harold Ober Associates Inc.), John Lane, 1918; the excerpt of Anderson's letter to Van Wyck Brooks used here (reprinted by permission of Harold Ober Associates Inc.), was originally published in* Story, *Vol. XIX, No. 91, September-October, 1941].*

BARRY D. BORT (essay date 1970)

[*Bort examines* Winesburg, Ohio, *tracing the recurrent theme of loneliness and desperation born of the failure to communicate.*]

A recurrent theme of the literature of recent times has been the difficulty and even impossibility of communication. . . .

Sherwood Anderson's **Winesburg, Ohio** is vitally concerned with the difficulty of understanding. The characters in that work are all desperately trying, in a strange variety of ways, to make meaningful contact with someone or something outside themselves. The opening chapter, **"The Book of the Grotesque,"** explains how each tried to live by one or perhaps several truths and closed his eyes to the immense world of reality beyond the margins of that province. (p. 443)

These distortions of reality labelled truths immure each character within the isolation of his selfhood but they do not preclude an attempt to escape from this inner loneliness. Any passion, any ideal, however genuine or commendable, is liable to the distortion that can destroy its living malleability. Even the man who understands this may fall victim to the rigidity of his conception.

Winesburg, Ohio opens with **"Hands,"** the story of ultimate frustration. Wing Biddlebaum sees himself reaching out to others, his marvelous hands complementing the truth of his words. As a school teacher he had "walked in the evening or had sat talking until dusk upon the schoolhouse steps lost in a kind of dream. Here and there went his hands, caressing the shoulders of the boys, playing about the tousled heads." . . . But a half-witted boy imagines "unspeakable things" and Biddlebaum narrowly escapes lynching by fleeing to his aunt's farm near Winesburg. George Willard, the town reporter and the unifying figure in most of the sketches, watches his hands perform the lovely ritual of their movement.

"A few stray white bread crumbs lay on the cleanly washed floor by the table; putting the lamp on a low stool he began to pick up the crumbs, carrying them to his mouth one by one with unbelievable rapidity. In the dense blotch of light beneath the table, the kneeling figure looked like a priest engaged in some service of his church." . . . The ritual has but one celebrant and the church no communicants.

"Paper Pills," the following story, stands in contrast to the first. Indeed the whole book centers around the contrast of these two stories. **"Paper Pills"** concerns itself with Dr. Reefy, also a figure of isolation, who expresses himself by writing gnomic bits of wisdom on paper. Understanding the futility of trying to communicate these truths to others, he stuffs them in his pocket. "After some weeks the scraps of paper became little hard round balls, and when the pockets were filled he dumped them out upon the floor." . . . His empty office, filled with cobwebs, is emblematic of the man. "He never opened the window. Once on a hot day in August he tried but found it stuck fast and after that he forgot all about it." . . . Such a man appears to differ from Wing Biddlebaum only in resignation to his fate, yet he has had an experience that sustains him in his loneliness. A tall dark unmarried girl, finding herself pregnant, came to his office for help and watched unmoved while he performed a particularly painful tooth extraction. (pp. 444-45)

"In the fall after the beginning of her acquaintanceship with him she married Doctor Reefy and in the following spring she died. During the winter he read to her all of the odds and ends of thoughts he had scribbled on the bits of paper." (p. 445)

Both Biddlebaum and Reefy are alone; each inhabits his dusty and solitary milieu. But the difference between them is immense. Biddlebaum is last seen furtively using his wonderful hands only to nourish himself. But Reefy has the sustaining memory of his understanding wife to whom he would read his bits of truth.

The book is full of memorable images of people desperately trying to reach outside themselves to achieve a moment of communication. Louise Bentley sits silently listening, cramped in a closet-like room of the parlor while "Mary Hardy, with the aid of the man who had come to spend the evening with her, brought to the country girl a knowledge of men and women." . . . Or Alice Hindman, possessed by a mad desire, runs naked in the rain trying to find "some other lonely human and embrace him." . . . She finds only a deaf old man who shouts, "What? What say?" . . .

The most grandiose attempt at communication is that of Jesse Bentley, a farmer who becomes wealthy through hard work and denial. Intent on validating the importance of his own life by setting it apart from the lives of others who, he says, live "like clods", he tries to relive the pastoral life of the men in the Old Testament days. (p. 446)

He takes his grandson to the woods in the hope that now "he could bring from God a word or a sign out of the sky, that the presence of the boy and man on their knees would make the miracle he had been waiting for almost inevitable. (p. 447)

But the effort is thwarted when the child runs away, terrified by the expression of fanaticism on the old man's face. He thinks some frightful spirit has come to inhabit the form of his kind grandfather. Some years later Jesse makes a second attempt. He plans to sacrifice a lamb and takes David with him, but the boy is again disturbed by the strange look in the old man's face and once more flees. When his grandfather gives chase he takes a sling and fells the old man with a stone.

Jesse Bentley's megalomaniacal idea of reliving the Old Testament results in a savage parody. Instead of hearing the voice of God he becomes a Goliath felled by David. The whole episode **"Godliness"**—to which Anderson devotes four sections of *Winesburg, Ohio*—chronicles the most gigantic failure of understanding in the entire book.

The deep need that so many characters feel to experience—if only for a moment—a sense of understanding that strips away all the barriers erected by society and self might seem to be satisfied by sexual communion. But such hope is illusory. Louise Bentley, neglected by her father, reaches out for someone who will comprehend her need. Living as a boarder in town, she finds no more understanding than among her family and, in her isolation, is attracted to John Hardy. (pp. 447-48)

But John Hardy mistakes her tentative gropings for erotic impulses. "Louise Bentley took John Hardy to be her lover. That was not what she wanted but it was so the young man had interpreted her approach to him, and so anxious was she to achieve something else that she made no resistance." . . . Their intimacy leads to her pregnancy and to marriage, but their misunderstanding only deepens. . . .

This is an iterated theme: sexual consummation holds out the promise of that profound communion when soul meets soul. But the search for a deeper intimacy is exchanged for a lesser one which fails to mitigate the loneliness of isolation. (p. 448)

Wash Williams is willing to forgive his unfaithful wife and take her back. "I thought that if she came in and just touched me with her hand I would perhaps faint away. I ached to forgive and forget." . . . Instead her mother, using sex as a substitute for understanding, displays the errant wife naked and Wash is angered beyond words. . . .

Enoch Robinson is an artist who finds that the difficulty of making others understand is an aesthetic problem. "He was afraid the things he felt were not getting expressed in the pictures he painted." . . . And so he invents "shadow people" to whom he can talk. He tells George Willard about his last real attempt to make someone see, and the compulsive need to make another understand it. "I became mad to make her understand me and to know what a big thing I was in that room. I wanted her to see how important I was. I told her over and over." . . . But he fails and, as a last resort, hopes that George will at least understand his failure. (p. 449)

People reach out to one another in bizarre ways as if they understand that the normal channels of communication are unavailing. The Reverend Curtis Hartman while preparing his sermon in the bell tower of Winesburg's Presbyterian Church sees Kate Swift in the window of a neighboring house and is irresistibly drawn to her. He preaches sermons meant only for her and finally decides that "God has manifested himself to me in the body of a woman." . . . He runs out in the wintry night to deliver this thwarted revelation to the puzzled George Willard while Kate Swift, completely unaware of the strange battle in Hartman's soul, fights her own raging inner conflict and vainly tries to make the young reporter see the importance of life's inner realities. . . .

There are also those characters immured in their own peculiarities who communicate only with themselves. Old Mook, the half-witted farmhand, when lonely, holds "long conversations with the cows, the pigs, and even with the chickens that ran around the barnyard." . . . Turk Smollet, the "half dangerous old woodchopper," gives himself directions as he balances a load of boards on his wheelbarrow. "'Easy there, Turk! Steady now, old boy!' the old man shouted to himself, and laughed so loud that the load of board rocked dangerously." . . . (p. 450)

Often the man with an immense burden of incommunicable truth is given to bursts of violence. These are verbal in Joe Welling, the Standard Oil agent who was "beset by ideas and in the throes of one of his ideas was uncontrollable. Words rolled and tumbled from his mouth." . . . Ironically, it is the compulsive—even violent—need to communicate that destroys its possibility. As critics have pointed out, "hands" is a recurring word, for characters try physically to reach others when words fail. But the greater the effort the greater the failure, and this only incites characters like Joe Welling, Enoch Robinson, and the Reverend Hartman to still more frenzied attempts.

Most of those who fail to communicate their inmost feelings to another understand that ordinary discourse is so debilitated by its continued exchange of commonplace sentiments that they must, out of desperation, find some aberrant manner of expression. But a more ordinary attempt is made by Hal Winters in **"The Untold Lie,"** who asks Ray Pearson whether or not he should marry the girl he has made pregnant. Years ago Pearson had a similar choice and finds himself tied down by the narrowness of his family life. Uncertain, he delays his answer, but later runs after Winters to tell him not to marry. But Hal has already made his decision and rejects the advice. The older man reflects, "It's just as well. Whatever I told him would have been a lie . . .". . . . He realizes that truth is only a personal possession. Moments of communion are not to be found in the imposition of one man's experience upon the other.

The lives of people in small towns seem to be completely open; virtues are paraded and vices difficult to conceal. Daily life is a series of prescribed rituals by which the townspeople reassure one another of the solidity of their shared reality. George Willard is the official recorder of the minutiae of collective existence. In his capacity as newspaper reporter, he represents what seems to be the town's essential life and people search him out hoping to make him see what others cannot.

But he is young and unformed. Life's deeper realities are hidden from him and he always fails of understanding. From his incomprehension arises the bleak comedy of the book. He only collects the meaningless mass of details which fill the newspaper and fail utterly to suggest the brooding essence of people's lives. As Kate Swift angrily says, "What's the use? It will be ten years before you begin to understand what I mean when I talk to you . . .". . . . (pp. 450-52)

Criticism of **Winesburg, Ohio** has recognized this desperate need to communicate, but what has not been understood about Anderson's work is that this continual frustration serves as the context out of which arise a few luminous moments of understanding. Precious anticipated communion is the real theme of the book. Wing Biddlebaum images such a communion in his vision of an Elysium of understanding in a pastoral golden age. (p. 452)

That paradise is only a dream, but there are a few characters whose experience stands out in contrast to the abortive efforts of the others. . . . [Anderson's] is the art of sudden revelation, not a private vision, but a moment of intense wordless understanding between people. (pp. 452-53)

Such moments are at the heart of **Winesburg, Ohio,** although they are few and evanescent. They are usually silent, or if they do involve talk, the words themselves take on a meaning deeper than any implied by the utterances. (p. 454)

Doctor Reefy and his young wife . . . have such a moment of wordless understanding and the remembrance of that communion is what sets his story apart from that of the hapless Wing Biddlebaum. In fact Doctor Reefy is the only character who is vouchsafed two such encounters, for, shortly before her death, Elizabeth Willard came to him. She talked to him and then "sprang out of the chair and began to walk about in the office. She walked as Doctor Reefy thought he had never seen anyone walk before. To her whole body there was a swing, a rhythm that intoxicated him." . . . She becomes for a moment "not the tired-out woman of forty-one but a lovely and innocent girl who had been able by some miracle to project herself out of the husk of the body of the tired-out woman." . . . He responds to her, but the moment is shattered and "the thing that comes to life in her as she talked to her one friend died suddenly." . . . (pp. 454-55)

After her death, her son George, about to leave Winesburg, has a similar moment at the deserted Winesburg fair ground with Helen White.

"In the darkness he took hold of her hand and when she crept close put a hand on her shoulder. A wind began to blow and he shivered. With all his strength he tried to hold and to understand the mood that had come upon him. In that high place in the darkness the two oddly sensitive human atoms held each other tightly and waited. In the mind of each was the same thought. "'I have come to this lonely place and here is the other,' was the substance of the thing felt." . . .

What Helen White and George Willard feel has nothing to do with conventional love, nor is it related to sex. Marriage would be only a distortion, for the attempt to hold this their precious and fleeting shared experience would only turn them into grotesques like so many others. Formal possession would not leave the "Thou" free.

The "I" meets "Thou" only in those unlooked for times when the burden of assumed selfhood society forced upon us drops away, when we have relinquished all desire to use people as means and can view them as ends. As Anderson says of that strange meeting at the fairground, "For some reason they could not have explained they had both got from their silent evening together the thing needed." . . . (p. 455)

What sets **Winesburg, Ohio** apart from the main stream of fiction and poetry dating from the beginning of the nineteenth century is that it is not concerned with the questing soul in search of experience and truth like the work of almost any author one can name in the last 150 years. It is not a chronicle of self discovery. It has as its goal the revelation of that rare ideal, the human community, even if that community be only two. (pp. 455-56)

> Barry D. Bort, "'Winesburg, Ohio': The Escape from Isolation," in The Midwest Quarterly (copyright, 1970, by The Midwest Quarterly, Pittsburg State University), Vol. XI, No. 4, Summer, 1970, pp. 443-56.

DAVID R. MESHER (essay date 1980)

[*Mesher examines Anderson's story* "The Egg," *one of the author's most accomplished short works.*]

Sherwood Anderson's two best stories, **"Death in the Woods"** and **"The Egg,"** share an odd but central detail: the narrator's open admission that he has fabricated the most important elements of the story he is telling. Irving Howe, discussing **"Death in the Woods,"** terms this the story's "one significant flaw: a clumsiness of perspective which forces the narrator to offer a weak explanation of how he could have known the precise circumstances of the old woman's death." (p. 180)

Nevertheless, in **"Death in the Woods,"** the narrator does attempt a realistic explanation of his knowledge. He had seen the woman's body in the snow, he says, and had heard "the whispered comments of the men" at the scene, and "later, in town . . . must have heard other fragments of the old woman's story." . . . The narrator of **"The Egg"** is much more straightforward about the story of his father and Joe Kane. "For some unexplainable reason," he claims, "I know the story as well as though I had been a witness to my father's discomfiture." . . . Yet as astute a reader as Irving Howe, who faults **"Death in the Woods"** for a lesser imposition on his willing suspension of disbelief, ignores this inexplicability and says only that "the narrator, deliberately avoiding a direct dramatic line, then tells what happened in the store below." **"The Egg"** has usually been treated, by Howe and others, as an autobiographical expression of Anderson's relationship with his father and, on a larger scale, "as a parable of human defeat"—meaning, of course, the defeat of the narrator's father. But, if the parallel with **"Death in the Woods"** holds, **"The Egg"** is a story about not the father but the son who, as narrator-turned-creator, projects the reality of his own psychology onto the history of his subject.

In **"Death in the Woods,"** Anderson prepares his reader for the coming departure from narrative conventions at the beginning of the story. Though the details of the woman's background are not such as would require a great deal of personal knowledge, the narrator makes a point of recalling them, or in [John S.] Lawry's term "recovering" them, with the justification that "all country and small-town people have seen such old women"; at the same time, however, the narrator also undercuts the most common details of his tale by continuing, "but no one knows much about them." . . . Obviously, the narrator knows a lot about one—as it turns out, in practical terms, too much. A different technique is employed in **"The Egg"** to achieve the same undercutting effect. The story begins with a romanticized portrait of the father's bachelorhood as a farm hand. At this early point, assertions like "he had then a horse of his own and on Saturday evenings drove into town to spend a few hours in social intercourse with other farm hands" . . . seem unremarkable. But as the narrator turns from father to mother, he passes from assertion to assumption, even though the specifics to be assumed about the mother are far more probable than the details presented as facts about the father. "At ten o'clock," we are told indicatively, "father drove home along a lonely country road, made his horse comfortable for the night and himself went to bed, quite happy in his position in life." But in discussing his mother and how, after marriage, "the American passion for getting up in the world took possession" of his parents, the narrator inundates us with subjunctives and conditionals:

> It may have been that mother was responsible. Being a school teacher she had no doubt read books and magazines. She had, I presume, read of how Garfield, Lincoln, and other Americans rose from poverty to fame and greatness and as I lay beside her—in the days of her lying-in—she may have dreamed that I would some day rule men and cities. . . .

The narrator's definite knowledge of the precise and orderly actions of a drunken farm hand, as opposed to his assumption that a school teacher has read books and magazines, has two effects. First, it immediately identifies the son with his father; second, it distances him from his mother, who has introduced ambition into her husband's previously idyllic existence.

Ambition, for the narrator, is always associated with the egg. The couple's first, ill-fated venture is a chicken ranch, and this early exposure to eggs and chickens, according to the narrator, is responsible for his adult fatalism. . . . (pp. 180-81)

The narrator then launches into the marvellous "digression" on "the many and tragic things that can happen to a chicken," which forms the crux of the story's symbolism. The various fates awaiting the egg, it turns out, are not only dismal but very much like those awaiting the human baby. "Small chickens, just setting out on the journey of life, look so bright and alert and they are in fact so dreadfully stupid. They are so much like people they mix one up in one's judgment of life." . . . The identification of chickens with people readily marks the hen as a symbol for the mother, and the egg as a symbol for the son and narrator. "My tale does not primarily concern itself with the hen," the narrator proclaims, though the mother's ambitions are the initial cause of trouble. "If correctly told it will center on the egg," . . . that is, on the narrator himself. That the story's "I" is linked with the egg is perhaps a pun on the narrative "ego."

And yet, one might argue, the story centers on neither mother nor son, but on the father, who carries the malformed chickens, "preserved in alcohol and put each in its own glass bottle" from the chicken ranch to the restaurant, the family's next venture. "The grotesques were, he declared, valuable. People, he said, like to look at strange and wonderful things." . . . Human grotesques are similarly valuable to Anderson, who uses them to depict alienation from modern society. But the father's attempt to exhibit his grotesques, especially later for Joe Kane, are futile. Instead, we have the narrator exhibiting his father as a grotesque, a human failure shaped by naive belief in the American dream—and Anderson depicting his own grotesque, the narrator himself. Thus, even when the narrator is discussing his father, the story is still focused on the son.

This is clearest in the crucial scene of the story—the father's disastrous attempt to entertain Joe Kane, which must be read primarily for its content about the son, not the father, because it is also the scene about which the narrator admits he can have no reasonable knowledge. He is only sure of the scene's aftermath, which he witnesses and therefore reports before the recreated scene itself. . . . The narrator [constructs] his version of the events out of that roar of anger, the bang of the door, his father's emotional state, the egg his father was carrying, his father's plan "to try and entertain the people who came to eat at our restaurant," . . . and, of course, his own *unrelated* memories of the chicken ranch, associations of eggs with failure, and sense of personal inadequacy.

The incidents that the narrator invents to explain his father's breakdown in the bedroom both involve eggs. The first is a parable of his father's grotesqueness, the second of his own. According to the narrator, the father begins with an attack on the legend of Christopher Columbus and the egg. "That Christopher Columbus was a cheat," the father says, because he broke an egg to make it stand on its end." . . . The father then attempts to do in fact what Columbus did only by trickery. "When after a half hour's effort he did succeed in making the egg stand for a moment he looked up to find that his visitor was no longer watching." . . . The American dream is not achieved by those innocent and sincere enough to follow the rules. Columbus, with whom that dream began, knew this; the father does not.

But the father's defeat is not that of the narrator, who knows of the treachery contained in "the American passion for getting up in the world," and had already warned the reader not to believe in the literature written about that segment of the American dream he has encountered. Indeed, the narrator has resisted attempts to force him into the American pursuit of success just as the egg—his symbol—resists the father's attempts to get it inside a bottle, the second trick; and like that egg, the narrator has been broken.

The key to the narrator's personality is given in the last line of the story, where he describes "the complete and final triumph of the egg—at least as far as my family is concerned." . . . He says "family" to include himself, even though the events of the story occur while he is a boy; in no direct way do we have a defeat of the narrator. The line only makes literal sense when we understand the events as reconstructions of a defeated mind seeking to place the seeds of his defeat—and the blame for it—as far from himself as possible. If the problem originates with his parents, then the solution would be an imaginative negation of their marriage—a wish that finds expression in the idealized bachelorhood of his father as described in the beginning of the story.

On another level, however, where the egg is the narrator's symbol, the triumph at the end is his as well. And the "defeat"—not "of" but only "concerning" his family—is ambiguous enough to allow for this. Not his parents but the system is the ultimate villain for the narrator, and his triumph against it consists simply of recognizing its dangers and refusing to become involved in it. Willed abstention may take a form no more consequential than an interruption in the cycle of the chicken and the egg; but in it, the narrator finds exoneration of his father and himself. According to Lawry, Anderson believed that "men must get rid of self, but at the same time the whole task of art is to gain knowledge of self." In **"The Egg,"** the negative attributes of self are characterized by the ambition the narrator forgoes; and through the telling of his largely invented story, the narrator has come not only to knowledge and acceptance of himself, but of others as well. (pp. 181-83)

> *David R. Mesher, "A Triumph of the Ego in Anderson's 'The Egg'," in* Studies in Short Fiction *(copyright 1980 by Newberry College), Vol. 17, No. 2, Spring, 1980, pp. 180-83.*

MARILYN JUDITH ATLAS (essay date 1981)

[Atlas examines with disapproval Anderson's treatment of his female characters in Winesburg, Ohio.]

Winesburg, Ohio has been studied biographically, geographically, historically, thematically, structurally, mystically, and mythically. However one enters the novel, attention is given to its characters. . . . But serious critical attention has not been paid to all of the individuals in Winesburg. The women, although they appear in almost every story, have not been studied collectively. Such a study can illuminate *Winesburg, Ohio* as well as Sherwood Anderson's understanding of and relationship to women. (p. 250)

As empathetic as Sherwood Anderson was toward the women he created in *Winesburg, Ohio,* he allowed neither Kate Swift nor any of the other women in Winesburg the escape that he hinted was possible for George Willard. While for George, Winesburg might become a background on which to paint his dreams of manhood, for even the most promising women of the town—for Kate Swift, Elizabeth Willard, Louise Bentley, Alice Hindman, and Helen White—Winesburg remained the foreground, if not the entire canvas of their lives. Even when Sherwood Anderson made George Willard and Helen White momentary equals and allowed them to find understanding and acceptance in one another, he ended his novel treating them

in vastly different ways. The last image the reader has of George is one of ascension. He is boarding a train that will take him away from his home town and ideally toward further understanding of himself; the last image that the reader has of Helen is one of misdirected energy. Helen chases the very same train on which George departs, hoping to have a parting word with him, herself having no thought of permanently leaving town. While Helen chases George, he is seated on the train preoccupied with himself and his future. Granted, it is George Willard, not Helen White, who is the main character of these stories, and it is his growth and escape which is central to *Winesburg, Ohio,* but since Anderson clearly portrayed that there was no salvation for those who remained in town and since he did allow a few other male characters—David Bentley, Seth Richmond, and Elmer Crowley—the possibility of beginning a new life elsewhere, one wonders why no woman leaves Winesburg.

Perhaps one of the reasons Anderson allowed no woman to leave Winesburg was because he created out of his own experiences, and his early experiences with women were with those who may have been sensitive but who were also clearly trapped. (pp. 250-51)

Anderson's mother and sister both had starved lives and their lives understandably left a strong impression on Anderson. Many of the frustrated lives in *Winesburg, Ohio* are very likely patterned on these women. . . .

[But there were many] independent, expansive women in Anderson's life by the time he began writing *Winesburg* in the fall of 1915. Margaret Anderson, editor of *The Little Review,* was one of Anderson's first connections to the literary world of Chicago. Edna Kenton, Harriet Monroe, and Agnes Tietjens were all part of Chicago's artistic community, the community which nurtured Anderson's own exploration and intellectual growth during that period of his life. (p. 252)

It is clear that while Anderson was writing *Winesburg, Ohio,* he was aware that women, even some from small towns, were escaping from their repressive environments and trying to live creative, self-directed lives. He even mentioned in **"Adventure"** that there was a "growing modern idea of a woman's owning herself and giving and taking for her own end in life." But Anderson was not interested in making any woman of Winesburg a carefully delineated, fully developed "modern woman." He began to make a number of his women strong but each one eventually catches herself in a traditional trap: Elizabeth Willard needs love first as does Louise Bentley. Alice Hindman can go as far as accepting economic independence, but she too prefers to live through her lover, even after he has obviously deserted her; Helen White shows potential: she is intelligent and seems capable of making choices, but Anderson finally chose not to develop her individuality, and presented her only through her relationships with others. At the end he was more comfortable leaving her safely at home.

While Anderson could be sympathetic to women, he could also unrealistically limit not only his presentation of them, but his understanding of what they needed. Too often he was comfortable assuming that what women wanted most was to give themselves away to an ideal lover. His belief that women wanted men and men wanted to create is depicted in the love relationships of Winesburg. (p. 253)

The women that Anderson created most sensitively in *Winesburg, Ohio* were those who posed no threat for either him or his male protagonists. Helen White is a potential threat to

George Willard's freedom and she is a possible competitor: leaving her behind with no solid aspirations of her own and only George Willard's wish that she not become like all the other women in Winesburg, was as much strength as Anderson was willing to allow her. Anderson created no overt power struggle between these two characters and he in no way dealt with the fact that he sacrificed Helen's potential in order to simplify George's exit.

But Anderson's unwillingness to allow his female characters the same amount of mobility as he allowed his male characters did not blind him to the fact that men's attitudes toward women can and do damage them irreparably. In "**Godliness,**" Anderson created a protagonist who succeeds in killing his wife, not out of cruelty but by watching her take on a role for which she is not sufficiently strong, and who succeeds in emotionally crippling his daughter because she was not the son who would help him "'pluck at last all of these lands out of the hands of the Philistines.'" In *Winesburg, Ohio* Anderson questioned some of the traditional myths; but he embraced others. Women, in Anderson's understanding, did not long to be worked to death, they did not long to be rejected because they were female, but they did long to be subsumed in a man.

If one journeys through *Winesburg, Ohio* looking carefully at the female characters that Anderson created, one senses that even if Anderson was not accurately or openly exploring all the various aspects of women in a small Midwestern city, he was seriously exploring them. The stories reflect both a deep sensitivity to female traps and an unwillingness to allow women the same choices, needs, and strengths that it allowed men. The first woman in Winesburg that Anderson presented in detail appeared in "**Paper Pills.**" She remained nameless throughout the story, hardly more than a sacrifice. The force of her powerlessness and of her accepting silence colored not only this tale, but all of *Winesburg, Ohio*. The reader is told little about her other than that her parents are dead and have left her a large fertile farm, and that this inheritance, coupled with the fact that she is dark, mysteriously attractive, and alone, interests suitors. One young man, the jeweler's son, talks constantly of virginity and another, a silent, black-haired boy, impregnates her. She is, in the context of Winesburg, a twisted apple, sweetest of all those in the orchard, and she sees herself in just such passive terms:

> At times it seemed to her that as he talked he was holding her body in his hands. She imagined him turning it slowly about in the white hands and staring at it. At night she dreamed that he had bitten into her body and that his jaws were dripping.

When the silent, dark-haired suitor seduces her, it is not without violence. In his moment of passion, he bites her. Shortly after this barbarous but brief encounter she realizes that she is pregnant and goes to see Doctor Reefy. In his office, she watches a woman whose tooth is being removed bleed. The woman's husband is also watching, and at the moment of extraction both the woman and her spouse simultaneously scream. The main female character does not react. She accepts the pain around her as simply as she accepts her own. The story quickly progresses and we are told that she falls in love with Doctor Reefy, and passively accepts the truths he shares. After a vague illness in which she loses her unborn child, she marries Doctor Reefy, and in the spring of that year, she quietly dies.

From this silent, bloody, dreamlike tale, the reader is introduced to Elizabeth Willard, George Willard's mother. She,

unlike the woman in "**Paper Pills,**" has the hunger to express herself, but she is no less silent and no more free. Elizabeth prays that her son be allowed to express something for them both. . . . When we are introduced to her, she is forty-five and broken. Her death hovers over the length of the novel and her wish for George Willard's creativity increases our own investment in it. In "**Death,**" one of the last stories in *Winesburg, Ohio*, we are told of her love relationship with Doctor Reefy and of her youthful aspiration to be an actress. As a young woman, her need of love stood in the way of her need of self. This, the narrator explains, is the way of women. But Elizabeth is less sure of this. She takes some responsibility for her defeat and states that she "let" the dream within her be killed. But more frequently she feels that she has been a victim. Anderson has her put down her head and weep when the Winesburg baker throws sticks and bits of broken glass at the druggist's cat who crouched behind barrels in an attempt to escape the abuse. Elizabeth eventually stops looking at the grey cat. The relationship between the cat and the baker seems too much like "a rehearsal of her own life, terrible in its vividness." (pp. 256-57)

[The story "**Godliness**"] is written in four parts. Through the development of Louise Bentley, the central female character, Anderson again explores how women are victimized by the society they live in and the people with whom they associate. When Anderson presents Louise Bentley's frustrated life and her inability to find the love she needs he has his narrator intrude with a statement indicting society and calling the writers of the period to action: "Before such women as Louise can be understood and their lives made livable, much will have to be done. Thoughtful books will have to be written and thoughtful lives lived by people about them." Ironically, it is also in "**Godliness**" that Anderson states his theory that what women want most is to be possessed: "Sometimes it seemed to her that to be held tightly and kissed was the whole secret of life, and then a new impulse came and she was terribly afraid. The age-old woman's desire to be possessed had taken possession of her. . . ." But in developing his character, Anderson shows that Louise Bentley wants more than someone to possess her: she wants spiritual communication with another human being. (p. 258)

In creating Louise Bentley and giving her a need for love which overpowers all her talents, Anderson is dooming her to an unhappy life. Wanting a friend, she takes John Hardy to be her lover, but sexuality does not satisfy her. John cannot understand what she wants and her frustration turns to bitterness. Her unhappiness does not cause her to reconsider the practicality of love as life's central solution. Instead it leads her to be an angry, ineffectual woman, and a hater of men. Interestingly, she does not reject women; for her they remain fellow victims, but she rejects all men and this anger negatively affects her relationship with her son whom she treats ambivalently. When her husband reproaches her for being a cruel mother she laughs: "'It is a man child and will get what it wants anyway,' she said sharply. 'Had it been a woman child there is nothing in the world I would not have done for it.'" But Louise Bentley does not have a woman child and she is given no opportunity to satisfy either her need to love or her need to be loved. She is clearly one of the female victims of Winesburg whose strength and creativity lead nowhere.

In the next story, "**A Man of Ideas,**" Anderson creates a strong female character, but he fails to develop her. Sarah King is an outcast of the town; she is neither beautiful nor a member of a socially acceptable family. While the story suggests that a meaningful relationship exists between her and Joe Welling, another outcast, and that this relationship is mutually fulfilling, he fails to support this. While the two characters nurture one another, the relationship seems to lack honesty. Joe Welling may tell her that she is intelligent, and Sarah King may allow him to talk to her about his ideas, but she is frightened when he decides to share these ideas with George Willard for she is convinced that Joe and George will quarrel over their worth. Her response implies that she finds Joe's ideas less intelligent than she privately encourages him to believe. Anderson, through the narrative tone, implies that Sarah is lucky that she is not more isolated being neither of fine breeding nor fine beauty, and certainly the town's people laugh at Joe's protestations of love, but the reader must question the degree of her luck, her happiness, and her strength.

Anderson is not allowing women many options. In his next story, "**Adventure,**" we are introduced to Alice Hindman who has good standing in her society, is strong and creative as well as beautiful. But he has her use that strength to repress herself rather than to love or create. (p. 259)

Alice Hindman tries to force herself to accept that many individuals live without love. She at no time considers finding a healthy outlet for her needs, but rather she demands that instinct be controlled; she does not consider being larger and learning to own the various parts of her nature, but rather demands that she be smaller and survive that smallness. (p. 260)

Kate Swift, the teacher, stern and cold toward her students, unable to communicate though passionate and sensitive, fares no better than her less intelligent, or less good, sisters. At thirty, she is considered a spinster, and has no outlet other than aborted attempts to communicate, and late night walks. Her mother, Elizabeth Swift, is angry when she stays out late. She reinforces her daughter to repress all instinct. . . . Kate Swift stays in Winesburg frustrated, unwilling to be sexual, unable to communicate, watching herself grow old. Once she was adventurous and travelled, but five years have passed since then, and there is no hint that she will search her fortune elsewhere.

Helen White, the woman with the most potential in *Winesburg, Ohio,* first appears in "**The Thinker.**" She is still young, a high school student, and, according to George Willard, has more "get up" than any other girl in Winesburg. She is attracted to George Willard, and to any young man, it seems, who has the least potential for leaving Winesburg and directing his own life. In "**The Thinker,**" Seth Richmond and George Willard compete for her attention. Rather than being shown her spiritual or intellectual complexity, we are shown her hunger for a worthy suitor. When Seth Richmond tells her that he is going to leave Winesburg and get some work, she is immediately impressed: "'This is as it should be,' she thought. 'This boy is not a boy at all, but a strong, purposeful man.'" She does not think of her own freedom, but rather is overcome by the sadness of losing the possibility to relate with Seth.

We meet Helen White again later, but we never see her actively working out her own goals. She is always caught between men, watching other characters define themselves and strike out new paths or she is simply the object of admiration and fantasy. In "**Drink**" Helen White appears as Tom Foster's fantasy. Tom works for her father, the town banker, and falls in love with her, but is afraid of sexuality and wants only to get drunk and verbalize his dreams of her. He tries to tell George Willard

about these fantasies, but succeeds only in aggravating him. Helen White appears as a fantasy in "**Death,**" the story that centers on the death of Elizabeth Willard. . . . George looks to Helen White for comfort less as an individual than as a nurturing woman. However, while he thinks of her, she is entertaining a young instructor whom her mother, the town organizer for poetry study groups, has invited down from college. Helen is also thinking of him. The main difference between George and Helen lies in the fact that George is caught between his thoughts of her and his thoughts of his own future, while she is much more involved in comparing two men than in seriously considering her independent existence.

When George and Helen next meet, George is more interested in telling her what he needs her to be than in listening to what she herself feels she needs:

> I want you to do something, I don't know what.
> Perhaps it is none of my business. I want you
> to try to be different from other women. You
> see the point. It's none of my business I tell
> you. I want you to be a beautiful woman. You
> see what I want.

Helen is neither offended nor satisfied. They part before either one of them is ready and they both want to somehow reestablish contact. George's solution is to go over to her house. Helen is less comfortable being so calculating and simply runs to her garden and calls his name. He is within hearing by then and they walk, successfully establishing mutual feelings of unity. But it is George Willard's feelings, the narrator tells us, which are reflected in Helen White. He is renewed and refreshed by her presence. While the narrator feels comfortable dealing with George's thoughts, at this point of the novel, the narrator refuses to deal with Helen's. He tells us: "There is no way of knowing what woman's thoughts went through her mind but, when the bottom of the hill was reached and she came up to the boy, she took his arm and walked beside him in dignified silence."

Helen White is thus reduced to an abstract figure whom we cannot know. She is the shadow of a strong woman and her major role at the end of *Winesburg, Ohio* is one of reflection rather than independent action. Here is Anderson's chance to develop a character who might try to break old patterns, find more life-giving categories, use her impulses and intelligence to form a balanced, self-directed life, but Anderson does not take it. We are given no evidence that Helen White will ever leave Winesburg or that she will ever transcend traditional roles. We have never seen her do so, and there is no suggestion that she can. (pp. 261-63)

For all the sensitive attention Anderson can pay to his female characters, for all the sympathy he uses to present the story of Louise Bentley, Alice Hindman, and Kate Swift, for all his tenderness toward Elizabeth Willard, he does not, even when the opportunity naturally presents itself, create a female character who wants, and is able, to form her own life. It is interesting that between 1915 and 1917 when *Winesburg, Ohio* was being created, Anderson was attempting to form an I-Thou relationship with a woman; he did not succeed. It may be that through the Helen White-George Willard relationship Anderson is also attempting to form this type of relationship, but again he does not succeed. He is not yet ready, even fictionally, to create a liberated woman with whom his protagonist must relate on equal terms. But Sherwood Anderson is aware that attitudes toward women must change, for the lives women are forced to live are unnecessarily cruel and destructive. If Anderson does prefer women to be reflections of men, he does not want them to be tortured or destroyed. *Winesburg, Ohio* does not satisfactorily portray the possibility of an active, independent, and creative woman who is also a survivor, but at least it portrays the women whose lives are limited because they live within a system which was never created for their benefit. By exploring the lives of the women in Winesburg we explore the biases of a period, the biases of a town, and the biases of an author, but we also experience moments of insight from which we may explore our own biases, our own potential, and our own alternatives. (pp. 264-65)

> *Marilyn Judith Atlas, "Sherwood Anderson and the Women of Winesburg," in* Critical Essays on Sherwood Anderson, *edited by David D. Anderson (copyright © 1981 by David D. Anderson), G. K. Hall & Company, 1981, pp. 250-66.*

ADDITIONAL BIBLIOGRAPHY

Anderson, David D. *Sherwood Anderson: An Introduction and Interpretation.* New York: Holt, Rinehart and Winston, 1967, 182 p.
 A critical study which holds that Anderson believed that love and understanding make life worthwhile.

Anderson, David D., ed. *Sherwood Anderson: Dimensions of His Literary Art.* Lansing: Michigan State University Press, 1976, 141 p.
 Centennial collection of critical essays by writers who view Anderson favorably.

Anderson, David D., ed. *Critical Essays on Sherwood Anderson.* Boston: G. K. Hall & Co., 1981, 302 p.
 A collection of reviews and recent essays. In his introduction, David Anderson provides an interesting overview of the most important critical and bibliographic items written on Anderson's work over the years.

Asselineau, Roger. "Beyond Realism: Sherwood Anderson's Transcendentalist Aesthetics." In his *The Transcendentalist Constant in American Literature,* pp. 124-36. New York: New York University Press, 1980.
 Examines Anderson as both a symbolist and an expressionist, interested in "the spiritual world of love."

Beach, Joseph Warren. "Auguries." In his *The Outlook for American Prose,* pp. 199-280. Port Washington, N.Y.: Kennikat Press, 1926.*
 Includes many comparisons to other artists and posits Anderson's superiority in writing American prose.

Chase, Cleveland B. *Sherwood Anderson.* Folcroft, Pa.: The Folcroft Press, 1927, 84 p.
 Critical biography which concludes that *Winesburg, Ohio* is the only one of Anderson's books which will endure.

Crane, Hart. "Sherwood Anderson." *The Pagan* IV, No. 5 (September 1919): 60-1.
 An enthusiastic review of *Winesburg, Ohio.*

Fagin, Nathan Brillion. *The Phenomenon of Sherwood Anderson: A Study in American Life and Letters.* Baltimore: The Rossi-Bryn Co., 1927, 156 p.
 A survey reflective of Anderson's popularity in the 1920s.

Frank, Waldo. "Laughter and Light." *The Dial* LXXIX, No. 7 (December 1925): 510-14.
 Favorably reviews *Dark Laughter.*

Hilbert, H. Campbell, and Modlin, Charles E., eds. *Sherwood Anderson: Centennial Studies.* Troy, N.Y.: Whitston Publishing Co., 1976, 275 p.
 Includes important source material and eleven critical essays by such essayists as David D. Anderson, Glen A. Love, and Walter B. Rideout.

Mencken, H. L. "Sherwood Anderson." In his *H. L. Mencken's "Smart Set" Criticism,* edited by William H. Nolte, pp. 272-78. Ithaca, N.Y.: Cornell University Press, 1968.
 Reprints three reviews of Anderson's books, written by Mencken while editor of *The Smart Set.* Mencken was an admirer of Anderson, though in time he came to rail against the "muddleheadedness" of Anderson's art.

Miller, Henry. "Anderson the Story-Teller." *Story* XIX, No. 91 (September-October 1941): 70-4.
 A discussion of Anderson's personality and his storytelling technique. This number of *Story* in which Miller's essay appears is a special issue devoted to Anderson and his work. It includes many valuable essays by his friends and literary descendents, including Ben Hecht, Gertrude Stein, Waldo Frank, William Saroyan, and many others. A short, elegaic essay by Theodore Dreiser is reprinted above.

Rideout, Walter B., ed. *Sherwood Anderson: A Collection of Critical Essays.* Englewood Cliffs, N.J.: Prentice-Hall, 1974, 177 p.
 Reprints sixteen important essays on Anderson's work. Contributors include Lionel Trilling, Gertrude Stein, Waldo Frank, Walter B. Rideout, and several others. A helpful bibliography is included.

Rogers, Douglas C. *Sherwood Anderson: A Selective, Annotated Bibliography.* Metuchen, N.J.: The Scarecrow Press, 1976, 157 p.
 Provides a brief survey and a most useful bibliography.

Rukeyser, Muriel. "Sherwood Anderson." *Decision* 1, No. 4 (April 1941): 12-13.
 An impressionistic elegy, written shortly after Anderson's death.

San Juan, Epifanio, Jr. "Vision and Reality: A Reconsideration of Sherwood Anderson's *Winesburg, Ohio.*" *American Literature* XXXV, No. 1 (April 1963): 137-55.
 An astute reconsideration of *Winesburg, Ohio.*

Sutton, William A. *The Road to Winesburg: A Mosaic of the Imaginative Life of Sherwood Anderson.* Metuchen, N.J.: The Scarecrow Press, 1972, 645 p.
 Loosely arranged biographical and critical data, of particular interest to the specialist.

Tanner, Tony. "Sherwood Anderson's Little Things." In his *The Reign of Wonder: Naivety and Reality in American Literature,* pp. 205-27. Cambridge: Cambridge University Press, 1965.
 Examines Anderson's quality of absorbing the many details of life and then recording them in his fiction, regardless of their importance to his plots.

White, Ray Lewis, ed. *The Achievement of Sherwood Anderson: Essays in Criticism.* Chapel Hill: The University of North Carolina Press, 1966, 270 p.
 Anthology which includes essays by Lionel Trilling, William L. Phillips, Irving Howe, and others of high critical repute.

Winther, S. K. "The Aura of Loneliness in Sherwood Anderson." *Modern Fiction Studies* V, No. 2 (Summer 1959): 145-52.
 A study of a pervasive theme as it appeared in Anderson's life and work.

Georg (Morris Cohen) Brandes

1842-1927

Danish critic, essayist, literary historian, biographer, and autobiographer.

Brandes is credited with leading Denmark out of its self-imposed cultural isolation into the mainstream of European philosophic and literary thought during the late 1800s. At a time when the philosophies of G.W.F. Hegel and Søren Kierkegaard dominated Danish thought, Brandes introduced the Danish people to other trends in the intellectual life of Europe. At the same time, his extensive critical writings on such authors as Henrik Ibsen, Bjørnstjerne Bjørnson, August Strindberg, and Kierkegaard, helped to make their names better known outside of Scandinavia. Brandes was one of the first critics to understand and encourage the innovative drama of Ibsen, and he virtually "discovered" Friedrich Nietzsche, providing the first serious critical attention that the German philosopher received. More than a critical interpreter of other writers and their works, Brandes was a man of original thought who had a profound influence on late nineteenth and early twentieth-century literature. Brandes's vision and comprehension of literary trends is most evident in his massive six-volume *Hovedstrømninger i det nittende aarhundredes litteratur (Main Currents in Nineteenth-Century Literature)*, in which he views nineteenth-century literary movements in terms of a struggle between reactionary and progressive forces.

Brandes was born in Copenhagen to Jewish parents. Educated at the University of Copenhagen, he was an excellent student, graduating with honors in 1864. Because of his Jewish background and his reputation as a radical and an atheist, Brandes was denied the chair of aesthetics at the University of Copenhagen, although it had earlier been promised him. Angered by the affront, Brandes left Denmark and lived abroad until 1883. During these years he came into contact with many of Europe's leading writers and thinkers. A meeting with Ibsen is considered to have been a significant event in the lives and careers of both men. Each found in the other reinforcement for his belief in an ideal of individuality. "The continually recurring theme of *Main Currents* is the individual versus society," Bertil Nolin has noted, and this also became a prominent theme of Ibsen's plays. The two Scandinavian writers further resembled one another in that both produced most of their works while living outside of their homelands, though both eventually returned. Brandes came back to Denmark when a group of wealthy admirers guaranteed his income as a private professor. He was elected to the chair of literature at the University of Copenhagen in 1902.

Brandes's most significant achievement in literary and cultural criticism is his *Main Currents in Nineteenth-Century Literature*. In this work, Brandes gives a comparative history of French, German, and English literary movements, which he views as a series of reactions against eighteenth-century thought. The remainder of Brandes's critical writings are a unique mixture of criticism and psychological studies of men whom he revered: not only writers, but statesmen such as Julius Caesar and Benjamin Disraeli, and philosophers such as Nietzsche and Kierkegaard. *Søren Kierkegaard* has been called a masterpiece of biographical and psychological criticism, and the two-vol-

Courtesy of Prints and Photographs Division, Library of Congress

ume study *William Shakespeare* was at the time of its appearance regarded by critics as one of the most important and original non-English language works on Shakespeare. Brandes's "cult of the individual" led him to a sometimes wholly non-critical admiration for the strongly individualistic men about whom he wrote; critics have especially noted that because of his great personal esteem for Nietzsche, Brandes was not able to provide objective criticism of the philosopher, despite his deep understanding of, and sympathy with, Nietzsche's ideas.

Brandes said of himself that he was more than a critic but less than a philosopher. In a letter to him, Nietzsche called Brandes a "missionary of culture." This is perhaps the best definition of Brandes's function within literature. He possessed the ability to view literary movements and the individuals who contributed to those movements within the broader context of virtually all of nineteenth-century European literature. This cosmopolitan outlook uniquely suited Brandes for his role of overseeing the exchange of ideas between Scandinavia and the rest of Europe.

PRINCIPAL WORKS

Dualismen i vor nyeste philosophie   (criticism)   1866
Den franske aesthetic i vore dage   (criticism)   1870

Emigrantlitteraturen (criticism) 1872
  [*The Emigrant Literature*, 1901]
Den romantiske skole i Tydakland (criticism) 1873
  [*The Romantic School in Germany*, 1902]
Reactionen i Frankrig (criticism) 1874
  [*The Reaction in France*, 1903]
Naturalismen i England (criticism) 1875
  [*Naturalism in England*, 1905]
Danske digtere (criticism) 1877
Søren Kierkegaard (criticism) 1877
Benjamin Disraeli (biography) 1878
  [*Lord Beaconsfield*, 1880]
Den romantiske skole i Frankrig (criticism) 1882
  [*The Romantic School in France*, 1904]
Det moderne gjennembruds maend (criticism) 1883
  [*Eminent Authors of the Nineteenth Century*, 1886]
Intryk fra Polen (essays) 1888
  [*Poland: A Study of the Land, People, and Literature*,
  1903]
Intryk fra Rusland (essays) 1888
  [*Impressions of Russia*, 1889]
Det unge Tydakland (criticism) 1890
  [*Young Germany*, 1905]
William Shakespeare. 2 vols. (criticism) 1895-96
  [*William Shakespeare*, 1898]
Henrik Ibsen (criticism) 1898
  [*Henrik Ibsen* published in *Henrik Ibsen. Bjørnstjerne
  Bjørnson*, 1899]
Samlede skrifter. 18 vols. (criticism, essays, and
  biographies) 1899-1910
Anatole France (criticism) 1905
  [*Anatole France*, 1908]
Levned. 3 vols. (autobiography) 1905-08
Reminiscences of My Childhood and Youth (autobiography)
  1906
Friedrich Nietzsche (criticism) 1909
Wolfgang Goethe. 2 vols. (criticism) 1914-15
  [*Wolfgang Goethe*, 1924]
François de Voltaire. 2 vols. (criticism) 1916-17
  [*Voltaire*, 1930]
Cajus Julius Caesar (biography) 1918
  [*Julius Caesar*, 1924]
Sagnet om Jesus (essay) 1925
  [*Jesus: A Myth*, 1926]

*These works are collectively referred to as *Hovedstrømninger i det
  nittende aarhundredes litteratur* (Main Currents in Nineteenth-Century Literature).

———————————————

BJØRNSTJERNE BJØRNSON (letter date 1869)

[*Soon after publishing a critical essay on Danish journalist Meyer
Goldschmidt, Brandes received a letter from Björnson, who attacked Brandes's critical approach. Of the portion of Björnson's
letter reprinted below, Brandes wrote: "This part of the letter
irritated me intensely, partly by the mentor's tone assumed in it,
partly by a summing up of my critical methods which was founded
simply and solely on the reading of three or four articles, more
especially those on Rubens and Goldschmidt, and which quite
missed the point."*]

I [must] touch upon a point that is distinctive of your criticism.
It is an absolute beauty worship. With that you can quickly

traverse our little literature and benefit no one greatly; for the
poet is only benefited by the man who approaches him with
affection and from his own standpoint; the other he does not
understand, and the public will, likely enough, pass with you
through this unravelling of the thousand threads, and believe
they are growing; but no man or woman who is sound and
good lays down a criticism of this nature without a feeling of
emptiness.

I chanced to read one of your travel descriptions which really
became a pronouncement upon some of the greatest painters.
It was their nature in their works (not their history or their lives
so much as their natural dispositions) that you pointed out,—
also the influence of their time upon them, but this only in
passing; and you compared these painters, one with another.
In itself, much of this mode of procedure is correct, but the
result is merely racy. A single one of them, seized largely and
affectionately, shown in such manner that the different paintings and figures became a description of himself, but were
simultaneously the unfolding of a culture, would have been
five times as understandable. A contrast can be drawn in when
opportunity arises, but that is not the essential task. Yes, this
is an illustration of the form of your criticism. It is an everlasting, and often very painful, juxtaposition of things apper-
taining and contrasting, but just as poetry itself is an absorption
in the one thing that it has extracted from the many, so comprehension of it is dependent on the same conditions. The
individual work or the individual author whom you have treated
of, you have in the same way not brought together, but disintegrated, and the whole has become merely a piquant piece
of effectiveness. Hitherto one might have said that it was at
least good-natured; but of late there have supervened flippant
expressions, paradoxical sentences, crude definitions, a definite contumacy and disgust, which is now and again succeeded
by an outburst of delight over the thing that is peculiarly Danish, or peculiarly beautiful. (pp. 224-25)

There are a thousand things between Heaven and Earth that
you understand better than I. But for that very reason you can
listen to me. It seems to me now as if the one half of your
powers were undoing what the other half accomplishes. I, too,
am a man with intellectual interests, but I feel no co-operation.
Might there not be other tasks that you were more fitted for
than that of criticism? I mean, that would be less of a temptation
to you, and would *build* up on your personality, at the same
time as you yourself were building? It strikes me that even if
you do choose criticism, it should be more strongly in the
direction of our educating responsibilities and less as the ar-
ranger of technicalities, the spyer out of small things, the drag-
ger together of all and everything which can be brought forward
as a witness for or against the author, which is all frightfully
welcome in a contemporary critical epidemic in Copenhagen,
but, God help me, is nothing and accomplishes nothing. (p. 225)

> *Bjørnstjerne Bjørnson, in an extract from his letter
> to George Brandes on April 15, 1869, in* Reminis-
> cences of My Childhood and Youth *by George Brandes
> (copyright, 1906, by Duffield & Company), Duffield,
> 1906, pp. 223-27.*

THE SPECTATOR (essay date 1890)

[In *Impressions of Russia*], written with an intensity and a
concentration that have kept it wholly free from the superfluous
matter and trivial personal details that load most books of the
kind, Dr. Brandes, well known in German and Scandinavian
countries as one of the ablest critics and publicists of the day,

has drawn a portrait of the Russian State that in depth of insight, range of knowledge, and vividness of presentation, surpasses every contribution we are acquainted with to our knowledge of the vast Empire which in England is still so little known, and, with insular heedlessness, too often slighted or neglected. (p. 696)

"A Continental View of Russia," in The Spectator *(© 1890 by* The Spectator*), Vol. 64, No. 3229, May 17, 1890, pp. 696-97.*

HJALMAR HJORTH BOYESEN (essay date 1895)

[*Boyesen discusses the influence of Auguste Comte, Herbert Spencer, John Stuart Mill, Charles Darwin, and Hippolyte Taine upon Brandes's approach to criticism. Though he praises Brandes's "linguistic excellences" Boyesen decries the anarchic tendencies Brandes exhibits in his endorsement of the "obscure German iconoclast named Friedrich Nietschke" (sic).*]

It is a greater achievement in a critic to gain an international fame than in a poet or a writer of fiction. The world is always more ready to be amused than to be instructed, and the literary purveyor of amusement has opportunities for fame ten times greater than those which fall to the lot of the literary instructor. (p. 199)

What I mean by a critic in this connection is . . . an interpreter of a civilization and a representative of a school of thought who sheds new light upon old phenomena—men like Lessing, Matthew Arnold, and Taine. The latest candidate for admission to this company, whose title, I think, no one who has read him will dispute, is the Dane, Georg Brandes. (pp. 199-200)

In his book, **"The Dualism in Our Most Recent Philosophy,"** . . . Brandes took up the dangerous question of the relation of science to religion, and treated it in a spirit which aroused antagonism on the part of the conservative and orthodox party.

This able treatise, though it may not be positivism pure and simple, shows a preponderating influence of Comte and his school, and its attitude toward religion is approximately that of Herbert Spencer and Stuart Mill. The constellation under which Brandes was born into the world of thought was made up of the stars Darwin, Comte, Taine, and Mill. These men put their stamp upon his spirit; and to the tendency which they represent he was for many years faithful. Mill's book on "The Subjection of Women" he has translated into Danish . . . , and he has written besides a charmingly sympathetic essay, containing personal reminiscences, of that grave and conscientious thinker. . . . (p. 201)

The three next books of Brandes, which all deal with aesthetical subjects [**"Aesthetic Studies," "Criticisms and Portraits,"** and **"French Aesthetics at the Present Day"**] . . . , are full of pith and winged felicities of phrase. It is a delight to read them. The passage of Scripture often occurs to me when I take up these earlier works of Brandes: "He rejoiceth like a strong man to run a race." He handles language with the zest and vigor of conscious mastery. There is no shade of meaning which is so subtle as to elude his grip. Things which I should have said, *a priori*, were impossible to express in Danish he expresses with scarcely a sign of effort; and however new and surprising his phrase is, it is never awkward, never cumbrous, never apparently conscious of its brilliancy.

I do not mean to say that these linguistic excellences are characteristic only of Dr. Brandes's earlier works; but, either because he has accustomed us to expect much of him in this respect, or because he has come to regard such brilliancy as of minor consequence, it is a fact that two of his latest books (**"Impressions of Poland"** and **"Impressions of Russia"**) contain fewer memorable phrases, fewer winged words, fewer *mots* with a flavor of Gallic wit. Intellectually these **"Impressions"** are no less weighty; nay, they are more weighty than anything from the same pen that has preceded them. They show a faculty to enter sympathetically into an alien civilization, to seize upon its characteristic phases, to steal into its confidence, as it were, and coax from it its intimate secrets; and they exhibit, moreover, an acuteness of observation and an appreciation of significant trifles (or what to a superficial observer might appear trifles) which no previous work on the Slavonic nations had displayed. It is obvious that Dr. Brandes here shuns the linguistic pyrotechnics in which, for instance, De Amicis indulges in his pictures of Holland and the Orient. It is the matter, rather than the manner, which he has at heart. . . . (pp. 201-03)

Having violated chronology in speaking of these two works out of their order, I shall have to leap back over a score of years and contemplate once more the young doctor of philosophy who returned to Copenhagen in 1872 and began a course of trial lectures at the University on modern literature. The lecturer here flies his agnostic colors from beginning to end. He treats **"The Romantic School in Germany"** as Voltaire treated Rousseau—with sovereign wit, superior intelligence, but scant sympathy. At the same time he penetrates to the fountains of life which infused strength into the movement. He accounts for romanticism as the chairman of a committee *de lunatico inquirendo* might account for a case of religious mania. The second and third courses of lectures . . . dealt with **"The Literature of the French Emigrés"** and **"The Reaction in France."** Here the critic is less unsympathetic, not because he regards the mental attitude of the fugitives from the Revolution with approbation, but because he has an intellectual bias in favor of everything French. Besides having a certain constitutional sympathy with the clearness and vigor of style and thought which distinguish the French, Dr. Brandes is so largely indebted to French science, philosophy, and art that it would be strange if he did not betray an occasional *soupçon* of partisanship. His treatment of Chateaubriand, Benjamin Constant, Madame de Staël, Oberman, Madame de Krüdener, and all the queer saints and scribbling sinners of that period is as entertaining as it is instructive. It gives one the spiritual complexion of the period in clear lines and vivid colors, which can never be forgotten. . . . And yet France has its romanticism too, which finds vent in a supercredulous religiosity, in a pictorial sentimentalized Christianity, such as we encounter in Chateaubriand's **"Génie du Christianisme"** and **"Les Martyrs."** It is with literary phenomena of this order that **"The Reaction in France"** particularly deals.

The fourth course of lectures, entitled **"Byron and his Group,"** though no less entertaining than the rest, appears to me less satisfactory. It is a clever presentation of Byron's case against the British public; but the case of the British against Byron is inadequately presented. It is the pleading of an able advocate, not the charge of an impartial judge. Dr. Brandes has so profound an admiration for the man who dares to rebel that he fails to do justice to the motives of society in protecting itself against him. It is not to be denied that the iconoclast may be in the right and society in the wrong; but it is by no means a foregone conclusion that such is the case. If society did not, with the fierce instinct of self-preservation, guard its traditional morality against such assailants as Byron and Shelley, civilization would suffer. . . . I cannot (as Dr. Brandes appears to do) discover any startling merit in outraging the moral sense of the community in which one lives; and though I may admit that a man who was capable of doing this was a great poet, I cannot concede that the fact of his being a great poet justified the outrage. Nor am I sure that Dr. Brandes means to imply so much; but in all of his writings there is manifested a deep sympathy with the law-breaker whose Titanic soul refuses to be bound by the obligations of morality which limit the freedom of ordinary mortals. Only petty and pusillanimous souls, according to him, submit to these restraints; the heroic soul breaks them, as did Byron and Shelley, because he has outgrown them, or because he is too great to recognize the right of any power to limit his freedom of action or restrain him in the free assertion of his individuality. This is the undertone in everything Dr. Brandes has written; but nowhere does it ring out more boldly than in his treatment of Byron and Shelley, unless it be in the fifth course of his **"Main Currents"** dealing with **"Young Germany."**

These four courses of lectures have been published under the collective title **"The Main Literary Currents in the Nineteenth Century"** (*Hovedströmninger i det Nittende Aarhundredes Litteratur*). . . . Barring the strictures which I have made, I know no work of contemporary criticism which is more luminous in its statements, more striking in its judgments, and more replete with interesting information. It reminds one in its style of Taine's "Lectures on Art" and the "History of English Literature." The intellectual bias is kindred, if not the same; as is also the pictorial vigor of the language, the subtle deductions of psychical from physical facts, and a certain lusty realism, which lays hold of external nature with a firm grip.

In Dr. Brandes's **"Impressions of Poland"** I found an observation which illustrates his extraordinary power of characterization. The temperament of the Polish people, he says, is not rational but fantastically heroic. When I recall the personalities of the various Poles I have known (and I have known a great many), I cannot conceive of a phrase more exquisitely descriptive. It makes all your haphazard knowledge about Poland significant and valuable by supplying you with a key to its interpretation. It is this faculty Dr. Brandes has displayed in an eminent degree in his many biographical and critical essays which have appeared in German and Danish periodicals; as also in his more elaborate biographies of [Benjamin Disraeli, Esaias Tegnér, Sören Kierkegaard, Ferdinand Lassalle, and Ludwig Holberg]. . . . They give in every instance the keynote to the personality with which they deal; they are not so much studies of books as studies of the men who are revealed in the books. Take, for instance, the essay on Björnstjerne Björnson, which I regard as one of the finest and most vital pieces of critical writing in recent times. What can be more subtly descriptive of the very innermost soul of this poet than the picture of him as the clansman, the Norse chieftain, who feels with the many and speaks for the many; and what more beautifully indicative of his external position than this phrase: "To mention his name is like running up the flag of Norway"?

It seems peculiarly appropriate to follow up this essay with one on Ibsen, who is as complete an antithesis to his great and popular rival as could well be conceived. . . . The summary of this poet's work and personality in Dr. Brandes's book is a masterpiece of analytical criticism. It enriches and expands the territory of one's thought. It is no less witty, no less epigrammatic, than Sainte-Beuve at his best; and it has flashes of deeper insight than I have ever found in Sainte-Beuve.

The last book of Dr. Brandes's that has been presented to the American public is his **"Impressions of Russia."** The motto of this work (which in the Danish edition is printed on the back of the title-page) is "Black Earth." . . . (pp. 203-09)

The whole of Dr. Brandes's book is interpenetrated with [a] consciousness of the vast possibilities hidden in the virgin bosom of the new earth, even though they may be too deeply hidden to sprout up into the daylight for centuries to come. The Russian literature, which is at present enchaining the attention of the civilized world, is a brilliant variation of this theme, an imaginative commentary on this text. The second half of Dr. Brandes's **"Impressions"** is devoted to the consideration of Puschkin, Gogol, Lermontoff, Dostojevski, Tourguéneff, and Tolstoï; of each of whom he gives, as it appears to me, a better account than M. de Vogüé in his book "Le Roman Russe," which gave him a seat among the Forty Immortals. (pp. 209-10)

[The] fifth volume of his lectures entitled **"Young Germany"** . . . betrays extraordinary intellectual acumen but also a singular confusion of moral values. All revolt is lauded, all conformity derided. The former is noble, daring, Titanic; the latter is pusillanimous and weak. Conjugal irregularities are treated not with tolerance but with obvious approval. Those authors who dared be a law unto themselves are, by implication at least, praised for flinging down their gauntlets to the dull, moral Philistines who have shackled themselves with their own stupid traditions. That is the tone of Brandes's comment upon such relations as that of Immermann to Eliza von Lützow.

But nowhere has he unmasked so Mephistophelian a countenance as in his essays on Luther and on an obscure German iconoclast named Friedrich Nietschke. . . . It is difficult to understand how a man of well-balanced brain and a logical equipment second to none, can take *au sérieux* a mere philosophical savage who dances a war-dance amid what he conceives to be the ruins of civilization, swings a reckless tomahawk and knocks down everybody and everything that comes in his way. (pp. 213-14)

In the essay on **"Martin Luther on Celibacy and Marriage"** Dr. Brandes derides with a satyr-like leer all traditional ideas of chastity, conjugal fidelity, and marital honor.

Though he pretends to fight behind Luther's shield the deftest thrusts are not the reformer's, but the essayist's own. Fundamentally, I fancy, this is an outbreak of that artistic paganism which is so prevalent among the so-called "advanced" Hebrews. The idea that obedience to law is degrading; that conformity to traditional morals is soul-crippling and unworthy of a free spirit; that only by giving sway to passion will the individual attain that joy which is his right, and that self-development which should be his highest aim, has found one of its ablest and most dangerous advocates in Georg Brandes. (pp. 215-16)

Hjalmar Hjorth Boyesen, "Georg Brandes," in his Essays on Scandinavian Literature *(copyright, 1895, by Charles Scribner's Sons), Charles Scribner's Sons, 1895, pp. 199-216.*

WILLIAM MORTON PAYNE   (essay date 1897)

[*In an early overview of Brandes's career, Payne voices the still-current critical belief that Brandes is responsible for introducing Denmark into the mainstream of contemporary European literary and philosophic thought at a time when Danish intellectual life was a half century behind the rest of Europe.*].

The list of [Brandes's] works includes upward of half a dozen volumes of miscellaneous essays and *impressions de voyage*, besides the separate monographs devoted respectively to Holberg, Tegnér, Kierkegaard, Lord Beaconsfield, and the socialist Lassalle. In addition to these books, of course, there is the monumental work entitled **Main Currents in the Literature of the Nineteenth Century.** This work, upon which the critical reputation of the author chiefly rests, is the outcome of a series of lectures begun in 1871 and extending over a period of about ten years. It fills six volumes, and the story which it tells has, as the author suggests, something of the sweep and the symmetry of a great drama. The six volumes of the work are the six acts of the play, and receive incisive characterisation in an introductory chapter. The first of the literary groups to be discussed is that which includes Chateaubriand, Senancour, and Madame de Staël—a group inspired partly by Rousseau, and partly by the vivifying influences of the emigration. To the study of this **Emigrant Literature** succeeds a study of **The Romantic School in Germany,** with its reactionary and catholicising tendencies. Then comes **The Reaction in France,** typified by Joseph la Maistre, Lamennais, and the young Hugo. The scene is now, midway in the play, transferred to another country, and Byron is the hero of **Naturalism in England**. . . .

The fifth volume has for its subject **The Romantic School in France,** and the liberal movement to which the July Revolution gave so powerful an impulse. Finally, the drama is worked out to as definite a close as any such drama can have in the volume entitled **Young Germany,** which shows us the effect of the liberal impulse upon Heine, Börne, Auerbach, and their associates.

It is evident from this outline that Brandes set himself a task calling for powers of a very high order. Something more than literary history and a body of aesthetic principles was needed for so large an exposition. The work called for philosophical grasp, an unerring instinct for what is typical in the intellectual development of a nation or a period, a resolute assumption of the cosmopolitan standpoint, and a frank acceptance of the conclusions of modern thought. Looking back upon the work as a whole, it may fairly be said that the requirements are met, and that the ambition of the plan is justified by the result. The ideas of the author may not always be our ideas, and his sense of relative values may differ widely from our own, but it is impossible to withhold the tribute of our admiration from a work so acute in its details, so illuminating in its general treatment, and so sincere from first to last. (p. 107)

"To bring literature back to life" is . . . the essential formula of our critic; a formula, be it observed, which has some points of contact with Arnold's "criticism of life" theory and with Taine's doctrine of the three influences that shape literature in all times and places, but which embodies a broader and deeper conception of what literature really is.

This new gospel of criticism was proclaimed by Brandes in so defiant a way that no little antagonism was aroused in the conservative Scandinavian camps. For the critic was not content with the quiet assertion of what he believed to be the principles of sound literary judgment, but felt constrained to add a good many things that could not fail to have an irritating effect. There was not only the implication that Denmark had never before produced any criticism worth mentioning, but also the very explicit statement that Danish literature and thought were still in the stage of the reaction—a stage outgrown by the rest of Europe for half a century. (p. 108)

[Brandes] has often shown himself a master of literary criticism in the narrower sense—in the sense in which it means a minute examination of the verbal texture of a piece of literature and the application of purely aesthetic tests—but his heart is not, nor ever was, in such work. He becomes his real self when the nature of his task permits the application of general ideas and philosophical principles, when he finds himself on the trail of some intellectual tendency in a people or an age, when the study of literature reveals to him the deep springs of human thought and action. The controversies of his early manhood have left their mark upon all of his work, although later years have given it more of urbanity and less of strenuousness, have softened its irony and relieved its oppressive earnestness. . . .

The same revolutionary sympathies which led him, many years ago, to an exaggerated estimate of Byron now lead him to an overvaluation of Nietzsche. His admiration for the strong man carries him into ethical vagaries not unlike those that have done so much to impair the influence of Carlyle. He still considers literature, as he did a quarter century ago, to be something that "brings problems up for debate.". . .

That the work of Brandes, taken as a whole, has been a contribution of great value to contemporary criticism can hardly be denied even by those the least in sympathy with his ideals. It more than makes up in light what it lacks in sweetness, and it has the stimulating quality that comes from freshness of thought and unconventionality of utterance. Here, says the reader who first makes his acquaintance, here is a man with an individual standpoint, who knows what he wants to say, and how to say it most directly and forcibly; a man, moreover, who has kept in touch with the chief spiritual movements of the age—with those "main currents" of thought the sweep of which he has so clearly marked out—who has been swayed by the *Zeitgeist,* yet who has a body of very positive opinions of his own. Those opinions are set forth in a strong and nervous prose that cares little for the subtler refinements of expression, but is fully adequate to the demands that the thought makes upon it. "The truly artistic style," he says in one of his essays, "is not that formal grace which spreads uniformly over everything." We shall find in his own style neither the superficial brilliancy of a Jules Lemaître nor the over-elaboration of a Walter Pater, but rather the garment of a thought too serious to care for external rhetorical adornment, and too eager in the pursuit of fundamental truth to waste its energies upon the niceties of verbal modulation and harmonious phrasing. (p. 109)

William Morton Payne, "Living Continental Critics: Georg Brandes," in The Bookman, *New York (copyright, 1897, by Dodd, Mead and Company), Vol. V, No. 2, April, 1897, pp. 106-09.*

ALEXANDER S. KAUN (essay date 1914)

[*Kaun provides a lukewarm review of* Friedrich Nietzsche.]

Friedrich Nietzsche, by George Brandes, . . . adds little new to the vast interpretative literature on the creator of Zarathustra. The book contains a moderate essay on Aristocratic Radicalism, written in 1889, a necrolog, a brief note on *Ecce Homo,* and a few letters interchanged between the philosopher and the critic. In the last twenty-five years life and literature (perhaps I ought to say art in general) have been so profoundly influenced by Nietzschean views that the source of those views has ceased to be discernable. (p. 15)

Yet this belated book in its somewhat belated English translation contains an invaluable feature—the correspondence between Nietzsche and Brandes. "The letters he sent me in that last year of his conscious life" says the famous critic, "appear to me to be of no little psychological and biographical interest." Indeed so, and what is more, they reveal a bit of the reserved personality of Brandes and provoke the reader to venture a comparison between the correspondents.

From the very first we mark the distinct characteristics of the Priest and the Prophet. The careful, correct, and clear interpreter, and the bewildering, cascading revaluator of life, or, to use Ben-Zakkay's metaphor, the plastered well that does not lose a drop, and the powerful spring ever shooting forth new streams; the earnest professor offering practical suggestions, telling of the book-binder, of the copyright business, and of the big audiences at his lectures, and the seething, "three parts blind" sufferer who swings his imagination on revolutionizing Europe, bringing "the whole world into convulsions." (p. 16)

George Brandes "discovered" Nietzsche in the last year of his conscious life, after he had written his greatest works, unrecognized, repulsed by his few former friends, suffering in solitude, yet with superhuman enthusiasm casting new worlds, slaughtering old gods, fighting mediocrity. His letters of that year reveal the final act of the greatest of world-tragedies—the Nietzsche-Tragedy; they grant us a glimpse into the torn soul of the joyous martyr. (p. 18)

> *Alexander S. Kaun, "The Crucified Dionysus," in* The Little Review *(copyright, 1914, by Margaret Anderson), Vol. I, No. 6, September, 1914, pp. 15-19.*

JAMES HUNEKER (essay date 1921)

[*Huneker praises the critic Brandes as the successor of Charles Sainte-Beuve and Hippolyte Taine.*]

Brandes is an iconoclast, a radical, a nonconformist born, and more often a No-Sayer than a Yes-Sayer. The many-headed monster has no message for him. (pp. 61-2)

[He] is brilliant and lucid, and steel-like, whether writing of Shakespeare or Lassalle. An ardent upholder of Taine and the psychology of race, he contends that in the individual, not in the people, lies the only hope for progress. He is altogether for the psychology of the individual. Like Carlyle, he has the cult of the great man. The fundamental question is—can the well-being of the race, which is the end of all effort, be attained without great men? "I say no, and again, no!" he cries. He is a firm believer in the axiom that every tub should stand on its own bottom; and in our earthly pasture, where the sheep think, act, or vote to order, the lesson of Brandes is "writ clear": To myself be true! that truth set forth with double facets by Ibsen in Peer Gynt and Brand. Also by Emerson. Beware of the Bogy—the cowardly spirit of compromise, with its sneaking prudent advice; Go around! For mobs and mob-made laws Georg Brandes has a mighty hatred. He, too, is a radical aristocrat whose motto might be: Blessed are the proud of spirit, for they shall inherit the Kingdom of Earth! . . . Not the polished writer that was Sainte-Beuve, not the possessor of a synthetic intellect like Hippolyte Taine's, Brandes is the broadest-minded man of the three, and upon his shoulders their critical mantles have fallen. (pp. 64-5)

> *James Huneker, "Roosevelt and Brandes," in his* Variations *(copyright, 1921 by Charles Scribner's Sons; copyright renewed © 1949 by Mrs. Josephine Huneker; reprinted with permission of Charles Scribner's Sons), Charles Scribner's Sons, 1921, pp. 57-66.**

ROBERT HERNDON FIFE (essay date 1922)

[*Fife praises Brandes for the freshness and eclecticism of his approach and work.*]

Some years ago, Georg Brandes declared of himself: "I am not a philosopher; for that I am too small. I am not a critic; for that I am too big."

It is certain that to call the great Danish writer merely a critic would be to limit too narrowly the position which he holds in the culture of Europe. To give an accurate definition of Brandes we should have to invent a new word; but it is not probable that we should need the word again, as it is not likely that the world will ever have another Brandes.

We associate the critic with literature, but Georg Brandes is bigger than literature. We expect the critic to sweep away the old and outworn and to adjust us to the new and practical. That has been Brandes' work, but only a part of it. We demand of the critic that he shall interpret for us what is real and lasting in works of art, thus revealing to the passing age the invisible spirit of itself and anticipating the verdict of posterity on the poet and artist of to-day.

All that Brandes has done, but something more besides. He has drawn together in himself all the streams of culture of the later nineteenth and earlier twentieth century as expressed in European letters and esthetics. He has not consciously created an esthetic or philosophical system. He has, however, fused together the million fragments of European culture and thrown over them the light of his own bright realism. What he has wrought and represents is not a brilliant mosaic of ideas, but a genuinely unique picture of the best in European culture during two and a half generations. (pp. vii-viii)

Georg Brandes' work on Shakespeare, the highwater mark of his critical insight, is the most brilliant esthetic study of the great Briton in any non-English tongue. His extraordinary linguistic equipment enabled him to break into the sealed world of the Slav. His journey into Poland and his studies of the Polish people brought the social and political problems of that race into the range of Western Europe. He pushed his studies further eastward into Russia. His appreciation of the genius of the Russian Byron, Puschkin; or Dostojewsky, and Tolstoy brought these great writers and their works in sharp outline to the knowledge of circles of the North and West when they had previously been little more than strange and hard names.

There are three great attributes which we have a right to expect of a critic: the courage to brave tradition, the willingness to accept the new, and a freedom from inherited and traditional bias. All of these Georg Brandes possesses in a high degree. There have been times when he seemed too ready for a fight and those who have attacked him have usually had reason to remember it. . . . He has never hesitated to change his theories nor to raise a new battle flag, and in his long life he has passed through many different stages. He has been a radical collectivist with Taine, a radical individualist with Michelangelo and Goethe, and a radical aristocrat with Nietzsche. He has been independent and international always, but reactionary never. (pp. xi-xii)

It is something like the role of chemical reagent that Brandes has played in the world, and which no man could play who came to his work loaded by such a weight of national, religious and social prejudices as most of us lap up with the milk of childhood.

It is not necessary to say that this freedom is joined with a very positive idealism. The man who can present the work of Michelangelo and Shakespeare and Goethe and Tolstoy and Zola and Strindberg with equal fairness and equal sympathy has within him a lofty ideal of humanity and a deep sense of the essential unity of all ages and all cultures.

Brandes adds to this a constant freshness of appreciation, eternally youthful and instinct with the spirit of a Columbus and a crusader. To master the genius of Shakespeare in his sixties, Goethe in his seventies and Michelangelo in his eighties indicates an ever fresh creativeness that time cannot fade nor custom stale.

Georg Brandes is unique in his contribution to the development of European thought. Certainly he is also unique in the history of Denmark. No other Dane has ever stretched himself like a great zone across the history of his country as Brandes has done. No Dane, and it may be assumed, no Scandinavian, has ever so thoroughly represented his people's cultural history. But he has done more than that. He is the only critic who has ever completely identified himself with the whole of Europe's culture and the entire spirit of the age. For such a man, then, the name of critic is merely too narrow—call him rather an apostle of culture. (pp. xiii-xiv)

> *Robert Herndon Fife, in his introduction to* Georg Brandes in Life and Letters *by Julius Moritzen (copyright, 1922, by Julius Moritzen), D.S. Colyer, Publisher, 1922, pp. vii-xiv.*

BEN RAY REDMAN   (essay date 1930)

[*Redman finds* Voltaire *to be a worthy biography, in the following review of the work.*]

Like Voltaire, [Brandes] was a fighter to the last. And when he came to write his story of Voltaire's long life he wrote as one who had himself lived three-quarters of a century; as one who had been persecuted for his opinions, but whose opinions had been heard around the world, even as those of the patriarch of Ferney. He wrote from a knowledge of men as well as from a knowledge of books. He wrote as one who knew that human character cannot be explained in terms of black and white, that the best of women are not always faithful and the best of men not always brave, and that the patterns of human action must often baffle the judgment of the wise. In short, he sat down to write the life of Voltaire in a mood of deep sympathy with his subject, and possessed of a personal experience that assured his understanding, tolerance and restraint. The result may, I think, fairly be called the most friendly life of Voltaire that has yet appeared.

Let there be no mistake. It is not a work of whitewashing, apology or ill-considered eulogy, but simply a work of understanding. The character which emerges from it is the one with which we have always been familiar, but the biographer is neither superior nor satirical in his presentation of this character. It has always been easy to poke fun at Voltaire's weaknesses, chicaneries and petty furies; and many minor critics have indulged themselves in the sport. This is a kind of fun that does not interest Brandes. He is content to say, without

sneering, moralizing or distorting his fact: This is what the man was like; take him for what he was worth. And we find him great. Others have dwelt with gusto upon the ignoble squabbles in which Volatire permitted himself to become involved, and have taken perverse pleasure in piling up examples of what they consider his cowardice, meanness or dishonesty. Brandes, preferring to linger upon the patience and generosity displayed in his relations with such unworthy creatures as Thiriot and Linant, speaks of "innate humanity" as the keynote of his character, and writes elsewhere: "It seems as though no unpleasant experience could change the inborn nobility of his nature." Brandes is right. I quarrel with him only when he refers to certain actions as being "unworthy" of Voltaire. The fact is, of course, that they were "worthy" in the sense that they were characteristic; just as characteristic as his tireless fight for justice, provoked by France's outrageous treatment of Calas, Sirven and the Chevalier de La Barre. . . .

Voltaire, in [Brandes's] biography, moves against a social background that is generously and vividly described; and his various writings, as they appear in the course of the narrative, are submitted to the acute intelligence of a critic who realized that the literary standards of one age are not those of another. Rich in history, anecdote, gossip and literary criticism, Brandes's life of Voltaire is a full book, a valuable one, and eminently readable; but it is not in itself a finished work of literature. The Danish critic did not trouble to give his materials a final artistic form: the pace of the biography changes; one portion has been polished at leisure, while another has been hurriedly chopped out from the rough mass. And one paragraph, which is very nearly a verbatim transcript of a paragraph in Morley's "Voltaire," is proof that Brandes sometimes made his scissors do service for his pen. But we have had so many "artistic" biographies of late that it is a relief to come upon one with homelier, sturdier virtues. Biographers of the "modern" school too often reveal more of themselves than they do of their subjects; they and their own heroes, and theirs is the glory. But this biography by Brandes is, as it should be, a revelation of Voltaire. That is what we may fairly seek in it and that is what we find in abundance.

> *Ben Ray Redman, "A Work of Understanding," in* New York Herald Tribune Books *(© I.H.T Corporation; reprinted by permission), November 23, 1930, p. 5.*

OSKAR SEIDLIN   (essay date 1942)

[*Seidlin concurs with the general critical concensus that Brandes "forced Denmark back into the stream of the intellectual life of Europe." Seidlin further analyzes Brandes's critical methods, and notes such faults as Brandes's inability to comprehend Symbolism, lyricism in poetry, and German Romanticism.*]

"My life, my books may be insignificant in themselves, but if taken symbolically, they are of interest as microcosms." Whatever the immense bulk of Brandes' literary activity may mean to us today, as an illustration of the intellectual movements in the last decades of the nineteenth century it is invaluable. In his writings, the revival of empiricism, the sweep of positivism, celebrate their triumphs; and even the countercurrents rather supplement than distort the picture of the nineteenth century.

His earliest ideas point in the direction of his future development. To be sure, they spring from very different sources. Kierkegaard and Hegel are his first teachers; but the young student is fascinated rather by their ''poetic'' qualities than by the real substance of their thought. Although in his early publications Brandes still followed the speculative method of his great masters, he was mentally prepared for the new tendencies embodied in the works of David Friedrich Strauss and Feuerbach, Comte and Taine, Renan and Mill. He went over to the camp of the positivists. . . . (pp. 2-3)

Liberation from metaphysics, from speculation, was the new slogan which Brandes now echoed. It was in the world of the exact sciences that the great revolutions of the human spirit took place; here were hidden the sources which nourished all the other forms of human expression. (p. 3)

Brandes could not possibly understand a religious genius like Kierkegaard, in spite of the fact that he admired him profoundly. If such a religious obsession, such a contempt for science, for history and psychology, could be excused at all, it was, Brandes believed, only by assuming that his was a mental case, that here was a man who through a deplorable education had been forced on the wrong track. Throughout his book on Kierkegaard there is a constant struggle going on between the biographer and his hero, except towards the end, when in the passionate fight of Kierkegaard against the present-day representatives of the Protestant church the two seem to have found a common platform; but Brandes overlooks the fact that the crusades of the free-thinker and the intense believer have nothing in common but the outer appearance. (pp. 3-4)

Darwin's theory of evolution was in the eyes of Brandes the cornerstone upon which the intellectual edifice of the nineteenth century rested. So axiomatic had this become to him that, in his *Goethe,* he followed up all the connections which lead from the poet to Darwin. It is not surprising that he emphasized in his discussion of the *Metamorphose der Pflanzen* and of Goethe's osteological studies the parallel between Goethe and Darwin, without recognizing how little Goethe's ''inneres Gesetz'' has in common with Darwin's ''survival of the fittest.'' And again, it is the natural law of evolution which provides the basis for his monumental work *Main Currents of Nineteenth-Century Literature,* the book which made him famous all through Europe, which was hailed by his friends as a revelation, abused by his enemies as heresy. The human mind constituting a unity, in all people and countries essentially the same, must necessarily everywhere obey the same laws of development, must traverse the same stages and find forms of expression whose parallelisms can be demonstrated without great difficulty. What he sets out to present is the ''six acts of a great play,'' a drama whose hero is the psyche of Europe; he has no doubt that the development as reflected in the literatures of France, Germany, and England must necessarily be a ''progressive'' one. Thus the division of the acts offers itself automatically. First act: the beginning of reaction in the French emigrant literature; second act: beginning and victory of reaction in German Romanticism; third act: the stabilization of reaction in France; fourth act: the rebirth of freedom in English Naturalism; fifth act: the liberal tendencies in French Romanticism; sixth act: the victory of liberal thought in ''Young Germany.'' At that point, the development has come to its close, the ''fittest have survived'', and a ''new species'' can originate.

He is permeated with the spirit of the new sciences, and wherever he discovers its essence in poetry, his enthusiasm is awakened. Being modern is Ibsen's foremost title to fame, and the scientifically cool attitude in which Flaubert approaches the phenomena of the outer world and the soul impresses him particularly. Even in Goethe's *Iphigenie* he suspects traces of

the doctrine of heredity, and he honestly wonders how it is possible that the model of pure humanity descends from a family of murderers and criminals. (pp. 5-6)

In his literary criticism are manifest also his almost religious reverence for activity and his negation of all those powers which might frustrate the activity of man. Shakespeare's *Hamlet* presents him with a difficult problem; and he does not rest content until he has succeeded in clearing Shakespeare's play of the ''reproach'' that it depicts the tragedy of inactivity. What he sees in Hamlet is not a tragedy of inactivity, but of disgust with the world, and Hamlet's hesitation is explained as a technical device to fill the five acts of the drama. Yes, Brandes whom one cannot accuse of yielding to compromises, who had chosen as his watchword: ''As flexible as possible when it is a question of understanding, as inflexible as possible if it is a question of speaking,'' raises his objections against Ibsen's rigorism, the passionate absoluteness of a Brand, because the rigid All or Nothing bars the way to action and the gradual realization of the ideal.

Here we have arrived at the crossroad where Brandes takes leave of scientific positivism. This passionate urge for action could arise only upon the basis of a philosophy of will, of an idealism of freedom in Brandes' *Weltanschauung.* In this connection it may suffice to point out that, in spite of being sincerely devoted to the spirit of the natural sciences, he was a fervent opponent of determinism, its legitimate child. So it was but natural that at times the attitude of the ideal scientist, his indifferent objectivity, his dispassionate observing and cool recording of facts, struck him as questionable and dangerous. (pp. 8-9)

Brandes' belief in the sciences is harmoniously and indissolubly tied up with his belief in reason. (p. 9)

He demands clarity and precision in poetry just as in the process of thinking. He was repelled by Hegel's philosophy, which devaluated and dissolved the logical opposites of thesis and antithesis by the superimposition of the synthesis. Like philosophy, poetry also is expected to furnish us with clearcut answers. It is not to be satisfied with just demonstrating the problems but it should work out a satisfactory and convincing solution. If his attitude towards Ibsen vacillates at times, it is because he realizes only too well that the playwright raised questions without intending to offer clear and distinct answers. (p. 10)

At times the rationalistic attitude results in a shallow prosaicness to which the vital and emotional contents of poetry are a closed world. The revolutionary antirationalism of the German Storm and Stress seems ridiculous to him, Maximilian Klinger is ''no artist, he lacks that sanity and balance indispensable to the creation of a character that does not act contrary to all principles of reason''; and his play, which gave the whole movement its name, is summed up as ''world-famous nonsense.'' But this aversion is not restricted to minor writers; ultimately Brandes is at a loss what to do with Goethe's *Werther.* He fails to grasp the central problem of the novel, the ruin of an individual caused by the superabundance of his emotions, and finds nothing but the story of an unhappy love whose high tension strikes the sober critic as exaggerated and unintelligible. (p. 11)

It is but natural that such a ''prosaic soul'' should have no spontaneous access to the deep enchantment of lyric poetry. It is true, he has tried again and again to capture the spirit of lyrics; and if we may believe the reports of his friends, he was even capable of losing himself in the music and magic of a poem with a fervor verging on a trance. But basically he is unmusical, and one will find in his works hardly any reference to music. Where he has to draw the musical element into his discussion, as in the instance of Kierkegaard's audacious *Don Juan*-analysis, one senses the helplessness of the critic who labels Mozart with the attributes "carefree and sparkling." Notwithstanding Brandes' ability to experience poetry intensely, the analyses he puts in writing sound astonishingly flat and uninspired. In so far as he ventures beyond the purely *Weltanschauliche* of a poem, he contents himself with noncommittal remarks on the beauty of the language, the audacity and accuracy of the metaphors, the richness of the rhyme. And his extensive quotations from the poems under discussion, particularly conspicuous in the case of Heine, seem to be an indication of his inadequacy and an attempt to unload the task of interpretation onto the shoulders of the reader. However, one must not jump to the conclusion that Brandes lacked a great sensitivity to the shades and potentialities of a language. On the contrary, it is admirable how he, the foreigner, succeeded in feeling his way into the subtleties of German, French, and English styles. Nevertheless, his works hardly contain a profound and creative analysis of lyrical poetry.

His basically rationalistic attitude shows up most conspicuously in his treatment of German Romanticism. The whole volume which he dedicated to this literary movement within the framework of his *Main Currents* is nothing but a protest against and a refutation of a poetic and human conception which he fails to understand, or as far as he does understand it, abhors. . . . Not once, throughout the whole book, has one the impression that he knew what the Romantic experiment really meant. . . . Romanticism is to him the great corrupting danger, a danger to which unfortunately even Kleist succumbed, whose "clearness and definiteness . . . was disturbed and deranged by the poetic insanity of Romanticism."

Is it then surprising that Rousseau, the father of European Romanticism, gets nothing but poor marks whenever his name is mentioned in Brandes' work? In spite of his own pantheism, he has not the slightest sympathy for this apostle of nature, because in Rousseau's struggle against civilization he sensed only too clearly the frontal attack on the organizing and constructive forces of reason. It goes without saying that in the Voltaire book Rousseau has no chance as the antagonist of the hero, though the weapons Brandes uses against his opponent can hardly be called fair. What must one think when the apologist for Voltaire, whose firmness of character was more than doubtful, reprimands Rousseau: "The champion of equality accepted the hospitality of a banker's wife"? (pp. 11-14)

We have already pointed out in a different connection how wrong it would be to see in Brandes exclusively the representative of empirical positivism. We shall have to show now to what a strong degree he was dominated by a radical philosophy of the will, by an idealism of freedom, which came constantly into conflict with his scientific deterministic attitude.

All his life long he remained loyal to the sentence which at the age of seventeen he put down in his diary:

> There is only one decisive factor on earth: the will, led by intelligence.

And the older he became, the more this sentence took on the character of his most personal confession. (pp. 14-15)

With Brandes extreme individualism assumed an almost religious form. For this very reason Byron and Shelley signified

a turning point in the whole of European literature, because in them forces were set free which made possible the emancipation of the individual from all ties and restrictions. With this deep religious belief in the freedom and emancipation of the individual from all external conditions, Brandes was bound soon to come into conflict with Taine and his theory of environment. . . . Individualism is the most precious possession of mankind; and the reason for the cowardly tameness of our culture he attributes to the "disintegration of individuality which the modern order of society involves." And do not also the poisonous invectives launched in his *Shakespeare* against the Baconian theory originate above all in the endeavor to save Shakespeare as an "individuality," and to protect him from the vilification which anonymity would mean from Brandes' point of view?

It is for this reason that the man of antiquity, who in noble harmony gives free rein to his instincts and abilities, and is not yet conscious of the Jewish-Christian "Thou shalt not," becomes the object of his intense admiration, carried over to the Renaissance, which, marked by the revolution of the individual against all restrictions, represents the period of highest human fulfillment. His autobiography, indeed all his works are filled with his allegiance to the Graeco-Pagan ideal of man; his *Michelangelo* is nothing but a hymn to the Renaissance. This Renaissance ideal of free human beings he rejoicingly rediscovers in Shakespeare; and with a biting sharpness he scorns Eduard von Hartmann, the "philosopher of Philistinism," who objected to the character of Juliet because he found in her only "purely sensuous passions."

To this gospel of the great personality, of the superman who does not stop short of full self-realization, corresponds a contempt for the masses which knows no bounds. He never misses an opportunity to expose the stupidity and inertia of the "compact majority"; and in reading his books, one can hardly rid oneself of the painful impression caused by the monotony of his fits of hatred. (pp. 16-18)

However, this *odi profanum vulgus* is again but one aspect of Brandes. The passionate admiration for the great personality, the violent contempt of the mob, are interspersed with an incredibly sensitive social conscience, with a bold defense of the rights of the oppressed and those neglected by fate. . . . It is true that this mixture of love and hatred expressed itself in the strangest forms: one day a desperate pessimism, the conviction that everything was futile, that belief in progress was nothing but a vain illusion; and the next a return to the battlefield, which would have been impossible had the outburst of despair really sprung from the depth of his heart. [*The World at War*] is full of these contradictions. On the one hand the belief that nations have been innocent victims of criminally irresponsible diplomats, on the other the conviction that the greed and stupidity of man had automatically to lead to this war. (pp. 18-19)

We who have been influenced by Croce's aesthetics, by the rigorous art of textual analysis practiced by the New Criticism, no longer believe in the separation of *life* and *work,* which nineteenth-century aesthetics assumed. (p. 21)

To Brandes, however, life and work constitute dual entities, which are only casually related to each other, two different substances which can be compared to each other, and in this way mutually clarified. He openly adopted Sainte-Beuve's method: "the works illuminating the life, the life supporting and determining the works." Particularly when direct biographical information about the poet is scarce, the work again and again has to furnish the missing data, and the interpretation gives way to guesses as to the ''hidden'' personal experiences. He explicitly states that it has been the purpose of his *Shakespeare*

> to declare and prove that Shakespeare is not thirty-six plays and a few poems jumbled together but a man who felt and thought, rejoiced and suffered, brooded, dreamed and created,

as though such proof were necessary, as though it helped us in the least to draw closer to the phenomenon Shakespeare. As he believes in the dualism of life and work, the construction of his books is not fundamentally different from the usual pattern of the nineteenth-century literary criticism which used to alternate monotonously one chapter of biography with one chapter of critical analysis. It is true that he arranges his material somewhat more tastefully; but the jumping back and forth from the biographical to the interpretative aspect is only thinly veiled.

To Brandes the world of the creative genius is not a cosmos resting in itself, obeying its own laws, but the everyday reality which he copies with the help of certain formal means, be they of a naturalistic, romantic or idealizing nature. The artist is nothing but a good observer who by a happy accident has also the capacity to give shape to his observations. (pp. 21-2)

Again and again Brandes applies the principle of causality, the gospel of all natural science, to the process of intellectual creativeness. With a simplicity sometimes bordering on the childish, the great work of art is interpreted as the direct sediment of a concrete experience. . . . [He] explains the young Heine's longing for death from the biographical fact that the boy Heine at this time was in love with Josepha, the daughter of an executioner. . . . Brandes was never able to free himself from this approach; the urge to ''explain'' scientifically is ingrained in him and pervades his whole work.

The positivistic aestheticians, obsessed by the idea that the growth of a work of art would be thus ''explained'' conclusively, had surrendered completely to the notorious hunt for original models, for those sources which they collected with minute accuracy, convinced as they were that they could grasp the secret of a work of art by dissolving it into its various elements like a chemical compound. Compared to the philological zeal with which the nineteenth century ferreted out sources, the work of Brandes signifies a tremendous progress. Still even he relapses at times into the dissection mania. For Shakespeare's *Tempest* he unearths no less than twelve sources, while, in the course of the discussion of Gretchen's prayer in *Faust,* he reminds us of five Goethean reminiscences which found their way into the poem. It would be unjust to overlook the surprising length to which Brandes had already gone beyond this hunt after sources. But the summative method, reflecting the atomistic mechanistic attitude of the nineteenth century, trying to dissolve the wholeness of a work of art and of life into particles derived from psychological and biographic data, is fundamentally the method of Brandes also. No doubt, it is to his great credit that he kept his mind open to great vistas of ideas, that he had the courage to write a literary history of Europe at a time when literary historiography exhausted itself in collections of philological material, concentrating its interest on minutely detailed inquiries. But the totalities, the great monuments which he tries to contruct, show only too blatantly the various single parts from which they have been put together.

Thus of the two great works of his old age, his book on Goethe is broken up into 140 small chapters representing almost as many fresh starts, and his *Voltaire* is anything but a well-integrated whole. To be sure, here he strives for a great unity; what he is after is not an isolated portrait but a monumental panorama of the period. Nevertheless, the long chapters which he fills with world history and petty court stories are unconnected with the figure of the hero. Again and again Voltaire disappears completely from the scene, and when we meet him again he seems to us an old acquaintance of whom we had lost sight. And are the *Main Currents,* the work of his mature manhood, essentially different? Do not these six volumes also fall apart into individual portraits, only superficially related to each other, and is the final product the truly comprehensive picture of the European spirit Brandes wanted to draw? Paradoxically, Brandes achieves his purpose only in the part dedicated to German Romanticism, for which he cared little and which he understood less. Here he does not place portrait next to portrait, but tries, by means of a topical arrangement, to do justice to the essential factors of an intellectual movement. (pp. 23-5)

So intimately had positivism related the work of art to chemical and physical phenomena that to assort, to register, and to explain facts, appeared to be the task of the literary critic. . . . Particularly in his younger years Brandes, too, saw strict detachment as the necessary condition of every critical effort. . . . In the course of years, however, Brandes more and more abandons this point of view. . . . [That] in his introduction to *Creative Spirits* he vigorously rejects Taine's thesis of ''criticism as an applied science,'' may be taken as valid proof. Here it dawns upon him that the real organ of literary criticism is not a cool observation which tries to maintain rigidly the distance between object and subject, but rather an intuitive process which, in a creative moment, merges object and subject into a real unity. (pp. 25-6)

His work belongs to the nineteenth century; and however high it may tower above the average, it lacks the touch of the immortal which might make us forget how closely it is tied up with a definite period, how inevitabley prone to the destiny of becoming ''dated.'' But the fire that burnt in him, his passion for truth, his enthusiastic willingness to serve the spirit in whatever form it revealed itself, are timeless, and will keep his name alive even if his work should sink into oblivion. His critical conceptions and analyses may be completely outmoded tomorrow; but his instinct for the truly great, his fight for the recognition of the new, will testify for him. That in spite of all his bias he was the first to raise his voice for Kierkegaard, that he made a stand for Ibsen, Nietzsche, Strindberg, at a time when they saw themselves confronted with cold indifference or violent opposition, weighs a hundred times more heavily than the fact that his critical arguments and methods may often fail to convince us. He was a great discoverer, and he had the courage of his discoveries. (p. 27)

Oskar Seidlin, ''Georg Brandes 1842-1927,'' in Journal of the History of Ideas *(copyright 1942, Journal of the History of Ideas, Inc.), Vol. III, No. 4, October, 1942 (and reprinted in his* Essays in German and Comparative Literature, *The University of North Carolina Press, 1961, pp. 1-29).*

HARALD O. DYRENFORTH (essay date 1963)

[*Dyrenforth discusses Brandes's drama criticism.*]

The fame of critics and *litterateurs* is a perishable commodity, unless, like Aristotle or Lessing, they are *very* great *sub specie aeternitatis*. Nowadays we may be more inclined to view Brandes as one of the great popularizers of knowledge, like Van Loon or de Kruif, combining their gifts with the—sometimes pseudo-scholarly—sweep and flashiness of Emil Ludwig and the showmanship and gossipy exuberance of Alexander Woollcott. (p. 143)

Brandes became the great importer and interpreter of foreign cultures to his compatriots. His principal work, the ***Main Currents in 19th Century Literature,*** began as a lecture series at the University of Copenhagen and grew into one of the most sensational successes in academic history. . . . Ibsen wrote about the ***Main Currents*** in a letter to Brandes: "Your revolt seems to me one great blasting and liberating expression of genius." (p. 144)

His weltanschauung was one of joyful worldliness, worship of beauty, and rationality. He was forever opposed to religiosity, transcendentalism, asceticism, and mysticism. Bergel calls him "a classic Greek, stranded in the North, a representative of the Age of Enlightenment who had strayed into the twentieth century."

Brandes' dramatic criticism is only a comparatively small part of his work. Most of it is found in his books [***William Shakespeare*** and ***Goethe***] . . . and a few scattered essays in various collections on Ibsen, Bjoernson, Strindberg, Schnitzler, and Kleist. His capacity for enthusiasm was probably one of the most attractive features of his writing. With all the wealth of detail and research, there is always a refreshing personal touch in Brandes' style. The first person singular, so studiously and anxiously avoided in our scholarly writing, was never suppressed by Brandes. (pp. 144-45)

In his *Hamlet* analysis Brandes showed how the character became a heightened, glorified version of Shakespeare, the man. (p. 145)

In the end of [the] chapter on "The Personal Element in Hamlet," Brandes . . . seemed to vent his own bitterness:

> And the Danish Court was only a picture in miniature of all Denmark—that Denmark where there was something rotten, and which to Hamlet was a prison. "Then is the world one?," Rosencrantz asks; and Hamlet does not recoil from the conclusion: "A goodly one," he replies, "in which there are many confines, wards and dungeons."

Brandes pointed out all this was obviously felt and expressed *from below upwards*, not from above downwards, and that a great many of these words are highly improbable, almost impossible, coming from the mouth of a prince. Hamlet comes to grip with the ultimate questions of good and evil, the existence of a just God and the world's relation to Him if He does exist. . . . Very emphatically, Brandes stated that the self-reproaches of Hamlet do not represent a condemnation of the character by Shakespeare. (pp. 145-46)

Very interesting and sound were his observations on the old question of Hamlet's sanity or madness. He quoted all of Hamlet's keen-edged sayings and witticisms and could find no trace of madness there. That Hamlet often concludes with a deliberately scurrilous remark such as "For yourself, sir, should be as old as I am, if, like a crab, you could go backwards," or "I am but mad north-north-west; when the wind is southerly, I know a hawk from a handsaw," is done only to lay down a smoke-screen and allay the suspicions of the watchful King and Polonius. "To see symptoms of insanity in all this is not only a crudity of interpretation, but a misconception of Shakespeare's evident meaning. . . . He [Hamlet] makes use of insanity; he is not in its power." (p. 146)

To Brandes, Hamlet is the genius of the Renaissance, Goethe's Faust (the medieval trappings notwithstanding) the genius of our time. Due to Shakespeare's marvellous power of transcending his time, Hamlet covers and bridges the whole span of time between him and us and has a significance in the twentieth century and the centuries to come to which Brandes could see no limit. Faust is probably the highest poetic expression of modern humanity—striving, investigating, enjoying, and mastering himself and the world. Of course, this was written in 1895-96; whether Brandes, after two world wars, Bolshevism, Nazism, Fascism, concentration and extermination camps, genocide, slave labor, and the atomic bomb, would still make this last statement about our "self-mastery" is highly questionable.

Just as fascinating are Brandes' comments on *Anthony and Cleopatra*. (p. 147)

A very brilliant piece of work, though, of necessity, mostly speculation, is Brandes' exegesis of Cleopatra as the dramatic version of the Dark Lady of the Sonnets. He started with pointing out the parallel in "darkness" of hair and complexion. Three times in Shakespeare's works, once in *Romeo and Juliet* and twice in *Anthony and Cleopatra*, the Egyptian is called "a gypsy" or "a right gypsy." She herself jests about her dark complexion and her "wrinkles":

> Think on me
> That am with Phoebus' amorous pinches black,
> And wrinkled deep in time.

To his friend Ibsen Brandes devoted only a few isolated essays, chapters in various collections of his such as [***"Moderne Geister," "Gestalten und Gedanken,"*** or ***"Miniaturen"***] . . . and a few articles in periodicals. In these, however, he shed more light on the withdrawn "giant of the North" than most other biographers and historians. (p. 149)

Brandes was probably the first to compare *Ghosts* in its firmness, simplicity, and delicacy with antique tragedy, such as *Oedipus Rex,* a comparison which has been repeated many times since then. . . . In Brandes' words:

> Thus we see him [Ibsen] at first, with all the living older writers of the day, standing waist-deep in the romantic period, then gradually working his way out of it to become the most modern of modern writers. This is his imperishable glory and will invest his works with enduring life.

When we consider that this was written in *1883,* while Ibsen was still in the middle of his production, and while Brandes was surrounded by so many other seemingly promising Scandinavian writers, this tribute to Ibsen is also a triumph of Brandes' artistic acumen, almost to the point of clairvoyance, and marks him as one of the freest, clearest, and most comprehensive minds of his time. (pp. 149-50)

Harald O. Dyrenforth, "Georg Brandes: 1842-1927," in Educational Theatre Journal *(© 1963 University College Theatre Association of the American Theatre Association), Vol. XV, No. 2, May, 1963, pp. 143-50.*

RENÉ WELLEK (essay date 1965)

[*Wellek's* A History of Modern Criticism *is a major, comprehensive study of the literary critics of the last three centuries. Wellek's critical method, as demonstrated in* A History *and outlined in his* Theory of Literature, *is one of describing, analyzing, and evaluating a work solely in terms of the problems it poses for itself and how the writer solves them. For Wellek, biographical, historical, and psychological information is incidental. Although many of Wellek's critical methods are reflected in the work of the New Critics, he was not a member of that group, and rejected their more formalistic tendencies.*]

The six volumes of Brandes' great work, *Hovedstrømninger i det 19de Aarhundredes Litteratur* . . . were a polemical work that caused an immense sensation in Denmark and later in Germany. . . . It is a comparative history of French, German, and English literature in the first half of the 19th century according to a scheme derived from the assumptions of European liberalism. The central topic is the reaction against the 18th century and the overcoming of that reaction. The Revolution is the thesis, the *Restauration* the antithesis, and the Liberal movement the synthesis that preserved and superseded, in good Hegelian fashion, the values of the romantic reaction. The six acts of the drama correspond to Brandes' six volumes: three on French, two on German, and one on English literature. . . . Nothing is said about Italy or Russia, but the application to Denmark is constantly in Brandes' mind. The whole country has missed the boat of progress: it is still stagnating in the backwaters of reaction.

Brandes calls his scheme ''psychological'' because he conceived of ''psychology'' as ''national psychology'' and wants to think of literature constantly as the expression of men, as a part of life. But basically his scheme is still the old romantic concept of history as the history of the national mind or minds: a history of ideas, mainly political and religious, as it was practiced by Hettner or Gervinus. Literature is judged by asking whether it ''put problems to debate,'' whether it contributes to progress, to political liberalization, to religious free thought and to sympathy for modern science and its deterministic and evolutionary doctrines. Brandes is perfectly sure of his standards of judgment: literature must be judged by its *Tendenz*, which is the ''spirit of the century,'' which in its turn is ''the lifeblood of genuine poetry.'' Political reaction is wrong; so is obscurantism, and any revealed religion. Feuerbach, Brandes believed, has settled for good the problem of theology: God is an invention of man. Theology is anthropology or psychology. Science has solved all other mysteries: belief in the freedom of will is as obsolete as belief in werewolves. The straight march of progress is assumed at every point. (pp. 357-58)

Brandes conceived of criticism as exhortation and propaganda. ''Criticism moves mountains: mountains which are called belief in authority, prejudice, and dead traditions.'' He always asks one question: did the writer contribute to the victory of liberalism, agnosticism, and the scientific outlook? Was he ''progressive''? As with present-day Marxists (who hold, of course, a different creed), there is, in Brandes, an inherent unresolved contradiction between the fervently held creed with which everything is judged and the pretention to scientific objectivity. He uses the well-worn image of the literary historian as a ''botanist'' who is just as concerned with nettles as with roses, but does not tell us that he considers nettles obnoxious and wants to weed them out. Brandes is thus no follower of Taine, in spite of his professions of indebtedness and his genuine admiration for the man and his work. There is no real attempt to explain literature in terms of *milieu, moment,*

and *race.* There is no literary sociology in Brandes, but literature is treated, in De Bonald's words, as ''the expression of society.'' A great writer must be permeated with the spirit of his time; he must be, or is assumed to be, representative. Occasionally Brandes makes rather naive correlations between literature and society. We are told, for instance, that there was ''no poetry in France during the Empire'' because epics and tragedies were being acted out in life. But mostly Brandes provides simply a political history as background, dwelling at length on events often entirely unrelated to concrete literary works or figures: we hear, for instance, much about the Irish rebellions in 1782 and 1799, or are provided with a fairly detailed account of the events in Berlin in 1848. At times we are given mere sketches of thinkers and their ideas—for example, of De Bonald's treatise on divorce, or of public figures who are assumed to be characteristic of the time or its mood. There is a whole chapter on Madame de Krüdener and another on Charlotte Stieglitz, who committed suicide in order to stimulate her husband to write great poetry out of suffering. In imaginative literature Brandes looks mainly for types: Werther is a great symbol in which ''the passions, desires, and sorrows of a whole era found expression.'' The next modern type was Chateaubriand's René, in whom the ''poetry of desire'' was replaced by the ''poetry of disillusion.'' René ''is a melancholiac and misanthropist. He forms the transition from Goethe's Werther to Byron's Giaour and Corsair.'' Constant's Adolphe is the next variation of the basic type. Balzac then discovered a new female type, *la femme de trente ans,* which rules over the whole of the modern French stage. Danish literature, Brandes laments, has no types, certainly nothing to compare to Nathan the Wise, Faust, Prometheus, or Marquis Posa. Oehlenschläger's heroes are ''abstract and ideal'': they ''mirror their age only imperfectly.'' They could not, as Brandes imagines, do anything like Posa running his sword through Phillip II, Prometheus rising from his rock and purging Olympus, or Faust subduing the earth with the help of steam, electricity, and methodical research.

With such ideas in mind we can predict the judgments on writers pretty easily. The volume on the German romantics is completely negative, though Brandes describes many writers with some care, often translating very closely and for long stretches from Haym and Goedeke. Brandes is particularly upset by the romantic disruption of illusion, the interest in the division of personality and the ''nature and night side of man.'' He wants ''striving, will, decision'' which make man a whole. The Reaction in France excites his indignation and distaste: he is amusingly satirical about Madame de Krüdener standing next to Tsar Alexander reviewing 150,000 Russian troops on the Champs des Vertus, or about Lamartine's highflown mixture of religiosity and eroticism. In the English volume the emphasis on naturalism gives a completely distorted picture of the visionary company of the great romantic poets. ''Naturalism'' is a term that covers Wordsworth's love of nature, Keats' sensualism, and Byron's revolutionary liberalism. (pp. 359-60)

The romantic group in France is Brandes' greatest love: ''Without exaggeration it is the greatest literary school that this century has seen.'' Brandes can reconcile his aversion for German romanticism with his boundless admiration for the French not only by the obvious political distinction, but by emphasizing the traditional character of the French. ''All French romantics are classicists. Mérimée, Gautier, George Sand, even Hugo, are classicists.'' (p. 361)

Brandes has fewer illusions about the poetic values of German liberal literature. But he is greatly interested in Börne, also as a converted Jew, and he must be one of the most fervent admirers of Heine on record. The account of Heine's poetry and prose surpasses most of Brandes' earlier essays in analytical and critical power: he gives close readings of individual poems, sensitively developing the implications of a passage; he can criticize the early poetry for its sentimentality and conventionality, and he praises the last poems addressed to Mouche, as they deserve to be praised. Brandes draws elaborate parallels to Rembrandt for Heine's attempts to achieve chiaroscuro and to Aristophanes for comic imagination, and he makes much of Heine's discovery of the sea as a theme of nature poetry hitherto missing in Germany. Heine is to him "the wittiest man who ever lived," and at the same time the finest lyrical poet, comparable only to Shelley; and, needless to say, Heine was a good fighter for the liberation of humanity, in spite of some backslidings.

The volume on the French romantics contains appreciative pages on Sainte-Beuve as the founder of modern criticism. Sainte-Beuve knew how to explain the genesis of a work, and to discover "the man behind the paper." He rightly chose as motto for his writings the words of Sénac de Meilhan: "Nous sommes mobiles et nous jugeons des êtres mobiles."

This could have been Brandes' motto also, for it is ultimately an injustice to pin him down to the ideological scheme of the *Main Currents*, a panoramic set of lectures often heavily dependent on secondary sources, indulging in glib comparisons and easy categorizations. The better Brandes is elsewhere. Brandes, we must not forget, has his roots in the Danish soil and is at his best as a critic of his native literature, in which he developed his art of portraiture before the lecture series. There, we see also that he had a well-defined taste and sense of beauty which often clashes with the ideology.

His first book, *Aesthetiske Studier* . . . , shows him a close student of Hegel and of F. T. Vischer, whom he opposes from a point of view that can be called Herbartian formalism. The essay on **"The Idea of Fate in Ancient Tragedy"** . . . argues in a scholastic manner that tragic guilt is neither metaphysical nor ethical, but must be conceived as purely aesthetic; and another study on **"The Theory of the Comic"** . . . develops the old idea of contradiction: the laughable must be illuminated by the idea of poetry to become comic. But the book contains also studies of Ibsen, against whose raw ugliness and moral harshness Brandes felt still much resistance.

The turn toward a positivistic point of view came with Brandes' two stays in Paris: in 1867 when he heard Taine lecture at the Ecole des Beaux Arts and in 1870, when he saw him frequently and met also Renan and Chasles. But the book *Den franske Aesthetik i vore Dage* . . . , written before his second stay, is by no means an uncritical exposition of Taine. It gives up speculative aesthetics in the Hegelian sense but makes many reservations against Taine's method. Brandes sees that Taine considers art as "psychology, as historical material. The work of art is a monument or a curiosity and never a revelation of beauty." He invokes Herbartian aesthetics in protest: Taine, he sees, is unable to distinguish between the beautiful and the ugly. "One feels how much they need in France the still unknown Herbartian aesthetics of measure." But Brandes recognized his own lack of clarity on these issues. A book published simultaneously with the volume of French aesthetics, *Critiker og Portraiter* . . . , contains mostly theatrical criticism and essays on Andersen, Mérimée and the piece on Sainte-

Beuve used so much later in the lecture series. Brandes advanced in both directions simultaneously: in adopting the historist method for which he had criticized Taine and in developing his taste for portraiture and individual psychology.

The book on *Søren Kierkegaard* . . . not only has a great historical merit but in German translation (1879) made Kierkegaard first known outside Denmark, and even in his homeland it was the first serious study. But it is also Brandes' first and most delicate psychological portrait, written with deep sympathy and penetration. The way Brandes traces the disguises of the unhappy love affair with Regina Olsen through Kierkegaard's writings—for example, in the interpretation of Antigone or the sacrifice of Isaac—is most ingenious and convincing. But of course Brandes' psychology has a reductive result: he cannot understand Kierkegaard's religion or philosophy. On the plane of ideas he sympathizes only with Kierkegaard's anticlericalism and with his fierce individualism. Kierkegaard, according to Brandes, discovered "the America of personality, of great passions and great independence," but it was his "incurable folly" to insist on calling it "the India" of tradition and orthodoxy. Kierkegaard is often criticized for not sharing Brandes' outlook: he "cannot and will not understand that the history of modern literature is identical with the liberation from the moral and religious conceptions of the tradition." This is a good description of Brandes' *Main Currents*: it is entirely alien to the ethos of Kierkegaard, who still appealed to something deep within Brandes. Kierkegaard helped Brandes to become the fervent expounder of Ibsen and the main architect of Ibsen's international fame. (pp. 361-64)

In 1887 Brandes had discovered Nietzsche: he entered into correspondence with him and gave the first public lectures on him in Copenhagen. He drew from them an essay on "aristocratic radicalism," a phrase that Nietzsche himself accepted as "the cleverest word which he had read about himself." The treatise was the first serious laudatory consideration given to Nietzsche's philosophy: it will strike us today as remaining on the surface of Nietzsche's thought, concentrating as it does on the *Genealogie der Moral* and on Nietzsche's psychology and immoralism. But Brandes does make some obvious and correct comparisons: with Schopenhauer, Eduard von Hartmann, Dühring, Rée, and, surprisingly, Kierkegaard, whom he recommended to Nietzsche; and he does make some judgments that seem to hold even today. Brandes, for example, cannot share Nietzsche's own preference for *Also Sprach Zarathustra*. (pp. 365-66)

Partly under the influence of Nietzsche and in the changed atmosphere of the *fin de siècle*, Brandes turned more and more to a worship of great men, supermen, Caesars, and away from his earlier, optimistic liberalism. Literary biography is the main form he cultivated in later life. The large book on *William Shakespeare* . . . was his major widely known achievement. It is now unduly neglected, though it is by no means mere fanciful speculation, as Frank Harris' *The Man Shakespeare*, but contains some well digested history, literary history, and simple exposition and criticism. This summary of Shakespeare lore obscures somewhat Brandes' central aim: to refute the idea of Shakespeare's impersonality. "It is the author's opinion that, given the possession of forty-five important works by any man, it is entirely our own fault if we know nothing whatever about him. The poet has incorporated his whole individuality in these writings, and there, if we can read aright, we shall find him." Brandes is aware of the problem of what "reading aright" means: he knows that it is "unreasonable to attribute conscious and deliberate autobiographical import to speeches torn from their context in different plays,'' but in practice he does, as does any other biographical interpreter of Shakespeare, play it by ear. He catches (like Dowden) the accent of Shakespeare in Biron, and is confident that Jaques' voice is Shakespeare's. ''Hamlet springs from within, has its origin in an overmastering sensation in the poet's soul.'' Shakespeare, he knows, has ''lived through Hamlet's experiences,'' a statement that is true and trite if taken as referring to Shakespeare's imagination, but surely unverifiable and unilluminating if it assumes, as Brandes does, that there must be empirical grounds for Hamlet's sentiments of humiliation, disillusionment, and thirst for revenge. How does Brandes know that Shakespeare met Iago in his own life, that Arthur's entreaties to spare his young life in *King John* are Shakespeare's prayers for his sick child, or that the death of Shakespeare's mother inspired the character of Volumnia in *Coriolanus*? Brandes accepts the Pembroke—Mary Fitton—Chapman theory about the Sonnets when he affirms that ''Shakespeare does here enter the confessional.'' But it seems plain bad taste for him to say, in reference to Cleopatra, that Shakespeare ''was a gentleman, a landed proprietor and tithe-farmer; but in him still lived the artist-Bohemian, fitted to mate with the gypsy queen.'' The most personal voice, the one that appeals most strongly to Brandes, is that of Troilus in his contempt for women and of Timon of Athens in his hatred for the human race in general. Brandes senses there ''the Anglo-Saxon vein in which flows the life blood of Swift's, Hogarth's, and even some of Byron's principal works'': the English spleen, which refutes the Merrie England myth. The admiration for Imogen, ''the most adorable woman Shakespeare has ever drawn,'' arouses speculations about her model in real life. *Cymbeline* puzzled Brandes enough to ask, ''What did Shakespeare mean by this play?'' and to become aware that he never answered this question directly; but always wanted to find out ''what impelled [Shakespeare] to write it.'' He solves the riddle by interpreting the play as an allegory of ''the ethics of intention.'' ''All the good characters commit acts of deception in violence and falsehoods, or even live their whole life under false colors, without in the least derogating from their moral worth. They touch evil without defilement.'' Brandes is sure that ''purely personal impressions'' have taught this to Shakespeare. He overcame his contempt of humanity and saw human worth in the mere existence of goodness and beauty. In substance, Brandes offers another version of the change from the dark bitter period of the tragicomedies to the hopeful serenity of the last plays.

It is most obvious that such a preoccupation with Shakespeare's presumed ethical development is alien to aesthetic considerations when Brandes disparages plays that do not lend themselves to this approach. In *Richard II* he sees ''the hand of the beginner in the way in which the poet there leaves characters and events to speak for themselves without any attempt to range them in a general scheme of perspective. He conceals himself too entirely behind his work.'' Even more damaging is Brandes' confession that *Macbeth* seems to him ''one of Shakespeare's less interesting efforts; not from the artistic, but from a purely human point of view. It is a rich, highly moral melodrama, but only at occasional points in it do I feel the beating of Shakespeare's heart.'' But the ''beating of Shakespeare's heart'' is clearly not a criterion that makes for good literary criticism.

Brandes' late books—on *Goethe* . . . , and on *Voltaire* . . .— keep the same pattern: the combination of history, biography, and literary criticism dominated by psychological standards of sincerity. The *Voltaire* book shows Brandes' complete iden-

tification with the rationalist and secular outlook (it made him write a book on Jesus that dissolves Him conveniently into mere myth). Brandes, for instance, assumes without question that Voltaire has refuted Pascal, and he does not see the flaws in Voltaire's character or the limits of his mind and art. This lack of distance is the more surprising because Brandes had just written a long book on Goethe that emphasizes Goethe's life as a model of self-culture free from supernatural ties, and still shows understanding for reaches of the mind and soul entirely inaccessible to Voltaire. There is a lively appreciation of *Westöstlicher Divan* and even of the second part of *Faust*, which is seen in terms of impressionism. The praise of *Die Natürliche Tochter* is unusual, and the genuine appreciation of Goethe's lyrics and ballads shows that there is a vein of feeling for poetry in Brandes that goes beyond the taste for Byron, Heine, and Musset. The Goethe book is often fragmentary, disorganized, and scrappy, but it makes an effort to show Goethe's development without paying attention to distinctions of genres and kinds. Goethe's work in natural science (interpreted too rigidly as anticipating Darwin) is shown as part of his concern for life, growth, and personal evolution. Much is perceptive, but the focus is again elsewhere than in literature. Brandes says himself programmatically: ''Literary history used to treat of books. The writer of these lines has the weakness and strength to be more interested in men than in books and to like looking into a man through the book.''

Brandes thus cannot be dismissed as a mere ideologist. His enormous energy and curiosity made him an important intermediary among several literatures. For his own country he became the pioneer of a new era. But even if he is taken outside of his historical context, we must, I think, grant him an original, effervescent sensibility, an insight into psychology, and a power of marshaling currents and movements, which, as he knew very well, is an art. Purely as a critic he must appear as a follower of Sainte-Beuve rather than Taine: a Sainte-Beuve of wider horizon but much less subtlety and finesse. (pp. 366-69)

> *René Wellek, ''The Lonely Dane: Georg Brandes,''*
> *in his* A History of Modern Criticism: The Late Nineteenth Century, 1750-1950 *(copyright © 1965 by Yale University), Yale University Press, 1965, pp. 357-69.*

BERTIL NOLIN   (essay date 1976)

> [Main Currents in Nineteenth-Century Literature *is examined at length and concluding remarks on Brandes's career offered, in the following sections excerpted from Nolin's* Georg Brandes.]

Main Currents was an attempt at writing a history of literature, including the contemporary literary developments of the main European countries: France, Germany, and England. Chronologically it dealt with the first half of the nineteenth century; politically, with the period between the French Revolution of 1789 and the February revolution of 1848. Considering the fact that Brandes began writing ***Main Currents*** in 1871, his proximity in time to the literature he dealt with in his lectures is clear. However, it took him about twenty years to complete his survey, and during this time his view of literature and society changed along with his literary methods. Nevertheless, his principle concepts were well established. Literature was a weapon in an ideological debate, an instrument for the continuous change of values and social situations. From this point of view it is obvious that literary works were judged in relation to Brandes' own radical way of looking at things, and to a great extent were evaluated on the basis of the degree to which they could contribute new arguments to the ongoing literary debate. While writing *Main Currents,* Brandes was also actively involved in the trends of modern literature as a critic and essayist. His two books on Poland and Russia may be regarded as a complement to *Main Currents.* His goal, a survey of the most important language areas of Europe, became even clearer.

Part one of *Main Currents* . . . was entitled *Emigrant Literature.* Here Brandes referred to the French emigrant authors, especially Mme de Staël and Chateaubriand. Both these authors were forced to emigrate during the revolutionary war and the Napoleonic era. Brandes meant them to exemplify a growing reaction, but this is actually valid only for Chateaubriand. In general, Brandes was not interested in authors as such nor in their works as structural units. Instead, he directed his attention to an assortment of fictional figures, or, as he put it, types. (p. 48)

Brandes attempted to apply a purely evolutionary viewpoint to literary material. The literary type went through certain predetermined changes, following a basic pattern, in much the same way that a part of the body changed in the struggle for survival. The analogy is, of course, absurd, but that does not mean that Brandes' technique in itself was totally unfruitful. Many of the comparisons he made among different literary figures are justified and were noted both before and after *Main Currents.* In a way one could say that Brandes applied pure comparativism in the first part of his work. (p. 49)

The continually returning theme of *Main Currents* is the individual versus society. . . . According to Brandes, the result of this discrepancy between the individual and society is melancholy, so characteristic of the "types" he discussed. (pp. 50-1)

Brandes surveyed the German Romantic period when he began the second part of *Main Currents: Den romantiske Skole i Tydskland (Romantic School in Germany* . . .). (p. 54)

The third part of *Main Currents, Reaktionen i Frankrig (The Reaction in France* . . .), was, as Brandes himself said in his autobiography, his most polemic work. He also admitted that he wrote it with reference to his own times. During these first years of the 1870s he was strongly influenced by socialism as formulated in the writings of Lassalle. In this part of the book, the literary material gave way to the social, political, and religious. The literary works discussed received only surface treatment. It was only in the latter part of the volume that Brandes got into real literature: Chateaubriand's *Les Martyrs,* Lamartine's *Meditations,* and the earlier works of Hugo and Vigny. Mme de Krüdener and her now forgotten novel *Valérie,* which can hardly be said to belong to French literature, received a thorough presentation.

The composition of the book was, however, well planned and built up around what Brandes called the growth and dissolution of the principle of authority. According to Brandes, worldly and religious authority were crushed in the French Revolution of 1789, and when the monarchy was abolished, the power of the Catholic Church was crushed and religious freedom was introduced. Naturally, Brandes was sympathetic to these developments during the time of the revolution. (p. 60)

Zola's interpretation of the concept of naturalism had not as yet been generally accepted when Brandes wrote *Naturalism*

in England. But both Zola and Brandes had already been confronted with a view that was fundamental for the conception of the book on true naturalism, namely, Taine's scientifically inspired literary criticism. Taine introduced his history of English literature by describing the countryside, the geological and topographical situation, and then proceeded to the political and social environment. Brandes took a similar approach in the introductory part of *Naturalism in England.* He began by speaking of "common traits in national character"—Taine's concept of race—and wished to consider what he called the Englishman's partiality for the worship, study, and adoration of nature as a racial characteristic. (p. 63)

Brandes' writings are full of definite sympathies and antipathies. He was clearly negative to Wordsworth and especially Southey, but this did not prevent him from giving full credit to Wordsworth's nature poetry. This was actually not so strange, since here we are dealing with a type of democratic realism that made Brandes think of Runeberg and his description of the poor peasants in Saarijärvi. But Brandes' knowledge of English was clearly not good enough to enable him to appreciate Wordsworth's poetic diction. He reacted to what he called the formlessness in Wordsworth's poetry and against his attempts at an everyday language. (p. 64)

[The] fifth volume of *Main Currents* came into being as a result of lectures delivered in Copenhagen and Berlin on a group of authors who were the focus of his interest at the time: Hugo, Balzac, Musset, George Sand, Stendhal, and Sainte-Beuve, to mention the most important ones. (p. 68)

The Romantic School in France begins with a presentation of the political background of the period between 1824 and 1848. The Restoration and the July monarchy are described critically. Thus even in this part of *Main Currents,* social and political characteristics are accentuated. . . . [Brandes] wondered whether French romanticism was not just naturalism in disguise. What Hugo demanded in his manifesto was simple nature, truthful descriptions, local color. In spite of the fact that Brandes was at this time familiar with French naturalism as Zola interpreted it, he used the term very generally, and gave it an almost Rousseau-like meaning: a unity with nature, a worship of nature and the natural. George Sand, he said, was the daughter of Rousseau, and Stendhal and Mérimée were "half brutal, half elegant nature worshipers." Nonetheless Brandes saw the French romantics largely through the eyes of a naturalist. (pp. 68-9)

In a special chapter of *The Romantic School in France* Brandes took up what he termed the sociopolitical ideological movement and its relation to poetry. Here he primarily examined pre-Marxist socialism stemming from Saint Simon. Several members of the romantic school were strongly influenced by it, especially George Sand. It was through her that Brandes himself came in touch with utopian socialism—in that way and also through his study of Sainte-Beuve's biography of Proudhon.

The Romantic School in France is the most substantial volume of *Main Currents.* Here Brandes wrote about authors he knew well, and his preparation for this book was more thorough than for the earlier volumes. (p. 75)

[The last part of *Main Currents: Det und Tydakland (Young Germany)*], was written with a great deal of inner resistance on Brandes' part. It was not published until 1890, almost two decades after his outline of the work as a whole. The European literary scene had changed very quickly during these years, especially because of the emergence of naturalism. "The young

Germany,'' including Heine, Börne, Immermann, Gutzkow, Laube, and Mundt, had aged very rapidly, and only Heine remained vital and important and still widely read. Originally the plan was that **Main Currents** would end by paying homage to that group of writers who created the literary and ideological basis for the revolution of 1848, the chronological endpoint. Seen literarily, **Young Germany** was an anticlimax. Nevertheless, Brandes maintained the political-revolutionary perspective that characterized the book as a whole. As in the earlier volumes, he began with a political exposition of the reactionary atmosphere in Germany during the years before the July revolution. Then the revolution came in 1830 and, with a sense of the dramatic, Brandes described how some of the authors in the ''young Germany'' group reacted to the news from Paris that the July revolution had broken out. In this way the reader was introduced to three of the most important authors later discussed: Gutzkow, Börne, and Heine. Later, in the last pages of the book, the outbreak of the February revolution was described along with its repercussions in Germany. The presentation was thus framed by these two revolutionary outbreaks, and this gave the last part of **Main Currents** a definite social and political character. (pp. 75-6)

The weakness in the design of **Main Currents** becomes clear in the last volume of the work. Poets like Hebbel and Mörike were left out of the mainstream of European literature. But **Main Currents** was not a history of literature in its ordinary meaning. Instead it was something between literary history and political history, something that functioned in the border area between these two, and that revealed tendencies toward the history of ideas and personal history. Pjotr Kogan, the Russian critic, stated in a valuable characterization that what Brandes had achieved was really what could be called the history of European intelligentsia. Brandes was interested not only in books but in the fruitful development of dynamic thought. From this point of view it was justifiable to include such figures as Schleiermacher, Gentz, de Maistre, Bonald, Lamennais, Börne, Jacoby, Rahel Varnhagen, Bettina von Arnim, and Charlotte Stieglitz. They could give an indication of the intellectual climate. . . .

Brandes was good at characterizing, at tracing the exchanges between countries, and his knowledge was extensive. But he was tendentious, unsure about details, and nonchalant in his choice of what was frequently anecdotal material. The part on Börne and Heine was judged best—a fairly accurate appraisal. (p. 78)

As a critic Brandes passed through different stages. Before 1870 he adopted a critical approach that can be traced to Hegel and his followers. As a spokesman for French naturalism he borrowed a number of terms from the natural sciences, with environment and heritage as the cornerstones. He saw a work of art in relation to the society in which it was created, and thus he can be considered an early representative of the sociological approach to literature. All the time, however, Brandes was a *comparatiste*, and that is perhaps his most distinguishing feature. He wished to use literature as an instrument for breaking through provincial isolation. (p. 185)

[One] remarkable trait was Brandes' versatility. His authorship included fiction, philosophy, religion, history, art history, and other closely related areas. His versatility did not always have a corresponding depth and originality. Actually, he was the great assimilator. He could have made Molière's saying ''je reprend mon bien partout où je le trouve'' (*I take up what is good for me wherever I can find it*) his own. In many cases

he functioned as a popularizer of others' ideas. This did not mean that he was lacking a conscious and well-thought-out philosophy. It was characterized by rationalism, passion for freedom, and a strong social commitment. His political views were rooted in the liberalism of the 1800s with John Stuart Mill as an important stimulus, but all political doctrines were too narrow for him. He had an avid interest in different varieties of socialism and was profoundly impressed by such different socialistic philosophers as Proudhon, Lassalle, Marx, and Kropotkin. His political profile is marked by a certain dualism. He did not succeed in bridging the gap between the democratic radicalism of Mill and the left-wing Hegelians, especially Lassalle, and the aristocratic radicalism developed from his studies of Nietzsche.

All of Brandes' activity was characterized by a tendency to take active part in the social, political and cultural debate. One of the mottos he adopted was ''To me, a book is an action.'' He was also attracted to definite men of action and will like Lassalle and Clemenceau. But this did not prevent him from appreciating writers who represented a versatile and often pronounced aesthetic educational ideal, such as Goethe. Brandes also spread his influence to a great extent as a critic in newspapers and magazines and through his essays. He continued the tradition of essay writing in European literature in the line of Sainte-Beuve, Taine, Renan, and Bourget. Brandes was almost exclusively interested in contemporary literature during the first decades of his work. His great book **Main Currents** is a survey of European literature up to the middle of the 1800s. As he grew older he came to deal with earlier periods, especially the Renaissance and the 1700s.

Brandes' style was characterized by clarity and lucidity and reflected his feeling for rationality and tangibility. His point of departure was often an illustrative anecdote or quotation. The scope of his reading was impressive, and his memory held an inexhaustible supply of thoughts and expressions he could mobilize quickly. His critical technique demonstrated great flexibility and ability to adapt to the theme he was treating. He was a critic of ideas who searched for the author's ethical and social philsophy. Involvement, vitality, and passion distinguish his way of writing. He was a perceptive critic who was primarily interested in originality, utility, and uniqueness. (pp. 186-87)

Bertil Nolin, in his Georg Brandes *(copyright © 1976 by Twayne Publishers, Inc.; reprinted with the permission of Twayne Publishers, a Division of G. K. Hall & Co., Boston), Twayne, 1976, 208 p.*

JAMES McFARLANE   (essay date 1979)

[*McFarlane sees an 1871 meeting between Brandes and Ibsen to have had a profound effect on the career of both. Brandes's early career is discussed.*]

[Henrik Ibsen had] a quietly conspiratorial encounter in the summer of 1871 with the Danish critic Georg Brandes. In itself, and on the surface, this latter occasion was undemonstratively private, domestic, social; it goes almost entirely unregarded in the literary and cultural histories of Europe. And yet, under more rigorous scrutiny, it reveals itself as an occasion within which much of what was significantly cultural in these years was curiously encapsulated. (p. 158)

As they took leave of each other, Ibsen called out after the departing Brandes: ''You go and stir up the Danes, I will stir up the Norwegians.'' As a recipe for achieving Ibsen's ''rev-olution of the human spirit'' this doubtless sounds an exces-sively modest and indeed rather negative programme. But be-hind the casual words, both men were conscious in their different ways of an urgent sense of crisis, of personal mission, and of a shared cultural conspiracy. (p. 160)

[Brandes had] a restlessly brilliant mind which, starting from the more familiar Danish orthodoxies of Kierkegaard in phi-losophy and of Heiberg in literary criticism, was eager to find a newer, more modern, more relevant set of values. He read insatiably—it is said, for example, that in his last year at school a passion for Goethe led him to the decision to read his works entire. He began as a student of law, but it was not long before his wider reading took him well outside the confines of his law books. The break with the prevailing orthodoxies came in two stages. First, in 1866, came his philosophical heresies, the assault on religious orthodoxy in a book called *Dualismen i vor nyeste Philosophie (On dualism in our most recent philosphy)*, a free-thinker's declaration directed against Rasmus Nielsen's claims to ''mediate'' between faith and knowledge. As for his literary criteria, for a long time they remained conventionally Heibergian, and solidly conservative. . . . But in the late 1860s a change came over his literary values: he found his admiration growing for the problem-centred plays of Dumas fils and Au-gier; he found himself drawn to the harder, thrusting Mérimée; and he discovered a new affinity with the criticism of St Beuve.

Finally, as the 'sixties drew to a close, he found himself greatly preoccupied first by Hippolyte Taine and then by John Stuart Mill. The direct positivism of their analytical method, the for-mer in literary and aesthetic matters, the latter more in phil-osophical and moral concerns, appealed to Brandes's forthright mind. Taine, who seemed to offer an escape from the abs-tractions of traditional German philosophy, was selected by Brandes as the central theme of his doctoral dissertation: *Den franske Æsthetik i vore Dage (French aesthetics in the present day)*. Eventually, however, it was Mill who above all came to represent Brandes's ideal, and who game him a design for conduct as well as stimulating him to a new attitude to life. It was an enthusiasm that led to his translating Mill's *The Sub-jection of Women* into Danish in 1869; and this he followed up by translating *Utilitarianism* in 1872. Above all, Mill ap-pealed to Brandes's own secret dreams of being a man of action. . . . He was, he insisted, determined not to be ''a mere scholar, an entertaining author, a literary historian, or anything like that'':

> I felt I was made to be a man of action. But
> the men of action I had come across hitherto
> had repelled me by their lack of ideas. . . . At
> last in Mill I made the acquaintance of a man
> in whom the power of action, of provocation,
> of perseverance were put wholly at the service
> of new social ideas.

This was the source of the ideal of the Thinker-agitator that fired Brandes as a young man—an ideal which he came in time to see supremely exemplified in Lasalle, on whom he wrote a monograph; an ideal which even today moves Danish com-mentators to describe Brandes not as a literary historian or critic but as a ''cultural politician''. It is a designation clearly invited by the opening phrases of his preface to *Hovedström-ninger i det nittende Aarhundredes Litteratur (Main currents in nineteenth century literature)*:

> *Main Currents,* by tracing the development of
> the literatures of the main countries of Europe

through the first half of the nineteenth century,
tells part of the history of the European Mind.
The design of the book is political, not literary.

It is his way—to adapt the terms he used of Mill—of trying to turn the academic lecture platform into a popular tribunal. Certainly, it was not by chance that for the terminal date of his comparative survey he chose 1848, that fateful and stormy year in Europe's destiny.

Life style and literary style fused together at this point. Delib-erately, consciously, he set out to perform the role of the man of action within his own self-acknowledged limitations: lob-bying, proselytising, establishing contacts, seeking out the in-fluential figures of the age. His visit to Ibsen in Dresden was part of the larger design, of which his lectures later that same year are in a sense a complementary manifestation. He formed groups, established periodicals; he developed a range of cor-respondence with other authors, thinkers, critics and scholars which in itself served as a kind of marshalling agency, pulling scattered individuals into concerted action. The title of one of his most influential books *Det moderne Gjennembruds Maend (Men of the modern breakthrough,* 1883) is completely attuned to the kind of concerted and aggressive cultural advance he sought to achieve. (pp. 165-67)

The history of the consequences, direct and oblique, of [the] meeting of minds in 1871 is a full and continuing one. The immediate result was that they both, in their own personal and indeed idiosyncratic ways, proceeded to make declarations which are startlingly dissimilar and yet strangely related: first Brandes in 1872 with the opening volume of his *Main Currents of Nineteenth Century Literature,* analytical, provocative, politi-cal; then, in 1873, Ibsen with his huge double ten-act drama *Emperor and Galilean,* prophetic, mystic, visionary. Brandes who, adopting the guise of a scholar's detachment, offered an analysis in depth of the development of European literature in France, Germany and England from the French Revolution of 1789 to the February Revolution of 1848, but who also in so doing succeeded in forging cultural history and literary criti-cism into a powerful weapon for use in the ideological conflicts of his own age. And Ibsen who, in a work historical in its setting but very deliberately contemporary in its relevance, made of it the repository of his own mature and pondered views on life and the world and the human situation. . . . Though outwardly and superficially greatly divergent, these two works of Brandes and Ibsen were nevertheless in large measure born of a shared vision and of a common sense of purpose.

And as it had begun, so in the subsequent careers and achieve-ments of the two men it continued. Both of them, in their own distinctive ways, came to dominate those areas of cultural en-deavour they had made their own: Brandes in the first instance to become the leading spokesman for ''problem literature'' and all that flowed from that, and destined in time to become the intermediary through whom, very largely, both Kierkegaard and Nietzsche won acknowledgement in the wider world as influential thinkers, and Ibsen who, though he abandoned his-torical drama after *Emperor and Galilean,* continued through the medium of his ''dramas of contemporary life'' to offer a comparable analysis of the nature of modern man and his pre-dicaments. (pp. 169-70)

James McFarlane, ''Cultural Conspiracy and Civi-lizational Change: Henrik Ibsen, Georg Brandes, and the Modern European Mind'' (a revision of a lecture originally delivered at the University of Ex-eter on February 23, 1978; copyright © 1979 by

James McFarlane), in Journal of European Studies, *Vol. 9, No. 35, September, 1979, pp. 155-73.**

ADDITIONAL BIBLIOGRAPHY

Clausen, Julius. "Danish Wit and Wisdom in Later Days." *The American-Scandinavian Review* XV, No. 6 (June 1927): 366-69.*
    Tribute to Brandes, calling him the "grand old man" of Danish intellectual life. Clausen also discusses Danish authors Sven Lange, Frederik Poulsen, and Louis Bobé.

Downs, Brian W. *Modern Norwegian Literature: 1860-1918.* London: Cambridge University Press, 1966, 276 p.*
    Survey of late nineteenth and early twentieth-century Norwegian literature. Throughout the book, Downs discusses Brandes's role in popularizing the works of Ibsen, Bjørnson, Kielland, and other Norwegian authors.

Gosse, Edmund. "1874." In his *Two Visits to Denmark: 1872, 1874,* pp. 141-366. London: Smith, Elder, & Co., 1911.*
    Personal reminiscence of Gosse's acquaintance with Brandes during a trip to Denmark. Gosse attributes to Brandes the beginning of a needed intellectual revival, and calls him the "one man whose mind had contrived to give shape to the idea of an intellectual revolution." He also recounts anecdotes which demonstrate the extreme disrepute in which Brandes was held in Denmark because of the revolutionary nature of his thought.

Lewisohn, Ludwig. "Georg Brandes." In his *Cities and Men,* pp. 194-99. New York: Harper & Brothers Publishers, 1927.
    Describes Brandes as "one of the great humanists of the age." Lewisohn characterizes Brandes as having prefigured Benedetto Croce's style of critical interpretation of literature as a "significant and concentrated expression of the entire inner process of civilization."

Liptzin, Sol. "Georg Brandes and Richard Beer-Hofmann." *Modern Austrian Studies* 12, No. 1 (1979): 19-29.*

Account of the friendship which developed late in Brandes's life between himself and the Austrian poet and dramatist Beer-Hofmann.

Moritzen, Julius. *George Brandes in Life and Letters.* Newark, N.J.: D. S. Colyer, 1922, 152 p.
    Important study of Brandes's chief critical works, including a biographical chapter.

"Brandes and His Detractors." *The Nation* XLVI, No. 1194 (17 May 1888): 402-04.
    Response to an article in the 26 April 1888 issue of *The Nation,* in which Dr. Puls, a German critic, charged that Brandes plagiarized large portions of *Main Currents in Nineteenth-Century Literature.* The anonymous writer argues that Brandes acknowledges his sources and that Puls's charges are unfounded.

Payne, William Morton. "A Critic Militant." *The Dial* XLI, No. 490 (16 November 1906): 323-26.
    Review of *Reminiscences of My Childhood and Youth.* Payne characterizes Brandes as "the critic who finds literature to be primarily the criticism and the expression of human life, and is all the time bent upon pointing out its relations to the political and social and intellectual environment of the men who are its producers." Payne assumes that Brandes's account of his childhood is perfectly objective.

Seccombe, Thomas. "Nature I Loved." *The Bookman,* London XXVIII, No. 166 (July 1905): 131-32.
    Review of *Naturalism in England.* Seccombe criticizes the translation of this volume and the coherence of the five volumes of *Main Currents* in relation to one another, but praises Brandes's "highly ingenious, well expressed, and creditable" literary generalizations about various authors. Seccombe also points out that the volume is somewhat dated, as it is comprised of thirty-year-old transcribed lectures.

Topsöe-Jensen, H. G. "The Modern Awakening: Denmark." In his *Scandinavian Literature,* pp. 13-35. New York: W.W. Norton & Co., 1929.*
    Credits Brandes first lecture at the University of Copenhagen, held on 3 November 1871, with establishing "a new period . . . in the intellectual life not only of Denmark, but of the entire North."

Valery (Yakovlevich) Bryusov

1873-1924

(Also transliterated as Valeriy, Valeri, Valerij, and Valerii; also Iakolevich; also Brjusov, Briusov, and Brussof) Russian poet, critic, novelist, short story writer, essayist, editor, translator, diarist, dramatist, and memoirist.

Bryusov was one of the leading figures of the Russian Symbolist movement. He translated the French Symbolists into Russian, promoted the development of Russian Symbolism in his journal *Vesy*, and, in *Stephanos*, created the purest representation of the themes and techniques of the Symbolist era in Russia. Also noted for his scholarship, Bryusov has achieved international acclaim for his insightful literary reviews and his studies of Alexander Pushkin's poetry.

During his childhood, Bryusov read widely from the numerous biographies, novels, and scientific books available in his home. In the early 1890s, he discovered French Symbolism and Decadence through reading and translating the works of Paul Verlaine, Arthur Rimbaud, and Stéphane Mallarmé. Believing himself destined for a literary career, Bryusov remarked of Decadence that "the future will belong to it, particularly when it finds a worthy leader. And that leader shall be I!" In 1894, he edited and published *Russkiye simvolisty*—three collections of translated French Symbolist poetry that also included many of his own poems. Bryusov's verse, particularly the one-line poem "O cover your pale legs," drew public indignation and critical scorn for its sensual imagery and self-conscious pretentiousness. But through their fervent mockery, critics unintentionally succeeded in focusing wide public attention on Symbolism and Decadence, and on Bryusov in particular. The poetry collections that followed—notably *Me eum esse, Tertia vigilia, Urbi et orbi*, and *Stephanos*—attracted many new readers and imitators, and helped establish Russian Symbolism as an important artistic school. The movement's adherents were concerned with the alienation of the individual from the secret unity of the cosmos, and viewed themselves as articulate intermediaries, who, through their art, were able to apprehend the essence of life and reality. They considered their doctrine and work to be less a literary school than a philosophy of life.

In 1904, Bryusov assumed a leadership role in the movement as editor of *Vesy*, an important literary review. Symbolist writers who failed to court Bryusov's friendship and advice found it difficult to get their work published. In spite of his supercilious personality, Bryusov proved to be an excellent editor, providing advice and direction for many prominent Russian poets, such as Aleksandr Blok, Andrey Bely, and Marina Tsvetaeva. In 1909, Bryusov published his most notable prose work, *Ognennyi angel (The Fiery Angel: A Sixteenth Century Romance)*, a veiled dramatization of his own rivalry with Bely for the love of the poet Nina Petrovsky, who appears in the novel as a witch. Praised for its beauty and power, *The Fiery Angel* was adapted for the opera by Sergey Prokofiev. This work and Bryusov's other novel, *Altar pobedy*—set in sixteenth-century Germany and in fourth-century Rome, respectively—have been found by Renato Poggioli to form "an archaelogical tableau in the manner of Flaubert's *Salammbô*." After 1909, Bryusov's theory and work became progressively

Ardis Publishers

more concerned with social and political themes—he was one of the few Russian artists of his generation who embraced the October Revolution of 1917. Bryusov accepted a post in the People's Commisariat for Enlightenment and Education, and spent his last years lecturing on poetry at the University of Moscow, writing literary criticism, and translating foreign works.

Poggioli has written that Bryusov's greatest contribution was that of giving "a Russian voice to the poetry of France." Echoes of Gustave Flaubert, Rimbaud, and Belgian dramatist Maurice Maeterlinck are found through much of his early work, particularly in "Poetu" ("To the Poet"). Here, in what is often considered the artistic credo of Bryusov's early career, the poet is encouraged to experience every possible situation, temptation, and sensation in life. The artist must be an amoral hero, who stands intellectually and aesthetically above the rest of humanity, and who progresses steadily toward artistic achievement, oblivious to persecution and misunderstanding by others. Bryusov himself was not an artist endowed with effortless creativity, but a literary workman; his art is based on the will—on painstakingly shaping beauty out of formlessness. In an oft-quoted poem, Bryusov likens his "dream" or artistic vision to an ox, and himself to a plowman.

Bryusov's work was most successful when treating subjects that are either mythological and classical or urban and modern. The poems of Bryusov's maturity, which include *Stephanos*, exemplify his skill in working with ancient themes and subject matter. His poetry of the city, which includes such works as "Slava tolpe" and "Gorodu," reflects the most important influence of his later career, the poetry of Émile Verhaeren. Like the work of this Belgian poet, these poems treat the menace, vitality, and movement of urban life. In addition to his poetry and novels, Bryusov wrote a number of short stories, which were collected in *Zemnaya os* and *Nochi i dni*. Many of these treat bizarre and fantastic subjects, evidence of the influence of Pushkin and Edgar Allan Poe.

When Bryusov left *Vesy* and abandoned Symbolism in 1909, the movement swiftly collapsed; for this reason Bryusov has been accused of opportunistically changing camps as new trends in poetry appeared. Much of the early criticism of Bryusov's poetry is colored by such reaction to the poet's personality and ways. But it is now commonly acknowledged that through his editorial advice and the example of his art, Bryusov gave new life to Russian poetry, which had hitherto fallen into lifeless imitation of works of the past.

(See also *Contemporary Authors*, Vol. 107.)

PRINCIPAL WORKS

Russkiye simvolisty 3 vols. [editor] (poetry) 1894
Chefs d'oeuvre (poetry) 1895
Me eum esse (poetry) 1897
Tertia vigilia (poetry) 1900
Urbi et orbi (poetry) 1903
Stephanos (poetry) 1906
Zemnaya os (short stories) 1907
Puti i pereputya. 3 vols. (poetry) 1908-09
Ognennyi angel (novel) 1909
   [*The Fiery Angel: A Sixteenth Century Romance*, 1930]
Dalekie i bliskie (criticism) 1912
Zerkalo tenej (poetry) 1912
Altar pobedy (novel) 1913
Nochi i dni (short stories) 1913
Polnoe sobranie socineniy i perevodov. 8 vols. (poetry, criticism, essays, novels, and short stories) 1913-14
The Republic of the Southern Cross and Other Stories (short stories) 1918
Posledniye mechty (poetry) 1920
Sobranie sochineniy. 7 vols. (poetry, criticism, novels, diary, essays, and memoirs) 1973-75
The Diary of Valery Bryusov (1893-1905) (diary) 1980

VLADIMIR SOLOVYOV (essay date 1894)

[*A highly respected philosopher, poet, and critic, Solovyov was largely responsible for the mystical turn taken by the Russian Symbolists. His sarcastic reviews of the three volumes of* Russkiye simvolisty *brought immediate attention to Bryusov and the young literary movement. In his review of the first volume, Solovyov noted several parodies of the Russian poet Afanasi Fet's verse. He then attacked the following poem by Bryusov:*]

> Golden fairies
> In a satin garden!
> When shall I find
> The glacial avenues?

> The silvery splashes
> Of amorous naiads!
> Where the jealous planks
> Bar the way to you?

> Incomprehensible bowls
> Illuminated by fire,
> The dawn is stultified
> Over the flight of fantasies. . . .

In spite of "the glacial avenues in a satin garden," the plot of this poem is as clear as it is reprehensible. Carried away by "a flight of fantasies," the author has become lost in the contemplation of fenced baths where persons of the female sex, whom he calls "fairies" and "naiads," are bathing. But can one expiate villainous actions with splendid words? . . . Let us hope at least that the "jealous planks" prove to be up to their calling. In the event this is not the case, then all that would be left for the "golden fairies" to do would be to douse the immodest Symbolist from those "incomprehensible bowls" which in the colloquial language are called washtubs and are used in the baths for the ablution of feet. (p. 32)

It is not possible to make a general judgment concerning Mr. Valery Briusov not knowing his age. If he is no older than fourteen then he might turn into a decent poet, and perhaps into nothing. But if he is a grown man, then, of course, any literary hopes are out of place. (pp. 32-3)

> *Vladimir Solovyov, in his extract, translated by Martin P. Rice (originally published in an essay in* Vestnik europy, *August, 1894), in* Valery Briusov and the Rise of Russian Symbolism *by Martin P. Rice (© 1975 by Ardis Publishers), Ardis, 1975, pp. 32-3.*

NIKOLAI GUMILEV (essay date 1908)

[*Gumilev offers high praise to Bryusov for the skill evidenced in the second volume of* Puti i pereputya. *At the time this review was written, Bryusov had long been recognized as a major literary figure, and he was now at the peak of his career.*]

Lately whole articles have been devoted to Bryusov, the best critics have been writing about him, and it would be strange in a short review to attempt to characterize his work, so complex and unified in its complexity. But then, another task presents itself to the critic: to note, if only in general outline, those peculiarities of form and thought which distinguish the second volume of *Paths and Crossroads* from the first. And most striking of all is the wholeness of the plan and the firm decision to follow the path of Symbolism, which in the first volume sometimes weakened with inclinations toward Decadence and Impressionism. Bryusov operates with only two quantities—"the self" and "the world" and in severe diagrams, devoid of anything fortuitous, gives the various possibilities of their interrelation. He reveals new horizons for elucidating the question of acceptance of the world, transferring events to a higher plane of thought, where the esthetic standard loses its validity and gives place to the ethical standard. At a wave of his hand, flowers again bloom in our world, which intoxicated the gaze of Assyrian kings, and passion becomes eternal, as in the times of the goddess Astarte. . . .

The distinguishing feature of Bryusov's ballads is their nobility.

Even in the circles most hostile to him, Bryusov earned the reputation of a master of form. He shares the dreams of Mallarmé and René Ghil about the return of the word's metaphysical value, but resorts neither to neologisms nor intentional syntactic difficulties. Through severe selection of expressions, sharpened clarity of thought and brazen music of phrase he achieves results which were not always the lot of his French colleagues. The eternally unsubmissive word no longer fights with him; it has found its master. (p. 39)

> *Nikolai Gumilev, "Bryusov" (originally a speech given on May 29, 1908), in his* Nikolai Gumilev on Russian Poetry, *edited and translated by David Lapeza (© 1977 by Ardis Publishers), Ardis, 1977, pp. 39-40.*

STEPHEN GRAHAM   (essay date 1918)

[Graham praises Bryusov's technical expertise as a short story writer and poet, but his criticism of the content of the Russian's work is somewhat guarded. He does, however, express a high opinion of Bryusov's literary criticism.]

Valery Brussof is a celebrated Russian writer of the present time. He is in the front rank of contemporary literature, and is undoubtedly very gifted, being considered by some to be the greatest of living Russian poets, and being in addition a critic of penetration and judgment, a writer of short tales, and the author of one long historical novel from the life of Germany in the sixteenth century.

He is a Russian of strong European tastes and temperament, a sort of Mediterraneanised Russian, with greater affinities in France and Italy than in his native land; an artificial production in the midst of the Russian literary world. A hard, polished, and even merciless personality, he has little in common with the compassionate spirits of Russia. If Kuprin or Gorky may be taken as characteristic of modern Russia, Brussoff is their opposite. He sheds no tears with the reader, he makes no passionate and "unmanly" defiance of the world, but is restrained and concentrated and wrapped up in himself and his ideas. The average length of a sentence of Dostoieffsky is probably about twenty-five words, of Kuprin thirty, but of Brussof only twenty, and if you take the staccato **"Republic of the Southern Cross,"** only twelve. His fine virile style is admired by Russians for its brevity and directness. He has been called a maker of sentences in bronze.

It is curious, however, that the theme of his writing has little in common with the virility of his style. As far as our Western point of view is concerned it is considered rather feminine than masculine to doubt the reality of our waking life and to give credence to dreams. Yet such is undoubtedly the preoccupation of Brussof in these stories [*The Republic of the Southern Cross and Other Stories*].

He says in his preface to the second edition of that collection which bears the title *The Axis of the Earth*, "the stories are written to show, in various ways, that there is no fixed boundary line between the world of reality and that of the imagination, between the dreaming and the waking world, life and fantasy; that what we commonly call "imaginary' may be the greatest reality of the world, and that which all call reality the most dreadful delirium." (pp. v-vi)

The Republic of the Southern Cross contains the best of Brussof's tales, and they all exemplify this particular attitude towards life. Six tales are taken from *The Axis of the Earth,* but **"For Herself or Another"** is taken from the volume entitled *Nights and Days,* and **"Rhea Silvia"** and **"Eluli, son of Eluli,"**

from the book bearing the title of *Rhea Silvia,* in the Russian Universal Library. (pp. vi-vii)

[*The Republic of the Southern Cross*] is an emotional study of reality and unreality cast in the form of brilliant tales. (p. vii)

In **"The Republic of the Southern Cross"** Brussof projects himself several centuries into the future and imagines an industrial community of millions of workers, so divorced from reality that they are living at the South Pole where no life is possible, in a huge town called Star City where no star is visible. . . . Star City, where the only refuge is the Town Hall where all earthly meridians become one, is all used with appalling power by Brussof to suggest his mental conceit. I once read outside a Russian theatre, "People of weak will are asked to refrain from taking tickets for this drama." A similar caution might be addressed to those who turn to read **"The Republic of the Southern Cross."** (pp. viii-ix)

What the new realists who dominate our Western schools of philosophy would say to Valery Brussof would be curious. He is not an hysterical type of writer and is not emotionally convinced of the truth of his writing, but wilfully persistent, affirming unreality intellectually and defending his conception with a sort of masculine impressionism. He drives his idea to the reader's mind clad in complete armour, no tenderness, no apologetics, no willingness to please a lady's eye in the use of his words and phrases.

The theme of several of the stories might have been worked out readily by our Mr. Algernon Blackwood, but so would have been more discursive, and the mystery of them better hidden. But Brussof, as it were, draws the skull and crossbones at the top of the page before he writes a word and then goes on. Inevitably the interest is reflected from the stories to the personality of the author. (p. xi)

Brussof's poetry, for which he enjoys a great reputation, is dedicated to the same ideas as his stories, though in them he is before all else a most polished craftsman and cares more for perfection of technique than for anything else.

His poetry is not difficult, and can be recommended for those who read Russian and prefer to study up-to-date matter. In my opinion, however, the best volumes of Balmont have more lyrical beauty than the best of Brussof. There is, moreover, a good deal of erotic verse which is bankrupt of real vital thought, as there are stories of this kind not by any means commendable for British consumption. Brussof evidently reads English, and one or two of his poems are reminiscent of better things at home.

In the midst of his wide literary activities Brussoff is also an interesting critic, and I know few more elucidative volumes than **"***Dalekie i Bliskie,* **Near and Far,"** a collection of essays on the Russian poets. (p. xiii)

> *Stephen Graham, in his introduction to* The Republic of the Southern Cross and Other Stories *by Valery Brussof, Constable and Company Ltd., 1918, pp. v-xiii.*

K. TCHUKOVSKY   (essay date 1920)

[A noted writer and authority on the Russian language, Korney Tchukovsky offers high praise to Bryusov's poetry, especially to Stephanos.]

[Bryusov's] poems have the strange quality of giving sternness, nobility, and a peculiar air of solemnity to everything they touch. You have the feeling of having read them long ago in old volumes. It seems as if every line of Bryusov's could live an independent life, so beautiful is it by itself, so perfect is it in itself, so finished is it in every way. It seems that if those lines were torn asunder, scattered, separated from each other, they would assemble by themselves and resume their former shape.

Bryusov is a crystallizing poet. Madness, storm, chaos becomes icy and lucid in his works. 'My poems are a magic vessel of poisons distilled in silence,' he spoke about himself. If you put into this vessel the most ecstatic, the most passionate experiences, how beautifully the process of purification will be completed, and what a thick, aromatic translucent wine will pour forth! (p. 178)

Stephanos is a great book. In it Bryusov is celebrating a victory over the elemental powers in his own spirit. In it he is a hero, a victor, a giant. It is a great radiant book of Russian poetry which is destined to make an epoch. . . . *Stephanos* is a book which carries a blessing. It knows the sorcery of purifying the human soul. From a high mountain you look over your life, and you reconcile yourself to all, and forgive all, and know that all is wise and all is quiet. (pp. 178-79)

> K. Tchukovsky, in his extract from "V. Bryusov," in A Guide to Russian Literature (1820-1917) by Moissaye J. Olgin (copyright, 1920, by Harcourt Brace Jovanovich, Inc.; reprinted by permission of the publisher), Harcourt Brace Jovanovich, 1920, pp. 178-79.

MARINA TSVETAEVA (essay date 1925)

[The poet Tsvetaeva describes Bryusov as a man who achieved artistry through willpower and struggle, rather than through refined natural talent.]

From age sixteen to age seventeen I loved Bryusov's poetry with a passionate and short-lived love. In Bryusov I contrived to love the most un-Bryusovian thing. I loved what he lacked in his very core, his very essence—song, the songful element. And this love of mine exists to this day for his *Fiery Angel,* more than for his poetry. I admired *Fiery Angel* then in both conception and execution, now only in conception and the memory of it—in its non-realization. I remember, however, that even at sixteen the word *interesting* on one of those pathetic pages struck me as something vulgar with a price tag on it, inconceivable either in Renata's epoch, in the narrative about the Angel, or in the general pathos of the thing. A master— and such a total miss! Yes, because craftsmanship is not everything. One needs an ear. And Bryusov was tone deaf.

Bryusov's antimusicality, in spite of the extrinsic musicality (in certain places) of a whole series of his poems, reflected the antimusicality of his essence, of his being: dry land, the absence of a river. I remember something that the unique and profound poet Adelaida Gertsyk (recently deceased) said about Max Voloshin and about me, then seventeen. "There is more river in you than shoreline, and in him there is more shore than river." Bryusov was comprised totally of shores—granite ones.

After everything just said, was Bryusov a poet? Yes, but not by the grace of God. A poet, a maker of verse, and, what is more important, maker of the creator in himself. Not the man in the Gospel, who buried his talent in the ground, but a man who by his own will forced it *from* the ground. Something created out of nothing.

"Forward, dream, my faithful ox." Oh, this motto was no accidental one, it was not inserted for rhyme. It is more like a sigh. If Bryusov was ever truthful to his core, it was in that very sigh. Made out of strength, of sinews, like an ox—what is this, the poet's labor? No, it is his dream! Inspiration plus ox-like labor equals poet. Ox-like labor plus ox-like labor equals Bryusov: the ox dragging the load. This ox is not devoid of majesty. But who else but Bryusov would have thought of likening dream to an ox? . . . If, instead of "dream," he had written "will," the line would have been a formula. A poet of will. (pp. 161-63)

Bryusov will appear in the anthologies, but not in the section "Lyrics." He will be found in that section—and there will be such a section in Soviet anthologies—"Will." In that section (of builders, conquerors, overcomers), his name, I want to believe, will be among the first of Russian names. And my heart, unjust but thirsting for justice, will not rest until there is in Moscow, in its most prominent square, a granite statue larger than life, with the inscription: To a Hero of Labor of the USSR. (p. 173)

> Marina Tsvetaeva, "From 'Hero of Labor: Notes on Valery Bryusov'" (1925), translated by Joan Delaney Grossman and Elissa Stern, in The Diary of Valery Bryusov (1893-1905), edited and translated by Joan Delaney Grossman (translation copyright © 1980 by The Regents of the University of California; reprinted by permission of the University of California Press), University of California Press, 1980, pp. 161-73.

V. F. KHODASEVICH (essay date 1925)

[A longtime acquaintance of Bryusov, the poet Khodasevich expresses admiration for Bryusov's verse. Elsewhere in this important essay, Khodasevich also describes Bryusov as an egocentric, imperious editor and artist, and as a drug addict.]

[Remembering] the young Bryusov, I felt that the chief piquancy of his [first published verses] consisted just in the combination of Decadent exoticism and the most simple-hearted Moscow bourgeois sensibility. It was an acrid mixture, a sharp disjunction; an acute dissonance, but for this reason Bryusov's early books (up to and including *Tertia Vigilia*) are nonetheless his best books: the most pungent. All that tropical fantasy— on the banks of the Yauza, the trans-evaluation of all values— in the Sretenka district of Moscow. And to this very day I much prefer to the recognized Bryusov that "unknown, mocked, peculiar" author of *Chefs d'oeuvre.* (p. 150)

Boris Sadovskoy, a clever and fine fellow, hiding a very good heart behind a rather dry exterior, was outraged by Bryusov's love lyrics, calling them bedroom poetry. But he was wrong. Bryusov's eroticism is deeply tragic, but not in an ontological sense, as the author liked to think; rather, in the psychological sense. Neither loving nor respecting human beings, he never once truly loved one of those with whom he happened to "share the couch" (to use his poetic phrase). The women in Bryusov's poems are as like one another as two drops of water. This is because there was not one of them he loved, or singled out from the others, or came to know. Possibly he really valued love in itself. But he hardly noticed his mistresses. "Like ministers of the altar we perform a rite . . . " Terrible words because if it is a rite, then it matters not at all with whom it is performed. "Priestess of love" was a favorite phrase of Bryusov's. But a priestess's face is covered; she has no *human* countenance. One priestess may be replaced by another—the "rite" remains the same. And not finding, not being capable of finding, the human person in all these priestesses, Bryusov shrieks with horror, "Trembling, I embrace a corpse!" Moreover, love for him always turned into torture: "Where are we? On a bed of passion / Or on the wheel of death?"

He loved literature, and only literature. He loved himself only in the name of literature. In truth, he fulfilled with holy zeal the precepts which he laid down for himself in his youth: "Do not love, do not give your sympathy, worship yourself alone and without bounds"; and "adore art, and only art, single-heartedly and without other goal." (pp. 156-57)

> *V. F. Khodasevich, "From Bryusov" (1925; originally published in an expanded form as "Bryusov," in his* Nekropoly: vospominania, Les Editions Petropolis, 1939), in The Diary of Valery Bryusov (1893-1905) *by Valery Bryusov, edited and translated by Joan Delaney Grossman (translation copyright © 1980 by The Regents of the University of California; reprinted by permission of the University of California Press), University of California Press, 1980, pp. 149-60.*

D. S. MIRSKY (essay date 1926)

[*Mirsky was a Russian prince who fled his country after the Bolshevik Revolution and settled in London. While in England, he wrote two important and comprehensive histories of Russian literature,* A History of Russian Literature *and* Contemporary Russian Literature. *In 1932, having reconciled himself to the Soviet regime, Mirsky returned to the U.S.S.R. He continued to write literary criticism, but his work eventually ran afoul of Soviet censors and he was exiled to Siberia. He disappeared in 1937. In the following excerpt, Mirsky provides a concise survey of Bryusov's career.*]

In 1894, together with A. L. Miropolsky, [Bryusov] published *Russian Symbolists* which had the success of a scandal. This and the books that followed it were for a whole decade the favourite laughing-stock of the whole press. Bryusov's name became the synonym of a literary mountebank, and while other Symbolists, like Balmont, Sologub, and Hippius, were more or less welcome guests in the literary press, Bryusov was forbidden its doors until at least 1905. Bryusov hardly answered to his first reputation: far from being the mountebank he was imagined to be, he is one of the most solemn and dead-serious figures in the whole of Russian literature. But his early poetry was so unlike the usual run of Russian magazine verse that the blockheads of criticism could account for it only as insolent tomfoolery. In reality it is only a rather youthful, immature imitation of the French poets of the day. For many years every new book by Bryusov was received with indignation or ridicule. But Bryusov persevered. His style matured. His following grew. By 1903 he was the recognized head of a numerous and energetic literary school; by 1906 his school had won its struggle; Symbolism was recognized as the whole of Russian poetry, and Bryusov as the first Russian poet. *Stephanos,* which appeared in 1906 at the height of the revolutionary excitement, was greeted with enthusiasm by the same critics who had ridiculed his early work. Its success is perhaps the most significant date in the history of the Symbolist march toward supremacy. (pp. 186-87)

From 1900 to 1906 Bryusov was the head of a compact and vigorous party on its march to success; after 1906 his position became even more influential. But his talent began to decline. *All My Melodies* . . . marked no progress as compared with *Stephanos;* the books that followed betrayed a steady and accelerating decline. Ever since the nineties Bryusov has worked with wonderful energy in the most various literary fields; in point of volume, his original poetry is only a small part of his whole output: he translated poetry with signal success; he wrote prose stories and plays; he reviewed almost every book of new verse; he edited classics; he worked in the archives, preparing material for the lives of Pushkin, Tyutchev, and others; he read enormously and was all the time the *de facto* editor of a magazine. (pp. 187-88)

Bryusov's poetry shares with Balmont's a general "foreign" air, the result of a more intimate connexion with French and Latin than with Russian poetical tradition. It has also in common with Balmont's a certain lack of refinement, of the "finer touch" and the finer shades. At its best it is gorgeous—all gold and purple—at its worst, gaudy. Like that of most Russian Symbolists, it is continuously solemn and hieratic, and big words are his stock material. In his early poetry . . . he tried to naturalize in Russia the "singing" accent of Verlaine and the early French Symbolists, and to revive and modernize the "melodies" of Fet. But, on the whole, Bryusov is not a "musical" poet, though, like all the Russian Symbolists, he often uses his words as emotional gestures rather than as signs with a precise meaning. Though his verse is saturated with the culture of ages, Bryusov is not a "philosophical" or thinking poet. At one time, under the influence of Ivan Konevskoy, he devoted himself to writing metaphysical poetry; some of it makes excellent rhetoric, but there is very little philosophy in it, only a succession of pathetic exclamations and juxtapositions. Bryusov's diction is terser and more compact than Balmont's, and at times he achieves excellent feats of poetical compression and expressiveness, but it lacks precision, and his words, often splendid, are never "curiously felicitous." His favourite subjects are meditations on the past and future of humanity, the representation of carnal love as a mystical ritual, and—in a favourite catchword of twenty years ago—the "mysticism of every day," that is to say, evocations of the modern big towns as a forest of mysteries and symbols. His best work is contained in *Urbi et Orbi* . . . and *Stephanos.* . . . The latter includes *Eternal Truth of Idols,* a series of magnificent variations of the eternal subjects of the Greek fable. Such poems as *Achilles at the Altar* (awaiting his fatal betrothal with Polyxene), *Orpheus and Eurydice,* and *Theseus to Ariadne* are the best achievement of the "classical" aspect of Russian Symbolism, which aimed at hieratic majesty and symbolical pregnancy.

Bryusov's prose is, on the whole, of a piece with his verse: it is solemn, hieratic, and academic. Its subjects are the same—pictures of the past and future, and the mysterious "abysses" of love, very often in its most perverse and abnormal aspects. Like his verse, it has a distinctly "translated" air. Bryusov felt this and often modelled it according to some definite foreign model of the past ages. One of his best short stories, *In an Underground Prison,* is in the style of a *novella* of the Italian Renaissance. His best novel, *The Fire Angel* . . . , is the narrative of a German mercenary of the age of Luther. This helped to save his prose from the dangers of "poeticalness" and of impressionism. On the whole, it is straightforward and manly, and free from mannerisms. The subject-matter and the construction of his stories were much influenced by Edgar Allan

Poe. Both the detailed and documented presentation of the future of civilization in *The Republic of the South Cross,* and the cold-blooded study of pathological states of mind in a story like *Now That I Am Again Awake,* bear the unmistakable impress of the great Southerner. There is coldness and cruelty in all Bryusov's prose, no sympathy, no pity, only a cold flame of sensual exaltation, and a desire to penetrate into the farthest recesses of human perversity. But Bryusov is no psychologist, and his visions of sensuality and of cruelty are only pageants of loud colour. His principal work in prose is *The Fire Angel,* which is perhaps the best Russian novel on a foreign subject. The story turns on witchcraft and the trial of a witch. Dr. Faustus appears, and Agrippa of Nettesheim. It is saturated with a genuine feeling for the epoch, and is as full of erudition as any of Merezhkovsky's novels, but it is free from that writer's puerile sophistications, and as a narrative it is incomparably better. In fact it is a very good and ably constructed romance. The *Lanzknecht's* leisurely manner of narrating the thrilling and mysterious events of which he was a witness, only adds to the tension of the reader's interest. Bryusov's second novel, *The Altar of Victory* . . . , a romance of fourth-century Rome, marks a definite decline: the book is long and tedious, and lacks every creative element. (pp. 189-91)

> D. S. Mirsky, "Bryusov," in his Contemporary Russian Literature: 1881-1925 *(copyright 1926 by Alfred A. Knopf, Inc.; reprinted by permission of the publisher), Knopf, 1926, G. Routledge & Sons, 1926, pp. 186-91.*

D. S. VON MOHRENSCHILDT   (essay date 1938)

[*Von Mohrenschildt finds Bryusov to be more important as an influence on other poets than as a great artist in his own right.*]

Briusov was first to introduce and popularize the aesthetic ideals of Poe and Baudelaire. As one of the founders of the publishing house, Scorpion (1899), and the editor of the Symbolist's principal review, *Vesy (The Scales),* his influence on the younger generation of poets was paramount. . . .

Briusov's own poetry fell short of the precepts he taught. His craftsmanship was always careful and often brilliant; but excessive erudition and lack of musical quality withheld it from the level of great poetry. At its best, it is gorgeous and majestic; at its worst, cold and rhetorical. His favorite themes were meditations on the history of civilizations, the mystical aspects of carnal love, and evocations of the life of modern industrial cities, similar to those of the Belgian poet, Verhaeren. Like his poetry, his prose is predominantly cold, erudite, academic. *The Fire Angel,* a semi-fantastic, historical novel of sixteenth century Germany, dealing with witchcraft trials and black magic, is a characteristic attempt to reproduce an historical epoch while at the same time endowing it with a general metaphysical significance.

Briusov was primarily an aesthetician. He had a sharp intelligence and a vast field of knowledge. His mystic and religious preoccupations were mostly ephemeral and academic, but his place in Russian literature as the initiator of an important literary movement is definitely assured.

Soon after the Revolution Briusov joined the Communist party . . . and occupied a number of important educational posts. In spite of what he himself called his "return home," he remained a typical representative of the *fin de siècle* generation of poets. To his last days he was preoccupied with literary and philosophical theories foreign to the spirit of Marxian ideology, but his poetry was long since dead. (p. 1195)

> D. S. von Mohrenschildt, "The Russian Symbolist Movement," in PMLA, *(copyright © 1938 by the Modern Language Association of America; reprinted by permission of the Modern Language Association of America), Vol. LIII, No. 4, December, 1938, pp. 1193-1209.**

GEORGETTE DONCHIN   (essay date 1958)

[*In this section from her key study* The Influence of French Symbolism on Russian Poetry, *Donchin explores the effects of Charles Baudelaire and Émile Verhaeren on Bryusov's verse.*]

Amoralism in Brjusov is usually connected with pronounced eroticism. The range of evils analysed by Baudelaire is equally narrow: for all his fascination with human vices, these are predominantly, though not exclusively, sexual. Brjusov's indebtedness to Baudelaire in this respect is apparent from his earliest poems. The first sadistic tones appear in [*Pro domo suo, Vestalis Virgo, O matuška, gde ty*]. . . . A certain Baudelairean reminiscence—details of the beloved's corpse—can be found in two poems of 1895: *I snova* and *Purpur blednejuščix gub.* The manner of the latter is almost typically Verlainean. Some details from *Fantom* . . . are also reminiscent of Baudelaire, especially the image of the swollen corpse of the woman. The erotic themes which started in *Chefs d'oeuvre,* subsided in *Me eum esse,* but revived anew after 1900. *Pytka* . . . illustrates a typically Baudelairean sadistic theme: love is compared to torture, to the agony on the cross. The more excruciating the pain, the greater the lovers' delight. . . . In a similar vein are many poems from *Iz ada izvedënnye* and the whole section *Mgnovenija.* Typical are the scenes of the lovers chained together in a hold (*V trjume*), or entombed in a crypt (*V sklepe*), or embracing on the wheel in a torture chamber (*V zastenke*). . . . Like Baudelaire, Brjusov also revelled in all the coarsest and most naturalistic details of passion. His interest in the physiological side of love is almost copied from Baudelaire. . . . Passion is represented as a self-inflicted suffering in many poems from *Stephanos,* especially in the cycle *Pravda večnaja kumirov.* The masochistic character of love reappears in *Vse napevy.* . . . Brjusov's delight in suffering connected with love is apparent even in some of his post-revolutionary poems.

Purely Baudelairean also is Brjusov's constant inclination to interrupt his ecstasy in order to know the sensation of bitterness hidden beyond it. The background to this attitude is provided by a certain masochism, by a conception of beauty as essentially sad or even tragic, and an awareness that there is beauty in evil and evil in beauty. Brjusov shared with Baudelaire the view that sensual pleasure is in the very knowledge of evil and that the extraction of beauty from evil provides an almost aesthetic pleasure derived from overcoming the difficulty of the task. . . . Brjusov seems to have taken over from Baudelaire the most superficial and the most debatable audacities of the French poet: namely his affectation for the macabre, his taste for mystification, and his conception of love both as a source of ecstasy and an object of execration (viz. especially *Le flacon* and *Une charogne*). (pp. 141-44)

The taste for the unusual and the artificial expressed itself not only in morbidity and perverted eroticism. The attitude of the symbolist poets to nature illustrates well their predilection for artificiality which, partly, was no more than the outcome of their aestheticism. . . . Brjusov openly acknowledged the French influence in this particular aspect of his philosophy: ''I read at that time Baudelaire and Verlaine. I imagined that I held in contempt [everything] young and natural, that paint was more beautiful to me than the bloom of youth, that naive love was ridiculous, that I wanted all the refined devices of artificiality.'' Further proof that Brjusov's reproduction of the French attitude was conscious, can be found in an early poem of his entitled *V duxe francuzskix simvolistov,* published only in 1935. . . . In his poetry Brjusov lived up to his theories. At first, in *Russkie simvolisty* the theme of nature still occurs, but has almost disappeared with *Chefs d'oeuvre.* In the rare cases where nature is depicted, it is treated in an impressionist manner. Fet had already used impressionist psychologisation of nature. Verlaine however goes further and turns nature into emotion, and the lyrical subject into *une machine à sensation.* Though influenced at first by Fet to some extent, Brjusov rather follows Verlaine in his treatment of nature. Thus many early poems are almost typically Verlainean, especially *Zvëzdy zakryli resnicy,* where nature is dissolved in emotion, and *Mračnoj pavilikoj,* where nature almost becomes a rationalist allegory. In the subjective manner of Verlaine are also the early poems [*Glaza, K bol'šoj medvedice, Duxi zemli,* and partly *Paporotnik*], . . . which is reminiscent of Tjutčev too. Not only does Brjusov forsake nature; he also transforms it and, like Baudelaire, tries to create his own artificial nature independent of reality, a kind of *paradis artificiels.* His manner here is undoubtedly influenced by Mallarmé, and poems like [*Prolog (Gasnut rozovye kraski), Ten' nesozdannyx sozdanij, Zolotistye fei*] . . . achieve such a degree of vagueness that even impressionism would seem substantial by comparison. Contempt of real nature is also characteristic of Brjusov's second volume of verse. His later poems are equally remote from nature as it exists. For instance *Orxidei i mimozy* describes a fantastic artificial world, while the whole cycle *U morja* (from *Tret'ja straža*) is composed of poems which may be termed a cerebral creation and not a description of nature. (pp. 145-47)

Brjusov and the other symbolists disregarded almost completely the *couleur locale* and the *couleur du temps* which were so treasured by the Parnassians. Historical exactitude was suspect in their eyes, and they leaned towards vagueness, often using legendary heroes merely as mouthpieces of their own feelings. Exoticism was for them mainly yet another expression of their intense dislike of ordinary life, yet another means of escape. Their fascination with medieval themes, partly inherited from the romantics, can be traced to the same origin. (p. 150)

Among the Russian symbolists no one was so constantly concerned with urban culture as Brjusov. He introduced the urban motif into his earliest poems and throughout his life was concerned with the town, whether seen through Baudelairean eyes, or through Verhaeren's prism. (p. 153)

One of Brjusov's earliest urban poems, *Mertvecy osveščennye gazom* . . . , is a typical echo of the French decadent manner. Like Baudelaire, Brjusov presents all his erotic poems against the background of urban culture. Themes devoted to the town are much more frequent between 1898 and 1899. The first urban cycle entitled *Gorod* (later changed to *V stenax*) is included in *Tertia vigilia.* Brjusov's treatment of the town in this cycle is in Verlaine's manner—impressionist and serving merely as a general ''musical'' background. Occasionally even in later poems Brjusov's attitude to the city seems to owe more to Verlaine than to Verhaeren. Against this ''musical'' background, the descriptions of human types connected with the city appear almost realistic.

A more profound approach to urban motifs starts with Brjusov's admiration for Verhaeren—an admiration which originated in 1899 and grew steadily with the years. In *Tertia vigilia* one can already discern a certain note and imagery reminiscent of Verhaeren. But the impact of the Belgian poet gains in strength after 1900, and his influence proves extremely important in Brjusov's mature work. Brjusov adopts the manner and *genre* of Verhaeren: he develops the *genre* of traditional lyrics, and follows Verhaeren's example in creating specific lyrico-descriptive poems and prophetic monologues. Such are many of Brjusov's 1900-1905 poems which can be characterised as having an objective content and a philosophic and social interpretation; some of them are written in *vers libre*. Thus, after his first contact with Verhaeren, Brjusov leaves behind him the city drawn in the soft, lyrical and impressionist tones of Verlaine, which was preponderant in *Tertia vigilia.* Verhaeren taught Brjusov to discard such a superficial view of the town, and to see it from within, in all its social and cultural complexity. Under the influence of Baudelaire, the terrible and frightening face of the great city had already appeared in *Chefs d'oeuvre,* but it was only later that Brjusov became fully aware of its significance.

Like Verhaeren who dreamt all his life of writing an epic of human destiny situated in the city of the future, Brjusov also conceived the idea of a city to come. In his interpretation he again followed the Belgian poet whose faith in the future set him apart from most French symbolists. Thus Brjusov reflects in his poems the beauty of the new city, its grandeur, its dynamism, its growing vitality. Such an interpretation of urban themes was entirely *terra incognita* in Russian poetry of the 1900's. Mirskij claimed that Brjusov's urban poems were based primarily on the poet's cult for everything great and powerful, that grandeur in all its forms was the main theme of Brjusov's poetry. It was the grandiosity of the city which impressed Brjusov foremost, hence his favourite vocabulary: *bezmernyj, neizmerimyj, vek, stoletie, gromadnyj gorod, edinyj gorod,* and so forth.

Brjusov was always aware of the new thematic range that Verhaeren had opened before him. He realised that the Belgian poet brought into poetry all the aspects of contemporary life and reflected its movement by picturing contemporary cities and factories and the social struggle. He had a deep respect for Verhaeren's search for new forms in poetry, designed to correspond to the introduction of the new subject matter. Like Verhaeren, Brjusov understood that the present epoch contained potentially all the developments of the future, and he called upon the poets ''to study closely their times'' (*vsmatrivat'sja v sovremennost'*). . . . Thus Verhaeren detached Brjusov from the narrow path of purely individualist experiences, and impelled him towards the universal and the all-human. But in a sense his influence on the Russian poet was limited. Vacillating between Baudelaire's pessimism and Verhaeren's faith, Brjusov did not always show a preference for the latter. His failure to translate successfully some of Verhaeren's poems throws an interesting light on Brjusov's psychology. On the whole his translations are masterly, but there are instances when the Belgian poet fails to inspire Brjusov. Thus his rendering of the symbolic blacksmith's dream of a socialist future (*Le forgeron*) falls quite flat: it is pale and almost sentimental. . . . All the subjective elements of the poem are missing in Brjusov's translation; the rhythm and the sweeping movement of the original are lost. This may be simply due to Brjusov's technical shortcomings. It is interesting to note however that Brjusov himself considered *Kuznec* to be a very faithful translation. His adaptations from Verhaeren reveal much better the affinity between the two poets. It is significant also that in his choice of Verhaeren's poems Brjusov omitted all those in which the Belgian poet figures as philosopher and thinker and expresses his mystical positivism. Brjusov is at his best in such poems as *Ženščina na perekrestke, Mor, London, Čisla, Mjatëž, Svin'i, Ne znaju gde;* these satisfied even Vološin who demanded from translators of poetry "an organic capacity for a miracle". Vološin maintained however that on the whole Brjusov's translations from Verhaeren were merely an expression of gratitude and respect for a poet who had been perhaps the greatest poetic revelation to Brjusov. The real Verhaeren in Russian is not to be found in Brjusov's translations—says Vološin—but in some of Brjusov's original poems which best embody the spirit of the Belgian poet; and the critic names in particular **Kon' bled** and **Slava tolpe.**

Slava tolpe is indeed the best illustration of Brjusov's profound affinity with Verhaeren. The poem is unmistakably inspired by *La révolte (Les villes tentaculaires)*: it has the same rhythm, the same colour tonality, the same force in the description of the mob. . . . Yet Černov's remark that **Slava tolpe** ought to have appeared in a volume of translations from Verhaeren and not in **Puti i pereput'ja** is not substantiated. The poem is not a paraphrase of *La révolte*: it succeeds in bearing the characteristic stamp of the Russian poet, though the model is just as characteristic of Verhaeren. Brjusov does not simply borrow from Verhaeren the image of the surging crowd and the objective passages relating to the streets soaked in the insurgents' blood. The movement of the city in revolt is similar in both cases, but Verhaeren concentrates on the rebellious crowd, while Brjusov introduces a note of modernity which is entirely absent from the French poem. He is not only interested in the crowd as such, but in the street with its offices buildings and its string of carriages and its prostitutes. . . . Brjusov is on the whole much more pessimistic than Verhaeren. What seems to be his own vision of the city of the future lacks the peaceful and clear notes of the Belgian poet. The image that rises before his eyes is dark and frightening and presages the decadence of a whole civilisation. . . . Brjusov often takes up a Baudelairean motif and develops it into a Verhaerenesque sociological prophecy. He tends however towards a Baudelairean mood. There is also a Baudelairean background of debauchery and vice in **Gorodu,** though the whole poem is clearly indebted to Verhaeren: Verhaeren saw the city as an octopus extending its grasping tentacles, sucking the life blood of humanity—Brjusov envisaged it as a dragon raising a poisoned knife over its own head.

What Verhaeren really did for Brjusov was to widen considerably his subject-matter range. He showed him that there were no themes unsuitable to poetry, that philosophical and sociological motifs could be treated by a poet. . . . With Verhaeren's example before him, Brjusov was the first Russian poet to incorporate within the bounds of poetry themes which had hitherto been considered utterly untranslatable into the language of poetic beauty. (pp. 154-61)

Georgette Donchin, "Themes in Symbolist Poetry," in her The Influence of French Symbolism on Russian Poetry *(© Mouton & Co., Publishers; reprinted by permission of the author), Mouton, 1958, pp. 120-63.**

V. SETCHKAREV (essay date 1959)

[*Setchkarev's essay is the most extensive English-language examination of Bryusov's prose to date.*]

Valerij Brjusov, the leader and to a certain degree the pioneer of Symbolism in Russia, is generally known as a poet and perhaps as a scholar. His studies in the poetry of Puškin, for example, having a lasting merit, as do his numerous articles on the theory of verse and his clever literary reviews and essays (e.g., those on Gogol' or Tjutčev). His narrative prose has never attracted too much attention. Seeking an explanation for this fact, we could point out the rather "daring" themes of his short stories and the sometimes very high erudition of **Ognennyj angel,** which might deter the ordinary reader. But **Altar' pobedy** should be generally much more appreciated, considering the fact that it is much better in every respect than the very popular historical novels of Merežkovskij. If, on the whole, Brjusov could not be expected to enjoy too great popularity, still the more discriminating reader will derive a great pleasure from his tales and novels, and the literary scholar will find in them a very stimulating example of a "knowing" way of telling tales, of an extremely conscious virtuosity in handling words, together with a passionate temperament and an astonishing range of knowledge and education. (pp. 237-38)

[In her preface to Brjusov's **Dnevniki 1891-1901,** his wife provides] a good description of most Brjusov's prose work—but to the earnestness of tone, the clarity and the light jest [she mentions], one factor should be added: this is his passionateness, the enormous tension of feeling which, combined with serious clarity and a touch of irony, is the perfect characterization of Brjusov's personal style, expressing his own truth in the genuine way he wanted. Unusual, extraordinary events, abnormally excited passions, reality on the verge of fantasy, the state of transition between wakefulness and dream—such are the favorite topics of Brjusov's prose. But in the same way as in his verse the heat of the contents is controlled by the icy form of presentation—they penetrate each other, and out of the tension between these two opposites results the aesthetic effect of Brjusov's prose. "I think that the task of a poet is to hand over to others the whole fullness of his soul. . . . A poet is not a person whose soul is higher in essence, more valuable than that of other people, but a person who can feel more clearly and retell his feelings. . . ." Without any doubt Brjusov had this gift. (p. 239)

In the preface to the first edition of **Zemnaja os'** Brjusov's awareness of what he does becomes perfectly clear. First of all, he states the most important literary influences on his art: he points out Edgar Allan Poe as responsible for **Respublika Južnogo Kresta** and **Teper' kogda ja prosnulsja;** for **V Podzemnoj Tjur'me,** it is Anatole France whose stylizations of the narrative manner of older epochs he has adopted; Stanislaw Przybyszewski's influence is to be found in **Sestry.** Then Brjusov declares that we have to distinguish in literature narratives of character and narratives of situation (*rasskazy xarakterov, rasskazy položenij*). While in the first category the outstanding or typical characters are important and the action exists only to offer the possibility of disclosing their souls to the reader, the second category presents exceptional events and the characters are important only in so far as they are involved in the basic action. As his own stories in this volume belong to the second category, he does not wish to be criticized because of his incomplete characterizations. He proceeds to explain that there are again two ways of looking at the narrated events: the first is the objective method, in which the author narrates from his own point of view; the second method "breaks the events in the prism of a certain soul", looks at the events with the eyes of an other person. It is the second method which Brjusov uses here and which accounts for some stylistic and ideological peculiarities of the tales.

In the preface to the second edition, which is much shorter, Brjusov points out the commonness of "manner", of the stylistic devices in the eleven tales and stresses the fact that they are still united by *one* thought, which is presented in each of them from a different side. This is the Hoffmannesque idea that there is no definite limit between the real and the imagined world, between "dream" and "reality", "life" and "fantasy". "What we usually think to be imagination is perhaps the highest reality of the world, and the reality recognized by all is perhaps the most terrible delirium." (p. 240)

In *Respublika Južnogo Kresta* Brjusov indulges in his love for utopias: he gives an account of an excellently organized totalitarian state of the future in Antarctica, the inhabitants of whose capital are suddenly seized by the "mania contradicens"—they say and do the contrary of what they really want. This naturally leads to the dissolution of order and complete decay of the huge city—a process which is described in all its details, illustrating the thesis that men without reins become worse than beasts. Sadism and sick eroticism of all kinds dominate the scene. Brjusov writes in the style of a journalist of coming centuries "who is not too well informed, rather indifferent to all events, but who endeavors to shine in exhibiting his scientific knowledge and to display a lot of feeling." . . . Brjusov's concern is again to oppose style and events, and he does it in a masterly way. By the contrast between the slightly sentimental, matter-of-fact prose of the reporter and the things narrated, he manages to make us feel in a symbolic way the dangers surrounding humanity, dangers from within, which are at their highest exactly in an environment of absolute order and apparent security.

The narrative *Zaščita* is particularly interesting. It is clearly an attempt to write in the style of Puškin. Brjusov wanted to do here what he had done in some of his poetry: to fuse the manner of Puškin, which he thought to be the pattern of genuine poetry in every respect, with the themes and feelings which were stressed by Romanticism and Symbolism. (pp. 241-42)

It is particularly of *Vystrel* and *Pikovaja dama* that we think when reading *Zaščita*. Brjusov treats a kind of Laodamia theme (an antique legend which inspired him for the tragedy *Protesilaj umeršij*). The dead husband of the heroine visits her, so that their love remains unshaken. In Puškin's manner it is a frame story: a colonel R. tells the young "I" what happened 25 years ago. They are both guests at a country-estate and the Colonel has remained silent during a general conversation on ghosts. But alone with the narrator he tells him how, as a young daredevil staying in a garrison-town, he fell in love with a Mrs. S. (the initials instead of names are indicative!) and managed to stay a night in her house. In answer to his declaration of love, she had told him that her husband still came to her, and he, sleeping in the dead man's room conceived the idea of disguising himself in his clothes and relying on a certain resemblance to him and on the darkness, appearing to his wife. He succeeded in penetrating into her room and was about to achieve his purpose, when suddenly he saw the real husband making a threatening gesture with his arm—whereupon he fled. There is of course a vague possibility of a natural explanation, as a mirror is mentioned before which Mrs. S. is sitting in her dressing room when things happen; but it is mentioned *en passant*. (pp. 242-43)

All the other stories in the first volume treat the contrast between reality and fantasy, and especially the border where they intersect; from subtle psychological studies they pass to psychopathology, which in the atmosphere created by Brjusov does not seem to be illness. (p. 243)

Brjusov's second volume, *Noči i dni,* contains six stories written between 1908 and 1912. The epigraph . . . [is] taken from Brjusov's own verse-volume *Me eum esse* indicates the pessimistic mood of boredom and indifference that pervades the atmosphere of the stories. Brjusov says in the short preface, that the aim of the volume is to present the society of our days and, above all, to "look closely at the peculiarities of the psychology of the feminine soul".

The bulk of the book is formed by a kind of short novel: *Poslednie stranicy iz dnevnika ženščiny.* The husband of the heroine has been killed without her knowledge by one of her lovers, the painter Modest. Her diary starts on the morning when the murder is discovered and closes with the conviction of the culprit and the acquittal of herself. The thesis is that a woman in love can be either a mother or a prostitute. In both cases the feeling is genuine, even if in the second case only short-lived and changing its object. Modern society, lost in unnatural conventions, ignores this truth; "cultured society plays at love" ("igrat' v ljubov'"), it ignores the freedom of love, tries to adapt it to conventionalities which deprive it of its genuineness. The attitude of man to woman is the result of these unnatural conventions. (pp. 248-49)

It is not very astonishing that in this story the manner of Tolstoj is widely used by Brjusov. The "estranging" of society—Tolstoj's usual device—was the natural frame for the presentation of the contrast between the truth of life and the lie of civilization. . . . The style of the story gets a peculiar touch by the large quantity of reminiscences from literature and painting, which at the same time differentiate it very distinctly from Tolstoj (Brjusov never merely imitates—he knows how to destroy the imitation as well). (pp. 249-50)

The first occupation with themes used in *Ognennyj Angel* goes back to 1897. Visiting Cologne and Aachen, Brjusov was "blinded" by the "golden splendor of their medieval cathedrals" and for the first time . . . the shapes of *Ognennyj Angel* appeared before him. . . . The first title intended for the novel was *Ved'ma*. Its genre is a combination of thorough historical scholarship, giving exact information, with a sweeping description of events in an ingeniously constructed plot. The result is certainly one of the best historical novels in world literature. (pp. 253-54)

It need not be mentioned that the artistic presentation of the epoch is correct in every detail. The splendid picture of Cologne and Düsseldorf is as glowing and persuasive as that of South America. Brjusov likes to mix normal, not very significant, but typical details with outstanding, unusual, exotic features into a concentrated description. The whole picture is made exotic by this calculated cumulation, and Mirskij is quite right in observing that even such unexotic topics as the social conditions in Russia in the unimaginative sixties of the nineteenth century look exotic if Brjusov presents them—a new kind of "estrangement" again! But where real exotism is inherent Brjusov feels in his element, and surely there is plenty of exoticism of every kind in the motifs of *Ognennyj Angel*. The main character, Ruprext, has a double aspect, like almost each one of Brjusov's heroes. He is perfectly aware of all he does, he knows it to be false, he sees clearly the means to avoid the dangerous ways—but he lacks the force to use them. When he tries to persuade himself into the belief that some of his actions are reasonable, he is perfectly aware of the fact that he is trying to deceive himself and as perfectly aware of the fact that still he will do what he knows is wrong. This always happens when passion is involved. Brjusov succeeds in depicting the power of love on his hero, his sufferings from a passion which he is able to analyze psychologically to its very details but which does not lose a bit of its devastating strength in spite of this cool analysis. A parallel to this attitude is the whole epoch vacillating between skepticism and belief.

The recurrent theme of Brjusov—the unity of the real and the unreal, whose borders are extremely indistinct—finds a fertile field in this novel dealing with the supernatural. There are no accidents in this world ruled by unknown but concrete forces. (pp. 255-56)

But the aesthetic effect of the novel seems to be due mostly to the fact that Brjusov uses almost exclusively one rhetorical figure: the simile, in its broadest sense. If, in spite of the coolness of tone, the novel never becomes monotonous, this is the result of the calculated distribution of comparisons, which are extremely frequent. Corresponding to the biography of the pretended writer, they are mostly related to nature, especially to the sea,—or to war. Brjusov likes to compare psychological facts with the phenomena of nature, which are always given in an unusual manner. . . . (p. 256)

Beside the enormous quantity of similes and metaphors Brjusov's style is characterized by the insertion of maxims, which are almost always interesting in essence and formulation. . . . (p. 257)

The sense of humor never leaves the author: he apparently enjoys the tricks of Mephistopheles and has a feeling for his fooleries on the spiritual and concrete level. The defense of Holy Church in the mouth of Mephistopheles is as amusingly described as his behavior after the swallowing of the impolite waiter. . . . Even the most positive characters are seen from an ironical distance. . . . (p. 258)

His excellent knowledge of Roman history—and on the whole of the history of the old world, as shown by his fragments of novels—may have induced Brjusov to write his second novel *Altar' Pobedy.* To the book-edition Brjusov attached an extensive commentary explaining all specific features of the time which might be unfamiliar to his readers. Here he also provides a list of his sources which cannot but impress by its completeness. Brjusov has chosen the end of the fourth century . . . , when the fight between the old Roman religion and Christianity was nearing a decision. It was, of course, neither Paganism nor Christianity that interested him, but the fact that one great culture was on the point of dying and being replaced by another. The ideological key to the novel is not to be found in the novel itself but in its continuation *Jupiter poveržennyj,* which remained a fragment: it is the dialogue between the hero Junij Norban and Father Nikolaj, in which the former declares that "a truth cannot die". But the solemn answer of the priest is: "You are mistaken, young man, truths die!" Christianity and its truth will die in its time, as the truth of Paganism is dying now. It is the same skepticism which gave its basic attitude to *Ognennyj angel* and which is illustrated here as there by an epoch of transition, by a changing world. Again, the writer is the hero narrating in retrospect, shortly after the events he describes, but after a violent shock which has changed his whole being. As a matter of fact, this change was only temporary in some respects, as in the continuation of the novel he is again the same weak boy in spite of the ten years which have passed. The final change seems to have been intended in his Christian conversion as shown in the introduction to *Jupiter poveržennyj.* The plot of the novel is the double passion of the hero—the eighteen-year-old Junij—for the beautiful cold, clever, calculating, and selfish Gesperija and the inspired, obsessed, glowing, and passionate Rea—the one striving for earthly power, the other for the realm of a mysterious and mystic sectarian God. Brjusov succeeds much better with the second character as Gesperija remains a sort of literary pattern in the first novel and gets living features only in the following fragment. But Rea—who is a variation of the hysterical Renata and who is repeated in a mysterious and significative way in Silvia, the second heroine of *Jupiter,* and to a certain degree in the heroine of the novella *Reja Silvija*—seems to be the character whose aspects interested Brjusov. Here he makes her the initiator of one of the strange orgiastic sects which modified and interpreted the Christian lore in their own way. The connection with the strong sect of the Ophites—the worshippers of the Serpent—is clearly established.

Again, as in the first novel, the hero knows what he is doing and disapproves of it but is unable to act otherwise. The motif of "two loves" is stressed in the décadence, and, being a strong argument against bourgeois morality, it was used in manifold variations. . . . Junij is always under the spell of whichever of the two women he sees at the moment.—The story of the two passions is joined to a vast picture of the historical events of the time, that of the Emperor Gratian, whose order to remove the Altar of Victory from the senate building and its consequences gave the novel its title. Real historical personages, like the Emperor himself, the poet and statesman Symmachus, and the bishop Ambrosius, give Brjusov the opportunity to draw historical portraits, of which that of Symmachus is especially successful. In an enthusiastic manner, by the way, Brjusov gives the description of his library—love and veneration for the book is certainly one of Brjusov's most genuinely cherished subjects, occurring again and again.

The secondary lines of the action are the love of the thirteen-year-old Namija for the hero, and the passion of his friend Remigij for the beautiful prostitute Leta. They end with the death of the lovers: Namija and Remigij commit suicide. The mystic eroticism which is opposed here to Gesperija's calculating passion for personal power is represented by Rea and her sect: the godlike boy Luciferat and the sexual orgy instigated by his naked beauty underscore once more the erotic trend of the symbolism as one of the mainsprings of human activity, subdued and mutilated by unimaginative mediocrity. Brjusov succeeds excellently in presenting the silly superstitions of Christianity and at the same time its enormous dynamic power. For the refined society of Rome the Christians are barbarians, but Brjusov knows how to make it perfectly clear that these barbarians will be the bearers of a new culture. Interesting from this point of view is the short fragment **"Telo Gektora"** (*Neizdannaja proza* . . .), in which the Greeks seem to be barbarians to the refined society of Troy.

The whole novel, as well as its fragmentary continuation, draws its characteristic aspect from its sustained "Latin" style. The ironical touch is explained here by the development of the hero, who looks back on himself in a somewhat condescending way and who now has the right distance to judge the events and their participants. (pp. 258-60)

To a certain degree the informative element in the novel becomes an artistic device too: with the large quantity of Latin designations of typically Roman objects or customs Brjusov achieves the feeling of a certain distance of the author from his subject and he manages to moderate the enormous suspense of some scenes by using special terms. The same part is played by the large number of quotations from Latin and Greek writers or at least of references to them. . . . [The] system of new similes remaining in the scope of the antique world would justify a special examination. (p. 261)

A kind of epilogue to the Roman novels and fragments in the charming short story *Reja Sil'vija. Rasskaz iz žizni VI. veka.* Brjusov's favorite theme—the floating limits between reality and dreams—is represented here in Maria, a girl on the verge of insanity who believes herself to be living in the times of Roman splendor, while actually living in the time of its final decay. Her belief that she is Rhea Silvia, the Vestal who bore the Roman twins to Mars, her discovery of Nero's Golden Palace, her love for the young Goth, who is soon killed, and her suicide in the Tiber are narrated without the slightest irony and with a deeply felt understanding for the heroine. . . . The Golden Palace becomes a symbol of the realm of dreams, and we believe in her happiness in spite of the real tragedy that happens to her.

The short story *Èluli syn Èluli,* still in contact with the old world, narrates the opening of an old grave by scientists and the revenge of the dead man on those who have disturbed his peace: a well-told anecdote on a menacing metaphysical background.

A big undertaking was intended by Brjusov in the novel: *Sem' zemnyx soblaznov.* It is a novel of life in the future, which was to have seven parts corresponding to the number of the mortal sins. It was to comprise "all aspects of human life and examine all basic passions of human soul". The seven parts would be united by the personality of the hero—again a weak youth writing his memoirs in retrospect. It is supposed that our world after a devastating catastrophe and nearly complete annihilation has reached again approximately the same cultural standard it has now—so it is the same and still different. (p. 262)

A complete new side of his talent is exhibited by Brjusov in *Obručenie Daši.* He describes the life and the customs of Moscow merchants in the sixties of the nineteenth century, a milieu from which he himself came. The hero of the tale, Kuz'ma, has some traits of Brjusov's father Jakov; the father of Kuz'ma, Vlas Terent'evič, is to a certain degree a portrait of Brjusov's grandfather, Kuz'ma Andreevič. It is again a transition period which Brjusov selected, perhaps as important for Russia as the fall of the Roman Empire has been for the world—the milieu of Ostrovskij shortly before its dissolution, "the dark realm" pierced by the first rays of the so-called enlightenment. (p. 263)

The tale is excellently written, in Brjusov's customary precise style. The description of the Moscow-merchant quarters in the beginning is a masterly tour de force of its kind, which seemed exotic to Mirskij. The personages are characterized by their language, and here Brjusov again shows himself a virtuoso. (p. 264)

But in spite of the beautiful words there is not one positive character among the "liberals"—the skepticism of Brjusov triumphs and, combined with his style, proves that even such a foreign task as the description of the Russian sixties should apparently be to "the poet of marble beauty"—is completely within his range. Brjusov's "academic coolness", for which he is so often reproached, seems to characterize his prose as well as his poetry; but this "coolness" is a literary attitude enabling him to see life in every form from a distance. He will never appeal to readers who seek the exhibition of strong emotions, but the subtlety of his seeming coolness proves that these emotions are still present and only controlled by an artistic judgment to which the clearness of the outlines means more than the appeal to immediate feeling. (p. 265)

> *V. Setchkarev, "The Narrative Prose of Brjusov,"
> in* International Journal of Slavic Linguistics and Poetics, *Vol. 1, 1959, pp. 237-65.*

RENATO POGGIOLI (essay date 1960)

[*Poggioli surveys Brjusov's career and examines his artistic theory in the following section from his* The Poets of Russia.]

When he was hardly more than twenty years of age, Brjusov had already translated Maeterlinck's *Pelléas et Mélisande* and Verlaine's *Romances sans paroles,* and had gathered around himself a group of youthful enthusiasts of the new poetry. In 1894, with some help on the part of his friends, he edited and published the pamphlet *Russian Symbolists,* which contained versions from a few French masters (Baudelaire, Verlaine, Mallarmé, Rimbaud, Maeterlinck), and original, although derivative, poems, mainly signed by himself. This first pamphlet, and the two which followed suit, had a *succès de scandale.* The daily and the periodical press treated Brjusov and his companions like knaves and fools, and chose as main objects of their scorn some of Brjusov's most daring images, like the one projecting "violet hands on an enameled wall," and especially a single-line poem of his, reading simply: "Oh cover your pale legs." (p. 97)

Those samples shocked public opinion by offending not only its standards of taste, but also its ethical norms, and for a while Brjusov was treated as a public enemy of both morality and art. The young poet took all this in his stride, and challenged even further his elders and all the upholders of respectability and tradition by entitling as *Chefs d'oeuvre* . . . the first collection of poems which appeared under his name. In the preface he added to the boastful insolence of that title by making assertions as outrageous as these: "In its present shape, this seems to me a perfect book. I never felt as sure of myself as I feel now, while bestowing it upon eternity." *Chefs d'oeuvre* was followed by [*Me eum esse* and *Tertia Vigilia*] . . . but it was only after the turn of the century that Brjusov published his two masterpieces, [*Urbi et Orbi* and *Stéphanos—Wreath*]. . . . While Brjusov's earlier books had been primarily influenced by the usual French models, Baudelaire, Mallarmé, and especially Maeterlinck, the poetry of his maturity found its formal ideals in Gautier, the Parnassians, and even in Pushkin, from whom he learned how to master pathos and to control words. From the viewpoint of thematic novelty, the later Brjusov was one of the first to follow the example of a more recent and lesser poet in French, who was a Belgian like Maeterlinck, and who was then heading the so-called Flemish Renaissance. That poet was Emile Verhaeren, whose works Brjusov translated into Russian, and whom he imitated, perhaps with greater success than the original model, in the attempt to celebrate in urban terms what Baudelaire had called *l'esprit de la vie moderne.* (pp. 97-8)

From 1904 to 1909, . . . [Brjusov] held the *de facto* if not *de jure* editorship of the *The Scales,* the magnificent review issued by that press. This leading editorial position made Brjusov the dictator of Russian literary life at the very time when his importance, if not his reputation, as a poet was already on the wane. If *Roads and Crossroads,* a revised and selected edition of all his previous poetry, which appeared in 1908, confirmed his standing without adding anything to his fame, the following collections, [*All Melodies* and *The Mirror of Shadows*] . . . , already marked the decline of Brjusov's creative powers.

Brjusov was not only a poet, but also a storyteller and a playwright. In 1907-1908 he published his important novel, *The Fiery Angel,* from which the composer Sergej Prokof'ev was later to take the libretto for the opera by the same name. The place and time of the novel is the Germany of the early Reformation; the narrator is a mercenary soldier with humanistic leanings, in whom Brjusov mirrored himself, as he reflected in the story a rather unsavory episode of his life, his rivalry with Andrej Belyj for the love of a strange, hysterical woman, who reappears in the novel in the shape of a witch. The plot itself deals with a case of witchcraft, evoked in an aura of reality and fancy, of history and legend. In the background of the novel there appear such shadowlike figures as Cornelius Agrippa and Doctor Faustus. Beautifully written, *The Fiery Angel* is not so much a historical novel as an archaeological tableau in the manner of Flaubert's *Salammbô*. The same can be said of another novel, *The Altar of Victory* . . . , set in the Rome of the fourth century; while *The Republic of the Southern Cross* . . . is a political fantasy not too different in spirit from the play *The Earth,* a verse drama written in 1905. In both of them the utopia of the future is treated as a nightmare, rather than as a dream.

Except for several stories, some of which are tales of horror and wonder in the manner of Edgar Allan Poe, the rest of Brjusov's literary heritage is taken up by translations and criticism. The translations, besides the items already mentioned, include versions of two Decadent tragedies, D'Annunzio's *Francesca da Rimini* and Wilde's *The Duchess of Padua,* as well as a late anthology of Armenian poetry, published in 1916. His outstanding contribution in this field is, however, a version of the *Aeneid*. Most of Brjusov's critical essays, the best of which are perhaps those on Pushkin and Tjutchev, were collected by him in *Far and Near Ones*. . . . Among his critical writings one should, however, also mention his reinterpretation of Gogol', strangely entitled *Man Burnt to Ashes* . . . ; the aesthetic manifesto **"Key of Mysteries,"** originally published in *The Scales* . . . ; and, finally, many technical studies about the structure of verse and rhyme, of meter and rhythm.

Brjusov composed most of these technical studies after the end of his creative period, which closed with 1917. . . . After issuing another collection of poems, sadly entitled *Last Dreams* . . . , Brjusov died in his native city in 1924, hardly more than fifty years of age, but already an old man, sick in body and spirit.

It is claimed that Brjusov could give his allegiance to the Red state only because no faith of any kind, whether religious or political, had ever attracted him. This is true; yet his decision to accept the new faith may have been dictated also by a sense of historical fatalism. If he bowed to the dictatorship of the proletariat, it was perhaps because his prophetic insight had anticipated it. He had done so at the time of the Russo-Japanese War and the Revolution of 1905, in one of the poems of *Stéphanos,* **"The Coming Huns,"** an apocalyptic vision announcing the imminent irruption from the East of a new barbaric horde. The poet foresaw that the invading conquerors would free the enslaved masses, and that the latter would show their joy by making bonfires of books. Then scholars and artists would save their treasures in caves and catacombs, knowing that sooner or later those treasures would be destroyed by the barbarians, but wondering whether chance would ultimately preserve any of their labors for posterity's benefit. Yet, speaking in the first person for all his peers, and sharing their terrors and doubts, Brjusov concluded his prophecy in the spirit of what the ancients called *amor fati,* greeting the coming Huns "with a hosanna and a hymn." (pp. 98-100)

Some of Brjusov's contemporaries, remembering that he came from a merchant's family, compared him to a tradesman's son, bringing home from Europe's emporia not only commodities but also *objets d'art*. Brjusov, however, was not a mere acquirer of culture, but a conqueror too. It was this aspect of his character that earned him the nickname of "little Napoleon," although he was rather a Peter the Great in miniature, who almost single-handedly westernized Russian poetry anew. He reduced this process of westernization almost exclusively to the reshaping of Russian literary culture after the pattern of French modernism. . . . (p. 101)

This was perhaps Brjusov's highest achievement: a fact obviously implying that for him formal values claimed precedence over all other ideals or concerns. One could almost say that he failed to take seriously any problems except those of form. He avowed as much in the poem **"I,"** where he proudly stated that his spirit had never languished "in the haze of contradictions": a not-too-oblique reference to the tendency of too many of his contemporaries to lose lucidity of vision and firmness of hand in the clouds of metaphysical speculation. In another poem he directly apostrophized the "God-seekers" of his age, telling them that he felt estranged from their controversies about God and Satan, Christ and the Anti-christ. Elsewhere he described this estrangement in terms of universality and open-mindedness, such as the desire to sail with the boat of his poetry on any sea, and to celebrate at once Jehovah and Lucifer. In **"I"** he expressed the same view, and painted himself as a spirit endowed with a gift for total understanding, with a many-sided ability to experience and feel everything: "I love all dreams, I hold dear all tongues, I consecrate one line to every god." Such an indiscriminate sympathy for all creeds is but the effect of a fundamental indifference to any form of belief, and the poet hastens to acknowledge, with great honesty, that he was born to play not the role of an apostle or teacher of truth, but merely of a student, eager to learn from his betters the secrets of thought and form: "I visited the groves of Lyceus and Academe, marking on wax the sayings of the wise; a faithful disciple, I was loved by all, while loving only the conjunctions of words."

Brjusov must have held very dear this closing formula, since he repeated it in **"To the Poet,"** a piece which is an *ars poetica* in a psychological key, and in imperative terms. The repetition occurs in the passage where Brjusov claims that life is but a pretext for the composition of resounding rhymes, and where he enjoins the poet to seek forever "the conjunctions of words." Among the other commands which Brjusov addresses there to the poet are those to be as proud as a flag and as sharp as a blade, and, above all, to follow Dante's example, by letting "the underground flame" burn one's cheek. Here Brjusov speaks with the voice of Baudelaire and Rimbaud: by the poet's duty to go through hell-fire he means that he must search for *paradis artificiels,* that he must strive after *le dérèglement de tous les sens*. In brief, Brjusov maintains that the artist must taste the fruit of the tree of knowledge, in order to experience good and evil, and thus to become an angel and a demon, a superman and a demigod. Yet in the following stanza Brjusov speaks rather with the voice of Flaubert, preaching on one side the gospel of artistic impassibility: "contemplate everything, but be a cold witness of all," and, on the other, the related and contradictory doctrine of the artist's sacrifice and martyrdom: "that your virtue be a readiness to climb the pyre where you will burn." The poem ends on this note, with the assertion that the secret wreath of the poet is but a crown of thorns.

Some of these views are but replicas of the literary commonplaces of the time (as shown by the morbid poem where, reshaping in decadent terms a Christian myth, Brjusov compares the sufferings of his soul to Saint Sebastian's martyrdom); and yet this does not mean that Brjusov restates them in a spirit of fashionable imitation or pose. If this poet ever believed in anything, it was in the ideas connected with aestheticism, which has already been defined as the attempt to lower existence to the status of the raw material of poetry and to reduce life to the condition of art. For Brjusov, it is not experience that determines creation, but creation that determines experience: the poet must go through a novel ordeal only in order to create a new form of art. All of Brjusov's psychological metamorphoses were due not to moral conversions or spiritual crises, but to the shifts of his own aesthetic interests, to the desire to carry out a rare experiment, to develop a theme still untouched.

It is quite significant that Brjusov achieved his most successful artistic effects at the opposite ends of his thematic range, by working on subject matters challenging him to become either as ancient or as modern as possible. In the first case we have to do with the cycle of poems which he collected in *Stéphanos* under the heading of **"The Everlasting Truth of the Idols,"** or more generally, with all the pieces he wrote on classical scenes or pagan myths. We find among them perhaps some of Brjusov's highest poetic feats, for instance, **"The Last Supper,"** which does not deal with Christ's passion, despite its title, but with the suicide of an old and tired Roman couple, who choose to die after an orgy, while their drunken guests are asleep. Other poems of this kind are **"Achilles at the Altar,"** depicting the Greek hero waiting for his fatal wedding with Polyxena; **"Medea,"** representing that barbarian heroine while she flees the scene of her crimes on her dragon-driven chariot; **"Orpheus and Eurydice,"** which, like many other of such pieces, is written in dialogue form. It was this group of poems, hammered or chiseled out of a hard and noble matter, that earned for Brjusov the label of "poet of marble and bronze" which Belyj awarded him.

When he followed, however, the example of Verhaeren's *Villes tentaculaires,* and wrote poems celebrating the throbbing life of the great modern centers in a spirit already anticipating Futurism itself, Brjusov worked instead, to use the words he employed in his poem **"To the City,"** in "steel, brick, and glass." Yet, unlike the Futurists, he used only rarely the new medium of free verse and preferred to sing of the beauty and horror of urban life in traditional meters. The most important of his urban poems are perhaps **"To the City"** and **"Eventide,"** both of which are written in regular rhythms. In the former Brjusov evoked the modern metropolis in a vision of fabulous realism, as a machinelike monster, devouring everything, and yet generating from its very entrails the poisons which will be the cause of its death. In **"Eventide"** (or, more literally, **"The Flow of Evening"**) Brjusov painted the gold and tinsel of the metropolis at dusk, with the crude light of its lampposts and shopwindows, with the "sheaves of fire" and "blue light-

nings" flung by its autos and streetcars; and closed the poem with a hymn to the real ruler of our urban civilization, **"Her Majesty the Dust."** If in his city poems Brjusov became for a while the poet of industrialism and capitalism, in his "factory songs" he sought instead to express the self-consciousness of the urban proletariat, of those masses building a civilization of which they were the slaves rather than the masters. Yet what led Brjusov to write these pieces was not a sense of sympathy for the working class, but perhaps the simple desire to attune the accents of modern poetry to the strains of the Russian folk song.

All this seems to suggest that the real muse of Brjusov was deliberation itself. Nothing better proves this truth than the lyric where, speaking in the first person, the poet compares himself to a plowman, and addresses his "dream" as his "faithful ox." Man and animal plod abreast along the field, toiling without rest or relief; and when the poet-plowman feels that his oxlike dream is failing in its effort, he incites it with his voice and excites it with his goad. This parable is almost symbolic of Brjusov's art, which is based on strenuous exertion, and on a constant will: a will ruling even over imagination or inspiration, which is what the poet here means by the word "dream." It was this quality of Brjusov's genius that led the critic Julij Ajkhenval'd to compare him to the protagonist of Pushkin's *Mozart and Salieri,* to that Salieri who had sacrificed all, with supreme devotion, to the art of music, and who could not comprehend why God had graced with an effortless creative power such a simple and naïve being as Mozart, unable to take seriously even his divine gift. Yet, precisely because he resembled Salieri, Brjusov felt the overpowering seduction of the Mozart-like wonders of Pushkin's art, up to the point of trying to complete a tale in verse and prose, *The Egyptian Nights,* which Pushkin had left unfinished. Brjusov did not do this to compete with the greatest of all Russian poets, but only to pay a tribute to his greatness, as a token of admiration and a sign of worship. The man who once said of himself, "I would rather not be Valerij Brjusov," sacrificed even his ego for the sake of his art. He never thought of himself as a god of poetry, but as one of its priests; he acted more like the servant than the master of his craft. Posterity may deny him lasting fame, but it will always respect his name at least for what Mallarmé, in his "Toast funèbre" to the memory of Théophile Gautier, called *la gloire ardente du métier.* (pp. 101-05)

> Renato Poggioli, "The Decadents," in his The Poets of Russia: 1890-1930 (copyright © 1960 by the President and Fellows of Harvard College; excerpted by permission), Cambridge, Mass.: Harvard University Press, 1960, pp. 89-115.*

VICTOR ERLICH (essay date 1964)

[*Erlich closely examines the poem* "To the Poet," *relating it to Bryusov's own artistic vision. The critic goes on to trace the influence of the French symbolists and to discuss certain of Bryusov's works, concluding that his greatest contribution to Russian literature is his literary criticism.*]

In 1907, at the height of his influence as literary pundit and pace-setter, Briusov produced his much quoted credo **"To the Poet."** Here is a rough English prose approximation of what the *maître* had to say to an imaginary apprentice:

> You must be proud as a banner / You must be sharp as a sword / Like Dante's, your cheeks must / Be scorched by subterranean flame.

Be an impassive witness of all / Encompassing all in your gaze / Let your supreme virtue be / Your readiness to mount the stake.

Perhaps, everything in life is but a means / To brightly singing verses. And from your carefree childhood on / [You must] seek combinations of words.

At moments of love embraces / Force yourself to be dispassionate. And in the hours of ruthless crucifixions / Sing the glory of frenzied pain.

In morning dreams and in the evening abyss / Seize the whispers of fate. And remember: for ages has the Poet's sacred wreath been made of thorns.

Let us note, at the outset, that Briusov's *ars poetica* is concerned with the poet rather than with poetry. The central question here is not what kind of verse the devotee ought to write, but what kind of life he should lead, what manner of man he ought to be.

The two adjectives featured in the opening lines of the poem have a characteristically, if not uniquely, Briusovian ring. To be sure, the cluster of attitudes suggested by "proud"—pride in one's calling, spiritual intransigence and a sense of superiority vis-à-vis the *profanum vulgus*—can be traced back to Pushkin, indeed to Horace. Yet the combative assertiveness of the military similes (banner, sword) is clearly reminiscent of the man who thought of himself—and was widely thought of—as a standard-bearer of the Movement. Nor will "sharp," with its intimations of definiteness and incisiveness, come as a surprise to anyone familiar with the tenor of Briusov's work. Though on occasions he paid lip-service to the Symbolist cult of "nuance," his rhetorical and cerebral bent was fundamentally incompatible with the Verlainian vagueness and languor.

The subsequent two lines are a homage to the *Zeitgeist*. Whether or not the "subterranean flame" image is in fact, as Renato Poggioli surmises, an echo of Baudelaire's "*paradis artificiels*" or Rimbaud's "*dérèglement des sens*" [see excerpt above], the phrase clearly points toward two interlocking turn-of-the-century themes—fascination with evil and the mystique of suffering. The latter emphasis is reinforced by "readiness to mount the stake" of the second stanza, the "ruthless crucifixions" in the fourth, and finally, the grim warning of the last quatrain.

On the face of it, [the pervasive] Christian symbolism seems to be oddly out of place in a poem whose key passage strongly suggests that "brightly singing verses" might be the only thing of value. Clearly, martyrdom as readiness to sacrifice oneself in behalf of what is generally recognized as a "cause," be it a religious or a secular one, is not at issue here. Are we thus justified in concluding that Briusov invokes the notion of sacrifice in vain? While the hyperbolical and hackneyed quality of Briusov's rhetoric is not to be gainsaid, such an inference might be a trifle premature.

Viewed at closer range, the semantics of **"To the Poet"** prove partly misleading. Briusov's argument does entail the motif of an ordeal, but characteristically, it is one which has less to do with the "hot" imagery (flame, stake) than with its opposite pole, notably the cluster revolving around the notion of coldness, detachment, noninvolvement.

"Be an impassive witness of all / Encompassing all in your gaze," these lines highlight two crucial aspects of the stance which Briusov is urging upon the novice. The repetition of the inclusive pronoun "all" reflects an insistence on an indiscriminately comprehensive attitude toward life. The poet cannot afford to be choosy or squeamish, he must not shun any facet of human existence, however sordid, grim or repellent. (This, incidentally, might be the minimum interpretation of the Inferno image: "subterranean flame,"—pain, suffering, degradation, vice—is "part of the game.") The poet worthy of the name must be prepared to take in his stride, or expose himself to, all dimensions of reality.

Expose himself to reality, rather than fully experience it. The importance of this distinction scarcely needs to be elaborated upon. Let us note that Briusov does not enjoin his imaginary disciple to plunge or leap into the flames. "Scorched cheeks" suggests surface contact, and properly so. For the poet is not expected here to be a full participant in the *agon,* but merely an "impassive witness." The code of behavior prescribed by Briusov rules out total emotional involvement.

The point is driven home with a somewhat chilling grimness in the fourth stanza: "At moments of love embraces force yourself to be dispassionate." Even in the most intimate experiences whose very integrity hinges on the participant's willingness and ability to let himself go, even in the moments of passion so assiduously celebrated by Briusov and his fellow Symbolists, the poet must not divest himself of his all-encompassing spectatorship. It is his duty—and his destiny—to withdraw a part of himself from the maelstrom of emotion in order to keep it cool, and thus available for observation, introspection, recording, mental note-taking. Otherwise, it seems, the encounter might go to waste, the love affair might fail to produce a love poem.

Experience is thus demoted to the status of mere raw material "for brightly singing verses," of a repertory of poetic themes. It becomes something to be manipulated, recorded, verbalized—in a word, used—rather than valued for its own sake. The Flaubert-Mallarmé life-for-art's-sake doctrine is proclaimed here with that relentless explicitness which is Briusov's trademark.

The keynote in this set of directives is self-discipline, a principle, we may add, which starts operating at a very early stage, as a matter of formative, existential choice. "And from your sorrow-free childhood on / [You must] seek combinations of words." For one who is not a poet, Briusov implies, childhood is indeed free of care and responsibility, a realm of unfocused, unpragmatic, disinterested play. But the child who is to be chosen cannot afford to play aimlessly, just for the fun of it. He must channel his natural proclivity for verbal play into a search for the best words in the best order, so that in the fulness of time they may glitter in his "brightly singing verses."

By now we may have a somewhat better idea as to the kind of sacrifice which Briusov has in store for the poet. It is a *sui generis* emotional asceticism, which plays havoc with natural impulses. The poet is regarded here as a member of a secular order. He is dedicated not to renunciation or withdrawal—since the life of the senses has to be fully explored for the greater glory of poetry—but to a ruthless self-restraint. What is surrendered here is emotional spontaneity, the right available to normal people to give in to one's emotions, to respond and experience freely, unencumbered by ulterior aesthetic designs, by the "stern commands of the Muse." (pp. 72-6)

Let the self-indulgent Philistine, Briusov is saying in effect, indulge his emotions; he has nothing better to do. The "guardian of Mystery'' must curb his common humanity in order to serve his demon the better. The credo culminates in a warning: Are you prepared to pay the price? Do you have the stamina which the poet's calling requires, the determination to subordinate your personal life to the stern demands of the Muse? If not, you need not apply. (p. 77)

The argument of **"To the Poet"** clearly presupposes the turn-of-the-century cult of experience—the belief that frenzied accumulation of variegated thrills is tantamount to living a full life, which in turn is incumbent upon the man of sensibility. Moreover, and, perhaps, more important, the notion of hoarding experiences with a view to subsequent poetic expression is predicated upon an unexamined Romantic assumption concerning the relationship between life and work. Only one who views the lyric as fundamentally a transcript of an actual emotional event can insist, as Briusov does in effect, that an indiscriminately wide range of experience is a necessary prerequisite for a variegated body of lyric verse. In fact, it might be argued that the Romantic and neo-Romantic view of the poetic process somewhere along the line tends to subvert the Parnassian tenet about the essential autonomy of art.

The difference between Briusov's and Mallarmé's Flaubertianism thus becomes apparent. Mallarmé withdrew into the ivory tower to keep his poetry pure and free from the vulgar distractions and blandishments of the market place. Briusov insisted on exposing himself, and his ideal poet, to any and all emotional and sensory stimuli. A full and thrill-packed life divested of spontaneity and of strong personal involvement is, from the standpoint of the poet's basic humanity, a flawed, indeed a self-contradictory affair. Was it also a self-defeating one? One wonders. Ironically, it is precisely the assumptions underlying Briusov's poetics that lend queries such as these special relevance and authority.

Yet to note the pitfalls and internal contradictions inherent in Briusov's mythology of the poet is not necessarily to bemoan the loss which may have resulted from his commitment to ''brightly singing verse.'' Judging by reliable testimony, on balance Briusov had little to lose and a great deal to gain by espousing a philosophy of life which set so much store by self-control. For Briusov was not merely a deliberate craftsman, a highly conscious ''maker'' rather than a ''natural,'' seemingly effortless, singer of Balmont's variety, or a possessed seer such as Blok. He was, in the literal sense of the word, a self-made poet, not that he came from the ranks —Briusov's solid merchant background lacked the intellectual luster of Blok's family tradition, but it was not exactly underprivileged—but in that he made himself a distinguished man of letters, a poet, a novelist, a critic, a leader of an important school of poetry, as a matter of a deliberate choice, of an act of will, by dint of painstaking, unremitting toil. For it took nothing less than a dogged effort at mastering unfamiliar techniques, at attuning oneself to uncongenial attitudes, to turn this sober, incisive, unbending, fundamentally unlyrical and ''unmusical'' man into the captain of a literary movement which favored the ineffable, worshipped ''music,'' and searched for a mystique. (pp. 81-3)

Briusov's prodigious industry and ever-widening literary culture, coupled with an incisive intelligence and some native poetic endowment, yielded an impressive image. His determination to absorb and to make his own the characteristic rhythms, strategies and attitudes of Russian modernism ushered in a number of poems so skillfully constructed, so ably orchestrated, so forcefully representative of the new sensibility as to be easily mistaken for masterpieces by some of Briusov's younger contemporaries, including poets finer than himself. Thus, after the publication of Briusov's widely acclaimed collection of verse, *Urbi et Orbi*, Aleksandr Blok, who was to develop into a lyrist of vastly superior suggestiveness and power, wrote reverently to his older colleague: ''I have no hope of ever finding myself next to you. I do not purport to know if what is known to you will ever become available to the rest of us or to speculate as to how soon this is likely to happen.''

Eventually some of this wide-eyed adulation gave way to a more critical assessment of Briusov's strengths and weaknesses. In his fascinating ''Reminiscences about A. A. Blok,'' Belyi claims that Blok was ''the first to realize that, that he [Briusov] is merely a mathematician, a calculator, a classifier and that there is no trace of a Magus in him.'' (pp. 84-5)

Yet even in his stridently risqué verses which were designed to shock the literary conservatives, Briusov was a decadent with a difference. If at a later stage, in spite of all the dutifully cryptic references to the esoteric revelations allegedly embodied in the poet's ''images, rhythms, words,'' Briusov's ''magic'' smacked to an intuitive contemporary of ''mathematics,'' his gestures toward weary overrefinement were never convincing. Lassitude and ennui were fundamentally alien to this energetic, imperious, hard-driven litterateur. He was much too curious and much too active to afford languor. His attitude toward the cultural heritage had none of the weary connoisseurship of one who ''has read all the books''; it had the freshness of an avid learner and the vigor of a tireless explorer and *Kulturtraeger*. Culture to Briusov was not a source of rarefied thrills for a jaded palate, but an enormous body of tradition, a heterogeneous cluster of intellectual and technical skills to be learned, assimilated, mastered, and transmitted. Few Russian poets, if any, could vie with Briusov in his insatiable thirst for knowledge, in his great, indeed indiscriminating, intellectual curiosity. In the course of his far-flung activity as poet, fiction writer, critic, and literary historian, he made the entire Western civilization his province. His sonnets, novels, and essays range over the vast expanse of cultural history, from classical antiquity through the Italian Renaissance and the German Reformation down to the latest trends or fads in French literature. Briusov's best work, I might add, testifies not only to the remarkably wide scope of his cultural receptivity, but to the vigor and relevance of his responses as well. His most distinguished novel, *The Fire Angel* . . . , set in sixteenth-century Germany, is a triumph of historical imagination. (pp. 86-7)

[Briusov] was not the only Symbolist to hail the November revolution, but he went considerably further in his support of the new regime than did either Belyi or Blok. In his post-1917 collections of verse, [*In Such Days, The Moment, Distances,* and *Mea*]. . . , he eulogized the universal sweep and the liberating mission of the proletarian revolution. . . . (p. 91)

Briusov did not offer his full support to the new regime until it demonstrated its ability and determination to subdue the ''people's wrath,'' to transform the revolutionary chaos into an increasingly autocratic cosmos and harness it to the leader's grand design. The triumph of organization over the principle of spontaneity *(stilchiinost)*—so dear to the heart of ''flabby'' liberals and democratic socialists—was bound to gain Briusov's assent and admiration.

But the primacy of discipline, the increasing efficacy of controls, was not the only aspect of the Bolshevik mentality and performance which Briusov must have found congenial. This tireless literary toiler was bound to respond positively to the Soviet regime's emphasis on work and productivity, to the Leninist drive against the traditionally Russian sloth, inertia, inefficiency—in a word, *Oblomovitis*. (p. 93)

Characteristically enough, the imagery of hard physical labor looms large in Briusov's metapoetry, more specifically in verse dealing with his own creative process. . . . Tsvetaeva is right; Briusov has the unique distinction of speaking of his inspiration in the accents of the Volga Boatmen's Song. (p. 94)

Though in some of Briusov's Bolshevik odes the discrepancy between the ultrarevolutionary tenor and the tired poetic clichés is very embarrassing indeed, the aging poet's literary conservatism should not be overestimated. Partly owing to his remarkable intellectual flexibility and sophisticated relativism in matters of versification, partly out of his determination to keep pace with shifting literary tides so as not to be outdistanced, Briusov as a critic showed more sympathy for Futurist innovations than did any of his fellow Symbolists, with the possible exception of Andrei Belyi. As a practitioner he bravely sought to absorb some of the *avant-garde* devices by extending his earlier experiments with inexact rhymes, by trying out various metrical patterns. Out of deference to what he felt to be the spirit of the New age, he labored to couch his metaphors in a cosmic, scientific vein. (This, incidentally, was not a totally new emphasis: some fifteen years earlier, when still editor of *The Scales,* Briusov featured prominently in his journal an abortive attempt by an obscure French Symbolist, René Ghil, at "scientific poetry.")

Yet none of these strenuous efforts could save the bulk of Briusov's post-1917 verse from vaporousness, stodginess, in a word, sterility. These polished but lifeless poetic exercises were produced in a vacuum. No one seemed to need them. They were too blatantly propagandistic and "conformist" for the unreconstructed intelligentsia, too conventional for the literary radicals, too learned and recondite, too cluttered up by the "archaistic" bric-a-brac of historical erudition (Maksimov) to be accessible to the workers and peasants to whom Briusov's "Bolshevik" poetry was allegedly addressed.

It would be a simplification to attribute the glaring weaknesses of Briusov's late verses to his inability to find an appropriate poetic pitch for his political "engagement." Symptoms of creative exhaustion had been apparent in his poetry well before 1917. As a lyrist Briusov reached his peak at the age of thirty-five, during the heyday of the literary school which he led so ably and forcefully. Perhaps, this "organizer of propaganda," this "leader and fighter" was too closely bound up with the inner dynamism of the movement to be able to survive its disintegration without losing much of his initial poetic thrust.

It is an interesting commentary on the nature and limits of Briusov's endowment that, in retrospect, the least vulnerable aspect of his legacy is the one which depends less on poetic imagination than on analytical intelligence. Briusov's most enduring contribution, I believe, lies not in his lyric verse or, with the significant exception of *The Fire Angel,* in his artistic prose, but in his literary criticism which encompasses many perceptive, well-documented and closely argued reexaminations of the Russian literary masters. In his most effective poetry he expressed the literary *ambiance* of the age with competence and authority such as to earn him those "two lines in the history of world literature" for which he toiled so strenuously. Yet it is possible to argue that, except for a few truly memorable poems, be it the apocalyptic **"Pale Horse"** *(Kon'*

bled) or the sharply etched mythological vignettes **"The Eternal Truth of the Idols"** *(Pravda vechnaia kumirov),* even the best of Briusov's poetry is often impressively second-rate. The virtues found here, e.g., sonority, eloquence, lucidity of the poetic argument, are many, but they are rhetorical rather than lyrical. What is missing time and again is "magic"—the haunting suggestiveness of the finest Symbolist verse, let alone the stunning verbal discoveries of the best post-Symbolist poets, of Mandelshtam, Maiakovskii, Pasternak. It is true that Briusov's reputation as a poet may suffer unduly from the contemporary reader's impatience with the hieratic and abstract quality of the turn-of-the-century vocabulary. Yet it is an earmark of a major poet to be able to survive the clichés of his age. Mallarmé, Rimbaud, Verlaine at his best, Blok and Belyi (especially as prose writer) speak to us above and beyond the vagaries of the Symbolist era. Briusov the poet remains primarily a purveyor of well-wrought period pieces. (pp. 95-7)

Though Briusov's debt to the Flaubert-Mallarmé tradition is undeniable, his brand of aestheticism shows at least as much affinity for the flamboyant Romantic Bohemian Gautier as it does for the austere *maître* of French symbolism. He was an indefatigable craftsman, but ultimately not a purist. He was too energetic, too mundane, too sensuous, too power-minded to shun the direct gratifications, the temptations and pitfalls of the life of action. Perhaps, when all is said and done, "craft" was not for Briusov a strictly aesthetic category. It was rather a generic notion, a principle applicable to life and art alike, though especially operative in the latter, notably one of shaping, molding, transforming recalcitrant matter, bending the non-human to human purposes, asserting the primacy of intelligence and skill, the superiority of culture to nature. In Tsvetaeva's words, "Briusov came into this world to show what the Will can and cannot do, but primarily what it can do." Few of those familiar with Briusov's achievement will deny that on both counts the demonstration was an instructive one. (pp. 98-9)

> *Victor Erlich, "The Maker and the Seer: Two Russian Symbolists," in his* The Double Image: Concepts of the Poet in Slavic Literatures *(© 1964, by The Johns Hopkins Press), Johns Hopkins Press, 1964, pp. 68-119.**

IRENE MASING-DELIC   (essay date 1975)

[*Masing-Delic examines the theme of pain and alienation in Bryusov's work, comparing it to similar currents in the work of Aleksandr Blok.*]

There exist several interesting comparisons between Brjusov's Parnassian and Blok's Dionysian poetry. (p. 388)

The aim of this paper is to compare two interrelated aspects in the aesthetics and world view of the two poets: the significance and function of pain in their poetic systems and the attitudes of the two poets towards limitation, Brjusov's system representing an aesthetic and psychological preference for limitation, where pain functions as a stimulant, whereas Blok's system represents a metaphysical protest against limitation, with pain functioning as a (last) link with reality. The term limitation is here broadly interpreted, so as to include the limitations of time and space, the limitations of man's access to knowledge of any reality beyond that given by the senses, and the spiritual and physiological limitations resulting from the limited reserves of emotional energy which man has at his disposal, reserves which are insufficient for a constant inner tension, a constantly inspired state. The term is used to include—in Brjusov's case—a preference for the clearly structured and a distaste for the diffuse and undefined or undefinable and—in Blok's case—a preference for the vague promise and a distaste for the too specific, concrete, and near.

The lyrical "I" of Brjusov's early poetry shows distinct if varied preferences. This voice often declares that it values something and then proceeds to define what it is that it values. A considerable number of poems by Brjusov begin with the words "I love," followed by a catalog, often of inanimate objects or abstract concepts. In the small cycle of poems characteristically entitled **"V stenax"** . . . this compositional device is used particularly often. . . . Consonant with the poet's preference for the limited and distinct are the objects of the ensuing catalog, which lists books, crystals, and "the sting of slender wasps" as pleasing. The reason for this preference is clear: crystals, although natural objects belonging to the category of "God's miraculous deeds," embody the principle of the limit in endless repetition, the endlessness of many confined facets (*grani*)—its *mnogogrannost'*. Similarly with the "sting of slender wasps": although it is found in nature, it attracts the poet as the epitome of thinness and sharpness, with the ability to penetrate a certain point in a limited area and cause live tissue a sharp, localized pain. A wasp sting is thus the ideal instrument for arousing a nerve center, for causing a distinct pain sensation. Other images in Brjusov's early poetry reflect the same preference for the crystal's fragmentation, e.g., the image of the poet's heart as "the whitekeys" (**"Belye klaviši,"** . . .), or the image of beauty as "rays" threatened by the more massive proportions of nature in its nonaestheticized state. . . . The principle of fragmentation may be extended to the poet's time consciousness and presented in a negative light, as in the image of minutes "heard" to pass, which are transformed into the sound of nails being driven into a coffin (from the cycle *Vejan'e smerti* . . .). . . . Perhaps it could be said that the fragmentation of time has both its negative and positive aspect to the poet; living for each moment makes the future nonexistent and therefore also death, but the intense awareness of each separate moment may also demonstrate the torment of gradual process towards an inevitable goal.

The poem **"Kogda sižu odin i v komnate temno"** . . . from the cycle *V stenax* offers a wide range of examples of the poet's attitudes towards limitation. The poem describes the mood of a certain time segment, an evening. The poet sits alone in his room at dusk; beyond the wall—the poet is always conscious of walls—which here safely separates him from other people, somebody "practices scales for a long time." This uniform repetition of notes apparently forms an essential factor in the poet's mood, because like the crystal it symbolizes for the poet segmentation and repetition. It is furthermore characteristic of the poet that although the time treated is dusk, as a Parnassian poet he is not interested in twilight effects but rather in the change from soft, blurred outlines to distinctness of contour. . . . This change is welcome to the poet, who feels however that there is still room for improvement. . . . The troublesome clouds dispersed, the poet can enjoy the aesthetic experience of a geometric shape being drawn before him, its outlines growing ever more distinct as they are filled in by the "pencil" of the moonbeam. In the wider context of the cycle the moonbeam can be seen as a variant of the wasp sting; it too can penetrate a surface as it passes through the window, a fact that is mentioned twice. Here also the function of the sting or the moonbeam becomes clear: these fine instruments wound the poet, pierce him and cause him to tremble, stirring

up his emotional and mental faculties with a sharp sensation of pain. . . . Pierced by the moonbeam the poet is stimulated to feel "friendship" for the streetlamp (masc. *fonar*) and "love" for the moon (fem. *luna*).

The same desire to be alone and to concentrate on some limited aspect of existence marks the poem **"Kogda opuskaetsja štora"** . . . from *V stenax*), where blinds and curtains shield the poet from the outer world and its multitude of unseparated and interwoven existential elements. It is interesting to compare this poet's affection for draperies with the desire of the younger Symbolists to tear down the "veils of Maya," to make the world "transparent" in order to see not only truth but also "supratruth" revealed. The poet here declares his indifference to visions; divine light, like divine miracles, is too much for him. . . . Perhaps feeling that he would not be able to cope with the impact of immediate experience, the poet prefers the structured experience found in books and poetry. . . . He gladly embraces even bondage and the pain of an ascetic discipline; chains (*verigi*) are sweet to him, he declares.

The poet's disinclination towards contact with fellow beings, his love for inanimate objects, and his confessions where he declares his soul to be "cold as the realm of snow" . . . indicate why sharp pain is needed in his poetic world. It helps him overcome indifference, stirs up suppressed feelings, and stimulates poetic activity. This function of pain is clearly shown in a poem written in 1910 entitled **"Na večernem asfal'te,"** where the image of the wasp sting is reintroduced. . . . Impressions of street life "penetrate" the observer like sharp, well-realized pain, and this quality transforms them into "quivering sensations." . . . (pp. 388-91)

An essential element in what might be called this acupuncture technique is its deliberateness. The epithet "slow" often appears in connection with sharp pain in Brjusov's poetry, for example, in the poem **"Sebast'jan"** which demonstrates the principle of deliberate pain slowly devastating area after area. The saint's sufferings clearly serve as an allegory of the poet's own martyrdom, as the saint is consumed in "slow fire" and wounded by arrows, which are likened to "tender wasp stings." The image of the poet at the stake recurs in Brjusov's poetry and is central in the well-known **"Poètu."** . . . It is perhaps not entirely just to imply that Brjusov's poet never is capable of suffering more than "surface exposure" to pain [as Victor Erlich suggests]. Not only is Blok's poet frequently "burnt to ashes" (e.g., in "Snežnyj koster" . . .), but so is Brjusov's, even though it takes him considerably longer. . . . The essential aspect of the poet's experience of pain is a full analytic perception of the sensation, with no obscuring, intoxicating, or ecstatic elements. (p. 391)

Consistent with Brjusov's preference for the clear and sharp outline, for the limited and narrow, is his vertical concept of space and time. Each day is to the poet a complete entity, separated from the next by a "thin but fine net" (from *Méditations,* the poem **"Tonkoj, no častoju setkoj"** . . .) The poet's glance may wander between the extremes of up and down but rarely moves sideways to cover a horizontal surface; rarely can one see the whole sky. He vizualizes an abyss, and to fall into it means to "fall eternally" (**"Svivajutsja blednye teni"** . . .). In this situation the poet asks where salvation is to be found, "from the abyss or from above," but while the alternatives appear to be open, he almost invariably favors descent. When he does undertake an ascent, as in the poem **"Lestnica,"** . . . it causes him great effort. . . . Secretly the poet would like to slip so that he might become "a falling star on the sky of being." In the poem **"V otvet,"** . . . with its famous image of the ox as a symbol of the poet's art, the poet moves on a horizontal surface, a field, but the movement takes place along the furrows of the field. . . . (pp. 391-92)

Brjusov's frequent descents into infernal regions have been noted by critics. Inferno, the labyrinth of the Minotaur, Hades—these are the termini for many journeys undertaken by Symbolists of both generations. (p. 392)

What is hell, Brjusov's terminus? Hell proves to be a place where clarity reigns and recognition is possible, to a certain extent. In the poem **"V restorane,"** . . . where the doors to the restaurant are the doors to hell, the scene is drenched in light, which keeps the patrons from losing their way. In the merciless blue light, contours are deepened and shadow effects are created, reminding one of the drawings of Toulouse-Lautrec. . . . A "ray of sunlight" emanating from a crystal wine glass and "frenzied whips" are thin cutting elements which heighten the poet's awareness. Recognition is therefore possible, and in one of "the children of Satan" the poet recognizes his beloved. . . . The poet begs his beloved to look at him at the moment of torture. . . . But—and here a negative attitude towards limitation is expressed—no amount of passion and torture can overcome the limitations of the "I"; here as in **"V damask"** the "eyes remain closed" apparently. Hell has no outlets, and it is only an external circumstance, daybreak, which releases the poet until the next visit to hell.

The poet thus has the mentality of a "man in a shell," where fear of open space is combined with uneasiness within the shell, as in the poem **"Sumasšedšij."** . . . The mental disorders described here could be diagnosed as agoraphobia combined with persecution mania. . . . This narrow existence is compensated for by grandiose and destructive dreams, which take the form of a gross misrepresentation of reality. Watching the sunset set the city aflame, the deranged protagonist of the poem regards himself as the cause of these "fires" and watches with pyromanic delight as walls are consumed. Hidden away in a coffin of snow which he has made himself, this would-be Nero delights in destruction until he is overtaken by the fear of persecution. . . . As Maksimov points out with reference to this passage, Brjusov is the first Russian poet to discover the horror, not of real danger, but of the lack of danger—the *horror vacui,* the feeling that the absence of real danger may be more terrifying than its presence. . . . This presentation of a deranged mentality may well be an allegory of the poet's situation, namely, the situation of the isolated poet who transforms nature into unreal visions and is persecuted by Nemesis for this attempt against God-given creation.

The poet who delights in visions of crumbling walls and discovers in "exitless hell" the limitations of knowledge seems to be ambivalent towards these limits, which elsewhere he praises. Whether he accepts it or not, he sees it as *the* existential condition of man. "Like animals we have made dwellings out of caves," the poet states in **"Oblegči nam stradanija, Bože!"** . . . , and he calls for a "last cover," a shroud, a final veiling of all perspective as a means of salvation.

In Brjusov's poetry one also finds a longing to forge the chain of separate moments and experiences into an uninterrupted line. In **"L'ennui de vivre"** . . . the poet confesses to being tired of living day by day, in a multitude of miniature prisons, of being fettered by the links of a heavy chain of memories and fragmented experience. The poet of consciousness and clarity of mind longs for oblivion or a road which leads to "the

majestic silence of wide fields"; he longs for a lonely freedom. If the poet reaches any solution at all to the contradiction between the inherent limitations of existence and the desire for freedom, it is in the hope that barbaric hordes, the "approaching huns" (**"Grjaduščie gunny"** . . .), may break through the isolation and decadent solipsism of the poet and his generation. Hoping for liberation in the future, it is, however, not the perspective of limitless freedom that entices the poet. In **"K sčastlivym"** . . . the poet hopes for a future which he views as a synthesis between freedom and the limit. . . . One could speak here of a Marxist solution, for it is this interpretation of freedom as the full achievement of one limited goal after the other, presumably ad infinitum (the thirst for knowledge will be "sleepless"), which perhaps casts some light on Brjusov's acceptance of a Marxist-Leninist world view, as well as on his prerevolutionary admiration for strong men capable of defining and reaching a goal. Freedom will be in man's possession when he (out of free will) limits himself and refrains from desiring the impossible, from wanting the unrealizable, from striving beyond himself—when he sees himself not as a link in a chain but as a stage towards a goal.

Brjusov's attitudes towards limitation, then, are several: a morbid delight in distinct sensations, which are heightened by pain and enjoyed in loneliness, within the confines of the poet's chamber and his ego; an uneasiness within the shell, where delight in pain is transformed into a sense of frustration; and the vision of a synthesis between limitation and freedom, achieved by strong men, where pain no longer has any place and limited desires find full expression in "realized beauty." These attitudes overlap, but the first attitude dominates during the poet's early period, the third in the later poetry. Although the poet in his typical pluralist fashion claims to have been open to a variety of aesthetic systems . . . and although he treated a great variety of themes (the lonely man as hero, madman and poet, the barbaric masses, refined pleasures and simple work, to mention but a few), it is in the poems based on the poetics of the limit where Brjusov achieves his best results. His most successful poems are small in format, expressing a single thought, mood, or sensation. (pp. 392-94)

[Between the poetry of Brjusov and that of Blok's, there are] some points of contact stemming from a shared acute awareness of the limitations of existence and the need for pain. Both poets try various ways of living with limitation, and both their systems include a protest against the system—the dissatisfaction with limitation in Brjusov's case, the disappointment with limitless freedom in Blok's. Both poets, in spite of their basically different existential attitudes, often find themselves in similar situations. As the "broad poet" splits into doubles or hides his wounds, he is pushed into a shell, just as the "narrow poet" finds himself there because of his fear of the void when he realizes that cosmos too is a prison. Both poets look to the future for a solution to their problems and those of their generation. But the differences remain even in similarity. The poet who accepts the limit and compensates for limitation within his shell, faces himself there and endures, as is manifested in his "portioning out" of experience and his acceptance of "slow pain." The poet who protests against the limit flees from an overly acute awareness of the self and transfers his quest for knowledge to another plane. Likewise, the "future solution" is similar on the surface only, as one calls for men who make the very principle of limitation their strength and the other for romantic heroes and criminals, whose very criminality is taken in a Dostoevskian sense as a guarantee that they will transgress the limit, presumably in the direction of good. The Romantic poet cannot reconcile himself to the limit, even when all evidence speaks against him. In spite of the emotionality of Blok's quest there is a great deal of analysis in it, and there is a great deal of emotion, however suppressed, in Brjusov's quest, in spite of its rationalism. (pp. 399-400)

> *Irene Masing-Delic, "Limitation and Pain in Brjusov's and Blok's Poetry," in* Slavic and East European Journal *(© 1975 by AATSEEL of the U.S., Inc.), Vol. 19, No. 4, Winter, 1975, pp. 388-402.**

MARTIN P. RICE (essay date 1975)

[*In the following section from his* Valery Briusov and the Rise of Russian Symbolism, *Rice discusses Bryusov's artistic theories, comparing and contrasting them with the theories of other Russian Symbolists and Decadents.*]

By 1905 the complexion of Modernism's mainstream . . . had undergone a fundamental transition, one that might be characterized as a transition from Decadence to Symbolism. (p. 70)

Although Briusov had abandoned Decadence, . . . it would be fallacious to assume that he was [by 1905] a Symbolist in the same sense as Bely, Viacheslav Ivanov, Ellis, and Blok himself, not to mention Merezhkovsky. It was precisely the absence of any mystical philosophy or metaphysics to be served by the new art that distinguished Briusov's brand of Symbolism from that of the above-named poets. As Victor Erlich points out, while Russian Symbolism—with the very prominent exception of Briusov—sought an "integrated world view . . . Verlaine, Laforgue, and Mallarmé were primarily concerned with evolving a new form of poetic expression." For Briusov, and this is of particular importance, Symbolism was rather Mallarméism (in Chulkov's expression), that is, "a new form of poetic expression" should indeed be its only concern, whether in Russia or in Europe. Briusov would never have been able to agree with Viacheslav Ivanov's famous maxim that Russian Symbolism "could not be, and did not want to be merely art." For Briusov there was no such thing as merely art, there was Art, and Art was not a metaphysic.

Certainly any consideration of Briusov's esthetic views must take into account which of his ideas were sincerely held and which were no more than "lip service" to the Symbolist "image." This is not an easy task; nevertheless, if we survey his critical and theoretical pronouncements over a longer period of time, say from 1895 to 1905, we are able to observe a decided degree of consistency in relation to certain views that would seem to have little bearing, if any, on the Symbolist "image" as such. We may, therefore, assume that these ideas and views are among those which were sincerely held by the poet and not maintained merely for propagandizing purposes.

Perhaps the fundamental difference between Briusov's estimation of Symbolism's place in art and that of his many opponents is to be found in his basic conception of art. In his opinion no literary school was an end unto itself, but only a way station along the road of art's eternal evolution. This view was made evident as early as 1897 when Briusov delivered an address entitled **"Toward a History of Symbolism."** In it he stated, ". . . individual literary schools—and among them Symbolism as well—are only stages, moments in this evolution [of modern poetry]." He sees Symbolism as continuing the work begun by the Romantics and furthered by the pre-Raphaelites who "judged and rejected the form and content of previous poetry" and "cleared the way for the new poetry."

. . . Now these movements have yielded to Symbolism, the mission of which "is to create a new poetical language, to rework the means of poetry anew." . . . For Briusov, poetry and art seem to be developing according to a natural progression, the eventual goal of which is "freedom in art." Symbolism is only a tool to be used in attaining this freedom; thus he writes in **"Toward a History of Symbolism"**: "I do not hope that Symbolism will develop further. It is only a transitionary stage [on the road] to the new poetry. Apparently it has already fulfilled its task. The old poetry is lying in ruins . . . At the same time, Symbolism has created a totally new organ (not yet put to the test) for the transmission of the soul's innermost dynamics." . . . (pp. 70-2)

The above remarks, to be sure, did not reflect Briusov's final views; they do, however, reflect his esthetic point of departure as far as Symbolism is concerned and this never changed.

We can see the continuity of his thought in the next statement of his artistic beliefs (and his first protracted one), *On Art,* which appeared in 1899. (p. 72)

In *On Art* Briusov maintains that art serves to "preserve for all time" the moment that has passed. It is the only means by which human experience may be preserved; but he who is able to recognize the fleeting moment as such, that is, as an important, never-to-be-repeated part of existence, also possesses the two most important traits of the true creator: the ability to recognize himself, his own soul, and the even more essential ability *to understand* his soul. What sets the artist apart from the others who may possess these abilities of self-recognition and self-understanding is his capacity to retell what he has understood in a manner that will make it accessible to the souls of other individuals. . . . (pp. 72-3)

We may here observe what—to Briusov's way of thinking—can be considered the only true justification of art; art is justified because it is an act of communication. The soul is ordinarily isolated because each man's perception of the world about him is unique. From an awareness of this isolation comes the need to communicate one's vision to the souls of other men, and, ideally, to find a unity with them. According to Briusov such a unity of souls is possible only through art . . . , however, never through "art for art's sake." . . .

Briusov, generally considered a "pure esthete," declares that "there is no sense in art for art's sake." . . . Real art—"utilitarian art" in the Briusovian sense—contains but one characteristic, originality; "art always creates something new." . . . And originality comes only at the time of inspiration, that is, during "a moment of greater feeling." . . .

It is important to note, however, that this "inspired originality" is not necessarily an originality of content. Purely innovative *form* has its own value. While defending Balmont's genius in a letter to Pertsov, Briusov simultaneously defends the integrity of the value of poetry in and for itself. Pertsov had attacked Balmont for the latter's deviations from reality. Briusov replied: "And don't you consider it worth anything that this deviation from reality makes it possible for Balmont to introduce unheard of words into his poetry, to become intoxicated by the exotic names? . . . Can it be true that you do not know how to enjoy verse as verse—exclusive of its content—only its sound, only its images, only its rhymes?"

In the same letter Briusov explicitly details his belief that the act of poetic communication is not attained solely through content, that is, through ideas expressed by words alone; there is no way of knowing if the ideas expressed by a lyricist are really his own sincerely held precepts or whether they came upon him while in an "alien mood." Better to become united with the poet's thoughts through his art than through the ideas expressed in his semantics, for "... in every verse, in the deployment of words, in the selection of epithets, everywhere the poet remains himself, preserves his individuality and, consequently, his world view, his philosophy. How can one find it there? How can one gather gleams in a wisp of light?" (pp. 73-4)

The above directs our attention to a further fundamental difference between Briusov's esthetic ideas and those of the St. Petersburg Symbolists; . . . this difference lies in Briusov's attitudes toward craftsmanship and toward the concept of "the literary school." In *On Art* he writes concerning the craft: "It is imperative to be acquainted with the external devices of an artistic creation, imperative to make oneself completely familiar with them. For in art there is much that is conventional and which will long continue to be conventional. *Mood* [that is, content] *and that in which it is expressed—words, sounds, and tints—are heterogeneous"* (. . . my italics).

With this passage in mind, we are better able to understand Briusov's devotion to technical mastery. We are also better able to understand why his intense study of the technical aspects of poetry was greeted with such contempt by many of his critics. Briusov's critics, chiefly other poets, were not aware that their conception of the nature of inspiration and Briusov's were fundamentally different. Content and form were "heterogeneous" for Briusov, for the others "homogeneous." Briusov finds the total work of art derived from three sources: 1) inspiration and resultant content come from within the artist himself, 2) images and coloring come from the epoch, and, 3) technique comes from the literary school. . . . (pp. 74-5)

[Briusov] saw Symbolism's contribution to art primarily as twofold: first, it continued the battle begun by Romanticism against artistic inhibition . . . , and second, it had "correctly evaluated the meaning of words for the artist." . . . And it is in this belief in the role of words that Briusov was a Symbolist, a Symbolist in the French sense, in the sense of impressions, moods, hints, and correspondences, in the sense of a continuation of Romanticism.

But Briusov's fellow Russian Symbolists, too, shared this respect for the power of words and their role in art. Their divergent path is to be found in their attitude toward the movement. For the others Symbolism was the one true faith, the faith without which art was unattainable. For Briusov, who was ready "to worship Christ and Satan," the essence of an artistic work was not to be found in the doctrine or metaphysics of the artist's school, rather, "the essence of an artistic work is the soul of its creator, *and it is all the same by what means one approaches it"* (. . . my italics).

Although Briusov was more than once to modify his esthetic theory, he never deviated in his attitude toward literary schools and their role. And in the end result it was precisely this attitude, which elevated the individual's pathos over that of the school, that was at the root of his subsequent split with the movement. Although Briusov eventually stopped preaching the doctrine of "extreme individualism" which characterized his earliest days, he never stopped believing in it and creating and working in accordance with it. (p. 75)

By the beginning of 1906, Briusov had reached his esthetic maturity and had overcome the narrow bias of parochial artistic

interests. Symbolism as a school had served its purpose, both for Briusov, by propelling him to the front ranks of Russia's literary luminaries, and for the advance of Russian literature in general, by finally freeing it from the tight strictures of the second half of the nineteenth century. (p. 89)

Martin P. Rice, " 'The Scales' Years (1904-1905)," (originally published in a different form as "The Aesthetic Views of Valerij Brjusov," in Slavic and East European Journal, Vol. 17, No. 1, Spring, 1973), in his Valery Briusov and the Rise of Russian Symbolism (© 1975 by Ardis Publishers), Ardis, 1975, pp. 65-89.*

JOAN DELANEY GROSSMAN   (essay date 1980)

[*The translator of Bryusov's diary, Grossman examines the often-neglected volume* Me eum esse, *providing much biographical background, and relating* Me eum esse *to the Caucasus tradition of Mikhail Lermontov and Alexander Pushkin.*]

Me eum esse, Briusov's second volume of poetry, was composed largely during his three month sojourn in Piatigorsk during the summer of 1896, following the disastrous critical reception of the two editions of his first collection, *Chefs d'oeuvre.* It has been usual to dismiss *Me eum esse,* along with much of what Briusov published before *Tertia Vigilia* in 1900, as either youthful folly or excessive zeal in the cause of baiting bourgeois taste. *Me eum esse* in particular, with its address to a young poet ("**Iunomu poetu**" . . .) advising him "do not love, do not sympathize, worship only yourself without limit," has been regarded as the peak of Briusov's individualism, one of the curiosities of the Decadent movement. During the next few years, as Briusov worked toward a more mature philosophical position, his individualism took other forms, less blatantly egoistic. Nonetheless, *Me eum esse* is more interesting and more important in Briusov's own work, and consequently in the development of modern Russian poetry, than most students of Symbolism and Decadence have recognized. . . . In his diary under February 6, 1896, smarting from recent criticism, he wrote: "My future book *It Is I* will be a gigantic joke on the whole human race. There will not be a single sensible word in it—and of course it will find admirers. *Chefs d'oeuvre* was weak in that it was middle-of-the-road: too poetic for the critics and for the public, and too simple for the Symbolists. Idiot! And I thought I was writing seriously!" (pp. 285-86)

Me eum esse, its largest part composed within a few weeks, offers a capsule history of the poet's soul over the previous year or more and a statement of his present beliefs and goals in art. It contains a foreword and thirty-six poems arranged in six cycles: **"Zavety," "Videniia," "Skitaniia," "Liubov'." "Veianie smerti,"** and **"V bor'be."** The last two are sub-titled **"Proshloe."**

The cyclical form is of the first importance. It should be mentioned, if only in passing, that *Me eum esse* seems to offer the earliest sustained example in modern Russian poetry of the kind of cyclization which was to become so important in the work of Blok, Pasternak, and many other Russian poets. Briusov conceived of a book of poems as a unified structure in which the poem within the section and the section within the book had a place as obligatory as chapters in a novel. (p. 287)

The cyclization of *Me eum esse* represented not only Briusov's esthetic conviction but his consciousness of completing a cycle of experience which demanded expression in some connected and unified form. This experience was to be rendered through an arrangement of poems which demanded sequential and continuous reading, from beginning to end. The programmatic poems of the first section, **"Zavety,"** represent his final position, while **"Videniia," "Skitaniia,"** and **"Liubov'"** retrace his pursuit of the ideal beauty he longs to worship, and the fifth and sixth sections portray the "dark night" through which his soul attained its present state of relative certainty and authority. All of this had to be seen as an ordered whole if the experience was to be conveyed at all. (p. 288)

The remarkable unity and coherence of the volume brought something new into Russian poetry. The quality of the poems themselves also merits some comment since they evidence Briusov's great and growing artistry with words. Not surprisingly they are uneven in value. Some of them were probably included for their relevance to a given cycle. They were also experimental in a modest but fruitful way. The sense of rhythm and rhyme and their relation to meaning, which was very soon a major concern of Briusov's theoretical work, is evident in many of these poems. So is the *vertical* interworking of sense with sound harmony, notable in poems like **"Kak tsarstvo belogo snega,"** where the play of combinations like *snega / strannaia nega / sna* and *neizmenno / nezemnoi / vselennoi* bind together the poem's sound and meaning. Briusov had abandoned the experiment with stanza form which marked *Chefs d'oeuvre*. The effect of *Me eum esse* is at once more severe and more polished, but that does not prevent some poems and even whole cycles, such as the final one, from being remarkably melodic. This, then, in summary is the book whose foreword acknowledged it far from finished. But its author hoped these hints would convey the rest of his intention to a "future friend," the symbolic "young poet" to whom the first poem is addressed. *Me eum esse* represents for most readers Briusov's defiant individualism of these years, a stance which most Soviet critics and others treat as a youthful aberration, from which he duly retreated in order to embrace "reality." The total picture is in fact more complicated. Briusov retained his individualism, but rejected "pure Beauty" as the object of the artist's pursuit. During the three years which separated *Me eum esse* from *Tertia Vigilia*, . . . he reformulated and developed his earlier conception of art. Art became for him a means of cognition, and the artist's soul was the instrument for attaining whatever knowledge lay beyond the generally accepted bounds of reality. The individual soul thus became an even more central feature of the artistic process, since it must absorb all reality into itself and transcend it. *Me eum esse* represented a false direction for Briusov, but insofar as it reinforced his individualism, it left its trace in the corpus of Briusov's mature poetry, from *Tertia Virgilia* on. (pp. 291-92)

> *Joan Delaney Grossman, "'Me eum esse': Valerii Briusov and the Caucasus Tradition in Russian Literature," in* The Russian Review *(copyright 1980 by The Russian Review, Inc.), Vol. 39, No. 3, July, 1980, pp. 285-300.*

MILTON EHRE   (essay date 1982)

[*Ehre summarizes Bryusov's career, concluding with comments on* The Diary of Valery Bryusov (1893-1905).]

[Bryusov] must be the only poet ever to have taken the lumbering ox as his Muse. The aim of his life, he said, was to win two lines in the history of world literature, and he set about it with frightening determination. . . . Primarily a poet, he also

made his mark as a critic, theoretician, and writer of prose fiction. The modernist reevaluation of the enigmatic genius of Gogol stems from Bryusov's reading, and, along with Andrey Bely, he inaugurated the systematic study of Russian versification. His novel, *The Fiery Angel* . . . , is one of the superior examples of Russian modernism.

Bryusov's major contribution may have been as the impresario of modernism—for this alone he has earned his two lines in history. In 1894-95 he issued three pamphlets under the title *Russian Symbolists* (in Russia the terms Symbolism and Decadence were used interchangeably). The collection gave the public a glimpse of recent French poetry—Baudelaire, Verlaine, Mallarmé, Maeterlinck—and included derivative exercises in the new style, most by Bryusov himself. It achieved a quick *succés de scandale*. Bryusov's one-line poem—**"O cover your pale legs"**—derided by the press, as was the entire enterprise, became notorious. Bryusov was not a man to be daunted by ridicule. By 1900 he had made himself the major force of the publishing house Scorpion, which was a focal point of the modernist movement, and from 1904 to 1909 he was the de facto editor of its magnificent journal, *The Scales* [Vesy]. Through indefatigable energy, a flair for promotion (and self-promotion), and organizational skills (which were dictatorial), Bryusov helped place Symbolism at the center of Russian literary culture.

His thirst for power was insatiable, and it has given him a bad name. Bryusov, however, had a keen intuition of the poetic needs of his age. He realized that the old literary manners had been exhausted. The mission of Symbolism, as he put it in an early essay, **"To the History of Symbolism"** . . . , was "to create a new poetic language, to rework the devices of poetry." Since the age of Pushkin poetry had languished in the shadow of the novel. Symbolism revived its energies and revolutionized its shape. Bryusov's own work was exemplary. (pp. 331-32)

As a poet Bryusov is cold and impersonal—"My soul is cold," he writes in one poem and "To be without people, to be alone!" in another. His finest poems are carefully chiseled, earning for him Bely's epithet, "poet of marble and bronze." The scandalous Decadent poems won him his notoriety, but he also composed some lovely nature lyrics in which a humanless landscape is frozen in the immutability of a moment and overlaid with "symbolist" nuance. His language is solemn, sonorous, richly colored, and humorless. Many poems are freighted with the furniture of world culture, so that reading him can be like walking through a museum of antiquities. Essentially, Bryusov is an academic poet—"the inventor of a poetic machine" in Ehrenburg's biting phrase. When the machine works well, it can be an impressive performance. His poetry is seldom inspired. The words may be right, but they fail to surprise us with the joy of discovery. Despite his insistence on pure poetry, Bryusov can be quite rhetorical, even didactic. As was the fashion, he proclaims the virtue of vice and heroic individualism—"To recognize my free 'I,'" as he says in a poem appropriately entitled, **"To Myself"** [**"K samomu sobe"**]. . . . For all his talk of the self, he stoically resists allowing felt experience to surface in his poetry. Mochulsky found "a certain grandeur" in his self-enclosed world. It is the icy and forbidding grandeur of a truly decadent mind.

Given the kind of man Bryusov was, it is not surprising that his *Diary* is so uninteresting. He has no curiosity about himself or others. Ideas apparently bore him. What consumes him is ambition—from getting top grades in school to scrambling to the top of the literary heap. In a famous poem, **"To the Poet"**

["**Poetu**"] . . . Bryusov asserted the Flaubertian doctrine that "all life is but a means / For brightly singing verses." A trip to Yalta incites a flash of excitement over the mountains and the sea, but he quickly cools, consoling himself that he got four poems out of the venture. . . . Venice appeals to him because its people are "not people"—only parts of an aesthetic landscape. . . . Writing of Bely . . . , Bryusov says that his fellow poet wanted "to behave as if unicorns actually did exist." This perhaps was the aim of Bryusov and his generation—to poeticize reality, to color life with the imaginings of art. In a backward and brutal country like Russia, "art for art's sake" might have served a civilizing purpose had history turned out differently. Did Bryusov ever stop to consider to what extent his unbridled individualism and aesthetic hedonism mirrored the values of the bourgeois society he held in such contempt? (pp. 332-33)

> *Milton Ehre, "Book Reviews: 'The Diary of Valery Bryusov (1893-1905)'" (reprinted by permission of the author), in* Modern Philology, *Vol. 79, No. 3, February, 1982, pp. 331-33.*

ADDITIONAL BIBLIOGRAPHY

Binyon, T. J. "Valery Bryusov and the Nature of Art." *Oxford Slavonic Papers* n.s. VII (1974): 96-111.
Clarifies Bryusov's poetic theories, relating them to the ideas of other Symbolists.

Grossman, Joan Delaney. Introduction to *The Diary of Valery Bryusov (1893-1905),* by Valery Bryusov, edited and translated by Joan Delaney Grossman, pp. 1-32. Berkeley and Los Angeles: University of California Press, 1980.
An excellent biocritical survey of Bryusov's life and work.

Gumilev, Nikolai. "Bryusov, Zenkevich, Kuzmina-Karavaeva, Ivanov" and "Bryusov, Severyanin, Khlebnikov, Komarovsky, Golike and Vilborg, Annensky, Sologub." In his *Nikolai Gumilev on Russian Poetry,* edited and translated by David Lapeza, pp. 105-08, pp. 129-39. Ann Arbor, Mich.: Ardis, 1977.*
Reprints translated contemporary reviews of Bryusov's work.

Maguire, Robert A. "Macrocosm or Microcosm? The Symbolists on Russia." *Review of National Literatures* III, No. 1 (Spring 1972): 125-52.*
Helpful survey of the theories and practitioners of Russian Symbolism, including a short discussion of Bryusov's contributions.

Maslenikov, Oleg A. "Andrey Biely and Valeri Bryusov." In his *The Frenzied Poets: Andrey Biely and the Russian Symbolists,* pp. 99-127. Berkeley: University of California Press, 1952.*
Recounts Bryusov's role in the Russian Symbolist movement and the story of his relationship with Bely.

Reeve, F. D. "Dobroljubov and Brjusov: Symbolists Extremists." *Slavic and East European Journal* VIII, No. 3 (1964): 292-301.*
Discusses the personal and artistic relationship between the two poets.

Struk, Danylo. "The Great Escape: Principal Themes in Valerij Brjusov's Poetry." *Slavic and East European Journal* XII, No. 4 (1968): 407-23.
Studies the unifying themes of "loneliness, love, and lore" in Bryusov's poetry.

Anton (Pavlovich) Chekhov

1860-1904

(Also transliterated as Chekov, Tchehov, Tchekhov, Čechov, Čexov, Čekov, Cecov, Čechov, Chekhoff, and Chehov; also wrote under pseudonym of Antosha Chekhonte) Russian dramatist, short story writer, and novelist.

In every respect Chekhov is the most significant Russian author of the literary generation to succeed Leo Tolstoy and Fedor Dostoevski. Preeminent for his stylistic innovations in both fictional and dramatic forms, he is revered for his depth of insight into the human condition. While Chekhov's most characteristic writings began in extremely personal feelings and observations, their ultimate form was one of supreme emotional balance and stylistic control. It is precisely this detached, rational artfulness that distinguishes his work from the confessional abandons of Dostoevski or the psychological fantasies of Nikolai Gogol. This artistic control makes Chekhov one of the masters of what has come to be a well-defined modern style of story-writing, and his works have been widely influential, especially among English and American writers.

Chekhov's grandfather was a serf who bought his freedom, and his father was the owner of a small grocery business in Taganrog, the village where Chekhov was born. When the family business went bankrupt in 1876, the Chekhovs, without Anton, moved to Moscow to escape creditors; Anton remained in Taganrog until 1879 in order to complete his education and earn a scholarship to Moscow University. There he studied medicine and, after graduation in 1884, went into practice. By this time he was publishing sketches, mostly humorous, in popular magazines. Chekhov did this to support his family, and although he wrote literally hundreds of these pieces, he did not take them very seriously. In 1885, however, Chekhov moved to St. Petersburg and became friends with A. S. Suvorin, editor of the journal *Novoe Vremja,* who encouraged the young writer to develop his obvious gifts. At this time, and for several years afterward, Chekhov was profoundly influenced by Tolstoy's ideas on ascetic morality and nonresistance to evil. But after Chekhov visited the penal settlement on the island of Sakhalin, which he would make the subject of a humanitarian study, he found Tolstoy's moral code an insufficient answer to human suffering. It was in the late 1880s that Chekhov began to produce what is regarded as his mature and most individual work in the short story form.

Chekhov's three periods in the short story genre—early sketches, stories influenced by Tolstoy, and later stories—comprise the major stages of his fiction. The early sketches display many of the traits of popular fiction: swift development of action, superficial yet vivid characterization, and surprise endings. But while many of these pieces were written as humor, they also contain qualities which led Maxim Gorky to call them "tragic humor." Gorky wrote of Chekhov: "One has only to read his 'humorous' stories with attention to see what a lot of cruel and disgusting things, behind the humorous words and situations, had been observed by the author with sorrow and were concealed by him." Chekhov's next major period was influenced by the later fiction and moral thought of Tolstoy, principally the older writer's ideas on sexual abstinence, devotion to the plight of others, strict antimaterialism, and

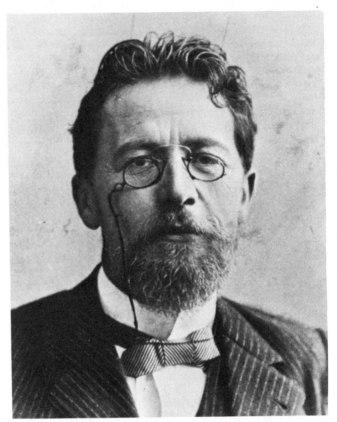

nonresistance to the natural evil of the temporal world. During this period Chekhov also believed that literature had the power to effect positive change in the world and that it was obliged to critique the lives of its readers. In consequence, stories like "Niscij" ("The Beggar") were written to convey a message, though this message is nonetheless delivered with the subtle artistry and restraint Chekhov cultivated throughout his career. This second period of Chekhov's fiction includes many features characteristic of all his works. "Step" ("The Steppe"), which was the author's first story to appear in a serious literary journal, substitutes for the mechanical tensions of plot a tightly-strung network of images, character portraits, and dense actionless scenes of commonplace tedium. Rather than detracting from reader involvement, these qualities contribute to an overall effect of tense realism which serves its author's private vision of art and morality, while also depicting a more general version of real life in an antisentimental manner. The banal tragedies of everyday existence form the substance of much of Chekhov's fiction. Even the more extraordinary tales—such as "Spat" ("Sleepy"), in which an overtired nursemaid strangles a baby so that she may rest undisturbed—are related in a tone of voice that betrays no deliberate intent aside from an objective, artistic rendering of events. "Skucnaja istorija" ("A Boring Story"), one of the masterpieces of Chekhov's Tolstoyan period, constructs a portrait of the author's most familiar character type: the unfulfilled, unproductive, ineffectual individual whose life remains dreamlike in its lack of purpose and direction.

In the final period of his fiction, Chekhov rejected and attacked his former master's ideas. "Duel" ("The Duel") critically examines the antisexuality message of Tolstoy's *Kreutzer Sonata*, and "Moya zhizn" ("My Life") elaborates on the adverse effects in general of the Tolstoyan dogma. In "Palata nomer 6" ("Ward Number 6"), a story of madness and misery, Chekhov opposed the doctrine of nonresistance to evil by depicting the downfall of one of its proponents. This is considered the period of Chekhov's full genius in the short story form, the era in which his art and insight achieved the perfection that placed him among the greatest figures in modern literature. As J. Middleton Murry wrote in 1920: "Tchehov is a standard by which modern literary effort must be measured, and the writer of prose or poetry who is not sufficiently single-minded to apply the standard to himself is of no particular account."

Chekhov's interest and participation in the theater has its origins in his schooldays at Taganrog, when he acted and wrote for the local playhouse. His first serious effort in drama was written during his residence in Moscow. This work, *Pyesa bez nazvaniya (That Worthless Fellow Platonov)*, is Chekhov's earliest surviving play and initiates the first of two major periods of the author's dramatic writings. The works of this first dramatic period are characterized by the theatrical conventions and subject matter of the times. *Platonov*, a long and somewhat declamatory social drama, features a leading character whose reformist ideals are negated by the indifference of others and by his own ineffectuality. Chekhov's next drama, *Ivanov*, is less bulky and more realistic than its predecessor, though critics still view it as a theatrically exaggerated and traditional period piece. Written during the Tolstoyan phase of Chekhov's works, *Leshy (The Wood Demon)* was his first attempt at the artistic realism fully achieved only in his later dramas. This didactic morality play on the theme of vice and virtue is criticized for the same dramatic faults as the other works of this period. *The Wood Demon* later reappeared in a revised version as *Dyadya Vanya (Uncle Vanya)*.

The dramas of Chekhov's second period comprise all of his major work in the theater. These plays are primarily noted for their technique of "indirect action," a method which assigns the most violent or intensely dramatic action to the intervals between the portions of the play actually seen by the audience. The main action, then, is made up of conversations alluding to the unseen moments in the characters' lives. In this way Chekhov was able to study and convey more precisely the effects of crucial events on a character's personality. The first drama done in this manner was *Chayka (The Seagull)*. Written seven years after *The Wood Demon*, *The Seagull* was a complete failure in its opening performance at St. Petersburg. Two years later, however, it was produced successfully in Moscow under the direction of Constantin Stanislavski, who emphasized, some critics say overemphasized, the more dismal aspects of Chekhov's "art of melancholy." The artistic success of *The Seagull* is attributed by critics to a subtle interweaving of theme and character. The resulting scenario is one in which viewed action is reduced to a minimum and in which nuances of pacing and mood become paramount to the full realization of dramatic tension. This work inaugurated Chekhov's association with the Moscow Art Theater, which staged the rest of his major dramas: *Uncle Vanya*, *Tri sestry (The Three Sisters)*, and *Vishnevy sad (The Cherry Orchard)*. In 1901 Chekhov

married Olga Knipper, an actress with the Moscow Art Theater. Because of his worsening tuberculosis, from which he had suffered since 1884, Chekhov was forced to spend a great deal of time in European health resorts and was often separated from his wife, who was performing in Moscow. Chekhov died in a Black Forest spa at the age of forty-four.

In *The Seagull* and the dramas that followed, the mood and meaning hovers somewhere between the tragic and the comic. *The Three Sisters* is the closest to tragedy among these works, the play which most heavily contributes to Chekhov's reputation as a portrayer of futile existences and a forerunner of the modernist tradition of the absurd. Among Chekhov's earliest plays are a number of comic farces, and he subtitled *The Cherry Orchard* "A Comedy," genuinely intending it to be viewed as such. Often interpreted as a nostalgic parable on the passing of an older order in Russian history, this late work again displays what is perhaps Chekhov's most persistent theme: the triumph of ignorance and vulgarity over the fragile traditions of elegance and nobility.

In comparison with the work of other great Russian authors, in particular the variety and vaulting ideological proportions of Tolstoy, Chekhov's stories and dramas are more uniform in mood and narrower in scope, frequently illustrating situations of hardship, boredom, and mundane suffering. The view of Chekhov as an utter pessimist, however, has always met with opposition, especially from those Soviet critics who see him as a chronicler of the degenerating land-owner classes during an era of imminent revolution. The exact relationship between Chekhov and his work has been a matter of interest for critics, and a distinction is often made to isolate the somber spirit of the stories and plays from the personal philosophy of their author. Chekhov in fact expressed optimism with regard to social progress, which he believed would be furthered by scientific advancements. Critics such as Ronald Hingley have attempted to modify the view of a pessimistic Chekhov, while at the same time avoiding the equally erroneous image of an optimistic one. In either case, Chekhov's prominent stature in world literature is not a consequence of his philosophy or worldview as much as it is based on fiction and dramas executed with a phenomenal artistry which permanently altered the literary standards for these genres.

(See also *TCLC*, Vol. 3 and *Contemporary Authors*, Vol. 104.)

PRINCIPAL WORKS

Pëstrye rasskazy   (short stories)   1886
Ivanov   (drama)   1887
   [*Ivanoff* published in *Plays*, 1912]
Nevinnye rechi   (short stories)   1887
V sumerkakh   (short stories)   1887
Leshy   (drama)   1889
   [*The Wood Demon*, 1926]
Rasskazy   (short stories)   1889
Chayka   (drama)   1896
   [*The Seagull* published in *Plays*, 1912]
*Dyadya Vanya   (drama)   1899
   [*Uncle Vanya* published in *Plays*, 1912]
Chekhov: Polnoe sobranie Sochineniy   (short stories and
   dramas)   1900-04
Tri sestry   (drama)   1901
   [*The Three Sisters*, 1922]
The Black Monk, and Other Stories   (short stories)   1903

Vishnevy sad (drama) 1904
  [*The Cherry Garden*, 1908; also published as *The Cherry Orchard*, 1912]
The Kiss, and Other Stories (short stories) 1908
Plays (dramas) 1912
The Darling, and Other Stories (short stories) 1916
The Duel, and Other Stories (short stories) 1916
The Lady with the Dog, and Other Stories (short stories) 1917
The Party, and Other Stories (short stories) 1917
The Wife, and Other Stories (short stories) 1918
The Witch, and Other Stories (short stories) 1918
The Bishop, and Other Stories (short stories) 1919
The Chorus Girl, and Other Stories (short stories) 1920
The Letters of Anton Chekhov (letters) 1920
The Horse-Stealers, and Other Stories (short stories) 1921
The Schoolmaster, and Other Stories (short stories) 1921
The Schoolmistress, and Other Stories (short stories) 1921
The Cook's Wedding, and Other Stories (short stories) 1922
Love, and Other Stories (short stories) 1922
**Pyesa bez nazvaniya* [first publication] (drama) 1923
  [*That Worthless Fellow Platonov*, 1930]
Polnoe sobranie sochinenii i pisem A. P. Chekhova (dramas, short stories, notebooks, diaries, and letters) 1944-51
The Oxford Chekhov. 9 vols. (short stories and dramas) 1964-80

*This work is a revision of the earlier *Leshy*.

**This work was written in 1881.

A. CAHAN (essay date 1899)

Chekhoff, who is neither a radical nor a conservative, but a man without convictions, . . . writes for no other "purpose" than the pleasure which he takes in his work. As a result, the applause which his genius received in the early days of his career was half-hearted and accompanied by howls of disapproval. (pp. 121-22)

[Since 1892,] Chekhoff has taken himself more seriously. His **"Ward No. 6,"** where a country physician—a lonely thinker and passionate reader, misunderstood by his neighbors—is locked up as a madman by his rival physician; **"The Black Friar,"** which portrays the picturesque hallucinations of an overworked professor and his misery upon recovering from his blissful megalomania; **"The Butterfly,"** which is the quiet tragedy of a good-natured man of science married to an unsuccessful painter, who, unable to appreciate her husband's gifts and the importance of his work, is abandoned to the recklessness of Bohemian life till she violates her plighted troth; **"The Kiss,"** which a shy bachelor received in a dark room from a charming woman, who mistook him for her lover, and the tragic-comic effect it had upon his psychology; **"The Peasants,"** where the grim truth of village life in Russia is laid bare—these and many other short stories and sketches are irresistible works of art, strong, deep, true, and beautiful. But they, too, are devoid of "underlying ideas;" and so, while the critics have come to agree that the appearance of a new story by Chekhoff is an

important event in the literary history of Russia, they still frown upon him as a kind of political heathen. (pp. 122-23)

"Chekhoff has talent and the power of observation," declares [Constantinovitch] Michailovsky, "but he lacks 'that which is called unifying idea or the God in the living man.' This is the key to the riddle why we all, who respect his gifts, are firmly convinced that he will never develop them to the full extent of their potential vigor."

The hero of **"A Dull Story"** and his author are representatives of a type which is quite common in Russia and Poland. Turgeneff has portrayed several varieties of this *Hamlet* of our times in his stories; and Sienkewitcz has made him the subject of his best psychological novel, "Without Dogma." As to Chekhoff, his **"Dull Story"** is not the only production in which his leading character is a man without a dogma. Several of his other tales have this type for their central figures. The rest treat of other types; each story "living by itself," and all of them reflecting the state of mind which is characteristic of their time. (p. 123)

Verisimilitude . . . is a first consideration; and no amount of cleverness and fine writing can atone for the lack of it. To win the attention of the educated Russian, it is absolutely necessary that the author should have the gift of making things seem real. Chekhoff possesses this gift in a marvellous degree. One of the striking features of his stories is their absolute naturalness. Korolenko, Potapenko, Gorki, and a score of lesser lights are endowed with a sense of character and can draw a lifelike picture; but Chekhoff, of all Russian writers of the younger generation, seems to tell a true story. It is impossible to read half a dozen sentences in any of his tales without beginning to feel that all was only spirited gossip about people with whom author and reader are personally acquainted. Chekhoff seems to be too keenly interested in these people, and too anxious to tell you about them, to indulge in a prettily turned phrase, a jest, or a piece of rhetoric. Indeed, his works teem with irresistible humor; his style is a model of grace; a few simple words sketch off the character so that it lives and moves before the reader; and, above all, almost every sentence exposes to view some interesting nook of the human soul. But all these results are achieved in a most casual way. The author enjoys his gossip too intensely to be aware of his own cleverness.

The stories mentioned, except **"The Peasants,"** have been selected, because they belong to those of Chekhoff's productions in which something happens, so that the "point" or the simple little plot can be presented in a nutshell. The typical Chekhoff story, however, the one which shows his genius at its best, is so absolutely storyless that there is not enough even to fill a nutshell. From five to ten thousand words are bestowed upon the most trivial bit of every-day life. But then it is life itself, not a mere *réchauffé* of it; and the plain, hum-drum people and things, to whom nothing out of the ordinary happens, turn out to be thrillingly interesting.

The great point of Chekhoff's genius is his wonderful artistic memory for the caprices and fleeting trifles of reality—for the wanton dissimilarities as well as for the similarities of life. Almost everything the author says sets the reader wondering how it ever occurred to him to mention such a thing at all. It seems to have so little in common with what writers, good or bad, usually put in their descriptions or dialogues. It is one of those evanescent flinders of life which one can neither remember nor invent, and which are as fresh and unexpected, in every instance, as they are characteristic of the period and place to which they relate. His stories are full of these little surprises, and the illusion is entrancingly complete. Tolstoy is the only writer who possesses this quality in a higher degree for psychical analysis; but even he yields first place to Chekhoff in the description of external phenomena. (pp. 123-24)

A. Cahan, "The Younger Russian Writers," in Forum and Century *(copyright, 1899), Vol. 28, No. 1, September, 1899, pp. 119-28.**

CONSTANTIN STANISLAVSKI (essay date 1924)

[*A prominent dramatic theorist and director with the Moscow Art Theater, Stanislavski staged* The Seagull *in Moscow with great success in 1898, after its failure in St. Petersburg two years earlier.*]

[After] my first acquaintance with Chekhov's **"Seagull"** I did not understand the essence, the aroma, the beauty of his play. . . . But some of the inner threads of the play attracted me, although I did not notice the evolution that had taken place in me. . . .

The Chekhov mood is that cave in which are kept all the unseen and hardly palpable treasures of Chekhov's soul, so often beyond the reach of mere consciousness. (p. 352)

Nemirovich-Danchenko and I approached the hidden riches each in his own way, Vladimir Ivanovich by the literary road and I by the road of the actor, the road of images. . . . Once we found that inner line of the play, which we could not define in words at that time, everything became comprehensible. . . . (pp. 352-53)

The conditions under which we produced **"The Seagull"** were complex and hard. The production was necessary to us because of the material circumstances of the life of our Theatre. Business was in a bad way. The administration hurried our labors. And suddenly Anton Pavlovich fell ill in Yalta with a new attack of tuberculosis. His spiritual condition was such that if **"The Seagull"** should fail as it did at its first production in Petrograd, the great poet would not be able to weather the blow. (p. 355)

I do not remember how we played. The first act was over. There was a gravelike silence. Knipper [Chekhov's wife] fainted on the stage. All of us could hardly keep our feet. . . . Then there were congratulations and embraces like those of Easter night, and ovations to Lilina, who played Masha, and who had broken the ice with her last words which tore themselves from her heart, moans washed with tears. This it was that had held the audience mute for a time before it began to roar and thunder in mad ovation.

We were no longer afraid of sending a telegram to our dear and beloved friend and poet. (p. 356)

At the special performance [Chekhov] seemed to be trying to avoid me. I waited for him in my dressing room, but he did not come. That was a bad sign. I went to him myself.

"Scold me, Anton Pavlovich," I begged him.

"Wonderful! Listen, it was wonderful! Only you need torn shoes and checked trousers."

He would tell me no more. What did it mean? Did he wish not to express his opinion? Was it a jest to get rid of me? Was he laughing at me? Trigorin in **"The Seagull"** was a young writer, a favorite of the women—and suddenly he was to wear torn shoes and checked trousers! I played the part in the most

elegant of costumes—white trousers, white vest, white hat, slippers, and a handsome make-up.

A year or more passed. Again I played the part of Trigorin in **"The Seagull"**—and during one of the performances I suddenly understood what Chekhov had meant.

"Of course, the shoes must be torn and the trousers checked, and Trigorin must not be handsome. In this lies the salt of the part: for young, inexperienced girls it is important that a man should be a writer and print touching and sentimental romances, and the Nina Zarechnayas, one after the other, will throw themselves on his neck, without noticing that he is not talented, that he is not handsome, that he wears checked trousers and torn shoes. Only afterwards, when the love affair with such "seagulls" is over, do they begin to understand that it was girlish imagination which created the great genius in their heads, instead of a simple mediocrity. Again, the depth and the richness of Chekhov's laconic remarks struck me. It was very typical and characteristic of him. (pp. 358-59)

Constantin Stanislavski, " 'The Seagull'," in his My Life in Art, *translated by J. J. Robbins (reprinted by permission of the publishers, Theatre Arts Books, 153 Waverly Place, New York, NY 10014; translation copyright, 1924, by Little, Brown, and Company; copyright, 1948, Elizabeth Reynolds Hapgood; copyright renewed 1952; also published as* Moia zhizn' v iskusstve, *Izd-vo. Gos. Akademii hudož mauk, 1926), Little, Brown, 1924 (and reprinted by Theatre Arts Books, 1948), pp. 352-59.*

VIRGINIA WOOLF (essay date 1925)

Our first impressions of Tchekov are not of simplicity but of bewilderment. What is the point of it, and why does he make a story out of this? we ask as we read story after story. A man falls in love with a married woman, and they part and meet, and in the end are left talking about their position and by what means they can be free from "this intolerable bondage".

" 'How? How?' he asked, clutching his head. . . . And it seemed as though in a little while the solution would be found and then a new and splendid life would begin." That is the end. A postman drives a student to the station and all the way the student tries to make the postman talk, but he remains silent. Suddenly the postman says unexpectedly, "It's against the regulations to take any one with the post." And he walks up and down the platform with a look of anger on his face. "With whom was he angry? Was it with people, with poverty, with the autumn nights?" Again, that story ends.

But is it the end, we ask? We have rather the feeling that we have overrun our signals; or it is as if a tune had stopped short without the expected chords to close it. These stories are inconclusive, we say, and proceed to frame a criticism based upon the assumption that stories ought to conclude in a way that we recognise. In so doing we raise the question of our own fitness as readers. Where the tune is familiar and the end emphatic—lovers united, villains discomfited, intrigues exposed—as it is in most Victorian fiction, we can scarcely go wrong, but where the tune is unfamiliar and the end a note of interrogation or merely the information that they went on talking, as it is in Tchekov, we need a very daring and alert sense of literature to make us hear the tune, and in particular those last notes which complete the harmony. Probably we have to read a great many stories before we feel, and the feeling is essential to our satisfaction, that we hold the parts together, and that Tchekov was not merely rambling disconnectedly, but struck now this note, now that with intention, in order to complete his meaning.

We have to cast about in order to discover where the emphasis in these strange stories rightly comes. Tchekov's own words give us a lead in the right direction. " . . . such a conversation as this between us", he says, "would have been unthinkable for our parents. At night they did not talk, but slept sound; we, our generation, sleep badly, are restless, but talk a great deal, and are always trying to settle whether we are right or not." Our literature of social satire and psychological finesse both sprang from that restless sleep, that incessant talking; but after all, there is an enormous difference between Tchekov and Henry James, between Tchekov and Bernard Shaw. Obviously—but where does it arise? Tchekov, too, is aware of the evils and injustices of the social state; the condition of the peasants appals him, but the reformer's zeal is not his—that is not the signal for us to stop. The mind interests him enormously; he is a most subtle and delicate analyst of human relations. But again, no; the end is not there. Is it that he is primarily interested not in the soul's relation with other souls, but with the soul's relation to health—with the soul's relation to goodness? These stories are always showing us some affectation, pose, insincerity. Some woman has got into a false relation; some man has been perverted by the inhumanity of his circumstances. The soul is ill; the soul is cured; the soul is not cured. Those are the emphatic points in his stories.

Once the eye is used to these shades, half the "conclusions" of fiction fade into thin air; they show like transparences with a light behind them—gaudy, glaring, superficial. The general tidying up of the last chapter, the marriage, the death, the statement of values so sonorously trumpeted forth, so heavily underlined, become of the most rudimentary kind. Nothing is solved, we feel; nothing is rightly held together. On the other hand, the method which at first seemed so casual, inconclusive, and occupied with trifles, now appears the result of an exquisitely original and fastidious taste, choosing boldly, arranging infallibly, and controlled by an honesty for which we can find no match save among the Russians themselves. There may be no answer to these questions, but at the same time let us never manipulate the evidence so as to produce something fitting, decorous, agreeable to our vanity. This may not be the way to catch the ear of the public; after all, they are used to louder music, fiercer measures; but as the tune sounded, so he has written it. In consequence, as we read these little stories about nothing at all, the horizon widens; the soul gains an astonishing sense of freedom.

In reading Tchekov we find ourselves repeating the word "soul" again and again. It sprinkles his pages. Old drunkards use it freely; " . . . you are high up in the service, beyond all reach, but haven't real soul, my dear boy . . . there's no strength in it." Indeed, it is the soul that is the chief character in Russian fiction. [It is] delicate and subtle in Tchekov, subject to an infinite number of humours and distempers. . . . (pp. 246-50)

> *Virginia Woolf, "The Russian Point of View," in her* The Common Reader *(copyright 1925 by Harcourt Brace Jovanovich, Inc.; renewed 1953 by Leonard Woolf; reprinted by permission of the publisher), Harcourt Brace Jovanovich, 1925 (and reprinted in her* The Common Reader, first and second series, *Harcourt Brace Jovanovich, 1948, pp. 243-56).**

JOHN GALSWORTHY   (essay date 1928)

Now, of Tchehov I would say that his stories have apparently neither head nor tail, they seem to be all middle like a tortoise. Many who have tried to imitate him however have failed to realise that the heads and tails are only tucked in. Just as one cannot see or paint like Whistler by merely wishing to, so one cannot feel or write like Tchehov because one thinks his is a nice new way. One young modern writer, Katharine Mansfield, has proved a definite exception to a fairly general rule of failure, not, indeed, because she was a better copyist than the others, but because she had the same intense and melancholy emotionalism as Tchehov, the same way of thinking and feeling, and died—alas!—of the same dread malady. I should say that Tchehov has been the most potent magnet to young writers in several countries for the last twenty years. He was a very great writer, but his influence has been almost wholly dissolvent. For he worked naturally in a method which seems easy, but which is very hard for Westerners, and his works became accessible to Western Europe at a time when writers were restless, and eager to make good without hard labour—a state of mind not so confined to writers that it cannot be noticed also among plumbers, and on the Stock Exchange.

Tchehov appeared to be that desirable thing, the "short cut," and it is hardly too much to say that most of those who have taken him have never arrived. His work has been a will-o'-the-wisp. Writers may think they have just to put down faithfully the daily run of feeling and event, and they will have a story as marvellous as those of Tchehov. Alas! things are not made 'marvellous' by being called so, or there would be a good many 'marvellous' things to-day. It is much harder for a Westerner than for a Russian to dispense with architecture in the building of a tale, but a good many Western writers now appear to think otherwise.

I don't wish to convey the impression of insensibility to the efforts and achievements of our 'new' fiction; which has so out-Tchehoved Tchehov that it doesn't know its own father. Very able and earnest writers are genuinely endeavouring with astounding skill to render life in its kaleidoscopic and vibrational aspects; they are imbued too with a kind of pitiful and ironic fatalism which seems to them new perhaps, but which is eminently Tchehovian, and can be found also in the work of many other writers whom they affect to have outgrown. There is that which is genuinely new in the style and methods of some of these adventuring new fictionists, but I do not think there is anything new in their philosophy of life. They have thrown over story and character, or rather the set and dramatic ways of depicting story and character; but they are no more philosophically emancipated than their forebears, Turgenev, De Maupassant, Flaubert, Henry James, Meredith, Hardy, France, Conrad. The kind of mysticism which these new writers claim as their own brand is no more mystical than that which lies at the back of the work of any of these older writers, all of whom have given ample evidence of recognising the mysterious and sufficing rhythm of creation, and the beauty, terror, pity and irony with which human life is shot through and through. The style and method in fact of these new "fictionists" are more arresting than their philosophy. I admire their adventurous industry even if it is a little too self conscious; but I cannot help wondering whether in their clever daring wholesale dismissal of shape and selected sequence they have not missed the truth that human lives, for all their appearance of volatility in these days of swift motion, are really tethered to deep and special roots. Now in his tales, unshaped though they seem, Tchehov never forgot that truth, nor is he ever over-sophisticated. (pp. 254-56)

There is no other of the older Russian writers with such an understanding of the Russian mind and the Russian heart, or such an intuitive sense of the typical Russian nature. He seemed to brood over its temperamental bonelessness as over a doom; and his work is one long objective revelation of it. . . . The Russian temperament, to speak rashly as if it were a single thing in a country containing many races, lays practically no store by time or place; it excels in feeling, still more perhaps in the expression of feeling, so that its aims are washed out by fresh tides of feeling before they can be achieved. The Russian temperament, in many ways very attractive, seems incapable of halting on a mark. That is why it has always been, and I think will always be, the prey of a bureaucracy. The Russian temperament flows and ebbs incessantly, the national catchword 'Nichevo'—'it doesn't matter'—expresses well the fatalism of its perpetual flux. Material things and the principles which they connote, do not matter enough to the Russian nature, emotion and its current expression matter too much. That is speaking, of course, from the English point of view. A Russian would say that to us material things and the principles they connote, matter too much; emotion and its expression too little. Well, it is just this contrast between national temperaments which makes the Tchehovian form so attractive to and so unsuitable for English writers. That form is flat as the plains of his country. And Tchehov's triumph was that he made flatness exciting, as exciting as a prairie or a desert is to those who first encounter it. How he did this was a secret, which many since have supposed they understood, but which speaking bluntly, they have not.

His plays, too, are never adequately performed on the English stage. Partly because they are written for Russian actors who are perhaps the best in the world; partly because of his method and temperament. English actors cannot render the atmosphere of a Tchehov play. But it is just the atmosphere—whether of play or story—which makes the work of Tchehov memorable.

Intuitive knowledge of human emotions gives to his stories a spiritual shape, which takes the place of the shape supplied by dramatic event. He never wrote a full-length novel, probably because the longer your story, the greater the need for something definite to happen. As for his characters, they are either too true to life or perhaps merely too Russian to be remembered by name. One recalls the figures in 'The Cherry Orchard' or in 'Uncle Vanya'—I can even clap a name to one or two—as very living, very actual, but so under the shadow of mood and of atmosphere, that they haunt the corridors rather than take their seats in the assembly house. Still, there is transcendent merit in Tchehov's writings, for he reveals to us the very soul of a great people, and that with a minimum of parade or pretence. (pp. 256-58)

> *John Galsworthy, "Four More Novelists in Profile"*
> *(originally an address given in 1928), in his* Can-
> delabra: Selected Essays and Addresses *(copyright,*
> *1932, by John Galsworthy; reprinted by permission*
> *of The Society of Authors as the literary represen-*
> *tative of the Estate of John Galsworthy), W. Hei-*
> *nemann, Ltd., 1932 (and reprinted by Charles Scrib-*
> *ner's Sons, 1933, pp. 249-69).**

JOHN MASON BROWN (essay date 1938)

Although Treplev is thinking in terms of dramatic abstractions when he condemns realism in *The Sea Gull*, there can be no

denying Chekov managed to turn realism itself into a new form of expression when he wrote his play. *The Three Sisters* and, even more particularly, *The Cherry Orchard* lay ahead, as final proofs of how superb was his genius for the stage. Yet already in *The Sea Gull* he had shown a magnificent mastery of an idiom which was fated to be his, and his alone.

He had abandoned the pretty moral, so dear to many dramatists both before and since his time. He had discarded plotting as plotting is ordinarily understood. With the eyes of a physician he had looked into the hearts of his characters—into their pasts, their presents, their futures. Then he had summoned these frustrated, tortured, antagonistic people into his play, and turned the theatre into their souls' confessional.

He had not, as Treplev dreamed of doing, avoided the commonplace phrases. He had only refused to use the *clichés* of the stage. The commonplace phrases of daily life were treasures which he seized upon in *The Sea Gull*. He did not record them as our dictophonic dramatists have done. He rearranged them into patterns of his own. He employed them to create that extraordinary illusion of reality which is so successfully achieved in all his long plays that no one is made aware of the unreality of the means by which these overpoweringly real effects are reached.

His concern was what lay beneath the surface rather than upon it. This was enough to set him apart from the majority of modern dramatists. It explains . . . the constantly enriching fascination of his plays. Speaking with what has been happily described as "the voice of twilight Russia," he gave expression to the hopes, the silliness, the vanity, the pathos, and the meanness of his country bourgeois. His genius was to let them seem to speak for themselves; to turn them into geysers of autobiography. Yet always he spoke for them as a superlative artist, transforming their prattle into significant revelation; putting inconsequentials to a large purpose; deriving plot from the mere friction of character upon character; and not only evoking a mood of rare luminosity but sustaining it with unerring surety.

Although he was to write dramas possessed of greater amplitude, *The Sea Gull* still stands out as a play of incredible fullness and depth. If it lacks the design of *The Cherry Orchard*, if it proves more elusive than *The Three Sisters* or *Uncle Vanya,* it is none the less to be treasured as a masterpiece.

It is an impossible play to synopsize. Its Chekovian virtue is that it is far larger than anything that happens in it. It is not merely about an older actress who is jealous of her playwright son. Nor does it limit itself to telling how a famous novelist, who is the actress's lover, destroys a young country girl who cares for the nearby lake as if she were one of the sea gulls which hover over it.

Its people are its story. What they do matters not half so much as what they think and feel and suffer and say. They are unhurried by any plot. They pause to ventilate their souls. They have plenty of time in which to talk as Trigorin does about the horror of being a famous novelist in one of the modern theatre's most probing scenes. Or they talk as Sorin does about what he had hoped for in vain from life. Or like Nina they tell us of their plans for tomorrow. But always their talk is action. It may speak despairingly for a vanished Russia. But always it speaks for more than that Russia. For what it lays bare are some of the eternal truths of human hope and suffering and character everywhere.

Then, too, Chekov of course never forgets his actors. By his amazing honesty in exposing his men and women, he manages to create in *The Sea Gull,* as in all his other long plays, a whole stageful of unparalleled acting parts. He challenges the truest talents of his actors and of his producers. (pp. 88-90)

> John Mason Brown, *"Old Wine in New Bottles: 'The Sea Gull' with the Lunts"* (originally published in a different form as *"'The Sea Gull' with the Lunts,"* in the New York Evening Post, *March 29, 1938), in his* Two on the Aisle: Ten Years of the American Theatre in Performance *(reprinted by permission of the Literary Estate of John Mason Brown; copyright © 1938 by W. W. Norton & Company, Inc.; copyright renewed © 1966 by John Mason Brown), Norton, 1938, pp. 88-91.*

JAMES T. FARRELL   (essay date 1943)

Anton Chekhov was wise in the understanding of the human heart; he was a man of deep humanity. Those who knew him give us much testimony concerning his simplicity of character, his modesty, his gentleness, his kindness, his quiet courage. . . .

Yes, this sick man surveyed his time with sadness, with humanity, with love of his fellow beings. His work is a record of that survey. (p. 60)

Gorky tells us: "In front of that dreary, gray crowd of helpless people there passed a great, wise, and observant man: he looked at all these dreary inhabitants of his country, and, with a sad smile, with a tone of gentle but deep reproach, with anguish in his face and in his heart, in a beautiful and sincere voice, he said to them: 'You live badly, my friends. It is shameful to live like that.'" [See excerpt in *TCLC,* Vol. 3.]

Chekhov raised the portrayal of banality to the level of world literature. He developed the short story as a form of literary art to one of its highest peaks, and the translation of his stories into English has constituted one of the greatest single literary influences at work in the short story of America, England, and Ireland. This influence has been one of the factors encouraging the short-story writers of these nations to revolt against the conventional plot story and to seek in simple and realistic terms to make of the story a form that more seriously reflects life. With the aid of Chekhov's inspiration, some of our own short-story writers have learned to tell us that there is too much dreariness, too much cruelty, too much banality in our own lives. Chekhov has not only influenced the form of the short story, but he also influenced its content.

Sometimes Chekhov is described as a complete indifferentist. Such an interpretation of him is incorrect. Chekhov was detached, but he was not indifferent. Educated as a doctor, his very training contributed to his detachment. In addition, he was ill—dying—and this protracted illness, which he bore with such fortitude, itself must also have contributed to this detachment. In a letter to a woman, in 1892, a remark of his reveals something of this detachment as it influenced his own writing. He advised her: " . . . when you depict sad or unlucky people, and want to touch the reader's heart, try to be colder—it gives their grief, as it were, a background against which it stands in greater relief." This observation should be treated very seriously by readers, by critics, and by writers. All too frequently the detachment and objectivity of realistic writers is falsely estimated as coldness, even as a lack of humanity. But far from being that, it is often an attitude that enables the writer to save himself from sinking into pits of facile sentimentality.

Chekhov wanted men to be free. In a sense, his stories were a protest that men were not free, because he found them unable to live a more noble and dignified life. (pp. 61-2)

Chekhov's comments on literature, in his letters to his friends and his family, help us to understand his work. In some of these letters he has explicitly stated his literary credo. He was a realist. Trained as a doctor, he made no qualitative distinctions between literature and science. To him, both served the same purpose. He conceived the artist and the scientist as specialists, and believed that when each performed his special tasks, he was serving humanity. Underlying these views there was an acceptance of materialism. (pp. 62-3)

It is not branches of knowledge such as poetry and anatomy, but errors—that is to say, men—that fight with one another."

Chekhov's ideal was that of freedom. There is another passage in one of his letters that suggests how he felt realistic literature could greatly assist in the attainment of more freedom:

> Let me remind you that the writers who, we say, are for all time, or are simply good, and who intoxicate us, have one common and very important characteristic. They are going toward something and are summoning you toward it, too, and you feel, not with your mind, but with your whole being, that they have some object. . . . The best of them are realists and paint life as it is, but, through every line's being soaked in the consciousness of an object, you feel, besides life as it is, the life that ought to be, and that captivates you.

In passing, I might add that this passage has on occasion been misused as a justification for attacks on realistic writers by those who possess an antimaterialistic, an antiscientific, bias and see literature as a means of the justification of abstract and generalized moral ideas. Understanding Chekhov's basic materialism and his advocacy of science, we can see clearly that such a use of this passage is unwarranted. (pp. 64-5)

Chekhov was never interested in critics or in formal criticism. He once told Gorky that, after twenty-five years of writing, he had not read one critical piece on his own work that he had found helpful, but that one critic had once predicted that he, Chekhov, would die in a ditch, drunk. However, he usually showed excellent literary taste, and his letters contain many illuminating observations on writers and writing. His advice to young writers was usually generous and helpful, and his letters to the young Gorky are particularly interesting in this respect. There was no snobbery in Chekhov's treatment of young writers; in fact, he often urged others to take a charitable view, arguing that in literature there is room for all honest craftsmen and that those who do even little work—if it be honest—are not to be hounded, attacked, castigated, for, after all, they are not Leo Tolstoy. In his letters, however, I do find but one serious judgment that I think was mistaken, even unfair: his opinion of the great Russian novel *Oblomov* by Gontcharev, of which he said:

> Oblomov himself is exaggerated and is not so striking as to make it worth while to write a whole book about him. A flabby sluggard like so many, a commonplace, petty nature without any complexity in it; to raise this person to the rank of a social type is to make too much of him. I ask myself, what would Oblomov be if

he had not been a sluggard? And I answer that he would not have been anything. And if so, let him snore in peace. . . . And the chief trouble is that the whole novel is cold, cold, cold.

These words almost shock one; they read as if they had been written by one of Chekhov's critics instead of by Anton Chekhov. Here Chekhov violates his own doctrine: that it is sufficient for the artist to see life truly, clearly, objectively, and to mirror what he has seen. For *Oblomov* is a profound social study of Czarist Russia in the period before the emancipation of the serfs. Gontcharev, in terms of literature, unmasks the social reasons why sluggards were developed, showing us that Oblomov had to be the son of sluggardly landowners before him, had to have a way of life oozed into his very soul before he could become a classic type and the subject of a great novel. However, a few days after writing this letter, Chekhov wrote of Gontcharev in another; "I am afraid that . . . I resemble Gontcharev, whom I don't like who is ten heads taller than I am in talent." (pp. 68-9)

While he was quietly writing and suffering at Yalta, the mighty forces of the Russian Revolution were gathering, and the winds of this tremendous historic movement blew into the little garden at Yalta and even found themselves reflected in his plays; for instance, in his character Trofimov of **The Cherry Orchard.** And the young Maxim Gorky also brought a breath of these winds with him when he visited Chekhov. Hope grew in the author of alleged hopelessness. . . .

Today, the work of Chekhov is part of the great tradition of world literature. It can said of relatively few men that had they not lived, the world would be spiritually poorer. Anton Chekhov was one such man. And the essential message of his stories and his plays remains the same for us today as it did in his lifetime. What he said then, he now says—with the same pertinency—to many of us, in many countries, and in many languages:

> You live badly, my friends. It is shameful to live like that.

(p. 71)

James T. Farrell, "On the Letters of Anton Chekhov" (originally published in The University Review, *Vol. IX, No. 3, Spring, 1943), in his* The League of Frightened Philistines and Other Papers *(copyright 1945 by James T. Farrell; copyright renewed 1972 by James T. Farrell; reprinted by permission of the publisher, Vanguard Press, Inc.), Vanguard Press, 1945, pp. 60-71.*

JOSEPH WOOD KRUTCH   (lecture date 1952)

Chekhov belonged to the age which followed the heroic generation of Tolstoi and Dostoevski. At times his characters live, or think that they live, in the world of his predecessors. One is tempted to say that they all seem to have read Tolstoi and Dostoevski and are trying to be Tolstoi and Dostoevski characters. But Chekhov has lost the passion of his predecessors because he has lost the faith which sustains it. He and often his characters are skeptics rather than believers. The soul searchings of his personages are not terrible but, frequently, ridiculous, and it is their futility rather than their tragedy which most impresses him. Whereas Tolstoi and Dostoevski were prophets, he is a critic and a satirist. They believed; he doubts. They saw tragedy; he sees, at most, pathos, usually tinged with absurdity.

Chekhov was, of course, well known as a short-story writer before he tried the theater. He would have been an important literary figure if the modern drama had never existed. It was, nevertheless, the foundation in Moscow of a theater consciously devoted to the "new" theatrical activity that led to his development as a dramatist and ultimately made his plays as well known as his stories. **The Sea Gull** had been first produced at the Imperial Russian Theater, where it proved so complete a failure that Chekhov vowed never to write another play. A few years later it was revived with great success at the "advanced" Moscow Art Theater and achieved the success which established it as a standard item in the repertory, where it remained for many years and even survived the Bolshevist revolution.

It is no accident that the title of **The Sea Gull** suggests at once *The Wild Duck.* Ibsen's "symbolism," his use of usually somewhat ambiguous objects or incidents to suggest a rather vague allegory, was one of the features of his style often imitated, as it was in France especially, by writers not particularly sympathetic to his sociological and realistic elements. The extent to which Chekhov was influenced is shown again in **The Cherry Orchard,** where the orchard symbolizes the grace and beauty of the past which is being sacrificed because it has no utilitarian value.

If the whole rather awkward business about the dead bird as a symbol of dead happiness is somewhat perfunctory and self-conscious Ibsen, most of the play is pure Chekhov, and nothing is more strikingly so than the two opening lines of the dialogue. The curtain goes up on two middle-aged people doing nothing on a country estate. "Why," asks the man, "do you always wear black?" And the woman replies, "I am in mourning for my dead life."

It is possible to play this opening scene and indeed the whole play with unrelieved solemnity. It has sometimes been so played in the United States. It would, however, also be possible to play it as well as various other scenes as pure farce. Chekhov's own remarks, especially in his letters, indicate that he himself was more aware of the comic aspect of his plays than were the Russian interpreters upon occasion. Yet **The Sea Gull** does end with a suicide; nearly everybody in it is miserable; and it can hardly be interpreted as though it were intended to be merely funny. Actually, it is both funny and sad, the chief characters both pathetic and ridiculous. They perpetually dramatize themselves and especially their unhappiness. They talk endlessly about Life with a capital L, about Love, about the Beautiful, and about all the other great abstractions which Anglo-Saxons are generally ashamed to mention. They see themselves and their fate as grandiose, but they are, in fact, never passionate enough to achieve Tolstoian or Dostoevskian dimensions, and their fates generally creep gradually upon them. They are hardly tragic. One can say only that they are pathetically ridiculous. Melancholy has marked them for her own. Almost from childhood they have known that they would be unhappy, and the most they generally hope for is that their unhappiness will be of a kind which others will recognize as an interesting unhappiness. They do have charm—a word we have never used in connection with Ibsen or Strindberg or Shaw—and so do the plays in which they figure. But the whole tone is elegiac and resigned.

Though it is clear that Chekhov often laughs at his characters, he nevertheless holds them in great affection. Perhaps he recognizes in their quiet bafflement something of himself. Undoubtedly he sees them as typical of something characteristic of his race and his time. But why are they like this? Offhand we may be inclined to answer, "Because they are Russians; this is what we have been told the Russian soul is like." Chekhov himself suggests a somewhat different answer.

They are, of course, recognizably "Russian," but the Russian soul had not always manifested itself in so passive and resigned a form. Moreover, the answer which Chekhov seems to give suggests immediately a connection with the theme of our discussion [of modernism in the drama]. The real trouble with these people is that they belong to the past. They are the surviving nobility and gentry of a dead age. They do nothing because there is nothing for them to do. Their political, social, and economic environment has disappeared, leaving them stranded. They are lost between two worlds, one dead, the other powerless to be born.

Now and then one of them expresses his realization of this fact in political or sociological terms. His futility takes the form of a futile idealism directed toward "the future." A great new day will dawn, he thinks. The world will be ruled by justice, and all men will be happy and prosperous. Our great-great-great-grandchildren will look back at us with pity and wonder.

In so far as Chekhov was political at all, he himself was a liberal. His plays were regarded by the Czarist government as mildly dangerous, and with the curious, hesitant repressiveness characteristic of it the authorities did put certain restrictions on the presentation of his plays without forbidding them entirely. Actually, of course, Chekhov was not very political, and it would be more unqualifiedly true to say of him than even of Ibsen that he was more a poet than a social philosopher. What absorbed him was not the future but the present. He was more interested in what the characters in his plays were like than in the question why they were like that.

It has become one of the characteristics of our time that when we find ourselves faced with any phenomenon, whether it be an animal, a social institution, or even a work of art, we immediately ask two questions: "What were its origins? What will be its future development?" Our interest in these questions concerning evolution and ultimate destiny has become so obsessive that we seldom bother to ask what a thing *is*—now and in itself. Possibly that is one result of a conviction that, being in transition, we have no significant present. But one of the reasons why Chekhov's plays have seemed so fascinating to so many is that they are, curiously, concerned primarily with what a special group of people is like rather than with how they got that way or what will become of them. Perhaps a thing can be loved only when it is thus accepted in its own terms, and perhaps the fact that Chekhov loved his characters is an important part of his uniqueness.

Nevertheless it is because he too was aware to some extent of the two abstractions, the Past and the Future, that he is relevant to our discussion and that he can give us as he does a glimpse at the problem from an angle somewhat different from any we have so far been afforded. If he had been simply unconcerned with the future and engaged in nothing but a defense of his dying aristocrat, he would merely have been a possibly interesting conservative and would not have come into our discussion at all. If, on the contrary, he had been, as the early Soviet critics tried to make him, a sort of John the Baptist of the Revolution preparing the way for the appearance of Lenin, he would be almost equally irrelevant. What he does exhibit is one of the characteristic features of what I have been calling modernism in the drama. He too ends with a dilemma.

The play which most directly and clearly illustrates this fact is *The Cherry Orchard*, where the situation is simplicity itself. A group of typically feckless and typically charming Chekhovian gentry are losing their estate to an up-and-coming Man of the Future. His first act is to lay an ax to their cherry orchard in order to make way for a more economic use of the land, and "Is this good or bad?" is the only question posed in the play. Characteristically, the aesthetic effect of the play does not depend upon any answers being given. Chekhov's tone is as usual elegiac, rather than philosophical or polemic. The one indisputable thing upon which the emotional attention centers is the fact that something beautiful is being destroyed—the useless cherry orchard itself and the useless lives of the people whom it symbolized. This destruction is in itself sad and pitiful whether one resents it as an evil or accepts it as something necessary and, in the end, productive of good.

Though the play is thus not primarily a problem play, both Chekhov himself and some of the characters recognize the problem implicit. One character in particular philosophizes the incidents and talks glowingly of the future, although one realizes that his talk, like that of nearly all Chekhov's characters, will never be anything but talk. Plainly Chekhov's own answer to the question posed is simply that no clear-cut answer is possible. The thing is both good and bad. No doubt it had to happen. But the present loss is at least as certain as any future gain. Whatever may be used in favor of the new world, one thing seems clear. There will be no place for Cherry Trees in it, at least for a long time to come. One cannot stand up against the Future. But one cannot be too happy about it either.

This is the dilemma in Chekhov, and I might add that the gentleness with which it is stated makes it a peculiarly Chekhovian manifestation of the tendency in modernism to reach such a dilemma. There is another reason why this particular play should be mentioned now. This is the first time that we have met the admission that the past is not merely something to grow away from, that something in itself worth having may be left behind when and if we cross the chasm. Nostalgia for the past is the very last thing one would expect to find in either Shaw or Ibsen. It is a very strong element in Chekhov.

One of the factors contributing to his purely artistic orginality and effectiveness is the peculiar dramatic form, the method of storytelling, which he developed in order to produce the effect intended and which one is tempted to call the method of the dramatically undramatic. Because of it a common complaint of his characters is that nothing ever happens to them, that life has passed them by; in a word, that their existence is without drama. To some extent this is true; to some extent on the other hand, it is a delusion cultivated as all their delusions are cultivated in order to make them seem pathetic to themselves. And if their creator is to make us share their mood, he must make us also feel that nothing is happening. That obviously creates a problem for the dramatist whose audience is going to expect that a good deal should happen in a play.

This problem Chekhov solved so successfully that, though something always does happen, critics as well as lay spectators often declare that nothing does, and the static character of his plays becomes a standing joke. Of the play *The Three Sisters* it has been said that the plot might be summarized as follows. In the first act three sisters living in the provinces wish that they could go to Moscow but are unable to do so. In the second act they again wish that they could go to Moscow and again do not do so. In the third act they still wish they could go to Moscow and they still do not go.

If one depends upon a general impression, it may seem that not much more actually happens in *The Sea Gull.* Yet, as a matter of fact, the action of the story told in that play includes among other things a seduction and a suicide—two events much relied upon by playwrights in search of something undeniably dramatic. The most obvious reason why Chekhov can keep them from seeming so is that they both take place off stage, and in general Chekhov tends to communicate to the spectators the characters' own conviction that their lives are eventless by exhibiting them during the eventless moments of their career.

In the mid-nineteenth century the exponents of what was termed "the well-made play" talked about what they called "the obligatory scene." Within certain limits the playwright, they said, is free to choose what parts of an action he will actually exhibit on the stage. In every story, however, there are crucial moments which the dramatist simply cannot refuse to face and which are "obligatory" in the sense that an audience will rightfully demand to see them happening before its eyes. The simplest description of Chekhov's method would be that he nearly always omits the obligatory scene which nearly always takes place either off stage or, like the seduction just referred to, between the acts and while the audience is chatting in the lobby. One agrees with the characters that nothing ever happens to them because one never sees it happen.

One specific illustration of how the matter is handled will suffice. *The Sea Gull,* you will remember, opens with the bit about the lady who is mourning for her dead life. Let us see how the play ends. A character enters in some agitation and whispers to another: "Don't say anything about it now, but the fact is that Constantine has shot himself." Curtain. (pp. 67-75)

Shakespeare presents the great passionate moments on the stage because he and his audience believe that in them the true meaning of life is revealed and the most noteworthy aspects of human experience exhibited. Chekhov avoids them because he seems to share, and expect his audience to share, the awareness of his characters that the most characteristic aspect of life is that under which it presents itself as a flat, melancholy, and featureless plain. It is this, of course, which serves to justify his plaintive and nostalgic tone.

Neither Ibsen, nor Strindberg, nor Wilde, nor Shaw commonly exhibits anything resembling this Chekhovian resignation. Even in the face of . . . his pessimistic implications, Shaw persists in proclaiming a sort of jaunty optimism. As an aesthete, Wilde believes in splendor and hopes for pleasure if not for happiness. Ibsen insists with a sort of somber optimism that something can be done about it. Even Strindberg responds to unresolvable conflict, not with resignation, but with Dionysian fury. Perhaps . . . there is some connection between the various aspects of Chekhov's uniqueness. Perhaps both the elegiac tone and the curiously undramatic dramatic method are both the result of the fact that he has not wholly committed himself to the future or willingly surrendered all of the past. He acknowledges, as none of the others do, a sense of loss, and instead of concerning himself exclusively with what the world is going to become, he looks back, sometimes longingly, towards what it once was. (pp. 76-7)

Ibsen denies the existence of absolutes. Strindberg denies the possibility of reconciling conflicting impulses. Shaw denies that man as he exists is capable of solving his problems. Now Chekhov denies, among other things, the significance of the drama. (p. 77)

*Joseph Wood Krutch, "Pirandello and the Dissolution of the Ego" (originally a lecture delivered at Cornell University in October, 1952), in his "Modernism" in Modern Drama: A Definition and an Estimate (copyright © 1953 Joseph Wood Krutch; copyright renewed © 1981 by Marcelle Krutch; reprinted by permission of The Trustees of Columbia University in the City of New York), Cornell University Press, 1953, pp. 65-87.**

W. H. BRUFORD (essay date 1957)

[*Bruford offers a survey of Chekhov's major fiction and dramas.*]

According to [D. S.] Mirsky, *The Party* . . . is the first story in the typical Chekhovian manner, the biography of a mood, developing under the pinpricks of life, but due in substance to a deep-lying physiological or psychological cause, here Olga's pregnancy. This description, one feels, does not do justice to *The Party.* It is far more than the 'biography of a mood'. It is a convincing picture of a day or two of crisis in Olga's life, in which we get to know her completely as she is to herself. . . . (p. 27)

In the great stories which follow, varying in length between 15 and 150 pages or so, two kinds of interest predominate, singly or combined: the psychological and the sociological. Sometimes, as in *The Party,* our attention is directed to a single character, fully displayed to us from within and without, and always depicted in a particular situation in contemporary Russia. An individual stands out 'like the moon among the stars', as Chekhov said about *The Party,* or as a 'round' character among 'flat' ones, to use Mr E. M. Forster's terms. Sometimes it is a group of people, or a member of a social group, in their typical relation to other groups. (p. 29)

From *The Party* onwards, we have Chekhov's work at its maturest and best in both types, and because he always sees his figures with 'the human mass out of which they came', all belong in some degree to both types. *A Nervous Breakdown* . . . is primarily a study of a temperament similar to that of the Russian writer Garshin, who had just died by his own hand, and for whose memorial volume the story was written, a man morally sensitive to a degree which finally made life in this imperfect world unbearable. . . . There is more than a question of individual psychology involved then in this story, and as so often before, without any direct pointing of the moral, Chekhov is drawing a contrast between the humane and the inhumane. So also in the longer stories [*A Dreary Story, The Duel,* and *Ward No. 6*]. . . . (p. 30)

In this lack of metaphysical interests Chekhov was clearly a child of the age of naturalism, as in several other respects: his insistence, when he theorised in his letters, on 'absolute truth' to life, including its seamy side, his concern in his stories with the causes, and not least the physical causes, of mental states (*The Party*), also in the social idealism. . . . When he tried to formulate his beliefs, they took the shape of a philosophical naturalism, a belief in a full and free natural life. (pp. 31-2)

Before writing *A Dreary Story,* the first of the three important longer stories mentioned above, Chekhov had twice attempted to write a full-length novel, but failed. (p. 32)

The longer stories with which Chekhov in the end contented himself, though they cannot be described as novels, are all concerned with questions of conscience and intended for a thoughtful reader. (pp. 32-3)

In the following longer stories, we see him attempting to get away from his accustomed method of presenting his characters in 'scenes', and at the same time to deal with serious ideas in fiction. By this time his Tolstoyan ideas were gradually losing their hold on him, and he usually contents himself with the negative aim of 'expressing the longing for a common idea and painfully admitting our need of one.' (P. N. Ostrovsky.) So in *A Dreary Story*. . . , he gives us the life of a famous scholar, a Russian professor of medicine of international reputation, movingly told by himself as he nears the retiring age and realises more and more clearly the tragic consequences of his inability to share the inner life of those dearest to him. (pp. 33-4)

One may discern a turning away from Tolstoy here, but it is clearer in [*The Duel,* and *Ward No. 6*]. . . . *The Duel* is the longest story of Chekhov's maturity. . . . The picture of a man and of his whole circle is built up slowly and deliberately, and it produces an effect of completeness. Again the 'hero' is an intellectual, a university graduate who, like the married woman with whom he runs away to the Caucasus, prides himself on his individual freedom. The effect on his character and on his happiness of living for freedom is so catastrophic that the story reads like a criticism of the central idea which Chekhov had earlier proposed for his novel. (p. 34)

In this story especially, we feel that out of consideration for the public at whom it was directed, the intelligentsia, Chekhov had allowed intellectual ideas too big a part, or rather, the emotional idea which was the starting point had not become flesh, so to speak, as it must in a completely satisfying story or play. . . .

Ward No. 6 could not be interpreted by anyone as conservative in feeling, and it was fittingly published in the liberal monthly *New Thought*. . . . *Ward No. 6* was, and still is, in Russia, one of the most discussed of Chekhov's stories. It may be taken as the first work of his in which Tolstoyan ideas are unmistakably weighed and found wanting, and the first of his markedly sociological stories. (p. 35)

When I had read this story to the end,' said Lenin, 'I was filled with awe. I could not remain in my room and went out of doors. I felt as if I were locked up in a ward too.' (p. 36)

Instead of the idealised picture of village innocence and contentment which had been current since the 'Populist' movement, we are shown the 'ignorant insensitive people, always thinking of money, quarrelling over a crust of bread, coarse and uncouth in their manners', of whom the deacon in *The Duel* had already spoken. . . . Yet it was only human nature if individuals like these Populists felt impelled to do what they could (*An Artist's Story* . . .), though they usually discovered, if they were honest with themselves, that in the hopeless struggle they had done little if anything beyond temporarily salving their own consciences (*My Life* . . .). There ought to stand at the door of every self-satisfied happy man someone with a hammer, to remind him continually by his knocking of the existence of unhappy people in the world' (*Gooseberries* . . .). Suffering is an inescapable element in life, against which it is morally dangerous to be too carefully cushioned. . . . (pp. 37-8)

Among the 'social' stories we may include also two or three which have as their subject the human results of the industrialism which was just beginning to develop in Russia, largely under foreign leadership, and one detailed study of a wholesale merchant's family during two generations: all presented to us, as usual, fictive individual characters, seen from within; but they are also social types with generic features. In *A Woman's Kingdom* . . . for instance, we see an engineering firm built up by two brothers, whose gifts are complementary to each other, the one supplying the technical skill and insight, without any thought of monetary gain, the other the organising ability energised by an ascetic love of power. The story asks what an intelligent young woman, inheriting such a show-piece of capitalistic enterprise from her father and uncle, would feel about it all, about the noisy engineering shop, the ill-housed workmen, and her own personal problems, having been brought up very simply and suddenly overwhelmed with wealth. *A Doctor's Visit* similarly poses a moral problem concerning a big industry, a cotton mill in the country, in which a young doctor from Moscow, who is asked to visit a patient there, finds something which he can only describe as diabolic. (p. 38)

In the long story *Three Years* . . . , finally, a kind of *Forsyte Saga* in miniature, we see the problem of the generations not in an industrial, but a commercial setting, one which Chekhov knew well from his own youth. . . . [The] unquestioning self-assertiveness of the father has given place to the religious escapism of one son and the vague fear of life of the other. The development is traced against this background, through the first three years of the younger son's married life, of the emotional relationships of a small group of people, nearly all frustrated in one way or another, and all incurably isolated as individuals. This is how Chekhov continues to see human relationships, in all the stories mentioned and also in some which develop on a larger scale the love stories discussed above, where the setting is of minor importance. Good examples are *The Teacher of Literature* . . . or Chekhov's last story, *The Betrothed* . . . , in both of which themes rather similar to those of the great plays Chekhov wrote in these later years are developed with all the resources of his mature art. He could afford now to take his own time over them, he knew his powers and his limitations, he gave free play to his fine sense of form, leaving no trace of the originating idea 'outside the characters' and providing models of artistic construction on which none of his countless imitators have been able to improve.

Summing up his merits as a storyteller, Mirsky says that 'in architectural unity he surpasses all the writers of the realistic age' and is only equalled among Russian writers by Pushkin and Lermontov. Henry James, who found the novels of Tolstoy and Dostoievsky not tasteless indeed, because of the mind and soul in them, but as regards form mere 'fluid puddings', saw in Chekhov's writings not only the imprint of a personality, but also the mark of a master-builder, a feeling for shape and artistic economy which give each work style as a whole as well as in the parts. (pp. 38-9)

Among Chekhov's plays . . . we have to distinguish a group of short humorous works, written quite frankly for money and little known outside Russia, from the serious longer works into which he put the best that was in him. . . .

Chekhov's first surviving attempt at a serious play was never acted, and published only after his death, because he soon came to see that its faults were incurable. It is a very interesting document for admirers of his later work and was therefore translated, and slightly adapted, by Basil Ashmore in 1952, under the title *Don Juan (in the Russian Manner)*. It is too long and complicated, it follows too closely the already old-fashioned Russian technique of the early 'eighties, but it possesses unmistakably the same bitter-sweet flavour as the most characteristic of the stories, the same preference for characters under the stress of unfulfilled desires, in the enervating conditions of everyday provincial life in Russia. . . .

Platonov himself, in particular, has much in common with the 'hero' of the first serious play of Chekhov's that was acted, *Ivanov.* . . . The theme is the inevitable fading of youth's generous ideals with the passing of the years. . . . (p. 40)

Chekhov spared no pains to make [*Ivanov*] a work of literary as well as theatrical significance, by avoiding the stereotyped both in content and form. Though for our modern taste it seems not startlingly novel but rather the reverse, the actors found it so difficult that Chekhov had to write long explanatory letters to even the best of them. They expected, following the accepted tradition, to be able to take sides with the 'hero', but Chekhov, aiming at truth to the life of his time, put in the centre of his play a man who could be neither whole-heartedly admired nor completely despised, a tired, confused and unsuccessful reformer, with the 'beautiful past' behind him which Chekhov considered typical for the intelligent Russian gentleman of that day. (pp. 41-2)

The ideal of drama which Chekhov no doubt already had at the back of his mind was the psychological naturalism which he brought to perfection in his later plays, a drama which should be content to make the spectator fully aware of complicated states of mind in a group of invented characters, without asking whether the result fitted in with any accepted notions about comedy or tragedy, so long as it interpreted convincingly the general sense of life as we know it. But in *Ivanov* Chekhov still follows the melodramatic tradition of his day in working up to strong act-endings. To end a play, he once complained, no one has ever invented any alternatives to a marrriage or a pistol-shot. Here he chose the latter not for the last time. What really interested him, however, is not the explicit action in the play so much as the lifelike presentation of character in dialogue and everyday incidents. He gives us a small number of characters in the round besides Ivanov, characters which do not develop in the course of the play, but reveal their complex but unchanging natures more fully in each successive scene. They are surrounded by a large number of 'flat' characters presented as types, with 'Leitmotiv' mannerisms and sayings of their own, which make them immediately recognisable. . . . The chief characters generally speak the normalised Russian of the intelligentsia, but the minor characters, especially the uneducated ones, are often given their own peculiar idiom, as in the stories. Chekhov had already perfected a method of presenting character in dialogue which he did not need to change later. (pp. 43-4)

Encouraged by the success of *Ivanov* when performed in St Petersburg, and the lively discussions which followed, Chekhov tried to get still further away from the conventional play constructed along a thin thread of plot, still closer to the unemphatic casual dialogue of everyday life, in the play he called *The Wood Demon.* . . . It was put on in Moscow and failed to please, and it was rejected by the Imperial Theatres in St Petersburg, so Chekhov laid it aside until seven years later he made out of it his *Uncle Vanya.* (p. 44)

The Seagull displays the same tendencies as *The Wood Demon,* and though it was better thought out and better adapted to stage performance, this play too, to his intense disappointment, was a complete failure when first produced, at the Alexandrovsky Theatre in St Petersburg, in October 1896. It was badly acted, partly because its form was altogether too novel for the ordinary actor, as well as for the playgoer. . . . In banishing violent

action from the stage Chekhov was, of course, only coming further into line with the classical tradition, which he had followed already in adopting an analytic type of construction, and the leading European dramatists of the 'nineties, Ibsen, Hauptmann and Maeterlinck, had provided many new examples of a drama concerned above all with the inner life. (pp. 44-5)

Yet the general effect of [*The Seagull*] is not naturalistic at all but profoundly poetical, lyrical in a dramatic way, in the sense that Chekhov does not express through the characters his own personal feeling, but seems to make the emotional life of a small group of people transparent for us, universalised, and therefore profoundly moving, as he does in his stories. (p. 45)

If we ask why love is always unhappy in Chekhov, one answer that might be suggested is that, like so many artists, he finds happiness undramatic, unproductive of tension. With this autumnal colouring he can achieve original effects. Biographical and sociological explanations might also be found for his preference for it, but they would not account for what he does with it. It belongs to his characteristic palette and like a good painter, he performs wonders within the limitations he imposes on himself, the unity of tone being unmistakable, in spite of what has been called the 'fragmentation' of his themes. (pp. 47-8)

The revised version of *The Wood Demon* was finished before the first performance of *The Seagull,* and is clearly by the same hand. It proved surprisingly popular in provincial Russian theatres, after its publication in the collection of Chekhov plays which appeared in 1897. It was given the title *Uncle Vanya* and styled 'Scenes from country life', instead of 'comedy', though there is more of the comic in it than in *The Seagull,* in the secondary characters like Telegin and Marina. The influence of prevailing economic and social conditions on everyday life in the country is strongly stressed, whereas in *The Wood Demon,* written in Chekhov's Tolstoyan period, it was the personal defects of the characters which were the root cause of their unhappiness. (pp. 49-50)

[In *The Three Sisters* the theme is] the passing of time and opportunity unused, the tragic waste of the best in life. . . . (p. 51)

Its themes are such things as the freshness of youth and its fading, happy memories of childhood and the longing to return to its scenes, the love of kindred souls bound by inescapable earlier ties, the first flush of joy in useful work, and later doubts of one's vocation—in a word, the plight of us all, who 'look before and after, and pine for what is not'. . . . Soviet criticism dwells on what it calls the optimism of the play, Chekhov's vision of humanity's triumphs to come. (p. 53)

[*The Cherry Orchard*], unlike *The Three Sisters,* is more or less analytic in its construction, the picture of a crisis, the end of a long story. (p. 55)

The dispute over the cherry-orchard is symbolic not only of the difference between landowners and businessmen, and the older and the younger generation—for Trofimov and Anya look forward to the ideal of making all Russia their garden, in the wonderful new life which is coming—but also of the final variation on what we have found to be a central theme in Chekhov's writings, the fate of beauty on earth, and its preciousness nevertheless to those who put good states of mind higher than the enjoyment of material prosperity. (p. 56)

If Chekhov's most devoted contemporary admirers sometimes failed so badly in interpreting his intentions, it is not surprising to find . . . that in Russia to-day he is still read in many different ways, or that English and Russian critics have usually stressed quite different aspects of his art. One of his most sensitive readers in this country, Virginia Woolf, wrote of him, for instance: 'Our first impressions of Chekhov are not of simplicity but of bewilderment', and her feeling has been widely shared. A recent Russian biographer on the other hand, Derman, finds it difficult to imagine a Russian reader to whom Chekhov would be incomprehensible, so great is the simplicity of his thought and expression, a directness comparable with Pushkin's. His effect on succeeding writers has been almost as revolutionary as was Pushkin's, for here were the beginnings of a 'democratisation of art'. To understand how such radical divergences are possible in the views taken of one writer, we must remind ourselves that the reader is himself responsible for half of the effect produced by what he reads. The same symbols evoke varying meanings in the minds that bring them to life again, for though the readers must have something in common to give the words any meaning at all, they may differ almost without limit in their dispositions, memories and habits of thought. As to English bewilderment, there was always a great deal in Chekhov, his stories of children and animals, for instance, that no reader can ever have found bewildering at all, and much of the rest has lost its first strangeness for readers familiar with his imitators. But with Chekhov, as with any foreign writer, we cannot feel quite at home without learning something about his world, and to do him justice as an artist, we must distinguish between the early sketches he threw off with careless ease and the finished masterpieces of his maturity.

Despite all differences of interpretation, few would now dispute Chekhov's claim to a place among the major writers of the nineteenth century. 'Genius can be bounded in a nutshell and yet embrace the whole fullness of life', said Thomas Mann, shortly before his death, with reference to Chekhov, whom he had recently come to admire as much as his own first models, Balzac and Tolstoy. He now held Chekhov's best stories to be just as perfect within their limits as the monumental works of these great novelists, for perfection is independent of size. There is certainly something uniquely impressive in the epic breadth of a Tolstoy, something for which Chekhov strove, we have seen, in vain, and though his own narrow angle pictures, put side by side, cover no less wide a span than Tolstoy's novels, they are not organized in relation to each other to form worlds of the imagination such as those that confront us in *Anna Karenina* or *War and Peace*. But against that consideration, to be just, we must set his mastery in the drama, where he is incomparably greater than Tolstoy. The acquired habit of extreme brevity, the lack of a unified philosophy, the interruption of his work by illness, all these things help to explain his abandonment of the projected novels, but what mattered most was probably the perfection of his sense of form, combined with the personal modesty and absolute honesty which endeared him to his friends and which those who know him well through his works and letters still find irresistible. Tolstoy the artist is magnificent, but from the would-be prophet we are often repelled by what Mann calls his 'colossal conceit'. The 'gentle ironist' Chekhov, with no gospel to offer but tolerance and humanity, by the reticence and purity of his art has a no less enduring appeal. (pp. 58-9)

W. H. Bruford, in his Anton Chekhov, *Bowes & Bowes Publishers Limited, 1957, 62 p.*

KENNETH REXROTH (essay date 1967)

Chekhov is the master of an art of such highly refined modesty that he can present his people in their simplicity on a stage and let life itself do the mocking.

He wanted a new theater, a theater that would tell it the way it really was. There has been plenty of realist and naturalist theater in Russia in his day and since, but there is only one Chekhov. The naturalist theater uses a whole armamentarium of devices to create an illusion of "real life" and then drive home its points, all derived from the storehouse of literary and dramatic morality.

There have been many more lifelike plays than Chekhov's. His is not a circumstantial naturalism of décor and talk and event—it is a moral naturalism. These lost people, off in the vast provinces of Russia, frustrated, aimless, hopeless, or full of utopian unrealizable hopes, all alike coming to trivial ends, actually make up a highly stylized theater of their own, as formal or classic as the Commedia dell' Arte or Plautus and Terence.

What is realistic, or naturalistic? What is "life as it really is"? This is the silent moral commentary that underlines every speech, like an unheard organ pedal. Is it a judgment? In the sense in which "Judge not lest ye be judged" is a judgment.

There is something intrinsically ridiculous about all the people in all the plays, Chekhov's is truly a theater of the absurd. Yet we never think of them as very funny—and we don't think of them as very sad, either. The play as a whole may sadden us, as life saddens us with all the massive pathos of mortality, but Chekhov's people we simply accept. (pp. 287-88)

Chekhov would have been horrified if anyone had cold-bloodedly accused him of teaching a moral—but so he does. We accept these tragic comedies, these sorrowful farces of Chekhov's the way we would accept life itself if we were gifted with sudden wisdom. Chekhov places us in a situation, confronting the behavior of a number of human beings in what seems to them, at least, an important crisis. We are so placed, so situated and informed, that we can afford to be wise. We can regard the affairs of men as they should be regarded, in the aspect of timelessness. But this is what Sophocles does.

Once we accept both the idiom of Chekhov and the idiom of Sophocles we can compare them, and we can see very clearly the great precision and economy with which Chekhov works. His plays are pre-eminently, in modern times, playwright's plays, a joy for a fellow craftsman to see or read. How right everything is! How little time or speech is wasted! How much every line is saturated with action! Sophocles, Molière, Racine—very few other playwrights have been as accurate and as economical.

It is this genius for stating only the simplest truth as simply as can be that makes Chekhov inexhaustible—like life. We can see him for the hundredth time when we are sick of everything else in the theater, just as we can read his stories when everything else, even detectives and science fiction, bores us. We are not bored because we do not feel we are being manipulated. We are, of course, but manipulated to respond, "That's the way it is." Since the professional manipulators of the mind never have this response in view, we are quite unconscious of Chekhov's craftiness—that he is always interfering on the side of suspended judgment.

Quite unlike those of Ibsen and Strindberg, who were tireless preachers and manipulators, Chekhov's people are not alienated. They have trouble, as men have always had, communicating, but the cast of each play forms a community nonetheless. They would all like to live in a society of mutual aid if only they could define the means and ends of aid itself. One feels that Ibsen and Strindberg didn't like any of their casts very much and made them up of people who wouldn't listen to Ibsen and Strindberg. Chevhov doesn't want to be listened to. He isn't there. He is out of sight, in the last row of the balcony, listening. "I imagine people so they can tell me things about themselves." This is an unusual, but certainly an unusually effective, credo for a playwright. (pp. 289-90)

> *Kenneth Rexroth, "Chekhov: 'Plays'" (originally published as "Chekhov's Plays," in* Saturday Review, *Vol. L, No. 27, July 8, 1967), in his* Classics Revisited *(copyright © 1965, 1966, 1967, 1968 by Kenneth Rexroth; used by permission of Bradford Morrow for the Kenneth Rexroth Trust), Quadrangle Books, 1968, pp. 286-90.*

SOPHIE LAFFITTE (essay date 1971)

> [*Laffitte's* Chekhov, 1860-1904, *from which the following introductory comments on the author's fiction and dramas have been excerpted, is a comprehensive study of Chekhov and his works.*]

In Chekhov's plays, complex and ambiguous characters perform their evolutions in a strange, almost realistic atmosphere, but one to which a subtle transposition gives an inimitable, characteristically Chekhovian undertone. And this transposition is created principally by the extreme precision of his stage directions in regard to seasons of the year, time, weather and the alternation of silences and various 'descriptive' noises, which are all woven into the psychological web of the play and invest it with an unexpected richness. The slow, extremely slow, outer life of the characters and their complex inner life unfold on several planes at the same time. The interior tension grows from scene to scene, invisible ties are forged between the different characters and grow stronger and stronger, until the suspense among the audience becomes intolerable.

His plays have fascinated generations of spectators by the deep, subtle, very musical truth, emanating from those slow movements and those silences. Its dramatic compositions are 'fundamentally musical'. Every moment has its own tenseness, but this tenseness does not reside in the dialogue but in the silence, in the life that is following its course. "What is the point of explaining anything to the audience? One must startle it and that is enough: then it will be interested and start pondering again." (pp. 4-5)

This is one of the keys to his aestheticism: a resolution not to explain, as 'old-fashioned' literature and theatre did, but to be content with administering shocks to the sensibility and imagination of reader or spectator. Both must collaborate with the artist, never remain passive. That is why Chekhov merely provided posts to indicate the way, and left gaps between them. These gaps, these pauses, became more and more frequent in his plays and their role more vital. He well knew the aesthetic value of these pauses: "I don't know why, but extreme happiness and misery are most often expressed by silence: lovers understand each other best when they don't speak."

There again, as in his stories, 'without beginning or end', Chekhov triumphs over the most solidly established conventions; there again, he ignores everything but his own inner imperatives, which never inclined him towards romantic or dramatic 'developments'. He never wrote novels because it was not in his temperament to portray the evolution of char-

acters at a particular time and in a particular setting, a complex evolution unfolding against the moving backcloth of life.

Chekhov lacked a certain form of creative imagination. He was never able to depict any action of long duration or an elaborate character, whose various facets would be displayed in various circumstances. Chekhov's art is not that of a novelist. He is epigrammatic, percussive, allusive, and expresses himself in brief jabs with a probe, delivered with a master's hand, at those points in the nervous system where the vital decisions affecting human destinies are formed. And plays should rightly stress those turning points, those privileged moments when certain mental impulses are starkly revealed. Chekhov's art was eminently suited to a poetical, psychological 'interiorized' type of play—and that is what burst on the audience with enormous impact at the first performance of *The Seagull*. . . . (pp. 5-6)

[It would] be incorrect to attribute Chekhov's aesthetic conceptions solely to his medical studies, though his scientific background had certainly enriched and disciplined a mind, already naturally inclined to objectivity and synthesis: "a writer should, above all, become a shrewd, and indefatigable observer, and should train himself in such a way that it becomes a habit, second nature with him. . . . A man of letters should be as objective as a chemist, he should abandon the subjectivity of everyday life." He should first and foremost be "an impartial witness".

Obviously, Chekhov was far from being solely a "witness". The personal element that enhanced the material supplied by direct observation of life was always depersonalized and sublimated until it acquired a general and superior quality. For instance, Treplev and Trigorin in *The Seagull* are both mouthpieces for the author, each incarnates one aspect of his personality; so does Dr. Astrov in *Uncle Vanya*; so, to a certain extent, does Vershinin in *The Three Sisters*; so does Gurov, the hero in *The Lady with the Dog*; so, more than all the others, does Monseigneur Peter in *The Bishop*. But Chekhov always carefully disguises himself behind his characters and his poignant lyricism never contains any trace of that subjectivism, which he loathed. ("Subjectivity is a terrible thing. . . . One must, above all, avoid the personal element.")

Nevertheless, lyrical passages appear with increasing frequency in his later writings. (pp. 16-17)

This abrupt irruption of the lyrical element, with its irresistible impact on the reader, is, as everything else with Chekhov, closely thought-out and deliberate. The poetry is there to compel the reader to think, to provoke him into doing what the author regards as essential—take a serious look at himself and the emptiness of his life: and, at the same time, to waken in him a longing for a better one. These are the twin objectives that Chekhov pursues in his work, they are the basis of it and always present in the background. (p. 19)

What becomes of the traditional divisions of a story—prologue, exposition or development and finally dénouement or conclusion—in Chekhov's work? The 'prologue' or introduction to the story is generally reduced to nil, or to a short sentence that immediately goes to the heart of the matter. This, for instance, is how his story *My Life* starts: "The bailiff said to me: 'I'm only keeping you on out of regard for your worthy father. Otherwise, I'd have sacked you long ago!'" This is the manner in which Chekhov cuts abruptly to the very core of his themes, and, throughout the actual development of his stories, the conciseness of the means of expression is equally striking. For instance, in *Ionich*, Chekhov is content to indicate Dr. Startsev's social advancement by means of a few scattered sign-posts. A young doctor at the start of his career, "Startsev walked unhurriedly, (he did not yet own any horses) and sang . . . ." A year goes by. The author does not go into detail but slips in, apparently casually: "By now, he owned a carriage and pair and a coachman, Panteleimon, in a velvet waistcoat." Four years later: "Startsev had a large practice. Every morning, he received his patients *with all possible speed* so as to be free to attend the ones who were expecting him to visit them in town: he no longer rode in his carriage, but in a troika with bells." And a few years later still comes the ultimate stage of his success: "Startsev had put on still more weight, had dif-ficulty in breathing and walked with his head in the air. When he passed by, corpulent and blotchy, in his troika with bells, with Panteleimon, equally corpulent and red-faced on the coachman's seat, it was a really imposing spectacle, and one felt it was not a man passing by but a pagan deity." That is all. But is not his social standing perfectly clear? As regards the third element, the dénouement or conclusion, Chekhov had always appreciated its vital role in the composition. He knew that it was in the ending that the impact produced by the whole work was concentrated, particularly when the work was as condensed and compact as a short story. (pp. 19-20)

The Chekhov of the final years ended his stories and plays abruptly, on a sort of musical chord. There is, strictly speaking, no longer an ending at all. On the contrary, a window is opened on to a distant vista. In *The Lady with the Dog*, the two leading characters are involved in an inextricable situation. And this is how the story ends: "What can I do, what can I do?—he wondered, his head in his hands. And he felt that a solution would crop up before long and that then a new and marvellous life would begin. But both of them were clearly aware that everything was far from being settled and that the most com-plicated, the most difficult part was only just beginning." One stage in the lives and the fortunes of the two characters had finished, but there was another to come, one that was only just beginning. That is what Chekhov is saying in this dénouement, which, in fact, is not one at all. This same form of ending is to be found in nearly all his works after 1894. (p. 21)

Music plays an immense part in Chekhov's work. The sonorous element is one of the most important in his method. If we analyse the various manifestations of this lyrical element, we see that the most outstanding is *the musicality of his style,* his way of altering his sentences so as to render them more har-monious and the precision with which he chooses and combines his words. Chekhov attached enormous importance to the mu-sical structure of his sentences. . . . (p. 22)

An innovator in his musical method, Chekhov is equally so in his visual one. His love of nature turns him into a great land-scape painter, whom his contemporaries often compared to Levitan.

The anthropomorphism, the bold painting and the colours, slightly blurred at the outset, gradually make way for a monochrome design of admirable simplicity. The original somewhat vague sentimentality becomes transformed into a virile, serene mel-ancholy. The austerity of the style accords well with the purity of the feelings it expresses and the final effect is one of ex-traordinary spirituality.

But the man of science, the doctor, watches over the lyrical poet. Alongside the beautiful, poetic descriptions are to be found others, both frightening and grotesque. His painterly naturalist's eyes enable Chekhov to observe the man he is

depicting, take him to pieces and reveal the deep-seated bru-tishness that sometimes forms a part of him. (pp. 23-4)

Beneath this art, so full of light and shade, lurked the tragic view of life, so characteristic of Chekhov in his maturity. This tragic view is expressed in his *Notebooks,* his letters and his best works. But there is an important distinction to be drawn here.

Actually, in Chekhov's eyes, the tragedy of life existed on two separate planes, on the higher plane it was metaphysical; on the lower, social. The former was, in its nature, eternal and irremediable. The second, temporary and susceptible to im-provement. One of Chekhov's favourite themes and unques-tionably the most characteristic and profound is that of solitude. A metaphysical solitude, inherent to the human condition. (pp. 25-6)

A Sad Story perfectly illustrates Chekhov's metaphysical pes-simism regarding the inevitable destiny of every human being, which, in the last analysis, is to be utterly alone both in life and in the face of death. (p. 27)

However, below this philosophical and inevitable tragedy there lies another plane, that of the social tragedy, which, unlike the former, offers hope of a cure. Culture, education, a relative prosperity can temper the horror of certain lives and certain situations, described by Chekhov in such stories as *The Mu-zhiks, In the Ravine* and *Vanka.* Society can be made better; men can become more disciplined, more refined, happier and more civilized. They will no longer torture children, they will become less coarse, less greedy, less cruel. In Chekhov's eyes, the social tragedy appears to be capable of improvement.

Who can forget the poetical endings to his plays, *Uncle Vanya* and *The Cherry Orchard,* from which there suddenly springs hope for a better future and a happiness, not only possible but certain, even though still far away? This hope, this faith are superimposed upon the fundamental theme of Chekhov's work—the constant assertion of man's inner, spiritual, moral and sen-timental solitude, face to face with his fellow-men. An eternal solitude, since it is rooted in the very foundation of human nature.

So how, then, can one reconcile the personal tragedy, the irremediable solitude (which was the lot of Chekhov, himself, and most of his heroes) with the illogical hope of a problematic, future happiness? One cannot, in fact, envisage any bridge capable of surmounting the gap between these two very con-tradictory conceptions. And Chekhov has not attempted to rec-oncile them in the abstract or in the absolute. Like a true stoic he is satisfied with confining himself to action, satisfied to struggle on, while abandoning any idea of that "personal hap-piness which does not exist, which should not exist." (pp. 27-8)

Sophie Laffitte, in her Chekhov, 1860-1904, *trans-lated by Moura Budberg and Gordon Latta (trans-lation copyright © 1973 Angus and Robertson; re-printed with the permission of Angus & Robertson (UK) Ltd Publishers and Hachette Littérature Gén-érale; originally published as* Tchékhov, 1860-1904, Hachette, 1971), *Angus and Robertson, 1974, 246 p.*

VIRGINIA LLEWELLYN SMITH   (essay date 1973)

[*Smith's* Anton Chekhov and the Lady with the Dog, *from which the following analysis of the title story is taken, is a study of the role of women in the author's life and work.*]

No other single work of Chekhov's fiction constitutes a more meaningful comment on Chekhov's attitude to women and to love than does 'The Lady with the Dog'. So many threads of Chekhov's thought and experience appear to have been woven together into this succinct story that it may be regarded as something in the nature of a summary of the entire topic.

Gurov, the hero of the story, may at first appear no more closely identifiable with Chekhov himself than are many other sympathetic male characters in Chekhov's fiction: he has a post in a bank and is a married man with three children. It is because he has this wife and family that his love-affair with Anna Sergeevna leads him into an *impasse*. And the affair itself, involving Gurov's desperate trip to Anna's home town, has no obvious feature in common with anything we know of Chekhov's amorous liaisons.

And yet Chekhov's own attitudes and experience have clearly shaped Gurov's character and fate.... As in general with early marriages in Chekhov's fiction, Gurov's has not proved a success. His wife seems 'much older than he' and imagines herself to be an intellectual: familiar danger-signals. She is summed-up in three words: 'stiff, pompous, dignified' (*pryamaya, vazhnaya, solidnaya*) which epitomize a type of woman (and man) that Chekhov heartily disliked.

Gurov's wife treats sex as something more complicated than it is, spoils it for him; and it is also spoilt for him by those mistresses of whom he soon tires. . . . It would seem that exactly some such sentiment inspired Chekhov when he depicted Ariadna, Nyuta, and the other anti-heroines.

Gurov has had, however, liaisons that were, for him, enjoyable—-and these we note, were brief. . . . (pp. 212-13)

Gurov cannot do without the company of women, and yet he describes them as an 'inferior breed': his experience of intimacy with women is limited to casual affairs and an unsatisfactory marriage. Chekhov also enjoyed the company of women and had many female friends and admirers: but he failed, or was unwilling, to involve himself deeply or lastingly with them. That in his work he should suggest that women are an inferior breed can be to some extent explained by the limited knowledge of women his self-contained attitude brought him—and perhaps, to some extent, by a sense of guilt concerning his inability to feel involved.

Gurov's behaviour to Anna Sergeevna at the beginning of their love-affair is characterized by an absence of emotional involvement, just such as appears in Chekhov's attitude towards certain women. There is a scene in 'The Lady with the Dog' where, after they have been to bed together, Gurov eats a watermelon while Anna Sergeevna weeps over her corruption. (pp. 213-14)

Gurov's egocentricity is dispelled, however, by the potent influence of love, because Anna Sergeevna turns out to be the ideal type of woman: pitiable, defenceless, childlike, capable of offering Gurov an unquestioning love. Love is seen to operate as a force for good: under its influence Gurov feels revulsion for the philistinism of his normal life and associates. Soviet interpreters have made much of the theme of regeneration, of the idea implicit in the story that 'a profound love experienced by ordinary people has become an enormous moral force'. In fact, although some idea of this sort is certainly implicit in the story, Chekhov is surely attempting above all to evoke what love meant to his protagonists as they themselves saw their situation. (pp. 214-15)

The point is that we are not seeing the lovers changed in relation to society, but in relation to their own inner lives. Gurov is shaken out of his romantic dreaming by a sudden recognition of the grossness of others in his stratum of society: but he does not give up his job or abandon his social life. Instead, he leads a double existence, and imagines that every man's 'real, most interesting life' goes on in secret. It is this life that Chekhov is interested in, not in Gurov as a representative of his class or his time.

That Gurov and Anna Sergeevna are alone amongst their fellow-men does not point a moral: but it is where the pathos of their initial situation lies. We are not impressed by their moral superiority, but moved by their loneliness. Love is the answer to this loneliness, and there is no need to bring morality into it. Chekhov, where love was concerned, wrote from the heart, not the head. . . .

As one might expect, Gurov's love for Anna Sergeevna has its romantic side. It is associated with the beauty of nature, for it is helped into existence by the view of the sea at Oreanda. When back in Moscow, Gurov thinks of Anna, he poeticizes her: the whole affair becomes the subject of a daydream, and ultimately an obsession. (p. 215)

[Chekhov's future wife], Olga Knipper, however, was no dream. And Anna Sergeevna is not seen solely in terms of 'poetry', even by Gurov.... The romantic heroine has become a creature of flesh and blood, and Gurov still loves her: 'she . . . now filled his whole life, she was his joy and his grief, the sole happiness that he now desired. . . .'

Gurov dreams—but dreaming is not enough for him. He has tasted happiness: the affair in Yalta was happy, in spite of Anna's sense of guilt. His love there developed from when, after Anna's self-recrimination and his irritation, they suddenly laughed together. This laugh denotes the beginning of communication: the tension relaxes and they behave normally, and find enjoyment in each other's company as well as in 'love'. Love, in fact, has come down to earth. Sex, communication, and simple companionship all play their part in it, in addition to 'poetry'.

And there the problem lies: the love-affair being rooted in reality, Anna and Gurov have to face the world's problems. . . .

The situation, indeed the entire plot of 'The Lady with the Dog', is obvious, even banal, and its merit as a work of art lies in the artistry with which Chekhov has preserved in the story a balance between the poetic and the prosaic, and in the careful characterization, dependent upon the use of half-tones. Soviet critics have a valid point when they regard Gurov as a sort of Everyman; 'The Lady with the Dog' is an essentially simple exposition of a commonplace theme. Unlike in 'The Duel' and 'Three Years', in 'The Lady with the Dog' Chekhov has made no attempt to investigate the problems of love: the conclusion of 'The Lady with the Dog' is left really and truly open: there is no suggestion, nor have we any inkling, of what the future may bring. (p. 216)

There can be no doubt but that the policy of expounding questions without presuming to answer them—that policy which Chekhov had declared to be the writer's task—suited his style best. A full appreciation of Chekhov's work requires of the reader a certain degree of involvement, a response intellectual, or, as in the case of his love-stories, emotional, that Chekhov invites rather than commandeers. Ultimately, all depends on how Chekhov is read; but much depends on his striking the delicate balance between sentimentality and flatness. . . .

The history of Gurov's relationships with women is a transmutation of Chekhov's history, and the essential point of the fiction was reality for him: true love had come too late, and complete happiness—poetry and communication and companionship—was impossible. (p. 217)

> Virginia Llewellyn Smith, in her Anton Chekhov and "The Lady with the Dog" (© 1973 by Oxford University Press; reprinted by permission of Oxford University Press), Oxford University Press, London, 1973, 249 p.

DONALD RAYFIELD (essay date 1975)

[*Rayfield's* Chekhov: The Evolution of His Art, *from which the following introductory statement has been excerpted, is an in-depth study of theme, style, and structure in the author's work.*]

The first stage in interpreting Chekhov is to bridge the gaps between the various Chekhovs that are brought out in any study of a particular aspect of his work. The most striking gap is that between Chekhov the dramatist, in particular the creator of *The Seagull, Uncle Vanya, Three Sisters* and *The Cherry Orchard,* and the Chekhov of the stories written in the 1890s, before and simultaneously with the major plays. Most critics of Chekhov's plays urge a reading based on one of three quite incompatible views of the dramatist's intentions. One view sees the plays as a requiem for the degenerate gentry, a prophecy of a new age of sanity and equality shortly to dawn. Another, more fashionable and sophisticated, takes the plays to be a statement of the absurdity of the human condition, in which there is no escape, no development, no reason. Thirdly, we are enjoined to look at the drama as ultimate realism—a minute recreation of what takes place in the pathology of human experience. Yet no one of these three Chekhovs—optimist, pessimist-decadent, or scientific impressionist—can be corroborated by the stories of the time, e.g. *My Life, The House with the Mezzanine, The Bishop.*

Chekhov was not a schizophrenic. The brave, muted optimism of the 'drop-out' Poloznev in *My Life,* the dissolution of all philosophies that we find in *The House with the Mezzanine,* and the extreme lyricism, as completely committed as Rimbaud's and Wordsworth's, of *The Bishop*—all this is as essentially Chekhovian as the off-stage noises, the speculation about life in two or three hundred years' time, and the tics of the characters in the plays. Nine-tenths of the perennial arguments on how to produce Chekhov's plays would be silenced for ever if only they were read together with the stories whose characters, situations, themes and techniques they continue. (p. 2)

[One] of the conflicting elements of Chekhov that cannot be accounted for by the changing outlook of a rapidly maturing and ageing writer is that between the lyrical and the comic. It is not quite enough to explain the conflict away by saying that Chekhov began with a comic approach to human quirks of behaviour and only with an increasingly close focus became lyrical rather than satirical; the comic element is always there, even in the ghastly hell of *In the Gully,* where the curate, as tradition demands, is a glutton; and in Chekhov's last play, *The Cherry Orchard,* the subtitle and everything Chekhov said about it insists on the word *comedy.* (p. 3)

Close examination of Chekhov's texts calls for the techniques of poetic analysis. Many of the typical features of prose narrative are often absent, such as intrigue and dénouement, even though there is a great deal of action; often the distinction between hero and narrator is blurred. Other elements dominate the structure: a recurrent, variable image, for instance of clear and contaminated water; or a senseless, half-conscious refrain uttered by one of the characters. Chekhov's sentences, especially in his landscapes or his interior monologues, have a rhythmic and intonational power just as important to the final effect as his handling of plot (or anti-plot). (p. 4)

Like some modern practitioners of linguistic analysis, Chekhov is not, perhaps, interested in metaphysical statements so much as in the chance stimulus and the words which make people formulate such statements. In some stories, notably *The House with the Mezzanine* and *The Duel,* Chekhov's characters expound conflicting philosophies: the point lies not in the viability of the philosophies themselves but in the forces that prompt characters to espouse them.

Similar problems arise when we try to distinguish between heroes and villains. To a certain extent, Chekhov's categories are aesthetic, not ethic; a complex, changing, responsive character is evidently far more attractive to him than a consistent monolith, who repeats the same actions and words. His criteria may be seen as those of a pathologist. Characters who are not diseased or in turmoil tend to bore him. Suffering-insufferable replaces good-bad. Whether this amounts to a morality is a question to be set out, if not to be answered.

The handle to Chekhov that is perhaps easiest to grasp lies in the theme of conservation. Throughout his work, but especially in the plays and the late stories, he sees human suffering as wastage of resources, and evil as destruction of the environment. Through the plays runs the symbol of chopped-down forests; through the stories the symbol of rivers polluted by brickworks or bone-processors. One of the most modern aspects of Chekhov is his feeling for the smallness and fragility of the earth, and to the idea of its conservation he subjugates all the old-fashioned, anthropocentric ethical systems of the past. In the plays, this fearful feeling comes out in the speeches of characters like Doctor Astrov [in *Uncle Vanya*]; in the stories it is expressed in innumerable symbols that colour an apparently straight-forward realistic narrative. (pp. 6-7)

Chekhov's irony is not the self-satisfied amusement of an author pulling his characters along on strings through a labyrinth; it is not the cynical resignation to fate of Greek tragedy; it is not just a manner that hints at gold reserves of knowledge to back the paper currency of talk. Chekhov's irony is much more modern, much closer to Samuel Beckett than to the great tradition of the European novel. What he knows and what his characters often ignore is that 'les choses sont contre nous' ["things are against us"]. His characters' statements not only get them nowhere, they are not even possible to complete, so insistent is the absurd importunacy of sand in the speaker's boots, the compulsion to fiddle with a sleeve, the banging of an iron rail outside the house. Not only the plays but also the stories are full of extraneous noises, physical tics and silences which give an ironic impotence to the sanest of rationalisations. (p. 7)

A unity of thematic resources and treatment . . . underlies Chekhov's evolution. For all the great variety of characters and settings, certain types and certain places recur throughout his work. The most noticeable character—participating or commenting—is an introverted doctor, whom Chekhov takes over from the traditional nineteenth-century portrayal of wisdom and sceptical foresight, and develops into a figure which is now an intermediary in the struggle of strong and weak, now the embodiment of man's struggle to find meaning in the cosmos. Less frequent, but also recurrent, is the schoolteacher, who demonstrates the corrupting force of decrepit institutions on a mind full of vapid idealism. The professor and the artist are likewise characters that exist outside any one story, and are incarnated at certain moments. The querulous, senile Professor Serebryakov of *Uncle Vanya* is only a degenerate form of the rough-hewn Faustian malcontent, the professor of *A Dreary Story:* their frail but ruthless dependence on others, even their fear of thunderstorms, identify them.

The ecclesiastic characters form an even stronger chain; from the unintellectual father Kristofor of *Steppe* to the naïve theology student of *The Student* to *The Bishop* stretches an unbroken thread; all are men with an aura of enchantment, who can encompass sorrow and who exemplify a lost human innocence.

It is the women in Chekhov's work, however, who give it the greatest consistency. Although Chekhov enjoyed the company of women on all sorts of bases and although he was unencumbered by any bitterness or fears, he characterises them in a far more schematic way than men. Quite early in his work a division of women into two types is apparent: one strong, self-deluding and often repellent—such as Ari Ariadna in the story of that name; the other more admirable and less predatory, passive and attractive. The division is very sharp in the two sisters of *The House with the Mezzanine,* or between Natasha and the 'three sisters, but it begins as early as the mid-1880s. On the few occasions that Chekhov's characterisations risk being caricatures, we find they are always of women. Not only occasional fits of misogyny but also the difficulty of showing total empathy with the other sex made Chekhov cast rather than forge women characters.

Chekhov's settings obviously reflect his own environment. All can be traced to places he knew well. But behind the variety of Moscow, country cottage, provincial town, country estate settings there lies a single purpose. Nearly all Chekhov's characters live in closed boxes, from which escape is not easy. They meet and conflict because they are unable to get away from each other, not because they want to discuss questions of life and death. The air of the closed box gives the plays their utterly convincing collisions of characters and their claustrophobia; but the stories use the same device to provoke clashes, for which other writers would use more elaborate settings.

The more mature the work, the more closely are both landscape and interior monologue rendered through the psychology of the characters. But many of Chekhov's techniques are established in early work. His landscapes. . . have a painter's quality, in that they are seen, not described. We feel an actual human retina and inner ear taking in sights and sounds, and the brain—at first of the author, then of the character—letting loose its irrational and imaginative responses. The prism of the senses in Chekhov's descriptions bends the perspectives and the priorities which conventional descriptions observe, giving his work a certain affinity with Impressionist painting. Furthermore, Chekhov presents nature description in terms of the psychology of the hero; though this sometimes gives his work a curious, outmoded Romantic quality of pathetic fallacy, his description of evening light, sea, storms lies at the heart of his world-outlook, in which human reflections and actions are only an ephemeral interruption of nature's continuum. (pp. 8-10)

For Chekhov as for other writers sexual love is the most important form of human involvement. Unlike Dostoyevsky and Tolstoy, he saw no need to incorporate the erotic into a scale of things in which Platonic love reigns supreme. In many of his later stories—*Ionych* or *The Lady with the Little Dog*—and in the plays, falling in love and acting on it amount to a brave self-fulfilment. Despite all the squalor of 'affairs'—hotel rooms and strewn underwear, which Chekhov found so distasteful, the commitment of one human being to another is one of the few ways in which the Chekhovian character can break out of his isolation and get round the uselessness of words for communication.

Chekhov came to accept without revulsion the animal in man, as had new trends in psychology, in which he was so interested. Here is one of the reasons for his modernity, for the appeal that his individualism still makes to us. His morality has an existentialist provisionality about it. He clearly believed human life to be an anomaly in a dead cosmos; his concept of man has no angelic pattern to live up to. Chekhov admires the human being who can make the most of his latencies. . . . In a meaningless world, each man overcomes the absurdity of the cosmos by expanding himself into a whole world. The innumerable remarks made by Chekhov and his characters about the oblivion which will swallow them up as soon as they die make all the clearer his ideal of living in the present, unchecked by habits of the past or fears of the future. The evil and depression that beset so much of his work can be equated with the dead weight of the past and the horror of the future. The desire to make the most of the present is not just a European hedonism; it is part of Chekhov's love of sense-impressions and dislike of ratiocination. It applies to the individual at a moment when a failure to act must imprison his life in the mould of his past, and it applies to humanity when failure to act must waste the beauty of the living earth. (pp. 11-12)

> *Donald Rayfield, in his* Chekhov: The Evolution of His Art *(copyright © Donald Rayfield 1975; by permission of Barnes & Noble Books, a Division of Littlefield, Adams & Co., Inc.), Barnes & Noble, 1975, 266 p.*

IEVA VITINS (essay date 1978)

Overlooked in discussions of Uncle Vanya's ineffectuality as a male protagonist is a textual network of emotional ties which bind him to his dead sister, her family, and his mother. To a great degree these ties serve to repress his masculinity and prevent him from establishing a family of his own or making an imprint on the outside world. Vanya has become a peripheral male figure, a veritable "Uncle Johnnie" who proudly supports his sister Vera's family and experiences the role of husband vicariously. It is only years after Vera's death and the recent remarriage of her husband that he becomes dissatisfied with his secondary role in life. He ceases temporarily to act the uncle and family provider; instead, he vents his hatred for the brother-in-law he formerly admired and assumes the role of self-dramatized suitor of the new wife Yelena. Querulous and aggressive, he suggests a man painfully out of character, whose impotence reflects the sterility of the dying gentry class. (p. 35)

Vanya is perhaps the most poignant example in Chekhov's plays of a man whose lasting attachment to a sister or mother has decisively affected his desire and ability to lead an independent life, but he is only one of several such ineffectual brothers and sons. Treplev's troubled relationship to his mother in *The Seagull* is recognized as a salient factor in his inability to cope with life and offers striking parallels to the family situation in **Uncle Vanya.** Andrey, in **Three Sisters,** is loved and looked up to by his sisters, but is cuckolded soon after his marriage and turns out to be a disastrous paterfamilias. Finally, the tearful Gayev in **The Cherry Orchard** (Lopakhin refers to him as "an old woman") adores his sister but can do nothing to save the family estate, nor lead a productive life. Each of these men, in his overrefined sensitivity and lack of physical and intellectual vigor, is somewhat of an "old woman," or perhaps an affable and harmless "uncle." (p. 44)

Ieva Vitins, "Uncle Vanya's Predicament," in Slavic and East European Journal *(©1978 by AATSEEL of the U.S., Inc.; reprinted by permission of the editor), Vol. 22, No. 4, Winter, 1978 (and reprinted in* Chekhov's Great Plays: A Critical Anthology, *edited by Jean-Pierre Barricelli, New York University Press, 1981, pp. 35-46).*

ANTHONY WINNER   (essay date 1981)

In Chekhov's characters the internalized hierarchy of social or cultural meanings central to the Balzacian tradition collapses. The absence of any sustaining, authoritative conviction—whether religious, social, or otherwise—brings with it a randomness of being. (pp. 142-43)

Chekhov's distrust of general organizing premises becomes a key to the frequent predicament of his characters. The disparateness experienced by many of his more fully developed figures is an almost bitter mirroring of the author's distrust of the prescriptive fixity of abstract positions, of his preference for the elusive truths of particular situations. . . . Chekhov's convictions help explain why he emerges as the true artist who heroically liberates Russian literature from the divisive social, political, and ideological position-taking demanded of writers by the liberal critics of the age. The same creed establishes him as the heroic liberator of short fiction from the heavy hand of novelistic expectations. Both estimates are wholly accurate, but both play down the doubts and ambiguities surrounding the relation between Chekhov's movingly expressed beliefs and the damaged characters who are so often the results of these beliefs, between the artist's rejection of labels and his characters' frequent inability to give public definition to their lives.

It is not paradoxical that a creator of imaginary worlds should abhor lies, but Chekhov's insistence on a scrupulously honest realism complicates his presentation of the illusions, fictions, or lies that are the staff of bearable life for many of his characters. (pp. 146-47)

The discrepancy between dream and fact is the traditional fare of realism. Yet Chekhov's commitment to both results in fictions that are at once pellucidly expressive and thematically opaque. . . . For Chekhov, the outer and the human dimensions exist in permanent mutual exclusion: each is true; each can be beautiful or uncouth. The characters thus become less victims than aliens. Finding privacy incomplete, they enter spheres beyond themselves only to lose the truths that define and sustain them. (p. 148)

[We] might expect Chekhov to seek solace or even solutions in nature. Certainly, he frequently contrasts human disorder with nature's bountiful beauty. But the contrast holds out no hope. Often, the solace of sky and landscape merely projects the human beholder's unreliable vision. In itself, nature is a thing apart, a separateness off which human desiring futilely rebounds. (pp. 148-49)

[His] idea of nature pursuing an indifferent life of its own wholly removed from man's purposes is constant. . . . Nature is a poem; the lives Chekhov narrates, a weary prose. (p. 150)

Chekhov's natural scenes almost always reflect, not external phenomena, but the sorcery of human need: the charm of happy moods, the disenchantment of pain. The emotions of the characters often seem equally deprived of objective meaning. Feelings are frequently expressed as poignantly as the glories of sunset or morning. But the force of Chekhov's evocations owes much to an accompanying implication of arbitrariness or unreality. (p. 151)

The external determinants of human existence—social status, occupation, geographic setting—are always clearly demarcated. The private content of character, on the other hand, is often a turbid flux in which mood and feeling, dreams, oddments of perceptions, and bits of ideas distort the outlines of fact. This inner region operates much like the linguistic concept of purely connotative, "phatic" communication. Phatic speech conveys no empirically verifiable message; its meaning lies in emotional tonalities. Would-be lovers speak of current events, of the weather, of food; they are saying, "Look, we're together, we're empathizing." Such a mode requires the shelter of intimacy; it cannot tolerate the intrusion of declarative realities. Lives lived under the aegis of free-floating sentiment tend to be blind to the approaching traffic of events.

There are always painful, sometimes fatal, collisions. But these usually produce an effect quite different from the mechanical crushing of individuals by the juggernaut of a world they never made. Chekhov's generosity of tone pervades the portrait of each character's perspective and modifies the pessimism typical of naturalistic determinism. . . . Never does he present private life as a unique source of authenticity. Outside the enclaves built by individual dreams is the great globe itself, and the very facts that now violate dreams may some day fulfill them, may even render them unnecessary. The rare balance between inner and outer truths Chekhov achieves derives from this belief. The writer's task is to depict the conditions of present disorder with a rational clarity and an absence of bias as committed as the presence of fellow feeling. . . . Chekhov's highly personal positivism, his belief in joint scientific and spiritual progress, is a fact of his biography. But his authorial laissez-faire is often so complete as to obscure all evidence of his hopes. For his characters, there is scant sign of directions to follow or structures to imitate; for his readers, rational skepticism can appear to be existential uncertainty, and the unwillingness to impose understanding can be confused with the loss of any dynamic, organizing vision.

Though Chekhov disclaims the superfluousness and decadence of purpose that become clichés of the Twilight, he feels his scope circumscribed by the absence of vast structures of meaning that is also typical of the age. . . . [The] conviction of diminishment is no passing mood. Its shadow darkens the lives Chekhov recounts and merges into the realities that harm them. Chekhov is one of the first modern masters of the turmoil of identity in the throes of fragmentation, one of the first to view self-creation as an alternative to the crude determinisms and false emphases of the Twilight. But his protagonists cannot share the high purposes and accomplishments of the art that gives them being. Flawed inheritors of no longer sufficient dreams, they are without the strengths that the writers Chekhov calls eternal lend to at lease some of their characters. The short novels contain no equivalent to the sustained emphasis on cosmic law and temporal decay in Hardy and Zola. No less aware of modern hazards, Chekhov is far less judgmental. Not only does he refuse to dramatize possible answers, he is bent upon conveying the pathos of badly framed questions. His narratives deal with characters at those times when private fabrications wear thin, when the artifices that have become the modus operandi of selfhood cannot protect their creators against the realities of "a precarious, sour, dreary period." Two modes of definition are always at war: the illusion each ego constructs and the external circumstances surrounding it. Illusion is necessary because culture and society no longer offer structures that can order and give stable value to individual aspiration. Compared to older faiths, illusions are arbitrary and short-lived. At best, in Chekhov's happier stories, the characters achieve only respite, moments when the impetus of fact is held at a standoff. And while the poignancy of fractured models and reductive distress is rarely held up for analysis or authorial comment, any representative collection of Chekhov's short novels will demonstrate the effects on character of a malady akin to Hardy's ache of modernism and Zola's malaise. (pp. 152-57)

The humanity with which Chekhov invests the course of failure simply renders the emptiness that is its consequence available to sympathetic scrutiny. Unconnected with an inner order of dreams and sentiments, scientific rationality becomes a realistic clarity that drains the blood from all of life. (p. 158)

The counterpoint between the limitations of a first-person narrator and the full-bodied art that expresses them recurs in many of the third person stories in a different but no less foreboding relation between character and art. Chekhov's use of the indirect free style, of narrated consciousness, mirrors the flailing attempts of separate lives to escape their hermetic plight. Immersing himself first in one consciousness and then in another, often without omniscient transition, Chekhov dramatizes self-imprisonment and the immense difficulty of transposing private melodies even into duets—let alone into social orchestration. The principle laid down by Rebecca West in one of her short novels some thirty years later provides an appropriate epigraph. "There is no such thing as conversation. It is an illusion. There are intersecting monologues, that is all. We speak; we spread round with sounds, with words, an emanation from ourselves. Sometimes they overlap the circles others are spreading round themselves. Then they are affected by these other circles, to be sure, but not because of any real conversation that has taken place." (pp. 168-69)

The intense psychological empathy and understanding that distinguish Chekhov from Hardy and Zola are transformed within the content of his characters' lives into an intense self-absorption resembling modern Laodiceanism and Empire neurasthenia. In several of the major short novels, moreover, the social bad faith and indifferent universal law typical of the other two writers enter the foreground of Chekhov's presentation. Edmund Wilson's contention that the stories and plays of Chekhov's later years "constitute a kind of analysis of Russian society, a miniature *Comédie Humaine*," clearly points to a more than psychological focus. The social, natural, and cosmic forces that intrude upon individuals are central to at least two of the studies of middle-class character, **Ward Six** and **An Anonymous Story**—both written slightly before the period Wilson specifies—and to two accounts of peasant life, **Peasants** and **In the Ravine**. (pp. 170-71)

Yet we remember the art more often than we do its characters, few of whom even approach the wholeness that Chekhov, like Hardy and Zola, desires to see reborn. The ethos of such wholeness, the synthesis of personality and cultural purpose that I have associated with the Balzacian model, does not survive the Twilight. Hardy, Zola, and Chekhov would find much to admire in the beliefs and techniques that enter into modern novelistic character, but they would deplore the passing of the moral imperatives they equated with their craft. (p. 194)

Anthony Winner, "Chekhov's Characters: True Tears, Real Things," in his Characters in the Twilight: Hardy, Zola, and Chekhov *(copyright ©1981 by the Rector and Visitors of the University of Virginia), University Press of Virginia, 1981, pp. 140-94.*

ADDITIONAL BIBLIOGRAPHY

Beckerman, Bernard. "The Artifice of 'Reality' in Chekhov and Pinter." *Modern Drama* XXI, No. 2 (June 1978): 153-61.*
Explains how Chekhov creates a sense of dramatic "reality" in terms distinct from those of conventionally naturalistic theater.

Bruford, W. H. *Anton Chekhov*. New Haven: Yale University Press, 1957, 62 p.
Examines Chekhov's work in relation to the social and political climate of the Russia of his time.

Bunin, Ivan. "Chekhov." *The Atlantic Monthly* 188, No. 1 (July 1951): 59-63.
Memories of the Russian novelist Bunin concerning his friendship with Chekhov.

Debreczeny, Paul, and Eeckman, Thomas, eds. *Chekhov's Art of Writing: A Collection of Critical Essays*. Columbus: Slavica Publishers, 1977, 199 p.
Essays from a predominantly formalist-structuralist critical perspective.

Gifford, Henry. "Chekhov the Humanist." In his *The Novel in Russia: From Pushkin to Pasternak*, pp. 125-34. London: Hutchinson University Library, 1964.
Introductory-level critical and biographical survey.

Hahn, Beverly. *Chekhov: A Study of the Major Stories and Plays*. Cambridge: Cambridge University Press, 1977, 350 p.
Sees Chekhov's work as highly psychological and claims he is "a more positive writer than even his strongest supporters often contend."

Hingley, Ronald. *A New Life of Chekhov*. New York: Alfred A. Knopf, 1976, 352 p.
Utilizes much significant documentary material which has become available since the publication of Hingley's *Chekhov: A Biographical and Critical Study* (see *TCLC*, Vol. 3).

Jackson, Robert Louis, ed. *Chekhov: A Collection of Critical Essays*. Englewood Cliffs, N.J.: Prentice-Hall, 1967, 213 p.
Collection composed primarily of essays translated from Russian, German, and French specifically for this appearance. Of particular interest are a number of essays by Russian scholars and critics, including Boris Eichenbaum, V. Yermilov, S. D. Balukhaty, G. Berdinov, A. Skaftymov, Vsevolod Meyerhold, and Dmitri Chizhevsky.

Jarrell, Randall. "Six Russian Short Novels." In his *The Third Book of Criticism*, pp. 235-75. New York: Farrar, Straus & Giroux, 1969.*
Reprint of an introduction to an anthology of Russian novellas, including *Ward No. 6*. The pages devoted to this story give a plot summary and some background information.

Kazin, Alfred. "Writing for Magazines." In his *Contemporaries*, pp. 469-74. Boston: Little, Brown and Co., 1962.
General evaluation praising Chekhov for showing "that prose could be as profound . . . an intimation of human existence as poetry."

Magarshack, David. Introductions to *The Real Chekhov: An Introduction to Chekhov's Last Plays,* by Anton Chekhov, pp. 9-18, 21-3,
79-81, 125-26, 187-96. London: George Allen & Unwin, 1972.
    Criticizes translators and directors of Chekhov's plays for their
misinterpretation of Chekhov as an artist who deliberately promoted despair. The introductions to *The Seagull, Uncle Vanya,
The Three Sisters,* and *The Cherry Orchard* give biographical and
literary background, including a long section from Chekhov's
letters concerning the writing of *The Cherry Orchard.*

Matual, David. "Chekhov's 'Black Monk' and Byron's 'Black Friar'."
International Fiction Review V, No. 1 (January 1978): 46-51.*
    Provides autobiographical documentation from Chekhov to sub-
stantiate Byron's influence on him.

Mirsky, D. S. "The Eighties and Early Nineties." In his *A History
of Russian Literature,* pp. 333-67. New York: Alfred A. Knopf, 1955.*
    Biographical sketch and introductory survey of Chekhov's work.

Nabokov, Vladimir. "Anton Chekhov." In his *Lectures on Russian
Literature,* edited by Fredson Bowers, pp. 245-95. New York, London:
Harcourt Brace Jovanovich, 1981.
    Analyzes Chekhov's narrative technique and discusses the inef-
fectual Chekhovian hero of the short stories.

O'Connor, Frank. "The Slave's Son." In his *The Lonely Voice: A
Study of the Short Story,* pp. 78-98. Cleveland: The World Publishing
Co., 1963.
    Thematic analysis of several plots of the short stories.

Slonim, Marc. "The Beginnings of the Moscow Art Theater." In his
Russian Theater: From the Empire to the Soviets, pp. 100-32. Cleveland: The World Publishing Co., 1961.*

    Plot outlines and theatrical history of the major dramas.

Speirs, Logan. "Chekhov: The Stories" and "Chekhov: The Plays."
In his *Tolstoy and Chekhov,* pp. 137-82, 185-223. Cambridge: Cambridge University Press, 1971.
    Sees the major similarity between Tolstoy and Chekhov in their
realistic recreation in literature of the world around them, and
their major difference in their divergent philosophical outlooks,
Tolstoy's that of dogmatic religiosity and Chekhov's that of agnostic materialism.

Winner, Thomas G. "Myth as a Device in the Works of Chekhov."
In *Myth and Symbol: Critical Approaches and Applications,* edited by
Bernice Slote, pp. 71-8. Lincoln: University of Nebraska, 1963.
    Points out archetypal patterns and characters in Chekhov's work
drawn from classical mythology.

Winner, Thomas [G]. *Chekhov and His Prose.* New York: Holt, Rinehart and Winston, 1966, 263 p.
    Critical study of the short stories divided into sections which
analyze Chekhov's themes, styles, and development as an author,
as well as his relationship to the artistic and social world of
nineteenth-century Russia.

Yermilov, Vladimir. *Anton Pavlovich Chekhov, 1860-1904.* Moscow:
Foreign Languages Publishing House, 1956, 415 p.
    Biography with an emphasis on developmental factors significant
to Chekhov's evolution as an author.

Young, Stark. "Gulls and Chekhov." *Theatre Arts Monthly* XXII,
No. 10 (October 1938): 737-42.
    Criticizes and corrects some English translations of *The Seagull.*
The critic also attempts to remedy Chekhov's widespread image
as an artist of gloom and morbidity.

Paul (Louis Charles Marie) Claudel

1868-1955

French dramatist, poet, essayist, apologist, and translator.

Claudel is considered the most important Catholic dramatist of the twentieth century. In his quest for a spiritual theater, he was one of the first French writers to revolt against the tenets of Naturalism and against the formal verse tradition best represented by his contemporary Edmond Rostand. The key to understanding Claudel, or the stumbling block, is his religious belief. All of his work, with the exception of the early play, *Tête d'or*, is in some sense an affirmation of his Roman Catholic faith. The strength of Claudel's drama lies not in its presentation of a divine universe, but in its passionate and lyrical portrayal of the individual's struggle to conform to the designs of Providence. Though his work was not widely performed until after 1925—when the panoramic scope and length of his plays became less intimidating to directors—Claudel had a significant effect on the French stage. He is remembered for his attempts to return drama to its religious origins as a mythic spectacle and a reenactment of the conflicts between God and humanity.

Claudel was born in the village of Villeneuve-sur-Fère to middle-class parents. He received his early education in the various provincial towns where his father worked as a civil servant, and eventually at the Lycee Louis-le-Grand in Paris. As a young man, Claudel rejected the vogue of Naturalism in literature and the prevailing philosophies of determinism and positivism. Instead, he studied the poetry of Charles Baudelaire, Paul Verlaine, and especially Arthur Rimbaud, who was a strong source of inspiration in Claudel's early years. In 1886, while studying for a diplomatic career, Claudel underwent a profound mystical experience at the cathedral of Notre Dame during Christmas Day Mass. The event shaped the rest of his life and formed the basis for his eventual conversion to the Catholic Church in 1890. The years preceding his conversion were marked by a spiritual struggle to reconcile the opposition between his intuition and his intellect. This spiritual crisis is evident in Claudel's first play, *Tête d'or*—a tragedy based on the life of an adventurer who seeks salvation solely through his own strength and intelligence. The play introduced a number of techniques Claudel was to utilize throughout his career: the use of symbolic rather than logical dramatic action, an emphasis on spiritual rather than psychological truth, and an innovative line of verse known as the *verset claudelien*, intended to reproduce the natural breathing or heartbeat of the poet or actor in order to indicate the emotional intensity of the passage. From 1893 to 1935 Claudel served in the French diplomatic corps and eventually held the office of ambassador to the United States. It was during these years that he wrote and published such major works as *Partage de midi (Break of Noon)*, *Le soulier de satin (The Satin Slipper)*, *L'annonce faite à Marie (The Tidings Brought to Mary)*, and the long lyric poems *Cinq grandes odes (Five Great Odes)*. Though the 1940s and 1950s saw the first productions of a number of his plays, Claudel wrote no poetry or drama during the last twenty years of his life; instead, he devoted himself entirely to lengthy reflections on various scriptural texts.

Most of Claudel's plays have historical settings and are concerned in part with great general themes, a major one being the conflict between the individual's earthly desires and his or her spiritual destination. The claims of God are often opposed to those of carnal love, and Claudel's favorite solution is for woman to serve as an instrument of salvation for man. This pattern is repeated in nearly all of Claudel's work, but it is most successful in *The Tidings Brought to Mary*, perhaps his best-known play. Here Claudel presents a moving drama set in the Middle Ages and based on human conflicts and religious sacrifice. In the end, Violaine—Claudel's prototypical heroine—reveals how love, separation, suffering, and even evil can lead humanity to understand both its role in the salvation of others and also the divine order of the universe. *The Satin Slipper* is considered by many critics to be Claudel's greatest play. It is a complicated drama of the Renaissance, a period Claudel believed to be the beginning of a new era of Catholicism. Against a background of violence and passion, the characters fulfill their destinies in a grand plot that covers four continents and demonstrates a number of Claudel's recurring themes: the individual's desire for the infinite, the limitations of human relationships, and the necessity of love as a means of reaching and understanding God. In a sense, *The Satin Slipper* is the culmination of all Claudel's poetic and dramatic works and a summary of his views on Catholic theology. Foremost among Claudel's poetic works is his *Five Great Odes*, a five-part poem based on the poet's meditations on the relationship between God and the created world, on the role of the poet, and on the function of love. In its final ode—"La maison fermée"—Claudel triumphantly affirms the presence of God in all things.

Criticism of Claudel's work is often very subjective. Those critics who share his faith tend to be enthusiastic in their appraisals, or afraid to criticize his work for fear they will be criticizing the Catholic faith. Those who oppose his religion are occasionally ignorant of the basic beliefs of Catholicism, and thus fail to give a meaningful account of his work. In general, most critics agree that as a poet and dramatist Claudel was a master lyricist who had a profound insight into the mysteries of faith and the history of Christianity. He has been praised for presenting the individual's existential struggle in a passionate style, rather than in the intellectual, detached manner of other Christian dramatists, such as T. S. Eliot. He is also credited with giving depth and substance to the Symbolist technique. On the other hand, many critics view Claudel as an uncompromising Catholic whose religious approach to human nature was anachronistic in a psychoanalytic age. They argue that his plays were often didactic, that his language was turgid, and that his unorthodox Catholicism, which stressed suffering and sacrifice, could not be appreciated by the general public. Despite the difference of critical opinion, Claudel's powerful literary style has led many critics to consider him the first truly dramatic poet in France since Racine.

(See also *TCLC*, Vol. 2 and *Contemporary Authors*, Vol. 104.)

PRINCIPAL WORKS

Tête d'or [first publication]   (drama)   1890
    [*Tête d'Or*, 1919]
La jeune fille Violaine [first publication]   (drama)   1892
La ville [first publication]   (drama)   1893
    [*The City*, 1920]
*L'arbre [first publication]   (dramas)   1901
L'echange [first publication]   (drama)   1901
Partage de midi [first publication]   (drama)   1906
    [*Break of Noon*, 1960]
Art poétique   (essays)   1907
    [*Poetic Art*, 1948]
Connaissance de l'est   (essays and prose poems)   1907
    [*The East I Know*, 1914]
**L'annonce faite à Marie   (drama)   1912
    [*The Tidings Brought to Mary*, 1916]
Cinq grandes odes   (poetry)   1913
    [*Five Great Odes*, 1967]
L'otage   (drama)   1914
    [*The Hostage*, 1917]
Protée [first publication]   (drama)   1914
Corona Benignitatis Anni Dei   (poetry)   1915
    [*Coronal*, 1942]
Trois poèmes de guerre   (poetry)   1915
    [*Three Poems of the War*, 1919]
La pain dur [first publication]   (drama)   1918
    [*Crusts* published in *Three Plays*, 1945]
La messe là-bas   (poetry)   1919
Le père humilié [first publication]   (drama)   1919
    [*The Humiliation of the Father* published in *Three Plays*, 1945]
Positions et propositions. 2 vols.   (essays)   1928-34
Le soulier de satin [first publication]   (drama)   1929
    [*The Satin Slipper*, 1931]

Le livre de Christophe Colomb   (drama)   1930
    [*The Book of Christopher Columbus*, 1930]
Jeanne d'Arc du búcher   (drama)   1939
Three Plays   (dramas)   1945
Oeuvres complètes. 26 vols.   (dramas, poetry, essays, and prose poems)   1950-67

*This work includes revisions of the earlier *Tête d'or*, *La jeune fille Violaine*, and *La ville*.

**This work is a revision of the earlier *La jeune fille Violaine*.

ANDRÉ GIDE   (letter date 1910)

[*The following excerpt is a portion of a letter from Gide to Claudel. The two writers were close friends for a number of years, and they often assisted each other with advice and editorial suggestions. Below, Gide comments on his reaction on first reading Claudel's L'otage.*]

[While] passing through Paris I received your admirable play [*L'Otage*] from Ruyters, read it at once, and gave it to be typed. I was only on my way through Paris (between Cuverville and Toulouse) and had just enough time to serve as a link between Ruyters and the typist. But when I had *L'Otage* in my hands I went at once to the post-office and telegraphed to Eugène Rouart that I should arrive twenty-four hours late. My yesterday was given over entirely to you. I travelled all night, with hardly a moment's sleep and this morning I can only tell you that I was deeply moved. The *urgency* of your play was beyond all my expectations—though you know that they were lively enough. The placing of your various characters is admirably effective; you give a new scale, a new dimension to yourself. (p. 135)

I am having three copies made: one for me—one for the *N.R.F.* [*La Nouvelle Revue Francaise*]. I can't help believing that the reverberation of this play will be as deep as it will be long; far from wishing (I am here speaking from your point of view—not that of the *N.R.F.*, for which I have no authority to speak) that it should appear in one single number, so that those who don't want it can easily ignore it, I think it an excellent idea that it should return to the charge. Besides, each act has its own persuasive power; and perhaps it's better to have digested the first two before taking the strain of the last act, which will antagonize more than one reader. Less so, however, if the first two acts have already imposed themselves on the public. (p. 136)

> *André Gide, in his letter to Paul Claudel on August 6, 1910, in* The Correspondence between Paul Claudel and André Gide, 1899-1926, *translated by John Russell (copyright 1952 by Pantheon Books Inc.; originally published as* Correspondence, 1899-1926 de Paul Claudel et André Gide, Gallimard, 1949), *Pantheon, 1952, pp. 135-36.*

PAUL CLAUDEL   (letter date 1910)

[*Below is a portion of a letter from Claudel to Gide. It continues a series of correspondences dealing with the publication of Claudel's L'Otage (see excerpt above).*]

Your letter, and one that I received a few days ago from my relation René Bazin, are of the sort that made it quite excusable for me to get something of a swollen head. I own that I was very pleased myself on reading my second Act, which comes off very well in print. *L'Otage,* for me, is a victory from two points of view: for the first time I've managed to hold in check the over-riding lyricism which is my great enemy: for the first time I've succeeded in creating objective and external characters, which means to say that the faculties of vision are beginning to develop to the same extent as the faculties of expression. But what trouble it takes one to reach that point! How often have I despaired and been on the point of dropping everything! And what a job the writer has! Past experience is no help; each new work sets new problems, in the face of which one feels as anguished and uncertain as any beginner, with the additional handicap of a certain treacherous facility which one must brutally suppress. . . . Anyway, our motto is that of the sardine firm Amieux ("One better each time"). (p. 144)

> *Paul Claudel, in his letter to André Gide on December 22, 1910, in* The Correspondence between Paul Claudel and André Gide, 1899-1926, *translated by John Russell (copyright 1952 by Pantheon Books, Inc.; originally published as* Correspondence, 1899-1926 de Paul Claudel et André Gide, *Gallimard, 1949), Pantheon, 1952, pp. 144-45.*

JOHN MIDDLETON MURRY   (essay date 1917)

[*In the following excerpt, Murry praises Claudel as one of the few poets who can effectively convey "a religious emotion" in his verse. He also calls his poetry "lyrical" and "universal," and says that it succeeds because its language is simple and direct. Other critics, such as Wladimir Weidlé, Wallace Fowlie, and Martin Turnell, have stressed the lyrical quality of Claudel's poetry (see excerpts below).*]

Claudel is a Catholic poet; he himself would doubtless say that he was before all else a Catholic poet. Yet by reason of his passionate sincerity, his poetry can make a deeper appeal to those who do not share his certitude than that of many poets who profess no faith. Deep in the souls of men, whose souls have depths to be reached, there is identity. Thus the most personal confession of a great man is impersonal and universal. Claudel's lyrical poetry has this impersonal quality, which is achieved not by any vagueness or comfortable generality, but by the extreme exactness of his own self-definition. 'Il n'est science que du général,' says the **'Art Poétique,'** 'il n'est création que du particulier' ["There is no knowledge except of the general; there is no creation except of the particular"]. Claudel has created himself and his poetry, according to this certain truth. Guided by it, he has been driven to abandon traditional forms of expression and to create for himself a means to the more complete delineation of his own soul.

In the **'Cinq Grands Odes'** he had reached a sure mastery of his new method. The opening poem to the Muses is a great ode, indeed, in which he evokes the Nine, each by the virtue she bears to those who understand her gifts. A new richness has been added to the poet's understanding of his privilege; he knows himself highly associated with the eternal work of creation. . . . [Claudel portrays] the rebirth of wonder in a world weary with much knowledge and a poetry enfeebled by words from which the immediate virtue has departed. The delight of recognition, the joy of the child in the revelation of existence, pours in . . . [**'Cinq Grands Odes'**], like a life-giving stream, into the exhausted fields of modern French poetry.

But Claudel himself is not naïve or child-like. The deliberate particularity of his vision is the goal of a long process in which

dialectic and intelligence have played their part. He has learned how to value his gift of sight and to perfect it to its purposes; and in the **'Cinq Grands Odes,'** armed with the instruments he has himself fashioned, adding new and resonant strings to the feebler lyre which he received, he halts in mid-journey, . . . and turns to make an acceptable music to the Lord. . . . (pp. 88-9)

The five odes are one splendid Magnificat, full of poetry that is deliberately great. It would have rejoiced Matthew Arnold to discover in Claudel a French poet who could so surely use the grand style. In this book Claudel becomes wholly and definitely himself, having conquered his freedom, alike in his life and his art. Everywhere he moves securely, by reason of his faith in God, and in himself as the poet and servant of God. He moves securely, but he moves away from his familiar things. The past slips from him like a garment. . . . As he comes to acquiesce in his isolation, so does his confidence in the spiritual quality of his remoteness increase, and more and more deliberately does he employ the simplest language of common speech. His images become yet more exact and realistic, and his desire to eliminate from his poetry the last vestige of an inherited grandeur apparent. (pp. 89-90)

Two books of Claudel's poetry have appeared since the beginning of the war. The one, **'Corona Benignitatis Anni Dei'** . . . , is a cycle of religious poetry; the other a slim volume containing three war poems. Although, when the poems which compose the larger book were written, Claudel can have had no premonition of the ordeal that was impending upon the world, they are complementary. In the religious poetry he has achieved the end of his evolution; he is not only certain, but he sees face to face. In so far as the progress of his belief was concerned, he could hardly hope to be more secure this side eternity. As with his faith, so with his art; the movement towards directness and simplicity of utterance could no further go. There are many poems in the **'Corona Benignitatis'** which confound by their apparent *naïveté;* and they confound not merely because the poet, in his newness of heart, delights in the unhesitating statement of the most enigmatic doctrines of his Church, but because he can confront the mysteries of death so simply that they are not mysterious any more. He is so familiar with the other world that he is not awed by it; he can be whimsical with his destiny. His heaven is homely to him and his God a friend. (p. 91)

[**'Corona Benignitatis'** demonstrates] that 'bonhomie de Claudel' of which a recent French critic has spoken; but this super-simplicity is the crown of a long and arduous struggle. It is a new victory for French poetry; almost it awakens a new emotion, or its unfamiliarity may be so strangely sweet because the secret pulse of the religious emotion is so seldom communicable to the profane. Claudel's triumph is that he can communicate this subtle tremor. He has cast away the obscurity which is the privilege of the adept, so that he almost persuades us that, if we should but open wide our physical eyes, from us too no secrets would be hid.

This surely is a mark of true poetry; and Claudel's **'Corona Benignitatis'** is not the less true poetry because it is the pinnacle reached by a slow and deliberate ascent. He knows well what he is doing; he can look back upon the path by which he came, and calculate his position by the stars. He knows well how long and solitary has been the journey away from familiar things before he stood near to them again, as a man who circles a mountain to gain the peak whence he can look down upon the world. He knows exactly what emotions his words will awaken in those whom he was forced to leave. (pp. 91-2)

'Corona Benignitatis' is a statement of belief; the 'Trois Poèmes de Guerre' . . . are a test of its efficacy. In a moment the war has set, to all those who have sought a solution and a certitude in life, their old problems once again, with a sudden swiftness that will admit of no delay. Claudel alone among French poets was prepared. He does not cheat himself, nor turn his eyes away from the awful truth that war is a name for the untimely death of innumerable men. His war poems are acceptable, because they satisfy the demand which the modern mind instinctively makes upon the poet whose theme is war. His words must be profoundly resonant with the sense of mortality. An army is no longer a nation within a nation; it *is* the nation. A war is the murder of a nation's youth. The easy gallantry and joyful adventure of the old war-songs belong to an epoch of history which was closed by the Civil War in America; and, when Whitman and Lowell and Lincoln sounded their clarion call to the dead, they magnificently gave out the note for the grave and Dorian music of modern war. Claudel had these notes within his compass; and he too has sounded them nobly. He speaks fearlessly to the dead, knowing that only thus he can speak to the living. It is the blood of the innocent dead which will rise up against the people of Cain, who can never fill the silence in their hearts, left by the voice of those whom they have killed. Therefore the poet is confident in his cause, for his hope of victory is no other than his eternal hope. The fight will endure so long as Might remains in arms against the mightier, which is Justice. But of the ultimate issue there is in his heart no doubt. It is sure as the march of the seasons, for it is one with that progression. . . . [The] opening lines of the elegy 'Aux Morts de la République' are a remarkable example of Claudel's poetical understanding. In the audacity of their movement, the delicate and inimitable acceleration which unites musical sense and spiritual faith into one triumphant certainty before the poet makes his unfaltering invocation to the dead, they mark the perfection of Claudel's peculiar gift.

Claudel is a great Catholic. His influence upon the religious ideal of an *élite* among the French youth has been already deep and may be incalculable. To some this will be a questionable title to their regard. But they cannot withhold it, if they reflect that he is a great Catholic because he is a great poet. He has held his craft so high that he has not been content by thought to become merely the master of poetical logic that he is. He has been impelled to justify his art to his own soul; and the justification he has found is one that restores to his country the true conception of a poet's dignity, and poetry to its high and fitting seat, remote from the meanness of petty rivalries and the turmoil of the market-place. (pp. 92-4)

> *John Middleton Murry, "The Works of Paul Claudel" (reprinted by permission of The Society of Authors as the literary Representative of the Estate of John Middleton Murry), in* The Quarterly Review, *Vol. 227, No. 450, January, 1917, pp. 78-94.*

DESMOND MacCARTHY   (essay date 1917)

[*L'Annonce Faite à Marie* opens] in France, sometime about the year 1420. It is night; the prologue takes place in the courtyard of the castle, or farm, of Comberon; Pierre de Craon, the builder of churches, is secretly stealing from the house. He has every reason to go quickly and quietly, for a double shame has fallen on him. In the first place, his passion for the eldest daughter of the house, Violaine, drove him when she

would not listen to him to try to kill her, and soon afterwards he discovered the white blotch of leprosy on his side. He is about to go when Violaine stops him. Then follows between them a dialogue which is lovely for many reasons. It is lovely because it is lyrical and profound; it is lovely because the feelings of both are true to human nature, and because these two human beings are set in a world which ratifies and explains what is best in them both. The beauty of goodness affects us differently, accordingly as we conceive it as something in itself, set in a hostile or indifferent or labouring universe, or as the expression of a universe finished in its inmost nature and sympathetic. In the first case, as in the second, it may be a pathetic beauty, or a beauty which is like a call to arms, or the mind may simply rest upon it and say, "This is enough." But in the second case it has a different pathos, carries a different encouragement, and in the place of the last satisfaction there is rather an expectancy of something more. Which beauty of the two a man will respond to most will depend upon his beliefs; but because he may love the one most, he need not be blind to the other. As an infidel, I prefer the first; but I confess that in art, though not in life, I am rather starved as far as that beauty is concerned. The world in which Claudel's characters have their being is a Theocracy. It is a world of miracles and saints (Violaine is going to be a saint and the miracle will be her miracle); a world in which each man has his own place like a stone in a building, a world in which sin is simply the refusal in one form or another to recognise the service of God as the end of life. Under pain and chaos, there is the force of virtue; over all ruin, the restoring charity of God. This is the world of Claudel, out of which this poem springs.

But that we are looking at a drama of character conceived as under a Theocracy, is true in a particular sense of the people in this play. Violaine's father is the peasant lord of the manor of Comberon. He has no suzerain above him; he is lord of the land, the house, and all the people about him. Combernon depends alone upon the nunnery of Monsanvierge, which rises somewhere (invisible from the stage) on a rock above the manor. The order of these people's lives, which is most solidly and beautifully suggested throughout, is secure because it has only one centre; there is no conflict of authority, there is nothing in their lives that does not tend directly to the one end, and all human passions and relations have in this order their fixed places. The Lord of Comberon is only the steward of his possessions, and the authority he wields rests, just as much as the life of the humblest servant on the estate, upon the idea of service. The idea which forms the framework of this world is that the individual is nothing and only derives worth from the order to which he belongs. It is the contrary of the idea [of] . . . Ibsen, that the individual is the test and measure of all values. In the world of Ibsen there is the thrill of an immense combative hope, however thwarted it may be; in the world of Claudel, peace. If one were to define the nature of the beauty of this play, one could not get nearer to it in a phrase than by calling it the beauty of peace. (pp. 254-55)

> *Desmond MacCarthy, "A Miracle Play," in* New Statesman *(© 1917 The Statesman Publishing Co. Ltd.), Vol. IX, No. 219, June 16, 1917, pp. 254-56.*

EDMUND GOSSE   (essay date 1921)

[*Gosse's assertion that Claudel represents "the neo-Gallic spirit of 'devotion' in its most arrogant and illiberal form" typifies the extreme opinion some critics have adopted toward the Frenchman's Catholicism. Contrary to such critics as John Middleton*

Murry, Wladimir Weidlé, and Wallace Fowlie (see excerpts above and below), Gosse believes that this intensely religious attitude often detracts from the quality of Claudel's work.]

I have been trying, with an open mind, to discover what is the real value of the poetry of M. Paul Claudel, whom Paris takes so seriously and London so imitatively. Let me confess that in past years I have not been able to join the choir of the maenads of West Kensington around the Claudelian altar, but I am constitutionally open to persuasion, and I have sought enlightenment from the Cymric deities, so propitious to a cloudy and oracular style in verse. (p. 241)

I have to admit that there is something in the very nature of M. Claudel, as he reveals himself in his writings, that repels me as an Englishman. I find it difficult to believe that his English admirers are quite honest with themselves in their raptures. M. Claudel, I believe an excellent Ambassador, is certainly not diplomatic as a poet. He loves to outrage the civilities, and in a way which does not amuse me. He wishes to sweep the immediate past out of existence; he has denounced Victor Hugo and Renan as "des infâmes."

Now, the young author who calls the noblest poet and the richest prose-writer of the age immediately preceding his own "infamous," does not appeal to my sympathy. He may be daring, but in this instance he seems to be stupid. M. Claudel is not stupid, but he is what I think is worse—he is bigoted. He represents the neo-Gallic spirit of "devotion" in its most arrogant and illiberal form. Hence the scorn poured on great precursors who wrote admirably but were Free Thinkers. In our Anglo-Saxon world we are accustomed to a broader toleration, and that is one reason why I cannot think the English worship of the poetry of M. Claudel and of his friend M. Jammes quite genuine. There is, or ought to be, a gulf fixed between our national temperament and the furious sacerdotalism of *La Messe là-bas* and the *Cinq Grandes Odes.*

The genius of M. Paul Claudel—and he possesses what can only be defined as genius—expresses itself in drama and lyric, but the lyrical poems are so theatrical and the drama so lyrical that the two are easily studied together. Nevertheless, it is better to approach M. Claudel on his dramatic side, because the faults which do so obstinately beset him are less obvious in his plays than in his canticles. When he abandons himself to his strange infatuated rhapsodies, he is apt to lose the thread of his intention, and to wander about in a cloud of noble words, from the midst of which proceed magnificent flashes of imagery and eloquent detonations of thought. But his plays are almost always clearer than his cantatas, more external, more vivid; there have to be characters in them who move and speak; there have to be localities which are made visual to us. Moreover, in his plays M. Claudel sometimes (not very often, but sometimes) forgets to preach, and when he is not thumping the dust with his fist out of some liturgical cushion he can be thrilling and even amusing. My knowledge of his work is, I confess, not exhaustive yet, but so far as I have advanced I have found nothing so thrilling as *L'Annonce faite à Marie,* and nothing so diverting as *Protée.* It cannot but be favourable to the reputation of M. Claudel to contemplate these two dramas.

There can be no question that *L'Annonce faite à Marie* is a production of extraordinary force. It is more than that, it is a work instinct with a sort of magnificence very rare indeed in modern literature. I have no hesitation in saying that I put it a full storey higher than anything else of its author which I have read. At the very threshold of it I gape at his incurable ecclesiasticism, because, so far as, after long meditation, I can

perceive, there is nothing in it from first to last which dimly suggests the miracle of the Annunciation to the Blessed Virgin. It is a realistic scene, slightly and casually supernatural, from the late mediaeval society of France. (pp. 242-43)

The landscape, the incidental movements of the persons, the strange and solemn symbols which appeal to a mediaeval conscience, all these are described with a vividness which is sometimes all the more blinding because of M. Claudel's explosive manner of expression, a manner quite peculiar to himself. Heroic passions, dolorous abnegations, turbulent and sterilising scruples, are illuminated throughout by an intensity of language which is sometimes almost terrifying, at other times exquisitely attractive.

The entertaining work I have mentioned is the drama of *Protée.* Here M. Paul Claudel forgets for once that he is a preaching friar, and only remembers to be the most fantastic and delirious of farce-writers. . . . It is not possible to mention a tithe of the incidents which enliven this boisterous and animated farce, one of the most exuberant and picturesque things in modern literature, quite worthy to take the place of that lost satiric play of *Proteus* which Aeschylus is known to have prefixed to his trilogy of the "Oresteia."

If all the writings of M. Paul Claudel were like *Protée* and *L'Annonce faite à Marie,* I should not be wandering disconsolate down the banks of the Wye; I should be building an altar of turves to his worship and trying to steal a Welsh lamb for the sacrifice. But, unhappily, in other of his works, while preserving in a very curious way his essential characteristics of intensity and spasm, he falls so far below his best as to fill the reader with alarm. The same volume which contains *Protée* presents us with a sort of choral drama called *La Cantate à Trois Voix,* in which there are splendid rhapsodies but, which, as a whole, I find entirely unintelligible. The obscurity is not merely one of language, but of thought. I read pages of *La Cantate* over and over again, and they remain completely incomprehensible. Now it is all very well for the French, with the infinite variety of their literature, to indulge themselves in any kind of experiment they please. Their poetry has been so limpid, so reasoned, so logical, that they can afford a burst of spasmodic obscurity. French literature has been good for so long a time that it must be excused for sowing its wild oats in Mallarmé and Rimbaud, and, even now, in Paul Claudel. But I hold it affectation and worse, in English readers, to profess a wild enthusiasm for these outlaws, until they have exhausted all the charm of the pure French classics. But this is too wide a subject to be expanded here.

Since the war M. Paul Claudel has produced three new works. . . . The new Claudels consist of a species of rhymed liturgy, *La Messe là-bas;* a farce for marionettes, *L'Ours et la Lune;* and a religious drama, *Le Père humilié.* The best of these is *La Messe là-bas,* a chain of sacerdotal reflections made by a solitary in Brazil. This work is written in a form hitherto unexampled, I think, in poetry, namely, in couplets of lines of uneven length, which wander on and eventually rhyme. We have comic analogies in Swift and Hood, but I recollect no serious example. Some of these rhapsodies are very beautiful, in the cloudy Claudelian manner; for instance, the luxuriance of the tropical scene in the piece called "In Principis" and the extraordinary vividness of "Lectures" are admirable. There is a good deal of Arthur Rimbaud in *La Messe là-bas,* and also of Coventry Patmore, whose ecclesiastical odes M. Claudel has closely studied.

Of the other new works less that is favourable can be said. *L'Ours et la Lune* is altogether beyond me; its incoherence borders upon lunacy; it seems to have a bearing upon the late war, but to my apprehension it is a specimen of *opéra bouffe* for maniacs.

The *Père humilié* is more serious. . . . (pp. 244-46)

This strange drama contains several scenes which are conceived and executed with skill. In the second act, where the arrogance of the Pope is broken down by the austerity of the familiar Franciscan monk who confesses him; the dialogue in which Orso and Orian, with a noble excess of loyalty, plead not each his own cause, but each that of the other; the close, where Pensée bends over the terrible basket ("Why is the odour of these flowers more intoxicating for me than that of laurel— laurel that speaks of victory?")—these and other individual passages, which are choral tirades rather than conversation, are of a high lyrical beauty. Their symbolism and their rhetoric intoxicate the reader, who, like Isabella when she "hung over her sweet Basil evermore," has "no knowledge when the day is done."

But the symbolism of M. Claudel, which was always perplexing, has never been more disconcerting, nor his purpose, underneath the intense Catholic suggestion, more uncertain. He is, like his blind heroine, the victim of obscure ardours and bewildered intuitions; while, in the midst of his rich imagery and the perpetual grandiloquence of his tirades, we are apt to lose sense of reality and nature. We wander by impassable streams in a vague but volcanic world of twilight superstitions. Such is the impression which M. Claudel's work continues to leave on at least one candid mind.

His new piece is entitled *Le Père humilié,* but if I am asked why, it is I who am humiliated, for I have not the least idea. (pp. 247-48)

> *Edmund Gosse, "Paul Claudel," in his* Books on the Table, *Charles Scribner's Sons, 1921, pp. 239-48.*

ANDRÉ MAUROIS   (essay date 1930)

In addition to being the French Ambassador to the United States M. Paul Claudel also is one of the three or four greatest living French authors. I would even say that he is the one whose "sense of grandeur" is best developed. If one were to attempt to explain the nature of his new drama, **"Le Soulier de Satin,"** by comparison with other works one could mention only such masterpieces as Goethe's "Faust," "The Divine Comedy" and the writings of Lope de Vega and Calderon.

To tell the story of this drama is almost impossible. It is an "action espagnole en quatre journées," laid in the Spain of the close of the sixteenth or the beginning of the seventeenth century. . . .

In many scenes which show us, in turn, the ocean, America, Spain, Japan and Africa, "that fiery spot on the belly of the earth," we watch Prouhèze and Rodrigue approaching death without yielding to their love. The end of Rodrigue, slave and hero at once, is of a beauty which recalls that of Velasquez's beggars.

In a remarkable American book, "A Preface to Morals," I have read that for many people the world is no longer an intelligible drama in which God and man are the players. But for M. Paul Claudel human life is still a divine drama. For him we are but the symbols with which God writes a history that is beyond our understanding. One feels that he is so sure of this that doubt would seem absurd to him. And hence his view of history is extraordinarily lofty and substantial.

That certainly gives him a love of life which our hesitant generation knows no longer. "Sad? How can one say without impiety that the truth of these things, which are the works of a perfect God, is sad? Is it not absurd to say that the world He has created in His image is smaller than we? I agree that youth is the time of illusions; but this is because youth imagines things to be infinitely less beautiful and varied and desirable than they are."

It is possible not to share M. Paul Claudel's faith. But it is difficult not to be touched by its force, by its sublime and tragic humor and profound humanity. (p. 7)

> *André Maurois, "Ambassador Claudel As a Dramatist," in* The New York Times Book Review (© *1930 by The New York Times Company; reprinted by permission), January 26, 1930, pp. 7, 26.**

G. K. CHESTERTON   (essay date 1935)

[*Chesterton suggests in the brief excerpt below the reason why Claudel's work seemed so fresh and original during the first decades of the 1900s. His statement that the modernist artist "has broken all [his] strings but one" represents the sentiment common to Catholic apologists of that era that modernism had run its course, and that a return of literature to its primary religious purpose, such as Claudel had done, was not only viable but necessary.*]

There is no space here even to suggest the sumptuous wealth of images and ideas in the work of Paul Claudel. It is only important to note the fact, as a fact of history rather than of literature, that it is on his side, and not on the other side, that the wealth of ideas can now be found. It might very well happen, at one time it probably did happen, that the historic culture he represents had dwindled down to narrow channels and rare and isolated notes; like the last pipe of the pastoral poets that sounded from the eighteenth-century clerics imitating the innocence of the Georgics; or that Irish harp of which a single string snapped whenever a heart had broken for liberty. But to-day it is exactly the other way. It is the rationalistic tradition of the nineteenth century that has narrowed into monotony and repetition. It is the artist who is an atheist that has taken refuge in a garden, to escape from the cry of all the ancient Christian civilization for the ploughing of all the fields of the earth. It is the musical instrument of the modernist that has broken all its strings but one, like the lute in the agnostic picture of Hope; and continues to strike the same few chords of truth remaining to it, but drearily and all on one note. Nobody denies, and certainly I do not deny, that the truths of the emancipated epoch are still true, even when thus isolated and irrelevant; just as the spiritual truths were still true, even when repeated mechanically by the court chaplains or stale preachers of the eighteenth century. But in the matter of fullness, of richness, and of variety, the whole advantage is now with the ancient cause. The thoughts that throng in a sort of hubbub, in a work like **The Satin Slipper,** are like a crowd of living men bursting the barriers of a deserted fortress. It is Claudel or the same type of man who is now storming the Bastille; a prison with all the harshness and inhumanity of a prison, except that it now contains fewer and fewer prisoners. An empty prison may be almost more depressing than a full prison; and such an empty prison is the tradition of academic scepticism to-day. Prejudice, the very spirit of a prison, alone shuts out the new generation from the full realization of the greater fruitfulness promised by the revival of Christendom. In one sense we may agree with all the old and weary journalists who say that the age is to be the age of Youth; but its most youthful manifestation is in something that renews its youth like the eagle. (pp. 114-15)

> G. K. Chesterton, "The Case of Claudel," in his *The Well and the Shallows (reprinted with permission from Andrews and McMeel, Inc.), Sheed and Ward, Inc., 1935, pp. 112-15.*

WALLACE FOWLIE   (essay date 1943)

[Fowlie is considered one of the major critics of twentieth-century French literature. In the excerpt below, he discusses the differences between Claudel—whom he calls "the poet of day"—and such other French poets as Baudelaire, Mallarmé, and Rimbaud—whom he calls those poets "obsessed with night." He also develops a point put forth by Wladimir Weidlé (see excerpt above) when he states that Claudel "rediscovers the old primitive vocation of a poet, the vocation of resurrecting the world." For negative criticism on the religious element in Claudel's work, read Edmund Gosse and Martin Turnell (see excerpts above and below).]

Paul Claudel appears as the most demanding of contemporary poets. To be understood and followed, he requires from the reader a total spiritual submission and attention. It is not only the ornate and complex part of his work which tyrannizes the reader's intelligence, it is above all the harassing and well-nigh unbearable unity of his books. This unity provides his reader with no rest, no dream, no immobility. Claudel hammers in his truth without breathing between the blows. Rightfully considered the most feared poet, he may also seem the most cruel. And yet, upon careful examination of his writings, it is impossible to discover precise examples of his cruelty. They give this general impression because they are unified in their criticism of the century's spirit. Paradoxically, Claudel is *par excellence* the poet of the world, the poet who has named the greatest number of objects in the world, the realist poet in his love for the humblest and most familiar objects; but he is also the most implacably hostile poet to the superficial world of our century. (p. 112)

After Baudelaire, who first stated the basic problem of modern poets; after Mallarmé, who was its master and theorist and whose brief work is a mine of secrets; after Rimbaud, who was its adolescent, that is, the one who underwent the experience in so personal and violent a way that we shall never be able to measure its profundity comes Paul Claudel, whom we make bold to call the "poet." He is a poet in a more vital and more complete sense than these other artists. He is the poet of day who comes after a long line of poets obsessed with night. (p. 115)

The difference between Claudel and the poets we call the poets of night springs from two needs apparent in both works: a need of negation with Claudel, which is a positive need with the other poets; and a positive need with Claudel, which is the contrary with the poets of night. The first need, of a negative principle for Claudel, is a desire to disappear from his work. It appears in his wish to be hidden by his work, his effort to give to his work the sole reality. (p. 117)

The second need, of a positive principle with Claudel, is the necessity which urges him to write integrally, to say everything at once, to sing in each verse the unity of his poet's credo. Experience with the night poets is divided and cut up into parts. They name separately their objects, their symbols, their sentiments. They exploit the refinement of grief. In Claudel we become aware of an incoercible need to say everything. His vocation of a poet is intense and necessary. He has called his work "une explosion intelligible." The impatience of his soul causes him to put everything into a single ode: the sun, the summer, the day, the harvest, the flowers sticky with honey. His poem is orchestrated as no other poem is. His lyricism is a form of delirium. . . . He is, in a word, the man who sings and thereby fulfils some hidden principle, as the tree is that object which bears branches and leaves. (pp. 117-18)

Before everything, before the entire world which waits like some inert matter, Paul Claudel rediscovers the old primitive vocation of a poet, the vocation of resurrecting the world. Everything must relive in a single work. As in Ulysses' voyage, as in the tragedy of human destiny sung by Sophocles, we find ourselves in Claudel's poetry in the presence of the primitive consecration of the earth and in the midst of the total movement of human effort. First, the entire world is in it: horizons, oceans, cities, houses, the furniture of each house. Then we find man in it, living at the very heart of the unbelievable richness of the world. And finally we see man in his relation with the universe, we follow his desire to utilize the universe in order to attain the First Source and total comprehension. All great poetry is by definition primitive because poets have never ceased being amazed at the universe. They have never forgotten their first vocation, formulated anew in the nineteenth century by Baudelaire, which is to seize the "profound and dark unity of things" (*la profonde et ténébreuse unité*).

Poetry of antiquity in its lyricism, in its epics, and in its tragedies, exalted man much more than the universe of man. The universe and man have equal places in Claudel's work, because the universe exists for man, and man, thanks to the universe, can begin to understand the reason for his existence. Man in antiquity is more tragic because he is less aware of this meaning of the universe. The works of antiquity, however beautiful and moving they may be, remain testimonials before man, whereas a truly Christian work must be a testimonial before God. Claudel is less easily comparable to the Greek poets, obsessed as they were with man's fatality, than he is comparable to the anonymous artisans and laborious philosophers of the French Middle Ages. In Claudel and in the mediaeval artisan we can discover the same effacement of self, the same desire to throw into relief man's work because the work testifies to something outside of man—to the eternal spirit of man, perhaps. (pp. 119-20)

The principal law for Claudel's poetic inspiration, as it was for all mediaeval arts, is the law of analogy. . . . It is perhaps true that only Christian poets, when they are Christian in the total dogmatic sense of the word, can explicitly obey this law of analogy. In logical sequence, their works must rest upon analogy because their faith makes it necessary. God, creator of all things, calls them back to himself at the end. He leaves them with us for a time and thereby reveals himself, although imperfectly, to us. Joy for the Christian poet is the discovery of God everywhere. (p. 121)

This poetry of the universe, which is a poetry of Christian faith, because everything named is attached to a metaphysical principle, is eminently in Claudel's work, and to a degree almost as powerful and continuous, in the work of the English poet who was a Jesuit priest, Gerard Manley Hopkins. Claudel and Hopkins maintain the principle of analogy more constantly than other Christian poets such as Crashaw, Eliot, Péguy. Their song is more robust. It attacks the classical rules of versification, the laws of syntax and vocabulary—that is, all the lesser laws, as the Gothic cathedral scorned the classical laws of architecture. Faith gives to some men a boldness which is very capable of irritating other men. Poetry is the universe for Claudel and Hopkins, and it is also a closed house because it contains everything. (pp. 121-22)

We named Claudel "the poet" who comes after certain artists in France, poets in their own right but not possessing the same total vigor and the same primitivism of the poetic talent. Then, we defined his heritage as being that of the entire world. It may be possible at this point to discover Claudel's secret and the key to his extensive work. For poets have secrets. The writing of each one is formed around a secret which is the *raison d'être* of the writing. It is the force which invokes the poetry, which demands the poetry, which belabors the mind of the poet, and which secretly invades all the verses and stanzas. Mallarmé's secret was the azure—the vast and unsounded purity of which each poem was an imperfection. Rimbaud's secret was intoxication, the state of the visionary, the physical and psychic state in which the poet could fix his attention upon his memory. Claudel's secret is something quite different. It is not like the azure of Mallarmé, which was an absence of images on which all the poetic images formed. It is not like Rimbaud's intoxication, which was the first dizziness of the adolescent facing all the universe and all that is not yet created. Claudel's secret is a problem in metaphysics. The essential word and key to his literary work is "knowledge." (pp. 122-23)

A poet like Claudel knows the things of the earth more intimately than most men, because he feels and longs for a birth with the first primitive universe, namely Paradise. Paradise was the first creation and man was born first with it. Claudel's secret seems to be his desire to be born with the first paradisaic universe and to lead the world back into its initial rôle of happiness and perfection. (p. 123)

The history of human thought and the history of art could be written in terms of the divers explanations of this word "knowledge." . . . We no longer hesitate to say that philosophical knowledge, so disastrously attacked by modern thinking, is going to survive thanks to what we might call poetic knowledge. Poets and critics of poetry have revindicated the rights of metaphysics. At all periods in history the bonds between philosophy and poetry have appeared close, but mysterious and difficult to define. This dilemma is vigorously rejected by Claudel, who appears as the great lover of the problem of metaphysics, as the conqueror of the problem. The unity of his entire work is the reprisal, in each part of the work, of the major themes of metaphysics. (p. 124)

After the secret of poets, comes the symbol of the secret. After Mallarmé's azure, after Rimbaud's intoxication, after Claudel's knowledge, comes the achievement in art, the poetic exploitation. Azure, intoxication, knowledge, are not susceptible of immediate translation: they have to be converted into another more symbolic language. Mallarmé's azure became a series of concrete symbols: a faun, a tomb, a swan. Rimbaud's intoxication was symbolized by hell, the domain where the soul becomes monstrous. And finally, Claudel's knowledge is translated by joy, by the religious sentiment of joy. It is not

necessary to share Claudel's faith in order to feel its expression in his work. Faith is experience for Claudel, as evil was for Baudelaire, as passion was for Racine, as religious suffering was for Pascal. A great art does not require us to undergo the same experience from which it has arisen; its only requirement is that we heed the form given to that experience. (p. 126)

Our world, tired of warfare and haunted by the perspective of still more complicated wars, has become the setting for Claudel's joy. It is a joy of superabundance and excess which will live longer than the wretched and sad history of our age. The place which Claudel occupies, his midway place, between the men who give themselves to the world and the saints who give themselves to God, will end perhaps in becoming the most radiant place in our world for the ages to come. The place of poets grows with time and ends by throwing into obscurity the lesser values of a period. This prophetic tone is pardonable on the basis that in Claudel's work we encounter not only the first essential lesson of the poet, which is the losing of oneself in the thing loved, but in addition we learn a second lesson, through the sanctification of joy, which is the losing of the thing loved in oneself. (p. 127)

Claudel gives us the portrait of a man who finds in his joy a better knowledge of himself. Each work of his is an explosion in which the poet seems bent upon overturning an entire system. He repudiates the most austere sentiments and denounces the most stable beliefs. But he pursues this work of demolition in order to rebuild afterwards, to reassemble, to reintegrate. And the new system, which is the old system reconstructed, reappears on a surer foundation. Claudel is both demolisher and builder. He is the poet of energy. Gerard Manley Hopkins is of the same race of poets. We are more accustomed to the poets whose work is better explained by the term "willfulness." The poetry of Mallarmé and T. S. Eliot, for example, grows laboriously and patiently by this force we call "willfulness" whereas the force which animates the poetry of Claudel and Father Hopkins is quite different. In the realm of painting, the canvases of Picasso can give the same effect as the poetry of Claudel. Picasso's energy, also, upsets the world and what remains on the finished picture is a delirious kind of joy, so intense that it ends by becoming the artist's personality.

Joy is Claudel's goal. It breaks out everywhere without revealing exactly its source or its manner. Joy in Claudel's work becomes the fact one accepts without explanation. We have seen how easy it is to understand in Claudel's conception the metaphysics of knowledge, and in it we have perhaps come upon a formula of art which teaches us that in the creative thoughts of a man of energy and valor, a total metaphysics of knowledge inevitably engenders joy. (p. 129)

> *Wallace Fowlie, "Paul Claudel: The Metaphysics of a Poet," in his* Clowns and Angels: Studies in Modern French Literature *(copyright, 1943, by Sheed & Ward, Inc.; reprinted with permission from Andrews and McMeel, Inc.), Sheed and Ward, 1943, pp. 112-29.*

WLADIMIR WEIDLÉ   (essay date 1948)

[Weidlé presents the most laudatory assessment of Claudel's work, asserting that "no other poet in our time has managed to fashion for himself a poetic instrument at once so new and so suited to the genius of his language."]

Our arts, our letters, are in an agony, and yet who would dare to speak of a general paralysis of the creative powers of man?

The waste land is still a volcanic soil. From time to time an eruption occurs, a genius appears, and the creative power of man reaffirms itself again. How could it reaffirm itself more magnificently than through the appearance in French literature, at the end of the last century, of Claudel? His work is a beginning, a renewal which nothing before him could have made us foresee. Our first astonishment as we read him is to find ourselves present at the birth of a new, free, living, spontaneous French, more so than it has ever been since the sixteenth century. Each word with him seems as if created afresh, exempt from all wear-and-tear, a direct link having been re-established between the meaning and the sound, between the form of the sentence and the hidden movement of emotion and thought. Here poetic language escapes rationalistic withering, purist distillation, oratorical swelling, and does so, one would say, by a simple, effortless springing-forth, by the pure act of creation. And in the same breath the versification is transformed, beyond all the prosodic innovations attempted for a century and all the experiments with free verse, in a more vigorous and at the same time a more natural manner. No other poet in our time has managed to fashion for himself a poetic instrument at once so new and so suited to the genius of his language, whose sources are, as the poet himself admits, along with the Bible, the prose of Rimbaud, of Maurice de Guérin and of Chateaubriand. The rhymed variations of this verse, with its strong final accent and its heavily emphasised caesura, resembles a greatly extended and more flexible alexandrine, but one which has kept its essential structure. And so Claudel's versification, like his poetic diction, though it keeps at a deliberate distance from traditional forms, never departs—and this is where it dissociates itself from the *Verslibristes*—from what in this tradition belongs to the very essence of French.

This reform of verse and diction has above all opened the way to establishing the foundations necessary for the renewal of the great poetic forms of the ode and the drama. . . . Claudel is the only modern poet who has learned how to amplify the lyrical style without mechanising it, who has achieved a kind of cosmic fullness without having lost any of the personal singularity of his genius. Moreover, scarcely had the dithyramb been born once again, when a much greater miracle happened under our very noses: the blossoming forth of drama.

Anyone who does not stop dumbfounded before the gulf which separates the Claudelian drama from everything called by this name for at least a hundred years and perhaps much longer in France and the rest of Europe, must have lost the faculty of astonishment. Not merely because this drama is quite different from the kind of plays that "hold the stage" and are good box-office; we must admit rather that it is utterly different from every recent dramatic production considered as literature: whether drama of ideas or problem drama, psychological drama, or poetic drama (in which poetry is only a layer of sugar covering the pill). . . . [The] dramas of Claudel seem to belong to an unknown species, to a new world. They come from heaven knows where; their source is no longer the same; to taste them is to lose one's taste for the kind that they reject by their very existence.

This rejection, moreover, is bound to be reciprocal, for from the point of view of habitual dramatic writing it is Claudel's that is no drama. He lacks action, movement, plot (on a level with the actions, movements and plots of daily life) and what the ordinary critic would call skill in dialogue. One does not find in his work well-known theatrical stratagems designed to keep the sleepiest spectator awake, or that kind of psychological display (within the reach of everybody) which gives us the flattering sense of knowing the human heart as well as the author. If it were only contemporary critics who were put out, it would be enough to remember that the Elizabethan critics were scarcely prepared to sacrifice Seneca to Shakespeare; but among the theorists of drama, not only from Boileau, but from Aristotle to our own days I can think of none who could decide in this dramatist's favour. Indeed to find a tradition which would suit him, we should have to go back beyond the age of Aristotle (or that of Euripides and Socrates) and link up with the initial impulse and the first expansion of Greek tragedy. The profound affinity between the work of Claudel and the drama of Aeschylus is due to the fact that the latter, like his own, never disowned its deep roots; the initial impetus, the lyrical surge from which it issued, continued to supply it with its principle of unity and balance, to constitute its nodal point and the central axis of its existence. The need the poet felt to adopt a dramatic form close to that of Aeschylus, far from enabling us to dismiss it as an arbitrary primitivism, was but the sign of a necessary return—even, we may say, an inevitable return—to the natural source of drama as such. The essentially lyrical character of the Claudelian drama, which no critic, whether enthusiast or adversary, has failed to underline, is by no means an accidental quality of his genius: it is the very condition without which genuine drama could not be re-created, re-established in a world used to ignoring it. . . . [If] there can be poetry without drama, there can be no drama without poetry. Without it what is left is only a play, a piece of work displayed before spectators who examine it with curiosity and recognise themselves in it with indifference. With Claudel it is always the poet who is there first, and it is from his soul that, along with hymn and great ode, the drama continually rises and pours forth. . . . (pp. 114-17)

"Springing forth", transport, the unfolding from one end of the work to the other of a rhythmical wave which lifts it up wholesale: that is what we find with Claudel, and the blossoming out of drama in his case transcends by this very fact—as was the case before him with the history of the Greek theatre—the distinction between the tragic and the comic. The stifling despair of *Tête d'Or*, the prolonged anguish of *Partage de Midi*, the happy excitement of *Protée*, were all equally able to give birth to drama. The deepest sorrow and the shout of laughter, farce and lyrical tragedy, make a happy marriage with each other among the Greeks as with Claudel, and together they are quite the opposite of the pleasant smile and the slender melancholy of the Greek "new comedy" (of Menander) or of a modern play. (p. 118)

The refusal to understand the nature of [lyrical] movement explains the accusation of immobility which has so often been thrown out against Claudel, just as the incapacity to distinguish between the laws of drama and the (photographic) conventions of the contemporary theatre has led people to misunderstand the structure of his characters. . . . Claudel's characters differ from nearly all other characters in the theatre by their absolute lack of conformity to external models. There is nothing in them which is anything like the words and the gestures which we observe in ordinary life. When we listen to them we never have the impression that we are hearing a conversation like other conversations. The inflexions of their voices are not the same; they have a sincerity and a spontaneity which our own never manage to acquire except at rare moments. It is not man's social being which is expressed in this way, it is his real being—that being which we commonly find so difficult to grasp in other people, and even in ourselves. This is true even for a

Coûfontaine or a Turelure, for what they stand for in the world of society cannot be separated from their deeper nature. The strange thing with Claudel is that it is only souls that speak, and nothing can get in their way, nothing can harm the unusual directness of their utterance. The beings he has created are as they are precisely because there is nothing in them that is brought from outside, because all comes from within, because everything is included in the initial impulse to which the whole work owes its life. We feel that the very intensity of the poetic fountain is making way for the creation of drama. . . . (pp. 118-19)

We have *L'Echange, l'Otage, The Satin Slipper;* we have that marvel of marvels, *The Tidings Brought to Mary.* The drama has gushed forth from the rock struck by Moses. And yet, is it possible for us to quench our thirst wholly from this living spring? Is it for us that the drama is played, is it we who play the drama? It seems not. Claudel's world is more genuine than the one we live in, Claudel's characters are more authentic than we ourselves—and that means in the end that his drama is further from us than that of Calderon or Shakespeare was from their contemporaries. All drama depends not only on the dramatic element within it but also on the element of the theatre, and the latter is always the result of not merely an individual but a collective creation and one which is achieved not merely upon the stage but with no less intensity among the audience. But in our days the sources of such a creation seem to be exhausted. In spite of many attempts, some of them relatively successful, Claudel, we must admit, remains if not unplayable upon the modern stage, at least theatrically unrealisable in respect of what is best in his work and most capable of quenching our thirst. In the last resort this is not the fault of the producers or of the actors, but of the spectators, since false familiarity or false declamation by the actors are usually only a reflection of the aesthetic incredulity or frivolity which pervades the audience. The new drama has been born, the new theatre is still in limbo; and the fault is not Claudel's—it is ours. (pp. 120-21)

> Wladimir Weidlé, ''Agony,'' *in his* The Dilemma of the Arts, *translated by Martin Jarrett-Kerr (originally published as* Les abeilles d'aristée, *Bruges, 1936), SCM Press Ltd, 1948, pp. 107-30.**

EDITH MELCHER (essay date 1949)

L'Annonce faite à Marie has so often been compared with Claudel's earlier play, *La Jeune Fille Violaine,* that it would be supererogatory to recall in detail the way in which the simple Cinderella-like folk drama of love and jealousy, with its modern setting and human message, developed between 1892 and 1912 into the medieval mystery-miracle play. The human elements in the story have an ageless familiarity: the father who must go on a long voyage to a distant land; one child Violaine, good, beautiful, and beloved, betrothed to Jacques Hury, the honest peasant who will look after the rich fields of her heritage; the other child Mara, angry, jealous, determined to have Jacques for herself; the mother taking the side of the unhappy Mara against her sister; the glamorous stranger Pierre de Craon, who enters their lives for a few hours, touching Violaine with a breath of the mystery and suffering that lie outside her sheltered world and leaving behind him the seeds of disaster. In the end, after the mother has died, Violaine has given up Jacques, and Mara's jealousy has finally consumed itself in the murder of her sister, the father returns and the stranger reappears to point the lesson of the tragic drama.

In *La Jeune Fille Violaine* this lesson is a condemnation of nineteenth-century materialism, of the scientific spirit that had substituted false gods for the true. The engineer Pierre decides to give up his bridge-building and to use his technical skill, not for the physical well-being of men but for the construction of churches to remind them that they have no being outside of God, that their souls are united in Him just as the waters of the earth penetrate and join all material substance. Because the modern setting does not suit the primitive story, the early play has philosophic as well as artistic inconsistencies. From a practical point of view it is impossible to understand why the father must abandon his family for many years without sending them an occasional message. Reflecting Claudel's own reaction to the uncongenial atmosphere of Boston, where he held his first consular post in 1894-95, Anne Vercors despises the American way of life and yet the goal of his efforts to help his brother's children is not to save their souls but to restore their fortune. And his attitude toward them is that of the typical nineteenth-century *bourgeois.* . . . (pp. 2-3)

It was not until Claudel turned to the Middle Ages that his play achieved the unity of spirit and action which makes it a great work of art. . . . The theme of leprosy is introduced, with its medieval significance not only as a symbol of sin but also as a proof of God's special grace. The kiss that the earlier Violaine had received as Pierre's farewell she now gives to him as a sign of forgiveness and compassion, thus impulsively jeopardizing her own mortal happiness and taking the first step toward salvation. The father sets forth, not on a business trip inspired by a sense of family responsibility, but on a Christian's pilgrimage to the Holy Land to do penance for himself and his contemporaries. His journey takes place against the background of the Crusades and the building of the gothic cathedrals. But the time of the play, vaguely indicated by Claudel as the ''fin d'un Moyen-Age de convention'' [end of the Middle Ages], includes also the years of the great Schism, and the progress of Violaine toward sainthood coincides with the last years of Jeanne d'Arc's life. The medieval atmosphere of faith in God's miraculous ways allows the poet to substitute the rebirth of Mara's child, which is one of the most moving episodes in the play, for the giving of sight to the little blind boy, which in the earlier play seems almost an act of witchcraft. The murder that in *La Jeune Fille Violaine* is a crime of jealousy and hatred as Mara sees her sister apparently entering her life again becomes in *L'Annonce* a gesture of liberation that ends the leper's earthly sufferings as her task is accomplished.

During the years between the last version of *La Jeune Fille Violaine* . . . and the appearance of *L'Annonce* . . . Claudel seems to have found gradually the themes and images that give the play its magnificent polyphony. The pattern of these *leitmotifs* can be traced through some of the other work of this period, especially the *Cinq grandes odes,* which are so close to the play in thought and imagery that they might almost be called a lyrical prelude to it. Thus the meaning of the play is often both simplified and enriched by a study of the odes. (pp. 3-4)

The revised version is only half as long as the original and ends as the stage performances have usually done with the death of Violaine. But there are other changes which make it more than merely a shortened form of the earlier text. The act opens with a scene between Jacques and Mara in which they discuss the mysterious recovery of their child, never understood by Jacques, and the possible return of Anne Vercors, seven years absent. They begin to imagine his arrival, Jacques taking the part of the father and Mara pretending to welcome him and give him news of Combernon. This curious dialogue has the familiar, almost humorous tone of the conversation between the mother and father at the beginning of Act I. Claudel's intention may have been to give the audience an emotional respite between the scene of the miracle and that of Violaine's death, and perhaps also to emphasize his favorite theme of continuity by showing that the father and mother exist always, whether they be named Jacques and Mara or Anne and Elizabeth. The return to homely realism seems incongruous, however, when we know that Mara has just tried to murder her sister. It is more fitting that she and Jacques should attain through their sense of suffering and sin, as they do in the original version, a dignity that raises them almost to the poetic level of Anne Vercors and Pierre de Craon.

The father does return at that moment, and it is he and not Pierre who carries back to Combernon the crushed body of Violaine. Pierre does not appear at all. The father tells that he too has made a pilgrimage, in gratitude for having been cured of his leprosy. This miraculous recovery convinces Jacques of Violaine's innocence, and he is overwhelmed to see his ring restored to her finger: Pierre had given it to the father in the Holy Land. Then Anne Vercors explains that Violaine had kissed Pierre deliberately, feeling within herself God's summons to sacrifice her own happiness that peace might be restored to France and to Christendom. . . . (pp. 7-8)

[This] is the first indication that Violaine's gesture of compassion in the Prologue was the conscious acceptance of her role as saint and martyr. It is difficult to understand why Claudel has chosen to introduce a new idea which seems to contradict a theme important throughout the play and first expressed by Pierre: "Ce n'est point à la pierre de choisir sa place, mais au Maître de l'oeuvre qui l'a choisie" [It is not the rock that chooses its place, but the master of the work who chooses it]. Does Claudel wish to identify Violaine with the Virgin, or with the Redeemer? Although she undoubtedly represents both of these, she is also a simple human incapable of realizing at first that she is the chosen agent of God's mysterious will. (p. 8)

The character of Mara is consistent to the end and seems in the new version even to have gained in dramatic force. On the contrary the role of Jacques has been weakened by the omission of the scene in which he forgives his wife.

Why did Claudel decide to omit also Pierre de Craon? Did he wish to emphasize the symbolic nature of Pierre's role by setting off the Prologue more clearly from the play itself? . . . It is true that Pierre takes no active part in the drama, representing rather the chorus which sets the stage in the beginning and comments on the tragedy before the curtain falls. And yet he is in a sense responsible for everything, his existence continues to be important throughout the play, and his construction of the cathedral is not completed until the end. When he fails to reappear in Act IV, when his church is left unfinished and there is no mention of the Justice which he and Violaine have understood and accepted, the play undoubtedly loses the perfect balance and harmony that it has in the earlier form. And Pierre's voice is needed in the contrapuntal sweep of the final scene, which Claudel has sacrificed completely. (pp. 8-9)

> Edith Melcher, "A Study of 'L'annonce faite à Marie'," in The French Review (copyright 1949 by the American Association of Teachers of French), Vol. XXIII, No. 1, October, 1949, pp. 1-9.

J. P. MANSHIP   (essay date 1955)

[*Along with Christopher Innes (see excerpt below), Manship is one of the few critics to discuss the influence Richard Wagner had on Claudel's conception of drama. In the following excerpt, he asserts that Wagner helped shape Claudel's "practical sense of the theater that has made his work capable of performance"; but he also believes that the Frenchman adopted the German's "incorrigible lyricism and verbosity." In the final assessment, Manship feels that Claudel used music in his drama much more effectively than Wagner.*]

It is curious that the critics of Claudel haven't—to my knowledge—dwelt much on [his debt to Wagner]. Perhaps it is that, as men of letters, they are incapable of seeing beyond that compartment. Perhaps it is too obvious an influence and, as such, one that is easily overlooked. In the case of the Frenchmen it may be due to an instinctive dislike of anyone as blatantly German as Wagner. Nor should we forget that Claudel himself has thrown dust in our eyes, by his many disparaging remarks concerning Wagner in his later essays.

But in the very number of these remarks, we have strong evidence of the facts. And the facts are that in Wagner he found a drama that was uncompromising to the weakness and frivolity of the audience; one that was richly poetic and that sprang entirely from the imagination: one in which the deepest of human passions could be treated nakedly. From Wagner came that practical sense of the theater that has made his work capable of performance—popular even—and which he could never have learned from the poetic plays of the symbolists. From Wagner too came his major faults: an incorrigible lyricism and verbosity.

The subject of *Tannhaeuser* is basically the same as that of *le Soulier de Satin* or *le Partage de Midi:* that of salvation through love, but how simple-minded Wagner seems as compared to Claudel! Tannhaeuser is a man addicted to *delectatio morosa*, who is saved by the love of a pure woman; but the mechanism of this is not at all clear, and, inartistically, Wagner depends too much on the miraculous. Mesa on the other hand is not a sensual but a proud man, whose heart is opened by his love for a sensual woman. The course of this love is clear, nor is there any trickery with grace, for Claudel perceived that Providence is in the very fabric of our passions and our sorrows.

This play follows closely the lines of *Tristan und Isolde:* in its structure (the first act on board ship, the love-duet in the second act, the *liebestod* in the third), even in the name of its heroine—Yse. But Claudel's play is richer in its symbolism than Wagner's. The latter strikes the notes of love and death: in the orgasm (what is the *liebestod* but a musical orgasm?) he sees a communion with death. But Claudel has torn from his heart—*Le Partage de Midi* is the result of a period of anguish and despair in his own life—a knowledge that is deeper than this—or perhaps it is only the hope—that love, no matter how impure, has a role in God's Providence. This insight—beyond the Manichaean German master—is elaborated, in *le Soulier de Satin,* into the skeleton of a new "Divine Comedy."

Claudel himself complained that Wagner dipped the whole of his work, indiscriminately, into his musical bath. He himself used music as an element in his drama with greater care. For music is a symbol of grace. The work becomes more musical with the development of grace, as in *le Soulier de Satin,* of which the last day is a pure lyric. In *le Pain dur,* from which grace is absent, music is as well: the horror of the play is intensified by the bareness of its prose. . . . In all of this he drew closer to the practice of the Greeks, for whom music was a subordinate element in the whole drama, and not as in Wagner an imperious one; but we must not forget that it was Wagner who fired him with the Greek ideal. (p. 202)

Le Soulier de Satin is, I think, the greatest work for the stage since Goethe's *Faust*. Claudel would not have liked this comparison, although perhaps only for the trivial reason that Goethe was a great favorite of Gide's, but there is a great similarity between the two poets and between them and Hugo. They are artists of a vast range—poets, dramatists, critics, philosophers. If Claudel never attempted the novel, neither of the others ever wrote a philosophical treatise like *l'Art Poètique,* nor anything like Claudel's Biblical exegesis. . . .

Of all the great artists with whom I have compared him, the one he is most like is, I think, Rubens. He was a modern Rubens, although a poet rather than a painter. He was a diplomat and man of the world, a family man and a Christian, robust and sensual, but, unlike Rubens, he lived in a time that seemed to contradict both his faith and his geniality. He did his work nonetheless—how could he not have?—for he was like a volcano of creativity, belching forth masterpieces, flowing over all other fields, warming his time with the heat of his passion and lighting it with his vision. (p. 203)

> *J. P. Manship, "The Universal Artist," in* Commonweal *(copyright © 1955 Commonweal Publishing Co., Inc.; reprinted by permission of Commonweal Publishing Co., Inc.), Vol. LXII, No. 8, May 27, 1955, pp. 201-03.*

MARTIN TURNELL   (essay date 1955)

[*Turnell offers perhaps the harshest criticism of Claudel's work. On the matter of Claudel's lyricism and "grandeur of vision" he is in complete agreement with such earlier critics as Wladimir Weidlé and Wallace Fowlie (see excerpts above); but contrary to those critics, he believes that the poet limited his verse to the "service of religion." Turnell concludes that compared to another Christian poet, T. S. Eliot, Claudel lacked the "intelligence" to form new patterns which can alter our ways of thinking and feeling.*]

While Claudel's letters and essays may outlast his poetry, it is on his poetic dramas and on the poems contained in the *Five Great Odes* or the *Cantata for Three Voices* that his reputation as a writer at present rests. (p. 205)

Claudel set out to write a *poesis perennis*—a poetry dealing with eternal themes in the created world. In his plays he chooses a critical moment in the spiritual evolution of mankind, but his procedure is the reverse of Eliot's. The setting is not a country house or a cocktail party. It is always far removed from contemporary civilization either in time or space. It is medieval France or Renaissance Europe, the Napoleonic era or the time of the Vatican Council, the Caucasus or China, or—most characteristic of all—a ship in mid-ocean.

The theme of the principal plays is the fortunes of the human couple in love. Claudel's conception of love clearly owes something to the "fatal passion" of the Tristan legend, but the handling is Christian. His lovers are "predestined" for one another, but they are always separated by an obstacle which may be either moral, psychological or physical. Ysé and Prouhèze have married "the wrong man"; Sygne de Coûfontaine gives up her cousin and marries the appalling Turelure in order to save the Pope; Violaine contracts leprosy. Violaine and Sygne are saintly figures, but with Ysé and Mesa, Prouhèze and Rodrigue, love becomes in fact or intention adulterous.

This is in keeping with the Tristan legend, but Claudel's aim is to show that good may come through sin, or that sin may be the means of finding God.

Love in Claudel, as surely as in the legend, is of its nature unhappy; but there is one serious flaw in the plays which has disturbed even Catholic critics. We have the impression that the lovers are unhappy in their love because God intends them to be unhappy, that God is engaged in a cat-and-mouse game with his creatures, dashing the cup from their lips at the very moment when the obstacles to happiness and a Christian life have been removed. There is something repellent about the arguments of the priest who persuades Sygne to sacrifice herself and abandon her widowed cousin; and though Ysé's husband is dead, the curtain falls "with a crash of thunder" as the house in which she and Mesa are hiding is blown to pieces. Whether they are saints or sinners, violent death following violent passion is the fate of nearly all these people. It is impossible to avoid the feeling not merely that Claudel's God has more in common with the tribal god of the Old Testament than with the Christian God of the New, but that He resembles the poet himself in one of his harsher moods.

Claudel described *Le Soulier de Satin* as a résumé of all his work. It is regarded by many of his critics as his most important play, and it is certainly his most ambitious. It is part poetic drama and part farce, part morality play and part fantasy. It opens in sixteenth-century Spain, but the setting expands to embrace Europe, Africa, America, the East, the whole world. It is one of the most striking productions of our time, but if it exemplifies Claudel's characteristic virtues, it also exemplifies his most serious weaknesses. There is little genuine dramatic tension; the characters are abstractions engaged in propagating the poet's ideas; and the exaggerated symbolism gives it an air of unreality. (pp. 205-06)

The plain fact is that it is much more a work of propaganda than a work of art. Claudel tried to create a Catholic world-conqueror, and to show him adding continents to the Church, but his eloquence could not breathe life into this phantom and the parallel between Rodrigue, who is stripped of his honors and sold as a slave, and Our Lord seems frankly grotesque.

In *Ma Conversion* Claudel pays tribute to the importance of the part played by Rimbaud in his spiritual development, but Rimbaud was also one of the major influences in his literary development. Claudel has explained his verse technique in a long essay in *Positions et Propositions*. This is not the place to discuss in detail the complicated theory of stresses and pauses, or the importance of the arrangement of words on the printed page. It is sufficient to say that Claudel introduced a personal form of free verse. His own word is *verset* which is the French word for a verse of the Bible. His verse was formed by a study of the Bible, the liturgy, the prose poetry of Baudelaire's *Petits poèmes en prose*, Rimbaud's *Illuminations* and, to a lesser extent, Whitman's free verse. His aim was flexibility and suppleness; he wanted to produce an instrument which though capable of the dignity and eloquence proper to poetry, remained close to the spoken word and was therefore suitable for drama. (p. 206)

[The] second of the *Five Great Odes* is a fair illustration of the strength and weakness of Claudel's poetry. We can hardly fail to be impressed by the loftiness of the voice, the marked liturgical movement, or the grandeur of the vision with its emphasis on words like "total," "entire," "span" and "octave of Creation," its conception of the hierarchy of being from

God down to the "fat sheep." Once again, however, the crucial word is the word "catholic." Claudel clearly intends it in the double sense of "Christian" and "universal," but his poetry is always at the service of religion and for me "catholic" in its present context is a word of limitation. Claudel does not forge new concepts out of theological terms as Eliot does in the *Four Quartets*—indeed, his theory of poetry plainly excludes anything of the sort—he uses them as a means of appealing to the beliefs of his readers in a manner which is both different from and less impressive than Eliot's. This is symptomatic of all his work. It means that his poetry is not creative in the full sense, that it does not possess either the intensity or the precision of the greatest poetry.

I think we must go on to conclude that what was really wrong with Claudel was a curious defect of intelligence. He was, as his fanaticism shows only too clearly, a man in whom powerful emotions were not matched by a correspondingly powerful intelligence. He did not possess the kind of intelligence—the intelligence that we find in a high degree in Eliot—which enables a writer to re-think traditional concepts, to sift and test his experience, and finally to introduce a fresh pattern which alters our ways of thinking and feeling. (pp. 206-07)

Claudel was a unique figure. There was no one remotely resembling him in contemporary literature, and it is difficult to think of anyone like him in the past. We are bound to admire the man and the grand design of his work, the uncompromising Christian whose faith was a constant reproach to the wayward, the laggards and the fainthearted. Yet in the last resort he seems to me to have been a great figure and a great Christian rather than a great writer. I do not think that he would have quarreled with this verdict. (p. 207)

> *Martin Turnell, "The Intolerance of Genius," in* Commonweal *(copyright © 1955 Commonweal Publishing Co., Inc.; reprinted by permission of Commonweal Publishing Co., Inc.), Vol. LXII, No. 8, May 27, 1955, pp. 204-07.*

ANNA BALAKIAN (essay date 1967)

[*Balakian examines Claudel's ties with the Symbolist theater between 1890 and 1900, a fact which is often overlooked by critics. In the excerpt below, she discusses Claudel's only two Symbolist plays—*Tête d'or *and* La ville—*as evidence of his early infatuation with the decadent spirit.*]

In considering the symbolist theater created between 1890 and 1900, the fact is often overlooked that Paul Claudel belongs to the group. So closely is his work connected with Catholicism that one often forgets that, like T. S. Eliot, he participated in a non-religious mysticism before his total conversion to the Church. In this respect, his two early dramatic dialogues, *Tête d'Or* and *La Ville,* demonstrate a sharp breach with the later and much better known works that place him clearly at the head of the Catholic coterie of the early twentieth-century French literature.

In 1890, however, Claudel was a young admirer of Mallarmé at the salon of the Rue de Rome, where he came into contact with all the practicing symbolists. He was not an unconditional convert to symbolism, as he has revealed in his correspondence with Jacques Rivière, for he was at the same time feeling the forces of Rimbaud and the attraction of Victor Hugo's later, cosmic poems. In the long run these non-symbolist forces were to dominate his writings, but the first dramatic works are distinctly symbolist in technique as well as in tone, revealing in

compelling intensity the decadent spirit. In 1893 he wrote to Mallarmé: "Let me congratulate myself for having had the good fortune to encounter at the beginning of my literary career your conversation, your example, and your friendship." (p. 144)

When, some thirty years later, upon reading the posthumously published *Igitur*, Claudel chided Mallarmé for having been a "decadent," he seems to have forgotten his own *Tête d'Or,* with its series of characters just as diffident toward life as Mallarmé's, as removed from the mainstream, as self-engrossed in their meditations, as inquisitive about the cross-purposes of life and death. The many voices that suggest answers to the fundamental question "Who am I and what is life?" present no conflicts of attitude. They are instead parts in a cantata in which they supplement each other, as they unfold an incoherent story of boredom, illness, old age, and death: Cébès, who has remained fixed to the native ground and has nursed his "ennui" like a long contemplation, without beginning or end; Simon, who has wandered to the four corners of the earth and comes back to observe that all roads, all cultures, all cities pass away, as we pass and are gone. Together they bury a woman who has just died, with the desperate finality, even brutality, of those who have no stakes in the hereafter. Later, Cébès, himself moribund, will meet his brother, Tête d'Or, who comes home as a conquering hero. But he who has conquered other men is equally powerless before death and before his brother's questions. There is only nothingness beyond the grave; man has only his hour and dies. . . . A desperate melancholy, nausea, a black flag, a stormy passage, the weight of chains—these are the marks of man's passage. His refuge lies in nursing his gross ignorance in "an august dream" where he has learned "to be married to himself." This is how Claudel, the young symbolist, viewed life: he envisaged the cult of the self as a wedding ring binding man to himself; it is a chain and yet a protection from the terrifying vulnerability to which he subjects himself when he diverts his vision to things outside of himself and is brought up sharp against the inevitable anonymity of non-self-consciousness. There is also a mysterious princess here, as in the plays of Maeterlinck, who once more represents the self that cannot find its identification: "I do not know who I am" is to be taken not only in its physical, but also in its spiritual sense. Again, as in all symbolist writing, time is the cruelest of enemies. . . . Instead of the pathetic fallacy, by which man applies to nature his inner thoughts or sentiments, here it is the sea, the trees, the wind, the dismal objectivity of the soil that create the fatal despair of man.

In his next play, *La Ville,* Claudel tried to give a few answers to the questions that persisted in tormenting him. He sought to arm himself with some weapons against the impending oblivion of death, which again is the recurrent theme. The narcissistic contemplation of the mortal plight becomes more universal as the characters find identification with the group condition (represented by the city), the group activity (represented by the enslavement to daily work), the interdependence which assuages the devastating reality of the total uselessness of the total effort. The drama here is the struggle of man against the void, whereas in the previous play there seemed to be submission without struggle. A character, Besme—so comparable to Beckett's Estragon that it seems unlikely that the resemblance is purely coincidental—repeats in hypnotic fashion: "Nothing is." When pressed to explain what he means, he defines "nothing" as the depth of all things, which totally eludes the capacity of our minds. But Claudel makes concessions to the poet's lyricism, admitting that it can partially overcome—at least temporarily—the bleak mystery in which man is engulfed: ''You will explain nothing, o poet, but through you everything will become explicable.'' At the end of the play, he goes so far as to lift his voice gently against the ''decadent'' spirit. . . . [To] the inaction of man in the ivory tower, Claudel responds with the efforts of man's hand and the calculations of his mind as challenges to the futility of all action and all thought. Yet in technique he is still very much the symbolist, condemning this play, as the previous one, to the repertory of unperformable theater. No action accompanies the spoken word, which takes the form of long monologues, or a most unconversational dialogue, interspersed with silences. These speeches are projected onto a vast, cosmic canvas where indeed nature is an open temple and its pillars—such as the tree, the vine, the wheat—are deemed to have meanings only partially revealed by the poet; even as the parts of the day form a meaningful parallel to the variations of human mood; to the end of his long career, Claudel was to attach a certain sense of spiritual crisis to high noon. There are also symbolic objects, such as the table, the ring, and mystical gestures, as of sharing or kissing. Lights and costumes could undoubtedly be used as special effects to highlight the critical moments of a drama that is in appearance so totally static.

Perhaps because so much of Claudel's future dramatic writings will be laden with emotional conflicts and intense confrontations of divergent human wills, these two early plays bring out the more strikingly all that distinguished symbolist theater. How shattering it was to conventional dramatic composition! How vulnerable it made itself, when it gave up the role of entertainment or of emotional catharsis, and instead put all its characters, as it were, into the same boat—or rather, shipwrecked vessel! (pp. 145-48)

> *Anna Balakian, ''The Symbolist Theater,'' in* The Symbolist Movement: A Critical Appraisal *(copyright © 1967 by Random House, Inc.; reprinted by permission of the publisher), Random House, 1967, pp. 123-55.**

E. M. BEAUMONT   (essay date 1973)

Order is an equivocal term, as is to a rather lesser degree adventure. Order may be barren, a mere convention, a timid conformity. Adventure may be only a disruptive breaking away. But order may also be a difficult patterning of a violent movement, the making sense of chaos; and adventure may be the pursuit of the worth-while, the staking of one's all on an activity whose outcome remains unknown, unpredictable. It is this latter sense of order and adventure that we find in *Cinq Grandes Odes,* though not in quite so simple and straightforward a relationship. In Claudel the poetic and the spiritual are indeed inseparable, since it is a basic tenet of the poet that his creative word participates in the creative Word of God. . . . Indeed, the odes reveal the discovery, most thoroughly explored in the fourth ode, that the writing of poetry and spiritual life are inseparably bound together, that is, to be authentic, poetry must express the innermost being of the poet, and that innermost life, to be itself authentic, must always move towards an ever more complete self-emptying. The poet realises that there is only one adventure, the search for and discovery of God and all that is associated with this, the task of redeeming and transforming the world. Ultimately he is to realise that the transformation of the self, the transfiguration which appears with such startling rapidity at the end of *Partage de Midi,* is what is needed of him. As there is fundamentally only one adventure,

so is there only one order, that of God's design, which Claudel considers it to be the poet's function to perceive and express. That is the aim of his poetry. There is the verbal order that the poet imposes on the disparate elements that he brings together and there is God's redemptive order for the salvation of the world. The difficulty arises with Claudel's claim that his poetic conferring of order on the world partakes essentially of the divine order, that his creative word is really an extension of the redemptive activity of the creative Word of God. The odes clearly express the notion that the poet's conception of order, the attempted redemption of the world through the ordering of poetry, was purely external, therefore superficial. That conception has to be rejected. Indeed, it was destroyed for him by the encounter with the woman whom we may call Erato or Ysé. In a sense, there was a period of disorder in the poet's life between 1900 and 1905. But this was also an adventure, an adventure fraught with extraordinary ambiguity, an adventure that brought new life to the poet's art. It is certainly not true to say that Claudel's finest poetry coincides necessarily with his most spiritual aspiration. In fact, in the intensely personal poetry of the odes the aspiration of the spirit, the call of a woman now gone, and poetic creativity are closely linked together. The odes bear witness to the painful restoration of order in the poet's life, an order at once spiritual and poetic, since Claudel sees no distinction between the two. Yet, though the order that we see emerging in the later odes may be more authentic than the first rather external notion of order that the poet had, it may not entirely satisfy us. The largely conjugal order of the fifth ode, for instance, may seem not only cold and joyless but also poetically unmoving and spiritually unenlightening.

In a sense, **'Les Muses'** is a prepatory ode, the one in which too purely a poetic order is sought and indeed achieved. Certainly, Claudel succeeds in ordering the most violent movements, the intense meaningful activity of all the nine muses brought startlingly to life from their sarcophagus, led by Terpsichore. . . . The whole poem is a violent act of parturition, the mysterious upheaval of the whole being from whom a new life bursts forth. . . . One may see in this bursting forth of a new life in parturition almost a prophecy of the adventure to come, the disruptive and yet extraordinarily creative appearance of Erato in the final verses, but at first the adventure is solely poetic. . . . Yet, even in **'Les Muses',** the poet recognises his affinity with Divine Wisdom participating in the creation of the cosmos. His poem confers order on the world, making meaningful relationships of the apparently disparate elements. It is at the point when he is claiming that he will reveal the meaning of the created world that the sudden rupture of the poem occurs. . . . [The] order we have seen in the earlier part of the ode, the careful categorising of the nine muses and the assignment to each of her rightful role in the birth of the poem, this skilful renewal of an old mythology in the contained violence of somewhat triumphal rhetoric, breaks down. Erato comes to life with a directness, an intensity, a frenetic quality, new to the poem. The order, it seems, was only provisional; it is now vanished. . . . (pp. 107-10)

Adventure is a dominant theme of the second ode, though the adventure is now lifted from the carnal presence to the invisible spirit; the ode was written in 1906. The sea, which made its appearance with Erato . . . in the closing lines of **'Les Muses',** remains in **'L'Esprit et l'eau'** a symbol of freedom, but also of ubiquity. . . . Yet, though the adventure of the spirit in its all-embracing quest is symbolised by the sea, breaking down the material earth, nonetheless, as always with Claudel, the creative spirit of the poet, sharing something of God's creative spirit breathing on the waters, brings order and meaning, limiting therefore the longing for freedom. . . . (pp. 110-11)

Much of 'L'Esprit et l'eau' is a magnificent prayer for a godlike spirituality, for freedom from the contingent, for freedom, as he says, from the weight of this inert matter. . . . Through the symbol of water, the water that God separated from the earth in the story of the Creation, the baptismal water that brings with it the life of the Holy Spirit, the figurative water that man desires in order to quench his spiritual thirst, the hypostatic water of the two natures united in Christ, human and divine . . . , the poet poignantly expresses his desire of total life in Christ. (pp. 111-12)

There is evident throughout this second ode too sharp a distinction between God and man, or in reality woman, between the spirit and the flesh. The year 1906 is still too close to the pain of loss, the loss not so much of God as of the woman. The words of Peter at the Transfiguration of Christ which Claudel makes his own . . . , like the transformation of Ysé in the final act of *Partage de Midi* and the transfiguration which seems to be implied in the closing lines of the ode, possibly that of the woman now speaking with the voice of Divine Wisdom . . . , occur perhaps rather too easily in 'L'Esprit et l'eau'. Darkness returns in the final section of the fourth ode. Yet these fluctuations of mood but emphasise the personal, human, quality of these poems, the movements of the spirit with the rebellious stirrings of the heart and flesh. The last twenty verses or so of this second ode clearly reveal that the one great adventure, the transfiguration of man in the love of Christ, has at least begun. Whether the verses are to be attributed to the resurrected Christ or to the woman perceived as the voice of Divine Wisdom, matters not at all. (p. 112)

'Magnificat' is poetically, in the opinion of the writer, one of the finest of the odes, in spite of some bombast and some unpleasant invective, for there is a complete merging of the liturgical and the personal in this hymn of praise and thanksgiving. The verses of the *Magnificat* itself and the birth of the Christ-Child, intermingled with the poet's joy in the birth of his own child and the memory of the birth of the new man in himself, also at Christmas, in 1886, clearly demonstrate that the human adventure, the life to be lived Godwards on earth, and the divine adventure, the taking of the manhood unto God, the life of Christ on earth which the Liturgy brings before us in the theophany of the Eucharist, are one and the same adventure. That the adventure is not purely a personal one, but that of the whole of the material world, for which the Redemption has to be actualised, the poet repeats again and again. . . . (p. 113)

One of the dominant images in 'Magnificat' is that of the priest. The poet holds his child in his arms, the real, living image of man now raised to the godhead by the Incarnation, just as the priest holds in his hands the bread of the Eucharist, the Body of Christ. . . . The image is so dominant that the ode ends with the evocation of the priest raising his eyes to the host in the monstrance at Benediction and the mingling of the *Nunc dimittis* and the *Magnificat*. The final section of the poem, with its images of light, of the sun rising, of refreshing waters gushing forth, in the setting of the basic analogy with Joshua entering the Promised Land, finely expresses once more the poet's function to evangelise the world by his word, to give back what he has received in a spirit of thanksgiving, to make all things new in the poetically creative word.

The familiar symbols of sea, opening doors and opening windows, introduce in 'La Muse qui est la Grâce' the continuing fluctuation of self-offering to God and the poetic evangelisation of the world by the word which we already see in the previous odes, but in this fourth ode these two alternating modes become completely identified. The poet comes to the final realisation that there is no alternative to total consecration to God, an understanding that brings with it a temporary resurgence of the old passion in the closing verses of the poem, which are the most poignantly moving of the ode. The order to which the poet has aspired, purely as a poet bringing creative form to the chaos of the world's diversity, is seen to be his own imperfect conception, to which he desperately clings. . . . [The] destruction of the world that took place with the encounter with Erato, also in a blaze of fire imagery, at the end of 'Les Muses', left something of the self which has to be destroyed by a more fully re-creative fire than the passionate love of a companion who seemed predestined. But, for the moment, the poet takes refuge from the blaze of the informing spirit in darkness, the darkness of a purely earthly memory of a woman's love. . . . This is the last time that she is evoked in the odes and it is also the last time, in the opinion of the writer, that Claudel succeeds in these poems in moving us deeply and, except in the final verses of the last ode, in achieving a high degree of poetic intensity. (pp. 114-16)

His poetic task of bringing God to mankind through his creative word is again developed at length in 'La Maison fermée', though with the emphasis now on the need for enclosure, for communication with God to be established. The open sea of 'L'Esprit et l'eau' seems far away. . . . The adventure is now purely interior, an adventure within the mind and heart of the poet, enclosed within his four-walled house, the abode of his family. Adventure and order are firmly one. God's creation of the world is now entirely seen in terms of conservation and order. . . . (p. 117)

Erato, who destroyed the old order, is at least for the moment effectively replaced by the more prosaic voice of the poet's wife. There are no more lyrical flights, no plunges into the carnal past, no lamentations over the spiritual darkness from which the poet is slowly and painfully emerging. All that is finished. . . . The poetry of 'La Maison fermée' is indeed largely free from the grandiloquence that mars so much of Claudel's writing; it is more dense and more restrained than in the previous odes, but the violence has departed, the tension has slackened. The poet is calm and self-possessed, within his newly restricted order, his recently established conjugal life, confident that he is giving God to the world. . . . (pp. 117-18)

The *Cinq Grandes Odes* remain a unique achievement in modern French poetry. The rich diversity of these poems has hardly yet been explored. This short essay only touches on one aspect of the odes, the expression of a personal anguish and the search for wisdom and enlightenment, above all, for a unifying harmony. These odes bear witness to a vital phase in the poet's life, both as poet and as man. From 1900 to 1908 the distance travelled is immense; yet certain factors remain constant, the poet's evangelising mission with a new kind of poetry of whose originality he is fully conscious and his fidelity to the experience which took place at Christmas 1886. The various extremes to which his reactions took him in these turbulent years are but the indications of his all too human nature. Even the rock-like affirmations and the cast-iron platitudes reveal that human weakness and fallibility in which Claudel, in common with every one else, participates. (p. 119)

E. M. Beaumont, "A Note on 'Cinq grandes odes':
Some Ambiguities of Order and Adventure," in Order
and Adventure in Post-Romantic French Poetry, E. M.
Beaumont, J. M. Cocking, J. Cruickshank, eds. (©
Basil Blackwell, 1973; by permission of Barnes &
Noble Books, a Division of Littlefield, Adams & Co.,
Inc.), Barnes & Noble, 1973, pp. 107-19.

CHRISTOPHER INNES   (essay date 1981)

[*In a larger discussion of* Christopher Columbus, *Innes mentions
the similarities in Claudel's "musical drama" with that of Richard
Wagner, but believes that Claudel used music toward a more
dramatic purpose than Wagner. For a similar opinion on this
point read J. P. Manship (see excerpt above).*]

On a technical level Claudel's plays, with their multiplicity of
short scenes and characters, their marvellously baroque, in-
cantatory language, and their shifting transformations of visual
imagery, provided a challenge that could only be met by radically new stage conventions. . . . Claudel labelled his theatrical work 'musical drama', but although it has general points
of resemblance to Wagner's *Gesamtkunstwerk* and includes
complex orchestral scores by composers like Honneger (*The
Satin Slipper*) or Darius Milhaud (*Christopher Columbus,* which
was originally conceived as an opera), 'music' is more a structural analogy than a formal description. Claudel rejected Wagner's concept because it subordinated setting, dialogue and
actor—and with the actor, drama itself and human emotion—
to a monochrome symphonic form that was self-enclosed and
tended to stasis. By contrast his idea was to use music to
amplify character and dramatic situation. And in ideal terms
this meant that instead of being pre-composed and pre-set, the
musical score would be orchestrated in direct response to the
performance, 'giving impulse and pace to our emotions through
a medium purely rhythmical and tonal, more direct and more
brutal than the spoken word . . . music not only in the state
of full realisation, as a cryptic language portioned out among
the pages of a score, but in the nascent state, rising and overflowing from some violent feeling'. In this concept music is
not simply a resonator. It also has an active function, to unify
the 'diverse voices' of a play into a harmonic 'enthusiasm',
transforming the conflict of dramatic action into a 'final hymn';
and this is paralleled by a type of structural composition which
weaves disconnected events into a single 'melodic' line.

Claudel's drama, which focusses on different varieties of religious conversion and sees human life in terms of the struggle
of the flesh ('the Ordeal of Sin') against the spirit ('the Ordeal
by Fire'), is yet another form of interior, mental drama. His
plays are autobiographical and, as he openly acknowledged,
in *Exchange* (*L'Echange* . . .), as in *Break of Noon*, all the
characters were projections of himself and reflected the 'painful
bondage' of his life, while *Break of Noon, The Satin Slipper*
and *Christopher Columbus* all repeat the same personal experience—sinful love for a married woman, who becomes the
instrument of the protagonist's salvation, since his desire, which
can never be consummated, leads to a victory over the self and
his emotion is transferred by a natural progression from the
woman, already idolised as an angel, to God. But instead of
the expressionist or surrealist stress on dreams, the stage here
represents the soul and the objects of the material world are
veils for spiritual realities. Nowhere is this clearer than in
Christopher Columbus. The play opens with Columbus on the
point of death, impoverished and rejected by the king, to whom
he has come to beg for the means to finance another voyage;

and the scenes are the past as he relives it in the continuous
present of his mind. The hero splits into two figures, the actor
in an epic of discovery and the spectator who holds judgement
on the temporal action from his standpoint on the threshold of
eternity. A voyage into a spiritual geography, in which the
materialistic preoccupations of social life in the form of greed,
envy and disbelief, creditors, sceptical courtiers and mutinous
sailors, is set against faith in the form of the luminous western
horizon or the revelations 'from beyond the tomb' that Columbus receives when he reaches the Azores, and the world's
ingratitude is balanced by one woman's saving love. The play
is bounded by the image of the dove, simultaneously the Holy
Ghost and standing for Columbus himself (through the double
meaning of his French name, *Colombe*), which brings a message of hope from across the ocean to the child in Genoa at
the beginning and carries the soul of man from a 'newly risen
world' to the bosom of Christ Pantocrator at the end. In this
world of symbols Columbus' life repeats the archetypal pattern
of the Passion, with him lashed by rebellious menials to the
mast of his ship. The stage is a metaphoric altar and the performance is a religious celebration, with a choir—adapted from
the classical Greek chorus—representing the collective awareness of subsequent generations and mediating between the 'sacred mystery' being re-enacted and the audience, who are conceived as a church congregation. (pp. 119-21)

*Christopher Innes, "Primitivism, Ritual and Cere-
mony," in his* Holy Theatre: Ritual and the Avant
Garde *(© Cambridge University Press 1981), Cambridge University Press, 1981, pp. 111-58.**

BETTINA L. KNAPP   (essay date 1982)

[*Knapp's* Paul Claudel, *from which the following discussion of*
The Satin Slipper *is taken, is an important study of Claudel's
major works. Knapp asserts that* The Satin Slipper *can be interpreted as a dramatization of the Sacrament of Penance and Sacrifice or even as a "staged sadomasochistic ritual." This reaction
typifies the religious approach many critics have undertaken in
evaluating Claudel's work.*]

The Satin Slipper is the most involved, ambiguous, and lengthy
play of Claudel's career. It dramatizes the Sacrament of Penance and Sacrifice: a spiritual flagellation and psychological
humiliation, a prolonged test of man's will to transcend the
flesh, to battle matter and the Devil in order to experience God
in His plenitude. It may also be considered a staged sadomasochistic ritual.

The Satin Slipper completes and resolves what had remained
unfinished and in a state of suspension at the conclusion of
Break of Noon. It is Claudel's nebulous answer to the question
plaguing him throughout his life: What is the meaning of love?
(p. 117)

Claudel's drama is divided into Four Days; not the Seven of
Creation, since man's job is incomparable to that of the omniscient and omnipotent God. Over a hundred characters inhabit
the stage. Were the play to be given in its entirety, it would
take nine hours. . . . Activity is forever altering structure and
texture in *The Satin Slipper;* tension is rampant, propelled by
his driving desire to break out of limited spheres and forms
into boundless realms. Some of the characters appear only
once, while others are occasional walkons. Still others play
significant roles. Some are essences, appearing as a vision or
a flesh and blood being acting as a device to contrast or harmonize with the prevailing mood surrounding the protagonists.

Passions from the most sublime to the most insidious ferment—spasmodically, spectrally, condensing, crystallizing—as each pursues the object of its search. The two main characters, Prouhèze and Rodrigue, weave their web throughout the globe, crossing continents (Asia, Africa, Europe, the Americas), communicating by means of waterways. *The Satin Slipper* is a giant conglomeration of disparate and fragmented factors—byroads and sideroads—networks of involutions and convolutions; it is an aggregate of genres and feelings—a storehouse of irony, comedy, tragedy, whimsy, parody, burlesque, satire—almost unending riches which a febrile imagination puts to good use.

The theme of *The Satin Slipper* is love: a love bond as colossal as that of Tristan and Isolde, a love destined and predestined to be unfulfilled. Powerful, consuming, abrasive, Prouhèze's passion for Rodrigue cannot be satisfied because she is married. To commit adultery would be to defile the sacrament—the Catholic Church and God. Her passion, therefore, must be dominated, repressed. At one point in the play, marriage would have been possible, but here, too, Claudel has fate intervene to prevent the completion of earthly love. It was Claudel's belief that to experience an all-embracing or total love on earth is to diminish humankind's love for God. To opt for a finite relationship is to consider salvation, which is infinite, of lesser importance. *The Satin Slipper,* then, is a network of events in which the protagonists are forever being punished, flayed, dismemebered; a willed refusal on the author's part to experience physical fulfillment and pleasure. Earthly love must be sublimated, energy dispelled and channelled in some other direction, drawn away from obsessive love. . . . Since Prouhèze and Rodrigue are forever repressing their feelings, dominating them, arming themselves with stoic and ascetic disciplines, they never experience the meaning of compassion, tenderness, or gentleness. Feelings are minimized, dismembered, flagellated. They must serve for larger purposes. The protagonists grow bitter during the travail that is their life. Love must be replaced with shame. A product of the will, humiliation, if earned, paves the way for redemption. Never is an action on the part of either Prouhèze or Rodrigue accepted for its own sake, but rather for a cause, a goal, whether it be for divinity or another. (pp. 119-22)

The Satin Slipper is an example of "total theatre." The action is being unraveled on all parts of the globe as well as among the elements. It is a living incarnation of the battle being waged within the author's psyche—personal and bloody. Prouhèze and Rodrigue are submerged in their passion for one another and intent upon dominating it. Their tension is continuous. Never do they experience the repose necessary to look at themselves directly, to understand the possessive, egotistical, and arrogant views of their intolerable goal. As Perseus needed a mirror into which he could peer while capturing the Medusa, so Claudel's beings look outward for help; angels, servants, captains, kings, husbands, anyone to prevent them from being submerged by their passion and losing sight of the real (or imaginary) goal of welding with divinity. Claudel wrote that the key to self-understanding lies in others: "it is our contact with the next person which enlightens our understanding of ourselves" and also helps us make ourselves understood.

Since neither Rodrigue nor Prouhèze is able to peer within their disparate psyches, their actions remain abrasive, constricting, grief-filled. Never will they know harmony or integration. Throughout they must flex their will, which takes on the contours of a muscle, bending, straining every so often in order to dominate the situation. Rodrigue and Prouhèze are undif-ferentiated and archaic beings. Their emotions are drained or sucked out spasmodically in protracted expulsions. Never are they decanted in understanding sequences. Prouhèze and Rodrigue are the proud possessors of anthropoid psyches; they are like stiff marionettes who fight, struggle, battle against each other's feelings, either destroying or being destroyed in the process. (pp. 137-38)

It is through [a] kind of incarceration that the protagonists carry out the Sacrament of Penance: the penalty each pays for being alive; the punishment each must endure to avoid joy, to know torture and humiliation in order to be worthy of Claudel's God. . . . Punishment serves the soul, Claudel suggests, by revealing man's pettiness, his shame. Dismemberment diffuses ignominious traits; it also gives meaning to life. Pain compels man to become aware of his function in the world, his relationship to others, his destiny. Such masochistic and sadistic overtones are replete in *The Satin Slipper,* each with powerfully sexual innuendoes: when Prouhèze rejects Rodrigue, the object of her lust, it increases his allure and dilates the excitement. The pathological connotations in *The Satin Slipper* are weighty; underlying them all is Claudel's corrosive and pervasive sense of guilt.

The Satin Slipper poses all types of theological problems. Claudel seems to believe that love plays little or no role in the sacrament of marriage; indeed, it is best that it does not, since if love were to be experienced between husband and wife, insufficient amounts would be given to God. (pp. 138-39)

Claudel's theological notions serve to separate man from God rather than unite him with divinity. For some believers, such views are contradictory and perplexing; for others, they are manifestations of a pathological condition. To know fulfillment in an earthly love experience, for many, allows the mortal to feel closer to God. The opposite is true for Claudel. Since God is excluded during an all too close relationship, a separation, therefore, exists, between the mortal and immortal sphere—man and God—the microcosm and the macrocosm. If this is true, the earth is no longer connected with the cosmos, the minute with eternity, space with spacelessness. God, then, is neither omniscient nor omnipotent! (pp. 139-40)

The Satin Slipper, an unwieldy and complex drama, is marred by too many tangential sequences, and many, many philosophical and dramatic asides. Claudel's religious ideas also pose a problem for the viewers. Some are irritated by his concept of evil, others consider the play a sado-masochistic orgy. Yet . . . when viewed symbolically as a dramatization of a vital theological problem, it neatly sets forth Claudel's viewpoint. Certainly not his finest play, *The Satin Slipper,* approached as a meditative work, is rich in thought-provoking material and powerful imagistic poetry. (pp. 140-41)

Bettina L. Knapp, in her Paul Claudel *(copyright © 1982 by Frederick Ungar Publishing Co., Inc.), Ungar, 1982, 287 p.*

ADDITIONAL BIBLIOGRAPHY

Beaumont, Ernest. *The Theme of Beatrice in the Plays of Claudel.* London: Rockliff Publishing, 1954, 102 p.
    Thematic examination. Beaumont discusses the similarities and differences of the role of Beatrice as developed by Dante and Claudel.

Beauvoir, Simone de. "Claudel and the Handmaid of the Lord." In her *The Second Sex,* edited and translated by H. M. Parshley, pp. 234-40. London: Jonathan Cape, 1953.

Thematic study. De Beauvoir discusses the role of woman—as both a source of evil and a means of salvation—in the plays of Claudel.

Berchan, Richard. *The Inner Stage: An Essay on the Conflict of Vocations in the Early Works of Paul Claudel.* Lansing: The Michigan State University Press, 1966, 118 p.

Biocritical study. Berchan examines Claudel's struggle over a religious and an artistic vocation and how this conflict affected his early work.

Birn, Randi Marie. "The Comedy of Disrespect in Claudel's *Soulier de Satin.*" *The French Review* XLIII, No. 1 (Winter 1970): 174-84.

Discusses the way in which Claudel satirizes those characters in *The Satin Slipper* who "are so locked within themselves that they miss the whole significance of existence."

Chaigne, Louis. *Paul Claudel: The Man and the Mystic.* Translated by Pierre de Fontnouvelle. Westport, Conn.: Greenwood Press, 1978, 280 p.

Biocritical account of Claudel's life and work by a personal friend and fellow writer. Chaigne also includes intimate anecdotes from the author's life.

Chavannes, Pierre. Introduction to *The Hostage,* by Paul Claudel, translated by Pierre Chavannes, pp. 1-20. New Haven, Conn.: Yale University Press, 1917.

General discussion of *The Hostage.* Chavannes focuses on the lyrical elements in Claudel's drama and suggests its similarities to the tragedies of the Greek dramatists.

Cunneen, Joseph E. "The Present State of Claudel Criticism." *Thought* XXVII, No. 107 (Winter 1952-53): 500-20.

Recapitulation of Claudel criticism. Cunneen reviews some of the major questions that enter into contemporary efforts at evaluating Claudel's work.

Hellerstein, Nina. "The Oriental Legends and Their Role in Claudel's *Connaissance de l'est.*" *Claudel Studies* I, No. 2 (1973): 36-46.

Comparative study. Hellerstein explores the relationship between the two poems "La cloche" and "La délivrance d'amaterasu" from *Connaissance de l'est,* as well as their relation to the work as a whole.

Humes, Joy Nachod. *Two Against Time: A Study of the Very Present Worlds of Paul Claudel and Charles Péguy.* North Carolina Studies in the Romance Languages and Literatures, vol. 200. Chapel Hill: U.N.C. Department of Romance Languages, 1978, 171 p.*

Comparative study. Humes compares and contrasts a common theme in Charles Péguy's and Claudel's work: the rejection of the modern world and a recreation of "a new time structure" which forms the basis to their separate doctrines of hope.

Maurois, André. "Paul Claudel." In his *From Proust to Camus: Profiles of Modern French Writers,* translated by Carl Morse and Renaud Bruce, pp. 122-41. London: Weidenfeld and Nicolson, 1966.

An account of Claudel's life plus a survey of his major plays. Maurois concludes by examining Claudel's philosophy of "salvation through sacrifice."

Merleau-Ponty, Maurice. "On Claudel." In his *Signs,* translated by Richard C. McCleary, pp. 314-18. Chicago: Northwestern University Press, 1964.

Examination of Claudel's Catholicism. Merleau-Ponty argues that what makes Claudel move so many readers "who are nevertheless alien to his beliefs is that he is one of the rare French writers who have made the din and prodigality of the world tangible."

Michaud, Régis. "Late Symbolism and the Cathedral of Paul Claudel." In his *Modern Thought and Literature in France,* pp. 32-51. New York, London: Funk & Wagnalls Co., 1934.

General criticism. Michaud discusses Claudel's work and its origins in the symbolism of Baudelaire and Mallarme.

Nagy, Moses M. "The Theme of Resurrection in Pirandello and Claudel." *Claudel Studies* VII, No. 2 (1980): 29-37.*

Thematic discussion. Nagy examines the idea of resurrection in Claudel's *L'annonce faite à Marie* and Pirandello's *Lazarus.*

Robinson, Christopher. "Collective Values: Intellectual Bankruptcy and the Catholic Revival." In his *French Literature in the Nineteenth Century,* pp. 171-89. New York: Barnes & Noble, 1978.*

In-depth analysis of *L'annonce faite à Marie.* Robinson suggests that all the Claudelian themes—"rejection of materialism, power of faith, virtue of suffering, separation of lovers, mystical significance of France"—are brought together in *L'annonce* "for the first time, and possibly to greater effect than in any later work."

Ryan, Mary. *Introduction to Paul Claudel.* Cork, Ireland: Cork University Press, 1951, 111 p.

Biocritical study. Ryan traces Claudel's spiritual journey biographically and through his lyric poetry, especially *Cinq grandes odes.*

Spitzer, Leo. "Interpretation of an Ode by Paul Claudel." In his *Linguistics and Literary History: Essays in Stylistics,* pp. 193-236. New York: Russell & Russell, 1948.

Detailed examination of a stanza from Claudel's *Cinq grandes odes.* Spitzer attempts a stylistic interpretation of the first stanza from "La muse qui est la Grâce" as a means of understanding the odes as a whole.

F(rancis) Marion Crawford

1854-1909

American novelist, short story writer, historian, dramatist, essayist, and journalist.

Crawford was one of the most prolific and popular novelists of his time. During the three decades of his literary career, he produced forty-four novels of romantic adventure, as well as several historical studies, a drama, and a volume of short stories. Many of his novels were best-sellers that pleased readers in search of light entertainment. During his lifetime Crawford was a literary celebrity on a par with Mark Twain, Henry James, and William Dean Howells. However, the advent of realism in late nineteenth and early twentieth-century American fiction led to a gradual decline in Crawford's popularity. Today, he is best remembered for the volume of horror stories, *Wandering Ghosts*, which was published after his death.

Crawford was born in Bagni di Lucca, Tuscany, to wealthy American expatriate parents. He received a cosmopolitan education at Cambridge, Harvard, and the universities of Heidelberg, Karlsruhe, and Rome, acquiring fluency in more than a dozen languages. While Crawford initially dreamed of becoming an operatic tenor, he first found work editing the *Allahabad Indian Herald*, after traveling to India to further his study of Sanskrit. He based his first novel, *Mr. Isaacs: A Tale of Modern India*, on his experiences in that country. The novel was an immediate critical and popular success, and Crawford quickly followed it with novels set in Germany, Italy, Turkey, Spain, Persia, and America—places familiar to him through his extensive travels. While he eschewed literary realism in favor of romanticism, Crawford sought to establish realistic backgrounds for his novels. For example, he learned silversmithing before he made the title character of *Marzio's Crucifix* a silversmith. Similarly, he studied glassblowing in Murano, Italy, before featuring a glassblower as a character in *Marietta: A Maid of Venice*. Crawford continued his world travels throughout his life, but after his marriage in 1884 he maintained a household in Sorrento, Italy.

Van Wyck Brooks has noted that Crawford "turned out novels at such a rate that critics lost account of them and failed to say how good they sometimes were." Critical attention, both past and present, has tended to focus on the first decade of Crawford's literary career. During this period, Crawford wrote the best known of his novels with Italian settings: *Saracinesca, Sant' Ilario,* and *Don Orsino*. He also wrote *Marzio's Crucifix* and *A Cigarette-Maker's Romance,* which exemplify his ability to give even the most improbably romantic plot a vividly depicted milieu. Most critics have praised Crawford's Italian novels as his best work. Crawford was skilled in his evocation of distant lands and foreign customs, and his familiarity with Italian history, topography, and law lent an air of authenticity to the twenty novels he set in that country. A few critics, however, have contended that Crawford's apparent intimacy with Italian ways is spurious. Joseph Pennell, the illustrator of *Salve Venetia: Gleanings from Venetian History,* stated that, despite a lifetime of residence in Italy, Crawford remained a foreigner living abroad and never understood the country or its inhabitants. More recently, Kenneth Churchill maintained that Crawford's Italian novels "are remarkable for the ab-

sence" of both literary power and psychological insight. Although the great narrative verve and richly depicted detail of Crawford's novels are undeniable, the novels dated quickly due to their romanticism, their complicated Gothic plots, and the sometimes ludicrous use of melodrama. The most common critical assessment of Crawford's career is that he wrote too much too rapidly, and therefore did not develop his talents. This conclusion has been challenged, though, by Donald Sidney-Fryer, who contends that Crawford "wrote some of his best books and some of his less distinguished ones with equal speed and fluency."

Crawford's few ventures into short fiction took the form of horror stories. These share with the novels effectively described settings and somewhat melodramatic action; unlike the novels, however, Crawford's horror stories have remained popular with readers and are frequently anthologized. "The Upper Berth," probably the most famous of the stories, was called by H. P. Lovecraft "one of the most tremendous horror-stories in all literature."

Crawford had been a popular novelist for nearly twenty years before he wrote three historical studies of Italian history: *Ave Roma Immortalis: Studies from the Chronicles of Rome, The Rulers of the South: Sicily, Calabria, Malta,* and *Salve Venetia: Gleanings from Venetian History*. Some critics believe that

Crawford resented the gradual decrease in serious critical consideration of his work, and that he wished to produce some enduring works of scholarship. His three studies have generally been regarded as informative and entertaining, though nonscholarly, pieces of research. Crawford's critical study, *The Novel—What It Is*, is primarily an explication of his own theory of the novel as pure entertainment.

For many years after Crawford's death, his work was virtually forgotten. However, there has been a recent revival of interest in the authors of romantic fiction whose reputations and popularity declined with the advent of literary realism in the late 1800s. A renewed enthusiasm for occult and fantastic literature has also contributed to the reevaluation of Crawford's efforts in this field, most notably his horror stories and *The Witch of Prague*. Today Crawford is receiving renewed critical attention as the preeminent romantic American novelist of his age, and is regarded as the author who most clearly gave expression to the theory of literature as entertainment.

(See also *Contemporary Authors*, Vol. 107.)

PRINCIPAL WORKS

Mr. Isaacs: A Tale of Modern India   (novel)   1882
Doctor Claudius   (novel)   1883
A Roman Singer   (novel)   1884
To Leeward   (novel)   1884
Zoroaster   (novel)   1885
A Tale of a Lonely Parish   (novel)   1886
Marzio's Crucifix   (novel)   1887
Paul Patoff   (novel)   1887
Saracinesca   (novel)   1887
With the Immortals   (novel)   1888
Greifenstein   (novel)   1889
Sant' Ilario   (novel)   1889
A Cigarette-Maker's Romance   (novel)   1890
Khaled: A Tale of Arabia   (novel)   1891
The Witch of Prague   (novel)   1891
Don Orsino   (novel)   1892
The Three Fates   (novel)   1892
The Children of the King   (novel)   1893
The Novel—What It Is   (essay)   1893
Casa Braccio   (novel)   1894
Katharine Lauderdale   (novel)   1894
The Ralstons   (novel)   1895
Corleone: A Tale of Sicily   (novel)   1896
Ave Roma Immortalis: Studies from the Chronicles of Rome.   2 vols.   (history)   1898
Via Crucis: A Romance of the Second Crusade   (novel)   1898
In the Palace of the King: A Love Story of Old Madrid   (novel)   1900
The Rulers of the South: Sicily, Calabria, Malta. 2 vols.   (history)   1900
Marietta: A Maid of Venice   (novel)   1901
Francesca da Rimini   (drama)   1902
Salve Venetia: Gleanings from Venetian History. 2 vols.   (history)   1905; also published as *Gleanings from Venetian History*, 1907
The Diva's Ruby   (novel)   1908
The White Sister   (novel)   1909
The White Sister   (drama)   1909
Wandering Ghosts   (short stories)   1911; also published as *Uncanny Tales*, 1911

*This drama is an adaptation of the novel *The White Sister*.

HENRY NORMAN   (essay date 1883)

The most interesting event in recent fiction was the *début* of Mr. F. Marion Crawford, who, previous to the publication of his first two books, was so unknown to the world that the critics could not make up their minds whether he was a man or a woman. *Mr. Isaacs* gave him at once a high place and a public of his own. It was seen to be a straightforward story, moving through a series of appropriate incidents, with constantly growing characters, told in a simple and powerful style, and permeated with a lofty view of life. It was felt to be a real novel, into which much of the life of the author had passed, not one of the familiar puppet-shows with someone turning the handle outside. It dealt with moving events in a new field, and introduced boldly an Indian adept and his doings, a subject on which most of those who know anything prefer being silent to being ridiculed. For to the readers who have been shocked at the appearance of Ram Lal's ''astral body'' it may be confidently said that there are people to whom such an appearance is by no means uncommon, as we shall all know when a few more of the things that exist in heaven and earth outside of our philosophy are revealed to Western omniscience. The two distinguishing merits, however, of *Mr. Isaacs*, apart from its attractiveness as a story, are, first, the loftiness of its sentiment, and second, the naturalness of the action, in which there are no puerile misunderstandings and no ingeniously contrived obstacles, but which moves on simply, logically, clearly, to the end. In this case the death of the heroine is not a loophole for an embarrassed author; it is fitting, and even necessary, to the development of the idea of the story. *Mr. Isaacs* is a tale which contains the promise of future great performances. *Dr. Claudius* shows a more finished literary style, and is proof that Mr. Crawford need not depend upon remarkable subjects to give power and interest to his work. It is simply the account of the falling in love of the Countess Margaret and Claudius, Ph.D., to whom the story of their own love is dedicated. It is full of good, both artistically and morally, and, though not on the high level of *Mr. Isaacs*, it is still much above most of its three-volume contemporaries. (pp. 878-79)

In his latest story [*To Leeward*] Mr. Crawford occupies new ground. . . . The sight of a soul beating to windward is always invigorating, but it is a question whether we are not so constituted as to be more impressed by the spectacle of one drifting to leeward, and it is upon this supposition that Mr. Crawford has described for us the life of Leonora Carantoni. It is not, however, a book which flaunts its moral before the reader; it tells its story and leaves him to draw a conclusion if he can find one. . . . But it is a faithful picture of life, and the moral is there plain enough. The book might have been called *ex nihilo nihil*, for it is based upon the fact that out of nothing nothing can come, or rather that out of a passive nothing there will arise an active chaos. In the mind of Leonora Carnethy there is nothing of sure knowledge or of definite conviction: in the life of Leonora, Marchesa Carantoni, there is the consequent wreck of all that is fairest and best. The action of the story goes steadily and relentlessly on from beginning to end. . . . *To Leeward* is probably in style and construction the best work that Mr. Crawford has yet done; the interest grows steadily from beginning to end, the leading characters are full of life and thought, and the environment is admirably drawn in proportion to form a significant and accurate *mise-en-scène*. Of this book, too, one may say that it is of equal interest and power, and the admirers of Mr. Crawford's previous work will be no less glad to mark the maturing of his talents, than to see that he is turning them to serious purposes. (p. 883)

> Henry Norman, "Theories and Practice of Modern Fiction," in The Fortnightly Review, n.s. Vol. XXXIV, December 1, 1883, pp. 870-86.*

HENRY JAMES   (essay date 1884)

What you tell me of the success of [Crawford's] last novel sickens and almost paralyses me. It seems to me (the book) so contemptibly bad and ignoble that the idea of people reading it in such numbers makes one return upon one's self and ask what is the use of trying to write anything decent or serious for a public so absolutely idiotic. It must be totally wasted. I would rather have produced the basest experiment in the "naturalism" that is being practised here than such a piece of sixpenny humbug. Work so shamelessly bad seems to me to dishonour the novelist's art to a degree that is absolutely not to be forgiven; just as its success dishonours the people for whom one supposes one's self to write. Excuse my ferocities, which (more discreetly and philosophically) I think you must share; and don't mention it, please, to any one, as it will be set down to green-eyed jealousy. (p. 104)

> Henry James, in his letter to William Dean Howells on February 21, 1884, in his The Letters of Henry James, Vol. I, edited by Percy Lubbock (copyright 1920 by Charles Scribner's Sons; copyright renewed 1948 William James and Margaret James Porter; reprinted with permission of Charles Scribner's Sons), Charles Scribner's Sons, 1920, pp. 103-05.

G. E. MEREDITH   (essay date 1888)

If we had been asked, half a dozen years ago, to point out the novelist of the moment whose interpretation of the facts of life, and whose theory of living seemed to us the most sober, rational and complete, we should certainly not have chosen the author of *Mr. Isaacs.* Yet it would be with the name of F. Marion Crawford that we should instantly respond to such a challenge to-day, passing over even that of the author of *Dr. Jekyl and Mr. Hyde.* For although the two writers have many points of what we may call moral likeness, Mr. Stevenson shows his rightness of judgment in regard to problems rather apart from the normal daylight side of life, leaving Mr. Crawford alone in the presentation, under a far from ordinary light of conscience and common sense, of the ordinary external world of the novelist. We do not mean that all the characters he draws are good and wise, nor even conscientious and sensible. On the contrary, many of them are bad and foolish, and all have faults—unless, perhaps, the good priest, Don Paolo, in *Marzio's Crucifix*—but what we mean is that all the men and women whom Mr. Crawford brings before us, he brings not as puppets, not as the toys of fate, not merely as natural curiosities to be observed, but as moral beings, creatures accountable to one above them, and possessing a power of choice and will. He writes, in short, as a Christian, and there is a certain novelty about it. (p. 343)

[Mr. Crawford] puts forward men who are neither stupid nor ignorant, but who are decided believers and do not at all aspire to that lofty flexibility of mind which enabled [George Eliot's]

Daniel Deronda to transfer himself from the Church to the Synagogue without, apparently, noticing the change. . . .

We have heard Mr. Crawford likened to Sir Walter Scott, and in this there is reason. The Waverley Novels were written at a time when popular thought was wholly under the influence of the Christian religion. Whether men did what that religion commands, whether they understood it rightly or not, still, it cannot be denied that it was then the constant basis of their theories of life, and the fixed standard to which they appealed. (p. 344)

The world presented in novels seems to have taken up the fashion of being bored at about the same time with the fashion of doing without religion. Both fashions are discarded in Mr. Crawford's pages, and herein lies his likeness to Sir Walter. The vigor of his style, the manly energy of life which he is capable of shewing in his characters, the hearty interest which he feels, and makes us feel, in them, their deeds and their experiences, all come from the *wholeness* of his conception of human life. He does not hide the evil, the baseness that is in the world, but neither does he ignore what is in it by reason of the facts of the Christian Faith. It is not that he chooses subjects more inspiring than those of other writers, nor that he is less able than they to understand the average man. *Marzio's Crucifix* . . . is a study, as sympathetic as condemnatory, of a type of character peculiar in time to the present half century, but peculiar to no country of the civilised world. He is everywhere, this fanatic possessed with the idea of destroying civilisation for the sake of an impossible equality between man and man. Marzio's untrained instincts of justice and pity, running wild in this manner, come near finding expression in a deed of murderous cruelty. He is an epitome of the faults, not of his nation only, but of his time, and if we can look on the picture without despair, it is because, in the Italian and the Anarchist, Mr. Crawford is still able to see the man, and the man's responsibility for the characteristics of the type. (p. 346)

[*Marzio's Crucifix* is not] equal to *Saracinesca* in plot, in variety of incident, and in the interest of the characters. The romance is prosaic compared with that of Giovanni and Corona, and there is no figure equal in humourous and pathetic charm to the dear, brave, old blundering gentleman who is Giovanni's father. But, looking beyond the mere story, it has more significance than the later book, and to the earlier is, in one respect, equal, in another superior. It is equal to *Saracinesca* in giving, of a special class of Roman society, a picture which, while not concealing the faults and dangers of these people, shows yet the good which remains in them, and through which they are united with all mankind in a great hope. It is superior in its clear indication of the nature and foundation of that hope.

We do not hear from Mr. Crawford of "the decadence of Italy;" we hear of an Italian who indulges himself in two very commonplace faults, vanity and ill-temper, at the same time laying aside his faith in, and obedience to, all religion. He cuts himself off from this at the point where it had brought him— as it has brought Christendom—to the enlarged power of imaginative sympathy of which we spoke above. But, separated from Christian Faith and obedience, this Christian instinct of compassion, growing—as some one has said—"as impatient of suffering as if it were sin," comes to believe "that poverty is the master-evil." After this there is a logic in Socialism, and it needs a clearer head than Marzio's to say where the line may be drawn, beyond which the tendency to Nihilism shall not proceed. (p. 348)

We have all felt the depression and perplexity with which one, on Dover Beach, heard "the melancholy long withdrawing roar" of the "sea of faith." But there are signs already that the tide has turned, and we welcome such work as Mr. Crawford's as spray, at least, from a mighty, in-coming wave. (p. 349)

G. E. Meredith, "Mr. Crawford's Latest Novels," in The Church Review, *Vol. LII, No. 189, October, 1888, pp. 343-49.*

OUIDA [pseudonym of MARIE LOUISE De La RAMÉE]   (essay date 1892)

[*Ouida was a leading popular novelist of the late nineteenth-century. Her romances with Italian settings were superceded by the work of Crawford.*]

I believe that the novels of Mr. Crawford of which the scene and the characters are Italian are not among those of his works which are the most generally popular. This fact, if it be a fact, must be due to the general inability of his English and American public to appreciate their accuracy of observation and delineation. Nearly all of them have qualities which cannot be gauged by those to whom the nationality of his personages in these works is unknown. In my own works, of which the scene is in Italy, I have dealt almost exclusively with the Italian peasantry. Mr. Crawford has devoted his attention to the middle and the higher classes. I do not think his portraiture of the Italian aristocracy always redolent of the soil, but that of the lower and middle classes is faithful to a wonderful degree. That side of Italian life which is given in *Marzio's Crucifix,* for instance, is drawn with an accuracy not to be surpassed. The whole of this story indeed is admirable in its construction and execution. There is not a page one would wish cancelled, and nothing could be added which would increase its excellence. It is to my taste the *capo d'opera* of all which he has hitherto done.

I think in his studies of the Italian aristocracy he has given them less charm and more backbone than they possess. He has drawn their passions more visible and furious than they are, and their wills less mutable and less feeble than they are in general. He seems to have mistaken their obstinacy for strength, while, if he have perceived it, he has not rendered that captivating courtesy and graceful animation which are so lovable in them, and which render so many of their men and women so irresistibly seductive. According to him they are a savage set of *berserkers,* always cutting each other's throats, and he does not in any way render that extreme politeness which so effectually conceals the real thoughts of the Italian gentleman, and which never deserts him except in rare moments of irresistible fury. (p. 719)

But in his Italian *genre* pictures, and in portraiture of the people whom we meet every day in society, Mr. Crawford has a delightful pencil; little side studies also of more humble persons, which many writers would neglect, are charming in his treatment; take, for instance, the old priest of Aquila in *Saracinesca;* with how few touches he is made to live for us. We only see him once, but he will always remain in our memory. . . .

[Mr. Crawford's] priests, by the way, are always excellently drawn, from the humble village vicar to the learned and imposing cardinal. He has penetrated alike their interiors and their characters with that skill which is only born of sympathy, and it is therefore perhaps only natural that he has not the faintest conception of the motives and views of the socialist and republican whom he dreads and hates. (p. 720)

[One] cannot forgive [Mr. Crawford] for ever beating the big drum of florid sensation.

Let me not be understood to mean that crime, or the impulse of crime, is not a perfectly legitimate subject for the novelist; both can be made so, but they are only so when treated as Mr. Crawford himself treats them in *Marzio's Crucifix.* When treated as he treats them in *To Leeward* and *Grieffenstein* and *Casa Braccio* they are merely coarse and inartistic. He has a leaning towards melodrama which is chiefly to be regretted because it mars and strains the style most natural to him, and does not accord with his way of looking at life, which is not either poetic or passionate, but slightly sad, and slightly humorous, modern and instinctively superficial, superficial in that sense in which modern society itself is so.

In *Marzio's Crucifix* he is perfectly natural, and one cannot but wish that he had never left that manner of treatment. Every motive therein is natural, every character consistent with itself. This naturalness in his characters is Mr. Crawford's greatest attraction, and when he departs from it, as he does in such detestable melodramas as the *Witch of Prague* and *Grieffenstein,* he is no longer himself. It is hard to understand that the same author can create the most delicate of aquarelles and the most glaring of posters, or why one who can draw so well and finely in silver-point can descend to daub with brooms in such gross distemper. If this be the price of versatility, it were best not to be versatile. But it is not versatility, because true versatility consists in possessing a many-sided power which flashes like a jewel of which all the facets are equally well cut. True versatility, moreover, does not consist in the mere change of subject, but in the change of style, of treatment of thought, in fact, the mutation of the entire mind of an author, such as brings it into entire harmony with its fresh field and its new atmosphere. There is no such change in these novels. Mr. Crawford is Mr. Crawford always. As he never loses himself in his creations, so he is always present in them to the reader; and his style never varies, whether he treats of horrible psychological mysteries in Prague or of pleasant carnival seasons in Rome.

He is not strong or forcible in tragedy. When it is incidental in his stories like the murder of Montevarchi, or the attempted assassination of Ser Tommaso, it is admirably sketched in; but when it forms the structure and essence of a romance he fails entirely to give it sublimity; it becomes in his hands a mere scarecrow, which makes us only smile as its wooden hands beat the empty air. One feels that it is not his natural element, that he does not like it or feel at home in it, and has merely lent himself to it from some wrong impression that the public requires it; due, perhaps, to the suggestion of some unwise publisher or friend. The coarse melodrama with which *To Leeward* ends is not in unison with the characters or the scope of the work. (pp. 720-21)

Mr. Crawford can draw men and women of the world so well that it is a pity he so often goes out of his way to spoil his portraits of them with the bowl and dagger taken from a different phase of life from that in which they move.

He is always a gentleman, and he is at his best when writing of gentlemen in the society which he knows so well. Duels are quite natural in good society everywhere, except in England, and no one since Charles Lever ever described them so well as Mr. Crawford; but murders are not general in the world of well-bred people, indeed are not very often heard of out of the lowest strata of plebeian life.

In *Casa Braccio* a fine motive, that of the peasant of Subiaco's long-cherished vengeance, with its final satisfaction, both based on a mistake, is wasted, because no one can care in the least for the man who is slain, and the original sin committed by this victim (marriage with a nun), although it seems so great to Mr. Crawford, appears to us no sin at all; so that his tragic end neither moves us nor satisfies us in any sense of justice. What are admirably rendered and true to life in *Casa Braccio* are not Griggs and Gloria, or Angus Dalrymple and Maria Addorata, but the peasants of Subiaco, Stefanone, with his long-cherished vendetta, and his wife, Sora Nanna, who wears her lost daughter's shoes because it would have been a sin to waste them. One regrets that two persons so perfectly natural and well drawn should be set on a pyre of flaring melodrama which obscures their portraits in its smoke and flame. . . . When I use the term melodrama, I mean by it that which mimics the tragic, but falls short of it; the tragic, imitated but so environed, that it loses dignity and has something of the inflated and grotesque. The melodrama in *Pietro Ghisleri*, in *Taquisara*, and in *The Children of the King* is this kind of melodrama; it does not move us for a moment; we are, on the contrary, impatient of it in a modern period and history, with neither of which it has any harmony. (pp. 721-22)

Another defect of Mr. Crawford's works is usually that their interest flags towards the close, that this close is too abrupt, and that it gives the reader the impression of the narrative being brought to an untimely end because the writer no longer cared about narrating it. This defect may be noticed in nearly all his stories, beginning with *Mr. Isaacs,* in which it is conspicuous; and is startlingly and irritatingly visible in one of his latest, *Adam Johnstone's Son;* indeed, in the last named story the conclusion is obviously totally different from what it was intended to be in the opening chapters. (pp. 722-23)

[Mr. Crawford] frequently introduces personages about whom he excites our liveliest interest, and whom he then forsakes or dismisses with an indifference which the reader does not share. It is as though a painter painted into his canvas numerous figures which he has never finished though he sends out his picture as a finished work. The only novels of his which are entirely free from this defect are the *Cigarette Maker,* the *Three Fates,* and *Marzio's Crucifix,* and here I cannot resist (though it is not within the scope of this article, since its venue is America) pointing out how delicate, subtle, and clever is that story entitled the *Three Fates.* There is little movement in it, no incident of any note, its interest lies entirely in the development of character and in the evolution of feeling, but these are so treated that they suffice to hold the reader's charmed attention. . . . (p. 723)

What to me is especially attractive in Mr. Crawford's novels is the atmosphere of good breeding which one breathes in them. One feels in the company of a well-bred man. Their philosophy, their experiences, their views, are all those of a man of the world; and there is in them a tolerance and a total absence of prejudice (except in religious and political matters) which are refreshing, and which are a fair approach to, if not an actual attainment of, unbiassed liberality. There is in them no enthusiasm for anything, no altruism, no deep emotion. They are unfortunately entirely lacking in any perception of those myriads of other lives not human, but as sentient as the human. . . . To Mr. Crawford as to Peter Bell, a primrose by the river's side is a primrose, and it is nothing more, and the thrush or the linnet which sings in the hawthorn above the primrose roots for him has no existence. He has the American's indifference to all created things which are not human. There are no animals in his books except two poor terriers (who have their necks broken by the odious lover in *To Leeward*), and the unhappy cat, introduced only to be poisoned in *Taquisara.* There is nothing which indicates that he cares for nature in any of its phases, and he calls the cicala a locust. (p. 724)

Mr. Crawford misses many opportunities of developing the capacity for analysis and deduction which he undoubtedly possesses. He is very observant but he is content to note a fact, he does not trouble himself to seek its origin or the influences which have made it the fact it is. (p. 728)

[In some of the stories of Mr. Crawford] there is an unfortunate tendency towards approval of what he calls hierarchical government, although a tendency not strongly enough insisted on by him for it to demand minute examination. The powers of Mr. Crawford, however, are limited by the narrowness of what is called religion, and the inability to see the higher side of these subversive opinions which he dreads, and which he has done his best to turn into ridicule by putting them into the mouth of the half-mad artist Marzio.

Indeed, his bigotry on religious subjects is very droll to see in these days; and he speaks of 'unbelievers' in a tone worthy of Puritans in the days of the *Mayflower* pilgrims. It does not agree with the tone of his books, which is invariably the tone of a man of the world; as such he should possess that liberality of thought which is the chief, perhaps the only, virtue of his generation; and if he had possessed it he would undoubtedly have reached a much higher level, a much finer ideal, than he has actually done. (pp. 730-31)

His religious prejudices have contributed to arrest his intellectual development, for they are puritanical and antiquated in a singular and lamentable degree. (p. 731)

Mr. Crawford, if he had 'let himself go,' might have been a satirist of no slight force. He has preferred to write charming stories, ingenious in construction, but slight in development, to amuse his generation; yet there is, I think, abundant evidence that he might have done stronger things, perhaps may do them still. . . . There is a regrettable inability in Mr. Crawford to perceive the ridiculous. He lacks humour, and the perception of the incongruous is not alive in him; nor is there needed poetic feeling in his way of regarding life. He is essentially a citizen of the world as the world exists in this last quarter of the fast-fading century, and the Sirens sing not for him. (p. 732)

> *Ouida [pseudonym of Marie Louise de la Ramée], "The Italian Novels of Marion Crawford," in* The Nineteenth Century, *Vol. XLII, No. 249, November, 1892, pp. 719-33.*

F. MARION CRAWFORD   (essay date 1893)

"What is a novel?" A novel is a marketable commodity, of the class collectively termed "luxuries," as not contributing directly to the support of life or the maintenance of health. It is of the class "artistic luxuries" because it does not appeal to any of the three material senses—touch, taste, smell; and it is of the class "intellectual artistic luxuries," because it is not judged by the superior senses—sight and hearing. The novel, therefore, is an intellectual artistic luxury—a definition which can be made to include a good deal, but which is, in reality, a closer one than it appears to be at first sight. (pp. 8-9)

Probably no one denies that the first object of the novel is to amuse and interest the reader. But it is often said that the novel should instruct as well as afford amusement, and the "novel-with-a-purpose" is the realisation of this idea. . . . Why not compound the words and call the odious thing a "purpose-novel"? The purpose-novel, then, proposes to serve two masters, besides procuring a reasonable amount of bread and butter for its writer and publisher. It proposes to escape from my definition of the novel in general and make itself an "intellectual moral lesson" instead of an "intellectual artistic luxury." It constitutes a violation of the unwritten contract tacitly existing between writer and reader. (pp. 11-12)

We [novelists] are nothing more than public amusers. Unless we choose we need not be anything less. Let us, then, accept our position cheerfully, and do the best we can to fulfil our mission, without attempting to dignify it with titles too imposing for it to bear, and without degrading it by bringing its productions down even a little way, from the lowest level of high comedy to the highest level of buffoonery. It is good to make people laugh; it is sometimes salutary to make them shed tears; it is best of all to make our readers think—not too serious thoughts, nor such as require an intimate knowledge of science and philosophy to be called thoughts at all—but to think, and, thinking, to see before them characters whom they might really like to resemble, acting in scenes in which they themselves would like to take a part. (pp. 22-3)

There is much talk in our day of the realistic school of fiction, and the romantic school, though not often mentioned, is understood to be opposed to it. . . . [The] realist proposes to show men what they are; the romantist tries to show men what they should be. It is very unlikely that mankind will ever agree as to the relative merits of these two, and the discussion which was practically begun in Plato's time is not likely to end so long as people care what they read or what they think. The most any one can do is to give a personal opinion, and that means, of course, that he who expresses it commits himself and publicly takes either the one side or the other. For my part, I believe that more good can be done by showing men what they may be, ought to be, or can be, than by describing their greatest weaknesses with the highest art. We all know how bad we are; but it needs much encouragement to persuade some of us to believe that we can really be any better. To create genuine interest, and afford rest and legitimate amusement, without losing sight of that fact, and to do so in a more or less traditional way, seems to be the profession of the novelist who belongs to the romantic persuasion.

That novel-writing is a business I am credibly informed by my publishers. And since that is the case, it must be taken for granted that it is a business which to some extent must be practised like any other and which will succeed or fail in the hands of any particular man according as he is more or less fitted to carry it on. The qualifications for any business are three: native talent, education, and industry. Where there is success of the right kind, the talent and power of application must be taken for granted. The education is and always must be a question of circumstance. With regard to novel-writing, when I speak of education I am not referring to it in the ordinary sense. Some people take a great deal of interest in concrete things, while others care more for humanity. The education of a novelist is the experience of men and women which he has got at first hand in the course of his own life, for he is of that class to whom humanity offers a higher interest than inanimate nature. He can use nature and art only as a scene and background upon which and before which his personages move and have their being. It is his business to present his readers with something which I have called the pocket-theatre, something which every man may carry in his pocket, believing that he has only to open it in order to look in upon the theatre of the living world. To produce it, to prepare it, to put it into a portable and serviceable shape, the writer must know what that living world is, what the men in it do and what the women think, why women shed tears and children laugh and young men make love and old men repeat themselves. While he is writing his book, his human beings must be with him, before him, moving before the eye of his mind and talking into the ear of his heart. He must have lived himself; he must have loved, fought, suffered, and struggled in the human battle. I would almost say that to describe another's death he must himself have died. (pp. 76-80)

> *F. Marion Crawford, in his* The Novel: What It Is, *Macmillan, 1893 (and reprinted by Books for Libraries Press, 1969; distributed by Arno Press, Inc.), 108 p.*

W. P. TRENT (essay date 1894)

[Mr. Marion Crawford] has displayed a versatility in choice and treatment of subjects that can hardly be predicated of any other novelist since Sir Walter. He has interested and amused and sometimes instructed a large and increasing number of readers on two continents. He has never written an absolutely dull book, save possibly **Doctor Claudius,** or an immoral one, and he has preserved a level of excellence which, in view of his fecundity, is decidedly remarkable. (pp. 239-40)

One who reads **Mr. Isaacs** a second time after having read the twenty volumes that have followed it in such rapid succession, can hardly fail to perceive that many of its author's most striking characteristics were plainly to be seen from the first in his work, or else were fore-shadowed in it. There is the same easy pleasant style that has carried so many readers smoothly along over thousands of pages, some of which have not been absolutely free from padding, but many of which have been vivacious, or humorous, or sometimes fairly poetic. There is the same fecundity of invention which has furnished an unfailing supply of incident to counterbalance a not infrequent returning upon his own traces of which our author, with the rest of his class, has been guilty. There is the same quite steady and unblushing adherence to the canons of the romancer,—the same reliance upon love as the true motive-spring of fiction. There is, let us acknowledge it gratefully, the same power of telling a story that shall be interesting—a story that is a story pure and simple. There are other characteristics, too, some of them not altogether admirable. There is the same very considerable power of characterization which yet, in the main, creates personages, not persons, and rarely deals with more than a small group of them. There is the same talent for description, the same eye for the beauties of nature, which though sharpened since, has been often that of the traveller mainly bent on seeing things worth describing on his return home—which has never made its observations with the penetrating sympathy of a poet (for he is a poet) like Thomas Hardy. There is, too, the thorough-going air of proprietorship over his characters that has never yet deserted Mr. Crawford—the same stage-manager air, for has he not himself likened his novels to little plays? There is, further, the same love for the bizarre and the curious that has constantly cropped up in subsequent stories, the same *penchant* for heroes and heroines provided with a plenty of this world's goods, the same fondness for having at least one character who is a "remarkable individual," and at least two characters who shall make a marriage somewhat out of the common. It would doubtless be hard to maintain successfully that in *Mr. Isaacs* one can find promise of the highly sustained power visible in *Greifenstein*, or of the careful workmanship and thought expended on the *Saracinesca* series, or of the poetical qualities that went to the making of *Khaled:* but it is hardly wide of the mark to say that few first books have ever had displayed in them so many of the traits that were destined to characterise their authors as *Mr. Isaacs.*

If this be admitted, it follows that there is less need than with most writers to examine Mr. Crawford's works in chronological order. It is an advantage, too, both to critic and reader that our author's productions readily lend themselves to classification. Somewhat too readily, perhaps, for Mr. Crawford is nothing if not versatile. . . . Still it would seem that nearly all his novels can be grouped as either *Cosmopolitan* or *National*. Under the first head will come those in which the characters, of various nationalities, change their habitat according to their own or the author's convenience, such as *Paul Patoff*, or in which a majority of the characters are foreign to the country they are residing in throughout the course of the narrative, such as *Mr. Isaacs*. Under the second head will come those in which a majority of the characters are inhabitants of the country in which the scene of the story is laid, such as *Saracinesca, Greifenstein,* and *Marion Darche*. It should be remarked that some of the novels to be hereafter considered as *Cosmopolitan*, might with advantage be classed as romances dealing with the uncommon or the extra-natural, such as *The Witch of Prague*, and that the classification adopted takes no account of the difference between such a novel of society and manners as *Pietro Ghisleri* and such a tragic idyl as *Children of the King*, between such a high-wrought romance as *Greifenstein* and such a simple character study as *Marzio's Crucifix*. It leaves out, also, all distinctions of realistic and romantic, for Mr. Crawford has dallied a little with realism, but this is of slight moment. . . . (pp. 241-43)

Of the twenty-one novels with which we have to deal, it would seem that five may be classed as *Cosmopolitan*. They are [*Mr. Isaacs, Doctor Claudius, Paul Patoff, The Witch of Prague,* and *A Cigarette Maker's Romance*]. . . . It may seem singular at first blush that the last two or certainly the last of the novels just named should appear under this classification, but it must be remembered that neither is, properly speaking, a study of local conditions. The chief characters are either nebulous like the "Wanderer," in *The Witch of Prague*, or of a foreign country like the cigarette maker of Munich.

Of *Mr. Isaacs* enough has already been said. When it was followed the next year by *Dr. Claudius* some at least of Mr. Crawford's admirers were disappointed not to say disillusioned. The sprightly ease, the *élan* of the first story seemed in the second to have given way to a quasi-smartness that degenerated into dullness before the book was finished. The characters seemed to be a set of overdressed puppets whose virtues the author was constantly proclaiming in a voice pitched on a superlatively shrill key. . . . [Some] readers at least shake their heads and regret that so talented a man as Mr. Crawford should have been ruined by the success of his first book. It is needless to add that these pessimists were mistaken and that not a few of the readers of 1883 managed to get some pleasure out of what its author proclaimed to be "A True Story." (pp. 243-44)

Paul Patoff is connected with *Mr. Isaacs* not merely through the fact that it is related by the same interesting Yankee, Paul Griggs, who told us the last named story, but also because it derives much of its interest from the same sources. Its hero is not quite such a remarkable character as Isaacs, nor is Balsamides (another Crichton) the equal of Ram Lal. But it describes another cosmopolitan love affair which this time ends happily after sundry ripples; it gives a picturesque description of a fascinating city, Constantinople; it is full of movement and adventure; and finally, it has a touch of the mysterious in the queer mental aberrations of Madame Patoff. While it does not display the maturity of thought and observation that became visible about the same time in *Saracinesca*, and while it can hardly be said to be an advance on *Mr. Isaacs* in point of interest and power, it still remains a story of love, adventure, and picturesque description that may be safely recommended in place of many of the dialect stories and realistic studies with which the novel-reading public of to-day regales itself.

The Witch of Prague is also the natural outcome of the mind that showed such interest in the wonders performed by Indian jugglers. The subject of hypnotic influence has of late years attracted the attention, not only of medical specialists and lawyers, but of nearly every reading man; it is no wonder, therefore, that a writer with Mr. Crawford's peculiar powers of imagination, should have made it the working idea of a new novel. He has not been alone in this, but it is safe to say that *The Witch of Prague* is one of the most remarkable stories of its kind ever conceived. . . . Here, then, we have at last something far removed from the light touch of *Mr. Isaacs* and *Paul Patoff. The Witch of Prague* may not be charming, it may be even to some minds revolting, but that it is powerful and daring and such a story as few living men could have written, is a claim that at least admits of argument.

Little need be said here of the story that closes the *Cosmopolitan* series—*A Cigarette Maker's Romance*. It is one of the most pathetic and charming pieces of work that has ever come from Mr. Crawford's prolific pen—much more charming than that other novelette dealing with the artisan class, *Marzio's Crucifix*, although not so powerful in its ending as that other idyl—this seems the only proper word—*Children of the King*. The scolding Frau Fischelowitz, the brawling peasant, Dumnoff, the exquisitely pure and self-sacrificing Vjera, and lastly that thorough gentleman, the Count himself, form a group of characters well worth the few hours needed for making their acquaintance.

Pausing for a moment before passing to the *National* novels we may note how in the eight years that intervene between *Mr. Isaacs* and *A Cigarette Maker's Romance*, Mr. Crawford has outgrown the tendency to make a more or less meteoric display of his versatility and brilliancy, how he is no longer content to tell a pretty love story dashed with adventure and a description of the many outlying countries he has visited. If *The Witch of Prague* still shows that the mysterious, the extranatural has a powerful hold upon his mind, it also shows that he has a more artistic control of his powers and that his imagination is as strong as his fancy is daring. (pp. 244-47)

The *National* novels include a decided majority of Mr. Crawford's works. Beginning with *A Roman Singer* and *To Leeward* . . . , they stretch to *Marion Darche*. . . . Of the thirteen stories that form the series, eight belong to Italy, one to England, one to Germany, and three to America. It will be most convenient to discuss them in this order.

The Italian novels embrace besides the first two named above, the well-known trilogy, [*Saracinesca, Sant' Ilario,* and *Don*

Orsino, besides *Marzio's Crucifix, Children of the King,* and *Pietro Ghisleri*]. . . . With the exception of *Greifenstein* and *Khaled* they contain within their number nearly all the works that a judicious admirer of Mr. Crawford would select in order to base and justify any praise of moment. (p. 247)

It can hardly be said that *A Roman Singer* and *To Leeward* were remarkable advances on *Doctor Claudius,* but they did show progress. (p. 248)

To Leeward is one of the very few stories in which Mr. Crawford touches on irregular relations between the sexes. Love is his constant theme, but it is always Love as the winged god is supposed, however erroneously, to be conceived by that patroness of the English and American novel, the blushing and innocent school-girl. For once, however, our author determined, it would seem, to write as if the schoolgirl patroness did not exist. His boldness did not, nevertheless, lead him very far, and there are few school-girls who need look with longing but unsatisfied eyes at *To Leeward* on account of its naughtiness. (pp. 248-49)

[*Saracinesca*] is one of the best studies that has been made in recent years of the aristocracy of a great capital. If the characters, more numerous than is usual with Mr. Crawford, are still personages, they are many of them interesting and admirable personages. (pp. 249-50)

Sant' Ilario if not equal to its predecessor, certainly does not show the falling off that is characteristic of sequels. . . . But the story is a very interesting one and much that has been said of *Saracinesca* might be said of it. Especially interesting and well executed is the description of the downward career of the old librarian who has murdered his hypocrite master. *Don Orsino* is the concluding member of this trilogy. . . . The plot is somewhat slow in developing, but does not lack interest or power. The novel, therefore, forms a not unworthy pendant to its predecessors.

Pietro Ghisleri, the last of the Italian novels . . . , should be mentioned here because, while the Saracinesca family are not important figures in it, its scene is laid amid the social surroundings with which the readers of the annals of that family are acquainted. Ghisleri, the hero, is one of the most complex characters Mr. Crawford has ever conceived, but his complexity is more hinted at by the author than shown in his own actions. . . . Altogether one feels that *Pietro Ghisleri* is well fit to rank with the *Saracinesca* series as one of Mr. Crawford's most powerful stories.

Marzio's Crucifix and *Children of the King* which conclude the Italian stories, demand only a word. Marzio is an interesting study of a talented artisan who has nearly lost his reason through dabbling in socialism and other dangerous modern isms. One feels, however, that the account of his madness and his recovery is not far removed from what Mr. Crawford has justly denounced in his little book, *The Novel—What It Is,* the purpose novel [see excerpt above]. Our author is nothing if not conservative in matters relating to religion, modern science, and politics, and his often promulgated views seem to find purposive expression in the story under discussion. Nothing of this sort, however, can be said of *Children of the King,* the loveliest of the Italian series. Here Mr. Crawford is at his best in his descriptions of the beauties of the southern coast of Italy. . . . (pp. 250-52)

[*A Tale of a Lonely Parish*] is the single story of English life that our versatile novelist has given us, certain chapters of *Paul*

Patoff alone excepted. It is a worthy connecting link between the earlier novels and *Saracinseca.* It is interesting, simple, and well told. The meteoric displays of **Mr. Isaacs** and *Dr. Claudius* have no place in it. There is, perhaps, a suspicion of thread-bareness in the plot, for the wives of convicts have been known before to be thrown into confusion by their husbands' unexpected return—indeed this happens in Mr. Crawford's very last novel—but we forgive this for the sake of the quiet style and the artistic character of the whole work. It is decidedly in Anthony Trollope's vein, and that veteran would not have blushed to own it. . . .

[*Greifenstein*] is by some considered Mr. Crawford's best work. It is certainly a romance of high power and originality. So much of a romance is it that somehow one wishes its scene had been laid a couple of centuries back. No one wishes that it should be removed from the Black Forest, so admirably described, or from the ruined castle that sheltered Hilda and her mother; but would not the almost Œdipean tragedy which took place in the gloomy forest have lost much of its repulsiveness if it had been somewhat removed from these days of the sensational newspaper with its daily budget of horrors? Be this as it may, we cannot deny that Mr. Crawford's imagination served him well throughout the whole course of his tragic romance. (p. 252)

In *The Three Fates* and *Marion Darche* Mr. Crawford has undertaken a study of New York society. Whether these stories fall below *Saracinesca* in interest because New York is less interesting than Rome or because Mr. Crawford is less at home there, must be left for others to determine. That he has not succeeded as well in his American as in his Roman novels is patent to most of his readers. *The Three Fates* has a special element of interest because the hero writes novels, and one is constantly wondering how far Mr. Crawford is speaking for himself and his own methods of work. It is also interesting as a study of a morbid girl who does not know her own mind when she is confronted with the problem of matrimony. But it may be doubted whether New York society will care to be judged by this story or by *Marion Darche,* which describes the woes brought upon a devoted wife by the rascality of a husband of a sort only too common at the present day.

We have now completed our survey of Mr. Crawford's works with the exception of three volumes still unclassified. They are [*Zoroaster, With the Immortals,* and *Khaled*]. . . . The first is an historical romance, the second is no novel at all, the third is an Arabian tale worthy of Scheherazade herself. (pp. 253-54)

It would be pleasant to dwell on many points that have suggested themselves in the course of our reading, such as his quaint but effective resuscitation of the elaborate Homeric simile, and the occasional bits of original poetry of some merit that he permits himself to insert in the body of his prose romances. But . . . readers are apt to grow weary even when so versatile and charming a writer as Mr. Crawford is the theme—a writer who has made thousands of friends and deserves to make thousands more. (p. 256)

> *W. P. Trent, "Mr. Crawford's Novels," in* The Sewanee Review *(© 1894 by The University of the South), Vol. II, No. 2, February, 1894, pp. 239-56.*

MAX [BEERBOHM]   (essay date 1902)

[If] Mr. Crawford's keynote seemed to me a proper one, **"Francesca da Rimini"** would seem to me quite a good entertainment—a play somewhat trite and vulgar in tone, but cleverly worked out, and provided with several thrilling moments. But alas! I, like everyone else whose opinion is or is not worth having, am obstinately convinced that Mr. Crawford ought to have thumped quite another keynote—the keynote of young and etherealised passion. Not that I have been yearning for yet another dramatic incarnation of "the two most memorable spirits that floated past Dante". D'Annunzio has given us their hearts' passion, Maeterlinck (changing but their names) has given us their souls' pathos, Mr. Stephen Phillips has given us their elegant and wistful winsomeness. If we had much more of them, just at present, they might get on our nerves. . . . We do not need the true Paolo and Francesca again, but still less do we need two other persons of the same names. The one pair would fatigue us, but would still illude us; the other revolts us, nor do we believe in it for one instant. Mr. Crawford, doubtless, would demur to the epithet "true" as applied to Dante's, not to his own, creatures. And I am not going to fly in the face of history (as learnt from Mr. Crawford's interesting preface and notes) by denying that there once lived in Italy a lady named Francesca da Rimini, and a gentleman named Paolo Malatesta, whose lives and characters have been grossly distorted by Dante and drawn with some measure of accuracy by Mr. Crawford. Yet will I not transpose the epithet "true" from the place I put it in. For who cares a wooden hoop what sort of people Paolo and Francesca were "when they were at home", or what sort of love they really had for each other? They simply don't exist for us. They never did exist, except for the scandalmongers of their period. But there is a very real and fiery existence for those two figments, Paolo and Francesca according to Dante. Them we accept, them we love (within reason), in them we believe with all our hearts. And there is a rude shock in store for anyone who, ignoring Dante—"Diabolo Dante Dedi": Mr. Crawford is welcome to this weird paraphrase of a famous motto—comes airily assuming that we shall not reject with scorn his revised version of the twain.

One phrase in that last sentence is not quite happy. Mr. Crawford is not a man to be conceived as "airily assuming" anything. He is painfully conscientious in the collection and verification of data. It seems that, before writing this play, he made a thorough examination of the castle in which Paolo and Francesca met their doom, and that he even succeeded in identifying beyond a doubt the very room in which that doom was met. Submissive to a famous precedent, "upstairs and downstairs and in my lady's chamber" wandered Mr. Marion Crawford, wasting that which his exemplar had not to waste—shoe-leather. If he had proceeded to put into his play the whole truth, as evolved by his various researches, and nothing but that truth, then perhaps the waste would seem to me to have been made good. If he had been frankly and consistently archaeological, then might his play, though giving no aesthetic pleasure to anyone, have had some value for some students. And I suspect that this is the line which Mr. Crawford, better versed in mediaeval Italy than in modern dramaturgy, would have preferred to take. But "j'ai usé la liberté du dramaturge", he says in apology for not showing us Paolo swinging to and fro, with his doublet caught by the hinge of an unfriendly trapdoor. Furthermore, Mr. Crawford wishes it to be distinctly understood that he has had regard only to the exigencies of drama, and has not attempted to make an historic study. So that this new version of Paolo and Francesca is not a really trustworthy version for the dry-as-dust. What, then, is it? Merely a painful fall between two stools, to serve as a warning for those about to write plays round obscure episodes which have

been transformed and immortalised by poetic genius. So salutary a warning deserves permanence. But I fear that **"Francesca da Rimini"** is doomed to very speedy oblivion. Nor can we be justly blamed for trying to forget this stodgy and sordid creation, which, though it is so unreal to us, does tend to mar the preconception which destroys it. It is unlucky for Mr. Crawford that his play was not produced some four years ago; for then these very columns would have been resounding with a paean in his honour. But I fancy that "G.B.S." [George Bernard Shaw] is the one and only person to whom Paolo, as a stout, middle-aged father of a family, stricken down untimely in the fourteenth year of his intrigue with Francesca, would appear as a reason for enthusiasm. (pp. 804-05)

> *Max [Beerbohm], "Crawford Versus Dante," in* The Saturday Review, *London, Vol. 93, No. 2434, June 21, 1902, pp. 804-05.*

EDITH WHARTON   (essay date 1902)

[*Wharton compares three dramas based on the story of Francesca da Rimini: Stephen Phillips's* Paolo and Francesca, *Gabrielle D'Annunzio's* Francesca da Rimini, *and Crawford's* Francesca da Rimini, *written expressly for Sarah Bernhardt. Wharton finds that of the three "Crawford has undoubtedly been most successful from the dramatic point of view. He has written the best 'acting' play."*]

The almost simultaneous production of three plays on the subject of Francesca da Rimini, by play-wrights of three different nationalities, illustrates in an interesting manner that impulse of the creative fancy which so often leads one imaginative writer to take up a theme already dealt with by another. (p. 17)

Before examining the plays separately, however, it is necessary to find some basis of comparison; since they are too different to be compared at all points. In form, for instance, Mr. Phillips has chosen blank verse, Signor d'Annunzio *vers libres,* rhymed and unrhymed, and Mr. Crawford (for special reasons) a prose simple to the verge of baldness. These vehicles of expression cannot be profitably compared, and one must seek elsewhere for an attribute common to the three versions. This is found in the fact that all three were written for the stage; and from this stand-point they must be considered.

In dealing with so well-known a theme, the dramatist's task is complicated by the fact that he must discount the suspense of his audience. From the first line they are in the secret with him: every spectator knows that Francesca and Paolo love each other, and that in the end their love will be found out and punished. The author, therefore, cannot play on the conjectures of his audience; and suspense being avowedly one of the most important factors in dramatic presentment, he must make up for this deficiency by keeping his characters in the dark and letting his audience become absorbed in their gropings through the labyrinth of fate. From the outset, the spectator knows the doom suspended over the house of Malatesta; and the chief interest in the play must lie in watching "the gods creep on with feet of wool" upon their unsuspecting victims. (p. 18)

[It] is to Mr. Crawford's credit that his skill in the construction of mechanical plots has not led him to turn a tragedy into a melodrama. He has preserved the simple outline which such a theme demands, and his dramatic instinct has saved him from clogging it with unessential detail.

His play was written for Madame Sarah Bernhardt, with the view of its being translated into French; and these peculiar conditions restricted Mr. Crawford to the use of the simplest prose. The English version necessarily suffers from this restriction. In a language which, like the English and the Italian, possesses a special poetic vocabulary, it is hard to render lofty situations in prose without running into colloquialism or bathos. Mr. Crawford has at least refrained from making his personages talk "prose poetry". They use the plainest and most direct English, and the play seems almost like the skeleton of a drama in blank verse.

This nudity makes the structure of the tragedy more salient. To turn from the crowded scene of Signor d'Annunzio's "Francesca" to the open spaces of Mr. Crawford's, is like passing from a modern English play with an elaborate stage-setting to the bare *mise-en-scène* of a classic drama at the Théâtre Français, where, if there is a glass of water on the stage, the spectator knows it has its special relevancy. Mr. Crawford, alone of the three authors, has turned to history for the chronology of his drama. According to the old chronicles, Paolo and Francesca loved each other for fourteen years before Giovanni discovered their secret; and, in the original version of Mr. Crawford's play, his heroine is the mother of a girl of thirteen when the action begins. A brief prologue, setting forth the fraud of Francesca's marriage, has been added to the French translation; but the addition, though cleverly made, detracts from the unity and simplicity of the original, and ought not to be included in its consideration. (p. 26)

Whatever the merits of the two other plays—and they are many— Mr. Crawford has undoubtedly been most successful from the dramatic point of view. He has written the best "acting" play. His action is more rapid and simpler than that of the other dramatists, and has a higher quality of dramatic inevitableness. He has been clever in letting the surprise of the lovers take place without the time-honored device of the feigned departure. The psychology of his principle characters is firmly drawn, and though his play is as bare of metaphor as a tragedy of Alfieri's, it does not lack high imaginative touches. . . . It is curious to note that the French critics, who have written much and favorably of Mr. Crawford's play, take exception at the two most characteristic *racial* traits in the drama: the long attachment of the lovers, and Malatesta's change from a violent and outspoken man to a stealthy smiling assassin. It is at these two points that Mr. Crawford has shown his insight into Italian character and his courage in departing from stage conventions. He has had the audacity to draw his characters as Italians of the Middle Ages, and not as scrupulous and sentimental modern altruists. Italian fidelity in love was for centuries the theme of wondering comment to French travellers. . . . To those who understand this tradition, the long affection between Paolo and Francesca gives an added dignity and pathos to their situation. . . . (pp. 29-30)

Edith Wharton, "The Three Francescas," in The North American Review, *Vol. CLXXV, No. 548, July, 1902, pp. 17-30.**

FREDERIC TABER COOPER   (essay date 1907)

[In contrast to the predominant critical opinion, Cooper finds Crawford's Italian novels lack the "artistic charm and unity" of Crawford's other works. While he singles out for praise novels written during the first decade of Crawford's literary career, Cooper notes that Crawford has maintained a fairly even and high "quality of interest" throughout his career.]

It would be futile to attempt to survey in detail any large number of Mr. Crawford's twoscore novels, nor would any very useful purpose be served were it practical to do so. There is a surprisingly large proportion of his books which a critic may quite safely ignore—books which one and all maintain an even quality of interest, yet add nothing to our estimate of him as a man or artist. As is well-nigh inevitable in a novelist who never allows himself to forget that "novel writing is a business," and who has the technique of construction down almost to a mechanical perfection, the difference between his earlier and later books is mainly a loss of spontaneity and an increased conventionality in plot and character. Mr. Crawford has not "written himself out," to use the phrase which he has declared is so terrible for any author to hear; nor is it likely that he ever will write himself out. His average standard to-day is far nearer to that of his best work than that of Mr. Howells, let us say, comes to *Silas Lapham*—nearer, indeed, than many another novelist whom the world has chosen to honour could come to his own best achievement after a quarter of a century of unremittent toil. It is nevertheless a fact that the volumes which one feels inclined to single out for specific discussion all belong to the first decade of Mr. Crawford's literary activity.

Mr. Isaacs of course must remain one of the volumes which will be read as long as Mr. Crawford continues to be remembered. Crude though it may be in construction, and uneven in style, it nevertheless remains a rather remarkable achievement, one of those rare first efforts that are nothing short of a sheer stroke of genius. It is usually an unwise experiment to read over in maturity a story which gave keen pleasure in early youth; yet if the present writer may be allowed to cite his own personal experience, *Mr. Isaacs* is one of the books that stand the test surprisingly well. Mr. Crawford himself admits that he was most fortunate in having begun his literary career with this particular book; theosophy was in the air, Kipling had not yet pre-empted the field of India for fiction, and there was, moreover, a certain mingling of poetry and cynicism, of mature experience and youthful enthusiasm, that went well with the strange theme and the vivid colouring. And one may seriously question whether any single volume written by Marion Crawford in the height of his powers could have duplicated the success of *Mr. Isaacs* if put forth as the first novel of an unknown author.

Dr. Claudius, which followed *Mr. Isaacs* within the year, may well be passed over with the comment that for a book so badly handicapped the wonder was that it succeeded at all. . . . Of the books which followed, at an average rate of two volumes a year, *A Roman Singer* was notable for that extreme simplicity of style which has since become one of Mr. Crawford's most effective assets: *Marzio's Crucifix,* as representing a long step forward in the technique of unity of plot; *Kahled,* as the most effective and artistic of all the author's purely fanciful efforts. But the volumes which it seems worth while to single out for more detailed comment are *The Three Fates, A Cigarette Maker's Romance,* and the *Saracinesca* trilogy.

It is a curious and unexplained fact that when the topic of Mr. Crawford's novels comes up in a company of fairly well-read men and women, and they have all expressed a more or less intelligent opinion about *The Ralstons* and *Don Orsino* and *Fair Margaret,* if you then make mention of *The Three Fates* you are likely to find that no one present has read the book nor one in ten even heard of it. Yet it is easily the best of Mr. Crawford's American stories; it is simply not in the same class with *Katharine Lauderdale* and *Marion Darche.* The people in it are all thoroughly alive; at times they tempt one to say that they are the most intensely alive of any characters Mr. Crawford has ever drawn. The principal character is a young and struggling author making the rounds of New York publishing houses and striving to win a hearing for his first novel. It takes no very profound intuition to guess that there is a modicum of autobiography worked into the pages of *The Three Fates* . . . and its author makes no attempt to deny it. If you ask Mr. Crawford which of his American stories he personally likes best, this is the one that he will name, adding with a reminiscent sigh of mingled satisfaction and regret, ''The fact is, I put a great deal of myself into *The Three Fates.*''

The personal touch is, of course, an all-sufficient reason to explain the author's preference, but a critic's choice should rest on sounder basis. And in this case that basis is to be found in the rather exceptional study it contains of some phases of love, where both the man and the woman are quite young. . . . And the task of interpreting these youthful crises with sympathetic understanding and just a touch of indulgent irony is one which just a few novelists successfully achieve. One recalls especially certain chapters in William Black's *Madcap Violet* and Mr. Howells's *April Hopes;* and to these may be added *The Three Fates.* Like so many of Mr. Crawford's earlier volumes, the construction is faulty. There is no clear-cut central theme. The most that can be said for the plot is that the author has sought to show how a young man of a keenly sensitive artistic temperament may, in those vital formative years when his life's career is just opening before him, find his ideals of women so subtly and yet so radically modified that in a comparatively brief space he has found himself able to love tenderly and sincerely three different women, and to receive from each in turn a permanent impression, a modification of his character which time will only strengthen. . . . [The] dénouement of *The Three Fates* is one of the most artistic and felicitous single touches to be found in Mr. Crawford's writings. (pp. 131-32)

It is customary to regard the cycle of Italian novels, beginning with the *Saracinesca* trilogy and continued in *Corleone* and *Tarquisara,* as the strongest and most finished work that the author of *A Roman Singer* has produced. This, however, is not the view held by those critics who have made the most careful study of his novels. . . . [While] they are his most ambitious efforts, even the best of them, even *Saracinesca* and *Sant' Ilario,* have not the artistic charm and unity possessed by several slighter works. . . . Nevertheless, oddly enough, *Don Orsino,* much inferior to its predecessors in human interest, is in point of structure much more logical and correct. In fact, it may be called an epic of the era of disastrous building speculation in Rome. . . . (pp. 132, 134)

In point of form, however, Mr. Crawford has never done anything more perfect than *A Cigarette Maker's Romance.* In dimensions it is a rather long novelette; in structure it obeys the rules of the short story rather than those of the novel. It contains no superfluous character or incident, and its time of action is confined within a space of thirty-six hours. (p. 134)

[Crawford's] real strength lies not in his mastery of technique or his originality of plot, but in his ability to picture for us honest gentlemen and noble women, whom we are the better for having known if only through the medium of the printed page. If there is room for choice, his men are better than his women, more finely drawn, with subtler understanding. There is a long list of them whom you cannot forget even if you would—even in *Saracinesca* alone there are a whole group whom it is a joy to remember. . . .

What place will be ultimately assigned to Mr. Crawford in the history of fiction it is somewhat early to predict. Excepting as a conservative force, it is doubtful whether he has influenced the development of the modern novel in any important degree. Yet few novelists of the present day have been more widely read or have had a more salutary influence in fostering a taste for what is clean and pure and high-minded in literature and in life. (p. 135)

Frederic Taber Cooper, ''Representative American Storytellers: Francis Marion Crawford,'' in The Bookman, *New York (copyright, 1907, by Dodd, Mead and Company), Vol. XXVI, No. 2, October, 1907, pp. 126-36.*

ELBRIDGE COLBY   (essay date 1917)

[Marion Crawford's] work was varied and cosmopolitan. He pictured Rome and he pictured the world; he pictured people and he pictured persons. The chief business of a novelist, according to his own definition, is to amuse and interest; and throughout his long career as a writer of fiction, this born story teller amused and interested the people of England and America. Versatile in his tastes, versatile in his abilities, romantic in his character, romantic in his picturesque art, he knew and represented life in facets of many colors. He was cosmopolitan. In quality he was now up, now down, in skill. Some of his work is good; some is very good, and no man can say until it has endured the trial of changing tastes and changing generations whether any or all of it has that universality of appeal which is the guarantee of greatness. He had a deftness in portraiture, a scenic gift for the essentials of a dramatic setting, and a pen that pierced to the heart of human nature in a few vigorous strokes. We may well imagine one of his readers thinking of him in the same phrases in which Corona Astrardente expresses her estimate of Don Giovanni Saracinesca:

> He never used the old worn subjects that the others harped on. She would not have found it easy to say what he talked about, for he talked indifferently about many subjects. She reflected that he was not so brilliant as many men she knew, only that she preferred his face above all faces and his voice beyond all voices.
>
> (p. 687)

Elbridge Colby, ''The Works of Francis Marion Crawford,'' in The American Catholic Quarterly Review, *Vol. XLII, No. 168, October, 1917, pp. 679-87.*

HUGH WALPOLE   (essay date 1923)

[*Walpole divides Crawford's oeuvre into three main classifications: the historical romances, upon which his discussion focusses; the Italian novels, which he finds overly melodramatic; and the novels of contemporary life. Walpole especially notes the great variety of realistic backgrounds portrayed in the historical romances, and makes extensive comparisons between Crawford and Trollope. Walpole finds that Crawford's skilled characterization often overcomes the melodrama which flaws many of the novels, and pronounces* Casa Braccio *Crawford's single great work. This opinion is contested by Arthur Hobson Quinn (see excerpt below).*]

Crawford's stories divide naturally into three divisions—the historical romances, the Italian novels, and the stories of contemporary life. From the vast number he wrote it is possible to select seven or eight in each division worthy of remembrance. In the historical romances there are: **"In the Palace of the King," "Marietta," "Stradella," "Khaled," "Zoroaster," "Via Crucis,"** and **"Arethusa."** Of the Italian novels there are: the four **"Saracinesca"** books, **"Saracinesca"** itself, **"Sant' Ilario," "Don Orsino,"** and **"Corleone."** To these may be added: **"Marzio's Crucifix," "A Roman Singer," "The Children of the King," "Casa Braccio,"** and **"Pietro Ghisleri."** In the modern series there are: **"Katharine Lauderdale,"** and its sequel **"The Ralstons,"** the famous **"Mr. Isaacs," "Greifenstein,"** and **"The Three Fates."** There is in these twenty-one novels everything in Crawford's work that need be remembered.

In looking at the historical romances, the first thing that strikes one is their variety of background. We have here ancient Arabia, the mediaeval Crusades, old Constantinople, seventeenth and eighteenth century Italy, and the Spain of Philip the Second. (p. 676)

Marion Crawford, of course, looked at his work from the very simplest ground. He published once a treatise on the novel [*The Novel—What It Is*] in which he showed that this art, now elaborated and sophisticated by the clever brains of our day to its very furthest limit, was, for him, something that could not possibly be too simple. He was a story-teller, first, last and all the time, and he was a story-teller, too, of the traveller's kind, standing beside Conrad, at least in this, that he had no ambition but to make his readers see, feel, and hear the things that he saw, felt, and heard. And these same things, unlike Conrad's, were often of the very last ingenuous naïveté. It was this same naïveté that led the critics to disregard so quickly anything that he had to say, and yet, when he was not dealing with the modern world, this simplicity had its merits. The Iliad and the Norse Sagas are in this fashion naïve; and although Crawford could not, of course, capture anything of their magnificent sweep of poetry and universal symbolism, he did succeed through the very simplicity of his characters in lending a certain heroic quality to his tales. He had also in these stories the great advantage of never attempting erudition. He never tried to tell the story from the contemporary standpoint. He was rather as a modern traveller about the world, who, having seen with his own eyes Rome and Sicily, the Arabian desert and the haunted palaces of Madrid, imagines for his own satisfaction and pleasure some picture of moving figures and swiftly passing events that it pleases him to tell to those, who, simple like himself, wish to listen. (pp. 677-78)

Brilliant he never was. You may search the pages of all his historical pictures and find in them nothing quotable. When he attempts an historical figure like Philip the Second of Spain or Queen Eleanor of England he definitely fails. Not for him the creation of Hewlett's Mary of Scots or James Branch Cabell's Falstaff. And yet there is a vividness here that cannot be denied. In the best of these historic histories, **"In the Palace of the King,"** he tells the story of one night; and simply as a story, for dark, exciting, and convincing narrative, it has as its only rivals in our time, Weyman's "House of the Wolf," and Haggard's "King Solomon's Mines." (p. 678)

Crawford, in [his] historical romances does more than tell a good story, without being for a single instant anything of a poet, or having the glorious fantasy of "Shagpat," the lyrical poetry of Morris, the gay erudition of Hewlett, the cynical charm of Cabell. He is not in the same world with these men as artists, but, presenting his incidents with the air of an honest man who tells the tale as an honest man sees it, he can be

found to have something in common, both with Conrad and with Trollope, without of course, the genius of either. His information in these romances as he gives us little facts about the times of which he is writing, is amusing, convincing, and never boring. In **"Marietta,"** for instance, he is concerned with the glass-blowers of Venice, and it is only when the reader looks back at the end of that very simple tale that he sees how many things he has learned, and in how easy a fashion he has learned them.

Again, in his **"Khaled"** he attempts that most difficult of all narrative forms, the imitation of Oriental imagery. (pp. 679-80)

With the Italian novels, Crawford enters into the country which is supposed to be especially his own. I say, *supposed,* because the critic of to-day, if he alludes to Crawford at all, is inclined to jest at his Italian knowledge. . . . [But] it must be remembered that Crawford was writing, for the most part, of an Italy that is now fast vanishing and that will very soon be so far behind us that we shall be able to speak of the Saracinesca series as themselves historical novels. In these four books, **"Saracinesca," "Sant' Ilario," "Don Orsino,"** and **"Corleone,"** Crawford has drawn a much more serious picture of society, changing from almost mediaeval conditions to modern ones, than is generally recognized. If the four books are read together it will be seen that the first three of them, at any rate, are planned with most careful and elaborate industry. (pp. 680-81)

It is a pity, of course, that Crawford's love of melodrama will continue to break in. He cannot leave his characters alone to work out their destiny, but must drive in upon them the old theatrical business of forged documents, murders in the dark, duels and the rest. It is indeed remarkable how the sure stability of these characters survives under these repeated sensational assaults. The plot of **"Sant' Ilario"** is enough to drive into the air the credibility of any number of characters, but Crawford shows something of Balzac's genius in mingling two worlds; only he has nothing, of course, of the magnificent bravado of a Vautrin, or the horrible midnight blackness of a Cousine Bette. But his little villain in **"Sant' Ilario"** has life, and contrasts pleasantly with the marble splendor of the immaculate Corona. (pp. 681-82)

The value of these four, then, consists almost entirely in the human existence of four or five figures and the change of the Roman scene. It is not for one who has never seen it to say whether Crawford's Rome of that period is accurate, or no; but it *seems* to be accurate, as one may judge from the independent witness of books like Henry James's "Story," and Mrs. Waddington's delightful "Letters." (p. 682)

Without having any philosophy of life that is not thoroughly commonplace, [Crawford] scatters his pages with little healthy aphorisms about love and marriage, good conduct, and what it is to be a Gentleman. We could well spare these things, and we look among the Italian novels for those in which Crawford's interest in his narrative is so strong that he forgets to moralize. There are three stories of this kind to be found, and in these he parts company entirely with Trollope because here he shows a romantic spirit of passion and almost intensity which was quite foreign to the spirit of that other writer. These three Italian stories—**"Marzio's Crucifix," "Casa Braccio,"** and **"The Children of the King"**—might, if Crawford had written only these and died or ceased to write, have left him as a potential novelist of far higher rank than he is now allowed. For the first third, indeed, **"Casa Braccio"** is a great work. (p. 685)

"The Children of the King" again is a remarkable piece of work. The Italian peasant hero would have been still more convincing had not Crawford himself so intensely admired him, but he is real, and so is the American girl whom he so passionately loves. The tragedy is a logical sequence, and all of the characters are fully realized.

It is noticeable, too, that here as in other passages of his Italian books the author succeeds in giving us real feeling of Italian heat and light and beauty without for a single instant becoming lyrical or indulging in any description of scenery. . . . Crawford is wise here. If he mentions the wind, it is from a yachtman's point of view; the coming of spring to him only means longer evenings and earlier morning risings. He sees Nature as the practical man sees her; never as a poet. And so it is by the real, deep feeling that he has for his characters in these three books that he gives us this true sense of Southern passion, love, and revenge. If anyone were tempted to try, in these latter days, to test Crawford once again as a possible artist, I would suggest that he read these three books, remembering, of course, the period, already distant, when they were written. I think he will be surprised at the impression that they make upon him.

When we come to the novels of Crawford that are neither of the past nor of Italy, the resemblance to Trollope becomes much more clear. I will omit the story in which he first made his name, "Mr. Isaacs"—a book that has now a faded interest, faded because the later Kipling stories and the romances of Mrs. Steele are of course so much more authentic and remarkable; also that fine romance, "Greifenstein," that, with all Crawford's fault of melodrama and sentimentalism piled up and flowing over, nevertheless has some admirable scenes and a picture of earlier student life in Germany never bettered by any English writer; and I will confine myself to three of his American novels—"Katharine Lauderdale," "The Ralstons," and "The Three Fates."

To take the last first, "The Three Fates" is the only novel of the long series in which Crawford is determined and persistently cynical to the very last page. This book has the interest, too, of being, I imagine, to a large extent, autobiographical, although, because there has never been a Life or volume of letters, one does not know enough of the author's private history to be sure of this. It, at any rate, tells the story of a successful novelist who is influenced by three women, falls in love with two of them, and misses the third—the only one he has really loved. There is a great deal that is amusing and true about the effect on a writer's character of popularity and success. There is nothing harder than to convey to the reader a conviction that your hero is really an artist; however strongly the author may affirm, the reader remains incredulous as to the great books the genius has written, the marvellous voice the heroine possesses, the wonderful picture that the artist has painted. . . . In "The Three Fates" Crawford succeeds in his difficult task because he lets us understand that his hero, in spite of his wonderful books, was not very much of a fellow. (pp. 686-88)

In one book, at any rate, [Crawford] avoided melodrama almost entirely. In "Katharine Lauderdale," and its sequel "The Ralstons," he began a long family history, intending, I imagine, to work out something in the manner of his Italian "Saracinesca" . . . . "Katharine Lauderdale" is a remarkable book. It tells quite simply how a girl of a good New York family loved a man who had the name of a good-natured wastrel; she is made to believe by a chain of tiny circumstances that her lover, after having given her a most earnest pledge that he

would change his life, is seen reeling helplessly drunk down Fifth Avenue. The circumstances are all probable. Crawford shows here his admirable talent for the accumulation of small convincing incidents. Both the girl and the man are human and alive, and the background of the New York life of that time is true and accurate. . . . "The Ralstons" is not so successful, chiefly because of the intrusion of quite ludicrous melodrama; but the two books convincingly show that [Crawford] was not limited to his Italian scenes, and had he only trusted to quiet life and the truth that he knew, he would have been a very fine artist. (pp. 689-90)

The writer of simple tales like Marion Crawford has gifts and talents that, although they are underrated to-day, equal in their value much modern cleverness and cynical skepticism. There are here stories that a man who runs may read. The author draws no conclusions that are novel or daring, but there is a spirit of gusto in his tales that is eternal. (p. 691)

> *Hugh Walpole, "The Stories of Francis Marion Crawford," in* The Yale Review *(© 1923 by Yale University), Vol. XII, No. 4, July, 1923, pp. 673-91.*

H. P. LOVECRAFT   (essay date 1927)

[*In his major work of criticism on supernatural fiction, Lovecraft singles out for praise Crawford's short story "The Upper Berth" as "one of the most effective horror-stories in all literature."*]

F. Marion Crawford produced several weird tales of varying quality, now collected in a volume entitled ***Wandering Ghosts***. ***For the Blood Is the Life*** touches powerfully on a case of moon-cursed vampirism near an ancient tower on the rocks of the lonely South Italian seacoast. ***The Dead Smile*** treats of family horrors in an old house and an ancestral vault in Ireland, and introduces the banshee with considerable force. ***The Upper Berth,*** however, is Crawford's weird masterpiece; and is one of the most tremendous horror-stories in all literature. In this tale of a suicide-haunted stateroom such things as the spectral saltwater dampness, the strangely open porthole, and the nightmare struggle with the nameless object are handled with incomparable dexterity. (p. 387)

> *H. P. Lovecraft, "Supernatural Horror in Literature" (1927), in his* Dagon and Other Macabre Tales, *edited by August Derleth (copyright 1965, by August Derleth; reprinted by permission of Arkham House Publishers, Inc.), Arkham House, 1965, pp. 347-413.**

ARTHUR HOBSON QUINN   (essay date 1936)

[*In a lengthy overview of Crawford's entire career, Quinn provides plot outlines of many of Crawford's novels. Like most critics, Quinn finds that Crawford's "most significant achievement, one in which he has not been surpassed by any writer in English, lay in the novels dealing with Italian life."*]

[Marion Crawford's] most significant achievement, one in which he has not been surpassed by any writer in English, lay in the novels dealing with Italian life. (p. 388)

Crawford's conversion to Catholicism, which took place in India, made it easier for him to understand the Italian nature and to appreciate the many shades of belief which permitted, for example, the Saracinesca family to remain good Catholics and still be political opponents of the Pope. Of the sixteen

Italian stories, fourteen are laid wholly or partly in Rome. *A Roman Singer* . . . is a charming novel of artistic life, with a striking character, Professor Cornello Grandi. It was based on years of acquaintance with the musical circles in Rome. *To Leeward* . . . is not so successful because the central character, Leonora Carnethy, an English girl who marries Marcantonio, Marchese Carontoni, without loving him truly and who leaves him for Julius Batiscombe, an English man of letters, is so supremely selfish that even Crawford could not make her very interesting. But Marcantonio is a fine picture of an Italian, who goes mad under the stress of grief at his wife's unfaithfulness; while the ending is sheer melodrama, there are several passages which showed the promise of the power that was coming.

In 1887 Crawford's art reached a high level in *Marzio's Crucifix*. Here he created the character of a silversmith, in whom "the gifts of the artist, the tenacity of the workman and the small astuteness of the plebeian were mingled with an appearance of something which was not precisely ideality, but which might easily be fanaticism." (pp. 388-89)

The unity of the novel, the perfect preservation of the tone, the art with which Crawford united the greatest symbol of Christianity and the love of beauty to bring peace to an unhappy heart, make it one of the finest novels in the language. (p. 389)

Crawford's versatility was shown by his turning from the ideal conceptions and the humble surroundings of *Marzio's Crucifix* to the reality of Italian social life in the series of novels [the Saracinesca group] dealing with three generations of a patrician Italian family. (p. 390)

Less definitely associated with the Saracinesca group, but dealing with the same order of society, *Pietro Ghisleri* . . . is one of his most fascinating stories. The plot is intricate, but it is the character drawing which makes the book important. Pietro Ghisleri is a complicated gentleman, who struggles out of the meshes of a liaison and ultimately wins the love of an English girl, Laura Carlyon, who is much more natural than Crawford's English characters usually are. Pietro, through his sensitiveness to his own defects and his high sense of honor in most directions, gains and keeps our sympathy. The description of the coming of second love to Pietro is in Crawford's best manner. Another remarkable character is that of Adele Savelli, Laura's half-sister, who does her best to ruin Laura by dexterously denying charges against her which Adele has herself invented. . . .

The first part of *Casa Braccio* . . . , dealing with the flight of Sister Maria Addolorata, some time in the 'forties, from her convent with Angus Dalrymple, a Scottish nobleman, is not so well done. But in the second part, which has to do with the fortunes of their daughter, Gloria Dalrymple, Crawford depicted a revenge of an unusual nature. (p. 392)

Some of Crawford's later stories of Rome, like [*Cecelia or A Lady of Rome*] . . . , while interesting, were hardly up to his earlier standard. *The Heart of Rome* . . . is well written and contains some of his shrewdest observations. The character of young Sabina Conti, who has inherited the courage if not the ruthlessness of her amusing mother, the Princess, is quite real, and is of more importance than the somewhat involved tale of the "lost water" of Rome. Still better was *The White Sister* . . . , in which he showed in his last year that he was still capable of inciting sympathy for human beings fighting against fate. Angela Chiarmonte enters the order of the White Sisters of Santa Giovanna d'Aza five years after her lover, Giovanni

Severi, a young engineer officer, is reported dead in Africa. On his return she makes every effort to keep her vows, even when he brings her to his rooms by a false message, and she escapes only by an appeal to his better nature. It is only when, in the hospital, he refuses to allow the operation which will save him until she agrees to apply through Monsignor Saracinesca for an annulment of her vows, that she weakens. It is this struggle to keep her self-respect which made the story so appealing and had led to its dramatization on the stage and in the moving pictures. Usually such a situation is distressing, and in *Casa Braccio* Crawford himself had not succeeded with it, but it was the character of Sister Giovanni and the unpolemical way in which Crawford treated the situation that made a fine story. He does not judge the right or wrong of the matter: he is interested simply in the dramatic value of a conflict between human love and religious duty in its strongest and most concrete form. . . . [*Children of the King*] is laid in Southern Italy, mostly in or near Sorrento. It has some good characters, especially Ruggiero and Sebastino, sailors who are by tradition descended from King Roger, and is more significant than *Taquisara* . . . , laid in Naples and concerned largely with the efforts of the Count and Countess Macomber to obtain their niece's estate.

Marion Crawford wrote seven novels in which the scene is laid in America, and one, *A Rose of Yesterday* . . . , in which the characters are American but the scene is Switzerland. His earliest effort in this field, *An American Politican* . . . , is hardly important. . . . Much better was *The Three Fates* . . . , for here Crawford was on familiar ground—the struggles of a young writer, George Wood, to gain recognition in New York. While Wood's career does not directly parallel Crawford's, the latter knew the intricate relations of publishing and newspaper criticism, and some of his shrewdest remarks about novel-writing are included in this book. The main plot, however, deals with Wood's love for three different women. . . . The ending is not convincing, but the revelation of the different ways in which a man may love or think he loves a woman, and the character portrayals of George Wood, Totty and Mamie Trimm make it the best of Crawford's novels dealing with American life.

Next best are [*Katherine Lauderdale* and its sequel, *The Ralstons*]. . . . They are studies of the reactions of the members of a wealthy New York family upon each other, and of the consequences of a secret marriage between Katherine Lauderdale and her cousin, Jack Ralston. The effect of money, both in the power it gives Robert Ralston, of the oldest generation, to determine consciously or unconsciously the actions of his family, and in the cruelty and avarice of his nephew, Alexander Lauderdale, is well portrayed. So, too, is the gradual development of resistance in Katherine Lauderdale to the tyranny of her father, Alexander. But Jack Ralston's willingness to tolerate for months after his marriage the arrangement which permits him only an occasional glimpse of his wife is inconceivable; the careful observance of the conventions of social life, even in the 'nineties, makes the characters run to types rather than individuals. There is some very good writing in both books, however. . . . But the novels are too long drawn out and their excellences lie in episodes and scenes rather than in the characters. They are more clearly distinct, however, than those in *Marion Darche* . . . , where the episodes are more melodramatic, especially in the scene in which Marion sets herself on fire to permit her husband, a convicted criminal, to escape. *A Rose of Yesterday* . . . , laid in Lucerne, has a strong situation, in which a woman discovers that her husband has caused the arrest of their son's mental growth. But the story is hardly worked out. Crawford's Americans, in general, are written about for themselves and not in contrast with other races. Like Crawford himself they were usually spirited people, and, if he limited himself largely to persons of wealth or to professional writers or painters, he was only following his invariable custom of writing about the life he knew. Certainly if George Wood or Jack Ralston have not the significance of Silas Lapham, they are red-blooded realities compared to the Americans of *Washington Square* or *The Bostonians*. He must have recognized, however, that his talent lay in other fields than in the analysis of moral values and social standards of America, for after 1894 he did not return to the American scene but treated American characters as individuals in a cosmopolitan *milieu*.

Of the three modern novels in which the characters are all English, *A Tale of a Lonely Parish* . . . is the only one of merit, and even it does not rank with his best. It is laid in a remote country parish in Essex; the interest arises from the natural way in which crime comes in from the outside to disturb its serenity. The similarity of the plot to Anne Brontë's *Tenant of Wildfell Hall* is apparent, but there is a charm in the picture of the quiet of an English community which reflects Crawford's life while he was preparing for Cambridge. *Adam Johnstone's Son* . . . is laid in Amalfi, though all the people in it are English, but neither it nor *The Undesirable Governess* . . . , a posthumous novel, a clever but extremely light story, need detail us. Crawford knew the English race, as he showed in *Paul Patoff*, but employed them best in contrast with others, or in his historical novels.

Much more significant were the two stories laid in Germany. *Greifenstein* . . . is one of the very few novels written in English and laid at a German university which has any resemblance to reality. The hero, a young *korps-student* at "Schwarzburg University," acts in that period of freedom which elapses between the strict regimen of the gymnasium and the more serious business of life just as his prototypes do. Crawford's experience at Karlsruhe made him choose this hero from the most picturesque of the three classes of German university students—those who are there to enjoy life, those who are there to study, and those who apparently do neither. (pp. 393-96)

Crawford proved in *A Cigarette Maker's Romance* . . . that he could make out of apparently unpromising materials one of the most charming love stories in fiction. Although the scene is Munich, the characters are all Slavs who are employed in a small tobacco workroom. Each character, however, is etched in with the art which could discover spiritual nobility even in the most humble economic life, and in the very recognition of caste could obliterate its outlines under the influence of a great love. . . . *A Cigarette Maker's Romance* is unimpeded in its movement, unified in time and place, and the tone is preserved with absolute fidelity.

Crawford was not so happy in his story of modern Constantinople and England, *Paul Patoff* . . . , although the study of insanity in Madame Patoff has some merit, and Paul Griggs reappears in an interesting rôle; nor in *The Witch of Prague* . . . , a fantastic tale of Bohemia in which hypnotism plays an important part. *With the Immortals* . . . is of more interest, since he brings to a group of people near Amalfi the figures of Heine, Frances I, and others, and his knowledge of literature and history comes into play.

It will be noticed that in his Italian, American, English, and German stories, Crawford is not so much concerned with international contrasts as with the interrelations of people of one race. There is another group of novels, however, in which the international flavor is more apparent. *Mr. Isaacs* belonged to this class, and so did his second story, *Dr. Claudius*. . . . In the latter, the hero, a Swedish privatdocent at Heidelberg, is contrasted with English and American characters in a series of adventures which bring them across the ocean to Newport. Toward the end of his career Crawford wrote a trilogy which centers around the character of Margaret Donne, an English girl of American descent, who becomes an opera singer. [*Fair Margaret, The Prima Donna,* and *The Diva's Ruby*] . . . are extremely readable books, but they do not add greatly to his reputation. (pp. 396-98)

It was in his historical novels that Crawford's wide cosmopolitan sympathy and his thorough knowledge of the past met to produce some creations of the first rank. . . .

[His first historical romance, *Zoroaster*,] a tale of Persia beginning about 550 B.C., is tragic in the unhappy outcome of the love story of Zoroaster, Persian soldier and scholar; Crawford paints with skill the movements of races and the contrasts of Persian and Jewish characters. The conquest of Babylon by Cyrus is especially well done. *Khaled* . . . , a tale of Arabia, is more fantastic. Khaled is a supernatural being who is to receive a soul when Zehowah, the Sultan's daughter, loves him. It is an unusual book, is said to have been Crawford's own favorite and it establishes the sense of the mystery of the East of which Crawford had given a modern treatment in *Mr. Isaacs*. . . .

[It was in *Via Crucis*], however, that Crawford wrote his masterpiece. For this story of the Second Crusade he created the character of Gilbert Warde, a young English noble of Norman descent, of whom his stepfather's enmity and the war between King Stephen and the Empress Maud had made an exile. He is not, however, the usual marvelous and precocious boy of eighteen. (p. 398)

Here is no fantasy of romance—here is reality, based upon Crawford's own periods of melancholy and the explanation, perhaps, of the curious melancholy of Abraham Lincoln at crucial moments of his life. The historical characters are vividly sketched, especially Queen Eleanor with her mixture of good and evil, the mother of Richard of the Lion Heart and of King John; and Henry Plantagenet, the boy who was to be King of England, already a man in his passion and ruthlessness. The Crusade is brought in sufficiently without tiresome details, and Crawford showed how great faith and courage were hampered by cupidity and jealousy. But even in his criticism of the weaknesses of the period, Marion Crawford shows his deep understanding and sympathy with the medieval spirit. (p. 399)

[*In the Palace of the King*], an historical romance of the time of Philip II of Spain, is hardly up to the standard of *Via Crucis*. It was planned first as a play for Viola Allen, then written as a novel, and later dramatized. This method of creation has resulted in remarkable unity, for all the events take place inside of a few hours, but it produces melodrama at times. . . .

Almost on a level with *Via Crucis* is *Marietta* . . . , a story of Venice about 1470. The characters, as usual with Crawford, are mainly fictitious, but the sense of the period is kept marvelously. (p. 400)

Marion Crawford possessed the two main requisites for the writing of historical novels. First he had a wide knowledge of history, so that whether the story is laid in England, France,

Italy, Spain, Arabia or Persia, the atmosphere has the illusion of verity. But this knowledge would not have been sufficient without his vivid imagination. This created living men and women under fictitious or historical names. It was his imagination which could survey the gathered facts in a broad vision and fuse them into those admirable descriptions of the movements of social progress or decay or those comparisons of racial characteristics which illuminate the pages of his romances. How much he can pack into one sentence! (p. 401)

To the same category belong his comparisons between the Norman and the Italian in *Via Crucis* and between the Persian and the Semite in *Zoroaster*. Sometimes this contrast is touched with satire as in the definition of a socialist in *Marzio's Crucifix*. I cannot quote it all, but the remark that "In England a socialist is equal to a French conservative republican" is as true today as it was then.

Crawford's short stories are usually concerned with the supernatural and were collected after his death under the title *Wandering Ghosts*. . . . The best is **"The Upper Berth"** . . . , which marks the next step in the progress made memorable by Fitz-James O'Brien's "What Was It?". In this earlier story, the senses of touch and hearing acted, but the ghost was invisible. In **"The Upper Berth,"** the being which enters the stateroom of the ocean liner can be felt and heard and smelt, with a strong odor of the sea. It is seen only dimly and the horror is measured in terms of the fear which has led three men to suicide in that stateroom. . . . [The] supernatural is very effective when the sense of sight does not act but the other senses do. Crawford has added one sense to O'Brien's two, and the result is correspondingly powerful.

It is this imaginative quality which impresses us most in the work of Crawford, whether historical or modern. In his forty-five novels, he repeats himself very seldom. When a character appears more than once, he bears the same name, but he is rarely the hero. And what a gallery of portraits he has created! Mr. Isaacs, Marzio, the three Saracinesci, San Giacinto, Count Boris, Vjera, Pietro Ghisleri, Paul Griggs, Gilbert Warde, Queen Eleanor, Zorzi, Marietta, and many others. How well he can describe the effect of one individual upon another, as he does in the scene in which Philip II dominates all in his presence except his brother. He is concerned principally with human beings, although there are remarkable pictures of scenery of which the description of the Himalayas in *Mr. Isaacs* will serve as an example. Above everything else he knew how to describe the relations of men and women. (pp. 401-02)

Another of Crawford's virtues is his liberal attitude toward all forms of belief and opinion. In each he sought what was best, although he never hesitated to criticize what was weakest. This liberality came of course from his extensive knowledge. Before he wrote *The Witch of Prague* he lived in that city long enough to learn Bohemian. It was the sixteenth language he had acquired. The final impression that he leaves is that of the supreme entertainer. He is rarely dull. The man who wrote forty-five novels could not always be at his best. But his really great inventive power, his unflagging industry, his sense of "the story in it," his belief in hearty romance, his powerful imagination, his grasp of material, ancient or modern—all these, combined with a style clear, forcible, and unaffected, make him an artist who may rank with any novelist of his day. (p. 403)

Arthur Hobson Quinn, "Francis Marion Crawford and the Cosmopolitan Novel," in his American Fiction: An Historical and Critical Survey *(© 1936,*

renewed 1963; adapted by permission of Prentice-Hall, Inc., Englewood Cliffs, New Jersey 07632), Appleton-Century-Crofts, 1936, pp. 385-407.*

VAN WYCK BROOKS   (essay date 1940)

[Marion Crawford] was an improvisator, a story-teller, natural, nonchalant, easy, and the art of the novel was always the last of his cares. Personally brilliant, he was anything but a brilliant writer, and problems of technique and social problems, which occupied the minds of James and Howells, were far from his intellectually simpler world. His fresh, brisk style was in no way distinguished, and his characterizations were general and somewhat blurred. His people were puppets in what he called a "pocket theatre," and one scarcely recalled their traits when the curtain fell. But his narrative gift was astonishing, and his interest in life was eager and inexhaustible, wide and observant. In his historical novels, about ancient Arabia and Persia, the Crusades or the Spain of Philip II, in his novels of modern life in many countries, Germany, Turkey, Bohemia, America, England, in the Saracinesca series, most of all, describing the Roman nobility in the decades after 1860,—the social world he had known from his earliest boyhood,—he seemed to possess in every case the special and accurate knowledge that created a perfect illusion of the *mise en scène*. He could tell you how life on the Bosphorus differed from life in Pera. . . . He knew the cry of the trumpeter swans when they pass overhead in the early morning in Iceland; he knew how a Cossack feels on a bench in exile, and he had at his tongue's end the proverbs and untranslatable phrases of Italians, Russians, Czechs, Arabs and Spaniards. Add to this versatility, which was truly astounding, his lucidity, his energy, his dash and the zest and the masculine charm that informed his writing, and one understood the vogue of Marion Crawford, with his tone of a clever, accomplished man of the world. He was the perfect romancer of the Tauchnitz series, born to be read on trains and in Swiss hotels, as one contemplated raids on Munich or Venice, on Prague, Rome, Heidelberg, Naples or Constantinople. Wherever one proposed to go, Marion Crawford had been there first and had written a charming story on the scenes in question, a story that gave a third dimension to Baedeker's dry notations and enabled one's fancy to share in the life of the people. (pp. 304-06)

Van Wyck Brooks, "Aldrich and His Circle," in his New England: Indian Summer, 1865-1915 *(copyright 1940 by Van Wyck Brooks; copyright renewed © 1968 by Gladys Brooks; reprinted by permission of the publisher, E. P. Dutton, Inc.), Dutton, 1940, pp. 296-315.**

GORDON HALL GEROULD   (essay date 1942)

[Francis Marion Crawford] was as candid as Trollope in admitting that he wrote for money and consequently must please his public. He was less cautious than Trollope, however, in that he made this sensible admission during his lifetime, including it in an essay, *The Novel. What It Is* [see excerpt above] . . . , which has been persistently misquoted ever since. As a matter of fact, no one has stated more adequately in brief form the essentials of a good novel and of a competent novelist. To say, as has been said repeatedly, that he regarded the novelist merely as a provider of light amusement does grave injustice to his words.

The foundation of good fiction and good poetry seems to be ethic rather than aesthetic. Everything in either which appeals to the taste, that is, to the aesthetic side, may ultimately perish as a mere matter of fashion; but that which speaks to man as man, independently of his fashions, his habits, and his tastes, must live and find a hearing with humanity so long as humanity is human.

This dictum is perhaps disputable, but it is not the utterance of a light-minded purveyor of ephemeral fiction.

Crawford had, indeed, far greater merit as a novelist than critics and literary historians have been willing to grant. He was extremely prolific, again like Trollope, publishing more than forty stories of some length in less than thirty years, besides several historical works; and often he did not allow his conceptions of people and events to ripen sufficiently in his mind before putting them into words. In the same fashion as Scott and the majority of nineteenth century novelists he improvised, with the result that only perhaps a quarter of his novels show him at his best. This should not blind us, however, to the superior quality of these. His record is not very different, after all, from that of most authors who have written many books. He seldom failed to invent a good story or to tell it interestingly; and when he took a line of his own with material that fired his imagination, his achievement was worthy of the high purpose which he attributed to the serious novelist. He spoke "to man as man." It is worth while to note that this usually happened, quite as in the case of Mark Twain, when he went back to impressions made upon him in boyhood and youth. (pp. 424, 427)

[Crawford] visualized persons and scenes with singular completeness, yet never painfully overloaded his descriptions with detail. Like Scott he heightened and to some extent simplified character, but not to the point of eliminating conflicting emotions and desires from the people whose lives were the subject of his stories. He has been accused, it seems to me quite falsely, of making his characters, whatever their backgrounds, behave and feel in the same way—of dealing with a standardized set of puppets. It is true that he believed—as why should he not?—in certain fundamental responses common to human beings everywhere; but it is not true that his Italians, though many of them were cosmopolitan in experience, lack national and even regional qualities. Crawford knew Italy better than those who have disparaged him, and he also had far more knowledge of mankind.

The close observation that underlay his novels is well illustrated by *A Tale of a Lonely Parish* . . . , the scene of which is rural England as he must have seen it while working with a tutor to prepare for Cambridge. The canvas is small, as the title implies; the tone is emotionally restrained; the manner is Trollopian rather than his own. Yet scarcely anyone else born and bred outside of England has caught so well the quality of English country life. It is not characteristic of his work, but it is an altogether excellent novel, independently conceived and soundly fashioned. With the same keen eye he looked at New York, which he knew somewhat casually as a youth and later from his annual sojourns there. Neither of the two novels dealing with the life of the circles later to be exploited in fiction by Mrs. Edith Wharton is so good as most of the Roman stories, but they give a notion of the period at least as satisfactory as hers. *Katharine Lauderdale* . . . suffers from a fault to which Crawford was subject in his weaker tales—a tendency to pro-

long conversations to undue length; but *The Ralstons* . . . is in my judgment superior to anything Mrs. Wharton created out of the same material. It is a novel the value of which has been grossly underestimated.

I have said that Crawford imagined persons and scenes with extraordinary distinctness and that he improvised. Evidently he heard his characters talking as he composed, for their conversation is almost invariably natural and unforced. Sometimes, as I have intimated, he reported what they had to say with unnecessary completeness, which gives an effect of prolixity quite out of keeping with the otherwise swift march of events. This did not occur when he was deeply stirred by the story he was telling, but it accounts for the relatively poor quality of some of his books. They are too easily imagined, too feebly controlled. On the other hand, so many of them are conceived and executed in the grand manner that only traditional prejudice can deny him a high place among the writers of his time. (pp. 428-29)

> Gordon Hall Gerould, *"Explorers of Varying Scenes," in his* The Patterns of English and American Fiction: A History *(copyright 1942, by Gordon Hall Gerould; copyright renewed © by Sylvia G. Loughnan; reprinted by permission of the Literary Estate of Gordon Hall Gerould), Little, Brown and Company, 1942, pp. 420-37.*

PETER PENZOLDT (essay date 1952)

[Penzoldt defines the "pure tale of horror" as a story "whose main motifs inspire physical repulsion as opposed to what [Algernon] Blackwood calls 'spiritual terror'." Penzoldt then discusses Crawford's "The Dead Smile" in Freudian psychoanalytic terms. He concludes that Crawford's obsession with and fear of death lead to the extensive descriptions of corpses in this and other stories.]

[Francis Marion Crawford] is the author of more than forty sensational novels, most of which were popular in their day. To-day he is chiefly remembered by two of his best stories **'The Screaming Skull,'** and **'The Upper Berth'**, which constantly reappear in anthologies. (p. 149)

[But it is in **'The Dead Smile'**] that Crawford concentrated more horror than in any other of his tales. The story is about Sir Hugh Ockram, an Irish noble, and a consummate villain, who, having betrayed his wife and his lover, dies while hoping to see the children of the two women, his own son and daughter, marry. They know nothing of their true relationship, but their monstrous father takes care to write down the secret which he will carry with him to the grave in the hope that it will be discovered when it is too late. Thus he dies smiling in gleeful anticipation of the torture inflicted both on the living children and on their dead mothers in hell. (pp. 149-50)

Fortunately young Ockram has the courage to descend into the crypt and wrench the written confession from the hands of the rotting corpse. The description of this descent and of the half-mummified, half-decayed body, forms the climax of the story—if climax there is, for the procession of horrors starts on the very first page. The paragraph . . . with which the tale opens is already a good sample of perverted taste, and from there on horror succeeds horror: the scene between the two lovers whose pure affection is marred by unconscious guilt feelings: the apparition of the banshee, who comes to announce Sir Hugh Ockram's death; the awful smile of the dead that twists the lips of the living; and the last moments of the hideous old villain, are only a few examples among many. The story ends with the scene already mentioned. (p. 150)

[The] whole tale is literally crammed with horror. This is in fact so exaggerated that the story would produce a laughable effect had not the author handled his theme so skilfully. His success is partly due to a specially fashioned style . . . , but principally to the realistic quality of the main motif.

The main motif, as always in Crawford, is the dead decaying body. Though particularly calculated to inspire horror and disgust it is not necessarily supernatural. But Crawford's corpses are in the habit of coming alive. They stand up headless in their coffins like Sir Vernon Ockram, or share one's bed like the slimy carrion thing in **'The Upper Berth'** or unfortunately forget that skeletons should be silent (**'The Screaming Skull'**). Crawford sometimes stresses the realistic description of decaying bodies, but often adds some purely imaginative features that make his tales true ghost stories.

The realistic and the supernatural treatments of the corpse theme have slightly different but closely related subconscious origins. Both are due to a neurotic fear of death which the author tries to symbolise and to overcome in his writings.

When Crawford describes a rotting corpse in the most realistic manner possible he tries to rid himself of his obsession by facing the problem directly and in its most hideous aspect. People who have a neurotic fear of certain animals are known to be attracted to them. Children moreover are observed to play games which symbolise and dramatise certain typical infantile fears. . . . Crawford behaves exactly like one of these children. His stories are the games that allow him to overcome his fears, to symbolise, or rather to objectify them. The nature of the symbol (the decaying body) is determined by the type of anxiety concerned. It has not changed since the childhood days of mankind.

Crawford's obsession with the 'living dead', 'the undead', is but another device of his subconscious to overcome the same anxieties. Apparently Crawford feared bodily physical death above all. This fear was so strong that it led him to wishful fancies about the survival of the body after death. Strange as it may seem, Crawford may have identified himself with his ghosts and sought eternal bodily life in the un-dead things he described.

Modern psychoanalysis has come to the conclusion that obsessions with the fear of death may have a very different origin in different individuals. It is merely a symptom which can have a variety of causes. The most frequent cause is the ancestral castration fear. The symbolical equation life equals penis is strong in the primitive mind and still appears in the subconscious of modern man. Crawford's fear of physical destruction may thus merely be symbolical of a deeply hidden castration anxiety. Life, the whole body and the fear of losing them express the still deeper fear of losing the one organ they symbolise.

It is a fact that people who suffer from a castration complex are often tormented by guilt-feelings concerning their sexual potency. To them the crime is being a normal male, the punishment castration. As long as they are not potent they have nothing to fear. This sort of guilt feeling may still persist even when the original castration fear has taken another symbolical form. In Crawford the primitive anxiety took the symbolical form of fear of death. Living on after death was thus for him equivalent to being sexually potent, and a punishable crime just as sexual intercourse is to the person with the more direct form of castration complex. As do many neurotic patients, he preferred to inflict the punishment himself, and this he did by the form he chose for his survival: his spectres are not angels nor glorious beings of eternal life, but hideous rotting creatures. If castration is a form of mutilation, decay is certainly another, and perhaps the worst sort imaginable.

To this rather orthodox Freudian explanation of Crawford's ghosts I should like to add another one, which, without impairing the first theory, may contribute something to the analysis of the phenomenon. Crawford's spectres may take such repulsive forms because unconsciously the author knew that physical existence after death is impossible. Reason told him that what he wished could not be. The spectre would then still represent the desire for eternal bodily life, while the decay would be the symbol of reason's categorical denial of such hopes. Whether in fact this is the case, and the putrefaction does reflect an almost conscious intervention of the superego, must remain an open question, but it seems probable.

So much has been written about Poe's necrophilia that some may expect to find similar tendencies in Crawford's tales. There is none of it. Necrophilia, erotic love of the dead body, implies descriptions of corpses belonging to the opposite sex which are nearly always beautiful. In the case of literary necrophilia a certain guilt feeling can lead to visions of horror as in Poe's 'Berenice', but, generally, stories springing from this particular perversity do not contain horrors. (pp. 151-53)

I have shown how fear of death accounts for Crawford's descriptions of horrors. But there is nothing particularly shocking in the subconscious origin of these horrors even if one admits that the basic complex was castration anxiety. (pp. 159-60)

> *Peter Penzoldt, ''The Pure Tale of Horror,'' in his* The Supernatural in Fiction *(copyright 1952 by Peter Penzoldt; reproduced by permission of The Hamlyn Publishing Group Limited), P. Nevill, 1952, pp. 146-90.**

JOHN PILKINGTON, JR.   (essay date 1964)

During the 1890's and the first decade of the twentieth century, any educated man conversant with literary matters in this country would probably have named F. Marion Crawford, William Dean Howells, and Samuel Langhorne Clemens as the leading professional men of letters in the United States. (p. 186)

On the level of popular appeal and the versatility of his talent, Crawford stood on an equal footing with Howells and in certain respects even possessed a slight edge. Aside from divergences in their approach to literature and in the artistic quality of their work, the major difference between Crawford and Howells lies in the powerful and direct influence which Howells exerted upon his contemporaries and the best writers of the younger generation. In Crawford's experience, there was no parallel to this relationship. (pp. 186-87)

Regardless of the variety of his literary activities, Crawford's major contribution, as well as his principal occupation, was the creation of a large shelf of entertaining and compelling novels. . . . The story—the moving ribbon of action, the continual answer to what happened—was the basis of Crawford's art.

Crawford never seems to have been aware that the ribbon of action could move so rapidly that it would become a source of weakness in his fiction. Nowhere is the validity of this observation more apparent than in the novels often grouped together as the Saracinesca series. In the opening trilogy, which comprises *Saracinesca, Sant' Ilario,* and *Don Orsino,* Crawford's desire to chronicle the impact of changing political and social events upon the members of an Italian family resulted in a concentration upon character, a faithful adherence to the realities of the Italian background, and at the same time a minimum of incident. As a result of these factors, Crawford achieved in this trilogy a balance and interdependence of character, of realistic detail, and of incident. These novels, together with *Katharine Lauderdale* and *The Ralstons,* which exhibit the same qualities in somewhat less degree, represent the peak of his artistic achievement. In writing the remainder of the Saracinesca series, however, Crawford no longer felt the constricting influence of theme and allowed his inventiveness free rein. Consequently, by subordinating character and Italian coloring to multiple incidents in the plot, Crawford gave additional evidence of his skill as an inventor of incident but failed to reach the artistic level of the earlier trilogy. (pp. 187-88)

The essential wholeness of Crawford's vast body of fiction and its inseparable connection with his own life is nowhere better seen than in his creation of an entire fictional society that spreads out over Europe and America in sixteen novels beginning with his first work, *Mr. Isaacs,* and ending with his last, *The White Sister.* Although the four novels primarily concerned with the Saracinesca family (*Saracinesca, Sant' Ilario, Don Orsino,* and *Corleone*) lie at the heart of this cycle, it also includes other Italian novels (*Taquisara, Casa Braccio, Pietro Ghisleri,* and *A Lady of Rome*), American novels (*Katharine Lauderdale* and *The Ralstons*), and novels that take place in several countries (*Paul Patoff, Fair Margaret, The Primadonna,* and *The Diva's Ruby*). In each of these novels, Crawford presented what was in every respect a complete story; but, by making a minor character in one novel become a major character in another, he gave his readers a feeling of participation with him as storyteller and with his characters as actors that carried over from one novel to another. The most prominent utilization of this device occurs in the novels of the Saracinesca family, but members of the family also appear in other novels, notably *A Lady of Rome* and *The White Sister.* (p. 189)

Crawford's method of composing his novels required the creation of a central or near-central character representing himself who functioned as a frame of reference or sounding board for the development of the action. In his first novel Crawford named this fictional representative of himself Paul Griggs and in private correspondence specifically identified himself with this character. In most of his subsequent fiction he gave his own spokesman other names, but in 1887 with *Paul Patoff* he re-introduced Paul Griggs. In the middle years of the 1890's he wrote three novels in which Paul Griggs once more played a role. In the first two of these, [*Katharine Lauderdale* . . . , and *The Ralstons*] . . . , Paul Griggs occupies a minor position; but, by mentioning "the strange story of Griggs' life" and leaving one of the threads of the plot plainly unresolved, Crawford sought to arouse the curiosity of his readers in the novel that was to feature Paul Griggs as hero. In *Casa Braccio* . . . , one of the longest novels Crawford ever wrote, he presented Griggs's story. After *Casa Braccio,* he made no further mention of Griggs until 1908 when Crawford gave him a part in [*The Primadonna* and in *The Diva's Ruby*]. . . .

The character of Paul Griggs thus in effect helps to bind together what would otherwise be widely separated parts of Crawford's total output of fiction. A novel set in India (*Mr. Isaacs*) and one set in Constantinople (*Paul Patoff*) are effectively joined to the body of Crawford's Italian and American novels. Moreover, by associating in a single volume (*Casa Braccio*) Walter Crowdie and Paul Griggs of his American novels with members of the Campodonico family and Pietro Ghisleri of the Italian series, Crawford effectively linked two other large segments of his work. Finally, by introducing Paul Griggs into the singer trilogy he tied it into the previous groups. In other words, the repeated appearances of Paul Griggs and other important characters constituted the major fictional device by which Crawford brought almost half of his novels together as one huge artistic canvas.

As Crawford's acknowledged fictional equivalent, Paul Griggs serves also to demonstrate the close relationship between the experiences of Crawford's own life and those of the characters in his novels; nevertheless, the novels in which Paul Griggs plays an important role (*Mr. Isaacs, Paul Patoff,* and *Casa Braccio*) are scarcely more autobiographical than many of his other volumes. Crawford's use of his own life in his fiction, however, cannot be explained merely on the basis of a method of composition which required his own participation in each novel as he wrote it. In a very real sense Crawford would have agreed with Thomas Wolfe's statement that "a man must use the material and experience of his own life if he is to create anything that has substantial value." On his part, Crawford never desired to confine himself to realities, and he never hesitated to invent incidents that had no relation to his own life for the sake of creating a more exciting and compelling story. Yet it is true that Crawford's novels were a projection of his own personality, and they did take their particular quality from his own experiences. His biography thus furnishes an indispensable commentary upon his novels.

Crawford's novels, which admirably suited the tastes of a generation of readers, were written according to a theory which may not have been entirely original with him but to which he assuredly gave classic expression. In advocating the claims of the literature of entertainment, Crawford was joined by such critics as Brander Matthews and Hamilton Wright Mabie and by such able and popular literary practitioners as Robert Louis Stevenson, Louise de la Ramée (Ouida), Henry Rider Haggard, Winston Churchill, Stanley J. Weyman, Agnes Repplier, and many others. Crawford spoke for them all, and during the 1890's he argued powerfully in their behalf against the claims of the already entrenched Realism of William Dean Howells and the incipient Naturalism of Stephen Crane.

In the light of the developments in the theory and practice of fiction since Crawford's lifetime, his theory seems rather the product of a value-system that was rapidly becoming outmoded than the work of a man who was opening new areas for literary exploration. Crawford's approach was comprehensible only in terms of a tradition that accepted without questioning the rationality and the moral responsibility of man. Neither Realism nor Naturalism exhibited any necessary connection with Christian humanism. Realism, whose strongest advocate and acknowledged leader in America was an agnostic, was in the strictest sense confined to a technique; nevertheless, the literary practice of Realism led very smoothly into the literary techniques of Naturalism, the basic philosophical premises of which must be regarded as antagonistic to the prevailing notions of Christian belief in Crawford's day. With the exception of Crawford's theory, the only other literary theory which received any vogue in the 1890's and which granted man the ability to improve himself by discriminating between right and wrong principles of conduct was that of Henry James. (pp. 189-91)

So far as the masters of fiction in the twentieth century are concerned, Crawford spoke with prophetic insight when he exclaimed: "The old fashioned novel is really dead, and nothing can revive it nor make anybody care for it again." Yet with certain changes necessitated by different social and moral standards, literature written according to the theory of entertainment has continued to flourish ever since Crawford's day.

Although Crawford's literary reputation will probably always rest upon his contributions in the novel and in literary criticism, during his lifetime he was also recognized as an acceptable playwright, as a very successful lecturer, and as a promising historian. Like many a successful novelist, Crawford tended to believe that a novelist's abilities to write effective dialogue and to capture the dramatic incident were talents that qualified him to write plays. After the failure of *Doctor Claudius* convincingly demonstrated the uncertainties and problems of playwriting, Crawford wrote *In the Palace of the King* more to silence his critics than to continue as a dramatist. Later his *Francesca da Rimini,* which he wrote mainly to please Sarah Bernhardt, proved only a qualified success; and he did not live long enough to witness the acclaim given Viola Allen in the dramatization of *The White Sister* or to enjoy the motion picture versions which starred Lillian Gish and Ronald Coleman in 1923 and a decade later Helen Hayes and Clark Gable. Compared to his record as a novelist, Crawford's efforts to write plays were not brilliant; however, he had the good sense to try his fortune in the theater only upon rare occasions. (pp. 192-93)

An appraisal of F. Marion Crawford's contribution to American letters should begin with recognition of the important fact that, although his position and experience were almost unique in the century and certainly foreign to most Americans, he was nevertheless very much the product of a value-system which dominated America (and England) throughout his lifetime. In fact, the combination of these two elements accounts for his extraordinary appeal to his generation and for his ultimate standing in literary history. (p. 194)

It was in fact the remarkable consonance of Crawford's beliefs with the aspirations of his generation that made him in the eyes of most Americans a major writer. His cosmopolitan outlook and consequent freedom from provincialism, his apparent conversancy with the cultures of the West and the East, his insistence upon Christian principles in the conduct of life, and his affirmation of the ideal in art made him seem to exemplify the qualities which American associated with the ideal life. To many of his admirers, he represented the life of art, culture, and the spirit at its best.

Howells is the most convenient measure of Crawford's position. In their emphasis upon the importance of discipline, self-realization, and Christian ethics and morality in the conduct of life, the principles of both men coincided; and in their insistence upon truth and reality as the base of all good fiction, both men were in substantial agreement. Howells, however, eventually became convinced that American literature must concern itself with peculiarly American institutions—specifically, American political, social, economic, and ethical problems. This conviction effectively separated Howells from the intellectual and ethical tradition in which he had begun his literary career and from the theory and practice of fiction represented by F. Marion Crawford. Even if he had desired to write in accordance with Howells' notions, Crawford's lack of familiarity with American attitudes and problems would have barred him from success. The literary practices advocated by

Howells gave enormous support to the Naturalists and their followers in the twentieth century. It would be ridiculous to assert that Crawford has been a powerful influence upon the major writers of twentieth-century America. Yet the thousands of novels written in the present century according to the guide lines expressed by Crawford furnish compelling evidence that literature of the type he wrote remains a vital part of our culture. (pp. 195-96)

John Pilkington, Jr., in his Francis Marion Crawford *(copyright © 1964 by Twayne Publishers, Inc.; reprinted with the permission of Twayne Publishers, a Division of G. K. Hall & Co., Boston), Twayne, 1964, 223 p.*

LARZER ZIFF (essay date 1966)

The novel, Crawford maintained, is an artistic luxury and the novelist a public amuser who should provide his reader with characters "whom they might really like to resemble, acting in scenes in which they themselves would like to take a part" [see excerpt above]. He should aim at the heart, and rather than writing for a specific doctrinal purpose, hold up ideals worthy to be imitated even though inimitable. Crawford had no theoretical opposition to realism, recognizing that if one examined the actual human community one was bound to find and portray at least as much vice as virtue, and he believed Zola to be a great man. But the French wrote for men and mature women, he said; those who wrote in English also wrote for the young. (p. 238)

[The] division between truth and art was developed by this witty and widely read author into a deliberate, conservative anti-intellectualism. His novels abound in gibes at modern theories, especially those of psychology. . . .

Crawford would invoke the hand of fate in his plots, rejecting opposition to this outmoded notion by saying that if he called it "the chemistry of the universe" the skeptics would be satisfied, though it comes to the same thing. (p. 239)

The values worthy to be imitated but inimitable, which Crawford held to steadily in his novels, whether they were about eloping Italian nuns, impoverished Russian counts, secretly married New York debutantes, or fifteenth-century Venetian glassworkers, were those of the gentleman, the man of heart, honor and conscience, whose every action sparkled with chivalry. The manners of this man were slightly formal, and he addressed all women as he would have addressed his mother, knowing that his deference and intense admiration for his mother were bred in him as a model of how he should regard her sex. Marriage he considered not as a contract but as a vow that he believed indissoluble because there was a God who every moment of his life would exact fidelity to the vow.

Together with his chivalric Christianity, the gentleman harbored extremely conservative notions. . . . In a Crawford novel socialism, divorce, and atheism are interchangeable. The enemies from without are those who are discontented with their stations in life and those unenlightened by Christianity. . . . The enemies from within are those made suddenly rich by commerce: "beings predestined never to enjoy, because they will always be able to buy what strong men fight for, and will never learn to enjoy what is really to be had only for money." . . . (pp. 239-40)

The romances of Crawford, regardless of the time and place in which they were set, were static illustrations of his version of the code of honor. The battle between vice and virtue was not as central to his fiction as was the nicety of the distinctions to be made among the virtues in the code. What to do when love and patriotism or honesty and family loyalty clashed? He constructed plots that would bring such virtues into conflict and force a choice—or at least an examination. But because virtues so conceived usually complement one another, he had to strain to concoct situations in which they would not, and his solution usually involved something incredibly brutal and tasteless. In the midst of opulent surroundings—New York mansions, Schwarzwald castles, and Neapolitan villas—a mother is both loving enough to deserve respect, yet cruel enough to drive her daughter to thoughts of suicide; a father is gentleman enough to honor the marriage vows, yet intemperate enough to beat his son into idiocy; a brother is loyal enough to shelter his outcast brother, yet zealous enough to murder his wife when he discovers that she has committed bigamy with that brother.

Crawford's novels seldom contain adventures, for all the exoticism of their settings; they are intensely descriptive as they minutely split the hairs of the code of honor. They were immensely popular because, to be sure, whatever the theme, they contained a great deal of inside information on how a Fifth Avenue drawing room was furnished, or what went on in a dueling corps in Germany, or the best way to picnic on the Bay of Naples—a function since assumed by the Technicolor camera. But they were not popular merely because of this. A generation dismayed at the shift in social values read them avidly because Crawford refused to accept any conflict in values between the new and the old except to dismiss contemptuously those who wanted change, and because he dwelt lovingly on a social code which he was the first to admit was ideal. He worked almost exclusively with the illusion of social stasis, with the notion that there were such things as good breeding and good manners, exemplified by the Christian gentleman, which were totally invulnerable to the operations of the market, the demands of labor unions, or the actions of discontented immigrants.

With the more impressive thinkers of his social circle, including Henry Adams, F. Marion Crawford in the nineties shared the dream of a unity that would withstand the untempered winds of multiplicity. The sale of his romances reveals that there were many who wished to believe in it, if only for the space of time it took to read the serialized chapters in the *Century*. (pp. 240-42)

> *Larzer Ziff, "Being Old-Fashioned: F. Marion Crawford and John Jay Chapman," in his* The American 1890s: Life and Times of a Lost Generation *(copyright © 1966 by Larzer Ziff; reprinted by permission of Viking Penguin Inc.), The Viking Press, 1966, pp. 229-49.**

KENNETH CHURCHILL   (essay date 1980)

[*Radically differing from earlier critics, Churchill maintains that Crawford's Italian novels "are distinguished neither for literary power nor psychological insight; indeed, in view of the number of times he returned to Italian themes, they are remarkable for the absence of both." During his lifetime, and by many critics since, Crawford has been thought to have admirably portrayed the Italian character.*]

Ouida was succeeded as the most popular 'Italian' novelist of the day by Francis Marion Crawford. . . . After travelling extensively, he settled at Sorrento in 1884, and for the next quarter

of a century poured out a stream of Italian fiction and occasional minor historical works on Italy. Fundamental to his work was his oft-repeated belief that only he was qualified to interpret Italy to the English-speaking world. . . . The work itself, however, can hardly be said to live up to Crawford's pretension. The novels are distinguished neither for literary power nor psychological insight; indeed, in view of the number of times he returned to Italian themes, they are remarkable for the absence of both. Crawford's feeling about the Italians was quite straightforward, and is more noteworthy for being consistent with the trend of English thought about Italy at this time than for any astonishing originality:

> The Italian habitually expresses what he feels, while it is the chief pride of Northern men that whatever they may feel they express nothing. The chief object of most Italians is to make life agreeable; the chief object of the Teutonic races is to make it profitable.

The novels are largely set in Rome during the last years of Papal government, a period of Roman history for which Crawford, like most people who had known it (as one sees throughout Henry James's *William Wetmore Story and His Friends*), was deeply nostalgic. Implicitly, there is a contrast with the feeling of Roman life in more recent years, but though he does sometimes discuss this, as in the first chapter of *Saracinesca* . . . , and does present one of his villains as a massive speculator in *Don Orsino* . . . , there is nothing of the force of Ouida's concern with the spreading malaise of Italy. Crawford's are thoroughly optimistic novels where the forces of good—true love and the Roman Catholic Church—always triumph in the end. Apart from his Catholicism and the greater sophistication of his style, Crawford recalls the Gothic novelists of the beginning of the century, sharing their crudely simple moral pattern of unfailing retribution and reward. Some of his villains, indeed, could almost have come straight out of those earlier novels: to such an extent that . . . one is struck by a curious sense of anachronism whenever one of them lights a cigarette or travels by train. Such novels do not develop the literary exploration of Italy; but their very feeling of old-fashionedness emphasises the changes in the literary treatment of Italy since the days when the Gothic image had been the normal convention. (pp. 165-67)

> *Kenneth Churchill, "Italy and the English Novel, 1870-1917," in his* Italy and English Literature, 1764-1930 *(© Kenneth Churchill 1980; reprinted by permission of Macmillan, London and Basingstoke), Macmillan, 1980, pp. 162-81.**

JOHN C. MORAN   (essay date 1981)

Mysticism, the occult, and the supernatural (although not in excess) appear in Crawford's very first novel, **Mr. Isaacs;** . . . his interest in the inexplicable began early in life, intensified during his residence in India, and never abated until his death. Therefore, no surprise is it that the incorporation of such elements into the corpus of his work occurred throughout his literary career; his classic **"The Upper Berth"** was written during 1885, and as late as 1908 **"The Screaming Skull"** appeared in *Colliers*. Crawford's work in the fields of fantasy and supernatural horror consists of the following: (1) the novels **With the Immortals, The Witch of Prague,** and **Khaled;** and (2) the short stories **"The Upper Berth," "By the Waters of Paradise," "The Dead Smile," "Man Overboard!"** (almost a novelette), "**For the Blood Is the Life**," "**The Screaming Skull**," "**The Doll's Ghost**," and "**The King's Messenger**."

Although "**The Upper Berth**" is Crawford's most famous story and the most often anthologized, in the present writer's opinion the most effective and artistic stories of this type dreamed by the great Romantist are "**For the Blood Is the Life**" and "**The Dead Smile**." The former is an uniquely-conceived story of female vampirism set in Italy with passages often lyrical, sensual, and even erotic (Crawford would never have intended any blatant sensationalism); the latter is a story that takes place in Ireland involving a thoroughly diabolical dying baronet and nocturnal adventures in a crypt.

There are a few themes that Crawford tended to weave into the fabric of his short stories. Because he was an avid sailor—the sea so often an attraction to the Romantic temperament—maritime aspects occasionally appear. "**Man Overboard!**" and "**The Upper Berth**" are outright sea stories, both narrated in the first person by alter-egos of Crawford. "**The Screaming Skull**," although not *per se* a sea story, is narrated by a retired naval captain (Crawford himself). "**The King's Messenger**" is narrated by Crawford himself while aboard his yacht *Alda* in the Gulf of Tunis. The vampire story "**For the Blood Is the Life**" is set near the Bay of Naples and contains a number of references to the sea, as does *With the Immortals*. This interest in the sea is not confined to Crawford's horror and ghost stories; it also appears in many of his other works, a good example being the novel *The Children of the King*. In that he loved the sea, Crawford was akin to Romantists Stevenson and Conrad.

Another thematic characteristic is the use of old Welsh [and] Scottish women as media through which Crawford voiced his respect for the seriousness of the supernatural in life via their fears and superstitions and credulity. In "**The Screaming Skull**" the two Scottish sisters who take domestic positions in the service of the narrator play such a role. In "**The Dead Smile**" the century-old nurse Macdonald is a convincing character who voices fears and beliefs in the devil and ghosts. Almost as memorable as nurse Macdonald is old Judith, the Welsh nurse who believes in and has seen the "unseen." The reason why Crawford did not develop these characters more than he did—and his pen could have done wonders with them—resulted from the simple fact that they appear only for the purpose of creating mood and hinting at impending horrors and terror; to a degree they are stage-props.

A third significant theme that recurs is that of vampirism. . . . In "**The Screaming Skull**" there is presented a very unusual form of vampirism; the skull itself is a murderous vampire. This animate, avenging skull bites the throat of two people including the narrator. In "**By the Waters of Paradise**" there is the hungry Woman of the Water—the ghost about whom old Judith speaks—who must be fed; she is a metaphysical vampire who never overtly vampirizes anyone during the story, the reader never being quite sure that she has fed upon the bride of the main character. . . . Crawford's use of vampirism in these . . . instances is unique; never does he present the now-standard Count Dracula-type vampires. (pp. 36-8)

Although Crawford's first novel, *Mr. Isaacs,* contains quite a number of fantastic and marvellous incidents, it cannot be properly classified as a fantasy. His first such novel was *With the Immortals* . . . which represents the one occasion when Crawford ventured into the realm of the scientific romance. At its beginning occur a number of scientific experiments with electricity which serve as a means through which the basic plot is introduced. Despite his only momentary interest in science-fiction, it is obvious that Crawford's imaginative genius could have excelled in that genre.

With the Immortals contains virtually no plot; structurally it consists of a series of conversations between the main character—an alter-ego of Crawford—and the ghosts of some famous men such as Dr. Samuel Johnson, Frederic Chopin, Julius Caesar, and Heinrich Heine, accidentally conjured up via the scientific experiments of Augustus Chard, the main character. In the mouths of these shades Crawford voices his own opinions (he has chosen historical figures from whom one could reasonably expect the various comments made) about life and the world. . . . *With the Immortals* contains a gold mine of insights into his personality. If not one of his greatest novels, it definitely is among the most important ones. (p. 38)

With the Immortals is important because it contains one of Crawford's occasional ventures into the realms of poetry—a long poem entitled "**Song of the Sirens**."

The great Romantist's masterpiece of the purely fantastic is of course the unique *Khaled*. . . . To describe this novel as a long prose-poem would not be hyperbolic. Subtitled "**A Tale of Arabia**," *Khaled* relates the adventures both cosmic and mundane of the genius Khaled, the purpose of which is for Khaled to win the love of a girl and thereby to receive a soul. Crawford's knowledge of the Near East and Islamic civilization pervades the entire story; one readily enters into another world teeming with the mysterious and enchanting spell of the *Arabian Nights*. If *Khaled* does not excell *Vathek*, verily does it equal that celebrated romance in both artistic conception and execution. (p. 39)

The Witch of Prague . . . undoubtedly is Crawford's most unusual novel—a fantasy, a Gothic novel, a horror tale, an occult novel; no one term can adequately classify this weird literary *tour de force*. . . . In writing *The Witch of Prague* Crawford removed any restrictions on his imagination, thereby creating a mosaic composed of many elements of weird and fantastic fiction. . . .

Difficult indeed it would be to describe adequately *The Witch of Prague* in a few words. Because of its originality of conception, its gallery of weird characters (the diabolical dwarf-wizard Keyork Arabian, the strange reanimated Old Man, the beautiful witch and medium Unorna of the differently colored eyes), its abundance of strange incidents, and its pervasive and overpowering atmosphere; *The Witch of Prague* must be *read* in order to be fully appreciated. Among its most interesting scenes are those involving the embalming of the living and the prolongation of life. Indeed Crawford deals with a subject quite relevant to contemporary ethical and medical problems: How long does one live after a doctor declares him dead? When does one die? What exactly is the relationship between the soul and the body? These questions pervade *The Witch of Prague,* not unintentionally. Crawford would have denounced the rapidity with which many modern physicians pronounce a person dead, especially the so-called hopeless cases in comas. This novel also provides the alienist with an abundance of psychological incidents worth his study. (p. 40)

["**By the Waters of Paradise**"] is difficult to interpret: If understood in one way, it is a failure (as a weird tale, that is); if viewed from another perspective, it is a powerful tale of psychic vampirism and astral projection. Although the present writer has never been completely convinced about Crawford's intention, he is inclined, based upon his knowledge of Crawford, toward the latter interpretation. . . . This factor of uncertainty makes the reader recall "The Turn of the Screw" by Henry James. (pp. 41-2)

A masterpiece of atmosphere, ["**The Dead Smile**"] relates the diabolical designs of a depraved Anglo-Irish baronet, Sir Hugh Ockram, upon his own son Gabriel. Thoroughly evil and apprenticed to Satan, Ockram is memorable especially for the description of his toad-red eyes and aged parchment-like face. . . . An atmosphere of impending doom and horror pervades the entire story, reaching an unforgettable climax with the scene in the family vault wherein Gabriel must remove a paper from the hand of dead Sir Hugh whose hideous death-smile sneeringly confronts him as does the headless corpse of long-deceased Sir Vernon Ockram. . . . "**The Dead Smile**" is one of the best tales of horror and evil ever written in English; it speaks for itself as does this description of Sir Hugh: "the falsest man that ever told a cowardly lie, and the cruelest that ever hurt a weak woman, and the worst that ever loved a sin." (pp. 42-3)

Man Overboard! is the story of twin sailors, Jack and Jim Benton, aboard the *Helen B. Jackson*. Jack is murdered by Jim during a vividly described storm. The ship is subsequently haunted by the ghost of the slain sailor. After returning to port, the dissembling fratricide Jim marries Jack's fiancée Mamie—almost, that is, because Jack decides to participate in the wedding, by touching his cold wet hand to that of Mamie. After realizing the truth and horror of it all, Mamie loses her mind. The story ends with Jack's ghost firmly leading Jim in a death-grip toward the ocean-tomb. Captain Torkeldsen is the sole witness to this avenging act of justice. Not only is *Man Overboard!* a superior ghost story, but it also is an excellent sea story vividly depicting the dangers confronting a storm-tossed boat—a subject with which the master-pilot Crawford was indeed quite familiar.

"**For the Blood Is the Life**" [is] one of the ten best vampire stories in the English language. . . . So unique and singular is its conception that "**For the Blood Is the Life**" cannot be compared to any other story of vampirism. . . . [The vampiress] is so vividly described that the blending of her erotic and dangerous nature almost exceeds even that of LeFanu's unforgettable Carmilla. (p. 43)

Structurally ["**The Screaming Skull**"] is a monologue although the narrator, Captain Charles Braddock, who eventually becomes mad and loses his mind at the story's end, seems at first to be talking with someone else; with consummate skill Crawford slowly transforms the captain into a monomaniac, progressively making the reader aware of it. . . . There are many well-written and effective scenes involving the skull, but the main factor in this story is the psychological one; it is a powerful tale of mental collapse resulting from an acute case of monomania compounded by complexes of guilt. (pp. 44-5)

["**The Doll's Ghost**"] does [not] involve malevolent specters; it is a rather sad tale which aims at the reader's heart. . . . Although not a terror-causing ghost story of the M. R. James type, "**The Doll's Ghost**" is nevertheless an originally-conceived and effectively-written example of the non-menacing type of ghost story. (p. 45)

It would be a misapprehension to consider Crawford's writings in the fields of fantasy and supernatural horror as mere incidental efforts. Both the quality and style of writing indicate a deliberate and serious approach on Crawford's part. The plots are quite original in each novel and story, in no way whatsoever

imitative. Long have his works in these fields been considered classics by *cognoscenti* of imaginative literature. One could not easily earn this critical acclaim by casually and rapidly writing these stories—not even a word-wizard and imaginative genius like Crawford, whose pen was indeed facile.

Chronology is another point to ponder. These few stories and three novels virtually span his entire literary career; Crawford never passed through any one period during which the fantastic interested him to the exclusion of all else. Like most people of a Romantic temperament, Crawford had a natural and life-long interest in the weird, the occult, and the mysterious; consequently no surprise is it that he manifested this interest in his writing. . . . Crawford could not earn his living simply confining his writing to this one limited field; but when he did, in the opinion of the present writer, Crawford consciously and intentionally strove for the literary immortality that these stories and novels have so long ago earned for him. (p. 59)

> *John C. Moran, "F. Marion Crawford: The Man and His Works," in his* An F. Marion Crawford Companion *(© 1981 by John C. Moran; reprinted by permission of Greenwood Press, a Division of Congressional Information Service, Inc., Westport, Connecticut), Greenwood Press, 1981, pp. 3-68.*

ADDITIONAL BIBLIOGRAPHY

Brumbaugh, Thomas B. "The Facile Francis Marion Crawford." *Markham Review* 4, No. 3 (May 1974): 70-1.
  Reprints a letter of 25 May 1892 from Crawford to his publisher. Brumbaugh finds the letter to be "a fascinating glimpse of a flamboyant personality of the period, going about the matter-of-fact business of his art." In the letter Crawford mentions the extremely brief periods of time he spent writing his early novels.

Chanler, Margaret. *Roman Spring: Memoirs.* Boston: Little, Brown, and Co., 1934, 324 p.*
  Autobiography, by one of Crawford's sisters, containing many anecdotes about Crawford's youth and early manhood.

Chapman, Grace. "Francis Marion Crawford: Some Observations on His Novels." *The London Mercury* XXX, No. 177 (July 1934): 244-53.
  Overview of Crawford's work, concentrating on the Italian novels.

Douglas, Norman. "Mr. Marion Crawford." In his *Looking Back: An Autobiographical Excursion,* pp. 401-07. New York: Harcourt Brace Jovanovich, 1933. Reprint. St. Clair Shores, Mich.: Scholarly Press, 1971.
  Describes Crawford as a "many-sided man, a linguist, scholar, and traveller," whose works, however, reveal him as a "rabid" Catholic "trying to thrust his antediluvian bigotry down the reader's throat."

"The Novels of Mr. Marion Crawford." *Edinburgh Review* 204, No. ccccxviii (July 1906): 61-80.
  Discusses *A Cigarette-Maker's Romance* at length, and thirteen of Crawford's other novels briefly. The anonymous critic praises Crawford's unsurpassed ability to "write books which give us the sense of being transported absolutely into a foreign country."

Elliott, Maud Howe. *My Cousin F. Marion Crawford.* New York: The Macmillan Co., 1934, 318 p.
  Biography containing the texts of many letters from Crawford to various family members.

Feeney, Sister Mary Hostia. "Crawford in the Near East: *Zoroaster* and *Arethusa*." *The Romantist,* No. 3 (1979): 15-17.
  Critical discussion of *Zoroaster* and *Arethusa.* Feeney notes the historical research that went into these novels, and provides plot

synopses of both, concluding that with these two novels Crawford met his stated objective of amusing and interesting readers.

Knight, Grant C. *The Critical Period in American Literature*. Chapel Hill: The University of North Carolina Press, 1951, 208 p.*

Study of the conflict between the defenders of Romanticism and the champions of Realism in American literature in the 1890s. Knight refers to Crawford throughout the book as a staunch romanticist; in chapter three, "The Search for Reality," Knight discusses *The Novel—What It Is* as a "classic presentation of the romanticist's dialectics."

Moran, John C. *An F. Marion Crawford Companion*. Westport, Conn.: Greenwood Press, 1981, 548 p.

Extensive handbook, dealing more with Crawford's work than with critical works on Crawford. This book contains lengthy biographical and critical essays by Moran, Edward Wagenknecht, Donald Sidney-Fryer, and Russell Kirk, as well as listings of Crawford's characters and every place-name that occurs in Crawford's works. Moran also provides biographical and literary chronologies, and detailed plot summaries of all of Crawford's novels. An excerpt from this book is included in the criticism above.

Pennell, Joseph. "Adventures of an Illustrator: With Hewlett and Crawford in Italy." *The Century Magazine* 104, No. 2 (June 1922): 293-300.*

Rare negative evaluation of Crawford's personality by the illustrator of *Salve Venetia: Gleanings from Venetian History*. Pennell claims that Crawford had no understanding of Italy or Italians, and that he was difficult to work with.

Sidney-Fryer, Donald. "Francis Marion Crawford: A Neglected But Not a Forgotten Master." *The Romantist,* No. 3 (1979): 43-50.

Overview of twelve of Crawford's novels. Sidney-Fryer opens with a discussion of Crawford's place in literature, and concludes by comparing him favorably with Arthur Conan Doyle, H. Rider Haggard, Robert W. Chambers, and William Dean Howells.

Tharpe, Louise Hall. *Mrs. Jack: A Biography of Isabella Stewart Gardner*. Boston: Little, Brown, and Co., 1965, 365 p.*

Makes recurrent mention of the close relationship between the young Crawford and Gardner, a Boston society figure. Tharpe for the most part presents Crawford as egotistical and selfish.

Tyler, George C. "Not That It Matters." *The Saturday Evening Post* 206, No. 33 (10 February 1934): 16-17, 32, 34, 38.*

Reminiscences of a theater director who worked with Crawford on productions of plays based on the novels *In the Palace of the King* and *The White Sister*.

Van Doren, Carl. "The Eighties and Their Kin: Francis Marion Crawford." In his *The American Novel*, pp. 238-45. New York: The Macmillan Co., 1921.

Praises the action of Crawford's novels as "Crawford's primary excellence." Van Doren writes that the ten novels of Crawford's first six years of writing typify his entire output.

Vedder, Henry C. "Francis Marion Crawford." In his *American Writer of To-Day*, pp. 141-57. Boston: Silver, Burdett and Co., 1895.

Early survey of Crawford's career. Vedder concludes that Crawford was "a man of genius" who had not yet produced a work of genius, but that he "has but to continue the progress he has already made to produce work that the world will never willingly let die."

Wagenknecht, Edward. "The Far-Ranging Novels of F. Marion Crawford." In his *Cavalcade of the American Novel: From the Birth of the Nation to the Middle of the Twentieth Century*, pp. 166-171. New York: Holt, Rinehart and Winston, 1952.

Characterizes Crawford as "the most versatile and prolific novelist of his day"; and further adds that "Crawford never wrote a book that was not worth reading." Wagenknecht goes on to cite critical recognition of Crawford's familiarity with Italy.

Theodore (Herman Albert) Dreiser

1871-1945

American novelist, essayist, autobiographer, journalist, short story writer, dramatist, and poet.

Dreiser was one of the principal American exponents of literary Naturalism. In spite of his numerous artistic failings, critics consider Dreiser one of America's foremost novelists. No other author has withstood so much vehemently negative criticism and retained such a high status—perhaps because no other author displayed such glaring faults of logic and style, while at the same time exhibiting such powerful characterizations and strong ideological convictions.

Dreiser was the twelfth of thirteen children born to a poor Indiana farm couple, whose family members were often separated when the parents and older children sought jobs in different cities. Dreiser was a poor student at the succession of schools he attended; however, he received encouragement from a high school teacher who offered to pay his tuition to the University of Indiana. The experience was not a beneficial one for Dreiser; he was acutely conscious of the differences between himself and wealthier, better-looking classmates. He left the university after one year to work as a journalist in Chicago, St. Louis, Pittsburgh, and finally New York, where his brother Paul helped him attain the editorship of *Ev'ry Month* magazine. During this period Dreiser wrote his first novel, *Sister Carrie*. Marital difficulties, together with the poor sales of *Sister Carrie*, left Dreiser deeply depressed. He lost his job and later recorded that for several years he suffered from hallucinations and seriously considered suicide. Paul again helped him find employment, and H. L. Mencken encouraged him to resume work on *Jennie Gerhardt*, his second novel. *Sister Carrie*, meanwhile, had been received favorably in England, and was reissued to mixed reviews in the United States in 1907.

Sister Carrie was unique in American fiction, departing sharply from the gentility and timidity of Howellsian realism. Many critics were shocked that Dreiser's heroine, a "fallen woman," remains unpunished at the novel's end, and this was the focal point of much early criticism. Dreiser's deterministic philosophy, developed more fully in the Cowperwood trilogy, is evident in what some critics call Carrie's "neo-Darwinian adaptability." She survives and prospers because of her willingness to adjust with equanimity to whatever advantageous situations develop. Conversely, the deterioration and death of her second lover, Hurstwood, is generally agreed to be one of the most powerful and moving portraits of human defeat ever written. Critics of *Sister Carrie* also noted an apparent contradiction, which persisted throughout Dreiser's works, between his determinism—his belief that individuals lacked the ability to shape their own destinies—and his sentimentalism—for though he portrayed their unhappy fates as inevitable, Dreiser evoked considerable pity and sympathy for his defeated characters. Popular legend, reinforced by Dreiser himself, holds that the original publishers of *Sister Carrie* attempted to suppress the book, and failing this, did not advertise it because of virulent early criticism. That Doubleday did not advertise *Sister Carrie* is true; however, the claim that it re-

ceived an overwhelmingly negative initial critical reaction is not borne out by an examination of the book's earliest reviews. The circumstances surrounding the first publication of *Sister Carrie* are still under examination.

Dreiser's next novel was *The Financier*, the first of the Cowperwood "Trilogy of Desire," detailing the life and career of successful businessman Frank Algernon Cowperwood. *The Financier*, and the second volume of the trilogy, *The Titan*, contain somewhat didactic illustrations of Dreiser's determinism, using crude Darwinian biological imagery. Dreiser's "chemicomechanistic" concept of life as little more than a series of chemical reactions is put forth for the first time in *The Financier*, primarily in the depiction of Cowperwood's relations with women. Cowperwood's rise, fall, and second triumph in the world of high finance are recounted with journalistic attention to detail—indeed, newspaper accounts of the life of streetcar magnate Charles Tyson Yerkes inspired the creation of Dreiser's financier. Dreiser worked on the third volume of the trilogy, *The Stoic*, intermittently for over thirty years. It was completed shortly before his death. Considered by most critics to be vastly inferior to the first two volumes of the trilogy, *The Stoic* concludes with the death of Cowperwood and the dispersal of his fortune. It ends on a note of Eastern mysticism, which was then a concern of Dreiser's second wife.

Dreiser's fifth novel, *The "Genius"*, aroused more genuine controversy than was fallaciously attributed to *Sister Carrie*. In this thematically scattered but important work, Dreiser portrayed the artist as Nietzschean superman, beyond conventional moral codes. Sales of *The "Genius"* were initially good and early reviews approbatory; however, in the year following its publication, *The "Genius"* came to the attention of the New York Society for the Suppression of Vice, which sought to block its distribution. Mencken, though he personally disapproved of the book, circulated a protest against the censorship of *The "Genius"* or of any literary work. The protest was signed by hundreds of American and British authors, including Robert Frost, Sinclair Lewis, Ezra Pound, and H. G. Wells. Though in retrospect critics find *The "Genius"* to be one of Dreiser's weakest novels, Charles Shapiro wrote that it "achieved historical importance as a result of the famed fight over its suppression, a struggle that ranks with the *Ulysses* case as a pivotal victory in the fight for American literary freedom." The legal issues surrounding the book's suppression are unclear. No formal action was taken against the book or its publishers; however, the influence wielded by self-appointed censors such as the Society for the Suppression of Vice was then considerable. The re-release of *The "Genius"* in 1923 was a decisive blow against such arbitrary and unqualified censorship.

Published ten years after *The "Genius"*, Dreiser's next novel, *An American Tragedy*, reaffirmed his standing as America's greatest Naturalist, and established him as the foremost American novelist of his time. Although critics deplored Dreiser's unwieldy, awkward prose, his stylistic and grammatical flaws—what Mencken called his lack "of what may be called literary tact"—they experienced in *An American Tragedy* an undeniable depth and power of vision. The novel is an indictment of the gulf between American ideals of wealth and power, and the provisions available for their realization. The entire American system is seen to be responsible for the destruction of Clyde Griffiths, a weak-willed individual who aspired to the American dream of success. Curiously, the journalistic tendency of Dreiser's prose, which was frequently the cause of critical complaint in the past, was found by some critics to benefit *An American Tragedy*. Grant C. Knight wrote "In his desire for veracity Mr. Dreiser does lapse into journalism"; and while it "is true that Mr. Dreiser is always at pains to spread out every fact that sometimes he even transgresses relevance, . . . in the instance of *An American Tragedy* . . . nothing short of full documentation would have been convincing." However, Dreiser's usual defender, Mencken, felt that the book was a failure and wrote that whole chapters of it should have been deleted—while Knight wrote that "not a chapter, hardly a page . . . could be deleted without injury."

Dreiser's final two novels, *The Stoic* and *The Bulwark*, were published posthumously. Dreiser devoted much of his time during his last twenty years to nonfiction writings and to *The Bulwark*, which remains something of a problem novel. In *The Bulwark* the moral scruples of a Quaker businessman, Solon Barnes, come up against the reality of American business dealings. In a reversal for Dreiser, Barnes, as the upholder of traditional mores and values, is portrayed sympathetically and without the usual implied charge of hypocrisy. Granville Hicks found in *The Bulwark* "a rejection of naturalism as a literary theory."

Dreiser produced four autobiographical works, *A Traveler at Forty, A Hoosier Holiday, A Book About Myself,* and *Dawn.*

He also wrote several dramas, which are generally agreed to be unactable; two volumes of poetry, *Moods, Cadenced and Declaimed* and *The Aspirant*, both harshly reviewed and little read; a volume of short stories, *Free,* and one of short stories and novellas, *Chains*. The volumes of essays *Dreiser Looks at Russia* and *Tragic America* reflect Dreiser's growing involvement with socialism. Several of his biographers believe that he joined the Communist Party late in his life. Dreiser's socialist activities included a trip to Russia in 1927 and investigation of labor conditions in Kentucky coal mines in 1931. The extensive press coverage of these activities, Dreiser's political writings, and the fact that he did not produce a novel for twenty-one years, led to the loss of his generally accepted reputation as America's greatest living novelist. Dreiser was critically evaluated as a novelist whose career ended with *An American Tragedy*, until the publication of the two posthumous novels, *The Bulwark* and *The Stoic*, demonstrated the need for reassessment.

Increasingly since his death, Dreiser's importance has been seen as chiefly historical. Critics such as J. Donald Adams and T. K. Whipple believe that Dreiser made his greatest contribution as a "trail blazer" in the field of modern Naturalist fiction, thus opening the field for other writers. Jack Salzman summarized Dreiser's current critical standing when he wrote that Dreiser's "significance in the history of American letters is no longer a matter for dispute. We may continue to debate his merits as an artist, but his importance to American literature has been well established."

(See also *Contemporary Authors*, Vol. 106; *Dictionary of Literary Biography*, Vol. 9, *American Novelists, 1910-1945;* Vol. 12, *American Realists and Naturalists;* and *Dictionary of Literary Biography Documentary Series*, Vol. 1.)

PRINCIPAL WORKS

Sister Carrie (novel) 1900
Jennie Gerhardt (novel) 1911
*The Financier (novel) 1912
A Traveler at Forty (autobiography) 1913
*The Titan (novel) 1914
The "Genius' (novel) 1915
A Hoosier Holiday (autobiography) 1916
Free and Other Stories (short stories) 1918
The Hand of the Potter [first publication] (drama) 1918
Twelve Men (sketches) 1919
Hey Rub-a-Dub-Dub: A Book of the Mystery and Wonder and Terror of Life (essays) 1920
A Book About Myself (autobiography) 1922; also published as *Newspaper Days*, 1931
An American Tragedy (novel) 1925
Moods, Cadenced and Declaimed (poetry) 1926
Chains (short stories and novels) 1927
Dreiser Looks at Russia (essays) 1928
The Aspirant (poetry) 1929
A Gallery of Women (sketches) 1929
Dawn (autobiography) 1931
Tragic America (essays) 1931
America is Worth Saving [with Cedric Belfrage] (essays) 1941
The Bulwark (novel) 1946
*The Stoic (novel) 1947
Letters of Theodore Dreiser (letters) 1959

*These works are collectively referred to as the "Trilogy of Desire."

[THEODORE WATTS-DUNTON]   (essay date 1901)

[*This early review by an English critic is representative of the reception* Sister Carrie *received in England. The novel is praised for its verisimilitude without the moral nature of the book or its author being called into question.*]

['Sister Carrie'] is the sixth of the volumes that have appeared in Mr. Heinemann's "Dollar Library"; and it is the most important. . . . [Throughout the book], the phrasing is of the streets and the bars—colloquial, familiar, vivid, slangy, unlovely, but intensely real. Of the manner of the book it is not easy to speak favourably; it is strikingly unworthy of the matter thereof. Whilst large, dignified, and generous, the scheme of the story here told is not pretentious, or complex, or ambitious. It is a very plain tale of a plain though eventful life. Between its covers no single note of unreality is struck. It-is untrammelled by any single concession to convention or tradition, literary or social. It is as compact of actuality as a police-court record, and throughout its pages one feels pulsing the sturdy, restless energy of a young people, a cosmopolitan community, a nation busy upon the hither side of maturity. The book is, firstly, the full, exhaustive story of the "half-equipped little knight's" life and adventures; secondly, it is a broad, vivid picture of men and manners in middle-class New York and Chicago; and, thirdly, it is a thorough and really masterly study of the moral, physical, and social deterioration of one Hurstwood, a lover of the heroine. Upon all these counts it is a creditable piece of work, faithful and rich in the interest which pertains to genuinely realistic fiction. It is further of interest by reason that it strikes a key-note and is typical, both in the faults of its manner and in the wealth and diversity of its matter, of the great country which gave it birth. Readers there are who, having perused the three hundred and odd pages which go to the making of 'Sister Carrie,' will find permanent place upon their shelves for the book beside M. Zola's 'Nana.' (pp. 312-13)

[*Theodore Watts-Dunton*], *"New Novels: 'Sister Carrie'," in* The Athenaeum, *No. 3854, September 7, 1901, pp. 312-13.*

H. L. MENCKEN   (letter date 1911)

[*Mencken was one of Dreiser's most persistent defenders and promoters. He was instrumental in revitalizing Dreiser's interest in writing after the early critical failure of* Sister Carrie. *In the following letter to Dreiser, Mencken offers enthusiastic praise for* Jennie Gerhardt.]

Dear Dreiser:—

When "Jennie Gerhardt" is printed it is probable that more than one reviewer will object to its length, its microscopic detail, its enormous painstaking—but rest assured that Heinrich Ludwig von Mencken will not be in that gang. I have just finished reading the ms.—every word of it, from first to last—and I put it down with a clear notion that it should remain as it stands. The story comes upon me with great force; it touches my own experience of life in a hundred places; it preaches (or perhaps I had better say exhibits) a philosophy of life that seems to me to be sound; altogether I get a powerful effect of reality, stark and unashamed. It is drab and gloomy, but so is the struggle for existence. It is without humor, but so are the jests of that great comedian who shoots at our heels and makes us do our grotesque dancing.

I needn't say that it seems to me an advance above "Sister Carrie". Its obvious superiority lies in its better form. You strained (or perhaps even broke) the back of "Sister Carrie" when you let Hurstwood lead you away from Carrie. In "Jennie Gerhardt" there is no such running amuck. The two currents of interest, of spiritual unfolding, are very deftly managed. Even when they do not actually coalesce, they are parallel and close together. Jennie is never out of Kane's life, and after their first meeting, she is never out of his. The reaction of will upon will, of character upon character, is splendidly worked out and indicated. In brief, the story hangs together; it is a complete whole; consciously or unconsciously, you have avoided the chief defect of "Sister Carrie".

It is difficult, just rising from the book, to describe the impression I bring away. That impression is of a living whole, not of a fabric that may be unravelled and examined in detail. In brief, you have painted so smoothly and yet so vigorously that I have no memory of brush strokes. But for one thing, the great naturalness of the dialogue sticks in mind. In particular, you have been extremely successful with Gerhardt. His speeches are perfect: nothing could be nearer to truth. I am well aware that certain persons are impatient of this photographic accuracy. Well, let them choose their poison. As for me, I prefer the fact to the fancy. You have tried to depict a German of a given type—a type with which I, by chance, happen to be very familiar. You have made him as thoroughly alive as Huck Finn.

These are random, disordered notes. When the time comes, I'll reduce my thoughts to order and write a formal, intelligible review. At the moment I am too near the book. I rather distrust my own enthusiasm for it. Perhaps I read my own prejudices and ideas into it. My interest is always in the subjective event, seldom or never in the objective event. That is why I like "Lord Jim". Here you have got very close to the very wellsprings of action. The march of episodes is nothing: the slow unfolding of character is everything.

If anyone urges you to cut down the book bid that one be damned. And if anyone argues that it is over-gloomy call the police. Let it stand as it is. Its bald, forthright style; its scientific, unemotional piling up of detail; the incisive truthfulness of its dialogue; the stark straightforwardness of it all—these are merits that need no praise. It is at once an accurate picture of life and a searching criticism of life. And that is my definition of a good novel.

Here and there I noted minor weaknesses. For one thing, it is doubtful that Jennie would have been able to conceal from so sophisticated a man as Kane the fact that she had had a child. Child-bearing leaves physical marks, and those marks commonly persist for five or six years. But there are, of course, exceptions to this rule. Not many readers, I suppose, will raise the point. . . . Again you give Kane $5,000 income from $75,000 at 6 percent. A small thing—but everywhere else you are so utterly careful that small errors stick out.

A final word: the least satisfactory personage in the book is Jennie herself. Not that you do not account for her, from head to heels—but I would have preferred, had I the choice, a more typical kept woman. She is, in brief, uncompromisingly exceptional, almost unique, in several important details. Her connection with her mother and father and with the facts of her life grows, at times, very fragile. But I can well understand how her essential plausibility must have reacted upon you—how your own creation must have dragged you on. (pp. 12-13)

But I go back to the effect of the book as a whole. That effect, believe me, is very powerful. I must go to Hardy and Conrad to find its like. David Phillips, I believe, might have done such a story had he lived, but the best that he actually wrote, to wit, "The Hungry Heart", goes to pieces beside **"Jennie"**. I mean this in all seriousness. You have written a novel that no other American of the time could have written, and even in England there are not six men who, with your material, could have reached so high a level of reality. My earnest congratulations. By all means let me see that third book. **"Jennie"** shows immense progress in craftsmanship. As a work of art it is decidedly superior to **"Sister Carrie"**. . . .

Yours,

H.L.M.

Reading this over it seems damned cold. [What] I really want to say is just—"Hurrah!" You have put over a truly *big* thing. (p. 14)

> *H. L. Mencken, in his letter to Theodore Dreiser on April 23, 1911, in* Letters of H. L. Mencken, *edited by Guy J. Forgue (copyright © 1961 by Alfred A. Knopf, Inc.; reprinted by permission of the publisher), Knopf, 1961, pp. 12-14.*

FREDERIC TABER COOPER   (essay date 1912)

[*Cooper, the longtime literary critic for* The Bookman, *offers a favorable appraisal of* The Financier.]

Mr. Dreiser's latest and most ambitious venture in fiction [is] *The Financier*. The type of story that it represents is one that has become fairly frequent since the novel of the business and financial world has come into vogue. It is the type that follows the hero through a promising career, as he rises through spectacular strokes of fortune to a dominant position, and then suddenly by one fatal blunder sends the whole carefully built structure tumbling, card-like, to the ground. . . . *The Financier* is a very unusual piece of work, a social and economic picture of American life that, in spite of certain crudities, must be recognized as a novel of the first magnitude. Its one real fault is that it is unwarrantedly long. Through nearly eight hundred pages of rather fine print, it surges forcefully on, in a mighty tide of words that the author himself seems to have been impotent to stay. Not that the structure of the story is loose and rambling, nor that the episodes are irrelevant or lacking in interest. It is simply that for the purposes of a clear, forceful picture, he has given us too much. That Mr. Dreiser should himself know all he has told us about his principal characters, and perhaps a good deal more, is as it should be; but he would have gained by practising a more rigid elimination. If Mr. Dreiser's structure had been of an epic variety, if it dealt with the destinies of a race, or summed up the psychology of an epoch, then space and amplitude, and crowding throngs of characters and incidents would all contribute quite properly toward the needed impression of vastness both of theme and of setting. But *The Financier* is distinctly the story of a single character, a certain Frank Algernon Cowperwood, from the time when as a small boy, he bought castile soap at auction and resold it to his father's grocer at one hundred per cent. profit, until a day twenty years later, when the doors

of the penitentiary open to give him freedom, and he starts once more to take up the broken threads of his life. In a certain broad sense, the book does give us, in addition to this central character, a picture of American business life, as it was during the Civil War and the reconstruction period, and in a veiled way it is a criticism of the same conditions, on a larger scale, existing in the financial world of to-day. But all this seems to interest Mr. Dreiser only as background. There is no dominant central symbol, like Wheat in *The Pit*, by Norris, or the Bourse, in Zola's *L'Argent*. The dishonesty of the local political ring in Philadelphia during the sixties and seventies, the juggling with city funds, the grabbing of street-car franchises, all of these things concern Mr. Dreiser only to the extent to which they react upon the character and the fortunes of his hero. And for that reason, the sheer mass of detail, the cumulation of names and incidents, people and situations glimpsed only for an instant, in a swift, bewildering panorama of life, have the effect of obscuring, instead of helping us to see. None the less, the personality of Cowperwood, born manipulator of money and colossal egotist, is a portrait not easily forgotten. (pp. 435-36)

> *Frederic Taber Cooper, "The Theory of Endings and Some Recent Novels," in* The Bookman, *New York (copyright, 1912, by Dodd, Mead and Company), Vol. XXXVI, No. 5, December, 1912, pp. 433-39.**

SINCLAIR LEWIS   (essay date 1914)

[*Writing six years before the classic* Main Street *established him as a master of satiric realism, Lewis was a little-known author when he offered the following review of* A Traveler at Forty.]

Three famous novelists, Howells, Dreiser and Bennett, have written three books of travel, in which they so mingle observations of foreign lands with glimpses of their own selves that the reader needs but little imagination to fancy himself traveling with them. . . .

Theodore Dreiser, whose **"Sister Carrie"** was widely hailed as the largest fruit of American realism, has in **"A Traveler at Forty,"** by far the most intimate of these three books. Not for a second does he write just travel only. He writes of Dreiser apropos of servants' buttons and Monmartre and Sir Secrop, the art critic. He is chatting familiarly with you all through the book. And this quality, precisely, has caused **"A Traveler at Forty"** to be ridiculed and praised about equally. One reviewer of some fame—at least among reviewers—declared that "Dreiser writes what the average Cook's tourist would like to describe and can't."

Actually, Mr. Dreiser is about as different from the average tourist as his **"Jennie Gerhardt"** is from the average ribbon-decked romance. For everywhere he goes he watches people with a terrible intentness and a curiosity about them that never rests until he has their secrets. (p. 165)

> *Sinclair Lewis, in his review of "A Traveler at Forty" (originally published as "Intimate Travel Talks by World-Famed Writers," in* St. Louis Republic, *February 21, 1914), in* Theodore Dreiser: The Critical Reception, *edited by Jack Salzman (copyright © 1972 by David Lewis, Inc.), Lewis, 1972, pp. 165-66.*

EDGAR LEE MASTERS   (essay date 1915)

[*Like Dreiser, Masters was a Midwestern realistic artist. The author of* Spoon River Anthology *favorably appraises Dreiser's work in general and* The "Genius" *in particular.*]

"**The Genius,**" by Theodore Dreiser is not the third part of his trilogy of desire tho it is so designated in some critical quarters. Yet it is a story of desire, the delineation of a man who simulated a genius, but was not one. The author puts the word genius in quotation marks, thereby conveying an intimation of his own judgment; at least by that method leaving the question to the judgment of the reader. In this book Dreiser's clear eye and patient, accurate hand display themselves in all the elaborateness that we have been taught to expect in his work. All his books, beginning with "**Sister Carrie,**" have this quality; and together they form a remarkable record of what a man of large experience and deep sympathy with his fellow beings has gleaned at first hand from a world that enthralls his imagination and bewilders his thought. As history these books are valuable—more valuable than the histories we have. For Dreiser knows Illinois and Indiana, Chicago and New York. He knows America, and he knows the people in villages and cities. He understands what a man almost a genius must contend with in this disorderly land of rhetorical freedom and societal tyranny and banality. He knows that the American soil is not productive of genius; and hence Witla, the hero, a name which connotes witless, goes thru the experience that would come to a genius, but fails in the main thing as a genius would not fail. Yet, so far as a chronicle of as well as against America is concerned, Witla suffices. The theme is bigger than Mr. Howells' "A Modern Instance," and Dreiser has gorged the book with things intimate and subtle and true to the life we know. His unique intellectual gifts show nothing more conspicuously than a zealous interest, a primal wonder, concerning the ironies and grotesqueries of life.

Over the book one can hear at times Gargantuan laughter; at other times a trembling sensitiveness seems to vibrate thru the pages. Life's phantasmagoric procession passes before his eyes. He sees its tragedies clearly; its comedies, fundamentally speaking, do not escape him. . . . He is therefore never done with explaining, and adding in touches and bringing forward facts. The reader must see what he sees. Nothing must be omitted, lest the picture lose the fidelity that he would portray—lest some less discerning eye fail of comprehension of the whole. Boundless curiosity, passion for life, immense strength and patience carry him beyond Browning in the endeavor to make the record complete. But, unlike Browning, Dreiser has no philosophy, unless it be a philosophy to see a cosmic force which concerns itself with great events, and cares nothing for the human souls bobbing like corks in its current. . . . America should awake to the significance of the fact that Dreiser is not striving for popularity or to make money. He is not writing to propitiate American standards. He does not see a power for righteousness moving thru the world, tho he is bound to see laws at work in every domain of human life, more clearly than he has seen them thus far. But he is admirable and to be acclaimed because he looks for truth and tells the truth. If America can boast of a novelist now living of greater power, insight, imaginative sweep, let him step forward and claim the laurel wreath. He seems to me our greatest novelist now writing, and destined in the wise judgment of posterity to be given a place among the noteworthy writers of this age. (pp. 221-22)

> *Edgar Lee Masters, in his review of "The 'Genius'"*
> *(originally published as "An American 'Genius',"*
> *in* Chicago Evening Post, *October 22, 1915), in*
> Theodore Dreiser: The Critical Reception, *edited by*
> *Jack Salzman (copyright © 1972 by David Lewis,*
> *Inc.), Lewis, 1972, pp. 221-24.*

STUART P. SHERMAN   (essay date 1915)

[*Sherman's is one of the most well-known and often-cited attacks on Dreiser and his work. "The Barbaric Naturalism of Mr. Dreiser" sparked the first intensive critical evaluation of Dreiser's work.*]

The layman who listens reverently to the reviewers discussing the new novels and to the novelists discussing themselves can hardly escape persuasion that a great change has rather recently taken place in the spirit of the age, in the literature which reflects it, and in the criticism which judges it. (p. 85)

The present age is fearless and is freeing itself from illusions. Now, for the first time in history, men are facing unabashed the facts of life. . . . Rejecting nothing, altering nothing, it presents to us—let us take our terms from the bright lexicon of the reviewer—a "transcript," a "cross-section," a "slice," a "photographic" or "cinematographic" reproduction of life. The critic who keeps pace with the movement no longer asks whether the artist has created beauty or glorified goodness, but merely whether he has told the truth.

Mr. Dreiser, in his latest novel ["**The Genius**"], describes a canvas by a painter of this austere modern school: "Raw reds, raw greens, dirty gray paving stones—such faces! Why, this thing fairly shouted its facts. It seemed to say: 'I'm dirty, I am commonplace, I am grim, I am shabby, but I am life.' And there was no apologizing for anything in it, no glossing anything over. Bang! Smash! Crack! came the facts one after another, with a bitter, brutal insistence on their so-ness." If you do not like what is in the picture, you are to be crushed by the retort that perhaps you do not like what is in life. Perhaps you have not the courage to confront reality. Perhaps you had better read the chromatic fairy-tales with the children. Men of sterner stuff exclaim, like the critic in this novel, "Thank God for a realist!"

Mr. Dreiser is a novelist of the new school, for whom we have been invited off and on these fourteen years to thank God—a form of speech, by the way, which crept into the language before the dawn of modern realism. He has performed with words what his hero performed with paint. He has presented the facts of life "one after another with a bitter, brutal insistence on their so-ness," which marks him as a "man of the hour," a "portent"—the successor of Mr. Howells and Mr. James. . . . He has laid reality bare for us in five novels published as follows: ["**Sister Carrie,**" "**Jennie Gerhardt,**" "**The Financier,**" "**The Titan,**" and "**The Genius**"]. . . . These five works constitute a singularly homogeneous mass of fiction. I do not find any moral value in them, nor any memorable beauty—of their truth I shall speak later; but I am greatly impressed by them as serious representatives of a new note in American literature, coming from that "ethnic" element of our mixed population which, as we are assured by competent authorities, is to redeem us from Puritanism and insure our artistic salvation. They abundantly illustrate, furthermore, the methods and intentions of our recent courageous, veracious realism. Before we thank God for it, let us consider a little more closely what is offered us.

The first step towards the definition of Mr. Dreiser's special contribution is to blow away the dust with which the exponents of the new realism seek to becloud the perceptions of our "reverent layman." In their main pretensions, there are large elements of conscious and unconscious sham.

It should clear the air to say that courage in facing and veracity in reporting the facts of life are no more characteristic of Theodore Dreiser than of John Bunyan. These moral traits are not the peculiar marks of the new school; they are marks common to every great movement of literature within the memory of man. Each literary generation detaching itself from its predecessor—whether it has called its own movement Classical or Romantic or what not—has revolted in the interest of what it took to be a more adequate representation of reality. No one who is not drunken with the egotism of the hour, no one who has penetrated with sober senses into the spirit of any historical period anterior to his own, will fall into the indecency of declaring his own age preëminent in the desire to see and to tell the truth. The real distinction between one generation and another is in the thing which each takes for its master truth—in the thing which each recognizes as the essential reality for it. The difference between Bunyan and Dreiser is in the order of facts which each reports. (pp. 85-8)

Let us, then, dismiss Mr. Dreiser's untenable claims to superior courage and veracity of intention, the photographic transcript, and the unbiassed service of truth; and let us seek for his definition in his general theory of life, in the order of facts which he records, and in the pattern of his representations.

The impressive unity of effect produced by Mr. Dreiser's five novels is due to the fact that they are all illustrations of a crude and naïvely simple naturalistic philosophy, such as we find in the mouths of exponents of the new *Real-Politik*. Each book, with its bewildering masses of detail, is a ferocious argument in behalf of a few brutal generalizations. To the eye cleared of illusions it appears that the ordered life which we call civilization does not really exist except on paper. In reality our so-called society is a jungle in which the struggle for existence continues, and must continue, on terms substantially unaltered by legal, moral, or social conventions. (p. 91)

The idea that civilization is a sham Mr. Dreiser sometimes sets forth explicitly, and sometimes he conveys it by the process known among journalists as "coloring the news.". . . Righteousness is always "legal"; conventions are always "current"; routine is always "dull"; respectability is always "unctuous"; an institution for transforming schoolgirls into young ladies is presided over by "owl-like conventionalists"; families in which parents are faithful to each other lead an "apple-pie order of existence"; a man who yeilds to his impulses yet condemns himself for yielding is a "rag-bag moralistic ass." Jennie Gerhardt, by a facile surrender of her chastity, shows that *"she could not be readily corrupted by the world's selfish lessons* on how to preserve oneself from the evil to come." Surely, this is "coloring the news."

By similar devices Mr. Dreiser drives home the great truth that man is essentially an animal, impelled by temperament, instinct, physics, chemistry—anything you please that is irrational and uncontrollable. Sometimes he writes an "editorial" paragraph in which the laws of human life are explained by reference to the behavior of certain protozoa or by reference to a squid and a lobster fighting in an aquarium. His heroes and heroines have "cat-like eyes," "feline grace," "sinuous strides," eyes and jaws which vary "from those of the tiger, lynx, and bear to those of the fox, the tolerant mastiff, and the surly bulldog." One hero and his mistress are said to "have run together temperamentally like two leopards." The lady in question, admiring the large rapacity of her mate, exclaims playfully: "Oh, you big tiger! You great, big lion! Boo!" Courtship as presented in these novels is after the manner of beasts in the jungle. Mr. Dreiser's leonine men but circle once or twice about their prey, and spring, and pounce; and the

struggle is over. A pure-minded servingmaid, who is suddenly held up in the hall by a "hairy, axiomatic" guest and "masterfully" kissed upon the lips, may for an instant be "horrified, stunned, *like a bird in the grasp of a cat.*" But we are always assured that "through it all something tremendously vital and insistent" will be speaking to her, and that in the end she will not resist the urge of the *élan vital.* I recall no one of all the dozens of obliging women in these books who makes any effective resistance when summoned to capitulate. "The *psychology of the human animal,* when confronted by these tangles, these ripping tides of the heart," says the author of **"The Titan,"** "has little to do with so-called reason or logic." No; as he informs us elsewhere with endless iteration, it is a question of chemistry. It is the "chemistry of her being" which rouses to blazing the ordinarily dormant forces of Eugene Witla's sympathies in **"The Genius."** If Stephanie Platow is disloyal to her married lover in **"The Titan,"** "let no one quarrel" with her. Reason: "She was an unstable chemical compound."

Such is the Dreiserian philosophy.

By thus eliminating distinctively human motives and making animal instincts the supreme factors in human life, Mr. Dreiser reduces the problem of the novelist to the lowest possible terms. I find myself unable to go with those who admire the powerful reality of his art while deploring the puerility of his philosophy. His philosophy quite excludes him from the field in which a great realist must work. He has deliberately rejected the novelist's supreme task—understanding and presenting the development of character; he has chosen only to illustrate the unrestricted flow of temperament. He has evaded the enterprise of representing human conduct; he has confined himself to a representation of animal behavior. He demands for the demonstration of his theory a moral vacuum from which the obligations of parenthood, marriage, chivalry, and citizenship have been quite withdrawn or locked in a twilight sleep. At each critical moment in his narrative, where a realist like George Eliot or Thackeray or Trollope or Meredith would be asking how a given individual would feel, think, and act under the manifold combined stresses of organized society, Mr. Dreiser sinks supinely back upon the law of the jungle or mutters his mystical gibberish about an alteration of the chemical formula.

The possibility of making the unvarying victoriousness of jungle-motive plausible depends directly upon the suppression of the evidence of other motives. In this work of suppression Mr. Dreiser simplifies American life almost beyond recognition. Whether it is because he comes from Indiana, or whether it is because he steadily envisages the human animal, I cannot say; I can only note that he never speaks of his men and women as "educated" or "brought up." Whatever their social status, they are invariably "raised." Raising human stock in America evidently includes feeding and clothing it, but does not include the inculcation of even the most elementary moral ideas. Hence Mr. Dreiser's field seems curiously outside American society. Yet he repeatedly informs us that his persons are typical of the American middle class, and three of the leading figures, to judge from their names—Carrie Meeber, Jennie Gerhardt, and Eugene Witla—are of our most highly "cultured" race. Frank Cowperwood, the hero of two novels, is a hawk of finance and a rake almost from the cradle; but of the powers which presided over his cradle we know nothing save that his father was a competent official in a Philadelphia bank. . . . Jennie Gerhardt, of course, succumbs to the first man who puts his arm around her; but, in certain respects, her case is exceptional.

In the novel **"Jennie Gerhardt"** Mr. Dreiser ventures a disastrous experiment at making the jungle-motive plausible without suppressing the evidence of other motives. He provides the girl with pious Lutheran parents, of fallen fortune, but alleged to be of sterling character, who "raise" her with the utmost strictness. . . . "Gerhardt and his wife, and also Jennie," says Mr. Dreiser, "accepted the doctrines of their church without reserve." Twenty pages later Jennie is represented as yielding her virtue in pure gratitude to a man of fifty, Senator Brander, who has let her do his laundry and in other ways has been kind to her and to her family. The Senator suddenly dies; Jennie expects to become a mother; Father Gerhardt is broken-hearted, and the family moves from Columbus to Cleveland. This first episode is not incredibly presented as a momentary triumph of emotional impulse over training—as an "accident." The incredible appears when Mr. Dreiser insists that an accident of this sort to a girl brought up *under the conditions stated* is not necessarily followed by any sense of sin or shame or regret. Upon this simple pious Lutheran he imposes his own naturalistic philosophy, and, in analyzing her psychology before the birth of her illegitimate child, pretends that she looks forward to the event "without a murmur," with "serene, unfaltering courage," "the marvel of life holding her in trance," with "joy and satisfaction," seeing in her state "the immense possibilities of racial fulfilment." This juggling is probably expected to prepare us for her instantaneous assent, perhaps a year later, when a healthy, magnetic manufacturer, who has seen her perhaps a dozen times, claps his paw upon her and says, "You belong to me," and in a perfectly cold-blooded interview proposes the terms on which he will set her up in New York as his mistress. Jennie, who is a fond mother and a dutiful daughter, goes to her pious Lutheran mother and talks the whole matter over with her quite candidly. The mother hesitates—not on Jennie's account, gentle reader, but because she will be obliged to deceive old Gerhardt; "the difficulty of telling this lie was very great for Mrs. Gerhardt"! But she acquiesces at last. "I'll help you out with it," she concludes—"with a little sigh." The unreality of the whole transaction shrieks.

Mr. Dreiser's stubborn insistence upon the jungle-motive results in a dreary monotony in the form and substance of his novels. Interested only in the description of animal behavior, he constructs his plot in such a way as to exhibit the persistence of two or three elementary instincts through every kind of situation. He finds, for example, a subject in the career of an American captain of industry, thinly disguised under the name of Frank Cowperwood. He has just two things to tell us about Cowperwood: that he has a rapacious appetite for money, and that he has a rapacious appetite for women. In **"The Financier"** he "documents" those two truths about Cowperwood in seventy-four chapters, in each one of which he shows us how his hero made money or how he captivated women in Philadelphia. Not satisfied with the demonstration, he returns to the same theses in **"The Titan,"** and shows us in sixty-two chapters how the same hero made money and captivated women in Chicago and New York. He promises us a third volume, in which we shall no doubt learn in a work of sixty or seventy chapters—a sort of huge club-sandwich composed of slices of business alternating with erotic episodes—how Frank Cowperwood made money and captivated women in London. Meanwhile Mr. Dreiser has turned aside from his great "trilogy of desire" to give us **"The Genius,"** in which the hero, Witla, alleged to be a great realistic painter, exhibits in 101 chapters, similarly "sandwiched" together, an appetite for women and money indistinguishable from that of Cowperwood. (pp. 92-9)

If at this point you stop and inquire why Mr. Dreiser goes to such great lengths to establish so little, you find yourself once more confronting the jungle-motive. Mr. Dreiser, with a problem similar to De Foe's in "The Apparition of Mrs. Veal," has availed himself of De Foe's method for creating the illusion of reality. The essence of the problem and of the method for both these authors is the certification of the unreal by the irrelevant. If you wish to make acceptable to your reader the incredible notion that Mrs. Veal's ghost appeared to Mrs. Bargrave, divert his incredulity from the precise point at issue by telling him all sorts of detailed credible things about the poverty of Mrs. Veal's early life, the sobriety of her brother, her father's neglect, and the bad temper of Mrs. Bargrave's husband. If you wish to make acceptable to your reader the incredible notion that Aileen Butler's first breach of the seventh article in the decalogue was "a happy event," taking place "much as a marriage might have," divert his incredulity by describing with the technical accuracy of a fashion magazine not merely the gown that she wore on the night of Cowperwood's reception, but also with equal detail the half-dozen other gowns that she thought she might wear, but did not. If you have been for three years editor-in-chief of the Butterick Publications, you can probably perform this feat with unimpeachable verisimilitude; and having acquired credit for expert knowledge in matters of dress and millinery, you can now and then emit unchallenged a bit of philosophy such as "Life cannot be put in any one mould, and the attempt may as well be abandoned at once. . . . Besides, whether we will or no, theory or no theory, the large basic facts of chemistry and physics remain." None the less, if you expect to gain credence for the notion that your hero can have any woman in Chicago or New York that he puts his paw upon, you had probably better lead up to it by a detailed account of the street-railway system in those cities. It will necessitate the loading of your pages with a tremendous baggage of irrelevant detail. It will not sound much like art. It will sound more like one of Lincoln Steffens's special articles. But it will produce an overwhelming impression of reality, which the reader will carry with him into the next chapter where you are laying bare the "chemistry" of the human animal.

It would make for clearness in our discussions of contemporary fiction if we withheld the title of "realist" from a writer like Mr. Dreiser, and called him, as Zola called himself, a "naturalist." While asserting that all great art in every period intends a representation of reality, I have tried to indicate the basis for a working distinction between the realistic novel and the naturalistic novel of the present day. Both are representations of the life of man in contemporary or nearly contemporary society, and both are presumably composed of materials within the experience and observation of the author. But a realistic novel is a representation based upon a theory of human conduct. If the theory of human conduct is adequate, the representation constitutes an addition to literature and to social history. A naturalistic novel is a representation based upon a theory of animal behavior. Since a theory of animal behavior can never be an adequate basis for a representation of the life of man in contemporary society, such a representation is an artistic blunder. When half the world attempts to assert such a theory, the other half rises in battle. And so one turns with relief from Mr. Dreiser's novels to the morning papers. (pp. 99-101)

Stuart P. Sherman, "The Barbaric Naturalism of Theodore Dreiser" (originally published as "The Naturalism of Mr. Dreiser," in The Nation, *Vol. 101, No. 2631, December 2, 1915), in his* On Contemporary Literature *(copyright © 1917 by Henry Holt and Company), Holt, Rinehart and Winston, 1917, pp. 85-101.*

H.L. MENCKEN   (essay date 1917)

[*Mencken and Stuart P. Sherman were bitter enemies in print; each held critical theories which were totally antagonistic to those of the other. Below, Mencken defends Dreiser against Sherman's earlier attack (see excerpt above), likening Sherman to Anthony Comstock, the founder and life secretary of the Society for the Suppression of Vice.*]

[What] is Sherman's complaint? In brief, that Dreiser is a liar when he calls himself a realist; that he is actually a naturalist, and hence accursed. That "he has evaded the enterprise of representing human conduct, and confined himself to a representation of animal behavior." That he "imposes his own naturalistic philosophy" upon his characters, making them do what they ought not to do, and think what they ought not to think. That he "has just two things to tell us about Frank Cowperwood: that he has a rapacious appetite for money, and a rapacious appetite for women." That this alleged "theory of animal behavior" is not only incorrect, but immoral, and that "when one half the world attempts to assert it, the other half rises in battle" [see excerpt above]. . . . (pp. 74-5)

Only a glance is needed to show the vacuity of all this irate flubdub. Dreiser, in point of fact, is scarcely more the realist or the naturalist, in any true sense, than H. G. Wells or the later George Moore, nor has he ever announced himself in either the one character or the other—if there be, in fact, any difference between them that anyone save a pigeon-holing pedagogue can discern. He is really something quite different, and, in his moments, something far more stately. His aim is not merely to record, but to translate and understand; the thing he exposes is not the empty event and act, but the endless mystery out of which it springs; his pictures have a passionate compassion in them that it is hard to separate from poetry. If this sense of the universal and inexplicable tragedy, if this vision of life as a seeking without a finding, if this adept summoning up of moving images, is mistaken by college professors for the empty, meticulous nastiness of Zola in "Pot-Bouille"—in Nietzsche's phrase, for "the delight to stink"—then surely the folly of college professors, as vast as it seems, has been underestimated. What is the fact? The fact is that Dreiser's attitude of mind, his manner of reaction to the phenomena he represents, the whole of his alleged "naturalistic philosophy," stem directly, not from Zola, Flaubert, Augier and the younger Dumas, but from the Greeks. In the midst of democratic cocksureness and Christian sentimentalism, of doctrinaire shallowness and professorial smugness, he stands for a point of view which at least has something honest and courageous about it; here, at all events, he is a realist. (p. 75)

As for the animal behavior prattle of the learned headmaster, it reveals on the one hand only the academic fondness for seizing upon high-sounding but empty phrases and using them to alarm the populace, and on the other hand, only the academic incapacity for observing facts correctly and reporting them honestly. The truth is, of course, that the behavior of such men as Cowperwood and Eugene Witla and of such women as Carrie Meeber and Jennie Gerhardt, as Dreiser describes it, is no more

merely animal than the behavior of such acknowledged and undoubted human beings as Dr. Woodrow Wilson and Dr. Jane Addams. The whole point of the story of Witla, to take the example which seems to concern the horrified watchmen most, is this: that this life is a bitter conflict between the animal in him and the aspiring soul, between the flesh and the spirit, between what is weak in him and what is strong, between what is base and what is noble. Moreover, the good, in the end, gets its hooks into the bad: as we part from Witla he is actually bathed in the tears of remorse, and resolved to be a correct and godfearing man. And what have we in **"The Financier"** and **"The Titan"**? A conflict, in the ego of Cowperwood, between aspiration and ambition, between the passion for beauty and the passion for power. Is either passion animal? To ask the question is to answer it.

I single out Dr. Sherman, not because his pompous syllogisms have any plausibility in fact or logic, but simply because he may well stand as archetype of the booming, indignant corrupter of criteria, the moralist turned critic. . . . What offends him is not actually Dreiser's shortcomings as an artist, but Dreiser's shortcomings as a Christian and an American. (pp. 75-6)

The Comstockian attack upon **"The 'Genius'"** seems to have sprung out of the same muddled sense of Dreiser's essential hostility to all that is safe and regular—of the danger in him to that mellowed Methodism which has become the national ethic. The book, in a way, was a direct challenge, for though it came to an end upon a note which even a Methodist might hear as sweet, there were provocations in detail. Dreiser, in fact, allowed his scorn to make off with his taste. . . . The Comstocks arose to the bait a bit slowly, but none the less surely. Going through the volume with the terrible industry of a Sunday-school boy dredging up pearls of smut from the Old Testament, they achieved a list of no less than 89 alledged floutings of the code—75 described as lewd and 14 as profane. An inspection of these specifications affords mirth of a rare and lofty variety; nothing could more cruelly expose the inner chambers of the moral mind. When young Witla, fastening his best girl's skate, is so overcome by the carnality of youth that he hugs her, it is set down as lewd. . . . Every kiss, hug and tickle of the chin in the chronicle is laboriously snouted out, empanelled, exhibited. Every hint that Witla is no vestal, that he indulges his unchristian fleshliness, that he burns in the manner of I Corinthians, VII, 9, is uncovered to the moral inquisition.

On the side of profanity there is a less ardent pursuit of evidence, chiefly, I daresay, because their unearthing is less stimulating. (Besides, there is no law prohibiting profanity in books: the whole inquiry here is but so much *lagniappe*.) On page 408, describing a character called Daniel C. Summerfield, Dreiser says that the fellow is "very much given to swearing, more as a matter of habit than of foul intention," and then goes on to explain somewhat lamely that "no picture of him would be complete without the interpolation of his various expressions." They turn out to be *God Damn* and *Jesus Christ*—three of the latter and five or six of the former. All go down; the pure in heart must be shielded from the knowledge of them. . . . Also, three plain *damns*, eight *hells*, one *my God*, five *by Gods*, one *go to the devil*, one *God Almighty* and one plain *God*. Altogether, 31 specimens are listed. **"The 'Genius'"** runs to 350,000 words. The profanity thus works out to somewhat less than one word in 10,000. . . . Alas, the Comstockian proboscis, feeling for such offendings, is not as alert as when uncovering more savoury delicacies. On page 191 I find an overlooked *by God*. . . . On page 720 there is *as God is my judge*. On page 723 there is *I'm no damned good*. . . . But I begin to blush. (pp. 76-8)

[Dreiser] is an American like the rest of us, and to be an American is to be burdened by an ethical prepossession, to lean toward causes and remedies. Go through **"The 'Genius'"** or **"A Hoosier Holiday"** carefully, and you will find disquieting indications of what might be called a democratic trend in thinking—that is, a trend toward short cuts, easy answers, glittering theories. He is bemused, off and on, by all the various poppycock of the age, from Christian Science to spiritism, and from the latest guesses in eschatology and epistemology to *art pour l'art*. A true American, he lacks a solid culture, and so he yields a bit to every wind that blows, to the inevitable damage of his representation of the eternal mystery that is man. (pp. 78-9)

Struggle as he may to rid himself of the current superstitions, he can never quite achieve deliverance from the believing attitude of mind—the heritage of the Indiana hinterland. One half of the man's brain, so to speak, wars with the other half. He is intelligent, he is thoughtful, he is a sound artist—but always there come moments when a dead hand falls upon him, and he is once more the Indiana peasant, snuffing absurdly over imbecile sentimentalities; giving a grave ear to quackeries, snorting and eye-rolling with the best of them. One generation spans too short a time to free the soul of man. (p. 79)

[Dreiser] is still, for all his achievement, in the transition stage between Christian Endeavor and civilization; between Warsaw, Indiana, and the Socratic grove; between being a good American and being a free man; and so he sometimes vacillates perilously between a moral sentimentalism and a somewhat extravagant revolt. *"The 'Genius,'"* on the one hand, is almost a tract for rectitude, a Warning to the Young; its motto might be *Scheut die Dirnen!* And on the other hand, it is full of a laborious truculence that can be explained only by imagining the author as heroically determined to prove that he is a plain-spoken fellow and his own man, let the chips fall where they may. So, in spots, in **"The Financier"** and **"The Titan,"** both of them far better books. There is an almost moral frenzy to expose and riddle what passes for morality among the stupid. The isolation of irony is never reached; the man is still a bit evangelical; his ideas are still novelties to him; he is as solemnly absurd in some of his floutings of the code American as he is in his respect for Bouguereau, or in his flirtings with New Thought, or in his naive belief in the importance of novel-writing. . . .

But his books remain, particularly his earlier books—and not all the ranting of the outraged orthodox will ever wipe them out. They were done in the stage of wonder, before self-consciousness began to creep in and corrupt it. The view of life that got into **"Sister Carrie,"** the first of them, was not the product of a deliberate thinking out of Carrie's problem. It simply got itself there by the force of the artistic passion behind it; its coherent statement had to wait for other and more reflective days. This complete rejection of ethical plan and purpose, this manifestation of what Nietzsche used to call moral innocence, is what brought up the guardians of the national tradition at the gallop, and created the Dreiser bugaboo of today. All the rubber-stamp formulae of American fiction were thrown overboard in these earlier books; instead of reducing the inexplicable to the obvious, they lifted the obvious to the inexplicable; one could find in them no orderly chain of causes

and effects, of rewards and punishments; they represented life as a phenomenon at once terrible and unintelligble, like a stroke of lightning. The prevailing criticism applied the moral litmus. They were not "good"; *ergo*, they were "evil."

The peril that Dreiser stands in is here. He may begin to act, if he is not careful, according to the costume forced on him. Unable to combat the orthodox valuation of his place and aim, he may seek a spiritual refuge in embracing it, and so arrange himself with the tripe-sellers of heterodoxy, and cry wares that differ from the other stock only in the bald fact that they are different. . . . Such a fall would grieve the judicious, of whom I have the honor to be one. (pp. 79-80)

> *H. L. Mencken, "The Dreiser Bugaboo" (copyright 1917 by* The Seven Arts), *in* The Seven Arts, *Vol. 2, No. 10, August, 1917 (and reprinted in* Dreiser: A Collection of Critical Essays, *edited by John Lydenberg, Prentice-Hall, Inc., 1971, pp. 73-80).*

SHERWOOD ANDERSON   (essay date 1918)

[*Anderson deeply admired Dreiser, who had encouraged the younger writer during Anderson's apprentice years in Chicago. Dreiser was touched by his friend's laudatory introduction to* Free and Other Stories.]

Theodore Dreiser is a man who, with the passage of time, is bound to loom larger and larger in the awakening æsthetic consciousness of America. Among all of our prose writers he is one of the few men of whom it may be said that he has always been an honest workman, always impersonal, never a trickster. (p. v)

Often I have thought of him as the bravest man who has lived in America in our times. Perhaps I exaggerate. He is a man of my own craft and always he has been a heroic figure in my own eyes. He is honest. Never in any line he has ever written will you find him resorting to the trick to get himself out of a hard situation. The beauty and the ironic terror of life is like a wall before him but he faces the wall. He does not mutter cheap little lies in the darkness and to me there is something honorable and fine in the fact that in him there is no lack of courage in facing his materials, that he needs resort to tricks of style to cover. (p. vi)

If there is a modern movement in American prose writing, a movement toward greater courage and fidelity to life in writing, then Theodore Dreiser is the pioneer and the hero of the movement. Of that I think there can be no question. I think it is true now that no American prose writer need hesitate before the task of putting his hands upon his materials. Puritanism, as a choking, smothering force, is dead or dying. We are rapidly approaching the old French standard wherein the only immorality for the artist is in bad art and I think that Theodore Dreiser, the man, has done more than any living American to bring this about. All honor to him. The whole air of America is sweeter to breathe because he had lived and worked here. He has laid a foundation upon which any sort of structure may be built. It will stand the strain. His work has been honestly and finely done. The man has laid so many old ghosts, pounded his way through such a wall of stupid prejudices and fears that today any man coming into the craft of writing comes with a new inheritance of freedom. (pp. vi-vii)

[Theodore Dreiser] has lived out most of his life as a comparatively poor man. He might have grown rich had he but joined the ranks of the clever tricksters or had he devoted his energies to turning out romantic sentimentalities. What amusing and clever men we have had in his time, what funny fellows, what masters of all the tricks of writing.

Where are they? What have they given us?

And what has Dreiser given us? A fine growing and glowing tradition, has he not, a new sense of the value of our own lives, a new interest in the life about us, in offices, streets and houses.

Theodore Dreiser's nature is the true artist's nature, so little understood among us. He is no reformer. In his work, as in the man himself, there is something bold, with all the health of true boldness, and at the same time something very finely humble. He stands before life, looking at it, trying to understand it that he may catch its significance and its drama. . . . He is the workman, full of self-respect, and—most strange and wonderful of all for an American writer—full of respect for his materials, for the lives of those who come close to him, for that world of people who have come into life under his pen.

As for my trying to make in any detailed way an estimate of the value of the man's work, that is beyond me. The man has done, is doing, his job, he has fought his way through darkness into the light and in making a pathway for himself he has made a pathway for us all. Because he had lived and worked so honestly and finely America is a better place for all workmen. As for his work, there it stands—sturdy, strong, true and fine and most of all free from all the many cheap tricks of our craft. (pp. ix-x)

> *Sherwood Anderson, "Introduction" (reprinted by permission of Harold Ober Associates; copyright © 1918, by Boni & Liveright, Inc.; copyright renewed © 1945 by Theodore Dreiser), in* Free and Other Stories *by Theodore Dreiser (copyright 1918, by Boni & Liveright, Inc.; copyright renewed © 1945 by T. Dreiser), Boni & Liveright, 1918, (and reprinted by Scholarly Press, Inc., 1971), pp. v-x.*

ALEXANDER WOOLLCOTT   (essay date 1919)

[*Woollcott, one of the most distinguished and hard-to-please drama critics of the early twentieth century, has little to say in praise of* The Hand of the Potter.]

"The Hand of the Potter," the tragedy of one marred in the making, is the name of an interesting and occasional dramatic narrative in play form by the author of **"Sister Carrie."** It tells, often in passages of great pathos, the story of a congenital degenerate's helpless battle with a tempting and uncomprehending world into which he does not fit. There is rehearsed then such a squalid and repellent murder as the sensational newspapers gloated over about a decade ago, when the body of little Ruth Wheeler was found.

However, it is not merely the fact that the story is hideous that makes Mr. Dreiser's play in its present form unsuitable for the theatre. It is also because he has written it with the spendthrift novelist's ignorance of the dramatist's enforced economy of means, relying lazily on long and archaic soliloquies to make himself clear, and indulging in his last act in such a symposium of windy and anti-climactic discussion as an older and better playwright named Shaw would have carefully put first and called a preface.

It is conceivable, however, that a neater artisan could prune the play into actable shape. He would begin by lopping off the last act, and it may be said that a play which can lose its last act without regrets is a defective play. The publishers of **"The Hand of the Potter"** bill it somewhat meretriciously as "Stark naked and unashamed"; but it really ought to be ashamed of its last act.

> *Alexander Woollcott, "Hand of the Potter," in* The New York Times Book Review *(© 1919 by the New York Times Company; reprinted by permission), October 26, 1919, p. 598.*

WALDO FRANK   (essay date 1919)

[*Frank's* Our America, *from which the following was excerpted, derided the stuffy "genteel tradition" in American letters. Frank saw Dreiser as an iconoclastic pioneer, who brought honesty and realism into American literature.*]

Perhaps the most majestic monument of this transition by which America needed to journey upward into birth is in the novels of Theodore Dreiser. Dreiser belongs to the same world as [Edgar Lee] Masters. . . . Unlike Masters he has professionally followed writing all his life, and has come East to New York. And yet, deeply, the two are brothers. And deeply, they express a muffled music of which Chicago is the tonal key.

Dreiser is the creator of a hero. Dreiser is a genius of epic reach, even if not of epic texture. . . . A burly giant with a face as tender as a little girl's. A body full of vast desire and a face in love with sweetness. In the disharmony of this, a great grief writ upon his face, and a stern anguish drenching his works.

The hero of Dreiser is the multi-millionaire. He has taken the complacent *pícaro* of the Broadway Play, the child-hero of Horatio Alger's "From Rags to Riches," and reduced him to the spiritual penury that must be his lot in a world full of gold and joyless, pent with activity and void of *being*. This great period of American life—the period which now awakes to the bankruptcy of pioneering—Dreiser has forevermore expressed.

But, like Masters, expressed unconsciously. Masters thought he was depicting life—all life—in his American town. And in reality he portrayed the spiritual dearth of his own outlook. Something was lacking, something that lived in Spoon River but not in Masters. Thus also, Dreiser paints the splendors of a man of might—Titan of Genius—and in sooth pens the confessional of his own failure to find true values of existence in the American world about him.

But the failure leads to an artistic triumph. Out of this spiritual void, Dreiser creates æsthetic *form*. For this inner lack of being, whose unconscious medium he is, is universal; is the pioneer's. This he has fixed and rendered memorable.

The stuff of Dreiser's novels corresponds with amazing clearness to the stuff of our American life. It is unlit and undifferentiated. His books have the crude form of simple massiveness. Some elemental force like Gravity holds them together and propels them. They are not integrated. The artist who is aware of the values of being touches his materials with that awareness and makes them live. Each element of his work will glow with an inner fire, quite as each quality of being is a flame. Such luminosity you will not find in Dreiser. Nor in America. His books move. But they move like herds.

And yet, they are vital. They lack characterization; often they seem, while one is plowing through them, mere heaped obstructions of reiterated incident. But when one has drawn away from them, one senses their slow, organic movement. They have a rhythm, huge, partaking of the Whole, like the rhythm of a glacier. The rhythm of inchoate, undifferentiated life. It is in this virtue that they are most like the American world.

Dreiser's principal hero, Frank Cowperwood, is like Dreiser's books and like his land. He does not seem to grow. He is not organic to that extent. Rather, he *accumulates*. He does not progress. He merely stirs. He is a reservoir of power, without synthesis of choice. . . . He never changes. For experience alone can change. And experience is precisely what he never reaches. He is like a molecule of matter that moves unaltered through eternity. Combining now with this being, now with that: but still the irrepressible and inalterable unit.

At the end of the excursions of his heroes, the sense of Emptiness weighs upon Dreiser. And, like Masters, he transfers this sense upon the world. Many of his novels end with metaphysical abstractions: protests of life against this void of being. The truth is, that lacking the virtue of experience, the measure of subjective being, Dreiser, filling his books with incident and facts, fills them only with symbols of vacuity. His Genius, Eugene Witla, goes through the welter of the world like a runner through a haystack. Come out at the other end, he shakes himself and looks at the daughter whom accident has somehow dropped into his hands, with a creeping sense of unreality. Witla has been a famous painter, a king of the publishing world, a failure, a laborer, a lover. But he has never for a moment created life out of the kaleidoscope of these occurrings. He has done everything: *been* not at all. No wonder he looks up at the stars like a lost lamb and unconsciously pleads for the warm flock.

In this longing, the Genius betrays the author. Dreiser, deep in his soul, yearns for the gods he has flung away: for the sweet comfort of a myth. If his Desire could face the actual world, it would soon warm it and make it glow. And since it does not, the cause can only be that it is facing elsewhere. Like the generation which he best expresses, Theodore Dreiser has cut away from the tradition and worship of the American past, only at the expense of the emotional energy which made that tradition and that worship live. The stuff of his books is not in flame, because the fire of his own soul is not free to ignite it. He is still caught in his own past.

From this circumstance, moreover, we may understand why Dreiser and Masters and their brothers spend such vehemence in attack upon the Past from which they should be free. They are not free. They attack because the Past is still so emotionally real; because it holds them back from full bestowal upon the Present. . . . The protest of Dreiser against American ghosts shows how fearfully America is still haunted by them. Masters' absorption in classical forms and classical allusions, Dreiser's rapt interest in the scientific formulae which twenty years ago seemed to promise a substitute for the vision of Genesis, point to their ancient yearnings.

The Past is still with us in this land. At best, the Present is a feeble growth. Dreiser and Masters mark the transition of revolt. They have denied the old gods. But we shall not be free of the old, till we have found the new. (pp. 129-33)

> *Waldo Frank, "Chicago," in his* Our America *(reprinted by permission of Liveright Publishing Corporation; copyright, 1919, by Boni & Liveright, Inc.;*

copyright renewed 1947 by Waldo Frank), Boni & Liveright, 1919, pp. 117-47.*

CLARENCE DARROW (essay date 1926)

[*Darrow, the famous criminal lawyer, offers high praise for* An American Tragedy.]

I finished Theodore Dreiser's latest story just before going to bed last night. I assume that I must have had some sleep during the troubled hours through which I tossed and dreamed after laying it down. But the haunted face of a helpless boy, strapped to an iron chair at Sing Sing, and the wan form of a dead girl floating on a lonely black lake surrounded by tall pine trees in Northern New York still were haunting me when I awoke. I presume the feeling will slowly fade from my consciousness and be blended with the other experiences, painful and pleasant, which make up life. I hardly can think of the eight hundred pages of **"An American Tragedy"** as a book. It does not leave the impression that goes with reading a story; the feeling is rather that of a series of terrible physical impacts that have relentlessly shocked every sensitive nerve in the body. (p. 1)

One who knows Dreiser's work could almost see the end from the beginning. One's feelings of resentment are almost turned from Clyde to Dreiser, who, with the relentlessness of fate and the logic of life, takes Clyde step by step from the city mission to the electric chair, and Roberta from the factory to the embraces of the deep, cold waters of the lake; and still one cannot get away from the fact that it is a true story of countless victims of fate.

"An American Tragedy" is a somber, gruesome tale. It is not relieved by a single flash of color or light of joy. Dreiser carries the story straight, honest and true to the inevitable end. One thing, at least, is sure: it is deadly interesting from the beginning to the last word. One hardly stops to realize that he is gripped in the hands of a master. Such a master of technique and tragedy as the world has seldom known. One is not reading; he is living—and dying! He is held in a spell from the first page to the eight hundred and thirty-fifth. When he has finished the book it lingers and haunts and plays with his emotions as few books have ever done.

Whether this book will sell, I cannot guess. In this weary world people want to be amused. They like pleasant pictures, however fantastic or impossible they may be. They do not dare to look at life. Mr. Dreiser will not lie. He will not use his marvelous powers to trick, deceive and please.

It is useless to discuss what form art should take. This depends on the artist. The crowd will turn to Harold Bell Wright and the rest. They wish to be fed on lies. Mr. Dreiser could no doubt do this if he would. For his honesty and fidelity the world will never give him a cash return. He must know this better than any one else. "One cannot eat his cake and keep it too." Even though Mr. Dreiser may live and die poor and neglected; even though his art and work may be criticized and derided, still that part of the public which thinks and feels will understand his fanatical devotion to truth and will recognize Mr. Dreiser as one of the few real writers who has never wavered nor been afraid; and he will one day be acknowledged one of the master artists of the world. (p. 2)

> *Clarence Darrow, "Touching a Terrible Tragedy,"*
> *in* The Literary Review *(copyright, 1926, by N.Y.*

Evening Post, Inc.; reprinted from The New York Post*), January 16, 1926, pp. 1-2.*

WILLIAM LYON PHELPS   (essay date 1926)

[*Phelps attacks* An American Tragedy, *providing criticism similar to that Stuart P. Sherman had earlier offered of* The "Genius" *(see excerpt above).*]

And now let me tackle that two-handed engine of naturalism, Theodore Dreiser's **"An American Tragedy"** where we follow the fortunes of a nincompoop from childhood to the chair. What A. E. Housman told in a page Mr. Dreiser tells in two volumes. Yet his steam-roller method gains, I suppose, by crushing out all this accumulated mass of detail. The style is clumsy and awkward; it has as much grace as an ichthyosaurus in a quagmire. But it is all true, unanswerably true. It is the naturalistic method of Zola. And if the novelist chooses to select from life a hero without brains or backbone or charm, and depict his unimportant career with patient microscopy, and bring in hosts of other characters none of whom one would ever wish to know in real life, that is his own affair. There are plenty of such persons and I suppose they spend their days in the manner herein described. One may justly admire Mr. Dreiser for sticking to his own theory of art, and for his dogged and truth-loving patience not in writing jewels five words long, but in scraping together pebbles and more pebbles.

It is properly called an American tragedy not because of the unfortunate career of this particular protagonist, but because he represents many Americans who lead equally tragic lives although not meeting an equally tragic end. The very commonplaceness of the vast number of characters in this story makes their representative quality more depressingly impressive. They are, alas, samples.

Yet it is strange that in this work and in others of the same author there should apparently be no hint that every town in America contains individuals of nobility, unselfishness, and idealism, people of intellect, resolution, and charm, who find and help to make life a splendid adventure.

The last thing Mr. Dreiser would wish to be called is a moralist or a preacher; yet this vast book resembles not a little the obvious sermon of Hogarth's Idle Apprentice.

It is quite easy for me to see and feel the qualities emphasized by his adorers, such as Mr. H. L. Mencken, Mr. Burton Rascoe, and the latest convert, Mr. Stuart Sherman. I remain outside this kneeling group, sceptical and unconvinced. For two reasons:

First, all great novels should have the element of transfiguration. People who are poor in health and brains and money may still be rich in significance. It would not be fair to compare Mr. Dreiser with Dickens; but it is easy to imagine how splendidly Dickens, with a knowledge of the seamy side of life fully equal to the American's, and with as much studiously realistic detail, would nevertheless have breathed into this ash-heap such a glow of life that it would have made a conflagration unquenchable by time. It would not be fair to compare Mr. Dreiser with Dickens, because Dickens was a man of genius. Let us then compare him with Mr. Arnold Bennett, who has perhaps no genius, but who is a literary expert, who has mastered the art of the novel, who is a shrewd, hard-bitten man of the world, and who loves life with a fervor both chronic and passionate. Compare **"An American Tragedy"** with ''The Old Wives'

Tale,'' or with ''Riceyman Steps.'' Mr. Bennett has transfigured the lives of the commonplace and of the downtrodden with a veritable glow of creative power, with the gift that belongs only to the true artist. Now if Henry James complained that Arnold Bennett's novels were simply an accumulation of bricks without ultimate significance, if what should have been the means had become the end, what would he say to **"An American Tragedy"**?

Furthermore, the great preservative is *style*. There *is* a literary standard, there is a difference between good writing and bad. I cannot believe that this work, hampered by such clumsy composition, will be read in the next century. To use William Sharp's phrase, it will float around awhile, a colossal derelict on the ocean of literature, and will eventually sink. (pp. 433-34)

William Lyon Phelps, "As I Like It," in Scribner's Magazine *(copyright 1926 by Charles Scribner's Sons; renewal copyright 1954; reprinted by permission of Charles Scribner's Sons), Vol. LXXIX, No. 4, April, 1926, pp. 431-38.**

ARNOLD BENNETT   (essay date 1926)

[*Bennett, one of Dreiser's most important English critics, provides a generally admiring appraisal of* An American Tragedy, *citing it as one of the greatest books published during 1926.*]

At the end of the year 1926 I recall that the most important large works of imagination which I have read in 1926 are both American. (p. 302)

The first of the two works . . . is Theodore Dreiser's *An American Tragedy*. (p. 303)

I am not going to recommend *An American Tragedy* to all and sundry dilettante and plain people. It is of tremendous length. It is written abominably, by a man who evidently despises style, elegance, clarity, even grammar. Dreiser simply does not know how to write, never did know, never wanted to know. Dreiser would sneer at Nathaniel Hawthorne, a writer of some of the loveliest English ever printed.

For this and other reasons he is difficult to read. He makes no compromise with the reader. Indeed, to read Dreiser with profit you must take your coat off to it, you must go down on your knees to it, you must up hands and say ''I surrender.'' And Dreiser will spit on you for a start.

But once you have fairly yielded to him he will reward you—yes, though his unrelenting grip should squeeze the life out of you. *An American Tragedy* is prodigious. Its characteristics are an absolutely fearless adherence to truth and a terrific imaginative power. Some pages are more exciting than others, but the sheer power is continuous in its spell; it never relaxes; it goes on and on; Dreiser determined to omit nothing at all, until the devastating end.

The story is the same old story that Dreiser has told again and again, the story of the passionate man determined to possess the woman whom society and his conscience utterly forbid to him; the background, a panorama of American life. Such stories are bound to be gloomy if honestly told. *An American Tragedy* is saved from depressingness, as every sound, sad tale is saved, by its beauty; but here the beauty is frightening, especially towards the close.

Twenty-six years have passed since I reviewed Dreiser's *Sister Carrie* with enthusiasm. *Sister Carrie* was marred by sentimentality. Dreiser is an intermittent creator. For ten years after *Sister Carrie* he produced nothing notable. Then *Jennie Gerhardt;* fine. Then *The Financier, The Titan,* and *The Genius,* quickly one after another—all long books. Of these *The Financier* is magnificent, the other two unsatisfactory. And now *An American Tragedy* has had an overwhelming popular success in The United States. I doubt whether any English novel so critical, so unsparing, so clumsy, and so sad, could have one quarter of such success in Britain. (pp. 304-05)

> *Arnold Bennett, "Books of the Year" (originally published in the* London Evening Standard, *December 30, 1926), in his* The Savour of Life: Essays in Gusto *(copyright © 1928 by Doubleday & Company, Inc.; reprinted by permission of the publisher), Doubleday, 1928, pp. 293-313.**

THEODORE DREISER   (letter date 1927)

[*Dreiser explains the purpose of* An American Tragedy.]

[In] so far as it is possible to explain the genesis of any creative idea, I shall be glad to tell you how *An American Tragedy* came to be.

I had long brooded upon the story, for it seemed to me not only to include every phase of our national life—politics, society, religion, business, sex—but it was a story so common to every boy reared in the smaller towns of America. It seemed so truly a story of what life does to the individual—and how impotent the individual is against such forces. My purpose was not to moralize—God forbid—but to give, if possible, a background and a psychology of reality which would somehow explain, if not condone, how such murders happen—and they have happened with surprising frequency in America as long as I can remember. (pp. 457-58)

> *Theodore Dreiser, in his letter to Jack Wilgus on April 20, 1927, in* Letters of Theodore Dreiser: A Selection, Vol. 2, *edited by Robert H. Elias (© 1959 by the Trustees of the University of Pennsylvania), University of Pennsylvania Press, 1959, pp. 457-58.*

G. K. CHESTERTON   (essay date 1929)

[*In what is primarily a discussion of the proper role and function of the literary critic, Chesterton offers some criticism of Dreiser's philosophy as he perceives it.*]

I dare say a great deal of the criticism I write really is moved by a mood of self-expression; and certainly it is true enough that there is a satisfaction in self-expression. I can take something or other about which I have definite feelings—as, for instance, the philosophy of Mr. Dreiser. . . . I can achieve for my own inner ego the grateful feeling of writing as follows:

"He describes a world which appears to be a dull and discoloring illusion of indigestion, not bright enough to be called a nightmare; smelly, but not even stinking with any strength; smelling of the stale gas of ignorant chemical experiments by dirty, secretive schoolboys—the sort of boys who torture cats in corners; spineless and spiritless like a broken-backed worm; loathsomely slow and laborious like an endless slug; despairing, but not with dignity; blaspheming, but not with courage; without wit, without will, without laughter or uplifting of the

heart; too old to die, too deaf to leave off talking, too blind to stop, too stupid to start afresh, too dead to be killed, and incapable even of being damned, since in all its weary centuries it has not reached the age of reason."

That is what I feel about it; and it certainly gives me pleasure to relieve my feelings. I have got it off my chest. (p. 67)

But what influence my feelings can be expected to have on Mr. Dreiser, or anybody who does not admit my standards of truth and falsehood, I do not quite see. Mr. Dreiser can hardly be expected to say that his chemistry is quackery, as I think it—quackery without the liveliness we might reasonably expect from quacks. He does not think fatalism base and servile, as I do; he does not think free will the highest truth about humanity, as I do. He does not believe that despair is itself a sin, and perhaps the worst of sins, as Catholics do. He does not think blasphemy the smallest and silliest sort of pride, as even pagans do. He naturally does not think his own picture of life a false picture, resembling real life about as much as a wilderness of linoleum would resemble the land of all the living flowers, as I do. He would not think it falser for being like a wilderness. He would probably admit that it was dreary, but think it correct to be dreary. He would probably own that he was hopeless, but not see any harm in being hopeless. What I advance as accusations, he would very probably accept as compliments.

Under these circumstances, I do not quite see how I, or anyone with my views, could have a *controversy* with Mr. Dreiser. There does not seem to be any way in which I could prove him wrong, because he does not accept my view of what is wrong. There does not seem to be any way in which he could prove himself right, because I do not share his notions of what is right. We might indeed meet in the street and fall on each other; and while I believe we are both heavy men, I doubt not that he is the more formidable. (pp. 67-8)

> *G. K. Chesterton, "The Skeptic As a Critic," in* The Forum *(copyright, 1929, by Events Publishing Company, Inc.), Vol. LXXXI, No. 2, February, 1929, pp. 65-9.*

JAMES BRANCH CABELL   (essay date 1930)

[*Cabell sarcastically applauds the would-be censors of Dreiser's works for bringing them to public attention.*]

I perceive some merit in Theodore Dreiser. Yet it is his luck which just now the more irresistibly woos my fancy—that irrational bit of luck which he has shared with others among the deciduous writers of the 'twenties. I mean, that more than once Mr. Dreiser has attracted the highly remunerative disfavor of those patrolmen of our literary morals who have also intermeddled at odd times with the work of Sherwood Anderson. (p. 77)

[Now] and then, as in the cases of Messrs. Dreiser and Anderson, the censor advertises a performance which merits assistance. Just now and then he averts from his daily fodder of the childishly salacious, and he gives over his innocent playing with rubber toys and picture post cards, so that he may cast the lime-light of moral reprobation upon a bit of sincere and talented writing. He then finds readers for his protégé where unaided merit could find none. He furthermore displays then, in his every act and speech, such fathomless asininity as provokes our instant championship for anyone whom he asperses. He is then entitled to our fervent applause.

I for one applaud even in the teeth of much which I myself have written at odd times. For here, I am afraid, in the novels of Sherwood Anderson and of Theodore Dreiser, is "realism" reasonably naked and unabashed; and my lack of love for "realism" has been expressed in several thousand pages. Yet here also is honesty; here is frankness; here is human tolerance: and these three one respects perforce. When a helping hand toward public applause is proffered to these three by the prude's dishonesty and by that wincing intolerance of all frankness which (through motives howsoever genuine) the censor embodies, then the considerate cannot but be delighted. (pp. 84-5)

> *James Branch Cabell, "Protégés of the Censor," in his* Some of Us: An Essay in Epitaphs *(copyright, 1930, copyright renewed © 1958, by James Branch Cabell; reprinted by permission of the Literary Estate of James Branch Cabell), Robert M. McBride & Company, 1930, pp. 77-88.**

DOROTHY PARKER   (essay date 1931)

[*Parker provides a stinging review of* Dawn *and attacks Dreiser's style.*]

There are times when images blow to fluff, and comparisons stiffen and shrivel. Such an occasion is surely at hand when one is confronted by Dreiser's latest museum piece, **"Dawn."** One can but revise a none-too-hot dialectic of childhood; ask, in rhetorical agressiveness, "What writes worse than a Theodore Dreiser?"; loudly crow the answer, "*Two* Theodore Dreisers"; and, according to temperament, rejoice at the merciful absurdity of the conception, or shudder away from the thought.

The reading of **"Dawn"** is a strain upon many parts, but the worst wear and tear fall on the forearms. After holding the massive volume for the half-day necessary to its perusal (well, look at that, would you? "Massive volume" and "perusal," one right after the other! You see how contagious Mr. D.'s manner is?) my arms ached with a slow, mean persistence beyond the services of aspirin or of liniment. I must file this distress, I suppose, under the head of "Occupational Diseases"; for I could not honestly chalk up such a result against "Pleasure" or even "Improvement." And I can't truly feel that **"Dawn"** was worth it. If I must have aches, I had rather gain them in the first tennis of the season, and get my back into it.

This present Dreiser book is the record of its author's first twenty years. It requires five hundred and eighty-nine long, wide, and closely printed pages. Nearly six hundred sheets to the title of **"Dawn"**; God help us one and all if Mr. Dreiser ever elects to write anything called "June Twenty-First"!

The actual account of the writer's early life, and of the lives of his mother, his father, and his nine brothers and sisters which colored and crossed it, is wholly absorbing; but, if I may say so, without that lightning bolt coming barging in the window, what honest setting-down of anyone's first years would not be? (pp. 600-01)

Nor should I cavil at the length, and hence the weight, of the book, were it all given over to memories, since if a man were to write down his remembrances and his impressions up to the age of five, much less of twenty, six hundred pages could not begin to contain them. But I do fret, through **"Dawn,"** at the great desert patches of Mr. Dreiser's moralizing, I do chafe at such monstrous bad writing as that with which he pads out his tale. I have read reviews of this book, written by those whose days are dedicated to literature. "Of course," each one says airily, "Dreiser writes badly," and thus they dismiss that tiny fact, and go off into their waltz-dream. . . .

But on second thinking, I dare to differ more specifically from the booksie-wooksies. It is of not such small importance to me that Theodore Dreiser writes in so abominable a style. He is regarded, and I wish you could gainsay me, as one of our first contemporary authors; it is the first job of a writer who demands rating among the great, or even among the good, to write well. If he fails that, as Mr. Dreiser, by any standard, so widely muffs it, he is, I think, unequipped to stand among the big.

For years, you see, I have been crouching in corners hissing small and ladylike anathema of Theodore Dreiser. I dared not yip it out loud, much less offer it up in print. But now, what with a series of events that have made me callous to anything that may later occur, I have become locally known as the What-the-Hell Girl of 1931. In that, my character, I may say that to me Dreiser is a dull, pompous, dated, and darned near ridiculous writer. All right. Go on and bring on your lightning bolts. (p. 601)

The booksy ones, with that butterfly touch of theirs, flutter away from Dreiser's bad writing and but brush their wings over the admission that he possesses no humor. . . . I am unable to feel that a writer can be complete without humor. And I don't mean by that, and you know it perfectly well, the creation or the appreciation of things comic. I mean that the possession of a sense of humor entails the sense of selection, the civilized fear of going too far. A little humor leavens the lump, surely, but it does more than that. It keeps you, from your respect for the humor of others, from making a dull jackass of yourself. Humor, imagination, and manners are pretty fairly interchangeably interwoven.

Mr. Theodore Dreiser has no humor.

I know that Mr. Dreiser is sincere, or rather I have been told it enough to impress me. So, I am assured, is Mrs. Kathleen Norris sincere; so, I am informed, is Mr. Zane Grey sincere; so, I am convinced, was Mr. Horatio Alger—whose work, to me, that of Mr. Dreiser's nearest approximates—sincere. But I will not—oh, come on with your lightning again!—admit that sincerity is the only thing. A good thing, a high thing, an admirable thing; but not the only thing in letters.

The thing that most distressed me in **"Dawn"** was the philosophising of its author. His is a sort of pre-war bitterness, a sort of road-company anger at conditions. (p. 602)

I think that Mr. Dreiser believes that the world is backward, hypocritical, and mean, and so, I suppose, it is; but times have changed and Mr. D. is not now the only advanced one. . . .

Early in this little dandy, you saw that I had been affected by the Dreiser style. That, maybe, is responsible for this plethora of words. I could have checked all this torrent, and given you a true idea of Theodore Dreiser's **"Dawn"** had I but succumbed to the influence of the present-day Nash and the sweeter-day Bentley, and had written:

> Theodore Dreiser
> Should ought to write nicer.
>
> (p. 603)

Dorothy Parker, "Reading and Writing: Words, Words, Words," in The New Yorker *(© 1931 by The New Yorker Magazine, Inc.), Vol. 7, No. 15, May 30, 1931 (and reprinted as her review of "Dawn," in* Theodore Dreiser: The Critical Reception, *edited by Jack Salzman, David Lewis, 1972, pp. 600-03).*

JOSEPH WARREN BEACH (essay date 1932)

[Beach discusses the characteristics of Dreiser's work in the following overview.]

One of the strongest of influences leading to the breakup of the well-made novel, at least in America, has been the movement toward extreme realism. This movement dates back into the nineteenth century, at least as early as Stephen Crane's "Maggie, a Girl of the Streets" (1893) and "The Red Badge of Courage" (1896). Its main exponent in the present century is Theodore Dreiser, whose career as a novelist is exactly contemporary with Edith Wharton's, **"Sister Carrie"** appearing in 1900 and **"An American Tragedy"** in 1925. Mr. Dreiser does not give the impression of being an author greatly concerned with questions of form as such; and if his novels constitute a reaction against the conventional pattern of the well-made novel, this is incidental. They are fundamentally a reaction against conventional ways of regarding human nature. They are one continuous protest against the prime assumptions of the genteel novel. (p. 321)

In the genteel novel the fact of wealth and social position is something taken for granted, something to start with, and carrying with it the notion of a certain degree of refinement, an ordered social status and a fixed standard of personal conduct. And all that remains is to plan out the social comedies and sentimental dramas suitable for production on this narrow stage. But Mr. Dreiser was born into a world in which none of these things was established. He was born into it and was himself a part of it. . . . (p. 322)

It was made up of men and women starting poor, vulgar, ignorant, emotionally starved, but—so far as they were strong—determined to win for themselves wealth, luxury, culture, social estimation, and the gratifications of love. They were not snobs—that was not at all the way they appealed to Theodore Dreiser—they were simply vital forces pushing forward irrepressibly to take their place in the sun. All about them were swarming millions of their kind, through the milling jam of whom they must force their way forward. The methods were the age-old methods of competitive business, never before perhaps displayed on so grand a scale as in the America of Dreiser's time: tireless work, organization, speculation, coöperation with those who can aid you, abandonment of those who cannot serve you, political graft and intimidation. The mental equipment was imagination, feline cunning, the gambling instinct, indomitable courage. . . . The race was to the strong.

Meantime the weak were striving, in their own ineffectual way, for much the same prizes—conceived with less imagination and pursued with less perseverance and ruthlessness. Most were doomed to envious mediocrity, and many heedless ones were destined to be caught in the toils of the law (Clyde Griffiths in **"An American Tragedy,"** Stener in **"The Financier"**) or to ignominious defeat and death (Hurstwood in **"Sister Carrie"**). (p. 323)

In his attitude toward this jungle life of human beings, Mr. Dreiser is not a satirist. He has neither the genial irony of a Thackeray nor the often smart and brittle mockery of a Sinclair Lewis. He is in deadly earnest. He does not take a tone of superiority or set himself apart from his characters. He does not regard them as philistines or as sinners. These people are, one feels, very much the sort he takes himself to be, with the same problems, ambitions, cravings, discouragements. And whether they are winners or losers in the struggle, he is pretty closely in sympathy with them, even though, in his wider vision, he may see them in their littleness, helplessness, and futility. . . . His tone is that of a brooding, compassionate, philosophical observer.

So far as there is a note of criticism in his picture, it is in reference to judgments and standards which he regards as conventional, artificial, and often—as he seems to imply—hypocritical. The one thing that moves him to impatience is the genteel assumption of the prevalence in society of standards which *do not prevail*, and the easy relegation to the background of selfish types of behavior which seem to him well-nigh universal. His great motivating passion as a writer is simply to tell the truth. Or to put it the other way round, his passion is to give the lie to the prevailing idealistic assumptions of fiction of his day in English. (p. 324)

Dreiser's realism does not exhaust itself upon the general outlines of action and motivation. There is plenty left over for the minutest details of psychology. Here again his aim is not to conventionalize, to simplify in the direction either of prettiness or meanness, but merely to record the natural facts of the case, without exaggeration or extenuation. (p. 325)

The genteel tradition Dreiser pushes aside altogether and goes straight back, for his models, to Balzac and perhaps the later French naturalists. His effort is to vision society not from the standpoint of a clique, but with the broad comprehensive view of a scientific observer, outside of all cliques and patterned societies. If I suggest a possible inspiration from the French naturalists, it is because his work is strongly colored by the terminology and deterministic assumptions of nineteenth-century science, which were so strong an element in Zola and his group. But it may have been direct from science, rather than from literature, that Dreiser took his disposition to regard human behavior as one manifestation of animal behavior in general, or even—to use his more frequently recurring term—as a chemical phenomenon. (pp. 325-26)

What is important, however, is not to point out the relative crudeness and exaggeration of Dreiser's realistic philosophy, but to emphasize what he has in common with the great French novelists—his fearlessness, his honesty, his determination to have done with conventional posturings and evasions. It was extremely important that we should have some one bold enough to set down in the English language just as he saw it the unvarnished truth about American business life, American social life in its major reaches, and the sex-psychology of American men and women. And every serious writer of the present day is deeply under obligation to the brave pioneering of Theodore Dreiser. It is he, more than any other writer, who has borne the brunt and odium of this ungrateful task. And he it is who should have the praise.

When we turn from the consideration of substance and ask what Mr. Dreiser has done for the novel as an art form, it is first to be noted of course that, if he has given adequate expression to his thought, he has met at least the minimum requirements of shaping art. And then it must be added that he has made no specific original contribution to novelistic technique, and is not among the most skilful of novelists when it comes to nice points of craftsmanship.

His books are solidly built around a central idea. They are documented in a manner worthy of his admired Balzac and even suggestive of the more colossal structures of Zola. (p. 327)

In two instances he has succeeded in giving a notably dramatic cast to his huge and copious material. **"The Financier"** is largely built round the great financial panic of 1871 following on the Chicago fire. . . . Another equally striking example is that part of **"An American Tragedy"** dealing with Clyde Griffith's murder of his sweetheart Roberta, which again, if we take into account the circumstances immediately leading to the crime, the detective work, the trail, the appeal, and the execution of Clyde, occupies considerably more than half of the story. All things considered, **"An American Tragedy"** is doubtless the most neatly constructed of all Dreiser's novels, as well as the best written. And it is always a satisfaction to find that an artist is gaining rather than losing with the passage of the years.

The solid documentation, which suggests Balzac, suggests a defect in technique which is even greater in Dreiser than it is in the French writer. He relies too much on formal exposition. (p. 328)

Again, he does not know how to get from one moment in his story to a later moment without giving an extensive summary of what was going on in the interval. In **"The Titan"** and **"The Genius"** chapter after chapter is given up to such perfunctory summaries, in which there is nothing to sustain us but the memory that there have been interesting times before and probably are interesting times ahead. (p. 329)

Mr. Dreiser, in short, is singularly defective in the faculty for conceiving his story in scenes. He has taken seriously his philosophic obligation to tell the truth, but has thought very little of his artistic obligation to "make us see." He is entirely innocent of any intention concerning point of view. He keeps himself, on the whole, pretty well out of the story. But he seldom considers from page to page whose story it now is. Whatever needs explaining must be explained at the moment it comes into his head, without regard to whether or not it will spoil an intimate effect for the imagination or the feeling. That is, his approach to his art is almost exclusively intellectual. He has so much matter to deliver from his mind to the reader's mind. For the reader's imagination he has no care. In keeping with his indifference to the scenical, he has no conception of what a chapter may mean in the way of imaginative composition of subject-matter. His chapters are chronological rag-bags rather than the imaginative units which Zola's chapters, for example, are.

His handling of dialogue is typical of his want of concern for the niceties of writing. Dialogue is one way of enlivening exposition, and he used it with the average frequency of serious writers. Of course there are moments of dramatic confrontation and struggle in which it would be practically impossible to avoid the spoken word. There is nothing remarkable about his dialogue. He is a plain realist, and does not attempt to make his people's talk pointed or witty. Neither does he attempt to signalize it as commonplace or vulgar. It is commonplace, but without intention. It is not slangy, racy, colloquial. It is ordinary speech, but without any special notation of the rhythms of ordinary speech. (pp. 329-30)

Much fault has been found by critics with Mr. Dreiser's style, and I do not mean to add anything here on that ungrateful subject. Only this: His style is all of a piece with his general want of concern for imaginative writing as such. As wholes, his books are of extreme interest because of the large spirit, the passionate intelligence which informs them. His writing does not bear too close inspection in detail, because he has not approached it with an esthetic intention. His people are true like historical personages. Intellectually we believe in them. We are certainly interested in them. We want to know how their stories come out. As imaginative creations, with some exceptions (Hurstwood, Jennie Gerhardt), they scarcely exist, and they move through scenes that scarcely exist, however conscientiously built up. There are in his books no *belles pages*, no enchanting moments, no passages that thrill us with minute precision of rightness, such as abound in Hardy, Gorki, Maupassant, Hudson, Thomas Mann.

For all that, he is one of the strongest forces tending to antiquate the well-made novel . . . and that *because of what he has to say*.

Dreiser is very unlike the new men, the modernists. He shows no interest in technical experiments and inventions. He makes no attempt to add a fourth dimension to the three dimensions of plain realism. He tells a simple story, straight forward. He is scarcely more interested in psychology as such than is Hardy. Like Hardy—much more than Hardy—he is literal, matter-of-fact, extravert, moving in a world of "substantial things." The lives of his people are made up of what they do and what happens to them. In his books there is no psychopathic divorce between thought and action, between motive and behavior. Compared with the new men, the generation of Joyce, he is a classical figure. (pp. 330-31)

Joseph Warren Beach, "The Realist Reaction: Dreiser," in his The Twentieth Century Novel: Studies in Technique *(© 1932, renewed 1960; adapted by permission of Prentice-Hall, Inc., Englewood Cliffs, New Jersey 07632), Appleton-Century-Crofts, Inc., 1932, pp. 321-31.*

GRANVILLE HICKS (essay date 1935)

[Hicks perceives the honesty and sheer power of Dreiser's works to be the hallmark of the author's genius.]

[Dreiser] had none of the faith in social reform that was hesitant in Norris, intermittent in London, and ineradicable in Upton Sinclair. He had studied the materialists too well to be able to justify any hope for mankind. But their honest contemplation of facts, however unpleasant, inspired in him a determination to be equally honest in recording the life about him.

Sister Carrie is the work of a bewildered man, willing to admit he is bewildered. One feels the man in the book, asking questions he cannot answer, recording his confusion, shaking his head with weary resignation over the course of his tale. One feels his effort, as he laboriously amasses detail, as he clumsily probes into motives, as he ponderously gropes for words. And one feels his honesty, his determination to present life exactly as he sees it. He may not approve of the deeds he describes; often he expresses his disapproval in ways that show how imperfectly he has conquered the prejudices of his boyhood; but the desire to understand triumphs over conventional morality, and the story of Carrie, Drouet, and Hurstwood is inexorably unfolded. One cries out against the author's clumsiness, his sheer stupidity, and yet one surrenders to his honesty and acknowledges in the end that he is a master. In *Sister Carrie* Dreiser not only shattered, in a single aimless gesture, a score of sacred conventions; he created living men and women in a world we recognize as ours.

It is a passion for truth, lodged in the deepest stratum of Dreiser's mind, operating in spite of conflicting interests, that gives his work its importance. *Sister Carrie* and *Jennie Gerhardt* came out of his observations, and in them he showed what happened to lower middle-class American families such as the Dreisers. For *The Financier* and *The Titan* he had to rely largely on research, but he succeeded in creating such a figure as had not previously appeared in our literature, a man of lusts so fierce that the ruthlessness of Van Harrington or John Barclay or Burning Daylight seems almost amiable by comparison, a man worthy of the exploits attributed to him. In each of his six novels Dreiser has touched the fundamental forces that shape American life. Whether he deals with poor girls who stray from the path of conventional virtue or with millionaires who dominate cities, whether he portrays the struggles of an artist or the tragedy of a factory-hand, he makes us feel the importance of his people because he shows us the forces that work through them. Despite innumerable faults, his six massive novels, built on the rocks of honesty and pity, stand while the works of shrewder architects crumble. (pp. 227-29)

> *Granville Hicks, "Two Roads," in his* The Great Tradition: An Interpretation of American Literature since the Civil War *(copyright © 1933, 1935 by Macmillan Publishing Co., Inc.; copyright © 1969 by Granville Hicks; reprinted by permission of Russell & Volkening, Inc., as agent for the author), revised edition, Macmillan, 1935, pp. 207-56.**

J. DONALD ADAMS (essay date 1944)

[*Adams, like T.K. Whipple (see bibliography), finds Dreiser's importance in the development of American fiction to be chiefly historical.*]

[Theodore Dreiser's] role in the development of American fiction was historically an important one, and it would be folly to minimize it. Better writers followed him who are in his debt for the courage and determination with which he fought his long battle against those who would have denied literature the freedom to range at will over the various levels of human life. So, too, it is only just to grant that, whatever may be lacking in Dreiser's novels, life itself is in them, however crudely and shortsightedly it is observed. They do not offer us the "smiling aspects" which Howells preferred as the "more truly American"; they are simply another part of the picture of which neither man painted the whole.

But if Dreiser contributed much to the widening of our literary boundaries, if he brought depth as well as scope to his writing, he also failed completely to bring to it elevation. His touch was heavy and earth-bound, and too many younger writers fell into step with his plodding gait. They did not copy his style, for, as even the least skilled could see, there was nothing there to emulate. . . . (p. 54)

Nor was it simply by his execrable craftsmanship, his stumbling, muddled, heavy-footed prose, that Dreiser failed as an artist. He could not think, and his lack of clarity and logic was not compensated for, as it sometimes is, by the power of intuition. Of the three great clarities—clarity of purpose, clarity of thought, and clarity of expression—Dreiser had only the first. His thinking is as heavy and confused as his prose.

All Dreiser's faults and limitations as an artist, as well as his shortcomings as a reflective observer of life—for his perception and handling of human relations were frequently weak—are plainly to be seen in the book which is commonly regarded as his masterpiece. *An American Tragedy,* which appeared in 1925, was the last book of consequence he published. The style had gained nothing over that of *Sister Carrie,* published a quarter of a century before; the one is as inept and fumbling, as weighted with banality, as the other. There is still no selective sense, no mastery of emphasis; like a powerful steam shovel, Dreiser's book scoops up in its capacious jaws everything that has the remotest bearing on the tale he has set himself to tell, and spews it forth again, still jumbled and indiscriminate.

What then, of its content? . . . Dreiser found the material from which he evolved his theme in the newspaper accounts of a trial for murder. That, certainly, is not to his discredit; a writer takes his material where he finds it, and shapes it to his purpose. Dostoevsky, surely one of the world's major novelists, more than once used a similar source. Dreiser's essential failure lies in his incapacity to transmute the material he had absorbed. He shovels it into the furnace of his creative energy, burning with the slow, steady heat of that human sympathy and compassion which, with his sincerity, are his finest qualities, and the product issues forth, not as shining and tempered steel, but as a dull and amorphous metal.

Dreiser took the bare bones of the sordid story set forth in the trial of Chester Gillette for the murder of Grace Brown in 1906 and, as his title indicates, tried so to expand and interpret the facts as to make a drama which could be regarded as typical of life in the United States, and which would have the dignity and inevitability associated with the proper use of the word "tragedy." I realize that I am one of a perhaps small minority in maintaining that he failed to do this. . . . (pp. 55-6)

In *An American Tragedy* Chester Gillette becomes Clyde Griffiths, and Grace Brown becomes Roberta Alden. In describing the childhood of his protagonist, Dreiser, as any reader of his autobiographical work is aware, draws heavily upon the experiences and yearnings of his own early years. He, like Clyde, grew up in poverty, amid drab surroundings; he, too, was negatively conditioned by a fanatically religious parent—in Dreiser's case, his father; in Clyde's, his mother. And here, at the outset, there is, I think, a fundamental flaw in Dreiser's psychology: a boy will resist and react against the excessive piety of his father much more readily than against that of his mother, just as a girl will submit more easily to the male parent's will. If Dreiser had given Clyde a conditioning paralleling his own in this respect, the boy's failure to absorb into his nature the moral stamina which his mother had, and tried to build in him, would have been more convincing. . . .

Like Clyde, the youthful Dreiser hungered for luxury and social position, and he endowed the boy with the same fickleness toward the opposite sex that he had observed in himself. He gave him the same shallow and trivial set of values, the same awe in the presence of material comfort. . . . (p. 57)

Young Clyde was to ditch the sweet and trusting little factory girl, whom he had made pregnant, when the glamorous Sondra Finchley and the dazzling world in which she moved came within his reach; he was carefully and coolly to plot her death by drowning when she had become an insuperable obstacle to the things he craved. (Dreiser emphasizes in his telling of the tale that the actual capsizing of the boat was an accident, while at the same time he tells us how the girl's frantic, imploring face was lifted toward Clyde as he turned and swam to shore.)

The only tragedy, as I see it, in Dreiser's story, is the girl's. She *was* caught in the web of inevitability. But Dreiser plainly meant his book to be the tragedy of two, and particularly the boy's, caught inexorably in the grip of forces which had made such an outcome possible. By implication, the quality of civilization in America must bear the burden of guilt. (It is not what you are, but what you have, that counts.) See, says Dreiser, how an attractive, life-loving, well-intentioned boy can, by force of the circumstances in which he was enmeshed, become a murderer—even a calculating, plotting murderer. See, too, how the course of his trial and punishment by death (on which Dreiser passes no judgment, direct or implied) is also determined by what this civilization has done to the people in whose hands his fate is laid.

I have read the book twice, but I have never, from the first reading, been able to believe that Dreiser's theme is valid. My unbelief does not derive, it seems to me, from harshness of judgment; with each passing year I find it more difficult to see human beings in black and white, and harder to sit in judgment on their acts. But I think that Dreiser was guilty of an enormous fallacy. Clyde's course was *not* inevitable; the boy hadn't the seeds of manhood in him. He had a better start in life than many thousands of boys who became effective citizens and decent men. What happened to him is pitiable (for the boy suffered torment before and after his crime), but not tragic. And I hold it to be a very partial and wrong reading of American life to place upon it the onus for the crumbling of character in Clyde. You can't forge steel out of milk and water.

Is it logical to take as your symbol of American youth, blocked and warped by the society which surrounds it, "one of those interesting individuals [as Dreiser describes the boy Clyde] who looked upon himself as a thing apart—never quite wholly and indissolubly merged with the family of which he was a member, and never with any profound obligations to those who had been responsible for his coming into the world." Why expect that such a lad, without his coming to grips with himself, should feel a sense of obligation toward other human beings outside his family?

Dreiser's thinking was never more confused and never more sentimental than it was in the writing of *An American Tragedy.* It is more serious here than in his earlier work, because this was the most ambitious theme he attempted. The results were deplorable, because Clyde Griffiths is the precursor of a long line of weak and rudderless young men who looked upon themselves as things apart. They were to multiply in our fiction like rabbits. (pp. 57-9)

> *J. Donald Adams, "The Heavy Hand of Dreiser,"*
> *in his* The Shape of Books to Come *(copyright 1944*
> *by J. Donald Adams; copyright renewed 1971 by*
> *Jacqueline Adams; reprinted by permission of Viking*
> *Penguin Inc.), The Viking Press, 1944, pp. 54-83.**

EDMUND WILSON (essay date 1946)

[*Wilson reviews* The Bulwark *and notes the difference in outlook between this and Dreiser's previous novels.*]

As you read "The Bulwark," . . . Theodore Dreiser's posthumous novel, you go through all the familiar experience of first groaning over the commonplace characters and the shoddy clichés of the style, then gradually finding yourself won by the candor and humanity of the author, then finally being moved by a powerful dramatic pathos which Dreiser has somehow built up. The people of "The Bulwark," when we start it, seem to be among the least promising that Dreiser has ever tackled: a family of Pennsylvania Quakers, hard-working and poor in the first generation, hard-working and well-to-do in the second, never adventurous, eccentric, or brilliant. Yet, even in its earlier and duller stretches, this is not one of Dreiser's most tedious books. He seems, by the time he wrote it, to have learned to cover ground more quickly. The language, too, is somewhat less oafish than it is in the worst of his work, and, here as elsewhere, the personal voice, the rhythm, carries off the vague and fumbling vocabulary. Yes, we say, when we come to the first love scene, Dreiser is still deeper and purer than most of the people who write so much more cleverly. . . . (p. 88)

It is interesting and unexpected that the point of view presented in "The Bulwark" should have apparently nothing in common with either Dreiser's early naturalistic materialism or his later combative Communism. When Solon Barnes, in his misery of guilt, finds, in his garden, a beautiful green insect devouring an equally beautiful rosebud, he does not, like the Dreiser of "The Financier," think of "Nature, red in tooth and claw;" he rises, on the contrary, to the realization that "there must be a Creative Divinity, and so a purpose, behind all of this variety and beauty and tragedy of life. For see how tragedy had descended upon him, and still he had faith, and would have." (p. 91)

It is thus a very old-fashioned America that reasserts itself in "The Bulwark." One finds even in the writing touches that seem to belong in such old, edifying novels as Dreiser must have read in his childhood. The chapter that tells of Solon's son's suicide is headed, for example:

> Oh what a tangled web we weave,
> When first we practice to deceive!

And the scene at Solon's deathbed is a nineteenth-century deathbed scene, in which the father passes on to his daughters, the psychologist and the Greenwich Villager, the only ones among his children who are able to appreciate what he has to give, the still-living Quaker faith. This seems to be their only hope: they must do with it what they can in the modern world. "If thee does not turn to the Inner Light," he says to one of them, "where will thee go?" (pp. 91-2)

> *Edmund Wilson, "Theodore Dreiser's Quaker and*
> *Graham Greene's Priest."* in The New Yorker (©
> *1946, copyright renewed © 1973, by The New Yorker*
> *Magazine, Inc.), Vol. XXII, No. 6, March 23, 1946,*
> *pp. 88, 91-2, 94.**

H.L. MENCKEN (essay date 1946)

[*Mencken offers a general appraisal of his old friend's career.*]

[Dreiser] was probably the most matter-of-fact novelist ever known on earth. It was seldom that he departed from what he understood to be the record, and he never did so willingly. I recall a curious example in the days when *The "Genius"* was under fire by the Comstocks, and all the friends of its author were cooperating in efforts to deliver him from their clutches. I was told off, at one stage, to enter upon negotiations with old Anthony's successor, a lawyer by the name of Sumner, in the hope of inducing him to let up on the book at the cost of a few minor changes. I found this Sumner an amiable fellow, and we quickly drew up a sort of protocol by which he waived most of his objections, but insisted that a word here or there should be expunged or a situation toned down a bit. One of these situations, as I recall it, depicted Eugene Witla, the hero, as thrusting an inquisitive hand up a girl's skirt. This was in 1922 and the case against *The "Genius"* had been going on for six long years, so I was glad enough to agree to stop the explorer at the patella in order to get the book released, and Dreiser restored to royalties and peace of mind. But I was reckoning without the conscience of a really implacable respecter of facts. He agreed under pressure to other changes that seemed to me to be quite as important to the flow of the narrative, but when it came to this one he was a stone wall. I could see no logic in his objection, which quickly became violent, and said so. "But that," he declared finally and immovably, "is something I simply *can't* consent to. It *really happened.*" So the episode remained in the book, and presently, when the Comstocks subsided, the presses began to roll again, and if the plates haven't worn out Eugene is still groping—an operation considered scandalous in 1922, but now somewhat shorn of its old horrors.

Here, as in many another place, Dreiser himself was his own hero. He had a mind closely packed with trivia that were not trivial at all, and he poured them into all his books. When he described a street in Chicago and New York it was always a street that he knew as intimately as the policeman on the beat, and he never omitted any detail that had stuck in his mind—a queer sign, a shopkeeper standing in his doorway, a leaky fireplug, an ashcan, a stray dog. (pp. ix-x)

I spent the better part of forty years trying to induce him to reform and electrify his manner of writing, but so far as I am aware with no more effect than if I had sought to persuade him to take up golf or abandon his belief in non-Euclidian arcana. The defects of his style, of course, have been somewhat exaggerated by a long line of literary popinjays, including myself; he was quite capable, on occasion, of writing simply and even gracefully, as you will discover if you turn to Chapter XIII of Book III of [*An American Tragedy*]. Nevertheless, his was predominantly viscous writing, and not infrequently its viscosity was increased by clichés and counter-words that pulled up the reader in an extremely painful manner. In *The "Genius"* he performed inhuman barbarities upon the dubious word *trig*, and in *An American Tragedy* he does the same with *chic*. (pp. xi-xii)

The massive effect that Huxley and Spencer had had upon him in early life sufficed to keep him hostile to the Catholic piety of his father to his dying day, but he remained of a generally believing cast of mind, and was easily fetched by secular theologies. When the Freudian revelation dawned upon the Republic he resisted it only faintly, and was presently suffering from what he himself once described in my presence as a complex complex. There are traces of it in *An American Tragedy:* he even tries to account for the imbecility of judges and district attorneys in terms of infantile suppressions. But the book is much more heavily marked by the "chemic" theory of human behavior that entertained him during the twenties. Where he picked it up I do not know: perhaps he invented it himself. Whatever its source, it made him, for a time, a com-

plete fatalist, even a sort of Calvinist, and hence a nihilist in the domain of morals. It was this nihilism, I believe, that brought down the Comstocks upon *The "Genius"* rather than any dirtiness in the text. That text, in truth, was extraordinarily free from indecent words and naughty innuendoes, as I discovered when I went through it word for word, seeking to get the Comstocks off his back. . . . It will probably astound posterity to hear that even *An American Tragedy* was forbidden as obscene in Boston. It is, in fact, no more obscene than a table of stock prices. But it is undoubtedly profoundly immoral, for if it teaches anything at all it is that committing a murder is a sort of biological accident, like breaking a leg or becoming a father. (pp. xiii-xiv)

Whether or not *An American Tragedy* will survive in the Dreiser canon is a question that can be answered only by time. It was, as I have said, his greatest success while he lived, but at least a part of that success, I suspect, was due to its sheer bulk. The reading public always embraces long and thick novels, for its members, on the lower and more numerous levels, read only one or two books a year, and they like something that will last them all Winter. If any reader of [*An American Tragedy*] is pressed for time, I advise him to begin his reading with the second volume. The first is a menagerie of all Dreiser's worst deficiencies, but in the second he becomes again the adept and persuasive reporter. The last scenes have in them all the plausibility that made *Sister Carrie* a memorable event in American letters. To be sure, they stick close to the record—but surely not overclose. It is Dreiser who is telling the story, not some commonplace reporter. It offers a picture of profound tragedy seen through a suitably melancholy temperament. The author's brooding, noted by so many critics incapable of inventing a better word, is all over it. It is not only a minutely detailed picture of one unhappy young man's life; it is a commentary upon human life in general. Dreiser, in the days when the story was written, saw that life as predominantly hopeless and meaningless. This was the note of all his earlier novels. In his old age, with his faculties dimming, he revolted against his own philosophy, and embraced the glittering promises of the Marxian gospel. But in *An American Tragedy* he was still content to think of the agonies of mankind as essentially irremediable, and to lay them, not to the sins of economic royalists, but to the the blind blundering of the God responsible for complexes, suppressions, hormones and vain dreams. (pp. xv-xvi)

> *H. L. Mencken, "Introduction" (copyright 1946 by The World Publishing Company; copyright renewed © 1973 by Mercantile Safe Deposit and Trust Company for the Surviving Estate of Henry L. Mencken; used by permission of The Enoch Pratt Free Library of Baltimore in accordance with the terms of the will of H. L. Mencken), in* An American Tragedy *by Theodore Dreiser, World Publishing Company, 1946, pp. ix-xvi.*

MALCOLM COWLEY (essay date 1947)

[Cowley reviews the concluding novel of Dreiser's "Trilogy of Desire."]

"The Financier" was published in 1912 and **"The Titan"** in 1914. These first two volumes in Theodore Dreiser's "trilogy of desire" had a lasting influence on American fiction, and they left many thousands of readers waiting for the volume to follow. Now that **"The Stoic"** has appeared, after more than thirty years, we can guess why Dreiser failed to publish it during his lifetime. He had worked on it patiently and had written two or three different endings, among which his literary executors were left to make their choice; but he had never succeeded in raising it to the level attained in the other two volumes.

The first of these remains the most impressive. **"The Financier"** is an interweaving of finance and politics with a love story that, besides being effective in itself, is also essential to the climax of the novel. There are two reasons, one public and one private, why Frank Algernon Cowperwood goes to prison. He has made and lost a fortune by gambling with the city's funds—that is the public reason—but he has also seduced the daughter of Edward Malia Butler, one of three political bosses who control Philadelphia. Butler, with his family affection and stubborn anger, is one of the most convincing figures in the whole trilogy—more convincing than Cowperwood himself, who is documented and philosophized, whereas Butler is presented almost without comments.

"The Titan," which came next, is inferior to its predecessor as a novel. Instead of being interwoven in the story, sex and finance are presented in alternate chapters—"to make a club sandwich," as Stuart P. Sherman said. The chapters about Cowperwood's successive mistresses have the monotony of variety, like the love life of a tomcat. One has to be more than ordinarily innocent and yearning to enjoy them today; but the business chapters are as good as ever, and they reach an overwhelming climax.

Look in "The Dictionary of American Biography" for the article on Charles Tyson Yerkes (1837-1905) and you will see how closely Dreiser has followed the life of that sturdy old pirate. Yerkes' story, like Cowperwood's, falls naturally into three volumes. . . .

[It provides] the ready-made plot of Dreiser's last novel, a book that should have been as impressive as the two others in his trilogy; but somehow the subject failed to touch his imagination. (p. 7)

Like Thomas Wolfe, he left piles of manuscript for his literary executors, who seem to be handling them conscientiously. It is true that they let two or three of Dreiser's historical errors slip past them in preparing **"The Stoic"** for publication. When they read that Cowperwood mourned at the tomb of Sarah Bernhardt, they should have opened the nearest encyclopedia, where they would have learned that Bernhardt outlived him by eighteen years. But this error—with others like it—is of little importance compared with mistakes in planning the novel that could have been corrected only by the author himself. Let me list what seem to be the worst of them:

1. The title leads us to believe that Cowperwood at the end of his life will find some inner dignity to match his outward success. But he never becomes a stoic; at most he develops from simple hedonism or cynicism into a sort of resigned epicureanism.

2. The story arouses other expectations in the reader that it fails to satisfy. Characters like Lord Ettinge and Abington Scarr, the promoter, are introduced with trumpets, as if they were destined to play an important role; but then they silently vanish. A scene in Chapter 15 suggests that Berenice Fleming, his ward and mistress, will destroy Cowperwood just as she destroyed the snow image of him, but instead she is unfailingly loyal.

3. The story lacks the careful documentation one has learned to expect in Dreiser's novels. Episodes that should have been central, like the struggle between Cowperwood and Drake (Yerkes and Morgan) or the melting away of the hero's vast estate are dismissed each in a single chapter.

4. The author misses almost all the opportunities for drama that he would have seized upon in his earlier novels. There is no confrontation of Drake and Cowperwood; or of Cowperwood and Lord Stane, who is courting Berenice; or of Berenice and Cowperwood's wife (although the last two exchange a single look that carries them both to the edge of hysteria). Cowperwood's death is another lost opportunity; it results from an illness that is unconnected—except in its results—with either his business projects or his love affairs. . . .

We feel after reading the treatise that Cowperwood's trilogy has simply broken off; it is ended but still unfinished. (p. 57)

> *Malcolm Cowley, "Ending Dreiser's 'Trilogy of Desire',"* in The New York Times Book Review *(© 1947 by The New York Times Company; reprinted by permission), November 23, 1947, pp. 7, 57.*

JAMES T. FARRELL (essay date 1955)

[Farrell, the creator of Studs Lonigan, was one of Dreiser's friends and literary consultants during the older writer's last years. Below, Farrell discusses Dreiser's best short stories.]

Due to the fact that his novels are so powerful and caused so much controversy, [Dreiser's] stories have been neglected by critics. But among them are some of the finest and most moving short stories written by an American in this century.

In these tales there is variety of scene and range and depth of emotion. . . . Dreiser paints and re-creates a broad human scene and, in each instance, he reveals his probing, searching mind, his ability to assimilate and make use of many details, and a compassion for humanity, its dreams and tragic sufferings, which is linked up with a sure insight into the nature of people.

During his entire literary life, Theodore Dreiser sought for a theory of existence. His mind seems constantly to have been filled with "whys." Why was life? Why was there this human spectacle of grandeur and misery, of the powerful and the weak, the gifted and the mediocre? Why did men drive and struggle for the prizes of this world—sometimes with little more than a jungle morality? And his fiction was a revelation of what he saw and how he felt about these questions. He found no answers, and most certainly he avoided cheap answers as he did the cheap tricks of commercial and plot short story writers. He was a deeply serious and brooding man, and in his writing he treated his characters with seriousness. They became intensely human in their dreaming, aspiring, and struggling as well as in their unhappiness, bewilderment, and moments of tragedy.

Dreiser saw a struggle between instinct and convention, and this was a major motif in both his novels and his stories. He saw how convention and conformity frustrates men and women. Here in [*The Best Short Stories of Theodore Dreiser*], there are several stories which deal with this subject matter. **"Free,"** the story of a gifted architect with definite artistic ability and of his dying wife dramatizes the frustrating role of convention in the life of a man with singular gifts. . . . This is a story of futility, but it is told with such sympathy and compassion that it acquires emotional force. Its simple tragedy becomes awesome, almost mysterious in the way that tragedy in real life is sometimes awesome and full of mystery. There are other stories of unhappy marriages, **"Convention,"** **"Marriage for One,"** and **"The Shadow."** These, again, are marked by a sympathy and understanding on a parallel with these same qualities that endow **"Free"** with such depth of feeling.

Along with **"Free,"** there are two other Dreiser stories in this volume that have already become acknowledged classics, **"The Lost Phoebe"** and **"Nigger Jeff."** . . . [In **"The Lost Phoebe,"**] it is as though life itself were speaking to us through the author. And it is a tale not only of the sad end which comes to us in old age; also, it is a tale of a lost dream, a dream that once endowed life with a beauty that was akin to poetry. Time, the enemy of all men, has eaten away beauty and rendered dreams obsolete. And yet the dreams remain. Dreiser's handling of this theme is truly poetic.

"Nigger Jeff" is a sympathetic and vivid account of a lynching. The main character is a reporter from a big city newspaper (undoubtedly a St. Louis journal) who is sent into a country district to cover a story where there might be a lynching. The description of the lynching, and the account of its impact on the young reporter, is presented so vividly and movingly that we feel that we are on the scene ourselves. And the "cruel sorrow" of the colored mother whose son has been hanged by a mob can only bring a choke in our throats. The young reporter says, in the last line of the story, "I'll get it all in!" Dreiser did get it all in and this means the human feelings, the terribleness of human sorrow that is caused by such a lynching.

Totally different is **"My Brother Paul,"** Dreiser's account of his older brother. The feeling he had of brotherly affection is finely and sensitively revealed. Also, the story is quite genuinely nostalgic. It creates the Broadway atmosphere at the turn of the century so well that I found myself longing to have lived in that era and in Paul Dresser's world. Often, Dreiser has depicted emotions of greed, and he has described how human beings can destroy one another. Here, he writes of generosity of feeling, of manly affection, of kindness and helpfulness.

But every story in this book bears the mark of genuineness and caliber. In every story, there is respect—deep respect for human beings. Great art reveals the importance of human feelings and emotions. This is what Dreiser achieved. He cut beneath the surfaces of conventional attitude and sought, painstakingly, carefully, and sensitively to see human beings as they are and to render and re-create them truly but with sympathy. (pp. 9-12)

Dreiser's lifelong quest for a theory of existence was bound up with his own answers to time and death, his own willingness to face them in a spirit of moral bravery. This is one of the sources of his pessimism. It is a healthy pessimism, and when we encounter it we can gain a deepened sense of and respect for life. And these fifteen stories are but some of the works which Dreiser left us in his own quest and journey through the world. They tell us of men and women dreaming, struggling, and becoming caught in tragic bewilderment; they create a sense of wonder about those feelings which are the common clay, the common ground, the common elements of our humanity. Often they are somber, but their somberness breaks out in a revelation of that wonder and mystery of life which Dreiser felt so deeply.

Theodore Dreiser was a great writer of our century, and these tales of his fully bear the mark of his greatness, his sincerity, and his genius. Written years ago, they remain vital today.

They belong to our literary tradition and they should long stand among the major short stories written in twentieth-century America. (p. 12)

> *James T. Farrell, "Introduction" (1955), in* The Best Short Stories of Theodore Dreiser *by Theodore Dreiser (copyright © 1918, 1919 by Boni & Liveright, Inc.; copyright © 1926, 1927 by Theodore Dreiser; copyright © 1947, copyright © 1956 by The World Publishing Company; reprinted by permission of the Literary Estate of Theodore Dreiser), World Publishing Co., 1956, pp. 9-12.*

KENNETH S. LYNN　(essay date 1955)

[*Lynn surveys Dreiser's career.*]

Theodore Dreiser asserted, with a blunt directness which no other American writer at the turn of the century could match, that pecuniary and sexual success were the values of American society, that they were his values, too, and that they were therefore worthy of his total attention as a literary artist. The indebtedness to Dreiser expressed by later American writers is a formal acknowledgment of the fact that his was the most significant exploration made by any novelist in his generation of the themes of money and sex, the two themes which have become so very much the major concern of our modern literature. (p. 13)

Dreiser sat down, in the fall of 1899, to write a novel about a woman who rises from obscurity to become a famous actress. What made the novel so different that it can be said to have inaugurated the twentieth century in American social fiction is exactly what outraged Mr. Doubleday's wife, the character of the heroine, Carrie Meeber. (p. 27)

Carrie has had, over the years, a host of friends. Dreiser himself was very fond of his "little soldier of fortune," his "half-equipped little knight," as he affectionately called her. Pretty, but not a great beauty, natively intelligent, but nothing more, a poor, inexperienced girl who feels so sorry for the downtrodden people she encounters in Chicago, and who is herself seduced and deceived by two city slickers, Carrie has caused two generations of critics to melt into tears at the thought of her.

The critics, however, should have listened to Mrs. Doubleday and saved their grief, for Carrie herself never wastes any tears on anyone. The sorrow she expresses for the poor is highly abstract and is constantly betrayed by her ruthless social selection, motivated by her desire to get ahead. As for her seductions, they have fazed the critics more than they ever did Carrie—never once in the novel does sex have any emotional effect upon her, except insofar as it leads to an augmentation of her living standard. Like Dreiser himself, who once admitted that he had never loved anyone, and that fame and power were the only objects of his heart, Carrie is characterized by a singular coldness of temperament. The author's sympathy for his heroine was the sympathy of self-recognition, not of pity—as the grief-stricken critics have assumed. . . . (pp. 27-8)

After finishing *Sister Carrie,* Dreiser had begun a second novel. Put aside and taken up again several times across these three years of failure, *Jennie Gerhardt* was abandoned altogether when Dreiser began to be plagued by hallucinations. The novel lay fallow for seven years.

The man who brought *Jennie Gerhardt* to completion in 1910 was very different from the underweight, shabbily dressed failure who had begun it. Seven years after his suicide attempt, Dreiser looked down at the world through a ribboned pincenez from an "enormous paneled office." Director of the destinies of the Butterick "Trio" of magazines—the *Delineator,* the *Designer* and *New Idea Woman's Magazine*—his salary was ten thousand dollars a year. (pp. 36-7)

Mencken, who felt that *Sister Carrie* contained two distinct plots (he failed to see that Hurstwood's and Carrie's careers were both integral aspects of the same up-and-down process), has said that Dreiser's first novel suffers from a "broken back." Actually, it is *Jennie Gerhardt* which has the broken back, the result of having been begun in desperation and finished in complacence. The writer who conceived the novel believed that life was a meaningless struggle in which man fought to stay alive for his brief span and then died. Because of the overwhelming nature of the struggle, man had a desperate need—in his cheap room in Brooklyn, Dreiser knew just how desperate—for comfort and reassurance. In the year of his failure, Dreiser created Jennie Gerhardt, the antisuccess heroine, a woman who, like Dreiser's own mother—on whom Jennie is based in part—could be a refuge for those fallen in the struggle. The man who in 1910 brought *Jennie Gerhardt* to a conclusion was cocksure that the world was an oyster ready to be eaten.

Jennie as we first see her is, like Carrie, eighteen years old, poor, and pretty. As a person, however, she is everything that Carrie was not—generous, unselfish, warm, and possessed of a sense of the possibility of a life of dignity in the face of poverty and disaster. As Carrie had been, Jennie is seduced by a man of the world, but the *quid pro quo* which she seeks is not clothes and money, but his influence to get her brother out of jail. When her seducer suddenly dies, Jennie is left to bear his child. Instead, however, of abandoning the baby, Jennie finds serene fulfillment in caring for it.

Going out to work as a maid in order to help pay the bills at home (her father is out of work), Jennie encounters a rich young man named Lester Kane in the mansion where she is employed. He is attracted to Jennie and persuades her to go to Chicago with him where he sets her up in an apartment. As the novel was originally planned, Jennie and Lester were to marry, but as Dreiser looked at the novel from the standpoint of Riverside Drive and 1910, he decided this would not do. He had lost interest in Jennie and now wanted to write only about Lester Kane. (pp. 38-9)

To generate reader-sympathy for Jennie—a sympathy which he no longer shared—Dreiser simply killed off her little girl. To conclude as quickly as possible his increasingly disproportionate concentration on Lester, he killed him off as well. (p. 41)

By means of this twin killing, Dreiser brought the novel to an end with some semblance of unity with its beginning. Jennie is reunited with the dying Lester long enough for him to tell her she is the only woman he ever loved; later, at his funeral, she sits humbly and unrecognized in the back of the church. An incorrigible homebody, Jennie has adopted two orphans to whom her life from now on will be dedicated. Like the heroines of Willa Cather of whom she is the forerunner, Jennie has constructed a mystique out of doing the dishes and raising children. Life is meaningless, but she accepts it all, in generous embrace. Although spuriously achieved, the tone of the novel's

conclusion is consonant with its beginning and Dreiser's real attitude toward life is nowhere in sight. The book sold better than *Carrie* had, and Mencken thought it, with the single exception of *Huckleberry Finn,* "the best American novel ever done," but Dreiser himself was glad to be done with mystical acceptances and the qualities of sweetness and mercy. Not for thirty years would he return to the original theme of *Jennie Gerhardt.*

Even while he was impatiently engaged in finishing *Jennie,* ideas for four other novels were boiling in Dreiser's brain—a three-volume study of the American business hero and a portrait of the artist. The trilogy was to be based on the career of a well-known American businessman, while the artist's portrait was to be palpably autobiographical, but in fact the heroes are essentially the same; both Frank Cowperwood of *The Financier, The Titan* and *The Stoic* and Eugene Witla of *The "Genius"* are full-scale embodiments of all that Dreiser had started to express through the character of Lester Kane.

Cowperwood and Witla, the business titan and the artist genius, are lonely individualists, cold of heart, like Carrie, but greatly exceeding Dreiser's first heroine in their ruthlessness of purpose and their will to power. . . . Dreiser's heroes are lucky . . . , but their possession of brains, energy and hypnotic power is what counts supremely. They occupy a superior position in regard to the rest of society because they are in fact superior. Cowperwood and Witla are, in sum, American versions of the Nietzschean superman. (pp. 41-2)

The "Genius" is a thinly veiled account of Dreiser's own life rendered in Nietzschean hard-guy tough talk. Eugene Witla, whose journey from a small Midwestern town to Chicago to New York paralleled Dreiser's own, is a painter. Because he is an artist, Witla is "not really subject to the ordinary conventions of life." (p. 43)

In addition to its basically Nietzschean tone, there is, in *The "Genius,"* a certain flavor of Mary Baker Eddy. Throughout his life, Dreiser was fascinated by Christian Science. . . . The Nietzschean superman, who realizes all struggle is eventually in vain, but whose superhuman immunity to all emotion, to all ideas of pleasure and pain, prevents him from ever being daunted, is quite close to the Christian Scientist's denial of pain. Buffeted by society and by his own emotions in his pursuit of sex and money, Witla finds Mrs. Eddy's spiritualizations as effective an instrument of his ambitions as the philosophy of the superman.

In Dreiser's favorite character, Frank Cowperwood, the influence of Nietzsche and Mrs. Eddy are readily discerned, but they play second fiddle to still another philosophy, one which Mrs. Eddy has denounced as leading to "moral and physical death," as "mental diabolism," in short, as "malicious animal magnetism." (pp. 45-6)

[It is] the colossal figure of Frank Cowperwood who is the grand illustration in Dreiser's work of the power of the individual mind and will. He is the Nietzschean hard guy, the sexual Svengali and the Mental Mazda who magnetizes his way to millions, all rolled into one. Dreiser's "rebellious Lucifer . . . glorious in his sombre conception of the value of power," is basically an Alger hero, but with all the modern twists. (p. 51)

Mencken, who read the novel in manuscript, liked *The Financier* well enough, but it did not compare in his eyes with the sequel, *The Titan.* Cowperwood in the former novel had not been completely hard—he had, after all, failed, the plot action had been more concerned with his rise to power than with his exercise of it, while despite his motto of self-indulgence, he had broken very few laws and committed adultery with only one woman. . . . The Cowperwood of the second novel, however, the fabulous man who builds an enormous mansion and stocks it with art objects looted from two continents, who scores countless business victories and has mistresses by the dozen, and who is sublimely indifferent to the whips and goads of society (''a law unto himself,'' around whom other men swing ''as planets around the sun''), was to Mencken ''radiantly real,'' the ''best picture of an immoralist in all modern literature.''

Yet *The Titan* is a fabulous bore. The structure of the novel is, as the critic Stuart Sherman has remarked, ''a sort of huge club-sandwich, composed of slices of business alternating with erotic episodes [see excerpt above].'' The faster Cowperwood changes his money and his women, the duller the novel becomes. (pp. 56-7)

In conceiving of Cowperwood, Dreiser chose as a model the robber baron Charles T. Yerkes, who had buccaneered his way to a traction fortune and whose collections of women and art were almost as notable as the size of his fortune. . . . In *The Titan,* Dreiser drew far loftier comparisons to Cowperwood than the Yerkes parallel in an attempt to heighten his hero's stature beyond that of a businessman. Cowperwood is a Prometheus, a Renaissance prince, a Hannibal, a Hamilcar Barca, a ''great personage of the Elizabethan order,'' a ''colossus,'' a ''half-god or demi-gorgon.'' Dreiser constantly emphasized in both *The Financier* and *The Titan* that finance was not merely a business, but an art. . . .

But try as Dresier might, the unavoidable fact remained: an artistic titan was still, after all, just a corner grocer who had made good. Unfortunately for a would-be transvaluer in America, the difference between him and the rest of society was merely one of degree, not of kind. (p. 59)

Cowperwood in *The Titan* tries for five hundred and fifty pages to be different; the effort, albeit abortive, is understandably exhausting; at the end of the novel he is beginning to feel somewhat old and tired—he is a little sick of trying. So too, for that matter, was Dreiser. . . . [Not] until the mid-forties, in the last months of his life, could Dreiser bring himself to take up Cowperwood again and finish out his career. (p. 60)

[In] *An American Tragedy* Dreiser returned to the Hurstwood theme, the anatomy of failure. (p. 61)

The theme of the novel grew out of Dreiser's recognition of ''the determination of so many young Americans, boys and girls alike, to obtain wealth quickly by marriage.'' . . . He was aware, too, that the magazines and newspapers continued to insist that ''we are all Napoleons, only we don't know it,'' whereas most people in the new age, he felt, were ''weak and limited, exceedingly so.'' Out of these reflections came the story of the white-collar hero, Clyde Griffiths.

In some respects Clyde is the typical Dreiser hero. Characteristically, he is burning with desire, yet his soul is ice cold. . . . Like Cowperwood and Carrie, Clyde has the instinctive faculty for sensing what he must do in order to capitalize a given situation to his advantage.

But in some respects Clyde is quite different from Dreiser's earlier protagonists. The general strategy for advancement which he formulates for himself while still in his teens is not, significantly, the lobster-eat-squid battle plan decided on by young Cowperwood, but the white-collar strategy of personality-selling. . . . Although clever at ingratiating himself with people who count, he is easily tempted into imprudent behavior, the unfortunate consequences of which he does not have the courage to face. (pp. 62-4)

That Dreiser could call the story of Clyde a tragedy has scandalized certain critics, particularly F. O. Matthiessen, who has insisted that Clyde has none of the stature or the greatness of an authentic tragic hero. To make such a criticism is, however, to miss the point. Dreiser's title does not stem from any false illusions of greatness which he entertained about his hero, nor did he intend any parallel to the Greeks. The title did not attempt to convey the idea that Clyde himself was great, but rather was intended to suggest how enormous his anguish was as the law closed in on him and he finally realized that the life he had dreamed of, and almost had, would never be his. In the glittering twenties the dream of success was to Dreiser as alluring as ever; therefore, the story of *any* American who had failed to succeed was, inevitably, a tragedy. (p. 67)

Perhaps the clearest-cut expression of his approval of the American system during this period of his greatest success came in 1927, upon the occasion of his visit to the U.S.S.R. at the invitation of the Soviet Bureau of Cultural Relations. (p. 69)

Dreiser Looks at Russia was published in 1928. Its adverse judgment of the Soviet experiment and its celebration of the principles of the success society were consistent with the vision of life to which Dreiser had given expression ever since he had assumed the editorship of *Ev'ry Month* some thirty-three years before. Then the crash of 1929 came and knocked the stuffing out of Dreiser and his life vision.

The depression absolutely convinced Dreiser that capitalism was through, that the American atmosphere of ''zest and go'' which he so loved was now only a memory. The great race up the ladder of success had been permanently canceled because someone had removed the ladder. *Tragic America,* published in 1931, shows how profoundly the depression had shaken Dreiser in just two years' time. The hard, grasping scheme of things which had worked so well a few years before had now suddenly produced ''the monopoly of everything by and for the few.'' (p. 71)

Turning his back on the faith of his whole life, Dreiser categorically denounced ''the Pluck and Luck, Work and Win theory of achievement.'' In place of Alger, he hastily substituted Marx. ''America needs a uniform, scientifically planned system which will divide work and the means of life's enjoyment and improvement among the people.'' Would such a system destroy ''the restless and creative individualism'' of the American people? To back up his negative answer to this question, Dreiser pointed to the Soviet Union: ''I saw no lack of individualism in Russia; creative or otherwise.'' On the record of *Dreiser Looks at Russia,* this was either a deliberate lie or amnesia—of the hysteria of a man who was dead certain that the end of the only world he had ever known was ''almost here and now.''

The depression was not merely something he read about in the newspapers. As the breadlines lengthened, Dreiser's own financial security was wiped out by the failure of his publisher; the Hoovervilles mushroomed while Dreiser's country place burned to the ground. The effect on Dreiser's art was catastrophic—in such a world a man whose only values were success values had nothing to say. For the first time since the beginning of the century, a decade passed without a book from Dreiser's pen. An isolationist polemic, **America Is Worth Saving,** appeared in 1941, but even this was partially ghost-written for Dreiser. The book's only significance was its further evidence that Dreiser still was convinced that the success dream had vanished from America forever. On into the forties, the river of his imagination ran drier and drier. Finally, in the last year of his life, Dreiser spoke again. (pp. 72-3)

[*The Bulwark* and *The Stoic*] are curious, hollow shells of books, utterly lacking in conviction. In the former, a rags-to-riches businessman with "clear bluish-gray eyes" forsakes success for the peace and tranquility which he finds in the contemplation of nature and in the Quaker doctrine of the Inner Light. The message of *The Bulwark* is partly, as Lionel Trilling has said, that "the sad joy of cosmic acceptance goes hand in hand with sexual abstinence," and partly that happiness can never be achieved on a big income.

In *The Stoic* Dreiser put the tired, aging Cowperwood through his paces once again. Although he had been an Episcopalian in *The Financier,* Dreiser now without explanation referred to him as a Quaker, nor was this the only sea change his hero had suffered across the years. For while Cowperwood's mind is "ever-telepathic," he finds it is no fun to win any more, no thrill to smash any more shams. Having lost his will to power, the Cowperwood of *The Stoic* shortly loses his will to live. Sick and weary, he is told by his doctor that only his mind can save his health, but Cowperwood is profoundly uninterested. . . . Like his dead hero . . . Dreiser seemed to have no real heart for what he was writing; the theme of acceptance had never really been his genre. With a final chapter of *The Stoic* still to be written, he died. (pp. 73-4)

> Kenneth S. Lynn, "Theodore Dreiser: The Man of Ice," in his The Dream of Success: A Study of the Modern American Imagination (copyright 1955, by Kenneth S. Lynn; reprinted by permission of the author), Little, Brown and Company, 1955, pp. 13-74.

ALFRED KAZIN (essay date 1959)

[*Kazin offers an insightful discussion of Dreiser's novels.*]

Dreiser is a particular example of the kind of mysterious strength, the strength with which a writer assimilates his environment, then recoils from it in order to tell a story, that makes the novelist's art possible. Although there were a good many possibilities in the novel that Dreiser never used and perhaps never understood, he grasped, in the symbol of his own drive for success and in the tragic careers of so many individuals in his own family, that the essence of narrative is the illusion of life, the suggestion of truth through the use of fact. However a novelist may create this illusion, it is indispensable. From his first novel, *Sister Carrie,* despite his *personal* commonness and proverbial lack of taste (we are told that Carrie "could scarcely toss her head gracefully" and that Hurstwood worked in "a truly swell saloon"), Dreiser was able to wheel into motion that enormous apparatus for suggestion and illusion that makes us lose ourselves in his books as if each were a profound and tragic experience of our own. The novel, as D. H. Lawrence said, is "the book of life." For more than two hundred years now it has been the only literary form able to suggest the ponderousness, the pressure and force, of modern industrial

society. More significantly, it has been the only form, as we can see from novels that have externally so little in common as *Moby-Dick, The Brothers Karamazov, The Sound and the Fury,* that has been able to find objective symbols for that increasing alienation from himself which man has come to feel in a society that is insensitive to the individual and a universe that is wholly indifferent to him.

On both these issues Dreiser is immense. In the wholly commercial society of the early twentieth century, Dreiser caught the banality, the mechanical routine, the ignorance of any larger hopes, precisely because he was able to recognize the significance of his own experience. Dreiser was never a "realist" in the pseudo-objective style that has been developed by American muckraking, advertising and sociology. The facts dredged up by impersonal "research" are often dubious and quickly dated, whereas the sheer web of fact that Dreiser put together about clothes, house furnishings and finance fifty years ago retains its interest for us today. Dreiser was an artist who operated with the *facts* of a new era because he saw them as instruments of human destiny. He saw man, man naked as he essentially is, playing with skyscrapers, trains, stocks and bonds, the costumes that man wears in our time. Only an imagination which can see the circumstances of life as significant accidents, which can portray the vulnerability of the human person under the pressure of social fact, can really portray the limited but unmistakable area of determinism within which we operate. What makes Dreiser's novels so extraordinarily "real" is his ability to make us aware that the world was not always like this, that it is not entirely like this even now.

The sense for the hidden dimension with which a true imagination always sees the present fills Dreiser's first novels with unforgettable images of the rawness of Chicago on the eve of the twentieth century. A recurrent symbol in Dreiser's work is the prairie left on the outskirts of Chicago, where the few houses look like sentinels. This is the picture of Chicago in *Sister Carrie,* which opens with a young girl on a train coming into the city; this is the Chicago that is seen by the magnate Frank Cowperwood, the millionaire hero of *The Financier* . . . and *The Titan* . . . , who, when he moves on to Chicago after his bankruptcy and imprisonment in Philadelphia, rises to the possibilities of the city with wonder and admiration. In *The "Genius,"* the dirty and tumultuous industrial scene around the Chicago River is the material which Eugene Witla discovers as a newspaper artist and which develops into his original and successful paintings of the modern city scene. This recurrent image of coming on the big city past lonely prairie houses has its most poignant expression in the second chapter of *Sister Carrie,* and expresses, in the innocence and awkwardness of its heroine, the experience of a whole generation. "The city had laid miles and miles of streets and sewers through regions where, perhaps, one solitary house stood out alone—a pioneer of the populous ways to be. There were regions open to the sweeping winds and rain, which were yet lighted throughout the night with long, blinking lines of gas-lamps, fluttering in the wind. Narrow board walks extended out, passing here a house, and there a store, at far intervals, eventually ending on the open prairie."

In such a passage we recognize that disproportion between man and his world which is one of the themes with which Dreiser is often able to create the sense of actuality. Only a writer who conceives of historical events in terms of personal sensation and emotion, who can describe the peculiar mercilessness of industrial society as an inarticulated experience in the human heart, can create for us a sense of the "times." . . . (pp. 88-90)

It is not Dreiser's laborious concern with external facts—the gas-lamps in the wind, the heaviness of clothes, the lights of the saloon in *Sister Carrie,* the brokerage business in *The Financier,* Chicago street-car franchises and big-city politics in *The Titan,* advertising and magazine publishing in *The "Genius"*—that creates this kind of "reality"; it is Dreiser's inability to take anything for granted: it is his usual sense of wonder at the dense, peopled, factual world itself. The great realists have always been those for whom the "real" world is always strange, who are fascinated by the commercial and industrial world because they know that this world is not *theirs.* For Dreiser the emotion of the provincial Carrie in the big city has become a powerful ingathering symbol of the interest and fascination of a society that, by reducing everyone in it to a feeling of complicity and powerlessness, makes *everyone* feel provincial. Only a writer like Theodore Dreiser, to whom success in the external world and some understanding of man's destiny were equal passions, could have created such unforgettable images of man's homelessness in both society and the universe at large as Dreiser did when he described Carrie rocking in her chair, or Cowperwood in prison looking up at the stars with a sense that he was no more strange to the world of infinite space than he felt himself to be to the conventional world of marriage and business. It has not always been noticed that it is precisely the imagination that sees modern society as a gigantic accident, as a paradigm of the infinite and indifferent universe, which creates, in the burning and vivid metaphors of Dreiser, Zola, Hardy, the feeling of truth about society. Without this necessary perspective, without some sense of wonder, or opposition, or fancy on the part of the realistic novelist, society gets so much taken for granted that it can no longer be fairly *seen;* and indeed this is exactly what has happened in many contemporary novels, where the concern with purely personal or sexual themes betrays a lack of perspective, of serious intention on the part of the novelist.

Dreiser's love of documentation, his naïve passion for "facts," recalls the poetic intent behind Whitman's "inventories" of modern city scenes. Dreiser attempts to create a sense of the material structure of modern life in much the same way that Whitman, in "Song of Myself," itemizes in quick detail the "blab of the pave, tires of carts, sluff of boot-soles, talk of the promenaders." As in Whitman, the external world is portrayed for its interest as *spectacle,* yet remains one to which man feels connected. Dreiser still writes in the spirit of the nineteenth-century discovery of evolution: nothing moves him so much as the realization that man has always been a part of nature. The concern with outward "reality" is one that contemporary novelists often reject in an age when the novel may seem as abstract as today's all-powerful science of physics. Dreiser was wholly under the influence of nineteenth-century biology and social philosophy. For him man is indissolubly part of the natural world itself: the order of nature reflects man's personal emotions in the same way that his fellow human beings, who belong to the same species as himself, reflect his longings and his weaknesses. Dreiser was able to portray modern society as an organism precisely because he recognized that although it did not always satisfy human aspirations, society itself was a natural growth: it expressed sexuality, greed, social ambition, in forms that are natural to man. In Dreiser's novels men like Drouet and Hurstwood, Frank Cowperwood and Eugene Witla can almost for the first time identify themselves with each other because they already identify themselves

with plants and animals. And they make the identification in a way that conveys both the truth of the resemblance and the uncertainty about its purpose which plagues man's awareness of the natural process.

This sense of modern society as itself biological and evolutionary attains in Dreiser's novels a glow of romantic exaltation, a suggestion that everything in the universe is alive and seeking new shape. It is hard to think of other American novelists who have described this as powerfully as Dreiser does when he introduces Carrie to Chicago, Eugene Witla to New York, and Clyde Griffiths to Kansas City: the sense we carry away of infinite reverberations in society is the greatest achievement of *The Financier* and *The Titan.* The bias of Dreiser's fellow "naturalists," as we can see in Stephen Crane's masterpiece, "The Open Boat," and in Frank Norris's best book, *McTeague,* was in favor of the *reductio ad absurdum:* life must be portrayed in such strong terms as to seem positively hostile to man. Dreiser, who shares their philosophy, nevertheless identified the world with his own ambition and his compassion, and this is why one recognizes a maturity of involvement in Dreiser's work that is very different from the self-conscious stylization in Crane and the essentially patronizing and abstract manner of Norris. The truth is that for many writers, the philosophy of naturalism was a way of rationalizing their own indifference and apathy, their typically modern sense of alienation. For Dreiser, on the other hand, this "scientific" philosophy actually played the role that evolution had for romantic pantheists like Emerson and Whitman: naturalism provided a way of binding himself more firmly to the world.

Dreiser sees the modern scene much as did the tender realists of the "ash-can" school of painters who discovered the beauty of the big city; he is not one of the pseudo-Nietzschean naturalists, like Jack London or Frank Norris, who mixed their toughness with romance; nor is he in the least a crusader, like Upton Sinclair and many proletarian novelists of the 1930s, for whom a novel was a description of things to be eradicated. Dreiser's loving realism is directed toward an urban world that is always various and colorful. Even Frank Norris's *McTeague* ends in a scene of such melodramatic claptrap—the hero in Death Valley chained to the enemy he has just killed—that we can see that for Norris the height of feeling was to show the world as the ironic enemy of man's hopes, tricking him. Dreiser, on the contrary, writes as a contemplative, one who finds the significance of the external scene through his personal attachment to it.

The nearest analogy to Dreiser's "personal" realism is to be found in the painter Edward Hopper, who shares Dreiser's passion for transcendentalist writers, for images of trains and roads. . . . It is one of the paradoxes of modern art that the more "external" and ordinary the object portrayed—a city street in Hopper, the complex record of a stock deal in Dreiser—the more personal is the emotion conveyed. The emotion consists in exactly this surprise of attachment to the world that so often dwarfs us. *An American Tragedy* begins unforgettably with a picture of a small missionary family in a big city, engulfed by the tall walls in its commercial heart; Sister Carrie is stupefied by the immensity of Chicago, and, when she asks for work at Speigelheim and Company, is looked over by the foreman "as one would a package"; even Cowperwood, magnetic and powerful as he is, is surrounded by "the endless shift of things," first in Philadelphia, then in Chicago. But it is the haunting feeling for objects that the hero of *The "Genius,"* a painter, conveys in his pictures of the Chicago River, the muddy industrial stream that significantly moves Witla to a "panegyric on its beauty and littleness, finding the former where few would have believed it to exist." Later in New York, Eugene does a picture of Greeley Square in a drizzling rain, catching "the exact texture of seeping water on gray stones in the glare of various electric lights. He had caught the values of various kinds of lights, those in cabs, those in cable cars, those in shop windows, those in the street lamp—relieving by them the black shadows of the crowd and of the sky." This might be a picture by Alfred Stieglitz. Despite the personal vulgarity and tinsel showiness in Dreiser's style, his fundamental vision of things is always the artist's.

Yet beyond this sensitivity to the once realized beauty of the modern city, Dreiser's greatest strength is as a dramatist of human relations. Although his narrative technique, especially in chronicle novels like *The Financier* and *The Titan,* often becomes mechanical, in alternating chapters describing Cowperwood's love affairs and business deals, Dreiser's curiously unconscious masterliness is emphasized by the way he virtually devours a subject. When Dreiser is bad, it is never because of the slowness or literalness of his technique; it is because of the imposition of a purely subjective emotion, as in parts of *The "Genius."* In Dreiser the writer was *always* wiser than the man. When his instinctive transformative powers fail him, when he imposes on the reader great blobs of incoherent personal emotion, one recognizes how silly the man Theodore Dreiser could be. An example is the tasteless endearments that Eugene Witla addresses to young Suzanne Dale. What made Dreiser powerful in *Sister Carrie* and *Jennie Gerhardt,* where he used the stories of his own sisters, was his ability to see his own family in historic and histrionic roles, exactly as if he had visualized them in dreams. In the Cowperwood novels, it was his candid self-identification with massive creatures of power, who represented the fulfillment of his own social yearnings to be, in twentieth-century terms, a hero. Even more, Cowperwood, of all Dreiser's many sensuous heroes, was able to convey best the humanity of Dreiser's own feeling for women, his exalted sense of their beauty—which Dreiser represented equally in Cowperwood's love of painting. In *The "Genius,"* however, Dreiser was writing too close to the bone of his marital troubles; the objective sympathy that had been available to him in describing his heroines, or in modeling Cowperwood on an American magnate of the period, Charles T. Yerkes, broke down because of his own notorious lack of humor. It is an interesting fact that one of the most powerful scenes in *The "Genius,"* the birth of Eugene Witla's child, seems to have had no parallel in Dreiser's life. On the other hand, Dreiser's maudlin descriptions of Eugene in love, even of Eugene's earlier breakdown and his odd success in advertising and publishing, *are* all based on Dreiser's life, and it is these scenes that are handled with that showiness of emotion which afflicted Dreiser's writing whenever he moved out of his natural orbit as a storyteller into too personal and confessional a tone.

It is this clumsiness in *The "Genius"* that explains why Dreiser's work is so often identified with pedestrian novelists of his own generation. Yet the theme of the book is significant, for Dreiser is always concerned with eroticism. Despite the many attacks on his books, this side of Dreiser's work is undervalued, for in his old-fashioned way Dreiser connects sex with money and social ambition. It is this connection that leads Clyde Griffiths to his death in *An American Tragedy,* as it is this that leads Hurstwood in *Sister Carrie* to rob his employer; one can see the connection even in Frank Cowperwood, who despite his immense personal authority, his fortune, his un-

deviating attraction to so many women, must himself go from woman to woman in a yearning for that "refinement," that ultimate "spell of beauty," which would represent a social victory higher than anything in Philadelphia or Chicago. The fact is that Dreiser is one of the most cogent novelists of sex we have had—so long as he sticks to the inescapable involvement of women, money and power, or can reveal a compassion for women that shows us such very different victims in Carrie, Jennie Gerhardt, and the utterly innocent Roberta Alden. In Dreiser compassion is as strong an emotion as lust. Compassion as a source of sexual emotion is so rarely expressed in contemporary novels that it is important to emphasize how different Dreiser is in this from the aggressive realists of our day. (John O'Hara in books like *A Rage to Live* imposes a masculine psychology on his women characters.) It is Dreiser's compassionate sense of what women themselves are likely to feel that explains why Carrie, who has seemed commonplace to many unsympathetic readers, and whose perverse success in life enraged old-fashioned moralists, figured for Dreiser himself as a true heroine of the modern world. "In your rocking-chair, by your window, shall you dream such happiness as you may never feel." Dreiser was able to portray not only the kind of woman who was the "prize," the "lure," for a man making his way up (Suzanne Dale in *The "Genius,"* Sondra Finchley in *An American Tragedy*), but he was able to show that a woman like Carrie could dazzle an ambitious man like Hurstwood and yet within herself remain a solitary and bewildered child still trying to understand the world that looked so inhuman when she first had come on it in Chicago.

The real objection that must be considered against Dreiser's work refers to more than his occasional vulgarity of style or to the naïveté with which he often furnishes a room. The force of the objection lies in the contrast between unassimilated actuality—the purely personal-historical portrait that Dreiser so often achieved—and what Henry James, who insisted on the novel as a wholly realized art form, called a "situation." James unfavorably compared fiction which gives us a "case" with fiction that presents a "situation," where the novelist can display so many connections with life at large that the form of the novel becomes a "reflection . . . to one's sense of life in general." Dreiser certainly does think of each of his novels as a "case." *Sister Carrie* is so rooted in reminiscent emotion, one critic has commented, that Dreiser wrote it as if he were taking down a vision; "it was something like translating the Golden Plates." *The Financier* and *The Titan* naturally became the case history of an individual in the setting of time which the hero helped to make. *The "Genius"* is again the portrait of a single man, and even *An American Tragedy,* though it is the one Dreiser title that might be taken to refer to more than an individual, is essentially the "history" of Clyde Griffiths. Henry James would not, in theory, have objected to Dreiser's material, or even to the style of a writer he might conceivably have accepted as "our American Balzac"—a type of which he saw the necessity, and from which he sadly excluded himself because of inadequate knowledge of American business. James's objection would have been that all of Dreiser's work, to use the titles of two books of Dreiser's stories, is either a gallery of men or a gallery of women. We feel the "case," the individual within the drama of history; the individual is surrounded by the actuality of experience, but we do not find the well-made novel that was James's ideal: one in which the plot and the subtlety of its development give us the sense that the situation is primary, and that everything which gives us pleasure in a novel—place, character, action—has been joined to bring about a singleness of effect.

Dreiser does not meet these specifications. When we read him, we are aware not only of the unevenness of style and intelligence that we get even in so strong a book as *Sister Carrie,* but we also discover that Dreiser's interest is in the individual within the immense struggle and pathos of historical circumstances. Sometimes, as in the Cowperwood novels, the individual has the strength to rise above these circumstances; usually, as in *An American Tragedy,* he falls entirely out of life. When we read Dreiser we are also aware of "extricable" meanings; we never forget the underlying pressure of life on him: there is always a sense of issues, of historical personages thinly disguised, of an actual murder trial and the newspaper reports of it, as in *An American Tragedy.* By the time we finish any Dreiser novel, the grit of actual life has got into the fine machinery of the novel, and we are left not with the worked-out "situation" but with case after case—Carrie, Hurstwood, Jennie Gerhardt, Frank Algernon Cowperwood, Eugene Witla, Clyde Griffiths, Roberta Alden. . . . In the end, the supposedly "pessimistic" novelist of determinism, of the ruthless social process, has really given us an extraordinarily large gallery of individuals who are symbolically divided from their society and who in one way or another evade its claim to full domination over them.

It is this essential solitariness that lingers in our imagination, and that gives us our conviction of Dreiser's lasting value. Undeniably, it is not the "situation" of art but the "case" of history itself, as it afflicts the individual, that is the ruling image in Dreiser. In fact, we cannot help admiring Dreiser for exactly those insights that James suggested were fundamental to the novel, when he said early in his career that the novelist succeeds to the "sacred office" of the historian. We think of Dreiser's work as a series of indelible episodes in the moral history of twentieth-century man; we cannot help being aware of an interest outside of the novelistic "situation" itself. But more than this, we are aware that we feel this historical interest because, when we read Dreiser, we are directed to it by his art. In the classic way of art, the issue, the moment, the historical drama, all have been fused to give us an image of the human person that has outlasted the issues themselves. Without the "case," we would by now have little sense of the times themselves; these individuals are by now out of time precisely because they have been caught so well in time. May it be, then, that the real objection we feel to the "case" technique is that Dreiser makes us feel the solitude of the individual even in society, the individual ultimately undetermined by "forces," outside the net of facts? May it be that in Dreiser we see the human soul, though almost crushed by circumstances, nevertheless irreconcilably free of them, its own freedom made clear in the light of inarticulate longing?

The truth is that Dreiser's books belong to a period of literature in which the individual is still large, epochal, heroic—not crushed. What gives his characters stature is not what *they* accomplish in history (only Cowperwood has creative force, but his actions are morally dubious) but what one may call their innocence: they can never become nonentities, for as provincials in the city they have too much to think about. More and more the contemporary novel is stocked with individuals who have nothing to think about except themselves, and who in their dullness justify the mechanical psychology with which they are conceived. They are engulfed, they have been taken over, they hardly exist. Dreiser's individuals are *large* because they still have an enormous capacity for suffering—and for realizing their suffering. In their defenselessness they recapture the reality of the human person. They are so alone that we watch with awe what is happening to them. We are entranced, because we are watching a social process that in Dreiser's novels, despite what he *says,* is not yet finished, that may turn out another way. We watch with admiration because we know that despite Dreiser's philosophy, Dreiser's novels prove that history does not simply ride over man but is in some sense an expression of him. In creating history, in suffering it, man becomes vivid; there, however we may change, is the unmistakable light of reality itself. (pp. 90-9)

> *Alfred Kazin, "Dreiser: The Esthetic of Realism" (originally published in his introduction to* An American Tragedy *by Theodore Dreiser, Dell Publishing Company, 1959), in his* Contemporaries *(copyright © 1924, 1946, 1952, 1955, ©, 1956, 1957, 1958, 1959, 1960, 1961, 1962 by Alfred Kazin; reprinted by permission of the author), Little, Brown and Company, 1962, pp. 87-99.*

IRVING HOWE   (essay date 1964)

[*Howe assays Dreiser's fiction, paying close critical attention to* An American Tragedy.]

In the first task of the novelist, which is to create an imaginary social landscape both credible and significant, Dreiser ranks among the American giants, the very few American giants we have had. Reading *An American Tragedy* once again, after a lapse of more than twenty years, I have found myself greatly moved and shaken by its repeated onslaughts of narrative, its profound immersion in human suffering, its dredging up of those shapeless desires which lie, as if in fever, just below the plane of consciousness. How much more vibrant this book is than the usual accounts of it in recent criticism might lead one to suppose! It is a masterpiece, nothing less. . . . [*Sister Carrie, Jennie Gerhardt* and *The Financier*] are crowded with exact observation—observation worked closely into the grain of narrative—about the customs and class structure of American society in the phase of early finance capitalism. No other novelist has absorbed into his work as much knowledge as Dreiser had about American institutions: the mechanisms of business, the stifling rhythms of the factory, the inner hierarchy of a large hotel, the chicaneries of city politics, the status arrangements of rulers and ruled. For the most part Dreiser's characters are defined through their relationships to these institutions. They writhe and suffer to win a foothold in the slippery social world or to break out of the limits of established social norms. They exhaust themselves to gain success, they destroy themselves in acts of impulsive deviancy. But whatever their individual lot, they all act out the drama of determinism—which, in Dreiser's handling, is not at all the sort of listless fatality that hostile critics would make it seem, but is rather a fierce struggle by human beings to discover the limits of what is possible to them and thereby perhaps to enlarge those limits by an inch or two. That mostly they fail is Dreiser's tribute to reality. (p. 143)

In Dreiser's early novels most of the central characters are harried by a desire for personal affirmation, a desire they can neither articulate nor suppress. They suffer from a need that their lives assume the dignity of dramatic form, and they suffer terribly, not so much because they cannot satisfy this need, but because they do not really understand it. Money, worldly success, sensual gratification are the only ends they know or can name, but none of these slakes their restlessness. . . . And Dreiser too, because he had in his own experience shared these values and struggled, with varying effectiveness, to burn them out of his system—Dreiser too lived out the longings and turmoil of his characters.

Yet there is usually present in his early novels a governing intelligence more copious and flexible than that of the characters. This governing intelligence is seldom revealed through direct statement, either by characters or author. Taking upon himself the perils and sharing in the miseries of his characters, he leaves the privilege of admonition to others. Yet there is never really a question as to what his novels "mean," nor any serious possibility that the characters will usurp control. Through the logic of the narrative, we are enabled to grasp with an almost visceral intensity how shallow are the standards by which the characters live.

In these early novels society figures largely as a jungle; and with good reason—the capitalism of the early 20th Century closely resembled a jungle. The characters may begin with a hard struggle for survival, but far more quickly than most of Dreiser's critics allow, they leave it behind them. Having emerged from the blunt innocence of their beginnings, they are now cursed with a fractional awareness. They can find neither peace nor fulfillment. In their half-articulate way, Dreiser's characters are beset by the same yearnings that trouble the characters of Fitzgerald and many other American novelists: a need for some principle of value by which to overcome the meanness, the littleness of their lives. To know, however, that the goals to which one has pledged one's years are trivial, yet not to know in what their triviality consists—this is a form of suffering which overcomes Dreiser's characters again and again. In all its dumb misery, it is the price, or reward, of their slow crawl to awareness. One sometimes feels that in the novels of Dreiser there is being reenacted the whole progression of the race toward the idea of the human.

The prose in these early novels is often as wretched as unsympathetic critics have said. Dreiser had little feeling for the sentence as a rhythmic unit (though he had a strong intuitive grasp of the underlying rhythm of narrative as a system of controlled variation and incremental development). He had a poor ear for the inflections of common speech, or even for the colloquial play of language. And worst of all, he had a weakness, all too common among the semi-educated, for "elegant" diction and antique rhetoric. Yet, despite the many patches of grey and the occasional patches of purple prose, Dreiser manages to accumulate large masses of narrative tension; he pulls one, muttering and bruised, into the arena of his imagination; and finally there is no recourse but surrender to its plenitude, its coarse and encompassing reality.

Not even Dreiser's philosophical excursions—bringing together nativist American prejudice with the very latest ideas of 1900—can break the thrust of these narratives. Dreiser's thought has by now been analyzed, mauled and ridiculed: his distortion of social life through metaphors of brute nature, his reduction of human motive to the malignant pressure of "chemisms," his toying with "the superman" in the Cowperwood novels. But it hardly matters. One brushes all this aside, resigned to the malice of a fate that could yoke together such intellectual debris with so much creative power.

Though surely Dreiser's major achievement, *An American Tragedy* is not the work of a master who, at the approach of old age, decides upon a revolutionary break from the premises and patterns of his earlier writing. For that order of boldness Dreiser lacked a sufficient self-awareness and sophistication as an artist; he was cut off from too much of the tradition of Western, even American, culture to do anything but continue with his version of naturalism. He was the kind of writer who must keep circling about the point of his beginnings, forever stirred by memories of his early struggles and preoccupations. All such a writer can hope for—a very great deal—is to mine his talent to its very depth; and that Dreiser did in *An American Tragedy*. Still, there are some changes from the earlier novels, and most of them to the good.

The prose, while quite as clotted and ungainly as in the past, is now more consistent in tone and less adorned with "literary" paste gems. Solecisms, pretentiousness and gaucherie remain, but the prose has at least the negative virtue of calling less attention to itself than in some of the earlier books. And there are long sections packed with the kind of specification that in Dreiser makes for a happy self-forgetfulness. . . . (pp. 144-46)

For the first and last time Dreiser is wholly in the grip of his vision of things, so that he feels little need for the buttress of comment or the decoration of philosophizing. Dreiser is hardly the writer whose name would immediately occur to one in connection with T. S. Eliot's famous epigram that Henry James had a mind so fine it could not be violated by ideas; yet if there is one Dreiser novel concerning which something like Eliot's remark might apply, it is *An American Tragedy*. What Eliot said has sometimes been taken, quite absurdly, as if it were a recommendation for writers to keep themselves innocent of ideas; actually he was trying to suggest the way a novelist can be affected by ideas yet must not allow his work to become a mere illustration for them. And of all Dreiser's novels *An American Tragedy* is the one that seems least cluttered with unassimilated formulas and preconceptions.

Where the earlier novels dealt with somewhat limited aspects of American life, *An American Tragedy*, enormous in scope and ambition, requires to be judged not merely as an extended study of the American lower-middle-class during the first years of the 20th Century but also as a kind of parable of our national experience. Strip the story to its bare outline, and see how much of American desire it involves: An obscure youth, amiable but weak, is lifted by chance from poverty to the possibility of winning pleasure and wealth. To gain these ends he must abandon the pieties of his fundamentalist upbringing and sacrifice the tender young woman who has given him a taste of pure affection. All of society conspires to persuade him that his goals are admirable, perhaps even sacred; he notices that others, no better endowed than himself, enjoy the privileges of money as if it were in the very nature of things that they should; but the entanglements of his past now form a barrier to realizing his desires, and to break through this barrier he must resort to criminal means. As it happens, he does not commit the murder he had planned, but he might as well have, for he is trapped in the machinery of social punishment and destroyed. "So well defined is the sphere of social activity that he who departs from it is doomed."

Now this story depends upon one of the most deeply-grounded fables in our culture. Clyde Griffiths, the figure in Dreiser's novel who acts it out, is not in any traditional sense either heroic or tragic. He has almost no assertive will, he lacks any large compelling idea, he reveals no special gift for the endurance of pain. In his puny self he is little more than a clouded reflection of the puny world about him. His significance lies in the fact that he represents not our potential greatness but our collective smallness, the common denominator of our foolish tastes and tawdry ambitions. He is that part of ourselves in which we take no pride, but know to be a settled resident. And we cannot dismiss him as a special case or an extreme instance, for his weakness is the essential shoddiness of mortality. By a twist of circumstance he could be a junior executive, a country-club favorite; he almost does manage to remake himself to the cut of his fantasy; and he finds in his rich and arrogant cousin Gilbert an exasperating double, the young man he too might be. Clyde embodies the nothingness at the heart of our scheme of things, the nothingness of our social aspirations. If Flaubert could say, *Emma Bovary, c'est moi*, Dreiser could echo, *Clyde Griffiths, he is us*.

We have then in Clyde a powerful representation of our unacknowledged values, powerful especially since Dreiser keeps a majestic balance between sympathy and criticism. He sees Clyde as a characteristic reflex of "the vast skepticism and apathy of life," as a characteristic instance of the futility of misplaced desire in a society that offers little ennobling sense of human potentiality. Yet he nevertheless manages to make the consequences of Clyde's mediocrity, if not the mediocrity itself, seem tragic. For in this youth there is concentrated the tragedy of human waste: energies, talents, affections all unused—and at least in our time the idea of human waste comprises an essential meaning of tragedy. It is an idea to which Dreiser kept returning both in his fiction and his essays. . . . (pp. 146-47)

The first half of *An American Tragedy* is given to the difficult yet, for Dreiser's purpose, essential task of persuading us that Clyde Griffiths, through his very lack of distinction, represents a major possibility in American experience. Toward this end Dreiser must accumulate a large sum of substantiating detail. He must show Clyde growing up in a family both materially and spiritually impoverished. He must show Clyde reaching out for the small pleasures, the trifles of desire, and learning from his environment how splendid are these induced wants. He must show Clyde, step by step, making his initiation into the world of sanctioned America, first through shabby and then luxury hotels, where he picks up the signals of status. He must show Clyde as the very image and prisoner of our culture, hungering with its hungers, empty with its emptiness.

Yet all the while Dreiser is also preparing to lift Clyde's story from this mere typicality, for he wishes to go beyond the mania for the average which is a bane of naturalism. Everything in this story is ordinary, not least of all the hope of prosperity through marriage—everything but the fact that Clyde begins to act out, or is treated as if he had acted out, the commonplace fantasy of violently disposing of a used-up lover. This is the sole important departure from ordinary verisimilitude in the entire novel, and Dreiser must surely have known that it was. In the particular case upon which he drew for *An American Tragedy*, the young man did kill his pregnant girl; but Dreiser must nevertheless have realized that in the vast majority of such crises the young man dreams of killing and ends by marrying. Dreiser understood, however, that in fiction the effort to represent common experience requires, at one or two crucial points, an effect of heightening, an intense exaggeration. Clyde's situation may be representative, but his conduct must be extreme. And is that not one way of establishing the dramatic: to drive a representative situation to its limits of possibility?

In *An American Tragedy* Dreiser solved the problem which vexes all naturalistic novelists: how to relate harmoniously a large panorama of realism with a sharply-contoured form. Dreiser is endlessly faithful to common experience. No one, not even the critics who have most harshly attacked the novel, would care to deny the credibility of Clyde and Roberta Alden, the girl he betrays; most of the attacks on Dreiser contain a mute testimony to his achievement, for in order to complain about his view of life they begin by taking for granted the "reality" of his imagined world. Yet for all its packed detail, the novel is economically structured—though one must understand that the criterion of economy for this kind of novel is radically different from that for a James or Conrad novel. In saying all this I do not mean anything so improbable as the claim that whatever is in the book belongs because it is there; certain sections, especially those which prepare for Clyde's trial, could be cut to advantage; but the over-all architecture has a rough and impressive craftsmanship.

The action of the novel moves like a series of waves, each surging forward to a peak of tension and then receding into quietness, and each, after the first one reenacting in a more complex and perilous fashion the material of its predecessor. Clyde in Kansas City, Clyde in Chicago, Clyde alone with Roberta in Lycurgus, Clyde on the edge of the wealthy set in Lycurgus—these divisions form the novel until the point where Roberta is drowned, and each of them acts as a reflector on the other, so that there is a mounting series of anticipations and variations upon the central theme. (pp. 147-49)

Reinforcing this narrative rhythm is Dreiser's frequent shifting of the distance he keeps from his characters. At some points he establishes an almost intolerable closeness to Clyde, so that we feel locked into the circle of the boy's moods, while at other points he pulls back to convey the sense that Clyde is but another helpless creature among thousands of helpless creatures struggling to get through their time. . . . Through these shifts in perspective Dreiser can show Clyde in his double aspect, both as solitary figure and symbolic agent.

In the first half of the novel Dreiser prepares us to believe that Clyde *could* commit the crime: which is to say, he prepares us to believe that a part of ourselves could commit the crime. At each point in the boy's development there occurs a meeting between his ill-formed self and the surrounding society. The impoverishment of his family life and the instinctual deprivation of his youth leave him a prey to the values of the streets and the hotels; yet it is a fine stroke on Dreiser's part that only through these tawdry values does Clyde really become aware of his impoverishment and deprivation. Yearning gives way to cheap desire and false gratification, and these in turn create new and still more incoherent yearnings. It is a vicious circle and the result is not, in any precise sense, a self at all, but rather the beginning of that poisonous fabrication which in America we call a "personality." (pp. 149-50)

Dreiser surrenders himself to the emotional life of his figures, not by passing over their delusions or failures but by casting all his energy into evoking the fullness of their experience. And how large, finally, is the sense of the human that smolders in this book! How unwavering the feeling for "the sensitive and seeking individual in his pitiful struggle with nature—with his enormous urges and his pathetic equipment!" Dreiser's passion for detail is a passion for his subject; his passion for his subject, a passion for the suffering of men. As we are touched by Clyde's early affection for Roberta, so later we participate vicariously in his desperation to be rid of her. We share this desire with some shame, but unless we count ourselves among the hopelessly pure, we share it.

Other naturalists, when they show a character being destroyed by overwhelming forces, frequently leave us with a sense of littleness and helplessness, as if the world were collapsed. Of Dreiser that is not, in my own experience, true. For he is always on the watch for a glimmer of transcendence, always concerned with the possibility of magnitude. Clyde is pitiable, his life and fate are pitiable; yet at the end we feel a somber exaltation, for we know that *An American Tragedy* does not seek to persuade us that human existence need be without value or beauty.

No, for Dreiser life is something very different. What makes him so absorbing a novelist, despite grave faults, is that he remains endlessly open to experience. This is something one cannot say easily about most modern writers, including those more subtle and gifted than Dreiser. The trend of modern literature has often been toward a recoil from experience, a nausea before its flow, a denial of its worth. Dreiser, to be sure, is unable to make the finer discriminations among varieties of experience; and there is no reason to expect these from him. But he is marvelous in his devotion to whatever portion of life a man can have; marvelous in his conviction that something sacred resides even in the transience of our days; marvelous in his feeling that the grimmest of lives retain the possibility of ''a mystic something of beauty that perennially transfigures the world.'' Transfigures—that is the key word, and not the catch-phrases of mechanistic determinism he furnished his detractors. (pp. 151-52)

> *Irving Howe, ''Dreiser and Tragedy: The Stature of Theodore Dreiser'' (copyright © 1964 by Irving Howe; reprinted by permission of the author), in* The New Republic, *Vol. 151, Nos. 4 & 5 and 8 & 9, July 25 and August 22, 1964 (and reprinted in* Dreiser: A Collection of Critical Essays, *edited by John Lydenberg, Prentice-Hall, Inc., 1971, pp. 141-52).*

HENRY NASH SMITH (essay date 1964)

[*Smith discusses the vision of Dreiser's Cowperwood trilogy.*]

Dreiser's trilogy about Frank Cowperwood contains by far the most impressive portrait of a big businessman in American fiction. No later writer has brought to the subject anything like Dreiser's commitment, no one else has dealt with it at such length or with such intensity. Yet in characterizing Cowperwood, Dreiser has in the main simply taken over the familiar catalogue of the businessman's vices and presented them as virtues. For example, Cowperwood resembles many of his predecessors in being an unsatisfactory husband, but Dreiser makes the failure of his two marriages turn upon his sexual prowess; Cowperwood is irresistible as a lover, and he refuses to be content with one woman at a time. The moral indictment brought against the businessman by earlier novelists becomes a blueprint for Dreiser's demonstration that Cowperwood is superior to the moral and legal codes binding the average of mankind. The characterization involves ideas drawn at second hand from H. L. Mencken's *The Philosophy of Friedrich Nietzsche* (1908). Cowperwood exerts the inexplicable charm of the superman because he is beyond good and evil; he has ''no consciousness of what is currently known as sin.''

Much of the vividness of Cowperwood as a character is due to Dreiser's evident sympathy with his protagonist's scorn for ''the conventional mind.'' . . . Virtually all Dreiser's allusions to morals carry the express or implied charge of hypocrisy. (pp. 99-100)

Dreiser, writing from the viewpoint of an outsider with a background of poverty, disorder, and early sorrow, takes at face value the state of affairs made explicit in Warner's *A Little Journey*, where the moral principles are affirmed by observers remote from the ''real'' world of business. Dreiser translates the older contrast between a virtuous, semi-rural New England and the wickedness of commercial-minded New York into a contrast between the families of established economic and social position in Chicago and aggressive newcomers like Cowperwood. He insists that traditional codes of conduct are rationalizations supporting the status of a ruling class; his admiration for Cowperwood expresses his own resentment of the silk-stocking crowd. Perceiving that the tradition supporting this class has lost its moral authority and become a mere ideology, the superman brushes it aside and makes his own rules. To put this another way, with the waning of the values linked with New England, the morally neutral enclave that apologists for business had declared to be controlled by the impersonal laws of trade has widened its boundaries to embrace the whole of Dreiser's fictive universe.

But Dreiser does not share the prevalent belief in inevitable progress resulting from the free play of economic forces. He makes little of the fact that Cowperwood's consolidation of the street-railway systems of Chicago and London benefits society by providing more efficient transportation at lower cost. Although he asserts that ''God or the life force, if anything, is an equation,'' the world of business is not a harmony maintained by an invisible hand but an anarchy of struggle. The collapse of Cowperwood's financial empire conveys the idea that such a man must sooner or later threaten the stability of society, whereupon an equilibrium of forces neither good nor bad will reestablish itself.

Both the Promethean accomplishments and the ultimate failure of Cowperwood link him with that other subversive, Mark Twain's Connecticut Yankee, and back of him with Emerson's conception of Napoleon as the representative figure of the commercial nineteenth century. Cowperwood's empire, like theirs, cannot survive him. It is dissipated amid the bickerings of heirs, creditors, administrators, and courts. (pp. 101-02)

> *Henry Nash Smith, ''The Search for a Capitalist Hero: Businessmen in American Fiction,'' in* The Business Establishment, *edited by Earl F. Cheit (copyright © 1964 by John Wiley & Sons, Inc.; reprinted by permission of Earl F. Cheit), Wiley, 1964, pp. 77-112.*

PHILIP L. GERBER (essay date 1964)

[*In his study* Theodore Dreiser, *Gerber presents a useful introduction to Dreiser's novels. The excerpt below is taken from a concluding chapter characterizing Dreiser as ''The World's Worst Great Writer.''*]

Of a major writer, one expects scope. And although he is known primarily—and rightly so—as a novelist, Dreiser labored with some distinction in every major genre of modern literature. His short stories are cut from the same fabric as his novels and share the same merits, the same defects. For a time he thought of himself as a poet, and surely there was a touch of the poet, at least of the mystic, in him; but it was heavy-handed and unlyrical. His *Moods* sacrifice image to philosophy, are overwhelmed by thought instead of feeling. His ideas found a more proper outlet in the essay form to which he turned increasingly. The enormous manuscript which was to have elucidated his final and complete vision of life, finishing what *Hey, Rub-A-Dub-Dub!* had begun a quarter of a century before, is indicative of his natural feeling for the prose form. Even so, the ideas in his essays seemed more vital and were projected with more impact when dramatized in his novels.

The same is also true of his books of sketches, such as those included in *The Color of a Great City*. ''Sketches'' is a good term for them, for while they are interesting in themselves, and some are semi-poetic, they are but groundwork for stories and become of significance only when incorporated in fiction. Between 1915 and 1920 Dreiser thought of himself as a playwright, and while some of his dramas were produced, the stage was not his métier. Outside of the novel form, it was as a writer of autobiography that Dreiser realized his greatest triumphs. His *Dawn* and *Newspaper Days* have been called unsurpassed. They read like novels, and perhaps that is the secret of their success. (pp. 172-73)

Dreiser was the first American to portray with truth and power our modern world of commerce and mechanization, the first to portray the dismal depersonalization of the individual which results from urbanization and intensifying societal pressure to conform, the first to draw us frankly and grimly as a nation of status-seekers. The measure of his success is marked by the persistent validity of his novels. And tame as his ''erotic episodes'' now read to a generation accustomed to stronger fare, he led the way in openly and honestly treating sex as a major force. (pp. 173-74)

Disappointingly few writers impress one as possessing a coherent philosophy. Hemingway had this quality, and perhaps to a lesser extent, Faulkner. They, like the nineteenth-century giants—Melville, Hawthorne, Whitman, Twain—saw life clearly and distinctly, if by necessity from limited vantage points. They seemed to examine life as through binoculars which allowed them to penetrate and yet at the same time restricted their fields of vision. We must be able to count on a great author not only to describe life but to interpret it. Dreiser, of all twentieth-century writers, belongs to this illustrious company. His works—poems, essays, dramas, as well as novels—are monolithic. In them life is everywhere seen through the same binoculars; it is a colorful, kaleidoscopic, unpredictable riddle, at bottom tragic. *Sister Carrie* of 1900 and *The Bulwark* of forty-five years later, aside from particulars, tell the same story about America. Man is a mechanism, his pitiful existence determined by factors of biology and social environment which Dreiser, for want of a better term, labels ''chemisms.'' The cosmos operating in his stories is uncaring, unfeeling; at bottom it is an unfair universe, controlled by gods who disdain involvement in their creation. We can nod in agreement with the writer or cavil at the darkness of his pessimism, but we are forced above all to stop, to consider, to think. (p. 174)

Probably because of his philosophy—we are all companions in the same sinking ship—Dreiser feels keenly the plight of each individual human soul at the mercy of chance and of forces beyond his control. It is significant that, though failures abound in his novels, there are no villains, only human beings who are more or less fortunate than their neighbors. In the Dreiser world, each life is necessarily a tragedy. One by one, from high to low, the objects of his pity are exposed to our view, trailing their stars of illusion into oblivion: Carrie, Hurstwood, Jennie, Cowperwood, Witla, Clyde, Solon Barnes. Man is a tool of the universe, at the mercy of hypnotic, incomprehensible drives for sexual conquest, for esteem, fame, power, money. Each life is a shooting star; and, as it burns itself out in the cold, unfriendly atmosphere, Dreiser's sympathy is with it.

The furor over Dreiser's subject matter, his handling of sexual matters in particular, has dropped below the level of a whisper; but the critical dispute concerning his other values as a novelist rolls merrily along. The river of Dreiser criticism runs, like the Mississippi, in an ever fluctuating channel, but it breaks clearly on the rock of fictional artistry and pours into distinct forks.

This is nothing new, but it has continued for well over half a century. The word we hear most often from those who lament his influence is ''barbarity.'' . . . Actually, a good case can be made for Dreiser's abilities as an artist, to demonstrate at the very least that the novels did not spew from his pen in an explosion of uncontrolled emotion. For there is much more to his work than the barbaric yawp which apparently has stymied the sensibilities of many critics.

The style in which a major author writes is a matter of natural concern to his readers and critics, and Dreiser's became a subject for heated controversy from the time of *Sister Carrie*. His disparagers found in it a flaw to cavil at; his admirers, a weakness to excuse. On more than one occasion it has been seriously questioned whether Dreiser has a style at all. (pp. 174-75)

Not completely insensitive to stylistic perfection, Dreiser was aware of his own limitations and trespasses—he could hardly avoid being, considering the critics' strident protests over his ''butchery'' of the language; and many times he professed a desire and intention of revising all his novels with style in mind. Only *The Financier* received this treatment, and then not entirely to its benefit; for if awkwardnesses and repetitions were deleted, so were a number of valuable commentaries. The fact is that, over and above his not being by nature a ''word man,'' Dreiser forever had too many projects in the works, too many statements to be made and books to be written to spare the necessary time for such revision. He had a choice to make, and he made it instinctively.

As a result, Dreiser produces a rough-hewn but solid and serviceable plank full of knots which, while not diminishing the plank's utility, add nothing to its beauty. (p. 177)

An American Tragedy contains sentences so muddied in progression and so awkwardly qualified as to assume almost the shape of a whirlpool. . . . But the novel also contains passages whose narrative function is clear, whose dramatic sense is unimpaired, and whose direction is straightforward rather than spiral.

One salient fact remains incontrovertible, however: the gaucheries are present and no amount of polishing in neighboring regions will remove them. There is, besides, an irritating playing of words to death, no doubt subconscious upon the writer's part. In *An American Tragedy,* for instance, Dreiser plays upon *chic* in the manner of a sophomore who, having just discovered the term, is determined to wrest a place for it in the unlikeliest situations. In the *Trilogy of Desire* it is *trig* which is ridden till it can no longer stand, and in *The "Genius"* the word *subtle* eventually cracks beneath a burden it should never be forced to bear—explaining every dark, mysterious force and act for which Dreiser cannot logically account. Also, he betrays an unfortunate tendency toward grandiloquence, and passages where this tendency gains control, sound as if another—and much less mature—writer has taken over. (p. 178)

Dreiser produces not the ''novel *démeublé*'' of Willa Cather, but a highly furnished, perhaps even overcrowded, room with a view of all outdoors. Such a method not only lends itself to but is based upon the piling up of background trivia. Often this appears to be done indiscriminately. Yet details which in many instances by themselves seem of no import do in the mass create the world of his stories. (p. 179)

If we are willing to overlook Dreiser's occasional lapses and excesses, we soon realize that it is precisely from their load of minutiae that the novels derive a good share of their remarkable sense of life. Enough detail of the right sort will eventually assume the shape of a mountain, and this is the image to which Dreiser's novels are most often compared—mountainous, craggy, rugged and ungainly perhaps, but solid and formidable. The proof of the method is found in those novels where its absence is conspicuous. *The Bulwark* and *The Stoic*—written out of a sense of obligation and necessity, long after the original stimuli and data upon which they were based had passed from the mind—seem sketches for novels to come, first drafts or outlines to be fleshed out later. They are bare trees upon whose limbs the leaf-buds have yet to burst. (pp. 181-82)

Without the full social background of its companion books, *The Stoic* provides a limp ending to the Cowperwood saga, while *The Bulwark* splits into a panel of separate incidents.

In shaping his novels, Dreiser prefers the method of straight chronology. He begins most characteristically with the birth of his protagonist and drives forward slowly, steadily until death or a more critical termination is reached. We feel impelled to comment upon the superiority—for Dreiser's type of story—of this method in supplying the fullness so woefully lacking in much of today's fiction. The infinite probing of a moment for every bit of light it can cast upon a sensitive personality has its very positive values and is not to be made light of. But Dreiser's themes of slow growth, of gradual personal disintegration, of life's inevitable reversals, require a different approach. The crucial events of his stories are the result of the passage of time and occur as the consequence of innumerable prior experiences. Being the result of time, Dreiser's most memorable denouements—Clyde's execution, Hurstwood's suicide, Frank Cowperwood's estate picked bare by legal vultures—can be arrived at effectively only by the presentation of extensive periods of time.

Only once, in *The Bulwark*, does he experiment with beginning a novel *in medias res* and then flashing back to the beginning. And every novel starting with youth pushes ahead, through that indispensable learning process, toward adulthood. But not for Dreiser is the modern story with its child or adolescent hero. The child lives in his own world, after all, a restricted and personal sphere. While this world may be of momentous significance to the child at its center, it of necessity puts limitations upon the broad social landscape whose depiction is one of the glories of Dreiser's achievement. Knowing that the child is but father to the man, Dreiser paints these formative years for their own sake, but always with the future in mind. His adults act in consistency with early experiences. So Carrie's life is conditioned by her schooling in Chicago's concrete jungle; Clyde's, by the tension between poverty and wealth; Frank's, by his observation and acute analysis of life's basic struggle; and Solon's, by his isolated and rigid Quaker upbringing. Looking from the last day, we can peer far back down the road to the inception of a particular life's journey; and the route is clear. These lives form patterns, are all of a piece, and, as such, achieve meaning. (pp. 182-83)

Even though Dreiser keeps his eyes, for the most part, upon his central actor, he reserves his right to omniscient authorship, so that he may if he wishes—and he often does wish—make a leap in time and space or enter the story to comment and interpret the action, particularly in its philosophical or sociological aspects.

Omniscience provides also for one of his most effective narrative devices—the portrayal of simultaneous action, generally for ironical counterpoint. We feel the effect of it in all his novels. One outstanding example is the continued tension set up in us between the rise of Carrie and the collapse of Hurstwood. . . . The device works brilliantly throughout *An American Tragedy*—for instance, in the flight of Clyde while the posse is dogging his trail, and even more effectively in the trial sequence. The advantage gained is in completeness of scene. A reader senses that he is dealing with a broad canvas of life rather than with the miniature of an isolated individual. He feels that nothing essential is being withheld, the machinery of society is stripped bare. And, while Dreiser avowedly cared only for the individual and nothing for the mass, there exists no individual except as a member of the crowd, formed by the crowd, pitted against the crowd.

Dreiser deals with a wealth of imagery and figure, but this artistry is often obscured by the moutain of realistic detail. The use of the rocking chair in *Sister Carrie* to indicate indecision, contemplation, stagnation, and restiveness is but one example. In the same book, water images are used consistently to portray the forces which sweep men forward, out of control; Carrie is described variously as ''getting into deep water. She was letting her few supports float away from her'' and as ''an anchorless, storm-beaten little craft which could do absolutely nothing but drift.''

Imagery from the animal world abounds. linking Dreiser with literary Darwinism; the jungle of nature overshadows human society. We think first of obvious instances, such as the lobster-squid duel in *The Financier* which sets young Cowperwood's notions firmly in the groove they are to follow until his death. (pp. 183-84)

A pattern of symbolism buttresses Dreiser's concepts; clothes and dwellings are the most prominent. Both serve to dramatize human beings trapped in illusory materialism—exterior symbols of show and display which furnish ultimately no nourishment for the soul. Without clothes as an emblem of status and achievement and worth, *Sister Carrie* would be hard pressed to convey the pointed comments it does upon American society. It is in this novel that clothes symbolism is sharpest. But the device carries over. Through her contrasting indifference to silks and ribbons we are enabled to perceive the more solid values of Jennie Gerhardt. And Clyde Griffiths places as much premium upon appearance as Carrie does; his delight in his bellhop's uniform tells us this at once. . . .

Dreiser is also fond of emphasizing human dwellings in order to heighten the impact of his stories. Any reader of the novels can at once call to mind a dozen or more localities which have lingered in his consciousness. From *Sister Carrie* we recall scenes which also represent the rise and fall of the characters: the shabby little flat on West Van Buren Street in which Carrie Meeber's sister is imprisoned; Drouet's apartment in Ogden Place with its green plush couch, pier-glass mirror, and Brussels carpet. . . . From these scenes we move upward until we reach the splendid hotels in which Carrie, without charge because of the publicity her presence lends the establishments, is furnished with every modern comfort except happiness and contentment. At the same time we slide downward with Hurstwood from home to flat to flophouse, to his narrow coffin-sized cubicle where he stuffs the cracks with his ragged clothes and turns on the gas jets.

The story **"Fine Furniture"** . . . is Dreiser's most pointed treatment of the furniture theme. (p. 185)

Or we might turn to the *Trilogy*, which of all Dreiser's works most depends upon house symbolism, and find here the pleasure domes of Frank Cowperwood, each one more extravagant than the last, more crammed with buccaneer's loot—and yet emptier. If any book rivals the *Trilogy* in emphasizing places, it is **An American Tragedy**. The book could almost be said to be structured in terms of dwellings: the Door of Hope Mission and the Green-Davidson Hotel; Mrs. Cuppy's rooming house and the Griffiths mansion on Wykeagy Avenue; Roberta's room and the death house. (p. 187)

Dreiser's *dramatis personae* exist in a material world, and by their material preferences we know them. . . . All of these dwellings, even more than they reflect the tastes of their inhabitants, shape the fears and joys, the frustrations and triumphs of those who live in them. They are little worlds over which they can rule, from which they can escape, or to which they will succumb.

Judicious foreshadowing again reveals the artist in control of his material. Carrie Meeber's success on the stage may astonish her, but it has been long prepared for. When it occurs, we remember her earlier triumph in Chicago in the Custer Lodge of the Order of Elks' production of "Under the Gaslight" when, almost single-handedly, she rescued that amateur theatrical from disaster. (pp. 187-88)

In later works, where Dreiser picks up the method and terminology of the psychoanalysts—when he first begins employing terms like "repressions" and "subconscious," "psychic sex scar" and "Freudianism"—we are also compelled to notice foreshadowing as it occurs. (p. 188)

The latter events of **An American Tragedy** are prepared for by the most extensive and artistically successful foreshadowing Dreiser was capable of. . . . Roberta's plight is seen in clear perspective when we recall the care with which Esta's shame—her elopement, pregnancy, and consequent abandonment—is described in Book One. Clyde's infatuation with Hortense Briggs—his naïve susceptibility to a pretty face and his eagerness to sacrifice all to gain it for his own—prepares the way for the Sondra-Roberta chapters which lie ahead. And when young Russell is introduced in the epilogue, we have the entire novel as a foreshadowing of his doom. Here the artist has clearly superseded the reporter.

The precise nature and degree of Dreiser's artistry will remain always a matter for sharp disagreement. His critics have cried down and his defenders shored up his reputation ever since 1900. (p. 189)

What has made his novels endure is, in the end, not the presence or absence of delicately balanced sentences or fine and precise diction. It is rather the tragic and real sense of life pulsing through their pages that causes his books to be read and reread. We feel that, whatever else is meritorious or crude, Dreiser's are portraits drawn straight from the varying strata of human existence; he is more Daumier or Goya than Raphael. Contributing to this effect is the effort expended on development of the *mise en scène*, the social panorama which ever reminds us of precisely what America was like while the action of any particular novel was unfolding.

Contributing even more grandly is the Dreiserian view of human existence. The artist becomes, not a camera obscura, but an interpreter. What is missing in lesser writers—the impression of life witnessed from a definite and stated viewpoint—becomes more and more with passing years a virtue that sets Dreiser above and apart. Whatever image we select to express the man's stand—whether it be the grim picture of life as a jungle with human beasts raging and clawing for survival, or of life as a maelstrom blindly, indifferently hurling human souls through the years on winds of chance—we recognize commitment to a philosophy.

And whether we join in that commitment or find it dismaying, there is pleasure and satisfaction in witnessing it, in having it elucidated, in having at least one window on life opened wide and clear so that we may all look, see, and judge for ourselves. More and more, the judgment of readers has exonerated Dreiser of the charges made against him in his early career. More and more, that judgment places him securely in the front rank of American fictionists; he becomes more solidly than ever what Mencken called him, "a crag of basalt." Whatever its beauty or grimness, the crag unmistakably marks our native landscape. (pp. 189-90)

> *Philip L. Gerber, in his* Theodore Dreiser *(copyright © 1964 by Twayne Publishers, Inc.; reprinted with the permission of Twayne Publishers, a Division of G. K. Hall & Co., Boston), Twayne, 1964, 220 p.*

JAMES LUNDQUIST   (essay date 1974)

[*In his discussion of "Dreiser's Philosophy and Politics," Lundquist mentions that Dreiser went "on occasional scientific and philosophical kicks" while working on a proposed, never-completed forty-chapter philosophical treatise. The conclusions to which Dreiser's philosophical ruminations led him are detailed by Desmond Tarrant (see excerpt below). Earlier chapters of Lundquist's book deal with biographical facts, Dreiser's characters, and an in-depth study of* An American Tragedy.]

The scene at the end of *The "Genius"* in which Eugene Witla walks out onto his yard one November night and looks up into endless space is emblematic of Dreiser's self-image. Dreiser thought of himself as a thinker, a brooder not only upon silences but also upon the whole welter of life. He was, in one sense, ill-prepared for such a task; he was poorly educated, his reading was erratic, and he often came to weighty conclusions without realizing that, despite their weight, they are the substance of clichés. . . . Yet in another sense despite his tendency toward superstition (Dreiser liked to consult fortunetellers, he worried over omens, and he did believe in the Ouija board) and a certain failure to realize the limitations forced upon him by his intellectual background, Dreiser's curiosity along with his compassion for the unfortunate made it possible for him to achieve reflective moments in his novels that sometimes suggest Melville, Dostoevsky, and Tolstoy. Moreover, Dreiser's compulsive brooding had manifestations outside of his fiction, especially in two often-neglected aspects of his life—his philosophic writing and his political involvement.

It is, of course, inexact to term Dreiser a philosopher. He had little training in the modes of formal philosophical discourse, and a logician would be able to read Dreiser's ruminative essays only with considerable irritation. As in his novels, Dreiser often writes too much and says too little, but in the one philosophic volume he published, *Hey, Rub-a-Dub-Dub!*, there are, along with many inconsistencies and much triteness, dozens of striking sentences, moods that are frequently charming, and reflections that occasionally make aspects of Dreiser's novels more understandable.

Hey, Rub-A-Dub-Dub! . . . is subtitled **"A Book of the Mystery and Wonder and Terror of Life."** The title and the subtitle suggest the sort of conflict present throughout Dreiser's thought. Dreiser explained the title by saying that it, like life itself, has no meaning. And this attitude is just what a superficial interpretation of Dreiser's writing would support. The subtitle, on the other hand, brings out another side of Dreiser—his deep involvement with the mysterious, with chemical relationships, dreams, the vagaries of human personality, crime and punishment, the meaning of sexuality, the courses of the stars. (pp. 106-07)

The eagerness to find and accept solutions is attacked again and again in Dreiser's novels and essays because it is, for him, a failure of nerve. To survive, as John Paradiso does [in the essay **"Hey, Rub-a-Dub-Dub!"**], amid the pressures of confusion, being reminded every time he opens a newspaper of the horror that is daily present in thousands of flesh-and-blood tragedies, and still not give himself over to illusion—that, for Dreiser, is true heroism. But the fact that there are no solutions does not mean that one should turn away from the mysteries of life. Solutions destroy mystery, and this is why Dreiser was so hesitant to believe in any of them. He wanted to sit and wonder about things. . . . (p. 109)

The subsequent chapters of *Hey, Rub-a-Dub-Dub!* (including three all but unreadable plays), while returning to the theme of illusion again and again, move Dreiser's philosophy toward comprehensiveness in outline if not in fact. One by one he considers such topics as the principle of change in the universe, man's place in nature, the makeup of the human personality, the importance of the sex impulse, the psychological consequences of manual labor, marriage and divorce, and the idea of progress. Although Dreiser does not stick to a chapter-by-chapter development of his thought, it is possible to put together a synthesis of his ideas, keeping in mind that in Dreiser's thinking there are no conclusions. . . . (pp. 109-10)

Dreiser argues . . . [that] in nature nothing is fixed and every individual is part of a vast restlessness. When we make up rules, such as those governing marriage, we fly in the face of external flux and only contribute to our own unhappiness. As a consequence, man's place in nature is severely limited—and even more severely limited if he continues to view nature in terms of rigid and illusory symptoms, such as the idea that each man possesses the potentialities of greatness. . . . Personality is determined long before birth and all life can do is to provide the opportunity for inherent capacities to develop within the scheme of universal and quite likely undirected change.

The development of these capacities is overwhelmingly influenced, however, by sexual drives that provide the major evidence for a chemical theory of human makeup. Unfortunately, human societies have organized themselves again and again to suppress or even ignore this dominant aspect of motivation, and the result (in the United States especially) is neurosis. (pp. 110-11)

Dreiser projects an image of secretive, mysterious Nature, seemingly indifferent to man's haphazard and fumbling progress (if progress it is), yet his Nature is a force or presence that seemingly abides by a principle of "swing," or balance—for every action there is a reaction, a condition of checks and balances—that Dreiser terms the "equation Inevitable." We are chemical beings, but "Nature has supplied us with certain forces and chemic tendencies and responses, and has also provided (rather roughly in certain instances) the checks and balances which govern the same." We are the victims of constant change, but change that can go only so far in one direction before an opposing force appears as a corrective.

Life is often painful, but we are physically prevented from suffering pain beyond a certain point. And it is here, in this equational conception of Nature, that an essential point concerning Dreiser's thinking is often missed—that his skepticism very readily turns into a tempered form of optimism. . . : Man's plight may be essentially tragic—he is a nonentity *and* aware of it—but out of the equational vise he is able to synthesize not only art but a reasonable idea of divinity. . . . This is not exactly a positive view, but neither is it the grim mechanism of despair often credited to Dreiser.

His reflections on "Nature," particularly in the essay **"The Reformer,"** but in many other chapters of *Hey, Rub-a-Dub-Dub!,* have an oddly Emersonian, if not exactly transcendental quality to them. Nature, to Dreiser, is thought of in relationship to pervading goodness; but he is not willing to give a conception of evil the upper hand either. To him Nature is wise, avoiding median conditions or strict balances between opposite forces because this would be nothingness. (pp. 111-12)

When we follow Dreiser's reasoning to its inevitable conclusions, we see that he is, like his near contemporary Hardy, something of a meliorist. This tendency is present in Dreiser's novels, even though none of them, not even *The Bulwark,* can be said to have a happy ending. Dreiser's "happier" characters—Carrie, Jennie, Eugene, Solon, and, not to be overlooked, John Paradiso—all learn how to stomach Nature and the eternal swing of forces. Others, Clyde Griffiths certainly, and Frank Cowperwood to a certain extent, are struck down by the pendulum. But all of these characters have a place in Dreiser's peculiar scheme of things, a scheme that is not mechanistic, naturalistic, Freudian, or behavioristic, although it involves related and often derivative ideas. Dreiser's philosophy is a partly scientific, partly mystic collection of thoughts that come out of his emotions as much as his intellect; its roots are in American Transcendentalism, the tough line of the Darwinians, the compassionate response of the Progressive era, and his own turn-of-the-century conglomeration of experience. (p. 113)

The melioristic turn in Dreiser's thought also explains his seemingly sudden interest in political theories after the publication of *An American Tragedy.* The standard conception of Dreiser as a despairing mechanist makes his direct involvement in social reform and his membership in the Communist Party appear at best contradictory, at worst intellectually dishonest. But Dreiser's inconsistency on this point is diminished considerably when one realizes that he increasingly came to blame social injustice on rigid political and economic attitudes and illusory conceptions of Nature's pendulumic swing. And it must be emphasized that Dreiser's thinking on these matters is not a consequence of either the attention focused on him by the success of *An American Tragedy* or of the awakened social consciousness that affected so many other writers in the late 1920s. Two essays in *Hey, Rub-A-Dub-Dub!*—**"Some Aspects of Our National Character,"** and **"More Democracy or Less?**

An Inquiry"—show that Dreiser's development as a pamphleteer on matters of national concern was not sudden or late.

In these essays Dreiser attacks American democracy as an illusion. The United States, given the enthusiasms of our founding ideologists, was to be a place of intellectual and spiritual freedom. . . . But this idea of democracy is an unrealized dream, Dreiser argues. Instead of freedom there is repression; and the chains of superstition and poverty still bind. The wealth is controlled by a small percentage of the population; the poor are taken advantage of and lied to; and we are falsely encouraged to believe that success is within our grasp if we will work hard enough. . . . But, given the eternal swing of Nature, the defects in American democracy cannot go unremedied, nor the drift toward ever greater money control go unchecked. Something must happen.

Dreiser more and more came to think that communism or some form of socialism was what would happen. There are many reasons—not all of them clear—why Dreiser arrived at this conclusion. His own conception of Nature is, of course, based on a dialectic not unlike that of Marxist thought. Dreiser's pulsating cosmos readily allows for Marx's dialectical materialism and the long history of class struggle. In addition, communism did not present itself as a closed system, and in the 1930s many liberals were convinced that it could more readily adjust to the calamities Dreiser's Nature was always forcing on helpless man. Soviet communism thus seemed to Dreiser to be based on a more accurate conception of reality than that of American democratic capitalism, with its apparently fatal susceptibility to illusory notions of morality or of a just and benign God. And in trying to account for Dreiser's leftward drift, one can neither overlook the Progressive elements in Dreiser's writing (*Sister Carrie,* it is remembered, came out of the same social climate that produced Upton Sinclair's *The Jungle*) nor the sympathy for the impoverished and powerless that runs all the way back to his childhood.

Dreiser obtained a firsthand look at communist society when upon the invitation of the Soviet Union's Bureau of Cultural Relations he toured the USSR during the last three months of 1927. Permitted considerable freedom of inquiry and movement, he was struck by the vitality of Russia and the promise its new society seemed to afford; but, as always he had his hesitations. . . . Nevertheless, when he returned to New York, he told the reporters who greeted him that, taking into account the breadlines forming in the United States even in that pre-Depression year, he preferred the Russian system. (pp. 114-16)

The Russian trip was followed by a long automobile journey across the United States in 1930, numerous magazine articles on social and political matters, and a greater interest in political activism. (p. 117)

Increasing age slowed his active participation considerably, but he retained, with characteristic hesitation and many doubts, his leftist stance even through such events as Stalin's purges and the Russo-German pact of 1939 that dismayed so many Soviet sympathizers. . . . Finally, in 1945, he formally joined the Communist Party.

Two of Dreiser's nonfiction books date from his 1930s political phase. The first, and most important of them, is *Tragic America* . . . , whose title echoed that of his most successful novel. Intended as Dreiser's outline for reform, *Tragic America* is one of his sloppiest books. . . . Bad as it is, *Tragic America* gives

us one more image of Dreiser the meliorist insisting that America need not be as tragic as it is, and holding to his central view that the belief in illusions is at the bottom of most of our economic and social problems. Though it is generally riddled with errors, portions of *Tragic America* lead the reader to wish that Dreiser had been able or willing to put the book together more carefully; it could have been an important document in American social history.

The same is not true of *America Is Worth Saving*. . . . It is a book designed to show the futility of America's entrance into another European war on the side of Great Britain. (pp. 118-20)

Dreiser's resistance to rigid systems often made his endorsement of communist programs impossible, and he was never considered an acceptable ideologist by the communist hierarchy in the United States. . . . Because of his belief in the pendulum of Nature, what Dreiser saw in communism was a leftward movement that at the time was not only necessary but inevitable. But he also believed that when Nature is ready the reverse tendency will begin, the pendulum will swing back, and we must avoid the kinds of illusions that result from dogmatic acceptance of a set of beliefs, be they philosophical or political.

There is little in Dreiser's thinking that can be called original, and he was certainly deceived in conceiving of himself as anything but a novelist. The time he spent on his nonfiction books . . . was not time well spent. . . . Throughout Dreiser's work there is something many critics have referred to as "clumsiness." But what this is, as his nonfiction writing certainly reveals, is a tendency toward laziness, a reluctance to revise, an impatience that pleases few readers. Though *Hey, Rub-A-Dub-Dub!* and *Tragic America* cast valuable light on Dreiser's work and time, they are for the extremely patient reader only—and this is unfortunate. (pp. 120-21)

The odd thing about the problem of explaining Dreiser is that he spent his whole life and much of his writing time trying to do the job for us. His autobiographical books are there, in all their frankness, for us to read. And all of his novels, especially *The "Genius,"* contain fragments of himself. Yet Dreiser remains mysterious and many formulas have been devised to categorize him. (p. 124)

In Dreiser we have a writer who cannot easily be understood in terms of his reading, his environment, or his education. He seems to have been born knowing things he did not have to learn. He knew little of literary history, yet his first novel became a turning point, a touchstone in American literature. Somehow, with nothing that can be read as a sense of direction, he found himself at "the crossroads of the novel." He set up a permanent roadblock for the older writers of the genteel tradition and went on to lead the fight for freedom of expression that made possible, to a certain extent, the achievement of the whole generation of writers that followed him. As Mencken wrote of him in a letter sent to be read at Dreiser's funeral, "the fact remains that he was a great artist, and that no other American of his generation left so wide and handsome a mark upon the national letters. American writing, before and after Darwin."

He was a man of contradiction and great inconsistency in his own output. He could weld together a giant novel like *An American Tragedy* and follow it up by botching what could have been an important book, *Tragic America*. . . . He could devote himself with great energy to contemporary developments in politics and science, yet his verse collections—[*Moods, Cadenced and Declaimed, The Aspirant,* and *Epitaph*] . . . show little awareness of what was happening in poetry at that time.

But the difficulty in understanding Dreiser is as it should be. He was forever suspicious of systems, of easy ways of getting light into dark corners, of accepting theories. He viewed himself as, and indeed was, a product of the Nature that figures so prominently in his philosophy. The mystery and wonder and terror that Dreiser in *Hey, Rub-A-Dub-Dub!* associates with all life are apparent in any reading of Dreiser's own life. And the restless swinging from one extreme to another that defines Nature in Dreiser's thought could be used to explain the significance of his place in the development of the novel. He was what he was, when he was, where he was, because that is the way things are. That is as close as Dreiser could come to understanding himself, and it is perhaps as close as we can come. (pp. 125-26)

> *James Lundquist, in his* Theodore Dreiser *(copyright © 1974 by Frederick Ungar Publishing Co., Inc.), Ungar, 1974, 150 p.*

DESMOND TARRANT   (essay date 1976)

[*Tarrant traces Dreiser's philosophical development toward mysticism.*]

During the fifteen years from 1930 until his death in December 1945, aged 74, Theodore Dreiser's thinking followed two main lines of development. One became externally interwoven with topical matters, social and political; the other led him inwards, finally to the well of the water of life in the garden of mystic comprehension.

The outcome was that he became a communist (although claiming complete freedom of thought and speech), a member of a proudly godless organisation, at the precise time when he was in his most religious frame of mind. . . .

But the route to the largest understanding of Dreiser's personal development is through his internal development. This took the form of a bridge from his scientific interests to his relations with everything created, comprising a scientifically-founded mystic awareness involving both head and heart in a Wordsworthian state in which is heard the still, sad music of the universe.

Previously, Dreiser had so read Spencer's philosophy that it had shattered and confused him by leaving him prone to a blind mechanical universe. Now, however, he fastened on Spencer's concept of immanence, the dwelling of the Creator within everything created. (p. 23)

Dreiser's development from narrow empirical enquiries to a larger religious comprehension may be seen in his introduction to *The Living Thoughts of Thoreau* (1939), published six years before his death.

He starts by reviewing the scope and development of philosophy from early Greece to his time, noting how science concentrates on *how* and philosophy and art on *why*. He observes that God is a word often used to describe Spirit, Brahma, Divine Essence, or Force, all expressing an "imaginary something", conforming to laws or "the essence or spirit otherwise assumed to inhabit or inform them". This is in accord with the Hindu concept whereby Force derives from Spirit, and during a process of change is reconverted into evolved Spirit.

The evolution, the greater refinement and complexity, is presumably the object of the exercise, the justification of the whole business, including the suffering.

This idea of a continuing process of evolution here and/or elsewhere is continually presented in Dreiser's selection of Thoreau's thoughts where all the later scientific findings of such an anthropology and psychology are projected to their natural conclusion by mystical and imaginative observation: including the idea of the "immanent creativity of nature", the concept that there are infinitely higher planes of life than exist here, and that poetry *is* all we do not know while most science but mimics it feebly at a distance. Dreiser concludes that if what is made can be creative and have a sense of purpose, so then can what made it.

Dreiser mentions on the basis of life being electrical—matter being only patterned energy as we would now say—the imaginative idea that is increasingly in the air, of man as a televised substance in a gigantic infinitely complex television programme. He refers to man "powered as a chemical and physical contrivance of external forces . . . responding to and synthesizing these inpouring and down-pouring stimuli. . . ."

He assumes that it could all be the work of a superior force in the matter-energy-space-time continuum; something inhabiting and directing what everywhere appears to be directed matter-energy; something—i.e. God—planning what it all does. This is his synchretism, his union of science and mysticism, of mind and emotion as he transcended his age by his imagination.

What Dreiser liked about Thoreau was that Thoreau's insight was rooted not in prejudiced dogma but in a clear, realistic, objective vision of the thing seen, the intermediary being "a gifted, almost telepathic, sensory reaction" as Thoreau seemed to tap "some marvellous, musical, lyrical source, which *was* life, which *is* a dream"

To see the full nature of Dreiser's final imaginative understanding, it is necessary to glance at the emotional ingredient that combined with his objective empirical enquiries. This may be summed up by his description of the same element in Thoreau of whom he writes that at no point is Thoreau willing to imply, "let alone admit, the absence . . . of a universal and apparently beneficent control, which, however dark and savage its results or expressions . . . is none-the-less, in some larger and realer sense . . . good—and more, artistically beautiful and satisfying, and so, well intended for all"

This is like saying that whatever the appearances, including the appearances of certain adults, whatever the screaming nightmare, that which made children could not but ultimately intend well for them.

The early Dreiser had thought man was abandoned, that Nature was indifferently cruel; now he thought the opposite. The reason for the change was a Wordsworthian experience Dreiser had in 1937. He was spending three months at laboratories on Long Island analysing scientifically the roots of life shown under the microscope. He came out into the sun and stooped to examine a cluster of small yellow flowers. He wrote in a letter: "Here was the same beautiful design and the lavish exquisite detail that I had been seeing all day. . . . Suddenly it was plain to me that there must be a divine, creative intelligence behind all this. It was after that, that I began to feel differently about the universe. I saw not only the intelligence, but the love and care that goes into all created things."

The higher the intelligence, the higher the purpose? Dreiser's suffering was the measure of his growth, an evolution now clearly visible as spiritual as he left the provincial to achieve the centre.

Dreiser's final mood is outlined in a long letter of July 18, 1940 to the Roman Catholic writer of a thesis on Dreiser who had gone so far as to say that Dreiser believed in God and the immortality of the soul while regarding it as ultimately unintelligible. In this letter, Dreiser referred to an "over" or universal soul and he considered that modern science and philosophy saw that this soul is "being" and contains all wisdom and all creative power. His scientific and philosophical studies, he wrote, compelled him to feel that there could be "but one primary creative force or soul", the laws of which are obeyed by all matter-energy. He sees all creation as manifestations of this all-pervading force. He added that to think that he may continue, in any form, as part of the process was enough for his well-being and peace of mind.

These ideas influenced the conclusion of **The Stoic,** while his final statement, **My Creator,** made in 1943, was written while he wrote **The Bulwark** and resembles the pacific Quakerism of that novel. In **My Creator,** Dreiser impartially sums up his final state of mind; he observed that he had at long last profound reverence for a process that might be eternal, and he prayed to remain the infinitesimal part of it that he was.

After a lifetime of struggle and despair, but of persistent enquiry, Theodore Dreiser's sense of drift and chaos had become a belief in necessity, orientation, and awe; he said that these qualities walk with deep, understanding serenity. (pp. 23-5)

> Desmond Tarrant, "The Mysticism of Theodore Dreiser" (copyright Desmond Tarrant), in World Union, Vol. XVI, No. 3, March, 1976, pp. 21-5.

YOSHINOBU HAKUTANI (essay date 1980)

[*Hakutani presents a biocritical study of Dreiser from his youth to the writing of his first novel,* Sister Carrie. *In two introductory chapters, Hakutani discusses Dreiser's contribution to American literary Naturalism and the influence of French Naturalist authors upon his work (see also Hakutani entry in bibliography). Also included are chapters on Dreiser's newspaper and magazine work, as well as a chapter on his early short stories, from which this excerpt is taken.*]

In the summer of 1899, shortly before the writing of *Sister Carrie,* Dreiser tried his hand at the short story, his first concentrated effort to write fiction. (p. 151)

During this period Dreiser managed to express himself on the concepts that had been latent in his mind for a long time. When he first read Herbert Spencer's work, Dreiser absorbed the technical theories of Spencerian determinism. . . . Seeing the proof of determinism in his own experience, Dreiser ignored Spencer's inherent theory of unending progress and chose to believe that man was a victim of natural forces. Dreiser's conclusion then was that "man was a mechanism, undevised and uncreated, and a badly and carelessly driven one at that." (p. 152)

Dreiser was a thoroughgoing determinist. He observed human behavior in terms of natural laws: the complexities of individual life were to be explained by physical and chemical reactions.

Despite the pessimistic conclusion at which Dreiser arrived in his interpretation of deterministic theory, it is still possible to find optimism in his belief that there is an inward, driving force, which is pushing mankind upward and onward. (pp. 152-53)

"**The Shining Slave Makers,**" Dreiser's first effort at fiction, is an allegory embodying a deterministic world view. What Dreiser tells by way of this allegory is reiterated in his short story "**Free,**" with which "**The Shining Slave Makers**" and the other early stories were later collected in a volume. . . . In another of his short stories, "**Butcher Rogaum's Door,**" Dreiser dramatizes a conflict between parent and child in much the same way as Crane deals with this conflict in *Maggie.* Unlike the first two stories, the other of Dreiser's stories in this group seem to mirror a considerable optimism and hope for man's condition. In "**Nigger Jeff**" the protagonist recognizes how a helpless man, a victim of natural forces within him and a prisoner of hostile forces in society, encounters his tragedy—his death. But this story by no means paints a hopeless predicament for man; man is also destined to ameliorate. "**Nigger Jeff**" ends with the hero's proclamation of his new ambition and hope not only for himself as an artist but for all men. And somewhat blatantly, in "**When the Old Century Was New,**" a fourth story, there is more social optimism than Darwinism, so that Dreiser looks upon life as an easy struggle for Utopia rather than as a bitter struggle for survival. (pp. 154-55)

The theme of "**The Shining Slave Makers,**" as might be expected from Dreiser's current preoccupation with deterministic philosophy, is the survival of the fittest. The setting of the story moves quickly from the human world to the world of ants. As Dreiser describes the environment and the action of the inhabitant, the ants' world is bizarre and fantastic yet turns out to be the same world with which he was familiar. That world is characterized by self-interest, greed, and the struggle for power. (pp. 155-56)

[The protagonist] McEwen, taking leave of the drudgery of the busy city life, comes out to take a seat under a soothing old beech tree. And for a while he sinks into his usual contemplative mood. Suddenly McEwen's meditation is interrupted by an ant crawling on his trousers. Shaking it off and then stamping on another ant running along the walk in front of him, McEwen now finds a swarm of other black ants hurrying about. At last, when one ant more active than the others catches his eye, McEwen follows its zigzag course while it stops here and there, examining something and considering the object's interest value. Suddenly, with a drowsy spell, McEwen discovers himself in an imaginary world in which, during a famine, the black ants are at war with the red ants.

Some critics have noticed a similarity between the setting of this tale and one of the interpolations Balzac makes toward the end of *The Wild Ass's Skin.* . . . In Balzac's story, however, the principal character, Valentin, is weary of his life and yet feels desperate at the thought of his approaching death. In order to divert his thoughts, Valentin tries to observe nature, thereby consoling himself with the equation of man and natural beings. . . . Balzac's vision, in his writing of *The Wild Ass's Skin,* is that of a human biologist. In writing "**The Shining Slave Makers**" Dreiser is not viewing man's life in terms of animal life. Rather, as in Thoreau's ant war in *Walden,* Dreiser is looking at ants in terms of man. (pp. 156-57)

McEwen, who is now a member of the same tribe—the black ants—cannot secure help from the ants of his own family. The persistent, reciprocal warfare among members of the family is more evocative of life in the animal kingdom than it is of the world of civilized man. Ironically, Dreiser intended to project an image of the survival of the fittest, not in the world of men but in the world of ants.

Dreiser's major motif here is man's selfishness as it is illustrated by the ants' behavior toward their fellow beings at the time of strife. . . . This is, to be sure, an allegory of life, but more importantly it is an allegory of Dreiser's own struggle in the past. In the newspaper experience of the early nineties, Dreiser viewed "life as a fierce, grim struggle in which no quarter was either given or taken, and in which all men laid traps, lied, squandered, erred through illusion." . . . (pp. 157-58)

Later in the story, when another ant is facing death, the compassionate McEwen attempts to offer him aid, but the ant, now overwhelmed by his own despair and resignation, declines. McEwen now realizes how helpless a creature can be under these circumstances. He cannot but simply look silently on the ant. "The sufferer," Dreiser remarks, "closed his eyes in evident pain, and trembled convulsively. Then he fell back and died. McEwen gazed upon the bleeding body, now fast stiffening in death, and wondered." . . . Dreiser's inference from the scene is clear: man, just like an insect, is powerless against those incidental forces that always surround him. This scene also resembles the aftermath of a train accident Dreiser reported a few years earlier in St. Louis. He then asked viewing the dead bodies that were twisted and burned beyond recognition, "Who were they? I asked myself. What had they been, done? The nothingness of man! They looked so commonplace, so unimportant, so like dead flies or beetles." . . . (pp. 158-59)

When a war breaks out between the black slave makers and the red Sanguineae (in Thoreau's ant war, between the black imperialists and the red republicans), McEwen, of course, sides with the black ants, but finally meets his own death. Dreiser seems to be telling himself: join the crowd, fight for the crowd, die for the crowd. The struggle for survival continues without purpose or a goal in sight. Only the fittest will survive; death alone is safe. After McEwen finally returns to reality, he is now possessed by a "mad enthusiasm." He tries to figure out the advantage of having met his recent comrades—the Shining Slave Makers—but, Dreiser writes, "finding it not he stood gazing. Then came reason, and with it sorrow—a vague, sad something out of far-off things." . . .

By projecting a serious and significant human dilemma onto minute subhuman life, Dreiser achieves detachment. But, in the allegory, though detached from the violent scene in which the struggle for survival is carried on, he can look at McEwen somewhat in the same way that McEwen looks at these ants in the insect Kingdom. In this way Dreiser does not reduce his life experience to a mere objective show but dramatizes it from a clumsy but instinctively derived point of view. By the solid material behind the theme and plot, the story became a powerful expression of his preoccupation at the time.

What Dreiser had to say in his first significant piece of fiction was exactly what brought about its rejection by the editor who first read the manuscript and returned it to its author with a letter protesting its "despicable philosophy." If this were the way the young author thought about man's life, the less he wrote about it the better. The editor thought that Dreiser was saying that men are cruel and deceptive just as nature is. The editor's reasoning was that Drieser enjoyed these qualities of man—the brutal, the deceptive, and the violent—and that Dreiser

was, therefore, dangerous to human society. However, Dreiser, who was blazing in those years with a strong passion for society and his fellow men, was still lined up against them. (p. 159)

In **"Butcher Rogaum's Door,"** Dreiser again justifies the value of Spencerian determinism. The events of the story happen with the mechanical consistency of the so-called chemisms. The story is a study of an incident that Dreiser sees as inevitable, granted the incipient milieu in which the character was placed.

The plot of **"Butcher Rogaum's Door"** first develops with the tension between an old father and his teenage daughter, Theresa, who has begun to be allured to the streetlights and the boys loitering outdoors on summer evenings. As the title suggests, the door to Rogaum's apartment above his butcher shop on Bleecker Street in New York City becomes significant. Old Rogaum tries to exhort against his daughter's going out after dark. . . . The stubborn German father's last restort is to threaten to lock her out, and indeed one night the determined old Rogaum does lock his daughter out when she fails to return by nine from dallying with her young friend. At the door, Theresa overhears her father talking savagely to Mrs. Rogaum, "Let her go, now. I vill her a lesson teach." Rattling the door again and getting no answer, she grows defiant. . . . And she walks back to her friend George Almerting. The night deepens; there is no sound of Theresa, and Rogaum starts searching for her. Returning in fear and without success, he sees at the door a young woman writhing in unmitigated pain as a result of her having drunk acid in a suicide attempt. Rogaum at first mistakes the woman for his daughter Therea. However clumsy the coincidence that Dreiser devises to suggest Theresa's possible fate, this story in the simple truth of its setting and characters mirrors the world Dreiser had grown to accept. The suicide, like Theresa, was once locked out, but Theresa, unlike the suicide, is never to become a prostitute or suicide, or both, like Crane's Maggie. Theresa obviously was written about as though she were one of Dreiser's own sisters. He was portraying the life of the people he knew by heart and what they could have become.

Fortunately, Theresa comes back safely, unlike the girl at the door who comes to a tragic end. But this was exactly his own family, since the religious old father, strict with the wanton daughter, locked her out one night and then worried, so that when he regained her unharmed, he refrained from beating her as he had intended. In the story, Dreiser, as elsewhere—*Dawn, Jennie Gerhardt, The "Genius", An American Tragedy*—treats the father with a sympathetic tone. A too Calvinistic German butcher, Rogaum emerges as a strangely appealing and rather pathetic figure. As in another of Dreiser's short stories. **"Typhoon,"** the father is a German immigrant with a heavy accent and has a moderately prosperous small business. The children in the Dreiser family, and indeed those in the Gerhardts' and Griffiths' families, attempted to run away from their oppressive poverty-stricken households. The chief difference between the Rogaum family and the other families is that it is not poverty-stricken. But here Dreiser's emphasis is upon the inability of parents to understand not only the social desires—in this case, money—but the natural desires and inclinations of their children.

Mrs. Rogaum, "a particularly fat, old German lady, completely dominated by her liege and portly lord" . . . , is warm-hearted but is in no position to advise her daughter. Dreiser's image of the mother is a significant departure from that of a modern American mother. What Dreiser depicts as a family situation in his fiction cannot be compared to that of today's America but to that of many an immigrant in the late nineteenth century. And this is exactly the scene of the family he knew in his youth. Thus Dreiser delineates not so much the social conditioning of his individuals, as critics maintain, but the historical complexities that make understandable the uniqueness of each individual's experience.

The city life to which Theresa is attracted is also important historically. Dreiser is here interested in the family in America in the 1880s and 90s, as in *Sister Carrie* and *Jennie Gerhardt*, which was changed and perverted by artificial lures. Theresa, like the children of the Dreiser family, is discontented with family ties and enchanted by the outside forces that separate her from her family. This is the same situation in which Dreiser describes Carrie's approaching the city in the summer of 1889 with the same "wonder and desire" he himself had felt in approaching Chicago two summers earlier. The role of the parent in the American family structure was diminishing; the truth of this becomes obvious when the family of Dreiser's fiction is compared with that of the present day. And this change, although important in the values of the children, was devastating in its effects on the parents.

In **"Butcher Rogaum's Door,"** the concepts of individual morality are bound to the larger, overall concept of man in a society where the artificial restraints of social position are removed and where the chemical urges of the blood are observed and respected. If Theresa could become enthralled with the lures of the city and meet a fine young man with "a shrewd way of winking one eye" . . . within the boundary of her household, she would not have gone out to the streets at night. Dreiser's point is that evil in man results not so much from an inherent tendency for evil in the individual as from the unreasonable and often unjust demands in society—in Theresa's case, the father, his customers, the police, and the townsmen on Bleecker Street. She is, first of all, the result of a home environment that has alienated her from life, so that when she faces its risks and might possibly be betrayed, it is the society that has provided such a milieu which is to blame. Likewise, whoever might exploit Theresa is not so much the result of a limitation of character as the result of society's failure to develop necessary virtues in the would-be exploiter. And these are represented less as the natural virtue of the passively innocent than as the qualities of aggression, selfishness, deceptiveness, and competition, which Dreiser perceives as the law of nature. In this sense **"Butcher Rogaum's Door"** is analogous to Dreiser's first story, **"The Shining Slave Makers."**

In both of these stories, the image of life that Dreiser presents is necessarily colored by a rather pessimistic frame of mind in accord with the philosophy of the gloomy determinism that accounts for human conditions. This is, perhaps, most obviously shown at the end of **"The Shining Slave Makers,"** where McEwen's vision of life as he is awakening from his recent dream is tinged with sorrow. This is also shown in the story of Rogaum and Theresa, but in this story the sense of sorrow is somewhat lightened by the hopeful tone that Dreiser gives to the outcome of the incident. The story, of course, does not say that one should lock out his daughter at night lest a dire fate befall her. Nor does it say that Theresa has learned a lesson so that she will not wander off at night again. For the author does not believe that man's life is only at the mercy of fate. Old Rogaum has learned that he must not be too harsh toward his daughter because he now recognizes the necessary demands of a young woman.

In his second story, then, Dreiser was to tell the reader that such a conflict between father and daughter could be adjusted. Since man's unreasonable environment was being ameliorated, man could learn. Dreiser was to weave this sign of hope into the third story, **"Nigger Jeff,"** in which he created patterns of action with architectonic skill. As a result, he achieved in the texture of the story a cumulative effect of no little significance. Because his two earlier stories derive from his own experiences (the characters in those stories are like himself, his family, and the people he knew, and the incidents are those he saw) his expression is spontaneous and markedly consonant with the feelings that were deeply rooted in his heart. Also in **"Nigger Jeff"** Dreiser was to express such congenial feelings as he remembered from an incident that occurred in his newspaper experience in St. Louis.

The story develops around a report of an apparently nefarious rape; it is not simply an illustration of man's conduct observed in terms of the deterministic philosophy but rather the process of revelation a newspaper reporter goes through. One day the reporter is sent out by the city editor to cover the lynching of a Negro rapist. The reporter, Eugene Davies, much like the young Dreiser in St. Louis, is portrayed as a naive youth. . . . The action of the story takes place in the hero's reaction to the dreadful violence and in his understanding of American society and himself as artist.

One of the most salient technical devices displayed in this story is the contrast in the images of man and nature. Although in the beginning the reporter is convinced that Jeff is guilty, he grows increasingly less certain. (pp. 160-64)

Later, visiting the room where the body is laid and seeing the rapist's sister sobbing over it, Davies becomes aware that all "the corners of the room were quite dark, and only in the middle were shining splotches of moonlight." For Davies, the climactic scene of his experience takes place when he dares to lift the sheet covering the body. He can now see exactly where the rope tightened around the neck. The delineation of the light against the dark is . . . focused on the dead body as Dreiser describes it: "A bar of cool moonlight lay across the face and breast." . . . Such deliberate contrasts between the light and the dark, hope and despair, suggest that man has failed to appreciate "transcending beauty" and "unity of nature," which are really illusions to him, and that he has only imitated the cruel and the indifferent that nature appears to symbolize.

At the end of the story, Davies is overwhelmed not only by the remorse he feels for the victim but also by his compassion for the victim's bereft mother he finds in the dark corner of the room. . . . The emphasis of the story is not, therefore, upon the process of the young man's becoming an artist; it is upon the sense of urgency in which the protagonist is compelled to act as a reformer. With his final proclamation, "I'll get it all in," the hero's revelation culminates in a feeling of triumph. Although, to Dreiser, man appears necessarily limited by his environment and natural feeling, Dreiser asserts that man can learn.

"Nigger Jeff," in disclosing true social conditions, can be construed as a powerful expression of Dreiser's hope for the better in American society. And it is quite reasonable to suppose that all this time there was in Dreiser as much optimism in viewing life as a struggle for Utopia as there was pessimism. For among his earliest short stories the last, **"When the Old Century Was New"**—though generally considered inferior—is clearly more a wistful Utopian picture than the others. In this story, Dreiser reconstructs one day in the spring of 1801 in New York City after the turn of the century. In such a world there is no misery, no struggle; the gulf dividing the rich from the poor is unimportant, and the friction between social classes is totally unknown. William Walton, a dreamer, taking a day off from his business engagements, strolls down the social center of New York. There he notices the celebrities of the city, even Thomas Jefferson and "the newly-elected President" Adams. (pp. 165-66)

F. O. Matthiessen can legitimately call **"When the Old Century Was New"** only a sketch "with nothing to distinguish it from other paper-thin period pieces." But it is worth noting that even in this slight piece of fiction we find Dreiser's dramatization of the American success story with his world of changing cities, where new careers and new fortunes are made daily. Despite the gloom hovering under the deterministic theory of life at his disposal, there was in Dreiser's mind during this period as much joy and optimism that influenced his writing. (p. 166)

[Dreiser's] short stories written before his novels are . . . closely related to his early novels. In subject matter these stories are various studies on the conditions of men and women in society, sometimes as individuals and at other times as groups. Man tends to be a victim of forces not only within him but about him. Dreiser, moreover, views men not only as social individuals but also, as in **"Butcher Rogaum's Door,"** as historical individuals. Much can be learned from the pages of *Sister Carrie* and *Jennie Gerhardt* about the nature and structure of American society and the American family in the years before the turn of the century. But, delineating the growth of cities, exhibiting the forceful lures of city life, and emphasizing the conflict between convention and individual demands, Dreiser shows one of the basic motifs of his early novels in such stories as **"Butcher Rogaum's Door"** and **"When the Old Century Was New."**

His early stories, like the ant tragedy developed in **"The Shining Slave Makers,"** give Dreiser a congenial means of expression, primarily because they contain characters, whether in an allegory or a historical romance, like Dreiser himself, personages he knew or events he remembered from his personal experience. It is arguable that Dreiser's early short fiction would have been more significant had he not been influenced by many of the specific technical concepts of the Spencerian world. More important for the argument here is that, as an artist, Dreiser transcends these technicalities and writes fiction with living individuals, whose personalities express their historical milieu and do not reflect merely the abstract motivations of "chemisms." . . . What prompted Dreiser to write fiction was his overwhelming desire to understand human beings. Unlike other literary naturalists, Dreiser attempted to discover an ideal order in man's life as he does in these stories. In this sense, Dreiser is more an idealist than a pessimist. And his understanding of humanity often goes beyond the deterministic philosophy he learned from Spencer.

This ambivalence in Dreiser's thoughts in the making of the early stories gave rise to his practice of applying the theory of determinism as well as designing his stories with a historical, and often personal, significance. This is why consistency in these stories is nearly impossible. Even though Dreiser's characters tend to be controlled by circumstances, the focus of his stories is upon the individual and the moral consequences of his actions, as shown by Eugene Davies in **"Nigger Jeff."** Dreiserian characters are sometimes larger than the author's

occasional philosophy, and they are able to speak for themselves. Dreiser the philosopher only gets in their way; Dreiser the artist remains true to them. In the end the interest of the story lies not in Dreiser's mind, but in his heart. Hence, his frequent tone of optimism, mingled, as it frequently is, with his pessimism, can be reasonably accounted for. (pp. 167-68)

> *Yoshinobu Hakutani, "The Making of Dreiser's Early Short Stories: The Philosopher and the Artist," in* Studies in American Fiction *(copyright © 1978 Northeastern University; reprinted by permission), Vol. 6, No. 1, Spring, 1978 (and reprinted in modified form as "Early Short Stories," in his* Young Dreiser: A Critical Study, *Fairleigh Dickinson University Press, 1980, pp. 151-68).*

JOSEPH J. KWIAT (essay date 1981)

[Kwiat examines Dreiser's early outlook on life and art.]

For Theodore Dreiser the great test was to practice in his novels what his literary predecessors, mainly Hamlin Garland, William Dean Howells, Frank Norris, and Stephen Crane had preached. Writing thirteen years after the heat of controversy over the publication, in 1900, of *Sister Carrie* had died down, Dreiser expresses his belief that the violent response to it at the time was "not so much the supposed immorality, as the book's straightforward, plain-spoken discussion of American life in general." . . . Many years later, he observes in a foreword to a bibliography of his works:

> On thinking back over the books I have written, I can only say: Ladies and gentlemen, this has been my vision of life. This is what living in my time has seemed to be like—life with its romance and cruelty, its pity and terror, its joys and anxiety, its peace and conflict. You may not like my vision, ladies and gentlemen, but it is the only one I have seen and felt, therefore, it is the only one I can give you.

Dreiser's contemporary, Frank Norris, seriously considered the relative importance of the emotions and the intellect for the creative artist in his essay, "Story-Tellers vs. Novelists"; and finally, after deliberation, he gave greater weight to feeling over against knowing. Similarly, Dreiser believes that feeling and not reason is the highest function of mankind. Life made a rational solution of its complexities futile. Dreiser, therefore, maintains that he preferred to take life "as a strange, unbelievable, impossible orchestral blending of sounds and scenes and moods and odors and sensations, which have no real meaning and yet which, tinkling and kaleidoscopic as they are, are important for that reason." He repudiates the idea of progress in his reflections on the great artists of the past, Homer, Euripides, and Shakespeare. . . . [In *A Hoosier Holiday*] Dreiser concludes his argument, an antirational one which obviously influenced his artistic theory and practice, on the following note:

> Why reason, anyway? And to what end? Supposing, for instance, that one could reason through to the socalled [sic] solution, actually found it, and then had to live with that bit of exact knowledge and no more forever and ever and ever! Give me, instead, sound and fury, signifying nothing. Give me the song sung by an idiot, dancing down the wind. Give me this

gay, sad, mad seeking and never finding about which we are all so feverishly employed. It is so perfect, this inexplicable mystery.

His awareness of "this inexplicable mystery" and his ambition to be a serious and accepted professional literary artist created an early crisis in Dreiser's literary career. In the late 1890s he contemplated quitting newspaper work in New York and he began the task of examining current magazines, *Century, Scribner's,* and *Harper's.* But all he could see was life portrayed with sweetness, beauty, success, and goodness. The split between the nature of reality as he observed it and the tastes of a popular audience which refused to recognize the relationship between life and art was brought home to him with a crushing weight which almost threatened to end his career. He persisted, however, and wrote his magazine articles and stories; in 1900 he managed to publish his first novel, *Sister Carrie,* which was almost immediately suppressed. An article in the St. Louis *Post-Dispatch* (January 26, 1902) reveals that Dreiser was aware of the consequences of his unconventional vision of the world. He is reported as saying, "I have not tried to gloss over any evil any more than I have stopped to dwell upon it. Life is too short; its phases are too numerous. What I desired to do was to show little human beings, or more, playing in and out of the giant legs of circumstance. Personally, I see nothing immoral in discussing with a clean purpose any phase of life. . . ." (pp. 265-67)

It is important to note that the novelist, early in his career, believed that the artist's primary function is pictorial rather than social. . . . When he arrived in New York in the late 1890s, his brother urged him to write about the luxury and extravagance he saw, for in this way the writer could inform the people in other sections of the country. But Dreiser's comment on this view is skeptical: "As though picturing or indicating life has ever yet changed it."

When, however, *The "Genius"* was suppressed in 1915, Dreiser gave a number of newspaper interviews. Many of these interviews indicated that he was now seriously concerned with the relationship between the censorship and its implications for American culture. . . . To the Chicago *Herald-Examiner* he defends his unconventional attitudes in his novel by arguing that since Heaven has proved unreliable for serving human needs, man "should unite and make war on the other forces of nature that now oppress him, reorganize his religious conceptions, as well as the theories of the state under which he lives, until he has brought all of them into tune with his own great needs." The artist, presumably, will play no small part in establishing this harmony. (pp. 268-69)

Many of Dreiser's works illuminate his ideas about the literary craft. His sketch, "De Maupassant, Jr.," is especially valuable for its insights into his artistic theories. Dreiser's major concern is to analyze the difficulties which plague an ambitious and serious writer, and he reveals "the prejudice against naturalness and sincerity in matters of the intellect and the facts of life. . . ." These literary values were the ones cherished and fought for by Dreiser, and they were the ones to which Guy de Maupassant gave allegiance in his preface to *Pierre and Jean* in 1887. In concluding his preface, Maupassant writes: "All the great artists are those who can make other men see their own particular illusion," and any theory "is simply the outcome, in generalizations, of a special temperament analyzing itself." The relationship between Dreiser's and Maupassant's general artistic theories is also seen in the American's book, *A Traveler at Forty.* Dreiser admires the French writer's insistence that

life is composed of the dissimilar, the unforeseen, the contradictory, and the incongruous. The artist can, therefore, select only characteristic details. Art for Dreiser, however, is not only *"life seen through a temperament"*; it is also something mystical and metaphysical. And it is, he continues, "the substance of an age" and, even more, "a time-spirit (the *Zietgeist* of the Germans) that appears on occasion to glorify a land, to make great a nation." (p. 270)

Dreiser analyzes his own work in *Dawn,* one of his autobiographies. He first considers himself more a "romanticist" than a "realist": "for all my modest repute as a realist I seem, to my self-analyzing eyes, somewhat more of a romanticist than a realist. The wonder of something that I cannot analyze!" But then he revises his self-appraisal and thinks of himself as both "realist" and "romantic," for "life, true life, by whomsoever set forth or discussed, cannot want utterly of romance or drama, and realism in its most artistic and forceful form is the very substance of both." (p. 273)

Dreiser's "philosophical" beliefs were sophomoric and experimental and his artistic theories were, admittedly, haphazard and contradictory. With all his limitations as a philosophical and esthetic thinker, nevertheless, the critic is impressed with Dreiser's struggle to discover a rationale for his early labors as a practicing novelist. There is the sense that he was seriously, albeit in a frequently fumbling style and uncertain artistic taste, aware of his literary-historical role. This role reflected his artistic efforts to translate the confusing and even traumatic changes in American society in the early years of the twentieth century into an expressive and appropriate form. It attempted to mirror those changes with uncompromising, if not always consistently successful, dramatic efforts. From another perspective, he assumed the role of a formidable figure who would be a forerunner of some of the major tendencies in twentieth-century American fiction and reveal himself as a significant historical force. He compels our continuing awareness and appreciation of his significantly looming stature and influence. (pp. 273-74)

> *Joseph J. Kwiat, "Theodore Dreiser's Creative Quest: Early 'Philosophical' Beliefs and Artistic Values,"* in Arizona Quarterly *(copyright © 1981 by Arizona Board of Regents), Vol. 37, No. 3, Autumn, 1981, pp. 265-74.*

ADDITIONAL BIBLIOGRAPHY

Bennett, Arnold. "The Future of the American Novel." *The North American Review* 195, No. 1 (January 1912): 76-83.*

> Discusses the then-current preeminence of the American novel over the English. Dreiser, James Lane Allen, Frank Norris, Gertrude Atherton, Edith Wharton, and Hamlin Garland are listed as the most popular American novelists in England. Bennett calls *Sister Carrie* a "fine and somber work," and notes that English reviewers, including himself, were ahead of American critics in praising the novel.

Brooks, Van Wyck. "Theodore Dreiser." In his *The Confident Years: 1885-1915,* pp. 301-29. New York: E. P. Dutton & Co., 1952.

> Finds in Dreiser's fiction an ability to recreate genuine American character types. Brooks writes that Dreiser's novels contain both "a sense of the wonder, the colour, and the beauty of life," as well as life's "cruelty, rank favouritism, uncertainty, indifference, and sorrow." These qualities, Brooks indicates, have to overcome

Dreiser's poor writing style, "occasional bad grammar [and] grotesque misuse of words."

Dreiser, Helen. *My Life with Dreiser.* Cleveland: The World Publishing Co., 1951, 328 p.
Noncritical biographical account by Dreiser's second wife.

Dreiser, Vera. *My Uncle Theodore.* New York: Nash Publishing, 1976, 236 p.
Noncritical biography by a niece of Dreiser's. The book reprints the texts of many letters from Dreiser to various family members.

Dudley, Dorothy. *Forgotten Frontiers: Dreiser and the Land of the Free.* New York: Harrison Smith and Robert Haas, 1932, 485 p.
Rambling, impressionistic account of Dreiser's life and career. Dudley incorporates comments from many of Dreiser's acquaintances.

Elias, Robert H. *Theodore Dreiser: Apostle of Nature.* Rev. ed. Ithaca: Cornell University Press, 1970, 435 p.
Investigates the apparent contradictions between Dreiser's espousal of Darwinian theories of determinism and his belief in the efficacy of social reform.

Frohock, W. M. *Theodore Dreiser.* Minneapolis: University of Minnesota Press, 1972, 48 p.
Brief overview of Dreiser's life and novels. Frohock terms Dreiser a "romantic realist" and notes his works of drama, poetry, and autobiography, but concludes that "we read the rest of his writing mostly because it illumines the novels."

Hakutani, Yoshinobu. "Dreiser and French Realism." *Texas Studies in Literature and Language* 6 (Summer 1964): 200-12.
Maintains that Dreiser, though influenced by early American realists who in turn were influenced by French realist authors, was not himself directly influenced by the French realists.

Hatcher, Harlan. "Theodore Dreiser." In his *Creating the Modern American Novel,* pp. 34-57. New York: Farrar & Rinehart, 1935.
Biocritical survey. Hatcher finds Dreiser to be a major figure in American fiction and a representative of the very elements in American life which earlier novelists had neglected.

Kazin, Alfred, and Shapiro, Charles, eds. *The Stature of Theodore Dreiser: A Critical Survey of the Man and His Work.* Bloomington: Indiana University Press, 1955, 303 p.
Collection of critical and biographical essays on Dreiser, including essays by Edgar Lee Masters, Ford Madox Ford, Sinclair Lewis, Lionel Trilling, Saul Bellow, and Granville Hicks. Several of these essays are excerpted above.

Knight, Grant C. "The Triumph of Realism: Theodore Dreiser." In his *The Novel in English,* pp. 338-46. New York: Richard R. Smith, 1931.
Brief overview of Dreiser's career. Knight agrees with the usual critical charge that Dreiser's style is journalistic, yet he argues that the novelist's compilation of sometimes barely relevant details provides convincing documentation. Knight concludes that Dreiser's novels have an epic quality.

Lehan, Richard. *Theodore Dreiser: His World and His Novels.* Carbondale, Edwardsville: Southern Illinois University Press, 1969, 280 p.
A study of Dreiser's life and novels.

Lydenberg, John, ed. *Dreiser: A Collection of Critical Essays.* Englewood Cliffs, N.J.: Prentice-Hall, 1971, 182 p.
Compendium of previously published critical essays on Dreiser, including articles by Alfred Kazin, Malcolm Cowley, H. L. Mencken, and Irving Howe. Several of these essays are excerpted above.

Masters, Edgar Lee. "Theodore the Poet." In his *Spoon River Anthology,* p. 41. New York: The Macmillan Co., 1916.
A poem which depicts Dreiser as a boy sitting on a riverbank, contemplating the ways of the crawfish. Masters likens the crawfish in his burrow to people living and hiding in cities.

Matthiessen, F. O. *Theodore Dreiser.* New York: William Sloan Associates, 1951, 267 p.
Biography which includes a discussion of Dreiser's major works and extensive delineation of the plots and themes of the major novels.

McAleer, John J. *Theodore Dreiser: An Introduction and Interpretation.* New York: Barnes & Noble, 1968, 180 p.
An able critical study of Dreiser's fiction.

Mencken, H. L. "Theodore Dreiser." In his *A Book of Prefaces,* pp. 67-148. Rev. ed. New York: Alfred A. Knopf, 1917.
Lengthy assessment of Dreiser's life and works by Dreiser's most noted critic.

Mencken, H. L. "Dreiser in 840 Pages." *The American Mercury* VII, No. 27 (March 1926): 379-81.
A scathing review of *An American Tragedy.* Mencken's appraisal of this novel ended his long friendship with Dreiser, though in later years the two were guardedly reconciled.

Moers, Ellen. *Two Dreisers.* New York: The Viking Press, 1969, 366 p.*
A biocritical study of Dreiser and his brother, Paul Dreiser. Moers examines Dreiser and his work as products of both nineteenth- and twentieth-century thought, and of both the provincial Midwest and the sophisticated East.

Morace, Robert A. "Dreiser's Contract for *Sister Carrie:* More Fact and Fiction." *Journal of Modern Literature* 9, No. 2 (May 1982): 305-11.
Extensively researched refutation of the popularly held belief, promulgated by Dreiser himself, that the 1900 edition of *Sister Carrie* was suppressed by Dreiser's publishers.

Nathan, George Jean. "Notebook I: Literary Personalities." In his *The Intimate Notebooks of George Jean Nathan,* pp. 3-124. New York: Alfred A. Knopf, 1932.*
Personal reminiscence, presenting Dreiser as flamboyant, eccentric, and naive.

Powys, John Cowper. "Theodore Dreiser: The Titan." In his *One Hundred Best Books,* p. 28. New York: G. Arnold Shaw, 1916.
Holds that "Of all modern novelists, Theodore Dreiser most entirely catches the spirit of America." Powys finds the writing in *The Titan* to be "simple, direct, hard and healthy—a very emptome of the life-force, as it manifests itself in America."

Purdy, Strother B. "*An American Tragedy* and *L'Etranger.*" *Comparative Literature* 19, No. 3 (Summer 1967): 252-68.*
Extensive comparison of *An American Tragedy* with Albert Camus's *L'Etranger.* Purdy notes the similarities of the protagonists, the anomalous nature of the two murders, and finds that "society is the villain of both novels . . . it is also the victor."

Rascoe, Burton. *Theodore Dreiser.* New York: Robert M. McBride & Co., 1926.
A sympathetic biocritical study.

Salzman, Jack, ed. *Theodore Dreiser: The Critical Reception.* New York: David Lewis, 1972, 741 p.
Comprehensive compilation of the book reviews which attended Dreiser's works upon publication. Several of the reviews are excerpted in the criticism above.

Schneider, John. "Theodore Dreiser." In his *Five Novelists of the Progressive Era,* pp. 153-204. New York: Columbia University Press, 1965.
Examination of Dreiser's life and works. Schneider compares Dreiser's apparent belief in "the essential innocence of the animal man" with eighteenth-century Enlightenment thought.

Shapiro, Charles. *Theodore Dreiser: Our Bitter Patriot.* Carbondale, Edwardsville: Southern Illinois University Press, 1962, 137 p.
Study of Dreiser's major novels. Shapiro traces Dreiser's recurrent theme: concern about a culture that creates unrealistic and purely materialistic goals and brings about a "crucial misdirection of

America's energies.'' Shapiro finds this theme treated in all of Dreiser's novels.

Swanberg, W. A. *Dreiser*. New York: Charles Scribner's Sons, 1965, 614 p.
    The definitive biography.

Tjader, Marguerite. *Theodore Dreiser: A New Dimension*. Norwalk, Conn.: Silvermine Publishers, 1965.
    Biographical reminiscences which reconsider Dreiser's philosophical beliefs. Tjader holds that Dreiser believed in an impersonal Creator, and that he was not the atheistic pessimist so often depicted by his critics.

Van Doren, Carl. ''American Literature: Dreiser.'' In his *What Is American Literature?* pp. 114-18. New York: William Morrow and Co., 1935.
    Briefly mentions the shock with which the American literary scene received Dreiser's brand of realism.

Wallace, Jack E. ''The Comic Voice in Dreiser's Cowperwood Narrative.'' *American Literature* 53, No. 1 (March 1981): 56-71.

Advocates a comic reading of Dreiser's ''Trilogy of Desire.'' Wallace feels that the extensive journalistic accounts of the career of Charles T. Yerkes, upon whom Dreiser based Cowperwood, display a great deal of comic irony, which found its way into Dreiser's work.

Warren, Robert Penn. *Homage to Theodore Dreiser, August 27, 1871-December 28, 1945: On the Centennial of His Birth*. New York: Random House, 1971, 173 p.
    Analysis of the plots and major themes of Dreiser's novels.

Whipple, T. K. ''Theodore Dreiser.'' In his *Spokesmen: Modern Writers and American Life*, pp. 70-93. New York: D. Appleton and Co., 1928.
    Finds Dreiser's importance to be chiefly historical, as does J. Donald Adams (see excerpt above). Whipple cites Dreiser's significance as a ''trail-breaker'' in modern fiction, but finds his shortcomings as a writer make ''the labor of reading Dreiser . . . too arduous and not sufficiently profitable.'' Whipple nonetheless concludes that ''the power and massiveness of his work'' secure Dreiser a place as a leader in American letters, possessed of ''distinct elements of greatness.''

(Johan) Nordahl (Brun) Grieg

1902-1943

(Also wrote under pseudonym of Fortinbras) Norwegian dramatist, poet, novelist, essayist, journalist, editor, and translator.

Grieg is best remembered as Norway's inspirational "war poet" of World War II and as one of its leading dramatists during the pre-war era. His indignation at social injustice and exploitation, together with his advocacy of militant activism, formed the basis for most of his works. These themes are best exemplified in two of his greatest works, the dramas *Vår aere og vår makt* and *Nederlaget: Et skuespill om Pariser-komunen (Defeat: A Play of the Paris Commune)*.

Grieg was born to a distinguished middle-class family in the seaport of Bergen. At the age of eighteen he postponed his university education to work as a deck hand on a ship bound for Australia. Grieg's experiences at sea provided the subject for his first volume of lyric poetry, *Rundt Kap det Gode Haab: Vers fra sjøen (Around the Cape of Good Hope: Poems of the Sea)*, and his important first novel, *Skibet gaar videre (The Ship Sails On)*, a frank portrayal of the perilous conditions of a shipboard life and the prevalence of venereal disease among sailors. The novel had a wide readership but earned Grieg a dubious reputation, for it offended many who viewed the work as a gross caricature of Norwegian sailors. Grieg interspersed his travels throughout Europe with studies in languages and literature at the University of Oslo and Wadham College at Oxford. In 1927, a career in journalism led him to China as a foreign correspondent. Grieg's impressions of the political and social struggles there were developed in his drama *Barabbas*. The play is important as his first dramatic attempt to examine the moral choice of violent versus peaceful means to justice. Grieg gained a reputation as a patriotic poet when he published the sentimental and spirited collection *Norge i vare hjerter*, a poetic tribute to his homeland. The book has often been compared with the patriotic works of Bjørnstjerne Bjørnson (author of the Norwegian national anthem) and the title poem of *Norge i vare hjerter* has been called Norway's "new national anthem." Representative of a more somber mood is Grieg's *De unge døde*, a volume of critical essays on six English poets who died young, including Rupert Brooke, Charles Hamilton Sorley, and Wilfred Owen. The essays also reflect Grieg's engrossing concern with the senselessness of wars that effect no lasting benefits in world affairs, and needlessly bring death to a generation in its prime.

Grieg's most successful and socially conscious period as a dramatist began in 1935 after a two-year stay in Russia. While there, he was impressed by the social and political aspects of Communism and was influenced by the artistry of the Russian theater. Grieg's most widely acclaimed dramas, *Vår aere og vår makt* and *Defeat*, are similar to Russian dramaturgy in their treatment of the collective mass rather than of individuals. *Vår aere og var makt*, a bitter protest against wartime profiteering by Norwegian shipping industrialists, created a controversial stir in Grieg's hometown of Bergen. *Defeat*, the more popular of the two plays outside Norway, is based on the 1871 insurrection of the Paris commune against the gov-

ernment of Louis Adolphe Thier. Both dramas reflect Grieg's socialist sentiments. But although his leftist sympathies were expounded in many of his works and in his monthly journal *Veien frem*, Grieg retained a unique pride in his homeland. During World War II, Grieg reached the height of his popularity, arousing the spirit of the Norwegians with the exuberant lyricism of his poetry, which he read over the radio. These "war poems," as they were called, are collected in *Friheten (All That Is Mine Demand: War Poems of Nordahl Grieg)*. Grieg was killed in 1943 while serving as a reporter on a bombing mission over Berlin.

Grieg's reputation as a writer of patriotic verse often overshadows his distinction as a dramatist. However, many critics believe that his dramatic works revolutionized the Norwegian stage. Borrowing techniques from the Russian theater and modern cinematography, Grieg used dramatic lighting and musical orchestration to suggest mood and theme. In addition, he has been praised for sustaining a detached point of view throughout his dramas that suggests the "epic theater" of Bertolt Brecht. Like Brecht, Grieg is concerned in his dramas with the brutal powers of a capitalist society, and like Brecht's "epic theater," Grieg's is more intent on engaging the audience in its didactic ideas than entertaining them with a theatrical illusion. Grieg is recognized as a versatile writer whose works call attention to social conditions under tyrannical governments, yet reveal humanity's enduring desire to overcome such forces. For these concerns and for the fervent patriotism of his verse, Grieg is an important writer to modern Norwegian literature.

(See also *Contemporary Authors*, Vol. 107.)

PRINCIPAL WORKS

Rundt Kap det Gode Haab: Vers fra sjøen   (poetry)   1922
   [*Around the Cape of Good Hope: Poems of the Sea*, 1979]
Skibet gaar videre   (novel)   1924
   [*The Ship Sails On*, 1927]
Stene i strømmen   (poetry)   1925
Barabbas   (drama)   1927
En ung mands kjaerlighet   (drama)   1927
Norge i vare hjerter   (poetry)   1929
Atlanterhavet   (drama)   1932
De unge døde   (essays)   1932
Vår aere og vår makt   (drama)   1935
Men imorgen   (drama)   1936
Nederlaget: Et skuespill om Pariser-komunen   (drama)
   1937
   [*Defeat: A Play of the Paris Commune*, 1944]
Ung må verden ennu vaere   (novel)   1938
Friheten   (poetry)   1943
   [*All That Is Mine Demand: War Poems of Nordahl Grieg*
   (partial translation), 1944]
Samlede verker. 7 vols.   (poetry, novels, dramas, and
   essays)   1947

THE NEW YORK TIMES BOOK REVIEW   (essay date 1927)

"The Ship Sails On" is both an intensely personal story of life aboard a Norwegian cargo boat in the course of a long voyage to South Africa and a philosophic exposition of the eternal continuity of human existence. Throughout the narrative of the seamen's physical and spiritual adventures runs the theme—the ship sails on—no matter what happens to any man, the ship sails on. It is better fiction than philosophy: the tale of fights and storms and breaking labor is superbly told. Grieg has a way of writing about the ocean that places him second to none. But his philosophic observations are rather trite. Hamlet taught us long ago that the Scandinavian is prone to speculation about the sorry scheme of things entire, and here is merely reiteration.

When young Benjamin Hall went aboard the Mignon for his first voyage as a seaman, the ship was lying in port and the crew was celebrating with a general debauch. He had just left a sweetheart, and that made the aspect of life which he had to view at once more loathsome and more poignant. Presently they were under way for Africa, and in the long days at sea Benjamin learned many things. (pp. 7, 12)

Benjamin learned to work unceasingly no matter how ill he felt, whether at his own job or at a job that some one else should be doing. . . . The life of the ship was integral: whatever affected one man affected the lives of all. Once Benjamin had to go below and work in the coal bunkers, and that nearly finished him off. At another time the whole crew was set to chipping rust from the ship's plates, and there was talk of mutiny.

It is in these brief significant pictures of details of the life at sea that Grieg achieves his best effects. They have a fresh sharpness that sets them apart from ordinary stories of a conventional sea pattern. (p. 12)

> "A Norse Freighter," in The New York Times Book
> Review (© 1927 by The New York Times Company;
> reprinted by permission), August 14, 1927, pp. 7,
> 12.

CYRIL CONNOLLY   (essay date 1927)

The Ship Sails On belongs to that horde of realist novels whose Nordic purity impairs the hybrid perfection of our literature by its translation. It is about a dismal and life-like tramp steamer that is being used as a brothel at its first port and a hospital by the last. It is hard to realise whether the author dislikes most the ship, the sailors, or the sea, or whether one is more provoked by his humour or his moralising. . . .

There are occasional moments of happiness in the dismal round of violence, meanness, squalor, and disease, and the book rattles on with a rusty vitality like the engines of the ship. It swells the growing quantity of slices of life that are turned out with drear efficiency ("on and on for ever, but why"?) and in degrees of thickness, like the fourteen grades of rasher offered the public by the bacon machine. There are so many of these at home that it seems a pity to import, like the depressions that move south from Iceland, these tales of cruelty and waste complicated by loose mysticism and the fawning whimsy of the inscrutable Scandinavian joke. (p. 782)

> Cyril Connolly, "New Novels: 'The Ship Sails On',"
> in New Statesman (© 1927 The Statesman Publishing
> Co. Ltd.), Vol. XXIX, No. 753, October 1, 1927,
> pp. 781-82.

HALVDAN KOHT   (essay date 1942)

[*As a friend and fellow Norwegian writer (the biographer of Ibsen
and other Norwegian authors), Koht holds Grieg in high esteem
for the nationalistic spirit inspired by his war poems and for his
literary contribution to Norway.*]

There is not much to say about [Grieg's first book of verses, ***Rundt Kap det Gode Haab (Around the Cape of Good Hope)***,] except that they are the natural outpourings of the easily affected sentiments of a youth of twenty. At least, they showed that it was his aim to be a poet. The prose novel [***The Ship Sails On***], which followed two years later . . . , was a far more serious work and drew more attention. Indeed, it roused a rather general indignation by its frank, some people thought exaggerated, pictures of the bane of the seaman's life, the reckless association with prostitutes in the ports. (p. 34)

In the same year that he completed his university studies . . . [Grieg] published a new book of verses [***Stene i strømmen***], filled with hot words about love, longing, and dreaming, and with not a little of juvenile embittered feelings, all of it fairly ordinary, without any strong mark of individuality. The best poem in the collection was the simplest one, fortunately concluding the book, "At home again." I presume the author was recalling a little ruefully his own experiences when, several years later, he wrote about the first poetry of John Keats: "It appears the eternal paradoxical law that the tempest of early youth always expresses itself in the character of weakness."

This is true also of his earliest dramatic venture [*En ung mands kjaerlighet*]. . . . To be sure, it revealed much more personality, a serious battle with the forces of life, a violent attempt to break through the contradictions and riddles of his own soul. His powers did not measure up to his intentions. Nevertheless, it is interesting to see his struggle, sympathetic even in its juvenile imperfections. (p. 35)

[Grieg's] primary urge was to saturate himself with the experiences of human life in its most tense and high-strung moods. He went to Russia, and was so fascinated by the colossal national experiment going on there that he remained in the country for several years. . . . When, later, the civil war in Spain broke out, he went down there, as a newspaper correspondent, but also as a helper behind the front, often risking his own life.

Those were years of rich development, of a deepening social conscience, of an enlargement of human sympathy, of enthusiasm transformed into indignation, which made his writings a succession of battles. During these years Grieg produced a series of dramas that put him in the foremost ranks of Norwegian dramatists of the last decade. They had a mighty appeal to some of the strongest and noblest cravings of the human will, the longing for justice, the desire to relieve suffering, the hatred of oppressors. They were constructed with great dramatic skill. In their technique they were influenced by the swift changes of the cinema and by the mass effects of the new Russian theater. Their heroes were not individuals, but whole classes of society.

First, in 1932, came *Atlanterhavet* (**The Atlantic**), a drama of modern sensationalism, in particular as evidenced by the juggernaut of journalism cold-bloodedly crushing personal happiness or life. Then, in 1933, *Våar aere og vår makt,* taking its title from a line of Björnson's poem: "Our honor and our power the white sails brought." It pictures how, during the former World War, the lives of the seamen were sacrificed for the profit of shipowners or for the avarice of spies. *Men imorgen—* (**But to-morrow—**), 1936, showing in somewhat obscure pictures, the conflict between on the one hand capitalistic war industry and ruthless Nazism, on the other hand pacifism and rebellious labor. At last, in 1937, *Nederlaget* (**The Defeat**), the drama about the Commune insurrection of Paris in 1871, presenting in imaginative wealth the ideals and the caricatures, the defeat and the hopes of the fight for a better world.

In particular the second and the fourth of these dramas were great theatrical success, evoking vehement discussions and disputes in wide circles. They were followed, in 1938, by the great novel *Ung må verden ennu vaere,* the title this time borrowed from a verse-line of Wergeland's: "The world must still be young." The subject is taken from the social upheaval in Russia and the civil war in Spain. It is a work parallel with and on a level with those of Hemingway or Dos Passos, perhaps even broader in its outlook. It presented in a side-show the superficial and ruthless hunting for profit and pleasure of a Norwegian business man with such scorn that people of his class forbade their wives to read the book. Essentially, however, it depicted the moral undermining of the man who, like a "gumanist" ["humanist"], wanted to remain outside the fight of humanity as a mere spectator. The pictures of life it gave from Russia and, in a more kaleidoscopic way, from Spain, were profound and vividly true, and the book might well merit being translated for a larger public.

Through all the most important of Grieg's works you will find the everlasting struggle between belief in the victory of good-ness and a compelling urge to fight for the ideals of justice. Evermore you see the urge to fight prevailing. (pp. 36-8)

The Norwegian nation has benefited greatly and will still benefit from the activities of Nordahl Grieg as its war poet. . . . He has told about his experiences in numerous articles in the Norwegian newspaper published in London since August 1939, communicating his courage to his fighting fellows. And he has interpreted his and their feelings in poems.

His first poem written in Great Britain, his "**Song to the Norwegian Legion**," July 1940, was a rather trivial piece, seeming to attest that the author's quality was not in composing songs for the use of masses. But he ascended true poetical heights with his next poem, *"Eidsvoll and Norge,"* August 1940, inspired by the tragic sinking of the two ironclads at Narvik. Here again was the virile passion of his poem from the Seventeenth of May, only still richer and deeper in its feelings. Then, in November, came the magnificent "**London.**" I cannot fancy a more superb hymn to the quiet, unflinching will to resist the brutal forces of destruction. And, in December, the most strongly moving of all his poems, the New Year greeting to the people at home, *Godt År fór Norge,* the letter that could not be mailed but would bear bitter witness to a deep-rooted love of home country never to be defeated. In all these poems a powerful mind, strengthened by suffering, speaks to us in stirring words. At the end of last year Nordahl Grieg surprised his countrymen by a national anthem intended for children, extremely simple in form, expressing and enhancing in brave and noble words the feelings of Norwegian children as shaped by the latest events. Indeed, Grieg's work in these years of struggle has given proof that here stands forth a true national poet. (pp. 39-40)

Halvdan Koht, "Nordahl Grieg," in The American Scandinavian Review *(copyright 1942 by The American-Scandinavian Foundation), Vol. XXX, No. 1, March, 1942, pp. 32-40.*

ALRIK GUSTAFSON   (essay date 1944)

Somewhere in one of Grieg's novels he refers in passing to "a living author, a person who has struggled violently with unfinished thoughts." These words describe Grieg's own work with considerable accuracy. This work reveals everywhere a youthful, daring, experimental spirit, full of an incorrigible appetite for life, searching constantly, at times desperately, for some solid bedrock of truth in a modern chaotic world, and always ready to try new literary forms in his eager desire to find *the* form in which the restless searchings of the modern spirit may be given their most adequate and satisfying expression. . . . His restless poetic temperament—stirred to its depths in later years by a burning social conscience of strong Marxist leanings—found its most satisfactory literary expression in a kind of loose, kaleidoscopic dramatic genre, largely Russian in origin, with free borrowings from modern cinematic techniques and propaganda devices. Of his first three plays [*Barabbas; En ung Mands Kjaerlighet (A Young Man's Love),* and *Atlanterhavet (The Atlantic)*] . . . , only *The Atlantic,* a satire on sensation-mongering in modern journalism, attracted any particular attention. Grieg was somewhat uncertainly feeling his way in these early dramas toward a content and a form which he did not find until 1935, when with the sensational antiwar play *Vår Aere og vår Makt (Our Honor and Our Power)* he at once became the most talked-of dramatist in the North. . . . Each of the scenes in *Our Honor and Our Power* deals only with essentials—there are no preliminaries, no slowly approached conclusions. The highly diversified tableaux are tied together by the employment of sharp dramatic contrasts, by appropriate incidental music, and by symbolistic devices frequently of ghastly suggestive power. Throughout the play mood and theme are skilfully reinforced by modern theatrical lighting effects, frequently of the most startling yet effective kind. Like the contemporary Russian drama, Grieg's play includes no individual character rôles in the usual sense of the term. He is concerned with groups rather than with individuals as such—primarily with the exploiter group (the shipowners) and the exploited group (the ordinary seamen), but also with a miscellaneous congeries of spies and foreign agents and other odds and ends of human material. To make his play as *aktuell* as a daily newspaper Grieg shifts the chronology of the later scenes from 1917 to our own day, providing us, first, with a gruesome picture of the final flophouse days of the "heroic" exploited seamen of 1917, and secondly, with a powerful closing protest against the actuality of a repetition of 1917 in terms of a present-day war industry prepared again to exploit the masses in order to gain its own selfish material ends. In its merciless exposé of the mentality of those preoccupied with capitalistic war industries *Our Honor and Our Power* is a grimly powerful antiwar pamphlet, but an antiwar pamphlet which rises at times in the intensity of its feeling and the skill of its human portraiture to really great dramatic art.

Neither the hectic tempo of the action nor the urgent immediacy with which the theme is forced home in *Our Honor and Our Power* is present in Grieg's second great drama *Nederlaget* (. . . *The Defeat*), but otherwise this latter play, whose theme is the final defeat of the French Commune in 1871, has much in common with *Our Honor and Our Power*. It employs the same mass effects and rapid change of scene; it deals with groups primarily, rather than with well developed individual characters; and it is motivated by the same rather oversimplified Marxist interpretation of human conduct, as exemplified in its negative forms by those who oppose the instincts of the masses. *The Defeat* is, however, much more loose and epic in its structure, less brutally concentrated in its dramatic focus. It permits, therefore, a more intimate poetic touch at times in the development of particular episodes, and a somewhat more detailed treatment of certain of its central characters. Though most of the action takes place in the streets and behind the barricades, we catch also occasional glimpses of interiors—the office of the leaders of the insurrection, the director's room of the Bank of France, and a room at the headquarters of Thiers, the man who finally crushed the insurrection. Thiers and the artist Gustave Courbet are among the historical figures who are treated in the greatest detail, the former as the vain and coldly calculating "villain" of the play, the latter as a sad example of the renegade type. The progress of action in the play is maintained with all the sense of movement and direction possible in a drama of mass motives and mass effects, but occasionally the introduction of political theorizing tends to drag upon the action and make the dialogue stiff and flat and inflexible. In the main, however, Grieg manages to control with more than acceptable dramatic effectiveness the vast machinery of political and military action which he has set into motion. Most of the scenes are vividly alive, and not infrequently the action is infused with a fine poetic quality which reveals how profoundly the dramatist has been stirred by the deeper human phases of the political conflict which the Commune uprising in the last analysis represented. The theme of the play is that, even though the Commune uprising was crushed in Paris in 1871, the only half-articulate faith of the masses in a society of love and justice

for all shall finally everywhere triumph. "Come, children," says Gabrielle, the fine feminine symbol of resistance, when the last pathetic group of rebels, including herself, are cornered like rats in the cemetery by soldiers of the execution squad—"we shall tell them of the future, of our uncompromising faith." (pp. 11-14)

> *Alrik Gustafson, in his introduction to* Scandinavian Plays of the Twentieth Century: Nordahl Grieg, Helge Krog, Kaj Munk, Kjeld Abell, second series *(copyright © 1944 by The American-Scandinavian Foundation; reprinted by permission of The American-Scandinavian Foundation), Princeton University Press, 1944, pp. 1-20.**

HARALD BEYER   (essay date 1956)

Of all the writers who streamed into Norwegian literature between the wars, none was more typical of the age than Nordahl Grieg. . . . In his indomitably lyric soul we meet the faith and the desperation of the times, their hopes and their doubts. . . . [He] was a great lyric poet, who created some of the finest poems of modern Norwegian literature, and a dramatist who brought an original turn to the Norwegian drama. In all his work he was a courageous, noble-minded personality. He was a lyricist above all, the poet of the grand emotions, the eternal youth.

His first collection of verse, **Round the Cape of Good Hope (Rundt Kap det gode Haab . . .),** resulted from a year at sea interspersed among his studies. It is romantic, both in its view of the sea and in its strongly expressed sympathy with the sailors. The novel that followed, **The Ship Sails On (Skibet gaar videre . . .),** was so realistic in its picture of the sailor's life in foreign harbors that many were offended, even though its purpose had been to call attention to the need for improving the sailor's lot. At the same time Grieg had his eyes opened to the "tragedy of the chief," "the immense loneliness he must wrap himself in if he is to rule over all." Grieg was something of a hero worshiper, and fell under the spell of Rudyard Kipling's poetry during a year of study at Oxford. He admired the wholehearted, unabashed patriotism of Kipling, on whom he wrote a thesis, and resolved to express some of the same enthusiasm for Norway in his own poems. A new collection, **Stones in the Stream (Stene i strommen . . .),** appeared at the same time as he took his advanced degree at the University of Oslo. But the patriotic note did not come fully into its own before his great collection **Norway in Our Hearts (Norge i vore hjerter . . .).** These poems are often verbose and pompous, but at their best they are matchless expressions of national feeling. He pays homage to nature and the people, to the postman and the pastor who cross the mountains on their rounds of duty, to the sailor and the fisherman and all who contribute to the welfare of their nation. (pp. 308-09)

[Grieg's] enthusiasm for Soviet Russia even survived the Moscow trials and the Trotsky episode, as we see from his novel **But Young the World Must Be (Ung ma verden ennu vaere . . .),** in which there are scenes from England, Russia, Spain, and Norway. While other Norwegian radicals had recoiled over the Moscow trials, Grieg attempted to justify them and even gave a psychological explanation of the confessions made. It is a fascinating book, enthusiastic, but loosely composed and hardly convincing. . . .

While actively on duty as an officer of the armed forces, [Grieg] used his literary talents in the service of his country. His poems and his radio speeches reached the Norwegian people and heartened them in their distress. His war poems included **"May 17, 1940,"** **"Good Year for Norway"** (**"Godt art for Norge"**), **"The King"** (**"Kongen"**), and many others. In these poems the primary theme is a warmhearted love for Norway which harks back to his earlier period, but now with an emphasis on the humanistic values her civilization represented. It is clear that in spite of the support Grieg gave to the use of force on behalf of good, he remained at heart the pacifist he had always been. In his poem **"The Nature of Man"** (**"Den menneskelige natur"**) he insisted that war was not a goal, not even a permanent part of human nature. (p. 310)

> *Harald Beyer, "New Trends Between the Wars," in his* A History of Norwegian Literature, *edited and translated by Einar Haugen (reprinted by permission of New York University Press; translation copyright 1956 by The American-Scandinavian Foundation; originally published as* Norsk litteratur historie, *Aschehoug, 1952), New York University Press, 1956 (and reprinted as "Citizen of the World," in* Masterpieces of the Modern Scandinavian Theatre, *edited by Robert W. Corrigan, Collier Books, 1967, pp. 308-10).*

HARALD S. NAESS   (essay date 1971)

[*This excerpt provides a representative survey of Grieg's literary works as well as a more detailed look at his important drama* Our Power and Our Glory. *Naess points out, as do most critics, the influence that the Russian theater had on Grieg's dramatic endeavors. He also states that Grieg's dramas are in the tradition of Bertolt Brecht's "epic theater," which sought an intellectual rather than an emotional response from the audience by using nonrealistic techniques that identified the drama as a blatant commentary on life rather than a conventionally realistic imitation of it.*]

[Grieg's first novel, **The Ship Sails On (Skibet gaar videre),**] was based upon actual memories and was received, partly as a social document dedicated to the exposure of venereal diseases among Norwegian sailors, partly as a vicious caricature. Unfortunately, to the surprise and sorrow of Grieg, this last view was shared by many of his shipmates. Sophisticated readers now will find the book repetitive and overly charged with melodrama and pathetic fallacies, but it was eventually translated into nine languages and already in its first year received eight printings in Norway. One reason for its popularity there can be found in the fact that this little giant among shipping nations had produced next to no literature describing life on board a steamer on the seven seas. Perhaps the greatest merit of Grieg's first novel was that in it the author changed the scene from Captain Marryat's distant territories to Norway and our own times. (p. 282)

[Grieg's second volume of poetry, **Stones in the Stream (Stene i strömmen),** is a] miscellany of love and nature poems, most of them low-keyed and less original than his first poems [in **Around the Cape of Good Hope (Rundt Kap det gode haab)**], though some contain interesting early versions of ideas which later became very central in Grieg's work: **"The Chapel of Wadham College,"** describing not architecture but the poet's sentiments during a memorial service, points to his lifelong preoccupation with the "Young Dead." Another important Grieg theme, The War, is often referred to, more particularly in the poem **"Woman, Death, and Jehovah,"** where a young expectant mother implores Jehovah to destroy the world, so

that her child will not be used in the war of revenge which her husband so eagerly waits for.

The problem of war continued to occupy Grieg's mind during a stay in Greece. . . . If war meant aggression, there was also a war to end aggression, and participation in this kind of war Nordahl Grieg came to view as the highest form of engagement, indeed—under the influence of Greek art and natural beauty—as a form of art. The first of Grieg's **"Greek Letters,"** which he published in *Oslo Aftenavis* during the summer of 1926, has the heading "Marathon" and the following passage: "For Aeschylus was not the only artist who fought there, they were all artists, whether they were themselves creative, or only loved art, in the theaters, in the temple square. Marathon means Art fighting. Beauty under arms."

On his return to Norway, Grieg published a play, *A Young Man's Love (En und mands kjoerlighet . . .).* The protagonist, Jan, is torn between his love of two women, Aimé, older and more experienced, whom he finally marries out of pity for her, and Berit, younger and more idealized, whom he forsakes with the result that she commits suicide. Outside the action, but actually its evil driving force, is Aimé's former lover, Bernhard, brutal and indestructible like the ship that sails on. As in the novel, where young Benjamin represented a humanity destroyed, Jan is another loser, continuing a line of Grieg characters who embody "the Christian love of defeat." In Grieg's wars between sexes, social groups, nations, Truth is bound to be beaten, though never in a way that destroys *all* hope. *A Young Man's Love,* though it has suspense and, in part, good dialogue, is a rather immature work. Grieg's love of melodrama and emotional language did not work in a technically conventional piece based upon as old a motif as a man's jealousy of his lover's past. But in his next play Grieg began the modernization which Norwegian drama had needed since the days of Ibsen. (pp. 283-84)

The title and subject [of Grieg's next play is **Barabbas**], symbol of war and violence, but Jesus is also in the play, representing the doctrine of love and conciliation. Although Grieg recognized the value and beauty of this doctrine, he was already moving toward an acceptance of violence, not the senseless brutality of Bernhard in *A Young Man's Love,* but the joy of battle which also goes with the revolutionary spirit. The play was written at a time when great changes took place on the Norwegian scene (the Socialist party was winning its first victory at the polls), and therefore, during its first production in 1928, proved to have considerable striking force. A poor performance in 1949, however, showed up the weakness of a play which was already dated, even though its chief technical merit had been the author's attempt to produce an atmosphere of timelessness: "The action can take place in China today. In India tomorrow. In Palestine 2,000 years ago."

In the fall of 1927 Nordahl Grieg was asked to write a cantata for a Bergen exhibition. The result was **"Norway in Our Hearts,"** which two years later became the title of a whole collection of patriotic verse [*Norge i våre hjerter*]. Grieg had spent most of this time in North Norway, but he also traveled in the western, southern and eastern parts of the country, since his aim was to write an opus honoring the land and its people. All provinces were to be represented and, if possible, all major professions. The emphasis on action as ultimate beauty, which Grieg had admired in Oxford and Greece, is unmistakable in this poem, written, as Grieg said, more in Björnson's than in Bull's or Wildenvey's style; that is to say, celebrating, not the colorful or sublime, but the homespun heroes of everyday life.

Although there are poems about the pleasures of a northern summer, the tone is mostly dark, as it should be north of latitude 60, but with the theme of hopeful waiting generally applied to characters both animate and inanimate: a mother over the cradle, fish spawning in winter, and the night train racing toward its goal. In retrospect *Norway in Our Hearts* can be seen as an attempt to write for the common people, a *biblia pauperum,* which was frowned upon by many critics, who found it too national or too sentimental. (pp. 284-86)

Perhaps the most striking poem in *Norway in Our Hearts* is Grieg's description of the stallion Sikil let loose among five dozen mares in a mountain valley. The poem, which is exuberant to the point of parody, touches Grieg's version of the *élan vital,* here as potency or pure power, and entirely nonpolitical (except, perhaps, as "male chauvinism"). But Grieg must have had second thoughts about his activity complex. In his next play *The Atlantic (Atlanterhavet . . .),* about the promotion and tragic end of a transatlantic flight, he shows how the press in its search for sensation helps disseminate a pathological restlessness, indeed the "Americanism" which Hamsun had exposed in his satire forty years earlier. Hamsun was also one of the few readers who received the play with enthusiasm; after *Norway in Our Hearts,* he and other conservatives had reason to look upon Grieg as a modern back-to-nature prophet. (p. 286)

It has been said of Grieg's two years in Russia that it was a period in which he studied, rested, and wrote nothing, which is not quite true. Both the play *Our Power and Our Glory* and the novel *Young the World as yet Must Be* were planned there, also the periodical *Veien Frem. Our Power and Our Glory,* which Grieg completed in Bergen in 1935, became his first stage success and helped him overcome his old fear—after three failures—of writing for the theater. His next play, however, in which he employed Ibsen's drawing-room technique, fell to the ground.

But Tomorrow (Men imorgen . . .) is about a Norwegian industrialist, forced by foreign shareholders to adapt his fertilizer plant to war production of poison gas. With the general acceptance of mass murder as background, a cold premeditated private murder is carried off, showing that in the author's mind one form of killing is no more objectionable than the other. The play, which is somewhat in the style of *Little Eyolf,* shares with Ibsen's work a topical theme and many moving scenes, but also some serious flaws. Although its more immediate meaning was plain enough for the Norwegian Nazis to boo during the Bergen performance, some of the liberals also criticized it for confusing characterization and poorly motivated action. Grieg explained his intentions in an angry article ("a sad and meaningless waste of my time"), which is extremely useful for an understanding of the play. Readers are told, for instance, that the industrialist's wife should not be seen as sympathetic. Under a surface of philanthropy and quasi-religion, she continues to cultivate her sexual appetites, and so, on the day of reckoning, will not be found on the side of Truth. If Grieg and Ibsen can be said to have shared one single quality, it must be the fact that neither of them thought much of sex. (pp. 287-88)

Some of the inspiration and background material for *The Defeat (Nederlaget . . .)* Grieg found in the family history of his friend Gerd Egede Nissen. Her grandfather Christian Nissen had fought for Garibaldi in the 1860s and her granduncle, Doctor Oscar Nissen, had been with the Paris Commune in 1871. In the play, which describes the Communists' last heroic stand against Thier's

government troops, Grieg gives a new version of the old Barabbas versus Christ theme. It uses all the theatrical devices he had learned in Russia and used effectively in *Our Power and Our Glory,* but it differs from it in having more fully developed characters, each of them representing, not only an idea, but a personal life. The philosophies of Barabbas and Christ seem to unite here in some strange dialectic. The young teacher Gabrielle, the peaceloving Varlin, and Delescluze, who has learned the bitter lesson that what is good can only survive through force—or even the boastful, cowardly Courbet, and Rigault, the cynical advocate of violence, all of these have the author's sympathy, but mostly Gabrielle, who, as the executioners approach, teaches her last lesson: "Come children, we shall tell the soldiers about the future, about our uncompromising faith. They shall see it in our smiles." What finally raises *The Defeat* above other Grieg plays is the beauty of its language. It was written in one of Grieg's more utilitarian periods, when what little verse he wrote was strictly revolutionary, conforming with his new esthetic theory: "A true work of art is precisely a product of its time. It will have the honor of being devoured completely by living beings who absorb it into their blood and tissue and use it in order to grow out of it. Happy and consummated, this work will be left behind like an empty crab shell." This is not true of *The Defeat,* whose characters and poetry are timeless, but it does apply—at least in some degree—to Grieg's next major work, a novel based upon his experiences in Russia and Spain.

Young the World as yet Must Be (Ung må verden ennu vaere . . .) has sex, suspense, violence and all the other ingredients of modern international fiction, it is both excellent journalism and forceful propaganda, but, for a work of art in the traditional sense, too superficial, particularly in details of characterization. Though it cannot now have the impact it must have had in 1938, the book is still readable as an exciting exposé of prewar political debate. It shows the defeat of western humanism and extolls the fervor of the young communist believer; it also demonstrates a new attitude to women. . . . (pp. 289-90)

Grieg's portrait of Kira Dimitrovna shows that he has left behind him the sailor's madonna concept of woman, but Kira is also idealized, and in a somewhat disturbing manner: because her attitude of no compromise is so devoid of human features, her personality often appears more Nazi than communist. *Young the World as yet Must Be* deals more particularly with the Moscow Trials, which were then attacked by all radicals in Norway, but which Grieg defended, even though his descriptions of them are frightening enough. Grieg was never a member of the Communist Party, but any attempt to deny or modify his communist sympathies would be futile. Thus, of the socioanarchist philosophy, which he had earlier admired in Shelley, he said it was nothing but bourgeois attitudes turned inside out. On the other hand, it is not certain what would have happened to Grieg's communism after Czechoslovakia and Hungary. His main concern was always war, the combination of business and war was the ultimate evil, and he sympathized with communism first and foremost because he considered this ideology to be the strongest power against war. (pp. 290-91)

A posthumous collection of speeches and articles, *The Flag (Flagget . . .),* contains an interesting miscellany of war impressions, and, judging from a note found after [Grieg's] death, he probably intended to work them into a complete volume of memoirs. (p. 291)

Ironically, the war, which Nordahl Grieg had foreseen more clearly and warned against more intensely than any other Norwegian, provided him with the perfect concluding years of a life dedicated to poetry and action. Not only was his verse technically more accomplished than before, but its dithyrambic qualities had the right setting. What had earlier seemed exaggerated or bombastic was now at one time deadly serious and uplifting. Among the poems in Grieg's posthumous collection, *Freedom (Friheten . . .),* perhaps the most striking are those dedicated to people he loved and admired: King Haakon VII, his wife Gerd, his friend Viggo Hansteen, and other men such as the actor Captain Martin Linge, whose life was truly consummated in death. . . . (p. 292)

That Grieg had profited from his study tour [in Russia] can be seen in his articles on Russian theater, but particularly in his new plays, which, like those of Bertolt Brecht, belong to the "epic theater" tradition. They do not depend on a "suspense of disbelief" in the audience, rather they demonstrate what Brecht calls "alienation," whereby everyday events are used in a manner that makes them strange, striking, and, above all, instructive. An interviewer who expressed concern about Grieg's use of living models, was told: "Since real life, in all its grotesque brutality, is so much more powerful than anything a person can think up, one would have to be very stupid not to use archives and old newspapers." Which is exactly what Grieg did [for his drama *Our Power and Our Glory (Vår aere og vår makt)*]. He searched for his material in the daily press from World War I, and in the papers of various seamen's organizations; he also stayed in a hotel on the waterfront, where he could observe and converse with shipping people and sailors. Some of them he invited to his hotel room, where they taught him the songs he used in the text of the play. As he completed the scenes—rarely in chronological order—he read them and discussed them with Hans Jacob Nilsen, also with his friend Gerd Egede Nissen, who approved of Grieg's sailors but criticized his shipowners for being too exaggerated: as an actress schooled in the naturalistic theater, she found them artistically and psychologically unacceptable. "But why," Grieg asked in an interview, "should I concern myself with a person's psychology in the bourgeois sense. What's the use of giving a psychological close-up of a shipowner in this connection? It may lead the person to various crises, for instance in his relationship to his wife, but interesting he is only in his societal emplacement." Rather than operating with complicated individuals, as Ibsen did and his followers, Grieg arranges his people in social groups, each character representing certain facets of the group spirit. The shipowners are ruthless, but sometimes jovial and sentimental (Ditlef Mathiesen), sometimes cold and calculating (Freddy), sometimes coarse and socially insecure (Konrad, Birger), sometimes full of law and order (Skipper Meydell). Their interests include gardening, playing with their children, cultivating the family tree, occasional orgies, and honoring the flag. What the sailors have in common is a basic sensitivity, even the robust Swiller has it, where he guards Alf against disturbing news, or the embittered Malvin, defending the informer's son. Ditlef's attitude to modern art, to his snowdrops, and even to his children, is seen as something artificial. The sailors, on the other hand, all belong in some sort of genuine relationship, usually to a woman—mother, wife, sweetheart—or, as in the case of the Swiller, to good companions in general. Otherwise the purpose of the social idea theater calls for a radical reduction of "character," whereby realistic action sometimes develops into allegory. This has been the case in the last of the fourteen scenes, where Grieg's two character groups are pitched in battle array around the soldiers. The shipowners with the stock broker to the left, preparing the war, the sailors to the right, retaliating with

general strike. Peace, however, is on the sailor's side, in the shape of a young woman. Probably her part should not be too stylized, but rather played with the force and warmth that colors most of the whole play: it is indeed remarkable that Nordahl Grieg, in spite of necessary simplifications, has been able to give so many characters life and individuality.

In its tone (character, language, use of dialect) *Our Power and Our Glory* is very much a Bergen play, in its ideas it is more generally Norwegian. Shipping has long been a major industry in Norway, contributing to the country's relatively high standard of living and providing a field—one of the few still left open—for large-scale free enterprise. Shipping has always been particularly profitable in times of war, especially for so-called neutral countries, which have everything to gain and nothing to lose, except the lives of their sailors. For a pugnacious playwright like Nordahl Grieg, the ruthless speculation in shipping during World War I was a remarkably fitting subject. Not only was he able to demonstrate a very palpable example of the War-Business complex, but, equally important, he could now prove his solidarity with Norway's seamen, whom he had partly estranged by writing *The Ship Sails On*. The title of the play is taken from Björnson's poem "The Norwegian Sailor" (". . . Our power and our glory / White sails have brought to us."), and used ironically: those who are really responsible for our power and our glory, the Norwegian sailors, are either killed in war, or left to die in poverty. Actually Björnson need not have been taken ironically; his poem, which honors the Norwegian sailor no less than *Our Power and Our Glory,* may even have inspired Grieg. . . . (pp. 293-96)

Perhaps the most interesting aspect of *Our Power and Our Glory* is its technique—Grieg's reliance on contemporary theater resources, more particularly his use of sound and lighting. The play departs from the naturalistic theater with its unified action and coherent character development, rather the effect is expressionistic, with a series of disconnected tableaux, making up a startling picture book of Norwegian shipping. The scenes shift from the shipowner's office to the agent's home, from the German submarine to the *Vargefjell* forecastle, from the Bergen restaurant to the lifeboat at sea, etc. The intention—to create contrast and thereby making Reality strange, striking, and instructive—is underlined by special light and sound effects. Much of this Grieg had learned in Moscow, not least the use of music for emphasis rather than ornamentation. In his articles about Russian theater he mentioned some of Nikolaj Okhlopkov's productions, where the conventional division of stage and audience was eliminated, making a kind of "total theater." In a somewhat modified form Grieg employs this method where, immediately following the curtain at the end of Act III, we have a Gentleman address the audience from a private box.

Grieg also wrote about Vsevolod Meyerhold with admiration (one scholar, overlooking Mischa Elman, suggests he is the model for Sascha Erdman!), in particular he commented on his ability to create sudden life and activity through his use of lights. This again points to Grieg's practice in the Epilogue, where, after the Gentleman's speech, we hear the gong, and then see 1935 projected on a curtain moving aside to reveal the Lodging for Homeless Men.

Grieg told Gerd Egede Nissen that he could not have written the play without having first watched Noel Coward's film *Cavalcade*. He did not want this to be known, however, since journalists would then say he had learned nothing in Russia, "And, by golly, that I have," he added. That he has also learned a lot from *Cavalcade* can be seen immediately by comparing the plays. Both consist of a chronological arrangement of scenes with a final 10-15 year jump. Both use light and sound, popular songs and music hall refrains as well as patriotic or religious hymns in much the same manner. . . . In spite of such corresponding features, *Cavalcade* and *Our Power and Our Glory* are very different in mood. Noel Coward is sentimental and patriotic, Grieg aggressively ironic: the warmongers cultivate snowdrops and Moral Rearmament; the sailors' death cries are silenced by chorus girls; the shipowners revel to the tune of Wergeland's moving song about the sailor's last voyage, arranged for a jazz band.

Naturally Norway's shipowners did not like the play. The Bergen Theater board of directors, hearing of the try-outs, voted to stop production immediately: "We have come to the conclusion that some demarcation is needed between tendentious literature and propaganda. This piece by Nordahl Grieg is the prototype of Russian propaganda theater. It will serve no purpose in Norway, but cause enmity and violate the neutrality of the stage, since art is here used in the service of propaganda." However, after director Hans Jacob Nilsen threatened to leave the theater and actress Gerd Egede Nissen to stop playing Hedda Gabler, the board rescinded its resolution. By that time the conflict had become nationally known, resulting in a sale of 40,000 tickets. The Bergen première took place on May 4, and Norway's leading critic wrote: "At long last a young poet who has something to tell us from the stage, so clear that it strikes us, so daring that we get new courage, so simple that we feel we have always thought exactly that. *Our Power and Our Glory* is straight out of our own times." (pp. 296-98)

Harald S. Naess, in his introduction to "Our Power and Our Glory," in Five Modern Scandinavian Plays: Carl Erik Soya, Walentin Chorell, David Stefansson, Nordahl Grieg, Par Lagerkvist, Vol. II, *edited by Erik J. Friis (copyright © 1971 by The American Scandinavian Foundation; reprinted by permission of Twayne Publishers, a Division of G. K. Hall & Co., Boston), Twayne, 1971, pp. 277-362.*

HALLVARD DAHLIE　(essay date 1975)

[*Dahlie analyzes Grieg's at one time controversial novel,* The Ship Sails On. *The novel reflects the pessimistic vision of Grieg's early works which, according to Dahlie, changed to "a more hopeful and dynamic vision of man's possibilities" in his later works.*]

Like the opening scene in a Shakespearean tragedy, the first chapter of *The Ship Sails On* establishes both a structural pattern of subsequent events and a thematic motif around which Grieg was able to document his deterministic vision of the human condition. The ship in this context fulfills two functions, a literal one in that it becomes the vehicle for destruction in the course of life, and a metaphorical one in that it represents the universe or life itself. The crew of the ship is steadily and irrevocably transformed through disease and death during the course of the novel, but the ship remains unchanged, and in its bleak indifference to its human cargo it is not unlike that other "master of the longitudes," E. J. Pratt's iceberg that destroyed the human world of the *Titanic*.

The initial opposition that Grieg establishes is between ship and shore, or perhaps more accurately between the ship and the seaport to which it is umbilically attached, although the larger world beyond the ship-seaport ambience is hinted at from time to time. Man, it seems, must choose one or the other of these two worlds, and once he makes his choice he is allowed no departure from its stern codes and regulations. The ship, ironically named the *Mignon*, offers, like life itself, either salvation or destruction, but in this bleak novel, the chances for salvation are rare, and man has to walk a strait and narrow road in order to achieve it. In effect, there are only two ways in Grieg's world to escape destruction: either to stay on board ship and never go ashore at all, or like Narvik, the only one of the crew who is eventually saved, to go ashore and escape immediately to the larger world which lies beyond the seaport. To partake of the seaport life and then return to the ship is in this novel tantamount to inevitable destruction, and one of the dramatic strengths of *The Ship Sails On* is the unfolding of the way in which, one by one, the ship-seaport world takes its toll of the crew. This spectacle operates effectively whether we view it in allegorical or realistic terms, although this depends in part on how one starts the novel: it does not shift readily back and forth from realism to allegory as does, for example, Melville's *Moby Dick,* Conrad's *Lord Jim,* or Lowry's *Ultramarine*. Its sparse prose and limited texture keeps it fairly rigidly in the one mold or the other, but whether realistic or allegorical, its informing impulse is determinism, and *The Ship Sails On* emerges very close in spirit to such naturalistic works as Zola's *L'Assommoir* or Hamsun's *Hunger*.

An appropriate sense of doom, therefore, attends the protagonist of *The Ship Sails On,* Benjamin Hall, as he approaches the *Mignon* for the first time at a Norwegian dockside. A chaste and innocent youth of nineteen, Hall reflects conflicting impressions of wonder, curiosity, and fear as he nears the ship, and Grieg's description here establishes the conflicts and illusions that are to operate dramatically and ironically throughout the novel.

> But one night a young face appears on the quay in the darkness; a new hand who knows nothing. He stares up at the mighty world of iron that rises up before him, and wonders within himself: What is there inside the ship, what does she conceal?

And this is what he guesses:

> She is a warehouse that moves about from port to port and sometimes visits lands of beauty. A community of human lives, with darksome clefts and ravines, but also with mountains rosy in the dawn. A Moloch that crushes the lives of men between its iron jaws, and then calmly turns its face to the solitudes, as though nothing had happened. All this the ship is, and a thousand things besides. And he feels drawn to her and afraid of her.

The ship by itself represents a kind of sealed off community which contains elements of both goodness and evil, but the ship in conjunction with the seaport ambience becomes something else again. Open to physical and moral contamination, it then becomes an arena of total life, which is more concentrated and inflexible than normal. And it is on this kind of restricted stage that Grieg sets in motion all the factors that move inexorably towards man's destruction.

On board the *Mignon*, the forces of destruction and disintegration from the seaport are already at work in the persons of the naked prostitutes who confront Hall in the forecastle bunks. Leering at him with all their vulgarity and filth, the prostitutes not only foreshadow the eventual path to his own doom, but they provide a vivid and frightening picture of what is entailed in the loss of paradise, as represented by Benjamin's ideal love, Eva. There is an animal savagery about the prostitutes, and the clawing, screaming fight between Normanna and Gunhild, with all its reptilian imagery, is reminiscent of that epic washhouse fight between Gervaise and Virginie in Zola's *L'Assommoir*. But the most poignant measure of the human degradation and loss involved here occurs when the fireman Anton confronts his own sister, whom the seaman Aaelesund has brought aboard; this dramatic revelation of the depravity that all on board, including Anton himself, have contributed to, proves too much for him, and shortly afterward he apparently takes his own life in his grief over what he has become.

Anton is a fireman and Aalesund a seaman, and the conflict between the two is therefore part of the polarization which in general operates on all ships between these segments of the crew. As fireman, Anton is in a sense invulnerable, but as a moral figure, his position is untenable in the world of Aalesund and Oscar, the most despicable of all the seamen. Benjamin, still fresh and innocent from Eva's world beyond the seaport, takes a strong moral stand here, in berating Aalesund for his action with Anton's sister, and in this act he is supported by Narvik, the oldest and most respected of the seamen. Narvik is like Anton in that he maintains a strong sense of order and morality, but both realize that they cannot maintain this position, and eventually both leave this corrupt world, Anton through apparent suicide, and Narvik by jumping ship in Capetown and heading for the goldfields of South Africa. But this opening scene of moral conflict suggests the inevitable course of destruction for those who remain on board, and though firemen and seamen soon come together to save the crew's dog from their captain, the hostility remains, and surfaces in the violent fight that breaks out between them near the end of the novel. An obligatory scene, it also parallels the fight between the prostitutes at the beginning, and again the prevailing animal imagery underlines the basic nature of man as Grieg viewed it at that time.

Grieg's faith in man, however, and his belief in man's ultimate goodness, which later in his career was to ring out loudly in his patriotic verse and drama, is even in this bleak novel never completely subdued. Like other naturalists, such as Zola or Crane or Dreiser, he could never write man off as a mere chemical or biological organism, for Grieg always saw in man the strong urge to prevail, even if in his social circumstances he was not always able to do so. As the *Mignon* leaves port, Sivert and Benjamin talk about what leaving home really means, and the values associated with their families and loved ones remain dimly in their consciousness even at the very moments of their transgressions. There is a strong bond between these two, though they are separated by experience and innocence, for Sivert is already infected by venereal disease. In one scene in the wheelhouse, Sivert is at the wheel, and Benjamin, polishing the brass, becomes agonizingly aware of the gulf that separates them: "[Sivert] was like a dark shadow in the joyous daylight." . . . Yet, ironically, he fails to heed Sivert's prophetic warning about going ashore in Cape Town, and it is on this excursion that Benjamin himself contracts venereal disease. (pp. 49-51)

There is a sharp distinction in this novel between the sea as a part of the natural world and the ship as both a molding and a destructive agent. Early in his voyage, Benjamin suffers a brief but agonizing bout with seasickness, which represents a kind of initiatory rite, for when it is over, he can laugh with the seamen and become a part of the crew. "He suddenly understood what the sea means to seamen," . . . he observed as he overcame his earlier self-pitying and loneliness, and assumed his manhood aboard ship. This manhood was put to a more severe test during the terrifying storm described in Chapters 13 and 14 which, like his seasickness and the fights in the forecastle, is couched in animal imagery: "Like a troop of frantic tigers with outstretched claws and foaming mouths the waves sprang upon the *Mignon*." . . . The storm, however, destroys no one, and for Benjamin, who wants a shipwreck, like the one Narvik survived, to test his heroism, it arouses mainly an ecstasy for living and action. As it was for Lowry, the sea for Grieg was generally a benign agent, as opposed to the ships themselves, which were frequently the vehicles for man's destruction.

This theme of destruction is realistically and dramatically expounded throughout **The Ship Sails On** by the simple method of documenting the disappearance of crewmen, one by one, both on board ship and ashore in the various seaports. And Grieg makes it clear that the loss of the individual makes no impact whatsoever upon the cosmic indifference of the ship: "Lives and destinies come and go in the forecastle, but the ship does not change. She is eternity." . . . (p. 52)

This drama of ship-board disappearances is paralleled by a kind of grotesque pilgrimage through Cape Town as Benjamin in his despair and bitterness leads the crew men on an orgy of drunkenness and lust. One by one the men disappear from the group into the dens of the prostitutes, until only Benjamin is left. Grieg here demonstrates a dramatic withholding of the moment of his fall, much the same as Milton did with the fall of Eve in *Paradise Lost*, where it is not until the last syllable of the final word, as it were, that her fall becomes irrevocable. So it is with Benjamin: the prostitute Rita reminds him of Eva, so he is momentarily hesitant, and he is at the point of heeding the crippled pianist's warning to him, when he reluctantly allows himself to be persuaded by Rita, and thus undergoes the final initiatory ritual into the full manhood represented by the rest of the crew.

The effect upon Benjamin and his universe is immediate; as he approaches the dock in the early hours of the morning, the depressingly grey dawn fills him with bitterness and emptiness, and again there is an echo of the parallel scene in *Paradise Lost* where the universe itself reflects the loss of innocence. Benjamin tries to rationalize his action by pretending that not much has changed: "Everything was as before; he had simply been initiated into a vulgar, trivial secret, which had left him poorer, or perhaps richer—richer for a disillusionment. His last dream was gone and life had no riddles left. That was all." . . .

But the terrible import of what he has done strikes him forcefully when he goes to the clinic to visit Little Bekhardt, another victim of "the dire disease" to disappear from the ship. Benjamin is confronted here by a vision of horror: a ward full of immobile and dying men, stricken by venereal disease—a surrealistic scene not unlike the hospital scene in Joseph Heller's *Catch-22*. This is a vision of Benjamin's ultimate destiny, for he goes from here to a specialist who confirms his worst fears, and thus he becomes one with Aalesund, Sivert, Little Bekhardt, and all the others who committed that simple transgression.

The final chapter of *The Ship Sails On* strikes the same structural and thematic note introduced in the opening chapter, with Benjamin once again approaching the ship, but this time of course he has no choice as he had in the first instance. He has moved from a state of innocence through a series of initiatory rites, both positive and negative, and he has now ironically discovered the answer to his earlier question of whether he would ever be the same as the rest of the crew. . . . Filled with despair, Benjamin is at the point of committing suicide, and is prepared to take the ship's dog with him. "Santos, this day shalt thou be with me in paradise," . . . he remarks, but he realizes that paradise is to be had only once, and that it exists now only in the world of Eva. As a result, he chooses to remain in the specific hell that his ship represents rather than to experience the uncertain hell of any after life; Grieg's characters are clearly made to suffer the punishments inflicted upon them for their transgressions.

In his later works, Grieg offered a more hopeful and dynamic vision of man's possibilities, especially in his plays and poetry which celebrated man's resistance against tyranny and oppression. In this early novel, however, written when he was only twenty-two, his vision was bleak indeed, but the picture of the world that he knew so well through his own seafaring experiences was a convincing and realistic one, and *The Ship Sails On* emerges even after fifty years as one of the more powerful naturalistic novels of its time. (pp. 52-3)

Hallvard Dahlie, "On Nordahl Grieg's 'The Ship Sails On'," in The International Fiction Review, *Vol. 2, No. 1, January, 1975, pp. 49-53.*

ADDITIONAL BIBLIOGRAPHY

Lehmkuhl, Dik. "Echo from the North: The Voice of Nordahl Grieg." *Transformation* 3 (1944) 164-71.
    Survey of Grieg's poetry, fiction, and drama.

Lehmkuhl, Dik. "Reviews: *All That Is Mine Demand: Nordahl Grieg's War Poems.*" *Life and Letters* 46, No. 97 (September 1945): 202-06.
    Review of an English translation of Grieg's nationalistic war poems.

Skavlan, Einar. "Drama with a Purpose." *The American-Scandinavian Review* XXIII, No. 3 (September 1935): 242-47.*
    Describes the early production of *Vår aere og vår makt*, the play for which Skavlan credits Grieg with introducing a new dramatic form to Norway.

Stork, Charles Wharton. "A Sea Hamsun." *New York Herald Tribune Books* (14 August 1927): 4.
    Favorable review of *The Ship Sails On*. The critic comments that "in no sea story that I know . . . does one get closer to the mind of the sailor."

Thomas Hardy

1840-1928

English novelist, poet, dramatist, short story writer, and essayist.

Hardy is considered one of the greatest novelists in English literature. His work resembles that of earlier Victorian novelists in technique, while in subject matter it daringly violated literary traditions of the age. In contrast to the Victorian ideal of progress, Hardy depicted human existence as a tragedy determined by powers beyond the individual's command, in particular the external pressures of society and the internal compulsions of character. His desire to reveal the underlying forces directing the lives of his characters led him to realistically examine love and sexuality in his fiction, a practice that often offended his readers and endangered his literary reputation.

Hardy was born and raised in the region of Dorsetshire, which he used as the basis for the Wessex countryside of his novels, short stories, and poems. Over the course of his career Hardy made of Wessex a self-contained literary world, one of the most extensive and minutely developed in all of fiction. Hardy initially sought recognition as a poet but turned to novel writing as a more realistic means to literary success. His unpublished first novel, *The Poor Man and the Lady,* was rejected for being overly satirical by George Meredith, then a reader for Chapman & Hall Publishing Company, who advised the young author to incorporate the plot devices of popular novels into his work.

Taking this advice Hardy wrote *Desperate Remedies,* a novel that defined many of the fundamental characteristics of his style. Because Hardy considered strict realism an insufficient method for creating interesting fiction, he created novels with artificially elaborate plots, highly unrealistic use of coincidence, and the frequently oppressive mood of Gothic melodrama. The first major novel to display the definitive strengths of Hardy's narrative art was *Far from the Madding Crowd.* The psychological portrait of Bathsheba Everdene in this novel demonstrates Hardy's genius for sympathetic portrayal of a feminine protagonist, which would most successfully display itself in *Tess of the d'Urbervilles: A Pure Woman Faithfully Presented.* Some critics have remarked that Hardy's strongest analysis of a male character is to be found in Michael Henchard, the protagonist of *The Mayor of Casterbridge: The Life and Death of a Man of Character.* This novel introduces Hardy's firm belief that "character is fate," and develops this theme into a tragedy of psychological determinism. The heroine of *Tess of the d'Urbervilles* is sometimes considered to be the single figure in Hardy to escape this determinism, her tragedy deriving largely from conflict with a restrictive social order. In addition to profound character studies, Hardy is esteemed for the vivid sense of natural forces in his novels, an intangible mood most dramatically symbolized by Egdon Heath in *The Return of the Native.*

Hardy achieved enormous success as a novelist, but his work was often compromised by the demands of popular taste. He consistently veiled the morally volatile situations in his novels with ambiguous description. Always subject to criticism, Hardy

incurred especially harsh attacks for his unidealized portrayal of human relationships in *Jude the Obscure.* His reaction to this criticism was to cease writing novels and devote himself to poetry, which he had written intermittently throughout his career.

Hardy's poems express the same pessimism that serves as the foundation of his novels. Critics have noted, however, that Hardy's emphasis on abstract ideas in the poems interferes with their literary value, with much of his poetry constituting a sermon on pessimistic themes. Though faulted for their sometimes clumsy structure, these poems are often praised for a lyric power unique in its particular blend of traditional and experimental forms. Critical opinion for the most part agrees that only a fraction of Hardy's poetry warrants serious consideration, though conceding this sufficient to rank him as a major poet. In addition to novels and poetry, Hardy also wrote several volumes of short stories. Like his poems, the stories are frequently concerned with grotesque situations in the lives of rural characters, and are often bitterly ironic. "The Three Strangers" and "The Withered Arm" exemplify Hardy's best work in this genre.

Hardy called his last major work, *The Dynasts,* an "epic drama" and designed it as a summation of his views on existence. Juxtaposing the historical drama of the Napoleonic wars with a Greek chorus made up of "Phantom Intelligences" such as the Spirits Ironic and Sinister, this work is the author's ultimate statement concerning the forces that influence life. Thematically central to this epic-drama is the concept of the Immanent Will, an all-pervasive force which is indifferent to human affairs and blindly generates conscious and nonconscious life as the result of an unknown, self-sustaining necessity. Many critics consider *The Dynasts* more successful as an examination of Hardy's philosophy than as a drama, finding it vital to a complete understanding of Hardy's ideas.

Criticism of Hardy has accommodated a diversity of interpretations. Early critics viewed the author as a consummate realist, while later evaluations by such critics as Albert J. Guerard suggest that Hardy may be recognized as a predecessor of anti-realist trends in twentieth-century fiction. Hardy's reputation has survived disparaging as well as excessively adulatory opinion. For the integrity of his moral and philosophical views, and for the imaginative achievement in creating the world of Wessex, he continues to receive undiminished acclaim from critics, scholars, and the reading public.

(See also *TCLC*, Vol. 4 and *Contemporary Authors*, Vol. 104.)

PRINCIPAL WORKS

Desperate Remedies (novel) 1871
Under the Greenwood Tree (novel) 1872
A Pair of Blue Eyes (novel) 1873
Far from the Madding Crowd (novel) 1874
The Hand of Ethelberta (novel) 1876
The Return of the Native (novel) 1878
The Trumpet-Major (novel) 1880
*A Laodicean; or, The Castle of the De Stancys: A Story of
    Today* (novel) 1881
Two on a Tower (novel) 1882
*The Mayor of Casterbridge: The Life and Death of a Man of
    Character* (novel) 1886
The Woodlanders (novel) 1887
Wessex Tales, Strange, Lively, and Commonplace (short
    stories) 1888
A Group of Noble Dames (short stories) 1891
*Tess of the D'Urbervilles: A Pure Woman Faithfully
    Presented* (novel) 1891
Life's Little Ironies (short stories) 1894
Jude the Obscure (novel) 1895
The Well-Beloved (novel) 1895
Wessex Poems, and Other Verses (poetry) 1898
Poems of the Past and Present (poetry) 1902
The Dynasts: A Drama of the Napoleonic Wars. 3 vols.
    [first publication] (drama) 1904-08
Time's Laughingstocks, and Other Verses (poetry) 1909
A Changed Man, the Waiting Supper, and Other Tales
    (short stories and novel) 1913
Satires of Circumstance, Lyrics and Reveries (poetry)
    1914
*Tess of the D'Urbervilles [first publication] (drama)
    1924
Winter Words, in Various Moods and Metres (poetry)
    1928
**An Indiscretion in the Life of an Heiress (novel) 1934

*This drama is an adaptation of the novel *Tess of the D'Urbervilles.*

**This work is a revision of *The Poor Man and the Lady,* an unpublished novel.

THE ATLANTIC MONTHLY (essay date 1892)

Brightly practical persons, it may perhaps have been noted, are wont to look on the novels of Mr. Thomas Hardy with an ill favor. This lack of approval they often dissemble through fear of being thought not to care for and understand what is "artistic;" but when the disapproval finds vent, it is commonly discovered to have its animus in an irritated feeling that fate is allowed an undue predominance over human will in the most delightful examples of later Victorian fiction. The irritation is not less that Mr. Hardy so seldom offers a point for direct attack: partly because he deals very much in the *vraie chose,* in his selections from life; partly as well because he never is so ill-advised as to preach a doctrine, whatever doctrinal teaching may be inferred from his books. True it is that "the sisters three and such branches of learning" have never been handicapped in the race of life which Mr. Hardy so skillfully reflects from reality, and Clotho, Lachesis, and Atropos have never had things quite so much their own way, even with Mr. Hardy, as in *Tess of the D'Urbervilles,* his latest work. It is a veritable tragedy, as the Greeks understood and practiced tragedy, and must be accounted the author's masterpiece until he surpasses it. The Fates have indeed always played the rôle eminent in the works of the author of *Desperate Remedies,*—Mr. Hardy's first book, and one to be recommended to younger craftsmen as a deeply interesting study in the novel,—but their part has never been quite so sharply relieved. **Under the Greenwood Tree,** in fact, shows them bland, flower-crowned, almost to be thought the three Graces instead of the three Fates; and in **The Hand of Ethelberta** they seem to have borrowed their cynical divinity from Momus. But throughout the great book which now so widely engages the attention of English-reading people they "path their native semblance on;" and no classic is more relentlessly executed than the work rather unhappily entitled *Tess of the D'Urbervilles.*

Tess makes one suggestion to English readers which is received in this country only by implication, and from the words "a pure woman faithfully presented" following the name of the heroine on the title page. This hinted defense of the singularly real creature of imagination, who has been finely described as an imperfect woman, nobly planned, is more explicitly (though still subtly) undertaken in a preface which the American publishers have seen fit to leave out, together with a chapter having much title to be called the most impressive of all the chapters in the book. "I baptize thee, Sorrow," the words spoken by poor Tess over the dying child of her misadventure,—a christening being beyond her reach,—will stand as the record of one of the most memorable episodes in modern fiction; and the chapter containing it should on every account be restored in a new American edition. The eliminated preface, on the other hand, is to be regretted only because authors are supposed to have rights, as it is by way of polemic, and hints at least a wish to dispute the justice of the punishment for sins of the flesh meted out by the world's law to men and women respectively. The question has been often mooted of late, not always savorily, and it is a disagreeable surprise to find a consummate artist wishing to make arguments of supererogation from the point of view of art, and not contenting himself with the noble plan of his imperfect, thrice unhappy woman.

But, this slight adverse comment once made, there is nothing save praise to be uttered, for the preface does not injure the body of the work, especially for the multitude of readers who will never see these preliminary words; and, however little the author should enter into the argument, the question of Tess's purity will inevitably (and fittingly) be discussed by readers. It is easy to imagine a reader of the Hardy temperament arguing the matter out with one of opposite characteristics, and there could be no better test of the difference in belief between fatalist and non-fatalist, no more pathetic opportunity for the Hopkins-ian attempt to reconcile predestination and free will,—if we may take refuge in theology,—than the story of *Tess of the D'Urbervilles*. Granted the girl's good instincts in the begin-ning, the strenuous non-fatalist will insist that a vigorous ex-ertion of the will should have kept them pure and delivered Tess from evil. But his interlocutor may meet him with the puzzling reply that the power to will, either in strong or weak degree, is as much a part of our inherited endowment as any other quality or any other defect. Mr. Hardy might well have made it more clear, not why Tess should have yielded in the first instance,—her youth and the power which circumstances gave D'Urberville over her explain that sufficiently,—but why she should have remained so long after her first submission to his wishes with a man whom she had never really loved. Whether, however, Tess's career justifies the aggressive sub-title of her history already quoted, there can be no doubt that all her in-stincts toward purity were as strong as those of many women in whom the quality is never questioned, either because temp-tation has never assailed them or because their lives are im-perfectly known. "To be honest, as this world goes, is to be one out of ten thousand," was spoken of the honor of men as men understand it, not of the honor of women as men and women understand it; but there are at least ten thousand out of this world's Lucretias who would conceal a past fault for the sake of making an honorable marriage. When, however, the marriage is to be made with a man whom the woman deeply and truly loves, as Tess loved Angel Clare, deceit assumes another complexion. And Mr. Hardy has not left this consid-eration unprovided for. The poor girl, having nerved herself to write to Clare, had every reason to believe that the letter had reached him, and that his unaltered demeanor was meant to tell her he forgave, if he could not forget. Then, after Tess had let her whole heart go out to him, came the crushing discovery that Clare had never received the letter of confession. Mr. Hardy might have baptized his story Sorrow, as Tess baptized her child; for it is only one of the piteous moments in a piteous tale, this moment when love had grown stronger than honor, and the woman allowed the man to marry her in ignorance of her fault.

It is a not insignificant testimony to the illusion of *Tess of the D'Urbervilles* that it has left at least one reader believing that many of the crimes served up morning and evening in the newspapers would seem less barbarous, less unintelligible, if there were at hand to explain the motives of them some seer of human nature, some Thomas Hardy. (pp. 697-99)

It must not be supposed that in Mr. Hardy's latest book scenery is out of proportion to character, drama, and narrative. Nothing is out of proportion, and everything lends itself to exhibit in the fullest light the central figure of the story. There is no one chapter, unless indeed it be the unhappily omitted one of the midnight baptism, which has the Old Testament grandeur of that chapter in *The Return of the Native* telling how the mother was turned away from her son's house, and went down the hill alone to die; but *Tess* as a whole definitely surpasses the rest of Mr. Hardy's books,—surpasses even *The Return of the Na-*

tive,—if only for its wider intellectual horizon, and its larger, sadder, less bitter irony. (p. 701)

"Recent American and English Fiction: 'Tess of the D'Urbervilles'," in The Atlantic Monthly *(copyright © 1892, by The Atlantic Montly Company, Boston, Mass.), Vol. LXIX, No. CCCCXV, May, 1892, pp. 697-702.*

THOMAS HARDY   (essay date 1892)

This novel [*Tess of the D'Urbervilles: A Pure Woman Faithfully Presented*] being one wherein the great campaign of the heroine begins after an event in her experience which has usually been treated as extinguishing her, in the aspect of protagonist at least, and as the virtual ending of her career and hopes, it was quite contrary to avowed conventions that the public should welcome the book, and agree with me in holding that there was something more to be said in fiction than had been said about the shaded side of a well-known catastrophe. But the responsive spirit in which *Tess of the D'Urbervilles* has been received by the readers of England and America would seem to prove that the plan of laying down a story on the lines of tacit opinion, instead of making it to square with the merely vocal formulae of society, is not altogether a wrong one, even when exemplified to so unequal and partial an achievement as the present. (p. ix)

Nevertheless, though the novel was intended to be neither di-dactic nor aggressive, but in the scenic parts to be representative simply, and in the contemplative to be oftener charged with impressions than with opinions, there have been objectors both to the matter and to the rendering.

Some of these maintain a conscientious difference of sentiment concerning, among other things, subjects fit for art, and reveal an inability to associate the idea of the title-adjective with any but the licensed and derivative meaning which has resulted to it from the ordinances of civilization. They thus ignore, not only all Nature's claims, all æsthetic claims on the word, but even the spiritual interpretation afforded by the finest side of Christianity; and drag in, as a vital point, the acts of a woman in her last days of desperation, when all her doings lie outside her normal character. Others dissent on grounds which are intrinsically no more than an assertion that the novel embodies the views of life prevalent at the end of the nineteenth century, and not those of an earlier and simpler generation—an assertion which I can only hope may be well founded. Let me repeat that a novel is an impression, not an argument; and there the matter must rest; as one is reminded by a passage which occurs in the letters of Schiller to Goethe on judges of this class: "They are those who seek only their own ideas in a represen-tation, and prize that which should be as higher than what is. The cause of the dispute, therefore, lies in the very first prin-ciples, and it would be utterly impossible to come to an un-derstanding with them." And again: "As soon as I observe that any one, when judging of poetical representations, con-siders anything more important than the inner Necessity and Truth, I have done with him."

In the introductory words to the first edition I suggested the possible advent of the genteel person who would not be able to endure the tone of these pages. That person duly appeared, mostly mixed up with the aforesaid objectors. In another of his forms he felt upset that it was not possible for him to read the book through three times, owing to my not having made that critical effort which "alone can prove the salvation of such an one.'' In another, he objected to such vulgar articles as the devil's pitchfork, a lodging-house carving-knife, and a shame-bought parasol appearing in a respectable story. In another place he was a gentleman who turned Christian for half an hour the better to express his grief that a disrespectful phrase about the immortals should have been used; though the same innate gentility compelled him to excuse the author in words of pity that one cannot be too thankful for: ''He does but give us of his best.'' I can assure this great critic that to exclaim illogically against the gods, singular or plural, is not such an original sin of mine as he seems to imagine. True, it may have some local originality; though if Shakespeare were an authority on history, which perhaps he is not, I could show that the sin was introduced into Wessex as early as the Heptarchy itself. Says Glo'ster to Lear, otherwise Ina, king of that country:

> As flies to wanton boys are we to the gods;
> They kill us for their sport.

The remaining two or three manipulators of *Tess* were of the sort whom most writers and readers would gladly forget: professed literary boxers, who put on their convictions for the occasion; modern ''Hammers of Heretics''; sworn discouragers of effort, ever on the watch to prevent the tentative half-success from becoming the whole success; who pervert plain meanings, and grow personal under the name of practising the great historical method. However they may have causes to advance, privileges to guard, traditions to keep going; some of which a mere tale-teller, who writes down how the things of the world strike him, without any ulterior intentions whatever, has overlooked, and may by pure inadvertence have run foul of when in the least aggressive mood. Perhaps some passing perception, the outcome of a dream-hour, would, if generally acted on, cause such an assailant considerable inconvenience with respect to position, interests, family, servant, ox, ass, neighbor, or neighbor's wife. He therefore valiantly hides his personality behind a publisher's shutters, and cries ''Shame!'' So densely is the world thronged that any shifting of positions, even the best warranted advance, hurts somebody's heels. Such shiftings often begin in sentiment and such sentiment sometimes begins in a novel. (pp. ix-xii)

> *Thomas Hardy, ''Preface to the Fifth (English) Edition,'' in his* Tess of the D'Urbervilles: A Pure Woman Faithfully Presented *(copyright © 1891, 1892, 1893, by Harper & Brothers; copyright © 1919, 1920, 1921, by Thomas Hardy), revised edition, Harper & Row, 1892 (and reprinted by A. L. Burt Company, 1921, pp. ix-xii).*

ERNEST BOYD (essay date 1927)

[*Boyd presents a lengthy study of Hardy's critical standing, written the year before Hardy's death. Much of the first part of this essay is devoted to an attack on George Moore's negative criticism of Hardy, and on Moore's own works. Boyd criticizes Hardy for allowing bowdlerized versions of his works to be serialized.*]

As a novelist Thomas Hardy is the living link between the modern literature of our own time and the literature of the past, to which the classics, by definition, belong. (p. 227)

It has often been said that if Thomas Hardy had died thirty years ago his position to-day would be very much what it is, in spite of his insistence during those years upon his superior claim to be a poet rather than a novelist. Strenuous efforts have been made by a few critics to recover from the first dismay created by the Napoleonic epic of *The Dynasts* and to lean so far forward in the other direction as to dismiss the Wessex novels as of little importance compared with that work and with his lyrics. Disputes on this point have something of the effect of thrusting the author, already retired from the world, so far back that he appears as remote as a classic should be. Were it not for the annual protest against the failure of the Swedish Committee to award him the Nobel Prize, Thomas Hardy would be regarded, not as an honored survivor of a departed epoch, but as a dead Victorian with a curious spark of life in his writings. (pp. 232-33)

In the circumstances discussion of Thomas Hardy becomes very much what it would be were Shakespeare to be raised from the dead and to submit an occasional verse for publication. Criticism would be silent and the mildest animadversions of his most orthodox exegetists in the past would be regarded as blasphemy. (pp. 233-34)

If Hardy could be dismissed because of clumsy writing and melodramatic plots, he would long since have gone the way of Wilkie Collins, or he might survive as a source of movie scenarios. . . . To outline the plot of certain masterpieces is often an easy way to be facetious. . . . But, even in his best novels, Hardy attains such heights of melodrama that in a perfectly sympathetic summary they sound ridiculous rather than impressive. He has a passion for plots, and plots that involve the maximum of incident, of coincidence, of incredible accident. . . . [One] recalls that a woman possessed of a vital secret occurs in *Desperate Remedies, A Pair of Blue Eyes, Tess of the d'Urbervilles, The Hand of Ethelberta, Under the Greenwood Tree, The Mayor of Casterbridge,* and *Two on a Tower.* The Enoch-Arden *motiv,* in its primitive or its slightly modified form, occurs in *Far from the Madding Crowd, Tess of the d'Urbervilles, Jude the Obscure,* and *Two on a Tower.* The secret wedding plays its part in *The Well-Beloved, Two on a Tower,* and *The Romantic Adventures of a Milkmaid.* The hero whose high station is obscured by poverty is found in *The Woodlanders, A Pair of Blue Eyes,* and *Waiting for Supper.* The villain as an illegitimate son works his nefarious way through *A Laodicean, Desperate Remedies,* and *Far from the Madding Crowd.* In most of these books one encounters all the other paraphernalia of melodrama, from the old-fashioned soliloquy, eavesdropping, mistaken identity, and undelivered messages to the neck-to-neck pursuit as practiced in the movies. Professor [Joseph Warren] Beach has pointed out that, in his last, his ripest, and his most intellectual novel, *Jude the Obscure,* the pattern of the story is a formula:

> Jude marries Arabella;
> Sue marries Philloson.
> Jude divorces Arabella;
> Sue is divorced by Philloson.
> Sue remarries Philloson,
> Jude remarries Arabella.

(pp. 237-39)

Thomas Hardy had none of [George] Meredith's superb indifference to public taste and opinion. Unlike the author who shares with him the honors of the Victorian literary *débâcle,* he did not wait until the public had caught up with him; he adapted himself to the public. He approached to the attack of Victorianism by Fabian methods, for it was not until *Jude the Obscure* and *Tess of the d'Urbervilles* appeared, at the close of his activities as a novelist, that he showed the cloven hoof of ideas. (pp. 239-40)

Thomas Hardy was very conscious of that condition of puerility and insincerity into which the English novel declined during the Victorian era. . . . Hardy's realization of the problem is apparent in his essay on **"Candour in Fiction."** . . . (p. 242)

[Hardy's] melodrama is old-fashioned, and his philosophy is now so much an accepted part of our modern point of view that, while it undoubtedly explains why he has not faded, its exposition may seem a little commonplace. An effort to evade this has been made by establishing parallels between Hardy's view of the universe and Schopenhauer's philosophy of the Will to live, with his corollary that renunciation of that Will is the only solution to the problem. Happiness is negative, as Schopenhauer once said; it consists in "the absence of pain."

Whatever the identity between their points of view (and Hardy confesses to many), it is not because of Schopenhauer that Hardy lives. His work belongs to our own time primarily because of the implied, rather than the expressed ideas that underlie his treatment of his characters. He is utterly untouched by didacticism, and even his wildest plots are relieved by touches of irony, a sardonic humor which saves them from the bathos of Dickens. (pp. 246-47)

Hardy has been accused of taking a "low" view of woman, that is to say, in the perversion of words to which rational idealists are prone, a view of women which accepts, admires, and understands her femininity. (p. 251)

Now that the possession of a vote has settled once for all the question of woman's equality with man, those who are attractive and intelligent have been quite resigned to the peculiar type of insult in which Hardy indulged in his delineation of their sex. He adopted instinctively the attitude which was to become the post-feminist attitude, and Sue in *Jude the Obscure* might have stepped out of a novel of 1927, and one, moreover, written by a woman with a vote and a college education. (pp. 252-53)

[In] spite of the obsolete machinery of his stories, the characters themselves are authentic human beings, truly observed, and however he may stretch coincidence, whatever melodramatic license he may take, he rarely does violence to the truth, because his men and women are not subservient to any preconceived dogma; they are not distorted by sentimentality. Herein lies the great contrast between Thomas Hardy and his eminent Victorian contemporaries. Dickens could realistically set his stage, but the people on it were grotesques. Hardy conceives the most improbable situation or setting, and then transfigures it by the sincerity and power of his characterization. In his ironical detachment and his sense of reality this last of the Victorians was preeminently un-Victorian. (pp. 254-55)

> *Ernest Boyd, "Thomas Hardy," in his* Literary Blasphemies *(copyright 1927, 1955, by Ernest Boyd; reprinted by permission of Harper & Row, Publishers, Inc.), Harper & Brothers Publishers, 1927, pp. 227-55.*

ARTHUR MIZENER   (essay date 1940)

I suppose no one will question Hardy's right to the title of "the first great tragedian in novel form," taking *tragedy* in its looser sense. Yet there seems to be a general feeling that somehow his novels are not successful, are not, for all their deep sense of the horror of ordinary life, really tragic. . . . The cause of that feeling is, I think, an attitude which is probably more the product of his age than of Hardy's own understanding. In a sense the courage of Hardy's profoundest conviction failed

him, precisely as Tennyson's did, under the pressure of the reasoning of his age.

Hardy, to be sure, refused to identify what he called "the ideal life" with the conventional views of his times, and this refusal saved him from the superior fatuousness of people like Tennyson and Browning at their worst. . . . Yet at bottom Hardy's attitude suffered from the same kind of fault as Browning's. Browning tried to convince himself that because God was in his heaven all must be right with the world. Hardy's objection to this view of things was that it believed in heaven at all; for Hardy, using Browning's logic in reverse, tried to convince himself that because all was obviously not right with the world, there could be no heaven. The only source of hope left him, therefore, was the belief that the world would, by a process of moral evolution, become a kind of heaven in time. This kind of hope was the only kind Hardy could discover, once he had denied any independent reality to the dream of perfection, and without some hope not only tragedy but life itself is impossible. (pp. 193-94)

Hardy, feeling profoundly the ingrained evil of human and animal life, thought that feeling committed him to a denial of heaven. (p. 194)

The code Hardy evolved as a description of the ideal life is a secularized version of the Sermon on the Mount, a thoroughly fumigated New Testament morality. The real subject of *Jude* is the evolution of this code in Jude's mind ("a species of Dick Whittington, whose spirit was touched to finer issues than a mere material gain"). . . . In so far as this code is a statement of the potentialities of humanity, it is the possibility of their realization somewhere, somehow, which gives Jude's death meaning. In so far as it is not a statement of the potentialities of humanity Jude is mad and his death meaningless: this alternative was obviously no part of Hardy's intention. But Hardy had no place outside of the actual world of time where he could visualize these potentialities as being realized; he saw no possibility that the nothing of death itself, when the long sickness of health and living begins to mend, would bring all things. So he ended by implying the realization of these human potentialities in this world; ended, that is, by denying his most profound conviction, that earth's conditions are ingrained. And if it is difficult to believe that life is evil and God good, it is even more difficult to believe that the evil of life is ingrained and that it will nevertheless presently come unstuck.

That Hardy produced such powerful novels, in spite of his inability to conceive an ideal life with an existence either very strong or outside of time and in spite of the formal limitations which this attitude inevitably imposed on him, is a tribute to his profound rectitude. The power of Hardy's novels is the power of Hardy's character; the consistency and purity of the feeling throughout both the novels and the poems proves that his vision of evil is, quite simply, what he saw. Such feeling cannot be faked. This power makes itself felt in spite of Hardy's fumbling inability to think his way through to an understanding of his personal impressions or to a form which would organize them in terms of their meaning.

About his idea in *Jude* Hardy was quite explicit: *Jude* was "to show the contrast between the ideal life a man wished to lead, and the squalid real life he was fated to lead. . . . [This] idea was meant to run all through the novel." It was to be a tragedy "of the worthy encompassed by the inevitable." Such an idea requires for its successful representation a form which is consciously an artifice, a verisimilar and plausible narrative which the novelist values, not for its own sake, but as the perfect vehicle for his idea. He must keep his narrative alive at every turn with his idea, for he cannot, once committed to it, afford the luxury of a meaningless appeal to his reader's delight in recognition and suspense. The characters of such a novel, as Aristotle said of the characters in the tragedy of his day, are there for the sake of the action, and the action or fable is there, ultimately, for the sake of the idea—*is* the idea.

Yet Hardy, with such an essentially tragic idea never freed himself wholly from the naturalistic assumption that narrative must be significant historically rather than fabulously. In the case of *Jude* this assumption forced him to identify himself as author with his hero instead of with the action as a whole. Jude is not a character in a larger composition, the dramatization of one of several presented points of view which go together to make up the author's attitude, because Hardy's attitude was not complex and inclusive but simple and exclusive. He therefore sought to contrast the ideal life with the real life, not of man but of *a* man. That is to say, he wrote a naturalistic novel, a history of his hero, in which the hero is the author, for Jude is obviously autobiographical in the general sense. The essential meaning of his fiction for Hardy is its narrative or "historical" meaning, and Jude's understanding of that history is Hardy's. (pp. 195-97)

Yet because Hardy had an idea he was not content simply to tell a story. If that idea was not finely enough conceived to drive him to discard the naturalistic form, it was strong enough to make him stretch that form to the breaking point by the use of devices which have no place in his kind of novel. There is, for example, nothing to be said against the use of a certain amount of coincidence in the novel which is consistently an artifice, but it only weakens a novel which depends for its acceptance on the reader's conviction of the distinguishably historical truth of its hero's career. In the same way Hardy's carefully devised contrasts fail of their full purpose because he is writing a novel at whose center there is no final contrast. These contrasts are not, therefore, means for enriching a central contrast between a vision of the ideal life and a vision of the real life; they are but means for contrasting a single view of things, which is true, with all other views of things, which are false. And this is the contrast of melodrama rather than of tragedy. In the same way, too, Hardy's use of symbolic incident, for all its immense immediate effectiveness, remains a kind of desperate contrivance in a novel which is not itself a symbol but "a true historie." These incidents do not, that is, have in them implications of contrasted views of experience; they are merely poetic projections of the hero's view of things. The result of all this is a novel which is formally neither fish, flesh, nor good red herring, a novel whose tremendous verisimilar life is constantly being sapped by a series of irrelevant devices and yet remains, as a systematic artifice, "a paradise of loose ends."

The nearest Hardy came to escaping from the strangling limitations of his attitude and the naturalistic form to which it committed him was in his pastoral idealization of the life of his Wessex peasants. He might, by completing this idealization, have produced profound romantic comedy. . . . (pp. 197-98)

Yet he did not know how to subdue the rational fact of the matter. The on-going of the world worked among the Wessex people too, if more slowly; and even if it did not, only the illusion of nostalgia could make one who knew that earth's conditions are ingrained suppose there had even been a felic-

itous moment in the past. The life of these peasants can be, for Hardy, only a charming anachronism; and their comments, though Hardy uses them chorically in his novels, are really irrelevant to any meaning which is possible for him. . . . For much as Hardy longed, however unconsciously, to make out of the world of his Wessex peasants an ideal pastoral world, the weary weight of its unintelligible actuality so burdened him that he was never able to see it as a type of Paradise, to make it a part of his means for "holding in a single thought reality and justice." It was indeed Hardy's tragedy as a writer that he never found any such means. Mrs. Edlin and the rest of his peasants remain meaningful only at the level of history; they are samples of the simpler and easier way of life in the past, preserved for Hardy's day by an eddy in time.

The moments of happiness which come in most of Hardy's novels just before the catastrophes are particular instances of his inability to make the country life a type of Paradise. Grace and Giles in Sherton Abbey while they still believe the divorce possible, Tess and Angel between the murder of Alec and the arrest at Stonehenge, Jude and Sue at the Wessex Agricultural Show, these felicitous moments are always moments when the protagonists believe they have won their way back to the Garden of Eden, to purity of heart and to a kindly country world which will be a satisfactory home for the pure in heart. Only a rather staggering amount of coincidence in the narrative or naïveté in the characters can provide moments of such delusion in a real world as Hardy knew it; and because Hardy was committed to a naturalistic form he not only had to produce these moments by coincidence and naïveté, but to demonstrate that, except as faint foreshadowings of a reformed humanity, they were fool's paradises. Thus Hardy's time-bound universe and the naturalistic form which it forced on him as a novelist prevented his imagining or presenting an artificial world which contained both reality and justice.

Committed as he was to the truth of abstract reason rather than the truth of imagination, Hardy therefore had no choice but to conceive his ideal life as a felicitous moment some place in the future of the real life, since this ideal life was the only kind which could be reached by strict reason from his premise. Hardy's faith in this kindly country world to which humanity would win in the course of history is seldom explicit in the novels, since to make it explicit is to make explicit also the contradiction between this faith and Hardy's overwhelming conviction that Earth's conditions are ingrained. That faith is, however, of necessity everywhere implicit in his presentation of the events of human and natural life; it is his only source for the light which reveals the horror of these events.

In that Hardy's novels rest, in this indirect fashion, on a belief in the world's progress toward a felicitous future, their meaning is the meaning of sentimental pastoral. (pp. 199-200)

The assumption which justifies the naturalistic novel is that there can be only one kind of reality, and this is Hardy's assumption. But if there is only one kind of reality there can be also only one kind of truth, and that truth, in *Jude,* is the melioristic view of the world which is the only belief Hardy can find. As author Hardy is therefore unable to represent justly in *Jude* those kinds of men according to whose ideas the world must be run if earth's conditions are ingrained. In his fictional world such people can be shown only in the light of the single true view of things which Hardy and Jude share. It is as if Shakespeare had first made Hamlet altogether incapable of believing the evil of the world incurable and had then shown us Claudius only as Hamlet saw him. Hardy's Claudiuses are not mighty opposites; they are inexplicable villains. At best he can give them credit for being better adjusted to the world as it is at the moment. And for the same reason the only irony he can direct against his hero is the irony to be derived from a demonstration of his temporary maladjustment in a world which, if it is not meaningless, will presently realize that hero's ideal. There is thus neither permanent justification in Hardy for the Arabellas nor permanent irony for the Judes. (p. 202)

But if the actions of the Arabellas are seen only as Jude saw them, they must remain for the reader what they were for Jude, the consequences of an inexplicable and brutal stupidity rather than of a different kind of wisdom to Jude's. Thus Hardy's attitude and the form it invoked excluded from his representation, despite the fact that no one knew them better than he did, the point of view of those men and women for whom "the defence and salvation of the body by daily bread is still a study, a religion, and a desire." It excluded, too, an understanding of how a woman like Sue might, not in weakness but in strength, deny the validity of Jude's humanitarian idealism. It is one thing, that is, for Jude to preach to Sue the horror of her final surrender to Phillotson and conventional conduct or for Hamlet to preach to his mother the horror of surrender to Claudius and a "normal" life. It is quite another for Hardy, who does, or Shakespeare, who does not, to commit himself completely as author to this sermon.

At the same time, however, that Hardy presents the almost universal opposition to Jude as inexplicably cruel, he is forced to present people and animals—of which there are a great many in Hardy—in such a way as to support Jude's view of them. In other words, Hardy presents the same kinds of objects at once unjustly and sentimentally. And this is the manifestation in the "verbal correlative" of Hardy's attitude of the contradiction inherent in that attitude. Because he can see only a single reality, that of the time-bound actual world, the life of that reality has to be at once incurably evil and potentially good. (pp. 202-03)

[*Jude the Obscure* is] not a tragedy, not a carefully devised representation of life the purpose of which is to contrast, at every turn, the permanently squalid real life of man, with the ideal life (or, if you will, man's dream of an ideal life). It is the history of how an obscure but worthy man, living a life which Hardy conceived to be representative, learned gradually "that the social moulds civilization fits us into have no more relation to our actual shapes than the conventional shapes of the constellations have to the real star-patterns" . . . , learned what the true morality of "unbiassed nature" is. In the process of learning this optimistic morality he discovered also that neither nature nor society even recognized it, to say nothing of living by it. In so far as Hardy gave him hope at the end that in time they would, he denied what he otherwise saw so clearly, that earth's conditions are ingrained; in so far as he did not give Jude this hope he denied the possibility of the only ideal life he could conceive and made his hero's life and death essentially meaningless.

The instructive comparison to *Jude* is of course *Hamlet*. For Shakespeare too saw most profoundly the horror of life's ingrained conditions. But because he could also understand and represent the attitude of those who sought to adjust themselves to life's conditions, he saw that the only hope he could give his hero was for that consummation he so devoutly wished, and death is the only felicity Hamlet ever deems possible. Hamlet's death is not death in a universe in which there is no place without bad dreams; neither is it a death justified by a

hope that some day the world's ingrained conditions will come unstuck. Jude's death is a little bit of both.

Hardy says in the preface to *Jude* that it "is simply an endeavor to give shape and coherence to a series of seemings, or personal impressions, the question of their consistency or their discordance . . . being regarded as not of the first moment." In that the feeling of the presented life in *Jude* has a powerful coherence this is a justified defense of it. But it is precisely because Hardy never really posed for himself the question of how the meaning of his impressions could be coherent without being consistent that *Jude*, for all the power of its presented life, is not a tragedy. (pp. 212-13)

Arthur Mizener, " 'Jude the Obscure' As a Tragedy" (copyright, 1940, by Arthur Mizener), in The Southern Review, *Vol. VI, No. 1, Summer, 1940, pp. 193-213.*

EVELYN HARDY   (essay date 1954)

[*In her critical biography of Thomas Hardy, Evelyn Hardy discusses the author's works chronologically in relation to one another and to Hardy's life. In her discussion of* The Mayor of Casterbridge, *Hardy examines the protagonist Henchard.*]

The Mayor of Casterbridge is unique in Hardy's work for more than one reason. For the first time he draws a protagonist who towers above the other leading characters in height and strength. Heretofore he has drawn a constellation of interrelated characters and no single one has dominated the others, as Henchard does, by sheer force of personality. It is the beginning of the epic conception and treatment, fulfilled in *Tess* and *Jude*, in which the interest centres on a single life. Henchard is drawn on the heroic scale: he stands six foot and more, he has eyes that 'dig into men's souls', and he moves 'like a great tree in a wind'.

Secondly, he is the most complex and subtly drawn [of] Hardy's male characters, a man at war with himself, who, ignorant of his motives, works against and destroys himself—a smouldering, volcanic fellow whose pattern is to cheat himself of success, companionship, happiness, love, to castigate and brand himself until he dies an outcast, self-excommunicate. Henchard is cruel, jealous, possessive; suspicious, vain, proud; dishonest, prejudiced and rigid; yet for all his villainy there is something lovable about him. He is a confusing mixture of good and evil. . . . Henchard is Lear-like in his tragic grandeur; but Hardy has consummately proved that such a tragic figure need not be a regal one: he evokes in us both terror and pity through his portrayal of a homespun trusser of hay.

Thirdly, Henchard is the most virile of all Hardy's men. Giles and Gabriel are male enough and they touch us by their staunchness, fidelity, sincerity and simplicity—the great Wessex virtues—but Henchard, like a wild bull roaming the hillside, triumphant in his prime, subdued and driven from the herd by a younger, more agile rival, attracts us through his animal strength. There is not another character like him in Hardy's work. (pp. 196-98)

The majority of Hardy's men stand aloof from, and are spectators of, even spies on, life which revolves round them, rather than active participants who intervene to shape life and the lives of others to their own ends. They are victims of the Victorian ethical convention which required that men, at least in fiction, must be virtually sexless. The self-effacing quality in his men makes Hardy's women all the more vital: the contrast is so marked that it has caused one writer to question whether this lack of virility in his masculine characters may not be unconsciously autobiographical. (p. 198)

If we turn to Hardy's poems and notes we may find something to explain the phenomenon of Henchard's character. The dated poems of this period in his life are scanty. Between 1872-82 there are only six dated ones. We know that some others of a descriptive nature were written. . . . Then suddenly in 1883 we find a beautiful poem, compact with certitude and decision, **"He abjures Love"** in which the writer shakes off love's enchantment. . . . Hardy was now forty-three and his disenchantment with love coincides with an increasing disillusion with life. Deeply romantic, he has hitherto made love the lodestar of his being: when this fails there is nothing left. Even though the poem may be merely the record of a passing mood (which Hardy later declared it to be: he also called it a love poem, adding 'and lovers are chartered irresponsibles') it contains a poignant admission. A deeply reticent man lays bare his heart. . . . (pp. 198-99)

Seven months after he had finished writing *The Mayor of Casterbridge,* in April 1885, Hardy states in his notes:

> . . . a tragedy exhibits a state of things in the life of an individual which unavoidably causes some natural aim, or desire, of his to end in a catastrophe when carried out.

The date of this note, so long after the novel's completion, implies that the latter was written in the white heat of inspiration and reflected on later; but the importance of developing character, rather than stressing incident, had occupied Hardy's mind for some time past. On the day of the tale's first appearance he had admitted his fears that *The Mayor* might not be as good as he had intended it to be. . . . (pp. 200-01)

Hardy's fear that this novel had been 'recklessly damaged' refers to the alterations which once again he had been forced to make to placate magazine editors and the squeamish public. He had had to tone down the portrait of Henchard and to introduce incidents, as he thought, far too freely. (p. 201)

Hardy found it difficult to get *The Mayor* published in volume form. The excuse which was given was that 'the lack of gentry among the characters made it uninteresting.' So much for Victorian taste. A more likely reason was that the publishers feared the reception that a novel seared with so much bitterness might win, for in book form Hardy 'made not the slightest concession' to public taste: *The Mayor* 'moves remorselessly to its remorseless close', and it 'exemplifies what had become Hardy's personal philosophy of life with a starkness to be found in none of his previous books'. (pp. 201-02)

> *Evelyn Hardy, in her* Thomas Hardy: A Critical Biography *(reprinted by permission of David Higham Associates Limited, as literary agents for Evelyn Hardy), The Hogarth Press, 1954, 342 p.*

A. ALVAREZ   (essay date 1961)

[In this examination of Hardy's last novel, Alvarez discusses the three leading characters and concludes that "Jude the Obscure is fundamentally a work without any heroines at all. It has only a hero." Alvarez criticizes the novel's dialogue and finds dialogue to be a weak point with Hardy generally. He especially praises those descriptive scenes with no dialogue.]

Jude the Obscure is Hardy's last and finest novel. Yet its publication in 1896 provoked an outcry as noisy as that which recently greeted *Lady Chatterley's Lover.* The press attacked in a pack, lady reviewers became hysterical, abusive letters poured in, and a bishop solemnly burnt the book. The fuss may seem to us, at this point in time, incredible and even faintly ridiculous, but its effect was serious enough: '. . . the experience', Hardy wrote later, 'completely cured me of further interest in novel-writing.' After *Jude* he devoted himself exclusively to his poetry, never returning to fiction.

What caused the uproar? It was not Hardy's fatalism; after *Tess* his public had learned to live with that and even love it. Nor was his attack on social and religious hypocrisy particularly virulent, though there was certainly a good deal of entrenched resentment of his criticism of those two almost equally venerable institutions: marriage and Oxford. Zola's name was invoked by one or two reviewers, but not seriously. The real blow to the eminently shockable Victorian public was the fact that Hardy treated the sexual undertheme of his book more or less frankly: less frankly, he complained, than he had wished, but more frankly than was normal or acceptable.

Despite the social criticism it involves, the tragedy of *Jude* is not one of missed chances but of missed fulfilment, of frustration. It is a kind of *Anna Karenina* from the male point of view, with the basic action turned upside down. Where Anna moves from Karenin to Vronsky, from desiccation to partial satisfaction, Jude, swinging from Arabella to Sue, does the opposite. For all his—and Hardy's—superficial disgust, Jude and Arabella are, physically, very much married: their night at Aldbrickham after years apart is made to seem the most natural thing in the world; Jude's subsequent shame is prompted less by the act itself than by his anger at missing Sue and fear that she will somehow find out. On the other hand, his great love for Sue remains at its high pitch of romance and fatality largely because she never really satisfies him. . . . So Jude's tragedy, like every true tragedy, comes from inner tensions which shape the action, not from any haphazard or indifferent force of circumstance. Jude is as frustrated by Sue, his ideal, intellectual woman, as he is by Oxford, his equally shining ideal of the intellectual life. Frustration is the permanent condition of his life.

I am not, of course, suggesting that the book has no theme beyond the sexual relations of Jude, Sue, Arabella, and Phillotson. (pp. 178-79)

Obviously, *Jude the Obscure* does have its declared social purpose: to criticize a system which could, for mainly snobbish reasons, keep out of the universities 'one of the very men', as Sue says, 'Christminster was intended for when the Colleges were founded; a man with a passion for learning, but no money, or opportunities, or friends. . . . You were elbowed off the pavement by the millionaires' sons.' (pp. 179-80)

Yet *Jude the Obscure* is clearly more than a criticism of the exclusiveness of the major English universities. Surprisingly early in the book Jude realizes that his Christminster ambitions are futile. After that, though the University remains an obsession with him, it plays very little part in the novel itself. Instead, it is a kind of sub-plot echoing the main theme in slightly different terms, just as Gloucester and his sons repeat on a smaller scale the tragedy of King Lear and his daughters. But with a crucial difference: Jude is the hero of both the main plot and the sub-plot. Christminster may drop out of the major action, but his continuing obsession with it repeats, in another tone of voice, his obsession with Sue. In the beginning, both Sue and the university seem objects of infinitely mysterious romance; both, in the end, land Jude in disillusion. Both seem to promise intellectual freedom and strength; both are shown to be at bottom utterly conventional. Both promise fulfilment; both frustrate him. All Jude's intellectual passion earns him nothing more than the title 'Tutor of St Slums', while all his patience and devotion to Sue loses him his job, his children and finally even his title of husband.

Hardy himself knew perfectly well that the Christminster, social-purpose side of the novel was relatively exterior to its main theme. Years later, when there was talk of turning *Jude* into a play, he wrote: 'Christminster is of course the tragic influence of Jude's drama in one sense, but innocently so, and merely as a crass obstruction.' There is, however, nothing exterior in the part Sue plays in Jude's tragedy. At times, in fact, she seems less a person in her own right than a projection of one side of Jude's character. . . . And, in harmony with the principle by which all the major intuitions in the novel are given to the men, Jude himself perceives the same thing: when he lends Sue his clothes after she has escaped from the training college and arrived, soaking wet, at his lodgings, 'he palpitated at the thought that she had fled to him in her trouble as he had fled to her in his. What counterparts they were! . . . Sitting in his only arm-chair he saw a slim and fragile being masquerading as himself on a Sunday, so pathetic in her defencelessness that his heart felt big with the sense of it.' The situation, in which the hero dresses in his own clothes his wet, lost, desperate double, is exactly the same as that of the masterpiece of double identity, Conrad's *The Secret Sharer*.

Considering the ultimate differences between Sue and Jude, Hardy perhaps thought that their similarities merely emphasized the contrasts of which, he wrote, the book was full: 'Sue and her heathen gods set against Jude's reading the Greek testament; Christminster academical, Christminster in the slums; Jude the saint, Jude the sinner; Sue the pagan, Sue the saint; marriage, no marriage; etc. etc.' But the geometrical neatness of Hardy's plan does not make his psychological insight any less profound or compelling. All through the book Sue is Jude 'masquerading as himself on a Sunday'. As even her name implies (Sue, Hardy says himself, is a lily, and Bridehead sounds very like maidenhead), she is the untouched part of him, all intellect, nerves and sensitivity, essentially bodiless. That is why her most dramatic and typical appearances have always something ghostly about them. When, for example, Jude suddenly and guiltily comes across her after his night with Arabella at Aldbrickham, 'Sue stood like a vision before him—her look bodeful and anxious as in a dream'. . . . It is this combination of non-physical purity with exaggeratedly sharp intellect and sensitivity which preserves her for Jude as an object of ideal yearning, hopeless and debilitating. It is a yearning for his own lost innocence, before his Christminster ambitions were diverted by Arabella. Even when he finally rounds on her, after all their years and tragedies together, he can still only call her 'a sort of fey, or sprite—not a woman!' Despite everything he can do, she remains a bodiless idea, an idea of something in himself.

Sue and Arabella are, in fact, like the white and black horses, the noble and base instincts, which draw Plato's chariot of the soul. But because Hardy too had a passion for Sue's kind of frigid purity ('She is', he wrote, 'a type of woman which has always had an attraction for me'), he exaggerated the case against Arabella almost to the point of parody. (pp. 180-82)

Where Hardy thought Arabella 'the villain of the piece', [D. H.] Lawrence tried to make her out the heroine. Both views are wrong, not because Sue is any more or less of the heroine than Arabella, but because *Jude the Obscure* is fundamentally a work without any heroines at all. It has only a hero. . . . Lawrence was, however, right when he said that Arabella survives Hardy's deliberate coarsening of her. The artist does her justice against the grain of his tastes. So it is she, not Sue, who shows flashes of real intelligence. . . . And it is also she, not Sue, who really wants Jude. . . . (p. 182)

Similarly, despite everything, it is Arabella whom Jude really wants physically. (p. 183)

Jude, after all, fell in love with Sue's photograph before he fell in love with Sue herself; and the first time she saw him 'she no more observed his presence than that of the dust-motes which his manipulations raised into the sunbeams'. So they are never really married because the connection between them is of the sensibility, not of the senses. The only real moment of ecstasy Jude shares with Sue is bodiless, precipitated by the scent and brilliance of the roses at the agricultural show. 'The real marriage of Jude and Sue was', as Lawrence said, 'in the roses.' So it is Arabella who gets the last word; however much Hardy may have disliked her in principle, artistically he acknowledged the sureness of her physical common sense, to the extent at least of allowing her to make the final, unqualified judgement of the tragedy:

> 'She may swear that on her knees to the holy cross upon her necklace till she's hoarse, but it won't be true!' said Arabella. 'She's never found peace since she left his arms, and never will again till she's as he is now!'

Yet although his final attitude to Sue may have been ambiguous, in creating her Hardy did something extraordinarily original: he created one of the few totally narcissistic women in literature; yet he did so at the same time as he made her something rather wonderful. Her complexity lies in the way in which Hardy managed to present the full, bitter sterility of her narcissism and yet tried to exonerate her.

Bit by bit, even Jude is made to build up the case against her: she is cold, 'incapable of real love', 'an epicure of the emotions', and a flirt; she wants to be loved more than she wants to love; she is vain, . . . she is even cruel, in a refined way, her deliberate, 'epicene' frigidity having killed one man before the novel even starts. Yet despite all this, Jude loves her. Part of his love, of course, is rooted in frustration: he wants her endlessly because he can never properly have her. And he loves her, too, because he loves himself; he has in himself a narcissism which responds to hers, a vanity of the intellectual life, of his ideals and ambitions, of the refinement of intellect and sensibility which he had first projected on to Christminster.

But the truth and power of the novel lie in the way in which Jude, in the end, is able to understand his love for Sue *without lessening it*. Until the closing scenes, he manages to make her conform to his ideal by a kind of emotional sleight of mind: he dismisses his glimpses of the unchanging conventionality below the bright surface of her non-conformity by invoking both his own worthlessness and that vague marriage-curse which has been the lot of his family. The turning-point is the death of the children. (pp. 183-84)

The novel's power . . . resides in that sustained, deep plangency of note which is the moving bass behind every major incident. This note is produced not by any single action but by a general sense of tragedy and sympathetic hopelessness which the figure of Jude provokes in Hardy. And the essence of his tragedy is Jude's loneliness. He is isolated from society because his ambitions, abilities and sensibility separate him from his own class while winning him no place in any other. He is isolated in his marriage to Arabella because she has no idea of what he is about, and doesn't care. He is isolated in his marriage to Sue because she is frigid. Moreover, the sense of loneliness is intensified by the way in which both women are presented less as characters complete in themselves than as projections of Jude, sides of his character, existing only in relation to him. (p. 186)

The power of *Jude the Obscure* is, then, less fictional than poetic. It arises less from the action or the fidelity of the setting than from the wholeness of the author's feelings. It is a tragedy whose unity is not Aristotelian but emotional. And the feelings are those which were later given perfect form in Hardy's best poetry. The work is the finest of Hardy's novels because it is the one in which the complex of emotions is, despite Father Time, least weakened by melodrama, bad plotting, and that odd incidental amateurishness of detail by which, perhaps, Hardy, all through his novel-writing period, showed his dissatisfaction with the form. It is also the finest because it is the novel in which the true Hardy hero is most fully vindicated, and the apparently fascinating myth of immaculate frigidity is finally exploded. But I wonder if Hardy was not being slightly disingenuous when he claimed that the treatment of the book by the popular reviewers had turned him, for good, from the novel to poetry. After *Jude the Obscure* there was no other direction in which he could go. (p. 187)

> A. Alvarez, "Novels: Thomas Hardy's 'Jude the Obscure'" (originally published as his afterword to Jude the Obscure *by Thomas Hardy, The New American Library, 1961), in his* Beyond All This Fiddle: Essays 1955-1967 *(copyright © 1968 by A. Alvarez; reprinted by permission of Random House, Inc.; in Canada by the author), Random House, 1969, pp. 178-87.*

BRIGID BROPHY, MICHAEL LEVEY, and CHARLES OSBORNE   (essay date 1968)

Perhaps it was Wessex clay that clogged Hardy's pen. Something certainly intervened between the sublime tragic ideas dimly in his head and the ludicrous results when set on paper. Or rather: nothing intervened. The spark of art refused to jump into existence. We are left standing futilely in the soggy wet fields of novels where the earth is the ravaged, bloodstained scene of dreary crimes and appalling mistakes, littered with frostbitten decaying vegetables and plentiful corpses. It is an almost Jacobean vision (where one might come on a severed hand while planting potatoes), except that it never touches the nerve of true intensity, and the pulse is more often quickened by laughter than by horror. Among the things butchered by Hardy is unfortunately the English language. You cannot make tragedy out of the life of Jude Fawley if you have no way to express its central theme except by throwing gobbets of raw diction at the reader. . . . As the plots deepen into hysterical gloom, the stilted inadequacy of the language becomes unbearable. Time has added an additional cruelty in making the sex in Hardy's Wessex simply funny. Or wasn't it always fairly silly? Hardy seems to be positively anxious to equate coition with destiny—and his idea of destiny is not at all cheerful.

This would not much matter did he not signal his approaching threats by destiny-motifs of such ponderous cosmic gloom and elephantine tread. The simplest action picture is framed by great bulbous gilt observations until one can't see the composition for the admonitions. . . . We are plunged into a world not of rustic reality but romantic opera, provided with a hack libretto which only the genius of Donizetti or Bellini could rise above. And underneath it all is a vein of deep cruelty, masquerading as factual, playing with the problem of a woman with a past. Angel Clare's behaviour, which Hardy is good enough to explain as rather conventional, is not only monstrous but—much worse artistic crime—unconscious. Not since medieval stories like that of patient Griselda had women been tortured as Hardy tortures Tess (and also Sue in *Jude*). Himself no president of immortals but the chairman of petty sessions, he is reluctant to let her receive the peace of death, and with sickening obtusity and deep moral conventionality, closes his book by hinting at Angel Clare's next marriage.

One final point must be made against Hardy. It is sometimes thought that his novels bring into literature a rural world that had not previously interested fiction writers. His pathetically inept Wessex is supposed to be particularly valid and true to the soil; applause greets the clumsy capers of the regional novel. But long before Hardy's lachrymose pomposities, George Eliot had created a wonderful rural world, artistically true, much more seriously ambitious in scope and much more far-ranging. Beside her achievement Hardy is the person who should be dealt with, and disposed of, not by the President of the Immortals but by us. We have finished with him. (pp. 95-6)

> *Brigid Brophy, Michael Levey, and Charles Osborne, " 'Tess of the D'Urbervilles',"* in their *Fifty Works of English and American Literature We Could Do Without (copyright © 1967 Brigid Brophy, Michael Levey, Charles Osborne; reprinted with permission of Stein and Day Publishers), Stein and Day, 1968, pp. 95-6.*

KENNETH MARSDEN   (essay date 1969)

[There is] sharp critical disagreement about Hardy's poetry and its somewhat anomalous standing in general esteem. The two problems are, to a large extent, one. The 'local' differences of opinion concerning poems play a large part in creating the peculiar repute of the poetry as a whole and are in turn affected by it. The typical symptom of this is the tone of grudging admiration which seems to be the prevailing attitude; this it is, I think, which is responsible for both the insistence on emphasizing the amount of inferior work and for the small number of poems which the critic really approves of. It seems that the critics are attracted against what they feel to be their judgement, perhaps against their will—certainly against their principles. (p. 211)

In some quarters there has been a hostility to the presence of explicit ideas in poetry ('preaching' is the usual label) and they do exist in Hardy in sufficient quantity to give him a bad reputation. (p. 212)

For much of this century the doctrine of organic or expressive form has been a potent and pervasive influence. Hardy was basically a 'formalist' and occasionally committed the 'crime' of contorting his verse to fit into prescribed and preordained patterns. This was made worse by his possession of a vague reputation as an innovator, which was found on closer inspection to be hollow. Allied to this was a claim, similarly exposed as largely sham, to be a dramatic poet, when powerful critical voices (Eliot, for instance) were holding that practically all great poetry was dramatic.

Hardy believed that 'the whole secret of a living style and the difference between it and a dead style, lies in not having too much style—being, in fact, a little careless, or rather seeming to be, here and there.' . . . Minor faults are common enough to make it look as if he put this doctrine into practice and this offends readers and critics in an age of close reading, analysis, and a general rise in technical standards of poetry. (p. 213)

Hardy's verse stands up to close scrutiny reasonably well; many of the weaknesses of vocabulary, rhythm, structure and so on exist only in the critic's understanding—or through a lack of it. . . . But close analysis is often only a partially effective instrument for dealing with many of these poems. One of the marks of this technique in the hands of its less able practitioners is a tendency to concentrate on one thing at a time; this makes it an effective method for determining the virtues and defects of vocabulary *or* rhythm *or* structure *or* ideas. But this very virtue often makes it much more difficult to respond to the poem as a unity, and the peculiar value of Hardy's best poetry lies in its pre-eminent possession of this unity (all good poetry has it, but other poets frequently have *local* strengths which are often lacking in Hardy).

I am convinced that the source of this unity in Hardy's poems is the personality which most poems disclose; many of the poems *are* unities, they *are* integrated because they have this common link or, rather, are expressions of it. Concentration on particular aspects can remove difficulties and misunderstandings; it does little, through its very nature, to help the reader to approach the central core since this is personal and indivisible. It is, of course, essential to avoid the error of identifying this poetic personality with that of the man Hardy. The difference between the two has been plain to many observers and critics, including Siegfried Sassoon, whose poem 'At Max Gate' is based on this contrast. . . . The poetic personality is the real source and centre and it exists only in the work. If, for any reason, the reader does not respond to this personality, then he will respond only to those poems which meet the critical criteria he brings with him; and, as we have seen, the number can be very small.

Critical theories about the necessary impersonality of poetry are likely to be a handicap when Hardy is being considered, and the inventor, or modern reviver, of the theory, T. S. Eliot, logically enough picked on Hardy as one of the outstanding examples of personality in modern literature. Admittedly, he considers only one example, a minor piece of prose, but the instinct was right. (pp. 213-15)

It would be easy to compile a long list of poets paying tribute to Hardy, but the critical harvest is very sparse. . . . Several critics . . . claim that Hardy influenced many poets. . . . No one, however, seems willing to give details or even ask some obvious questions. For instance, Pound who says that Hardy taught him something does not show very obviously what it was (since it is hard to believe that he needed to learn the importance of subject-matter from Hardy) and Graves, while recommending Hardy to young poets, has apparently kept to other paths himself.

Scattered examples of influence are, it is true, easy enough to find, though they usually come from a poet's very early work (W. H. Auden for example). . . . It is also true that close

imitation, amounting to pastiche, can be found; see, for example, de la Mare's 'Thomas Hardy' and C. Day Lewis's 'Singing Children: Lucca della Robbia' (from *An Italian Visit*); the latter, in particular, seems a Hardy poem that, by some accident, Hardy forgot to write. Furthermore, no lover of parody should miss William Plomer's 'A Right of Way: 1865.'' . . . (pp. 216-17)

Most of these resemblances, of varied strength and seriousness, have one thing in common; they imitate him where he is most imitable, usually in idiosyncrasies of vocabulary and rhythm. It should be fairly obvious, however, that for another poet to be *seriously* influenced by Hardy is rather unlikely, because as the real Hardy, the one who is worth being influenced by, started from subject, the poet being influenced would do the same. He might well take over, or rather perceive anew, Hardy's subject-matter, but since he would be attempting to render *his* perception it is not likely that he would employ Hardy's peculiarities of vocabulary. (pp. 217-18)

Although the theories and assumptions which constitute Hardy's 'philosophy' are still alive, they are also to some extent 'historical' and will become increasingly so. They will, therefore, lose much of their power to irritate, but also their full and immediate impact on the mind and spirit. His readers will have to rely increasingly upon notes, commentators and background reading, and so he will come to the public on the same footing as his great predecessors whose work and reputation have overcome similar obstacles. He will, of course, always have some readers whose contact with his work is a kind of naked encounter, creating sympathy and comprehension without the need for intermediaries. It seems likely, too, that in the future, as in the past, their number will be increased in times of stress. The First World War was one such period when Hardy's stock rose and there was a similar, if less marked, movement during the Second.

Q. D. Leavis, after quoting a statement that only a disenchanted sophomore could be impressed by Hardy's view of Life, admits that there is always a generation of such readers. (pp. 220-21)

Conversely there will always be readers whose temperaments will clash with Hardy's. Any kind of self-satisfaction is likely to produce this, the situation then being as he described it in **'In Tenebris II'**. Furthermore, despite his reputation for intrusive and repeated expression of ideas, the true Hardy is a poet of the intimate whisper; and it is very easy for some people to get the tone wrong. (p. 221)

The best approach [to Hardy's poetry] appears to be by way of a book of selections, though it is impossible to recommend any existing volume without considerable reservation.

There are, in addition to the danger inseparable from *any* anthologizing, two approaches which must be avoided by any editor of Hardy's verse: the "cross-section' and the 'jewels from rubbish-heaps'.

The first sounds plausible, especially when advocated in the cause of honesty, since it is claimed that in this way we have the verse as it really is, warts and all. But Hardy's verse is already inextricably various; nearly every poem has its quota of dross, even if it is dross transmuted temporarily to gold, and there is no need to display more of it. In any case the deliberate republication and dissemination of inferior verse is a heavy responsibility for an editor to shoulder. Such material should be allowed to lie dormant in its author's collected works.

On the other hand, the editor who sees himself as a dauntless prospector sieving malodorous heaps for a few nuggets is a danger too. Critical uncertainty is so marked at present that it is doubtful whether a satisfactory short selection is possible at all; too many serious candidates would be left out. . . . Furthermore, one poem often throws light upon another if only by contrast. Lastly, and most importantly, Hardy should be read, if not complete, at any rate in bulk; there is a large quantity of verse, both relatively and absolutely which needs to be read sympathetically and with the understanding gained by reading the better work, which is similar to it in essence anyway. It is common knowledge that his verse grows on the reader, but there is less chance of this happening if the cream—assuming it can be identified—is to be strained off into a 'recognized' anthology.

Ultimately, however, the reader who is trying to enjoy what Hardy has to offer will have to make the effort . . . to see the poems as the poetic unity that many of them are, to be in contact with the poetic persona revealed there. If Hardy seems a little tentative, clumsy or indiscriminate, they should remember the remark of Joubert: 'Those who have no thought beyond their words, and no vision beyond their thoughts, have a very decisive style.' . . . (pp. 222-23)

It is a truism that great literature is in the last resort ineffable; Pound must have felt this when he was discussing Hardy: 'Given those specifications, poem after poem of Hardy's leaves one with nowt more to say. Expression coterminous with matter: Nothing for disciples' exploitation.'

All this can be seen in, for instance, **'Proud Songsters'**; the personal rhythm, expression coterminous with matter, the lack of anything for disciples' exploitation; all ensuring that there is 'nowt more' to say, that an attempt to say anything would be impertinence or anti-climax. (p. 223)

Kenneth Marsden, in his The Poems of Thomas Hardy:
A Critical Introduction (© Kenneth Marsden 1969),
Athlone Press, 1969, 247 p.

F. R. SOUTHERINGTON　(essay date 1971)

[*In his critical study of Hardy's prose works, excerpted below, Southerington notes especially "the presence of autobiographical features embedded deep in the fabric of the novels." Unlike most critics, Southerington finds a strong tendency toward optimism in Hardy's work, and finds* The Dynasts *"to be more a cry of hope than of despair."*]

[*Desperate Remedies*] is a strange work, and it deserves attention; but those qualities in it which are most remarkable are all foreshadowings of later techniques, and they are best seen in relation to the later prose. Moreover, in *Under the Greenwood Tree* we have an early work which displays an assurance which Hardy scarcely equalled in his later works. The concern with change, with the natural environment, and with feminine sexuality and passivity are all present; but they carry with them a mastery of prose which was scarcely intimated in *Desperate Remedies*. Undistorted by irrelevant generalisation, free from self-conscious literary references, and using its few symbols discreetly and naturally, it marks a consistency of sensibility never again equalled in Hardy. It is Hardy at his lightest, but in many senses it is Hardy at his best too. That the treatment of the rustics is occasionally patronising or facetious is admitted; yet such passages play a minor part in the novel and I do not propose to do more with them than note that they are

there. It seems more fruitful to point to the qualities of proportion which belie the critical judgement that this is a slight work—a judgement which Hardy regrettably seems to have accepted without demur. (p. 44)

[In *Under the Greenwood Tree*], a nostalgic tale of the decay of rustic life, Hardy infuses his theme with an idyllic delicacy which stresses the dignity of the disappearing way. He strikes a balance between awareness of the value of the past and awareness that decline has, in fact, occurred. Landscape plays its part in this balance, since the rural sights and sounds which are Hardy's *métier* are not only closely allied with the human activity which goes on amidst them, but are also lovingly and precisely handled. The tiny rural community is given its home and natural environment with tact and the minimum of self-consciousness, and we see rural life as being in itself a delicate and coherent organism. . . . (pp. 44-5)

But of course that environment is insecure, and it is the insecurity which is Hardy's theme. For however idyllic Mellstock may be, it is not Arcady, and the impermanence of the ways of life is gently underlined, even as the community is presented to us. As the characters are introduced they are given an air of unreality, and we are reminded that what we see is no more than a *picture* of the past, a loving reconstruction of ways now dead and gone. (p. 45)

[In *A Pair of Blue Eyes*] we have a novel in which there is continual stress on circumstance and the power of accident, but which can be read as an illustration of false choice; and at the heart of the novel as its most dramatic incident, we have a scene which stresses man's place in the evolutionary pattern, the power of the elements, and the power of circumstance—and yet places its final stress on the defeat of those forces by human ingenuity. . . .

[There is] a tentative attempt to establish a pattern of imagery and symbol which would reinforce the 'circumstance motif' if it were successful, and in particular there are the beginnings of a scheme of proleptic imagery foreshadowing Elfride's eventual decline and death. In the greater novels, where its success is more apparent, we cannot ignore it—in *Tess* above all. Much of the schematic pattern attempted in *A Pair of Blue Eyes* would lend weight to those who believe that Hardy's characters are without a defence against circumstance; but if read in this way it would make little sense of the action of the book, concerned as much as it is with motivation and relationships between one person and another. *A Pair of Blue Eyes*, seen alone or in common with the later novels, shows the superiority of the human intelligence in the evolutionary pattern, and attempts to show the strength of the forces which intelligence can, at its best, defeat. Elfride's tragedy is that her intelligence serves her only at a physical crisis, and then on behalf of the man who is primarily responsible for her defeat. In moral crises she has no intelligence at all. (p. 59)

Each of Hardy's earlier novels had been written under special circumstances which occasionally interfered with success, and which certainly justify us in regarding them as experimental works. *Desperate Remedies* was a reaction against the first, unpublished work, *The Poor Man and the Lady;* and its adherence to the advice of George Meredith, with the consequent debt to Wilkie Collins's sensational works, is not much to its advantage. *Under the Greenwood Tree* is successful because Hardy was not drawn too deeply into an analysis of rural decline, nor did he become too morbidly involved with his own personal affairs. In a *Pair of Blue Eyes* autobiographical elements are again present, the young Tryphena Sparks disguised under the features of Hardy's first wife, for example, and Cornwall selected as the setting. Even here, though, Hardy's chief problem was not personal, but was one of expression and setting: his feeling for the Cornish landscape, whatever it may have become *after* the death of his first wife, does not appear to be very deeply engaged, while his search for a way of expressing his conclusions about human conduct and choice is hampered because he is still dogged by a youthful conception of Chance and Coincidence, and has not yet absorbed it into a larger scheme. Against all this, *Far From the Madding Crowd* marks the end of an apprenticeship, and it has rightly been seen as the 'most characteristic' of Hardy's successful novels. It has all the ingredients of a ballad tale, it strikes a balance between rural strength and rural weaknesses, its lovers are the three stock types—the staunch, rejected lover, the passionately unstable man, and the philanderer; and in its attention to the great consequences of trivial beginnings it focuses most clearly upon one of the central preoccupations of Hardy's novels. If the book lacks the power of some of Hardy's later work, this may be because his perspective here is more consistently maintained. Neither autobiographical matter nor ideological matter is allowed to dominate the tale. . . . [It] is to the moral point of view and to Hardy's success in finding a correlation between individuals and the environment that the book owes its coherence. Although so strongly rooted in the 'ballad' tradition, *Far From the Madding Crowd* is a moral work. (pp. 60-1)

Henry James [said] that the book is essentially a tale made inordinately long by superfluous padding. . . .

James, in failing to see the organic nature of Hardy's rural society, failed to see the relevance of many of the rustic scenes. . . . (p. 61)

It seems perfectly accurate to say that Hardy does not take sides with his characters: but to say that he does not *judge* them is a different thing, and is refuted by the text. Judgement is made frequently, and in the same terms: to what extent is there control of the emotions by reason or by the will? To what extent do characters comply with nature, to what extent do they resist, and on what degree of understanding is their choice to comply or resist founded? To what extent is choice taken deliberately and with forethought? Finally, to what extent are human skills used for the benefit of man and the improvement of the conditions in which man lives? These are the questions posed in *Far From the Madding Crowd,* and they are asked of society as well as of individuals. The notion of equilibrium is common to both, and Hardy's detailed study of the rural environment is not thus an attempt merely to create a solid social background for his plot; 'solidity of specification' here does have that function, of course, but it also stresses the communal effects of individual effort, and the part which even one individual may play in the reinvigoration of society. The 'mere padding' which James saw is in fact one of the principal features which gave proportion to the work, because it establishes the mutual relationship between the nature of man and the nature of the environment in which he lives and works. (p. 67)

Far From the Madding Crowd is the first of Hardy's works to make a claim to greatness. The basis for its claim is its treatment of an abiding moral problem, man's relation to his environment and to others; and the claim may be respected, and finally conceded, on the grounds that an old philosophy of the necessity of the dominance of reason over passion is not merely re-stated, but is renewed in terms of a modern vision of nature

in which the role of man is reduced, but his significance enhanced. (p. 75)

The real cause of its failure was that Hardy was not by nature a social satirist', writes Evelyn Hardy of *The Hand of Ethelberta* . . . . Without wishing to defend the book against the charge of failure, one can only say that this judgement is wrong: *The Hand of Ethelberta* is not primarily a social satire. It reflects Hardy's further attempt to analyse problems already raised in *Far From the Madding Crowd,* and as an attempt, albeit an unsuccessful one, at a more subtle analysis of the nature of human reason and the emotions, it deserves an important place in any study of Hardy's work. Had Hardy shown more awareness of his own developing attitude to the problems he was facing it might even have played a vital part in our understanding of him, and been a turning-point in his achievement; whereas we are compelled by its failure to see it only as a faltering step towards ideas which he carried out more successfully elsewhere. (p. 76)

The Return of the Native is an imaginative, and in some senses allegorical, study of the 'mutually destructive interdependence of spirit and flesh'. Seen in these terms the relative failure to transform local gentility into figures of Promethean grandeur matters less: Thomasin, Mrs Yeobright, Wildeve, Diggory Venn, all lose significance, it is true, because they are scarcely adequate to the framework which Hardy depicts. But if we look for a tragedy of chance and fate then Eustacia and Clym sink into insignificance also. . . . But if we look for a drama of the spirit and the flesh . . . then Clym and Eustacia not merely gain enormously, they also become vitally integrated with the author's personal observations. The lengthy discursive passages imbedded in the description of the heath, and the portraits of Clym's face, also take on a new freshness and significance for the work.

The Return of the Native is concerned with Time, and the evolution of consciousness within Time, It is concerned with the demands of the mind and the spirit, and the incompatible demands of the flesh. And Hardy's method of dramatising this is notably close to his method in the poem **'The Convergence of the Twain'**, where concrete realities, the 'Titanic' and the iceberg, signify cosmic abstractions. The realities of *The Return of the Native* are Egdon, Clym, and Eustacia. Without wishing to schematise the plot too rigidly, it is none the less possible—indeed, essential—to regard the heath as representative of the background of Space and Time, and Clym and Eustacia are representative of different phases of existence within Time—Clym representing the 'modern type', Eustacia representing 'that zest for existence which was so intense in early civilizations'. One is, of course, aware of what actually *happens* to Eustacia, and so far from weakening this case her fate strengthens it. (pp. 90-1)

[*The Return of the Native*] dramatises the death of older forms of perception in the struggle for survival in the modern world. It dramatises the evolution of consciousness and if there are moments when the evolution appears to be a tragic process, it is so not of itself but because of the nature of the perception that it brings. It is because they objectify these abstractions that Clym and Eustacia achieve grandeur, and it is this additional and systematically contrived stratum of the book that gives impressiveness to the novel. Despite crudities in dialogue . . . , despite weaknesses of characterisation (Thomasin and Wildeve especially), the ambitious structure of the book, and the careful attention to the Promethean and classical allusions, are justified because Hardy has chosen a modern theme whose grandeur approaches, if it cannot equal, the inquiries of his classical forebears. (pp. 94-5)

If *The Return of the Native* marks a new departure, so too does *The Mayor of Casterbridge.* Of all Hardy's works it is probably the most individual, and it stands in contrast to the other novels, where he attempts to give a partial explanation of his characters, either in terms of environment or of heredity, or of both. Thus Clym may be partly understood as a product of his upbringing on Egdon Heath, Eustacia by her Mediterranean ancestry; the same sort of explanations occur in *Tess* and *Jude.* In these works not only does the environment affect the events in which the characters are involved, but the very nature of the characters derives in part from their environment. Yet when we first meet Michael Henchard, and in all our subsequent dealings with him, we find a hero who is rootless, scarcely integrated—if at all—with the social environment, and totally without antecedents. Certainly his environment influences the events of his career, but his character is none the less a given entity, and remains unexplained however much it may be explored. Despite the indication that the action takes place 'before the nineteenth century had reached one-third of its span', the opening of the book possesses a deliberately-rendered timelessness: the scene is one that might have been matched at almost any spot in any county in England at this time of year', the road is featureless, 'neither straight nor crooked, neither level nor hilly', and the only sounds are the murmur of mother and child and 'the voice of a weak bird singing a trite old evening song that might doubtless have been heard on the same hill at the same hour, and with the self-same trills, quavers, and breves, at any sunset of that season for centuries untold'. In this detached objective opening one senses Hardy's warning that whatever may take place in this work, and whatever social forces operate, we are to study a character in isolation, not only from others but from himself, not only from his own time but from any time. And the structure of the opening of the novel, with its swift dramatic prologue to an action of twenty years later, implies that the laws of cause, effect, and retribution may also play a major part.

For though his character remains unexplained, the social, moral, and spiritual isolation of Henchard are revealed to be the consequences of his own actions, and even more of his own nature. In his frequent stress on heredity and environment Hardy faces the mystery behind the formation of human personality: and the fact that he so clearly *chooses* not to attempt an explanation here, as he partly attempts it in his other works, suggests that his purpose is more than an analysis of character. Indeed, we find an analysis of the influence of character upon events, and of the slowly strengthening hold of Consequence over character. In a very real sense the theme of this work is closely related to the theme of *The Dynasts,* and despite its attention to a specific individual in a specific, named and localised society, it is also a study of human history whose conclusions match the conclusions of *The Dynasts* in several major respects. (pp. 96-7)

In *The Return of the Native* Hardy had dramatised the role of two modes of perception in the modern world, and *The Mayor of Casterbridge* is capable of similar 'allegorical' interpretation; but it should be noted that in these works his representative types are creatures of high sensitivity. In *The Trumpet-Major* and *A Laodicean* Hardy's concern with Time and the role of man in Time is still present, although his power is muted, and *The Trumpet-Major* confines itself specifically to the past, a past seen through a veil of nostalgia but none the less positive

and productive. *A Laodicean* is con[ce]... and the future, and it expands its con[c]... type to contrast with the sensitivity [of] their kind. Potentially it is a greater [book than *The Trumpet-] Major,* yet it is more subjective and [more] and for this reason, as well as through [the illness] of 1880-81, when the book was writte[n it is a notice]able failure. In some senses both novel[s]...... self: the attitudes expressed are his, [and they] illustrate his perplexity at his position as the last scion of a noble but decayed stock. (p. 106)

[There] are autobiographical elements in *Under the Greenwood Tree* and *A Pair of Blue Eyes.* Their full relevance will only be completely clear when seen in relation to *Tess of the D'Urbervilles* and *Jude the Obscure.* In these novels it will be apparent that throughout his career as a novelist Hardy more and more frequently touched upon personal issues which finally grew into obsessions, and which destroyed his artistic objectivity. *Tess* survives, but *Jude* is very close to being wrecked as a work of art, though it remained a powerful personal document. In a sense it represents Hardy's complete disintegration as a novelist, though perhaps as a thinker it may have been his salvation. After *Jude* he shows himself capable of clear and objective thought, and the intellectual strands of the novels, shorn of disturbing and personal influences, are gathered into a finely-woven thread of argument, which subtly and artistically presents the role of humanity in an environment of Time and Chance. My point here is that *A Laodicean,* perhaps because of Hardy's severe illness, foreshadows that disintegration. The influence of heredity, though powerful, is never followed through to any conclusion. Nor, ultimately, is it more than a side-issue in the resolution of the plot. (pp. 111-12)

Biographical elements are also present in *Two on a Tower,* though they contribute little to its failure, which is simply due to the farcical nature of the plot. (pp. 112-13)

It is extremely difficult to take *The Woodlanders* seriously if we regard it as Hardy appears to ask us to regard it, a drama of 'grandeur and unity truly Sophoclean'. The death of Giles, the essential pettiness of Grace Melbury's tastes, and the melodrama centring on Fitzpiers, Felice Charmond, and the gentleman from South Carolina, are all distractions, and unconvincing. Sometimes, indeed, there is a note of cynicism in the author's treatment of his plot, most especially in the reunion of Grace and her erring husband. . . . (p. 119)

More openly than in any previous work Hardy establishes a sense of the organic unity between man and nature, in terms which question the possibility of happiness within any human or natural society. The novel is the most overtly Darwinian of Hardy's books, and a pattern of struggle throughout nature is applied to man and his environment. Hardy frequently uses the same terminology for man and for his surroundings: just as the branches of the woodland trees disfigure each other, or hollow oaks become afflicted with tumours, so time brings in its strains and spasms for men, 'hiding ill-results when they could be guarded against for greater effect when they could not'. The eternal presence of decay and the purely temporary nature of the recuperative powers is made ironic by human insistence on those recuperative powers. . . . This is not a theme which *The Woodlanders* directly states, but it may lie beneath the almost carelessly cynical approach which Hardy takes towards his plot, and it seems certain that ideas expressed more directly in *Tess* and *Jude* are already moving beneath the surface. (p. 120)

Woodlanders places more stress on the hostility of man's natural and social environment than any of the previous novels; there is indeed a darkening of the vision. (p. 122)

Hardy's view that if Grace 'would have done a really self-abandoned thing (gone off with Giles) he could have made a fine tragic ending of the book' implies . . . [a] conflict between natural conduct and social restraint. Yet this conflict never takes life in the work. Hardy was too embarrassed by his public, too trammelled by the conventions of his medium, or too confused in his thinking at this point; for whatever reason, a degree of condemnation is reserved for the sexual exploits of Fitzpiers, and to perhaps a lesser extent of Mrs Charmond. The conflict is never adequately resolved. (p. 123)

The same conflict appears in a more drastic and potentially more damaging form in *Tess of the D'Urbervilles,* a work which appears to me to present the most crucial critical problem raised by Hardy's novels. It is a great book. Yet as a work of art it falls more clearly into two levels than any of his novels: the ballad tale of the maiden seduced by the dashing young squire forms the basis for the book; this basis is overlaid by a sombre moral commentary which cannot be ignored. Hardy's sub-title [**"A Pure Woman Faithfully Presented"**] makes a moral claim for the heroine, and his appeals to our judgement in the text make the same claim from varying points of view. (pp. 123-24)

In *Tess of the D'Urbervilles* the moral commentary is an integral part of the order of discourse, which imposes upon us a standard of judgement through which we are obliged to see the heroine. (p. 125)

Tess of the D'Urbervilles is based, as was *The Return of the Native,* on a knowledge of an inevitable conflict in nature: the conflict between sentient man and insentient forces. But it steps beyond that knowledge to question the appropriateness of social institutions and social concepts as weapons in that conflict. Hardy uses a set of irreconcilables to point to parallel irreconcilables in nature. A social code which regards sexuality as in itself evil, and holds men and women responsible for impulses for which they hold no responsibility is contrasted with a view of sexuality as an instinctive, irresistible force. In this sense *Tess* is a work about determinism. Sexuality is neither condemned nor praised; it is merely accepted. There are times when the 'appetite for joy' appears to be synonymous with sexuality; there are moments, too, when the 'well-judged plan' of the mating of men and women is described as 'ill-judged' in its execution. These conflicting attitudes are unreconciled. Nor is it clear to what extent Hardy regards sexuality as uncontrollable. . . . One could wish for greater clarity here since the degree to which man can or cannot regulate sexual passions is relevant to our judgement of the characters in *Tess.* The basic discrepancy, however, between social laws and natural conduct is drawn clearly enough. So too is the parallel discrepancy between a universe in which man is irrelevant, and a consciousness through which he becomes the centre of that universe. Tess's tragedy is that her consciousness is trapped by its growing awareness of the irrelevance of social ordinances, and the mastering influence of her natural being. (pp. 131-32)

[In] addition to sexual determinism, this work goes far to postulate hereditary determinism also. (p. 132)

Tess of the D'Urbervilles rejects determinism as a creed. Yet it is the work in which 'proleptic' images are most consistently fulfilled, one in which little chance appears to be offered to either Tess or Clare, and a novel in which the illusion of inevitability is most clearly maintained. The only real opportunity which is given to Tess to escape from the trap in which she is caught is ruined by the loss of courage which hinders her from appealing to Clare's parents. The remaining opportunities are negated by innate qualities; so too, however, are our judgements of the failings of both Tess and Clare. One may fairly say that if Tess's career is not predestined, it certainly appears so. (pp. 132-33)

In parts *Tess of the D'Urbervilles* fails to balance its narrative against its commentary; in parts the commentary appears querulous and ill-judged. But in its portrait of an innocent sensibility violated by social ignorance it becomes a passionate appeal for sanity in a difficult and confusing world. (p. 133)

To search for objective comment in *Jude the Obscure* . . . becomes an almost vain attempt. Hardy was not writing objectively; he was pouring his heart's blood into the work. When *Jude* was complete there were no more novels to write, for the almost obsessional reflections of the previous years found their fulfilment. . . . Its effect is startling. Few novels in the English language have a more powerful impact, yet few major works are so ill-defined in their aims. *Jude* is almost wrecked by its subjective elements; yet were they absent *Jude* could not exist.

What is the theme of *Jude the Obscure?* Hardy himself defined it in his preface as:

> . . . the fret and fever, derision and disaster,
> that may press in the wake of the strongest
> passion known to humanity, . . . a deadly war
> waged between flesh and spirit; . . . the tragedy
> of unfulfilled aims . . .
>
> (pp. 140-41)

But it is perhaps *Jude's* greatest merit that it cannot be reduced to a formula. For it is in its portrait of two struggling and sensitive souls against a whole range of obstacles that the success of *Jude the Obscure* lies. Despite its apparent fragmentation of themes the book is saved by its contrast, at times explicit, between man's aspirations and his opportunities. The sexual and scholarly sides of Jude's nature are linked by a parallel between his ambition for learning and his love for Sue. . . . Jude and Sue stand in relations very similar to those of Clym Yeobright and Eustacia Vye, the men representing an adjustment to the modern environment, the women a tradition which can no longer survive. That Jude adjusts slowly, and only with self-knowledge, and that the self-knowledge involves virtual self-annihilation, is the measure of Hardy's development—if that is the right word—since *The Return of the Native.* In *Jude* all that a consciousness of the modern environment can lead to is 'the universal wish not to live'.

Discussion of Hardy's debt to Schopenhauer and von Hartmann would suggest that this is a logical development of Hardy's thought, and that the evolutionary meliorism which he came to adopt is a partial and inadequate answer to pessimistic notions to which he was more deeply committed. The evidence is against such a view. There is no doubt that his reading of philosophy influenced Hardy. . . . But his responses, as his literary notebooks, the comments in the *Life,* and the surviving letters all suggest, were conditioned by mood and subjectivity. Hardy was a feeler first, only secondarily a thinker, and his reading was often an attempt to confirm impressions already formed. Nor did he claim otherwise. *Jude the Obscure* is an almost total negation of the message of Hardy's other work.

It would be difficult, to say the least, to make a case for *Jude* as optimisitic or melioristic philosophy; it is equally difficult to make a case for it as philosophy at all. More than anything else he wrote, this work, despite philosophical asides—many fewer than in *Tess*—is an 'impression', a 'seeming', highly subjective, highly emotional, even unbalanced. . . . Hardy's previous works, while accepting the intimidating nature of the universal environment, had none the less shown a refusal to be intimidated. The following works, *The Dynasts* above all, explore methods of resisting irrevocable universal forces. *Jude,* and *Jude* alone, appears to admit wholly negative impressions.

Superficially, Jude, like Tess, is at the mercy of social disadvantages; yet one is hard put to see Jude content in any society. The breakdown of his marriage and his life with Sue are so clearly, even if incompletely, paralleled with the turbulent lives of their common ancestors that they cannot be seen as purely local and temporary features: there is something fundamental here, a force possessed by the blood alone. This force is never clearly explained, and Hardy, as his poems show, did not know the explanation himself. He may have derived something from Weismann's *Essays on Heredity.* . . . [In *Jude*] Hardy successfully brought to life the psychology of his characters to a degree surpassing any of his previous attempts. Sue Bridehead is perhaps the most remarkable feminine portrait in the English novel. (pp. 142-45)

> *F. R. Southerington, in his* Hardy's Vision of Man, *(© F. R. Southerington 1971; by permission of Barnes & Noble Books, a Division of Littlefield, Adams & Co., Inc.), Barnes & Noble, 1971, 290 p.*

A.O.J. COCKSHUT (essay date 1977)

Hardy's tone, we know, varies. Perhaps the most difficult question that can be asked about him (and one of the most important) is this: do his ideas vary with his tone? Is he, fundamentally, saying the same thing in the semi-pastoral of *Far From the Madding Crowd,* as in *Tess* and *Jude*? Is the effect on him of the changes in his personal experience between 1874 and 1895 deep enough to cause a revolution in his thinking on the relation of the sexes? In an attempt to answer, I shall dwell especially on the earliest and the latest of his major works, since, by common consent, the first, *Far From the Madding Crowd* is the most cheerful, and the last, *Jude,* is the most sombre.

The rather vague term, semi-pastoral, which has just been used is intended to suggest the contrast of which every reader is aware in *Far From the Madding Crowd.* There is a strong sense of the richness of country life and its satisfactions, yet the book is full of setbacks and disasters. Gabriel Oak is an archetypal shepherd, whose love endures through all vicissitudes, yet his response to his first impression of Bathsheba's charm reminds us more of Mr Guppy than of Theocritus—he drenches his dry, sandy hair in hair-oil. Graceful traditions, like the sending of valentines, end in violence and madness. Bathsheba is both naïve and coquettish.

Reading with the hindsight denied to the first readers, we can easily find light-hearted adumbrations of themes later to be tragic. This is how Hardy introduces us to the idea that the marriage-bond kills love by commanding it to endure:

> 'Coggan,' he said, 'I could never wish for a handsomer woman than I've got, but feeling she's ticketed as my lawful wife, I can't help

my wicked heart wandering, do what I will.' But at last I believe he cured it by making her take off her wedding-ring and calling her by her maiden name as they sat together after the shop was shut, and so a' would get to fancy she was only his sweetheart and not married to him at all. And as soon as he could thoroughly fancy he was doing wrong and committing the seventh, a' got to like her as well as ever, and they lived on a perfect picture of mutel love.

Yet, of course, there is more than a difference of tone between this and anything in *Jude.* The comic point here lies in man's sly power of adjustment of his wayward, wilful nature to the moral requirements of society. Here, no one stops to wonder what happens when the adjustment is beyond people's strength.

Before Troy appears on the scene, we have got to know Bathsheba. The interesting and unusual thing about her, for the readers of the 1870s, was that she was an independent, modern woman, entirely her own mistress, confidently giving orders to men, and yet remote from all feminist issues of the time. She might come under moral criticism, but it would certainly be criticism of a traditional kind. She could be called 'forward', 'capricious', 'unreasonable', 'vain'. She could not be supposed by anyone to be unfeminine. With unconscious cleverness she blends the role of the woman in charge of a business, giving orders and paying wages, with an old-fashioned feminine 'imperiousness' more like that of the 'cruel fair' of the seventeenth-century poets. Like them she is commanding to men, not because she is really independent of them, but because she feels she would be nothing without them, and had better make the most of the brief opportunities granted by youth and beauty. Until Troy appears, she betrays a touch of surprise that strong men can be so obedient to a woman's caprice and so easily cowed by her displeasure.

The power of the scenes describing her encounter with Troy springs from a happy blending of three different modes of writing. Hardy is at the same time particular, general and symbolical. He is particular, since Bathsheba has attained the status of a full feminine portrait, and general since Troy is not a true portrait, but a typical masculine presence, felt by the woman as answering to her yearning to submit. It is symbolical, perhaps almost by accident, since Troy's military accoutrements, the spur and the sword, become types of masculine dominance, and hence by implication, of feminine submissiveness. (pp. 116-18)

[The] polarity of male and female is emphasized as much as possible and similarities are forgotten or denied.

And this polarity is so complete that personality is forgotten too, merged in masculinity and femininity. Naturally, this cannot last. . . . The story of the death of Fanny Robin, and of her child, who is also Troy's, is impressive in establishing the unexpectedness of known characters. Hardy achieves the kind of surprise that we sometimes feel about people we know well, when we say 'I would never have thought he would have done that, but I see now it was in character.' (p. 120)

These last scenes figure strongly in T. S. Eliot's *After Strange Gods,* supporting the indictment that Hardy was deliberately morbid, and satisfying perverse emotions of his own rather than tracing the real history and feeling of his characters. Morbid or not, the message is certainly simplistic, and one may be inclined to ask whether the doctrine that all women are alike is not a simple logical muddle. Naturally, all women are alike in that which makes them women; and all men in that which makes them men. But just as some men, faced with the strange situation which confronted Troy, would have behaved quite differently, with tenderness or self-reproach or horror, so, it seems fair to suggest, would some women have behaved quite differently from Bathsheba, with anger, hysterical or controlled, with feigned indifference, with contempt.

But it seems to me that a few chapters later Hardy goes far to defend himself against Eliot's charge, and at the same time to throw doubt on his own generalization that women are all the same. Alone, deserted by Troy, who is now believed to be dead, she opens the case of his watch, which contains the lock of Fanny's hair:

> 'He was hers and she was his; they should be gone together,' she said. 'I am nothing to either of them, and why should I keep her hair?' She took it in her hand, and held it over the fire. 'No—I'll not burn it—I'll keep it in memory of her, poor thing!' she added, snatching back her hand.

The surprise we feel here is salutary. The utter oppositeness of male and female has been stressed throughout. Here we suddenly move into another realm, one of creative generosity. Bathsheba is still feminine, and still recognizably in character. But without forfeiting that, she has reached a place where 'there is neither male nor female', where forgiveness is blest and charity is triumphant. To assert the polarity of sex as powerfully, imaginatively and memorably as Hardy has throughout, and especially in the swordflash scene, and then to assert, just as memorably, a deeper level of the soul whose moral grandeur is essentially human, and as some, unlike Hardy himself, would say, divine in its origin—this is magnificent, and not morbid at all. One can only regret that the melodramatic ending blurs the effect.

At all stages, Bathsheba's history is told by an author oblivious of all feminist arguments. *Qua* woman, she is predictably like all other women, yearning, pleading, submissive, even masochistic. In her great moment, when she treasures Fanny's hair, she is beyond all sexual differences, acting as Man, *homo*, not as man or woman.

This leads on to the case of Marty South in *The Woodlanders*. . . . In a book full of flirtations, passions of varying degrees of egoism and carnality, she stands alone. Her love for Giles is sexual, certainly, in the sense that it is essentially the love of a woman for a man. But Hardy takes care to separate it from all other passions by assimilating it to love that is not sexual but filial. There are two moments of sad dignity and repose in Marty's life. In each she is mourning for the dead; in the first, silently for her father, in the second, with eloquent words for her lost love, Giles Winterborne. . . . (pp. 121-23)

In order to become unselfish and truly generous, love, for Hardy, must almost cease to be sexual. It must be essentially like filial love. Marty's love is simple, enduring, impervious to change. Sex, in Hardy's world, is inescapably self-regarding. Passionate feminine abasement is as much so, in its way, as the predatoriness and inconstancy of the male. The most startling statement of this view comes when the kind, gentle Tess, whose love for Angel Clare seemed so pure and generous, actually commits a murder in order to achieve her return to him. Venus is a cruel goddess, even in the case of the 'pure

woman'. Marty stands apart; she has escaped the clutches of the cruel goddess by 'rejecting with indifference the attribute of sex'. And Giles, the man she loves, perhaps approaches her pinnacle of generosity in the unselfishness of his love for another woman.

The sadness of Marty (and Giles) is in a sense one of the least sad things in Hardy's work. Hardy's worst fear, as can be clearly seen in some of his poems, was not that life was painful (though his sensibility to this fact was exceptionally acute) but rather that it might be meaningless. Marty's grief is self-justifying; it has value in itself. It is also one-sided. No happy, mutual love, either erotic or affectionate, exists in Hardy's work to embody a similar positive value. For Hardy sexual love and moral sublimity are almost strangers; and Marty South has to abandon the turmoils of the one before she can fully attain to the other.

Jude the Obscure is a by-word for pessimism; and so it is important to observe that it contains several different kinds of pessimism. The first kind is a permanent feature of Hardy's work, and might be called ballad-pessimism, the experienced countryman's wry corrective to idyllic dreams of the country:

> Every inch of ground had been the site, first or last, of energy, gaiety, horseplay, bickerings, weariness. . . . Under the hedge which divided the field from a distant plantation girls had given themselves to lovers who would not turn their heads to look at them by the next harvest; and in that ancient cornfield many a man had made love-promises to a woman at whose voice he had trembled by the next seed-time after fulfilling them in the church adjoining.

The second pessimism, perhaps the least convincing one might be called the pseudo-Greek. There are vague mutterings about a family curse affecting both Fawleys and Brideheads, so that in each generation marriages are unhappy. The idea is never developed or explained, and it really amounts to little more than a desultory justification for some of the more unlikely strokes of bad luck the characters suffer.

The third pessimism might be called social-critical. Hardy attacks, more fiercely than in earlier works, the assumptions of society, the law and the customs of marriage. To do this, he makes a neat reversal of some time-honoured literary conventions. As we have seen, frankness about sexual desire and action had tended to omit marriage. Marriage had to do with 'love', and 'love' came to seem far removed from sexual satisfaction. One could read a lot of novels by Hardy's immediate predecessors, and be led to suppose that sexual desire, even sexual awareness, was something shared out between men and immodest women. Good girls and good wives were exempt. Hardy sets out to undermine these assumptions—which like many very influential assumptions in all periods, were all the more influential for being unstated, and so impervious to rational criticism—by a simple and effective device. He makes the lawful wife, Arabella, full-blooded, fleshy and philistine. He makes the mistress, Sue, ethereal, intellectual and apt to dismiss the realities of sex as crudely animal. And he does this, as he does many things in a book dominated by anger and tending to shrillness, with a heavy hand, associating Arabella from the first with pigs' flesh, provocatively thrown at Jude as he is thinking high thoughts of scholarship and divinity. More, he carries the reversal of literary assumptions into the next generation; instead of bastard Edmund and legitimate Edgar, we have the misshapen, and ultimately murderous and suicidal Time, as legitimate issue, while the illegitimate are innocent victims.

Arabella traps Jude into marriage by a seductive trick, followed by a lie about a non-existent pregnancy. It is Arabella, not Sue who recalls Fielding's Molly Seagrim and Mrs Waters. To a certain extent, all this is telling. The law that wives should be less carnal than mistresses, and illegitimate children morally inferior to legitimate is a law of literary convention, not a law of nature; and an author has a right to subvert such laws. But there are two points that Hardy did not sufficiently consider. Jude's troubles spring not from following accepted moral principles, but from mixing incompatibles. Had he been chaste, Arabella could not have deceived him into marriage. Had he been a carefree disciple of the wild oats school, her trick would likewise have failed. That Jude should be inconsistent, influenced by lust, by credulity, by a wish to be decent, is credible enough. But Hardy is illogical in attempting to lay blame for the sad consequences of these manifest inconsistencies upon any of the principles which Jude has confused and muddled. (pp. 124-26)

The other point is less obvious. Hardy is more bound than he knows by the convention he is attacking. Arabella's carnality is treated as repulsive. It is not always easy to disentangle the different principles by which she is condemned; but it is clear that dishonesty in tricking Jude into marriage mingles in Hardy's mind with considerations that lack the same moral force. Her open sexual invitation to Jude, of wife to husband, is clearly regarded as an obscenity. Yet, it could well be argued that since marriage is a sexual relationship, Arabella, for all her vices, her lying and coarse insensitiveness, is more in harmony with the spirit of marriage *in this respect* than her rival Sue is. Hardy's argument tends to rebound upon himself. He conceives himself to be showing that marriage is a fraud, since wives may be coarsely physical and sexually provocative. Actually, he is showing that he himself is really very like the literary predecessors he is supposed to be refuting. Like them, he finds it shocking that a wife should have the slightest interest in sex.

Now we come to a type of pessimism which Hardy was the first to voice, and which has an abiding interest. The character and destiny of Sue is Hardy's bitter, intelligent and intensely personal reaction to the fashionable ideas of the nineties about the 'New Woman'. He was quick to form his opinions. . . . [Some] readers must have read Hardy's refutation of the new ideas before being fully aware of them. One book in particular, published in the same year as *Jude*, and probably not one which Hardy had in mind, may be used as typical of a whole current of new ideas. This is Grant Allen's *The Woman Who Did*. Here we have a young woman, handsome, well-educated, sincere, affectionate and constant, who refuses to marry the man she loves and is free to marry, simply from a preference for free union (conceived to be as solemn and permanent as marriage.) . . . Herminia is unlike her fictional predecessors in preaching a frank sexual enjoyment, for women as for men. But promiscuity and loveless intercourse are most severely reproved; Herminia's aim is to be a highly moral, frankly enjoying, passionately loving, monogamous mistress.

In some ways Sue is very like this, with the important proviso that a complex being like Sue cannot be wholly like a simple one. She has a similar sense of quasi-religious awe about the supposed joys of sexual union, and the same dislike of the marriage ceremony. ('Somebody *gives* me to him, like a she-ass or she-goat').

But she is much more aware than Herminia of dark and primitive forces. She turns to Greek paganism, just as Swinburne had done, to buttress her rejection of Christianity. To some extent she is aware of the divisions and contradictions in her nature and in her theories. She likes to present herself as a new woman, yet claims to be 'more ancient than mediaevalism'. Her statue of Venus, which she worships secretly, is more than a symbol. It has a fetishistic quality for her. And gradually we come to see why. She has taken the Christian ideas of mortification and self-discipline, and transferred them to the service of her pagan deity. Just as many a Christian through the centuries has felt a conflict between his sexual desires and his belief in chastity as a religious duty, so does Sue feel a conflict between her belief in the flesh, and her instinctive distaste for it. Admittedly, she finds sexual intercourse with Jude more tolerable than it had been in her marriage to Phillotson. But this is only a matter of degree. She can never be self-forgetfully carnal, as her paganized conscience tells her she should be.

Or rather one part of it does; for she is simultaneously under the influence of quite a different current of ideas, stemming from feminist writers like J. S. Mill. In this vein, she regards sex differences as unimportant, talks of Venus Urania (a spiritualized deity of intellectual companionship), and speaks scornfully of the philosophy of the respectable world as recognizing only 'relations based on animal desire'. In her strange correspondence with her husband, when she is pleading to be allowed to separate from him, the contrasts of her nature are well shown. For a time she writes, with copious quotations, like an excessively priggish, blue-stocking disciple of the high Victorian agnostic tradition. Suddenly her urgent personal fears break in, and she expresses the wish that sex did not exist and that the world could have been peopled by 'some harmless mode of vegetation'.

There is, however, one thread of consistency in Sue's contradictions. She is always in some sense a feminist. Whether she is devotedly praising the joys of a carnal passion from which her own instincts rebel, or attacking the marriage bond, or speaking of a rarefied, intellectual companionship between people of different sex, she is constant to her theme of the slights and wrongs immemorially endured by women, and in her claim that they are equal to men. This is a claim that Hardy cannot admit. Here is his description of the dormitory in the Training School at Melchester:

> . . . they all lay in their cubicles, their tender feminine faces upturned to the flaring gas-jets which at intervals stretched down the long dormitories, every face bearing the legend 'The Weaker' upon it, as the penalty of the sex wherein they were moulded, which by no possible exertion of their willing hearts and abilities could be made strong while the inexorable laws of nature remain what they are.

Hardy decisively rejects the whole feminist argument of the preceding generation, which was the soil for the growth of the idea of the 'New Woman' à la Havelock Ellis and Grant Allen; and this is his final word on the matter. The feminists saw the natural disabilities as trivial compared with those caused by bad traditions and false theories. Hardy reversed this, and he did so feelingly. The phrase 'inexorable laws of nature' was no cliché for him. It represented the slowly-garnered fruits of his deepest meditations on life. It was an epitome of what found full imaginative expression in memorable descriptions, like that of Egdon Heath. The attempt to turn Hardy into a feminist is altogether vain.

It is not merely deliberate statements like this one that undermine Sue's feminist position. More cunningly, Hardy shows that beneath a veneer of new ideas, and old, rebellious pagan ones revived, Sue is not the New Woman at all, but the Old in disguise. Her sexless coquettish style is as tantalizing and self-centred as the most obvious provocation. Even Jude, who is slow to understand, comes to see that she is jealous of Arabella, and will yield her body to him if he pretends to more interest in Arabella than he really feels. His comment 'Jealous little Sue! I withdraw all remarks about your sexlessness' clearly carries the author's endorsement.

La Rochefoucauld said that women did not understand their own coquetry. Sue's whole treatment of Jude might have been invented to illustrate this saying. The austere feminist doctrines of Mill and the sickly pseudo-pagan deliriums of Swinburne become new weapons in the old game, the game of provoking male interest and desire by refusal. And in case we should miss the point, Hardy has an impartial observer describe her as 'a little hussy' and 'a tantalizing, capricious little woman'.

What are we to make then of Sue's last phase, when under the influence of the shock of finding her children murdered, she returns to Phillotson, her original and lawful husband, though her fear of his caresses is stronger than her fear of spiders? This certainly does not seem to be the act of a heartless and teasing flirt. Nor is it. Hardy's conception of her character includes this but it includes much more. Bathsheba, too, could be a teasing flirt, and yet she was reduced to the abasement of begging for a kiss that was denied her and given only to the dead. Hardy tends to see feminine nature in layers. The flirtatious and provocative is a superficial layer, which is fully in evidence only in a civilized setting when men agree to play the woman's game. Beneath, in all Hardy's women potentially, and in many actually, is an irrational and passionate animal force. It turns Tess into a murderess, Bathsheba into a humiliated slave, and Sue into a creature embracing what is most horrible to her at the bidding of a superstitious guilt. [In a footnote, the author states, ''I call her guilt superstitious not because I think it superstitious to treat the marriage bond as sacred, but because she regards her children's death as a punishment for her sin.'']

Hardy was never likely to go very far along the path marked out by Havelock Ellis [, D. H. Lawrence, and other optimists]. . . . However much he sympathized with their criticism of marriage laws and traditional moral views, he disagreed fundamentally with their contention that natural forces are beneficent, and will lead us to happiness if we passively follow them. But the ferocity of his reaction is nevertheless surprising. He combines the idea that 'all women are alike at heart' with an indictment of the new ideas for making them worse. It is something like a secular variant of Sancho Panza's 'Man is as God made him and often a great deal worse.' Woman is as nature made her, but worse if feminism gets a hold on her. By attempting to be advanced, intellectual and rational, Sue suppresses for a time what, in Hardy's view, can never be suppressed for ever, the irrationality and weakness of the female, decreed by 'inexorable laws of nature'. When the long-suppressed feminine forces break out at last, they are more savage and destructive than ever. Sue is both more unhappy and more harmful to others than Hardy's other women.

All this should hardly surprise us. Like most pessimistic people Hardy was intensely conservative. There is not much happiness in his world. Such as there is, is enjoyed by people well-rooted in traditional ways:

> For a moment there fell on Jude a true illu-
> mination; that here in the stoneyard was a centre
> of effort worthy as that dignified by the name
> of scholarly study within the noblest of the col-
> leges. But he lost it. . . This was his form of
> the modern vice of unrest.

Sue's form of the same vice consists in denying the natural limitations of the feminine; in attempting to substitute theory for sensation. Hardy ends where he began; the tone varies but the ideas are the same. (pp. 126-30)

> *A.O.J. Cockshut, "The Pessimists," in his* Man and Woman: A Study of Love and the Novel 1740-1940 *(© 1977 by A.O.J. Cockshut; reprinted by permission of Oxford University Press, Inc.; in Canada by William Collins Sons & Co., Ltd.), Collins, 1977 (and reprinted by Oxford University Press, New York, 1978), pp. 100-35.* *

D. H. FUSSELL   (essay date 1981)

[In Cryil Clemens's *My Chat with Thomas Hardy*] when Mr. Clemens asked Mr. Hardy, '''Did Poe influence your work?''' and Hardy replied: '''Yes, without hesitation I say that Poe has influenced my work . . . ,''' we may ask in what way, then, was this influence exerted or felt? (p. 214)

Poe's ''The Raven,'' first published in January 1845, is capable of a variety of interpretations. Beneath the Gothic surface lies a very real sense of horror located in the word ''nevermore,'' a word whose similarity of sound with the name Lenore indicates the inextricable fusion of feeling: the loss of the ''rare and radiant maiden.'' . . . There is, I think, much in this poem which would strike a chord in Hardy's imagination, but for the moment I shall concentrate upon one particular point. The poem is, as I have suggested, about a complex of feelings set up around the experience of lost love, a recurrent theme in both Poe and Hardy. But what seems to me to be of particular significance is that [Hardy's] poem **"Dawn After the Dance,"** which . . . follows Poe's meter, was written at Weymouth in 1869. Eighteen sixty-nine was a significant year in Hardy's emotional life for the relationship with Tryphena Sparks was about to come to an end—she was to enter college to become a teacher in January 1870, and it was important for her career that an unblemished character should be maintained. In February, Hardy gave up his rooms in Weymouth. This period in which there was a small but intense revival in Hardy's writing may well mark the breakdown of Hardy's relationship with Tryphena, a relationship which, for all the controversy which surrounds it, was indisputably of critical importance to him. As F. R. Southerington comments [in his *The Poetry of Thomas Hardy*], ''From the poems of this date I get the general impression of a firm relationship slowly crumbling.'' And Robert Gittings in his biography *Young Thomas Hardy* stresses the sense of deprivation which Hardy felt. It is perhaps not without reason then that Hardy would find Poe's poem on lost love particularly appealing. (pp. 214-15)

Thus one might well suggest that Tryphena Sparks is associated in Hardy's mind with ''The Raven'' and, more generally, that there is a fusion of interest between the two writers at significant and impressionable points in Hardy's career, points which predate much of his major work. Thus Poe's influence is not to be measured in superficial trappings of Gothic horror which sometimes form a part of his settings, nor simply in technique, but in a shared preoccupation which is an organic part of Hardy's vision and a major element in his work. (p. 216)

Poe and Hardy have a common sense of the destructive capacity of the human consciousness—the way in which feelings remain as a carrion presence in the individual psyche. More important, however, is, I think, the similarity between the two writers in the way in which the carrion presence becomes powerfully associated with the theme of the beloved. The most obvious image of destruction linked with the woman figure in those stories of Poe which Hardy says he read is, of course, "The Fall of the House of Usher." It is a story which may well have much in common with Hardy's last published novel, *The Well-Beloved,* with which it has, I think, certain important similarities. And equally important, one can argue that Hardy's novel, subtitled "a sketch of a temperament," approaches very close to admitting Hardy's personal biography entrance into his fictional world in a novel whose narrative outline can scarcely be described as realistic in any obvious way. (p. 218)

Superficially, Hardy's novel has a certain similarity with "The Fall of the House of Usher." Its hero, Jocelyn Pierston, is, like Roderick Usher, an artist, an artist who compulsively returns to his house on the Isle of Slingers. It is an island which forms a landscape "apt to generate a type of personage like the character imperfectly sketched in these pages." . . . There is a suggestion of that connection between place and person which is reminiscent of the earlier stages of Poe's tale, which correspondingly begins with the return of the narrator or principal character, if we take Usher as a projection of the narrator, to the landscape of his childhood. If "The Fall of the House of Usher" is partly about art, it is also about the relationship of the artist with his sister Madeleine. And Roderick Usher, having withdrawn into the House of Usher with his sister, with whom there exists a sympathy of a very special kind, is gradually wasting away. It is the tension between him and his sister which in part ultimately destroys both his artistic and his human creativity; there is no child for Usher, no child for Jocelyn Pierston, perhaps no child for Hardy. Usher, then, is bound to his sister not simply in affection but also in terror. There is every suggestion of an incestuous relation, a love which is vampiristic, a relationship which brings ultimate destruction.

In *The Well-Beloved* the importance of an enclosed community is of paramount importance; it brings a peculiar significance to the interrelations between the various characters, a significance which is strengthened by the fact that there is a further narrowing down. Jocelyn falls in love with a girl, Avice; twenty years later he falls in love with her daughter, and then after another twenty years he falls in love with her granddaughter. The rationale for all this lies in the intensely self-aware protagonist's admission that he pursues "the migratory, elusive idealisation he called his love who, ever since his boyhood, had flitted from human shell to human shell an indefinite number of times. . . ." . . . This, of course, if clearly related to the pursuit of the soul mate. It is a theme which Hardy had treated with a strong sense of irony in the character of Fitzpiers in *The Woodlanders,* and Jocelyn's surname may well be a faint recollection of his predecessor. The more positive presentation of this character in *The Well-Beloved* suggests that the contrasting treatments mark a central ambivalence in Hardy toward the motivations which direct their actions. The theme is also

recurrent in the work of Hardy's favorite poet, Shelley. (pp. 219-20)

[Throughout] the novel each "reincarnation" of the well-beloved is accompanied both by delightful expectation and fear. And the failure which succeeds each failing vision is marked by a sense of horror which is not perhaps only casually reminiscent of Poe's "The Raven." . . . (p. 220)

Thus, in Poe's writing—in all the manifestations of the One, of her who is born and dies so many times, Ligeia, Madeleine, Ulalume, Helen, and Lenore—perhaps Hardy recognized, as he did in Shelley's work, versions of his own Well-Beloved. (p. 223)

> *D. H. Fussell, "Do You Like Poe, Mr. Hardy?," in* Modern Fiction Studies *(© 1981 by Purdue Research Foundation, West Lafayette, Indiana 47907, U.S.A.), Vol. 27, No. 2, Summer, 1981, pp. 211-24.*

ROBERT LANGBAUM (essay date 1982)

Hardy and Frost are worth comparing because they occupy equivalent positions on the current poetic scene. They converge, first of all, because of their adversary relation to modernist poetry—the kind of poetry represented by Yeats, Pound, and Eliot; so that a taste for Hardy and Frost becomes for many readers a vote against modernism. Hardy and Frost also converge in that they are known as nature poets at a time when modernist poets have largely rejected nature as a subject for poetry. Yet Hardy and Frost write a new kind of nature poetry, which they define through its *resistance* to the pathetic fallacy—to the idea, as Wordsworth puts it, that mind and nature are admirably suited to each other so that the landscape can validly give back the meaning the poet projects into it.

As an example of the new nature poetry, let us look at one of Hardy's best poems, **"Neutral Tones,"** which was written as early as 1867. Here is the first stanza:

> We stood by a pond that winter day,
> And the sun was white, as though chidden of God,
> And a few leaves lay on the starving sod;
> —They had fallen from an ash, and were gray.

It is clear from the very title that **"Neutral Tones"** makes its impact through resistance to the pathetic fallacy. The *neutrality* of Hardy's landscape suggests that nature is indifferent and alien. Yet later in the poem nature comes to seem downright malevolent. The movement is from "And the sun was white, *as though* chidden of God"—where God's intervention is clearly an illusory projection of the lovers' desolation—to the poem's last two lines where the association with the lover's hated face causes the speaker to drop "as though" and speak simply of "the God-curst sun": "Your face, and the God-curst sun, and a tree, / And a pond edged with grayish leaves." Here and elsewhere Hardy achieves powerful ironies by invoking the pathetic fallacy, in order to suggest its inapplicability but also its inevitability—in order to suggest that under the pressure of emotion we inevitably conceive nature's neutrality as malevolent. This oscillation between nature's neutrality and malevolence runs through Hardy's poems and novels. The oscillation or contradiction has given rise to the quip that Hardy could not forgive God for *not* existing. (pp. 69-70)

Both Frost and Hardy refrain from projecting themselves into nature in Wordsworth's manner, as a way of giving meaning to nature. Instead of projection, Hardy often uses the preromantic, traditional devices of personification and allegory to make nature yield meaning. In **"The Darkling Thrush,"** dated Dec. 31, 1900, the landscape is "The [Nineteenth-] Century's corpse outleant." Here and elsewhere Hardy's blatant anthropomorphism, as compared to Wordsworth's gentle animation of nature, is used as the only way to make us understand how utterly *non*anthropomorphic nature really is. Design of any kind, even malevolent design, says Hardy in **"Hap"** —and we are reminded here of Frost's poem "Design"—would be a consolation. Instead there is only "Crass Casualty"—note the personification—which would as readily strew "blisses" in my path as the pains I encounter. Hardy's bleakest statements about nature are often expressed as a dialogue of personified natural forces—as in "The Subalterns," where the forces of Cold, Sickness, Death afflicting the narrator complain that they are as much victims of nature as he. Hardy presumably felt that realistic rendition of nature, especially of nature's beauty, would inevitably bring back Wordsworthian feelings that nature might be alive with purpose and meaning. (pp. 71-2)

Donald Davie begins his book *Thomas Hardy and British Poetry* (1972) by declaring that "in British poetry of the last fifty years (as not in American) the most far-reaching influence for good and ill, has been not Yeats, still less Eliot or Pound, not Lawrence, but *Hardy*." In speaking of Philip Larkin's significant "conversion . . . from Yeats to Hardy," Davie makes clear that the movement of post-World War II British poetry has been away from modernism. Similarly in America, the critics committed to modernism have consistently downplayed Frost in the interests of Eliot and recently Wallace Stevens. Hardy and Frost have themselves attacked the modernist poets (Hardy lived long enough into the 20th century to do so) for their obscurity and free verse. Readers who prefer Hardy and Frost to the modernists prefer them for their lucidity and because they do not—like Yeats with his occultism and Eliot with his Anglo-Catholicism—ask us to believe what we do not really believe. Hardy and Frost make poetry out of our scientific, common-sense view of the world.

The general line of modernist critics has been that Hardy and Frost are excellent *minor* poets. And indeed, the way to reconcile a taste for Hardy and Frost, on the one hand, and the modernists, on the other, is to put them in different niches— to say, as I have elsewhere, that Yeats and Eliot are major and that Hardy, at any rate, is minor. Frost's position is questionable. But Hardy seems to me to be an important influence on younger poets just because minor poets are less oppressive as influences than are major poets. In order to find their own voices, the younger British poets have had to *save* themselves from Yeats and Eliot just as Keats had to save himself from Milton ("Life to him," wrote Keats, "would be death to me"). Hardy's function has been to adapt and revise the major innovations of the great 19th-century poets—especially Wordsworth and Browning, his principal influences. Hardy hands on to 20th-century poets what is still usable in 19th-century poetry. (pp. 77-8)

Hardy's poems are, with a few splendid exceptions (such as **"Transformations"** and **"The Self-Unseeing"**), successes in a distinctly minor way because they make their points *completely*, as in **"His Immortality"**; whereas major poetry gives the impression of unfathomed depths, leaving us with the desire to *re*read as soon as we have read. Even in **"The Darkling Thrush,"** which moves for three stanzas like major poetry through intensification of the imagery and irony, even here Hardy retreats in the end to minor poetry by shrugging off the

impasse he has created—with a pat remark. "So little cause for carolings," he reflects, "That I could think there trembled through" the bird's

> happy good-night air
> Some blessed Hope, whereof he knew
> And I was unaware.

The thrush's song is so distinctly unrelated to the landscape or the poet's feelings that the poet—whatever he might wishfully fancy the bird to be saying—*knows* there is no Hope. Here as elsewhere Hardy *chooses* to write a minor poem in order to avoid the pathetic fallacy—the transforming vision of significance in the bird's song. It can also be said of the British poets who follow Hardy—Larkin is a prime example—that they have chosen to be minor poets in order to be true to quotidian reality. (pp. 79-80)

In balance I am inclined to think that Hardy is on the whole a minor poet for the reasons given above, and that Frost may be a major poet for the following reasons. His best poems are enigmatic, repaying endless rereadings. He has managed to make a new music out of the modern flatness of voice cultivated by Hardy; and this is a prosodic feat equal to Eliot's in *Prufrock* and *The Waste Land*. . . . But whether major or minor, Hardy and Frost matter at this point in the 20th century when the mighty modernist movement seems to have run its course and young poets are looking for another direction. Hardy and Frost are important just now, because they show how to be modern without being modernist. (p. 80)

Robert Langbaum, "Hardy, Frost, and the Question of Modernist Poetry," in The Virginia Quarterly Review *(copyright, 1982, by* The Virginia Quarterly Review, The University of Virginia), *Vol. 58, No. 1 (Winter, 1982), pp. 69-80.*

ADDITIONAL BIBLIOGRAPHY

Bailey, J. O. *The Poetry of Thomas Hardy: A Handbook and Commentary*. Chapel Hill: The University of North Carolina Press, 1970, 712 p.
   Supplies literary and personal background to Hardy's complete poems. Bailey maintains that knowledge of Hardy's life is the key to a full understanding of his poetry.

Blunden, Edmund. *Thomas Hardy*. London: Macmillan and Co., 1942, 286 p.
   Critical study of the novels, poetry, and *The Dynasts*.

Brown, Douglas. *Thomas Hardy*. London: Longmans, 1961, 194 p.
   Focuses on Hardy as the literary voice of English agricultural society, examining how the author's "unserviceable, even shoddy" prose style effectively expresses this way of life.

Brown, Suzanne Hunter. " 'Tess' and *Tess*: An Experiment in Genre." *Modern Fiction Studies* 28, No. 1 (Spring 1982): 25-44.
   Demonstration of how knowledge of generic, as well as historical, contexts governs a reader's experience of literature. Brown presents a section of *Tess of the D'Urbervilles* as a short story. She then discusses how various elements of the passage function differently when the passage is regarded as a short story rather than as a segment of a novel.

Cecil, David. *Hardy the Novelist: An Essay in Criticism*. London: Constable and Co., 1943, 157 p.
   Compilation of essays originally delivered as lectures. Cecil devotes chapters to the "Scope," "Power," "Art," and "Weak-

ness'' of Hardy's novels. In a concluding chapter Cecil discusses Hardy's style.

Cox, R. G., ed. *Thomas Hardy: The Critical Heritage*. New York: Barnes & Noble, 1970, 473 p.
Useful compendium of early magazine reviews of Hardy's novels and poetry. Several of these reviews are excerpted in *TCLC*, Vol. 4.

Deutsch, Babette. ''A Look at the Worst.'' In her *Poetry in Our Time*, pp. 1-27. New York: Columbia University Press, 1952.
Discussion of Hardy's poetry, which Deutsch finds ''bridges the gulf between the Victorian sensibility and our own.''

Drabble, Margaret, ed. *The Genius of Thomas Hardy*. New York: Alfred A. Knopf, 1976, 191 p.
Essays divided into sections on Hardy's life and works, with special studies devoted to specific aspects of the author's writing such as architecture and history. Critics in this collection include J.I.M. Stewart, Elizabeth Hardwick, Sir John Betjeman, and Lord David Cecil, among others.

Draper, R.P., ed. *Hardy: The Tragic Novels: ''The Return of the Native,'' ''The Mayor of Casterbridge,'' ''Tess of the D'Urbervilles,'' ''Jude the Obscure.''* London: The Macmillan Co., 1975, 256 p.
In three sections presents (1) Hardy's comments on his own work gathered from various sources; (2) a chronological sampling of criticism, including essays by Lionel Johnson and D. H. Lawrence; and (3) modern thematic perspectives on the major novels.

Duffin, H. C. *Thomas Hardy: A Study of the Wessex Novels, the Poems, and ''The Dynasts.''* Manchester: Manchester University Press, 1937, 356 p.
Primarily devoted to thematic and technical analysis of the novels, with a chapter on ''Hardy's Use of the Marvelous.''

Gittings, Robert. *Young Thomas Hardy*. Boston: Little, Brown and Co., 1975, 259 p.
Noncritical biography. Gittings maintains that Hardy wrote the biographical works published under his second wife's name. In an appendix Gittings produces evidence to disprove the theory that Hardy and Tryphena Sparks had an illegitimate child.

Grimsditch, Herbert B. *Character and Environment in the Novels of Thomas Hardy*. New York: Russell & Russell, 1962, 189 p.
Analyzes Hardy's characterizations with regard to environmental influences contributing to a given character's psychology and development, inferring from this the author's philosophical views of humanity and existence.

·Guerard, Albert, ed. *Hardy: A Collection of Critical Essays*. Englewood Cliffs, N.J.: Prentice-Hall, 1963, 180 p.
Includes essays by Guerard, D. H. Lawrence, A. Alvarez, W. H. Auden, Samuel Hynes, and Delmore Schwartz, among others.

Hardy, Florence Emily. *The Early Life of Thomas Hardy: 1840-1891*. New York: The Macmillan Co., 1928, 327 p.
Biography of Hardy's first fifty-one years, comprised largely of diary entries, as well as letters and conversations with Hardy. Robert Gittings (see above) believes that the biographical works purportedly by Florence Emily Hardy, Hardy's second wife, were actually written entirely by Hardy.

Hardy, Florence Emily. *The Later Years of Thomas Hardy: 1892-1928*. New York: The Macmillan Co., 1930, 289 p.
Lengthy noncritical account of Hardy's later years. This book incorporates the texts of many letters from Hardy to various correspondents. Gittings (see above) believes Hardy heavily edited the letters before allowing their inclusion.

Hawkins, Desmond. *Thomas Hardy*. London: Arthur Barker, 1950, 112 p.
Survey of the novels.

Jacobus, Mary. ''Hardy's Magian Retrospect.'' *Essays in Criticism* XXXII, No. 3 (July 1982): 258-79.

Discussion of Hardy's ''literary posthumousness''—his seeming obsession, in the poems from *Wessex Poems* onward, with the form of immortality a writer of lasting literary merit can attain.

Lee, Vernon [pseudonym of Violet Paget]. ''The Handling of Words: Hardy.'' In her *The Handling of Words and Other Studies in Literary Psychology*, pp. 222-41. London: John Lane, The Bodley Head, 1923.
Analysis of Hardy's stylistic flaws in a passage selected from *Tess*, concluding that these flaws are an expression of the author's particular genius.

Lucas, John. ''Hardy's Women.'' In his *The Literature of Change: Studies in the Nineteenth-Century Provincial Novel*, pp. 119-91. Sussex, England: The Harvester Press, 1977.
Analysis of the ways Hardy employed his fictional women characters to focus on issues of class and separation. Lucas finds that Hardy is ''unique in the ways he gives prominence to his women.''

Millgate, Michael. *Thomas Hardy: A Biography*. New York: Random House, 1982, 637 p.
Lengthy noncritical biography. Millgate presents a comprehensive account of Hardy's life, drawing upon diaries, notebooks, letters, and local records previously inaccessible to biographers. Millgate devotes an appendix to the theory that Hardy had an illegitimate son with his cousin Tryphena Sparks. This theory is disputed by Robert Gittings (see above).

Moore, Marianne. ''Memory's Immortal Gear.'' *Chicago Review* IV, No. 1 (Autumn 1949): 15-19.
Brief assessment of Hardy's poetry. Moore praises Hardy's aesthetic vision and technical idiom.

Orel, Harold. *Thomas Hardy's Epic-Drama: A Study of ''The Dynasts.''* Lawrence: University of Kansas Publications, 1963, 122 p.
Contains chapters on the writing of *The Dynasts*, its philosophical foundations, its relationship to Milton's *Paradise Lost*, and ''Hardy's Attitude toward War.''

Pinion, F. B. *A Hardy Companion: A Guide to the Works of Thomas Hardy and Their Background*. London: Macmillan, 1968, 555 p.
Survey of Hardy's work and its major influences, with biographical background. This study contains an insightful chapter entitled ''Aspects of the Unusual and Irrational.''

Roberts, Marguerite. *Hardy's Poetic Drama and the Theatre: ''The Dynasts'' and ''The Famous Tragedy of the Queen of Cornwall.''* New York: Pageant Press, 1965, 10 p.
Examines Hardy's interest in the theater and considers the purely dramatic aspects of these two works.

Rutland, William R. *Thomas Hardy: A Study of His Writings and Their Background*. Oxford: Basil Blackwell, 1938, 365 p.
Examines influences on Hardy's writings and philosophical outlook; gives biographical and literary background to his works.

Sankey, Benjamin. *The Major Novels of Thomas Hardy*. Denver: Alan Swallow, 1965, 59 p.
Examination of major themes, characterization, and some aspects of style in Hardy's novels.

Spivey, Ted R. ''Thomas Hardy and the Tragedy of Neoromanticism.'' In his *The Journey Beyond Tragedy: A Study of Myth and Modern Fiction*, pp. 41-56. Orlando: University Presses of Florida, 1980.
Characterizes Hardy and George Eliot as the creators of the first fully modern English novels. Spivey terms Hardy's fiction ''neo-romantic tragedy.''

Taylor, Dennis., *Hardy's Poetry, 1860-1928*. New York: Columbia University Press, 1981, 204 p.
Traces the development of skill and maturity in Hardy's lyric poetry.

Taylor, Richard H. *The Neglected Hardy: Thomas Hardy's Lesser Novels*. New York: St. Martin's Press, 1982, 202 p.
Thorough critical study of each of Hardy's novels usually considered ''minor,'' including *Desperate Remedies, A Pair of Blue Eyes, The Hand of Ethelberta, The Trumpet-Major, A Laodicean, Two on a Tower*, and *The Well-Beloved*. Taylor places each novel

in the context of Hardy's developing career and establishes its relationship to the major novels.

Wagner, Geoffrey. "*Tess of the D'Urbervilles*: The 'Pure' Woman." In his *Five for Freedom: A Study of Feminism in Fiction*, pp. 183-211. Rutherford, N.J.: Fairleigh Dickinson University Press, 1972.

Presents the character of Tess as an archetypal Earth Mother image. Wagner interprets Tess as a modern, liberated woman seeking to become the social and political equal of the two men in her life.

Weber, Carl J. *Hardy in America: A Study of Thomas Hardy and His American Readers*. Waterville, Maine: Colby College Press, 1946, 321 p.

Study which proposes "not to write a criticism of Hardy's books but to tell the story of his American readers." Weber discusses Hardy's American publishers and critics, and his effect on American readership and criticism since his death.

Weber, Carl J. *Hardy of Wessex: His Life and Literary Career*. New York: Columbia University Press, 1965, 324 p.

Biography drawing in large part on Hardy's letters, which this prominent Hardy scholar edited for publication.

Winner, Anthony. "Hardy's Moderns: The Ache of Uncertain Character." In his *Characters in the Twilight: Hardy, Zola, Chekhov*, pp. 28-72. Charlottesville: University Press of Virginia, 1981.

In-depth analysis of some characters from Hardy's major fiction. Winner stresses that Hardy's treatment of female characters, in particular Sue Bridehead, attests to Hardy's lack of feminism.

A(lfred) E(dward) Housman

1859-1936

English poet, critic, essayist, translator, and editor.

Although in his lifetime Housman was a renowned classicist, well-known among European scholars for his brilliant emendations of Latin texts, it was as the author of *A Shropshire Lad* that he achieved widespread popularity and critical recognition. At a time when the trend in poetry was increasingly toward the recondite and obscure, Housman produced verse that was clear, intelligible, and direct in its emotional impact. *A Shropshire Lad*, his first collection, was published in 1896. Within a few years, in spite of provoking a critical controversy that prompted George Meredith to dismiss it as "an orgy of naturalism," it had attained the status of a minor classic, and it is still regarded as such. Today, Housman's poems are among the most widely read in the English language.

Housman was born at Catshill in the county of Worcestershire, England, within sight of the Shropshire hills. He was the eldest son of a remarkable family that was also to produce a famous dramatist—Housman's youngest brother, Laurence—and a novelist and short story writer, his sister Clemence. As a young man Housman attended Bromsgrove School, where the curriculum emphasized Greek and Latin studies. There Housman developed the talent for precise translation that would later earn him a reputation as the most formidable classical scholar in Europe. When Housman was twelve years old, his mother died. This tragedy affected him profoundly and set in motion the slow erosion of his religious faith. Years later Housman wrote to a friend that he "became a deist at thirteen and an atheist at twenty-one." Housman's religious disillusionment was reflected in his poetry in the form of a stoic despair renouncing all hope of personal salvation and welcoming death as a release from life's sufferings.

In 1877 Housman matriculated at Oxford. While there, in addition to continuing his classical studies, he helped to found *Ye Round Table*, an undergraduate magazine featuring humorous verse and satire. His contributions to this periodical demonstrate not only his wit, but his talent for nonsense verse, which he kept well-concealed in later years. Although a well-qualified scholar, Housman inexplicably failed his exams at Oxford in 1881. He did not earn a degree until 1892 when he was made professor of Latin at University College, London. The cause of Housman's Oxford failure was for many years a subject of speculation among critics and biographers. Today it is known from Housman's diaries that the reason for his failure at Oxford was his despair over his relationship with a young science student named Moses Jackson. The realization of his homosexuality and his ultimate rejection by Jackson embittered Housman, and transformed his life. He became a repressed and melancholy recluse. His contemporaries thereafter saw him only as an "enigmatic personality burdened by a private grief," who declined all honors he was offered, including the poet laureateship of England and the Order of Merit, one of the loftiest distinctions bestowed by the British government.

It was shortly after the crisis at Oxford, during what Housman many years later described as "a period of continuous excite-

ment," that he wrote all of *A Shropshire Lad*, most of *Last Poems*, and all but about twenty of the posthumously published verses in *More Poems*. Many of the latter, such as *"Shake hands we shall never be friends, all's over"* and *"Because I liked you better"* make direct reference to his relationship with Jackson, and it was for this reason that they were suppressed by the poet during his lifetime. Housman's well-known verse *"Oh who is that young sinner with the handcuffs on his wrists?"* with its ironic refrain—"they're taking him to prison for the colour of his hair"—was written on the occasion of Oscar Wilde's imprisonment. This poem probably goes furthest in expressing Housman's anger over his own fate and the contempt that he felt for social conventions that victimize individuals for traits over which they have no control.

In writing *A Shropshire Lad*, Housman adopted the persona of a young Shropshire yeoman, whom he called Terence Hearsay, in order to conceal the poems' autobiographical aspects. This fact, combined with the colloquial diction and the simple ballad meters that Housman employed often make his verses seem deceptively simple. However, the sophistication of their author is betrayed by the finesse with which Housman uses irony, by his many latinate inversions, and by the precisely antithetical poetic structure he designed to heighten the effect of emotions in conflict and to lend drama and tension to the verse. Critics agree that Housman was a master of subtle poetic technique, and while many dislike the sparseness of his verse, with its absence of simile and metaphor, and others feel that he over used certain mannerisms of speech, most agree that technically his verses possess the classical beauty, the conciseness, and the restraint of Greek and Latin poetry.

Housman produced only a small body of poetic works, and his themes and techniques never varied. Nothing he ever wrote would have been out of place in *A Shropshire Lad,* because everything that appeared after it reiterated the philosophy and the moods evoked by the poems in that volume. While this was due in part to the fact that Housman wrote most of his poems in a relatively brief span of time, it was also a reflection of Housman's limited range as a poet. Critics never fail to note the extreme narrowness of his choice of themes. Although his poetry is forceful, passionate, and possesses remarkable vigor, critics now agree that he was a great minor poet who was preoccupied almost exclusively with adolescent themes. Edmund Wilson described him as "always the poet of bitter youth who managed to grow old without ever coming to maturity." Critics cite this inability to deal with mature themes as Housman's most serious poetic failing.

Housman, in his famous lecture, *The Name and Nature of Poetry,* cited Shakespeare's songs, Heinrich Heine's poetry, and the Scottish border ballads as his major poetic influences. Metrically, his poems stand midway between the lyric and the quatrain form of ballad, while the influence of Shakespeare is apparent in Housman's favorite theme: the dominion of time over love, friendship, and everything mortal. Irony and surprise endings are important elements in the work of Heine, and Housman uses them in much the same style as the German poet. *The Name and Nature of Poetry* represents the only statement that Housman could ever be induced to make about his personal theories of poetry, and as such it is an important key to the understanding of his work. However, some critics feel that Housman's remarks on this occasion were designed to be deliberately misleading and to provoke controversy. They base their conclusions on Housman's lifelong reticence on the subject of his poetry. Nevertheless, *The Name and Nature of Poetry* is interesting for what it reveals about Housman's taste in poetry, primarily the importance he attached to the presence of a strong dramatic element capable of "raising the hackles on the back of the neck".

Housman was, in his lifetime, a controversial literary figure, and there is still an element of controversy surrounding him. Over the years some critics have charged that he gained his reputation dishonestly by deliberately surrounding himself with an air of "persistent silence and mystery." There is no question that, as Christopher Ricks said of him, he was "a man whose reticence, arrogance and will-power are fascinating and unforgettable." However, although the enigma of his life has undoubtedly contributed to the interest in his work, his poetry has merits of its own. The magnitude of Housman's despair and disillusionment, as expressed in his poetry, elevates his experiences beyond the realm of the merely personal. His poems become, by virtue of their emotional force, a statement on the fate of humankind.

(See also *TCLC*, Vol. 1 and *Contemporary Authors*, Vol. 104.)

PRINCIPAL WORKS

A Shropshire Lad (poetry) 1896
Last Poems (poetry) 1922
The Name and Nature of Poetry (criticism) 1933
More Poems (poetry) 1936
Collected Poems (poetry) 1939
Complete Poems (poetry) 1959
A. E. Housman: Selected Prose (essays and criticism) 1961
The Letters of A. E. Housman (letters) 1970

FRANCIS THOMPSON   (essay date 1898)

[*Thompson, himself a noted poet of the 1890s, praises Housman as a unique voice in modern poetry. He discusses the sternness and stoicism of Housman's philosophy, and although he acknowledges that Housman's simple approach occasionally fails, in contrast to Edith Sitwell (see excerpt below), he believes it more often succeeds due to a "fulness of feeling which creates art."*]

Because we have very earnest praise to give Mr. Housman, we shall begin by certain protests, not against him, but against his critics, or rather some excesses of his critics. He comes upon reviewers with a surprise of novelty; and under such circumstances the reviewer is all too apt in extremes of reaction, as though the new thing were not only a right thing, but *the* right thing. Directness is not the note of most modern poetry. It is emphatically a note of Mr. Housman; and accordingly critics write as though directness *à la Housman* were your only wear in song, and his predecessors like sheep had gone astray. We can see in Mr. Housman's directness an excellent thing for Mr. Housman's aims, without repudiating all other modes of excellence. . . . One reviewer is so grateful for Mr. Housman's directness that he tries to make him out what emphatically he is not—the simple, wholesome, manly, rural singer, who loves football and cricket, and can drink beer and break a rival's head as well as make rustic love. . . . Strangely surprised would the reader be who adventured upon *A Shropshire Lad* with such a preconception. He sings of cricket, it is true, but in this fashion:

> Now in Maytime to the wicket
>   Oft I march with bat and pad;
> See the Son of Grief at cricket
>   Trying to be glad. . . .

Clearly, nothing can be more misleading than to regard this poet as a specimen of the healthy, life-enjoying, country bard.

Mr. Housman, as a matter of fact, is a peculiar combination, and the originality which has attracted reviewers arises from that peculiarity. On the one hand is the sweet breath of the fields, on the other the stern and sombre endurance of the dweller in cities. It is the note of the caged thrush, the scent of the unforgotten copse and hedgerows still haunting with wildness its enslaved voice. No more iron philosophy has been sung in this day than that which some reviewers acclaim as rustic and homely. Just so men listen delighted to the rustic note of the caged bird, missing its inward tragedy. Or rather, the combination is piquant to them in poet as in bird, and they do not stop to analyse the source of a delight. Mr. Housman is, in no disparaging sense, a monotonous singer, "a poet of one note in all his lays." In all his poems is present the contrast between his happy country youth and the grim realities of his adult city life. . . . That is one aspect of Mr. Housman. The other is the philosophy with which he encounters his "lost content." It is a grim and pessimistic philosophy. Your pessimist, according to temperament, either whines or "grins and bears it." On the latter there are variations. Mr. Housman mourns and bears it. Man is thrown together from pre-existent elements, and dislimns like a summer cloud, again to be brought together in fresh combinations. We are swayed by ancestral passions, and our ancestors live in us again. As what has been, so what shall be; and each must take his portion while it lasts—having drunk the little sweet, he must drink also the much sour. And for consolation—a living ass is better than a dead lion. It is a familiar position; the philosophy of Ecclesiastes, as Ecclesiastes is usually read, *plus* the doctrine of heredity. It is made impressive by the downright sincerity of the poet and his power of expression. Expression—that is what it all comes back to. This union of remembered country sights and scents and sounds with most urban pessimistic philosophy, is dignified by virility, and brought home to us through a fulness of feeling which creates art. On the whole, it more creates art than is guided by it. Like all modern poets of the truly direct kind, apart from the eloquent Byronic school which is not really direct, Mr. Housman is unequal. He is unequal as Wordsworth was unequal, and from the same cause. Where his feeling is not strong enough to inspire him, he lapses into mere rhymed prose. Where his feeling is acute, he pierces to the quick. And he seems quite ignorant when he is inspired or uninspired.

At the same time, as will have been gathered, nothing could be less Wordsworthian than this poet's general style. It seems rather founded on the old ballads. (pp. 120-23)

["**From far, from eve and morning**," No. XXXII in *A Shropshire Lad*,] contains Mr. Housman's philosophy and attitude towards life in a nutshell. This one insistent note, like the cry of a bittern, sounds lonelily throughout the book. Sometimes he frankly repeats a *motif* in several poems. Thus two successive poems sing the folly of giving "the heart out of the bosom." The second is superfluous, for the first has said the thing once for all, and the repetition is distinctly weaker. More often the iteration is disguised by the varying form of utterance. The haunting cry of fate, heredity, and passing away is presented over and over again with striking skill in variation. (p. 124)

We like Mr. Housman least in the few poems where he attempts a lilting metre, which he does not seem to us to handle skilfully. But allowing this, allowing a proportion of poems where simplicity becomes insipidity, this is yet the annunciation of a new and valuable voice in present poetry. Sometimes grim, strong, close-knit, commanding attention by its virile pessimism; sometimes haunting and melancholy; sometimes taking us by a piercing and Heinesque surprise at the poem's close; monotonous, but not wearying; grave, sad, sincere, unsuperfluous, with a latter-day simplicity, less simple than it seems; it is individual work, to which the reader will return with deepening interest and admiration. For it is rarely that simplicity is combined, as it is here combined, with the self-consciousness of the modern poet, yet a simplicity without affectation. (pp. 125-26)

Francis Thompson, "Mr. A. E. Housman's Poems" (*originally published in* The Academy, *Vol. LIV, No. 1379, October 8, 1898), in his* The Real Robert Louis Stevenson and Other Critical Essays, *edited by Terence L. Connolly (copyright © 1959, by University Publishers Incorporated), University Publishers Incorporated, 1959, pp. 120-26.*

WILLIAM ARCHER   (essay date 1902)

[Mr. A. E. Housman's book, *A Shropshire Lad*,] is a very small one. It contains some sixty brief lyrics, occupying not quite one hundred pages in all. You may read it in half an hour—but there are things in it you will scarce forget in a lifetime. It tingles with an original, fascinating, melancholy vitality.

Mr. Housman writes, for the most part, under the guise of "A Shropshire Lad"—the rustic namefather of his book. But this is evidently a mere mask. Mr. Housman is no Shropshire Burns singing at his plough. He is a man of culture. He moves in his rustic garb with no clodhopper's gait, but with the ease of an athlete; and he has an Elzevir classic in the pocket of his smock frock. But it is not Theocritus, not the Georgics or the Eclogues; I rather take it to be Lucretius. Never was there less of a "pastoral" poet, in the artificial, Italian-Elizabethan sense of the word. The Shropshire of Mr. Housman is no Arcadia, no Sicily, still less a courtly pleasaunce peopled with beribboned nymphs and swains. It is as real, as tragic, as the Wessex of Mr. Hardy. The genius, or rather the spirit, of the two writers is not dissimilar. Both have the same rapturous realisation, the same bitter resentment, of life. To both Nature is an exquisitely seductive, inexorably malign enchantress. "Life's Ironies" might be the common title of Mr. Hardy's long series of novels and Mr. Housman's little book of verse. (pp. 184-85)

Mr. Housman has three main topics: a stoical pessimism; a dogged rather than an exultant patriotism; and what I may perhaps call a wistful cynicism. (p. 186)

In a few of Mr. Housman's poems, however, there is no touch of that bitterness of feeling which I have named, or misnamed, cynicism. **Bredon Hill** . . . seems to me almost unrivalled in its delicate, unemphatic pathos. It exemplifies one of Mr. Housman's strongest and rarest qualities—his unerring dramatic instinct. (pp. 191-92)

It is long since we have caught just this note in English verse—the note of intense feeling uttering itself in language of unadorned precision, uncontorted truth. Mr. Housman is a vernacular poet, if ever there was one. He employs scarcely a word that is not understood of the people, and current on their lips. For this very reason, some readers who have come to regard decoration, and even contortion, as of the essence of poetry, may need time to acquire the taste for Mr. Housman's simplicity. But if he is vernacular, he is also classical in the best sense of the word. His simplicity is not that of weakness, but of strength and skill. He eschews extrinsic and factitious ornament because he knows how to attain beauty without it. It is good to mirror a thing in figures, but it is at least as good to express the thing itself in its essence, always provided, of course, that the method be that of poetic synthesis, not of scientific analysis. Mr. Housman has this talent in a very high degree; and cognate and complementary to it is his remarkable gift of reticence—of aposiopesis, if I may wrest the term from its rhetorical sense and apply it to poetry. He will often say more by a cunning silence than many another poet by pages of speech. That is how he has contrived to get into his tiny volume so much of the very essence and savour of life. (pp. 192-93)

There is no reason why Mr. Housman should not put off his rustic mask and widen the range of his subject matter. I trust he will do so in other and larger volumes. But even should he be content to remain merely "A Shropshire Lad," his place among English poets is secure. (p. 193)

William Archer, "A. E. Housman," in his Poets of the Younger Generation, *John Lane, 1902 (and reprinted by Scholarly Press, 1969), pp. 183-95.*

F. L. LUCAS (essay date 1923)

[*In contrast to the vast majority of critics, Lucas accepts Housman's pessimism as a necessary aspect of his poetry. While most critics label as puerile Housman's negative view of existence, Lucas recognizes it as the poet's entirely valid and dignified reply to the questions posed by his experience.*]

Professor Housman has given us his "last" poems; so that we can see his work, it is to be feared, already as a whole, if not so steadily as posterity. For that posterity will read him, seems to me as (humanly) certain, as it is dubious if there are more than two other living English poets of whom the same can be said. When *Last Poems* appeared, the reviews paid, indeed, their tributes to his verse and style and beauty—such tributes as adorn the wrappers of half a hundred other poets, in the inflated currency of to-day; but when it came to certain other characteristics, there appeared in their criticisms a tone ludicrously like the reluctant testimony of conjured devils. The view of life that breathes through these poems, the essence of their being, was passed gingerly over, with a mild deprecation, perhaps, of some particularly defiant utterance, or a pious wish that Professor Housman were less pessimistic—much as one might sigh what an agreeable play *Hamlet* might be without that depressing prince. . . .

But one cannot believe that posterity, if statesmen allow us that luxury, will fall into this half-hearted, impertinent folly. Wondering what the Georgians really thought and felt about existence—turning wearily from piles of little poets who busied themselves scrabbling illuminated miniatures in the margin of the book of life . . .—they will find here one answer to their question, one personality among so many echoing masks, one reading of life, wrong maybe, but blurred and corrupted at least with no optimistic emendations, and rendered into English of a purity that English literature has not surpassed. Some, rejecting his interpretation, will yet recognise, if they are human, that in moods, at least, they too have felt the same, and will hope, if they are wise, that though differing they enjoy him none the less; and some, sharing his view of life, will know that they enjoy him yet the more. And nobody will deprecate. (p. 45)

[Matthew Arnold] is Professor Housman's nearest kin in English literature; and for a third to join with these, we must look to the disdainful yet tender brevity of Landor. In no other three of our poets have the spirits of Greece, Rome, and England found that happy mixture of their elements which lives in them— the grace and lucid sadness of the flutes of Hellas, the proud glitter and the stab of the short Roman sword, the sweetness and strength of the English countryside. Arnold doubted more, and wailed because he doubted, till harder men lost patience with his "nibbling and quibbling" about belief; he was sometimes prim; and, unsurpassed as his best work is, and far wider in its range, he had not, technically, the sureness of the later poet's touch. Landor was less subtle and, likewise, less sure. It is a curiosity of literature that so late in the development of English poetry it should have been possible to bring harmonies so new, so invariably perfect out of some of its most hackneyed metres. Swinburne produced many of his miracles by brilliant modifications of old metrical forms. Beddoes recaptured, as no one since has done, the secret magic of Elizabethan blank verse. But Professor Housman modifies little and recaptures nothing; though the Carolines used some of his verse-forms to perfection, they are not like him. And when one sits down and puzzles where one has seen anything really akin to this Melchizedek, there comes only the unexpected half-answer: "In

Heine." The belief that there is here more than coincidence is strengthened when one recognizes in the flower of "Sinner's Rue" no other than the German's Armesünderblum—the blue floweret that grows at cross-roads on the mounds of the slayers of themselves.

But this does not go far towards explaining how his effects are produced; it is easy to docket the artifices he so boldly and openly uses. . . . But the charm endures where these devices are not; there are so many strings to this bow with its sweet swallow-song—pause and shift of stress, fingering and vowel-play, and, above all, the skill which keeps the diction of these lyrics so simple and close to the directness of prose, without ever transgressing that fatal boundary, by its perfect intermingling of the unexpected word with the speech of everyday, of the unexpected thought with the looked-for conclusion. (pp. 45-6)

These things produce their complete effect just because the power to contrive them is controlled with a rigid economy; so that the general impression these lyrics leave is of a strength that never needs to strive or cry, a beauty whose quality is never strained. "Schiller," observed Coleridge, "sets you a whole town afire. But Shakespeare drops you a handkerchief." And, as there is no strain, so there are no collapses; if we could spare anything, it would be some of the poems on soldiers and on gallows. But such exceptions are few, and the most serious challenge to Housman's position will be his want of bulk. I do not think that need trouble us greatly; these poems, as Meleager said of Sappho's, are "few, but roses." The poems of Catullus are likewise few.

But the spell of this poetry does not live merely in its technical perfections, in its pure beauty, in the happy way it has won a province of its own, like Hardy's Wessex, in the heart of England, in the flowery grace with which it wears its ancient learning, so that the reader recognises on Shropshire lips, with a stab of spiritual homesickness, the well-known accents of Sarpedon and Achilles or some echo of the laconic fortitude of Rome; and the water, not of "Nile" only, but of Simois and Scamander, Ilissus and Tiber,

> spills its overflow
> Beside the Severn's dead.

It is, as Milton demanded, not only "simple" and "sensuous," but "passionate" also, as the perfect in style often fails to be; and it is "criticism of life" after Arnold's heart. Not popular criticism, indeed; pessimism so unflinching and inflexible is to be found in few English poets apart from Hardy and James Thomson. And even Mr. Hardy has sometimes wavered and of late grown mysteriously to resent the name; there is nothing in Professor Housman's work that could lend itself to such irony as the recent spectacle of babes and sucklings chanting a judiciously selected chorus of *The Dynasts* in honour of the Prince's visit to Dorchester. (p. 46)

Pessimism is not depressing to those who have faced it, and pride may be one of the deadly sins, but it gives not the ignoblest human answer to the menace of eternity. (pp. 46-7)

F. L. Lucas, "Few, But Roses," in New Statesman (©1923 The Statesman Publishing Co. Ltd.), Vol. XXII, No. 549, October 20, 1923, pp. 45-7.

EDITH SITWELL (essay date 1934)

[*Sitwell compares Housman unfavorably to T. S. Eliot. She concedes that Housman's verse expresses genuine feeling, but like*

Conrad Aiken (see excerpt below) she feels that it is "thin and threadbare in texture," and generally lacks the sort of sensory appeal that she believes is the means through which poetry enhances the reader's experience of life.]

I have the greatest respect for the integrity of Professor Housman, and I am not intending any discourtesy to him when I say that to my feeling, the cramped and rheumatic eight-syllable lines, the threadbare texture in which he finds, as a rule, his expression, are not suitable to his themes. Ploughboys never moved so elegantly, men about to be hanged never expressed their sentiments with such neatness; the broken-hearted groan or they whisper, but they do not confine their outpourings to the brevity of such epigrammatic quatrains as these. In short, life and death are not like that. Yet, strangely enough, in Marvell's great poem "To His Coy Mistress," T. S. Eliot's great poem "Whispers of Immortality," the vast imagination of these is preserved within the prim eight-syllable line, and this, indeed, even heightens the effect in both these poems, shows us, in its narrow grave, the eternal skeleton. Wherein lies the difference? In the fact that we feel a controlled and terrible passion underlying Marvell's and Eliot's verses, an explosive force heaving beneath the surface of the lines.

"**The Shropshire Lad**" is claimed to be great poetry because of the bareness of the line, the absolute lack of decoration. But to my feeling, that bareness is due as much to lack of vitality as to anything else. It is certain that the greatest impressiveness of emotion is gained by an absolute simplicity. But in Professor Housman's poems one reader, at least, feels that this simplicity is not invariably the result of passion finding its expression in one inevitable phrase, inhabiting it as the soul inhabits the body, but is sometimes the result of a thin and threadbare texture. This texture is not strong enough to contain an explosive force, or the possibility of a passionate upheaval under the line. The rigidity of the structure does not seem like the rigidity of grief; it seems to arise from stiffness, from an insufficient fluidity. The verse is for the most part rhythmically dead. (pp. 14-15)

> *Edith Sitwell, "Pastors and Masters," in her* Aspects of Modern Poetry *(reprinted by permission of the Estate of Edith Sitwell), Duckworth, 1934, pp. 9-50.**

CONRAD AIKEN (essay date 1936)

[Aiken was one of the first critics to level the often repeated charge that Housman's poetry was adolescent in outlook. Edmund Wilson (see excerpt below) concurs with Aiken in this view up to a point, while continuing to praise much of Housman's poetry. Like Edith Sitwell (see excerpt above), Aiken also maintains that the celebrated simplicity of Housman's lyrics may be more a result of the aridity of the poet's "sensory equipment for poetry" than his devotion to classical form. This essay first appeared only three weeks after Housman's death. Aiken's insensitivity in publishing such a harsh indictment at such an inopportune time provoked normally moderate critics like John Sparrow to condemn him as a publicity seeker. Sparrow remarked that although Aiken was "late for the funeral" he had arrived in time to "spit on the grave."]

The **Last Poems** of Housman have now been succeeded by **More Poems**, chosen from among the completed verses which he left behind him at his death, and thus the total number of lyrics given to the world by this most reticent and self-denying of poets grows to the total of one hundred and fifty-three; but one can say at once that it is an addition which does not change,

that the addition of the third volume, like the addition of the second, extends slightly, if at all, the range, does not alter the character, and that the three books are really one, are really **The Shropshire Lad**. It is more or less true that the third collection is very slightly inferior to the second, just as the second was very slightly inferior to the first. The thinnesses and barenesses are more noticeable, the repetitions of theme and tone more staring, the genuine felicities are certainly fewer. Nor are there whole poems, as many of them, which attain to quite the cool completeness of the best in **The Shropshire Lad**. . . .

That [Housman] is limited, no one in his senses would deny. The actual range, when one stops to consider it, is extraordinarily narrow, and the perhaps too-well-disposed critic wonders whether he is not wish-thinking in supposing that many of Housman's restrictions were self-restrictions. It is one thing—one may say—to be limited, another to *impose* limitations on oneself; and somehow or other the myth has grown up that Housman's limitedness, like the smallness of his output, was the result of an iron-discipline and restraint, a process of selection and elimination at a very high degree of tension, and that the product was accordingly, *ipso facto*, severely and beautifully classic. Housman himself did a good deal to encourage the growth of this notion. . . . (p. 223)

Just the same, it is permissible perhaps to question whether the narrowness of the range and the smallness of the output were not actually implicit in the nature of Housman's talent, and imposed from within rather than from without; and to question in parallel fashion whether the often-praised "classic" perfection and severity of his style might not more justly, now and then, be termed pseudo-classic.

And that, for better or worse, and at the risk of being considered guilty of something perilously like *lèse majesté*, the present reviewer has always thought, and still thinks, thinks more than ever after a rereading of the three little books. It is idle to deny the charm, the grace, the dexterity, the neatness, whether of form or thought, just as it is idle to deny the wistful and brave individuality which everywhere shows in these poems; but it seems equally idle to deny that the classic should be made of sterner and deeper stuff than this, and that if it is not to be profounder, then it must at least be more richly and variously wrought.

And even taken at its best, the texture of Housman's verse tends to be thin. Nor is this wholly a matter of choice. Simplicity is aimed at, to be sure, but there is always, also, a little *more* simplicity than was aimed at, and this looks as if it arose from the fact that Housman's sensory equipment for poetry was definitely somewhat arid. The range of mere perception is very narrow indeed—it is a world in which the grass is green and the sheep are white, as simple a world as that of W. H. Davies, for example, but with almost nothing of Davies' sudden felicities of observation or quick aptnesses of statement. Housman conventionalizes, and that would be all right if the conventionalization were itself more interesting; but for this reader at least the constant reliance on a pretty threadbare and perhaps deliberately anachronistic kind of martial imagery, joined with a bucolic imagery just as deliberately "quaint" or "homely," becomes in the end both barren and defrauding.

That one should cease to believe might not matter, provided the *playing* at poetry, the playing at profundity or skepticism, were itself more richly and ingeniously managed; but this Housman only seldom achieved. The result is a charming but incomplete and essentially adolescent poetry—the questionings and despairs and loyalties are alike adolescent, and so are the thoughts and the bravenesses and the nostalgic gayeties; and what makes it sometimes worse is one's suspicion that this adolescent note, this boyishness, is a cultivated thing, a calculated falsetto. It has been pointed out that one of the longest of the new poems—**"Down the waterway of sunset drove to shore a ship of gold"**—is a little Kiplingesque. But the truth is that something very like the Kipling note is always lurking just round the corner, in these poems, both in the tone and the text. The slightly too dactylic dittylike use of the octosyllabic quatrains, coupled with the characteristically too-thumping use of Universals, an attitudinizing orotundity, produce now and then an effect perilously close to that of the *Barrack Room Ballads*.

But no, that is perhaps being too hard on a very fine poet, and to overdo our point that at least a part of Housman's charm grew from his very limitations. Greatness? No. Epigrammatic, lovely, light-colored, youthfully charming above all. . . . (pp. 224-25)

Conrad Aiken, "Housman, A. E." (originally published as "A. E. Housman," in The New Republic, *Vol. 89, No. 1145, November 11, 1936), in his* Collected Criticism *(copyright © 1935, 1939, 1940, 1942, 1951, 1958 by Conrad Aiken; reprinted by permission of Brandt & Brandt Literary Agents, Inc.),* Oxford University Press, New York, 1968, pp. 223-25.

RANDALL JARRELL   (essay date 1939)

[*Jarrell's essay, excerpted below, is widely regarded by critics as representing one of the most astute estimations of Housman's poetry. Jarrell offers valuable insights into Housman's poetic technique by demonstrating how the poet, through his masterful use of language, used ambiguity as a device for adding a dimension of meaning to his poems that transcends the particular incidents they describe. Jarrell was the first critic to observe the divergence between what Housman says and the manner in which he says it. This approach is reflected in the essays, excerpted below, by Richard Wilbur, Christopher Ricks, and John Bligh, as well as forming the substance of a controversy between T.S.K. Scott-Craig and Cleanth Brooks (see excerpts below). Jarrell's essay has in general led to a reevaluation of Housman's role in twentieth-century literature.*]

I am about to analyze [Housman's **"Crossing alone the nighted ferry,"** No. XXIII in *More Poems*]. . . .

> Crossing alone the nighted ferry
> With the one coin for fee,
> Whom, on the wharf of Lethe waiting,
> Count you to find? Not me.
>
> The brisk fond lackey to fetch and carry,
> The true, sick-hearted slave,
> Expect him not in the just city
> And free land of the grave.

The first stanza is oddly constructed; it manages to carry over several more or less unexpressed statements, while the statement it makes on the surface, grammatically, is arranged so as to make the reader disregard it completely. Literally, the stanza says: *Whom do you expect to find waiting for you? Not me.* But the denying and elliptical *not me* is not an answer to the surface question; that question is almost rhetorical, and obviously gets a *me*; the *not me* denies *And I'll satisfy your expectations and be there?*—the implied corollary of the surface question; and the flippant and brutal finality of the *not me*

implies that the expectations are foolish. (A belief that can be contradicted so carelessly and completely—by a person in a position to know—is a foolish one.) The stanza says: *You do expect to find me and ought not to* and *You're actually such a fool as to count on my being there?* and *So I'll be there, eh? Not me.*

Some paraphrases of the two stanzas will show how extraordinarily much they do mean; they illustrate the quality of poetry that is almost its most characteristic, compression. These paraphrases are not very imaginative—the reader can find justification for any statement in the actual words of the poem. (Though not in any part considered in isolation. . . . [Most] of the important meanings attached to the first stanza do not exist when the stanza is considered in isolation.) And the paraphrases are not hypertrophied, they do not even begin to be exhaustive.

Stanza I: Do you expect me to wait patiently for you there, just as I have done on earth? expect that, in hell, after death, things will go on for you just as they do here on earth? that there, after crossing and drinking Lethe and oblivion, I'll still be thinking of human you, still be waiting faithfully there on the wharf for you to arrive, with you still my only interest, with me still your absolutely devoted slave—just as we are here? Do you really? Do you actually suppose that you yourself, then, will be able to expect it? Even when dead, all alone, on that grim ferry, in the middle of the dark forgetful river, all that's left of your human life one coin, you'll be stupid or inflexible or faithful enough to *count* on (you're sure, are you, so sure that not even a doubt enters your mind?) finding me waiting there? How are we to understand an inflexibility that seems almost incredible? Is it because you're pathetically deluded about love's constancy, my great lasting love for you? (This version makes the *you* sympathetic; but it is unlikely, an unstressed possibility, and the others do not.) Or is it that you're so sure of my complete enslavement that you know death itself can't change it? Or are you so peculiarly stupid that you can't even conceive of any essential change away from your past life and knowledge, even after the death that has destroyed them both? Or it is the general inescapable stupidity of mankind, who can conceive of death only in human and vital terms? (Housman's not giving the reasons, when the reasons must be thought about if the poem is to be understood, forces the reader to make them for himself, and to see that there is a wide range that must be considered. This is one of the most important principles of compression in poetry; these implied foundations or justifications for a statement might be called *bases*.) Are you actually such a fool as to believe that? So I'll be there? Not me. You're wrong. There things are really different.

One of the most important elements in the poem is the tone of the *not me*. Its casualness, finality, and matter-of-fact bluntness give it almost the effect of slang. It is the crudest of denials. There is in it a laconic brutality, an imperturbable and almost complacent vigor; it has certainly a sort of contempt. Contempt for what? Contempt at himself for his faithlessness? contempt at himself for his obsessing weakness—for not being faithless now instead of then? Or contempt at her, for being bad enough to keep things as they are, for being stupid enough to imagine that they will be so always? The tone is both threatening and disgusted. It shivers between all these qualities like a just-thrown knife. And to what particular denial does this tone attach? how specific, how general a one? These are changes a reader can easily ring for himself; but I hope he will realize their importance. Variations of this formula of alternative possibilities make up one of the most valuable resources of the poet.

The second stanza is most thoroughly ambiguous; there are two entirely different levels of meaning for the whole, and most of the parts exhibit a comparable stratification. I give a word-for-word analysis:

Do not expect me to be after death what I was alive and human: the *fond* (1. *foolish;* 2. *loving*—you get the same two meanings in the synonym *doting*) *brisk* (the normal meanings are favorable: *full of life, keenly alive or alert, energetic;* but here the context forces it over into *officious, undignified, solicitous, leaping at your every word*—there is a pathetic ignoble sense to it here) *lackey* (the most contemptuous and degrading form of the word *servant:* a servile follower, a toady) *to fetch and carry* (you thought so poorly of me that you let me perform nothing but silly menial physical tasks; thus, our love was nothing but the degrading relationship of obsequious servant and contemptuous master), *the true* (1. *constant, loyal, devoted, faithful;* 2. *properly so-called, ideally or typically such*—the perfectly slavish slave) *sickhearted* (1. cowardly, disheartened in a weak discouraged ignoble way, as a Spartan would have said of helots, "These sick-hearted slaves"; 2. sick at heart at the whole mess, his own helpless subjection. There was a man in one of the sagas who had a bad boil on his foot; when he was asked why he didn't limp and favor it, he replied: "One walks straight while the leg is whole." If the reader imagines this man as a slave he will see sharply the more elevated sense of the phrase *sick-hearted slave*) *slave* (1. the conventional hardly meant sense in which we use it of lovers, as an almost completely dead metaphor; this sense has very little force here; or 2. the literal *slave:* the relation of slave to master is not pleasant, not honorable, is between lovers indecent and horrible, but immensely comprehensive—their love is made even more compulsive and even less favorable). But here I leave the word-by-word analysis for more general comment. I think I hardly need remark on the shock in this treatment, which forces over the conventional unfelt terms into their literal degrading senses; and this shock is amplified by the paradoxical fall through *just city* and *free land* into *the grave.* (Also, the effect of the *lackey/carry* and versification of the first line of the stanza should be noted.)

Let me give first the favorable literal surface sense of *the just city and free land of the grave,* its sense on the level at which you take Housman's Greek underworld convention seriously. The house of Hades is the *just city* for a number of reasons: in it are the three just judges; in it are all the exemplary convicts, from Ixion to the Danaïdes, simply dripping with justice; here justice is meted equally to the anonymous and rankless dead; there is no corruption here. It is the *free land* because here the king and the slave are equal (though even on the level of death as the Greek underworld, the horrid irony has begun to intrude—Achilles knew, and Housman knows, that it is better to be the slave of a poor farmer than king among the hosts of the dead); because here we are free at last from life; and so on and so on.

But at the deeper level, the *just* fastened to *city,* the *city* fastened to *grave,* have an irony that is thorough. How are we to apply *just* to a place where corruption and nothingness are forced on good and bad, innocent and guilty alike? (From Housman's point of view it might be called mercy, but never justice.) And the *city* is as bad; the cemetery looks like a city of the graves, of the stone rectangular houses—but a city without occupations, citizens, without life: a shell, a blank check that can

never be filled out. And can we call a land *free* whose inhabitants cannot move a finger, are compelled as completely as stones? And can we call the little cave, the patch of darkness and pressing earth, the *land* of the grave?

And why are we told to expect him not, the slave, the lackey, in the just city and free land of the grave? Because he is changed now, a citizen of the Greek underworld, engrossed in its games and occupations, the new interests that he has acquired? Oh no, the change is complete, not from the old interests to new ones, but from any interests to none; do not expect him because he has ceased to exist, he is really, finally different now. It is foolish to expect *anything* of the world after death. But we can expect nothingness; and that is better than this world, the poem is supposed to make us feel; there, even though we are overwhelmed impartially and completely, we shall be free of the evil of this world—a world whose best thing, love, is nothing but injustice and stupidity and slavery. This is why the poet resorts to the ambiguity that permits him to employ the adjectives *just* and *free:* they seem to apply truly on the surface level, and ironically at the other; but in a way they, and certainly the air of reward and luck and approbation that goes with them, apply truly at the second level as well. This is the accusation and condemnation of life that we read so often in Housman: that the grave seems better, we are glad to be in it.

We ought not to forget that this poem is a love poem by the living "me" of the poem to its equally living "you": *when we are dead, things will be different—and I'm glad of it.* It is, considerably sublimated, the formula familiar to such connections: *I wish I were dead;* and it has more than a suspicion of the child's *when I'm dead, then they'll be sorry.* It is an accusation that embodies a very strong statement of the underlying antagonism, the real ambivalence of most such relationships. The condemnation applied to the world for being bad is extended to the *you* for not being better. And these plaints are always pleas; so the poem has an additional force. Certainly this particular-seeming little poem turns out to be general enough: it carries implicit in it attitudes (aggregates of related generalizations) toward love, life, and death. (pp. 20-4)

Randall Jarrell, "Texts from Housman" (originally published in The Kenyon Review, *Vol. I, No. 3, Summer, 1939), in his* Kipling, Auden & Co.: Essays and Reviews 1935-1964 *(reprinted by permission of Farrar, Straus and Giroux, Inc.; copyright © 1939, 1980 by Mrs. Randall Jarrell), Farrar, Straus and Giroux, 1980, pp. 20-8.*

J. BRONOWSKI (essay date 1939)

[*Bronowski's* The Poet's Defence *includes one of the best known critical attacks to appear after Housman's death. See also Conrad Aiken's essay excerpted above.*]

Swinburne believed that the worth of poems lies in their manner. His belief in 'pure' poetry has been well put to-day by A. E. Housman. It is worth our while to study it as Housman puts it in his one essay, *The Name and Nature of Poetry.*

We shall best understand how Housman is putting it if we begin with a sentence from the middle of his essay.

> When I hear anyone say, with defiant emphasis, that Pope was a poet, I suspect him of calling in ambiguity of language to promote confusion of thought.

This clears the air. We know what we are not talking about. We are not talking about poetry in the meaning in which the *Oxford Book of English Verse* is a book of poetry. We are talking only about some poems chosen for some one grace; and we are putting aside all the poems which have long been judged to be good which are without this grace. So Housman puts aside the poems of the Metaphysicals and of the Augustans. They are not poetry. Then what is poetry?

> 'But no man may deliver his brother, nor make agreement unto God for him', that is to me poetry so moving that I can hardly keep my voice steady in reading it. And that this is the effect of language I can ascertain by experiment: the same thought in the bible version, 'None of them can by any means redeem his brother, nor give to God a ransom for him', I can read without emotion.
>
> Poetry is not the thing said but a way of saying it.

The sentences carry the belief of Swinburne: 'something in the mere progress and resonance of the words, some secret in the very motion and cadence of the lines'. But they give it a new air. The judgment which leads Housman to Swinburne's belief is a judgment from the feelings and from the body, 'I can hardly keep my voice steady'. Housman blurs the question whether these feelings are indeed made by the way of saying it, or whether they are merely made unbearable by the way of saying it. Like Swinburne, he finds the worth in the way of saying it: but he judges the way by his feelings. (pp. 209-10)

Housman's feelings are bodily feelings: 'Poetry indeed seems to me more physical than intellectual'. They grow from the bodily life of the senses. Have such feelings a place in the judgment of poetry? Housman quotes the *Book of Common Prayer*, and says,

> That is to me poetry so moving that I can hardly keep my voice steady in reading it.

Very well. But there are sentences which shake the voices of other readers: sentences from love letters, the news of a friend's death, the number of men who were blinded in the War. Does their unsteadiness make these sentences poetry? Or would it make them poetry only if it were caused by the way of saying it? Housman is not clear. He holds that a poem should move the feelings. He holds that the feeling gives the poem worth, and that the feeling at last is the poem. But he holds that the poem and therefore the feeling is not the thing said but a way of saying it. Since this is not true of every feeling, we learn suddenly that Housman is not speaking of the feelings as one. He is speaking only of some feelings: those which are ruled by words, those which shake the voice. We now understand his dislike of the Metaphysicals and of the Augustans. He does not dislike them for their lack of feeling. He dislikes them for their lack of one feeling, the sadness and longing which shake the voice. When he blames Pope he writes,

> But not even in the Elegy to the memory of an unfortunate lady does the fire burn clear of smoke, and truth of emotion do itself full justice in naturalness and purity of diction.

But why choose the *Elegy to the Memory of an Unfortunate Lady*? Why not choose *Windsor Forest*? Because Housman is only looking for elegies and sadness. He is looking not for

'truth of emotion' but for that emotion which shakes the voice. . . . To him sadness *is* poetry, and the only poetry.

I study some sentences which search for this sadness.

> In these six simple words of Milton—
>
> Nymphs and shepherds, dance no more—
>
> what is it that can draw tears, as I know it can, to the eyes of more readers than one? What in the world is there to cry about?
>
> (pp. 211-13)

> Experience has taught me, when I am shaving of a morning, to keep watch over my thoughts, because, if a line of poetry strays into my memory, my skin bristles so that the razor ceases to act. This particular symptom is accompanied by a shiver down the spine; there is another which consists in a constriction of the throat and a precipitation of water to the eyes.

I stop here, because the words 'a precipitation of water to the eyes' sum the false seriousness and the manliness-ill-at-ease of Housman's essay. They warn us that Housman is speaking in a mood at once sprightly and shamefaced, in which he will shirk his meaning. And they throw a cruel light on his test, 'not the thing said but a way of saying it'. Housman's way of saying tears is 'a precipitation of water to the eyes'. (p. 213)

There are good poems which carry the sadness which is Housman's Poetry. There are more bad poems which carry it. And there are good poems which do not carry it. The *Ancient Mariner*, the *Intimations of Immortality* are poems which carry beyond measure more tragedy than anything which Housman quotes. They carry none of his petty sadness. (p. 216)

Housman's theory fences off a small plot of feeling and calls it Poetry. This is more than a theory: it is a cast of mind. (p. 218)

The matter of Housman's poems is simple. It holds to a few feelings: the feelings of love, of friendship, of honour, of bravery; and the feeling that we must look at these bravely and know that they are pointless. These feelings are not praised and they are not debated. It is taken for granted that they are in all men. And it is not debated that they are at odds with themselves. We see that they are at odds. If love, friendship, honour, bravery are worthy feelings which give point to living, why does Housman write

> Lie down, lie down, young yeoman;
>   What use to rise and rise?
> Rise man a thousand mornings
>   Yet down at last he lies,
>   And then the man is wise.

If they are pointless feelings and death is their pointless end, why does he write

> If it chance your eye offend you,
>   Pluck it out, lad, and be sound:
> 'Twill hurt, but here are salves to friend you,
>   And many a balsam grows on ground.
>
> And if your hand or foot offend you,
>   Cut it off, lad, and be whole;
> But play the man, stand up and end you,
>   When your sickness is your soul.

The brunt of these two sets of feelings makes the sadness of Housman's poems. This is the sadness which Housman calls Poetry. And it is the point of his sadness that it shall be at odds within itself. It shall grow from holding two feelings at once which no force can hold together. When Housman chooses to hold at once the feeling for love, friendship, honour, bravery, and the feeling that these feelings are pointless, he makes sure that he shall fail. It is a foreseen defeat and a planned sadness. (pp. 219-20)

We therefore learn to see deeply into Housman's sadness. He is sad because he writes in an aimless welter of standards which he cannot hold together. Not only two standards are at odds. Every standard is called on, now in this poem, now in that. Every poem is at odds with every other. For every poem has a standard and makes a judgment of living: but Housman has no standard. Housman can judge the acts of life with one sentence only: that we must die. But death is not a standard for life. It may be, as Housman thought, that man is helpless and worthless. But man is not worthless because he is helpless. He is not helpless and worthless because he must die. (pp. 221-22)

If one poem is glad that a young man has left life before honour, the next will say that silly lads always want to leave their life. And whatever the standard, Housman feels that he himself who is without a standard is smaller by it. The lads who have gone off to play, to war, and to be hanged are always better lads than Housman. (p. 223)

This is more bitter than to call himself coward: Housman is belittling his feelings more. And this is Housman's most tender sadness: to belittle the very feeling which makes the poem. It gives irony to the sadness, it makes it rueful as well as wistful. Housman is ashamed of the tear which he drops, and yet he must show the tear and show the shame. This is the shamefaced manliness of 'a precipitation of water to the eyes'. (pp. 223-24)

This is Housman's most subtle tool of sadness: to make the reader pity him for a weakness which the reader is also asked to despise, and which Housman despises. (p. 225)

The poems damn themselves. They have no standards. They despise their own feelings. They move the reader only by their own self-belittling. They judge themselves, and find themselves little. They leave Housman only two defences, which he took in *The Name and Nature of Poetry.* One defence is that sadness and longing makes a worthy poem however they are got. This makes Housman plead for tearfulness in a blithe and gay poem of Milton. This make him boast that 'I have seldom written poetry unless I was rather out of health'. He is claiming that maudlin feelings are poetry, whether we get them from Milton, from ill-health, or from the self-pity and belittling of his own poems. (p. 227)

> *J. Bronowski, "Alfred Edward Housman," in his* The Poet's Defence, *Cambridge at the University Press, 1939 (and reprinted by Hyperion Press, Inc., 1979), pp. 209-28.*

JOHN PEALE BISHOP   (essay date 1940)

[*For Bishop, the suppression of the "secret cause" of Housman's sufferings obscures the meaning of his poems. Bishop's assumption, without overt statement, of Housman's homosexuality is later incorporated into Norman Marlow's biographical reading of the poetry (see excerpt below).*]

The posthumous poems will not much change the estimation in which Housman has been held. They are work worthy of that proud mind. The *Additional Poems,* while they increase the sum of his poetry, add no poetic quality that was not there before. This they could hardly do, for it is apparent from the list of dates . . . that they were composed along with the poems we already know. Some of them are contemporaneous with *A Shropshire Lad;* the latest, as far as anyone knows, is from 1925. What they do is to let us see the poet plain. Now that we have his poetry whole, we know what his personal plight was, and that is bound to affect our reading of all the poems. To know **"Oh, who is that young sinner with the handcuffs on his wrist?"** is to know something that we should have known all along about those culprits of *A Shropshire Lad.* We have known and long known those hanged boys who hear the stroke of eight from the clock in the tower on the market place and never hear the stroke of nine. We know now for what crime all of them have been condemned. We have known when the noose went round their necks, but not whose head stood above the rope. They have many names and all have one name. Their features are not beyond recognition. The head is A. E. Housman's.

Romantic poetry as Housman received it was in need of correction. He corrected it. The romantic conflict of man against society, of man against immutable laws is still there, but presented by a man who had the classic craftsman's respect for both himself and his craft. The form is concise and accurate; but, for all their lightness, his poems never lose the sense of earth; for all their grace, they are tough enough to sustain a considerable irony. The limits within which Housman was able to feel at all were strict, but within them he felt intensely, and both strictness and intensity are in his verse.

His style has in it nothing strange. It is not unconventional; it is extremely careful never to affront conventional ideas of what a poetic style should be. The truth was quite strange enough. Poetry that pardons the poet nothing less than the truth, once the truth is assured, pardons him everything. The passion for truth was in Housman. He could, in his poetry, condemn himself as contemporary opinion—in the very year *A Shropshire Lad* was written—had condemned Wilde. When almost all others had abandoned him, Housman sent Wilde a copy of *A Shropshire Lad* to prison; Wilde's answer was *A Ballad of Reading Gaol.* (pp. 138-39)

No matter where we open Housman's poems, we are almost sure to be struck with how young are those who suffer in them, how brief and sure their suffering—its course predictable, since all has been known before:

> These, in the day when heaven was falling,
>   The hour when earth's foundations fled,
> Followed their mercenary calling
>   And took their wages and are dead.
>
> Their shoulders held the sky suspended;
>   They stood, and earth's foundations stay;
> What God abandoned, these defended,
>   And saved the sum of things for pay.

Whatever the occasion that gave rise to them, these moving lines can scarcely be read without bringing to mind the part played by the professional soldiers of the British Army in the retreat from Mons. They are called, however, simply *Epitaph on an Army of Mercenaries,* and, as they stand, are as applicable to the soldiers of some desperate and remote army in some forgotten war of antiquity as they are to the men of 1914. Here, a particular situation has produced a tragic emotion; whatever is lacking we can supply, so that the event behind the lines is adequate to the emotion. But this is not always so in Housman. If—to follow Joyce's excellent and convenient definitions—pity is present in poetry whenever what is grave and constant in human sufferings is united with the human sufferer; terror, whenever what is grave and constant in human sufferings is united with the secret cause, then pity and terror should scarcely be lacking from anything that Housman wrote. And pity and terror do not lack in this noble and completely successful poem. And yet, in Housman's poetry as a whole, something is lacking. Despite an apparent clarity such that almost any poem seems ready to deliver its meaning at once, there is always something that is not clear, something not brought into the open, something that is left in doubt. Housman knew very well what he was doing. He could always put himself in the reader's place. You must, he wrote his brother, "consider how, and at what stage, that man of sorrows is to find out what it is all about. You are behind the scenes and know all the data; but he knows only what you tell him." What Housman told the reader is clear. But there is much that he would not, and while he lived could not, tell him. Of the suffering we have no doubt, but something, it seems, has been suppressed that it is essential to know of the particular situation of the human sufferer. There is an emotion here that is unaccounted for. It is apparently united to the secret cause.

> Ay, look: high heaven and earth ail from the prime
> 　foundation;
> All thoughts to rive the heart are here, and all are vain:
> Horror and scorn and hate and fear and indignation—
> Oh why did I awake? When shall I sleep again?

There is much here that is moving; but again the essential is not evident. Sophocles also believed that a man's best fate would be never to be born and that, failing this, it was best for him to perish young. But Sophocles' pessimism does not, as Housman's seems to do, exist in a void.

The passion of the lad on the scaffold is made appallingly present to us; but for what crime he is being punished is not, in any of the poems in which he occurs, made clear. What had he done, that other lad who lay dead, never to rise, never to stir forth free. . . . Or those lads so in love with the grave, why are they so attracted to that unfeeling solitude? It is not enough to blame the primal fault. Death has its attraction, and it is possible for a poet to put it in a moral framework so that we know, not only how strong it is, but its motivation. Yeats has done it, not once, but many times. But in Housman we move so rapidly from the personal situation to an impersonal despair that we cannot but feel that something has been left out. What has been left out is his personal plight, which did not find a perfect solution in poetry and probably could not, so long as no place could be found for it in any moral scheme of which Housman's mind could approve. The facts are clear; the meaning is not. "Even when poetry has a meaning, as it usually has, it may be inadvisable to draw it out," Housman wrote. "Perfect understanding will sometimes extinguish pleasure."

It is possible that Housman did not want his meaning drawn out; but about that I am not certain. Perfect understanding of his poems depends upon knowledge of his personal plight, for until that is known, the emotion must seem in excess of its object. Now that we know from the posthumous poems what that plight was, all slips into place. The despair is explained; the scholar's abandonment of Propertius for Manilius; the ret-

icence that at last seemed to fix his mouth in a perpetual snarl; the churlish silence which made the poet who had written the poems which above all others in our time have been loved into the least lovely of men. There is point to his philosophy. And we are at last in a position to understand the special pathos of *A Shropshire Lad.*

What Housman did in *A Shropshire Lad* was not to create an object of desire. That he had found, presumably in London, and none can doubt the intensity, the reality, the impossibility of his love. What he did was to make himself into a proper lover, or at least into one of an appropriate age, and to create in a country called Shropshire conditions where that love—without ceasing to be what it was—could come into its own. He became young, but with such a youth as he had never known. The hands which for almost twenty years had scarcely left their Greek and Latin texts, were put to the plow. He was a young yeoman, complete with an ancestry, which Housman made up, perhaps without knowing it, since he seems presently to have persuaded himself that it was his own. The heart of the youth was his, the temper was his own, and, what is most remarkable, the voice he found for him had the vibration of very youth.

The country of *A Shropshire Lad* is so created that it is with surprise that we learn, not only that Housman was not native to Shropshire, but that he had seldom been there. But once we begin to think about it, we see, not only that no such countryside exists in England, but that there could have been none like it in the last century. It is a country that belongs to the dead. What was important to Housman about Shropshire was that it lay on the western horizon of the Worcestershire in which his own boyhood was passed. The West has long been in popular imagination where the dead dwell, and, at the very time that Housman was writing, English soldiers did not die—they went West. (pp. 140-43)

It is underworld. And to Housman, with his mind on the classical poets, it is probable that the West is identified, not only with their underworld of the nerveless dead, but also with a classical world, long dead, in which loves such as his would not have found all the laws of God and man against them. . . . Just as in *A la Recherche du Temps Perdu,* Proust's narrator has never such conviction of completely possessing Albertine as when he sits motionless by her side and looks at her lost in sleep, so, in Housman's poetry, there is no complete consummation of desire until the lad he loves lies dead. The body that lust demanded must be all bone and contemplation before he is finished with fear and condemnation. Even then, Housman cannot delude himself into believing that any love, least of all a love like his, can long survive on the contemplative satisfactions of the grave. (pp. 143-44)

To Housman, all loves are frustrate or faithless. The best a girl can do is to listen to a boy's lies and follow him into the leafy wood; the best the boy can do there is not work her ill. The conception is, of course, prejudiced. Still, what Housman sets down is not so far from the actual conditions under which love is made in youth. The youth Housman reverted to was an imaginary one, his charm is factitious, and yet because he is so often true to the imagination, he seems to speak, not merely for himself, but for all who are, or have ever been, young. What we should know from our own responses to Housman's poetry, if we have not already learned it more explicitly from Proust's prose, is that such desire as his, while it differs from others in its object, is most painfully distinguished from them by the brevity of time in which it is possible, even as unrequited desire. The youth's garland is always briefer than a girl's. And it is this constant present and inescapable pressure of time that constitutes the special poignancy of Housman's poetry.

But if his personal plight is responsible for much of the poignancy of the emotions that went to the making of Housman's poetry, it also placed serious limitations on his emotions. And what nature had not limited, Housman himself thwarted. He is the poet of the end of an age in England, and he is the best poet that could be produced at the end, as he is probably, in England, the purest poet of the whole age. His range is small. We have only to look largely at poetry to see that there is an honesty, a humanity, that simply is not in Housman, any more than it was in the world that made him. What was left in that world was enough for him to perceive how impossible is the achievement of all desire, how vain the search for honor and happiness, and yet what pathos, what beauty, what grandeur even, man releases in their vain pursuit. (pp. 144-45)

> *John Peale Bishop, "The Poetry of A. E. Housman,"* in Poetry *(© 1940 by the Modern Poetry Association; reprinted by permission of the Editor of* Poetry*), Vol. LVI, No. 3, June, 1940 (and reprinted in* The Collected Essays of John Peale Bishop, *edited by Edmund Wilson, Charles Scribner's Sons, 1948, pp. 138-45).*

MORTON DAUWEN ZABEL   (essay date 1940)

Silence is the initial condition of Housman's poetry, as it was the token of a painful diminution of personality that befell him at the outset of adult life. His verse was set from the beginning, by an almost violent mandate, in a fixed and deliberate mold. It offers no characteristic modern pattern of growth, experiment, and discovery. Only Hardy's shows as undeviating an identity from first to last. His distance from the great poets of tragedy or pessimism—agonized, rebellious, impressionable—is great: not only from Baudelaire, Verlaine, and Villon, for whom he expressed a distaste, or from Heine, whose continuous influence brought so little of the German's critical wit and exhilaration into his lyrics, or from Arnold and Hardy, whom he admired above all his contemporaries, but from Pascal and Leopardi, those two stricken witnesses of the dark abyss and the frightening heavens, whom he "studied with admiration" and whose anguished vision and starlit shudders are sometimes caught in his own finest songs. Beyond any of these brothers in darkness he stifled his agony before the mystery and fatality of life. His lyrics speak from the threshold of silence itself. Had their discipline become as absolute as the one he imposed on his practical emotions, his poems would have receded wholly into the reserve that marked Housman's outward character.

That discipline was as final as any poet, short of the defeat of his gifts, could make it. Housman's first problem as a lyrist was to perfect a form and language exactly expressive of the extreme mandate of will he imposed on his sensibility. He once admitted Heine, Shakespeare's songs, and the Border ballads as his models but was "surprised" at the imputation of Latin and Greek influences. But these cannot be slighted. Housman's whole temper, recognizing its suspension between an active poetic impulse and a willed surrender of it, between an instinctive fervor for life and a tragic denial of its value, sharpens toward irony, seeks resolution in the ambiguity of epigram, and tends to express the ingrowth of its forces and the tension of its faculties in a salient virtue of the Latin lyric style—its

integrity of structure, its verbal and tonal unity, its delicate stasis of form. What it gave him—as did the Elizabethans, among whom he once called Jonson his master—were the interlocking balances and inversions of phrase, the distributed reference in nouns and pronouns, the hovering ambiguity of particles, the reflexive dependence of verbs and subjects that give his stanzas their tightness and pith. Had he coerced a purely modern and explicit English into these structures he would have produced a language continuously—instead of intermittently—stilted. But here one of his strongest sympathies came to his rescue—his love of folk speech. The aphoristic tang and irony of peasant idiom, grafted to the sophistication of the Horatian style, relaxed his temper, freed it from formulated stiffness and cliché, and gave Housman his true and single medium as a poet—a verse style marked by a subtle irony of tragic suggestion, a tensile integrity of phrasing, a sense of haunting human appeals playing against the grim inexorability of law. In that medium, rising above the inertness of a formula and the desperate repression of his impulses, he wrote his finest poems.

These, now that his work stands complete, no longer appear in some of his most quoted lyrics, those that cast his thought into the inflexibly didactic form that is always the bane of a negative temperament. The lesser Housman, the one most vulnerable to parody, imitation, and personal attack, is seen wherever his lyric style hardens into such inflexibility and his pessimism into the hortatory despair that becomes by inversion sentimental. Originally, it appears, Housman had an extremely uncertain taste in words and meters. He was fond of the sing-song lilt or chant used in rather tawdry and superficial poems like **"Atys," "The Land of Biscay,"** and **"Far known to sea and shore."** Of **"Atys"** ("Lydians, lords of Hermus river, Sifters of the golden loam") he once said that he was so fond of the rhythm that he always doubted the merit of any poem in which he succumbed to its attraction. He came to guard himself from that music as he guarded his emotional impulses from the appeals of common life and friendship. At both ends of his narrow lyric range, as at both ends of his emotional character, he exercised a ruthless vigilance: here from the spontaneity of feelings that had to be canceled, there from the violence of a censorship so strong that it could end not merely in silence but in emotional paralysis and the logic of suicide. Recoiling from instinctive music or feeling, he produced poems of an opposite extreme: of a deadly and inverted romanticism, of a pessimism so imperative and bare of realistic qualities that they produce a repellent travesty of his talent. Here the Latinized concentration bristles with guards to emotion, and starkness of vision becomes as cloying as the lines in which he rings changes on the ale, the lads, the night, the noose, and the gallows to the point of comic surfeit. It appears at its worst in **"Think no more, lad," "The Welsh Marches," "Say, lad, have you things to do," "Others, I am not the first," "The laws of God," "Yonder see the morning blink," "The Immortal Part,"** and **"The Culprit."** The authentic part of his talent demanded escape from confines as laming as these, and it is only when he gives some voice to the instinctive delight of his senses, to memories of lost youth, or to responses to nature, that he arrives at the finer sincerity of **"With rue my heart," "On Wenlock Edge," "Far in a western brookland,"** and **"The Merry Guide."** He succeeds best of all when the repressed emotion becomes externalized, released from an iron-clad vigilance, adopts a dramatic mask or situation, and so takes on the life and pathos of genuine lyric realism: when, in **"Bredon Hill," "Hughley Steeple," "Is my team ploughing," "To an Athlete," "I to my perils," "In valleys green and** still,'' and "**With seed the sowers scatter,**" he resolves the hostilities of his nature to their finest delicacy and harmony, avoids both the curt asperity and the occasional Aeschylean pomp of which he was capable, and contributes exquisite poems to the English lyric tradition. (pp. 124-26)

[Housman] was complex obviously and an eccentric certainly, a personality of laming deficiencies and self-persecuting logic; a lyric artist of the most limited order. He lends himself almost naively to J. Bronowski's attack (in *The Poet's Defence*) [see excerpt above] as a victim of inverted sentiment from whose "welter of standards" little emerges but a cancelation of feelings almost antiphonal in regularity and as a self-belittler who took evasive refuge in negations of life, of emotion, of the nature and meaning of poetry itself. Housman's admirers have done him the disservice of blind adulation; his detractors, with the added cooperation of his own perverseness and inconsistency of temperament, will go to inevitable extremes. There are even severer measures of his stature. The cry of despair has sounded in modern poetry, as in ancient, with an anguish but also with an illumination that Housman seldom or never attains. (p. 127)

Yet as we now see Housman in his full stature, as the obscurity of his temperament begins to wane, so also the exacerbation of his emotion and his evasion of responsible feeling begin to take on the alleviation of what at its best becomes a subtle and ennobling lyric dignity, a mastery of selfhood and of style that surmounts the imposed denials of his life and the implacable tragedy he saw there but, having seen and faced it, refused to disguise from himself. What that tragedy was is too much a part of the complex of his nature and his poems to bear crude expression, but this much he makes unmistakable: it was his realization that he was destined to live a life deprived of human love. . . . Whatever irresolution exists in his book is a reflection of the contradiction imposed on his faculties by nature itself; the pervading frustration resulted from an intelligence that permitted no blinkers before the fact. But concealed in Housman's nature, masked by his forbidding exterior and his scholarly isolation, existed the true stuff of the poet, once free and impulsive but surviving even its later curtailment, and he was strong enough to make of that conflict the strength and charm of his poems. The science and realism that permit us to see the errors or defects of men also impose the responsibility of understanding them. Outside his poems Housman made that understanding difficult enough, and even inside his verse the slightest comparison with Baudelaire and Hopkins, Yeats and Rilke, immediately gives the measure of his lower station. Yet if he ate of the shadow so long that he became something of the shadow of a man, he at least refused to lapse into sullen silence over the whole wretched business of existence. His endurance was the sign of his character, and the lyrics he wrested from grief and discipline are the mark of his true, if minor, genius. He is one of the most complete instances in literature of the man determined to live by will alone, and his lyrics too often reveal what the discipline of will does to a poet. Yet the discipline was real, and its reward came when his suppressed forces broke from him in the form of an exact and exquisite art. It saved him from languor and annihilation, and in the complete book of his songs, standing between the perils of sense and insistence of death, are the lyrics that hold their permanent beauty. (pp. 128-29)

> *Morton Dauwen Zabel, "The Whole of Housman"*
> *in* The Nation *(copyright 1940* The Nation *magazine,*
> *The Nation Associates, Inc.), Vol. 150, No. 22, June*
> *1, 1940 (and reprinted in* A. E. Housman: A Col-

lection of Critical Essays, *edited by Christopher Ricks,*
Prentice-Hall, Inc., 1968, pp. 123-29).

T.S.K. SCOTT-CRAIG   (essay date 1944)

[Scott-Craig's straightforward, pious reading of the poem "1887" is contested by Cleanth Brooks (see excerpt below)].

What is the religious tone of "**1887**"? Sentimental religious poems are as easy to recognize as commercial Christmas cards; but this poem has breadth and strength. Genuine religious poetry is somewhat more difficult to interpret, since it tends to have an element of high paradox in both content and style; for, when the creature speaks to or of the Uncreated, he must contradict himself; but such, surely, is not the opening note of a volume that plans to leave us tasting the poison of Mithridates. Our task is to interpret a poem which uses the language of religious paradox to describe the antinomy of Man and Nature, and which, somewhat incongruously, employs images and rhythms whose harmonies are grandiose and sonorous. In other words: in what sense are we to take it that God saves the Queen?

Some critics claim to see in "**1887**" the affirmation of the religious paradox, the antinomy of God and Man, Saviour and Sinner. In this view, the dead men in the poem solemnly "shared the work with God" and are one with the suffering Christ whom of old the bystanders taunted to save Himself; and the living, if they continue faithful, may be of good courage, may take to themselves (like the Shepherds) the comfortable words of the angel: Fear ye not. Such an interpretation could be rejected as pious message-hunting were it not the obvious correlative of the universal imagery and resilient rhythm of the poem. Clee is so near to Heaven, almost as near as Francis Thompson's Charing Cross; answering beacons illumine the ample quietude of the night and touch the skies; the stately dawn comes up over Asia and silently bathes the restingplace of those whose strife is over. The beat of the poem is sonorous and regular; its ringing tones are those of the church-bells on occasions of solemn rejoicing. A pious reading of "**1887**" is, indeed, almost inevitable if we allow our sensuous responses to the poem to control the clear intention of the other meanings.

In order to clarify those other meanings, suppose we conjure up a situation where the religious paradox usual in the words "God" and "save" will be more apparent: a sermon to the lads of Clee, by the very Catholic rector of the parish, on the occasion of the Jubilee Eucharist. The priest reminds these Shropshire lads that the candles on the altar are burning from Clee to Heaven; however dark the World may be, there is Light in the Church. Their time as acolytes and choristers is brief; indeed, their whole life in the Church Militant is brief, and may be suddenly shortened if they have taken the Queen's shilling; yet they must never forget that always they are one with the lads of the Church suffering in Purgatory and the lads of the Church Triumphant in Heaven. He recalls that when all mankind could not save themselves, God took humanity upon Him and as the God-man saved them; that He returns in each Mass to re-present Himself to the Father as the one, true, pure, immortal sacrifice; that He returns not only on the altars of Clee by the Severn, but wherever it dawns in Asia, and on the native as well as the imperial altars of the Nile. He exhorts them to pledge their sacramental loyalty to the Saviour returning in the Mass, and to sing the National Anthem in prayer to the Almighty, that He may be pleased in His inscrutable wisdom to grant salvation to the Queen, continuing to Her Majesty long life and prosperity, and finally bringing her to the beatific vision of Himself: God save the Queen!

With this picture in mind we can see perhaps more clearly the role of the poet, and of the words "God" and "save," in **"1887."** In the middle of some Jubilee ceremonies, the poet intervenes (somewhat in the manner of Shaw's sententious anchorite) to address a sort of sermon to the assembly, pitching the tone as religiously as he honestly can. But there is no Heaven for him to appeal to, just heaven or the right-knitting skies. There are no dim, religious altar lights, but flaring beacons in the open air to dispel the physical darkness and announce the start of a human and social ritual. The dead are gone and in danger of being forgotten, those dead who at first seem to share the work of salvation with God but who very soon are themselves called the real saviours; in distant battle they saved their country but could not save their own lives, and the pitiless dawn of Asia shows up their barren tombstones; they cannot even now be said to keep a sacred vigil in the shades, for "the flame they watch not." Everything devolves upon the living; it is they who must create social solidarity by busily lighting beacons and making pledges; they must take what courage they can from poetry and song; they must act as well as they have in the past; above all they must beget their kind—they must get the sons their fathers got that *they* (rather than God) may save the Queen.

The relentless humanism beneath the God-save-the-Queen piety of the poem is doubtless partly concealed from view by the too magnificent harmonies; **"1887"** does not have the stark perfection of Hardy's "Darkling Thrush," that miracle of congruous thought and expression. But the all too common misunderstanding of the poem throws into bold relief not so much certain inadequacies in Housman's statement as the widespread refusal to let texts mean first of all what they say to the mind.

> *T.S.K. Scott-Craig, in his essay in* The Explicator, Special Issue: A. E. Housman *(copyright 1944 by Helen Dwight Reid Foundation; reprinted by permission of Heldref Publications), Vol. II, No. 5, March, 1944, No. 34.*

CLEANTH BROOKS (essay date 1944)

[*Brooks replies to T.S.K. Scott-Craig (see excerpt above) regarding the degree of irony contained in the poem "1887." For a similar discussion of this poem see Richard Wilbur's essay excerpted below.*]

I am surprised to read Mr. Scott-Craig's statement that "a pious reading of **'1887'** is . . . almost inevitable if we allow our sensuous responses to control the clear intention of the other meanings" [see excerpt above]. My personal experience with the poem would indicate that the ordinary reader is much more likely to err by reading the poem as a too bitter and too heavily ironic attack on the conventional pieties of the Jubilee occasion. If there is any danger of a pious misreading, then Mr. Scott-Craig's analysis constitutes a proper makeweight; and, in any case, it provides a useful starting point for a discussion of the poem.

I use the term "starting point" advisedly, for I believe that Mr. Scott-Craig's analysis is not complete: it hardly does justice to Housman's strategy, or to the complexity of the irony which that strategy involves. A complete account of the poem would not, I believe, finally contradict Mr. Scott-Craig's attribution to Housman of what he calls a "relentless human-

ism," but it would qualify the term "relentless." It would certainly indicate more carefully the dramatic development of the theme, the elements of parody, and the special process employed in order to lead up to a revelation of the speaker's "real" attitude. In doing these things, it might succeed in indicating why this poem is so much richer than other poems of Housman's in which Housman's "relentless humanism" is more nakedly and directly set forth.

> *Cleanth Brooks, in his essay in* The Explicator, Special Issue: A. E. Housman *(copyright 1944 by Helen Dwight Reid Foundation; reprinted by permission of Heldref Publications), Vol. II, No. 5, March, 1944, No. 34.*

NESCA A. ROBB (essay date 1948)

[*In her essay on Housman, Robb traces the themes, characters, situations, and other features which make* A Shropshire Lad *an "ordered sequence" of poems and a unified work of literature.*]

A Shropshire Lad is an ordered sequence. One might almost go farther and call it a poem, for the more one studies it the more intimately do its component parts appear to be related to one another. They are arranged with extreme deliberateness, so that not only does one theme follow another in logical sequence, but the themes prophecy, recall and intertwine with each other so that, as one grows familiar with the whole, one comes to feel the closest organic connection between the individual poems. The feelings expressed in *The Immortal Part* **(No. XLIII)** add a new content to the phrase "the lover of the grave" in **No. XVI.** The exile's dream of the "high snowdrifts" on the hawthorns of his native shire recalls inevitably "the cherry hung with snow" and makes one feel more strongly what a capacity for pain is already implicit and stirring in the poet's delight. The casual love-making of **"Oh, see how thick the gold cup flowers"** emphasises the gulf of human experience that lies between its light-hearted falsehood and the tortured sincerity of **"If truth in hearts that perish."** They are correlated moments of a single spiritual process, which is accomplished in the individual soul as well as being worked out on the larger stage of the world. The book has unity as the cycle of man's awakening from the illusions of youth, his passing through the agony of loss, failure and disillusionment, and his emergence from that agony with such strength and wisdom as he can muster; and this unity is made concrete in the person of the imaginary Shropshire Lad, Terence. By a process analogous to that by which the athlete in **No. XIX** is transformed from an individual country boy into an image of the universal tragedy of early death, the slight rustic accent that marks many of the poems passes, by an almost imperceptible transition, into the delicately restrained and classical utterance of others, so that two worlds, the individual and the universal, are kept continuously but unobtrusively before us. (pp. 12-13)

If the history of Terence and his friends was intended to be no more than an outpouring of sentiment, a *cri du coeur* exquisite but with no implications beyond itself, one doubts if the author would have claimed for it the kind of universality he does. . . . [If] the sorrow is not individual but general and typical, so the figures of the sufferers—the soldier, the criminal, the lover, the exile—seem to gather about them hints of a larger significance and to embody truths more various than would appear on the surface. (p. 16)

It is useless to speculate on how far, if at all, directly autobiographical elements may be traced in the poems, and where and how the distinctive images of the Shropshire yeomen first came to haunt the poet's thought, until that "continuous excitement" in 1895 gave them a perdurable form. Yet it is easy to imagine something of their possible history. The prominence given to the soldier for instance, seems natural to a youth growing up during the latter part of last century, who would probably absorb ideas of the glamour and nobility of the military life that find less welcome to-day. No doubt too, those very ideas, would attract many of those whom such a youth would most admire; and their way to death or short-lived fame might easily become for him symbolic of the highest human life. So the strange preoccupation with hanging may well date from some personal association, if only from a local tale of horrors that tormented a child's imagination long before the dark figure of the condemned felon took on the significance it held for the man. Whatever their origins, such figures grow with their creator. They may have at the beginning little more than their face value, and come in the end to hold for the writer as for the reader, fold upon fold of implicated suggestions, as the correspondence between outward and inward, image and reality, becomes closer and more vital, enriched by the phases of spiritual growth. So the figures of soldier and felon may appear as types of the accepted and rejected of life, diverse forms of the human tragedy, struggling powers of the soul, and what is true of them on the simplest interpretation is equally true on the most complex. Shropshire is no "minor county"; it is a microcosm of infinite potentialities.

It is to a world of youth that the first poem introduces us. "'Tis fifty years to-night that God has saved the Queen" and Shropshire is celebrating the Jubilee of 1887. To the poet, as he watches the beacons leaping on the hills, and cheers and drinks with his fellows, the festivities are a celebration of present friendship and of the valour and delight of young manhood. Even regret for the soldier friends who will not return holds a note of exaltation. These "friends of ours who shared the work with God" have died well, and the thought of them, though sorrowful, is illumined by gratitude for the honour they have brought to their native soil, and by hope for the future in the recurrence of the great qualities of the race. . . . Directly after this assurance comes *Loveliest of trees* which sets the transience of the individual against the relative permanence of his kind, much as each year's bloom might contrast its own frail beauty with the continued existence and fertility of the tree. There is a freshness of morning and spring in these quiet lines where melancholy and delight interpenetrate like the lights and clouds of an April sky. They depict the moment when youth, emerging from the strange timelessness of childhood, first grows aware of the lapse of hours, and instinctively reaches out to clasp life's joys more closely and to live the hurrying moments with a new and trembling intensity. The two poems that follow repeat the exhortation in varying forms. In *The Recruit* the young man is called to seek the military glory that has dignified his fellows; in *Reveillé,* though the military idiom is preserved, the summons comes from life itself, bidding man cast off sloth and taste all the experience he may while the day lasts. The two poems, taken together, confirm what has already been suggested as to the real significance of Housman's idealisation of the soldier. (pp. 17-19)

After *Reveillé* with its call to the full experience of life a new theme is introduced; the love of man and maid. It is first treated humorously in the dialogue between the indiscreet wooer and the prudent young woman who so neatly disposes of him; and then takes a darker colour in the contrasting picture of the girl whose weakness has earned her only "the wan look, the hollow

tone" that formerly marked the unrequited lover. Neither poem is distinguished by any very personal note. They seem rather, if one may so express it, to be reflections on two items of parish news. They have this in common with the other introductory poems that they suggest the spectator rather than the actor. The poet is looking from the outside upon experiences which he, or those dearest to him, are to pass through in their turn. He has felt the joy of friendship, but not yet its pain. He has seen change and death, but they have not struck him nearly. He has not known exile, but his thoughts have flown to where the Severn's dead lie buried on the banks of the Nile. He is aware of love and grief, remorse and sin, but they have not yet been sovereign in his soul. He gazes, a little troubled, at all these things, but they are still half hidden in the morning mist.

So, as if suggested by the lover's ills, and prophetic of the darkness to be, the note of mortality sounds again. Death breaks in upon the country sweetness, forces itself upon the young man in his health and vigour, and insinuates into the unscathed heart a more troubling sense of life's uncertainty and of the vanity of man's endeavour. The blackbird pipes from the coppice and its voice is that of a death-ridden world. . . . Once heard that refrain cannot be silenced. The listener may kill the bird, but the song passes into his own consciousness and "the heart within him" repeats that to which he would deliberately close his ears.

Then, while his thoughts are thus preoccupied with the shortness of life, the real drama opens. Suddenly death stands before him in a new and terrible form. Grim as any ballad of fratricide the story of Maurice's murder is told in twenty-four short lines that, for all their brevity, suggest the many-sided horror of the tragedy; death and desolation and ruin, and the breaking up of friendship and home, and all the charities of work and fellowship. . . . Retribution follows; and once more we look on death, but this time it comes in a guise whose dreadfulness haunts the poet ever after like a nightmare. Death at the hands of the law, deliberate, punctual, remorseless, shaming and defiling sufferer and spectator alike, and—cries the young man agonising over his friend—somehow fundamentally unjust. In the huge, irresponsive universe, made, he suspects in his dark hours by some superhuman "brute and blackguard," man is cast adrift without chart or compass, laden with unruly passions that he never implanted in himself, but subject, if they break loose, to harsh laws not of his devising. It is chance weakness rather than special depravity that makes the criminal. (pp. 19-21)

The poem *On an athlete dying young* has been criticised by Professor Garrod for the clumsiness of its opening lines. Clumsy they are, no doubt, but it may be that their clumsiness is deliberate and not a mere failure of taste or technique. The language of the opening stanzas has a suggestion of rustic speech that vanishes completely as the poem mounts to its climax. The image before one's eyes at the beginning is that of a country lad, carried shoulder-high through the streets of an English market town. At the end it is that of an Olympic victor, borne garlanded to his pyre. The change of diction corresponds with the passing from local, individual life with its limitations, small triumphs, petty defeats, into the august universality of death. In dying the athlete becomes a personification of youth going down to the shades with promise unfulfilled, but with hope untarnished. He is a timeless figure, crowned with the mingled glamour and pathos of early death. . . . Enviable that fate, thinks the survivor, as he loiters by the waterside, and, like the companions of Maeldune at the under-sea isle, longs to plunge in and lose himself in the crystal mirage at his feet, while from the same depths there gazes up at him "a silly lad that longs and looks and wishes he were I"—the self that clings to life even while it suffers. The protagonists of a long struggle have met in the divided heart; the hunger for death and the tenacious principle of life that reasserts itself after every disaster, and that, as it feels one support knocked away, still grasps with bleeding hands at another. In *Bredon Hill* the scale dips heavily to the side of death. The beloved herself is snatched away, almost in the moment of possession, and the lover cries out to the funeral bell that should have rung his wedding peal "I hear you, I will come." But how true is the vow? Life goes on with its claims and affections, and time brings the swift onset of forgetfulness and the betrayal of the dead by the living. The long anthem of mortality whose individual notes are the brief glory of the cherry tree and "the beautiful and death-struck year," the athlete and the maiden, the felon in his shame and the soldier in his magnificent futility, includes nothing so heart-rending as the inconstancy of man's heart. The very passions that most ennoble it and that there seem most enduring are themselves ephemeral. It is a discovery so bitter that it shakes the poet as death itself has not had power to do. In some of the *Last Poems* he returns to this theme of life's ruthless continuance, and accepts the necessity of new ties and some measure of forgetfulness, even while he knows that something is gone from him that can never be quite replaced. . . . With numbers **XXV-XXVII** we find three variations on the same motive. In the first and poorest of the three it is Rose Harland who walks with the survivor, but not the winner, of the pair of rivals who had fought for her the previous summer. In the second it is the youth who, after just the same interval, has found consolation and is haunted by half-guilty forebodings of how he himself will be superseded in the favours of his new love. . . . This leads on to the third poem with its double betrayal and its pathetic undertone of man's inability to imagine the world pursuing its way without him. In a few lines, but with sure dramatic strokes, the climax is built up, and one feels unmistakably through the bald words, the varied emotions of the speakers: incredulity, growing realisation, and the incapacity to stop rubbing salt on a wound, in the questions of the ghost: increasing shame and pain in the reluctant answers of the living. . . . From the picture of treachery in action, we pass to the thought of subtler and deeper treachery within. The borderlands of Wales and Shropshire appear to an eye quickened by suffering as a country so saturated with old woes that the very changes of day and night seem to re-enact them in savage pageantry. The ancient wars of England and Wales become an image of the internecine strife of passions, the fierce incongruities of the soul. The conqueror's lust and the stunned submission of the vanquished, from which were born the mingled races of the border, live on in the spiritual malady of their remote descendant. . . . What the contending forces are is not specified, but some of them may be surmised from other poems. There is the fundamental strife of the insatiable energy that clutches at life and the despair that repudiates life as evil, of the Saxon and the slave, the busy flesh and the sullen bones. There may be something of the remorse towards the dead that has lately been pursuing the writer. But chiefly there is the suggestion of some new shattering of the spirit's integrity, the emergence of passions whether of love or of hate,—or it may be of both,—that fill their victim with horror. Conscience stands among the rebel powers trying to subdue them to the "alien laws of God and man" but they spring up continually with dreadful vigour. The spirit ravens on itself and can find no

place of rest among its own antagonistic and mutually loathing forces which can neither escape from, nor destroy, each other. . . . After [*The Welsh Marches*] it is a little surprising to find the lilting stanzas of *The Lent Lily* interposed between this poem and the next two which are obviously so closely akin to it. Probably the slight thing has been placed here for two reasons. It comes as a brief interlude of refreshment at a moment of painful tension, and, by its echo of *Loveliest of trees* it serves to remind us how far we have travelled since that first self-counselling, grave, yet heavy with delight as the cherry tree with bloom.

Indeed some relief is welcome, for one feels that the writer of the next poem [**No. XXX**] might well, like Oedipus, put out his own eyes. The war goes on, but the insurgent passions have almost conquered. The hard-pressed soul, though it tries to check them and to remember that these things also have an end, is very near the limit of its strength. The words come gaspingly out of the black and bitter isolation of self-loathing. Friends fail, for the sufferer is convinced that others would find him as hateful as he finds himself. Death that has often lurked at his elbow now seems too remote to offer him a hope of peace. . . . It is a terrible poem; and sad though much of the remainder of the book is, it nowhere else touches such a bedrock of despair.

For, as the poet stands watching the storm swirling over Wrekin and Severn, the blackness lifts a little and shows him that he is not alone in his anguish and that after all he struggles in a mirage. The Roman, now "ashes under Uricon" had tasted a like bitterness. He is gone; the Englishman will go; and the woods and cities are no more permanent than the men who inhabit them. Only the wind and "the gale of life" continue unchanged through the ages and link one with another. A sudden kindling of imagination universalises the individual tragedy. The sufferer is not a man but all men. The agony he partakes is old as humanity; in his short, tormented life he is one with all created things. At one flight he has bridged the centuries and taken the Roman by the hand, for he sees in him a common nature and a common pain. So in spite of evil and death, he finds a point of rest in the windy vastness of the universe—a sense of human comradeship so potent that it can embrace even men unseen and unknown. It recalls him to the chief solace that remains to him: the love of living friends. Compassion, and the need to serve and spend himself call him from his isolation. Let him make haste to give such treasure as he has to these others, sentenced like himself, before the night engulfs him again. . . . "But no man may deliver his brother, nor make agreement unto God for him." Even while he pleads he attains the bitter knowledge of love's powerlessness, in any supreme crisis, to succour the beloved. Simplicity of metre and language in the beautiful *If truth in hearts that perish* serve only to emphasise the intensity of pain brought by that realisation. Passionate tenderness, faced with the gulf between its will to serve and its power of serving, makes of that final entreaty *To this lost heart be kind* an agony of self-giving.

We are not told very clearly whether this love was rejected or accepted, but from the fact that the poem is immediately followed by *The New Mistress* we are perhaps intended to believe that it was unfortunate. Yet it is difficult to accept *The New Mistress* as the true sequel. Love of such quality as that which animates *If truth in hearts that perish* would hardly, even in its utmost abandonment, express itself in cheap recriminations and diluted Kipling. The suggestion is a pure conjecture, but it seems not unlikely that **Nos. XXX** and **XXXI** of *More Poems* were originally intended to follow here. They are not on the same artistic plane as *If truth in hearts that perish,* but they are on a similar emotional plane, and their style is in keeping with that of the finer poem, instead of being in almost ludicrous contrast with it, as the style of *The New Mistress* is. Moreover they are true not only to the psychology of devotion but to the ultimate significance that Housman attaches to the love of friends. It may be worth noting that if one were to look upon *The New Mistress* as the true response of the lover to his misfortune, one would naturally expect the later poems of the sequence to be more bitter than the early ones, whereas they are on the whole considerably less so. One finds not cynicism but larger sympathy, and that though it might logically follow on the renunciation in the two poems just mentioned, seems a very unlikely development from the sentiment of *The New Mistress,* which speaks the language of wounded vanity and not of the self-surrender which even in its last renouncement of joy, may be a liberation to the soul that makes it.

The probability of a substitution here is strengthened by the fact that—apart from the difference of sentiment and the strong indications in the posthumous poems that the object of devotion is a man and not a woman—the two pairs of poems (*Shropshire Lad,* XXXIV, XXXV, *More Poems,* XXX, XXXI) convey the same ideas and could equally well fill this place in the sequence. Both suggest the rejection of the lover by the loved one, and, as a prelude to the poems of exile introduce the thought of departure from the native place and of some deeper spiritual upheaval. (pp. 24-30)

In *The Merry Guide* poetic inspiration and natural beauty are joint workers in a single enchantment. Departure from Shropshire means also a cleavage with the world of early experience, and the first of the exile poems makes the parting from the beauty of earth a central factor in the exile's unhappiness. If nature and poetry are so intimately connected in the poet's mind it looks as if in the severing of youthful ties he includes that sense of being exiled from poetry itself which has so often marked a similar turning point in the lives of other poets.

The exchange of Shropshire for London is a passing from a natural life to an artificial and unfriendly one. If poetry means— as we know that for Housman it *did* mean—living from the depths of one's being, surrendering the superficial self to "obscure and latent" forces of intenser life, then Terence's heartsick longing for his "homely comforters" is true not only for every country man at odds with urban surroundings, but for every human being who, in whatever degree, has felt the deeper elements of his nature choking in the grasp of circumstance. It is a common experience for one whose early life, whether happy or unhappy, has been inwardly rich, to feel, as those first ties are broken and the world's concerns claim him more and more, that he is in reality exchanging a profound life for an empty one, and that the world's offer of so-called larger interests is a lie. (p. 33)

The Merry Guide and its sequel [*The Immortal Part*] close the exile cycle. (p. 34)

In *The Immortal Part*—placed so ironically after the spirit's dream of fulfilment—the exuberance of life is contrasted with the hidden revolt of the bones, which lurk in the flesh like imprisoned conspirators awaiting their hour. (p. 35)

[**No. LI**] picks up naturally the theme of the poems of exile. Is not the whole quest for the solution of life's mystery the yearning of the tormented spirit for some home and place of rest?

The gracious *Far in a western brookland* leads back from this universal nostalgia to the wistful remembrance of home and vanished youth; and its still atmosphere of starlit summer darkness and whispering boughs, passes on into the succeeding ballad, that ghostly tale of suicide and faithless love whose ancestors were *Clerk Saunders* and *The Demon Lover.* Then the whole history of early death, and waste and sorrow passes into the melancholy sweetness of *With rue my heart is laden,* and it would seem that the tragedy is over, distilled away in a fading breath of music.

Yet these sorrows can be closed only for the individual. . . . [From] **No. LVI** to **No. LXI** a series of echoes recalls, with a new cadence, the substance of that sumless tale. Here again are the soldier, the lover, the young man early stricken by death, the suicide and the felon, and to each of them the poet turns with the warmth of friendship in his voice and the counsel of brave acceptance on his lips. These closing poems are still sad, for he must still suffer in his brothers' pain, but they are no longer desperate, for something has been won from his own struggle and may be won from theirs—love for all fellow-sufferers, and courage that can face, though it cannot penetrate, the irresponsive dark. . . . To know that we shall share the vastness of night and peace with the beloved who shared our blind wanderings is to have the promise of perfect rest even if we must forgo the hope of perfect happiness. In accepting life with all its painful mystery, the spirit receives a measure of wisdom and even of consolation.

There remain only the two poems in which Terence offers a justification of his verses. His book is neither a pleasant entertainment nor a philosophical treatise. He cannot pretend to solve the dark problems of the universe. He cannot weave for his readers a web of rosy illusions. All he has to offer is the companionship of his sufferings. The knowledge of what others have endured in the past has brought strength to him and so the record of his own struggle may do something to strengthen those who come after him. (pp. 38-40)

In his own fate he sees man's lot in miniature; and from the tenderness of individual friendships he learns a large compassion for others to whom he can never be more than a voice in the darkness. It has generally been taken for granted that his final word to them [in **No. LXII**] is an exhortation to the grim fortitude of unmingled despair. I believe myself that he offered something more subtle. If *A Shropshire Lad* and its sequels are a history of the mind's growth in disillusionment they are equally, though less obviously, a history of the heart's progress in love. (p. 42)

Nesca A. Robb, "A. E. Housman," in her Four in Exile, *Hutchinson & Co. (Publishers) Ltd., 1948, pp. 11-54.*

EDMUND WILSON   (essay date 1948)

[Wilson examines the relationship between Housman's poetry and his classical scholarship. He believes that it was Housman's poetic sensibility that enabled him to "give the [classic poets] back their lines as they had written them" with "a miraculous sureness." Wilson also believes that the same repressive tendencies that limited the range of emotion Housman was able to express in his poetry led him to devote years of his life to a translation of Manilius, whom Housman regarded as "a facile and frivolous poet." For further discussion of the role emotional repression

*plays in Housman's poetry see the essays by Conrad Aiken and
John Peale Bishop excerpted above.*]

[Housman's **Introductory Lecture** delivered in 1892 'Before
the Faculties of Arts and Laws and of Science in University
College, London'] is curious in largely evading the questions
it raises and taking the direction of a piece of special pleading
for the author's own pursuits. Both the sciences and the arts,
says Housman, are ordinarily defended by arguments which
make their interests appear mutually antagonistic. But the arguments on both sides are mistaken. Science is said to be useful;
but what is the use, for example, of a great deal of astronomical
research? And the businessmen who make practical use of the
results of scientific study are usually not scientists at all. (They
do make use of them, nevertheless; and the results of the most
gratuitous researches are always likely to turn out to be useful.)
The Humanities, on the other hand, are supposed to 'transform
and beautify our inner nature by culture.' Yet the proportion
of the human race capable of being benefited by classical studies is certainly very small, and these 'can attain the desired
end without that minute and accurate study of the classical
tongues which affords Latin professors their only excuse for
existing.' Not even the great critics of the classics are genuine
classical scholars: 'When it comes to literary criticism, heap
up in one scale all the literary criticism that the whole nation
of professed scholars ever wrote, and drop into the other the
thin green volume of Matthew Arnold's *Lectures on Translating Homer*, which has long been out of print because the
British public does not care to read it, and the first scale, as
Milton says, will straight fly up and kick the beam.' (We shall
look into the assumptions here in a moment.)

The arts and the sciences alike are only to be defended, says
Housman, on the ground that the desire for knowledge is one
of the normal human appetites, and that men suffer if they do
not have it gratified. . . . If a certain department of knowledge
specially attracts a man, let him study that, and study it because
it attracts him; and let him not fabricate excuses for that which
requires no excuse, but rest assured that the reason why it most
attracts him is that it is best for him.'

This is certainly true in so far as it means that we should follow
the direction of our aptitudes; but it seems to imply that there
is no difference in value between one department of learning
and another or between the different points of view from which
the various kinds of research can be conducted. There is no
conception in Housman's mind, as there would have been in
Whitehead's, for example, of relating the part to the whole,
understanding the organism through the cell. Knowledge seems
to be regarded by Housman as a superior sort of pastime—
'good for man' because it gives him pleasure and at most
because 'it must in the long run be better for a man to see
things as they are than to be ignorant of them; just as there is
less fear of stumbling or of striking against corners in the
daylight than in the dark.' . . . The disillusionment of western
man in regard to his place in the universe, finding 'that he has
been deceived alike as to his origin and his expectations, that
he neither springs of the high lineage he fancied, nor will inherit
the vast estate he looked for,' is described in an eloquent
passage; and the activities of the 'Arts and Laws and Science'
are finally characterized as 'the rivalry of fellow soldiers in
striving which can most victoriously achieve the common end
of all, to set back the frontier of darkness.'

In other words, there is no role for creation in Housman's
scheme of things. Indeed, if one had read only his poetry, one
might be surprised to find that he even believed that it was
possible or of any importance to set back the frontier of darkness. In this poetry, we find only the realization of man's
smallness on his turning globe among the other revolving planets
and of his own basic wrongness to himself, his own inescapable
anguish. No one, it seems, can do anything about this universe
which 'ails from its prime foundation': we can only, like Mithridates, render ourselves immune to its poisons by compelling
ourselves to absorb them in small quantities in order that we
may not succumb to the larger doses reserved for us by our
fellows, or face the world with the hard mask of stoicism,
'manful like the man of stone.' For the rest, 'let us endure an
hour and see injustice done.' And now we learn that for Housman knowledge itself meant at most the discovery of things
that were already there—of those sharp corners which it was
just as well not to bump into, of facts that were as invariable
and as inert as the astronomical phenomena which are always
turning up in his poems and which form the subject of the
poem of Manilius to which he devoted so much of his life. He
does not look to the sciences and arts for the births of new
worlds of thought, of new possibilities for men themselves. It
is characteristic of him that he should speak, in this essay, of
Milton as a greater artist than Shakespeare, of Shakespeare, in
fact, as not 'a great artist'—as if the completeness and richness
of Shakespeare's dramatic imagination, a kind of genius which
Milton, by comparison, seems hardly to possess at all, were
not important enough to be taken into account in estimating
his greatness as an artist—as if those stretches of *Paradise Lost*
where everything is dead but the langauge were not the result
of artistic deficiency. Again, the creation of life has no place
in the universe of Housman.

Housman's practice in his own field of scholarship is an astonishing proof of this. The modern English classical scholar
of the type of A. W. Verrall or Gilbert Murray is a critic not
merely of texts but of the classics in their quality as literature
and of literature in its bearing on history. This school on one
of its sides sometimes merges with the anthropology of J. G.
Frazer; and it deals with ancient Greece and Rome in relation
to the life of its own time, restates them in terms of its own
time. The danger, of course, with a Verrall or a Murray is that,
with something of the poet's imagination himself, he may give
way, in the case of Greek drama, for example, to inventing
new plays of his own and trying to foist them on Euripides or
Aeschylus. With Housman we do not run this danger. Housman
is the opposite kind of scholar; he is preoccupied with the
emendation of texts. He could never have been guilty of the
extravagances of a Gilbert Murray or a Verrall, but he was not
capable of their kind of illumination. Note his assumption, in
the passage quoted above, that 'the minute and accurate study
of the classical tongues,' with which he himself is exclusively
preoccupied, 'affords Latin professors their only excuse for
existing.' Have those classical scholars who write history, who
write criticism, who make translations—Gibbon and Renan and
Verrall and Murray and Jowett and Mackail (to take in the
whole field of the classics)—no excuse for existing, then? Is
it so certain that, if their literary criticism were put into the
scales with Matthew Arnold on Homer, the scholars would
kick the beam? Or are such persons not scholars at all? In either
case, it is plain that, for Housman, their activities lie outside
the periphery of the sphere which he has chosen for himself.

Not, however, that Housman in this limited sphere has left the
poet of *The Shropshire Lad* behind him. On the contrary, the
peculiar genius which won him a place beside Porson and
Bentley, which established him in his own time as almost
supreme, with, apparently, only Wilamowitz as a rival, was

derived from his ability to combine with the most 'minute and accurate' mastery of language a first-hand knowledge of how poets express themselves. 'The task of editing the classics,' he wrote in his preface to Juvenal, 'is continually attempted by scholars who have neither enough intellect nor enough literature. Unless a false reading chances to be unmetrical or ungrammatical they have no means of knowing that it is false.' And he himself seemed able with a miraculous sureness to give the authors back their lines as they had written them. . . . Several of his readings, I understand, have been confirmed by the subsequent discovery of manuscripts which Housman had never seen.

To this rescue of the Greek and Roman poets from the negligence of the Middle Ages, from the incompetence and insensitivity of the scholars, A. E. Housman brought an unremitting zeal which may almost be described as a passion. It has been said of the theorems of Newton that they cause the pulse to beat faster as one follows them. But the excitement and satisfaction afforded by the classical commentary of Housman must be unique in the history of scholarship. Even the scraping of the rust from an old coin is too tame an image to convey the experience of pursuing one of his arguments to its climax. It is as if, from the ancient author, so long dumb with his language itself, his very identity blurred or obliterated, the modern classicist were striking a new spark of life—as if the poet could only find his tongue at the touch across Time of the poet. So far is Housman the scholar a giver of life—yet it is only as re-creator. He is only, after all, again, discovering things that were already there. His findings do not imply a new vision.

It was a queer destiny, and one that cramped him—if one should not say rather that he had cramped himself. (Not to dispute, however, with Housman, who thought that human beings were all but helpless, the problem of natural fate and free will.)

The great work of A. E. Housman's life in the field of classical scholarship was his edition of the five books of Manilius, the publication of which alone extended from 1903 to 1930. (pp. 60-5)

The elegist of *The Shropshire Lad* . . . deliberately and grimly chose Manilius when his real interest was in Propertius. There is an element of perversity, of self-mortification, in Housman's career all along. . . . And his scholarship, great as it is in its way, is poisoned in revenge by the instincts which it seems to be attempting to destroy, so that it radiates more hatred for his opponents than love for the great literature of antiquity. Housman's papers on classical subjects, which shocked the sense of decorum of his colleagues, are painful to the admirers of his poetry. The bitterness here *is* indecent as in his poetry it never is. (pp. 65-6)

[Yet] some acquaintance with the classical work of Housman greatly increases one's estimate of his stature. One encounters an intellectual pride almost Dantesque or Swiftian. 'You would be welcome to praise me,' he writes, 'if you did not praise one another'; and 'the reader whose good opinion I desire and have done my utmost to secure is the next Bentley or Scaliger who may chance to occupy himself with Manilius.' His arrogance is perhaps never more ferocious than when he is judging himself severely: when a friend who had ventured to suggest the publication of a paper on Swinburne which Housman had read before a college literary society had been told by Housman that he was leaving directions to have it destroyed after his death and had retorted that if the writer really thought it so

bad, he would already himself have destroyed it, Housman replied: 'I do not think it bad: I think it not good enough for me.' And he put on the title page of his edition of Juvenal, *editorum in usum edidit,* to indicate that this feat of erudition—according to his own announcement, unprecedented—was merely intended as a hint to future scholars who might tackle the subject as to how they might accomplish their task in a thoroughgoing fashion.

Is this the spectacle of a great mind crippled? Certainly it is the spectacle of a mind of remarkable penetration and vigor, of uncommon sensibility and intensity, condemning itself to duties which prevent it from rising to its full height. Perhaps it is the case of a man of genius who has never been allowed to come to growth. Housman's anger is tragic like Swift's. He is perhaps more pitiable than Swift, because he has been compelled to suppress himself more completely. Even when Swift had been exiled to Ireland, he was able to take out his fury in crusading against the English. But A. E. Housman, giving up Greek in order to specialize in Latin because he 'could not attain to excellence in both,' giving up Propertius, who wrote about love, for Manilius, who did not even deal with human beings, turning away from the lives of the Romans to rivet his attention to the difficulties of their texts, can only flatten out small German professors with weapons which would have found fit employment in the hands of a great reformer or a great satirist. He is the hero of *The Grammarian's Funeral*—the man of learning who makes himself impressive through the magnitude, not the importance, of his achievement. After all, there was no need for another Bentley.

It is only in the Latin verses—said to have been called by Murray the best since the ancient world—which Housman prefixed to his Manilius, in his few translations from Latin and Greek, and in his occasional literary essays, that the voice of the Shropshire Lad comes through—that voice which, once sped on its way, so quickly pierced to the hearts and the minds of the whole English-speaking world and which went on vibrating for decades, disburdening hearts with its music that made loss and death and disgrace seem so beautiful, while poor Housman, burdened sorely forever, sat grinding and snarling at his texts. Would he have called back that voice if he could, as he recalled, or tried to recall, so much else? There are moments when his ill humor and his pedantry, his humility which is a perverse kind of pride, almost make us think that he would. (pp. 68-9)

Edmund Wilson, "A. E. Housman," in his The Triple Thinkers: Twelve Essays on Literary Subjects *(reprinted by permission of Farrar, Straus and Giroux, Inc.; copyright 1938, 1948 by Edmund Wilson; copyright renewed © 1956, 1971 by Edmund Wilson, and 1976 by Elena Wilson, Executrix of the Estate of Edmund Wilson), revised edition, Oxford University Press, New York, 1948 (and reprinted by Noonday, 1976), pp. 60-71.*

NORMAN MARLOW   (essay date 1958)

[*Marlow's* A. E. Housman: Scholar and Poet *contains chapters on the poet's literary influences, stylistic features of his work, and, excerpted below, a biographical reading of the poems.*]

We must begin with a statement of Housman's own in a letter to a French student. 'The Shropshire Lad is an imaginary figure, with something of my temperament and view of life. Very little in the book is biographical.' This is borne out by further remarks in the same letter: 'I have never had any such thing as a "crisis of pessimism". In the first place, I am not a pessimist but a "pejorist" (as George Eliot said she was not an optimist but a meliorist); and that is owing to my observation of the world, not to personal circumstances. Secondly, I did not begin to write poetry in earnest until the really emotional part of my life was over; and my poetry, as far as I could make out, sprang chiefly from physical conditions, such as a relaxed sore throat during my most prolific period, the first five months of 1895. He says much the same thing in the introductory poem of *More Poems:*

> They say my verse is sad: no wonder;
>   Its narrow measure spans
> Tears of eternity, and sorrow,
>   Not mine, but man's.

Yet in the very next verse he goes on to imply that part at least of the world's sorrow he had made his own, and in the last poems of [*A Shropshire Lad*] he shows that it is from his own bitterness that he has learned to write what may comfort others. . . . (p. 150)

What then, is autobiographical? To begin with, the preoccupation with death, which had come upon him when his mother died on his twelfth birthday and never left him. We have early evidence of this preoccupation in the poems he wrote at school, in the Dürer woodcuts which were the only pictures to adorn his rooms in Oxford, in such poems as *Alta Quies* which he wrote as an undergraduate but which in its maturity has misled many into thinking it was one of his last. . . .

It is not without significance that Housman's father died in the winter before the 'prolific period of 1895', and the death of his younger brother in the Boer War produced two profoundly moving poems, [*Last Poems* iv and xvii]. Against this dark incoming tide of death Housman saw himself as pathetically striving to erect his sand-castle of scholarship. . . . (p. 151)

Housman professed to be a Cyrenaic: that is, an egoistic hedonist, for whom the pleasure of the moment is the only possible motive of action; but his inherited seriousness of outlook, the urge to redeem the time, to make a name, to work while it is day, these are the mark of the Stoic and the Christian. One can sense in Housman, as in Huxley, Romanes and other agnostics of the late nineteenth century, the underlying bewilderment and anguish of a soul naturally Christian which finds itself 'in the position of one who has been reared from his cradle as the child of a noble race and the heir to great possessions, and who finds at his coming of age that he has been deceived alike as to his origin and his expectations; that he neither springs of the high lineage he fancied, nor will inherit the vast estate he looked for, but must put off his towering pride and contract his boundless hopes, and begin the world anew from a lower level.' To call Housman a Christian, as some have done, is of course nonsense, but the bitterness at death and oblivion are more natural to one whose anger is because Christianity ought to be true and who can no longer believe in it than to a Cyrenaic in pursuit of the pleasure of the moment. (p. 152)

The love of landscape and of Worcestershire is as certainly biographical as anything in his poetry. 'Nature', he once said, 'intended me for a geographer', and certainly his sense of place was very strong. (p. 153)

Presumably the early craving for

> The happy highways where I went
> And cannot come again

a craving repeatedly expressed in one way or another in *A Shropshire Lad,* never died in his heart. The fact that on holidays he went not to Shropshire but to Paris strengthens the probability that this was so, for like Heraclitus Housman knew that one cannot enter the same river twice. This is the most truly personal note in all his poetry, so that for the last half-century the Shropshire hills have been invested with more potent magic because of their association with a genuine and poignant experience.

It is characteristic of the hedonist that he cannot keep the bitter tang from the cup he drinks, for the time is short. This sense of urgency is everywhere in *A Shropshire Lad.* . . . (p. 154)

Even in the London **Introductory Lecture** there is the same insistence on living now rather than tomorrow. 'Live while you live, the epicure would say,' wrote Dr. Doddridge, and we find Housman inveighing against those who spend their lives in amassing worldly goods or on putting something aside for a rainy day. . . .

There is of course another meaning to the poems urging the shortness of life. It was not merely or even mainly that Housman wished to see the cherry hung with snow: there was the building of the monument of scholarship. 'I see no hope', he wrote in 1888, 'of completing a presentable commentary on Propertius within the next ten years.' (p. 155)

Coming across T. E. Lawrence's self-portrait in *Seven Pillars of Wisdom,* Housman wrote against it 'this is me'. There is an instructive similarity between the two in their awareness of tension between opposites, their craving for friendship which ruined all naturalness in their approach to others, in the element of the self-tormentor in their natures which went with an Epicurean sensuousness. In both thinking killed the natural man.

Housman, I believe, was always sensitive to his failure at Oxford and to the apparent failure in his friendship. [A.S.F.] Gow significantly speaks of what friendship had once meant for Housman: 'a whole-hearted devotion which its objects were not always able to repay in kind'. Some have seen in this devotion a sign of sexual perversion. They point to various facts and fancies in support of their view: to the frankness of some of the posthumous poems:

> Because I liked you better
>   Than suits a man to say,
> It irked you, and I promised
>   To throw the thought away.

to Housman's open enjoyment of the works of Corvo and Frank Harris and to the evident satisfaction with which he explains obscene jokes in the Greek and Roman poets, as witness the notorious article *Praefanda* in *Hermes* for 1931; to a supposed and probably legendary collection of pornography which he is alleged to have made at Cambridge; to his occasionally expressed intention of writing an autobiography to be kept at the British Museum under lock and key for fifty years (this project never came to fruition); and to the acute horror and anguish of mind to which some of the poems bear witness. Here, they say, must be some twist or flaw in the character, something which its possessor views with loathing but of which he cannot rid himself.

All this may be true. Housman was always tender to those who had made moral shipwreck of their lives, and [*A Shropshire Lad xliv*] was evoked by the suicide of a young cadet who wrote that he had absolutely ruined his own life and was sure that if he lived another five years he would involve another in his own ruin. There may have been an element of guilt in the friendship between Housman and Jackson at Oxford, though everyone who knew them in London scouted the idea. It is much more likely that the continence of Housman's life was not achieved without terrible struggles and that these struggles left an outward trace in the poems. If Housman felt homosexual tendencies, he repressed them. When he left the Patent Office for University College the letter written to him by one of his colleagues is one of the most moving tributes ever paid by a man to his colleague and contains the words, 'There is, so far as I could ever discover, absolutely no flaw in your character as a man, and no one would ever hope for a better friend.' When Jackson left for India in 1887 Housman was grieved, but they met on occasion throughout Jackson's life and corresponded regularly. It is quite enough to say that Housman deliberately determined from 1881 onwards to make a name in scholarship and that he pursued this aim relentlessly in spite of temptations that a man of coarser fibre would not have felt; and that the poems, born as they were of unaccountable though pleasurable emotional agitation, were physical concomitants of his suppression of one part of his life (it is significant that he always felt poetry to be something physical rather than intellectual). His emotions, expelled by one door, came in by another. (pp. 156-57)

The soldiering is only biographical to the extent that soldiers had always fascinated Housman by their colourful uniforms and by their destiny. They were men paid to die, so that he could not expel them from his imagination and perhaps found relief in his poems, just as he found relief in writing of the criminal's last moments on the scaffold and in picturing the Shropshire hills and rivers which he would not visit in reality. In this again he may have resembled T. E. Lawrence, who once spoke of pain as a great stimulus. The hills of Shropshire could only evoke profound poetry if they were viewed as boyhood's land of lost content. (p. 158)

> *Norman Marlow, in his* A. E. Housman: Scholar and Poet *(© 1958, Norman Marlow; reprinted by permission of Routledge & Kegan Paul Ltd), Routledge & Paul, 1958, 192 p.*

RICHARD WILBUR (essay date 1961)

[*Wilbur's comments on "Epitaph on an Army of Mercenaries" reflect some of the methods indicated by Randall Jarrell's essay (see excerpt above): that to properly understand Housman, one must be alert to the undercurrents of meaning conveyed by the poet's evocative use of language. Wilbur argues that with Housman's verse in particular, tone, rhythm, and allusion must be weighed against the poet's apparently straightforward statements if one is to fully apprehend the meaning of any given poem. For a more recent example of this approach, see John Bligh's analysis of a famous Housman image, excerpted below.*]

One of my favorite poems of A. E. Housman is called **"Epitaph on an Army of Mercenaries,"** and because it is a soluble problem in tact that I want to discuss it here. Let me say it to you a first time in a fairly flat voice, so as to stress by *lack* of stress the necessity, at certain points, of making crucial decisions as to tone:

> These, in the day when heaven was falling,
> The hour when earth's foundations fled,
> Followed their mercenary calling,
> And took their wages and are dead.

> Their shoulders held the sky suspended;
> They stood, and earth's foundations stay;
> What God abandoned, these defended,
> And saved the sum of things for pay.

Perhaps the main decision to be made is how to say those last two words, "for pay." Should they be spoken in a weary drawl? Should they be spoken matter-of-factly? Or should they be spat out defiantly, as if one were saying "Of *course* they did it for pay; what did you expect?" Two or three years ago, I happened to mention Housman's poem to a distinguished author who is usually right about things, and he spoke very ill of it. He found distasteful what he called its easy and sweeping cynicism, and he thought it no better, except in technique, than the more juvenile pessimistic verses of Stephen Crane. For him, the gist of the poem was this: "What a stinking world this is, in which what we call civilization must be preserved by the blood of miserable hirelings." (pp. 21-2)

I couldn't accept that way of taking the poem, even though at the time I was unprepared to argue against it; and so I persisted in saying Housman's lines to myself, in my own way, while walking or driving or waiting for trains. Then one day I came upon an excellent essay by Cleanth Brooks [see excerpt in *TCLC,* Vol. 1], which supported my notion of the poem and expressed its sense and tone far better than I could have done. Mr. Brooks likened Housman's Shropshire lads, so many of whom are soldiers, to those Hemingway heroes who do the brave thing not out of a high idealism but out of stoic courage and a commitment to some personal or professional code. Seen in this manner, Housman's mercenaries—his professional soldiers, that is—are not cynically conceived; rather, their poet is praising them for doing what they had engaged to do, for doing what had to be done, and for doing it without a lot of lofty talk. If we understand the poem so, it is not hard to see what tones and emphases are called for. . . . (p. 22)

But now suppose that the distinguished author who thought the poem wholly cynical should not be satisfied. Suppose he should say, "Mr. Brooks's interpretation is very enhancing, and makes the poem far less cheaply sardonic; but unfortunately Mr. Brooks is being more creative than critical, and the poem is really just what I said it was."

There are a number of arguments I might venture in reply, and one would be this: Housman was a great classical scholar, and would have been particularly well acquainted with the convention of the military epitaph. His title refers us, in fact, to such poems as Simonides wrote in honor of the Spartans who fell at Thermopylae, or the Athenians who fought at the Isthmus. Those poems are celebratory in character, and so is Housman's. The sound and movement of Housman's poem accord, moreover, with the mood of plain solemnity that the convention demands. The tetrameter, which inclines by its nature to skip a bit, . . . is slowed down here to the pace of a dead march. The rhetorical balancing of line against line, and half-line against half-line, the frequency of grammatical stops, and the even placement of strong beats make a deliberate movement inescapable; and this deliberate movement releases the full and powerful sonority that Housman intends. It is not the music of sardony.

The distinguished author might come back at me here, saying something like this: "No doubt you've named the right convention, but what you forget is that there are *mock* versions of every convention, including this one. While Housman's mock use of the military epitaph is not broadly comic but wryly subtle, it does employ the basic trick of high burlesque. Just as Pope, in his mock epic *The Rape of the Lock,* adopts the tone and matter of Milton or Homer only to deflate them, so Housman sets his solemn, sonorous poem to leaking with the word 'mercenary,' and in the last line lets the air out completely. The poem is thus a gesture of total repudiation, a specimen of indiscriminate romantic irony, and it is what we might expect from the poet who counsels us to 'endure an hour and see injustice done,' who refers to God as 'whatever brute and blackguard made the world,' and who disposes of this life by crying, 'Oh, why did I awake? When shall I sleep again?' "

From now on I am going to play to win, and I shall not allow the distinguished author any further rebuttals. The answer to what he said just now is this: while Housman may maintain that "heaven and earth ail from the prime foundation," he consistently honors those who face up manfully to a bad world; and especially he honors the common soldier who, without having any fancy reasons for doing so, draws his mercenary "thirteen pence a day" and fights and dies. . . . The mercenaries of the poem I've been discussing are enlisted from all these other soldier poems [which include **"Lancer"** and **"Grenadier"**], and though their deaths exemplify the world's evil, Housman stresses not that but the shining of their courage in the general darkness.

The poem is not a mock version of the military epitaph; however, the distinguished author was right in feeling that Housman's poem is not so free of irony as, for instance, William Collins's eighteenth-century ode "How sleep the brave . . ." These eight short lines do, in fact, carry a huge freight of irony, most of it implicit in a system of subtle echoes and allusions; but none of the irony is at the expense of the mercenaries, and all of it defends them against slight and detraction.

If one lets the eye travel over Housman's lines, looking for echo or allusion, it is probably line 4 that first arrests the attention. . . .

> And took their wages and are dead.

This puts one in mind of Saint Paul's Epistle to the Romans, Chapter 6, where the Apostle declares that "the wages of sin is death." The implication of this echo is that paid professional soldiers are sinful and unrighteous persons, damned souls who have forfeited the gift of eternal life. That is certainly not Housman's view, even if one makes allowance for ironic exaggeration; and so we are forced to try to imagine a sort of person whose view it might be. The sort of person we are after is, of course, self-righteous, idealistic, and convinced of his moral superiority to those common fellows who fight, not for high and noble reasons, but because fighting is their job. Doubtless you have heard regulars of the American army subjected to just that kind of spiritual snobbery, and one readily finds analogies in other departments of life: think of the way professional politicians are condemned by our higher-minded citizens, while shiny-faced amateurs are prized for their wholesome incapacity. Spiritual snobs are unattractive persons under any circumstances, but they appear to especial disadvantage in Housman's poem. After all, they and their civilization were saved by the mercenaries—or professionals—who did their fighting for them, and that fact makes their scorn seem both ungrateful and hypocritical. (pp. 22-5)

[In] the poem **"1887,"** Housman says this of the soldiers who have helped God save the Queen by dying in battle:

> To skies that knit their heartstrings right,
> To fields that bred them brave,

The saviours come not home to-night:
>   Themselves they could not save.

As Mr. Brooks points out in his essay [in *A Shaping Joy*], those last lines "echo the passage in the Gospels in which Christ, hanging on the cross, is taunted with the words: 'Others he saved; himself he cannot save.' " It appears, then, that in his **"Epitaph on an Army of Mercenaries"** Housman may be bestowing on his soldiers the ultimate commendation; he may be saying that their sacrifice, in its courage and in the scope of its consequences, was Christlike. (pp. 26-7)

I would uphold Housman's poem as a splendid demonstration of the art of referring. The poem requires a literate reader, but given such a reader it is eminently effective. I selected the poem for discussion precisely because, unlike most of Housman, it is capable of misinterpretation; nevertheless, as I have pointed out, a reader *can* arrive at a just sense of its tone and drift without consciously identifying any of its references. It *all but* delivers its whole meaning right away. (pp. 30-1)

Housman's allusions, once one is aware of them, are not decorative but very hard-working. Their chief function is to supplement Housman's explicit praise of the mercenaries with implicit dispraise of their detractors, and so make us certain of the poem's whole attitude toward its subject. To achieve such certainty, however, one need not catch every hint, every echo; any *one* of Housman's references, rightly interpreted, will permit the reader to take confident possession of the poem. I like that. A poem should not be like a Double-Crostic; it should not be the sort of puzzle in which you get nothing until you get it all. Art does not or should not work that way; we are not cheated of a symphony if we fail to react to some passage on the flute, and a good poem should yield itself more than once, offering the reader an early and sure purchase, and deepening repeatedly as he comes to know it better. (pp. 31-2)

> *Richard Wilbur, "Round About a Poem of Housman's" (1961; originally published in* The Moment of Poetry, *edited by D. C. Allen, The Johns Hopkins University Press, 1962), in* Responses: Prose Pieces, 1953-1976 *by Richard Wilbur (copyright © 1962 by Richard Wilbur; reprinted by permission of Harcourt Brace Jovanovich, Inc.), Harcourt Brace Jovanovich, 1976, pp. 16-38.*

CHRISTOPHER RICKS (essay date 1964)

[*In this much-praised essay Ricks further develops the idea, which was also explored by Randall Jarrell (see excerpt above), of a characteristic tension in Housman's poems between the bald pessimism of the poet's overt statements and the complex and contradictory aspects of the poet's manner of expressing them. Ricks also applies his insights into Housman's verse to the poet's famous lecture,* The Name and Nature of Poetry. *Rick's analysis in this section of the essay reveal concurrences between Housman's poetry and the theory of poetry he expressed in his famous lecture.*]

Housman thought that literary critics were even rarer than poets or saints, so he would not have been surprised that we are hard put to say why we like or dislike his poems. His admirers usually offer little more than pious generalities, and his detractors say 'adolescent'—a word used by critics as different as Edmund Wilson, George Orwell, Cyril Connolly, R. P. Blackmur, and Conrad Aiken. . . . [Everyone] seems to take it for granted that Housman's poems unwaveringly endorse the pessimistic beliefs which they assert. To me his poems are remarkable for the ways in which rhythm and style temper or mitigate or criticise what in bald paraphrase the poem would be saying. Rhythm and style never abolish the beliefs, and this for the good reason that the beliefs (the urge to pessimism, the need to strike a strong pose) are not abolishable—we can call them adolescent or childish or puerile or immature only if we also concede that there has never been a man adult enough not to feel some magnetic pull from them, some wish to succumb to them, some uncertainty as to whether they are temptations or aspirations.

Housman has often been compared to a child, and not always by those who dislike his poems. . . . His poems often assert positions that are inadequate in ways suggested by calling them adolescent—inadequate not as utterly alien to our experience, or wilfully thought-up, but in the sense that we ought not to be in one mind about them, and should fear that they might be sirens. There are usually three reactions to this 'adolescence' of attitude. We may say that what a poem asserts, its attitudes or beliefs, has no bearing on its poetic quality. And here we might call up Housman, who seems at times (but only at times) to be saying this in *The Name and Nature of Poetry.* Or we may say that a poem's beliefs are inseparable from its quality, and that his poems suffer because of the childishness of what they say. Such is the opinion of the most articulate of his detractors. Or we may agree that the beliefs of a poem are inseparable from its quality, but argue that the relationship between belief and the final total meaning may be strange and oblique. This is to argue that in the best of Housman's poems, the childishness of what is said is part of the effect, but only part, and is absorbed to produce something fine and true—though often something that is, quite legitimately, in two minds. Clearly this does not apply to many of his most attractive and simple poems; these I rate less highly not because they are simple but because they are not profound.

A straightforward example. In paraphrase, the poem **'I to my perils'** says that if you look on the black side you will never be disappointed. Childish, in the narrow sense that it expresses an attitude commoner in children than in adults. Taking an exam at 16, one said 'I'm sure I've failed'. Childish, too, in the larger sense, that later on one couldn't but see how little use it actually was in the face of troubles—indeed, one had a reluctant sense of that all along. On the other hand, it is also an inextinguishable attitude; I have not met a man so mature as never to glance wistfully towards it as a possible bolt-hole from what is intolerable. There is no reason why a poem shouldn't express the attitude, but, yes, there would be something un-thinkingly shallow about a poem which found this advice adequate to the troubles of life. But if we go from paraphrase (not a rigged one) to the poem itself, we find something different. . . . The poem says a dour glum cramping thing, but how does it say it? With gaiety and wit that are, if you like, utterly inappropriate. Instead of the 'steady' tramp of military fortitude, there is the exquisite interlacing of a dance; instead of granite rhymes, there is a supple effrontery and insouciance that links 'charmer' and 'armour', and in so doing surely opposes something to the simple sturdiness, the indurated hope-lessness, of armour. It says that 'The thoughts of others / Were light and fleeting' while 'Mine were of trouble', but whatever the poem may say (in its natural human wish to find armour for itself, to find steadiness), this cannot be the case. The movement itself is light and fleeting, and not just in the lines about others. Just how much difference the movement makes to what in the end is *said,* can be seen when Edmund Wilson, in his excellent essay (*The Triple Thinkers*) [see excerpt above],

quotes these lines but prints them as prose, as a parenthetical gloss on a pessimistic bit of Housman's prose. Housman in this poem may have tried to be a philosopher, but cheerfulness was breaking in. That the poem is not resting smugly in shallow pessimism is borne out by its emphatic closing words: 'When trouble came'. The Biblical figure who endured all that life could inflict, but who was sustained by something other than a habit of looking on the black side, would have retorted harshly. 'Job curseth the day of his birth' (Ch. 3)—a chapter which ends emphatically: 'I was not in safety, neither had I rest, neither was I quiet; yet trouble came'. If Housman (as Norman Marlow noted) tacitly invokes Job, it is not because he thinks he has found a moral stance which could cope unrepiningly with all that Job suffered, but because he knows he has not. 'An ill-favoured thing, sir, but mine own.' Housman's position may be inadequate, but it would be ignoble only if he thought it was adequate. (pp. 268-71)

Christopher Ricks, "The Nature of Housman's Po-etry," in Essays in Criticism, *Vol. XIV, No. 2, April, 1964, pp. 268-84.*

TOM BURNS HABER   (essay date 1967)

[*Haber's* A. E. Housman, *from which the following section on stylistic features of Housman's poetry is excerpted, is a complete biocritical study and one of the best introductions to the poet and his work.*]

The main characteristics of [Housman's] poetry are its formal simplicity, its emotional thrust, and its pessimistic tone. All three of these are, in varying degrees, present in his numerous ballad-lyrics. A reader looking for the first time through a volume of Housman's poetry cannot help observing the frequency of the ballad stanza of four short lines and alternating rhyme. Many of the other short poems also suggest that the writer was trying for ballad compactness rather than for the expansion of his poetic idea. But the impersonality of the folk singer is poles apart from Housman's attitude and method. Even before the meaning of the poem is apprehended, the reader might surmise the poet's involvement by his frequent use of the first personal pronoun, which occurs, by the way, in the opening line of forty-eight (more than one-fourth) of the pieces in the *Complete Poems.* Housman's mastery of the re-sources of the ballad and his expansion of it go far to make the reader feel the presence of the writer in his story and hear the accents of his lyric cry, which almost invariably sounds a note of sadness and defeat.

But these generalizations must be illustrated and qualified, particularly since they relate to poetry as carefully fashioned as Housman's. Consider his language. It is a richly varied texture woven of many ancient and modern literatures and employed with masterly skill. Echoes of Classical mannerisms, for example, may be seen in his many compounded words: *amber-sanded, rainy-sounding, steeple-shadowed, silver-tufted, many-venomed, death-struck, light-leaved*—a list that could easily be tripled. The chief prompter in verbal coinages of this kind may be Lucretius, whose influence is a vital element throughout Housman's poetry.

Another Classical borrowing is seen in such phrases as these from **"When Israel out of Egypt came"** . . . : *"The realm I look upon and die"* and *"the heaven that I / Perish and have not known."* These lines sound un-idiomatic to the English reader—and they are because they are intentional transfers from Greek syntax. Peculiarities of this nature abound in Housman's famous **"Fragment of a Greek Tragedy,"** first published in *The Bromsgrovian* (June, 1883). (pp. 69-70)

An independent element in the language of Housman's poetry, one from which its tone of simplicity derives, is his large stock of provincial and dialectal words; *shaws, haulms, mayhap, liefer, tun, hap, tedded, sprack* ("brisk"), *hie, amidmost, thorough* ("through"), and *frore* are among the more familiar examples. A much larger group consists of colloquial expressions common to the man of the street and the lane—speechways that contribute most effectively to the realism of the sayings and doings of Housman's characters. This element in his poetic language may, because of his artful use of it, pass without notice, as in real life his Ned Lears and his Rose Harlands may pass unnoticed by us; it is seldom perceived by those who think of **"Loveliest of trees . . ."** as Housman's finest lyric. But his poetry would lose much savor without the salt of expressions of this kind: *guts in the head, and sure enough, as I hear tell, miles around, no heart at all, free for nothing, never fear, man, lay me low, no use to talk to me, luckless aye, no harm in trying, the like on earth, lads for the girls, enough as 'tis, till they drop, long time since, little 'twill matter, for all they try, 'tis truth you say, what's to pay, 'tis little matter. . . .* Even out of context, each of these expressions speaks from the page with something of the still, sad music of humanity—unlettered and unspoiled. (pp. 70-1)

A poet with these resources at his disposal, believing lucidity to be an excellent thing, has it within his power to achieve a style that is succinct, unmystical, and unmistakably clear. This style is the essence of Housman's poetry. . . . Housman has nothing in common . . . with the aims and methods of that segment of modern poetry that consists of abstract musings which the reader is invited to endow with what intelligibility he will or can. Clarity meant to Housman the poet what accuracy meant to Housman the scholar; and one main reason for the scantiness of the selections made by him from his four notebooks can be attributed to the fact that the standard of clarity in some of the lyrics he passed over was not—could not be—satisfactorily met.

Housman declared in his **"Name and Nature of Poetry"** that his test of poetry was the emotional disturbance it produced in him, an effect accompanied by certain physical reactions. These reactions were also present during the composition of his own poetry. Emotion, then, was at the heart of the poetic experience, and his lyrics strike home to the hearts of his readers because of their power to transfuse emotion: we are led to feel his griefs and resentments as if they were our own. The volcanic turmoil within him was the generating process, objectifying in his Shropshire creations his disgust at himself and the blind fate that, in the words of Thomas Hardy, made the human condition "a general drama of pain." (pp. 71-2)

Poetry, even Keats's "ditties of no tone," is for many readers primarily an address to the ear, and critics have found harsh things to say about the aural effects of Housman's serious poetry. It cannot be denied that many of his pieces—and some of his most popular—are burdened with lines that are distressingly heavy. This unhappy effect is sometimes the result of Housman's fondness for alliteration that invariably puts an extra weight on the accented syllables. Perhaps his plodding line, with its strong iambic rhythm, is a carry-over from the ballad stanza. He had an invincible fondness for these formal simplicities, and his notebooks show repeatedly how, after jotting down his alternatives for a line that would not come

out right, he often—but not usually—fair-copied into it an alliterative phrase. (pp. 73-4)

Housman abhorred obscurity, intentional or not, as a mark of incapacity that no literary virtues could atone for. He wanted his poetry to be widely read, indeed; but, above all, he wanted it understood. To write such poetry was not always easy. One of the early drafts of his lecture, **"The Name and Nature of Poetry,"** contains a sentence which ought to be better known than it is, for it is the key to understanding his poetic method: "Not only is it difficult to know the truth about anything, but to tell the truth when one knows it, to find words which will not obscure or pervert it, is in my experience an exhausting effort." It is on this plane, to repeat, that Housman the poet and Housman the scholar come together: their common business is to find the truth and properly relate it. Housman would have concurred with Alexander Eliot's declaration: "The greatest poetry, it seems to me, is always spontaneous and invariably precise. It occurs where the meaning and the music merge; it stands clear as mathematical equations. . . ." (p. 77)

> *Tom Burns Haber, in his* A. E. Housman *(copyright ©1967 by Twayne Publishers, Inc.; reprinted with the permission of Twayne Publishers, a Division of G. K. Hall & Co., Boston), Twayne, 1967, 223 p.*

B. J. LEGGETT (essay date 1970)

[*Here Leggett defends Housman from the charge of such critics as Conrad Aiken and Edith Sitwell (see excerpts above) that the philosophy expressed in his poems is adolescent. Leggett sees Housman's use of the Shropshire lad persona as a device similar to W. B. Yeats's theory of the mask. Picking up the critical theme of duality in Housman, Leggett insists that a fundamental, yet unrecognized duality in Housman's work is the split between poet and persona. He goes on to argue that, therefore, one cannot assume that statements Housman makes in the poems in which he employs this poetic persona are accurate reflections of the poet's own beliefs.*]

What has concerned Housman's critics since the publication of *A Shropshire Lad* in 1896 is the enigma of Housman the man as it is reflected in his verse. He has suffered, like Byron, from the fact that his personality is of more interest to many readers than his poetry, and that for some scholars the poetry is valuable only as a key to the personality. (pp. 5-6)

It is ironic, in view of Housman's own conception of the business of criticism, that his poetry should have suffered its present fate of being subordinated to the critics' preoccupation with extra-literary matters. Housman wrote in 1915 while reviewing a study of the English literature of the period of the French Revolution, "Now the centre of interest in a poet is his poetry: not his themes, his doctrines, his opinions, his life or conduct, but the poetical quality of the works he has bequeathed to us." It was decided, however, soon after Housman's death, or perhaps before, that there was very little to be said about the poetical quality of his simple verse, and that criticism must be content with his life, his opinions and doctrines, and, to a lesser extent, his themes. But, in truth, much remains to be said about the poetical quality of the works he has bequeathed to us. What, specifically, is the nature of Housman's art and of his achievement as a poet?

First, one must consider seriously the matter of his infamous "simplicity." . . . [The] artless, uncomplicated manner of Housman's verse is more apparent than real. His poetry is not entirely free from punning and a certain ambiguity of statement.

It is characterized to a greater extent by conceit, paradox, irony—in short, the qualities which have been viewed by much modern criticism as the marks of a necessary complexity in poetic texture. Added to these devices is a use of allusion that one might well call modern. Housman's allusive technique frequently serves to complicate the seemingly simple statement of a poem by echoing and reversing a commonplace expression or a passage from another work so that the resulting tone is a complex one. This statement is not to imply that Housman is "modern" in any real sense, only that his directness is often a matter of metrical form and of the tradition of the pastoral and the ballad, as distinguished from a threadbare texture. It is the subtlety with which Housman employs these techniques that suggests a distinction between his poetry and that of the moderns. It may also help to account for the fact that his ironies have been mistaken for literal statement, his paradoxes for perversity, and his conceits for personal belief.

But in spite of his use of many of the devices of wit, Housman's poetic mode is more akin to the Romantic tradition than to the modern. Wordsworth he considered "the chief figure in English poetry after Chaucer," and he declared that "no poet later born . . . entirely escaped his influence." Whether he considered Wordsworth a strong influence on his own poetry will never be known; Housman was not given to discussions of his art. But it is nevertheless true that his verse owes much to the tradition of Wordsworth. This debt is manifested not only in the rural setting and the pastoral persona, but in such persistent themes as the city-country antithesis, the loss of harmony with nature, and the nostalgia for lost innocence. (pp. 131-32)

One would not wish, however, to push Housman's debt to the tradition of Wordsworth too far. If he owed something of his lyric impulse to the Romantics, he also disavowed the Romantic doctrine of nature and the essentially spiritual view of the universe as a force in harmony with man's own nature. It is Housman's post-Darwinian conception of the natural world that alienates him from the Romantics and allies him with the moderns, so that, finally, his poetry lies between two traditions, one defunct, the other not yet fully developed. And his unique position in the history of nineteenth- and twentieth-century English poetry explains, in part, the failure of scholarship to do justice to a poetry which combines the simple lyricism of one tradition with the complex attitudes of another.

But even if Housman anticipated to some degree the course of English literature, his work failed to influence the direction that poetry was to take in the twentieth century. He remains a minor figure whose fame rests on the solid achievement of one volume of poems. Furthermore, he has suffered the fate, as Ian Scott-Kilvert notes, of "a minor poet thrust by popularity into the role of a major one." The suspicion persists that the popular poet is, at best, second rate; but Housman's achievement, however minor, deserves to be more correctly assessed.

Such a reassessment must begin with the recognition of the art of *A Shropshire Lad*. It has long been regarded as a collection of short lyrics which voice a *fin de siècle* pessimism. But *A Shropshire Lad* is clearly more than a collection; it is unified in theme and tone, and its force derives from the effect of the whole work, not merely from isolated lyrics. Housman was undoubtedly correct in prohibiting during his lifetime the divorcing of individual poems from their context, for the modern practice of excerpting single poems from *A Shropshire Lad* for anthologies has obscured the essential unity of the work. It has also obscured the fact that, thematically and structurally, *A Shropshire Lad* is a self-contained work, a factor that has some implications for Housman scholarship.

It means, in short, that scholars must turn from Housman's life to his art in seeking to explain the nature of his achievement as a poet. For example, the dramatis personae of *A Shropshire Lad*—the soldier, the young sinner, the forsaken lover, the rustic—may be defined more exactly in terms of the over-all thematic design of the work than in terms of the personal inadequacies of the poet. No one would deny the value of biographical and historical scholarship; but after it has finished its task, the aesthetic problems of a work of art remain untouched, a fact of which Housman scholarship serves as the classic example.

The problem is illustrated by the question of the ordering of the poems of *A Shropshire Lad*. A number of early reviewers detected a consistent order in the arrangement of the poems, but in the last twenty years no one has examined the work closely from this point of view. Professor Haber has attempted to solve the problem of the ordering of the poems by reference to Housman's notebooks and his "nature," not by an analysis of the finished work. He found, as might be expected, that the notebooks do not yield any evidence of a thematic arrangement. . . . This is surely a dangerous line of argument. To contend that it was "contrary to Housman's nature" to give order to his art is to question seriously his abilities as an artist. But perhaps even more difficult to accept is the implication that our knowledge of the character of a poet is ample evidence of the kind of work he will produce. (pp. 134-36)

If the work does reveal some evidence of order, what is the nature of that order? The structure of *A Shropshire Lad* is narrative only as far as it involves a clearly defined persona, the record of his discoveries of the nature of his world, and his journey from the place of his birth to the alien city. By far the most significant structural elements are thematic. That is, one may identify in the work, as it is ordered, the growth and development of one predominant theme which corresponds to a configuration of emotion or feeling in the mind of the persona. What has not been recognized is that the theme evident in the individual lyrics is reinforced by the structure of the work as a whole.

Evidence of this structural pattern can be noted, first of all, in the frame poems. The introductory poem and the final two lyrics of the work are important to the design of the whole by virtue of the fact that they define and clarify the purpose and scope of *A Shropshire Lad*. Through allusions to another poetic tradition, these poems provide the necessary context for Housman's own treatment of one of the most pervasive themes of Western literature. Furthermore, Housman uses this framework to justify the theme and tone of his poetry and to suggest its ultimate value. This structural element of *A Shropshire Lad* is too obvious to have been completely overlooked, and even Haber admits that the "appropriateness of 'I hoed and trenched and weeded' to be the final poem is beyond dispute."

But it is difficult to accept the notion that Housman carefully ordered one portion of his work and gathered the remaining lyrics indiscriminately. Even though his account of the genesis of the individual poems implies a doctrine of spontaneous and passive creativity, it must not be forgotten that Housman was not only a poet but an editor and critic as well. It has been traditionally held that Housman represents the classic case of the bifurcation of emotion and intellect, an argument that is supported by his own statements on the divergent nature of poetry and criticism. Yet it is impossible to conceive of the complete separation of the two faculties, even in a man who attempted throughout his career to divorce his poetry from his scholarship. How could the classical scholar avoid seeing the potentialities of the genre which informed his work? The pastoral tradition provided the conventions for unifying the separate poems, which were themselves the product of the union of classical learning and personal insight. If, in Housman's theory of poetics, creation is, on the whole, a passive process and an end in itself, he also held that the business of the critic is to impose order on that which is created. Furthermore, Housman never held that his art was entirely divorced from his intellectual faculties. Although, he says, a poem may have originated as a purely emotional activity, sometimes it "had to be taken in hand and completed by the brain. . . ."

One might well conjecture that this was the process of *A Shropshire Lad.* The individual lyrics began as "secretions" of emotions, to use Housman's own terminology; but when this activity was done and the poet was faced with the task of arranging the poems for publication, they "had to be taken in hand and completed by the brain." This is perhaps the simplest explanation for the consistency of the structure of *A Shropshire Lad*—the Shropshire-London arrangement, the pattern of growth and knowledge evident in the persona of the poems, and the final resolution of the theme. But to conjecture about the poet's process of creation is dangerous. The most that one can conclude is that the view of *A Shropshire Lad* as an ordered whole is not as inconsistent with Housman's nature and his doctrine of poetry as earlier criticism has suggested.

Housman's theory of the name and nature of poetry does, however, cast some light on the lasting appeal of his art. He held that the ultimate strength of poetry lies in the fact that it deals with unconscious, archetypal patterns of thought and feeling. He states, for example, that the words of a poem "find their way to something in man which is obscure and latent, something older than the present organization of his nature, like the patches of fen which still linger here and there in the drained lands of Cambridgeshire." And he repeated as praiseworthy a statement made about Wordsworth: "his indisputed sovereignty . . . lies in his extraordinary faculty of giving utterance to some of the most elementary and at the same time obscure sensations of man confronted by natural phenomena." One might amend this statement to suggest one reason for the continued appeal of a work which, by all rights, should not have survived far into the twentieth century. Clearly, a part of Housman's achievement as a poet was to give coherence to the elementary and obscure sensations of man confronted by natural phenomena, but these phenomena reveal that the Wordsworthian affinity with nature has been lost; what remains is the realization of the transience and mortality of an essentially alien world. (pp. 136-38)

> *B. J. Leggett, in his* Housman's Land of Lost Content: A Critical Study of "A Shropshire Lad" *(copyright © 1970 by The University of Tennessee Press; reprinted by permission of the publisher), University of Tennessee Press, Knoxville, 1970, 160 p.*

NORMAN MARLOW (essay date 1974)

[*Marlow's article, excerpted below, is a scholarly and perceptive discussion of Housman's prose style. It briefly outlines and examines most of Housman's major influences, including Juvenal's and Selden's* Table Talk.]

[Housman's] prose has the same sustained excellence as his verse and often closely resembles it; of no author is it truer that 'le style, c'est l'homme même' ['style is the man himself'].

In his very first writings, whether nonsense verse or letters, there is an incisiveness, a mastery of everyday words and situations, an almost defiant pragmatism that remained with him throughout life and which, together with a very lively streak of satire, is responsible for some of his happiest effects. We know that he professed to have no time for metaphysics or German philosophy and that he showed up no answers to many of the questions on political economy in his Greats examination at Oxford. In the preface to the last volume of his major work of scholarship, the edition of the fifth book of the astrologer-poet, Manilius, are these words: 'Unable to soar in the void, I creep upon the earth; and there I make the acquaintance of stony facts.'

Percy Withers reports him as saying, 'I always keep Selden's *Table-Talk* at hand, often turn to it, and always find it serviceable and cleansing. When engaged in writing I have made constant use of it as a corrective both of slipshod and flummery, as a guide to follow as faithfully as can be.' If we turn to Selden we very soon find examples of the sort of pithy downrightness that would appeal to Housman: in particular Selden delights to transpose an abstract argument into everyday terms and thereby to expose its essential folly or its inner nature. . . . (p. 20)

For many readers the chief attraction of Housman's prose is the shock of amused enlightenment which accompanies the reading of passages such as the following:

> A textual critic engaged upon his business is not at all like Newton investigating the motions of the planets: he is much more like a dog hunting for fleas. If a dog hunted for fleas on mathematical principles, basing his researches on statistics of area and population, he would never catch a flea except by accident. They require to be treated as individuals; and every problem which presents itself to the textual critic must be regarded as possibly unique.
>
> In enquiring whether a given reading of P's is right, we behave as if we really wanted to know, and we ask whether it is probable: they ask only whether it is possible, and unless it is impossible they believe it to be right; much as if you should believe that every Irishman is a Roman Catholic unless he knocks you down for looking as if you thought so.
>
> If Lachmann, having no good MSS., used a bad one, is that a reason why Lachmann's disciples, having two good MSS., should use it still? Parisians ate rats in the siege, when they had nothing better to eat: must admirers of Parisian cookery eat rats for ever?

We have evidence that ammunition of this kind was stored up in notebooks and never used: 'If Mr. ——— were a postage-stamp he would be a very good postage-stamp; but adhesiveness is not the virtue of a critic. A critic is free and detached.' (p. 21)

Housman's own finished style was arresting, shapely, and always characterized by formality even when he was using homely metaphor. He can incorporate phrases from the poets or the King James Bible and their setting is worthy of them. (p. 24)

Housman calls upon authors from Homer to Herbert Spencer, from the Bible to W. S. Gilbert, from Pliny to Goethe; never choosing a hackneyed quotation, never overdoing it, but always appearing to choose the exact phrase to illustrate his point, whether it is the endurance of Priam or the hardness of the parrot's head or man's distaste for thinking or a lame man's attitude to men of sound body. This ability to choose the exact parallel is even more striking in his learned works and makes his edition of the unread poet Manilius a mine of information for scholars working in the field of Latin poetry and astrology.

A word here of Housman's Latin style, which reminds us of a phrase he himself used of Scaliger. 'No commentary', he wrote, 'is brisker reading or better entertainment than these abrupt and pithy notes, with their spurts of mockery at unnamed detractors, and their frequent and significant stress upon the difference between Scaliger and a jackass.' Except that Housman did not forbear to name his detractors, these words might have been written of the Manilius. Indeed the vituperative style which Housman affected was seen as a return to the polemical methods of Scaliger, Salmasius, Milton, and Bentley, with their *odium scholasticum* over pedantic trifles.

A device which Housman employed very effectively was the deliberate use, as it were, of a steam hammer to crack a nut. These pedantic trifles are dignified with majestic metaphors so that we may be let down with a bigger bump at the end, and the incongruity of the anticlimax may strike home. This device was well known to ancient satirists from the Homeric mock-epic to Juvenal. . . . (pp. 24-5)

Housman spoke of one of the greatest achievements of the eighteenth century as 'the invention and establishment of a healthy, workmanlike, athletic prose, to supersede the cumbrous and decorated and self-admiring prose of a Milton or a Jeremy Taylor, and it is perhaps of the eighteenth rather than of any other century that his prose reminds us. Sometimes it rises to the stateliness of Gibbon. . . .

But [Housman's] formality never degenerates, as it often does with Gibbon or Samuel Johnson, into a mannerism. Each phrase is worked out with an exact choice of word, a right balance of Greek and Latin polysyllables with Saxon monosyllables, like Shakespear's 'Multitudinous seas incarnadine, Making the green one red', and a supreme mastery of all subtle metrical devices which enhance the satirical effect. . . . (p. 25)

Like [Housman's] poetry, his prose has a crystal clarity, but is on so high a level of simplicity and straightforwardness that on that very account it occasionally seems artificial—one's only criticism is it is *too* perfect. (p. 26)

> *Norman Marlow, "The Prose Style of A. E. Housman" (reprinted by permission of the author), in* Housman Society Journal *(© The Housman Society 1974), Vol. 1, 1974, pp. 20-6.*

JOHN BLIGH   (essay date 1981)

> [*Bligh's commentary indicates that critics continue to discover new complexities in Housman's poetry, particularly with regard to ambiguities of tone and literary allusion. These devices are examined at length in Richard Wilbur's essay (see excerpt above).*]

To regard Housman's lyric ["**The night is freezing fast,**" No. XX in *Last Poems*] as formulating a highly complex attitude to death is to take it too seriously. The little poem records a frost-at-midnight meditation, ending, not with a prayer or blessing, but with a joke—which is one of its attractions, for do we not often break off our more serious meditations with a smile? A Christian, recalling how Dick would hate the cold, might say to himself: "I hope he hasn't gone some place where he complains of the heat!" But the unbelieving meditator in Housman's poem does not accept the Christian eschatology. He tells himself that Dick has mocked not Death but Winter by making himself "a winter robe . . . the turning globe." James R. Kreuzer in *Elements of Poetry* . . . regards this as ironical because actually Dick is lying in a cold grave "and the cold of death is upon him." But in fact he feels neither the cold of death nor the warmth of the overcoat. The speaker knows well that he is soothing himself with illogical comfort. Dick is as insentient as Wordsworth's Lucy who "neither hears nor sees; / Rolled round in earth's diurnal course, / With rocks, and stones, and trees." But Housman rejoices in his play of wit and leaves serious thoughts to others.

For those who know Greek there is another, more secret turn of wit to savour here. Housman uses the imagery of St. Paul's eschatology in the very act of rejecting it. The image of the overcoat occurs in the Second Epistle to the Corinthians, 5:2-4, where St. Paul says that the Christian, looking forward to the world to come, does not desire to take anything off *(ek-dusasthai)*, but rather to put on an additional garment *(epen-dusasthai)*: Christians who are alive at the Second Coming will not die; they will not shed the garment of the body, but will, as it were, put on an overcoat *(ependuten*, as in John 21:7) of heavenly glory. Housman's Dick put on, when he died, his "overcoat for ever," an overcoat made of "earth and sea," not of heavenly glory. In both texts what the wearer wears is not only a garment but a dwelling, in the one text an eternal mansion not made with human hands, and in the other "the turning globe." If the image of the overcoat is borrowed from Second Corinthians, the speaker is playfully rejecting St. Paul's eschatology.

> *John Bligh, in his essay in* The Explicator *(copyright 1981 by Helen Dwight Reid Foundation; reprinted by permission of Heldref Publications), Vol. 40, No. 1, Fall, 1981, p. 48.*

ADDITIONAL BIBLIOGRAPHY

Brashear, William R. "The Trouble with Housman." In his *The Gorgon's Head: A Study in Tragedy and Despair*, pp. 49-58. Athens: The University of Georgia Press, 1977.

> Discussion of the theme of despair in Housman's poetry. While agreeing with Housman's detractors that the poet's attitude often seems "puerile," Brashear cites examples of poems in which Housman transcends the emotional limitations imposed by his "cynicism and detachment."

Brown, Stuart Gerry. "The Poetry of A. E. Housman." *The Sewanee Review* XLVII, No. 3 (Summer 1941): pp. 397-408.

> Discussion of Housman's poetic technique. Brown examines Housman's style and analyzes the influence of Shakespeare, Heine, and the Scottish border ballads on Housman's poetry.

Friedman, Ellen. "The Divided Self in the Poems of A. E. Housman." *English Literature in Transition* 20, No. 1 (1977): 27-34.

Psychological criticism. Friedman employs examples from Housman's poetry in an attempt to prove that, by his attitude, he reveals himself to be a schizoid personality as psychologist R. D. Laing has defined the term.

Garrod, H. W. "Housman: 1939." In *Essays and Studies by Members of the English Association: Vol. XXV, 1939*, edited by Percy Simpson, pp. 7-21. Oxford: The Clarendon Press, 1940.
   Critical essay. Garrod was personally acquainted with Housman at Oxford. In this review of the *Collected Poems*, he speculates as to the nature of the emotional crisis that precipitated Housman's poetry.

Graves, Richard Perceval. *A. E. Housman: The Scholar Poet*. London: Routledge and Kegan Paul, 1979, 304 p.
   Frank modern biography of Housman. Graves had access to a number of documents containing confidential information about the poet that was unavailable to previous biographers.

Hawkins, Maude. *A. E. Housman: Man behind a Mask*. Chicago: Henry Regnery Co., 1958, 292 p.
   Biography. Hawkins corresponded with and visited the poet's brother, Laurence Housman, many times before publishing her Housman study. She was the first to document the true nature of Housman's relationship with Moses Jackson.

Housman, Laurence. "A. E. Housman's 'De Amicitia'." *Encounter* XXIX, No. 4 (October 1967): pp. 33-41.
   Article written by Laurence Housman to accompany the official release of his brother's diaries.

Leggett, B. J. "The Poetry of Insight: Persona and Point of View in Housman." *Victorian Poetry* 14, No. 4 (Winter 1976): 325-39.
   Argues that the point of view affected by Housman in his poems is not necessarily a reflection of the poet's own attitudes.

Pound, Ezra. "Mr. Housman at Little Bethel." In his *Polite Essays*, pp. 17-26. Norfolk, Conn.: New Directions, 1937.
   Discussion of Housman's *The Name and Nature of Poetry*. Pound praises Housman's prose style while disagreeing with his critical conclusions.

Robinson, Oliver. *Angry Dust: The Poetry of A. E. Housman*. Boston: Bruce Humphries, 1950, 71 p.
   A critical survey of Housman's poetry. Robinson's essay provides "a descriptive analysis of the form and content of [Housman's] work," including the mechanics of the poetry, its sources of influence, and the poet's manner of composition, as well as his fatalistic philosophy.

Scott-Kilvert, Ian. *A. E. Housman*. Writers and Their Work Series, edited by Bonamy Dobree, no. 69. London: British Council, 1955, 40 p.
   Concise and well-researched survey of Housman's work.

Sparrow, John. "The Housman Dilemma." In his *Controversial Essays*, pp. 71-88. London: Faber and Faber, 1966.
   Textual criticism of Housman's *More Poems*. This is a reprint of a running dispute between Sparrow and Tom Burns Haber that was originally published in the letter column of *The Times Literary Supplement*. In it, Sparrow questions Haber's ethics in publishing material from Housman's notebooks that Laurence Housman, the poet's brother and literary executor, had elected not to publish. He also feels that Haber's editorial skills were not equal to the task.

Sparrow, W. Keats. "The Structure of Housman's *The Name and Nature of Poetry*." *The Housman Society Journal* 3 (1977): 38-42.
   Analysis of Housman's controversial lecture. Sparrow argues in support of B. J. Leggett's claim that far from being an "impressionistic hodge-podge of Housman's . . . reactions to poetry," the lecture is actually "a frontal attack on the scientific criticism of [I. A.] Richards and his school."

Watson, George L. *A. E. Housman: A Divided Life*. London: Rupert Hart-Davis, 1957, 234 p.
   A well-known biographical work. At the time Watson's book appeared, most of the salient facts about Housman's relationship with Moses Jackson were still being conscientiously suppressed by his family. The controversial conjectures Watson made in this biography were later corroborated by facts that appeared in Maude Hawkins's Housman biography, published one year later.

Whitridge, Arnold. "Vigny and Housman: A Study in Pessimism." *The American Scholar* 10, No. 2 (Spring 1941): pp. 156-69.*
   Explains that the appeal of Housman's poetry is a result of the spare artistic style, moral stoicism, and love of the physical world which were the by-products of his pessimism.

Henry Kuttner

1915-1958

(Also wrote under pseudonyms of Paul Edmonds, Will Garth, Keith Hammond, Kelvin Kent, Lawrence O'Donnell, Lewis Padgett, Woodrow Wilson Smith, among others) American short story writer and novelist.

Kuttner was a major contributor to science fiction's "Golden Age"—a period during the 1930s and 1940s when some of the genre's most notable authors, including Isaac Asimov and Robert A. Heinlein, were beginning their careers. While the tendency of the era was toward technical stories with an emphasis upon "science," Kuttner was one of the earliest science fiction authors to write less about future technology than about the effects of possible technological advances upon individuals and society. He wrote extensively about human mutations, treating the concept seriously in the "Baldies" stories (later consolidated in *Mutant*) and humorously in the long-running series of stories about the Hogben family. Despite his early development of these now standard science fiction themes, Kuttner is not as widely read as he was during his lifetime. After his death his reputation was quickly overshadowed by those of his contemporaries who went on writing, and in many cases improving, on his themes.

Like many science fiction writers of his generation, Kuttner developed an early interest in fantasy literature through reading the Oz books of L. Frank Baum, the works of Edgar Rice Burroughs, and pulp magazines such as *Amazing Stories* and *Weird Tales*. It was in these magazines that Kuttner published his first stories, including "The Graveyard Rats." This and other of Kuttner's early tales of supernatural horror indicate the influence of H. P. Lovecraft, who corresponded with Kuttner and offered helpful commentary on his fictional efforts. To support himself at the beginning of his career, Kuttner wrote westerns and detective novels under various pseudonyms. His first work of science fiction, the short story "When the Earth Lived," published in *Thrilling Stories* in 1937, utilized an idea that recurs in much of his fiction: the animation of inanimate objects.

Thereafter, Kuttner wrote primarily science fiction, under a variety of pseudonyms; as many as seventeen have been attributed to him. Under these pen names, Kuttner wrote many works that became quite popular with readers. The revelation, in 1943, that these authors were all in fact Kuttner caused a stir among science fiction fans. In 1940 Kuttner married Catherine Lucille Moore, who was at that time one of the very few women who regularly wrote and published science fiction. All of Kuttner's subsequent work was written in collaboration with Moore. Sometimes they would write in relays, particularly when working on a novel; at other times, one would write the rough draft from which the other would produce a finished story. In 1950 Kuttner entered the University of Southern California to resume studies which had been interrupted by the Depression. He graduated in 1954 and was doing postgraduate work when he died of a heart attack.

Kuttner displayed great ingenuity in his handling of themes common to science fiction, such as time travel, alternate worlds, and robots. He was especially innovative in his treatment of telepathy. His "Baldies" series was one of the first attempts

Courtesy of University of Southern California

to portray the sociological aspects of a world in which some people could read the minds of others. Kuttner later explored the humorous possibilities of human mutations in a series of stories about the Hogbens, a hillbilly family whose members possess dozens of paranormal abilities. Kuttner also wrote what is regarded as one of science fiction's most notable stories with a child protagonist: "Mimsy Were the Borogoves," included in *A Gnome There Was, and Other Tales of Science Fiction and Fantasy*. In this story, a brother and sister use educational toys from the future to transport themselves into another dimension. Critics generally agree that Kuttner's best novel is *Fury*, which deals insightfully with the differences in outlook between normal humans and mutated humans whose lives last several hundred years, and with the inevitable ennui of life in a utopia.

Within the ever-growing body of science fiction criticism, Kuttner is the subject of some controversy. Between two of the genre's primary critics, Sam Moskowitz and James Blish, there has been a sharp divergence of opinion regarding Kuttner. In an early critical study of science fiction, Moskowitz dismissed Kuttner as an imitative author, a "proficient literary mimic" who "usually wrote like whoever was in demand at the time." However, since many of his early works, including his detective fiction, sword-and-sorcery fantasies, and even some sex horror and science fiction stories, were written to the specifications of editors, some resemblance between Kuttner's stories and those of others was inevitable. Blish argues that a study of Kuttner's works, beginning with his earliest magazine fiction, which Moskowitz does not discuss, demonstrates that Kuttner's technical proficiency was developed and not "borrowed." Many newer critics of science fiction concur with Blish; even Damon Knight, who agrees with Moskowitz that Kuttner imitated the writing styles of other authors, notes his versatility with plot. While the amount of criticism devoted to Kuttner is still comparatively slight, critics recognize him as one of the first pulp writers to forsake futuristic gadgetry and examine the effects on humanity of technological developments of the future.

(See also *Contemporary Authors*, **Vol. 107** and *Dictionary of Literary Biography*, **Vol. 8:** *Twentieth-Century American Science-Fiction Writers*.)

PRINCIPAL WORKS

"The Graveyard Rats"   (short story)   1936; published in journal *Weird Tales*
Lawless Gun [as Will Garth]   (novel)   1937
The Brass Ring [with C. L. Moore under the joint pseudonym of Lewis Padgett]   (novel)   1946; also published as *Murder in Brass*, 1947
Fury [as Lawrence O'Donnell]   (novel)   1950; also published as *Destination Infinity*, 1958
A Gnome There Was, and Other Tales of Science Fiction and Fantasy [with C. L. Moore under the joint pseudonym of Lewis Padgett]   (short stories)   1950
*The Fairy Chessmen [with C. L. Moore under the joint pseudonym of Lewis Padgett]   (novel)   1951; also published as *Chessboard Planet*, 1956; and *The Far Reality*, 1963
*Tomorrow and Tomorrow [with C. L. Moore under the joint pseudonym of Lewis Padgett]   (novel)   1951
Robots Have No Tails [with C.L. Moore under the joint pseudonym of Lewis Padgett]   (short stories)   1952
Ahead of Time: Ten Stories of Science Fiction and Fantasy [with C. L. Moore]   (short stories)   1953
Mutant [with C. L. Moore under the joint pseudonym of Lewis Padgett]   (novel)   1953
Well of the Worlds [with C. L. Moore under the joint pseudonym of Lewis Padgett]   (novel)   1953
Beyond Earth's Gates [as Lewis Padgett; with C. L. Moore]   (novel)   1954
Line to Tomorrow [with C. L. Moore under the joint pseudonym of Lewis Padgett]   (novel)   1954
No Boundaries [with C. L. Moore]   (novel)   1955

**These works were published together as *Tomorrow and Tomorrow. The Fairy Chessmen* in 1951.*

HENRY KUTTNER   (essay date 1939)

[*The following excerpt is taken from an article Kuttner contributed to* Writer's Digest *offering guidelines for the composition of science fiction stories and commenting on trends and techniques in the genre.*]

Science-fiction has its trends. A few years ago writers, having apparently exhausted every idea remotely possible, went hog-wild and wrote stories so extremely imaginative that they were in some cases pretty silly. Characterization, atmosphere, plausibility—all the factors that go to make up a yarn were sacrificed to the frantic attempt to create something stupendously novel. Since readers, in the last analysis, want to read about human or at least understandable beings, reaction set in, and writers discovered there was still plenty of story value in such prosaic themes as the crack-up of a rocket ship on the moon. Characterization came back with a bang.

It is a mistake to think that readers of science-fiction are juvenile, and that the Buck Rogers type of hero is necessary. The jimber-jawed, steely-eyed interplanetary cop, with a blazing ray-gun in each hand, has pause to hoist a slug of Martian rye, swap wisecracks with the villain, or indulge in nostalgic retrospection about the far green hills of earth a few light-years away. The characters can even be human! (pp. 34-5)

Indeed, the trend in science-fiction today is away from super-colossal characters and ideas and toward the sort of story H. G. Wells used to write. The reader has grown up, unfamiliar with fantasy and unwilling to swallow a story that begins with an intelligent octopod in Alpha Centauri creating a machine to speed up the entropy of the universe. Such a yarn, if written today, would begin, perhaps, with an ordinary, normal chap in New York or London or Pasadena discovering a fallen meteor that is in reality a spaceship, and extricating the intelligent octopod from the device. Modern science-fiction utilizes the springboard device, in which the board is our own familiar, understandable *milieu*, and the pool into which we dive is the fantastic element. (p. 35)

Henry Kuttner, "Selling Science Fiction," in Writer's Digest *(© 1939 by Writer's Digest Magazine; reprinted by permission of Writer's Digest Books), Vol. 19, No. 11, October, 1939, pp. 34-8.*

J. FRANCIS McCOMAS   (essay date 1952)

There's a sharp contrast in the quality of ["**Tomorrow and Tomorrow**" and "**The Fairy Chessman**."] Both deal with a not too remote future and with the impact of atomic warfare on human culture. But "**Tomorrow and Tomorrow,**" while good, competent science fiction, offers nothing new on such fascinating themes as the idea of alternate worlds or the possibility of man mutating into superman. Happily, however, "**The Fairy Chessman**" gives us Padgett's imagination at its brilliant best. He has concocted a system of variable "truths" and "logics"—a wondrous Lewis Carroll kind of logical illogic. Against this the normal mind cannot stand and retreats into insanity. Padgett describes such retreats with superb visual sense of surrealist nightmare. Most readers would be content with such a theme but Padgett also presents some really new ideas on time travel and blends all his ideas into a story whose melodramatic plotting is first rate.

J. Francis McComas, "Spacemen's Realm: After the Bomb," in The New York Times Book Review *(© 1952 by The New York Times Company; reprinted by permission), February 10, 1952, p. 21.*

J. FRANCIS McCOMAS   (essay date 1953)

First published in the magazines of 1945, Lewis Padgett's famed series of "Baldy" stories rank today as the classic exploration of all the ramifications of that inevitable conflict between man and—not superman, but psi-man. Those tales of the hairless telepaths are now gathered together and published as a novel ["**Mutant**"]; this novelistic unification does not seem at all strained, since each story was originally a single episode in a general history. In fact, when read in sequence they add up to such a brilliant total that the connecting device added in ["**Mutant**"] seems an awkward, distracting appendage.

It is obvious that telepaths, particularly those who possess marked physical differences from the norm, will be people set apart. Not ghetto-sized, perhaps, but certainly distrusted, often hated by their neighbors. Less obvious—and here Padgett is impressively intuitive—is the postulate that telepaths will be otherwise quite ordinary human beings, with a basic need for complete integration with their society. And the drive and tension of Padgett's novel stem from the obstacles to this urge for acceptance: the non-telepath's dread of assault on his mental privacy, the occasional paranoid mutant's lust for conquest, the ultimate need to make all men sensorily equal.

So perfect, so complete is this study of people with extra talents that all writers who have tried the theme since Padgett's first story have been confined within his all-embracing framework. And, as always, Lewis Padgett propounds his ideas in a beguiling story rich in reading entertainment.

> *J. Francis McComas, "Spaceman's Realm: Hairless Telepaths," in* The New York Times Book Review *(© 1953 by The New York Times Company; reprinted by permission), December 20, 1953, p. 17.*

WILLIAM ATHELING, JR. [pseudonym of JAMES BLISH] (essay date 1964)

[*In this brief discussion of "Humpty Dumpty," one of the "Baldies" stories, Blish analyzes a pattern which he discerns in the story, and which he finds evident in many of the stories written as "Lewis Padgett." James Gunn refers to this pattern in his discussion of "Piggy Bank" (see excerpt below).*]

The reappearance of Lewis Padgett in the September, 1953 *Astounding*—and with that Baldy story, at that—provides a fresh reminder of those of us who need it of how many worlds the Kuttners are away from the technical universe occupied by most of the new writers. "**Humpty Dumpty**" is not, to my eyes, the best Baldy story of the series, partly because it has its share of the symbols of resignation and defeat which have been creeping into the Kuttners' most recent writings, but it is an object lesson in how to construct a science fiction novelette.

It manages to be so in spite of the fact that its basic construction follows a plan developed by the Kuttners a long time ago, and follows it rather mechanically at that. Padgett stories for years have begun in just this way: The narrative hook, almost always dealing with incipient violence, madness, or both; enough development of the hook to lead the story into a paradox; then a complete suspension of the story while the authors lecture the reader on the background for a short time, seldom more than 1,000 words. The lecture technique is generally taboo for fiction, especially in the hands of new writers, and only two science fiction writers have managed to get away with it and make the reader like it, Heinlein being the other. "**Humpty Dumpty**" is no exception; it follows the pattern so predictably as to suggest that the Kuttners do not have their entire attention on their work.

And yet, automatic though some of the writing seems to be, the story is beautifully rounded as a structure, and, as is usual

with the Kuttners, does not contain an unnecessary word. As a writing team the Kuttners evidently subscribe to Chekhov's principle of plot economy (the Russian writer once remarked that if in a story he mentioned that an ornamental gun hung on the wall of a room, that gun must go off before the story is over). For a single example, note the mention in "**Humpty Dumpty**" of the way Cody perceives the minds of the goldfish [quoted in Aldiss excerpt below]. Any other writer would have been so pleased with this as a bit of coloring matter—for, while it's logical enough that a telepath should be able to read the minds of animals, few other writers in the field would have conveyed the point in so bizarre a way—that he would have let it stand just as it was. Not so the Kuttners; that bit of color has to be for something, not just color for its own sake, and so toward the end of the story the goldfish are used as a springboard into understanding the mind of the child. This, gentlemen, is story-telling; and if more than half of [editor John W.] Campbell's current stable could be forced to drink from the Kuttners' goldfish pond, *Astounding* would be a hell of a lot more readable than it is these days. (pp. 78-9)

> *William Atheling, Jr. [pseudonym of James Blish], "Negative Judgments: Swashbungling, Series and Second-guessing," in his* The Issue at Hand: Studies in Contemporary Magazine Science Fiction, *edited by James Blish (copyright, © 1964, by James Blish; reprinted by courtesy of Advent:Publishers, Inc.), Advent, 1964, pp. 71-80.**

SAM MOSKOWITZ (essay date 1966)

[*Moskowitz provides a detailed survey of Kuttner's early short stories, citing first magazine publication dates. He presents Kuttner as a derivative author who never formulated his own plots or even writing style—an interpretation which is contested by James Blish (see excerpt below).*]

Select in your mind any of today's science-fiction writers you consider third-rate, and imagine what the effect might be on you if he suddenly confessed to being the real genius behind the published efforts of Theodore Sturgeon and Clifford D. Simak, and, for good measure, coyly owned up to responsibility for the Mark Clifton, Cordwainer Smith, and Christopher Anvil stories, and you will approximate the impact when Henry Kuttner admitted for publication that he was Lewis Padgett and Lawrence O'Donnell, and was also willing to accept credit for Keith Hammond, Kelvin Kent, Paul Edmonds, and sundry other names that had been regarded as science-fiction writers to bear watching. (p. 319)

Many writers had catapulted to overnight fame on the strength of a single outstanding story. Kuttner was the first in the science-fiction world to rise to glory incognito. (p. 320)

Unlike his close friend, Ray Bradbury, who has bared endless anecdotes concerning his tender years, Henry Kuttner in personal conversation and in print studiously bypassed the subject.

His interest in fantasy followed traditional lines. He began with the Oz books, graduated to Edgar Rice Burroughs, and at the age of 12, found himself "hooked" when the first *Amazing Stories* appeared in 1926.

As the years passed his interest shifted from science fiction toward weird-fantasy and as a devoted reader of *Weird Tales* he became a correspondent of H. P. Lovecraft and other members of the "Lovecraft Circle," particularly Robert Bloch.

Kuttner's first professional sale was a poem *Ballad of the Gods,* done in the pulsating rhythms of Robert E. Howard. . . . Kuttner is best remembered for his immense versatility, but in all evaluations his verse has been forgotten. True, most of it worshipped at the shrine of Robert E. Howard and some of it made obeisance to H. P. Lovecraft, but all of it is eminently readable. . . . (pp. 320-21)

Kuttner's fictional debut, *The Graveyard Rats,* in *Weird Tales* for March, 1936, marked the appearance of what is undoubtedly one of the half-dozen most truly *horrifying* short stories in the entire gamut of literature, *all* of literature. A ghoulish cemetery caretaker in New England's old Salem crawls after immense rats through underground tunnels to reclaim a newly buried body they have dragged from the coffin. His nightmarish struggle against the rats and an ancient cadaver still instinct with the reflexes of life build to a denouement of such revolting terror that the reader must almost drive himself physically to complete it.

In background, theme, buildup, style, and intent the story owes everything to H. P. Lovecraft. While no evidence has been uncovered to show that Lovecraft helped in the writing of the story, it would be hard to conceive that he had not read it and offered suggestions before publication. *The Graveyard Rats* is so powerful an exercise in fear, so basic in striking the chord of all that man holds abhorrent, and it rears so monstrously in effectiveness above any other weird tale that Henry Kuttner subsequently had published (indeed, when the final evaluation is made, it may be the best thing he ever wrote), that one finds it difficult to attribute it to a fledgling 21-year-old, his first time out. (pp. 321-22)

In later years, Kuttner grew literally to hate *The Graveyard Rats.* He resented requests for reprint rights and contemplated violence when an endless parade of readers kept telling him it was the best thing he had ever written. He regarded praise of the story as an insinuation that the decades had taught him nothing about the technique of storytelling. . . .

In *The Secret of Kralitz* (*Weird Tales,* October, 1936), a young baron becomes a member of the living dead; the theme of *It Walks By Night* (*Weird Tales,* December, 1936) involves the dead who feed on the bodies of the dead. Both of these tales were outright imitations of Lovecraft, and *The Eater of Souls* (*Weird Tales,* January, 1937) imitated Lovecraft's imitation of Lord Dunsany! (p. 322)

[There would] be other Lovecraft imitations, *The Salem Horror* (*Weird Tales,* May, 1937) and *The Jest of Droom Avista* (*Weird Tales,* August, 1937), for while Kuttner wanted to change he seemed unable to bring to bear any qualities that were fundamentally his own.

One of the most interesting and successful stories of this period was his collaboration with his close friend Robert Bloch, *The Black Kiss* (*Weird Tales,* June, 1937). A tale of a sea creature that lures a man in his dreams to partake of its kisses, resulting in a transfer of bodies, this story employed a combination of the methods and styles of H. P. Lovecraft *and* C. L. Moore, the girl Kuttner was destined to marry. Another literary collaboration, in which Henry Kuttner and C. L. Moore united in one story her two famous characters Northwest Smith and Jirel of Joiry (*Quest of the Star Stone, Weird Tales,* November, 1937), symbolically anticipated their marriage some three years later.

During the thirties an outgrowth of the mystery magazines were publications like *Thrilling Mystery, Horror Tales,* and *Terror Tales,* which specialized in stories of sadism, torture, flagellation, and satanism, heavily flavored with sex. These stories were developed as though they related supernatural events, but it was the policy of the magazines to have normal, logical explanations for the erotic and sometimes debased content of the stories. Henry Kuttner sold regularly to *Thrilling Mystery* such tales as *Laughter of the Dead, The Dweller in the Tomb,* and *Lord of the Lions.* It is likely that he used pen names for stories in *Horror Tales* and *Terror Tales,* for these publications were the most blatantly titillating of the group.

Julius Schwartz, his agent, convinced Kuttner that he should divert some of his energies toward science fiction. Kuttner was reluctant at first, because though he liked science fiction his scientific background was so skimpy that he felt inadequate to the job. (pp. 323-24)

When the Earth Lived (*Thrilling Stories,* November, 1937) is said by Schwartz to have been the first science fiction written by Kuttner, though *Raider of the Spaceways* (*Weird Tales,* July, 1937) was published before it. *When the Earth Lived* employed the fairly original idea of rays, projected by scientists in the macrocosmos, bombarding the earth and investing such unlikely objects as automobiles, boats, coffee pots, and jewelry with life, thereby raising hob. The treatment was corny, the writing amateurish, and the idea unbelievable, but Kuttner had launched his science-fiction career.

In *Raider of the Spaceways,* Kuttner used Stanley G. Weinbaum's *Lotus Eaters* as a model. In *The Lotus Eaters,* a male and female adventurer discover an intelligent talking plant in the twilight zone of Venus. In *Raider of the Spaceways,* a male and female adventurer discover an intelligent talking plant in the twilight zone of Venus. Kuttner gave it "his own" twist, however: Weinbaum's plant was friendly, Kuttner's wasn't. (pp. 324-25)

Kuttner got his first big writing break in science fiction. *Thrilling Wonder Stories'* editor, Mort Weisinger, asked him to write a series of novelettes based on the motion picture industry of the future. The first, *Hollywood on the Moon,* appeared in the April, 1938, issue. Hollywood was something Kuttner knew, so he could write with some authenticity, but the stories were to be formularized Stanley G. Weinbaum. The principal characters, Tony Quade and Gerry Carlyle, were copied from Ham Hammond and Pat Burlingame of Weinbaum's *Parasite Planet, Lotus Eaters,* and *Planet of Doubt.* Each story featured strange, weird, lovable, or outré alien creatures of the type popularized by Weinbaum, and each story attempted to imitate the modern, swift dialogue characteristic of Weinbaum's writing.

In a magazine oriented toward the juvenile market, Kuttner's series on the Hollywood of the future had the virtue of being readable and mildly entertaining. No one realized it then, but the single element that enabled Kuttner to lift those yarns out of the cellar was that they required humor, an ingredient he had in abundance.

Almost simultaneously with *Hollywood on the Moon,* Henry Kuttner started another series for *Weird Tales.* . . . [Kuttner created] a heroic character titled Elak, brawling and loving in the manner of Conan (and in the style of Robert E. Howard), but with supernatural settings from H. P. Lovecraft and stylistic hyperbole *à la* C. L. Moore.

The first in the series was *Thunder in the Dawn,* a two-part novel beginning in the May, 1938, *Weird Tales.* It was good fun, but in Howard's stories the character of Conan was bigger than life. Elak, however, was overshadowed by the events of the story. The series terminated after four widely spaced stories.

When *Marvel Science Stories'* initial issue, dated August, appeared on the newsstands in May, 1938, it was the first new science-fiction magazine in seven years. Henry Kuttner had been writing sex-horror stories for its companion, *Mystery Tales.* The editor of *Marvel Science Stories,* Robert O. Erisman, had decided to experiment with a little sex in science fiction. . . . Since Henry Kuttner was experienced at both the writing of science fiction and the horror magazine concept of what constituted sex, he was a logical man for the task.

Kuttner took two unsold short novels, *Avengers in Space* and *Time Trap* and inserted a few "racy" passages involving nude women and monsters with high libidos. The stories were fast-action science fiction and the "sex" by today's standards was rather tame, but they elicited a symphony of reader protest. Kuttner's never-high reputation skidded to a new low. Kuttner had two other decidedly second-rate stories in the first issue under pen names, *Dark Heritage* as Robert O. Kenyon and *Dictator of the Americas* as James Hall, the latter the most sex-laden story in the issue. (pp. 325-27)

Kuttner's best story of the year, *Hands Across the Void,* a poetic tale of the self-sacrifice of a Titanian to save Earthmen from destruction at the hands of their giant "servants," appeared in the December 1938, *Thrilling Wonder Stories* under the Will Garth name, so he received no credit for it.

His lack of popularity, combined with circumstance, forced Kuttner further and further into adopting pseudonyms as 1939 progressed. "Keith Hammond" originated as a device for running two stories in the same issues of *Strange Stories.* . . . Most of the stories under the Hammond name were imitations of Lovecraft and may even have been rejects from *Weird Tales.*

"Kelvin Kent" was used at first in collaboration, then alternately, with Arthur K. (for Kelvin) Barnes for a series of humorous stories in *Thrilling Wonder Stories.* The stories revolved around Peter Manx, side-show concessionaire in an amusement park, whose consciousness is shunted back in time into the bodies of ancient Romans, Greeks, Egyptians, and other residents of historical and legendary lands, where through his crude but native cunning he cons his way to success. The first, *Roman Holiday,* in *Thrilling Wonder Stories* for August, 1939, was the most popular story in the issue, ensuring a fairly long run for the series. (pp. 327-28)

[Henry Kuttner married Catherine Lucille Moore in June of 1940] and the career of the most famous writing team in science-fiction history was launched. (p. 329)

It would be nice to say that Kuttner's transformation to a top-rank author began at the moment of matrimony, but the evidence indicates that his ability was growing immediately before that.

Thrilling Wonder Stories in its April, 1940, number, ran the memorable *Beauty and the Beast,* which tells of an intelligent creature from Venus who is killed because of his monstrous appearance, as he attempts to deliver a message that would have saved Earth from disaster from lovely but deadly alien plants.

The May-June, 1940, issue of *Famous Fantastic Mysteries* carried his touching, well-told fantasy *Pegasus,* concerning a boy who catches and tames a flying horse. Though possibly inspired by Edmond Hamilton's masterpiece, *He That Hath*

Wings, in the July, 1938, issue of *Weird Tales . . .*, Kuttner's story has sufficient difference and quality to stand on its own.

Unknown for April, 1940, contained Kuttner's humorous fantasy *All Is Illusion,* whose subject is revealed by the title. In combining humor and fantasy Kuttner was in his element, but the speed at which he wrote divested this story, and a majority of his subsequent fantasies for *Unknown,* of all believability. Even the flashes of cleverness and the author's increasing skill at turning a phrase failed to rescue them. Most of his science fiction, though based on tenuous premises, was momentarily believable. Virtually none of his deliberate fantasies possessed this essential. (pp. 329-30)

More and more, writing became a symbiotic relationship [between Kuttner and Moore]. They frequently wrote in relays, one taking over sometimes in the middle of a sentence, helping the other past a writing block. Often one supplied the idea and the other wrote the story. Just as frequently Henry Kuttner would write the first draft and C. L. Moore would put it into final form. Kuttner was better than Moore at plotting, but Moore was a far more accomplished stylist.

Pearl Harbor played an unexpected role in their lives. For his magazines *Astounding Science-Fiction* and *Unknown Worlds,* John W. Campbell, Jr., had developed a crack team of writers. Now, what with military service and war work, he lost Robert A. Heinlein, Isaac Asimov, Theodore Sturgeon, L. Sprague de Camp, and L. Ron Hubbard. He had to develop a new team of authors who would continue to produce the quality and style of fiction his readers had come to expect. His bright young men were in the Army. The only answer was to recruit and work with some of the second stringers.

Henry Kuttner was one of those approached, but because of his tarnished reputation a pen name was considered essential. He chose "Lewis Padgett." (p. 330)

The first story under the Padgett name, *Deadlock (Astounding Science-Fiction,* August, 1942), obviously was intended to emulate Asimov's highly popular series of amusing robot stories, but it barely passed muster. *The Twonkey,* in the September issue, struck a highly original note; a radio which is really a robot censors reading matter, drinking habits, and other things possibly harmful to its owner, while obligingly pitching in to wash the dishes. The style, reading like something new to the science-fiction audience, was actually simulated John Collier. The result was widely praised. This story could have been the inspiration of *"With Folded Hands . . ."* and *". . . And of Searching Mind,"* the Jack Williamson stories about robots which never, under any circumstances, will permit humans to do anything that might be harmful to themselves.

The third story, *Piggy Bank,* in the December, 1942, issue of *Astounding Science-Fiction,* reverted to the Asimov robot formula, but the fourth, *Time Locker (Astounding Science-Fiction,* June, 1943), was not a robot story and was a small masterpiece involving a locker that emptied into the future, and the man who killed himself using it. It was slickly written with an adroit twist that could not have been anticipated by the readers. Kuttner's own name appeared on a second story in that issue, *". . . Nothing but Gingerbread Left,"* the title from a verse of Lewis Carroll. No one linked it with the Padgett story in the February issue carrying the Carrollian title, *Mimsy Were the Borogoves.* It dealt with toys from our future projected back in time to the present; they are found by youngsters who devise from them a formula for entering a non-Euclidean universe, disappearing forever from the sight of their parents. Immediately recognized as a classic in the field, it is quite obvious that this story served as the inspiration for *The Veldt* by Ray Bradbury, and possibly for his whole series of childhood-centered stories. (p. 331)

Shock, in the March, 1943, *Astounding Science-Fiction,* is about a genius out of time who develops to be an escapee from a padded cell of the future, set the pattern for similar tales to come, including Gore Vidal's TV and stage play *Visit from a Small Planet.*

The same issue saw Lawrence O'Donnell's debut with *Clash by Night,* plot derived and expanded from Clifford D. Simak's *Rim of the Deep* dealing with a Venusian culture where all civilization survives in the "keeps," giant domes beneath the seas. This one Kuttner wrote on his own, but he had the help of Moore for the novel-length sequel *Fury* (1947), dramatizing the conflict between the long-lived and short-lived Venusians. Though primarily action stories, both proved very popular.

When the news eventually broke that Henry Kuttner was both Lewis Padgett *and* to some degree Lawrence O'Donnell, all past transgressions were forgiven if not completely forgotten by the readers. Their enthusiasm was partially predicated on superior craftsmanship, partially on the desire to see the underdog come out on top, but predominantly because Kuttner usually reminded them of someone they liked. A superbly proficient literary mimic, Kuttner usually wrote like whoever was in demand at the time. (p. 332)

In the cold light of critical appraisal, detaching oneself from the man's likability as a human being, the introduction of the John Collier type of sophisticated fantasy into the science-fiction magazines was Kuttner's major contribution. (p. 333)

Kuttner felt, and many agree, that his best story in this vein was *Don't Look Now* (*Startling Stories,* March, 1948), in which a man at a bar warns his drinking companion to be on the lookout for Martians, who can be recognized by a third eye in their forehead. As he walks away the listener opens his third eye and stares at him. The story has since been done frequently on television.

The Shock, The Twonky, and *Time Locker* . . . are essentially in the same category with the addition of a diverting potpourri of fantastic elements, too rich for the blood of the uninitiate but grist for the mills of the science-fiction fans.

Kuttner's A. E. van Vogt kick, most obviously apparent in his well-done "Baldies" series, . . . are variations on *Slan.* **The Fairy Chessman** and **Tomorrow and Tomorrow,** though creditable, are also attempts to duplicate the methods of van Vogt. (pp. 333-34)

The Lancelot Hogben series, which ran in *Thrilling Wonder Stories* in 1947-49 (the last of which, *Cold War,* was completely written by Moore from a plot supplied by Kuttner), dealing with a family of hillbilly mutations, were ludicrously unbelievable comedies blatantly drawn from a series which Murray Leinster wrote under the name William Fitzgerald in the same magazine, about a character called Bud Gregory.

The popular A. Merritt imitations, beginning with *Earth's Last Citadel,* serialized in *Argosy* in 1943, reached a height of popularity with *Dark World* in the Summer, 1946, *Startling Stories* with its obvious echoes of *Dwellers in the Mirage.* The group obtained a note of authenticity from the contributions of Moore, whose colorful style at times was reminiscent of Merritt.

Who was the real Henry Kuttner? We will never know. The man had discipline, technical brilliance, immense versatility, and ingenuity, and these betrayed him. Lured by opportunism, suffering from an acute sense of inadequacy, he refused to

stand alone, but leaned on others for support: H. P. Lovecraft, Robert E. Howard, Stanley G. Weinbaum, A. Merritt, John Collier, A. E. van Vogt, and, of course, C. L. Moore. (p. 334)

> *Sam Moskowitz, "Henry Kuttner," in his* Seekers of Tomorrow: Masters of Science Fiction (*copyright © 1966, 1964, 1963, 1962, 1961 by Sam Moskowitz; reprinted by permission of the author*), *World Publishing Co., 1966, pp. 319-34.*

DAMON KNIGHT (essay date 1967)

[*Knight echoes Moskowitz's contention (see excerpt above) that Kuttner's style "is frankly borrowed," and attributes elements of two of Kuttner's novels to his use of themes from science fiction authors A. E. Van Vogt and Ray Cummings. Knight, however, praises Kuttner's versatility in matters of plot, as does Lin Carter (see excerpt below).*]

When Kuttner married Catherine Moore in 1940, two seemingly discordant talents merged. Kuttner's previous stories had been superficial and clever, well constructed but without much content or conviction; Moore had written moody fantasies, meaningful but a little thin. In the forties, working together, they began to turn out stories in which the practical solidity of Kuttner's plots seemed to provide a vessel for Moore's poetic imagination. Probably the truth is a good deal more complex; the Kuttners themselves say they do not know any more which of them wrote what (and I've always been uncertain whether to review them as a single or double author); at any rate, the two elements still seem to be present, and separable, in their work. (p. 144)

[*No Boundaries*] gives only a taste of this blending: of the five stories, I take one, "Vintage Season," to be almost entirely C. L. Moore's, and two, "The Devil We Know" and "Exit the Professor," to be equally pure Kuttner.

To dispose of these first: "Vintage Season" is the hauntingly memorable story . . . about the brief visit of a group of cruel pleasure-seekers from the future, which fairly drips with a blend of love, luxury and fear—a specific emotional color, so intense that you can almost taste it. The story is a rounded whole, complete and perfect in itself, except for a rather awkwardly prolonged ending. In an unfolding puzzle story like this one, the argument and the physical action ought to come to a point at once, like the intersection of a fist and a chin.

"The Devil We Know" is a deplorable potboiler . . . with one paragraph of good writing in it—the description of the demon . . . ; the rest is bromides and desperation. "Exit the Professor" is one of the funniest of the unfailingly funny Hogben series; these . . . belong in a book of their own. (pp. 144-45)

Both ["Home There's No Returning" and "Two-Handed Engine"] are about robots, a subject which has intrigued the Kuttners separately before.

Here it's no longer possible even to guess what part is Kuttner's and what Moore's: the hypnotically deft treatment of Deirdre's robot body in "No Woman Born" is clearly echoed in these stories, but so is the ingenious improvisation of ENIAC in "The Ego Machine." The result is a series of brilliant and penetrating images, in which the robot, that clanking servitor of hack writers, becomes a vehicle for allegory and symbol. The blunt weapon suddenly has a point so sharp and fine that it tickles you at the heart before you know you have been touched.

"Home There's No Returning" deals with the robot as savior, and has a stiff little moral at the end: **"Two-Handed Engine"** deals with the robot as destroyer—the Fury of Greek myth, who pursues a malefactor to his doom. Which of the two stories you like better probably depends partly on the meaning these symbols have for you, and partly on how far the emotional experience succeeds in distracting you from the details of the plotting. Stripped of their elaborations, both plots are banal; the sociological backgrounds are no better than they should be, and the other sciences are worse; in one, the physical action of the story is so arbitrarily arranged as to be flatly incredible. Yet these are stories you won't soon forget: probably because science fiction is so full of stories in which the technical data are correct and soundly handled, but the people are so many zero-eyed integers—as blankfaced, but not a hundredth part as meaningful, as the Kuttners' shining robots. (p. 145)

> *Damon Knight, "Genius to Order: Kuttner and Moore," in his* In Search of Wonder: Essays on Modern Science Fiction *(copyright, © 1956, 1967, by Damon Knight; reprinted by courtesy of Advent: Publishers, Inc.), revised edition, Advent, 1967, pp. 139-45.*

JAMES BLISH　(essay date 1972)

[*Blish, a friend of Kuttner's for ten years and a noted science fiction critic, refutes Moskowitz's charges (see excerpt above) that Kuttner wrote only stories with borrowed plots, in styles imitative of other authors. Blish contends that an examination of Kuttner's earliest magazine fiction demonstrates that his later style was carefully developed and not summarily "borrowed."*]

Sam Moskowitz's book *Seekers of Tomorrow* . . . is subtitled "Masters of Modern Science Fiction," and as this subtitle suggests, all but one of the twenty two authors to which it gives major attention were alive in 1966. . . . The exception is Henry Kuttner, who died in 1958.

Moskowitz's chapter (number 18) on Kuttner contains a strikingly just and funny line: "Kuttner was the first in the science-fiction field to rise to glory incognito" [see excerpt above]. . . . It also exhibits one of his major critical weaknesses, the overclaim, as when he characterizes . . . a 1936 Kuttner story as "undoubtedly one of the half-dozen truly *horrifying* short stories in the entire gamut of literature, *all* of literature" [his emphases]. In order to arrive at this judgement Moskowitz would have been obliged to read the entire literary output of the human race, in some six thousand languages. . . .

The chapter's account of Kuttner's career is radically incomplete, particularly of Kuttner's early years as a writer. Kuttner's output of non-science fiction and non-fantasy from 1936 to 1941 was enormous, and included detective, adventure, and Western stories, as well as horror stories. Moskowitz is primarily concerned with science fiction, of course, and is not obliged to mention these predecessors, though he does mention the part of this output which went to the mystery and horror magazines, citing three titles. . . . But Moskowitz's picture of Kuttner as a lifelong imitator of other writers shows in a rather different light when one realizes that Kuttner was technically proficient and versatile almost from the start. Furthermore, the germs of Kuttner's literary preoccupations are buried in this mass of early work, which is all the more important because, as Moskowitz says . . . , Kuttner rarely talked personally or in print about his formative years. Moskowitz has made no attempt to run down these titles, as is revealed in his statement,

"It is likely that he used pen names for stories in *Horror Tales* [correct title, *Horror Stories*] and *Terror Tales*." . . . (p. 140)

Kuttner did indeed use a plethora of pen names, particularly in these early years, but ferreting them out doesn't require much effort; the Day Index alone lists seventeen of them. Among those unmentioned by Moskowitz are Edward J. Bellin, Noel Gardner, Hudson Hastings, Peter Horn, K. H. Maepen, Scott Morgan, Woodrow Wilson Smith, and Charles Stoddard, two of them house names, signed to a total of eight science-fiction stories, plus stories of other kinds. Above all, he does not mention C. H. Liddell, which was a pen name Kuttner used for seven additional science-fiction stories, one of them a novel, in his *last* years (though most of the material published under this name had been written quite early). . . .

Moskowitz's assessment of Kuttner, like that of C. M. Kornbluth, contains elements of direct personal attack which even the most callous historian might hesitate to inflict upon a living figure.

Moskowitz's overall view of Kuttner's achievement, as noted above, is that of a writer who never attained to a voice of his own, but who instead spent his whole life imitating others. Moskowitz in fact views all of literature as a spectacle of successive imitations, which he calls "influences" and "derivations." . . . (p. 141)

He concludes:

> Who was the real Henry Kuttner? We will never know. The man had discipline, technical brilliance, immense versatility, and ingenuity, and these betrayed him. Lured by opportunism, suffering from an acute sense of inadequacy, he refused to stand alone, but leaned on others for support: H. P. Lovecraft, Robert E. Howard, Stanley G. Weinbaum, A. Merritt, John Collier, A. E. van Vogt, and of course C. L. Moore. . . .

The remark about "an acute sense of inadequacy" is gratuitous mind-reading. As a friend of Kuttner's for the last ten years of his life, I can describe him as a sensitive, self-questioning, but basically confident man—but I could no more read his mind than Moskowitz can, nor does such parlor psychoanalysis in any way illuminate what he wrote for publication.

As for "opportunism," this is libel pure and simple: it accuses Kuttner in print of misconduct in his chosen profession, and holds him up to opprobrium to his peers. Taken together, these two slurs—and indeed the whole of Moskowitz's final paragraph—are not criticism at all, but defamation of the dead.

At this point, let me introduce Kuttner speaking for himself:

> . . . for the writer to modify a clinical-necessity story for the market would be awfully bad for his innards. Which may be a yardstick. The stories one feels most strongly about are the ones that should be reworked only when the inward critic thoroughly approves. Stories with which I'm emotionally involved can be reworked effectively only after a considerable time has elapsed, whereas technical jobs can be tinkered with—and seen clearly—very quickly. For an even more practical yardstick, I suggest that the stories one has trouble changing at an editor's request are the ones to leave alone pro tem . . . 100% of the stories written to please

the writer first of all invariably sell. The more compromises on such stories, the worse the results. You've got to accept the validity of criticism and suggestions before you can use them well on a story.

(Personal letter, March 21, 1950)

These are not, I submit, the opinions of an opportunist or of a man with any sense of inadequacy . . . nor of one whose achievement should be patronised, and his memory defamed. . . . (pp. 142-43)

> *James Blish, "Moskowitz on Kuttner," in* Riverside Quarterly *(© 1972 by Leland Sapiro), Vol. 5, No. 2, 1972, pp. 140-44.*

BRIAN W. ALDISS   (essay date 1973)

[Kuttner] was lyrical and gave the impression of seeing the whole picture.

Henry Kuttner's was a sensuous world, non-diagrammatic, blurred at the edges. Whereas Asimov concerned himself with robots and androids which men could not tell from fellow men, Kuttner's universe rejected such non-resonant themes. He posited a human society in which there was a sub-species of telepaths, all linked to each other by thought and sensation. They could be distinguished from ordinary men by their bald heads (hence the series was known as "The Baldies"). In Kuttner's world, people marry and have babies and cry and upset milk. They enjoy the Earth and the Sun. Donne-like, they understand that no man is an island, not even a mechanical island. "Each time a telepath dies, all the rest within minds' reach feel the blackness close upon an exhausted mind, and feel their own minds extinguish a little in response."

Even at a time of tension, Kuttner's telepathic minds are open to random impressions. In **"Humpty Dumpty"** in a 1953 *Astounding* we read:

> By now Cody was at the little park before the long Byzantine building. Trees were wilting above brownish lawns. A shallow rectangular pool held goldfish, who gulped hopefully as they swam to the surface and flipped down again. The little minds of the fish lay open to Cody, minds thoughtless as so many bright, tiny, steady flames on little birthday candles, as he walked past the pool.

An image like that can burn in a reader's mind for decades after he has read it. (pp. 236-37)

Kuttner was exceptional. (p. 237)

> *Brian W. Aldiss, "The Future on a Chipped Plate: The World of John W. Campbell's 'Astounding',"* in his Billion Year Spree: The True History of Science Fiction *(copyright © 1973 by Brian W. Aldiss; reprinted by permission of Doubleday & Company, Inc.; in Canada by the author), Doubleday, 1973 (and reprinted by Schocken Books, 1974), pp. 215-43.**

LIN CARTER   (essay date 1973)

[*Carter is a noted author and critic in the fields of supernatural horror and sword-and-sorcery fiction.*]

[In 1938 an] important and talented figure entered the [sword and sorcery] field with a magnificent yarn about a wandering rogue called Elak, an Atlantean prince whose throne had been usurped out from under him. The first of these Elak yarns was a two-part serial called **"Thunder in the Dawn,"** which began in the 1938 issue of *Weird Tales,* and the author's name was Henry Kuttner. (pp. 66-7)

[Kuttner was] a superb craftsman—a born writer—a story-teller par excellence in much the same way that [Robert E.] Howard had been; however, Kuttner was capable of a truly remarkable variety, unlike Howard. Kuttner could (and did) write every sort of story, from the Lovecraftian brand of slithering horror, the Howardian fantastic swashbuckler, or the delicately lyric Dunsanian fable, to space opera, coldly cerebral science fiction of the type that John W. Campbell, Jr., preferred for his *Astounding Science Fiction,* or the sort of wacky humor with which Thorne Smith made his mark. He was, simply, a "writer's writer," the envy, despair, and idol of his colleagues—able to turn out such a voluminous number of stories that he employed sixteen pen-names in order to sell them.

Kuttner sold four novelettes about Elak of Atlantis to *Weird Tales*—splendid, rousing yarns filled with color and whirlwind action and spectacular magic. They were, however, written during his apprenticeship as a fictioneer and are not without their flaws. The characterization is hardly developed at all, and Elak remains a cardboard figure, little more than a stereotype. (p. 67)

> *Lin Carter, "Lost Cities, Forgotten Ages: The Rise of Fantasy in the American Pulp Magazines," in his* Imaginary Worlds: The Art of Fantasy *(copyright © 1973 by Lin Carter; reprinted by permission of the author and Henry Morrison, Inc., his agents), Ballantine Books, 1973, pp. 49-69.**

RAY BRADBURY   (essay date 1975)

[*At the beginning of his career as a science fiction writer, Bradbury received literary advice from Kuttner and the two became close friends.*]

Move around in high schools and colleges, in various semiintellectual circles high and low, and listen to the names spoken there when books come into the conversation. A great deal of the time you'll hear:

Tolkien. Lovecraft. Heinlein. Sturgeon. Wells. Verne. Orwell. Vonnegut. And, you should excuse the expression, Bradbury.

But not often enough—Kuttner.

Why is this so?

Why has Henry Kuttner been so unfairly neglected since his death back in the late fifties?

Was he as good a writer as the others?

Yes.

Did he write as much?

In some cases more.

Was he a pomegranate writer—popping with seeds, full of ideas?

He was.

Was he as flamboyant as the others mentioned?

Perhaps not enough.

Did he sound his own horn?

Rarely.

Perhaps he was too diversified, working in too many sub-areas of the science-fiction and fantasy genres.

That may well be. (p. vii)

Leafing through the contents of this present volume [*The Best of Henry Kuttner*], I find, to my dismay, that there are no convenient handles by which to pick Kuttner up. He wrote serious stories and light stories. He was not a science-fiction writer or a fantasist or a humorist, and yet he was all of these. If he had lived much longer he might have been troublesome to critics and librarians who like to slap precise labels on authors and file them neatly on shelves.

Kuttner was also troublesome to himself. His first published story, "**The Graveyard Rats,**" became an instant classic when it appeared in *Weird Tales* when he was still a teen-ager. This swift fame for what is in essence a grisly, but finally brilliant, story caused Henry to fall into uneasy silences in later years when the story was mentioned. He did not really want to become a minor-league Lovecraft.

He went through a long period of trying and testing himself. During this time he wrote dozens of undistinguished tales for the various science-fiction pulps, until Thorne Smith out of John Collier out of Robert E. Howard became the at-last-remarkable Henry Kuttner.

Where was the turning point? When did the pulp writer become the writer of quality? I imagine we could point to a half dozen stories that appeared in Campbell's incredible magazine *Unknown*. But I prefer to select two which popped our eyes and dropped our mouths agape in *Astounding*. I feel a deep personal response to them because, in the weeks during which he was finishing "**The Twonky**" and "**Mimsy Were the Borogoves,**" Kuttner gave me copies of the stories to take home, read, and study. I knew then what everyone else knows now; I was reading two stories that would become very special in their field.

It would be hard to guess the impact of these two stories on other writers in the genre. But in all probability hundreds of imitations were written by struggling as well as by published authors. I count myself among them. I very much doubt that my "Zero Hour," or for that matter "The Veldt," would ever have leaped out of my typewriter if Kuttner's imagination had not led the way.

All of this makes it dreadfully sad to consider Henry Kuttner's early death. He had what we all admire and respond to: a love of ideas and a love of literature. (pp. ix-x)

I wish he could have lived into the Kennedy-Johnson-Nixon years, the years when the computers really arrived on-scene, the years of incredible paradox when we footprinted the moon and inched toward the stars. Kuttner, being nonpolitical, thank God, would have given us insights into our political-technological cultures that most of our "in" writers lack because they lean right or left. Kuttner never belonged to anything. He belonged, finally, to all of us. In a polarized world, we need fewer Mailers and many more Kuttners.

This brings us back to the problem of why Kuttner's name remains semi-obscure in our genre.

Apolitics is certainly part of the answer. When you mention Vonnegut, you polarize on the instant. Orwell, similarly. And Heinlein and Wells, and even Verne. (pp. x-xi)

Most science-fiction writers are moral revolutionaries on some level or another, instructing us for our own good. (p. xi)

Here, I think, we may find Kuttner's flaw—if flaw it is, and I for one do not consider it so. One cannot be polarized all the time, one cannot think politically from noon to night. That way is the way of the True Believer—that is to say, finally, the Mad Man.

Kuttner is not mad, nor especially kicking up his heels with joie de vivre. He is wryly calm. If he celebrates anything, it is within his head.

I cannot recall any particularly violent ideas he put forth on politics or politicians. He seemed never to have gone through one of those nineteenth or twentieth summers when we all go a bit amok on Technocracy or Socialism or Scientology. When the fever passes and the smoke clears we wonder what happened to us and are puzzled when our friends don't speak to us for a time, until they discover that the hair has fallen off us and we have given up being a political gorilla and are back being human again. If Kuttner had such a year, or month, I never knew it. And it doesn't show in his work.

So because much of what he wrote is not, in modern terminology, Relevant with a capital R, he is probably graded by some as ten degrees down from Orwell, and twenty below Vonnegut—which is, needless to say, a damned and awful shame. What we need is not more political cant and polarized bias, but more traffic engineers, with no particular traffic in mind save survival, to stand on the highroads leading toward the future, waving us on creatively but not necessarily banging our ears when we, children that we are, misbehave.

Kuttner, then, was no moral revolutionary or political reformer. He was an entertaining writer. His stories are seeded with ideas and moralities, yes, but these do not cry out, shout, shriek, or necessarily ask for change. This is the way we are, Kuttner says, what do you think of us?

And so, the more I think of it, the more I feel Kuttner has been cursed by the great curse of our time. People have too often asked: Well, how do we *use* Kuttner? What's he good for? What kind of tool is he? Where does he fit? What is the appropriate label? Will people look up to me if I carry "**Mimsy Were the Borogoves**" around campus rather than *The Gulag Archipelago*?

If this is not the complete explanation, it leans toward it, in any event. In what tends to be a practical Kleenex culture, if you can't clean out your ears with an author, you tend, because others bully you about it, to leave him alone. (pp. xi-xii)

[If you] look to Kuttner for religious instruction, secular improvement, or moral renovation, save with certain exceptions you had best retreat to *Siddhartha* and other forms of literate navel-lint plucking with which the sophomores of the world bug each other. Kuttner will not kick, bite, beat, much less kiss, hug, stroke, or improve you. And thank God for that. I have had enough improvement, just as I have had too much cotton candy at too many circuses. (p. xii)

Ray Bradbury, "Henry Kuttner: A Neglected Master" (reprinted by permission of Don Congdon Associates, Inc.; copyright © 1975 by Ray Bradbury), in The Best of Henry Kuttner *by Henry Kuttner, Nelson Doubleday, Inc., 1975, pp. vii-xii.*

JAMES GUNN   (essay date 1976)

[*In this lengthy discussion of Kuttner's work, Gunn provides comprehensive background to the state of science fiction during the early years of World War II, and details Kuttner's considerable contributions to the genre at that time. Writing primarily about Kuttner and C. L. Moore as a team, Gunn finds they were instrumental in introducing mainstream fiction techniques and a concern for literary excellence to science fiction.*]

What the Kuttners brought to science fiction, which broadened it and helped it evolve, was a concern for literary skill and culture. The Kuttners expanded the techniques of science fiction to include techniques prevalent in the mainstream; they expanded its scope to include the vast cultural tradition available outside science fiction, just as, in their ways, Heinlein would draw upon and bring into his fiction the engineering and military education he received at Annapolis, Asimov would open to science fiction the concepts and methods of the working scientist, and Hal Clement and Larry Niven would expand science fiction into the physical sciences in such works as *A Mission of Gravity* and *Ringworld*. The significance of the Kuttners' work rests in the fact that much of the development in science fiction over the past twenty years has come along the lines they pioneered.

This is not to say that everything the Kuttners wrote (not even the stories they wrote for *Astounding*) was without precedent: certainly man's cultural heritage and a concern for style were a part of science fiction in its beginnings, in the work, for instance, of Mary Shelley and Edgar Allan Poe, both of whom, directly or indirectly, benefited from a classical English education. And there was H. G. Wells. But those classical and literary traditions were lost in the science fiction ghetto created by Hugo Gernsback in 1926; they were replaced by newer pulp traditions of action and adventure, and eventually of scientific accuracy and informed speculation about one science after another, beginning with geography and mesmerism and progressing through chemistry, electricity, physics, and mathematics to computers, psychology, sociology, and biology.

Many areas of human experience, as contrasted with human knowledge, were considered unimportant or inappropriate to science fiction, either consciously—as in the case of sexual relationships and such other basic functions as eating and excreting—or unconsciously in areas in which writers were unaware or uneasy, such as cultural traditions and stylistic methods.

In the latter areas the Kuttners moved with growing skill and familiarity. Insofar as one can disentangle the gestalts they created, Moore seems to have contributed most of the unusual romantic involvements and perhaps all the classical references to myth, legend, and literature which served to expand and enrich the Kuttner's best work. Kuttner provided insights into the minds of children—he seemed to have a particular fondness for what has become known as the generation gap—and his literary references, perhaps appropriately, were almost entirely restricted to *Alice in Wonderland* and *Through the Looking Glass*. (pp. 194-95)

As fantasy writers, the Kuttners were attracted first to the new *Unknown*, introduced by Campbell as a companion fantasy magazine to *Astounding* with the issue of March 1939. (p. 195)

But after their marriage the Kuttners turned most of their efforts toward science fiction, particularly during the 1942-1945 period. (pp. 195-96)

"**The Twonky**" was a memorable story frequently anthologized and adapted for other media. What makes it distinctive is its domestic setting and matter-of-fact tone; into this situation is introduced a console radio-record player. Kerry Westerfield, a likeable professor at the university, does not know that it is actually a Twonky, manufactured by a workman from the future who was caught in a temporal snag and, while under partial amnesia, created a Twonky with the materials at hand in a radio factory. The Twonky analyzes Westerfield, performs services for him—such as lighting his cigarette and washing the dishes—and then begins to censor his reading and his personal habits. Westerfield's reactions run through amazement, interest, and finally consternation. In the end, the Twonky blocks his friend's memory, destroys his wife when she starts toward it with a hatchet, and then disintegrates Westerfield when he attacks it, saying, "Subject basically unsuitable. Elimination has been necessary." And then, "Preparation for next subject completed." The story ends with a newly married couple looking over the house and admiring the console.

The story is pleasantly and efficiently told, with some effective references to music and literature (including *Alice in Wonderland*). "**The Twonky**" suggests one other observation: without its introductory exposition about the Twonky's origin, "**The Twonky**" would have a Kafkaesque mainstream quality; explanations seem to be one aspect which distinguishes science fiction from mainstream stories. The mainstream cherishes its ambiguity. (p. 196)

Kuttner's "**Clash by Night**" introduced, for the first time, the concept of a Venus on which the land and its various life forms were so deadly that man had built his cities under impervium domes in the oceans. It contained, also, one of the early suggestions that an atomic accident might consume the Earth. Earth had been turned into another sun. . . . (p. 198)

The concept would be used again by Kuttner, not only in *Fury*, the novel built upon the same background, but in the two-part 1947 serial, "**Tomorrow and Tomorrow**." In response to the catastrophe on Earth, scientists on Venus had outlawed atomic research and adopted a peculiarly modern "Minervan Oath":

> . . . to work for the ultimate good of mankind . . . taking all precautions against harming humanity and science . . . requiring permission from those in authority before undertaking any experiment involving peril to the race . . . remembering always the extent of trust placed in us and remembering forever the death of the mother planet through misuse of knowledge. . . .

However accidental the choice of the O'Donnell pseudonym, in the first of these stories some of the characteristics are apparent which would be developed and enlarged in later work to be published under that name: the use of chapter epigraphs, literary quotations, and mythological references (in this case to Greek gods Mars, Minerva, and Aphrodite); relatively complex characterization (in "**Clash by Night**," Captain Scott is torn between two different kinds of life and between his loyalty to his Free Companions and the military life and his knowledge that it is meaningless and doomed); and conflict and complication which are not altogether linear. The usual Kuttner story, even the customary Padgett narrative, is slick and controlled; "**Clash by Night**" approaches the texture of real life. Moore, in a private letter, attributes this first O'Donnell story to Kuttner, but internal evidence suggests that she may have had a significant hand in it.

In 1943 *Astounding* also published one of the Kuttner classics, the story which placed seventh for inclusion in *The Science Fiction Hall of Fame*, "**Mimsy Were the Borogoves**." "**Mimsy . . .**" introduced one of Kuttner's favorite notions: children are aliens. This quiet, controlled story begins with a scientist in the future stuffing into a time-travel device some of the toys which had helped his son "pass over from Earth"; Scott, the son of Dennis and Jane Paradine, discovers the faulty device, extracts the toys, and, along with his younger sister, Emma, begins to play with them. The toys teach Scott and Emma how to perceive and manipulate different kinds of space and relationships because, unlike adults, they're "not handicapped by too many preconceived ideas." Eventually, while their parents puzzle out what the children are doing, learning, and becoming, the children discover the way to pass over into a larger world through a strange physical parallel to the equation described in the *Through the Looking Glass* quatrain beginning "'Twas brillig. . . .''

Science fiction and fantasy have discovered many ways to achieve conviction; science fiction, in particular, has struggled for verisimilitude. One fantasy technique is the final triumphant display of the key artifact, as in many a tale of horror. . . . Science fiction refined and sophisticated the technique. Kuttner used it almost unchanged in "The Third Eye"—also called "Don't Look Now"—the frequently anthologized and dramatized 1948 *Startling Stories* tour-de-force which ends with the Martian opening his third eye and looking after the man leaving the bar. In "Mimsy . . ." Kuttner does it more subtly. A series of references to *Through the Looking Glass* leads to the revelation that Alice Liddell also had found a box of toys from the future (and the reader realizes that the opening section describes *two* time travel experiments) and that she had told Charles Dodgson the songs and verses which he sprinkled through the book he would later write.

Kuttner brought in other references: Hughes' *High Wind in Jamaica*, the nature of education, the spawning patterns of eels and salmon. And the quiet tone builds to a final climax in which the sensible father sees his son and daughter disappear like smoke. We feel his horror and his wife's horror yet to come, as well as the potential horror of the children when they arrive in a larger world where there are no adults and where they will be alone, possibly helpless, and afraid. (pp. 198-200)

"When the Bough Breaks" by Lewis Padgett plays upon the notion introduced in "Mimsy . . ." that children are aliens. Almost as soon as Kuttner has introduced Joe and Myra Calderon (Joe is a favorite Kuttner character, a reasonable, rational university professor) as the new parents of the infant Alexander, he insinuates that "babies are a great trial. Still they're worth it." But then goblin-like men from the future arrive at their door and acclaim Alexander as a mutant, the father of their race, and a long-lived "x-free superman" of the future. They have traveled through time to his childhood so that they can remove the frustrations Alexander suffered as a child and begin his education early enough that he can attain still greater feats of intellect and insight. Joe and Myra are unable to discipline Alexander, at first because of the powerful gadgets of the dwarfs from the future and then because of the growing powers of the infant superman. His parents can only watch nervously as Alexander grows more powerful but not more mature. He teases and torments his parents through his abilities of teleportation, telekinesis, and energy control, with "a child's normal cruelty and selfishness." . . . Driven beyond endurance, they allow Alexander to play with a blue ovoid his dwarf mentor has forbidden him, and Alexander destroys himself.

Besides the insights into infant irritation and parental patience, the story is enriched with references to biology ("parthenogenesis, binary fission") and mythology ("Deucalion and what's

her name—that's us. Parents of a new race"; "I feel more like Prometheus. . . . He was helpful, too. And he ended up with a vulture eating his liver.") And the story includes comments about riddles, the nature of humor, and comic strips. Moore estimates that "When the Bough Breaks" was seventy per cent Kuttner. (pp. 200-01)

"The Piper's Son," "Three Blind Mice," "The Lion and the Unicorn," and "Beggars in Velvet" [belong] to Kuttner's "Baldies" series about mutant telepaths trying to remain a part of human society through restraint and good manners while they cope with paranoia among themselves: effective stories, competently done, sensibly conceived, but seldom touched with greatness or special insights. (p. 204)

["The Fairy Chessman" and "Tomorrow and Tomorrow" both begin with] scenes in which a man with overpowering responsibilities fears that he is beginning to lose his sanity. In "The Fairy Chessmen," the protagonist is Robert Cameron, Civilian Director of Psychometrics in Low Chicago. (Life on the surface is no longer possible in a United States which has been at war for decades with "the Falangists.") Cameron fears he is losing his mind when reality begins to change around him; the story opens with a great line: "The doorknob opened a blue eye and looked at him." In "Tomorrow and Tomorrow," Joseph Breden has nightmares about blowing up the atomic pile of which he is a guardian; he lives in a world the antithesis of "The Fairy Chessmen": a Global Peace Commission, set up after an abortive World War II, has kept peace for one hundred years, but the price of peace has been a stern maintenance of the status quo, including a ban on new research.

The stories have more similarities than differences: both involve mutations caused by proximity to radiation; both include interaction with strange, extra-temporal forces (in "Chessmen" a genetically bred and conditioned warrior from the future named Ridgeley, whose nation has been defeated in his own time, has escaped by means of one-way time travel to Cameron's world and is manipulating the war on both sides, while in "Tomorrow" a mutant called "the Freak" perceives alternate worlds created by decisions made during World War II); and both progress by means of plots and counter-plots. Both have some nice touches, including in "Chessmen" effective description of Low Chicago; and both have well calculated surprises at the end. In "Chessmen" Cameron solves his problem, but now fears that what he must do will bring about Ridgeley's world. Before his aide can propose an alternative to a world continually at war by directing man's need for an Enemy toward the stars, the hostile universe, Cameron goes mad; the final sentence repeats the first. In "Tomorrow" Kuttner suggests that the world should have its atomic war and then get on to a beneficent, peaceful world where progress is possible (compare H. G. Wells's utopian novels). But the two short novels, though readable enough, do not represent major additions to the science fiction canon, possibly because they never suggest universals. (pp. 205-06)

An immediate sensation when it appeared, the novelette ["Vintage Season"] still retains its evocative appeal, as evidenced by its inclusion in *The Science Fiction Hall of Fame*, volume II, where it was ranked sixth among the novelettes. The narrative is relatively simple: a young man named Oliver Wilson rents his house to three foreigners, Omerie, Klia, and Kleph Sancisco; they are perfectly dressed but as if for a part, they are arrogantly assured, and they look "expensive." The complication comes through Oliver's fiancée, who wants him to get out of his lease and accept a better offer from another "foreigner." The substance of the story involves the Sanciscos, who move into the house with him and conduct themselves strangely, and Oliver's growing involvement with them and gradual understanding of what they are: time-travelers, dilettantes of the future making a sort of pilgrimage of the seasons—Canterbury in autumn in the 14th century, Christmastime in Rome at the Coronation of Charlemagne in 800, and May in Oliver's house and time. (p. 206)

At the end all the Sancisco's friends from the future gather in the three front bedrooms of the house to watch a small meteor strike the city. The city burns; Oliver falls ill; the character who has been largely an observer becomes the central figure as he awakens to find the future's great composer of music and visual images, Cenbe, finishing his composition from the inspiration of the city's destruction, with Oliver's death-marked face one of the major motifs. Fatally ill, Oliver writes down a message about the time-travelers who might be captured and forced to warn about impending disasters, but six days later the house is dynamited as part of a futile attempt to halt the relentless spread of the Blue Death.

The impact of the story comes from two elements: the gay mood of the pilgrims in time contrasted with the cataclysmic events involving the protagonist and his city; and the distancing effect from contemporary man—which lies at the heart of all good science fiction—achieved through Oliver's inability to understand the Sanciscos: what they do and why, their pleasures, their lives, their values, and their attitudes toward his present. (p. 207)

Oliver had succumbed to the lure of the delightful and the unknown, including Kleph, who had seemed more human than the others but was only weaker and more foolish; he now realizes that "all of them had been touched with a pettiness, the faculty that had enabled Hollia to concentrate on her malicious, small schemes to acquire a ringside seat while the meteor thundered in toward Earth's atmosphere. They were all dilettantes, Kleph and Omerie and the others. They toured time, but only as onlookers. Were they bored—sated—with their normal existence?" Stories are great as they exhibit uniqueness of idea; specificity of character, setting, and action; suitability of diction and style; and universality of theme. All of these qualities can be found in **"Vintage Season."**

Similar statements, though more qualified, might be made about the Kuttners' 1947 *Astounding* serial **Fury,** another story by O'Donnell. The novel was eighty-per-cent Kuttner. The setting, a watery Venus still in its ravening Jurassic period, has been rendered improbable, perhaps impossible, by recent scientific observations and unmanned rocket explorations. But the storyline, the driving of a decaying humanity out of its undersea paradise onto the hostile surface, retains its universality. The Kuttners attack the problem that defeats most utopias, how to make people do what is good for them.

The story begins seven hundred years after the undersea Keeps were created, six hundred years after Earth was turned by atomic holocaust into a star, and three hundred years after **"Clash by Night."** The Keeps are ruled by immortals—tall, slim, aristocratic mutants who outlive normal humanity by centuries and can make their plans for the long term. For lack of a challenge, because life is too easy, the Keeps have become "the tomb, or womb, or both for the men of Venus."

To a couple of immortals, at the cost of the mother's life, is born a child. Turning insanely on the infant, the father has the child operated upon and converted, by endocrinological tampering, into someone who will grow up fleshy, thick, and bald—

obviously not an immortal. The child grows up to be Sam Reed; as a street urchin he comes under the tutelage of a master criminal named the Slider and learns to live ruthlessly and savagely, using others before they can use him. He lives with fury, in constant rebellion against the shortness of his life measured against his needs and ambitions, not knowing that he is immortal. The plot brings him into contact with his own Harker family of immortals (he has an affair with a woman who may be his great-great-grandmother); with Ben Crowell, a one-thousand-year-old immortal who can predict the future and has become the Logician at the Temple of Truth; and with Robin Hale, an immortal who is the last surviving Free Companion and wishes to persuade the people of the Keeps to go landside. Sam uses Hale to work a stock swindle based on conquering landside, but in the moment of his triumph his mistress, bribed by the Harkers, gives him dreamdust. Normally dreamdust is fatal, but Sam is nursed through forty years of unconsciousness. He awakens to the realization that he, too, is immortal. The remainder of the novel consists of Sam's efforts to force the people of the Keeps to the land surfaces, deadly with Venusian life forms though they are; his plans culminate in a simulated rebellion which turns radioactive the impervium domes of the Keeps.

Woven through the plot is the kind of insights seldom found in science fiction novels: immortals view life differently (they can take up occupations that require fifty or one hundred years of preparation; they have time to let their enemies die); a workless society provides limited alternatives (a person can be a technician, an artist, or a hedonist); an unrelenting search for pleasure must go continually further for satisfaction (deadly "happy clocks" and "dream dust"); foreknowledge has built-in difficulties (which is why the utterances of oracles are always cryptic).

The novel is rounded with literary touches which satisfy the reader looking for some extension of the work beyond the here-and-now (or there-and-then): epigraphs, a prologue and an epilogue, quotations, mythological references. In the prologue the word "fury" is applied to the deadly, teeming land surface of Venus; later the word describes Sam Reed. After Sam awakens, a character comments, "Someone had fed him dream-dust forty years ago. *The voice is Jacob's voice, but the hand is the hand of Esau.*"

Finally, wounded, defeated through treachery, Sam is spirited away by Ben Crowell, who tells him:

> '. . . Up till now we've needed you, Sam. Once
> in a long while a fella like you comes along,
> somebody strong enough to move a world. . . .
> There's nothing you wouldn't do, son, nothing
> at all—if it would get you what you want. . . .
> If you hadn't been born, if Blaze hadn't done
> what he did, mankind would be in the Keeps
> yet. And in a few hundred years, or a thousand,
> say, the race would have died out. . . . But
> now we've come landside. We'll finish colo-
> nizing Venus. And then we'll go out and col-
> onize the whole universe, I expect. . . . All
> you could think of was repeating the thing that
> made you a success—more fighting, more
> force. . . . You had the same drive that made
> the first life-form leave water for land, but we
> can't use your kind any more for a while, Sam.
> The race has got immortality, Sam, and you
> gave it to 'em. . . .'

Ben Crowell puts Sam to sleep where he will stay until he and his "fury" may be needed again. (pp. 207-10)

The novel concludes with an epilogue which, in spite of its gimmickery, opens up the novel for further speculation and suggests eternal principles at work rather than the special circumstances which so often weaken the endings of science fiction novels: "Sam woke—" (p. 210)

Both stories were very nearly fifty-fifty collaborations; both are rich plum-puddings of stories. In **"Private Eye"** the fullness comes in large part from psychology; in **"Two-Handed Engine,"** from legend and literature. Even the titles are revealing: **"Private Eye"** is a psychological pun; **"Two-Handed Engine"** is a quotation from Milton:

> But that two-handed engine at the door
> Stands ready to smite once, and smite no more. . . .
>
> (p. 211)

The Kuttners did not deal with such themes as "the wonderful journey," or man and the future (in any extrapolative sense, with the possible exception of *Fury*, **"Judgment Night,"** and— in lesser ways, because they are not extrapolative but thematic—**"The Fairy Chessmen"** and **"Tomorrow and Tomorrow"**); cataclysm (they dealt entirely with precataclysm or post-cataclysm, and never in a cataclysmic vein); and only in a limited way with man and his environment, man and alien, and man and religion.

The Kuttners concerned themselves principally with man and society; how is man going to function in the new worlds that will be created by changes in technology, science, and social restructuring? To this theme they brought perceptions and techniques refined by their fantasy writing. (pp. 213-14)

What the Kuttners brought to science fiction from fantasy were the qualities of literature: the quest for conviction through characterization and individualization, through setting, through symbol and myth. Fantasy always has been close to mainstream literature, if not indistinguishable from it; in our times, at least, both are concerned with private visions rather than the public— or shared—visions of science fiction. The mixture of the two brought back from beyond the grace of years what might be called literary science fiction, or science fiction which attempted to meet the standards of mainstream literature. It was not an easy task, for elements on both sides are antagonistic. At best, an uneasy balance could be struck: too much science fiction convention, too much explanation, and the characters seem manipulated by the story. The non-initiated reader is lost. Too much concern for style, for myth, for the individual, and the heart of science fiction—the idea—is buried beyond recall. In the 1940's the Kuttners provided the best mixture. (p. 215)

> *James Gunn, "Henry Kuttner, C. L. Moore, Lewis Padgett et al.," in* Voices for the Future: Essays on Major Science Fiction Writers *(© 1976 by The Pop-* *ular Press), Bowling Green University Popular Press, 1976, pp. 185-215.**

MARK ROSE (essay date 1981)

Henry Kuttner's and C. L. Moore's **"Vintage Season"** . . . deals with travelers from the future on a packaged tour of the most perfect seasons in history. Part of the appeal of the present moment is the weather—the loveliest May on record—and part is the disaster that concludes the season when a great meteor strikes the earth bringing fire and plague. The travelers are artists and connoisseurs who relish human spectacles. For them both the delight and the pain of the past are, like works of art, simultaneously real and not real. Built upon the analogy between temporal and aesthetic distance, **"Vintage Season"** becomes a parable of engagement and disengagement, a suggestive exploration of the processes that transform the immediacy of human experience into material for contemplation.

The visualization of time as a line generates the idea of time travel and it also generates the paradox of the time loop, the line bent back into a circle. Kuttner's and Moore's travelers remark that they are forbidden to intervene to ease the sufferings of the past because interference might alter their present. But what if a time traveler murdered his grandfather? Would the traveler himself cease to exist? If so, how could he have murdered his grandfather? Again and again, time-travel stories play with such paradoxes, working witty or bizarre variations on the theme. (pp. 107-08)

> *Mark Rose, "Time," in his* Alien Encounters: Anatomy of Science Fiction *(copyright © 1981 by the President and Fellows of Harvard College; excerpted by permission), Cambridge, Mass.: Harvard University Press, 1981, pp. 96-138.**

ADDITIONAL BIBLIOGRAPHY

DeBolt, Joe, and Pfeiffer, John R. "The Modern Period: 1938-1980." In *Anatomy of Wonder: A Critical Guide to Science Fiction*, 2d ed., edited by Neil Barron, pp. 125-35. New York: R. R. Bowker, 1981.*

> Includes annotated entries for six of Kuttner's works: *The Best of Henry Kuttner, Fury, Mutant, Robots Have No Tails, Tomorrow and Tomorrow* and *The Fairy Chessmen*. The publisher and publication date of each work is given, along with information about pseudonyms and collaborations. A brief summary of the plot of each work is appended.

Lovecraft, H. P. *Selected Letters: 1934-1937*. Edited by August Derleth and James Turner. Sauk City, Wisconsin: Arkham House Publishers, 1976, 436 p.*

> Letter to Kuttner of November 30, 1936, indicative of the close relationship that had developed between the correspondents. Lovecraft praises Kuttner's "Hydra" as a "vivid" story which he read "with the keenest enjoyment."

(Joaquim Maria) Machado de Assis

1839-1908

Brazilian novelist, short story writer, poet, critic, dramatist, essayist, and journalist.

Machado is recognized as a master of the psychological novel. His works are especially praised for their modernity of theme and technique. Throughout his fiction, which has been called bitterly pessimistic and sardonic, Machado used satire to illuminate the trivial vanities and selfishness of humanity. His novels, which are more concerned with character examination than with plot development, have been compared to those of Henry James.

Machado was born in Rio de Janeiro, the son of a black house painter and Portuguese mother. His mother died when he was young and his mulatto stepmother, Maria Ines, is credited with introducing the youth to literature. At seventeen, Machado was apprenticed to a printer and became a proofreader and typesetter. This provided him with the opportunity to associate with many important literary figures, who in later years would help get his initial works published. Machado was an early success and his work was widely acclaimed by the time he was twenty-five. Some critics, noting a preoccupation in Machado's initial works with the inevitable sacrifices one makes to succeed, find this to be evidence of guilt the author felt over his abandonment of his stepmother when he was on the threshold of success. The pessimism throughout his works has similarly been attributed to strong feelings of inferiority about his black heritage and his lifelong epilepsy. However, several commentators, including his most important English-language critic, Helen Caldwell, feel that there is no indication in his fiction or in the facts known about his life to support this view. Nevertheless, it is still a point of critical contention. After his printing apprenticeship, Machado joined the civil service and spent most of his life as a middle-level bureaucrat. Popular with readers and critics, Machado, in 1897, was made president for life of the newly founded Brazilian Academy of Letters.

Machado's earliest literary works were dramas and poetry. Most of his dramatic work was unpublished or unproduced, and was quickly ignored. Like his dramas, Machado's poetry is now largely forgotten; however, his best work in this genre is found in his collection *Occidentais,* which was published in *Poesias completas.* Although criticized for their mundane style and their lack of emotion, these poems faithfully represent Machado's belief that life is meaningless, while conveying both his characteristic attitude of ironic resignation and his disenchanted examination of human illusions. These traits are displayed more extensively and with greater artistic success in his novels.

Machado's first four novels—*Resurreiçáo, A mão e a luva (The Hand and the Glove), Helena,* and *Yayá Garcia*—are generally characterized as products of the Romantic movement in Brazilian literature, and are considered inferior to his later fiction. Like other works of this movement, Machado's novels are guided by Romantic plot conventions centering upon thwarted love or ambition, and are often criticized for their unrealistic situations and lack of proper character motivation. An interesting exception to this criticism is made by Alfred J. MacAdam, who believes that all of Machado's novels should be considered satires, a viewpoint that gives new importance to the early novels by stressing their satiric elements and thus justifying their lack of conventional realism. In these early novels, Machado meticulously examined the moral and social implications of the marriage of convenience, while he presented detailed portraits of female characters. In his later works he abandoned both female protagonists and his concern with the delineation of class and social distinctions.

Memórias pósthumas de Braz Cubas (Epitaph of a Small Winner) initiates what has been called Machado's realistic period. Critics often note that the fictional devices he used in the psychological novels of this period—self-reflection, unreliable narrators, time shifts, and constant irony—foreshadow the techniques of literary modernism. Throughout this period Machado was concerned with the effects of egotism, with extremes of self-love, and with the absurdity of life and inevitability of death. Machado did not believe that individual existences were guided by any transcendental forces. He also viewed human nature as fundamentally irrational, finding self-love to be the only consistent motivating force in human behavior. While characterizing this world-view as pessimistic, critics also note that Machado's fiction conveys amusement rather than bitterness toward the folly of selfish, passion-driven humanity.

The Granger Collection, New York

Throughout his novels, and particularly in *Epitaph of a Small Winner*, Machado challenged the accepted beliefs of society through his disillusioned mocking. For this reason Richard J. Callan has stated that "at the heart of his criticism of mankind lies the hope that he can move his readers to a reform of manners." Similarly, William L. Grossman believes that *Epitaph of a Small Winner* affirms several important values by destroying many false gods and illusions.

Like *Epitaph of a Small Winner, Dom Casmurro*, considered Machado's masterpiece, is told by an unreliable narrator. Casmurro's deception, admitted omission of facts, and intentional ambiguity are so skillfully executed that critics still disagree about the author's intent. The narrator's self-destructive conviction that his wife and best friend cuckolded him, and that his son is in fact theirs, was long accepted as a central fact of the novel. But in recent years critics have questioned whether Santiago's conclusion was perhaps based on suspicion, circumstantial evidence, and unfounded jealousy—all prevalent themes in Machado's novels. In *Dom Casmurro*, as in all his major novels, Machado examined the unreliability of human perception and the tenuous nature of "truth," which Machado believed were motivated and shaped by self-interest. In her closely argued *The Brazilian Othello of Machado de Assis*, Helen Caldwell points out that Shakespearean symbols and allusions throughout the novel are important in analyzing the work and in understanding the various manifestations of guilt and innocence. Ultimately, what critics find important in the novel is not the truth of Dom Casmurro's assertions, but the reasons for his desire to believe them. Most later critics agree that Santiago seems to be pleading his case before a jury of readers in an attempt to let them decide for themselves, and for him, if his cruelty toward those closest to him was justified.

Machado's last two novels, *Esaú e Jacob (Esau and Jacob)* and *Memorial de Ayres (Counselor Ayres' Memorial)*, are read by critics as extended allegorical interpretations of contemporary Brazilian social conflicts. The warring twins of the title *Esau and Jacob*, for example, have been seen as symbolic of the emancipation period in Rio de Janeiro, representing conflicts between liberal and conservative factions, between tradition and modern values, and between colonial life and the birth of an independent Brazil. In *Counselor Ayres' Memorial*, Brazil is again metaphorically evoked, but this time Machado expresses hope for the future of his country if it can learn to be guided by selfless love—the force which rejuvenates the jaded ambassador Ayres in the novel. The affirmations of life and love found in this novel are regarded as the alternatives to total pessimism that were so artfully hidden in Machado's earlier works.

In addition to his skill as a novelist, Machado is considered a master of the short story. Although he dealt with the same preoccupations found in his larger fictions—such as the revelation of hidden or unconscious motives and a critique of human egotism and inadequacy—his range as a short story writer was much broader. In his more than two hundred stories, Machado experimented with a variety of styles and forms. This diversity of subject and technique, described in detail by Donald M. Decker, suggests why Machado's stories are considered as important as his novels—in briefer form they wholly encompass his vision of life.

In Machado's fiction, many aspects of modern life are treated satirically. It is this pervasive satire which allows for the diversity of opinions regarding the nature of Machado's pessimism. As Waldo Frank noted: "Within the quiet, courses a

complex fugue: innocence cruelly punished and revealed as guilt; pleasure pleasurably crushed; the 'good' and the 'beautiful' on the wrack and dissolving into their contraries. The blood, indeed the core, of the fictive world of Machado de Assis is ambiguity—ambiguity raised to a principle and a substance."

(See also *Contemporary Authors*, Vol. 107.)

PRINCIPAL WORKS

Desencantos [first publication]   (drama)   1861
Teatro   (essays)   1863
Crisálidas   (poetry)   1864
Quáse ministro   (drama)   1864
Os deuses de casaca   (drama)   1866
Phalenas   (poetry)   1869
Contos fluminenses   (short stories)   1870
Resurreiçáo   (novel)   1872
Histórias de meia-noite   (short stories)   1873
A máo e a luva   (novel)   1874
    [*The Hand and the Glove*, 1970]
Americanas   (poetry)   1875
Helena   (novel)   1876
Yayá Garcia   (novel)   1878
    [*Yayá Garcia*, 1976; also published as *Iaiá Garcia*, 1977]
Tu, só tu, puro amor   (drama)   1880
    [*You, Love, and Love Alone*, 1972]
Memórias pósthumas de Braz Cubas   (novel)   1881
    [*Epitaph of a Small Winner*, 1952; also published as
      Posthumous Reminiscences of Braz Cubas, 1955]
Histórias sem data   (short stories)   1884
Papéis avulos   (short stories)   1884
Quincas Borba   (novel)   1891
    [*Philosopher or Dog?* 1954; also published as *The
      Heritage of Quincas Borba*, 1954]
Várias histórias   (short stories)   1895
Dom Casmurro   (novel)   1899
    [*Dom Casmurro*, 1953]
Páginas recolhidas   (short stories)   1899
Poesias completas   (poetry)   1901
Esaú e Jacob   (novel)   1904
    [*Esau and Jacob*, 1965]
Reliquas de casa velha   (short stories)   1906
Memorial de Ayres   (novel)   1908
    [*Counselor Ayres' Memorial*, 1972]
The Psychiatrist, and Other Stories   (short stories)   1963
What Went on at the Baroness': A Tale with a Point   (short
    story)   1963
The Devil's Church, and Other Stories   (short stories)
    1977

ISAAC GOLDBERG   (essay date 1922)

[*Goldberg's* Brazilian Literature *is often praised as the pioneering work which introduced readers of the United States to the literature of Brazil.*]

[Machado de Assis] is not of the sort that dissolves into ecstasies before a wonderful sunset or rises to the empyrean on the wings of song; for such self-abandonment he is too critical, too self-conscious. In him, then, as a poet we are not to seek for passion; in his tales we must not hunt too eagerly for action; in his novels (let us call them such) we are not to hope for adventure, intrigue, climax. Machado de Assis is, as far as a man may be, sui generis, a literary law unto himself. His best productions, which range over thirty years of mature activity, reveal an eclectic spirit in whom something of classic repose balances his innate pessimism. It has been written of him that he was "a man of half tints, of half words, of half ideas, of half systems. . . ." Such an estimate, if it be purged of any derogatory insinuations, is, on the whole, just; if Machado de Assis seems to miss real greatness, it is because of something inherently balanced in his make-up; he is never himself carried away, and therefore neither are we. (pp. 143-44)

The poetry of Machado de Assis appears in four collections, all of which go to make up a book of moderate size. And, if the truth is to be told, their worth is about as moderate as their size. If critics have found him, in his verse, very correct and somewhat cold; if they have pointed out that he lacked a vivid imagination, suffered from a limited vocabulary, was indifferent to nature, and thus deficient in description, they have but spoken what is evident from a reading of the lines. This is not to say that a poem here and there has not become part of the national memory—as, for example, the well-known *Circulo Vicioso* (**Vicious Circle**) and *Mosca Azul* (**The Blue Fly**)—verses of a broadly moralistic significance and of little originality. His *Chrysalides* [was] the first collection . . . ; already his muse appears as a lady desirous of tranquillity (and this at the age of twenty-five!) while in the poem *Erro* he makes the tell-tale declaration: "I loved you one day with that transient love which is born in the imagination and does not reach the heart." There you have the type of love that appears in his poetry; and there you have one of the reasons why the man is so much more successful as a psychological ironist in his novels than as a poet. Yet close study would show that at times this tranquillity, far from being always the absence of torment, is the result of neutralizing forces; it is like the revolving disk of primary hues that seems white in the rapidity of its whirling.

These early poems dwell upon such love; upon a desire for justice, as revealed in his *Epitaphio do Mexico* (**Mexico's Epitaph**) and *Polonia* (**Poland**); upon an elegiac note that seems statement rather than feeling. "Like a pelican of love," he writes in one of his poems that recalls the famous image of de Musset, "I will rend my breast and nurture my offspring with my own blood; my offspring: desire, chimera, hope. . . ." But read through the verses of *Chrysalides* and it is hard to find where any red blood flows. The vocabulary is small, the phrases are trite; his very muse is named *Musa Consolatrix,* bringing solace rather than agitated emotion.

Phalenas (**Moths . . .**) is more varied; the collection shows a sense of humour, a feeling for the exotic, as in the quasi-Chinese poems, which are of a delicate pallor. But there is little new in his admonitions to cull the flower ere it fade, and his love poetry would insult a sensitive maiden with its self-understanding substratum of commentary. His reserve is simply too great to permit outbursts and like the worshipper of whom he speaks in his *Lagrimas de Cera,* he "did not shed a single tear. She had faith, the flame to burn—but what she could not do was weep." He is altogether too frequently the self-observer rather than the self-giver; nor would this be objectionable, if out of that autoscopy emerged something vital and communicable to the introspective spirit in us all. He can sing of seizing the flower ere it fades away, yet how frequently does he himself seize it? (pp. 144-47)

More successful is *Uma Oda de Anacreonte,* a one-act play in verse, in which is portrayed the power of money over the sway of love. Cleon, confiding, amorous youth that he is, is disillusioned by both love (Myrto) and friendship (Lysias). There is a didactic tint to the piece, which is informed with the author's characteristic irony, cynicism, brooding reflection and resigned acceptation. Of truly dramatic value—and by that phrase I mean not so much the conventional stageworthiness of the drama's technicians as a captivating reality born of the people themselves—there is very little.

In *Americanas* . . . the poet goes to the native scenes and legends for inspiration; *Potyra*—recounting the plight of a Christian captive who, rather than betray her husband by wedding a Tamoyo chief, accepts death at the heathen's hands—is a cold, objective presentation, unwarmed by figures of speech, not illuminated by any inner light; *Niani,* a Guaycuru legend, is far better stuff, more human, more vivid, in ballad style as opposed to the halting blank verse of the former; for the most part, the collection consists of external narrative—feeling, insight, passion are sacrificed to arid reticence.

Thus *A Christã Nova* (**The Converted Jewess**) contains few ideas; neither colour nor passion, vision nor fire, inhere in it. There is a sentimental fondness for the vanquished races—a note so common in the "Indian" age of Brazilian letters, and in analogous writings of the Spanish-Americans, as to have become a convention. The poem tells the story of a converted Jewess who is betrothed to a soldier. She is met by her betrothed after the war, with her father in the toils of the Inquisition. Rather than remain with her lover, she chooses to die with her parent; father and daughter go to their end together. Chiefly dry narrative, and perhaps better than *Potyra,* though that is negative praise. (pp. 147-48)

It is in the *Occidentaes* . . . that we find more of the real Machado de Assis than in the series that preceded it. The ripened man now speaks from a pulsing heart. Not that any of these verses leap into flame, as in the sonorous, incendiary strophes of Bilac, but at least the thoughts live in the words that body them forth and technical skill revels in its power. Here the essence of his attitude toward life appears—that life which, rather than death, is the corroding force, the universal and ubiquitous element. The *Mosca Azul* is almost an epitome of his outlook, revealing as it does his tender irony, his human pity, his repressed sensuality, his feeling for form, his disillusioned comprehension of illusions. His resigned acceptance of life's decline is characteristic of the man—part, perhaps, of his balanced outlook. One misses in him the rebel—the note that lends greatness to the hero in his foreordained defeat, raising the drama of surrender to the tragedy of the unconquered victim. But this would be asking him to be some one else—an inartistic request which we must withhold. (pp. 148-49)

What is this poem of the fly, but the tale of the man who killed the goose that laid the golden eggs, retold in verses admirable for colour, freshness,—for everything, indeed, except originality and feeling? Those critics are right who find in Machado de Assis a certain homiletic preoccupation; but he is never the preacher, and his light is cast not upon narrow dogmas, with which he had nothing to do, but upon the broad ethical implications of every life that seeks to bring something like order into the chaos we call existence,—a thing without rhyme or reason, as he would have agreed, but what would you? . . .

Companioning the search for roots of illusion is the theme of eternal dissatisfaction. This Machado de Assis has put into one of the most quoted of Brazilian sonnets, which he calls *Circulo Vicioso* (**Vicious Circle**). . . . (p. 152)

Between the loss of illusion and eternal dissatisfaction lies the luring desert of introspection; here men ask questions that send back silence as the wisest answer, or words that are more quiet than silence and about as informing. The poet's tribute to Arthur de Oliveira is really a description—particularly in the closing lines—of himself. "You will laugh, not with the ancient laughter, long and powerful,—the laughter of an eternal friendly youth, but with another, a bitter laughter, like the laughter of an ailing god, who wearies of divinity and who, too, longs for an end. . . ." This world-weariness runs all through Machado de Assis; it is one of the mainsprings of his remarkable prose works. It is no vain paradox to say that the real poet Machado de Assis is in his prose, for in his prose alone do the fruits of his imagination come to maturity; only in his better tales and the strange books he called novels does his rare personality reach a rounded fulfilment. Peculiarly enough, the man is in his poetry, the artist in his prose. The one is as revelatory of his ethical outlook as the other of his esthetic intuitions. What he thinks, as distinct from what he feels, is in his verse rather than in his novels or tales.

He was haunted, it seems, by the symbol of a Prometheus wearied of his immortality of anguish,—by the *tedium vitae*. This world-weariness appears in the very reticence of his style. He writes, at times, as if it were one of the vanities of vanities, yet one feels that a certain inner pride lay behind this outer timidity. His method is the most leisurely of indirection,—not the involved indirection of a Conrad, nor the circuitous adumbration of a Hamsun. He has been compared, for his humourism, to the Englishman Sterne, and there is a basis for the comparison if we remove all connotation of ribaldry and retain only the fruitful rambling. Machado de Assis is the essence of charming sobriety, of slily smiling half-speech. He is something like his own Ahasverus in the conte *Viver!*, withdrawn from life not so much because he hated it as because he loved it exceedingly. (pp. 153-54)

[In the work of] Machado de Assis, description and sensation are fairly one; like so many ironists, he has a mistrust of feeling. (p. 157)

So much for the weariness of the superhuman,—an attitude matched among us more common mortals by such a delirium as occurs in a famous passage of Machado de Assis's *Braz Cubas,* one of the mature works of which *Dom Casmurro* is by many held to be the best. What shall we say of the plots of these novels? In reality, the plots do not exist. They are the slenderest of strings upon which the master stylist hangs the pearls of his wisdom. And such a wisdom! Not the maxims of a Solomon, nor the pompous nothings of the professional moralist. Seeming by-products of the narrative, they form its essence. To read Machado de Assis's central novels for their tale is the vainest of pursuits. He is not interested in goals; the road is his pleasure, and he pauses wherever he lists, indulging the most whimsical conceits. For this Brazilian is a master of the whimsy that is instinct with a sense of man's futility. (pp. 158-59)

[Take for example the] whole of Chapter XVII of *Dom Casmurro*. What has it to do with the love story of the hero and Capitú? Nothing. It could be removed, like any number of passages from Machado de Assis's chief labours, without destroying the mere tale. Yet it is precisely these passages that are the soul of the man's work.

The chapter is entitled The Worms (*Os Vermes*).

> . . . When, later, I came to know that the lance of Achilles also cured a wound that it inflicted, I conceived certain desires to write a disquisition upon the subject. I went as far as to approach old books, dead books, buried books, to open them, compare them, plumbing the text and the sense, so as to find the common origin of pagan oracle and Israelite thought. I seized upon the very worms of the books, that they might tell me what there was in the texts they gnawed.
>
> "My dear sir," replied a long, fat bookworm, 'we know absolutely nothing about the texts that we gnaw, nor do we choose what we gnaw, nor do we love or detest what we gnaw; we simply go on gnawing."
>
> And that was all I got out of him. All the others, as if they had agreed upon it, repeated the same song. Perhaps this discreet silence upon the texts they gnawed was itself another manner still of gnawing the gnawed.

This is more than a commentary upon books; it is, in little, a philosophical attitude toward life, and, so far as one may judge from his works, it was Machado de Assis's attitude. He was a kindly sceptic; for that matter, look through the history of scepticism, and see whether, as a lot, the sceptics are not much more kindly than their supposedly sweeter-tempered brothers who dwell in the everlasting grace of life's certainties.

Machado de Assis was not too hopeful of human nature. One of his most noted tales, *O Infermeiro* (**The Nurse or Attendant**) is a miniature masterpiece of irony in which man's self-deception in the face of his own advantages is brought out with that charm-in-power which is not the least of the Brazilian's qualities. (pp. 159-60)

I have ommitted mention of the earlier novels of Machado de Assis because they belong to a romantic epoch, and he was not of the stuff that makes real romantics. How could he be a genuine member of that school when every trait of his retiring personality rebelled against the abandonment to outspokenness implied in membership? He is as wary of extremes, as mistrustful of superlatives, as José Dias in *Dom Casmurro* is fond of them. "I wiped my eyes," relates the hero of that book, when apprised of his mother's illness, "since of all José Dias's words, but a single one remained in my heart: it was that *gravissimo*, (very serious). I saw afterward that he had meant to say only *grave* (serious), but the use of the superlative makes the mouth long, and through love of a sonorous sentence José Dias had increased my sadness. If you should find in this book any words belonging to the same family, let me know, gentle reader, that I may emend it in the second edition; there is nothing uglier than giving very long feet to very short ideas." If anything, his method follows the reverse order, that of giving short feet to long ideas. He never strains a thought or a situation. If he is sad, it is not the loud-mouthed melancholy of Byronic youth; neither is he the blatant cynic. He does not wave his hands and beat his breast in deep despair; he seems rather to sit brooding—not too deeply, for that would imply too great a concern with the silly world—by the banks of a lake in which the reflection of the clouds paints fantastic pictures upon the changing waters. (pp. 163-64)

*Isaac Goldberg, "Machado de Assis," in his Bra-
zilian Literature (copyright 1922 by Alfred A. Knopf,
Inc.), Knopf, 1922, pp. 142-64.*

CLOTILDE WILSON (essay date 1942)

[*In a brief but important essay, Wilson disagrees with Brazilian
biographers and critics who attribute Machado's preoccupation
with insanity to a personal fear of going insane. Wilson sees this
preoccupation as an outgrowth of the author's "pessimistic, often
cynical philosophy" and illustrative of his desire to escape the
misery of reality.*]

[Machado de Assis's] preoccupation with mental derangement
was but another manifestation of his pessimism. It has even
been suggested that Machado de Assis may have been afraid
that one day he himself might lose his mind and that that may
have been why he found a peculiar fascination in the subject
of insanity. This explanation seems improbable, however, if
one realizes the irony with which the subject is treated. Machado de Assis wrote of madness not as one who feared it, but
rather as one who would welcome it as an outlet from the
intolerable sadness of reality. . . .

That Machado de Assis was convinced of . . . 'the sanity of
insanity,' and that like Erasmus he found it a subject for irony
is apparent from a study of his writings. We know that Machado
de Assis was familiar with Erasmus' *In Praise of Folly,* since
he makes several references to it. . . . [We] see its concept,
glossed by the novelist's artistry, developed in the novels *As
Memorias posthumas de Braz Cubas* . . . and *Quincas Borba*. . . .
(p. 198)

Megalomania was . . . the form of madness that most interested
the pessimistic Machado de Assis, since, as Erasmus had in-
sinuated and as psychologists recognize today, it offers an
avenue of escape from the often humdrum and unhappy realities
of life.

Braz Cubas, Quincas Borba, and Rubião live miserable, futile
little lives from which they can escape only by letting their
minds wander into an hallucinatory world, which finally becomes for Quincas Borba and Rubião more real than the world
of actuality. (p. 199)

Quincas Borba dies content in the delusion that he is Saint
Augustine, whom he has always so admired and with whom
he has felt a close affinity, and Rubião, who is really the
protagonist of the novel *Quincas Borba,* dies in exultation as
Napoleon III. He has suffered financial loss, the woman whom
he loves is the wife of another, but as Napoleon III he dies
with a glittering crown on his head, a crown that the novelist
tells us was not even so much as an old hat or a basin—merely
nothing at all, which the dying man picks up and puts on and
which he alone sees, murmuring "Keep my crown. To the
victor . . ." Thus, through madness, he whose life was one
of insignificance and frustration enjoys a final moment of complete triumph. (pp. 199-200)

In the unforgettable passage in which Machado de Assis describes the delirium of Braz Cubas, a turbulent vision in which
the past ages file before the sick man's fevered eyes, wretched
mankind, forsaken by an indifferent universe, appears in eternal
pursuit of that nebulous, elusive thing that he calls happiness.
Thus does the novelist portray the 'pleasure principle' of the
modern psychologist. Perhaps no other passage more clearly
reflects the author's deeply pessimistic philosophy, for here
we see humanity struggling in vain against a relentless fate and

seeking with frantic eagerness a chimerical happiness, which
may fall within his grasp for one brief moment only to vanish
the next with mocking laughter.

For Machado de Assis life is a thing of unbearable sadness and
disenchantment, and since this is so he would seem to imply
that only he can avoid despair who can escape from this life
into a world of dreams. And since the often cynical humor that
imbues the works of Machado de Assis is allied to the bitterness
with which he contemplates the sorrows of mankind, he, like
Erasmus, found in the lunatic's gratification of the 'pleasure
principle' a theme for ironical laughter—or perhaps tears. . . .

Surely, then, the pessimism of Machado de Assis reaches its
ultimate expression in the implication that only through madness may one attain the illusion of happiness. (p. 200)

*Clotilde Wilson, "Machado de Assis, Encomiast of
Lunacy," in Hispania (© 1942 The American As-
sociation of Teachers of Spanish and Portuguese,
Inc.), Vol. XXXII, No. 2, May, 1942, pp. 198-201.*

SAMUEL PUTNAM (essay date 1948)

One would have said that life had given Machado de Assis all
that he could have asked of it, yet in his writing he reveals a
boundless disillusionment with humankind. The taste of life is
a bitter one to him, there is no doubt of that, though his bitterness never breaks forth in imprecations, wailings, or manifestations of self-pity, but is cloaked, rather, in an Olympian
serenity, the serenity of one who has learned to smile at his
own lost illusions and shattered dreams.

There have been numerous attempts to explain this seeming
paradox. For one thing, much has been made of the afflicting
disease from which he suffered: epilepsy. It is possible that
this had something to do with the matter, but it is well not to
overstress such a factor in the formation of a writer's personality; for in Machado de Assis's case there was the deeper soul
sickness that the modern psychoanalyst would probably label
an inferiority complex—the consciousness of having had a
black father. True, he had overcome every color prejudice,
had received during his lifetime every recognition, every honor
that his countrymen could bestow upon him, yet the scars of
that inner conflict remained with him still. (pp. 180-81)

Machado de Assis, despite the fact that he had been born and
reared almost in sight and sound of the old slave market of
Valongo, had not a word to say upon the subject, not a word
of reproach for slavery as an institution, but instead devoted
himself exclusively to the finely nuanced art of fiction, which
he brought to so high a degree of perfection.

The racial factor, however, like the physiological one is not
to be overstressed in an attempt to find a reason for the life
view of a writer of the stature of Machado de Assis. (p. 182)

All of which brings us up short before that ultimate indefinable
residue of individual temperament that can only be described
as the mystery of genius. A genius that endows the work of a
writer with universal in place of merely parochial or national
significance. A universality of time as well that renders him
the property of all succeeding ages. Machado de Assis is possessed of that kind of genius, that universal appeal. There are
writers who mirror their age more or less directly and concretely, and many of them are justly called great, but there are
others for whom any epoch, any land that may be traced upon
a map is too small, and who claim as their own country no

less a domain than the cramped, confined, yet constantly re-belling and expanding spirit of man. These latter are the greatest as distinguished from the great, and Machado de Assis is of their company.

This it is that gives him his pre-eminence in Brazilian literature. Writers before him had striven a little too consciously, often a little too zealously to "be Brazilian," to be of their time. He comes bringing the gift of temperament, a highly person-alized view of life and the world which still is broad as the world, as deep and dark and mystery-laden as life itself. A point that those with an eye for social propaganda in the guise of literature commonly overlook is this: that the greater includes the less, and that writers like Machado de Assis—writers like James, Proust, Joyce—in taking man as their subject and por-traying him *as they know him,* are inevitably portraying their age and the society in which they live as part of that larger cosmos they recognize as their own and which they endeavor to depict.

There is a danger always in a period when propagandists invade the literary domain that writers of this type, a Machado de Assis in Brazil, a Henry James in our country, will be dis-dainfully shelved, elbowed aside, in favor of those with far less talent but with a more obvious or readily discoverable social message. Yet if one looks closely one will find in a work like the Brazilian novelist's *Posthumous Memoirs of Braz Cubas* a fine picture not only of society under the Second Empire, but of the forces that were engaged in undermining the old patriarchal slaveholding regime of former days. Freyre, for instance, draws attention to the manner in which the creator of Braz Cubas has portrayed the sadism of young masters of the Big House toward the plantation slaves, and one might also refer to *Iaiá Garcia, Dom Casmurro,* and other novels and short stories by the same pen.

Much the same might be said of Henry James and of the relation of his art, "the pale little art of fiction," as he called it, to the society in which he lived and from which he fled. It all depends upon what we ask of the artist: a sermon, a blueprint for revolution, or that profound apprehension of life through the lens of a creative personality to which alone the name of art may properly be applied.

Different as they are in many ways, Henry James and Machado de Assis have much in common. Both are novelists who deal in ideas; not ideas in the repellent abstract, but clothed in human form, made over into characters. Both are concerned with psy-chological analysis, with the nebulous action that takes place behind the curtained consciousness of men. If there is a dif-ference between them it is largely one of depth. James, not too far beneath the surface, is apt to be content with the delicate shading, the subtle nuance that illuminates the fragile moti-vation of his figures as they move about in an atmosphere of aristocratic aloofness, while Machado de Assis goes on down to those forbidden regions of the soul where man may only venture at his peril. The North American will pause to find significance in a gesture or a piece of furniture, but the Bra-zilian is not satisfied until he has confronted his own familiar demon, one that we all may recognize as being actually or potentially ours. In other words, where the former is above all delicate, the latter is at once sensitive and strong, sensitive and strong and wise as few other novelists in the world have been.

But there is one resemblance that anyone who reads these two authors cannot fail to note, and that is the comparative absence of action or plot in their pages as those terms are commonly understood. (pp. 182-84)

In his view of man as the helpless victim of a cruel fate, the Brazilian has in him something of the ancient Greek. Man for him is a lost being, as he is for the Catholic Mauriac, but there is no redemption, no Christian heaven, only the "voluptuous-ness of nothing." He is a humorist of a high order, but his humor is that of Laurence Sterne, whom he had read. His *Dom Casmurro* and *Quincas Borba* have been compared to *Le Rouge et le Noir* and *Madame Bovary.* But in the end he remains Machado de Assis and none other. He must be read to be appreciated, and if he is to be fully appreciated he must be read not once but many times.

It has been remarked that this storyteller who despairs so ut-terly, if so tranquilly, of humankind has given us in all his gallery of portraits but one picture (in *Quincas Borba*) of a man who can be described as good—and he is a madman! With it all the author never once rails any more than he weeps, but looks on with a perfect detachment when not with a grim, sardonic humor. The one thing that he abhors, and here too he resembles the Greeks, is excess of any kind. He will have none of that eloquence, that verbosity, of which the Latin, the man of the tropics, and the Negro are so fond. But a writer with this view of life and his fellow men must have a refuge of some sort, and with Machado de Assis the haven is that of beauty, aesthetic form, as reflected in a carefully hewn literary style that is all but flawless. An Apollonian style, some have called it, marked by a "Mediterranean clarity." A style that is the man. (p. 185)

As regards literary schools, Machado de Assis is commonly looked upon as a romanticist who became a realist. He is seen as the romantic in his earlier novels (1872-1878): *Resurrection, Helena,* and *Iaiá Garcia,* while his realistic period, properly speaking, is dated from the publication of the *Posthumous Memoirs of Braz Cubas,* a period that culminates in his mas-terpiece, *Dom Casmurro.* . . . However, I am inclined to agree with such critics as the late Olivera Lima and Professor Mon-tenegro who hold that any such distinction is not in reality valid and that the realist was at work from the very start, being constantly engaged in correcting the traces of romanticism that are to be discerned in the first novels. (p. 187)

Brazilian literature had now come of age. Thanks to its writers of the naturalist school, and above all to that great realist Machado de Assis, it was prepared to confront those deep moral, social, and psychologic problems that the man of the twentieth century finds it impossible to evade. (p. 192)

Samuel Putnam, "Machado de Assis and the End-of-the-Century Realists," in his Marvelous Journey: A Survey of Four Centuries of Brazilian Writing *(copyright 1948 by Alfred A. Knopf, Inc. and re-newed 1975 by Riva Putnam; reprinted by permission of the publisher), Knopf, 1948, pp. 176-92.**

WILLIAM L. GROSSMAN   (essay date 1952)

[Epitaph of a Small Winner, *Grossman's translation of Machado's* Memórias póstumas de Braz Cubas, *marked the first appearance of a novel by Machado in English. The following essay discusses Machado's pessimism; for contrasting opinions, see the essays by Anthony West and Richard J. Callan excerpted below.*]

For all his restraint and good humor, Machado de Assis hurls at his readers a fierce challenge, unrecognized by many, of-fensive to some, a joy to those who are strong enough to accept it. The challenge lies in Machado's vast iconoclasm, which is likely to involve destruction of the reader's own icons. In his best work, Machado is perhaps the most completely disenchanted writer in occidental literature. Skeptics generally destroy certain illusions in order to cling to others. Machado rejects everything mundane. (p. 11)

[*Epitaph of a Small Winner*] sets forth Machado's pessimism with a fastidious minuteness that leaves the reader only two alternatives: to reject Machado or, with Machado, to reject the world. The latter alternative still permits affirmation of certain supramundane values which Machado does not touch. Many religious persons regard agnostic Machado as a great writer—perhaps because, by destroying so many false gods, he leaves room for none but the true.

Braz Cubas, the protagonist of this novel, is spiritually and psychologically a very ordinary man. Machado endows him with wealth, good looks, and health, doubtless to avoid dwelling upon the frustration occasioned by the lack of these characteristics. For Machado has more esoteric game in mind than the sources of unhappiness that everyone recognizes as such. Braz's pursuits embrace sex, politics, philosophy, even "doing good." Yet in the final chapter, when he comes to calculate the net profit in his life, he finds it to be zero—until he remembers that, having had no children, he has handed on to no one the misery of human existence. And so, he concludes, he is a little ahead of the game, a small winner.

The abject and ironic pessimism of the book is based on nature's indifference and man's egoism. Indeed, virtually all of Braz's interests can be reduced to one: the affirmation of Braz. In the other two of Machado's three great novels—*Quincas Borba* . . . and *Dom Casmurro* . . . , Machado emphasizes a third factor, which is perhaps implicit in egoism: the indifference of the human environment to the individual's welfare. Braz Cubas betrays himself; the chief character in *Dom Casmurro* is betrayed by the indifference (to him) of his wife and of his friend. A commonplace triangle becomes, in Machado's hands, a tragedy of the frustration of a sensitive man's love by the ruthless but natural lust of two stronger persons. In a sense, the human environment takes on much of the aspect of the physical environment, leaving the individual without recourse. (pp. 11-12)

[Machado's] poor health may have been in part responsible for the Machadian irony, but it cannot account for—rather it makes all the more unaccountable—his rejection of the superman; there are surely Nietzschean elements in Quincas Borba's philosophy, which Machado ridicules in the latter part of this book. As for the source of Machado's classic taste, implicit in his rejection of false models and explicit in some of his critical writings, we are even more at sea and can hardly avoid reliance upon undiscovered, possibly undiscoverable, subjective factors. (pp. 13-14)

Without denying the tragic power of *Dom Casmurro,* the present translator chose *Epitaph of a Small Winner* because the creative release of Machado's inhibited (by compliance with romantic conventions) sentiments makes it the liveliest and most inventive of his novels and because, as a cogent and nearly complete statement of Machado's attitude, it provides a suitable introduction to his work. (p. 14)

> *William L. Grossman, in his introduction to* Epitaph of a Small Winner *by Machado de Assis, translated by William L. Grossman (reprinted by permission of Farrar, Straus and Giroux, Inc.; translation copyright 1952 by William L. Grossman; copyright renewed © 1980 by Mignon S. Grossman), Noonday Press, 1952, pp. 11-14.*

FRANK GETLEIN   (essay date 1952)

Certainly Machado is to a considerable extent in the Cervantes tradition. The most immediate evidence of this is the first-person style. Cervantes [in *Don Quixote*] never hesitates to draw conclusions and to argue them with the reader as they proceed together through the fantastic events of the narrative. Machado does the same [in *Epitaph of a Small Winner*], and does so with much the same wry humor. Two things are going forward at once: the story of the characters and their adventures, and the relating of that story, as it were, and our interest is requested as much for one as the other. This device obviously enjoins a certain detachment essential to the full enjoyment of both Cervantes and the Brazilian. We can make—indeed we cannot avoid making—identification with the various madnesses of the characters, but we never become so closely involved as to lose sight of the paramount fact that the whole proceeding is, after all, quite mad.

The "small winner" for whom the novel is the epitaph is one Braz Cubas, a wealthy citizen of Rio who lived from 1805 to 1869, a lifespan covering the liberation of Brazil and the several independent experiments in politics that make the history of the period exciting. It is a key to the nature of Braz, which in turn is a pretty fair reflection of the nature of man, that although he is a political writer by trade, a figure in the government from time to time and always the close associate of those who are experimenting in rule, the book almost ignores the revolutions and evolutions of the period. As a child, Braz took part in the celebration of Napoleon's fall, but on that occasion his consuming interest was in his own little sword, a gift from an uncle. He concludes, correctly, that most of us have our own little swords beside which the blade of an emperor seems unimportant. (pp. 417-18)

The life of Braz encompasses early wild oats, university education, a long melancholy torpor after the death of his mother, literature, politics, uplift and organized charity and above all a deep affair with the wife of a friend. In all these activities the ghost [of Braz] discerns the canker in the rose, the vanity of human endeavor, the amazing ability of mankind to lie and to come to believe the lie as truth.

The novel well deserves its established place in world literature. (p. 418)

> *Frank Getlein, "Rediscovery of a Classic," in* Commonweal *(copyright © 1952 Commonweal Publishing Co., Inc.; reprinted by permission of Commonweal Publishing Co., Inc.), Vol. LVI, No. 17, August 1, 1952, pp. 417-18.*

WALDO FRANK   (essay date 1952)

The structure of [Machado de Assis's] art, beneath its flat surface, is always contrapuntal. Within the quiet, courses a complex fugue: innocence cruelly punished and revealed as guilt; pleasure pleasurably crushed; the "good" and the "beautiful" on the wrack and dissolving into their contraries. The blood, indeed the core, of the fictive world of Machado de Assis is ambiguity—ambiguity raised to a principle and a substance. (pp. 5-6)

Dom Casmurro . . . is a deceptive book—and means to be. The language is limpid and light; far indeed from the heavy-laden voices of the nineteenth century masters: Balzac, overfreighted with mass material; Flaubert static and hard as burnished gems; Pérez Galdós, open like the parabola of a comet;

Zola, turgid with choking fires. The language of Machado de Assis resembles the simplicities of the eighteenth century, whose various rump-rationalist schools were fondly certain that the beheading of kings, the mechanics of constitutions balancing property with the rights of man, and the advance of science, would presently exile injustice and terror from the earth. The design of the book at once recalls Laurence Sterne: there is a similar play of tiny chapters, digressions, parentheses, cut-backs, verbal jests; the same discursiveness and casualness and innuendo, by which Tristram Shandy, gentleman, mirrored the expansiveness and the security of his class in William Pitt's England. . . . The Sternean style of *Dom Casmurro* and *Memórias Póstumas de Braz Cubas* [*Epitaph of a Small Winner*] lends itself to the conveying of an obsessive spatiality, a human lostness within it, making men and women huddle close together: an emotion that belongs to Brazil and which Brazil's second great master of prose, Euclides da Cunha, author of the epic *Os Sertões*, achieved by a totally distinct stylistic method.

But the Sternean whimsy has here a deeper purpose: *to deceive*. Machado de Assis aims to entice us lightly to a storm center; to drift us into it, lazily lulled, beyond any eighteenth century scope, to a depth that we do not grow aware of until we find that our feet have lost bottom!

The book is a treacherous stroll. Each detail on the way, casual and slight, is perfect, leading us on. We know these characters as closely—and as little—as if we were sipping coffee with them. We idle onward. Suddenly, behind us, the tide has come in! We must swim to get back! (pp. 9-10)

And the humor: is it like Sterne's? Enough like, to make one ask: is a box containing a bright kaleidoscope like the telescope which makes the eyes touch the infinite black spaces between stars?

I wish I could be sure that this Introduction will not be read at all (the usual fate, I am informed, of introductions) or read only after the book. I should then feel free to discuss the central ambiguity of *Dom Casmurro:* Capitú's innocence or guilt, without harming the innocence of the reader's stroll from chapter to chapter. What exquisite details he will find as he meanders! The delicious wit of the sonnet whose twelve middle lines are never written; and the shift of the last line from *Life is lost, the battle still is won!* to *Life is won, the battle still is lost*.

I must refrain from discussing the final question, since the reader should first encounter it *on his stroll*.

But when he has come out of it all—*swum back*, the reader will understand that the true answer of Machado de Assis to the great question, as to all the others, is *that he has no answer*. Ambiguity is the book's texture and life vision. And this no-answer is built with a happiness of detail that the reader can only truly relish upon a second reading. The ambiguity begins, indeed, with the first pages. (p. 11)

Dom Casmurro is no mystery story about a marital triangle; no psychological novel about jealousy. This much can be said. Bento cites *Othello*. But Othello was not jealous; he killed from conviction and certainty of justice. There is no triangle in *Othello;* the duologue is between evil and virtuous folly. Bento is also convinced. But the stuff of his life is *the ambiguous;* and the author shares it. Whatever conclusion the reader comes to about the superbly drawn heroine and the friend and the boy, Machado will not disagree; He "knows the answer" no more than we do. What he knows is Ambiguity. This is

not enough: he limns it with the sure hand of the master goldsmith.

At the turn of the last century, a Brazilian writes a novel that presages Proust and Kafka. A profound religious culture gave to all three artists insight into man's tragic marrow; but all three had lost the revelation and the subsequent faith that resolve tragedy into Wholeness. . . . Proust sang his hymn to Ambiguity in a vast novel; Machado de Assis in a short one. Of the two, it could be that the Brazilian's will be read longer. (pp. 12-13)

> *Waldo Frank, "Introduction" (1952), in* Dom Casmurro *by Machado de Assis, translated by Helen Caldwell (reprinted by permission of Farrar, Straus and Giroux, Inc.; translation copyright © 1953, 1981, by Helen Caldwell), Noonday Press, 1953, pp. 5-13.*

RAYMOND S. SAYERS (essay date 1956)

[*Sayers defends Machado, a mulatto, against critics who contend that he did not use his works to further the cause of black liberation, as did many of his contemporaries, because he was ashamed of his black heritage. In the excerpt below, Sayers cites examples of Machado's sympathetic treatment of blacks where they do appear in his works, but points out that the established rules of satire and the urban novel to which the author adhered do not lend themselves to an examination of social or economic issues.*]

One of the strange paradoxes of literature is that the greatest Brazilian novelist, Joaquim Maria Machado de Assis (1839-1908), was a mulatto who wrote very little about his fellow Negroes and their lives but instead drew most of his material for his novels from the lives of the upper classes of Carioca society, which were predominantly white. Yet in his formative years he must have been surrounded almost exclusively by other Negroes or mulattoes. (p. 201)

During his first twenty years . . . Machado de Assis owed almost all the affection he received, almost all the opportunities he was given, to people of his own race, to other mulattoes. It might be expected that in return he would strive to lend his talents to the cause of the Negro, to the struggle against slavery. . . . Or he might at least develop the theme of Salomé Queiroga and Bernardo Guimarães, that the genuine Brazilian type is the Negro mestizo, and write novels with mulatto protagonists. That he did not do so is common knowledge. His Negro personages are slaves or servants, and in only one of his novels and four of his short stories are there Negro characters of more than secondary importance. (pp. 201-02)

Machado de Assis was not indifferent to the plight of the slaves or to the injustice of slavery. There is enough in his writings to show that he sympathized with the Negroes and hated all injustice. However, his sympathy for the Negroes did not cause him to take any part in the struggle against slavery. Why he did not do so is a moot question. . . . Was it because of his rise in the Brazilian bureaucracy, which in time brought him an excellent salary and an important official position? Perhaps it was because of his growing literary fame, which led to his being the first President of the *Academia Brasileira de Letras*. It may have been his epilepsy, which caused him to shrink from conflict and, for that matter, from any activity that would attract the attention of others to his person. (pp. 202-03)

Or it may be that his failure to take an emphatic stand on the question of abolition is to be explained on other grounds. His life seems to have been guided by the philosophy of enlightened egotism which is the predominant characteristic of so many of his creatures, an egotism which may have caused him to feel that he would be justified in making any sort of sacrifice to attain the goals that he had set for himself. . . . He was not an upstart who was dazzled by luxury or by the friendship of bankers, ministers and the diplomatic set that gathered around the intellectual D. Pedro II. His novels demonstrate, on the contrary, a constant skepticism about all the qualities for which that society has been praised: the integrity of the bankers, the intelligence of the statemen, the selfishness of the diplomats, the virtue of the women. It is not that he believes that these people or their world could have been improved; indeed, he seems to believe that people are a rather sorry lot and they are unlikely to change. His satire does not envisage a finer race or a happier world, but at its mildest, in his last book, *Memorial de Ayres,* suggests the need for a resigned acceptance of the banalities that constitute our existence. (p. 203)

His goal was not an important position in his world but perfection in his art. He took for his own the urban novel about the upper middle classes, a very small segment of the Brazilian human comedy, it is true, which Macedo and Alencar had developed, and he distorted, twisted, polished and refined it until he had made it the vehicle of his pessimistic view of life. Influenced by his wide reading in English literature, . . . in which he probably preferred Thackeray to Dickens, he chose Rio de Janeiro's Vanity Fair for his subject. His reason for this choice was not the superficial one that English manners and ideas were the mode, for the more democratic, proletarian French influence was also strong, as is evident in the writings of the *condor* poets, but rather that, in writing about the upper classes, with their money and their assured position in the world, he was able to deal with the group of people who were least subject to economic pressures and who should therefore have been best able to live independently and to emerge from the mean dimensions that form the world of most men—and who failed to do so.

From two points of view, then, it is hardly to be expected that he would choose the slave or even the free Negro as a subject. In the first place his models, if one may use the word for writers like Alencar and Macedo, or even Thackeray, do not deal with the proletariat in their novels of urban life, and in the second place even the free Negro was not able to move unhampered through life as Machado de Assis wanted his characters to do. The question is not one, here, of Brazilian prejudice or lack of prejudice toward people of colored blood. There is no doubt as to the great part played in Brazilian history and the arts by Negroes and mulattoes. On the other hand, the Negro, even if he was a wealthy intellectual, was always in an ambiguous position in the society of the latter days of the Empire. . . . The Negro could not serve as a subject for the irony of Machado, for the Negro could never determine his own conduct or fix his own position in society; he was not a free agent, and therefore he could not be made a subject for satire.

Nevertheless Machado de Assis has more Negro characters than any other writer of the urban school, and to the gallery of Negro types found in Brazilian literature he adds some studies that are more complete and satisfying than any previous ones. Furthermore, he almost always treats the Negroes and their problems with sympathy. . . . In 1876 he satirized a man who sighed for the good old days when slaves were whipped, and in 1877 he ridiculed one who had emancipated a sixty-five year old slave and then had written to the papers about his meri-

torious act. . . . In these chronicles, which are often in a light or humorous vein, he is always serious or satirical in his references to slavery. In 1887 he wrote a satirical poem in Negro dialect criticizing the Parliamentary debates about the subject; in it a Negro says that all the talking does not improve his position. . . . (pp. 203-05)

In four stories and two novels Negro characters have a rather important role. In "O Caso da Vara" . . . he shows his pessimism about human nature. . . . There is no other story in pre-Abolition Brazilian literature that gives so revealing a glimpse as this of the life of the urban slave child. Nor is there any more affecting tale of the fugitive slave than the one that Machado de Assis published in his *Reliquias de Casa Velha* . . . , eighteen years after the passage of the *Lei Aurea.* (p. 205)

There are significant references to slavery and its pernicious effects upon slave and master in Machado's first great novel, *Memorias Posthumas de Braz Cubas.* . . . (p. 206)

Machado's only full length portrait of a Negro is found in his novel *Yayá Garcia.* . . . Raymundo is the Faithful Slave whose loyalty continues after he has been granted his freedom. In "Encher Tempo," a short story published in his posthumous *Historias Romanticas,* Machado has a sketch of the faithful freedwoman. . . . But since she is a secondary character in a short story, the author cannot develop her personality as he does that of Raymundo in *Yayá Garcia.* This African might be considered as Machado's tribute to the Negro and as the most complete study that he could make of a member of that race, within the limits that he had set for his subject matter, the upper classes of Rio de Janeiro. He is the contrary of the Machadean hero—the ingenuous Dom Casmurro, the insane Rubião, the egotistic Braz Cubas—for he represents a healthy if instinctive acceptance of life, with its necessary requisites of honesty, integrity and good sense in human relations. At the beginning of the book the author describes him as an African type, of medium size, strong in spite of his fifty years. . . . Unlike the romantic conception of the Faithful Slave, he is not a melancholy being, fond of singing sad songs about his native land. On the contrary, when he plays the marimba at night in the garden, he sings happy, warlike songs, and when he has an opportunity, he plays merrily with the young heroine of the story. He is quite sure of his place in the family, and he does not hesitate to act as he thinks best to protect the people he loves. . . . If Machado did not depict another character like Raymundo, it is probably because as an artist he did not want to repeat himself, for except for the servant, there was no Negro type that could be logically introduced into a novel about the upper classes of Rio.

Machado de Assis disapproved of slavery and felt that its effects upon Brazilian society and the Brazilian character were harmful. Yet although he praised anti-slavery novels and plays in his literary criticism, he himself did not attempt to produce works of propaganda, for the type of novel in which he could best express himself could hardly be twisted to the needs of the anti-slavery campaign. He did not write much about Negroes, just as in general he did not write about the lower classes of Rio, because he could only illustrate his theme of man's essential puniness by using as his personages members of the upper classes, people who did not have enough imagination to use their privileged economic position as a means of obtaining spiritual freedom. (pp. 207-08)

Raymond S. Sayers, "The Negro in the Novels of Machado de Assis and the Naturalists," in his The Negro in Brazilian Literature *(copyright, 1956 Ray-*

mond S. Sayers; reprinted by permission of the author), Hispanic Institute in the United States, 1956, pp. 201-22.*

ANTHONY WEST   (essay date 1957)

[*In the following review of* Epitaph of a Small Winner, *West disagrees with William L. Grossman's interpretation of the novel as a nihilistic attack on all forms of belief (see excerpt above).*]

Superficially [*Epitaph of a Small Winner*] is a formal exercise in imitating the technique Sterne perfected in *Tristram Shandy,* but it is Sterne's technique strengthened with the psychological realism of the French novel. This combination of alien influences in a necessarily provincial milieu could easily have produced something pedantic and dead, but Machado had a psychological insight of his own, an incisive wit, and, surprisingly, an aristocratic toughness of mind that saved him from any imitative woodenness. *Epitaph of a Small Winner* has the experimental and inventive vitality that one associates with the writing of the 'twenties, and it seems to belong much more in spirit to that lively period than to the 'eighties, in which it was first published. If it has to be given a category, it should be placed alongside such successful modern *jeux d'esprit* as Hemingway's *The Torrents of Spring* and Montherlant's *Pity for Women*—jokes that are all the better for being savage and, like all good jokes, wholly serious. (pp. 142-43)

Machado's joke has [a] . . . slightly suicidal edge, since its attack on romantic idealism is so absolute that it can be taken for a nihilistic attack on all forms of belief, including the values that produced it. Dr. Grossman does so take it, and refers to Machado as "perhaps the most completely disenchanted writer in Occidental literature" [see excerpt above], but this seems to disregard the very deliberate, classical use of irony that is part of Machado's technique. . . . The ironist constantly uses a double-edged weapon, and he generally cannot resist giving an edge to the hilt as well, so that anyone who grasps the thing in the wrong way will get a third cut from it; the attack on the naïve reader is just as strong as it is on the targets inside the book. Machado seems to be playing this rather elaborate teasing game. The final words of *Epitaph of a Small Winner* sum up the extent to which its hero, Braz Cubas, is ahead of the game at the end of his life: "I found that I had a small surplus. . . . I had no progeny, I transmitted to no one the legacy of our misery." To Dr. Grossman, this is a definite statement of the author's absolute pessimism, but it can be read as a diagnosis of what is, or was, incurably wrong with Braz Cubas.

Braz Cubas is . . . an average member of a fortunate class of people. He has enough money to free him from all pressures and an almost unlimited opportunity to make his life what he chooses. He lives timidly and uncertainly on the fringes of literature, always intending to write something really good someday, and on the fringes of politics, always intending to make a splash someday. His complete lack of will or tenacity, and of intellectual discipline, insures that his life boils down to a series of dim affairs with women in which he flirts in a scared way but with a certain intensity of feeling. Machado follows him through his ineffectual romances, ruthlessly describing their empty reality, and allows him to make these shallow, negative experiences the basis of his nihilist philosophy of despair. The contrasts between his intellectual self-importance and his incapacity for living produce some extraordinary effects, of both comedy and pathos. In his first affair, he is taken for what the traffic will bear by a hardheaded little

gold-digger called Marcella. It is the only episode in his life that he really understands, because it all turns on the girl's simple appetite for hard cash. Love comes his way as a genuine emotion when he meets Eugenia, who loves him, but before it is too late he notices that she has a slight limp—she has limped from birth—she is a cripple—marry a cripple—impossible—he bolts in a fright from the situation that has so nearly betrayed him into a world of valid experience.

The remainder of his life is taken up with a long-drawn-out adultery with the wife of a friend. This is described in a series of tours de force of realistic writing, episodic and exact. Everything superfluous is pared away, and only the vital episodes are presented. Machado had a remarkably sure sense of what was important—at least when he was writing this novel—and the whole of the relationship is there, from its origin to its last ramifications. In a sequence of the briefest scenes, he shows the affair at the stage of private rapture, shows it branching out and becoming the subject of gossip, shows its effect on Braz Cubas' family and on local society. He shows, too, its diminution of intensity, its deterioration into habit, and its final extinction under the weight of social expediency. It is an absorbing story about that most deadly of diseases, the incapacity to love, and about the intellectual dishonesty of the shallow-hearted. When the affair has collapsed, and become so meaningless that Braz Cubas can boast of its secret delights in casual conversation (the death of the spirit is complete), he settles into a cozy round of puttering and waiting to die in the shade of his gray pessimism. To liven things up for him, an old school friend, the most promising and brilliant of his classmates, turns up, flat broke and a total failure, but ready, all the same, to state a richly optimistic philosophy of existence—rather akin to Blake's and Whitman's—called Humanitism, which has as its center an unlimited belief in the human power to create happiness and to enrich life. Machado's ironic last chapters describe the way in which the pallidly defeated Braz Cubas shelters and cherishes his friend, whom he considers to be a lunatic. So does Dr. Grossman, who takes it that Machado is laughing at the idea of the Nietzschean superman in the person of Braz Cubas' friend. It may be that he is right, but it does not seem likely that the wholly negativist outlook he attributes to Machado could have produced such a sparkling and enjoyable comedy. It is easier to believe that if Machado is in the book at all, he appears as the suspected friend; it takes a robust mind to write real tragedy in the form of comedy. Yet even if one has to disagree with Dr. Grossman about the content of the book, one can only be grateful to him for introducing a classic comedy of ideas, as fascinating as it is delightful, to the English language. (pp. 144-47)

Anthony West, "Machado de Assis," in his Principles and Persuasions: The Literary Essays of Anthony West *(reprinted by permission of Wallace & Sheil Agency, Inc.; copyright © 1957 by Anthony West),* Harcourt, Brace and Company, 1957, pp. 141-47.

KEITH ELLIS   (essay date 1962)

[*In the following essay, Ellis summarizes various critical interpretations of* Dom Casmurro, *including the works of many critics which have never been translated into English, and he offers a new interpretation.*]

Since its publication . . . , Machado de Assis' *Dom Casmurro* has occupied a prominent place in Brazilian literature. There has been, nevertheless, a very wide divergence of views expressed concerning this work. . . .

For more than forty years the critical approach to *Dom Casmurro* has been based upon the judgment that Capitú betrayed her husband, Bentinho, with his best friend, Escobar. In 1961, José Veríssimo established the position in his *História da Literatura Brasileira* that *Dom Casmurro* is the story of a simple, but undeniably intelligent man who even from his boyhood allowed himself to be deluded by Capitú whom he eventually marries. She fascinates him with her calculated coquetry, with her deceitfulness, to which he gives himself up hopelessly. She deceives him with his best friend, Escobar, also a childhood friend, without his suspecting.

This interpretation of the novel, involving a total acceptance of the point of view established by the narrator, was essentially continued by Lúcia Miguel Pereira and Barreto Filho. For these writers the impact of Capitú's guilt is softened by a consideration of responsibility. Miguel Pereira sees one of the central problems left by the author as that of determining whether Capitú, by betraying Bantinho, was indeed a hypocrite or whether she obeyed indomitable hereditary instincts. . . . For Barreto Filho the falseness of Capitú is a manifestation of Machado's view of life itself. . . . This is an indication of the tendency of criticism to see the novel within the frame of a naturalistic *Weltanschauung* established for the author.

It is possible to derive from Machado's treatment of the theme of deception in the earlier novels, *Memórias Póstumas de Bráz Cubas* and *Quincas Borba,* a tendency to generalize from the guilt presented in these two novels to the conclusion that Capitú did in fact betray her husband's trust in *Dom Casmurro.* The tendency to generalize is strengthened by resemblances in the novels. The mysterious eyes of Capitú, for instance, are reminiscent of Sofia's in *Quincas Borba.* . . . Moreover, the persistent reference to *Othello* that is to be found in *Dom Casmurro* had a weaker correlative in *Quincas Borba.* (p. 436)

It is likely, too, that if the interpretation of *Dom Casmurro* is influenced by the other works of Machado whose tendencies are predominantly naturalistic, Capitú's guilt will be accepted; and we should look for the influence of indomitable drives in her nature to account for this deception. All these external conditions may contribute to the acceptance of the narrator's point of view in Dom Casmurro, but they depend little on an analysis of the work itself.

Helen Caldwell's *The Brazilian Othello of Machado de Assis* [see annotated bibliography] contains the most detailed attempt at an exposition of Machado's novel to date. It is distinguished by its departure from traditional Machado criticism in arguing strongly, against a background of formidable opposition, the case for Capitú's innocence.

Helen Caldwell, in effect, has not differed greatly from her predecessors as far as the broad outline of approach to the novel is concerned. . . . [The] main question of Helen Caldwell's study is whether or not Capitú was guilty of adultery. Thus, the question of Capitú's fidelity is the central point from which both [she and Barreto Filho] set out to appraise the novel. Where the earlier critics have in a brusque, sweeping manner accepted the narrator's point of view and fitted *Dom Casmurro* within a definite frame of Machado's philosophy, by a patient attention to fine details and careful choice of material Helen Caldwell ultimately fits the novel into a general frame of the novelist's view of life as she conceives it.

In both her case and that of the earlier critics the judgment passed on Capitú and the determined view of life are in harmony. The pattern of love and self-love that Helen Caldwell establishes in Machado's novels supports the case for her connected theme of Dom Casmurro's self-love and Capitú's innocence. Within the text itself she adduces arguments for her case by carefully analysing names, characters, images and passages. In addition she relies on Machado's other works, notably *Ressurreição* and *Esaú e Jacob,* as well as on Shakespeare's *Othello* for substantiation of these arguments. The sum of her conclusion is that the Othello-Casmurro, Desdemona-Capitú parallels form the key to the interpretation of the novel.

Helen Caldwell has been most effective when she works within the text itself, and her establishing of the essential jealously of Bentinho by tracing his development into the jealous, self-centered Casmurro, constitutes a valuable part of her work. Indeed, there are sufficient instances of our protagonist-narrator's manifestation of jealousy to evoke the possibility that it could be at the root of his final accusation of Capitú. Moreover, our narrator never really understands either his wife or his best friend; their behavior spins a web of mystery for him which he is never able to penetrate. With them he feels an underlying current of mystery that prevents a real union of personalities. In the darkness of his incomprehension, there lies a vague mistrust of his wife and his friend which can court disaster, and if jealousy attaches itself to the insecurity that results from misunderstanding, he may go to the extent of conjuring up his own ocular proof of his wife's infidelity without its real existence.

Now in all this, our narrator shows some similarity to Othello, and indeed he himself professes a high degree of concordance with the situation, conduct and character of Shakespeare's tragic hero. Once this has been done, it provides grounds for an extension of the affinity between *Dom Casmurro* and *Othello.* There is much in the text of *Dom Casmurro* that can be cited to substantiate further parallels in characterization, but while these affinities must be taken into account in the criticism of the novel, they form a weak basis for objective critical interpretation.

Helen Caldwell, going beyond the text, relies greatly on resemblances in *Othello* as well as in Machado's other works in her attempt to prove Capitú's innocence; for within the novel itself nothing more definite than the possibility of her innocence can be determined, and little of what she cites for her case for Capitú amounts to more than conjecture. (pp. 436-38)

Having admitted the possibility that Capitú may not be guilty, we may not conclude that she is innocent. Helen Caldwell has follows the narrator's tendency to present a definite verdict, but readers of *Dom Casmurro* have no need to make a judgment on Capitú. It would seem that, in *Dom Casmurro,* Machado has discredited the effectiveness of either the provable guilt or provable innocence of Capitú, and has indelibly branded this aspect of the novel with the mark of ambiguity.

In accounting for Machado's success in creating this ambiguity, attention must be focused on his choice of point of view in the novel. By presenting the point of view of a narrator who speaks in the first person and who reveals deficiencies in his own character that cause his view of things to be mistrusted, the author has managed to demonstrate the point made by the narrator that "nem tudo é claro na vida ou nos livros." As Henry James observed, narrative in the first person can lend itself to effecting obscurity by preventing the possibility of a center and preventing real directness of contact with objectivity. . . .

In *Dom Casmurro,* the death of Escobar is well devised at once to create and preserve a veil of obscurity. While the sorrow that it brings to Capitú sets off the chain of Bentinho's suspicions, at the same time it eliminates a possible means of clarifying the question of infidelity. Hereafter, Capitú is scrupulously noncommital in word and action. Ezequiel [her son], too, is kept well out of contact with the other characters of the story, preventing the possibility of their commenting on his appearance.

In the use of narrative in the first person, in general, nothing is done that might prevent the narrator from presenting a picture of events as *he* sees them. He looks back on events with a fixed view. His description represents the aspect that the facts in their sequence turned towards him; his field of vision is defined with perfect distinctness and his story does not stray outside it. . . . And yet, although Machado works within this frame in *Dom Casmurro,* he has transcended its normal use by subtly managing to convey to the reader a lack of confidence in the real existence of what the narrator sees.

There are sufficient instances of Bentinho's manifestation of disruptive jealousy to convince us that it could be at the root of his final accusation of Capitú. (p. 438)

Despite the concentration of criticism on the determination of Capitú's guilt or innocence, the verdict of "guilty" or "innocent" has had little to do with the total evaluation of the novel as a literary work. The fundamental element that gives the novel its prominent place in Brazilian letters may well have its source in the extent to which Machado has managed to promote a deep human awareness by means of a technique that marks an expansion of the possibilities of the art of the novel. The basis of this technique lies in the author's distinctive use of the first person narrator. The narrator's authority being lessened by the revelation of his character, his narrative becomes at once a presentation of what he sees and an invitation to the reader to determine why he sees it. Thus the novel *Dom Casmurro* is intensely, intimately, about the first person narrator who is revealed to be a highly sensitive, imaginative, jealous man—insecure with those to whom he should have been closest. Representing the pathetic, archetypal image of bewildered man before mysterious woman, he evokes profound responses. As narrator he has constant, direct contact with the reader, and yet this closeness of contact, by revealing his character, serves to deny the objective reality of what he relates.

But, the novel being primarily concerned with Dom Casmurro, the important aspect of the Capitú question is not whether or not he was in fact betrayed: it is that he came to believe himself betrayed. By making this question ambiguous, Machado has achieved a subtle suggestion of possibilities more artistic than the revelation of either guilt or innocence. He brings the reader to an awareness of the relativity of point of view and, by forcing us to contemplate the question of Capitú's guilt or innocence, increases our scope for imaginative participation in developing these possibilities.

Machado's achievement in employing the first person narrator in this manner as early as 1900, is especially remarkable. (pp. 439-40)

The question of Capitú's guilt is clothed in an ambiguity that resists clarification. It is ambiguity that is a deliberate literary device, contributing greatly to the central effect of the work. The alternatives that it suggests engage the reader to reflect on the complex possibilities of human nature that Machado has implied, thereby promising for the novel that continuing interest which the great literary creations engender. (p. 440)

Keith Ellis, "Technique and Ambiguity in 'Dom Casmurro'," in Hispania *(© 1962 The American Association of Teachers of Spanish and Portuguese, Inc.), Vol. XLV, No. 3, September, 1962, pp. 436-40.*

WILLIAM L. GROSSMAN (essay date 1963)

An increasing number of readers are coming to share Helen Caldwell's opinion that [Machado de Assis's] *Dom Casmurro* is "perhaps the finest of all American novels of either continent." His *Epitaph of a Small Winner* has been included in great-books courses and enshrined in a library list of One Hundred Great Novels.

According to an eminent Machadian (the late Lúcia Miguel Pereira), however, "it was undoubtedly as a short-story writer that Machado de Assis wrought his masterpieces." Another scholar, Renard Perez, points out that the short story was the ideal form for so meticulous and concise a writer, who liked to attack his themes "vertically." "It is the acuteness of his analyses," says Perez, "together with the originality of his themes and his perfection of form, that make him a world master of the short story." (p. vii)

In Brazil, probably the most celebrated of the stories here presented is **"Midnight Mass."** Readers are captivated by its typically Machadian combination of insight, simplicity, and subtlety. It brings to mind a passage in an essay on Machado by the dean of Brazilian intellectuals, Alceu Amoroso Lima: "He writes more between the lines than on the lines. He suggests more than he says. He evokes more than he manifests. And he never writes without an ulterior meaning."

In one of the forty-odd books on Machado de Assis written by Brazilians, Agrippino Grieco remarks the dream-like quality of **"Midnight Mass."** In another, Gondin da Fonseca notes its "suffocating atmosphere of excitement and frustration," but to him any dreaminess would doubtless be a consequence of the "onanistic sublimation" that he finds in both this story and **"A Woman's Arms."** He maintains that young Nogueira, the narrator, "although deftly provoked by Conceição, pretends not to recognize her desires and does not possess her, no matter how much she offers herself." But can we be so sure that the narrator was merely pretending? He himself tells us otherwise. And can one be wholly precise about Conceição's objective? Is it so certain that she would have permitted herself to be possessed? The charm of the story derives in part from its mixture of clarity and elusiveness in the interplay of inexplicit desires and restraints. One who tries to make them wholly explicit may tell more about himself than about the story—a danger often encountered in efforts to interpret Machado's stories and novels, especially those told in the first person.

"Education of a Stuffed Shirt" is one of the several works in which Machado ridicules the dedication of men to the superficial, the inauthentic, the mediocre. The formula for success prescribed here by the father—essentially, conformity plus publicity—is chillingly up-to-date. (p. viii)

In temperament and basic emphasis . . . Machado was [close] to Kierkegaard—whom he doubtless never read. With much the same intensity and sometimes with similar thrusts of caustic wit, these two strange prophets remind us that we must be judged as individuals, not as parts of the crowd, that merger into the mass cannot free us of our responsibility to choose the true and the authentic. (p. ix)

Like others of Machado's works, ["**The Psychiatrist**"] means somewhat different things to different exegetes. According to Augusto Meyer, its satire is aimed at "mental activity itself" and especially at pure rationalism, represented in the story by Dr. Bacamarte. Barreto Filho finds in "**The Psychiatrist**" not only Machado's contempt for "scientific rationalism" and for "scientific dictatorship" but also an attack upon specifically Brazilian ways of thinking. "Anyone," he writes, "who knows our receptivity to everything that presents itself in the guise of science, our readiness to plunge into improbable projects, anyone who observes how little resistance we have to imported theories of politics or pedagogy—in brief, our delight in panaceas—knows what Machado de Assis was seeking to stigmatize. . . ."

Without denying the validity of these interpretations, so far as they go, I wonder whether the central thought of the story is not in an observation by Pascal: "Men are so necessarily mad, that not to be mad would amount to another form of madness." (pp. ix-x)

Taken together, these . . . stories provide a fair, although of course not wholly representative, sample of Machado's concepts and methods. We see his economy of means and his sometimes deceptive simplicity. We see his hatred of cruelty, his sympathetic understanding of young people (rarely reciprocated), his perception of hidden and even unconscious motives, his lack of interest in inanimate nature ("Where are the trees?" complained one reader), his curiosity about the relationship between good and evil—and always his critique, now biting, now compassionate, of human inadequacy. (p. x)

> *William L. Grossman, in his introduction to* The Psychiatrist and Other Stories *by Machado de Assis, translated by William L. Grossman & Helen Caldwell (translation copyright © 1963 by The Regents of the University of California; reprinted by permission of the University of California Press), University of California Press, 1963, pp. vii-x.*

RICHARD J. CALLAN   (essay date 1964)

[*In an interesting divergence from the standard reading of* Epitaph of a Small Winner, *Callan disagrees with William L. Grossman and interprets the satiric vision of the novel as Machado's attempt to reform the petty evils of humanity.*]

[*Memórias pósthumas de Braz Cubas* was published] when Machado de Assis was forty-one, nearly twenty years before **Dom Casmurro**. At first sight the two novels are similar; each is told in first person narrative by a wealthy old man whose long life has been dedicated to himself; each reveals by ironic indirection the narrator's selfish and cynical nature, aggravated by his indolent existence. One of the chief differences, however, and herein lies the superiority as a novel of **Dom Casmurro** over the other, is that Casmurro begins life with some chances of being human, since the purpose of the novel is to show the tragedy of his decadence; whereas it is evident that Braz Cubas has a perverse nature from the start, and that given his upbringing and his circumstances, he will be quite unable to change. Moreover, the temptation to do so never presents itself. . . .

Braz Cubas gives much emphasis to his childhood background, stressing the hopelessness of his outlook for the future. Little Braz was adored and spoiled by his father, while his weak and unintelligent mother taught him nothing beyond the recitation of prayers. His childish pranks were malicious and spiteful and

he had more than the natural cruelty of children, but his father, loving himself in his son, beamed on the mischief as if it had been the expression of genius. . . .

The plot which follows is relatively bare and serves chiefly to provide illustrations for Machado's ideas and maxims on the baseness of human motives. (p. 530)

[Braz Cubas] mocks everything indiscriminately: the beauty of Marcella who became pockmarked, and her money-grasping that did not keep her from the poorhouse; Borba, the cheerful philosopher of logic and reason who lost his reason; his own father, who died of despair over Braz's failure of which he himself had been the chief cause. . . . And above all he mocks vanity, every one's and especially his own, which had been the mainspring of his life. . . .

Each of the seven deadly sins, and many of their corollaries, are illustrated by the life of Braz Cubas. . . .

Braz Cubas' struggles with his conscience (for he has one in spite of all) are specious debates which he usually wins. . . . There are times, however, when Braz does follow the dictates of conscience, and that is when he is confronted with two temptations. He will resist one (the easier one) in order to compensate for yielding to the other. (p. 531)

Reason comes in for a lot of ridicule throughout the book. Besides serving to outwit one's conscience, it can help us to gratify with equanimity many of our deepest instincts, especially in the philosophy of Quincas Borba. *Humanitismo*, an application of the principles of the survival of the fittest to human relations, easily demonstrates the necessity of self-love; to wit: every man is humanity in miniature, everything that benefits him benefits humanity—hence, man owes it to humanity to love himself. By further lucid reasoning in this vein, one can arrive at such gratifying conclusions as, Envy is a virtue . . . , Gratitude is an aberration . . . , Pride benefits humanity . . . , etc. When Braz Cubas talks with Nature in his delirium, she says that Egoism or Self-preservation is her law. . . . The panther eats the calf because it must live. Throughout the novel it is demonstrated that this universal law is natural to man too, and that if man does not transcend this animal law, he necessarily falls beneath the level of animals, because he adds to it his own ingredients, vanity, pride, and malice, vices which are not seen in animals.

But how should man transcend the law of Nature? This the novel does not state. But perhaps the answer is suggested. The last chapter . . . is entitled "Das negativas." It lists the events of Braz Cubas' life that did not happen. Can we not push the negatives further, into the realm of the abstract, and add that he did not love? In fact he never experienced any genuine emotion; he had tried to when his mother died, but unable to discern between grief and melancholy, he had deceived himself. . . . His feelings are strictly self-centered. *Humanitismo* taught that it is better to give than to receive, because the benefactor enjoys the feeling of superiority, and that feeling is the most agreeable emotion that a human being can experience. This is the deepest emotion Braz Cubas ever felt. The most brilliant phase of his life according to him was the time he devoted to philanthropy, when he really came to know his worth. . . . (pp. 531-32)

Machado liked to depict this sort of inhuman character, the suspicious type, always curled in on himself like a sowbug, unable to let go or to love. . . .

It has been said that Machado is a writer of pessimism and despair. This may be true of his character, Braz Cubas: certainly the best thing Braz ever did was not to bring any more little Braz Cubas like himself into the world. But the pessimism of Machado himself is debatable. It seems more likely that at the heart of his criticism of mankind lies the hope that he can move his reader to a reform of manners. As Zola probed into vice and degeneracy with the intention of awakening the public to the need for social regeneration, so did Machado when he portrayed the strait jacket of self-seeking, sloth, and vanity into which Brazilian boys are thrust from early youth, and the calamitous life which inevitably, or almost inevitably, must follow.

By restricting his characters to the ruling classes, government officials, cabinet ministers, and the like, Machado de Assis wished to focus the attention of these very people on the mirror he was teasing them with and jolt them into self-perception. His intention seems to have been modest and specific. He wanted to move every man who read him, but most of all he wanted to reach the man in the *Casa-Grande* and move him to set his house in order. Machado was very much aware of the force that the example set by the upper class had on the rest of society. (p. 532)

If there was any solution for the sad state of society, it was not in religion (at least not in religion as it was popularly misunderstood), not in politics, not in the science of sociology, or any such sweeping generalization. But it might be found within the heart of each man. The suggestion of progress which is to be found in the theory of human editions . . . , the solitary note of optimism in the book, lends itself to this interpretation. Each period of a man's life is—or should be—like a new edition which corrects the preceding one, and so on until the final edition at death.

It seems to me that in this case, Machado de Assis wrote a pessimistic novel with an idealistic, and therefore hopeful purpose. (p. 533)

> Richard J. Callan, "Notes on 'Braz Cubas'," in
> Hispania (© 1964 The American Association of
> Teachers of Spanish and Portuguese, Inc.), Vol.
> XLVII, No. 3, September, 1964, pp. 530-33.

DONALD M. DECKER (essay date 1965)

[*In the excerpt below, Donald M. Decker discusses the cohesive elements in the short stories of Machado, concentrating on recurring themes and techniques.*]

The themes of Machado's short stories are subtopics of one broad basic concept of human life and the world in which men live. If there is a purpose in Machado's writing, other than simply to entertain his readers, it is to reveal to them this concept by combining fantasy, irony, and reality, blended in innumerable and original juxtapositions.

In **"Adão e Eva"** a judge explains that the earth was really created by the Devil, not by God. In **"Viver!"** the last man on earth, being weary of the world's ills, is happy to have reached the end of his existence. Although Machado appears to view the world as the Devil's creation, he does not find it perfect in its evil. In the story **"A igreja do Diabo"** the Devil establishes his own Church on earth, but its success is tempered by followers who "practice virtues on the side." (p. 76)

In **"Trio em lá menor"** the writer refers to the "technique of destiny," which proves in this case, as usual throughout his stories, to be utterly absurd. In **"Viver!"** man's vigorous hope for a better life proves to be but a foolish fancy. Thus, Machado does not envision a completely evil world, but rather one which is basically incongruous.

In her article "Machado de Assis, Encomiast of Lunacy," Clotilde Wilson refers to the writer's "deeply pessimistic philosophy" which sees "humanity struggling in vain against a relentless fate and seeking with frantic eagerness a chimerical happiness, which may fall within his grasp for one brief moment only to vanish the next with mocking laughter" (see excerpt above). Machado's characters frequently have specific yearnings for happiness both in material forms—such as, a uniform (**"O espelho"**), a pair of shoes (**"Último capítulo"**), or coins (**"Anedota pecuniária"**)—and in longings for fame (**"Fulano"**) or social success (**"Teoria do medalhão"**). Whether or not these are achieved, however, is purely a matter of incongruous fate. In any case, disease or death soon dissolves all human yearnings.

With unremitting frequency Machado's characters suddenly fall ill and die. It is evident that he had a broad knowledge of physical ailments. Never dealing emotionally with death, he briefly states that a character dies. The only commentary which he may imply is that death serves well to end a life of absurdities. Machado has Ahasverus savor this idea in **"Viver!"**. . . . (pp. 76-7)

The senseless world of man is revealed by Machado in tales both fanciful and realistic. Most of these are based on curious variations of sociological and psychological phenomena.

In considering the social aspects of an incongruous world, Machado humorously depicts the sharp contrasts between lofty sociological ideals and basic individual self-interests. He commonly deals with government, science, and philosophy in their relationships to the functioning of society.

The institution of government is mocked in **"A Sereníssima República"** through satire directed at election procedures. In **"O alienista"** a governmental institution becomes subservient to "sacred" science. . . .

Science provides the basis for satire and ironic humor in many of Machado's stories. In **"Conto alexandrino,"** for example, scientific methods of experimentation lead to utter folly. (p. 77)

Imagined or existing philosophical notions are often presented in Machado's stories. In **"O segrêdo do bonzo"** the theory that belief is the equivalent of truth is treated humorously. **"Idéias de canário"** deals with the concept that a man's philosophy is entirely dependent upon his own limited experience. Most of the philosophical elements in Machado's stories are related to his idea of an incongruous world. For example, in **"Lágrimas de Xerxes"** he points out that both life and love are fleeting in spite of the strong human yearning for permanency.

The stories most nearly approaching literary realism, as it is generally regarded, are those which illustrate individual psychological phenomena. These are clearly of special interest to Machado and his writings reveal a remarkable understanding of them.

That quirk of human nature which renders love between man and woman so impermanent is an incongruity which fascinated Machado. It is the most common theme of his stories—generally cast in "eternal triangle" plot structures. A usual "triangle'' consists of husband and wife and a third man (usually the husband's friend) who in time becomes the wife's ''true love.'' In **"A canomante"** a husband shoots his wife's lover; in **"Mariana"** a wife completely forgets her love for her original suitor; in **"A senhora do Galvão"** a wife fights for her husband's faithfulness; in **"Um erradio"** Tosta steals Estrellita from his poet friend while in **"Três tesouros perdidos"** the main character loses his wife, friend, and a large sum of money all in one day.

Illicit love affairs appropriately constitute an essential element in Machado's inconsistent and diabolical world. (pp. 77-8)

Other human traits vividly depicted in the stories are: sadism (**"A causa secreta"**), envy (**"Verba testamentária"**), compensation (**"Último capítulo"**), selfishness (**"Na arca"**), fickleness (**"Dona Benedita"**), vanity (**"Elogio da vaidade"**), love of fame (**"Fulano"**), and aversion to marraige (**"A desejada des gentes"**). These are but a few of the stories illustrating clear-cut psychological phenomena or ''cases,'' as Machado sometimes calls them. . . .

There is a timelessness and universality in Machado's realistic stories. He constantly eschews descriptions of settings and elements of local color. The interpersonal problems which he deals with occur principally among members of the middle or upper classes of Rio de Janeiro and could easily be applicable to life in any large city of the Occident.

Another thematic source from which many of the stories are drawn is the matter of the superiority of spontaneous creativity to studied art. In **"Cantiga de esponsais"** a newly-wedded bride impulsively provides the musical phrase which a composer has sought all his life. In **"Ex cathedra"** a godfather sets up classes in love for two young persons who succeed in becoming enamored of each other on their own outside the classroom. In **"Um homem célebre"** a musician meets with success through his popular compositions in spite of a strong personal preference for classical music.

Machado's writings are a testimony of his own possession of the talent of spontaneous creativity which he admired so much. Many of his stories are pure fancies—highly original and entertaining. One marvels at his ability to conjure up an imaginary situation and to follow it along from association to association in a bold and bizarre progression. (p. 78)

An ancient Greek returns to earth in modern times in **"Uma vista de Alcebíades"** and cannot tolerate the wearing of hats. In **"O dicionário"** the king's ministers decide to invent a dictionary with entirely new words. The protagonist of **"Idéias de canário"** is a bird that informs its owner about its concept of the world. The statues of saints in a church described in **"Entre santos"** come to life and engage in a discussion. In **"O cônego"** a writer supposes that nouns and adjectives occupy opposite sides of the brain, that they may come to love one another, and that their marriages produce style. (pp. 78-9)

These and many similar samples of Machado's remarkable flights of fancy show that he clearly champions the literary value of make-believe, as well as of realism, to develop his themes.

In designing the structure of his tales, Machado often uses the straightforward, chronological pattern of an anecdote—especially in illustrating an irony of fate or an incongruous social or psychological phenomenon. While narrating in the third person, he sometimes takes the liberty of interjecting his own remarks. . . .

Some of the realistic-type stories take the form of a straight dialogue in which one character relates his own or another's experiences to a second person. . . .

The more fanciful narratives, such as **"O alienista," "Idéias de canário,"** and **"O cônego,"** are usually written in the third person with highly improbable plots.

Another group of stories are allegorical in form, such as **"A Sereníssima República"** (a republic of spiders), **"A igreja do Diabo," "Adão e Eva"** (a new version of the biblical account), **"Elogio da vaidade"** (in which Modesty and Vanity address an audience), and **"Viver!"** (in the form of a stage play).

Taking the form of documents or manuscripts, some stories are supposed to be ''additions'' to existing works: **"Na arca"** is an addition to the Bible; **"O segrêdo do bonzo,"** to Fernão Mendes Pinto's *Peregrinação;* and **"Lágrimas de Xerxes,"** to Shakespeare's *Romeo and Juliet*. . . .

Several stories are disguised as wills and the final writings of men about to die. Some examples of these are: **"Verba testamentária,"** the will of an envious man; **"Último capítulo,"** a suicide note; **"Galeria póstuma,"** a posthumous diary; and **"O enfermeiro,"** a final document of confession. . . .

Like the Peruvian Ricardo Palma, Machado often breaks into the structure of his stories to discuss openly the methods and purposes of his story fabrication. He usually does this in a whimsical manner—as one might speak when telling a tale to a group of listening friends. (p. 79)

Allusions to well-known literary works occur in scattered form throughout Machado's stories. Most frequent references are those made to Shakespeare and the Bible. These works, dealing with universal human traits, evidently led Machado away from a purely ''local'' view of life—or perhaps they coincided with a universal viewpoint which appealed to him from the outset. He was never a ''regionalist'' writer.

With regard to general attitudes reflected in Machado's stories, one notes a tendency toward equanimity. Although dealing with weird aberrations, strange incongruities, and discouraging twists of fate, the author never openly expresses despair or strong emotions. If there is a trace of attitude, it is usually that of humor born of irony. The follies of fate do not seem greatly to perturb Machado as he describes their ironic absurdities.

In the handling of his themes, therefore, he strives for ''objectivity'' in refraining from subjective evaluations of that which he relates. The touch of humor, evident from time to time, usually appears in the guise of light satire. Like William S. Gilbert (of Gilbert and Sullivan operetta fame), Machado often uses a topsy-turvy situation to produce such humor. **"A igreja do Diabo"** is perhaps the best example of this. In **"O alienista"** first the insane, then the sane, and finally the doctor himself are committed to the asylum. . . .

As to the language element in the author's style, highly literary or abstruse terms are infrequent. Machado writes concretely, tersely—one might say, almost in a journalistic fashion. He avoids an excessive use of adjectives and affective expressions. His language is clear, straight-forward, and restrained. It provokes thought, enjoyment, and often amusement in the reader—as the concise writings of the Chinese have done for centuries

Although varied, the short stories of Machado de Assis, taken as a whole, have a basic unity—reflecting the same general concept of the ''Devil's world.'' They are products of an ingenious craftsman gifted with a deep understanding of human motives, a flair for a spontaneously fanciful and original treatment, and a clear and restrained manner of expression. Reading them affords an enjoyable literary experience. (p. 80)

> Donald M. Decker, "Machado de Assis: Short Story Craftsman," in Hispania (© 1965 The American Association of Teachers of Spanish and Portuguese, Inc.), Vol. XLVIII, No. 1, March, 1965, pp. 76-81.

THE TIMES LITERARY SUPPLEMENT   (essay date 1966)

[Machado de Assis] wrote a series of novels and short stories which have an appeal to the modern reader comparable with those of Stendhal or Sterne. Both these writers he admired, and he shared their psychological penetration and their sense of detachment. It is this detachment which brings him near to our own viewpoint, for he seems as if he were living in the twentieth century and looking back on the society of Rio de Janeiro humanely but from a distance, not personally involved.

For Machado de Assis the life of society was a human comedy, an immensely diverting spectacle of folly which he frequently compared to a play or—in his novel *Dom Casmurro*—to an opera. . . .

In this human spectacle, Machado de Assis played the part of observer and critic. The fluid state of nineteenth-century Brazilian society ensured him of an opera of great variety and vigour, but it was not one in which he could take part as a performer of conviction. He was, indeed, an outsider by birth and temperament. . . . His novels brought him literary recognition and he was appointed first president of Brazil's Academy of Letters.

Under the surface of this success story, there lurked a darker side at which the novels and short stories hint. During his literary apprenticeship he wrote four romantic novels which have little appeal to the modern reader; but one of these, *Helena* . . . , gives some indication of the price of social acceptance; in it, social success is equated with personal frustration. The heroine is believed to be the illegitimate offspring of a wealthy man. Under the terms of his will, she is accepted into his family and succeeds in winning their respect and affection. But she wins this family acceptance only by suppressing the fact that she is not the wealthy man's daughter and that her real father is alive and living in poverty. The real human relationship, based on affection, has to be hidden and stifled in order to give the girl a chance in life. One can easily see a parallel here with Machado de Assis's own life, for he too obtained acceptance only by suppression and by forgetting his early origins. On his marriage, relations with his mulatto stepmother seem to have been allowed to drop, and the paucity of facts about his early life is almost certainly attributable to his own wish to forget this period.

Machado de Assis's output was enormous; nine novels, more than 200 short stories, many poems. But between the first poem, published when he was fifteen, and his first important novel, *Memórias Póstumas de Brás Cubas (The Posthumous Memoirs of Brás Cubas)* . . . there was a long apprenticeship in which his genius seems to have been hampered by romantic plot conventions. After 1881, the influence of Sterne, Xavier de Maestre and Stendhal permitted him to adopt a freer form more suitable to his discursive, detached approach. It is in this freer form that all his outstanding novels, [*Memórias Póstumas de Brás Cubas, Quincas Borba, Dom Casmurro, Esaú e Jacó* and *Memorial de Aires*] . . . , were written. But in his own

introduction to *Brás Cubas,* while acknowledging his debt to Sterne and de Maestre, he adds that there was a "bitter and harsh sentiment" in his own novel that was not to be found in his models.

Machado de Assis's attitude to life was indeed harsh and bitter. Like Schopenhauer, the novelist believed that men were irrational creatures, actuated by will and that individual existence had no transcendental design. . . .

Schopenhauer's philosophy dominated the thinking of many Brazilians of the period, including many prominent philosophers and writers, but with Machado de Assis the influence extended even to the moral and aesthetic. Like Schopenhauer he saw in self-denying love and in art two ways of escape from the individuation principle. The genius alone could achieve a certain tranquillity through the contemplation of universal ideas.

But although Machado de Assis's personal philosophy was pessimistic it was not dismal, for the spectacle of passion-driven humanity was immensely diverting. . . . True, each of the novels describes a circle of defeat and despair. Brás Cubas, Rubião (the protagonist of *Quincas Borba*), Dom Casmurro, all lead wasted lives. Brás Cubas spends his youth and energies in a long adulterous affair with the wife of a friend, a woman he could have married in the first place if he had really set his mind to it. Life slips by in plots, intrigues and secret meetings and he suddenly realizes that he is fifty years old. . . .

Human lives, then, are spent in vanities; human relationships are treacherous. "Winner takes all" is the leitmotif that runs through *Quincas Borba*. Nevertheless, in all the novels the humour and not the pessimism triumphs; it is the spectacle of the human comedy not its bitter end that claims the reader's interest.

Esaú e Jacó (Esau and Jacob) was published . . . only four years before Machado de Assis died. In spirit it resembles the three preceding novels, but perhaps it has less immediate attraction for the English reader since the characters are not so much individuals as allegorical figures in a political fable. . . .

The novel shows us a society in transition from a patriarchal slave-owning society of the Empire to the new republican society with its anxiety to reproduce in Brazil the liberal democracies and the industrial progress of Europe. The quarrelling twins represent the political discords of this new society, a discord which never arises from matters of principle but simply from mutual envy. The issues of slavery and republicanism were no doubt serious issues, but what Machado de Assis suggests is that people's attitudes on such issues are not rationally motivated and have really very little to do with the issues themselves. *Esau and Jacob* is thus a political fable which though about Brazilian society can be applied to the political game in any liberal democracy.

Indeed all through the novel the frivolity and senselessness of political partisanship is brought out, and in case the reader should have any doubt about his intention Machado de Assis introduces a mouthpiece for his own views, the Counsellor Ayres, an ex-diplomat who sometimes acts as wise arbiter in the twins' disputes. Ayres, like the author, is an onlooker in life's comedy. . . .

The momentous events of contemporary history are all treated in [a] lighthearted way. The passing of the Empire is described through the reactions of the confectioner who is afraid he might lose business if he does not change the name of his shop from the "Imperial Confectionery" to something more in tune with the times. Another character, the conservative politician Baptista, is faced with years in obscurity when the liberals come to power, but soon argues himself into believing that he has always been liberal at heart.

Machado de Assis sees a sacrifice of principles as one of the inevitable consequences of living in society. . . . In many of the short stories he expounds the view that human beings have two selves, a public self and a private self, and that the public self may flourish at the expense of the private one. In *O Espelho (The Looking Glass)*, the reflected image of the narrator is dim until he puts on his lieutenant's dress uniform, when the outlines of his reflection become sharp and clear. In *Teoría do Medalhão* (or *How to become a Pillar of the Establishment*), a father gives his son advice on how to achieve success. He should have no original ideas, avoid exercising his mind and, if he enters politics, he should either do battle over trivial issues or deal only in abstractions.

These wry comments on social man might suggest that Machado de Assis was a political cynic. He was not. But he refused to accept the sentimental and self-deceiving view. His attitude to slavery illustrates this. The one story he wrote on the topic (*Pai contra mãe—Father Against Mother*), is one of the most brutal exposures of the inhumanity of slavery ever written. The protagonist is a poor white who pursues runaway slaves in order to get the reward for their capture. Desperate from poverty and with his own family in danger of dispersal, he hunts down a pregnant slave who aborts when he captures her. Slavery is not presented here as an abstract question of principles but as an economic system which degrades people and does not allow them to have "finer" feelings.

Esau and Jacob is, therefore, not simply a political fable but a fable about what politics really are—a game in which men exercise their passions and in which issues are decided not on intrinsic merit but according to the temperament and situation of the players. Not for nothing does Machado de Assis bring in the analogy of the chess game. . . .

In this game the devil wins when men are moved by self-interest, God when they transcend egoistic love. But those who transcend egoistic love are rare. In *Esau and Jacob* only Flora and Counsellor Ayres achieve this. Both are detached from the social game around them, both have a superior penetration that enables them to see beneath the surface of strife. They alone understand that Pedro and Paulo are "one and the same . . . and have been from the womb". And perhaps ultimately this is what Machado de Assis wanted to say about humanity in general.

    "Winner Takes All," in The Times Literary Supplement (© *Times Newspapers Ltd. (London) 1966; reproduced from* The Times Literary Supplement *by permission), No. 3338, February 17, 1966, p. 122.*

LEO L. BARROW   (essay date 1966)

[*Barrow disagrees with many critics (in particular Helen Caldwell) by stating that a study of Machado's life is invaluable in understanding his work. Barrow sees in the novels a reflection of Machado's personal problems and moral dilemmas.*]

Machado's universality must be intimately linked to his Brazilian heritage. Just as the universality found in Cervantes cannot be divorced from its Spanish origins, it is also essential I believe, to link Machado's life—the life of a poor Brazilian mulatto who stuttered and had epilepsy—to his works and study the close and complex relation which exists between them. This relation consists primarily of those actions and traumatic moments in Machado's life which reveal his moral essence and reflect in his novels and short stories. In this relationship lies the key to his narrative art and what Machado hoped would be the reader's reaction to it.

To try to explain every author's production and craft by investigating the most important facets and most dramatic moments of his personal life would be an absurd step, a step backwards towards the nineteenth century. However, in Machado's case, little bits of his moral self which can be easily traced to episodes of his personal life, appear and reappear with such frequency that it is difficult to ignore them. Some of these moral themes crop up in such a casual manner that the reader can hardly be expected to relate them to the author's personal life. Others, which appear more often, are veiled by the humoristic tone of the prose, its highly original style, and the author's reserve. Machado urges us to read attentively, digesting slowly all the contents of the prose. . . . The theme of ingratitude must surely strike the attentive reader forcibly because of the number of appearances and the incisive impression it makes on his sensitivity.

The significance of ingratitude in Machado's life can be, and has been, traced to one person, his stepmother Maria Inez. . . . Machado de Assis owed the beginnings of his education and of his culture to his stepmother, Maria Inez. (pp. 211-12)

Maria Inez was a most deserving and loving mother to Machado; and no one understood this better than he himself. She had, however, one or two shortcomings: she was a mulatta and of very humble origin. One day he felt he had to choose between her and his career as a writer and a public servant, between her and his marriage to the cultured Portuguese woman, Carolina. Machado's problem [was] strictly a moral one. . . . (p. 212)

The novel [*A mão e a luva*] is an excellent example of the close relationship between his personal life and his literary works. Here his style—the cup which contains the bitter wine of Machado's personal life and moral essence—lacks the delicate charm and distinction which will later serve to disguise and obfuscate this relationship. If we read *A mão e a luva* carefully, we will see that it contains all the principal elements of Machado's life. Guiomar, the heroine, is of humble origin, but her mother gave her the rudiments of an education. She loses her mother when she is thirteen and is taken in by her rich and aristocratic godmother. Is this merely a romantic convenience? In any case, Machado also sought the protection of the more powerful at an early age.

Everything that Guiomar does reflects a strong will and ambition, a desire to flee from vulgarity. She has to choose between three suitors: Estevão, sentimental, deeply in love, but weak and doomed to obscurity; Jorge, the nephew of her godmother who is lacking in ambition and content to vegetate; and Luís Alves, not very romantic but strong-willed, ambitious, and very sure of himself. The conflict, clearly stated and felt by the author, is between the head and the heart. . . . Although true sentiment wasn't lacking, [the marriage of Guiomar and Luís Alves] was a wedding of two ambitions. . . . It is cruel but necessary to point out that Machado's marriage to Carolina, five years before the publication of this novel . . . , was a marriage which helped him considerably in his flight from obscurity. Without Carolina his greatest literary achievements might have been impossible. Although Machado had achieved some renown as a writer before his marriage to Carolina, without her, the mate to his strong will and ambition, he still might have been lost in the dark sea of the nameless multitude. This is the fate of the rejected suitor, Estevão. (pp. 212-13)

Ingratitude is only mentioned in the novel in connection with Guiomar's debt of gratitude to her aristocratic godmother. The Englishwoman, Mrs. Oswald, thinks that this gratitude will cause her to choose Jorge, her godmother's nephew. Guiomar's decision is against gratitude, but she is able to protect her self interest because the Baroness is generous and good and loved her truly as a mother. Although gratitude is overtly mentioned in this connection only, Machado makes the reader feel it in almost all the human relationships. Guiomar's real mother, who struggled so hard to raise and educate her, receives no word of praise, in fact is scarcely mentioned. When Estevão falls desperately in love with Guiomar he confides in his friend and schoolmate, Luís Alves, who promptly takes her for his own and forgets his friend without the least bit of remorse.

The earlier manifestations of gratitude and ingratitude, treated in a somewhat open manner, show clearly the intimate relationship between this theme and Machado's personal life. This relationship isn't lessened when in *Brás Cubas* and all the subsequent works it suffers a highly stylized and artistic fragmentation. Moreover, the theme remains intimately Brazilian since gratitude is one of the moral values which the mestizo must often sacrifice in order to improve his position in society. . . .

In the masterpiece *As memórias póstumas de Brás Cubas* and in subsequent works, ingratitude, along with other moral shortcomings, is delicately fragmented, veiled, and made to seem incidental. In Chapter XXI Brás Cubas tells how the muleteer saved his life and how generously he was going to reward him. The reader watches the size of the gratitude shrink. As the muleteer fixes the harness, Brás Cubas decides to give him three gold coins, then decides two will be enough, or perhaps one. He finally gives him a silver coin. (p. 213)

The episode does more than reveal a facet of Brás Cubas' moral character. It does more than measure his gratitude. The episode is a delicately disguised confession of the size of Machado's gratitude and through it Machado has crept slyly into the hearts of his "dear readers" and given the exact measurement of our own gratitude. The author's moral confession is essential here since one cannot penetrate into the heart of Brás Cubas or of a "dear reader" through the objective study of literary models. Neither is such keen penetration possible through realistic or naturalistic observation. Machado rejected this type of observation as superficial and slavishly photographic in his essay on *O Primo Basílio* by Eça de Queiroz. (pp. 213-14)

Thus the relationship between certain dramatic moments in his life and certain episodes in his works becomes quite obvious. There are a number of episodes which clearly strengthen our belief in this relationship. . . .

Another episode in the life of Brás Cubas intimately connected with Machado's struggle with gratitude is found in the two chapters called "A borboleta preta" and "Coxa de nascença." Both chapters tell the same story of how we hurt those who love us because of some quality, perhaps being crippled or black, which may offend us or may not be accepted by others. The black butterfly comes to visit Brás Cubas while he is dressing. Annoyed, he kills it with a towel. In his moment of pity he reflects that the butterfly sought to please him by kissing him on the forehead. (p. 214)

The chapter foreshadows what is going to happen in his relations with Eugênia. He is falling in love with her when he notices that she has a slight limp. The problem is the same as the problem in "A borboleta preta." Why should she have this defect? He is also concerned about her origin since he thinks she is the result of an amorous affair which took place in his own gardens. . . . It is easy to link these two episodes to Maria Inez. Brás Cubas' concern with color, origin, and other physical defects are very significant here.

The basic conflict seems to be between social, political, and intellectual preeminence and gratitude. We remember the advice given Brás Cubas by his father. "Teme a obscuridade, Brás; foge do que é ínfimo. Olha que os homens valem por diferentes modos, e que o mais seguro de todos é valer pela opinião dos outros homens." . . . ["Fear obscurity, Braz; flee everything that isn't big. Look here, there are different ways for a man to amount to something, but the surest of all is to amount to something in other men's opinions." (Translated by William L. Grossman.)] This has been considered by many critics the sustaining motto of Machado's life and the basic reason for his ingratitude towards Maria Inez.

Once the connection between the author's ingratitude and its fragmented moral substance in his work is established, it is fascinating to see the many subtle variations on this basic theme. Some of these variations can be grouped around the advice given Brás Cubas by his father. . . .

Other variations can be grouped under the heading of *bel ami* stories. In the longer story, **"Almas agradecidas,"** the title is of course significant. Oliveira takes Magalhães off the street and into his home, gets him a job, and introduces him to his circle of friends. Magalhães shows his gratitude by stealing his girl. Oliveira generously gives up the girl. (p. 215)

Some of the more subtle variations deal with the strange relationships which exist between the person who proffers gratitude and its intended recipient. In one of Machado's best short stories, Gouveia is seriously wounded by bandits and during his convalescence a stranger named Fortunato cares for him with rare and seemingly disinterested dedication. Once he recovers he is eager to show his gratitude, but is brusquely rejected. At the end of the story the reader discovers that "A causa secreta" which prompts Fortunato to care for the sick and wounded is his delight in human suffering. In **"Galeria póstuma"** the recipient of gratitude considers it a nuisance. (p. 216)

Gratitude seems to be a delicate moral sensation which is easily crushed or dissipated by other motives. It also seems to be an exterior truth or value imposed upon man from the outside. The human heart seems to have difficulty in echoing it with any force or in sustaining the echo for any length of time.

In every one of these episodes the reader should find a bit of his own heart, a parallel episode, a confession which reads, "I have or would have done the same thing." The reader should become a member of a very intimate triangle composed of himself, the character, and the author. Machado strives constantly to strengthen the bonds of this triangle, always speaking to his readers in an intimate tone, giving them choices to make in almost every paragraph, and constantly asking them to participate in the literary creation. (pp. 216-17)

Leo L. Barrow, "Ingratitude in the Works of Machado de Assis," in Hispania *(© 1966 The American Association of Teachers of Spanish and Portuguese, Inc.), Vol. XLIX, No. 2, May, 1966, pp. 211-17.*

CARMELO VIRGILLO (essay date 1966)

[*Virgillo agrees with Helen Caldwell's observations in* The Brazilian Othello of Machado de Assis *that true love versus self-love is a predominant theme in Machado's fiction. But Virgillo finds, even in the author's depiction of true love, an examination of ulterior motives of self-interest.*]

It has been observed [by Helen Caldwell] that Machado de Assis' fiction reveals the author's preoccupation with the theme of true love versus self-love. One can add, however, that excluding perhaps *Memorial de Aires,* his last novel, true love generally appears in his works as a device concealing an ulterior motive deeply rooted in self-love. This motive Machado himself has called the "causa secreta," or the ugly side of human beings, which his fictional characters try to conceal behind a mask of selfless humanity. Machado's denial of true love, furthermore, can be observed in his short stories as well as his novels, and even in those early tales commonly taken as emotional, sentimental stories supposedly aimed at the immature, love-starved reader who delights in the triumph of true love. These earlier tales, assigned to his so-called romantic period, seem to be filled with sentimental clichés very much in keeping with the literary conventions of the times. As one looks more closely, however, at the stories in *Contos fluminenses* and *Histórias da meia noite,* his first collections, one finds paradoxes and ironies that should dispel the notion that these early tales among Machado's works are uncharacteristically romantic, hence inferior to his later production. The mating game is depicted, to be sure, but as an ironical battle of wits, and a strenuous one at that, at the conclusion of which it is uncertain whether the winner really enjoys the spoils or merely gets stuck with them. In these tales Machado seems to be asking: Who is to tell what lies hidden behind people's actions even when they seem most sincere? What guarantees that love can reform self-centered people?

Self-centered love appears in a number of these early stories in the form of greed, vanity, pride, jealousy, envy, lust or any combination of these. In **"Frei Simão"** selfish parents destroy their son's life out of greed and pride. Simão's parents, wishing their son to marry a wealthy heiress, more likely for a financial gain of their own than for their son's welfare, deceive Simão by telling him that Helena, the destitute orphan girl with whom he is in love, has died. Machado describes Simão's parents in a way that leaves no doubt as to their character. . . . [Their] egoism eventually kills Simão, who after he has become a Benedictine monk discovers that Helena is alive and married to a peasant. Soon after, he goes out of his mind and dies. (p. 778)

In **"O segrêdo de Augusta,"** the "cause secreta" is envy on the part of a parent, who should be the last person to be suspected. Augusta is envious of her daughter Adelaide's youth and beauty, which she conceals behind a mask of motherly zeal. Fearing that if her daughter were to marry and have children of her own it would make her look old, Augusta discourages her daughter's suitors by magnifying their slightest faults while feigning parental concern.

Lust is the "causa secreta" which triggers the seemingly sincere actions of a number of Machadian lovers. Machado, however, does not usually allow lust to triumph unmolested over honor. His unscrupulous lovers will get away with just about anything except with a deception leading to moral degradation. In **"Confissões de uma viúva moça,"** for instance, Eugênia is led to believe by handsome Emilio that she is deeply loved by him and that she should give in to his demands. But when her husband dies and she is free to marry, her young man suddenly leaves, revealing his true, dishonorable intentions. **"Casada e viúva"** depicts an outwardly ideal husband, Meneses, very much in love with his wife Eulália although he deceives her constantly. Eulália, however, going through her husband's papers, unearths some incriminating love letters that give away the man's escapades and his true character. He ends up losing his wife's love forever. . . . The lustful husbands who seem to collect mistresses to inflate their male ego while pretending to adore their wives are frequently encountered in Machado's short stories. They are insensitive, selfish creatures who are usually punished by their own "causa secreta" which gives them away.

Machado de Assis often portrays women as selfish creatures incapable of self-denial, with the result that they seem to create more problems for the men who fall in love with them than they solve. However, men in Machado's fiction cling to these women desperately as a salvation from their miserable existence or, as is usually the case, as a liberation from themselves. But when a misanthrope meets a conceited woman and expects her to reform him, the results are all but good. Indeed, many of Machado's males are weak individuals who seek in women financial and moral support. (pp. 778-79)

Machado is far from presenting his readers with uncomplicated stereotypes. Everyone of his characters conceals a "causa secreta," an intimate secret triggering actions anything but altruistic.

Machado de Assis' pessimistic philosophy of life becomes even more apparent in his third collection of stories, *Papéis avulsos.* Here one difference is noticed immediately in his concern with the subject of love. Machado concentrates his efforts on a number of other aspects of this emotion, consistently tearing it down to expose the real side of his characters. The latter are portrayed as either consciously hiding a "cause secreta" or as acting according to a subconscious selfish urge. This is readily apparent in his constant presentation of seemingly legitimate acts of affection concealing self-love, frustrated love succumbing to egoism, or in the proclamation of the superiority of opportunism over altruism. (p. 780)

Many of Machado's characters seem to be affected by what the Brazilian writer refers to as "o enjôo" or "tédio"—boredom with life leading to apathy and withdrawal from reality. The character is usually described as an inconsistent, unreliable individual who unconsciously cannot help but think of himself. Such is D. Benedita, the protagonist of the homonymous tale. She loses her husband because, too busy thinking of herself, she cannot make up her mind to follow her magistrate husband where his new job has taken him. Her concern for her children, a son and a daughter, is quite superficial: she is more worried about what other people think of her than she is about her own children. D. Benedita hardly interferes with their lives. She ignores the boy and goes along with her daughter's every wish. As for her friends, they too serve only to inflate her ego, only to be soon forgotten when they cease to be of use to her. Following her daughter's marriage and the husband's death, D. Benedita is left to face a life of loneliness and frustration with no one to flatter and worship her.

Jealousy hidden behind a seemingly selfless act is encountered in **"Verba testamentária."** Here Nicolou B. dies holding a grudge against humanity, particularly against those whose earthly accomplishments overshadowed his. His grievance against his fellow human beings is based on the competitive role of man in society. Everyone strives for importance on earth without regard to religion or moral values. Failure to achieve importance generates hate for the luckier ones. It is for this reason that Nicolau's will and testament insists that he be given burial by the least known and least successful casket maker in town. (pp. 780-81)

Machado's continued denial of altruistic love and his exposé of man's constant attempt to hide egocentricity behind a mask of generosity reaches paradoxical proportions in "A causa secreta." Here what has all the appearances of a humanitarian act by Fortunato conceals instead a gruesome reality. Fortunato's only reason for caring for a wounded man and for later opening a hospital is that he enjoys watching others suffer. When he cannot observe human beings suffer he takes great pleasure in vivisecting guinea pigs in the pretext of doing scientific research. (p. 781)

Whenever he does not deny that man is actually capable of noble acts, Machado appears to ridicule the very essence of altruism by satirizing legitimate philanthropists. These are portrayed in his stories as lunatics or wild visionaries who take upon themselves the courageous task of saving humanity through seemingly worthy feats which in true quixotic tradition defeat their own purposes. . . . [A] paradoxical situation is encountered in **"Conto alexandrino"** where Herophilus appoints himself a savior of mankind and discovers the science of anatomy, which is to spare his fellow human beings the pain of malady. To carry on his merciful work our great humanitarian asks the state for and obtains live human guinea pigs whom he vivisects unmercifully in the name of science. (p. 782)

In later stories one notices almost immediately that Machado has dropped the romantic veil of pretense which may have previously masked his sentiments on love. His new treatment of passion brings to light all kinds of illicit love affairs. Only the writer's characteristic *bienséance* rescues some of his stories from immorality. Here the "causa secreta" is more present than ever. Under a coat of marital faithfulness spouses either deceive one another or wish they did. Many a time matters are greatly facilitated if the lover or the mistress is a friend of the house not likely to be suspected. (p. 783)

In **"Mariana"** Evaristo returns to Brazil to resume his love affair with Mariana whose husband has, in the meantime, passed away. He finds her thoroughly uninterested in him, not out of love for her deceased husband whom she had loved for only a short while, but out of the desire to pass in the eyes of friends and relatives as a faithful wife. Machado's ever-present subtlety is clear in the concluding lines of this tale where his sentiments toward love seem to be clearly manifested. In short, love does not deserve to be glorified. Like anything else in life it is fickle, perishable. Only life continues unmolested and indifferent to man's suffering. To this end, he informs all those readers who may feel sorry for Evaristo that the latter, far from being crushed by Mariana's *volte-face*, returns to France to resume the life he has temporarily interrupted. (pp. 783-84)

Love is not worth sacrificing one's life for. One should only try to prove the contrary, and he will discover how senseless it is to pit something ephemeral—love—against something quite concrete, death. This theory is evidenced in **"Maria Cora"** where Correia risks his own life for the love of a married woman, only to be scorned and miserably rejected by her after killing on the field of battle and quite honorably a husband she despised. Theoretically Correia should be driven to desperation, Machado seems to suggest ironically. He should punish

Maria Cora for first motivating the combat and then scorning the winner. But what good would it do? Is life going to stop because of the ingratitude of a fickle woman? Indeed not; Correia will just have to remember to wind his watch, a thing he seems to have overlooked the very night he thought he had finally met his true love.

People in love commonly think that love is eternal; it survives time and should not bow even to death. The marriage vows are a trifle more realistic, for the spouses promise one another love and devotion only as long as both shall live. A close examination of Machado's views on the subject as observed through his many tales appears to contrast radically with both of these views. He seems to question the validity of any institution created by human beings who are by nature selfish and inconstant. Time changes everything including love, which, like people, must also be selfish and fickle. Machado's married and unmarried lovers either give the impression of being faithful or are actually faithful as long as nothing better appears on the horizon. When time sends along a more advantageous situation they do not hesitate to trade spouses, lovers, and even their children for what they think is an improvement in their situation. . . .

It seems to me that selfless love, as opposed to self-love, is represented in Machado's stories as an illusion devised to conceal man's natural instinct of self-preservation in a world full of uncertainty and contradiction. A pessimist and a true fatalist, the Brazilian writer sees in beauty and goodness something superficial and ephemeral designed to counteract the ugliness of a basically evil life. Like life itself, nearly all Machadian lovers are deceivingly ideal individuals: good-looking, healthy, well-off, yet tragic, unpredictable, often ugly in truth. Men are many a time misanthropes who expect to find in heterosexual love a way out of their misery, thus seeking a cure-all in their relationship with the opposite sex. They fail miserably in their intent, most of the time. The Machadian woman is no better than her male counterpart, if anything, worse. (p. 784)

If life is conceived by Machado's dialectical philosophy as basically contradictory, and if man is nothing but a part of life, or life itself, then one must conclude that there must be two sides to every person. To this end the Brazilian writer presents selfless love, generosity, and a number of other positive attributes of man only to prove that they represent but one of the two sides of the individual. The other side is represented by self-love, opportunism, and all the vices imaginable which constitute the invisible "causa secreta." Therefore, assuming that Machado's fictional creations seek in beauty an escape from the ugly side of life, and if love is synonymous with beauty and everything that is good, then one must concede that behind the beautiful human beings in love or behind the altruists in Machado de Assis' fiction there must be ugly creatures in love with themselves. The two sides: the superficial, or the beautiful, and the invisible, or the ugly, complete the individual. Man, claims Jacobina, a Machadian character in **"O espelho,"** is, metaphysically speaking, nothing but an orange: there are the peelings covering the orange and then, underneath, there is the orange itself. It seems to me from a close examination of a number of the Brazilian writer's most representative short stories that his denial of selfless love as symbolic of all good in man is very real; it is Machado's way of saying that human beings must not be taken at face value. Man is basically sinful, evil, and if he expects to survive he must create the beautiful part of himself with his own hands for everyone to see. This second soul will enable others not to detect the "causa secreta'' which motivates his selfish actions and which is, as I see it, his only true self. (p. 785)

Carmelo Virgillo, "Love and the 'Causa Secreta' in the Tales of Machado de Assis," in Hispania (© 1966 The American Association of Teachers of Spanish and Portuguese, Inc.), Vol. XLIX, No. 4, December, 1966, pp. 778-86.

HELEN CALDWELL (essay date 1970)

[*Helen Caldwell is Machado's most important English-language critic as well as translator of several of his works. Her* Machado de Assis: The Brazilian Master and His Novels, *excerpted below, presents a detailed study of all of Machado's novels.*]

[In Assis's criticism] of Eça de Queiroz's *Cousin Bazilio* and the Naturalist school of fiction, he put forth as the proper aim of the novel the displaying of action caused by passions and ideas arising from within the natures of the characters. His complaint against the Naturalistic novel was that, playing on the surface, it is false and artificial. (pp. 40-1)

This concern with "character" might lead one to think that Assis's ambition was to write tragedy rather than comedy, in which the action does not necessarily result from conflicts of emotion or will. . . . Felix, the protagonist of *Resurrection,* has in his nature the seeds of tragic conflict: a strain of tenderness and desire to love that warred with a cynical distrust. We find in him the refusal to yield that typifies the Sophoclean hero, even though the essence of Felix's nature was doubt.

The title of the novel explains its action. Felix's dead heart or capacity for love came to life in the warming flame of a woman's love, then sank back into the tomb again, snuffed out by jealousy. The jealousy was engendered and fed by distrust and fear of being deceived by himself and others. His doubt downed all other emotions, all arguments, all reason, all truth. It is a trait common to us all in greater or less degree, so that the fate of Felix has a certain sinister universality.

The other personages of the novel are no match for Felix's tragic nature. They have little of the tragic about them. They are out of other media. (pp. 41-2)

All the women in this novel are possessed of a submissiveness (to men and life) that almost passes belief. The abandoned mistress Cecilia and the adoring but unloved Rachel are of an unrelieved magnanimity in their relinquishment of Felix to "another." . . .

The men too, all except Felix, are out of comedy. (p. 42)

Vianna, Livia's conniving brother, "was born a parasite as others are born dwarfs. He was a parasite by divine right." Chief among the comedians is Baptista—and this is a name Assis reserved for characters with a Shakespearean flavor. Baptista, a plain-dealing villain like Don John of *Much Ado About Nothing,* mapped a definite campaign of treachery. . . .

The author and his heroine took a serious view of the problem facing their hero—a life without love. Not all the characters shared their feeling. Needless to say Baptista and Vianna saw everything through eyes distorted by self-interest. Others found it hard to be completely serious about Felix. A newspaper man, "a friend of his, used to compare him to Achilles' shield—a mixture of tin and gold—'but much less solid,' he would add." (One sees here the beginning of the narrative method that Assis brought to such perfection in the later novels *Dom Casmurro* and *Esau and Jacob*—a method by which the characters push

the author aside, write their own lines, and act out their own play.)

Resurrection's odd assortment of personages—from various walks of literature—makes a tragic struggle on the hero's part scarcely worth the trouble, so that the story becomes by turns either comic or sentimental, with only the specter of tragedy peering from the shadow of Felix's soul. (p. 43)

Assis's second novel, *Hand and Glove,* . . . has no hero of tragic proportions, or of tragic possibilities. And yet the novel is concerned with "will"—will in the Stendhalian sense. *Hand and Glove* contains no less than two Julien Sorels: one male, one female. If Stendhal's Sorel was a travesty of the Napoleonic hero, Guiomar and Luiz are little tin Sorels. There is no murder, no seduction, no melodrama, however; *Hand and Glove* is romantic comedy, with more comedy than romance. The protagonist, Guiomar, was a beautiful, intelligent, elegant young lady; she was also poor, orphaned, and the foster daughter of a wealthy widow, a baroness. (p. 44)

The widow's nephew Jorge, attracted by Guiomar's charms and egged on by his aunt's officious paid companion, Mrs. Oswald, made Guiomar a proposal of marriage. . . . There was, however, the matter of the second "Sorel" to be dealt with—Luiz Alves, a successful young lawyer with political ambitions, who had a house next door to the widow's estate. Although his will to succeed had led him to exclude romance from his thoughts as a waste of valuable time, he became convinced that Guiomar would furnish him added strength in his ascent to glory. He too made her a proposal of marriage—a lawyer's proposal, a standing offer so couched that it required neither acceptance nor refusal.

These are comic types and they find themselves sooner or later in embarrassingly comic predicaments. Guiomar had still another admirer, Estevam, a romantic lover who never had a chance with this female Sorel: he was easily disposed of at the proper time by the male of the species. As far as the plot is concerned this man could be dispensed with; but, for the comedy, he is indispensable: in himself he is a complete satire on romantic love—a lovesick egotist who builds dreams out of air, making an ass of himself before the lady, firing up his melancholy with thousands of pages of *Werther,* and serving as a constant butt for both Assis's and Alves's wit. A companion piece of fatuous love is the nephew Jorge, a vain, idle, empty-headed stuffed shirt. (pp. 44-5)

[The] story appears to bear out the implications of its title: a pair of strong wills appear to win out. Since the hero and heroine are spiritual twins, their wills do not clash but join forces in a silent entente cordiale. Like Julien Sorels with preconceived ambitions and with a certain amount of sangfroid and detached determination, they exert their wills over other people's. Though not ruthless they get their way because their opponents' wills are flabby and their owners more stupid than not. This is what seems to be the case. Actually, Guiomar and Alves were trapped by their own better natures—by "love"—as happens in romantic comedy. They thought they were attracted to each other by an identity of interest—for the better furthering of their individual ambitions; but this was only partially true, as the author makes apparent on the last page of the novel, where, I believe, he laughs at this delusion of theirs. (p. 47)

[The] theme of this second novel is seen to be no more than a variation on that of the first. In *Hand and Glove* we have the reverse of the coin: it is will, where the obverse, in *Resurrec-*

tion, was doubt. There tragedy demanded the defeat of love, here comedy contrives love's triumph.

As a comedy, **Hand and Glove** is not flawless; still it is a gem—a slight satire on various manifestations of human vanity. Only the baroness is spared: she has no vanity. When Jorge referred to her ''saintly qualities,'' she replied, ''Only one, Jorge, only one: that of loving you both—you and her.'' (p. 48)

Whereas **Hand and Glove** is pure comedy, Assis's next novel **Helena** skirts tragedy and ends in melodrama. It too is shot through with threads of satire on human desires and mental aberrations. And its opening paragraph is out of low comedy:

> Counselor Valle died at seven o'clock in the evening, April 25, 1859. He expired of a thundering stroke of apoplexy . . .

The paragraph goes on to explain that because of the sudden nature of his taking off he was obliged to die without any assistance from the medical profession and even without the consolation of religion. On the other hand, his funeral, the following day, was one of the best attended ever seen in all that neighborhood. (It might be noted that Machado de Assis was partial to apoplexy as a *deus ex machina* to dispose of unwanted and embarrassing persons. In the short story, **''The Rod of Justice''** *(O Caso da Vara),* he refers to this device as the ''apoplectic solution.'')

In spite of its almost frivolously macabre opening, this novel marks a big step forward in Assis's early avowed artistic purpose of presenting the drama resulting from the emotional conflicts of his characters. The personages of the novel **Helena** are more true and far more complex, more fully developed, than those of either **Resurrection** or of **Hand and Glove.** In a tragic situation they could have been tragic characters of heroic stature. But the situation is not truly tragic: it is, in a sense, false and trivial. As a result, the whole novel takes on an air of impossible romance. The characters' emotions are extreme for the ultimate situation. The theme, which could be tragic, suffers the same dislocation as the characters.

The book starts with a theme not unlike that of Aeschylus's *Oresteia*—the idea that crime begets crime. There is a curse on the aristocratic and wealthy house of Valle as there was on the house of Atreus. A wealthy man's caprice and his extramarital adventures not only brought about the suffering and early death of his wife, but it was also to foster ungovernable passions in his children, destroying his daughter Helena in the bloom of youth and ruining the happiness of his only son.

The Counselor's will disclosed that he had a natural daughter, Helena, a young lady of sixteen whose widowed mother, now dead, had been his mistress. The girl was in school in a suburb of Rio de Janeiro. The will directed that Helena be recognized as a legal heir and brought to live in the family mansion, where she was to be treated with all the honor and indulgence of a legitimate daughter. (pp. 49-50)

Estacio [the son], without being aware of it, began to fall in love with Helena. His passion for his sister was revealed to him by the family priest, Melchior. Helena already knew that she was in love with Estacio. She knew also that she was not the Counselor's daughter but only treated as such from childhood when her mother became Valle's mistress. (pp. 50-1)

Estacio's possessive love of Helena refined his powers of observation. Suspicion finally led him to the old house that lay in the path of Helena's [horseback] rides: he thought she was visiting a lover; he found her father. Estacio's first impulse was to throw family reputation to the winds and marry Helena; but all opposed him: his aunt, the priest Melchior, the family physician Camargo, Helena, and even his own ideas of ''society's law.'' (p. 51)

In her despairing struggle to repress her love for Estacio and conquer her feelings of remorse and shattered pride, [Helena] died.

That Machado de Assis had wanted to write a novel of real incest is not impossible. If he had done so, the emotions of the novel's personages would probably strike a more sympathetic response in the present-day reader. As it is, Helena's struggle against her passion is motivated primarily by respect for the Valle family's position in society and by her own understandable, but excessive, pride, and this strains our credulity a little, and our patience. (p. 52)

Helena and Estacio are in essence tragic characters, but the situation is a matter of nineteenth-century Rio de Janeiro etiquette, and the proper narrative framework would be the comic. If Estacio and Helena had been brother and sister, the outcome could have been tragic; as it is, it is melodramatic. The unhappy ending seems forced, and the characters overacting. Unlike the novel **Resurrection** in which the situation had tragic possibilities but the characters fell short of their destiny, here it is the situation that is meretricious; the characters' struggle could have had universal implications. Indeed, as the book stands, one closes it with that sensation of being in a world fallen apart such as tragedy engenders; but the feeling is momentary, for this little world had no real substance in the first place, and on second thought one perceives that the story was only an exciting series of events with no implications beyond themselves—in short, a melodrama. The author knows it. By way of holding our emotions in subjection he inserts into the ending a poetic burst of romance that might have come out of Goethe—with wind, beating rain, and a hero toiling under the weight of a heroine's almost lifeless body.

As if to offset the tale's romantic improbability, or in revulsion against it, Assis introduced into the narrative an instance of true incestuous love. It is not given tragic treatment, however, but satiric. Camargo, the family physician, is portrayed as a cynical, avaricious, ambitious man who schemed to marry his daughter to Estacio do Valle for the sake of wealth and family aggrandizement. (p. 58)

Camargo is Assis's caustic comment on the marriage of convenience, which is, in a sense, the subject of this novel. The story ends on a note of fierce comedy. Helena's love was selfless. Estacio's became so, as did Dona Ursula's, Melchior's, and Mendonça's; even Eugenia was affected by Helena's death, but Camargo's love was and remained selfish. As Assis explains more than once, it was himself he loved in his daughter. (p. 60)

As tragedy reveals the soul of the individual hero, so comedy reveals the common, the all-too-human beneath the individual mask. Camargo's humanity is ludicrous and we laugh, but our laughter is not hilarious. The comic villain and his marriage of convenience win out. But it is Helena's pride that is the determining factor in the plot of this novel. Without it, the wills of the others—Estacio, Melchior, Ursula—would have given way to their love for her, and Camargo would have been powerless; but pride was a part of the beauty of her nature.

Along with its characters of larger stature and the almost-tragic theme, we suddenly find developing in this novel the symbolism that was to become an integral part of Assis's later novels, with its subtle, poetic, pervasive strength. The symbols are as yet few and barely hinted, but they add their bit to the book's atmosphere of deceit, menace, and love. (pp. 60-1)

With his fifth novel, *Posthumous Memoirs of Braz Cubas* . . . , Machado de Assis returned both to the simple theme sounded in his first novel, *Resurrection,* and to the comic genre of his second, *Hand and Glove.* After tracing the intricacies of the feminine psyche . . . , he abandoned the female protagonist for good and all and resumed his exploration of the male heart and the basic problem of love and self-love, life and death, good and evil. In *Posthumous Memoirs of Braz Cubas* he gave self-love a thorough going-over. Consequently death enters its every page; even life takes on the role of death at times; and death, of life. There is no gentle Raymundo in this narrative—practically nothing in the way of unadulterated love, or of unadulterated good or evil or life or death, although self-love does hold the scene, assuming many masks, as greed, vanity, envy, ambition, and so on.

For all its concern with dead and half-dead souls, *Posthumous Memoirs of Braz Cubas* is cast in the form of a comedy, with comic personages and comic action arising out of their comic natures. It is a little strange, therefore, that it has generally been regarded as a work of profound pessimism.

It was probably the hero-narrator himself, Braz Cubas, who put ideas of pessimism into the critics' heads in the first place, with his prefatory note, "To the Reader."

> If I have adopted the free form of a Sterne or of a Xavier de Maistre, I am not sure but what I have also inserted a certain cantankerous pessimism of my own.

And, finally, there is his remark on the last page of the novel, the remark that no critic neglects to quote, the remark from which William Grossman coined the title for his translation, *Epitaph of a Small Winner.* When he balanced his life's accounts, says Braz, the good against the credit side: he discovered he had a small amount on the credit side: he had never had a child, had transmitted to no living being the legacy of our human wretchedness. True, there seems to be a bitter taste here, but if we have followed the narration closely, this remark will invite an amusing as well as a pessimistic interpretation. (pp. 73-4)

As Sterne in *Tristram Shandy* borrowed from, and at the same time burlesqued and parodied, the epics, romances, comic epics, and picaresque tales of his predecessors, Machado de Assis in this novel did the same for Sterne. Sterne, in order to satirize the long romance that begins with the birth or childhood of the hero and gradually takes him up to maturity, or beyond into middle age, began his *Life and Opinions of Tristram Shandy* before his hero's birth, with his begetting. It took the first three of the novel's nine volumes to get him born, almost another volume to get him through the first day of his life, another half-volume or so to get him into breeches, and, so far as the narrative goes, it is difficult to determine whether he ever did come of age.

Machado de Assis, in his turn, parodied the older romances, and *Tristram Shandy* into the bargain. Only, he went about it from the opposite direction. *His* hero-author, Braz Cubas, begins his story with his own death notice. . . . (pp. 75-6)

Braz Cubas's method is a refinement on Shandy's. It too progresses through digressions, and even through retrogressions, that are economical and dramatic. (p. 76)

[The] title's second half perhaps bears a trace of that picaresque novel par excellence, *Gil Blas de Santillane* by Le Sage. The name Braz is the Portuguese form of the Spanish *Blas,* and Assis, who frequently mentions Le Sage's hero in his writings, always refers to him as Gil Braz. Conversely, the Spanish translations of *Posthumous Memoirs* have been titled *Memorias Póstumas de Blas Cubas.* (p. 77)

Braz could say at the end of his memoirs that as a hero of romance and even as a picaresque hero he was something of a failure. He listed his defeats: no page with blood on it; he suffered no remorse; with Don Quixote he did not win fame, although, like him, he had tried to win it—through his medicinal plaster to cure melancholy, the disease of which Don Quixote was thought to have died. He never became "caliph" or "minister," never knew marriage, had no children—not even the two-child minimum, the boy and girl of a Gil Blas or Tom Jones. Finally he adds in a tone between regret and perhaps genuine relief the phrase that has been taken ever so seriously and applied to Machado de Assis as well as, or even more than, to his creature Braz Cubas—the remark about leaving no legacy of our human misery to a child of his.

In spirit, however, Braz was a Gil Blas, though an unsuccessful one. Wide-awake, witty, handsome, reckless, light-minded, of an easy virtue and adaptable morals, accepting all situations and turning most of them to his own advantage, tolerant of vice in himself and in others, yet not completely vicious—he gradually learned something as he made his "circuit of life"; but, unlike the more conventional, the true picaro, he never got around to reforming or having any regrets. Yet his story contains traces of pessimism, he says: he warns of it in his prefatory note, "To the Reader," and frequently reminds us in the course of the narrative that his is a lugubrious tale, that it reeks of death; and he will drive home a point by saying, "I assure you of this from the depths of my tomb." Although he thus insists on his pessimism, his manner is far from pessimistic. He is about as carefree a corpse as one is likely to come across. Even the worm of his dedication, that is, death (perhaps his critics also), is patted on the back, so to speak, with a certain camaraderie, and one suspects that Braz's tomb was a snug affair with hot and cold running water and a good library.

Life, as well as death, is given the comic treatment. The butt of the comedy is in all cases the same—human vanity. All the characters suffer from it, some more than others, none more than Braz, except, perhaps, his father. The elder Cubas is the incarnation of vanity—a simple, unaffected, undisguised, harmless, and inoffensive vanity. . . . (pp. 84-5)

Vanity is the backbone, the very viscera, not only of silly and of vicious acts on the part of the characters, but of their good and generous actions as well. Take charity for example: nothing could have induced Cotrim to make donations to charity except to get his generosity written up in the newspaper or to have his portrait painted in oils and hung on the wall of a benevolent society.

Vanity begets ambition, which in Braz's world is what stokes the engine of human progress. Ambition, he shows us, promotes science (exemplified in his invention), politics and letters (to cite himself, Neves, and Luiz Dutra) and snobbery, or social distinction if you prefer, like Bento Cubas's.

Vanity is the very essence of sexual love and fidelity: it was in great measure responsible not only for Braz's love of Virgilia but also for his faithfulness to her over so many years. (pp. 86-7)

Vanity is responsible for honesty; and it is honesty, we are told, that gives rise to dishonesty. . . .

When vanity is stifled, it is replaced by some less amusing form of self-love. . . . (p. 87)

It is not often that Braz's vanity fails him. He is such a thoroughgoing egoist, so sure in his superior wisdom, so indulgent toward his own imperfections, that it is no wonder he can view with Olympian calm the slips and errors of the less than perfect mortals that bask in the sun of his presence. The villain of the piece is not any of the personages. It is human nature, life itself. (pp. 87-8)

Humanitism, the philosophy invented by the mad Quincas Borba, is a kind of exuberant development of Pandora—a thoroughgoing egoism. According to Quincas Borba's explanation, humanitas, the principle of all things, is Man shared by and summed up in every man. Each man is not merely humanitas's vehicle; he is at one and the same time vehicle, driver, and passenger.

Quincas Borba's Humanitism has been interpreted variously by various critics—as a satire on Leibnitz, Nietzsche, evolution, and so on. Probably there are shafts at these and some other philosophies in it; but there is little doubt that superficially Assis was poking fun at Auguste Comte and Positivism with its professed aim of securing the victory of altruism over egoism. . . . Machado de Assis delivered many a body blow to Positivism in the columns of his journalism, and in other writings also. (p. 89)

Humanitism has the all-embracing quality of Positivism: it covers metaphysics, ethics, science, literature, economics, and has a religious dogma with liturgies. Quincas spent a great deal of thought and perspiration over his liturgies for the Church of Humanitism. Humanitism, he explained to Braz, was to be the church of the future, the only true religion; Christianity was all right for women and beggars, and other religions in his opinion were no better. (p. 90)

All these resemblances, however, are more apparent than real. Assis is poking fun not only at Positivism but at all other illusory *isms,* and particularly at materialistic ones. In addition, I believe, he is poking fun at himself, as though to say, "The opinions Braz Cubas spouts and this Pandora I inserted into his delirium are the same as Quincas Borba's philosophy; they are as crazy as Positivism. I am as crazy as Quincas Borba, that is, I am as crazy as Auguste Comte." Perhaps it is worth noting that Quincas is the nickname for Joaquim, which was Assis's first name as well as Borba's. (pp. 90-1)

Finally, the determinism to be found both in Positivism and in Quincas's Humanitism is also a part of the Cubas philosophy, and as such is turned to artistic purpose: it becomes a dramatic device in the novel. Quincas Borba constantly maintains that since humanitas is in all men, and vice versa all men are a part of humanitas, every man has a stake in every other man's life, thought, and actions. (p. 91)

Braz's determinism is much less complex than Quincas's. He calls it his "theory of rolling balls." . . . Braz likens himself and others to rolling balls: the ball Marcella rolled against the ball Braz; it, set in motion, rolled against Virgilia. Thus one may say Marcella changed the course of Virgilia's life, and even of Lobo Neves's without coming into contact with either

of them. . . . In the same way, the purpose of Dona Placida's birth and existence, and of the unlovely coupling of her parents, was to foster an illicit love affair between Braz and Virgilia. The witty Braz remarks that the principle of the rolling balls is responsible for the "solidarity of human boredom."

Although Braz laughs and blames everything on Nature, the projection of his rolling-balls theory into the novel's action does inject a moral tone—a suggestion of human responsibility. Thus a combination, or interlocking, of human will and chance seems to close round the characters with the vicelike grip of inescapable Fate, and is perhaps one more reason for critics calling this novel "pessimistic." The individual cannot escape his own past and that of his parents and ancestors, nor even from acts—present and past—of strangers. (pp. 92-3)

Like Tristram Shandy, Braz gives minute analyses not only of his own thoughts, but smells out the secret opinions, feelings, and ambitions of all the other characters as well. It is through these opinions and sentiments, rather than through their actions, that Assis's personages, like Sterne's, come alive, grow on our affections, and move our pity or laughter. More often than not it is our laughter, for that, after all, is Braz's purpose. (p. 96)

In the novel itself [Assis] leaves Braz to shift for himself and make what impression he will with his memoirs. This is a far cry from *Resurrection,* into which the author frequently entered without ceremony to explain the faults, virtues, and doubts of his characters. . . . Although the least personages of Braz's *Memoirs* vibrate with a life of their own, still we must never forget that we see them in the mirrors of Braz's mind.

Another point of difference between Braz and his creator is this matter of Humanitism. Although Braz seems to subscribe to Quincas Borba's mad philosophy, there is no reason to believe that Assis did. There is some reason to believe he did not. . . . Positivism's literary outgrowth, Naturalism, on the whole, [Assis] loathed. He particularly condemned a writer's use of shocking physical details with little or no motivation, and implied that Zola sometimes followed such practices with a view to increasing his income. (pp. 112-13)

His criticism of the Naturalist novel was that it aimed at representing superficial appearance—content to be an "inventory of events and fortuitous" actions unmotivated by human passion and, in its most extreme form, a photographic and slavish reproduction of the low and ignoble—sordid details related for the purpose of politico-social propaganda or with nothing more than a view to arousing momentary physical sensation in the reader, and with no meaning beyond. (p. 117)

Assis's seventh novel, *Dom Casmurro,* is the culmination of the six that preceded it. Not only does it surpass the others as an artistic work, but elements of the first six novels appear here in more perfect form: composition of characters, narrative structures, theme developments—the whole novelist's art. In particular, Assis's ever-increasing strands of symbolism send subtle threads all through these other elements and weave a wonderful thing. (p. 142)

Dom Casmurro's hero, Bento Santiago, . . . has two men within him, but his is a . . . sinister combination: Othello and Iago. In addition to superior passion, Santiago was possessed of attributes essential to a tragic hero . . . namely, those of high degree. . . . Santiago was born to wealth and position; he was handsome, well educated, and by no means stupid. Since he narrates his own story, he not only manages to convey the impression that he is the aristocratic descendant of a long line of great plantation owners with countless slaves, he also contrives to envelop himself in an aura of superstitiously religious, almost divine, eminence. This he does by dwelling on a special relationship between his mother and God and by insinuating that his very birth was a miracle, and so regarded by the family priest. He informs us that his story was Othello's—except that his Desdemona was guilty. But soon, however, we discover the hidden Iago. With a criminal's urge to talk, he discloses, in carefully guarded metaphor, that his jealousy was rooted in aboriginal evil, that it antedated its object, groped until it found an object, than pursued and clung to it with obdurate blindness. (p. 143)

The titles of Assis's novels are in every instance an important element of the whole. Each is what he called in his preface to *Esau and Jacob* a resumé of the *matter*. . . . In *Dom Casmurro* he went so far as to permit his hero-narrator to deliberately mislead us.

Santiago tells how the nickname Dom Casmurro had been given him by an irate neighbor, and explains that *casmurro*, as applied to him means a morose, tight-lipped man withdrawn within himself, a definition not to be found in dictionaries. Since those days, however, Portuguese dictionaries have expanded their definition to include the meaning Santiago gives. In Assis's day, they defined casmurro as "obstinate, stubborn, wrong-headed." And this, perhaps is the more important definition for the understanding of the novel. Santiago did become casmurro by *his* definition, but he also had in his nature that "resistance to persuasion" found in Sophocles' tragic heroes.

The dom, Santiago informs us, was intended to make fun of his aristocratic airs, for this word is a titular prefix to the name of a member of the higher nobility. (pp. 144-45)

The superficial story Santiago would tell us is of his betrayal by Capitu with his friend, Escobar. Through the language of metaphor, however, he tells a different story. . . . *Dom Casmurro*'s tragedy takes place within Santiago's own psyche, the war of passions, the exercise of moral freedom. It is he who makes the choice between good and evil, and, although time hardens his cold heart, he cannot rid himself of twinges of guilt. That is why he tells his story. The interplay of natures is within him—his generous, loving nature fighting against and finally overcome by the strong powers of evil. Although these latter are within himself, he projects them upon others—especially upon Capitu; but, as he himself tells us, he carried "death on his own retina." Good in this novel is equated with love, and love with life; evil with self-love and death. Santiago's struggle with his destiny resembles that of Felix, the hero of *Resurrection,* who tried to revive his dead heart. "I appear to be alive but am not," Santiago tells us. I am a corpse painted and made up to look like life, but the "inner structure will not take dye." He repeats this theme louder and more clearly: "I tried to connect the two ends of my life—restore adolescence (love) in old age (lack-love), but the middle, myself (the essential part, love, life), is missing." He tore down the old house (his heart) and had the original duplicated in another part of town. He tried to bring ghosts to life. He could not fill in the sonnet "battle of life," between the first and last line, because love failed him. . . . All these symbols tell the same story: living death, death in life. Although he lived on, his soul, like Dante's traitorous Alberigo's, was in the icy depths of hell. . . . (pp. 146-47)

Evil assumes a . . . terrifying aspect in *Dom Casmurro*. The death of Santiago's heart is enveloped in an atmosphere of mystery and ominous suggestion: ghosts, revenge, guilt, torture, broken vows, Faust and Macbeth—both of whom were in league with the powers of darkness; the libretto of his life's "opera" was written by God, music by Satan—and Santiago danced to that music. These innuendos give one a feeling that unholy murder has been done. Santiago insinuates that it was his wife Capitu and his friend Escobar who murdered his heart with their cruel betrayal. But his own words give him the lie: his metaphors tell the more forthright tale. He himself murdered the loving Bento and projected that murder upon Capitu and Escobar. Many readers, convinced by Santiago's cunning, believe implicitly the plain Portuguese of his clever insinuations. But even if Capitu were guilty of adultery with Escobar, the tragedy of Dom Casmurro would remain: it is *in him*. Santiago's "heart" had been killed long before the supposed betrayal—his jealous cruelty manifested itself before Capitu ever saw Escobar. If Capitu deceived him, it was not the loving Bento she deceived: it was Dom Casmurro. The title of the book is *Dom Casmurro,* not *Capitu;* the tragedy is his—the terror of a life without love, and Santiago was formed for love. Yet his life, like Macbeth's, became "a tale told by an idiot." When we finally recognize the fate that has closed in upon him we are struck with awe and horror; and, as in great tragedies, we have a feeling that there has been a "change in the face of the universe." Our sadness over the sacrifice of Capitu's love and beauty is not unmixed with a kind of joy. She won life's battle: her self-love, her original vanities and jealousies, were driven out; only love remained in her life. This victory of hers was mirrored in the soul's battles of the other characters—José Dias, Dona Gloria, Cousin Justina, and the rest.

But all these personages, and even the portraits on the wall, who seem to speak with their mute eyes and gesture, are melded into the life of the principal character, Santiago, into his very brain, so to speak. It is he who tells us of them; they are, or become in the telling, aspects of his personality. It is he who dominates the story, dominates the mystery-charged atmosphere, dominates our emotions—on which he leaves a mark that never completely fades away. He stands at the center of the whole structure; everything—plot, symbolism, characters, theme—all converge in him, making this Assis's most emotionally powerful work. (pp. 148-49)

Both Braz and Santiago, given a free hand by Machado de Assis, explored their own psyches and those of their friends and relations for the benefit of their readers. The purpose of the two authors, however, was quite different. Braz Cubas's aim was to amuse and instruct, both himself and his reader, by recounting his travels around life and his tilts with society and with his own nature. The result is comedy. Santiago on the other hand had a more specific aim, a deadly serious one—to do away with his own guilt feelings, to convince himself, by convincing the reader, that he had not committed a crime. We are not amused for long by his narrative. He arouses our pity, and our horror at the enormity of the change in a human being who once had the love of all about him and the reader's affection as well. (p. 154)

As had become usual with Assis, the keynote [of *Esau and Jacob*] is sounded on the first page with these words, "Not everyone can say he knows a whole city." For "city," read "society," because Rio de Janeiro was Brazil's capital—political, financial, cultural—and in this novel it is to be taken as the whole people. Brazil, in all its history, resides in the personages of this "city"—in the flesh and blood individuals and in what Ayres called their "souls," that is, in what each represents in essence or metaphorically.

Immediately, upon the above pronouncement, author Ayres proceeds to show us "the whole city," that is, its "soul" as well as its outer physical aspect. He shows it to us in a multitude of brief scenes and tableaux that fuse, superimpose, and change almost imperceptibly. To start us off spiritually on the right foot, he placed a posy at the very beginning, a verse from Dante's *Inferno* (V, 7): *Dico, che quando l'anima mal nata* . . . ("I say that when the ignobly born soul . . ."). . . . *Anima mal nata* designates an individual born with a nature capable of accomplishing a great destiny but predestined by God not to fulfill the destiny promised by his nature. Minos, the judge of Hell, assigns such *mal nate* souls to their proper circle of Hell by the number of times he lashes his tail. Later in our novel, Santos himself "lashed his tongue seven times," thus landing himself in the seventh circle with the bankers and usurers—where, in fact, he belonged. (pp. 163-64)

In chapters xxxii and xxxiii we are told Ayres's experience on his return to his native city and retirement from the foreign service. . . . [The narrator] alludes to the psalm in which David returned after fighting the Philistines and "saw the City all full of wickedness and contention," and "in the marketplace nothing but usury and fraud." (p. 164)

The moral fiber of this society was on a par with its religious practices—not conspicuously vicious but frivolous, foolish, contemptuous of its heritage, and not averse to the practice of dishonesty. Nóbrega . . . was a thief; he became a millionaire. Santos had a distinct talent, we are told, for making money and making other people lose theirs. Baptista's ethical standards in the matter of political patronage also appear to have been questionable. The times were propitious to crooked dealings; but, as Ayres tells us, the occasion makes the theft, it does not make the thief. The thief (he says) is born not made— and we are back with the *anima mal nata* and a city filled with sinners "doomed to go astray from the moment they leave their mother's womb." Ayres was not dishonest: he was discreet and diplomatic. He shared some of the other weaknesses of the age, however.

The women of this society are less offensive than the men, at least to our narrator Ayres, but he was not blind to their faults. Although he was charmed by Natividade in particular, he does not conceal from us that she was vain, passionate, selfish, snobbish, unreasonable, and somewhat mean to start with. Motherhood and time gradually changed her. (pp. 168-69)

Flora, the heroine, is an exception among the women of this novel, as her third suitor, the young bureaucrat-poet Gouvêa is an exception among the men. Love is what distinguishes these two. But, Flora is more than a lover; she is more than a human being. As our narrator presents her, she appears a charming Portuguese-Brazilian-Catholic girl of the time: innocent, modest, sweet, gentle, artistic, poetically romantic, superstitious, and subject to vapors like a true Victorian lady. The character Ayres, however, found something strange about her: a will, an ambition, and a more than human desire for perfection. She loved the identical twins Pedro and Paulo equally; because for her their "souls" were also identical, except that each had "something indefinable" that the other lacked. Paulo's dreams for the future stirred her; she found peace and contentment in Pedro's satisfaction with the way things were. Dante saw the double nature of incarnate love in Beatrice's eyes, now as wholly divine, now as wholly human, but could not see the two as one thing and one person until the beatific vision at the end of the *Paradiso*. So Flora, just before her death, saw the twins as one. (p. 169)

This is more than a real girl—sane and lovely in spite of her hallucinations and her strange desire. Our narrator gives a key to her identity, especially with his metaphors. Her name was Flora—goddess of flowers. She was "Orpheus the sweet singer," a will-o-the-wisp, a "fragile vase," "flower of a single morning," fit subject "for a tender elegy," a "rose growing beside a crumbling wall," ruins of a partly-built house that was never finished, a spring that never had a summer. She did not resemble her parents—the unenlightened Imperial politicians Baptista and Dona Claudia; she was the spiritual child of the literary, career diplomat Ayres. Ayres—the intellectual, the free-thinking man of European culture—read in the classics, suave, kindly, moderate, urbane, and eternally youthful. She was born in the year 1871, which marked the struggle over the law of *free birth* in the Chamber of Deputies—the law that declared every child born, free. Her intellectual progress in speaking, reading, writing, was dated by ministries. All these symbols, facts, and images connect her with the establishment of the Brazilian Republic—the ideal republic. . . . During the first troubled days of Floriano Peixoto's regime Flora died; "her funeral passed through a city in a state of siege." The ideal republic was dead. Her pallbearers, listed for us by Ayres, were Baptista, Santos, Ayres, Pedro, Paulo, and Nóbrega (government, finance, diplomacy, the conservative and liberal parties of the new era, and the new wealth). (pp. 170-71)

Brazil it would seem, was destined never to realize her dreams, never to enjoy a present, but only a future that would be identical with her past. That is what all the personages of the book secretly wanted. Time is a specter that stalks this novel's pages just as it did **Dom Casmurro**'s; but here the bouts with the invincible antagonist are for the most part comic, and the old fellow is often knocked out and put in chains—though not for long. His opponents tried to escape his grasp by clinging to the past: a letter written by the Marquis de Pombal, an antique inkwell, an old signboard. Or they fortified themselves with other weapons and stratagems. Baptista would have turned back the clock if he could. Nóbrega rubbed imported toilet waters on a face already badly battered and bruised by time. (p. 172)

Flora's concern with time was of another sort. She tried to escape the present through her music. "For her, music had the advantage of not being past, present, or future: it was a thing outside time and space, pure idea." Nevertheless, there was in her music "a kind of harmony with the present hour." That is, there is only one way of holding "Time captive"—through love. Love for Assis is the present moment, and its major symbol a flower. Flora was the present, she was the Republic, which was also a symbol of love—born out of the emancipation movement, with its ideal of brotherhood. In contemporary prints, the Republic was regularly represented as a beautiful young woman, or girl, with roses and rose petals all about her. Flora too was a "rose growing beside a crumbling wall," and the "red rose of dawn"; her mother gathered flowers for her to wear at the republican ball. In other of Assis's writings roses are "God's thoughts"; these flowers, it is plain, are political ideals or ideas that "keep growing." As republic, Flora died; as love, as present, she disappeared; but her brief presence and strangely beautiful death drew the other main characters of the novel together: what she had stirred in their hearts lingered on as a sainted memory symbolized by "immortelles" and "forget-me-nots."

But there are no consistent allegories for Machado de Assis— no *Pilgrims' Progresses*. Flora is as paradoxical as the other characters, and she too was tainted with the weakness of the age. The only person truly flesh of her flesh and spirit of her spirit was the young, obscure, poetic government employee Gouvêa, from whose worshipful glances she steadily averted her eyes. . . . She too preferred the past's illusions. She chose candles rather than gaslight, so that she could not see clearly when Pedro and Paulo appeared to her (past and future).

Machadean allegory does not embalm the characters into fixed attitudes, nor slow their action: it infuses life and vigor. This novel's real plot scarcely moves, even on place: where will the mediocre talents and halfhearted bickering of a couple of rich boys lead? and the answer, nowhere. Not much there to raise the blood pressure. But, an age, a great country, human progress itself, missing a rendezvous with its destiny? The thematic action is poignant, suspenseful, and witty. The wit is not made leaden by allegory: it is given wings. Santos's fads in religion, financial speculation, beards, and governments are funny in an individual banker or banker type; they are still more ridiculous in the Bank of Brazil. Our mild amusement over the childish hopes and superstitions of the banker's wife deepens when these are seen to be the illusory dreams of Imperial Brazil, whose womb teemed, not with "royal kings," but with republican political parties—conservative and liberal—which were indistinguishable twins. (pp. 173-74)

Every person in the book has a universal essence. Narrator Ayres early advises us that the epigraph from the *Inferno,* *"Dico, che quando l'anima mal nata"* will help round out the characters. As Dante's *Divina Comedia* is filled with "souls," so *soul* is the keyword repeated on every page of the novel. Not only human beings but also animals (donkeys, horses), inanimate objects (a signboard, an inkwell, the stones of the street, the walls of houses; the sea, winds, and sky), and even activities like the soothsayer's rites, all have a "soul," an impelling spirit, an essence, a metaphorical life. (p. 176)

Flora's beauty had promised to be "long-lasting" like Natividade's and "possessed of a life that might be great," but the ephemeral republic never blossomed into summer. Even the old Brazil, spirit of illusory hopes, daughter of Portugal, was not given "the kiss of eternity." She died. "She should have lived much longer" (here we feel the Machadean irony), but she was cut off in one of the city's frequent epidemics. Her belief in the predicted greatness of her sons (Ayres tells us with dramatic irony) was "an illusion." This society was not to fulfill its destiny. Brazil was always to pursue, never to achieve its glorious future. The old Brazil was dead. There was no reason to expect anything of her sons: the frivolous bickering between political factions that were essentially alike would continue. Ayres was left, however, and he too believed in the future, he too believed in time, and he kept forever young with his European springs of wisdom. We feel that Brazil will live: *it* will not die between its past and future, as the republic died; it will perdure as long as Ayres does, and *he* shows no signs of buckling at the knees. As the novel ends, the flower of youth is still fresh in his buttonhole. Brazil will continue to look forward to its future. (pp. 180-81)

> *Helen Caldwell, in her* Machado de Assis: The Brazilian Master and His Novels *(copyright © 1970 by The Regents of the University of California; reprinted by permission of the University of California Press),* University of California Press, 1970, 270 p.

ALFRED J. MᴀᴄADAM (essay date 1977)

[*In* Modern Latin American Narratives, *MacAdam, relying on the genre theories of E. D. Hirsh and Northrop Frye, determines that*

what has been called the Latin American novel can only be read and understood from its intended perspective when classified as the Latin American satire. In the following excerpt he examines the satiric elements and narrative techniques of Memórias Póstumas de Brás Cubas (Epitaph of a Small Winner).

A narrative is the deployment of words to represent the passage of time. It is of no consequence whether the temporal flow is circular or linear; all narratives are committed to time, which is of their essence. But there is also built into narrative, into words used as narration, a contrary activity, one that concentrates the reader's attention on a timeless moment. These two notions, derived from the notions of synchrony and diachrony in Saussure's linguistics, constitute the basic structure of all narratives. Furthermore, they may be seen as identical to the distinctions Jakobson makes between metaphor and metonymy in *Fundamentals of Language:* "The development of a discourse may take place along two different semantic lines: one topic may lead to another either through their similarity or through their contiguity. The METAPHORIC way would be the most appropriate term for the first case and the METONYMIC way for the second, since they find their most condensed expression in metaphor and metonymy respectively." . . . While metaphor (or selection) and metonymy (or combination) are the basis of all discourse, one tends to predominate in the various sorts of literary discourse. . . . [Poetry] tends toward "epos" or recurrence, while prose tends toward continuance and flow: what we shall see in the works examined in this essay is the conflict between metaphor and metonymy, between closure and extension, between synchrony and diachrony.

When we consider Machado de Assis's **Memórias Póstumas de Brás Cubas** . . . in the light of this opposition, we find the conflict first expressed as a struggle between the flow of life and the metaphorizing tendency of autobiography. This is the problem of unity in any first person narrative, the one Don Quijote presents . . . : how can a picaresque narrative end— that is, have unity—unless the life of the *pícaro* is over. Machado resolves this difficulty by locating his narrator outside of time, in eternity. From the privileged vantage point of death, to which, presumably, the past conceals no secrets, Brás presents the reader with the events that constitute his life. To prove he will have no difficulty finishing his story, Brás begins by describing his death: "Life was shuddering within my breast with the power of an ocean wave, awareness faded, I sank into physical and moral immobility, and my body became vegetable, stone, mud, nothing." . . . This passage marks a moment in Machado's literature in which he is consciously liberating himself from the resolutions to certain narrative problems presented to him by his immediate literary tradition. First, the narrator makes us see that it will be impossible for us to identify ourselves with him. That is, he demands that we never forget either his fictional identity or his being "on the other side" of time. All writers of autobiographies, as Olney points out, claim some sort of special point of view with regard to their own lives, and it is one of the standard fixtures of the Spanish picaresque that the hero comment on himself, as he was, as if that other self were dead. Here however we find no such ethical posturing; the difference between the narrator's two selves is the relationship each has to time.

The ramifications of this temporal status for determining the text's genre are serious. An omniscient narrator can tell things about which the characters themselves are ignorant; character-narrators, located simultaneously within and beyond the action they describe, can reveal things they themselves do not suspect.

But both of these types of narrator exist primarily as shapers of temporal flow. Their purpose is to organize linear narrative into a particular shape. Brás Cubas, to be sure, does exactly this, but he does it in such a way, from such an alien perspective, that we must consider what he says not only as flow but also as icon, not only as metonymic narrative flow but also as metaphor.

When we say that a text is metaphoric, that it has, in Jakobson's sense, drifted away from metonymic scene linking, we are admitting that the text is discourse à propos of something else. It is of the nature of satire and romance to be accumulations of metaphors: the great problem of interpreting metaphoric texts involves locating the referent, the meaning which would "close" the open gap of metaphor. This, clearly, is impossible, and it is the peculiar nature of metaphor, of all signs in fact, to be eternally elusive, always suggesting something which they can never be.

Brás Cubas, from his first words, knows what he is doing, and he explains why he is doing it by confessing a life-long desire for fame and glory. He hopes to gain immortality, after death, by writing a text, and in doing so renders ironic a traditional apology for writing. The text will be his life story, his autobiography, but a reading of the book reveals that it can in no way be taken for an exemplary life. The saint's life is a model to be emulated: even Saint Augustine offers himself as an example, implying that what happened to him can happen to the reader. The lives of great men are called "inspirational" precisely because they spur the reader on to imitate the hero's life. Brás Cubas falls into neither category, unless we think of him as we would of Lazarillo De Tormes, as a negative saint whose ironic life is a model to be avoided rather than copied. (pp. 11-13)

Society in Brás's book is a projection of man himself; therefore it contains the same bizarre mixture of ideals and perversities as its creator. If Brás is a pessimist, it is not because he is horrified by man as a social animal, but because he sees life as a series of futile exercises leading to an end identical for the good and the bad, the foolish and the wise. Brás is a pessimist, not on an ethical or social level, but on a biological level. To act, to be idle, to move, or to stand still often turn out to be synonyms instead of antonyms. When Brás strives for something, for Virgília the woman he loves, for example, he loses. Later she becomes his mistress without his having to fight at all. That this is a parody of Augustinian grace may be true, but it is certain that whatever man's plans may be, they lead inexorably to the grave. Antiexistentialist from the outset, Brás's discourse mocks even itself: his is a voice from the grave telling us we have nothing to lose.

In the perspective of the ideologically "committed" literature of the same era, from the point of view of naturalism, for example, Machado's text is reactionary. Its radical skepticism, which discredits all notions of progress and history, and all hopes of altering human nature, runs contrary to the spirit of the age, but not, of course, to the spirit of satire. Just as he had done in his first extended narrative, *Ressurreição* . . . , Machado extracts his protagonist from the "struggle for life," releasing him thereby from any involuntary contact with the world around him. It is in this liberation of the protagonist from the world of contingencies that we see Machado's desire to present his subject as an ethical or psychological type rather than as a "real" person living in a real world.

It is in this attitude that we see Machado turning away from a representation of time as history, metonymical realism (in Ja-

kobson's sense), and turning toward the presentation of time as metaphorical scene. The "free form of a Sterne, or of a Xavier de Maistre," that Brás posits as a model in his first paragraph is in reality not free at all, but an abandonment of plot as an imitation or metaphor of history. Machado's work proceeds by accumulation . . . and it is in this subjective sorting that we see the author turning toward satire. We may wonder why Brás thinks of Sterne and de Maistre—he is presumably referring to *Tristram Shandy, The Sentimental Journey,* and *Voyage autour de ma chambre*—as utilizing a free form, and we may simultaneously ask what texts he would think of as not being "free." It would seem that freedom for Brás is the ability to digress, to abandon plot, while the opposite, keeping to a linear flow and adhering to a plot, constitutes imprisonment. And yet this seems too vague a distinction. *Tristram Shandy* has a plot, its own particular kind, and it would seem that Brás's story also possesses one. The type of plot neither has is one based on history, on a Hegelian concept of history which postulates a goal in the historical process.

Nothing typifies Machado's attitude toward history better than the celebrated chapter 7, "Delirium." Brás begins the chapter with another "first" (he is already the first dead man to become an author): he will describe his own delirium. But this mental disorder is peculiarly iconic in its development. It begins with a series of metamorphoses by the subject himself: he becomes a Chinese barber and a morocco-bound edition of the *Summa Theologica* before returning to his own shape. Both of these seemingly bizarre transformations may be images of the artist—the barber who shaves a capricious mandarin, who punishes and rewards his servant at the same time, and the text which is the writer once he has died or ceased to exercise any control over it. Neither of these interpretations is far fetched when we think of Kafka's hunger-artist, who starves himself to entertain his public, or Borges's "Borges and I" (1960), where the living author acknowledges that the Borges whose name appears on the spine of books, who is somehow different from the man who lives in Buenos Aires, is "more real" than he is. (pp. 14-15)

The problem of universal history enters the chapter when Brás, in his own shape, is whisked away to the "origin of the centuries" by a hippopotamus. There would seem to be at least three other literary texts in the background of the scene: the *Divine Comedy,* an influence which pervades all of Machado's work; *Gulliver's Travels,* especially the scenes with the Brobdingnagians; and Camões's *Os Lusiadas,* particularly the Adamastor episode. Machado's relationship with Dante is a complex matter, but in *Memórias Póstumas* the *Commedia* may be seen as an ironic analogue to what Machado's text is. Dante, in life, is granted a trip to the tripartite other world, and is then told to publish his vision. Symbolically, he dies and is resurrected so that he may die and again be raised, this last time for eternity. His text is a message of hope for all Christians, but unlike Saint Augustine's, it gives testimony to a miracle, something more spectacular than an individual's receiving grace.

Brás is mad (delirious) when he has his vision (his madness is the result of illness, however, not divine inspiration), and his experience is a kind of affirmation of the nothingness which awaits him and has awaited all those who came before. There is no hope in Nature's (or Pandora's, the female figure who instructs Brás) message to Brás; the only hope she bears is the one nurtured by all men, a hope which is naturally fatuous. Unlike Dante, who also visits the "origin of the centuries" when he enters the Earthly Paradise in *Purgatory* 28, Brás is presented with a vision of the centuries in the form of an endless parade of identical beings: all the ages of mankind are one in ethical terms and all pursue a Harlequin-like figure. . . . Both happiness and hope are verbal fictions, like Brás's vision, and exist only as figments of the imagination.

Brás's Nature/Pandora, a colossal female figure combining aspects of the Brobdingnagians, of Adamastor, and of Baudelaire's giantess, is a grotesque. She is a kind of eternal feminine, a parody of both Matelda and Beatrice, anthropomorphic but not human, whose sole function is to show man (Brás) an objective picture of the universe. She gives no explanations, makes no promises, instills no hopes: she *is,* and her existence, together with the spectacle of the procession of the ages, all set in an ice-bound wasteland "beyond Eden" instead of a garden, moves Brás to see the insignificance of human life.

In a sense, Brás's delirium vision, an echo of the Erasmian blend of reason and folly, represents a systematic negation of the transcendental significance assigned to space in the *Divine Comedy.* Dante begins his journey on a plane located above, physically and morally, Hell, and below, in the same senses, Purgatory. In the all-important phase of mediation, Purgatory, his physical and moral motion acquires a certain logic: the past is evil; the present is a removal of the past and a lengthening of the distance from that past. The privileged present from which Dante writes what he has experienced is a metaphoric representation of what his present time will be in the future, the absence of time. Brás's space and time are equivocal, false, because they never go beyond esthetic representation. The Dantesque tripartite division is mocked here in the two metamorphoses and the vision-journey. The transformations, as we have seen, are of an esthetic nature: Brás becomes an artist and then a book. The vision reveals to him what he has always known, that the universe has no human dimension; but it reveals it in such an ironic fashion—the hippopotamus used as magical means of conveyance, for example . . .—that attention is diverted from the content of the vision to the spectacle itself. (pp. 15-17)

Dante had something to say after his experience; Brás, very literally, has to talk about nothing. Dante had a vision, Brás has a dream, and if there is any transcendental significance in the dream, it emanates from within Brás's psyche, this scene being the only one in which a visionary, albeit a mock visionary, mode is utilized.

That the function of the dream-delirium is to make a grotesque statement about a grotesque reality may be seen by comparing it with another eschatological episode, the death of Brás's mother. Here we find no dream framework, and it would seem that we are to take the event literally: this is how Brás reacts to his mother's death. The difference between action and metaphoric representation seems to be Brás's inability to comprehend the former: "What? Was it absolutely necessary that so docile, so mild, so devout a creature, who had never caused anyone to shed a tear of grief, die in such a way, tortured, mauled by the tenacious jaws of a merciless affliction? I confess that all of it seemed dark, incongruous, insane." . . . Brás's reaction is so "natural," his meditation on death as the end of social conventions is itself so conventional, that we are apt to forget the context in which it occurs. In effect, the scene is highly sentimental, recalling similar passages in Sterne and de Maistre, but we must recall what sort of character Brás is in order to see just what function the ruminations on death fulfill. If Brás were a novelistic character, we might expect some sort of

transformation in his personality. Because he is a satiric character, however, the scene has a different value. Brás's life up until that moment had been a series of egoistic, selfish actions: his childhood greed and cruelty, his ambition to "own" a beautiful courtesan (Marcela), his scapegrace student life, and his adventures on the grand tour. Now the mirror is held up to his face: in his mother's death he sees his own. But does this change him? Only to the extent that he is now incapable of dedicating himself body and soul to any vital project since he knows where it will end. . . .

Brás is now ready to become a wounded soul, incapable of taking direct action, incapable of acting on his own desires, wishing for fame and glory but unable to seize them. He is now himself, sick with the incurable malady of nihilism combined with an egoistic incapacity to place himself in any social context.

What seems difficult to grasp is why Machado chose to repeat the same message. It is true that the dream is more applicable to history itself, that an event like the death of Brás's mother provides a cause, an explanation for the narrator's later relationships. It is almost as if the two events were the opening and closing of a life composed of reiterations, of a life which could "go" nowhere. What Brás may have understood, what the reader may also have understood, as a "personal tragedy" is revealed in the text to have been nothing more than the common fate of all men. Brás must be thought of as a kind of Everyman, but with this difference: he exists in a world devoid of metaphysical possibilities where salvation in the Christian sense is impossible. This transforms him into an abstraction camouflaged with personality, a name only, totally devoid of reality. And it is this abstract quality which links him with the character-types of traditional satire instead of making him a novelistic "person."

This same generalized status is manifest in all of the characters in Brás's narration. Abstraction and repetition are the hallmark of the *Memórias Póstumas.* We should remember that Brás is an author "for whom the graveyard was a cradle" . . . , that beginnings and ends in his life are peculiarly affinal. In chapter 51, Brás pronounces his "law of the equivalence of windows" (repeated in chapter 105), which for him is an ethical posture: "the way to compensate for a closed window is to open another so that one's morals can constantly ventilate one's conscience." This ironic passage may also be taken as a structural postulate: Brás cannot change or develop after his mother's death; his life consists of a number of repetitions. The people around him are really permutations of his own personality, all versions of himself.

That birth and death, creation and destruction, and many other traditionally opposed terms are actually opposite faces of the same process is a commonplace of metaphysical speculation. It is a commonplace taken ironically throughout Machado's work. The very title of his earliest long narrative, *Ressurreição* [**Resurrection**] . . . , points to the hero's inability to be truly reborn, and it is this persistence of character which marks all of Machado's protagonists. In the *Memórias Póstumas* the rebirth is, again, esthetic, and there is no possibility of transcending that category. Brás can never be a part of life because he was always dead. His world too is devoid of real life, locked in a permanent state of flux. Only a few social roles possess a rudimentary sort of identity: people are rich or poor, slaves, beggars, or priests. All are narcissistic; all are either victims or oppressors; and, most importantly, because of this, all are mad.

That the characters are all mad is consistent with the generic identity of the text. There may be a statement about Machado's attitude toward Brazil in this reduction of character to type, and the name of the protagonist here certainly invites an identification of him with the country in which he lives. This may further suggest that the text is in fact a true-to-life representation of life in Brazil in the nineteenth century. All of this is possible; however, it seems more useful, especially after considering the *Memórias Póstumas* in the context of Machado's other satires, where character is reduced to stereotype and society is reduced to a cardboard stageset, to think of Machado as a writer who could produce only satires.

The final cause for this sort of literary output as opposed, say, to the writing of novels may be social in that Machado's act of *mimesis* may actually be accurate for a society devoid of those elements necessary for writing novels (a specific sense of history for example). And if it is so, then one would have to say that the same kind of society is still in existence in Latin America and that the same kind of relationship that exists between Machado's texts and his world exists between the other texts examined here and their worlds. Be that as it may, it may be concluded that the novel as a genre has never manifested itself in Latin America, where writers of narrative have turned either to satire or to romance. (pp. 17-20)

> Alfred J. MacAdam, "Machado de Assis: Satire and Madness," in his Modern Latin American Narratives: The Dreams of Reason *(reprinted by permission of The University of Chicago Press; © 1977 by the University of Chicago), University of Chicago Press, 1977, pp. 11-20.*

V. S. PRITCHETT (essay date 1979)

Assis said that his simple novels were written 'in the ink of mirth and melancholy'. The simplicity is limpid and delightful, but it is a deceptive distillation. One is always doubtful about how to interpret the symbolism and allegory that underlie his strange love stories and his impressions of a wealthy society. The picture of Rio could not be more precise, yet people and city seem to be both physically there and not there. The actual life he evokes has gone, but it is reillumined or revived by his habit of seeing people as souls fluttering like leaves blown away by time. In this he is very modern: his individuals have the force of anonymities. His aim, in all his books, seems to be to rescue a present moment just before it sinks into the past or reaches into its future. He is a mixture of comedian, lyrical poet, psychological realist and utterly pessimistic philosopher. We abruptly fall into dust and that is the end. But it would be quite wrong to identify him with the sated bankers, politicians, sentimental roués and bookish diplomats who appear in the novels. His tone is far removed from the bitter-sweet mockery and urbane scepticism of, say, Anatole France; and it is free of that addiction to rhetorical French romanticism which influenced all South American literature during the nineteenth century. He eventually became an Anglophile.

Epitaph for a Small Winner was a conscious break with France. . . . To get a closer idea of Assis, one must think chiefly of Sterne, Swift and Stendhal. He is an exact, original, economical writer, who pushes the machinery of plot into the background. His short chapters might be a moralist's notes. Like Sterne, he is obsessed with Time, eccentric, even whimsical; like Stendhal, accurate and yet passionate; like Swift, occasionally savage. But the substance is Brazilian. (pp. 158-59)

It is said that [Assis] is even more admired in Brazil for his short stories than for his novels and from the small selection called *The Psychiatrist,* one can see why: here the dreamy monotone of his novels vanishes. From story to story the mood changes. He astonishes by passing from satire to artifice, from wit to the emotional weight of a tale like **'Midnight Mass'** or to the terrible realism of **'Admiral's Night,'** a story of slave-hunting which could have come out of Flaubert. In a way, all the novels of Assis are constructed by a short-story-teller's mind, for he is a vertical, condensing writer who slices through the upholstery of the realist novel into what is essential. He is a collector of the essences of whole lives and does not labour with chronology, jumping back or forward confidently in time as it pleases him. A man will be described simply as handsome or coarse, a woman as beautiful or plain; but he will plunge his hand into them and pull out the vitalizing paradox of their inner lives, showing how they are themselves and the opposite of themselves and how they are in flux.

In *Esau and Jacob* there is a fine comic portrait of the pushing wife of a wobbly politician who has just lost his governorship. She is a woman who kisses her friends 'as if she wanted to eat them alive, to consume them, not with hate, to put them inside her, deep inside'. She revels in power and—a quality Assis admires in his women—is innocent of moral sense. . . . The grotesque, Assis says in one of his epigrams, is simply ferocity in disguise: but here the beauty of the grotesque comes from tolerance. Sometimes people are absurd, sometimes wicked, sometimes good. Timidity may lead to virtue, deception to love; our virtues are married to our vices. The politician's wife gets to work on her husband and skilfully persuades him to change parties. He is morally ruined but this stimulates his self-esteem. The pair simply become absurd. This particular chapter of comedy is very Stendhalian—say, from *Lucien Leuwen.*

Esau and Jacob is, on the face of it, a political allegory, observed by an old diplomat. He has been the unsuccessful lover of Natividade, the wife of a rich banker, a lady given to a rather sadistic fidelity and to exaltation. She gives birth to identical twin boys and consults an old sorceress about their destiny. She is told they will become great men and will perpetually quarrel. And so they do. As they rise to greatness, one becomes a monarchist and defender of the old stable traditions, the other a republican and a believer in change and the future. They fall in love with the same girl, Flora, who can scarcely tell them apart and who, fatally unable to make up her mind about them, fades away and dies. (People die as inconsequently as they do in E. M. Forster.) The meaning of the allegory may be that Natividade is the old Brazil and that Flora is the girl of the new Brazil who cannot decide between the parties. But underlying this is another allegory. One young man looks to the Past, the other to the Future; the girl is the Present, puzzled by its own breathless evanescence, and doomed. All the people in Assis seem to be dissolving in time, directed by their Destiny—the old sorceress up in the *favela.*

The theme of *Esau and Jacob* is made for high-sounding dramatic treatment; but Assis disposes of that by his cool, almost disparaging tenderness as he watches reality and illusion change places. . . . The concern with exchanged identities and doubles—very much a theme of the Romantic movement—is not left on the level of irony or paradox: Assis follows it into our moral nature, into the double quality of our sensibility, and the uncertainty of what we are. We are the sport of nature, items in a game.

One sees how much Assis has in common with his contemporary, Pirandello. With the growth of agnosticism at the end of the nineteenth century, people played intellectually with the occult—one of the Assis bankers consults a spiritualist—and amused themselves with conundrums about illusion and reality, sanity and insanity. . . . But there is something heartless and brittle in Pirandello. The Brazilian is warmer, gentler. One does not feel about him, as about Pirandello, that intellect and feeling are separate. At his most airily speculative and oblique, Assis still contrives to give us the sense of a whole person, all of a love affair, a marriage, an illness, a career and a society, by looking at their fragments. There is a curious moment in the **Epitaph for a Small Winner** when we are told that the poor, wronged, unhappy woman who is used by the clandestine lovers as a screen for their affair was perhaps born to have just that role and use in their lives: the reflection is good, for if it conveys the egoism of the lovers, it also conveys the sense of unconscious participation which is the chief intuition of Assis as an artist, and which makes his creatures momentarily solid. (pp. 160-63)

> *V. S. Pritchett, "Machado de Assis: A Brazilian" (originally published in a different version as "Machado de Assis," in* New Statesman, *Vol. 71, No. 1824, February 25, 1966), in his* The Myth Makers: Literary Essays *(copyright © 1979 by V. S. Pritchett; reprinted by permission of Random House, Inc.), Random House, 1979, pp. 158-63.*

ADDITIONAL BIBLIOGRAPHY

Bandeira, Manuel. "Machado de Assis." In his *Brief History of Brazilian Literature*, pp. 101-06. Washington, D.C.: Pan American Union, 1958.
  Brief survey of Machado's career.

Caldwell, Helen. *The Brazilian Othello of Machado de Assis: A Study of 'Dom Casmurro'*. Berkeley and Los Angeles: University of California Press, 1960, 194 p.
  The first comprehensive analysis of Machado's *Dom Casmurro*. Caldwell debates the question of the heroine Capitu's guilt, the reasons behind the author's ambiguity, and explores the author's unity of theme and his allusions to Shakespeare.

Loos, Dorothy Scott. *The Naturalistic Novel of Brazil*. New York: Hispanic Institute of the United States, 1963, 163 p.*
  Traces historical roots of the Naturalistic movement in Brazil, with scattered references to Machado as exemplar of Realism and predecessor of Naturalism.

MacAdam, Alfred J. "Rereading *Ressurreição*." *Luso-Brazilian Review* IX, No. 2 (December 1972): 47-57.
  Finds that Machado's first novel, *Ressurreição*, has been inappropriately labeled a novel. MacAdam reexamines *Ressurreição* as a masterpiece of satire, exhibiting different aims and formal characteristics than those attributed to the novel form.

Param, Charles. "Machado de Assis and Dostoyevsky." *Hispania* XLIX, No. 1 (March 1966): 81-7.*
  Examines the similarities in the works of Machado and Dostoyevsky, with biocritical analysis.

Param, Charles. "The Case for *Quincas Borba* As Confession." *Hispania* L, No. 3 (September 1967): 430-41.
  Discusses the dog, Quincas Borba, in the novel of the same name, as a symbol of his master Rubiao's various moral compromises. Param sees the psychological makeup of Rubiao as analogous to that of Machado. This, the critic feels, allowed the author to defend himself against his critics and examine several personal moral dilemmas.

Param, Charles. "Jealousy in the Novels of Machado de Assis." *Hispania* LIII, No. 2 (May 1970): 198-206.
  Discusses the large number of Machado's works which examine the theme of jealousy. Param agrees with Helen Caldwell, who found this to be a dominant concern of Machado's fiction.

Verissimo, Erico. "Yes, But Snakes and Slaves Too." In his *Brazilian Literature: An Outline*, pp. 55-73. New York: Macmillan, 1945.
  Examination of the style, theme, and biographical influences in Machado's first three novels.

F(ilippo) T(ommaso) Marinetti

1876-1944

Italian novelist, dramatist, poet, essayist, and critic.

Marinetti was the founder and chief activist of Futurism, one of the most influential artistic movements of the twentieth century. While technically allied with the multiple perspectivism of the Cubists and temperamentally of a kind with the nihilism of the later Dada movement, Futurism was more concerned with inciting action than with the abstractions of aesthetics or ideology. The Futurists especially valued physical and political might, as represented by the Italian Fascist party. Originally a follower of Stéphane Mallarmé and the French Symbolists, Marinetti eventually came to repudiate the cloistered alienation of this tradition in favor of a life and an art defined by intense activity. Marinetti abhorred all literature of the past, particularly Romanticism, and extended this contempt to the past itself. The catchwords of his movement were new, modern, dynamic, fast, violent. The primary objects of its hatred were tradition, reason, and romantic love. Calling for the destruction of the masterpieces of former literary schools, along with their symbols, was one of Futurism's characteristic and most frequently indulged pastimes, concisely illustrated by the slogan: "Let's murder the moonlight."

Marinetti was born in Alexandria, Egypt, to wealthy Italian parents. He received his early education at a Jesuit school in Alexandria, where the classes were conducted in French, the language in which he subsequently wrote many of his works. As a young man he studied in Paris at the Sorbonne and attained an undergraduate degree from the University of Paris. He moved to Italy and studied law at the University of Genoa. The thesis he wrote on parliamentary government gave Marinetti the background for his satire on this subject in *Le roi Bombance*, a sensational farce similar to Alfred Jarry's *King Ubu* plays. In 1905 Marinetti settled in Milan and founded the journal *Poesia*, which later served as a forum for the *grands poètes incendiaires*, the "incendiary poets" of Italian Futurism. Marinetti's 1909 *Manifeste du Futurisme (The Founding and Manifesto of Futurism)*, however, was first published not in *Poesia*, but in the Paris newspaper *Le Figaro*, where it was more likely to receive the exposure and provoke the widespread reaction that its author desired. A deluge of manifestos—some by Marinetti, some by other writers, artists, composers, filmmakers, and architects—followed and refined upon the 1909 proclamation, but Futurism's basic ideas and sentiments are adequately contained in the first manifesto. In this work Marinetti officially introduced the Futurist ideals of speed, machinery, war, and aggressive modernity, while at the same time denouncing several obstructions to a Futurist utopia: human reason, respect for tradition and culture in its institutionalized forms, and the romanticization of women expressed by the term *amore*.

The subsequent history of Marinetti—and of the artistic movement that was largely an extension of his character—is one of scandal, radical politics and aesthetics, public spectacles, and a comparatively intense but short-lived notoriety in the world of European arts and letters. In 1909, in *Mafarka le futuriste*, Marinetti constructed a portrait of his new man—a celebrant of mutilation, rape, confrontation with the unknown, and the

general mystique of danger and pain. For this work Marinetti was tried for pornography and received a prison sentence, though there is some doubt whether or not he actually served time. Having openly advocated war as a fundamental principle of Futurism, and a reflection of its unrestrained nationalism, Marinetti served in the infantry and as a bombardier during World War I. His egocentric record of wartime experience, *L'alcòva d'acciaio*, describes war and aggression as intrinsic to human existence—a reality that cannot be denied and should in fact be welcomed for its "hygenic" effects on stagnant periods of history. Marinetti wrote: "War—Futurism intensified—obliges us to march and not to rot in libraries and reading rooms."

After the war Marinetti allied himself with various militant anti-Socialist factions in Italian politics. Included among his associates was Benito Mussolini, and in 1919 Marinetti and the future leader of Italy together razed the offices of a Socialist newspaper. In *Futurismo e Fascismo*, Marinetti explained the connections between the Futurist imagination and Fascist politics. Though he came to realize that Fascism was not the political fulfillment of Futurist aesthetics—he abandoned the party in 1920—there was never any question that their ambitions were at least complementary, and in the political sphere identical. As Benedetto Croce stated in 1924: "For anyone who has a sense of historical connections, the ideological origins of Fascism can be found in Futurism, in the determination to go down into the streets, to impose their own opinions, to stop the mouths of those who disagree, not to fear riots or fights, in this eagerness to break with all traditions. . . ." Marinetti was later reconciled with Mussolini, who named him to the Italian Academy in 1929. After fighting in the Ethiopian war and on the Russian front in World War II, Marinetti returned to Italy and died at Bellagio.

While there is general agreement among critics that Marinetti possessed a greater talent for leadership than literature, he is nonetheless recognized for codifying, if not initiating, a number of literary concepts that formed the basis for much of twentieth-century avant-garde writing. Marinetti's idea of *parole in libertà* ("words in freedom") moved poetry further along a course whose starting point was the free verse of the nineteenth century. His experimentation with typography, word order, and disjunction of verbal logic displayed in *Zang tumb tuum* later became commonplace principles in modern poetics. His emphasis on spontaneity in verbal expression, no matter how seemingly erratic the results, anticipated by several years the disjointed outpouring of images and ideas that was the foundation of Surrealism in the late 1920s.

Futurism had something to contribute to almost every art form—literary, visual, or musical—but it was in the theater that its most radical and enduring contribution was made. Antiliterary, antirealist, and antilogical, the kind of drama described in the 1913 manifesto *Il teatro di varieta (The Variety Theatre)* was reiterated and developed in the decades to come by dramatists and theorists such as Antonin Artaud, Eugene Ionesco, and numerous other representatives of nontraditional dramatic techniques. Like everything Futurism produced, the Variety Theatre was intended more to disturb than to amuse. Actors raging wildly at the audience, contrived mishaps, and various other shock tactics were designed to force the spectator's sensibility "to the very brink of madness." Later manifestos proposed the "Synthetic Drama," which was for the most part an exaggerated and concentrated form of its predecessor. It also exemplified Marinetti's concept of "simultaneity" in drama: an anachronistic and incongruous interlocking of one time and place with another. This technique is perhaps best represented by the play *Simultaneità (Simultaneity)*, in which a middle-class family at home shares the stage with a young prostitute at her dressing table.

Critical interest in Marinetti and Futurism has undergone a revival in the last few decades. Both were ignored for years and regarded as somewhat infamous for their advocacy of a world view that so easily lent itself to the terrors of Fascism, which culminated in the Second World War. Also, many have found Futurism either immature or immoral in its enthusiasm for technological novelties and its lack of a true human concern for social progress. However, as the Futurists repeatedly indicated in their manifestos, their struggle was for liberation at all levels, regardless of the consequences that arose. Futurism did not look forward to a well-made society, but rather to one in which the social, political, and psychological traumas of human existence would be embraced and celebrated as occasions for physical heroics and creative expression. Perhaps the ultimate definition of the Futurist sensibility, then, was uttered in Marinetti's first *Manifesto*, when he wrote: "Except in struggle, there is no more beauty."

(See also *Contemporary Authors*, Vol. 107.)

PRINCIPAL WORKS

La conquête des étoiles (poetry) 1902
Destruction (poetry) 1904
La ville charnelle (poetry) 1908
Mafarka le futuriste (novel) 1909; also published as
    Mafarka il futurista, 1910
Manifeste du futurisme (manifesto) 1909; published in
    newspaper *Le Figaro*
    [*The Founding and Manifesto of Futurism* published in
      Marinetti: Selected Writings, 1972]
Poupées électrique (drama) 1909
Le roi Bombance (drama) 1909
Il teatro di varietà (manifesto) 1913; published in journal
    Lacerba
    [*The Variety Theatre* published in newspaper *Daily Mail*,
      1913]
Zang tumb tuum (poetry) 1914
Simultaneità (drama) 1915
    [*Simultaneity* published in journal *The Drama Review*,
      1963]
Le théâtre futuriste synthetique [with Emilio Settimelli and
    Bruno Corra] (manifesto) 1915
    [*The Synthetic Futurist Theatre* published in *Art and Stage
      in the Twentieth Century*, 1968]
Manifesti del futurismo. 4 vols. (manifestos) 1919
Elettricita sessuale (drama) 1920
L'alcòva d'acciaio (memoir) 1921
Futurismo e Fascismo (essay) 1922
Gli indomabili (novel) 1922
    [*The Untamables* (partial translation) published in
      Marinetti: Selected Writings, 1972]
Il tamburo di fuoco (drama) 1922
Prigionieri (drama) 1925
Vulcani (drama) 1926
Canto eroi e macchine della guerra Mussoliniana (poetry)
    1942
Marinetti: Selected Writings (essays, manifestos, memoirs,
    and novel) 1972

*This work includes manifestos by a number of other authors.

F. T. MARINETTI (essay date 1909)

    [*The following is excerpted from Marinetti's first* Manifesto *of Futurism.*]

1. We intend to sing the love of danger, the habit of energy and fearlessness.

2. Courage, audacity, and revolt will be essential elements of our poetry.

3. Up to now literature has exalted a pensive immobility, ecstasy, and sleep. We intend to exalt aggressive action, a feverish insomnia, the racer's stride, the mortal leap, the punch and the slap.

4. We affirm that the world's magnificence has been enriched by a new beauty: the beauty of speed. A racing car whose hood is adorned with great pipes, like serpents of explosive breath— a roaring car that seems to ride on grapeshot is more beautiful than the *Victory of Samothrace.*

5. We want to hymn the man at the wheel, who hurls the lance of his spirit across the Earth, along the circle of its orbit.

6. The poet must spend himself with ardour, splendour, and generosity, to swell the enthusiastic fervour of the primordial elements.

7. Except in struggle, there is no more beauty. No work without an aggressive character can be a masterpiece. Poetry must be conceived as a violent attack on unknown forces, to reduce and prostrate them before man.

8. We stand on the last promontory of the centuries! . . . Why should we look back, when what we want is to break down the mysterious doors of the Impossible? Time and Space died yesterday. We already live in the absolute, because we have created eternal, omnipresent speed.

9. We will glorify war—the world's only hygiene—militarism, patriotism, the destructive gesture of freedom-bringers, beautiful ideas worth dying for, and scorn for woman.

10. We will destroy the museums, libraries, academies of every kind, will fight moralism, feminism, every opportunistic or utilitarian cowardice.

11. We will sing of great crowds excited by work, by pleasure, and by riot; we will sing of the multicoloured, polyphonic tides of revolution in the modern capitals; we will sing of the vibrant nightly fervour of arsenals and shipyards blazing with violent electric moons; greedy railway stations that devour smoke-plumed serpents; factories hung on clouds by the crooked lines of their smoke; bridges that stride the rivers like giant gymnasts, flashing in the sun with a glitter of knives; adventurous steamers that sniff the horizon; deep-chested locomotives whose wheels paw the tracks like the hooves of enormous steel horses bridled by tubing; and the sleek flight of planes whose propellers chatter in the wind like banners and seem to cheer like an enthusiastic crowd.

It is from Italy that we launch through the world this violently upsetting incendiary manifesto of ours. With it, today, we establish *Futurism*, because we want to free this land from its smelly gangrene of professors, archaeologists, *ciceroni* and antiquarians. For too long has Italy been a dealer in second-hand clothes. We mean to free her from the numberless museums that cover her like so many graveyards.

Museums: cemeteries! . . . Identical, surely, in the sinister promiscuity of so many bodies unknown to one another. Museums: public dormitories where one lies forever beside hated or unknown beings. Museums: absurd abattoirs of painters and sculptors ferociously slaughtering each other with colour-blows and line-blows, the length of the fought-over walls!

That one should make an annual pilgrimage, just as one goes to the graveyard on All Souls' Day—that I grant. That once a year one should leave a floral tribute beneath the *Gioconda*, I grant you that. . . . But I don't admit that our sorrows, our fragile courage, our morbid restlessness should be given a daily conducted tour through the museums. Why poison ourselves? Why rot?

And what is there to see in an old picture except the laborious contortions of an artist throwing himself against the barriers that thwart his desire to express his dream completely? . . . Admiring an old picture is the same as pouring our sensibility into a funerary urn instead of hurling it far off, in violent spasms of action and creation.

Do you, then, wish to waste all your best powers in this eternal and futile worship of the past, from which you emerge fatally exhausted, shrunken, beaten down?

In truth I tell you that daily visits to museums, libraries, and academies (cemeteries of empty exertion, Calvaries of crucified dreams, registries of aborted beginnings!) are, for artists, as damaging as the prolonged supervision by parents of certain young people drunk with their talent and their ambitious wills. When the future is barred to them, the admirable past may be a solace for the ills of the moribund, the sickly, the prisoner. . . . But we want no part of it, the past, we the young and strong *Futurists*!

So let them come, the gay incendiaries with charred fingers! Here they are! Here they are! . . . Come on! set fire to the library shelves! Turn aside the canals to flood the museums! . . . Oh, the joy of seeing the glorious old canvases bobbing adrift on those waters, discoloured and shredded! . . . Take up your pickaxes, your axes and hammers and wreck, wreck the venerable cities, pitilessly! (pp. 21-3)

> *F. T. Marinetti, "The Founding and Manifesto of Futurism," translated by R. W. Flint (1909), in* Futurist Manifesto, *edited by Umbro Apollonio, translated by Robert Brain and others (translation copyright © 1973 by Thames and Hudson Ltd; reprinted by permission of Thames and Hudson Ltd and Nuove Edizioni Gabriele Mazzotta; originally published as* Futurismo, *edited by Umbro Apollonio (copyright © 1970 by Verlag M. DuMont Schauberg, Cologne, and Gabriele Mazzotta editore, Milan), Gabriele Mazzotta, 1970), Thames and Hudson, 1973, pp. 19-24.*

RUBÉN DARÍO (essay date 1909)

Marinetti is an Italian poet writing in French. He is a good poet, a notable poet. The intellectual élite, the world over, knows of him. I know that personally he is a nice boy and is a socialite. In Milan he publishes a polyglot and lyrical review, luxuriously put out, *Poesía*. His poems have been praised by the best lyric poets of France. His principal work, so far: *Le Roi Bombance,* which is rabelaisian, pompously comic, tragically burlesque, exuberant, had a deserved success, on publication. . . . His book against D'Annunzio is so well done and so malevolent that the "Imaginifico—the panache on his hat, eh, Lugones?"—must be gratified by the satiric homage. (p. 147)

Marinetti's poems are violent, noisy, and unbridled. This is the effect of Italian vehemence on a French instrument. And it is curious to note that the poet most like him is the Flemish Verhaeren. But my speaking to you now about Marinetti is occasioned by an experiment he is making these days, with a new literary school he has founded, or whose principles he has proclaimed with all the trumpets of his powerful utterance. (p. 148)

[One] must recognize the priority of the word Futurism, though not that of the whole doctrine.

What is this doctrine?

We shall see.

1. "We want to sing the love of danger, the habit of energy and of temerity." In the first proposition it seems to me that Futurism changes into Pastism. Isn't all that in Homer?

2. "The essential elements of our poetry will be bravery, audacity, and rebellion." Isn't all that already in the whole classical cycle?

3. "While literature, until now, has made much of contemplating immobility, ecstasy, and dreaming, we wish to exalt instead aggressive movement, feverish insomnia, the gymnastic gait, the death-defying leap, the slap and the punch." I think many of those things are already in Homer himself, and that Pindar is an excellent poet of sports.

4. "We declare that the splendor of the world has been enriched with a new beauty: the beauty of speed. A racing car, its rear adorned with thick tubes like serpents breathing explosions . . . , a roaring automobile that seems to run on blasts of grapeshot is more beautiful than the *Victory of Samothrace*." I do not understand the (terms of) comparison. Which is more beautiful, a naked woman or a tempest? A lily or an artillery barrage? (pp. 148-49)

5. "We want to celebrate the man at the wheel, whose ideal beauty passes over the earth, which is itself launched on the track of its orbit." Even if not in the modern form of comprehending (man in flight), one might still return to antiquity in search of Bellerophons and Mercuries.

6. "The poet must expend himself with heat, brilliance, and prodigality, to increase the enthusiastic brilliance of the primordial elements." Quite plausible. In that case it is an impulse of youth and of a mentality, of one's own vigor.

7. "There is no beauty but in fighting. There is no masterpiece without an aggressive character. Poetry should be conceived as a violent assault on unknown forces, to impose upon them the sovereignty of man." Apollo and Amphion inferior to Herakles? Unknown forces are not tamed by violence. And, in any case, for the poet there are no unknown forces.

8. "We are upon the final promontory of the centuries. . . . Why look behind us, when we have to unlock the doorways of the Impossible? Time and Space died yesterday. We are already living in the Absolute, since we have now created eternal omnipotent speed." Oh, Marinetti! The automobile is a poor sleepy beetle, compared to eternal Destruction, manifested, for example, in the recent horror of Etna.

9. "We want to glorify War—the only hygiene of the world—militarism, patriotism, the destructive gesture of the Anarchists, beautiful Ideas which kill, and contempt for women." The innovating poet exposes himself as oriental, nietzschian, of an ungoverned and destructive violence. But why the articles of dogma and the regulations? As for War being the one and only hygiene of the world, Pestilence protests.

10. "We want to demolish the museums, the libraries, to combat moralism, feminism, and all forms of opportunistic and utilitarian cowardice."

11. "We shall sing of the great masses agitated by work, pleasure, or revolt; the many-colored and polyphonic surges of revolution in the modern capitals, the nocturnal vibration of arsenals and shipyards under their violent electric moons; greedy railroad stations that swallow smoking serpents, the acrobatic bridges leaping over the diabolical blades of sunlit rivers; adventurous steamers nosing into the horizon; chesty locomotives that whinny on the rails, like enormous horses of steel, bridled with long tubes, and the gliding flight of aeroplanes, whose propellor whips and snaps like a flag or an enthusiastic multitude." All this is beautifully enthusiastic and,

more than anything, beautifully juvenile. It is a platform of youth at its full; because it is, it has its inherent qualities and its inevitable weak points.

The futurists say, through the voice of their principal "leader," that he launches that proclamation in Italy—though it is in French, like all self-respecting manifestos—because they want to rid Italy of her gangrene of professors, archaeologists, guides and antiquarians. They say Italy has to stop being the great market of curio collectors (the *grand marché des brocanteurs*)." (pp. 149-50)

So museums are cemeteries? Let us not think too much like Peladan. [In a footnote the translator notes that Sar Peladan (1859-1918) was a Catholic mystic who wrote against the materialism of the time and material things in general.] There are dead men in marble and bronze through our parks and promenades, and if it is certain that some esthetic ideas are offended by the agglomeration in those official buildings, nothing better has been discovered so far to replace those orderly and catalogued exhibitions. (p. 150)

Marinetti's principal idea is that everything is in what is to come and almost nothing in the past. In an old painting he sees no more than "the painful contortions of the artist struggling to break the barriers which his desire to express his dream completely cannot pass." But has modern painting accomplished this? If it is a spray of flowers, once a year at most, that one must carry in funereal homage to the Gioconda, what shall we do about the contemporary painters of automobiles and golf? And "Forward!" But where to? If Time and Space do not exist now, will not going Forward be the same as going Backward?

The oldest of us, says Marinetti, are thirty years old. That covers it all. They give themselves ten years to fulfill their work, and then voluntarily yield to those who will come later. "They will rise up—when the Futurists will be forty!—they will rise up around us, in anguish and indignation, and all exasperated by our proud untiring valor they will rush to kill us, with all the more hatred the more their hearts will be inebriated with love and admiration for us."

And on this tone the ode goes on with the same speed and impetus.

Wonderful youth! I feel a certain nostalgia for that impulsive springtime, considering I would be among those devoured, since I am over forty. And, in its violence, I applaud Marinetti's motive, because I see it in its aspect of a poetic work, by a much concerned and valiant poet who desires to drive the sacred horse toward new horizons. You will find in all this much that is excessive; the sound of warfare is too impetuous; but who except the young, they who have their primary strength and constant hope, can express impetuous and excessive motives?

The only thing I find useless is the manifesto itself. If Marinetti with his vehement works has proved that he has an admirable talent and that he knows how to fulfill his mission of Beauty, I do not think his manifesto does more than incite a good many imitators to do "Futurism" to the very limit, many of them, certainly, not having the talent nor the style of the originator. In the good epoch of Symbolism there were also manifestos by chiefs of schools. . . . What did all that come to? The Naturalists too "manifested" and their transitory chapel had resonance, like Positivism in Brazil. Since then there have been other schools and other esthetic proclamations. The oldest of all those literary revolutionaries were not yet thirty.

I do not know how old the bald D'Annunzio is now, and let Marinetti take notice that the glorious Italian is enjoying good health after the fine bomb with which he tried to demolish him. The gods depart, and in doing so they do well. If that were not so there would not have been room for all of them in this poor world. Now D'Annunzio too will depart. And other gods will come who likewise will have to depart when their turn comes, and so on until the final cataclysm blows to pieces the globe on which we all spin towards eternity, and with the globe all the illusions, all the hopes, all the impulses and all the dreams of the transitory king of creation. The Future is the incessant alternation of Life and Death. It is the past in reverse. One must take advantage of what energies there are in the instant, united as we are in the process of universal existence. And afterwards we shall sleep untroubled and forever after. Amen. (pp. 150-52)

Rubén Darío, "Marinetti and Futurism," translated by Donald Sutherland (1909; reprinted by permission of the Literary Estate of Donald Sutherland), in The Denver Quarterly *(copyright © 1977 by The University of Denver), Vol. 12, No. 1, Spring, 1977, pp. 147-52.*

F. T. MARINETTI   (essay date 1913)

[*The following is excerpted from Marinetti's statement of 1913 which explains his concepts of words-in-freedom, the imagination without strings, and expressive orthography.*]

Futurism is grounded in the complete renewal of human sensibility brought about by the great discoveries of science. Those people who today make use of the telegraph, the telephone, the phonograph, the train, the bicycle, the motorcycle, the automobile, the ocean liner, the dirigible, the aeroplane, the cinema, the great newspaper (synthesis of a day in the world's life) do not realize that these various means of communication, transportation and information have a decisive influence on their psyches.

An ordinary man can in a day's time travel by train from a little dead town of empty squares, where the sun, the dust, and the wind amuse themselves in silence, to a great capital city bristling with lights, gestures, and street cries. By reading a newspaper the inhabitant of a mountain village can tremble each day with anxiety, following insurrection in China, the London and New York suffragettes, Doctor Carrel, and the heroic dog-sleds of the polar explorers. The timid, sedentary inhabitant of any provincial town can indulge in the intoxication of danger by going to the movies and watching a great hunt in the Congo. He can admire Japanese athletes, Negro boxers, tireless American eccentrics, the most elegant Parisian women, by paying a franc to go to the variety theatre. Then, back in his bourgeois bed, he can enjoy the distant, expensive voice of a Caruso or a Burzio.

Having become commonplace, these opportunities arouse no curiosity in superficial minds who are as incapable of grasping any novel facts *as the Arabs who looked with indifference at the first aeroplanes in the sky of Tripoli.* For the keen observer, however, these facts are important modifiers of our sensibility because they have caused the following significant phenomena:

1. Acceleration of life to today's swift pace. Physical, intellectual, and sentimental equilibration on the cord of speed stretched between contrary magnetisms. Multiple and simultaneous awareness in a single individual.

2. Dread of the old and the known. Love of the new, the unexpected.

3. Dread of quiet living, love of danger, and an attitude of daily heroism.

4. Destruction of a sense of the Beyond and an increased value of the individual whose desire is *vivre sa vie* ["*to live his life*"], in Bonnot's phrase.

5. The multiplication and unbridling of human desires and ambitions.

6. An exact awareness of everything inaccessible and unrealizable in every person.

7. Semi-equality of man and woman and a lessening of the disproportion in their social rights.

8. Disdain for *amore* (sentimentality or lechery) produced by the greater freedom and erotic ease of women and by the universal exaggeration of female luxury. Let me explain: Today's woman loves luxury more than love. A visit to a great dressmaker's establishment, escorted by a paunchy, gouty banker friend who pays the bills, is a perfect substitute for the most amorous rendezvous with an adored young man. The woman finds all the mystery of love in the selection of an amazing ensemble, the latest model, which her friends still do not have. Men do not love women who lack luxury. The lover has lost all his prestige Love has lost its absolute worth. A complex question; all I can do is to raise it.

9. A modification of patriotism, which now means a heroic idealization of the commercial, industrial, and artistic solidarity of a people.

10. A modification in the idea of war, which has become the necessary and bloody test of a people's force.

11. The passion, art, and idealism of Business. New financial sensibility.

12. Man multiplied by the machine. New mechanical sense, a fusion of instinct with the efficiency of motors and conquered forces.

13. The passion, art, and idealism of Sport. Idea and love of the 'record'.

14. New tourist sensibility bred by ocean liners and great hotels (annual synthesis of different races). Passion for the city. Negation of distances and nostalgic solitudes. Ridicule of the 'holy green silence' and the ineffable landscape.

15. The earth shrunk by speed. New sense of the world. To be precise: One after the other, man will gain the sense of his home, of the quarter where he lives, of his region, and finally of the continent. Today he is aware of the whole world. He little needs to know what his ancestors did, but he must assiduously discover what his contemporaries are doing all over the world. The single man, therefore, must communicate with every people on earth. He must feel himself to be the axis, judge, and motor of the explored and unexplored infinite. Vast increase of a sense of humanity and a momentary urgent need to establish relations with all mankind.

16. A loathing of curved lines, spirals, and the *tourniquet*. Love for the straight line and the tunnel. The habit of visual foreshortening and visual synthesis caused by the speed of trains and cars that look down on cities and countrysides. Dread of slowness, pettiness, analysis, and detailed explanations. Love

of speed, abbreviation, and the summary. 'Quick, give me the whole thing in two words!'

17. Love of depth and essence in every exercise of the spirit.

So these are some elements of the new Futurist sensibility that has generated our pictorial dynamism, or antigraceful music in its free, irregular rhythms, our noise-art and our words-in-freedom.

Words-in-freedom
Casting aside every stupid formula and all the confused verbalisms of the professors, I now declare that lyricism is the exquisite faculty of intoxicating oneself with life, of filling life with the inebriation of oneself. The faculty of changing into wine the muddy water of the life that swirls and engulfs us. The ability to colour the world with the unique colours of our changeable selves.

Now suppose that a friend of yours gifted with this faculty finds himself in a zone of intense life (revolution, war, shipwreck, earthquake, and so on) and starts right away to tell you his impressions. Do you know what this lyric, excited friend of yours will instinctively do?

He will begin by brutally destroying the syntax of his speech. He wastes no time in building sentences. Punctuation and the right adjectives will mean nothing to him. He will despise subtleties and nuances of language. Breathlessly he will assault your nerves with visual, auditory, olfactory sensations, just as they come to him. The rush of steam-emotion will burst the sentence's steampipe, the values of punctuation, and the adjectival clamp. Fistfuls of essential words in no conventional order. Sole preoccupation of the narrator, to render every vibration of his being.

If the mind of this gifted lyrical narrator is also populated by general ideas, he will involuntarily bind up his sensations with the entire universe that he intuitively knows. And in order to render the true worth and dimension of his lived life, he will cast immense nets of analogy across the world. In this way he will reveal the analogical foundation of life, telegraphically, with the same economical speed that the telegraph imposes on reporters and war correspondents in their swift reportings. This urgent laconism answers not only to the laws of speed that govern us but also to the rapport of centuries between poet and audience. Between poet and audience, in fact, the same rapport exists as between two old friends. They can make themselves understood with half a word, a gesture, a glance. So the poet's imagination must weave together distant things *with no connecting strings,* by means of essential *free* words. (pp. 96-8)

The imagination without strings
By the imagination without strings I mean the absolute freedom of images or analogies, expressed with unhampered words and with no connecting strings of syntax and with no punctuation.

Up to now writers have been restricted to immediate analogies. For instance, they have compared an animal with a man or with another animal, which is almost the same as a kind of photography. (They have compared, for example, a fox terrier to a very small thoroughbred. Others, more advanced, might compare the same trembling fox terrier to a little Morse Code machine. I, on the other hand, compare it with gurgling water. In this there is an *ever vaster gradation of analogies,* there are ever deeper and more solid affinities, however remote.)

Analogy is nothing more than the deep love that assembles distant, seemingly diverse and hostile things. An orchestral style, at once polychromatic, polyphonic, and polymorphous, can embrace the life of matter only by means of the most extensive analogies. (p. 99)

The imagination without strings, and words-in-freedom, will bring us to the essence of material. As we discover new analogies between distant and apparently contrary things, we will endow them with an ever more intimate value. (p. 100)

Free expressive orthography
The historical necessity of free expressive orthography is demonstrated by the successive revolutions that have continuously freed the lyric powers of the human race from shackles and rules.

1. In fact, the poets began by channelling their lyric intoxication into a series of equal breaths, with accents, echoes, assonances, or rhymes at pre-established intervals (*traditional metric*). Then the poets varied these different measured breaths of their predecessors' lungs with a certain freedom.

2. Later the poets realized that the different moments of their lyric intoxication had to create breaths suited to the most varied and surprising intervals, with absolute freedom of accentuation. Thus they arrived at *free verse,* but they still preserved the syntactic order of the words, so that the lyric intoxication could flow down to the listeners by the logical canal of syntax.

3. Today we no longer want the lyric intoxication to order the words syntactically before launching them forth with the breaths we have invented, and we have *words-in-freedom.* Moreover our lyric intoxication should freely deform, reflesh the words, cutting them short, stretching them out, reinforcing the centre or the extremities, augmenting or diminishing the number of vowels and consonants. Thus we will have the *new orthography* that I call *free expressive.* This instinctive deformation of words corresponds to our natural tendency towards onomatopoeia. It matters little if the deformed word becomes ambiguous. It will marry itself to the onomatopoetic harmonies, or the noise-summaries, and will permit us soon to reach the *onomatopoetic psychic* harmony, the sonorous but abstract expression of an emotion or a pure thought. But one may object that my words-in-freedom, my imagination without strings, demand special speakers if they are to be understood. Atlhough I do not care for the comprehension of the multitude, I will reply that the number of Futurist public speakers is increasing and that any admired traditional poem, for that matter, requires a special speaker if it is to be understood. (p. 106)

F. T. Marinetti, "Destruction of Syntax—Imagination without Strings—Words-in-Freedom," translated by R. W. Flint (1913), in Futurist Manifestos, *edited by Umbro Apollonio, translated by Robert Brain and others (translation copyright © 1973 by Thames and Hudson Ltd.; reprinted by permission of Viking Penguin Inc.; in Canada by Thames and Hudson Ltd and Nuove Edizioni Gabriele Mazzotta; originally published as* Futurismo, *edited by Umbro Apollonio (copyright © 1970 by Verlag M. DuMont Schauberg, Cologne, and Gabriele Mazzotta editore, Milan), Gabriele Mazzotta, 1970), The Viking Press, 1973, Thames and Hudson, 1973, pp. 95-106.*

BLACKWOOD'S MAGAZINE (essay date 1914)

[*The following excerpt represents some of the objections to Futurist writing among Marinetti's contemporaries: that it was unintelligible and anarchistic without any redeeming artistic effect.*]

[Signor Marinetti], the apostle of Futurism, has arrived at what he fondly believes to be a new kind of poetry. And he has arrived at it by outraging the accepted canons of grammar and sense. His ideal is an ideal of anarchy. Other poets have admitted such obvious distinctions as exist between nouns and verbs. He will bear none of the old restraints. His words, as well as his mind, must be "at liberty." They must not be bound together by the common links of construction. He has a special and inveterate spite against verbs and adjectives. He flings his words together like stones in a rubble-heap, and he comes no nearer to the making of a poem than an architect would come to the building of a house who should refuse to weld his bricks together with mortar or to cut his planks to suit their proper space.

His style, therefore, if style it may be called, resembles nothing so much as a telegraphic despatch. Where you are asked to pay so much a word, you may be excused if you practise a verbal economy. To save your pocket, you rely cheerfully upon the quick understanding of your audience. You employ a code of signals, which is intelligible at a moderate cost. In other words, you reduce the language to its lowest terms, and hope that your meaning will be effectively conveyed. You do not boast yourself a poet for your economy; you do not claim that your enforced concision has the merit of a discovery in style. And here it is that Signor Marinetti proves his vanity. He is not asked to transmit his poems by wire. He can plead no material cause for their formlessness. He is enchained only by a superstition of purposed originality. "Other men," says he in effect, "have used verbs and adjectives; they have bent their neck beneath the yoke of grammar; they have accepted the foolish conventions of commas and full stops. I am wiser than they. I have set my words at liberty, and what does it matter that I have enchained my mind in a fiercer convention than man ever did before?"

That Signor Marinetti, a declared anarchist, should set forth his themes in intelligible pamphlets, proves that he has escaped also from the bonds of logic. It should be enough for him to run a steam-roller over the past, and for the rest to give full play to his taste for expletives. The war which he has declared upon all libraries is ridiculous and ineffectual. The war which he has declared upon style and grammar proves how little he understands their purpose and limitations. He seems to think that style is a thing that you can put on or off like a hat, and that when you have put it off there is an end of it. But style is organic. It is part of the blood and bone of all good writing, and when it is omitted, as by Signor Marinetti, what is left is a mere shapeless mass of unlettered letters. Here, for instance, is a passage from his poem, to which, in defiance of his principles, he has given the title, **"Train of Sick Soldiers"**:—

> Hohohohowling of 1500 sick men
>   at the carriage-doors
> locked up before 18 Turkish gun-
>   ners battered to pieces
> rags   tatters   caps
>   officers thrown upon the
> network of iron wire pass pass at
>   all costs anguish writhe
> with the short bayonet tear the
>   mails rage mouse trap.

It is not illuminating. It has no beauty of phrase or vision that we should desire it. It is not even original. The style of the Futurists was practised nearly a hundred years ago with far better effect than Signor Marinetti can hope to attain. Do you remember the rapid sketch of Rochester made by Alfred Jingle, Esq.? "Ah! fine, glorious pile-frowning walls—tottering arches—dark nooks—crumbling staircases—old cathedral too—earthy smell—pilgrims' feet worn away the old steps—little Saxon doors— . . . buff-jerkins too—match-locks—sarcophagus—fine place—old legends too—strange stories—capital." There is here a note of interest, of enthusiasm even, which Signor Marinetti's masterpiece seems to lack. But there is no doubt about the style. We know that our Futurist is a faithful pupil of Alfred Jingle, and we only regret that he has not studied his model with a deeper attention.

The passage which we have quoted above shows Signor Marinetti in his closest adherence to convention. When he keeps the future full in view, he attains to a lyrical height of onomatopoeia. Here is a specimen, which the fervents of the Future may interpret as they will:

> tlactlac ii ii gaiiii
> trrrrrrtrrrrrr
> tatatatôo—tatatatatôo
> (Wheels)
> currrrrr
> cuhrrrr
> gurrrrrrr
> (Locomotive)

The use of brackets appears a useless convention. For the rest, this gem of eight lines owes nothing to the outworn traditions of the past. It came from nowhere; it will go nowhither. Even as a representation of the clank and rattle of a train it is imperfect, though it makes a concession to realism, of which we thought the true Futurist incapable. And if this is a fair sample of the poetry of the Future, we may take comfort to ourselves that we shall not live to see it widely popular. In truth, Signor Marinetti need not be taken very seriously. It is easy enough to break the rules, and that so far is the sum of his achievement. (pp. 139-40)

"Musings without Method," in Blackwood's Magazine *(© William Blackwood & Sons Ltd 1914), Vol. CXCV, No. MCLXXIX, January, 1914, pp. 138-48.*

D. H. LAWRENCE (letter date 1914)

[The following excerpt is taken from a letter of D. H. Lawrence to Arthur McLeod.]

I have been interested in the futurists. I got a book of their poetry—a very fat book too—and a book of pictures—and I read Marinetti's and Paolo Buzzi's manifestations and essays—and Sofficis essays on cubism and futurism. It interests me very much. I like it because it is the applying to emotions of the purging of the old forms and sentimentalities. I like it for its saying—enough of this sickly cant, let us be honest and stick by what is in us. Only when folk say, 'let us be honest and stick by what is in us'—they always mean, stick by those things that have been thought horrid, and by those alone. They want to deny every scrap of tradition and experience, which is silly. They are very young, infantile, college-student and medical-student at his most blatant. But I like them. Only I don't believe in them. I agree with them about the weary sickness of pedantry and tradition and inertness, but I don't agree with them as to the cure and the escape. They will progress down the purely male or intellectual or scientific line. They will even use their intuition for intellectual and scientific purpose. The one thing about their art is that it *isn't* art, but ultra scientific attempts to make diagrams of certain physic or mental states. It is ultra-ultra intellectual, going beyond Maeterlinck and the Symbolistes, who are intellectual. There isn't one trace of naïveté in the works—though there's plenty of naïveté in the authors. It's the most self conscious, intentional, pseudo scientific stuff on the face of the earth. Marinetti begins 'Italy is like a great Dreadnought surrounded by her torpedo boats'. That is it exactly—a great mechanism. Italy has got to go through the most mechanical and dead stage of all—everything is appraised according to its mechanic value—everything is subject to the laws of physics. This is the revolt against beastly sentiment and slavish adherence to tradition and the dead mind. For that I love it. I love them when they say to the child 'all right, if you want to drag nests and torment kittens, do it, lustily'. But I reserve the right to answer 'all right, try it on. But if I catch you at it you get a hiding.' (pp. 180-81)

> *D. H. Lawrence, in his letter to Arthur McLeod on June 2, 1914, in* The Letters of D. H. Lawrence: June 1913-October 1916, Volume II, *edited by George J. Zytaruk and James T. Boulton (copyright 1932 by the estate of D. H. Lawrence; copyright 1934 by Frieda Lawrence; copyright 1933, 1948, 1953, 1954, © 1956, 1957, 1958, 1959, 1960, 1961, 1962, 1967, 1969 by Angelo Ravagli and C. Montague Weekley, executors of the estate of Frieda Lawrence Ravagli; © the estate of Frieda Lawrence Ravagli 1981), Cambridge University Press, 1981, pp. 180-82.*

ANNE SIMON (essay date 1914)

[Simon believes that Mafarka (the novel which led to Marinetti's conviction for pornography) *contains a serious, decent, and humane intent beneath its surface celebration of violence. For a contrasting interpretation, see J. C. Squire's essay excerpted below.]*

In [**'Mafarka il Futurista'**] is described most impressively the ascent of an African hero, a man of temerity and cunning, who after exhibiting an unbridled desire to live, the desire for victory in battle, who after having had all sorts of experiences and adventures, suddenly raised himself from this vain-glorious military heroism to philosophic and artistic heroism. In this novel he describes the glorious evolution of life, life which was first vegetal, then animal and then human, and which should finally manifest itself in a miraculous being, winged and immortal. With great beauty of idealism, he brings to man unbounded hope for his ultimate physical and spiritual perfection. He wants to liberate man from lust, from that lust which slowly consumes and devours. He wants to assure man of his speedy liberation from sleep, fatigue and death.

And this is the man they call a pornographer!

The prevailing idea in this book is of Nietzschean origin, that man shall surpass himself. It is more a poem than a novel, in which is portrayed the approaching liberty of man through spiritual conquest. It is full of contrasts between brutal instinct and the development of the spiritual nature. It is full of rich and strange images—images of love and of victory—of desire for lust and for chastity—of rebellion and of sacrifice. It is both tragic and lyric, and compels us to realize the author's clairvoyant and exalted vision. Marinetti loved **'Mafarka'** more than any of his other books, because he used it to convey his great Futuristic dream. He considered it an African poem, illuminated by unbounded fantasy. And it is a poem, utterly incomprehensible though to the majority of intelligences, so disgracefully unfamiliar with poetry.

In order to be true to African customs and life he found it necessary to lay a certain stress on things regarded as indecent to civilized eyes; for he says that 'Africa may be symbolized in three words: heat, filth and lust.' He did not write of the Africa of Pierre Loti, nor did he try to prettily adjust it for the academic and private salons of Paris. In the one chapter of **'Mafarka'** which really led to its incrimination, his motive was ethical. He wanted to suggest that even out of the seething cauldron of lust and brutality, a finer being might emerge. He wanted to prove that man can conquer his carnal instincts. He used the incidents in this chapter to show his violent disgust of man's brutalities and brutishness. It is easy for anyone of even fairly broad vision to see his purpose, through the very crudeness of the vocabulary, through his exactness of vulgar detail. It gives his hero the opportunity to denounce a race that could be so frequently guilty of the crime stated there. One should rather be moved by the artistic power of the representation of that orgy. In defending his book at the trial, Marinetti said: 'I have tried to show, according to the law of contrast, the ascent of the human spirit when freed from the tyranny of love and the obsession of woman; how it detaches itself finally from earth and opens its great wings, which lay folded and asleep in the flesh of man.'—Can man have a finer motive than this? (pp. 455-56)

Marinetti is an artist, and not a man of sensual vision. In his art, he persistently deals in contrasts, considering it legitimate to use any details which will make the contrasts more prominent. There is a vast difference between a book that incites a person to sensuality, and a book just as repulsive in plot and description, but in which the writer makes evident the repulsion in his heart. A few critics suggested that he at least might have eliminated certain harsh, crude, ugly words, or that he might have used the mask a little more freely. We answer that by saying, when a great writer is in the anguish of creation, he cannot be anything but sincere, and is far removed from word-coquetry.

With Marinetti, the thought is often so colossal, that language can hardly sustain it, and the imagery so subtle, that one feels it cannot be translated into language. He is not polished in his work, but we cannot fail to admire the truly extraordinary force of his creation.

He thinks one of the principles of the highest type of literature is to consider the images not as accessories or decoration, but as really essential elements of expression—unconscious instruments to fix the elusive truth, and to indicate the indefinite and the undefinable. (p. 457)

His art is barbaric, impulsive and opulent. His ideal, like that of Novalis, is the search for the transcendental self. (p. 459)

> *Anne Simon, "An Appreciation of Marinetti," in* Poet Lore *(copyright, 1914, by Poet Lore, Inc.; reprinted by permission of Heldref Publications), Vol. XXV, No. V, Autumn, 1914, pp. 453-59.*

SOLOMON EAGLE [pseudonym of J. C. SQUIRE] (essay date 1920)

[Squire finds Mafarka *to be a straightforward exercise in violence. For a contrasting interpretation, see Anne Simon's essay excerpted above.]*

[**Mafarka, Le Futuriste**] was suppressed in France. It certainly deserved to be. An English translation would not have a lifetime of five minutes. The iridescent hues of [D. H. Lawrence's] *The Rainbow* pale and fade before it.

The book has several prominent characteristics, some of which I need not mention, but undoubtedly the dominant theme is the panegyric of savagery, ferocity, and blood. There is more carnage to the square inch in this book than in any other that I have read; and though it is conceivable that the novels of the Marquis de Sade—to which I have never had access—are still more gruesome, I am inclined to doubt it. I will not sketch the plot—for there is no plot. But I may indicate one or two of the details, so as to give an idea of what Signor Marinetti finds beautiful and amusing. In one chapter there is a great battle between King Mafarka and his brother and an innumerable host of wild desert dogs, which are pounded into a pulp by large stones flung from catapults. Later on, Mafarka's brother, who is newly married, disappears. Mafarka, very concerned, goes to look for him, and finds on the floor of his bedroom a few strips—which are all that is left of the bride—whilst the bridegroom, who has been infected by hydrophobia, sits like an ape on the top of a pillar with strings of foam hanging from his jaws.

But the most striking episode—the most striking mentionable episode—is that in which Mafarka shows a decadent and timid world how it really ought to deal with its enemies. He assembles his Court in a dimly lit underground chamber. One wall of this chamber is of glass, and forms one side of an enormous tank, communicating, by means of gratings, with the sea overhead. In this tank are collected sharks, octopuses, and all the ugliest and most uncanny fish which infest the oceans of the world. There is a meal; and then, reclining on luxurious cushions, and feeding their senses on the most languorous of scents, the guests watch a somewhat torrid Oriental dance. The chamber is then darkened—though the tank is not—and two of the king's enemies, a fat old man and a thin young one, are shot into the top of the tank struggling. The sharks float up, twist them down, and bite off portions; the bits float up again and bump against the top, whilst the sharks sail round below wondering what has become of their prey. Soon they track it again, and the process recommences. The details of the disintegration, the lines and colours made by the "remains" as they drift and toss through green waters, the horrible quiet movements of the fishes—these are all described with a revolting accuracy which makes one's blood cold. It still haunts my dreams. (pp. 44-6)

In the end the hero, if he may be so described, goes to something that appears to be heaven in something that looks like an aeroplane—but about here Signor Marinetti's lyricism gets too confused for my understanding. This was, I believe, the first manifesto of the Futurist School which, before the war, some people took almost seriously. The world before the war must indeed have been a barren place to its author; he had to get what poor sustenance he could out of watching fights with fists at public meetings. Let us hope that he has found slaughter as invigorating and enjoyable as he always said it was. (pp. 46-7)

Solomon Eagle [pseudonym of J. C. Squire], "Signor Marinetti's Masterpiece," in his Books in General, *second series (copyright 1920; reprinted by kind permission of J. C. Squire's son, Mr. Raglan Squire), Alfred A. Knopf, 1920, pp. 44-7.*

JAMES JOLL (essay date 1960)

[Marinetti's] epic *La Conquête des Etoiles* appeared in 1902, and has little original about it, though it already shows a taste for vigorous battle scenes. Soon, however, he began to think of himself as a writer of the twentieth century, looking to a future in which all would be possible, provided that what was old and stale could be destroyed quickly and radically enough. His second volume of poems was dedicated to D'Annunzio and called, characteristically, *Destruction.* Marinetti's mind was already full of universal disasters that would purify the world. . . . (p. 135)

Marinetti's most ambitious work of this period was a play, *Le Roi Bombance* . . . , a tedious and laboured satire in which a style that echoes that of his friend Alfred Jarry's *Ubu Roi* is used to attack Socialist ideals of a Utopia in which all men's material needs will have been met. None of Marinetti's writings are very interesting or very original; but certain ideas were already emerging which, ever more stridently repeated, were to be the main themes of the Futurist movement—violence, destruction, hatred of the past and its values, and, at the same time, intense excitement about the prospects of the new century that was just beginning, an awareness of the beauty of machines which could replace the more traditional objects of aesthetic satisfaction, and a realisation of the heightening of experience which new sensations of speed and mechanical power could give.

There was nothing very new in all this. The admiration for destruction was common enough at a moment when Nietzsche's influence in France and Italy was at its height, and when Georges Sorel was elevating violence into a political doctrine. Indeed, a group of minor writers and artists, who had founded in Paris a group called *Compagnons de l'action d'Art,* based on a mixture of anarchist and Nietzschean ideas, had already gone so far as to publish a Manifesto in 1907—two years before the Futurists—in which they proclaimed the necessity of resorting to violence to preserve the dignity of art, declared the inequality of man, and exclaimed 'Long live violence against all that makes life ugly!' (pp. 135-36)

Futurism was only one of the paths that led to Fascism; and, if it had been the only one, Fascism would not have had to be taken so seriously. The Fascist movement was a success because it combined the systematic use of terrorism as a political weapon with an ability to appeal to the desperate and disillusioned elements of the organised working class, as well as to the disappointed nationalism of middle class intellectuals and ex-officers. What Mussolini learnt from the Futurists was a certain technique of invective, a means of publicity and popular agitation, together with a set of phrases that would give his supporters the sense of moving with, indeed ahead of, the times. (Marinetti would have been right in claiming Mussolini as a Futurist on the strength of his repeated use of Futurist language alone.) As a destroyer of orderly, 'bourgeois' values Marinetti had been unequalled, and the Fascists were the chief people to profit by it.

Yet the revolt against the past had an importance beyond its immediate political effects and consequences. Although there are moments when the whole Futurist movement seems little more than an expression of misguided Italian youthful exuberance—a sort of revving-up of intellectual and artistic Vespas—its effects were widespread, and extended far beyond Italy. Its effect in Italy is well expressed by [Giovanni] Papini: 'Marinetti, even if he did nothing else, obliged a large part of the somnolent and rheumatic Italian *bourgeoisie* to interest itself in new problems of art and literature, and to enter into violent contact with the researches of the new European spirit'. And, in fact, the Futurists made their own contribution to this new European spirit. If the art and literature of the twentieth century have learnt to deal with the phenomena of a mechanised age, if writers and artists have learnt to try the boldest technical innovations and to use the most violent juxtaposition of images and ideas to achieve their effects, then it is to the Futurists that this is in part due. As the painter [Gino] Severini put it—and he himself was to give up the practice of strictly 'Futurist' art—'We cannot deny that Futurism has infinitely enlarged the horizon of the creative act and given a fine example of boldness in its passionate search for what is authentically new—an example of which all the art of our time, from Dadaism to Surrealism and recent Abstract Art, shows traces'. If, in the second half of the twentieth century, these phases of our art are taken for granted and have passed into our day-to-day surroundings—the advertisements we see, the furniture we use, or the films we look at—this is partly the achievement of the Futurists. And, even if Europe and the United States have perhaps outgrown the childish nationalism of Marinetti, we may yet, by studying his techniques and ideas, understand a little more clearly the pathology of extreme nationalist feeling with which we are faced in other parts of the world. Finally, on the threshold of the Space Age, perhaps we may grant a certain prophetic gift to those who, in 1909, 'standing aloft on the world's summit launched an insolent challenge to the stars'. (pp. 176-78)

> *James Joll, "F. T. Marinetti: Futurism and Fascism," in his* Intellectuals in Politics: Three Biographical Essays *(© 1960 by James Joll; reprinted by permission of A D Peters & Co Ltd), Weidenfeld and Nicolson, 1960, pp. 133-78.*

MICHAEL KIRBY (essay date 1971)

[*Kirby shares the viewpoint of many later critics, who acknowledge Futurism's notorious sympathy with Fascist ideals, but who also recognize the movement's great contribution to twentieth-century avant-garde literature and the performing arts. For a similar reevaluation of Marinetti, see R. W. Flint's introduction to* Marinetti: Selected Writings *excerpted below.*]

As with any movement, Futurism may best be understood in terms of certain works that most accurately represent its achievement and contribution; other works, equally substantial or even more substantial as productions, may safely be ignored.

It is not necessary to go further than the work of Marinetti to establish this point. From a purely technical point of view, all of Marinetti's plays written after 1909 may be considered as Futurist. But on stylistic grounds, his longer plays such as [*Il Tamburo di Fuoco, Prigionieri,* and *Vulcano*] . . . seem to relate much more clearly to Symbolism and Expressionism than to the movement he headed. They contribute little or nothing to our understanding of the important contributions of Futurism to performance. In a brief note introducing *Il Tamburo di Fuoco,* Marinetti wrote:

> I have not been able to achieve my goal with a synthetic drama. I then wrote this impressionist drama with comparable theatrical development. No concession to your traditional tastes! You shall soon have new ultrafuturist theatrical *sintesi!*

The truth may be read clearly through Marinetti's bravado: *Il Tamburo di Fuoco* was one of his concessions to somewhat traditional tastes. . . . But Marinetti himself did create "ultrafuturist" theatrical works of great originality and impor-

tance. Even as late as the nineteen-thirties when he was producing his "Radio Sintesi," he was able to create performance pieces that were pure and powerful examples of Futurist concerns. (pp. 10-11)

[In **"The Variety Theatre"** manifesto] can be found almost all of the major concerns of Futurist performance.

In considering the manifesto, it is very important, first of all, to realize that the variety theatre—music halls, cabarets, night-clubs, and circuses—was not intended to be taken literally as an example of Futurist theatre. It was the "only theatrical entertainment worthy of the true Futurist spirit," but it was only "the crucible in which the elements of a new sensibility that is coming into being are stirring." Although many of the facets and components of the variety theatre were used to exemplify Futurist concerns in a vivid way, Marinetti did not say that the works should be emulated. He was concerned with the spirit or content rather than with the details of style or form. The variety theatre became a giant and expanded metaphor for the Futurist theatre; it was not intended as a representation of it.

What were these "elements of a new sensibility" that could be seen in the variety theatre and that were proposed as the basis for true Futurist performance? In essence, they involved an emphasis on concrete or alogical presentation, on the use and combination of all modes and technical means of performance, and on the physical involvement of the spectators and the destruction of the "fourth wall" convention. They were manifested in two relatively distinct styles: the illogical or absurd and the mechanical or objective.

The single most important aspect of Futurist performance was to be its establishment of the concept of the *concrete* or the *alogical* in theatre. If a thing is experienced for its own sake rather than for its references and implications, it may be considered to be concrete: it is "there" rather than referring to something that is not there. A performance or an element of that performance, therefore, can be thought of as being concrete to the extent that it maximizes the sensory dimensions and minimizes or eliminates the intellectual aspects. (pp. 20-1)

One of the main things that attracted Marinetti to the variety theatre was its basically alogical nature. The variety theatre does not deal in illusion as a play or opera does. It does not tell a story or represent anything. It tends to *be* rather than to refer. The female singer or dancer does not pretend to be someone else: she does not, in the words of **"The Variety Theatre"** manifesto, wear a "mask" of "sighs" and "romantic sobs" like an actress but presents directly all of her "admirable animal qualities." The acrobat and juggler do not aid in the development of a narrative or pretend to be anywhere other than where they really are. Nor do they generally embody abstract ideas and concepts: the trapeze artiste flies without representing flight. The actions of such variety performers are not symbolic but complete and self-sufficient. The immediate presence of a certain physical activity or action is enough to create a rewarding experience for the spectator. There is no intellectual elaboration, but there is the possibility of "new significations . . . in the most unexplored parts of our sensibility."

The distinction that Marinetti sets up in **"The Variety Theatre"** manifesto is between "psychology" and what he calls *"fisicofollia"* or "physical madness." "Psychology" in this case refers to "the internal life" of drives, ambitions, conscience, feelings, emotions, and so forth; it also includes the intellectual discussion and analysis of life. The "madness" that he prefers and contrasts with it is both intense and nonrational—an absolute involvement with the qualities of direct experience. He opposes the elaboration of interpretation with an "anti-academic" and functionally "primitive," alogical response. (In this "madness," as well as in his "significations of light, sound, noise, and speech with their mysterious and inexplicable prolongations," Marinetti prefigures Artaud.)

The variety theatre also was used by Marinetti to illustrate what he considered to be a more viable audience-performance relationship. The "fourth wall" conventions of drama, in which the actor performs in a room with three real walls and an imaginary fourth wall, while, theoretically, taking no cognizance of the audience, implicitly asked the observer to remain politely passive so as not to intrude on the "reality" of the work. The variety theatre was diametrically opposed to the conventions and implications of the "fourth wall." Just as the smoke-filled nightclubs created a single undivided ambience for performers and spectators, Marinetti wanted to remove the separation between audience and presentation.

Perhaps thinking of how a singer in a nightclub sometimes walks among the tables singing to individual customers or clowns in a circus sometimes perform their antics with and among the spectators, Marinetti asked for a less rigid audience-performance relationship. He wanted the physical presentation to surround and involve the observers. He wanted "the necessity of acting among the spectators in the orchestra, the boxes and the gallery."

Such a change in the spatial relationship between the viewer and what is viewed does not necessarily make the spectator more active (except perhaps by requiring him to shift position frequently) or more involved physically. Yet the actual physical involvement of the spectator was Marinetti's intent. He admired the variety theatre because its spectators actively responded during the performance with indications of approval or disdain, rather than waiting passively until the curtain went down to applaud. They yelled comments and sang along with the music. There was an energetic exchange between performers and spectators. The audience helped to create the particular quality of the theatrical experience, rather than pretending that the experience would be the same without them.

But Marinetti wanted something more specific than a lively and demonstrative audience. In **"The Variety Theatre"** manifesto he made several suggestions for forcing the spectators to become a part of the performance whether they wanted to or not—the use of itching and sneezing powders, coating some of the auditorium seats with glue, provoking fights and disturbances by selling the same seat to two or more people. It should be noted that, like the juggler and acrobat, these devices are alogical. Marinetti was not suggesting that the incidents of a story be placed in and around the audience or that actors speak to the spectators "in character." The occurrences were to be sufficient in themselves without representing or symbolizing anything.

A third major aspect of **"The Variety Theatre"** manifesto was its emphasis on the utilization and combination of various theatrical media, means, or elements. Marinetti pointed out that variety theatre made use of motion pictures whereas "legitimate theatre" did not. As implied by the phrase already quoted—"light, sound, noise, and speech"—each had its own "significations," and no performance possibilities were to be excluded. The variety of the variety theatre was seen as one of its most important characteristics.

There was also the suggestion in the manifesto that these various performance elements be presented at the same time. Like the three rings of a circus that are all employed at once, the Futurist performance was to make simultaneous presentations, creating a "dynamism of form and color."

Marinetti admired two distinct stylistic qualities of the variety theatre: its illogical absurdity and its speed, energy, and power. He saw humor as an antidote to "the Solemn, the Sacred, the Serious, the Sublime of Art with a capital *A*," and wanted to ridicule and parody accepted dramatic masterpieces in order to destroy the attachment to traditional values. There was a cleansing, purgative aspect to the incongruous and absurd. It was a way to "air the intelligence" and to destroy "all our conceptions of perspective, of proportion, of time and of space." In this sense, the illogical can be seen as a stage in a progression toward the alogical. It was "absolutely necessary to destroy all logic in the spectacles" so that things could be perceived for their own sake without intellectual elaboration.

The other stylistic characteristics of variety theatre that interested Marinetti were more obviously related to the basic concerns of Futurism as established in the **"Foundation and Manifesto of Futurism"**: Dynamism was the focus of Futurist style. Just as the earlier manifesto extolled the "aggressive movement, feverish insomnia, the running step, the somersault, the insult and punches," **"The Variety Theatre"** manifesto exalted "jugglers, dancers, gymnasts, vari-colored riding troupes, spiraling cyclones of spinning dancers on points." Where the earlier publication said, "No work can be a masterpiece without an aggressive character," the later pointed out that the variety theatre was able to "create a strong and healthy atmosphere of danger upon the stage."

Like athletes, the acrobats and related artistes of the variety theatre set standards of accomplishment that were objective: whether or not they were equaled or surpassed could be determined by anyone and did not depend upon personal, subjective judgment. Marinetti admired this objectification of standards and wrote of the "relentless emulation by brains and muscles in order to surpass the various records of agility, velocity, strength, complexity and grace." (pp. 21-5)

The most important plays of the Futurists took the form of very short pieces called *sintesi*. Marinetti, [F. Balilla] Pratella, Pino Masnata, and others wrote plays and operas of extended length, but the *sintesi* embody all of the major Futurist contributions in this area. . . . Once again, the basic concepts of this type of performance were elucidated in a manifesto: **"The Futurist Synthetic Theatre,"** written by Marinetti, Emilio Settimelli, and Bruno Corra; it is dated both January 11, 1915, and February 18, 1915.

The most obvious characteristic of the *sintesi* was its length. "Synthetic," it was flatly stated in the manifesto, meant "very brief": although most were somewhat longer, some of the scripts would take only a minute, or even less, to perform. This could be considered their one defining characteristic; however, the term became very popular, at least among the Futurists, and was occasionally attached to rather long works.

As explained by the manifesto, brevity was, most simply, a distillation, condensation, or compression of traditional drama. In keeping with the Futurist concern with speed and motion, the proper work of the playwright was seen as "synthesizing facts and ideas into the least number of words"; his pieces were to be "rapid and concise."

Actually, this compressed brevity was one of the aspects of nightclubs, circuses, and music halls that had been praised two years earlier in **"The Variety Theatre"** manifesto. The variety theatre, it had been pointed out, "explains in an incisive and rapid manner the most sentimental and abstruse problems," and there one sees "heaps of events dispatched in haste." Not only did Marinetti approve in **"The Variety Theatre"** of "the execution of *Parsifal* in forty minutes that is now in preparation for a large London music hall," but he suggested "representing, for example, in a single evening all the Greek, French and Italian tragedies condensed and comically mixed up" and reducing "the whole of Shakespeare to a single act."

When **"The Synthetic Theatre"** manifesto specifically advised the world to "abolish farce, vaudeville, sketches, comedy, drama, and tragedy, in order to create in their place numerous forms of Futurist theatre," the concepts of brevity and condensation had become more subtle and elaborate. The distillation or compression of existing dramatic works was only the crudest and most obvious form of synthesis. Now what was to be compressed and synthesized was the diversity of life itself, a diversity "present *for a moment* in a tram, in a café, at a station, and which remains filmed on our minds as dynamic, fragmentary symphonies of gestures, words, noises, and lights." The writers of **"The Synthetic Theatre"** might have been talking about the well-established *parole in libertà* rather than drama.

As with all Futurist art, the Synthetic Theatre can be clarified and, at least in part, explained in terms of its rejection of traditional forms. In this case, it was the conventions of exposition, structure, and characterization that, among other things, were rejected. In an extended analysis of the current techniques of playwriting, **"The Synthetic Theatre"** manifesto scorned the practice of "introducing only a tenth of the conceptions in the first act, five tenths in the second, four tenths in the third"; it claimed that it was "STUPID to be subjected to the impositions of *crescendo, exposition,* and *the final climax,*" and it mocked the public that "from habit and by infantile instinct, wishes to see how the character of a person emerges from a series of events." The age-old dichotomy between heroes and villains and the contingent processes of projection and identification were dismissed as "the primitiveness of the crowd that wishes to see the agreeable person exalted and the disagreeable one defeated." But most important of all the Futurists rejected the "minute logic" that holds together traditional theatre and is the binding force in its structure; they dismissed the notion that the public must *"always completely understand the whys and wherefores of every scenic action."*

Like the other aspects of Futurist art and performance, however, the Synthetic Theatre was not merely a rejection of traditional concepts. If the brevity of the *sintesi* can be seen in part as a reaction against a theatre that was considered "monotonous and depressing" and in which the public was "in the disgusting attitude of a group of loafers who sip their distress and their pity, spying on the very slow agony of a horse fallen on the pavement," the short length of the new plays also had its positive side. Above all, the compression of the *sintesi* was seen as a means of intensifying the direct impact of the performance. **"The Synthetic Theatre"** manifesto might well have influenced Artaud's thought when it called for "synthetic expressions of cerebral energy" creating "a specialized reality that violently assaults the nerves." Unlike the "long-winded, analytical, pedantically psychological, explanatory, diluted, meticulous, static" traditional theatre, the new Synthetic The-

atre moved away from information and logic and toward direct sensory appeal. According to the Futurists, "reality vibrates around us, hitting us with *bursts of fragments* with events amongst them, embedded one within the other, confused, entangled, chaotic." Although there is a somewhat telegraphic list in the manifesto indicating how these goals were being achieved in practice, the best way to understand how they were to take actual theatrical form is to look at the *sintesi* themselves.

There is a tremendous formal and stylistic diversity among so-called *sintesi*. In part this diversity is intentional and programmatic. Marinetti himself was quite catholic and eclectic, and the Futurists saw no need to develop a single style of performance. **"The Synthetic Theatre"** manifesto spoke of their discoveries in a variety of areas: "in the subconscious, in undefined forces, in pure abstraction, in pure cerebralism, in pure fantasy, in breaking records, and physical madness." The acceptance of one avenue of investigation—that of the unconscious, for example, that would eventually lead to Surrealism—did not preclude the investigation of other areas. But along with the more original forms, almost every trend that was then current in playwriting can be found represented in the *sintesi*. Calling a piece a *"sintesi"* was not a stylistic qualification.

Traditional standards of "verisimilitude" and "the photographic" were among those attacked in **"The Synthetic Theatre,"** and, with very few exceptions, the *sintesi* rejected literal reality and naturalism. This in itself was no innovation, however: many of the *sintesi,* as well as some of the longer Futurist works, were influenced by Symbolism. But all of the *sintesi,* the innovative as well as the derivative, did tend to be nonnaturalistic. In their stylistic diversity, this tendency and their "very brief" length are the only defining characteristics that we have. Of course the common nonrealistic approach was not a rejection of reality itself, like all nonrealistic artists, the Futurists felt that imitation was superficial and that they were in touch with "reality" of a more meaningful kind. (pp. 41-4)

A second important tenet of Futurist theory that formed certain *sintesi* was the emphasis on simultaneity. The earliest example, published in 1915, was a play by Marinetti himself with the simple title of *Simultaneity (Simultaneità).* Two entirely different places and their particular inhabitants occupy the same stage at the same time. The life of a beautiful cocotte "penetrates," to use Marinetti's word, the life of a bourgeois family. For most of the play, the occupants of one "world" are completely unaware of those in the other, although the cocotte's dressing table occupies part of the family's living room.

The following year Marinetti developed the concept of simultaneity even further in *The Communicating Vases (I Vasi Communicanti).* (Later the same title was used for a book by André Breton, the leader of the Surrealists.) In this play, three different, unrelated locations occupy the stage, which is divided by two partitions, and the action goes on in all three at the same time. It is interesting that in both of these plays Marinetti chose to fuse the disparate ambiences at the end: the cocotte suddenly enters the other world of the bourgeois living room, and, in *The Communicating Vases,* soldiers actually break through the partitions between the areas, moving from one to the other. **"The Synthetic Theatre"** manifesto had spoken of the "race with cinematography," and the use of simultaneity undoubtedly derived in part from an attempt to parallel in stage terms the way in which motion pictures moved instantaneously from one locale to another, eliminating distance while compressing time. (pp. 46-7)

The creation of a "Tactile Theatre" that focused primarily upon the sense of touch was also proposed by Marinetti. He actually created displays, which he called "tactile tables," that were intended to be felt rather than seen and which presented an organized variety of textures and surface qualities. In "Tactilism," a manifesto read at the Théâtre de l'Oeuvre in Paris and published in January, 1921, Marinetti described his theoretical distribution of tactile qualities into categories and scales that were somewhat similar to Russolo's organization and grouping of various kinds of noise. As explained in a short section of the "Tactilism" manifesto, Marinetti's Tactile Theatre was to be composed of long moving bands or turning wheels that were to be touched by the spectators. Time was an element in the performance, and other senses besides that of touch were to be involved. As the bands flowed smoothly or the wheels revolved, providing different textual rhythms as well as a variety of tactile qualities, there would be "accompaniments of music and light."

Of course it cannot be claimed that tactile elements have been completely absent from contemporary theatre. Several attempts to involve the audience more directly and immediately have employed physical contact between performers and spectators: Audience members have been touched, stroked, physically led or moved, and have had various things dropped or thrown on them. The involvement of the sense of touch in these cases, however, has been episodic and limited, whereas Marinetti had proposed that central importance be given to the tactile elements.

Marinetti's Tactile Theatre should not be confused with his "tactile *sintesi*" such as **The Great Remedy** and **The Tactile Quartet (Il Quartetto Tattile)**. There is no direct contact in the plays between the spectators and the presentation. As has been mentioned, when "The Sensible One" goes into the auditorium in **The Great Remedy,** she "almost grazes . . . with her hands" the "very beautiful women" in the front row of seats: she looks at them, smells them, but does not actually touch them. Tactile elements abound in the plays, but they are to be experienced imaginatively by the audience, rather than directly. The dilemma faced by "The Sensible One" opposes two contrasting images—a slanting wall bristling with sharp blades and a "marvelous semi-nude woman"—that are tactile to a high degree. The texture of paper, the eating of fruit and fruit skins, and the feel of bare skin play important parts in **The Tactile Quartet.** Both plays employ the violent physical contact of blows, kicks, and falls, but all of these tactile elements must be understood and experienced by the spectator through imagination, projection, and empathy. (pp. 148-50)

In drama, the Futurists compressed represented time and space and originated techniques of simultaneous staging in which two or more unrelated actions were presented at the same time. Stylistically, they developed in several directions, including the symbolic and subjective, the irrational and "absurd," and the formalistic. They wrote and presented plays that were antipsychological and antiliterary, and that made use of semi-alogical and alogical structures. They experimented with various psychological and physical relationships between the spectators and the performance, developments that involved both purposeful confrontation with the audience and acting in the auditorium as well as on the stage.

Futurist scenography was, to some extent, influenced by concepts that had already been clearly established by others. . . . They used light for its dynamic rather than its atmospheric qualities, and, both in practice and, more elaborately, in theory

they developed the concept of the actorless abstract scenographic presentation. On the other hand, they worked extensively with the mechanization of the performer both in costuming and in acting style.

In *Vita Futurista,* the one motion picture they produced, the Futurists helped to establish the tradition of the independent film made noncommercially by artists for their own purposes. They made early use of unusual lenses, curved mirrors, and other means of achieving expression through visual distortion. Certain sections of their film seem to have been imagistic rather than narrative in structure, and, by combining different unrelated scenes or segments of various styles, they produced a film based on an alogical progression through time: these developments helped to establish the basic principles of abstract cinema.

Futurist music made use of atonality and improvisation. It contributed to the development of the field in the twentieth century by opening musical composition to impure "nonmusical" sounds or "noise." The Futurists invented and produced their own musical instruments and developed new kinds of musical notation for their scores. (pp. 152-53)

The presentations of the Futurists both broke down the distinction between performance forms by combining them and extended the concept of performance itself. Readings, visual displays, dance, sound effects, and representational actions were mixed at one moment of a production or followed each other in close sequence. . . .

These developments had little effect on the mainstream of theatre that progressed in a generally realistic direction, and encompassed both stylization and naturalism. But Futurism did have a great influence on practically every nonrealistic approach to theatre. It stimulated Pirandello in Italy and Wilder in the United States. It influenced the Russian Futurists and, eventually, the Constructivists. It led directly to Dada in almost all its manifestations. It was an impetus to pre-Surrealists like Apollinaire, demi-Surrealists like Cocteau, Surrealism itself, and to the entire French avant-garde theatre. In Germany, it contributed to the development of the theatre of the Bauhaus in an entirely different direction. (p. 153)

Although Futurism had a clear personality and identity, it also produced aesthetic products of great diversity. Its theories and presentations in almost every area of performance were significant contributions to the history of the performance art. (p. 154)

> *Michael Kirby, in his* Futurist Performance *(copyright © 1971 by Michael Kirby; reprinted by permission of the publisher, E. P. Dutton, Inc.), Dutton, 1971, 335 p.**

R. W. FLINT (essay date 1972)

[*Like Michael Kirby (see excerpt above), Flint believes that Marinetti's Fascist sympathies should not prevent critics from recognizing his original qualities as a man and as an artist.*]

Of all the theorists and instigators of aesthetic modernism's heroic age, Marinetti has been dealt with most harshly by time, and this neglect, though firmly grounded in his character and action, foreseen and even somewhat courted by the man himself, can now be taken as an inevitable result of his radical program for renewal. The experience of ends makes possible the understanding of beginnings; the cycle of modernism has come around to a point where its origins can finally be detached from the politics that submerged them so soon after their birth. Futurism can now be enjoyed in its comedy, its haphazard profundity, its welter of crazily naïve, exuberant paradox and divination. (p. 3)

In his role as "the caffeine of Europe," Marinetti was a dramatic break in the smooth evolution of Italian elegiac pessimism from Leopardi to Pascoli, Carducci, Gozzano, and D'Annunzio. A monster sprung, apparently, from D'Annunzio's loins who nevertheless kept his distance from the Divine Gabriele, a man who during his best years seemed to have no inner life at all, certainly not by the reigning standards of polite letters, the first wholesale Italian enthusiast for American promotional techniques, the first important Italian disciple of Whitman and yawper of the barbaric yawp, Marinetti became one of the great intuitive sleepwalking impresarios of Europe. His scale of operation was so original that it seems out of place to call his later submergence as an Accademico d'Italia under Mussolini tragic; pathetic is the better word. It was the revenge of history on a man who tried to destroy history in the name of art.

To define what sets him apart from a dozen contemporary rivals in anarchy and artistic utopianism is not easy. As soon as you dip below the surface of his dream of himself as the caffeine of Europe begetting "an anarchy of perfectionisms," an "association of desperate ideas"; as the liberator of the machine and prophet of "the metalization of man"; as the scourge of "psychology," scorner of lechery and D'Annunzian *amore* (but he was in and out of exotic beds no less than his repudiated master); as a self-proclaimed "primitive of a new sensibility," discoverer of "the proletariat of gifted men," the "madness of becoming," and "the extrinsicated will"; as soon as you apply the normal procedures of the history of ideas, you find the ghost of Futurist originality—even though events prove that it was there—dissolving backward and sideward into the bubbling acids of that prewar world. Nietzsche clearly hovers in the background, but Marinetti, in response to the German's own directives, intended to convert everything private, fugitive, and driven in Nietzscheanism into the hearty noonday bustle of optimistic Milanese enterprise; failing that, into genial farce. (pp. 6-7)

As a middle-aged American, conscripted and politically half-awake during the Axis war, I dislike Marinetti's strident bellicosity. . . . Certainly the Futurist cult of "synthetic" verbal violence, of "war, the world's only hygiene," the appalling innocence about war, as it seems now, of the whole European prewar world, is the greatest obstacle to the understanding of Futurism. Yet its forthrightness in the matter, like Tennyson's in the opening sections of "Maud," is appealing and radical. And this belligerence was fundamental, an energizing theme that reaches back to the oldest springs of Italian action, that fuses the farcical immoralism of D'Annunzio or Casanova with a wildly accelerated Viconian philosophy of action and creativity at any price.

Moreover, this ferocious antihumanitarian bristling was naïve enough in the Futurists to be enjoyable in its accidents, if rarely in its essence. (pp. 7-8)

Marinetti's nature, in other words, contained many of the sturdier ingredients of Renaissance *virtù*: a true valor behind the clownish urbanity, a good soldier's kind of loyalty, the Hemingway type of courage (which sent him out to a dangerous sector of the Russian front in 1944) and strength to openly oppose his "friend" Mussolini, in 1920 when he left the Fascist party, and in 1938 when, after years of uneasy support of the regime, he published an open letter condemning anti-Semitism in the arts.

In the final accounting, Marinetti *was* Futurism. (p. 8)

R. W. Flint, in his introduction to Marinetti: Selected Writings *by F. T. Marinetti, edited by R. W. Flint, translated by R. W. Flint and Arthur A. Coppotelli (reprinted by permission of Farrar, Straus and Giroux, Inc.; translation copyright © 1971, 1972 by Farrar, Straus and Giroux, Inc.), Farrar, Straus and Giroux, 1972, pp. 3-36.*

DAVID MITCHELL   (essay date 1975)

Marinetti's muscular aestheticism produced a poorish crop of results in the arts; and the shock items of Futurist soirées, including some of his own verses, now figure as amusing nonsense ditties in Italian primary school anthologies. Yet many of his targets were ones of which Carlyle, Ruskin and Morris would have approved. He was convinced that intellectuals had a duty not to loiter impotently on the political sidelines, not to shrink from what Morris called 'the river of violence', since the willingness to cross it was, for both men, the acid test of their sincerity. His manifest eagerness to do so gives Marinetti a kind of balefully heroic stature. In an overpopulated, increasingly bureaucratized and resentful Europe, his revolutionary slogans—'better a splendid disaster', 'the world needs only heroism', 'go against the current'—rank with d'Annunzio's battle cry—'every insurrection is an act of creation'—as summaries, and, it may be, inspirations of the mood of *squadrismo* that has been growing for two decades and is likely to intensify. Dandy, poseur, and egomaniac, he yet showed the courage of his expressed convictions—among them the belief that a life of routine is worse than death—and deserves to be recognized as a patron saint of the multiplying mystics of action who to an aesthetic of filthy lucre seek to oppose one of violence and of blood. (p. 711)

David Mitchell, "Marinetti, Futurist and Fascist," in History Today *(© History Today Limited 1975), Vol. XXV, No. 10, October, 1975, pp. 704-11.*

CHRISTOPHER WAGSTAFF   (essay date 1976)

[*Wagstaff examines* L'alcova d'acciaio *in the context of writings about the First World War and as an expression of Futurist poetics and ideology.*]

Marinetti received from the war little that he did not bring to it. The Futurist movement, founded by him in 1909 as an aesthetic avant-garde in literature, the visual arts, music, drama and the cinema, was from the moment of its foundation politically active. Marinetti propagated the ideas of industrial and technological development, imperial expansion, aggressive military and cultural nationalism, the heroic palingenesis of the individual and of the nation, distrust of socialism and contempt for the corruption and inefficiency of liberal democratic parliamentarianism. These ideas, in various guises, had been the property of middle-class intellectuals in Italy since the 1890s, and they contributed to an ideology which saw in war the chance of achieving the goals to which they aspired. Behind Marinetti's version of the ideology lie Nietzsche, Darwin, Sorel, Bergson, Pareto, Morasso, Corradini and D'Annunzio. In *L'alcova d'acciaio*—his account of his experiences in the last few months of the war—this ideology emerges coherently and artistically complete, and stands as a clear cultural signpost pointing from the war to Fascism.

There are three aspects of the novel to be examined: memoir, propaganda and ideology, all merging together, but with the latter predominating, and subordinating the entire narrative to a vision of human existence that pre-existed the historical reality of the war.

The novel is its flimsiest at the level of memoir; Marinetti wishes to glorfiy his sensibility rather than communicate his experiences. He writes about his sexual conquests both at the front and while on leave, and about his participation in the defence against the Austrian assault at Asiago in 15 June 1918, the crossing of the Piave at the end of October, his helter-skelter advance in an armoured car through retreating and surrendering Austrian armies and his triumphal entry the following week in the vanguard of the Italian advance into villages like Vittorio Veneto, where he received a liberator's welcome from the female Italian populace.

Marinetti was a seasoned war correspondent, but his dispatches had always said more about his 'futurist genius' than about the wars he was covering. *Alcova* is no exception. A comparison between this novel and Norman Gladden's memoir, *Across the Piave*—which covers the same events up to the entry into Vittorio Veneto—shows us how little Marinetti is telling us. Gladden was a machine-gunner, and tells us how he shot, at what, in what situations. Marinetti, in the Asiago episode, was in charge of a mortar unit. He tells us nothing about mortaring activities, but he does carry on a lyrical elaboration of a poetic conceit, begun in a previous war narrative, concerning machine guns and erotic women:

> Then we hear the furious dance and the ta-ta-ta-ta-*ta*—capricious, merciless, ironic and feminine—of the Saint-Étienne machine-gun, six yards off to the right, like an Andalusian woman spitting out passionate fire and red carnations from her balcony masked with foliage. . . .

He describes with aesthetic detachment and enthusiasm the Austrian bombardment. The reader needs another source to discover that it was a bombardment of terrifying and unprecedented magnitude. Nevertheless, Marinetti's elated band of an élite few individualists speeding through the abandoned Austrian lines, capturing prisoners without firing a shot—even capturing an entire corps of four thousand—probably describes what actually happened. What few details he allows to loom from the rhetorical fog tally with Gladden's account. It is, however, extraordinary that a man who had his hernia operated on so that he could join up in 1915, fought through the Alpine campaigns, was wounded and decorated in 1917, and returned to the fray to remain there to the end, could come through such a war and in three hundred and eighty pages on the subject show almost no trace of having been touched by it, or of even having noticed what was actually going on.

Desertion was widespread and harshly punished. Marinetti does not suppress the matter; he transforms it. An officer tells him about two Italian deserters he has shot: one wanted only to punish his wife for infidelity, and the other to kill his father for sleeping with his fiancée. The officer concludes: 'With deserters like that we are bound to win the war'. . . . The force that drives men to war (which, as we shall see, is sexual) also motivates them to fight a 'war' on the home front against sexual rivals. The appalling reality of self-mutilation and desertion is

transformed into warrior propaganda. This is a consequence of Marinetti's techniques of characterisation. He has only one way of portraying characters in his writings: the moral portrait. Women are voluptuous and capricious, men virile and robust. Any visual adjective is merely a peg on which to hang the moral quality. Morality is a matter of psychology, however: and psychology is a matter of drives. A character either manifests these drives (which are really only one drive: sexual aggression) or else is frustrated. There is a third category, of people who do not belong in the same 'species' as Marinetti, and are pacifists, neutralists, traditionalists, cowards, rational, Germanic or old. A deserter must either be suffocated beneath the weight of the past or else he is driven to desert by his drive. Since he is part of the glorious Italian front line, he belongs in the latter category.

While recovering in a hospital from wounds in 1917, Marinetti wrote a short treatise to raise the moral of the troops called *Come si seducono le donne* (**'How to Seduce Women'**), in which there is a chapter exhorting women to respond to the superior sexual attractions of mutilated men. In *Alcova*, wounds are 'flesh yearning to become metal' . . . , and beautiful women are excited by the wounded. . . . If you want young men to get themselves blown apart, it makes sense, in Marinetti's psychological system, to suggest that it makes women desire to be laid by them. It makes sense in 1917, but less so in 1921, unless Marinetti is attempting to justify a war whose value was being questioned.

Italy needed a victory to justify the war, and Vittorio Veneto was to be that victory. The fact that the advance was a hasty decision to assure bargaining power at Versailles, that any real fighting to get across the Piave was as much Allied as Italian, and the fact that the Austrian army disintegrated in mutiny before the Italians could get to it were an embarrassment to the government, which suppressed the facts. Marinetti, however, does not suppress them; he transforms them, rhetorically. In his narrative, the fact that he arrives after the fighting is over, and the fact that the Austrians have mutinied and fled, or simply surrendered without resistance, are perfectly plain. He gives as a reason for this the indomitable will to victory of the heroic Italians: 'We bear on our faces the crushing defiant arrogance of victory and our eyes are invincible projectors of forces'. . . . For Marinetti, this is an *explanation*.

In the very coherence and completeness of Marinetti's ideology lies the denial of the reality of the war, and indeed the very intensity of his visionary aspirations produces an almost totally rhetorical representation of human existence. In order to take control of reality, which he has to do if he is to make of it a language for his ideology, Marinetti renders abstract the real, concrete world and concrete the world of his own subjective feelings. Marinetti is hungry and describes his dream: 'My hunger dreamed of a supremely elegant tablecloth, an infinite silken flight of soft, fluctuating, pearly reflections'. . . . The mighty Austrian bombardment of 15 June 1918 evaporates into Decadent aestheticism as a shell explodes: 'The soft, nonchalant sloth of its smoke, rising, becoming dishevelled and gracefully twining round an early star'. . . . 'Isms', in the plural, abound. Marinetti is full of 'optimisms', Italian soldiers are full of 'heroisms', women of 'ironies', the letters soldiers receive are 'too many postal sentimentalities (*sentimentalismi*) on the eve of a decisive battle'. . . . Conceits are taken to extraordinary lengths. . . . The whole novel is to a certain extent a conceit on the analogy of the will dominating reality and being invincible like machines: 'I feel the material of my heart become transformed into metal, into an optimism of steel'. . . . But by now we are in the realm of making concrete the abstract. In chapter XXVII his feelings of joy, of invincibility at victory are expressed by describing in vivid prose the eleven erupting volcanoes which are their 'concrete' expression. Marinetti, in 1912, told poets to glorify 'matter' in their poetry, and to destroy their own ego. What this often meant, in Marinetti's case, was to glorify his own ego as though it were matter, so that by 1913 he is defining 'the sole concern of the narrator, to convey all the vibrations of his ego'.

Marinetti is not just using ordinary language in a rhetorical manner. Reality becomes language and language becomes 'pure' rhetoric, so that the real world becomes part of a basically musical instrument of self-expression. The stylisation is at times that of grand opera, and the novel must be read as a kind of modulated bellow (if not read that way, it soon becomes intolerably monotonous). (pp. 150-53)

The 'lived' story that Marinetti is telling us is not really 'lived', for much of what is told is a rhetorical structure designed to induce a certain response in the reader. If it is read out loud, declaimed as it was no doubt composed (Marinetti generally dictated, and he first became known as a reciter of poetry), its powerful histrionic nature is immediately effective. The effect is part of the ideology:

> I want this book to dance, dance, dance, alive
> and throbbing with joyful rhythm in the reader's
> hands. . . .

The book is an *action,* and it is carried out on the reader: to narcotise him or to assault him. It is written on a monotone, in which 'inebriation', 'madness', 'joy' are one set of key words and the other set is summed up by the word *spavaldo,* meaning 'arrogant and defiant'. Various blends of these two motifs are the obbligato theme of the novel. . . . (p. 154)

The reader is to respond with precisely the feelings that Marinetti attributes to himself in the novel. Reason and rationality are anathema in this activist world. Marinetti must communicate his state of mind intuitively, through a rhetoric of contagion. The *arditi* (crack assault troops, later the backbone of the Fascist squads) are portrayed as being without minds: 'A confusion of bare arms can be seen pumping like pistons and pouring like taps bottles of wine and glasses of beer amid a fantasmagoric flickering of blue lights and grotesque shadows.' . . . Their non-humanness is conveyed not only by the way they are mechanised, but also by the way in which their surroundings are made unreal, so that the activity of these *arditi* is deprived of any sense or purpose. Marinetti is not despising the common soldiery; he associates himself with this anti-rationality. . . . The novel carries a number of attacks on the general staff who want to run the war with logic: 'War . . . is the one thing in the world which does not admit of habit. You have to make your play. Whoever wins wins, whoever loses loses, and that's the end of it!' . . . The narcotic frenzy of vitalism, mechanical metaphors applied to men, sporting metaphors applied to carnage, are rhetoric, not war. Marinetti, in his manifestos, has used military metaphors to describe literary polemic. In this novel he produces a simile in which he compares military aggression with literary polemic: Austrians surrender 'like idiotic professors in love with the past who, feeling our futurist boots in their behinds, reluctantly give up their old dictionaries of Austria's worn-out glory'. . . . (pp. 154-55)

If the *arditi* are machines, other troops are 'like cogs in the great machine of battle.' . . . The workers in the port of Genoa

are dehumanised, while the machines are humanised. Barges are 'unloaded by microscopic little men who swiftly carry on their heads baskets of coal running on the elastic swaying of hung planks. To and fro of the little men between the barges and tall heaps of coal scattered with glinting lights. The sweating torsos glisten too.' . . . On the other hand, 'a firm solidarity of will in war swells the biceps of the cranes who swivel proudly on their joined feet to be admired as good patriots by all the attentive houses in the amphitheatre-port.' . . . The war is an expression of the will of the cranes, whom the men serve and fuel. Men are industrial fodder. Marinetti's war is the earthly paradise of the machine; it is futurist war, aesthetic spectacle and experience, the total work of modern art. Rather than the individual feeling himself submerged in monotony or a passive target for shrapnel, a feeling expressed by many witnesses, for Marinetti 'forces predisposed everything in favour of our typically swift and personal victory.' . . . Regressive dehumanisation of man—irrationality, mechanisation—is a positive factor for Marinetti, it is progress, wherein the machine is measure of man. (pp. 155-56)

The only mention of trenches in the novel comes in a speech Marinetti makes to Genoese women who are seeing troops off to the front from the station: 'barrack and depot life is so stifling with stupidity and cowardice that it turns the trench into paradise'. . . . When, in the scene in which the women give themselves to the war-wounded, one of the virgins, pausing from voluptuous intimacy with a metal thigh, says to Marinetti: 'You know I am a good patriot, but I don't understand, I can't admit, try as I might, the necessity for this eternal, brutal carnage', he reacts quickly: 'I shut my friend's mouth with a long kiss'. . . . He then makes her listen to a speech in which he says that war and life are synonymous, and goes on:

> In the distant origins of humanity we see dogged
> peoples offering bloody corpses to their Gods.
> Then a Hebrew God also hungry for human
> flesh. The earth in its envelope of atmospheres
> contains forces of domination, extremely intricate and difficult to decipher, which we define
> with inadequate words such as: spring, youth,
> heroism, will to ascendancy of races, revolution, scientific curiosity, thrust of progress,
> civilisation, record. All these undoubtedly telluric Forces adore human blood, in other words,
> struggle, our need to destroy one another. . . .

The crude social and biological Darwinism, echoes of the *Golden Bough* and of Nietzsche, fused with the ideals and fetishes of competitive free enterprise, are here explicitly used to defend the ideology of war as a *natural* expression of vitality. So fundamental is this ideology of violent struggle to the novel that Marinetti has allowed doubt to be voiced by a character just so that he can make his point antagonistically, by sexually and intellectually dominating the woman.

With the removal of inhibitions, natural, instinctive man is released, his 'forces' greater than those of reason. Many in Europe thought the war a necessary regressive step to prepare for a better world. For Marinetti regression *was* that better world. Being a poet, he needed images for this regenerate natural man, and he took from his Decadent heritage the analogy of sex. *L'alcova d'acciaio* is *all* sex: there is not a cloud, not a hill, not a machine that is not described in sexual terms. The 'steel alcove' is his armoured car, ready for the divine, naked female body of Italy; it is a woman too, whom he dominates by controlling. The rhetoric falls apart when the female armoured car, dominated by Marinetti, is described as dominating in turn the female road with 'lesbian virility'. . . . Sex too is just a language. (pp. 156-57)

The image Marinetti has chosen to convey natural man's drive, his instinct, is an aggressive sexual drive. But since natural man is an heroic *individual*, his sex act has to be free of emotion, it has to be humanly alienated. Women are elegant, capricious, small-breasted to differentiate them from the ties associated with females—maternity, family, marriage: one quick lay and away. In 1910 Marinetti wrote: 'We are convinced that love—sentimentality and eroticism—is the least natural thing in the world. The only thing that is natural and important is coitus . . .'. In *Alcova* he says that love would destroy 'the ultimate aggressive activity of coitus'. . . . The language sex speaks in *Alcova* is the language of the mystical ideology of natural man, who exists on a higher sphere than rational, peaceful, loving man. (pp. 157-58)

Alcova is perhaps the best example of Marinetti's putting into effect two statements from the original 1909 Futurist Manifesto: 'There is no beauty except in struggle. No work of art that is not of an aggressive nature can be a masterpiece'; and: 'We want to glorify war—the world's only hygiene—militarism, patriotism, the destructive act of the anarchists, beautiful ideas for which one dies and contempt for woman'.

'War, the world's only hygiene' became one of Marinetti's favourite slogans. The word 'hygiene' suggests a sort of purging; and the slogan is often accompanied by a condemnation of sexual love. The purging that Marinetti undergoes in his sexual encounters in *Alcova* is also an exorcism; it is exorcising death. (p. 158)

In an industrial age, in which each man must compete alone for personal gain and self-affirmation, by identifying with the machine each man defends himself against annihilation. In the rut, he enters death's abode, defies death, transcends time and space and affirms the primeval indestructibility of his drive; he is the hero of a myth. If love, or any human tie, calms his aggression, it destroys his drive, his life, his heroism. Hence Marinetti's 'solution to the problem of love' is the brothel, and is described in these terms: 'Mechanisation of love. I can feel the house vibrate with an uninterrupted, mechanical piston-like pumping of violent instincts stripped of all civilisation'. . . .

Marinetti began his literary career as a Decadent poet, seeing in the barbarism of the industrial age, which trampled over traditional cultural values, the possibility of rejuvenation. Marinetti insisted that, to survive, culture had to embrace the menacing barbarism, and produce a mass culture of the machine age, dominated by a new élite of artists—the futurists. Rather than bewail the passing of human values Marinetti would have men purge themselves of them. Men would undergo the 'hygiene' of war and emerge purified of everything except their elemental drive. The reward that awaited such heroes was a state of mind: 'intoxication', 'arrogant defiance', 'joy'; the condition of one who does not fear death.

When once the reader reflects that the machines to which men are urged to surrender their humanity are owned by somebody, and earn somebody a profit (the machines of war as much as any others), then the implications of Marinetti's ideology become clear. Marinetti's war novel is significant because it expresses what the industrial age requires from culture: a vision of existence in which the machine does not submerge the individual, but rather offers him release from the very inhibitions with which previous culture had suppressed his drive. For this

reason, the ideological perspective that Marinetti imposes on the war, while concealing the superficial realities of suffering, monotony, dirt and disease, reveals the deeper reality of the social and economic forces that brought it about. (p. 159)

> *Christopher Wagstaff, "Dead Man Erect: F. T. Marinetti, 'L'alcova d'acciaio'" (© The Macmillan Press Ltd 1976; reprinted by permission of the author), in* The First World War in Fiction: A Collection of Critical Essays, *edited by Holger Klein, Macmillan, 1976 (and reprinted by Barnes & Noble, 1977), pp. 149-59.*

JUDY RAWSON   (essay date 1976)

The *Futurist Manifesto* first appeared in *Le Figaro* for 20 February 1909. (p. 243)

In the preamble to the first *Manifesto* [Marinetti] claimed that 'soon we will see the first angels fly'. In his novel *Mafarka le Futuriste,* contemporary with the first *Manifesto,* the climax comes when Mafarka, the African king, dies in the act of creating his own son Gazurmah, an Icarus Superman figure, who successfully defies the sun and makes 'total music' with his wings as he flies off into the heavens at the end of the novel. Beneath Gazurmah the mountains topple, towns are ruined and the sea is cloven into an abyss with the facility of a scene from Walt Disney's *Fantasia,* while he bandies erotic nothings with the breezes and shouts defiance at the sea and the sun. So far as any metaphysics is implied it is an amoral exaltation of action for its own sake—as prescribed in the first three points of the *Manifesto.* 'Dynamism' was in fact a name that was contemplated for the movement during these early days. Again one can see how this easily-communicated ideal foreshadowed Fascism's cult of action and drive. In *The Technical Manifesto of Literature* (1912) the motor car is replaced by the aeroplane flying two hundred metres above Milan. (pp. 244-45)

[In the *Technical Manifesto of Literature* the] call is for a new poetry of intuition: to hate libraries and museums, to repudiate reason, to reassert that divine intuition which is the gift of the Latin races. Their poetry is to depend on analogy instead of logic; the old Latin grammar is to go, and nouns are to be placed as they come; verbs are to be used only in the infinitive; adjectives, adverbs and punctuation to be abolished (though mathematical and musical signs are allowed); and human psychology is to be replaced by a lyrical obsession with matter. He writes of an intuitive psychology or 'physiology' of matter. They will invent Wireless Imagination; they will give only the second terms of analogies, unintelligible though this may sometimes be. The result will be an 'analogical synthesis of the world embraced at one glance and expressed in essential words'. These are the *'Parole in libertà',* or *'Parolibere'*: 'After Free Verse'—the invention of Gustave Kahn whom Marinetti much admired—'we have at last Free Words.' In his *Replies to the Objections* to this *Manifesto* (11 August 1912), Marinetti describes the intuitive act of creation almost as if it were automatic writing: 'The hand that writes seems to detach itself from the body and reaches out independently far away from the brain . . .' It reads like some early foreshadowing of Breton's 'magic Surrealist art'.

Marinetti's *Zang Tumb Tuum* (dated Adrianople, October 1912) is in Free Words. Published in 1914, prefaced by a further Manifesto written the year before, and entitled *Destruction of Grammar—Wireless Imagination—Free Words,* it decrees that the new style is only to be used for the lyric, and not for philosophy, the sciences, politics, journalism or business, or indeed for Marinetti's own *Manifestos*. The basis of the new Futurist art forms—pictorial dynamism, noise-music, Free Words—lies in the new sensibility which has been conditioned by the new speed in communications. He held, as he put it, that a great daily paper is the synthesis of one whole day in the world. Each individual has multiple and simultaneous consciousnesses. He needs to see everything at a glance, to have everything explained in a couple of words. A war correspondent (before the age of television, which would presumably have delighted Marinetti) will need to explode the mechanism of Latin grammar in order to communicate in essential words his impressions—which will be largely sense impressions—and the 'vibrations of his *ego*'. Like wireless, he will link distant things through his poetry. Typographic revolution will help to express different ideas simultaneously. Twenty different types and three or four different colours can be used on one page if need be, to express ideas of differing importance and the impressions of the different senses. Molecular life, for instance, will always be expressed in italics.

This is the style of *Zang Tumb Tuum*. The impact of the new typography is immediate, particularly when contrasted with what Marinetti called the 'mythological greengroceries' of the *art nouveau* decorative style he was replacing. Words in a variety of types are splayed out over the pages, interspersed with mathematical signs, and sometimes arranged in graphic designs as in the very explicit 'hanging'. The spelling too bears witness to the liberation advocated in the opening Manifesto and to some extent achieves the marriage with onomatopoeia that Marinetti was hoping for. The 'sssssssiii ssiissii ssi-issssssiiii' of the first page, describing a train journey to Sicily while correcting the proofs of the book, expresses both the positive hopes he has for Futurism and the whistling of the train. The 'chapters' of the book are impressionistic vignettes with titles such as 'Mobilization', 'Raid', 'A Train full of Sick Soldiers'. This last is a very graphic and telegraphic account of the smells and sounds, the hopes, dreams and anguish, and the medical conditions of 1500 soldiers being taken in a locked train, under fire, from Karagatch to Istanbul. It is remarkably successful if one can break through the intelligibility barrier. (pp. 246-48)

The last technical literary *Manifesto* of the pioneering days was contemporary with the publication of *Zang Tumb Tuum;* it uses passages from this book as examples. (Later literary *Manifestos* such as the introduction to the anthology of *New Futurist Poets* [Rome 1925] and the 1937 article on *The Technique of the New Poetry* do little more than summarize the history of the movement and reiterate the definitions of Free Words.) With the baffling title *Geometric and Mechanical Splendour and Numerical Sensitivity,* it first appeared in *Lacerba* in March and April 1914. Here the technique of Free Words is brought even closer to the aesthetics of the machine; first it is likened to the controlling of a Dreadnought at war, and then to the control panels of a hydro-electric station with the sparkling perfection of their precise machinery representing the synthesis of a whole range of mountains. The depreciation of human psychology which had been noticeable in the *Technical Manifesto* of 1912 ('The warmth of a piece of iron or wood is now more exciting to us than the smiles or tears of a woman') . . . has become much more pronounced. At the front in 1911 Marinetti had noticed 'how the shining aggressive muzzle of a gun, scorched by the sun and by rapid firing, makes the sight of tortured and dying human flesh almost negligible'. In this way 'the poetry

of the human is to be supplanted by the poetry of cosmic forces. The old romantic, sentimental and Christian proportions of the story are abolished'.

Another theme taken up from the earlier *Manifestos* was the use of the verb in the infinitive, instead of in the forms related to persons or tenses. This gave 'action' to the new lyric, using the verb like the wheel of a train or the propeller of an aeroplane, and reduced human representation. As with a number of his linguistic suggestions, one is conscious that the language Marinetti is dealing with does not lend itself to this kind of experiment. English or American might have proved a much more malleable instrument for his purposes than Italian. The new 'numerical sensitivity' derives from a love of precision which prefers to describe the sound of a bell in terms of the distance over which it is audible—'bell stroke distance 20 sq. km.'—rather than by 'imprecise and ineffectual' adjectives. Similarly, the formula $+ - + - + + \times$ describes a car changing speed and accelerating.

It is natural to concentrate on *Manifestos,* partly because they give the essence of the Futurist movement as its founder saw it, but also because they were the movement's literary form *par excellence*. Marinetti possessed the flair for setting out his ideas attractively and aggressively in this form. (pp. 248-49)

Futurism had always had a political side. As early as 1909 a short political *Manifesto* with an anti-clerical message had been published for the elections. In 1911 a second *Manifesto* appeared in favour of the Libyan war. For the elections of 1913, a more evolved *Futurist Political Programme* was brought out, its first phrase reiterating, from the 1911 *Manifesto:* 'The word Italy must dominate the word Liberty'. The ideological basis was anti-clerical and anti-socialist, and what constructive proposals there were supported modernization in industry and agriculture, Irredentism, and an aggressive foreign policy. These three *Manifestos,* with other politically aggressive writings, were published together in *War the only Cure for the World* in 1915—the year of Italy's entry into the First World War. (p. 252)

[The] alliance with Fascism has ever since been the greatest stumbling block to an appreciation of Futurism. Futurism certainly contributed to the aggressive rhetoric of Fascism that allowed Mussolini to speak with pride of 'punching the stomach of the Italian *bourgeoisie*', as also to the Fascist programme of toughening up the Italians. The 'Fascist Saturday' was to be given over to gymnastics and physical training, and Mussolini wanted the Appennines reforested to 'make Italy colder and snowier'. Other ideas actually detrimental to the national cause are traceable to Futurist sources. For instance: 'Italy did not have aircraft carriers since Mussolini had proudly announced that Italy herself was a huge aircraft carrier extending into the Mediterranean'. As early as 1911 Marinetti had said in his *Second Political Manifesto*: 'Today Italy has for us the shape and the power of a Dreadnought battleship with its squadron of torpedo-boat islands'. Again during the war, when economic collapse was imminent, Mussolini apparently thought he would avoid trouble by selling off Italian art treasures—a proposal in line with the early Futurist dream of destroying museums and art galleries, as well as a later idea of capitalizing on works of art. (p. 254)

Critics have pointed out that many of the ideas of Futurism were in the air during the early years of the century, and Pavolini writing in 1924 could say that there would have been some kind of Futurism without Marinetti. But the synthesizing and aggressive publicizing of these ideas in the Futurist style was important. Many of them were taken up and fought over by other movements, particularly the Dadaists. It has also been suggested, with reference to Dos Passos, that perhaps the most important discovery of the Futurists was the realization that fragmentation, contrast, and the interplay of apparently discordant materials constituted a direct expression of the speed and diversity of modern life'. Certainly the technique of the newspaper headlines and the 'Camera Eye' in Dos Passos's *U.S.A.* recalls Marinetti's remarks about the daily paper being the synthesis of a day in the life of the world. It is perhaps time that the literary and theatrical experiments of Futurism were revalued and not allowed to be entirely overshadowed by the work of the painters and sculptors. (pp. 254-55)

> *Judy Rawson, "Italian Futurism," in* Modernism: 1890-1930, *edited by Malcolm Bradbury and James McFarlane (copyright ©1976 by Penguin Books; reprinted by permission of Penguin Books Ltd), Penguin Books Inc., 1976, pp. 243-58.*

ADDITIONAL BIBLIOGRAPHY

Apollonio, Umbro, ed. *The Documents of Twentieth-Century Art: Futurist Manifestos.* Translated by Robert Brain, R. W. Flint, J. C. Higgitt, and Caroline Tisdall. New York: The Viking Press, 1973, 232 p.
   Anthology of the most important Futurist manifestos on literature, art, music, architecture, clothing, and other subjects.

Clough, Rosa Trillo. *Futurism: The Story of a Modern Art Movement: A New Appraisal.* New York: Philosophical Library, 1961, 297 p.*
   Study of Futurist art, literature, and music, with a lengthy section on Futurism's post-World War II influence in these areas.

Dashwood, Julie R. "Futurism and Fascism." *Italian Studies* XXVII (1972): 91-103.
   Examines the social and political climate in Italy that enabled the rise of both Futurism and Fascism.

Goldberg, Isaac. "Italy: Francesco T. Marinetti." In his *The Drama of Transition: Native and Exotic Playcraft,* pp. 160-72. Cincinnati: Stewart Kidd Co., 1922.
   Denigrates Futurist theater, concluding that the sensation-seeking dramatic theories of Futurism "are as false as any that seek to encompass all creation in a dogma; their performances add strangeness to that inherent falsity.

Payne, Richard M. "Marinetti's *Le Futurisme* and Apollinaire's *Les Peintres Cubistes.*" In *Studies in Comparative Literature,* edited by Waldo F. McNeir, pp. 173-85. Baton Rouge: Louisiana State University Press, 1962.*
   Discusses aesthetic differences and similarities between Marinetti's 1909 manifesto of Futurist principles and those of Apollinaire's critical study of the Cubist movement and its leading artists.

Simon, Anne. "F. T. Marinetti and Some Principles of Futurism." *Poet Lore* XXVI, No. 6 (November-December 1915): 738-41.
   Defines the general principles of Futurist aesthetics and philosophy. Following this essay are several of Simon's translations of Marinetti's poems.

"Forward with Futurism." *The Times Literary Supplement,* No. 3695 (29 December 1972): 1578.
   Criticizes the scholarship and translation of the editor of Marinetti's *Selected Writings.*

Vinall, Shirley W. "Marinetti and the English Contributors to *Poesia.*" *Modern Language Review* 75, No. 3 (July 1980): 547-60.
   Article that examines "Marinetti's relationships with the English writers whose work he published in his magazine *Poesia,*" discussing such contributors as W. B. Yeats, Arthur Symons, and John Masefield.

Wilkins, Ernest Hatch. "Writers of the Twentieth Century." In his *A History of Italian Literature,* pp. 478-95. Cambridge: Harvard University Press, 1954.*
   Brief sketch of Marinetti's life that also discusses the chief traits of the Futurist movement.

Sōseki Natsume

1867-1916

(Pseudonym of Kinnosuke Natsume; also wrote under pseudonym of Gudabutsu) Japanese novelist, essayist, poet, and critic.

Sōseki is considered the first major novelist of modern Japan. His greatest novels are concerned with the effects of Japan's transition from an insular, feudal culture to a modern society based on Western models. This was the primary concern of the Meiji period (1868-1912), when Japanese writers sought to unite the best values of East and West while still retaining a national identity. Sōseki examined the more painful consequences of this era, exploring the agony of that transition and the moral dilemmas of individuals caught in the historical conflict between Japanese traditions and the influence of Western individualism. Sōseki believed that the Westernization of Japan was forcing his country to digest in a few decades what had evolved in the West over centuries, and that the pressure of this change was creating a sense of emptiness and alienation in the Japanese people. In his most important works Sōseki examined the resulting isolation of individuals in modern society, while also experimenting with the form of the Japanese novel, especially narrative point of view.

Sōseki was born in Tokyo to a well-to-do family. However, loss of the family fortune forced Sōseki's parents to place him in a foster home when he was two years old. When his foster parents were divorced seven years later, he was returned to his family. Some critics have contended that Sōseki's later feelings of loneliness and alienation stem from his early experience as an unwanted child. However, it is just as often noted that late nineteenth-century Japan was involved in a turbulent period of vast cultural changes, and Sōseki's sense of personal isolation can be explained by the rapid deterioration of traditional Japanese values and the growing impersonality of modern culture.

As a young man, Sōseki became a student of English literature and received a degree in English studies from Tokyo Imperial University. He taught school for several years thereafter in various provincial towns. During this period he began composing essays and stories, and became quite proficient in haiku poetry. In 1900, Sōseki was awarded a scholarship by the Ministry of Education to study in England. His two years in London were spent in overwhelming isolation, attended by intellectual and emotional strain that resulted in an emotional breakdown. This experience is vividly described in his most autobiographical novel, *Michikusa (Grass on the Wayside)*. It was during this time of personal pain and intense study of English literature that Sōseki realized the impossibility of imitating Western art, and became interested in developing a novel that combined the methods of the Western psychological novel with the traditional lyricism of the Japanese novel.

In 1903, upon his return from England, Sōseki became the successor to Lafcadio Hearn for the chair in the English Department at Tokyo University. Four years later, after the serialization and popular success of *Wagahai wa neko de aru (I Am a Cat)*, Sōseki resigned his chair to become literary editor of *Asahi*, the largest daily newspaper in Japan. All of his

subsequent novels were serialized in *Asahi*. During this time his home became a major artistic salon for a group of artists and writers who came to be called the Neo-Idealists. The Neo-Idealists were reacting against the romantic literature of the previous generation, which presented noble characters devoid of human failings. They also opposed the contemporary school of Naturalism, which was completely devoid of idealism and seemed preoccupied with the ugliest aspects of human nature. The solution of the Neo-Idealists was to create a literature that examined characters who could serve as models for behavior, who understood their own worst impulses and tried to control them. Many of Sōseki's late novels fit this mold.

Sōseki began writing novels in 1905. By the time of his death in 1916, he had published more than a dozen. In his early works, which were influenced greatly by his readings in English literature, Sōseki was concerned with the effect that egotism and a quest for individuality have on individuals and society. In both realms he felt that egotism destroyed the possibility for any completely honest human relationships. His earliest novels satirized the egotistical. In *I Am a Cat* the narrator, a tomcat, mocks the pretense found in a professor's life and in the lives of his circle of friends. *Botchan*, drawn from Sōseki's experience as a teacher, satirizes the corrupt atmosphere of a provincial school, as well as Sōseki's own youthful idealism, as personified by a quixotic schoolteacher seeking to reform petty hypocrisies. It was with *Kusamakura (The Three-Cornered World)* that Sōseki tried to formulate an individual solution to the problems of hypocrisy and alienation in the modern world by promoting a more radical form of egoism—the deliberate cultivation of an aloof egocentricity and the negation of all emotional ties. This remedy is also explored in three other important novels of the period, all of which realize Sōseki's desire to create a Japanese psychological novel; *Sanshirō, Sorekara (And Then),* and *Mon.* In each of these novels the protagonists are disillusioned men who have betrayed or been betrayed by others, and who seek to remove themselves from the pain of existence by noninvolvement with others. All three novels depict, to some extent, the failure of this ideal of aloof egocentricity as a practical solution to the pain of living. In the last of these, the protagonist seeks consolation in Zen and cultivates an attitude of resignation rather than rejection, a solution that typifies Sōseki's later and greater novels.

Sōseki termed his new approach to the problems of alienation *sokuten kyoshi,* a philosophy that called for individuals to model themselves after heaven in order to transcend the self and its attendant pains. This philosophy was embodied in the lives of several characters in his later novels, with varying degrees of success. The most important work of this period is the trilogy of novels *Higan sugi made, Kōjin (The Wayfarer),* and *Kokoro.* Of these, *The Wayfarer* is considered one of Sōseki's most mature works. The novel examines both a domestic impasse—a husband and wife who question their love for each other are bound by tradition to their "arranged" marriage—and the effects of encroaching Western values on Japanese traditions.

Sōseki died before he could complete *Meian (Light and Darkness),* which many consider to be the triumph of his psychological method. In this novel Sōseki examines in detail the personalities of six characters who inhabit varying degrees of moral development on a spectrum ranging from egotism (darkness) to complete peace and self-abnegation (light). V.H. Viglielmo notes that in these six characters Sōseki deftly described the discord in modern Japanese life, and suggested its resolution in the character of Kiyoko, the embodiment of light and *sokuten kyoshi.* Though he saw no resolution to the multiple dilemmas of modern Japan, Sōseki held out hope for individual resolution through complete abnegation of the self. As Viglielmo notes: "Sōseki's entire artistic life may be represented as a progression from a view of man as ridiculous to a view of man as infinitely precious, from a standpoint of satire verging on cynicism to one of deepest compassion, or in symbolic terms, from his nameless cat's impudent grin to Kiyoko's beatific smile."

Although most of Sōseki's characters, according to Edwin McClellan, never attain faith, *sokuten kyoshi* remains an important ideal that aids them in realizing that individual isolation is something that can only be accepted, not transcended. There is no escape from the human condition but death, no peace but through resignation. Critics note that, through his novels, Sōseki illuminated a major problem of modern Japan and of modern life in general. In his greatest works he illustrated the problems of transition that individuals in all modern societies encounter.

(See also *TCLC,* Vol. 2, and *Contemporary Authors,* Vol. 104.)

PRINCIPAL WORKS

Wagahai wa neko de aru. 3 vols.   (novel)   1905-07
   [*I Am a Cat.* 2 vols., 1906-09]

Botchan   (novel)   1907
   [*Botchan (Master Darling),* 1918]
Bungakuron   (criticism)   1907
Kusamakura   (novel)   1907
   [*Unhuman Tour (Kusamakura),* 1927; also published as
      The Three-Cornered World, 1965]
Gubijinso   (novel)   1908
   [*Red Poppy* published in journal *Japan Magazine,* 1918]
Nowaki   (novel)   1908
Sanshirō   (novel)   1909
   [*Sanshiro,* 1933]
Sorekara   (novel)   1910
   [*And Then,* 1978]
Mon   (novel)   1911
   [*Mon,* 1972]
Higan sugi made   (novel)   1912
Kōjin   (novel)   1914
   [*The Wayfarer (Kojin),* 1967]
Kokoro   (novel)   1914
   [*Kokoro,* 1941]
Michikusa   (novel)   1915
   [*Grass on the Wayside (Michikusa),* 1969]
Meian   (unfinished novel)   1917
   [*Light and Darkness,* 1971]
Sōseki zenshu. 14 vols.   (novels, essays, poetry, and
      criticism)   1924-25

OKAZAKI YOSHIE   (essay date 1955)

[*In this brief survey of Sōseki's career, Okazaki describes him as an innovative writer who embraced, then developed beyond, several twentieth-century Japanese literary movements. Okazaki is particularly concerned with delineating Sōseki's development from a romantic to a proponent of the Neo-Idealism movement.*]

At about the same time as the rise of Naturalism, the activity of Natsume Sōseki (Kinnosuke), who is the founder of Neo-Idealism, attracted the attention of the literary world. It was in January 1905 that Sōseki's first works, *Wagahai wa Neko de Aru (I Am a Cat)* and *Rondon Tō (The Tower of London),* were made public. . . . Sōseki's emergence preceded Naturalism somewhat, and occurred at a time when the afterglow of Romanticism had not yet disappeared. Thus, the fact that the beginning of Sōseki's writing career should have such deep romantic overtones can be said to be one reflection of the current of the time. Another reason Sōseki is considered to be the source of Neo-Idealism is that he was a writer who held an anti-Naturalist position. (p. 268)

Wagahai wa Neko de Aru is a *haiku*-type *shaseibun* piece, but its core is the satire and humor derived from English literature, particularly that of the eighteenth century prose writers. On top of this is reared even a scholarly, idealistic superstructure. Disguised as a tomcat, the author criticizes his own life, and satirizes the world of vanity and pretense that surrounds him. This book is certainly the work of an intellect of genius, and underneath it runs a deep current of ethical idealism. We can say that the ideal of his later life, *sokuten kyoshi* (to model oneself after heaven and depart from the self), is already present here in foetal form. Together with violent humor and an almost excessive introspection, there is the evident zeal to penetrate to the very heart of existence.

But this Sōseki, who as a realist turns his penetrating glance at the various aspects of human life, for several years did not develop in a straight line. *Rondom Tō,* which appeared at the same time, can be thought of as a realistic travelogue-like account of his London sightseeing during his stay abroad, but there are many scenes where he calls up the past history of the Tower which are exceedingly romantic in tone. Both *Maboroshi no Tate (The Phantom Shield)* and *Kairokō (The Song of Evanescence),* which next appeared, derived their material from European medieval legend, and giving free rein to his imagination, he attempted to describe in a mystic atmosphere the power of an undivided love. *Koto no Sorane (The False Sound of the Lute)* and *Ichiya (One Night)* have their setting in Japan, but they are still attempts at evoking a fantastic, mystic, and romantic beauty. (pp. 269-70)

Botchan, Kusamakura, and *Nihyakutōka (The Two Hundred Tenth Day)* further indicate the development of Sōseki's romanticism.

Kusamakura has as its setting the Oama Hot Spring in the vicinity of Kumamoto where he taught before going abroad, and while creating a peaceful Oriental poetic world in the midst of a pastoral nature and Zen adherents, he describes the mind of a painter who is attempting an aesthetic discipline of isolation from the world, and the character of a strange, beautiful girl, Nami, as reflected in this painter's eyes. (p. 270)

For *Botchan* Sōseki gathered his material from his teaching experience at a middle school in Matsuyama, and the principal character, a forthright and naive teacher, who is really the author himself, suffers in the corrupt school atmosphere, and finally returns to Tōkyō after having visited a just punishment on a group of sycophants and hypocrites centering around Red Shirt, the nickname that Botchan has given one of the teachers. Its plot and style, and the fact that it is filled with satire and ethical concern, appear to put it in direct opposition to the aesthetic, transcendental tone of *Kusamakura;* yet both of them deeply reflect the author's subjective spirit, and we can see his strong emphasis on a romantic ideal. *Kusamakura* demonstrates the union of beauty and religion in the union of the painter and Nami, while *Botchan* tries to show, in the conflict of Botchan and Red Shirt, the loneliness that results when the spirit of justice and simplicity has to struggle in vain in a world of injustice and vanity. Both of these works are the reflection of the author's inner spirit, and they are simply expressed as a romantic dream. (pp. 270-71)

[In *Gubijinsō (The Red Poppy)*] he gives final synthesis and unity to the romantic qualities that had appeared in his works until then. Its main female character, Fujio, is similar to Nami of *Kusamakura* in that she is a woman of strong will, but she demonstrates a personality of rather modern feminity, and the novel is an account of how this proud, egocentric personality and behavior are finally destroyed and how Fujio meets a sudden death. Surrounding her there move Munechika, who is a natural man removed from the self, the philosopher Kōno, who endeavors to depart from the world of vanity and enter into the truth, and the brilliant Ono, who even though he is tempted by Fujio, returns to the world of moral law. The author here shows for the last time his brilliant colors. The construction is also elaborate, with one dramatic scene following another, but the central idea appears to be a kind of idealism that teaches the truth that when the modern ego separates itself from a moral foundation a terrible tragedy occurs. At the same time it indicates that the final destination of the self is nothing other

than a truthful and undefiled naturalness which is in the direction of Sōseki's ultimate ideal of *sokuten kyoshi.*

With this work Sōseki's romantic period ends, and in the following year he advanced strikingly toward realism; however, from one viewpoint, he was unwilling to allow these early ideals to remain only in the world of romantic fancy, and seeking them anew in actual life, he embarked upon his career of intense experiment.

Sōseki first published *Kōfu (The Miner),* attempting, with a detailed realistic method, an analysis of the psychology of a youth who agrees to work in a mine. He approaches the Naturalistic position at the end of the novel, when he looks at the semi-light, semi-dark, indecisive world as the true picture of life. And yet in this novel also there burn the ethical ideals which prize human sincerity.

Sanshirō, which followed, represents the author's characteristic realistic method, and in it he gives a penetrating analysis of the psychology of the late Meiji youth that was awakening to a recognition of self. The main character, Sanshirō, leaves the country and enters Tōkyō student life, where he is perplexed by the new atmosphere and where he is unable to assess the complex personality of a young woman of the new era, Mineko, and is disturbed at not knowing whether he is loved by her or is being made a fool of by her. The author himself calls Mineko an unconscious hypocrite, and as one of the characters, the philosopher Hirota, says, she is the embodiment of the modern woman whose personality is a riddle. Later in O-Nao of *Kōjin (The Passerby)* he adds even further complexities to the modern woman as a wife, but in *Sanshirō* we are able to see one facet of Sōseki's view of women. Sanshirō is the embodiment of the modern egoism that is in the process of losing all sincerity, and Mineko is his female counterpart, although the process in her case is further advanced.

Sanshirō depicts young men and women who have awakened to the modern ego but who on account of it fall into the evils of individualism, and are unable easily to cast themselves into an altruistic situation. It is a picture of unfulfilled love. Daisuke, the principal of *Sore Kara (And Then)* which appeared in the following year, endeavors to recover Michiyo, the only woman he can truly love, whom he has handed over to his close friend Hiraoka, but since love also is placed in society, he must receive as well the punishment that accompanies this gift. He finally despairs of ever recovering Michiyo from Hiraoka. This work is an account of how even a person who can feel the will of Heaven in the midst of the pretensions of the self is unable to accomplish his love.

Mon (The Gate), which together with the above-mentioned two works constitutes a trilogy, appeared in the following year, 1910. This work is the story of Sōsuke, who has betrayed his best friend to marry his wife and who enjoys this sad love secretly while living with her almost as a recluse in a corner of society; when, however, the friend who has disappeared for awhile reappears, Sōsuke falls into a state of uneasiness, and without telling his wife anything, goes alone to knock at the gate of a Zen Buddhist temple to seek peace of mind. The gate (hence the title), however, does not open, and Sōsuke knows he is fated to stand forever outside it. One who has bravely achieved his love also must bear the burden of a life of anxiety. And yet this trilogy which treats of the spiritual struggle that comes from love, is not a denial of love.

After having produced this trilogy, Sōseki underwent a serious illness, and in 1911 he published only a series of essays entitled

Omoidasu Koto Nado (**Random Recollections**), which told of his experiences during his illness. This illness, however, further deepened the mind of the author, and after having faced death, his eyes, which searched the patterns of existence, became even sharper. He looked now beyond temporary falseness, and never ceased to seek a religious enlightenment. *Higan Sugi Made* (**Until after the Spring Equinox**), which appeared in the following year . . . , marks a new starting-point.

This work has a novel construction in that it is made up of several independent stories linked together; in this group, "Sunaga's Story" is the most significant, and in it he probes most deeply the sickness in the modern ego. (pp. 271-74)

In order to pursue further the fate of the egoist who is entangled by his ego, Sōseki continued to write full-length novels after the beginning of Taishō, and finally, by means of his philosophy of *sokuten kyoshi*, he arrived at the threshold of a world of divine purity. These later Meiji works at first glance appeared to be Naturalistic, but actually they were stages on the road to his final ideal. (p. 274)

> Okazaki Yoshie, "The Rise of Neo-Idealism," in Japanese Literature in the Meiji Era, *edited by Okazaki Yoshie, translated by V. H. Viglielmo, Obunsha, 1955, pp. 268-316.*

EDWIN McCLELLAN   (essay date 1958-59)

[*In the following excerpt McClellan, a major critic of modern Japanese literature and important translator of Sōseki's work, examines in detail the novel* Kokoro. *For a more extended discussion of Sōseki's work by McClellan, see* TCLC, *Vol. 2.*]

Kokoro appeared in 1914, two years before Sōseki's death. The novel is told in the first person all the way through. Sōseki must not, of course, be identified with the narrators in *Kokoro.* Yet we feel, when reading the novel, that the power which moves the characters to their end manipulates the author himself with equal force and inevitability. And perhaps it is because Sōseki seems to share this helplessness with his own characters that *Kokoro* is so convincing a novel.

The construction of the novel deserves at least a cursory examination, for it significantly reflects the intention of the novelist. It is divided into three parts. The first two are narrated by Sensei's young friend, and the third by Sensei himself. In Part I, we see Sensei through the young man's eyes, and with the narrator, we begin to see that some tragic event in Sensei's past has overshadowed his life. Part II is outwardly concerned with the young man's relationship with his family, though throughout, we feel the shadowy presence of Sensei in the background. Part III is the central part of the novel. For it is here that we discover Sensei's terrible secret: his betrayal of K, and the latter's suicide. At the end of the novel, we know that Sensei also will kill himself.

It may be objected that Parts I and II form too long an introduction to Part III. . . . When we read Parts I and II carefully, we find that everything the young man tells us has a place in the scheme of the novel. And if we regard *Kokoro* as not only the story of Sensei's despair, but of the growing sense of isolation of his young friend, then surely the first two parts are crucial to our understanding of the novel as a whole.

The young man is far from being a static bystander. He grows in the course of his own narrative. And as he leaves adolescence and enters manhood, we see that he too will suffer from the deep sense of isolation that has been the curse of his mentor's life. (pp. 116-17)

Slowly the sunlight fades away from his life, and evening sets in. The pain of the older man's life is gradually transmitted to his young friend. Never again does the young man make similar references to the bright sun. The world around him does not lose its beauty for him, but it becomes somehow grey and tranquil, and the emotions it evokes in him are hauntingly sad. (p. 117)

Sensei would lose much of his significance as a human being if we did not see him first, in his full maturity, as he appeared to another man. Moreover, it is the young man's love for him that forces Sensei to write his letter. And, most important of all, it is through our understanding of the young man's suffering that we are asked to see the tragedy of Sensei's life as something which is not unique, but which is human.

Regarded in this light, even Part II, which is concerned solely with the young man and his family, becomes an important part of the novel. Here, what Sōseki seems to be stressing is the young man's gradual alienation from his father, mother, and his elder brother, which culminates in his sudden departure for Tōkyō when his father is dying. (p. 118)

His family will never forgive him for deserting his father's bedside. And Sensei, his only friend, is about to kill himself. We cannot but notice the implied parallel between the fate of the young man and that of Sensei.

It is possible that in Part II, Sōseki intended to stress the contrast between the relative contentment of the young man's conventional parents and the suffering of his friend and mentor, Sensei. But there is a certain obviousness in this interpretation. It would lead us to suppose, for instance, that Sōseki's primary intention was to remind us of the happiness of those who humbly and unthinkingly accept convention as opposed to the unhappiness of those who, like Sensei, seriously question it. . . . [But what] is really crucial to our understanding of the father's place in the novel is the manner of his dying. In Sōseki's eyes, his death is more ignoble than that of either Sensei or K. (pp. 119-20)

The old man, however, is far from being a mere figure of contempt. Despite his lack of imagination, despite his slavish regard for convention, he retains a certain dignity even on his sickbed. This dignity is little more than that which any man might possess who has lived his life in a formally decent and dutiful manner. It is there nevertheless, and Sōseki's subtle art can be seen in the way he makes such a person as this affect us deeply. (p. 120)

Though the old man differs from Sensei and K in that he feels his loneliness because he is dying, while the other two kill themselves because of their loneliness, he does nevertheless share with them the same experience of isolation from other human beings. Despite the presence of his family around his deathbed, he is absolutely alone as he faces death.

Simply because we understand death to be the cessation of life, many of us have come to regard life and death as opposite conditions, negating each other. But to the author of *Kokoro,* death is not merely the only escape from loneliness in life, as in the case of Sensei and K, but the clearest confirmation of the truth about every man's life; namely, that the profoundest experiences which each of us undergoes are not communicable to others. There will always be an insurmountable wall between two people, no matter how much they may love each other. (p. 121)

We are reminded here of that question of Ichirō's in *Kōjin*: "What is it that brings your heart and my heart together? And what is it that parts them?"

It is only by recognizing the supreme importance of the theme of isolation in Sōseki's major novels that we may understand their significance. It is really not their sense of wrong-doing that brings the protagonists together; it is their sense of loneliness. True, the protagonists of *Sorekara, Mon,* and *Kokoro* are all conscious of having betrayed other men; and Ichirō in *Kōjin,* though not betrayer himself, is equally guilty of unjust conduct, for he suspects his innocent wife and brother of having betrayed him. However, the significance of betrayal in these novels lies not so much in the sense of guilt or sin involved, as in the fact that it sharpens the sense of loneliness of the protagonists. To say that guilt plays no part in Sōseki's novels would of course be an exaggeration. But for Sōseki, the recognition of man's sinfulness is not the key to the understanding of man's essential condition. The suffering of Sensei, caused by his own betrayal of K, gives him insight not into man's capacity for evil-doing, but into his loneliness. . . . (pp. 121-22)

Sōseki speaks often as though loneliness were peculiar to modern man. The question is whether loneliness is primarily a contemporary social phenomenon for Sōseki, or an eternal human condition. Perhaps the answer lies in the fact that a tragic writer of Sōseki's perception and sensitivity would not view man's suffering wholly as a product of some particular set of social or historical circumstances. (p. 122)

At any rate, it was his opinion that because of the very rapid social change, the Japanese were fast becoming a nation of neurotics: "We have had to do in ten years what the West took a hundred years to accomplish." There could be no relaxation, he said, amidst such hurried progress. (p. 123)

But it would be wrong to conclude from this that Sensei's loneliness, or Ichirō's, stems from their having being born in the modern age. Accidents of time and place may increase one's sense of isolation, but they do not create it. The accidental and essential are sometimes confused in the minds of Sōseki's protagonists. Sensei, for example, seems to take some comfort in the thought that he is separated from the young man by their difference in years: "You and I belong to different eras, and so we think differently. There is nothing to bridge the gap between us." But what he says right after this is significant: "Of course, it may be more correct to say that we are different simply because we are two separate human beings."

Finally, the construction of those novels which precede *Kokoro* and of the only completed one which follows it bears a significant relationship to the spiritual condition of their protagonists, in that none of the novels have what one might call a satisfactory ending. There can be only one explanation for this; which is that only death will end the suffering of the protagonists. . . . Faith or madness cannot really provide an alternative for Sōseki's protagonists therefore; and if they do not kill themselves, they must, like Kenzō or Sōsuke in *Mon*, live the rest of their lives in bitter resignation, waiting each year for the winter to come. (pp. 123-24)

Edwin McClellan, "Implications of Sōseki's 'Kokoro'," in Monumenta Nipponica, *Vol. XIV, Nos. 3 & 4, October, 1958 & January, 1959, pp. 110-24.*

SAKUKO MATSUI   (essay date 1967)

[*Matsui discusses the influence of English and American literature on Sōseki's work. In particular, he notes how Sōseki borrowed the structure of the English novel to extend the possibilities of the traditional Japanese novel.*]

[Soseki's] formative years fell in the Meiji period, and he was among the few writers who successfully expressed the agony of living in a changing period, although his problems were shared, consciously or unconsciously, by all other writers and to some extent by the educated youth of the time. Yet his interests extended to something more universal, so that his writing has great intrinsic merit and continues to have a significance even for contemporary readers. (pp. 282-83)

Soseki published two works while he was at the university. *On poems of Walt Whitman, a representative egalitarian writer* . . . begins: 'It is the French who tried politically to realize Revolutionalism. It is the English who displayed it in literature.' He welcomes the appearance of egalitarian poems even more powerful than those of Shelley and Byron. Whitman is the true representative of America, the only nation that could have given him birth. Soseki's discussion of Whitman's conception of an ideal republic based upon 'manly love of comrades' goes little beyond simple exegesis. Yet his understanding and appreciation were remarkable for a young man of twenty-five, still a university student. Soseki shows a deep sympathy with Whitman's egalitarianism, independence and optimism. Independent and individualistic by temperament, Soseki came gradually to form from western literature an ideal for his individualism. But optimism, if he ever had any, was to be shattered as he inevitably realized the gulf between his ideal and the reality of life in Meiji Japan.

As a man of his time, Soseki found in Whitman some points hardly admirable for a Japanese with a background of a thousand years of Confucian thought. (p. 287)

His second university work, *English poets' ideas of Nature,* is a treatise on the development of the idea of Nature in 18th and 19th century poets such as Pope, Addison, Thomson, Goldsmith, Cowper, and in particular, Burns and Wordsworth. Though it is not clear whether Burns's 'emotional intuition' or Wordsworth's 'philosophical intuition' appealed more, Soseki's own attitudes towards Nature seem to have been somewhat closer to Burns's. . . .

In spite of his reputation as a scholar of English literature he was not happy. His later confession in the Introduction to *On Literature* is bitter. He feels as if he 'may have been deceived by English Literature' which he had taken up in the hope that 'it might not be a matter for regret to spend even a lifetime in its study'. (p. 288)

Soseki stayed in Kyushu [on Shikoku Island] for four years until the Ministry of Education ordered him abroad to study in England. During this Kyushu period, besides writing *haiku* and Chinese poems, he published three essays. The first on *Tristram Shandy,* was an introduction to Lawrence Sterne for Japanese readers. Soseki's sympathy with this extraordinary novel of learned wit led him to write, eight years afterwards, his own novel of learned wit, *I am a Cat,* which immediately won general recognition and went through thirty-five impressions in the author's lifetime.

The second essay, **'English men of letters and newspapers and magazines,'** a brief sketch of the rise and development of journalism in England and its relationship to literature, shows that

Soseki had considerable interest in the social background of literature and in English writers' concern with politics. Journalism and political concern by writers were virtually unknown in pre-Meiji Japan.

The third essay, **'On the Novel *Aylwin*,'** is a critical introduction to W. T. Watts-Dunton's *Aylwin,* which had been published with great success in England, in 1898. This essay gives an impression that Soseki had read by this time most of the major works of the English novel from the 18th century onwards. That Soseki chose so contemporary works as *Leaves of Grass* and *Aylwin* for the subjects of his early essays suggests that he had a stronger inclination to literary pursuits than to academic research. Had it been his sole aim to become a distinguished scholar of English literature it seems more likely he would have been devoting himself to, say, Shakespeare or English poetry. (p. 289)

[What] his study in London yielded, besides a nervous breakdown and the rumour that Soseki had gone mad, was *On Literature,* written originally as lecture notes immediately after his return and published in 1907. The book, an analysis and criticism of the content of English literature, is very systematic, perhaps too systematic, and very dry. It merits respect, however, as an early attempt by a Japanese scholar based on honest and independent inquiry. (p. 290)

His greatness is that he made his country's spiritual conflict the starting point of his own writing, and developed his work out of his own struggle with the problem. (p. 291)

His lectures [given at Tokyo University], published later as *Literary Criticism,* were on the General Background, Addison and Steele, Swift, Pope and Defoe. The book remains interesting and useful for present-day students. Characteristically, Soseki had the greatest sympathy with Swift. But the frustration and impatience with which Soseki writes is particularly noticeable. By the time he wrote those lectures, he had begun his own creative work—novels and short stories, 'products of my nervous breakdown and madness'. *Haiku* and Chinese poems had long ceased satisfactorily to express his ideas and feelings. The only academic work he wrote for publication during this period was **'On the Ghost in *Macbeth*'**, which has been called 'such an excellent essay for its fine logic and original ideas that had it been written in English, it would have been compared with De Quincey's "On the Knocking at the Gate in *Macbeth*"'.

It is generally accepted that Soseki was 'influenced' by George Meredith and that he found his ideal model in Jane Austen. But the influence on Soseki of western literature is of a more general and profound nature.

Soseki wrote four novels and several short stories while teaching at the university, and ten novels and a few short stories during his nine years as a professional novelist, between 1907, when he resigned from the university at forty, and 1916, the year of his death.

His early novels give the impression of the release of a flood of pent-up ideas. His mastery of language enabled him to write incredibly quickly. Some of these novels have a stylistic basis in the *Rakugo* storyteller's technique; the mode of expression of others is drawn from his early training in *haiku* and Chinese poems. Yet while ***Pillow of Grass*** (recently translated into English as **'The Three-Cornered World'**), claimed by the author to be 'a novel of detachment' and 'a *haiku*-like novel', is a vindication of the tradition of eastern aesthetics, Soseki was unable to remain 'detached', and his essential involvement

produced the satire of ***Botchan*** and ***I am a Cat*** and the criticism of modern Japan in ***Winter's Wind***.

Botchan still remains one of the most popular Japanese novels. The story is written in a terse and vigorous style, using the vernacular speech of Tokyo. The narrator is a headstrong young man of rather conventional morals. In the country school where the adventures of the naïve and comic hero take place, Soseki detects many of the characteristics of modern Japanese life— such legacies of feudalism as a lack of individualism and independence and an undue emphasis on loyalty to superiors. The English satirical tradition, no doubt contributed to Soseki's ***Botchan*** and ***I am a Cat***.

In his next novel, ***Winter's Wind*** . . . , Soseki attempted even more direct social criticism, but as a novel it is not a great success and cannot compare with the achievement of ***And Then*** . . . , the fourth novel of his professional period. ***And Then*** . . . , is a mature and successful treatment of the problem of a young intellectual in late Meiji Japan.

Soseki was seriously concerned with the right conduct for a modern man caught in the conflict between western individualism and Japanese traditions based on 'the national polity' and the family system. Like many other writers of his time, however, Soseki's pursuit of this problem did not lead him to a consideration of broad social issues. He held, of course, that individual morality was higher than stage morality. But gradually he turned to the investigation of individual personality. This was probably due to an intense interest in himself, and to the tragic fact that the individualist in Japan of his time was fated to stand isolated from the great mass of the people. The 'loneliness' of human existence became the theme of his later novels such as ***Until after the Autumn Equinox, Passers-by*** and ***Kokoro***. This can make his later novels of great interest to the West in its present obsession with the inevitable isolation of the individual.

Soseki was always interested in the structure of the novel. He had learnt from his English studies what the novel is and how to write it. Interest in structure had been totally absent in the Japanese tradition since the 12th century. Now Soseki felt obliged to treat each of his novels as a new experiment. At the cost of some awkward and pathetic failures, Soseki advanced towards the creation of the modern Japanese novel.

Light and Dark, his last work, is a long unfinished novel of more than 600 pages which stands out in the history of the modern Japanese novels. In this psychological novel Soseki describes the discord between a young Tokyo white-collar worker and his newly-married wife. The incidents of this tightly constructed work take place within a space of two weeks. In contrast to his former works, in almost every one of which Soseki had an intellectual hero, the protagonist of this novel, although a university graduate, is a mediocre salaried man. And quite unlike his earlier female characters, the wife is a very vivid and interesting woman, unusual in modern Japanese fiction— at least, as written by men. The conflicts, therefore, between them and between each and a third party, depicted with penetrating insight, appeal to us with a force rare in Japanese novels. Soseki had finally achieved in the novel form, originally developed in England, a near perfect expression of the reality of modern Japanese life. (pp. 292-94)

Sakuko Matsui, "East and West in Natsume Soseki: The Formation of a Modern Japanese Novelist" (originally a paper delivered at the University of New

England in January, 1967), in Meanjin, Vol. XXVI, No. 3, September, 1967, pp. 282-94.

V. H. VIGLIELMO (essay date 1967)

[*Viglielmo provides a detailed analysis of Sōseki's* Light and Darkness, *with particular emphasis given to a discussion of the novel's characters and how they reflect Sōseki's personal dilemmas.*]

Grass on the Wayside, his last complete work, is Sōseki's only clearly autobiographical novel, although it is written in the third person and all of the names, together with many of the details, are changed from what they were in actuality. This work can be viewed as providing a complete catharsis for Sōseki in that he unsparingly dissected his own egoism in the same way that he had dissected that of his other principal characters in his earlier works. It is almost as if he was intent on cleansing his own spirit before embarking on his most ambitious portrayal of egoism, **Light and Darkness,** the very ambitiousness of which may have been responsible for his not living to complete it. (pp. 377-78)

How then did Sōseki culminate his work as an artist in this last mammoth novel, **Light and Darkness?** At first reading this work may appear commonplace, for it certainly cannot be denied that it treats lives and events which are ordinary in the extreme. Yet Sōseki has achieved an extraordinary work while thus utilizing the most ordinary material.

The action of the novel covers some ten days during which Tsuda Yoshio, a company official, enters the hospital for treatment of a fistula and after the operation goes off for a few days to a hot spring to recuperate. This is practically the entire substance of the external action of the novel. Quite obviously, therefore, Sōseki's attention is directed towards the workings of the minds and hearts of the principal characters. For around Tsuda revolve five persons who are related to him in various ways: O-Nobu, his wife; O-Hide, his younger sister; Mrs. Yoshikawa, the wife of the president of the company where he works; Kobayashi, his 'friend' from school days; and Kiyoko, his former sweetheart who is now married.

The main theme of the novel is the operation which is performed on Tsuda, and its outcome. Komiya Toyotaka, the foremost critic of Sōseki and author of the definitive biography, was the first to point out the symbolic significance of the opening section which deals with the necessity of Tsuda's undergoing an operation. Komiya states, and all succeeding critics have agreed with him, that while Tsuda must undergo an operation on his body, he must also undergo a much more basic and far-reaching operation on his soul. There can be no doubt that Sōseki intended this interpretation, for without it **Light and Darkness** becomes merely another 'medical' novel. . . . (pp. 381-82)

The necessity for the operation is clearly indicated and Tsuda dutifully undergoes it, that is, the physical phase of it. The spiritual operation cannot be performed so simply, and there are certain critics who feel that the major aspect of it was yet to be treated at the time the novel was broken off. I feel, however, that there is ample proof in the section which exists to state that Tsuda's operation was already begun and, indeed, that he was responding to treatment. (p. 382)

It is, I think, profitable in an analysis of this novel, to see the five major characters who revolve around Tsuda as each performing a part of the operation. And yet it must be remembered that the five have, in varying degrees, their own 'illnesses'

which must similarly be treated. We can see these five characters as constituting a hierarchy of value from dark to light, to use the standards of the novel itself. At the end of the spectrum nearest to Tsuda in the 'darkness' of her soul is O-Nobu, who is of course also closest to him physically. In the second position on the road to 'light' stands Mrs. Yoshikawa, who displays at every turn a worldliness and a sense of her social superiority which could hardly be termed humble or directed towards religion but who still makes a rather astute appraisal of Tsuda's essential cowardice and vanity. At a stage somewhat more advanced stands Tsuda's younger sister, O-Hide, who brings to bear in her excoriation of her brother and sister-in-law a penetrating mind and a highly evolved morality, but who, at the same time, is not wholly free from self-righteousness and an inability to forgive, and who is eaten away by jealousy of O-Nobu's freedom. Beyond the half-way point between 'light' and 'darkness' stands Kobayashi, who, though he is in abject poverty and practically begs for assistance from Tsuda and O-Nobu, displays a depth of compassion towards all suffering humanity and a quasi-prophetic insight into Tsuda's true problem. He further acts as a catalyst in speeding up the action between O-Nobu and Tsuda. At the very end of the spectrum, bathed in light, stands the beautiful figure of Kiyoko, 'the child of purity' as the Chinese characters of her name could be rendered. Significantly, also, Kiyoko appears towards the end of the work, and we thus have moved along in one direction from the 'darkness' of Tsuda's 'unoperated' condition to Kiyoko's naturalness, calm, and forgiveness.

I shall begin, then, with an analysis of the position that O-Nobu occupies in the novel, and especially of her function *vis-à-vis* Tsuda. There is a fierce controversy over her role: the pro-O-Nobu faction, the major proponents of which are younger critics such as Ara Masahito and Etō Jun, see O-Nobu as a woman maligned and consider the major culprit responsible for such defamation to be none other than her creator, Sōseki himself, for they accuse him of 'stacking the cards against her'; the anti-O-Nobu faction, which includes the late Komiya Toyotaka, see O-Nobu as the feminine counterpart of Tsuda, suffering almost as acutely from the disease of egoism as Tsuda himself. Those favouring O-Nobu have pushed the controversy quite openly into the realm of value by attaching the adjective *kindaiteki,* or 'modern', to O-Nobu; conversely, her detractors within the novel, Mrs Yoshikawa and O-Hide primarily, and outside the novel, Sōseki and the anti-O-Nobu group, are described as *hōkenteki,* or 'feudal'. Thus, O-Nobu, much more than Kiyoko, has become a symbol: to those critics who approve of her, of individualistic integrity, courage in the face of the deadening and stultifying opposition of centuries of traditional, family- or class-centred ethics; and to those critics who indict her she has become a symbol, together with Tsuda, of the egoism that eats at the moral fibre of man in no matter what century and in no matter what land, of that egoism which Sōseki sought to overcome, or perhaps more accurately, to exorcise, through his philosophy of *sokuten kyoshi.*

The major point of conflict lies, I believe, in the different emphasis—and therefore, in a sense, value—which each camp places on the will. For O-Nobu is manifestly a woman of will, a will so strong that her emergence in a Japanese novel of 1916 gives the lie to the all-too-facile assessment of the Japanese woman delivered by both native and Western authorities. (pp. 382-84)

O-Nobu reminds me of such heroines of popular Western fiction as Scarlett O'Hara, who moves through *Gone With the*

Wind with the same vigour and unquenchable vitality—in short, with the same dynamic will. And just as not one of the millions of readers of the American work begrudges his admiration of Scarlett O'Hara's strength so too do I feel that all who read *Light and Darkness* must, of necessity, admire O-Nobu. (pp. 384-85)

It cannot be denied by the most ardent of O-Nobu's admirers that her actions are scarcely motivated by altruism or that her will is employed for sheer self-gratification. Her major goal, namely the forcing of her husband to love her, and her alone, is sought by methods which may appear to be a glorification of the individual as opposed to the family or class but which, on closer analysis, reveal themselves as crassly selfish. (p. 385)

O-Nobu suspects that Tsuda is still emotionally attached to someone else, as indeed he is to Kiyoko, who suddenly on the eve of their engagement broke off relations with him and married, shortly thereafter, a man named Seki, who never appears in the novel. . . . Once roused, O-Nobu's mind, usually alert, becomes an exquisitely sensitive antenna to gather more information on which to base her actions. She accepts the challenge almost with eagerness, and moves forth to do battle. . . . The 'one word' which O-Nobu wishes to hear, namely that Tsuda loves only her, is of course not forthcoming, and she must continue her struggle alone. (pp. 385-86)

Although O-Nobu is sick with the same disease as Tsuda, the symptoms are entirely different. Also, I definitely do not think that her case is as serious as her husband's. Within the terms of the symbolism of the novel in Section 1 she is even less susceptible to becoming 'tubercular' than Tsuda, for 'being tubercular' is tantamount to hopelessness. These two factors, then, provide that margin of light which enables O-Nobu to lead Tsuda. It is a case of 'the partially blind leading the almost totally blind', which is hardly an impossibility.

O-Nobu's egoism and Tsuda's differ qualitatively primarily in that O-Nobu is still 'open' whereas Tsuda is almost completely 'closed'. Such openness is magnificently revealed in the section . . . where O-Nobu is not afraid to bare her soul, to admit her weakness (she who is so strong), and to beg for help, whereas Tsuda retreats even further into himself, and shows at every turn his affinity with Sunaga of *Until After the Equinox,* Ichirō of *The Wayfarer,* and Sensei of *Heart.* (pp. 387-88)

Tsuda, then, is able to gain greatly from a comparison of his spiritual condition with that of his wife. He can see in her the first stages of recovery through which he will have to pass if he is to emerge from darkness. The very least that is required of him is that he become as open as O-Nobu, and I feel that there is ample reason to believe that her influence in this regard is already working on him, albeit slowly and subtly. For he can hardly remain wholly indifferent to her endless acts to bind him more closely to her and extort his love. Every evasion, every retreat or hesitation, every closing up on his part, such as the one we have seen in the face of her plea, brings him closer to the moment when he will have no place to retreat to, when he will either have to open up or seal himself in forever in the utter darkness of his soul. O-Nobu's very existence, then, is a challenge he cannot indefinitely spurn.

Yet another area where O-Nobu can heal him, or at least assist in the healing, is in her shaming him into action and out of cowardice by her own formidable courage. How long can Tsuda continue in the knowledge that his wife is the stronger, and more courageous, and still maintain his self-respect? (pp. 388-89)

[If] Tsuda reflects sufficiently on the difference between O-Nobu and himself, and sees why it is that Kiyoko fled from him, he will be able to love, or, in other words, he will be healed. For to learn to love is to be freed from the prison of the self. It is the only known antidote to the poison of egoism. (p. 389)

[Mrs. Yoshikawa] stands next, after O-Nobu, on the road to light. . . .

If she had been a member of the aristocracy, instead of the *bourgeoisie,* I could almost have substituted Proust's Duchesse de Guermantes, who is an exact fictional contemporary of Mrs Yoshikawa, as indeed Proust is of Sōseki. Mrs Yoshikawa's freedom of action, her lack of reserve in her relations with Tsuda, her meddling officiousness, her wit and banter which emerge from a life of complete leisure—all of these again would hardly seem to be in keeping with the image that we normally receive of the wife of a Japanese capitalist during the early years of this century. (p. 390)

[If] Tsuda is vain in desiring to be known as a special friend of the Yoshikawas, Mrs Yoshikawa is just as vain in accepting and basking in Tsuda's adulation. She thoroughly enjoys her role of Lady Bountiful dispensing advice and charity to her impoverished tenants from her ample store. Since Tsuda is a handsome young man of twenty-nine (we actually first learn his age when she banteringly asks him) her role becomes that much more pleasant; indeed at times she even appears to be flirting with him, secure in the knowledge she cannot possibly be rebuffed, for Tsuda 'knows his place' and is perfectly content to be thus condescended to by her. . . .

She fully believes that her actions are altruistic and that she is actually being very useful in her various schemes for Tsuda's betterment. Her vanity, therefore, is not at all as complex or as deleterious as Tsuda's. Indeed in their two characters we can see the essential difference between vanity and egoism, which Sōseki is endeavouring to make, the one being naïve (for all Mrs Yoshikawa's external sophistication) and almost healthy, the other being deep-seated and malignant.

Mrs Yoshikawa makes one of her characteristically quick assessments of the causes of the unhappiness which Tsuda manifests on his visit to her: Tsuda is responsible for part of his unhappiness (as indeed he is, although not in the way that she imagines), and O-Nobu is responsible for the remainder. (p. 391)

Just to assess the difficulties in Tsuda's and O-Nobu's marriage is hardly enough for such a practical-minded, bustling woman as Mrs Yoshikawa. She must set about to correct those difficulties, and she is not slow in devising schemes which she feels will do precisely that. Her next meeting with Tsuda is at the hospital where she then broaches both of them. (He is of course extremely flattered that the wife of the company president would actually deign to visit him, and she thus makes it impossible for him to refuse co-operation with her plans.) He must see Kiyoko once more and settle his relationship with her, once and for all, in a manly manner. . . . Tsuda complies with Mrs Yoshikawa's request, although not without considerable reluctance, so that half of her plan is realized, or, at any rate, is to be realized. (p. 392)

[Mrs Yoshikawa] is precisely correct in contending that his unwillingness to accept the fact of Kiyoko's rejection of him is one facet, and an important one, of his distress and marital unhappiness. As I have shown, O-Nobu provides an object lesson in courage for Tsuda, but it is Mrs Yoshikawa who actually prods him into action. It is ironical (and Sōseki is wholly aware of his having produced such irony) that these two women, who in their goals are diametrically opposed and outright enemies, should unconsciously co-operate, and complement each other, in their influence on Tsuda. (pp. 392-93)

I now turn to Tsuda's younger sister, O-Hide, who, despite her self-righteousness, is clearly Mrs. Yoshikawa's moral superior, and thus yet one step closer to light. If O-Nobu affects Tsuda by her mere existence, and Mrs Yoshikawa by her half-humorous taunts and jibes, O-Hide affects Tsuda by her stinging excoriation. . . . [She] firmly believes Tsuda to have changed radically since his marriage to O-Nobu, and thus she condemns her sister-in-law more than her brother; but nonetheless much of what she says is valid, if we overlook her initial bias.

The crisis which brings to a head the always indifferent relationship between O-Hide and her brother and his wife is a matter of money. . . . With the added expense for his operation, Tsuda is indeed in a quandary. O-Hide learns of his embarrassment and brings him a certain amount on her visit to the hospital. It is this act which arouses the emotions of both donor and recipient, and which involves O-Nobu too when she arrives on the scene.

This quarrel is the climax of the novel. For sheer emotional intensity it has few equals in Eastern or Western literature. That such a commonplace event as a money matter between sister and brother should have been exalted and transformed into a piercing flash of insight into the soul of man, that his baseness and ugliness should have been so brilliantly exposed, represent the triumph of Sōseki's psychological method, and indeed of his entire literary art. Here, as it were, all of Sōseki's 'cards are on the table', and *Light and Darkness,* which moves more often in accordance with the inward processes of man, for a few brief sections explodes into action, with much of the tension that has built up dispelled by the blast. (p. 393)

As O-Hide asserts, Tsuda is indeed unable to be grateful for anything: not just for his sister's gift but for every spiritual and material endowment. Exactly as she says, it is a tremendous misfortune for Tsuda to be unable to accept the kindness of others, and it is not only 'as if' Tsuda were deprived of the ability to be happy but rather that such is his actual spiritual state. . . . It is significant that Tsuda can accept O-Hide's indictment of him as being concerned only about himself 'with composure because he did not doubt that it was a statement of a general human characteristic rather than specifically of one of his own'. He truly feels that selfishness and lack of concern for others is the common state of all human beings, and thus, arch-conformist that he is, he sees no reason to change.

And yet if Tsuda were wholly unaffected by O'Hide's impassioned denunciation he would be an extraordinary individual indeed. The effect on him is extremely subtle but still considerable. (pp. 393-94)

O-Hide's gadfly function is reinforced by Kobayashi, the penniless socialist journalist. Even the severest critics of Sōseki have been unstinting in their praise of this remarkable character who appears to have strayed from the pages of an unpublished Dostoyevsky novel at the same time that he is, paradoxically, unmistakably Japanese. Every word, every minor action of his is so absorbing, so essentially new, so alive that it is only with the greatest regret that the reader can say farewell to him. . . . (p. 394)

No two individuals could ever be more different than Tsuda and Kobayashi. Tsuda is, as I have said, an arch-conformist;

Kobayashi's every bone is violently non-conformist. Tsuda is calculating and suspicious; Kobayashi cares nothing about the results of his actions for he has absolutely nothing to lose, and he is suspicious of no one for he has nothing to defend. Tsuda is an egoist of the first order while Kobayashi yearns for the day when all human beings have banished egoism and its concomitant loneliness in a society of perfect love and justice. The banishment of loneliness for Kobayashi is not just an abstract ideal but a keenly felt personal need, for, as he laments to Tsuda in one of the most touching scenes of the novel, he himself is appallingly *sabishii* (lonely).

Kobayashi thus stands in direct opposition to everything that Tsuda represents, and he is not slow in verbalizing this opposition. He flays Tsuda as strongly as does O-Hide but without a trace of the latter's self-righteousness. His denunciation of Tsuda at times seems almost as merciless as O-Hide's, and yet the reader is quickly aware that he is not rejecting Tsuda outright but rather attempting to transform him into a person who will at once be able to banish his own loneliness and enter into true brotherhood with him. Ironically, Kobayashi is trying to make Tsuda his brother while O-Hide, despite her protestations to the contrary, is casting Tsuda off and breaking the blood ties of actual brotherhood. . . . (p. 395)

[Kobayashi] is a far more appealing character than O-Hide, his morality is not so rigidly legalistic, he is closer to love and thus to truth than O-Hide, but he is by no means without faults. He appears to have a kind of inverted vanity in his poverty and in his being a social outcast. Moreover, his excoriation of Tsuda is not only of Tsuda as an individual but of Tsuda as a member of the bourgeoisie. Yet egoism, and certainly Tsuda's, is independent of economic status. Nevertheless, Kobayashi firmly believes, and here he is a doctrinaire Marxist, although he is never so defined, that if Tsuda's economic margin were removed he would be in large measure healed. Precisely in this mistaken diagnosis do we see the darkness in Kobayashi's soul which places him at one remove from Kiyoko, who stands, by common consent, at the pinnacle of the moral hierarchy of *Light and Darkness.*

While Sōseki's death deprives us of a conclusion to the novel, the 188 existing sections give us well-rounded portraits of five of the six major characters. Whatever else Sōseki might have written, the main lines and even most of the details of the personalities of Tsuda, O-Nobu, Mrs. Yoshikawa, O-Hide, and Kobayashi are drawn so as not to allow any dispute as to their roles in the work. . . . It is only in the case of Kiyoko that we are lacking in sufficient material to describe her role with any precision, for she makes her appearance only in Section 176, at the very end of the novel.

Nevertheless so great is the economy of Sōseki's style that many things can be said about Kiyoko with the reasonable certainty that they would not have to be revised if we miraculously could acquire the remainder of the novel. Her actions reveal a soul that is pure, natural, and calm. She neither attacks nor condones Tsuda. Her physical beauty is but the complement to her greater spiritual beauty. This beauty informs her every motion so that we find Tsuda looking transfixed as she peels an apple. (pp. 395-96)

I feel that in many ways she holds the key to the entire novel and even more to the entire art and thought of Natsume Sōseki.

Surely it cannot be an accident that Kiyoko's beauty, selflessness, and serenity should be the last creation of Sōseki's pen. (p. 396)

Even if it is open to doubt as to whether Kiyoko will save Tsuda, it is in no way open to doubt that Kiyoko represents a state of blessedness. To the reader who has toiled and suffered through five hundred pages of egoistic hell the figure of Kiyoko at the end can only be interpreted as a sign to him that all hope is not yet lost, that the gates of hell may yet be broken, and that the imprisoned spirits may yet rise to a purer, nobler realm.

Light and Darkness ends with Kiyoko's smile. The very last sentence that Sōseki ever wrote is: 'Tsuda returned to his own room, while trying to explain to himself the meaning of her smile.'

Indeed Sōseki's entire artistic life may be represented as a progression from a view of man as ridiculous to a view of man as infinitely precious, from a standpoint of satire verging on cynicism to one of the deepest compassion, or, in symbolic terms, from his nameless cat's impudent grin to Kiyoko's beatific smile. (pp. 396-97)

> V. H. Viglielmo, "Afterword" (1967), in Light and Darkness: An Unfinished Novel *by Natsume Sōseki, translated by V. H. Viglielmo (translation © 1971 Peter Owen), Owen, 1971, pp. 376-97.*

BEONGCHEON YU (essay date 1967)

[*Yu's* Natsume Soseki *is the only book-length discussion of Sōseki's work in English (see* TCLC, *Vol. 2). The following discussion of* Kojin *(from an introduction to that novel) focuses on Sōseki's technical accomplishments, his skill at characterization, and his examination of the character Ichiro as a modern Hamlet in hopeless isolation from family, society, and culture. Ichiro's acceptance of Zen as a solution to his metaphysical crisis is an example of Sōseki's ideal of* sokuten kyoshi—*modeling oneself after heaven to transcend the self.*]

In Sōseki's use of varying points of view, his deliberate unfolding of plot, and above all his intense psychological probing, *Kojin* has much in common with *Until After the Spring Equinox* and *Kokoro,* the other two works of the second trilogy. In all these three novels Soseki deals with situations which are potentially violent, yet he always has them well under artistic control. As a result they achieve both beauty of form and depth of theme. All this is noteworthy in view of the fact that Soseki rarely took the pains to revise his novels once they were off his pen—excepting only those simple mechanical matters which might obscure the general context.

Like many of his fellow artists, Soseki drew heavily on his own experiences. He had that enviable gift for weaving into the very texture of his literary fabric anything significant that was happening to him, to his mind, and even to those around him. For instance, it is known that some of the settings in *Kojin,* such as Osaka, Wakanoura, and Benigayatsu, were drawn from Soseki's recent experiences. . . . Far more important to us is the fact that Soseki is an impersonal artist through and through, not merely because, as with *Kojin,* he keeps mum about his source, but also because all his works, including *I Am a Cat,* take on an air of impersonality, a mark of a genuine art. Such impersonality is indeed rare in modern Japanese literature, which has often indulged in the confessional *watakushi shosetsu* ("I" novel).

Yet *Kojin* is by no means a perfect work; it has many flaws when judged by our standards. To those who are used to European fiction, especially contemporary fiction, *Kojin* may appear to be but a series of sharply-etched tableaus which lack the dynamic rhythm of action. However, in fairness to Soseki, it is well to point out that this static quality of *Kojin* is due in part to the very tradition of Oriental fiction and in part to the peculiar circumstances under which a novelist labors when writing his work serially for a daily newspaper. In fact, there is much evidence that Soseki was conscious of this problem and did his utmost to make virtue of necessity.

Aside from such an over-all objection, there are still more specific points to be weighed. For example, some, if not all, readers may complain of the apparent cleavage between the first three parts and the fourth and last part, although this apparent flaw can be easily justified as a thematic turning point. Others might wish that Soseki had been more specific about Ichiro's and Jiro's professions, and also about the previous relationship between Jiro and Onao; and that Soseki had not dropped Jiro's own problem unsolved. Also, some may express dissatisfaction with the denouement itself which is only suggested in H's letter in the last part. And so on. Some of these criticisms may well be sound; however, one must bear in mind that a *perfect* work is usually an artist's dream and a critic's hypothesis. It would be more profitable for us to probe into those qualities which make *Kojin* a significant piece of literature, whatever may be the defects that seem to draw attention away from its architectonic import.

In believing in fiction as art, Soseki was as firm as James, his western contemporary. And much like James Soseki experimented with its possibilities, selected what might be called a point-of-view technique, and shaped his structural pattern so that the theme might emerge out of his central situation. In *Kojin,* as in the other two works of his second trilogy, Soseki attempts a novel which consists of short stories or pieces. And in fact in tightening his work without damaging its organic wholeness Soseki here is more successful than in *Until After the Spring Equinox.* His narrative method in *Kojin* is unmistakably modern, akin to what we might call an oblique method. In the present work Soseki employs it in two ways: First, to unfold the whole story Soseki creates Jiro, who is sympathetic toward Ichiro because they are brothers, and at the same time prejudiced because he himself is intimately involved in the situation. Until he receives H's missive, Jiro remains imperceptive. Then, to complete Jiro's broken vision, Soseki introduces H and places him in an inner circle—far closer to Ichiro than Jiro, and far closer than any other character, for that matter, can ever be. It is by way of H's detailed report concerning Ichiro that Soseki heightens this basically domestic issue to the level of an intellectual, cultural, and even metaphysical issue. By the same means Soseki is able to dispose of what he once regarded as an important but difficult matter in modern fiction, namely the treatment of religion or a religious state. In *Kojin* Soseki deals with this very state quite successfully. And his success is due largely to this oblique method which enables him to offer just sufficient indications as to the direction of Ichiro's ultimate salvation.

Commensurate with Soseki's technical consciousness is his sense of structure. On both points Soseki stands apart from many of his Japanese contemporaries, as does his art from the native tradition of fiction. Nurtured in one of the finest traditions of European fiction, Soseki knows how to make those seemingly unrelated episodes and anecdotes function organically, centering on the principal situation. As one whose ambition once was to become an architect, Soseki knows how to bring into play his sense of balance—contrast as well as parallel—to make intricate the pattern of symmetry and thereby enrich and accentuate rather than confuse or obscure the basic theme of the novel. First, the impossible relationship between Ichiro and Onao is made sharper by introducing Okada and Okane, and Sano and Osada, two pairs, one established, and the other in process, who should exemplify the norm of traditional matrimony. These two pairs, indeed are made to serve as the very norm set down by long feudal tradition they all accept matter-of-factly. Presumably Ichiro and Onao married by arrangement, just as did Okada and Okane, and just as Sano and Osada do, but their marriage resulted only in deviation from the social norm, for Ichiro and Onao are a classic example of an incompatible couple forced to live together by tradition. Furthermore, they are, unlike their foils, new man and new woman dissociating their individual selves from society and seeking to value their hearts on their own individual terms. Yet the trouble is that they are and cannot be completely free or modern. In the world where everything is in transition, a very sudden and rapid one, their selves and hearts know only their conflict. What worsens their situation is that Ichiro, instead of quitting in compromise, tries to settle once and for all his personal problem on the absolute level, whereas Onao is not as forthrightly free a woman as, say, Ibsen's Nora. (pp. 16-20)

Onao's tragedy lies precisely in the fact that, by virtue of her own egotism, she can never be insane . . . and thereby release her passion; at the same time she is just sufficiently freed from tradition to keep her heart in silence. . . . She is thus aligning herself with the long lineage of Soseki's heroines, who are all self-assertive in one way or another, and yet unlike their feudal counterparts, sufficiently awakened to their individual selves. Especially Onao, as Jiro describes her, is extremely elusive because she accepts the dictates of tradition, an acceptance which is in her case a silent defiance, and almost by instinct she keeps her heart to herself—as her only measure of self-protection.

Ichiro also is typical of the Soseki hero in that he suffers from his excessively cultivated intellect and introspective sensibility. He has his own share of passion toward Onao but, like her, he is also incapable of discarding his self. Neither Ichiro nor Onao knows an easy compromise; nor is divorce conceivable. Thus theirs is in a sense the battle of the sexes, a case similar to that of Strindberg's characters. What makes the situation worse still is that in their society the battle cannot be brought out into the open; it is a constant duel of two minds which allows for no finality.

It is true that the domestic impasse of Ichiro and Onao is the common tragedy of a new man and a new woman caught in the violent transition of Japan from feudal to modern society. Yet in *Kojin* this domestic tragedy is not the cause of Ichiro's plight; it is really a symptom of the general malady of an age Ichiro happens to represent. This point is vital for our correct reading of the novel. For this reason Soseki first depicts the personal situation by way of Jiro, and then by way of H's letter places it in a larger supra-personal perspective. Thanks to the latter device *Kojin* becomes something more significant, more profound than a mere domestic tragedy.

And that significance is first of all socio-cultural, in the sense that in Ichiro Soseki creates a modern Japanese intellect, a product of Meiji Japan, which is comparable not only to the Russia during the second half of the 19th century, but also to Renaissance Europe still trying to escape the shadow of the medieval world. Only in these terms can we view the socio-cultural dilemma of Meiji Japan as an impossible hybrid of eastern and western civilization. In this sense Ichiro is more germane to Hamlet than to Raskolnikov, for instance. Ichiro is a modern Japanese Hamlet to whom the world is out of joint. (pp. 20-2)

''Why, then, 'tis none to you; for there is nothing either good or bad, but thinking makes it so: to me it is a prison.'' What Hamlet here says about himself may also apply to Ichiro. Ichiro's plight is the plight of the intellectual. He excels in the abstract, but fails in the concrete. As when he recreates a night scene of Osaka he is incapable of grasping the idea of people, places, and events in their proper context. His memories of these, graphic as they may be, still remain totally fragmentary. Take for instance those foreign names scattered all through the novel, an aspect which once more reminds us of those Russian novels by Turgenev, Dostoevski and Tolstoi. . . .[The] allusions are completely functional in the context. (Besides, the novel teems with unspecified allusions to western masterpieces, especially some well-known situations. . . . [More] signifcant is that in the novel all these foreign names, with a few exceptions, are supposedly an integral part of Ichiro's own thinking process. All his references, while highly functional in their respective context, take on an air of outlandishness. These names appear as alien to the novel itself as, according to Soseki's speech of 1911, western civilization in the culture of Japan. They are not completely blended; it is this failure in interfusion that indicates the root of Ichiro's tragedy.

Yet Ichiro's plight has a further significance, a universal one. His is also the plight of the modern intellect, and modern man in general. His plight is symbolic of the predicament of modern man in the hopeless isolation from his family, society, culture, and ultimately his own cosmos. This deeper implication becomes clearer when Ichiro interprets his personal case in the light of modern science which knows no moment of rest, only driving him on and on. . . . The theme, we know too well, has been one of the major themes of western literature since the later 19th century. The significance of Soseki's art here is, then, that while treating of the most concrete domestic situation, he can also expand its implication across many layers of human existence in the modern world, without losing its immediacy. And this is what he accomplishes in *Kojin*. Though Soseki's own favorite work was apparently *Kokoro* (in his announcement he urged those seeking their own hearts to read the work which did grasp the heart of man) it appears that *Kojin*, thematically and artistically, is more representative of Soseki the man and the artist. (pp. 22-4)

Soseki designated the dilemma of modern Japan as a tragedy with no hope of solution. Soseki might have believed this to be still the case—at least on the collective level. On the individual level, however, it is certain that Soseki had by now come to see some possibility of it. This is suggested in *Kojin*. It is Ichiro himself who said in unequivocal terms: ''To die, to go mad, or to enter religion—these are the only three courses left open for me.'' To Ichiro the absolutist of all or nothing, any practical expediency is out of the question from the outset. Yet no ordinary human solution is possible in his tragedy of self. It calls for some sort of transhuman measure which alone could deal with self to any satisfactory degree. And Soseki suggests that the only possible solution is the last of the three, namely religion as the only human way in which man can surpass himself—by surrendering his self to something larger than himself. (p. 24)

Just as in modern literature so many heroes in this dilemma have returned to their traditional religion, so does Ichiro seem to tend toward his own. The solution suggested in *Kojin*, unsatisfying and incomplete as it may appear to the western reader, is authentically Oriental. Soseki's hints as to this matter are given when H suggests that Ichiro resolve his plight by surrendering rather than asserting his small ego. The crab scene is a case in point. Soseki seems to agree with H in suggesting self-absorption as the only possible human solution—at least to Ichiro who knows no God he may turn to. This solution, however, is not the counterpart of Rousseau's return to nature; it simply points to the possibility of releasing the accursed self by way of aesthetic union, for in this basically mystic union there is no longer any difference between "Thou" and "I." True, this kind of solution might appear to the western reader no better than an escape from the issue itself or, worse still, the obliteration of self. But the traditional Orient has viewed the problem in a different light, always asserting this kind of self-absorption as a divine state for the reason that it simply means to expand, not obliterate, self as large as nature, the way which is the divine source of individual life. In other words, it is something comparable to what Christian mystics term one's total surrender to God. Nature is as much Ichiro's birthright as those foreign names are alien to him. Thus considered, Soseki's solution in terms of union with nature would be as valid as say Dostoevski's solution in terms of return to Christ.

It must be remembered that in *Kojin* Soseki is content with only offering this hint of solution. The solution here, vague as it may seem to some, is unmistakably in that direction. . . . Soseki's solution suggested in *Kojin* is therefore doubly meaningful: first, he is now able to take a positive forward step; second, his forward step is not in the direction of formalism which is often not free from its own theoretical or dogmatic basis, even though it be Zen. Furthermore, Soseki's solution here definitely points to his much-discussed philosophy, *sokuten kyoshi* ("Conform to Heaven and forsake Self"). Whether Soseki personally attained this state is a matter of little consequence. It will suffice to say that in it Soseki finally saw the possibility of salvation for his hero, Ichiro. And here is the significance of *Kojin* in the long cycle of Soseki's novels. (pp. 24-6)

> *Beongcheon Yu, in his introduction to* The Wayfarer (Kojin) *by Natsume Sōseki, translated by Beongcheon Yu (reprinted by permission of the Wayne State University Press; translation copyright © 1967 by Wayne State University Press), Wayne State University Press, 1967, pp. 9-28.*

EDWIN McCLELLAN　(essay date 1969)

When we read the autobiographical *Grass on the Wayside*, we see how much of himself Sōseki had put into the heroes of the preceding novels.

Sōseki was a sick man when he wrote *Grass on the Wayside*. After 1910, when he very nearly died from stomach ulcers, he seems to have felt that death was not far away. He wrote the novel in 1915, when he was forty-eight; the following year, before he could complete *Light and Darkness (Meian)*, he died.

The period dealt with in *Grass on the Wayside* is very short. It begins soon after the author's return from London in 1903 and ends as his career as a writer is about to begin. (*I am a Cat* was published in 1905.) Kenzō (the name Sōseki gives himself) is at this time in his middle thirties, and his wife in her middle twenties. It was then, presumably, that relations

between Sōseki and his wife became strained and he began to be acutely conscious of his loneliness.

The novel has its shortcomings. It is not devoid of self-pity or naiveté and it is so introspective that the reader may find it at times rather slow-moving. Nevertheless, it is all in all his most serious work. And of the countless number of autobiographical novels that have been written in Japan since the early 1900's, it is perhaps the most distinguished.

One of the most curious aspects of the history of modern Japanese fiction after the turn of the century is the important place occupied by the autobiographical novel, which was made fashionable by the so-called naturalists who flourished at about the same time as Soseki. In their attempt to introduce realism into the Japanese novel, these "naturalists" were inclined to regard the novel as a means of describing their own experiences, to think of it more or less as an extended essay form.

Sōseki's conception of realism was not so literal, and much of what is most imaginative and daring in modern Japanese fiction is due largely to his example and influence. In his entire career, he wrote only one autobiographical novel. And when he did, he brought to the genre qualities which had never been seen in it before.

What *Grass on the Wayside* manages to avoid is the rather obvious lyricism of most Japanese autobiographical novels, their annoying reticence and vagueness. Its people are alive and refuse to get lost in the misty Japanese scene. No modern Japanese novelist before Sōseki ever wrote so movingly about his childhood, or created so real a woman as Kenzō's wife. And Kenzō himself remains one of the most fully developed characters in Japanese fiction. (pp. ix-x)

The original title of this novel is *Michikusa*, the literal meaning of which is "grass on the road." But when used idiomatically, as in *michikusa o kuu*, "to eat grass on the road," it means to waste one's time or to be distracted. The title seems to suggest, therefore, that the novel is about distractions. But perhaps Sōseki intended it to be understood in another sense, that his private life had been that of an outsider, like a weed growing beside the main road. (p. xi)

> *Edwin McClellan, in his introduction to* Grass on the Wayside (Michikusa): A Novel *by Natsume Sōseki, translated by Edwin McClellan (reprinted by permission of The University of Chicago Press; translation © 1969 by UNESCO), University of Chicago Press, 1969, pp. vii-xi.*

NORMA MOORE FIELD　(essay date 1978)

[Sōseki's] life undeniably furnished some of the major themes of his art, and a brief glance at this connection may add perspective to a discussion of the novels.

The first, most obvious theme taken from his life is that of abandonment. Many Sōseki characters are literally or figuratively abandoned children, who must therefore grapple with basic questions of identity.

Another important theme is ambivalence, if not outright skepticism, toward modernity and Westernization. . . . His anguish when it came to choosing a career was really an anguish over whether to cast his lot with the future or to desist from taking part in the "struggle for survival" (a phrase which recurs throughout his writings) altogether. This ambivalence about modernity is also a dimension of the abandonment theme. (p. 265)

Finally, and most importantly, all these concerns are part of the theme of alienation. If there is one characteristic that all Sōseki heroes share, it is a sense of discomfort in the world. They are all anxious outsiders. (pp. 265-66)

It is in the first trilogy, consisting of [*Sanshirō, And Then (Sorekara),* and *The Gate (Mon)*], . . . that we see the emergence of the mature novelist. In these works his style solidifies; he identifies the questions he wishes to investigate; he chooses the characters he will employ for that investigation.

Before discussing these three works, it may be wise to consider the basis for calling them a trilogy. After *Sanshirō* had appeared in the newspaper, Sōseki explained in an advance notice that he was titling the next work **"And Then,"** first, because *Sanshirō* was about a university student, and the new work would be about what "then" happened; second, because Sanshirō was a simple man, but the new main character would be in a more advanced stage; and finally, because a strange fate was to befall this character, but what "then" followed would not be described. *The Gate,* the last novel in the trilogy, is about what "then" might have followed. Obviously, these are only the most schematic links between the novels. The progression of age and situation of the central characters provides a framework for the complex interaction of Sōseki's lifelong themes. The three novels anticipate and harken back to each other in such a way that a consideration of them as a group becomes valuable. (p. 266)

Sanshirō is Sōseki's sweetest novel, the culmination of one level of his art before he attempts to climb to another. Here, the bald comedy of his earlier works has been refined into a more subtle humor that adds just the necessary touch of irony to his compassionate treatment of Sanshirō. Because Sanshirō is young and lacking in both internal and external experience, the novel does not have the dark staying power of the later works. Perhaps it will finally be remembered for its series of beautifully wrought scenes which are as eloquent a testimony to Sōseki's artistry as anything else in his work. How can any reader forget Sanshirō's night with a strange woman on his way to Tokyo, when he rolls up the sheet from his half of the bed to make a boundary in the center? Or his hopeless ventures into the library, where he checks out book after book, hoping to find one that no one else has read? The encounters with Mineko ache with suppressed longing, fulfilled only by a brush of the sleeves here, a glance there. Is it not a quintessentially Japanese passion—wordless and almost gestureless—that Sōseki has described in the scene in which a beautifully dressed Mineko appears to Sanshirō in a mirror while his back is turned to her? Or when the two of them, seeking refuge from the rain under a cedar tree, inch closer and closer as the rain falls harder and harder, until they are almost standing shoulder to shoulder?

These are among the scenes that make *Sanshirō* memorable, but there are other dimensions that help lead us to the subsequent works. I have characterized *Sanshirō* as a "sweet" novel, but its sweetness does not preclude shadows. Despite its being a story about youth, the novel begins in late summer and ends with the onset of winter; the recurrent death images are delicate and beautiful, but nonetheless ominous. As his later works will show, for Sōseki, love and death are never far apart.

We must look to the characters of Mineko and Hirota to anticipate the concerns of the next two works and, in addition, to clarify Sanshirō's plight. Mineko is important first of all for the elegiac note she lends to the narrative. If *Sanshirō* is a tale about youth, Mineko represents the dying of youth. The portrait for which she chooses to pose in the attire in which Sanshirō first sees her is the death mask of her youth.

There is a second, more significant function for Mineko. It is she who articulates a central Sōseki theme when she describes herself and Sanshirō as "stray sheep." Mineko is clearly a new type of woman, and this is reason enough to make her stray. In her reaching out to Sanshirō, she is seeking something—something that she had apparently sought in the scientist Nonomiya and failed to find. Her portrayal is incomplete and ambiguous, thus we cannot specify what she is seeking—perhaps simply some form of meaningful communion, some sympathetic understanding of what it means to be an intelligent young woman in a society that tantalizes her with new horizons but will not permit her to explore them. In any case, we cannot miss the punitive quality of her fate, for she is quickly married off to a man whom her less independent, less attractive friend Yoshiko had refused. In Mineko's last words to Sanshirō, she quotes from Psalm 51: "For I acknowledge my transgressions: and my sin is ever before me." Mineko's fate dimly prefigures the sanctions society will impose on the aberrant lovers of *And Then* and *The Gate.*

Hirota, perhaps a more important "stray sheep" in the Sōseki genealogy, will find his way into almost all the subsequent Sōseki novels. Here, in keeping with the overall tone of the novel, he is a bemused, benign spectator-critic, not yet driven by the vanity and hypocrisy surrounding him to the obsessive bitterness of his heirs. (pp. 267-68)

These two brief sketches are rich in suggestions about the nature of the relationship between love and society. One such thought is that an ideal love cannot exist within society; at the same time, it leaves its subject unfit for more mundane attachments. Another is that a deep disillusionment in love, whether filial or romantic, may leave one permanently incapable of serious intercourse with society. In both cases, the result is alienation.

In contrast to Mineko and Hirota, Sanshirō has little understanding of himself as a stray sheep. Early in his Tokyo life, he identifies three worlds at his disposal: the world of his mother, which he has left behind but will not jettison altogether because of its comfortable familiarity; the world of learning, represented by Hirota and Nonomiya and the library; and, most exciting of all, the world of action and beautiful women. He thinks that he was meant to play a central role in the last, yet somehow, he cannot find his way in. In fact, he belongs to none of these worlds. He will never be able to go home again, and he is not dedicated enough to occupy the scholar's world. His timidity, if nothing else, bars him forever from the third world. At the end of the novel, we sense that Sanshirō has been touched in some fundamental, unalterable way by his experience with Mineko. We also sense that he is one of those destined to stand wistfully between worlds, never able to step in. What we cannot tell is how much of this he will ever understand. This is what keeps him from being a great Sōseki character, and this is why Mineko and Hirota make better guides to the world of *And Then,* whose hero Daisuke is an acutely self-conscious stray sheep.

And Then opens ominously with a red double camellia falling on the floor. The camellia flower, which drops as a whole rather than petal by petal, was distasteful to samurai because it reminded them of falling heads. Daisuke is introduced to us as a healthy young man neurotically concerned with his physical well-being—so much so, in fact, that he cannot take for granted the life that flows through his body day after day.

It is not just his body, of course, that Daisuke views with detachment; he stands outside every aspect of his life—his family, society at large, and most importantly, his own heart and mind. What is responsible for this state of affairs?

Daisuke himself would probably point to the state of Japan and the world as the principal cause. The novel is set four or five years after the Russo-Japanese War (1904-1905), perhaps the Meiji government's proudest international moment. The Japanese victory was widely taken to mean Japan's coming of age, its right to stand shoulder-to-shoulder with the nations of the West for the first time since the humiliating years of the forced opening. The postwar years were a bombastic, ostentatious period for the nation as a whole, and Daisuke's skepticism and disaffection may be taken as an accurate reflection of his creator's views.

It is not so much the question of Japan's standing in the world that troubles Daisuke and Sōseki but rather the dislocation of values brought on by the breathtaking changes since 1868. . . . Still, there is a perceptible vacuum in him, and this vacuum is dangerous, not only for Daisuke but for all Japanese, because industrialization—that is, Westernization—has dazzled the eye with the possibility of hitherto undreamed of material comfort. This is the content of what Daisuke refers to as the conflict between the life appetites and the moral appetites.

These passages of social commentary, pedantically written and awkwardly interpolated, are part of what sustains Sōseki's reputation as a social critic. They are convincing as a partial explanation for Daisuke's disaffection; but in order to truly understand his malaise—and Sōseki's wisdom as an artist— we must go further. Sōseki himself encourages us to do so by saying to Daisuke through Michiyo, ''I think you're cheating a little.''

Let us look first at Daisuke's relationships with his father, Hiraoka, and Michiyo. . . . We are told that Daisuke ceased to have temper outbursts at his father from about the time he graduated from the university. Perhaps this marks the beginning of Daisuke's alienation. Recognizing and accepting one's parent's shabbiness of character is a serious business. Moreover, Daisuke can easily generalize from his father to the society around him, for his father is more the rule than the exception. (pp. 269-71)

These circumstances constitute part of the answer to Michiyo's poignant question, ''But why did you let me go?'' when Daisuke at last declares his love. It is something of a vogue nowadays to posit a homoerotic relationship between Sōseki's characters. . . . The homosexual theory is debatable on two grounds. First, it is hard to imagine that Hiraoka, even before the changes brought on by his downfall, had any deep, enduring appeal for Daisuke. He is too much of a philistine, a member of Daisuke's father's and brother's camp. Secondly, there are many specific suggestions of Daisuke's longing for Michiyo. . . . No, Daisuke did love Michiyo at the time he gave her up, but only within the limits of his ability to love. He let Michiyo go because he simply did not have it in him to take the initiative to marry her; moreover, he threw himself into arranging the match with Hiraoka in order to avoid having to confront that vacuum in himself.

In the three years following Hiraoka's and Michiyo's wedding, these circumstances—his ambiguous position with his father,

and his (unacknowledged) inability to admit his love for Michiyo—have had a cumulatively debilitating effect. Add to this the more concrete reasons for which society at that time should appear repugnant to a thoughtful, sensitive individual like Daisuke, and it becomes only too natural that he should be neurotically incapable of action.

Yet, having said this, I am still unconvinced that we have truly understood Daisuke. Is it not possible that Daisuke would have been much the same even had he lived in a more sympathetic age and even had his father been warm and admirable? Has Sōseki given us in Daisuke a portrait of the most irredeemable stray sheep, the most radical form of alienation of all—that is, the individual who is burdened with an acute awareness of the impossibility of existence such that nonexistence appears more real and more natural? And, finally, what of the possibility that Daisuke is, after all, just a decadent coward? Let us examine what happens with Michiyo.

Daisuke's declaration of love to Michiyo, with its implications of ostracism by family and society and consequent financial disaster, has usually been read as a redemptive, regenerative act. For one thing, it is beautifully written; the image of the lovers sitting opposite each other, motionless and wordless, has a secure place in the collection of memorable Sōseki scenes. Daisuke himself says that he is in heaven. Michiyo is undeniably a revitalizing force. This is emphasized by the recurrent water imagery, such as the water she drinks from the flower bowl or the rain that brings her to Daisuke's and then shields and isolates the lovers. It is also unquestionable that acknowledging his love has a restorative effect on Daisuke. Still, in what way is Michiyo revitalizing, and to what is Daisuke restored?

Once the blissfulness of declaring himself to Michiyo is past, Daisuke is beset with anxiety over the future. He is worried about money. In his mind he casts an eye over that region of life called work but finds nothing until he comes upon the domain of beggars. Indeed, it is virtually impossible to imagine Daisuke working to stave off starvation. Here the question of cowardice presents itself. Is Daisuke losing his recently earned redemption when he discloses his financial worries to Michiyo, or when he cancels his arrangements with the secondhand bookseller after receiving Umeko's check? It is possible, of course, that Sōseki has taken such pains to present us with an interesting moral coward; still, the work suggests greater richness.

It can be no accident that Daisuke is able to commit himself to a woman with a heart problem, a woman from whom no children will issue, a woman who repeatedly states her readiness to die. In the very act of returning to his original self, Daisuke is embracing death. In fact, he was never seriously interested in existence; that is why he cannot fight for it, unlike his university friend Terao, or Hiraoka, or, for that matter, his father and brother. There are a number of indications (e.g., the flower-scented sleep in which he drowns himself when the ''stimuli of the universe'' become too much for him) that nonbeing was always attractive to him. Even his obsession with health is the other side of the coin of a fascination with death (evident, for example, in the delicious horror with which he contemplates the execution scene from Andreev). For Daisuke, to be consumed with Michiyo in the flames of society's wrath is indeed an act faithful to his original being.

The end of the novel is unclear; it is unnecessary to specify whether Daisuke goes insane, commits suicide, or is destroyed passively. In any case, it is difficult to postulate a reunion with

Michiyo. The ominous signs throughout the book—the surrealistic train rides at night, the earthquake, the motionless gecko above Hiraoka's door—reach a climax in the brutal red imagery of summer, which blindingly reflects the red camellia at the opening.

The contrast between the burning sun with which we leave *And Then* and the lingering warmth of the autumn sun with which *The Gate* begins accurately indicates the distance between the worlds of the two novels. *The Gate* is a quiet tale about Sōsuke and his wife Oyone, who live in a house beneath a cliff. During their student days, Oyone had been with Sōsuke's friend Yasui (as his wife? the novel does not say), but a moment of indiscretion drives her and Sōsuke to the edge of society. Rather than support the possibility that Daisuke and Michiyo take up life together after his declaration of love, *The Gate* graphically illustrates the implausibility of that idea. Daisuke could not have endured for one minute Sōsuke and Oyone's existence.

If *Sanshirō* was a novel about youth and *And Then* a novel about troubled adulthood, *The Gate* is a novel about middle age. Sōsuke and Oyone live without any dreams for the future in a shabby house on which the sun rarely shines. . . . They are Sōseki's happiest couple, and it is with good reason that this work has often been characterized as idyllic. (pp. 271-74)

Although they do not understand very well what happened, they accept their punishment and ask merely to be left alone.

There are two crises in the book. The first comes when Oyone falls acutely ill. She has never been healthy; the strain of trying to deal graciously with Koroku, her husband's brother, who clearly blames her for her brother's and therefore his own downfall, proves to be too much. After this seizure has passed, Oyone discloses to Sōsuke that she visited a fortuneteller after her last unsuccessful pregnancy. He confirmed her suspicion that she would never give birth to a healthy child and attributed it to her having wronged someone.

The second crisis comes when Sōsuke discovers, almost by accident, that Yasui, the friend whom he had betrayed, is to visit Sōsuke's landlord's home. The news is so shaking that he takes ten days off from work to go to a Zen temple. He knows nothing about Zen and has no idea what to expect, but he goes with desperate hopes for a miraculous reordering of his life. Needless to say, the venture is unsuccessful. He is told to consider the nature of his soul before the birth of his parents, but he fails to come up with any thoughts.

Sōsuke returns home looking more spent than when he left. On the surface, however, things are not bad. He manages to to hold on to his job through a personnel review and even gets a raise. Still, when his wife happily remarks on the coming spring, he can only think about the next fall.

Sōsuke's and Oyone's flaw is, essentially, lack of self-knowledge. Each is driven to a crisis, each seeks help, and each returns unenlightened. When Sōsuke hears about the fortuneteller episode, he tells Oyone never to go again, that it is foolish to pay money to hear such things. Oyone agrees that she never will, for it is too frightening. When Sōsuke returns from the Zen temple, he wishes he could change his name to lessen the chances of accidental encounter with Yasui. Both he and Oyone want to escape from their past, and, by extension, from themselves. They are stray sheep lost not only to society but to their own souls. The Zen temple episode is crucial in clarifying this theme. The seemingly irrelevant kōan assigned to Sōsuke was

in fact directing him to think about a most urgent issue—the essence of his being, indeed, of life; but Sōsuke's unexamined fear blinds him and he does no know that he must look into himself to right his skewed universe.

The question of self-knowledge raised here adds a new dimension to the trilogy as a whole. At the end of *The Gate*, as Sōsuke prepares to leave the temple, he is described as a man fated to stand at the gate, knock, and receive no answer. At the same time, he is not one of those permitted to go through life without seeking the gate. Might this not describe Sanshirō as well? Daisuke, on the other hand, is one who chooses not to seek the gate. Being far more introspective and analytically acute than the other two, he consciously shuns self-knowledge in order to make life tolerable. Yet, in the end, he, too, finds himself at the gate—with the door flying open in his face.

Sōseki is not severe with the patiently cowardly Sōsuke. His compassion is evident in the quiet love, the enduring devotion of the couple that permeates the novel. It is not a love to have satisfied the young Sanshirō, much less Daisuke. It is a love granted to a pair who have lost everything else. Sōsuke and Oyone are, in a sense, dead to society. We might think of this as Sōseki's final comment on love in this trilogy.

In retrospect the trilogy can be seen as a web spun around the points of love, death, self-knowledge, and society. These points are linked to one another in a complex series of relationships that are examined from a different angle in each novel. Sōseki continued to examine these same ideas in his later works— what else is there for the novelist to explore?—but from a darker and darker perspective. (pp. 275-76)

Norma Moore Field, in her afterword to And Then: Natsume Sōseki's Novel "Sorekara" *by Natsume Sōseki, translated by Norma Moore Field (reprinted by permission of Louisiana State University Press; translation © 1978 by Louisiana State University Press), Louisiana State University Press, 1978, pp. 258-78.*

J. THOMAS RIMER (essay date 1978)

[*Rimer provides a comprehensive discussion of the novel* Kusamakura.]

[In] Natsume Sōseki's remarkable 1906 novel *Kusamakura* (translated by Alan Turney as *The Three-Cornered World*), traditional literary techniques are recast in the light of Sōseki's own modern sensibility to produce not only a satisfying novel in its own terms but a virtual handbook of traditional aesthetic attitudes and methods. (p. 38)

The word *kusamakura* Sōseki chose for the title might be translated as "the traveller's pillow," and, in traditional Japanese poetic vocabulary, the term suggests a journey, possibly a search. Sōseki provides both. The Western reader who stumbles on the novel unaided may feel at first that he is wandering around in a maze, somewhere between art criticism and a mystery story. Fortunately, *Kusamakura* explains itself as it goes along, and what it is "about" becomes clear as the narrative progresses. Sōseki himself considered his novel an experiment; he called it a *haiku*-novel and commented that his experiment involved having the protagonist stand still as events moved around him, rather than following a more normal pattern of moving a protagonist through those external events. Such a structure, worked out so carefully in the course of the novel, brings with it new demands on the reader, whose own sense of relationships between thought and action must alter. themselves accordingly. . . .

Sōseki chose to write *Kusamakura* in the first person. . . . [In] the case of *Kusamakura,* Sōseki uses a traditional narrative technique with a considerable lineage in order to suggest to his readers the atmosphere of certain classic works. This atmosphere helps thrust the reader into the interior—but not too far into the interior—of the narrator's mind. Sōseki's aim here is to project an artistic and creative consciousness, mixing observation, action, and reflection. In such a construction, style is of the utmost importance. *Kusamakura* is widely regarded as a model of elegant modern Japanese prose. (p. 39)

Sōseki's "I" is an artist who paints in oils, in the Western style increasingly practiced in Japan by the turn of the century. This very fact sets the artist at some objective distance from past tradition. His journey takes him deep into the country in southern Japan, in an attempt to experience the traditional aesthetic vision of which his own art is no longer a part. The artist wishes to find in his own responses an objectivity without emotional ties: not, as he puts it at one point, an "inhuman tour," but a "non-human" one. Sōseki uses this tour to construct a novel that performs three functions at once. *Kusamakura* is at the same time a working out in modern prose of traditional Japanese aesthetics, an examination of the necessity for human relations, and a commentary on the spiritual crisis of modernizing Japan. All three themes are sketched out with a light hand, as is entirely appropriate for a book of this sort. Nevertheless, Sōseki's seriousness of purpose is powerfully conveyed. (pp. 39-40)

The protagonist does, psychologically at least, stand still as he responds to the various events around him. The first chapter of the novel is a *tour de force,* presenting the thoughts of the artist on a mountain walk, ranging over Eastern and Western art and philosophy. The treatment given is elegant, psychologically astute, and lightly ironic, in Sōseki's finest fashion.

Art, muses the artist, involves transcendence. . . .

Tranquillity, above the mundane and vulgar world, is the goal sought. The artist goes on, however, to remind himself that to know life must inevitably require a knowledge of sorrow; and that knowledge as well is at the beginning of all art. . . . (p. 41)

The quality of the relationship of man to nature is also crucial. Man exists as a part of nature in the traditional Japanese view, and his best means of living is to accommodate himself to it. (p. 42)

Distance from mundane concern permits worldly values to be set aside. For the protagonist, it is the lack of such distance that sets off Western art from Eastern art. . . . (p. 44)

This essential desire for transcendence and tranquillity, then, becomes the object of the artist's tour. "I wish," he concludes, "if only for a brief period, to wander at will through a land which is completely detached from feelings and emotions."

Such are the aesthetic boundaries sketched out by Sōseki in his opening chapter, and he uses the rest of his novel to let the protagonist, and the reader, decide what the real limitations of such a trip might be.

Throughout the course of the narrative Sōseki provides short and vivid glimpses into the traditional aesthetic processes behind the creation of art and literature. To discuss the hundreds of examples he provides would require a book as long as the

novel itself, but a few examples may suffice to show the gratifying range of his sympathies. . . .

In the second chapter, for example, the artist meets an old woman who runs a dingy shop by the side of the road. She points out to him a local landmark, a large rock shaped like a Japanese goblin. He defines the woman in terms of art and the scenery. . . . (p. 46)

The old woman is seen (at least at this juncture of the narrative) in terms of such relationships, not in terms of her own personality; indeed what the protagonist is seeking is a larger propriety outside the realm of the individual.

Such assimilation of the individual into art and nature is an important principle in traditional Japanese aesthetics. . . . (p. 47)

Sōseki uses the concept of the great assimilating powers of nature as a means to provide a lyric rhythm in his narrative. Nature frames each incident presented and places each in a larger perspective. (p. 48)

The fact that the protagonist senses these proportions shows that he is an artist. For, as Sōseki indicates in a later passage in the novel, the artist is not afraid to abandon his own preoccupations to join with nature. Such an attitude of mind is fundamental to the aesthetics of the traditional poetic arts, especially for the writing of *haiku.* (p. 49)

Later in the novel, the artist composes a whole sequence of *haiku* poems, thereby showing the relation of one succeeding sensation to another. In each case, a glimpse of beauty produces an instantaneous vision that results in a poem. (p. 50)

The relationships that link one *haiku* to another vary widely: season, hour, some small detail of nature, color, or any other point that provides for an emotional movement, even if not a strictly logical one. What a Western mind terms the "association of ideas" is so expanded in the world of *haiku* composition that, for most Western readers at least, the reasons for the linkages often seem difficult to determine at first glance. . . . Sōseki often uses this seemingly random means to connect paragraphs in his narrative. Lying in his bath, the artist hears the sound of a samisen, which quickly suggests to his half-dreaming consciousness a neighbor girl who played the samisen when he was a child. . . . As does Proust, Sōseki uses the seemingly arbitrary workings of the mind to conjure up a whole childhood. His technique in doing so (although not unlike Proust's) is traditionally Japanese.

The central role of poetry in the literary conception behind *Kusamakura* is paramount. The artist never finishes a painting during his "non-human" tour. Yet, as Sōseki is at great pains to suggest, all forms of art are interrelated, and a visual or aural stimulation may produce a poem as easily, and as appropriately, as a picture. The protagonist writes many poems in traditional styles, both in Japanese and in classical Chinese, a form of poetry much favored in most periods of Japanese literary history for certain modes of philosophically directed expression. (pp. 50-1)

The beauty and efficacy of many other Japanese artistic forms are discussed throughout the book, ranging from calligraphy to *nō* and the tea ceremony. (p. 51)

Kusamakura is by no means merely a plea for traditional Japanese attitudes. The artist, like Sōseki, is trained in and committed to Western methods of art, and the trip remains an experiment on the traveller's part. Throughout the novel Sōseki shows he is well-versed in Western art and Western attitudes, and his Western examples are often most appropriately chosen. (p. 52)

Kusamakura is a remarkable attempt to define traditional Japanese aesthetics at least in part by contrasting them with those inherent in the kinds of lives led by Sōseki and his contemporaries. Such contrasts are never presented in any pejorative fashion, yet are sharply rendered nevertheless. The non-human is set against the human, ironic detachment against human involvement, leisure against speed, the aristocratic against the democratic. In particular, the sense of contrast shown between the painter's attempt to ''stand still'' and the throbbing vitality of Onami in her search for self-realization gives the book, through Sōseki's careful structuring, its narrative energy and turns what might have been a treatise into a novel.

The protagonist of *Kusamakura* does make discoveries as the novel progresses. Despite his desire to remain uninvolved (almost a passion in itself), he manages to come closer and closer to understanding the character of Onami, the mysterious young woman. . . . His mental "sketch" of her, which he feels must precede any actual sketch, remains unfinished until the last page of the novel. Sōseki creates an atmosphere of suspense that provides a certain ironic perspective on the mental world of the protagonist: his doubt about the nature of Onami serves to render arbitrary many of his other suppositions as well. He is slowly drawn into human involvements despite himself, and the movement of the narrative shows that such a course is inevitable. (p. 53)

The artist learns other views concerning Onami at various points in the narrative. For Gembei, the packhorse driver, she is a madwoman, from a long line of madwomen; for the barber, she is a harlot; for the Abbot of a nearby Zen temple, she is a wise and enlightened woman. Such widely divergent images are constantly juxtaposed against the artist's own discoveries about Onami, discoveries that also serve as a means to self-discovery for him. (p. 54)

Later in the novel, the protagonist sorts out his thoughts on Onami and tries to compare them with the wildly different accounts he has heard. He realizes that he has not yet grasped her personality and cannot yet understand what is lacking in her expression, something missing that prevents him from painting her beautiful face. . . .

The protagonist cannot see what Sōseki shows the reader: the deficiency of perception may be on the artist's part. Sōseki's ironies now become more obvious. (p. 56)

[The] reader begins to understand that Sōseki has set up the artist and Onami as parallel cases. Her study of Zen is an attempt to withdraw and to transcend, just as the artist is making a similar attempt on his ''non-human'' tour. The rhythm of their encounters, reinforced by Sōseki's ironic treatment of the pair, suggests that, to him, withdrawal from human concerns is not finally possible. . . .

The last image of the novel ties all the strands together. The artist's trip is over, and he accompanies Onami, her father, and the unfortunate Kyuichi [Onami's cousin] down to the city, where the young man will take a train to join the army. As the train departs, there is a last surprise [as Onami sees her ex-husband also departing on the train]. . . .

Onami has shown compassion and the painter has seen it. Emotion has entered the non-human world. Significantly, the Japanese word employed by Sōseki for ''compassion'' is *aware*,

that term defined earlier as perhaps the highest virtue that can be mirrored in literature. . . . (p. 58)

In bulk if nothing else, *Kusamakura* may seem more a sketch than a serious work. There is nothing remotely portentous about the text. . . . Yet Sōseki's humor and delicacy do not make his novel merely slight; indeed, Sōseki's artist begins his journey in the same way that Dante's hero does his. And the return journey from the mountain to the railroad, with the hint of the coming slaughter in the Russo-Japanese War, seems planned, artistically, to serve the same purposes in *Kusamakura,* as does the final descent from the mountain in Thomas Mann's *The Magic Mountain.* Both show war and the end of a civilization. For Sōseki, the modern world exists and we must simply live in it, with whatever wisdom and compassion we can muster. (pp. 58-9)

Kusamakura, however, maintains a peculiar charm because Sōseki's serious concerns are so concealed in the structures of the book. Both the artist and the reader are educated to understand that any escape into the past is at best a tour, a spree; the present must command our attention, and our compassion. Sōseki's artist comes to this awareness only at the end of the novel, but the reader is shown from the beginning the disparity between what the artist thinks and what he feels. This gap becomes a source of humor for Sōseki, who often makes fun of that disparity. (p. 60)

Irony is a coloration found throughout much of his best work and in *Kusamakura,* too, irony is the usual means to suggest larger perspectives. The reader feels an ache, of course, as the party leaves the delights of the mountain village for what seems the inevitable pain to follow. Sōseki wanted that ache to be felt. The novel serves as a farewell to the author's younger enthusiasms and to his own love for his traditional culture. How fitting that Sōseki should render so clearly a multitude of traditional literary attitudes, using so many traditional techniques, in this slight, profound, and very modern novel. (p. 61)

> *J. Thomas Rimer, ''Natsume Sōseki, The Past As Style: 'Kusamakura','' in his* Modern Japanese Fiction and Its Traditions: An Introduction *(copyright © 1978 by Princeton University Press; reprinted by permission of Princeton University Press), Princeton University Press, 1978, pp. 38-61.*

HISAAKI YAMANOUCHI   (essay date 1978)

[*The following essay examines a theme common to all Sōseki's major works—the possibilities for individual freedom and the difficulty of its realization in modern Japanese society.*]

Out of Sōseki's lectures, on a variety of authors from Shakespeare to George Eliot, grew two substantial critical works, [*A Theory of Literature (Bungakuron)* and *Literary Criticism (Bungaku Hyōron)*]. . . .

Of these two critical works the former is a product of the painstaking effort that he made in London in the midst of his neurosis. . . . Sōseki was seriously worried about the difficulties that confronted him and Japanese students of English literature in general. The cultural barrier that existed between England and Japan undeniably prevented Japanese students from understanding English literature with the same ease and sensitiveness as English scholars did. Japanese students might follow in the wake of English scholars and study English literature, adopting their methods of approach to it, but so long as they did this, they would never overtake English scholars.

The alternatives, then, would be either to express a uniquely personal view or to establish some objective standard similar to that of science. In conceiving of a plan to systematise literature in analogy to science, Sōseki was probably inspired by the frequent dialogues he had with Dr Ikeda Kikunae, a Japanese chemist, who was also studying in London at the time. In *A Theory of Literature* Sōseki thus tried hard to lay down a scientific theory of literature. The product that he made available to us is not very successful, but still his intention should be appreciated. In *Literary Criticism,* too, Sōseki is as keenly aware of the difficulties confronting Japanese students of English literature. However, while *A Theory of Literature* consists of a theoretical system, *Literary Criticism* is a survey of eighteenth-century English literature, dealing with individual authors such as Addison and Steele, Jonathan Swift, Alexander Pope and Daniel Defoe. Of these writers especially important to Sōseki is Swift, with whom he shares a deep-seated misanthropism and pungent satire. *Literary Criticism* differs from *A Theory of Literature* in another respect. In *A Theory of Literature* Sōseki aims at scientific objectivity, while in *Literary Criticism* he boldly expresses his personal and Japanese views although he incorporates, where relevant, English scholarship with exemplary exactitude. In brief, he demonstrated here an attitude which he was later to call 'inner-directed'. (pp. 51-2)

During the last ten years of his life, from about the age of forty, Sōseki produced more than a dozen long novels and some shorter works of varying content and form. Some results of his experiences in Britain and his knowledge of English literature are projected into the earlier works written before he resigned from the university. ['The Tower of London' ('Rondon-tō) and 'The Carlyle House' ('Kārairu Hakubutsukan')] . . . , for instance, are the by-products of his stay in London. 'The Tower of London' is a short piece narrated with historical and topographical accuracy. For the pathetic episode of the little princes murdered by order of Richard III Sōseki is indebted to Shakespeare's play and for the figure of an executioner to W. H. Ainsworth's *The Tower of London.* Even more interesting than these historical details, however, is the way in which Sōseki fuses the past and the present. Such an ingenious overlapping of 'a real character with a historical figure in the story effects the willing suspension of disbelief in the reader's mind. In the same year Sōseki wrote two stories with their settings in the times of King Arthur, 'A Shield of Phantom' ('Gen'ei no Tate') and 'An Elegy' ('Kairo-kō'). The latter is indebted to Malory's *Morte Darthur* and Tennyson's *Idylls of the King.* Sōseki's tale, however, differs from these sources in stressing the sinfulness of Lancelot's and Guinevere's illicit love and their consequent deaths. It seems possible that under the guise of medieval romance Sōseki represented the theme of tangled love relations and associated states which he was to elaborate in his later realistic novels.

The striking feature of *I am a Cat (Wagahai wa Neko de Aru. . .)* is that the whole novel is narrated by a cat. Consequently, Sōseki very amusingly tricks, or forces, us to look at the world through the eyes of this cat. The model for this omniscient creature was his own cat, which had strayed into his house and became the family pet. Likewise, the cat's master named Kushami-sensei or Professor Sneeze is a self-caricature of Sōseki, whom the cat wryly observes in a self-detached tone rare in modern Japanese novels. . . . [There] is very little development of the plot, and the whole novel consists of a series of episodes combined by free association as in Laurence Sterne's *Tristram Shandy.* . . . Similar allusions to English literature are innumerable all through *I am a Cat.* A striking feature of this novel is the fact that the hostility between the professor's circle and the surrounding world, which otherwise could be depressing, is enveloped by the sense of humour permeating the rest of the novel. While writing this novel, Sōseki suffered from persistent neurotic melancholy. Obviously repression is a conscious method of containing melancholy. But humour, as Freud noted, is a less conscious and more automatic mechanism of defence against depression. This literary and psychological device is exactly what Sōseki exercises in *I am a Cat,* a novel which, by virtue of its narrative technique, has no distinguished equivalent in modern Japanese literature.

Humour is also the keynote of *Little Master (Botchan. . .).* The hero is a teacher of mathematics arriving from Tokyo at a school in Matsuyama where Sōseki once taught English. But, unlike Sōseki and Professor Sneeze, the main characteristic of the protagonist of *Little Master* is not intellectual sophistication but a straightforward, and even reckless, bravado with which he fights for justice and against hypocrisy. Perhaps Quixotic is a suitable epithet for his character and behaviour. In this novel Sōseki is very skilled at vividly depicting the crudity, vulgarity, absurdity and boredom of life at a local school, from which the hero becomes more and more alienated. At the end of the novel the hero confronts his enemy, the deputy headmaster nicknamed Akashatsu (red shirt), coming out of a brothel, and thus exposes his hypocrisy. Instead of berating this pedant, the hero gives 'red shirt' a gratifying thrashing. Consequently, the little master resigns his post and goes back to Tokyo. Despite their obvious differences in other respects, the hero shares with Sōseki at least a deep sense of justice and outrage against hypocrisy. If Professor Sneeze is a caricature of Sōseki the introverted scholar, the hero of *Little Master* is perhaps a projection of the other side of Sōseki's character, a moral integrity, striking furiously against bureaucrats and other meddling fools.

Pillow of Grass (Kusamakura . . .) is a novel entirely different in kind from the two playful works just discussed. Sōseki calls it 'a novel in the manner of a *haiku',* or in more general terms one may call it 'a poem in prose'. The narrator is a painter, who leaves Tokyo for a remote mountain village to paint its scenery. The novel consists of the painter's reflections on art, scenic descriptions, encounters with people such as a Zen priest, and Nami, the daughter at the inn where he stays. The whole work is pervaded by some kind of ethereal other-worldliness stemming partly from the inherent qualities of the objects described and partly from the artistic detachment with which the painter eyes his subjects including Nami. . . . The name Nami, written in Chinese characters, can signify beauty. The painter's relationship to Nami as portrayed so far suggests that beauty is an elusive entity which becomes intangible at the very moment when it looks tangible. Nami is thus presented in a heightened tension between the tangible and intangible, concrete and abstract, real and unreal, and image and idea. . . . Towards the end of the novel, a way is prepared for the painter to be brought back to mundane reality. . . . In the last scene of the novel people go to the station to see Nami's cousin off, a conscript about to be sent off to Manchuria to fight in the Russo-Japanese War. When the departing train passes alongside the platform, Nami notices her husband is also on the train. They gaze upon each other for an instant; an instant which becomes an epiphany when 'compassion' betrays itself on her face. And the painter cries out, 'That's it! That's it! That makes a picture!' His journey to the village has been a conscious escape from the real to the ethereal. The whole process is now reversed, as, through this 'picture', he is made ready to return to the reality of Tokyo. Similarly Sōseki returned by leaving behind the quasi-romantic world of *Pillow of Grass* and moving to the more realistic one of *Autumn Wind (Nowaki . . .).* (pp. 53-9)

In *Autumn Wind* Sōseki contrasts Nakano who represents the social establishment, with two poor and socially alienated outsiders, Shirai and Takayanagi. Shirai devoutly believes in the cause of social reform, whereas Takayanagi, tubercular and depressed, is merely bitter about his own unhappiness. . . . Both Shirai and Takayanagi are alienated from society; but for Shirai the existing world is unreal or 'derealised' while he preserves his integral self. In Takayanagi's case, it is not only the external world but his self that is unreal. In other words, Takayanagi suffers a dissolution of his self, a loss Shirai has never experienced. This pair of characters may tell us of the conflict in Sōseki's own mind. Takayanagi may partly be a product of Sōseki's own sense of alienation and insecurity, which, however, he had to surmount like Shirai; such was the task Sōseki imposed on himself by choosing the career of a professional writer.

[*Wild Poppy (Gubijinsō)*], Sōseki's first novel serialised in the *Asahi Shimbun,* draws heavily on English literature for the characterisation and plot convention. Fujio, the arrogant and self-centred heroine who is proud of her own beauty and eventually commits suicide, is modelled on Cleopatra, the philosopher Kōno, her half-brother, on Hamlet and his friend Munechika on Horatio. The echoes of Meredith are also obvious. . . . Far from enriching the novel these echoes from English literature are responsible for the stereotyped characterisation.

[*Sanshirō, And Then . . . (Sorekara)* and *The Gate (Mon)*] are regarded as Sōseki's trilogy. . . . Some of the characters in *Sanshirō* are modelled partly on the people who gathered round Sōseki as his disciples from 1905 onwards. . . . The novel centres round Sanshirō's innocent but unrequited love for Mineko. In some respects the novel is like a comedy of manners, but its ultimate theme proves to be a tragic one. There is nothing intentional about Mineko's thwarting of Sanshirō's naïve affection, nor is there any bitterness in the latter's reaction to his lost love. . . . Thus from *Sanshirō* emerges the theme of man's vulnerability in love relationships, which is reiterated in the other two works of the trilogy.

In the second of the trilogy, *And Then* . . . , the tragedy originates from two men loving one woman, just as in a later work, *Kokoro.* In the earlier novel Daisuke renounces love for the sake of his friend Hiraoka, but within a few years all three find themselves unhappy. Daisuke, noticing that there no longer exists any love between his friend and his wife, asks his friend to give her away. . . . [Daisuke is] a rebel against the social code of the late Meiji period in two respects, first in his determination to marry the wife of his friend and secondly in his unwillingness to put his talents to the use of society. Though immoral from the point of view of society, he is nevertheless true to his heart's desires and embodies some kind of moral integrity. . . . Daisuke represents Sōseki's awareness of a tragic situation in late Meiji Japan, where the chasm between the moral vision of the ineffectual intellectuals and the rapidly 'modernised' society was becoming ever greater.

What would have happened to Daisuke and Michiyo later? This question is dealt with in the third of the trilogy, *The Gate,* in which the protagonist Sōsuke has betrayed his friend Yasui by snatching away his wife O-Yone. Sōseki begins the story in *medias res* and only halfway through gives a minimal and

retrospective account of how Sōsuke betrayed Yasui. As a consequence of his act of betrayal Sōsuke suffers from insecurity, both social and psychological. With only limited prospects in his career as a low-rank bureaucrat he is another example of a character who feels himself redundant. (pp. 59-62)

The insecurity of Sōsuke's life can also be attributed to another factor beyond his control. He lost his father while still a child, and then his uncle's mismanagement dissipated the legacy to which he and his younger brother Koroku were entitled. The theme of betrayal converges in Sōsuke, who is at once the betrayed and the betrayer. . . . Sōseki so constructs this novel that the passage of time from autumn to winter coincides with the aggravation of Sōsuke's insecurity and O-Yone's declining health. At the end of the novel O-Yone celebrates with a touch of hope the coming of spring, to which Sōsuke responds only with anticipation of another winter: 'Yes, but it will be winter again.'

Sōseki's concern with the theme of the difficulty of communication between individuals reappears in the novels he wrote in his last years. In *The Wayfarer (Kōjin . . .),* for instance, the protagonist Ichirō is tantalised by his wish and inability to love and to be loved heart and soul by his wife Nao. He represents the type of unhappy intellectual whose abstract attitude to life lacks emotional suppleness. Alienating and alienated from Nao, Ichirō even becomes susceptible to a paranoiac phantasy that Nao bears illicit love desires towards his younger brother Jirō. When Ichirō asks Jirō to test her by giving her an opportunity to let her heart out, Jirō declines his brother's request, but at least agrees to talk to Nao so that her relationship with Ichirō could be improved. . . . This novel then could be linked with the earlier works in which Sōseki dealt with triangular love relationships. *The Wayfarer,* however, clearly differs from the earlier works. In *The Gate,* for instance, the protagonists become alienated from society through their guilt but the emotional ties between them are strengthened as a result. By contrast, in *The Wayfarer* Jiro's virtuousness prevents him from committing a sin with Nao but this does not facilitate communication between them, nor does it improve the relationship of Nao with her husband.

In *The Wayfarer* Sōseki provides an interesting psychological study. . . . [It emerges] that by the word 'wayfarer' is meant a person who is eternally harassed by the lack of purpose in life, by perpetual insecurity and by estrangement from external reality. (pp. 64-7)

The contents of *The Wayfarer* cannot be discussed separately from the novel's structure. It centres round the psychology of alienation in neurotic Ichirō. Sōseki has so deftly constructed the novel that it contains multiple points of view, even though throughout the novel Jirō serves as the narrator. The episode of the mad woman in part I, for instance, is meant to parallel and contrast with Ichirō's state of mind. Part II leads up to the dramatic situation in which Jirō as the narrative point of view becomes fully involved in the task of investigating unsuccessfully what Nao really feels towards Ichirō. Jirō continues to function as the point of view in part III. The last twenty-five chapters in part IV consist of the letters written by Mr H, who accompanies Ichirō on his trip. While revealing the symptoms of Ichirō's acute neurosis, they also show the limits of Jirō's knowledge and understanding. There is therefore every reason for Mr H to supplement what has been narrated by Jirō. Because of the complexities of Ichirō's psychological state, it is natural for the author to adopt these multiple points of view without imposing an interpretation of his own. Looked at in this way

The Wayfarer is an example of Sōseki's experiment with the psychological novel, a form which he developed in *Kokoro* and finally in *Light and Darkness*.

In *Kokoro* (*Kokoro* . . .) Sōseki abandons the position of an omniscient author and has the first two parts narrated by a first person. The third part consists of the suicide note of Sensei, the mentor of the narrator for the first two parts. Sōseki constructs the novel so that the conflicts of value in the narrator's mind coincide with the bifocal structure of the novel. The narrator is attracted to Sensei because of his intelligence and sage-like detachment from the world. In Sensei Sōseki has created another of those characters who is intellectually powerful but socially ineffectual. The narrator's parents are a kind of landed gentry of the provincial countryside who can conceive of his future career in nothing but pragmatic terms. Just when his own father is lying on his death-bed, the narrator receives by post a thick envelope containing Sensei's suicide note. He rushes to Tokyo without even saying goodbye to his dying father. Sensei's suicide note discloses two main causes for his misanthropism and eventual suicide. First, as a young man he was cheated of part of his legacy after his parents' death. Secondly, and more important, his marriage to a woman with whom both he and his best friend were in love drove the latter to suicide. Because of his feelings of guilt he could never again establish perfect rapport with his wife. Having been the victim of evil, Sensei in turn inflicted it upon another. Sōseki is thus concerned with moral evil stemming from egotism.

The narrator loses both his actual and his spiritual fathers. Their deaths further overlap with the decease of the Emperor Meiji and General Nogi. In comparing his own suicide with that of General Nogi, Sensei says that he is going to kill himself because of the spirit of Meiji. What is implied by this testament? The assertion of ego was one of the major concerns in Japan's modernisation along Western lines. The failure of personal egotism in his own case makes Sensei look back with mixed feelings upon the ideals of the early Meiji, when forward-looking modernisation and right spiritual values appeared inseparable, indeed identical. By the end of the Meiji this coherence was breaking apart, with the spiritual ideals increasingly overshadowed and atomised by the material progress of an impersonal industrialisation. Sensei's suicide then represents one answer to the predicament of perceptive intellectuals in a post-Meiji Japan. (pp. 69-70)

Among Sōseki's works *Grass on the Wayside* (*Michikusa* . . .) is unique as an explicitly autobiographical novel, although it differs from the works of the I-novelists. Kenzō, the main character, is pestered by his foster-parents and their relatives for the money to which they claim to be entitled. He has thus to deal once again in flesh and blood with people who have been continually present in his subconscious as ghosts from the past. His childhood experience of the pettiness of his foster-parents, of their discord leading to separation and of his being sent back and forth between three households are factors that later cause his psychological insecurity. All these correspond more or less to what happened to Sōseki himself. Another theme of the novel centres round the tense relationship between Kenzō and his wife, the causes for which are various. The reminders of the past when he was pestered by his foster-parents cannot exert anything but a baleful influence upon Kenzō and his wife. The straitened financial state of her parents' family helps to engender further tension. These external circumstances might have had little adverse effect but for Kenzō's character which only serves to complicate the relations between him and

his wife. His attitude to women inherited from Meiji Japan does not allow him to acknowledge his wife as an independent person. Besides, his tendency to intellectual abstraction serves as an obstacle to establishing a rapport not only with his wife but with the world at large. Failing to attain authenticity in his mode of life, he is insecure.

All these themes are recurrent in other works of Sōseki's later period. *Grass on the Wayside,* however, is quite distinct. Kenzō's afflictions in his present life are tightly bound up with those in the past. . . . In writing *Grass on the Wayside,* Sōseki projected a great deal of his own life history not only by dealing with his present sufferings but also by tracing their origins in his childhood. It is an autobiographical novel unique in modern Japanese literature. Unlike many of the I-novelists Sōseki is free from self-pity or masochistic probing into his own malady; he penetrates into the depths of his subconscious, observes what he sees with objective detachment and represents it in an artistic form.

In Sōseki's last and unfinished work, *Light and Darkness (Meian* . . .), the action develops slowly and uneventfully round the protagonist Tsuda and his wife O-Nobu. As the major characters in the novel they have nothing very distinctive about them. Their married life is peaceful on the surface, but there exists a barrier beyond which they cannot get through to one another. Instead of O-Nobu, Tsuda might have married Kiyoko, who suddenly left him to marry another man without giving any explanation. This may be partly responsible for Tsuda's inability to love O-Nobu totally. Other characters intrude to complicate their relations. O-Hide, Tsuda's younger sister, for instance, meddles with the arrangement for Tsuda to receive financial assistance from his father. Kobayashi pesters Tsuda with requests for alms. Mrs Yoshikawa, the wife of Tsuda's superior, arranges things so that, under the pretext of convalescence from an operation on a fistula, Tsuda goes to a hot spring where Kiyoko is staying on her own. Left unfinished owing to Sōseki's untimely death, *Light and Darkness* allows little room for conjecturing how it might have developed further. (pp. 70-2)

Sōseki was trying to project all his major concerns into this novel. Estrangement or lack of communication between individuals is the central theme as in *And Then . . . , The Gate, The Wayfarer, Kokoro* and *Grass on the Wayside.* It also shares with these works the theme of tangled love relations although there is no shadow of guilt in this work. There is also the problem of money which alienates relatives and friends as in *Kokoro* and *Grass on the Wayside.* . . . The alienation of the main characters in *Light and Darkness* arises not so much from any particular external circumstances but from their personalities. (p. 72)

In *Light and Darkness* everybody is shut up within his or her own cell partitioned off from one another by impenetrable walls. In presenting this theme Sōseki expanded more than ever the range of the psychological novel with which he had experimented in *The Wayfarer* and *Kokoro*. That the psychological analysis of the characters is much more detailed is evinced by the short period of time. All the events take place in one week, which, if not comparable with the one day of James Joyce's *Ulysses,* is nevertheless a short time for a novel of several hundred pages. (p. 73)

These characters are so much divorced from one another that the author is not in a position to provide a unified, omniscient point of view in which every character is grasped as part of a totality. In conceiving such a structure for the novel, Sōseki to some extent transcended nineteenth-century realism and came a step closer to the psychological novels of Henry James and after.

In August 1911 Sōseki gave a talk in Wakayama entitled **'The Enlightenment of Modern Japan'** (**'Gendai Nihon no Kaika'**), which together with another of his talks given three years later, **'My Individualism'** (**'Watakushi no Kojinshugi'**), evinces his insight into the cultural milieu of modern Japan. The gist of his talk is that the Enlightenment in the West was a process of self-awakening, whereas in Japan it was brought about by external forces. For this growth and reaction Sōseki coined, respectively, the words *naihatsu-teki* (inner-directed) and *gaihatsu-teki* (outer-directed). . . . Sōseki had no illusion about the fact that under the overwhelming influence of the West modern Japanese culture was inevitably bound to be derivative or parasitic. . . . Out of this derived Sōseki's ultimate criticism of the Enlightenment of modern Japan: that it is superficial. Anybody with as sensitive a perception as Sōseki's must have found himself under heavy strain . . . . (pp. 76-7)

'My Individualism', given at the Peers' School on 25 November 1914, can be read as a supplement to **'The Enlightenment of Modern Japan'**. Sōseki elaborates his argument by referring to his own experiences of studying English literature. In his account he introduces the word *tanin-hon'i* (reliance on other people). What he means by this word is that as a Japanese student of English literature, he had for a long time no choice but to rely on the achievements of English scholars and critics. Reliance on Western scholars and critics was part of the phenomenon which Sōseki previously described as 'outer-directed'. . . . Sōseki's dilemma was greater because of his conscientious attitude towards the study of English literature. . . . The 'self-reliance' Sōseki thus attained is a variation of what he described in the previous talk as 'inner-directed'. After explaining the process by which he attained this notion, Sōseki discusses it in a general, social context. He extends the notion of 'self-reliance' to the fulfilment of individual potential in society. This concept is what he means by 'individualism' in the title of his talk. There are additional noteworthy features of Sōseki's individualism. First, it must be distinguished from mere selfishness. . . . In other words, Sōseki's individualism is a 'moralistic individualism', something similar to Kantian 'autonomy'. Secondly, it stands out distinctly against the factionalism or group behaviour characteristic of Japanese society. . . . Sōseki goes on to delineate the third and final trait of his concept of individualism—its priority to nationalism although the two need not conflict with each other. . . . It emerges from the foregoing discussion that one of the major themes of Sōseki's work is his concern for individual freedom and the difficulty of its realisation in modern Japanese society. Instead of attaining fully integrated personalities, many of his characters often suffer from alienation, insecurity and other abnormal states of mind. Individual freedom is the basis on which interpersonal communication should be established, and yet in actual fact it is bound to bring about the conflict of interest and to lapse into selfish egotism. Everybody is then estranged from everybody else and all become enemies of one another. Sōseki was especially aware of two cases in which egotism entails moral evil: tangled love relations and man's acquisitive desire for properties. His preoccupation with complex love relations may have originated in his aspiration to the eternal female figure, either real or imaginary. His concern for the money problem derived from his involvement with his foster-parents and other relatives. Notably enough, it is not only that the characters he created to represented these themes often undergo the disintegration of personality, but also that the way in which he was preoccupied with these themes is obsessively neurotic.

Inseparable from his personal suffering was Sōseki's cultural confrontation with the Western world. The anxieties and worries he endured as a scholar of English literature might never have disturbed a less scrupulous and less perceptive person. To overcome the difficulties of English literature he proposed two solutions for Japanese scholars: to aspire to scientific objectivity and to cultivate one's personal taste in literary studies. Neither, in fact, proved entirely successful. Sōseki's attempt to base literary criticism on his personal taste was a declaration of independence from English scholarship, and yet, ironically enough, it was a Japanisation of an essentially English attitude. In this instance as well as in his defence of individualism he showed that Japanese culture should be an 'inner-directed' synthesis, for which neither jingoism nor superficial imitation of the West would do.

Sōseki demonstrated all this in the process by which he became a professional writer during the last decade of his life. His earlier works echo to the sounds of English literature in such forms as allusions, character types and plot conventions. These ostensible echoes became less apparent as he matured into a realistic novelist. This does not mean, however, that he discarded English literature. On the contrary it had been assimilated and had become part and parcel of his writing in a most fruitful way. His expert knowledge of the English novel as well as his psychological studies enabled him to achieve the kind of realism which distinguishes itself from that of the Japanese naturalist I-novelists. While the latter were concerned with self-exposure in their naïvely autobiographical novels and stories, Sōseki rendered his experiences into an authentic form of literary art. (pp. 77-81)

Hisaaki Yamanouchi, "The Agonies of Individualism: Natsume Sōseki," in his The Search for Authenticity in Modern Japanese Literature *(© Cambridge University Press 1978), Cambridge University Press, 1978, pp. 40-81.*

JOHN UPDIKE (essay date 1983)

Sōseki's was a wan talent, given to affectionate descriptions of the weather and drifting accounts of conversational impasse within the paper walls of Japanese homes. **"Mon"** takes place in 1909-1910, and **"I Am a Cat"** shortly after the conclusion, in 1905, of the Russo-Japanese War—a lopsided triumph for the Japanese that signalled their arrival as the newest of the world's imperial powers and that on the other side helped trigger czarist Russia's slide into revolution. Yet Sōseki's characters take small comfort from Japan's international burgeoning and remind us of Chekhov's gentle, dithering, futile gentry. The debilitating effects of Westernization are one of Sōseki's themes, and one he was well qualified to understand: a student of English literature, he lived in England for the first three years of the century and returned in 1903 to succeed Lafcadio Hearn as lecturer in English literature at Tokyo's Imperial University. (p. 66)

"I Am a Cat" was Sōseki's first novel and made his fame. Written by a teacher, it is bookish; it is riddled with the lore and tag names of Western culture, from Aeschylus and Seneca to Leibniz and Nietzsche and Carlyle and right up to date with William James and Henry James and George Meredith. "Tristram Shandy'' gets mentioned, and readers who relish that work's stalled action and endless playful quibbling might find the discourses of **"I Am a Cat"** less tedious than did this reviewer, who lost track, often, of who is talking and what is being talked about. A nameless cat, a stray tossed by a student into the household of a disgruntled, dyspeptic, jam-loving, poem-writing schoolteacher called Mr. Kushami, gives a narrative account of what he overhears there and in a few neighboring houses, chiefly that of a businessman called Kaneda, his big-nosed wife, and a marriageable daughter. . . . The cat, though born in ''a gloomy damp place'' and destined to drown in a rain barrel at the age of two, spices his account with an unexpected knowledgeability: he knows that ''Chikamatsu is considered as the Shakespeare of Japan'' and observes of Mrs. Kaneda that her eyes are ''thinner than the eyes of a whale,'' though where a Tokyo alley cat would have seen a whale is left to the imagination. The narrator seems very much a cat at places, chasing insects and climbing trees and falling in love with other cats, and at other places scarcely distinguishable from the woolgathering human riffraff that visits and heckles Mr. Kushami. A certain carelessness in regard to its central premise prevents **"I Am a Cat"** from developing the wit and force of such zoomorphic fables as Kafka's ''Report to an Academy,'' Orwell's ''Animal Farm,'' and the Houyhnhnms section of ''Gulliver's Travels.'' The panoramic possibilities of a prowling cat as silent, intelligent witness are oddly stunted; beyond a few forays into the Kanedas' house next door, our feline commentator seems content to take the human comedy as it arrives, with monotonous talkiness, in Mr. Kushami's six-mat room.

Several passages do, however, develop a sustained interest. The author has closely observed pet cats, and the protagonist's preening upon ''the plum-blossom marks of my paws on the porch'' and interrogations of his own twitching tail gratify us with specificity, and even with poetry. . . . Sōseki also knew students and the discomforts of discipline, and the chapter on the campaign of teasing launched upon poor Mr. Kushami by the pupils of the nearby Raku-unkan (Descending Cloud) Junior High School has enough authority and embodied emotion to induce us to stop counting the pages as we read. The second half of the book is better than the first; it takes Sōseki too long to bring Mr. Kushami into focus. We are told repeatedly that he is a fool, but the core of his foolishness is not laid bare. Is it that he, like Molière's *bourgeois gentilhomme*, is obsessed by an inappropriate aspiration? Or is he meant to be made rigid, like one of Shakespeare's peripheral clowns, by a dominant humor? ''My master has always been too rigid. He is as crusty as coke and terribly intolerant besides,'' the cat claims at one point; but the behavior we see is characterized by a certain sullen passivity rather than any dynamic crustiness. He is a hypochondriac—''an idiot and an invalid,'' the cat confides—but not much is done with the farcical possibilities of *un malade imaginaire*. His comic flaw seems to consist, at bottom, in being merely human—''He wants the luxury of being an invalid but not of being sick enough to die. If he were told that his illness were fatal, he, being timid, would most probably tremble.'' The cat likens his master to ''a spent arrow shot from a strong bow,'' a phrase that perhaps sums up much of Sōseki's unease about the society around him. Westernization threw a harsh light into the cloisters of traditional Japanese culture; it brought doubt, followed by a vulgar busyness of imitation. Without overwhelming conviction but with a poignance of wounded feeling, Sōseki articulates a reactionary easing of this doubt. The Zen master, Dokusen, though ridiculed

elsewhere in the novel, is allowed to frame a shrewd critique of the West:

> I believe the Japanese of old were much more clever than most Westerners. Westerners want to be positive and this is quite the fashion in Japan today, but being so positive has a great defect. In the first place, there's no limit to the craving for satisfaction. A state of thorough completeness is never attained. Do you see those cypress trees over there? Well, you say to yourself that they're unsightly so you clear them away; then it would be the boarding house beyond them that irritates you. There would be no limit to your search for the perfect view. Westerners are like this. . . . One cannot stop the sun from setting nor can one reverse the flow of the Kamo River. But what we can all manage to control is our own mind.

The novel ends with an abrupt prayer to Buddha and the assertion ''Peace cannot be had without dying.'' Throughout this diffuse and feebly organized tale, Sōseki shows a fine gift for aphorism, that recourse of resigned minds. . . . (pp. 66-7)

"Mon," which translates as ''The Gate'' but has been allowed to stand as the translation's title, tells of a couple, Sosuke and Oyone, who married in haste and amid disapproval, as they six years later worry through some minor difficulties in their isolated, chastened life together in Tokyo. (p. 67)

As with **"I Am a Cat,"** but less exasperatingly, this short novel is stabbingly sketched, with blank places a Western novelist would have felt obliged to fill in. The exact incidents of the couple's original fall into disgrace and marriage are left vague. . . . Yet as a portrait of domestic life and daily discontents, Japanese style, **"Mon"** is pleasant to read, and its very diffidence serves to pique our interest. As with Mr. Kushami, it is hard to know exactly what is wrong with Sosuke, that he is incapable of either action or contentment. ''As he walked through the black night, he thought of his desire to escape from his poverty of spirit. He felt himself weak, restless, fearful, uncertain, cowardly and mean.'' When he goes to ''the gate''—the path of Zen, as disclosed during his retreat at the temple—the result is neither illumination nor drastic disillusion and consequent resolve. ''He had come here to have the gate opened to him, but its warden had remained obstinately within.'' The temple head—the *roshi*—sets Sosuke a *koan* with a casualness that borders on contempt:

> ''I suppose it doesn't make much difference what you begin with,'' the *roshi* told Sosuke. ''How about trying to work on 'What was my Face before my parents were born?' ''

The wry religious comedy of the novice's inexpert and distracted meditation follows: ''It even occurred to him as he sat there trying to meditate that this was all very silly.'' We are never told what answer to the *koan* Sosuke comes up with, but the *roshi* pronounces it unsatisfactory:

> The *roshi* spoke only one sentence to Sosuke, who sat before him, drained of all spirit. ''If you haven't more to offer than that, you shouldn't have come; anyone with even a little education could say as much as you said.''
>
> Sosuke left the room feeling like a dog whose master had died. Behind him the gong clanged loudly.

"Drained of all spirit" he remains—a kind of "spent arrow" in a world where enterprise belongs entirely to others and religious impulse has been reduced to an objectless longing. When the pale but patient Oyone remarks that it is at last spring, her husband replies that it will soon be winter, and keeps cutting his fingernails. Natsume Sōseki's refusal to force his material toward pat conclusions or heightened climaxes represents a kind of negative power, that surrender to irregularlity which is one of art's maneuvers of renewal. Sosuke does not struggle against his "fate" (a recurrent word), and his creator does not struggle to give his little novel more shape than the untransfigured lives within it deserve. A certain Western restlessness has penetrated these lives, but no concomitant hope. (pp. 67-8)

Sōseki seems present in his passive, baffled protagonists—embodied wistfully in the youthful Sosuke, and erratically parodied in the figure of Mr. Kushami. Both novels left this reader, at his several removes in space and time, with the sensation of music heard fitfully across the water; that both appeared beguiling and relevant to their contemporary audience is a historical fact, but the secret of their beguilement lies well below the surface of these rather dusty, stiff translations. (p. 68)

John Updike, "Spent Arrows and First Buddings" (©1983 by John Updike), in The New Yorker, *Vol. LVIII, No. 46, January 3, 1983, pp. 66-70.**

ADDITIONAL BIBLIOGRAPHY

Griffith, Charles Q. "*Kokoro* and *The Setting Sun*." In *Sôseki and Salinger: American Students on Japanese Fiction,* edited by George Saitô and Philip Williams, pp. 25-32. Tokyo: The Eihôsha, 1971.*
    Comparison of the two novels in regard to theme, tone, and major and minor characters.

Hibbett, Howard S. "Natsume Sōseki and the Psychological Novel." In *Tradition and Modernization in Japanese Culture,* edited by Donald H. Shively, pp. 305-46. Princeton: Princeton University Press, 1971.
    Examines Sōseki's later novels.

Japan National Commission for UNESCO. *Essays on Natsume Sô-seki's Works.* Tokyo: Japan Society for the Promotion of Science, 1970, 143 p.
    Collection of critical material by contemporary scholars and writers.

Jones, Sumie. "Natsume Sōseki's *Botchan*: The Outer World through Edo Eyes." In *Approaches to the Modern Japanese Novel,* edited by Kinya Tsuruta and Thomas E. Swann, pp. 148-65. Tokyo: Sophia University, 1976.
    Examines the extent to which Natsume uses the colloquial speech of the Edo period.

Oughton, Robyn. "Suicides in Salinger and Sôseki." In *Sôseki and Salinger: American Students on Japanese Fiction,* edited by George Saitô and Philip Williams, pp. 11-24. Tokyo: The Eihôsha, 1971.*
    Comparison of the lives and deaths of two characters: Seymour Glass in Salinger's "A Perfect Day for Bananafish" and Sôseki's Sensei in *Kokoro.*

Takeo, Doi. *The Psychological World of Natsume Sôseki.* Cambridge: East Asian Research Center, Harvard University, 1976, 161 p.
    A psychological interpretation of Sôseki's major characters.

Friedrich (Wilhelm) Nietzsche

1844-1900

German philosopher, essayist, poet, and autobiographer.

Nietzsche is considered one of the most important philosophers of the nineteenth and twentieth centuries. His thought has influenced nearly every aspect of modern culture. Among his many achievements, he is credited with being a forerunner of existentialism, the first philosopher to recognize nihilism as a historical phenomenon and to utilize it as a source for positive values, and an important psychological theorist to whom Sigmund Freud was admittedly grateful, especially for the psychoanalytic concepts of sublimation and repression. Nietzsche was a master stylist, reintroducing the aphorism to German prose, and he had a profound effect in the field of epistemology, particularly in his assaults on the reliability of language. Besides his impact on philosophy and psychology, Nietzsche significantly shaped the development of twentieth-century literature. Such writers as Rainer Maria Rilke, Stefan George, Gottfried Benn, Thomas Mann, Hermann Hesse, André Gide, William Butler Yeats, and Bernard Shaw were all influenced by Nietzsche's works. In general, Nietzsche has had a crucial effect on the intellectual development of Western society: his thought signified the disintegration of the nineteenth century's social, religious, and scientific optimism and anticipated the nihilist sensibility of the modern world.

Nietzsche was born in Röcken, Prussia. His father and both of his grandfathers were ministers and Nietzsche's early childhood was spent in a devoutly religious environment. When Nietzsche was four years old, his father suffered a serious fall, injured his head, and died soon after. Two years later his mother moved the family to Naumburg, where Nietzsche grew up in a household of five women: his mother, his grandmother, two maiden aunts, and his younger sister, Elizabeth. His relationships with these women, critics suggest, accounts for some of Nietzsche's prejudicial comments about women in later years. Between 1858 and 1864 he attended the Schulpforta, a famous boarding school outside Naumburg, where he acquired a thorough education in classical literature and history. Upon graduation he entered the University of Bonn, where he studied theology and classical philology, but in 1865 he decided against theology and transferred to the University of Leipzig. There he studied under the noted philologist Friedrich Ritschl and discovered the works of Arthur Schopenhauer and Richard Wagner, the two greatest influences on his early thought. It was as a student that Nietzsche supposedly contracted syphilis after visiting a Cologne brothel, a claim that has never been validated. This illness has been the focus of much debate because of Nietzsche's eventual madness—which most experts agree was probably caused by tertiary syphilis—and because of Thomas Mann's treatment of it in his novel *Doktor Faustus*, wherein the protagonist, Adrian Leverkühn, contracts syphilis and follows a path into insanity similar to Nietzsche's.

After a brief military service between 1867 and 1868, Nietzsche was recommended by Ritschl for the chair of classical philology at the University of Basel. Though he had not yet written a doctoral thesis, nor the dissertation required before a doctor of philosophy becomes a university lecturer, Nietzsche was

appointed associate professor at the age of twenty-four. While at Basel he occasionally visited Wagner at his home in Tribschen, Switzerland. The two became close friends, though for Wagner the friendship assumed a more practical purpose: in Nietzsche he found a young, responsive scholar who could lend authority to his artistic vision—the rebirth of German myth in drama and music. For his part, Nietzsche greatly admired Wagner and believed that his music was the modern incarnation of Hellenic tragedy. Out of this association came one of Nietzsche's most important works: *Die Geburt der Tragödie aus dem Geiste der Musik (The Birth of Tragedy)*. The final sections of the book, added to the original draft after Wagner befriended Nietzsche, consist of a rhapsody on the rebirth of tragedy in Wagner's operas. Following the publication of *The Birth of Tragedy*, the Nietzsche-Wagner friendship began to suffer; a second book on Wagner was postponed several times until the publication in 1876 of *Richard Wagner in Bayreuth*—a slender volume which completed Nietzsche's four-volume *Unzeitgemässe Betrachtungen (Thoughts Out of Season)*. These volumes all focus on the deterioration of German culture following the Franco-Prussian war.

Throughout his life Nietzsche's health was poor. He suffered from a number of ailments, including severe headaches, gastric pains, diarrhea, and partial blindness. In 1879 his poor health forced him to retire from his post at the university. Yet he continued reading and writing. During the late 1870s and early 1880s he published three books—*Menschliches, Allzumenschliches: Ein Buch für freie Geister (Human, All Too Human: A Book for Free Spirits), Die Morgenröte: Gedanken über die moralischen Vorurteile (The Dawn of Day)*, and *Die fröhliche Wissenschaft (The Joyful Wisdom)*—each of which noted a shift in his interests from art and aesthetics to science and "the free spirit," an individual unfettered by conventions or history. These works were soon followed by Nietzsche's most renowned publication: *Also sprach Zarathustra: Ein Buch für Alle und Keinen (Thus Spake Zarathustra: A Book for All and None)*. Published in four volumes, *Thus Spake Zarathustra* contains the first presentation of Nietzsche's mature philosophy. It is here that he introduces his concepts of the will to power, the *Übermensch* (the "overman" or "superman"), and the eternal return. All of Nietzsche's subsequent works, especially *Jenseits von Gut und Böse: Vorspiel einer Philosophie der Zukunft (Beyond Good and Evil: Prelude to a Philosophy of the Future)* and *Zur Genealogie der Moral (The Genealogy of Morals)*, support and elaborate the ideas put forth in *Thus Spake Zarathustra*. Nietzsche wrote his final works during an extended period in 1888 when his health seemed to improve. Of these the most significant are *Die Götzendämmerung; oder, Wie man mit dem Hammer philosophiert (The Twilight of the Idols)* and *Der Antichrist (The Antichrist)*. In both works Nietzsche violently attacked Christianity, proclaiming the superiority of his own philosophy of heroic vitalism. In January 1889, Nietzsche collapsed on a street in Turin, Italy. His mind was completely disoriented, and he grew progressively worse until he became a complete mental and physical invalid. He lived for eleven years before his death at Weimar.

Many critics divide Nietzsche's work into three periods, each one representing a different stage in the development of his thought. The first, from 1872 to 1876, culminates in a philosophy based on the Dionysian, or destructive, aspect of music; the second, from 1878 to 1882, is noted for its break with metaphysical speculation and its emphasis on nihilism and a pragmatic approach to the world; the third, from 1883 to 1889, contains Nietzsche's three-point perspective of the will to power, the *Übermensch,* and the eternal return, and is recognized for its prophetic and polemical character. Though some critics argue that the sudden shifts in Nietzsche's philosophical thought demonstrate the erratic nature of his intellect, others, such as Rudolf Steiner, Eric Bentley, and Peter Heller, believe a single idea passes through and unifies each stage. For Steiner this idea is the concept of the *Übermensch;* for Bentley it is Nietzsche's concept of power; for Heller it consists of Nietzsche's dedication to the Dionysian process.

Nietzsche's first important essay, *The Birth of Tragedy*, deals specifically with the deterioration of Greek culture following the rise of rationalist Socratic thought. Nietzsche believed that before Socrates Greek culture consisted of two tendencies: the Apollonian—the process of restraint, harmony, and measure that found expression in Greek sculpture and architecture—and the Dionysian, a savage longing to resist all norms that found its outlet in the drunken orgies of the Dionysian festivals and the music associated with them. In *The Birth of Tragedy*, Nietzsche challenged the prevalent conception of Greek art by positing the idea that Hellenic tragedy was essentially the outcome of the Apollonian-Dionysian synthesis—the Dionysian captured in the chorus and the music and the Apollonian represented by the actors and the text. Essentially, Greek tragedy—at its very beginning—sought to affirm life in the presence of the terrors of nature and history. After Socrates, when the quest for rational rather than mystical truth became the preoccupation of philosophers, Greek culture began to deteriorate; the Dionysian was suppressed in favor of the Apollonian, and art, as well as culture, became obsessed with the beauty of form. Nietzsche took up this theme of cultural decadence again in his next work, *Thoughts Out of Season*, but this time with respect to Germany in the 1870s, which he believed was following a course similar to the Greeks in its attraction to systems of external forms and empirical thought. Following attacks on David Strauss, whom Nietzsche considered a "cultural philistine," and the German educational system, he praised Schopenhauer as a relentless thinker who possessed the courage to form his own vision of the world—one which attacked the same optimistic spirit and facile rationalism of the nineteenth century that Nietzsche also deplored.

The second period in Nietzsche's development, which begins with *Human, All Too Human,* signified a dramatic shift in his philosophy. He rejected Schopenhauer and Wagner for Voltaire and Socrates; he attacked art and metaphysics and, instead, espoused science and free thinking. All of the works in this period—*Human, All Too Human, The Dawn of Day,* and *The Joyful Wisdom*—demonstrate the meaninglessness of the world and the decadent origin of religion, especially Christianity. Nietzsche constructed a portrait of the human being as an animal devoid of free will, acting strictly out of fear or desire. He also suggested a number of concepts which are more fully developed in his final works, such as the will to power and the contrast of master and slave moralities. Here power is defined as the individual's ability to give "style" to his or her character. Master and slave moralities are tied directly to Nietzsche's critique of Christianity, the former born out of affirmation and a desire to live, the latter born of resentment and fear. Essentially, the works of this period served to free Nietzsche from the influence of Schopenhauer and Wagner—a separation which had to occur before he could completely control the direction of his thought.

The third and final period in Nietzsche's career consisted of seven books, but none are as prominent as *Thus Spake Zarathustra*. This imaginative work alternates between essay and parody, epigram and dithyramb, wit and bathos. Here, through the persona of his prophet Zarathustra, Nietzsche set forth his concept of the will to power as the essence of all beings. According to Nietzsche, what every living being wants more than anything else is a higher, more powerful state of existence in which the inertia of the present state is overcome. Power is a process of becoming; it never achieves its end, but is always seeking to surpass its present state. From the concept of power Nietzsche constructs his ideal individual: the *Übermensch*. The *Übermensch* is the highest type to which humanity should strive; he is the human being who has organized the chaos of his passions, given style to his character, and become creative. Aware of the meaninglessness of life, the *Übermensch* affirms life without resentment. What sets the *Übermensch* apart from general humanity is the ability to endure the implications determined by Nietzsche's most mystical doctrine: the "eternal return of the same." This hypothesis states that the universe evolves in gigantic cycles, repeating itself at distant intervals. To Nietzsche the ramifications of such a concept are obvious: if one's life is to be endlessly repeated throughout eternity, it is extremely important—in order to endure this phenomenon—that one accept and affirm existence without resentment. In this scheme, which can be viewed as an antithesis to the Christian conception of time and history, the world no longer has a purpose; it is an eternally repeated senseless play of forces and it takes someone of the spiritual stature of the *Übermensch* to affirm life in the face of such a gruesome prospect. The remainder of Nietzsche's works after *Zarathustra* more or less elaborate on these concepts, with the exception of his caustic autobiography *Ecce Homo: Wie Man wird, was Man ist (Ecce Homo)*. This book is the most controversial of Nietzsche's final works. With such chapter titles as "Why I Am So Wise" and "Why I Write Such Excellent Books," *Ecce Homo* was attacked by many critics as self-serving and without literary merit, and Nietzsche was called a megalomaniac. However, the autobiography offers an insightful account of Nietzsche's philosophical development; and what early critics considered self-aggrandizing was later considered Nietzsche's sense of humor and irony. Nietzsche's last major work, published after his death, is *Der Wille zur Macht (The Will to Power)*. This book consists of some of the notes Nietzsche accumulated from 1884 to 1888, systematically arranged by his sister. Although the systematic arrangement makes it easy to see what Nietzsche had to say about religion, morality, epistemology, art, and so forth, it is not generally regarded as Nietzsche's magnum opus, as some critics and scholars have argued. Though Nietzsche planned to write a book called "The Will to Power"—later changed to "Revaluation of All Values," of which *The Antichrist* was to be the first volume—most critics agree that the version published by his sister in no way approximates what the author himself might have accomplished.

The history of Nietzsche criticism is nearly as diverse and complex as the author's work itself. Early critics found it difficult to assess Nietzsche's philosophy. Some argued that he was pathological and that his work was the result of a sick mind. Although most critics were not this extreme, many felt that Nietzsche's thought was at best interesting, but hardly demanded serious consideration. However, there were a few interpreters, in particular Georg Brandes and Rudolf Steiner, who understood the significance of Nietzsche's ideas, both for their own times and for the twentieth century. They praised the author for his awareness of the cultural decay in Europe, for his insights into individual psychology, and for his studies in ethics and morality. As a result of Brandes's lectures and work on Nietzsche, the philosopher's popularity increased steadily during the 1890s, reaching its peak at the outbreak of World War I. After the war Nietzsche fell out of favor, but his ideas were taken up again, with even more vigor, during the 1930s by the National Socialists in Germany. With the encouragement of Nietzsche's sister, the Nazis systematically perverted his thought for the purpose of propaganda, particularly Nietzsche's concept of the will to power, which the Nazis interpreted exclusively in terms of military superiority. They also attributed to Nietzsche feelings of anti-Semitism and nationalism which are the precise opposite of his stated views. Because of his erroneous association with Nazi ideology, Nietzsche was unjustly attacked during and immediately following World War II. Some critics tried—as did Thomas Mann—to reevaluate Nietzsche's work in the light of contemporary events, but it wasn't until the 1950s and 1960s that Nietzsche once again received favorable international attention. New interpretations of his work came to the forefront: Walter Kaufmann published the first edition of his landmark study on Nietzsche, and Martin Heidegger attempted to demonstrate the integrity of Nietzsche's philosophy—a philosophy, Heidegger argued, designed to answer the question of being. Today Nietzsche is considered one of the most imposing figures of the nineteenth and twentieth centuries. He is often praised for his theories on Greek culture, many of which were derided

in his lifetime; for his views on decadence and nihilism; for his experiments with language, which were later developed by the phenomenologists and deconstructionists; and for his contribution to the field of psychology. At the same time, Nietzsche has been criticized for his failure to develop a systematic philosophy, for his dogmatism, for his glorification of power, for the impracticality of many of his ideas, and for his attacks on metaphysics, though he was probably one of the most metaphysical thinkers of his age. Ultimately, critics agree that Nietzsche is most important for the influence of his ideas—for the effect of his thought rather than the validity of its presentation.

Although there are more than four thousand books and articles on Nietzsche, critics and scholars have only begun to assess his impact on twentieth-century thought. More than seventy-five years after his death, his life and work have lost none of their fascination. Nietzsche's appeal is confined to no single group; it crosses all boundaries. To use the word he applied to himself in *Ecce Homo*, he became a "destiny" for many people, including some of the leading artists and thinkers of our century.

(See also *Contemporary Authors*, Vol. 107.)

PRINCIPAL WORKS

Die Geburt der Tragödie aus dem Geiste der Musik (essay) 1872
  [*The Birth of Tragedy* published in *The Complete Works of Friedrich Nietzsche*, Vol. 1, 1909]
*Unzeitgemässe Betrachtungen. 4 vols. (essays) 1873-76
  [*Thoughts Out of Season* published in *The Complete Works of Friedrich Nietzsche*, Vols. 4 and 5, 1909-10]
**Menschliches, Allzumenschliches: Ein Buch für freie Geister. 2 vols. (essays and aphorisms) 1878-80
  [*Human, All Too Human: A Book for Free Spirits*, 1908]
Die Morgenröte: Gedanken über die moralischen Vorurteile (essays and aphorisms) 1880
  [*The Dawn of Day*, 1903]
Die fröhliche Wissenschaft (essays and aphorisms) 1882
  [*The Joyful Wisdom* published in *The Complete Works of Friedrich Nietzsche*, Vol. 10, 1910]
Also sprach Zarathustra: Ein Buch für Alle und Keinen. 4 vols. (prose) 1883-85
  [*Thus Spake Zarathustra: A Book for All and None*, 1909]
Jenseits von Gut und Böse: Vorspiel einer Philosophie der Zukunft (essays and aphorisms) 1886
  [*Beyond Good and Evil: Prelude to a Philosophy of the Future*, 1907]
Zur Genealogie der Moral (essays and aphorisms) 1887
  [*The Genealogy of Morals* published in *The Complete Works of Friedrich Nietzsche*, Vol. 13, 1910]
Der Fall Wagner: Ein Musikanten-Problem (essay) 1888
  [*The Case of Wagner* published in *The Complete Works of Friedrich Nietzsche*, Vol. 8, 1911]
Die Götzendämmerung; oder, Wie man mit dem Hammer philosophiert (essays) 1889
  [*The Twilight of the Idols* published in *The Complete Works of Friedrich Nietzsche*, Vol. 16, 1911]
Nietzsche contra Wagner: Aktenstücke eines Psychologen (essay) 1889
  [*Nietzsche Contra Wagner* published in *The Complete Works of Friedrich Nietzsche*, Vol. 8, 1911]
Dionysus Dithyramben (poetry) 1891

Der Antichrist (essays) 1895
[*The Antichrist*, 1920]
Ecce Homo: Wie man wird, was man ist (essays) 1908
[*Ecce Homo*, 1911]
Der Wille zur Macht (notebooks, essays, and aphorisms)
1909-10
[*The Will to Power* published in *The Complete Works of
Friedrich Nietzsche*, Vols. 14 and 15, 1909-10]
The Complete Works of Friedrich Nietzsche. 18 vols.
(essays, aphorisms, notebooks, and poetry) 1909-13
Gesammelte Werke. 23 vols. (essays, aphorisms,
notebooks, and poetry) 1920-29
Selected Letters of Friedrich Nietzsche (letters) 1921
Fifty Poems (poetry) 1965

*This work includes the essays *David Strauss, der Bekenner und der
Schriftsteller (David Strauss, the Confessor and the Writer)*, *Vom
Nützen und Nachteil der Historie für das Leben (On the Uses and
Disadvantages of History for Life)*, *Schopenhauer als Erzieher (Scho-
penhauer As Educator)*, and *Richard Wagner in Bayreuth*.

**This work includes the essay *Der Wanderer und sein Schatten (The
Wanderer and His Shadow)*.

F[RANZ] LISZT (letter date 1872)

[*The excerpt below is taken from a letter to Nietzsche by the
composer Franz Liszt.*]

Mounting obligations have until now prevented me from conveying to you my most sincere thanks for sending a copy of
your captivating book **The Birth of Tragedy,** which I have read
twice. The mighty spirit storming and blazing within it has
stirred me deeply. I must, of course, confess I lack the training
and the knowledge to appreciate your book to the full: Hellenism and the idolatry scholars practise towards it have remained more or less foreign to me. I used to regard the raising
of the altar "*deo ignoto*" as the highest spiritual act of the
Athenians—the moment Paul proclaimed the unknown God the
whole of Parnassus fell into shattered ruin. My gaze is not
tempted to linger in the shades of Parnassus and Helicon—but
Tabor and Golgotha, to them my soul gladly cleaves.

So forgive me, dear Sir, if I only manage to express my admiration in an imperfect manner, though I do so without hesitation or reserve. Your important and penetrating exegeses of
the "Apollonian and Dionysian" elements in myth and tragedy
are amazingly illuminating and magnificently expressed. Nowhere have I found such a beautiful definition of art as this:
"Art is the completion and consummation of existence, se-
ducing us to a continuation of life." And such aphorisms! "A
people, or any individual for that matter, is valuable only to
the extent it succeeds in imprinting its experiences with the
stamp of the eternal." Sayings like this find a deep echo in
my heart.

Let us pray God that the delusion and the woe of the world
may succumb more and more to the will!

> F[ranz] Liszt, in his letter to Dr. Nietzsche on Feb-
> ruary 29, 1872, translated by David S. Thatcher
> (reprinted by permission of David S. Thatcher), in
> The Malahat Review, *No. 24, October, 1972, p. 7.*

H. TAINE (letter date 1886)

[*French philosopher, critic, and historian Hippolyte Taine was,
along with Georg Brandes (see excerpt below), among the first
leading thinkers of the nineteenth century to recognize Nietzsche's
genius.*]

On my return from a journey I found the book that you were
good enough to send me; as you express it, it is full of thoughts
that pierce behind the veil. Its vivid literary style and often
paradoxical expression will open the eyes of the reader who
wants to be initiated.

I shall recommend to philosophers what you say upon philosophy . . . but historians and critics will also find a store of
new ideals. . . .

What you say upon national character and genius in your eighth
essay is infinitely suggestive. I shall re-read this passage, although it speaks far too flatteringly of myself. (p. 262)

> H. Taine, in his letter to Friedrich Nietzsche on Oc-
> tober 17, 1886, in his Life and Letters of H. Taine:
> 1870-1892, *Vol. III,* edited and translated by
> E. Sparvel-Bayly, Archibald Constable & Co Ltd,
> 1908, pp. 262-63.

AUGUST STRINDBERG (letter date 1888)

[*The following letter was part of a brief correspondence between
Nietzsche and Strindberg. This exchange was initiated by Nietzsche,
who was seeking translators in four languages for* Ecce Homo.
Strindberg's reply expresses his appreciation for Zarathustra, *one
of the books Nietzsche had sent to him.*]

There is no doubt that you have bestowed upon humanity the
deepest book that it possesses, and moreover, have had the
courage and possibly also the urging to spit these magnificent
words straight into the faces of this pack of rogues! For that I
thank you! Nevertheless it appears to me that in your liberality
of spirit, you have to some degree flattered the criminal types.
If you regard the hundreds of photographs which illustrate
Lombroso's types of criminal, you will be convinced that the
felon is a low sort of animal, a degenerate, a weakling who
does not possess the necessary faculties to enable him to evade
the more powerful laws which oppose themselves to his will
and power. Just observe how stupidly moral most of these
brutes really appear! What a disillusion for morality!

And you desire to be translated into our Greenlandish tongue!
Why not into French or English? You may judge of our intelligence by the fact that there was talk of putting me into an
asylum because of my tragedy, and that this mob-majority has
succeeded in imposing silence upon so fine and lofty a spirit
as Brandes.

I conclude all my letters to my friends; Read Nietzsche! That
is my *Carthago est delenda!*

At all events your greatness will decline from the very moment
when you become known and understood, and the dear mob
begins to acclaim you as one of its own kidney. It is better
that you preserve that aristocratic aloofness, and permit us other
ten thousand spirits of finer fire to make pilgrimages to your
holy of holies in order to refresh ourselves to the full. Let us
guard the esoteric truth in order to keep it pure and whole, and
not allow it to become common property save by means of
devoted disciples—in whose name I sign myself,

> "AUGUST STRINDBERG."
> (pp. 199-200)

August Strindberg, in his letter to Friedrich Nietzsche in 1888, in The North American Review *(reprinted by permission from* The North American Review; *copyright © 1913 by the University of Northern Iowa), Vol. CXCVIII, No. 693, August, 1913, pp. 199-200.*

FRIEDRICH NIETZSCHE   (essay date 1888)

[*The criticism below is taken from Nietzsche's autobiographical essays in* Ecce Homo, *written in 1888 shortly before his collapse but not published until 1908. It is perhaps this work, more than any other, which led critics to consider Nietzsche a megalomaniac and a madman.*]

In order to be just to **'The Birth of Tragedy'** . . . one will have to forget a few things. It made its *effect* and even exercised fascination through what was wrong with it—through its application to *Wagnerism*, as if this were a symptom of a *beginning*. That is what made this book an event in Wagner's life: it was only from then on that great hopes surrounded the name Wagner. Even today people remind me, sometimes in the middle of *Parsifal*, that it is really *I* who have it on my conscience that so high an opinion of the *cultural value* of this movement has come to predominate.—I have often found the book cited as 'the *Re*birth of Tragedy out of the Spirit of Music': people have had ears only for a new formula for the art, the intention, the task of *Wagner*—what of value was concealed in the book was thereby not listened to. 'Hellenism and Pessimism': that would have been a less ambiguous title: that is to say as a first instruction in how the Greeks got rid of pessimism—with what they *overcame* it. . . . Precisely tragedy is the proof that the Greeks were *no* pessimists: Schopenhauer blundered in this as he blundered in everything.—Taken up and viewed impartially, the **'Birth of Tragedy'** looks very untimely: one would not dream it was *begun* amid the thunders of the battle of Wörth. I thought these problems through before the walls of Metz, in cold September nights while serving in the medical corps; one would rather believe the book to be fifty years older. It is politically indifferent—'un-German' one would say today—it smells offensively Hegelian, it is in only a few formulas infected with the cadaverous perfume of Schopenhauer. An 'idea'—the antithesis dionysian and apollonian—translated into the metaphysical; history itself as the evolution of this 'idea'; in tragedy this antithesis elevated to a unity; from this perspective things which had never before caught sight of one another suddenly confronted with one another, illuminated by one another and *comprehended* . . . for example opera and revolution. . . . The book's two decisive *novelties* are, firstly the understanding of the *dionysian* phenomenon in the case of the Greeks—it offers the first psychology of this phenomenon, it sees in it the sole root of the whole of Hellenic art—. The other novelty is the understanding of Socratism: Socrates for the first time recognized as an agent of Hellenic disintegration, as a typical *décadent*. 'Rationality' *against* instinct. 'Rationality' at any price as dangerous, as a force undermining life!—A profound hostile silence with regard to Christianity throughout the book. It is neither apollonian nor dionysian, it *negates* all *aesthetic* values—the only values the **'Birth of Tragedy'** recognizes: it is in the profoundest sense nihilistic, while in the dionysian symbol there is attained the extreme limit of *affirmation*. (pp. 78-9)

The four *untimely essays* [**'David Strauss, The Confessor and Writer'**; **'On the Use and Disadvantage of History for Life'**; **'Schopenhauer as Educator'**; and **'Wagner in Bayreuth'**] are altogether warlike. They demonstrate that I was no 'Jack o'

Dreams', that I derive pleasure from drawing the sword—also, perhaps, that I have a dangerously supple wrist. The *first* attack . . . was on German culture, which even at that time I already looked down on with remorseless contempt. Without meaning, without substance, without aim: a mere 'public opinion'. There is no more vicious misunderstanding than to believe that the Germans' great success in arms could demonstrate anything in favour of this culture—not to speak of *its* victory over France. . . . The *second* untimely essay . . . brings to light what is dangerous, what gnaws at and poisons life, in our way of carrying on science—: life *sick* with this inhuman clockwork and mechanism, with the '*im*personality' of the worker, with the false economy of 'division of labour'. The *goal* gets lost, culture—the means, the modern way of carrying on science, *barbarzied* . . . In this essay the 'historical sense' of which this century is so proud is recognized for the first time as a sickness, as a typical sign of decay.—In the *third* and *fourth* untimely essays two pictures of the sternest *selfishness, self-discipline* are erected against this, as signposts to a *higher* concept of culture, to the restoration of the concept 'culture': untimely types *par excellence*, full of sovereign contempt for all that around them which was called 'Reich', 'culture', 'Christianity', 'Bismarck', 'success'—Schopenhauer and Wagner *or*, in *one* word, Nietzsche. . . . (p. 84)

That the untimely essays designated with the names Schopenhauer and Wagner could contribute very greatly to an understanding of these two cases, or even to the posing of psychological questions about them, I would not like to assert—a few things in them of course excepted. Thus, for example, what is elemental in Wagner's nature is even here with profound certainty of instinct designated as an actor's talent the methods and objectives of which are only consequences of it. What I really wanted to do in these essays was something quite other than to pursue psychology—a problem of education without its like, a new concept of *self-discipline, self-defence* to the point of harshness, a way to greatness and to world-historical tasks demanded its first expression. What I did by and large was to take two famous and still altogether undetermined types by the forelock, as one takes an opportunity by the forelock, in order to say something, in order to have a couple more formulas, signs, means of expression in my hands. This is, with perfectly uncanny sagacity, even indicated on page 183 of the third untimely essay. It was in this way that Plato employed Socrates, as a semiotic for Plato.—Now, when I look back from a distance at the circumstances of which these essays are a witness, I would not wish to deny that fundamentally they speak only of me. The essay **'Wagner in Bayreuth'** is a vision of my future; on the other hand, in **'Schopenhauer as Educator'** it is my innermost history, my *evolution* that is inscribed. Above all my *solemn vow*! . . . What I am today, *where* I am today—at a height at which I no longer speak with words but with lightning-bolts—oh how far away I was from it in those days!—But I *saw* the land—I did not deceive myself for a moment as to the way, sea, danger—*and* success! Great repose in promising, this happy looking outward into a future which shall not always remain a promise!—Here every word is experienced, profound, inward; the most painful things are not lacking, there are words in it which are downright blood-soaked. But a wind of the *great* freedom blows across everything; the wound itself does *not* act as an objection.—How I understand the philosopher, as a fearful explosive material from which everything is in danger, how I remove my concept 'philosopher' miles away from a concept which includes in it even a Kant, not to speak of the academic 'ruminants' and other professors of philosophy: as to this the essay offers an invaluable instruction, even admitting that what is being spoken of is fundamentally not **'Schopenhauer as Educator'** but his *opposite,* 'Nietzsche as Educator'.—Considering that my trade was at this time that of a scholar, and perhaps too that I *understood* my trade, an astringent piece of psychology of the scholar which suddenly appears in this essay is not without significance: it expresses *feeling of distance,* my profound certainty as to what can be my *task* and what merely means, interlude and extra. It is my sagacity to have been many things and in many places so as to be able to become *one person*—so as to be able to attain *one thing.* For a time I *had* also to be a scholar. (pp. 87-8)

'Human, All Too Human' is the memorial of a crisis. It calls itself a book for *free* spirits: almost every sentence in it is the expression of a victory—with this book I liberated myself from that in my nature which *did not belong to me.* Idealism does not belong to me: the title says: 'where *you* see ideal things, *I* see—human, alas all too human things!' . . . I know humanity *better* . . . The expression 'free spirit' should here be understood in no other sense: a spirit that has *become free,* that has again seized possession of itself. The tone, the sound of the voice has completely changed: one will find the book sagacious, cool, sometimes harsh and mocking. A certain spirituality of *noble* taste seems to be in constant struggle to keep itself aloft above a more passionate current running underneath. In this connection there is significance in the fact that it is actually the hundredth anniversary of the death of Voltaire with which the book as it were apologizes for being published in 1878. For Voltaire is, in contrast to all who have written after him, above all a *grandseigneur* of the spirit: precisely what I am too.—The name of Voltaire on a writing by me—that really was progress—*towards myself* . . . If one looks more closely, one discovers a merciless spirit who knows every hiding-place in which the ideal is at home—where it has its castle-keep and as it were its last place of security. With a torch in hand which gives no trembling light I illuminate with piercing brightness this *underworld* of the ideal. It is a war, but a war without powder and smoke, without warlike attitudes, without pathos and contorted limbs—all this would still have been 'idealism'. One error after another is calmly laid on ice, the ideal is not refuted—*it freezes* . . . Here for example 'the genius' freezes; on the next corner 'the saint' freezes; 'the hero' freezes into a thick icicle; at last 'faith', so-called 'conviction', freezes; 'pity' also grows considerably cooler—almost everywhere 'the thing in itself' freezes . . . (pp. 89-90)

With [**'Daybreak'**] begins my campaign against *morality.* Not that it smells in the slightest of gunpowder—quite other and more pleasant odours will be perceived in it, provided one has some subtlety in one's nostrils. Neither big nor even small guns: if the effect of the book is negative, its means are all the less so, means from which the effect follows like a conclusion *not* like a cannon-shot. That one takes leave of the book with a cautious reserve in regard to everything that has hitherto been honored and even worshipped under the name morality does not contradict the fact that in the entire book there is no negative word, no attack, no malice—that it rather lies in the sun, round, happy, like a sea-beast sunning itself among rocks. In the end it was I myself who was this sea-beast: almost every sentence in the book was thought, *tracked down* among that confusion of rocks near to Genoa where I was alone and still shared secrets with the sea. Even now, when I chance to light on this book every sentence becomes for me a spike with which I again draw something incomparable out of the depths: its entire skin trembles with tender shudders

of recollection. The art in which it is preeminent is no small one in making things which easily slip by without a sound, moments which I call divine lizards, stay still for a little—not with the cruelty of that young Greek god who simply impaled the poor little lizard, but nonetheless still with something sharp, with the pen . . . 'There are so many daybreaks that have not yet dawned'—this *Indian* inscription stands on the gateway to this book. Where does its author *seek* that new dawn, that hitherto still undetected tender roseate sky with which another day—ah, a whole series, a whole world of new days!—breaks? In a *revaluation of all values,* in an escape from all moral values, in an affirmation of and trust in all that has hitherto been forbidden, despised, accursed. This *affirmative* book pours its light, its love, its tenderness upon nothing but evil things, it restores to them their 'soul', the good conscience, the exalted right and *privilege* to exist. Morality is not attacked, it only no longer comes into consideration. . . . This book ends with an 'Or?'—it is the only book which ends with an 'Or?' . . . (pp. 95-6)

[**'Beyond Good and Evil'**] is in all essentials a *critique of modernity,* the modern sciences, the modern arts, not even excluding modern politics, together with signposts to an antithetical type who is as little modern as possible, a noble, an affirmative type. In the latter sense the book is a *school for gentlemen,* that concept taken more spiritually *and radically* than it has ever been taken. One has to have courage in one even to endure it, one must never have learned fear. . . . All the things of which the age is proud are felt as contradictions of this type, almost as bad manners, for example its celebrated 'objectivity', its 'sympathy with all that suffers', its 'historical sense' with its subjection to the taste of others, with its prostration before *petits faits,* its 'scientificality'.—If one considers that the book comes *after* Zarathustra one will also perhaps divine the dietetic *regime* to which it owes its existence. The eye grown through a tremendous compulsion accustomed to seeing *afar*—Zarathustra is more farsighted even than the Tsar—is here constrained to focus sharply on what is close at hand, the age, what is *around us.* In every aspect of the book, above all in its form, one will discover the same *intentional* turning away from the instincts out of which a Zarathustra becomes possible. Refinement in form, in intention, in the art of *keeping silent,* is in the foreground, psychology is employed with an avowed harshness and cruelty—there is not a single good-natured word in the entire book. . . . All this is recuperative: who could in the end divine *what* kind of recuperation is needed after such an expenditure of goodness as Zarathustra is? . . . Speaking theologically—pay heed, for I rarely speak as a theologian—it was God himself who at the end of his labour lay down as a serpent under the Tree of Knowledge: it was thus he recuperated from being God . . . He had made everything too beautiful . . . The Devil is merely the idleness of God on that seventh day. . . . (pp. 112-13)

The three essays of which [**'The Genealogy of Morals'**] consists are in regard to expression, intention and art of surprise perhaps the uncanniest things that have ever been written. Dionysos is, as one knows, also the god of darkness.—Each time a beginning which is *intended* to mislead, cool, scientific, even ironic, intentionally foreground, intentionally keeping in suspense. Gradually an increasing disquiet; isolated flashes of lightning; very unpleasant truths becoming audible as a dull rumbling in the distance—until at last a *tempo feroce* is attained in which everything surges forward with tremendous tension. At the conclusion each time amid perfectly awful detonations a *new* truth visible between thick clouds.—The truth of the *first* essay is the psychology of Christianity: the birth of Christianity out of the spirit of *ressentiment, not,* as is no doubt believed, out of the 'spirit'—essentially a counter-movement, the great revolt against the domination of *noble* values. The *second* essay gives the psychology of the *conscience*: it is *not,* as is no doubt believed, 'the voice of God in man'—it is the instinct of cruelty turned backwards after it can no longer discharge itself outwards. Cruelty here brought to light for the first time as one of the oldest substrata of culture and one that can least be thought away. The *third* essay gives the answer to the question where the tremendous *power* of the ascetic ideal, the priestly ideal, comes from, although it is the *harmful* ideal *par excellence,* a will to the end, a *décadence* ideal. Answer: *not* because God is active behind the priests, which is no doubt believed, but *faute de mieux*—because hitherto it has been the only ideal, because it had no competitors. 'For man will rather will nothingness than *not* will' . . . What was lacking above all was a *counter-ideal*—until the advent of Zarathustra.—I have been understood. Three decisive preliminary studies of a psychologist for a revaluation of all values.—This book contains the first psychology of the priest. (pp. 114-15)

This writing of fewer than 150 pages ['**Twilight of the Idols'**], cheerful and fateful in tone, a demon which laughs—the work of so few days I hesitate to reveal their number, is the exception among books: there exists nothing more rich in substance, more independent, more overthrowing—more wicked. If you want to get a quick idea of how everything was upsidedown before me, make a start with this writing. That which is called *idol* on the title-page is quite simply that which has hitherto been called truth. *Twilight of the Idols*—in plain terms: the old truth is coming to an end. . . .

There is no reality, no 'ideality' which is not touched on in this writing (—touched on: what a cautious euphemism! . . .). Not merely *eternal* idols, also the youngest of all, consequently weakest with age. 'Modern ideas', for example. A great wind blows among the trees and everywhere fruits fall—truths. There is the prodigality of an all too abundant autumn in it: one trips over truths, one even treads some to death—there are too many of them. . . . But those one gets one's hands on are no longer anything questionable, they are decisions. Only I have the standard for 'truths' in my hand, only I *can* decide. As if in me a *second consciousness* had grown, as if in me 'the will' had turned on a light for itself over the *oblique* path on which it had hitherto been *descending.* . . . The *oblique* path—it was called the 'path to truth' . . . All 'obscure impulse' is at an end, it is precisely the *good* man who has known least what was the right path . . . And, in all seriousness, no one before me has known the right path, the *ascending* path: only after me are there again hopes, tasks, prescribable paths of culture—*I am the bringer of the good tidings of these* . . . Precisely therewith am I a destiny. (pp. 116-17)

> *Friedrich Nietzsche, in his* Ecce Homo: How One Becomes What One Is, *translated by R. J. Hollingdale (translation copyright © R. J. Hollingdale, 1979; reprinted by permission of Penguin Books Ltd; originally published as* Ecce Homo: Wie Man wird, was Man ist. Insel Verlag, 1908), *Penguin Books, 1979, 140 p.*

GEORGE BRANDES (essay date 1889)

[*The following excerpt is drawn from Brandes'* Friedrich Nietzsche, *the first full-length study devoted to Nietzsche's life and work. In*

it he praises the philosopher for his accute observations on the detrimental effects of historical education.]

Four of Nietzsche's early works bear the collective title, *Thoughts out of Season (Unzeitgemässe Betrachtungen),* a title which is significant of his early-formed determination to go against the stream.

One of the fields in which he opposed the spirit of the age in Germany is that of education, since he condemns in the most uncompromising fashion the entire historical system of education of which Germany is proud, and which as a rule is everywhere regarded as desirable.

His view is that what keeps the race from breathing freely and willing boldly is that it drags far too much of its past about with it, like a round-shot chained to a convict's leg. He thinks it is historical education that fetters the race both in enjoyment and in action, since he who cannot concentrate himself on the moment and live entirely in it, can neither feel happiness himself nor do anything to make others happy. Without the power of feeling unhistorically, there is no happiness. And in the same way, forgetfulness, or rather, non-knowledge of the past is essential to all action. Forgetfulness, the unhistorical, is as it were the enveloping air, the atmosphere, in which alone life can come into being. . . . [For] Nietzsche, there exists a certain degree of historical knowledge which is destructive of a man's energy and fatal to the productive powers of a nation. (pp. 15-16)

[What] is interesting and significant of Nietzsche's whole intellectual standpoint is his inquiry as to how far life is able to make use of history. History, in his view, belongs to him who is fighting a great fight, and who needs examples, teachers and comforters, but cannot find them among his contemporaries. Without history the mountain chain of great men's great moments, which runs through milleniums, could not stand clearly and vividly before me. (p. 17)

Nietzsche's quarrel is ultimately with the broken-winded education of the present day. That *education* and *historical education* have in our time almost become synonymous terms, is to him a mournful sign. It has been irretrievably forgotten that culture ought to be what it was with the Greeks: a motive, a prompting to resolution; nowadays culture is commonly described as inwardness, because it is a dead internal lump, which does not stir its possessor. (p. 18)

Significant of Nietzsche's aristocratic tendency, so marked later, is his anger with the deference paid by modern historians to the masses. Formerly, he argues, history was written from the standpoint of the rulers; it was occupied exclusively with them, however mediocre or bad they might be. Now it has crossed over to the standpoint of the masses. But the masses—they are only to be regarded as one of three things: either as copies of great personalities, bad copies, clumsily produced in a poor material, or as foils to the great, or finally as their tools. Otherwise they are matter for statisticians to deal with, who find so-called historical laws in the instincts of the masses—aping, laziness, hunger and sexual impulse. What has set the mass in motion for any length of time is then called great. It is given the name of a historical power. When, for example, the vulgar mob has appropriated or adapted to its needs some religious idea, has defended it stubbornly and dragged it along for centuries, then the originator of that idea is called great. There is the testimony of thousands of years for it, we are told. But—this is Nietzsche's and Kierkegaard's idea—the noblest and highest does not affect the masses at all, either at the moment or later. Therefore the historical success of a religion, its toughness and persistence, witness against its founder's greatness rather than for it. (pp. 19-20)

[For Nietzsche] history is not so sound and strengthening an educational factor as is thought: only he who has learnt to know life and is equipped for action has use for history and is capable of applying it; others are oppressed by it and rendered unproductive by being made to feel themselves late-comers, or are induced to worship success in every field. (p. 21)

What kind of a writer is it who warns us with such firm conviction against the dangers of historical culture? A philologist obviously, who has experienced them in himself, has felt himself threatened with becoming a mere aftermath and tempted to worship historical success. What kind of a nature is it that so passionately defines culture as the worship of genius? Certainly no Eckermann-nature, but an enthusiast, willing at the outset to obey where he cannot command, but quick to recognise his own masterful bias, and to see that humanity is far from having outgrown the ancient antithetical relation of commanding and obeying. The appearance of Napoleon is to him, as to many others, a proof of this; in the joy that thrilled thousands, when at last they saw one who knew how to command. But in the sphere of ethics he is not disposed to preach obedience. On the contrary, constituted as he is, he sees the apathy and meanness of our modern morality in the fact that it still upholds obedience as the highest moral commandment, instead of the power of dictating to one's self one's own morality.

His military schooling and participation in the war of 1870-71 probably led to his discovery of a hard and manly quality in himself, and imbued him with an extreme abhorrence of all softness and effeminacy. He turned aside with disgust from the morality of pity in Schopenhauer's philosophy and from the romantic-catholic element in Wagner's music, to both of which he had previously paid homage. He saw that he had transformed both masters according to his own needs, and he understood quite well the instinct of self-preservation that was here at work. The aspiring mind creates the helpers it requires. Thus he afterwards dedicated his book, *Human, all-too-Human,* which was published on Voltaire's centenary, to the "free spirits" among his contemporaries; his dreams created the associates that he had not yet found in the flesh. The severe and painful illness, which began in his thirty-second year and long made him a recluse, detached him from all romanticism and freed his heart from all bonds of piety. . . . This illness made a philosopher of him in a strict sense. His thoughts stole inquisitively along forbidden paths: This thing passes for a value. Can we not turn it upside-down? This is regarded as good. Is it not rather evil?—Is not God refuted? But can we say as much of the devil?—Are we not deceived? and deceived deceivers, all of us? . . .

And then out of this long sickliness arises a passionate desire for health, the joy of the convalescent in life, in light, in warmth, in freedom and ease of mind, in the range and horizon of thought, in "visions of new dawns," in creative capacity, in poetical strength. And he enters upon the lofty self-confidence and ecstasy of a long uninterrupted production. (pp. 22-3)

> *George Brandes, "An Essay on Aristocratic Radicalism" (originally published as "Friedrich Nietzsche: En Afhandling om aristokratiek Radikalisme," in his* Essays: Fremmede Personligheder, *Vol. 2, 1889), in*

> *his* Friedrich Nietzsche, *translated by A. G. Chater, William Heineman, 1909, pp. 1-56.*

MAX NORDAU　(essay date 1892)

[*Nordau's study represents an extreme example of the psychological approach adopted by many early critics when interpreting Nietzsche's thought. In it he considers Nietzsche's philosophy as the result of a sick mind. Nearly all twentieth-century critics have refuted the idea that Nietzsche's thought was greatly influenced by his eventual insanity, though some, including James Huneker and Stefan Zweig (see excerpts below), argue that his feverish philosophical quest could have contributed to his insanity.*]

From the first to the last page of Nietzsche's writings the careful reader seems to hear a madman, with flashing eyes, wild gestures, and foaming mouth, spouting forth deafening bombast; and through it all, now breaking out into frenzied laughter, now sputtering expressions of filthy abuse and invective, now skipping about in a giddily agile dance, and now bursting upon the auditors with threatening mien and clenched fists. So far as any meaning at all can be extracted from the endless stream of phrases, it shows, as its fundamental elements, a series of constantly reiterated delirious ideas, having their source in illusions of sense and diseased organic processes. . . . Here and there emerges a distinct idea, which, as is always the case with the insane, assumes the form of imperious assertion, a sort of despotic command. Nietzsche never tries to argue. If the thought of the possibility of an objection arises in his mind, he treats it lightly, or sneers at it, or curtly and rudely decrees, 'That is false!' . . . For that matter, he himself contradicts almost every one of his violently dictatorial dogmas. He first asserts something and then its opposite, and both with equal vehemence, most frequently in the same book, often on the same page. Now and then he becomes conscious of the self-contradiction, and then he pretends to have been amusing himself and making sport of the reader. (pp. 416-17)

Nietzsche's assertions are either commonplaces, tricked out like Indian caciques with feather-crown, nose-ring, and tattooing (and of so mean a kind that a high-school girl would be ashamed to make use of them in a composition-exercise); or bellowing insanity, rambling far beyond the range of rational examination and refutation. (p. 417)

Rarely is a thought developed to any extent; rarely are a few consecutive pages connected by any unity of purpose or logical argument. Nietzsche evidently had the habit of throwing on paper with feverish haste all that passed through his head, and when he had collected a heap of snippings he sent them to the printer, and there was a book. . . . [Each] one of Nietzsche's assertions is contradicted by himself in some place or other, and if it be resolved, with barefaced dishonesty, to pay regard to dicta of a definite kind only, and to pass over those in opposition to them, it would be possible at pleasure to extract from Nietzsche a philosophical view or its sheer opposite. (pp. 419-20)

Nietzsche's ranting includes some ideas which, in part, respond to a widespread notion of the age, and in part are capable of awakening the deception that, in spite of all the exaggeration and insane distortion of exposition, they contain a germ of truth and right; and these ideas explain why many persons agree with them who can hardly be reproached with lack of clearness and critical capacity. Nietzsche's fundamental idea of utter disregard and brutal contempt for all the rights of others standing in the way of an egoistical desire, must please the generation reared under the Bismarckian system. . . . His doctrine shows how Bismarck's system is mirrored in the brain of a maniac. Nietzsche could not have come to the front and succeeded in any but the Bismarckian and post-Bismarckian era. He would, doubtless, have been delirious at whatever period he might have lived; but his insanity would not have assumed the special colour and tendency now perceptible in it. It is true that sometimes Nietzsche vexes himself over the fact that 'the type of the new Germany most rich in success in all that has depth . . . fails in "swagger,"' and he then proclaims: 'It were well for us not to exchange too cheaply our ancient renown as a people of depth for Prussian "swagger," and the wit and sand of Berlin.' But in other places he betrays what really displeases him in the 'swagger,' at which he directs his philosophical verse; it makes too much ado about the officer. . . . Nietzsche cannot consent to that—Nietzsche, who apprehends that there can be no God, as in that case he himself must be this God. He cannot suffer the 'good German' to place the officer above him. But apart from this inconvenience, which is involved in the system of 'swagger,' he finds everything in it good and beautiful, and lauds it as 'intrepidity of glance, courage and hardness of the cutting hand, an inflexible will for dangerous voyages of discovery, for spiritualized North-Polar expeditions under desolate and dangerous skies,' and prophesies exultingly that for Europe there will soon begin an era of brass, an era of war, soldiers, arms, violence. Hence it is natural that 'swaggerers' should hail him as their very own peculiar philosopher. (pp. 470-71)

> *Max Nordau, "Friedrich Nietzsche," in his* Degeneration *(originally published as* Entartung, *second edition, 1892), fourth edition, D. Appleton and Company, 1895 (and reprinted by Howard Fertig, 1968), pp. 415-72.*

HJALMAR HJORTH BOYESEN   (essay date 1895)

[*The following remarks on Nietzsche are taken from Boyesen's study of Georg Brandes. Boyesen, like Max Nordau (see excerpt above), considers Nietzsche's philosophy the work of a "crackbrained visionary." Nietzsche's name is misspelled.*]

[Nowhere has Dr. Brandes] unmasked so Mephistophelian a countenance as in his essays on Luther and on an obscure German iconoclast named Friedrich Nietschke. . . . It is difficult to understand how a man of well-balanced brain and a logical equipment second to none, can take *au sérieux* a mere philosophical savage who dances a war-dance amid what he conceives to be the ruins of civilization, swings a reckless tomahawk and knocks down everybody and everthing that comes in his way. There must lie a long history of disappointment and bitterness behind that endorsement of anarchy pure and simple. (pp. 213-14)

It is the more to be wondered at that an evolutionist like Dr. Brandes, in his impatience at the tardiness of social progress, should lose his philosophic temper and make common cause with a crackbrained visionary. The kind of explosive radicalism which Nietschke betrays in his cynical questions and explanations is no evidence of profundity or sagacity, but is the equivalent of the dynamiter's activity, transferred to the world of thought. His pretended re-investigation of the foundations of the moral sentiments reminds one of the mud geysers of the Yellowstone, which break out periodically and envelop everything within reach in an indeterminate shower of mud. To me there is more of vanity than of philosophic acumen in his

onslaught on well-nigh all human institutions. He would, like Ibsen, no doubt,

"Place 'neath the ark the torpedo most cheerfully;"

but torpedoes of his making would scarcely do the ark much harm. They have not the explosive power of Ibsen's. There are in every age men who, unable to achieve the fame of Dinocrates, who built the temple of the Ephesian Diana, aspire to that of Herostratos, who destroyed it. To admire these men is as compromising as to be admired by them. (pp. 214-15)

> *Hjalmar Hjorth Boyesen, "Georg Brandes," in his* Essays on Scandinavian Literature *(copyright, 1895, by Charles Scribner's Sons), Charles Scribner's Sons, 1895, pp. 199-218.**

RUDOLF STEINER   (essay date 1895)

[*Steiner suggests that from his very first works Nietzsche expressed the concept of the* Ubermensch, *though in a crude form and in a language influenced by Schopenhauer. This idea attributes a unity to Nietzsche's work which many early critics failed to recognize.*]

At the very beginning of his writing career, Nietzsche did not express his thoughts in their most characteristic form. At first he stood under the influence of German idealism, in the manner in which it was represented by Schopenhauer and Richard Wagner. This expresses itself in his first writings as Schopenhauer and Wagner formulas, but the one who can see through these formulations into the kernel of Nietzsche's thoughts, finds in these writings the same purposes and goals which come to expression in his later works. (pp. 121-22)

[Nietzsche] looked to Schopenhauer's world of concepts for the ladder upon which he could climb to his own world of thought.

Our entire world knowledge stems from *two* roots, according to Schopenhauer's opinion. It comes out of the life of reflection, and out of the awareness of will, namely, that which appears in us as doer. The "thing in itself" lies on the other side of the world of our reflections. For the reflection is only the effect which the "thing in itself" exercises upon my organ of knowledge. I know only the impressions which the things make upon me, not the things themselves. And these impressions only form my reflections. . . . However, the human being does not merely reflect the world, but is also *active* within it; he becomes conscious of his own will, and he learns that what he feels within himself as *will* can be perceived from outside as movement of his body; that is, the human being becomes aware of his own acts twice: from within as *reflection*, and from outside as *will*. Schopenhauer concludes from this that it is the will itself which appears in the perceived body motion as reflection. And he asserts further that not only is the reflection of one's own body and movements based upon will, but that this is also the case behind all other reflections. The whole world then, in Schopenhauer's opinion, according to its very essence, is will, and appears to our intellect as reflection. This will, Schopenhauer asserts, is uniform in all things. Only our intellect causes us to perceive a multitude of differentiated things. (pp. 126-27)

If we assume that as he came to know Schopenhauer's philosophy, the thought of the superman already existed unconsciously, instinctively in Nietzsche, then this teaching of the will could only affect him sympathetically. In the human will Nietzsche found an element which allowed man to take part directly in the creation of the world-content. As the one who wills, man is not merely a spectator standing outside the world-content, who makes for himself pictures of reality, but he himself is a *creator*. Within him reigns that divine power above which there is no other.

Out of these viewpoints within Nietzsche the ideas of the *Apollonian* and of the *Dionysian* world conceptions form themselves. He turns these two upon the Greek life of art, letting them develop according to two roots, namely, out of an art of representation and out of an art of willing. When the reflecting human being idealizes his world of reflection and embodies his idealized reflections in works of art, then the *Apollonian art* arises. He lends the shine of the eternal to the individual objects of reflection, through the fact that he imbues them with *beauty*. But he remains standing within the world of reflection. The *Dionysian artist* tries not only to express beauty in his works of art, but he even imitates the creative working of the world will. In his own movements he tries to image the world spirit. He makes himself into a visible embodiment of the will. He himself becomes a work of art. . . . In this way Nietzsche interprets the festivals which were given by the servants of Dionysus in honor of the latter. In the Dionysian servant Nietzsche sees the archetypal pictures of the Dionysian artist. Now he imagines that the oldest dramatic art of the Greeks came into existence for the reason that a higher union of the Dionysian with the Apollonian had taken place. In this way he explains the origin of the first Greek tragedy. He assumes that the tragedy arose out of the tragic chorus. The Dionysian human being becomes the spectator, the observer of a picture which represents himself. The *chorus* is the self-reflection of a Dionysically aroused human being, that is, the Dionysian human being sees his Dionysian stimulation reflected through an Apollonian work of art. The presentation of the Dionysian in the Apollonian picture is the primitive *tragedy*. The assumption of such a tragedy is that in its creator a living consciousness of the connection of man with the primordial powers of the world is present. Such a consciousness expresses itself in the myths. The mythological must be the object of the oldest tragedies. When, in the development of a people the moment arrives that the destructive intellect extinguishes the living feeling for myths, the death of the tragic is the necessary consequence.

In the development of Greek culture, according to Nietzsche, this moment began with Socrates. Socrates was an enemy of all instinctive life which was bound up with powers of nature. He allowed only that to be valid which the intellect could prove in its thinking, that which was teachable. Through this, war was declared upon the myth, and Euripides, described by Nietzsche as the pupil of Socrates, destroyed tragedy because his creating sprang no longer out of the Dionysian instinct, as did that of Aeschylus, but out of a critical intellect. Instead of the imitation of the movements of the world spirit's will, in Euripides is found the *intellectual* knitting together of individual events within the tragic action. (pp. 127-30)

Nietzsche's description of Greek culture can be compared to the picture a man gives of a landscape which he observes from the summit of a mountain; it is a philological presentation of a description which a traveler could give who visits each single little spot. From the top of the mountain many a thing is distorted, according to the laws of optics. (p. 130)

What task does Nietzsche place before himself in his *Geburt der Trägodie*, **Birth of Tragedy?** Nietzsche is of the opinion that the older Greeks well knew the sufferings of existence. . . . He considers it a superficiality when one presents

the Greeks as a continually merry, childishly playful people. Out of the tragic feeling of the Greeks had to arise the impulse to create something whereby existence became bearable. They looked for justification of existence, and found this within the world of the Gods and in their art. Only through the counter image of the Olympic Gods and art could raw reality become bearable for the Greeks. The fundamental question in the *Geburt der Trägodie*, **Birth of Tragedy,** and for Nietzsche himself is, To what extent does Greek art foster life, and to what extent does it maintain life? Nietzsche's fundamental instinct in regard to art as a life-fostering power, already makes itself known in this first work.

Still another fundamental instinct of Nietzsche's is to be observed in this work. It is his aversion toward the merely logical spirit, whose personality stands completely under the domination of his intellect. From this aversion stems Nietzsche's opinion that the *Socratic* spirit was the destroyer of Greek culture. Logic for Nietzsche is merely a form in which a person expresses himself. If no further modes of expression are added to this form, then the personality appears as a cripple, as an organism in which the necessary organs are atrophied. Because in Kant's writings Nietzsche could discover only the pondering intellect, he called Kant a "mis-grown concept cripple." Only when logic is the means of expression of deeper fundamental instincts of a personality does Nietzsche grant it validity. Logic must be the outflow for the *super-logical* in a personality. (pp. 130-32)

Nietzsche believed that in Richard Wagner he recognized a restorer of the Dionysian spirit. Out of this belief he wrote the fourth of his *Unzeitgemässen Betrachtungen, Untimely Observations, Richard Wagner in Bayreuth*. . . . During this time he was still a strong believer in the interpretation of the Dionysian spirit which he had constructed for himself with the aid of Schopenhauer's philosophy. He still believed that reality was solely human reflection, and that beyond the world of reflection was the essence of things in the form of *primordial will*. And the *creative* Dionysian spirit had not yet become for him the human being creating out of himself, but was the human being forgetting himself and arising out of primordial willing. For him, Wagner's music-dramas were pictures of the ruling primordial will, created by one of those Dionysian spirits abandoned to this same primordial will.

And since Schopenhauer saw in music an immediate image of the will, Nietzsche also believed that he should see in music the best means of expression for a Dionysian creative spirit. To Nietzsche, the *language* of civilized people appears *sick*. It can no longer be the simple expression of feelings, because words must gradually be used more and more to express the increasing intellectual conditioning of the human being. But, because of this, the meaning of words has become abstract, has become poor. They can no longer express what the Dionysian spirit feels, who creates out of this primordial will. The Dionysian spirit, therefore, is no longer able to express himself in the dramatic element in words. He must call upon other means of expression to help, above all, upon music, but also upon other arts. The Dionysian spirit becomes a *dithyrambic dramatist*. . . . Nietzsche revered Richard Wagner as a Dionysian spirit, and Richard Wagner can only be described as a Dionysian spirit as Nietzsche represented the latter in the above mentioned work. His instincts are turned toward the beyond; he wants to let the voice of the beyond ring forth in his music. . . . [But Nietzsche] had originally misunderstood Wagner's art because he had misunderstood himself, because he had allowed his instincts to be tyrannized by Schopenhauer's philosophy. This subordination of his own instincts to a foreign spirit power appeared to him later like a sickness. He discovered that he had not listened to his instincts, and had allowed himself to be led astray by an opinion which was not in accord with his, that he had allowed an art to work upon these instincts which could only be to their disadvantage, and which finally had to make them ill.

Nietzsche himself described the influence which Schopenhauer's philosophy, which was antagonistic to his basic impulses, had made upon him. He described it when he still believed in this philosophy, in his third *Unzeitgemässen Betrachtung, Schopenhauer als Erzieher,* **Untimely Observations, Schopenhauer as Educator** . . . at a time when Nietzsche was looking for a teacher. . . . Through the study of Schopenhauer's philosophy, Nietzsche found himself nevertheless, even if not yet in his most essential selfhood. Nietzsche strove unconsciously to express himself *simply* and *honestly,* according to his own basic impulses. Around him he found only people who expressed themselves in the educational formulas of their time, who hid their essential being behind these formulas. But in Schopenhauer Nietzsche discovered a human being who had the courage to make his personal feelings regarding the world into the content of his philosophy: "the hearty well being of the speaker" surrounded Nietzsche at the first reading of Schopenhauer's sentences. . . . What attracted Nietzsche to Schopenhauer was that he heard a human being speak who expressed his innermost instincts.

Nietzsche saw in Schopenhauer a *strong* personality who was not transformed through philosophy into a mere intellectual, but a personality who made use of logic merely to express the super-logic, the instinctive in himself. . . . Already in those days the striving after the idea of the superman who searches for himself as the meaning of his own existence was working in Niezsche's mind, and such a searcher he found in Schopenhauer. In such human beings he saw the purpose, indeed, the only purpose of world existence; nature appeared to him to have reached a goal when she brought forth such a human being. Here "Nature, who never leaps, had made her only jump, and indeed a jump of joy, for she feels herself for the first time at the goal, where she comprehends that she must abandon having goals." . . . In this sentence lies the kernel of the conception of the superman. When he wrote this sentence Nietzsche wanted exactly the same thing that he later wanted from his Zarathustra. . . . (pp. 132-37)

> *Rudolf Steiner, in his* Friedrich Nietzsche: Fighter for Freedom, *translated by Margaret Ingram deRis (translation copyright © 1960 by Rudolf Steiner Publications, Inc.; reprinted by permission of Rudolf Steiner Publications, Blauvelt, N.Y.; originally published as* Friedrich Nietzsche: Ein Kämpfer gegen sein Zeit, Weimar, 1895), Rudolf Steiner, 1960, 222 p.

BERNARD SHAW   (essay date 1896)

[*Shaw's remarks on Nietzsche balance the typically positive and negative assessments of his work. Though he praises Nietzsche for his "pungency" and his "rare spirit," he also points out the practical failings of many of his ideas.*]

Nietzsche is worse than shocking, he is simply awful: his epigrams are written with phosphorus on brimstone. The only excuse for reading them is that before long you must be pre-pared either to talk about Nietzsche or else retire from society, especially from aristocratically minded society (not the same thing, by the way, as aristocratic society), since Nietzsche is the champion of privilege, of power, and of inequality. Famous as Nietzsche has become—he has had a great *succès de scandale* to advertise his penetrating wit—I never heard of him until a few years ago, when, on the occasion of my contributing to the literature of philosophy a minute treatise entitled "The Quintessence of Ibsenism," I was asked whether I had not been inspired by a book called **"Out at the other side of Good and Evil,"** by Nietzsche. The title seemed to me promising; and in fact Nietzsche's criticism of morality and idealism is essentially that demonstrated in my book as at the bottom of Ibsen's plays. His pungency; his power of putting the merest platitudes of his position in rousing, startling paradoxes; his way of getting underneath moral precepts which are so unquestionable to us that common decency seems to compel unhesitating assent to them, and upsetting them with a scornful laugh: all this is easy to a witty man who has once well learnt Schopenhauer's lesson, that the intellect by itself is a mere dead piece of brain machinery, and our ethical and moral systems merely the pierced cards you stick into it when you want it to play a certain tune. So far I am on common ground with Nietzsche. But not for a moment will I suffer any one to compare me to him as a critic. Never was there a deafer, blinder, socially and politically inepter academician. He has fancies concerning different periods of history, idealizing the Romans and the Renascence, and deducing from his idealization no end of excellences in their works. When have I ever been guilty of such professorial folly? I simply go and look at their works, and after that you may talk to me until you go black in the face about their being such wonderful fellows: I know by my senses that they were as bad artists, and as arrant intellect-mongers, as need be. And what can you say to a man who, after pitting his philosophy against Wagner's with refreshing ingenuity and force, proceeds to hold up as the masterpiece of modern dramatic music, blazing with the merits which the Wagnerian music dramas lack—guess what! "Don Giovanni," perhaps, or "Orfeo," or "Fidelio"? Not at all: "Carmen," no less. Yes, as I live by bread, as I made that bread for many a year by listening to music, Georges Bizet's "Carmen." After this one is not surprised to find Nietzsche blundering over politics, and social organization and administration in a way that would be impossible to a man who had ever served on a genuine working committee long enough— say ten minutes—to find out how very little attention the exigencies of practical action can be made to pay to our theories when we have to get things done, one way or another. To him modern Democracy, Pauline Christianity, Socialism, and so on are deliberate plots hatched by malignant philosophers to frustrate the evolution of the human race and mass the stupidity and brute force of the many weak against the beneficial tyranny of the few strong. This is not even a point of view: it is an absolutely fictitious hypothesis: it would not be worth reading were it not that there is almost as much evidence for it as if it were true, and that it leads Nietzsche to produce some new and very striking and suggestive combinations of ideas. In short, his sallies, petulant and impossible as some of them are, are the work of a rare spirit and are pregnant with its vitality. It is notable that Nietzsche does not write in chapters or treatises: he writes leading articles, leaderettes, occasional notes, and epigrams. He recognizes that humanity, having tasted the art of the journalist, will no longer suffer men to inflict books on it. And he simplifies matters, quite in the manner of the leading article writer, by ignoring things as they are, and dealing with things as it is easiest, with our prejudices and training, to think they are, except that he supplies the training and instils the prejudices himself as he goes along, instead of picking up those that lie about the street as one does in writing leaders for the daily press. (pp. 373-74)

Bernard Shaw, "Nietzsche in English," in The Saturday Review, *London, Vol. 81, No. 211, April 11, 1896, pp. 373-74.*

JAMES HUNEKER   (essay date 1904)

[*In the following excerpt, Huneker states that Nietzsche's intensity of vision contributed to his eventual insanity. Many critics believe that Nietzsche's insanity and Faustian spirit are intimately linked, though there are some, including Thomas Mann, who believe that it was caused by his contracting syphilis during his university years.*]

It is in *Also sprach Zarathustra* that the genius of Nietzsche is best studied. Like the Buddhistic Tripatka, it is a book of highly colored Oriental aphorisms, interrupted by lofty lyric outbursts. It is an ironic, enigmatic rhetorical rhapsody, the Third Part of a half-mad *Faust*. In it may be seen flowing all the currents of modern cultures and philosophies, and if it teaches anything at all, it teaches the wisdom and beauty of air, sky, waters, and earth, and of laughter, not Pantagruelian, but "holy laughter." The love of earth is preached in rapturous accents. A Dionysian ecstasy anoints the lips of this latter-day Sibyl on his tripod, when he speaks of earth. He is intoxicated with the fulness of its joys. No gloomy monasticism, no denial of the will to live, no futile thinking about thinking,—so despised by Goethe,—no denial of grand realities, may be found in the curriculum of this Bacchantic philosopher. A Pantheist, he is also a poet and seer like William Blake, and marvels at the symbol of nature, "the living garment of the Deity"— Nietzsche's deity, of course. It is this realistic, working philosophy—if philosophy it be in the academic sense—that has endeared Nietzsche to the newer generation, that has set his triumphant standard on the very threshold of the new century. After the metaphysical cobweb spinners, the Hegels, Fichtes, Schellings, after the dreary pessimism of the soured Schopenhauer,—whose pessimism was temperamental, as is all pessimism, so James Sully has pointed out,—after many negations and stumblings, the vigorous affirmations of this Nihilist are stimulating, suggestive, refreshing, especially in Germany, the stronghold of philosophical and sentimental Philistinism. Not reward, but the sheer delight of living, of conquering self, of winning victories in the teeth of defeat,—thus spake the wisdom of Nietzsche.

For English-speaking readers the many attacks on Nietzsche have placed the philosopher under the cloud of a peculiar misconception. Viciously arguing that a man in a madhouse could only produce a mad philosophy, his assailants forgot that it was Nietzsche's very intensity of mental vision, his phenomenal faculty of attention, his hopeless attempt to square the circle of things human, that brought about his sad plight. If he had not thought so madly, so strenuously, if he had put to slumber his irritable conscience, his insatiable curiosity, with current anodynes, Nietzsche might have been alive to-day.

In *Also sprach Zarathustra* he consciously or unconsciously vied with Goethe in *Faust*; with Wagner's *Ring*, with Balzac's *Comédie Humaine*, with Ibsen's *Brand*, with Tolstoy's *War and Peace*, with Senancour's *Oberman*, with Browning's *Paracelsus*. It is the history of his soul, as *Leaves of Grass* is

Whitman's—there are some curious parallelisms between these two subjective epics. It is intimate, yet hints at universality; it contains some of Amiel's introspection and some of Baudelaire's morbidity; half mad, yet exhorting, comforting; Hamlet and John Bunyan.

Nietzsche then is a critical mode of viewing the universe, rather than creator of a formal philosophy. He has set his imprint on all European culture, from the dream novels of that Italian of the Renaissance, the new Cellini, Gabriele d'Annunzio, to the Pole [Stanislaw] Przybyszewski, who has transformed Nietzsche into a very Typhoon of emotion. The musician Heinrich Pudor has imitated the master in his attacks on modern music; while Gerhart Hauptmann, Richard Dehmel—all young Germany, young France, has patterned after the great Immoralist, as he chose to call himself. Among the composers affected by him we find Richard Strauss, not attempting to set the philosophy of Nietzsche to music—as many wrongfully suppose—but arranging, as in a huge phantasmagoria, the emotions excited by the close study of *Also sprach Zarathustra*. And a many-colored piece of music it is, full of frowning mountains, fragrant meads, and barren, ugly, waste places.

Nietzsche met the fate of all rebels from Lucifer to Byron— neglect and obloquy. With something of Heraclitus, of Democritus, of Bruno Giordano, of Luther in him, there was allied a sensitivity almost Chopin's. The combination is a poor one for practical purposes; so the brain died before the body,— humanity cannot transcend itself. Notwithstanding all his contradictions, limitations, cloudland rhapsodies, aversion from the banal, despite his futile flights into the Inane, his wordweaving, his impossible premises and mad conclusions, the thunder-march of his ideas, the brilliancy and polish of his style—the greatest German prose since Schopenhauer's—have insured Nietzsche immortality. . . . (pp. 116-20)

James Huneker, "Nietzsche the Rhapsodist," in his Overtones, a Book of Temperaments: Richard Strauss, Parsifal, Verdi, Balzac, Flaubert, Nietzsche, and Turgénieff *(copyright, 1904, by Charles Scribner's Sons), Charles Scribner's Sons, 1904, pp. 109-41.*

PAUL ELMER MORE   (essay date 1912)

[*More argues that Nietzsche's attempts to escape the decadence of modern civilization failed and that his philosophy never freed itself from the constraints of nihilism. More's interpretation that Nietzsche sought to overcome a nihilistic vision of the world is similar to that of Richard Schacht (see excerpt below), but opposes the work of Arthur C. Danto and Albert Camus (see excerpts below)—both of whom consider Nietzsche the foremost nihilist. For a third interpretation of this question, see Martin Heidegger's essay excerpted below.*]

One may begin the perusal of the life of Nietzsche with a feeling of repulsion for the man,—at least that, I confess, was my own experience,—but one can scarcely lay it down without pity for his tragic failures, and without something like admiration for his reckless devotion to ideas. And all through the reading one is impressed by the truth which his ardent worshipper, Madame von Salis-Marschlins, had made the keynote of her characterization: "He—and this is the salient point— condemned a whole class of feelings in their excess, not because he did not have them, but just because he did have them and knew their danger." That truth is as important for judging the man as for understanding his philosophy. He was a man terribly at war with himself, and in this very breach in his nature lies the attraction—powerfully felt but not always clearly understood—of his works for the modern world. No doubt, if we look into the causes of his growing popularity, we shall find that a considerable part of his writing is just the sort of spasmodic commonplace that enraptures the half-cultured and flatters them with thinking they have discovered a profound philosophical basis for their untutored emotions. But withal he cannot be quite so easily disposed of. He may be, like Poe, "three-fifths of him genius and two-fifths mere fudge"; but the inspired part of him is the provocative and, it might be said, final expression of one side of the contest between the principles of egotism and sympathy that for two centuries and more has been waging for the polity and morals of the world. (pp. 154-55)

[There] is this to be observed in regard to Nietzsche's works: to one who dips into them at random, they are likely to seem dark and tangled. His manner of expressing himself in aphorisms and of uttering half-truths in emphatic finality gives to his writing an appearance of complexity and groping uncertainty; but a little persistence in reading will show that his theory of life, though never systematized, was really quite simple, and that he had in fact a few master ideas which he repeated in endlessly diversified language. It soon becomes easy to disentangle this main current of his ideas from the sporadic observations on life and art, often sound and extremely acute, which have no relation to it. Any one of his major works will afford a fairly complete view of his central doctrine: it will be found in *Human All-Too-Human* to implicate pretty fully the Bergsonian philosophy and two or three other much-vaunted philosophies of the self-evolving flux; in *Beyond Good and Evil* the ethical aspects of the new liberty are chiefly considered; in *Zarathustra,* on the whole the greatest of his works, he writes in a tone of lyrical egotism and prophetic brooding on his own destiny; in *The Will to Power* there is an attempt to reduce his scattered intentions to a logical system, but unfortunately that work was never finished, and is printed largely from his hasty notes. What probably first impresses one in any of these books is Nietzsche's violent antipathy to the past— " 'It was'—so is named the Will's gnashing of teeth and loneliest tribulation. Impotent before the thing that has been done, of all the past the Will is a malicious spectator." In this apparently sweeping condemnation of tradition all that has been held sacred is denounced in language that sounds occasionally like the fury of a madman. (pp. 172-73)

But as we become better versed in Nietzsche's extreme manner of expression, we find that his condemnation of the past is by no means indiscriminate, that in truth his denunciations are directed to a particular aspect of history. In the classical world this distinction takes the form of a harsh and unreal contrast between the Dionysiac principle of unrest and growth and creation for which he expresses the highest regard, and the Apollonian principle of rest and renunciation and contraction for which, as Platonism, he has the deepest aversion. The same distinction really holds in his attitude towards religion, although here his feelings are not so clearly defined. For the Old Testament and its virile, human poetry, for instance, he admits great reverence, reserving his spleen for the New Testament and its faith. (pp. 173-74)

[We] must remember that there are two elements in Christianity as it developed in the early centuries: on the one hand, the strong aspiring faith of a people in the vigour of youth and eager to bring into life fresh and unworn spiritual values, and, on the other hand, the depression and world-weariness which haunted the decadent heterogeneous people of Alexandria and the East. Now it is clear that for the former of these Nietzsche had no understanding, since it lay quite beyond his range of vision, whereas for the latter he had a very intimate understanding and a bitter detestation. Hence his almost unreserved rejection of Christianity as a product of corruption and race impurity. (pp. 174-75)

[Nietzsche's] mind was really concerned with certain aspects of society as it existed about him, and his hostility to the past was not to the dead centuries in themselves, but to what remained over from them in the present—for what, after all, is there for any man in the past to hate or fear, except as it lives and will not be put away? In the sickness of his soul Nietzsche looked abroad over the Western world, and saw, or thought he saw, everywhere futility and purposelessness and pessimistic uncertainty of the values of life. An ideal, as he sees it, is embraced only when a man's grip on the real world and its good has been weakened; in the end such supernatural ideals, as they are without foundation in fact, lose their hold on the human mind, and mankind, having sacrificed its sense of actual values and having nursed the cause of decay, is left helpless and joyless. This condition he calls Nihilism. . . . The restless activities of our life he interprets as so many attempts to escape from the gloom of purposelessness, as so many varieties of self-stupefaction. No one can read this list of these efforts without shuddering recollection of what decadent music and literature and painting have produced. . . . (pp. 176-77)

The attempt to maintain Christianity amidst a nihilistic society which has lost even its false ideals, can have only one result. As these supernatural ideals were evoked by the weaker mass of the race to cover its subjection to the few stronger individuals, so when belief in the other world has perished, the only defence that remains is the humanitarian exaltation of the humble and common and undistinguished in itself as a kind of simulacrum of Christianity, the unideal sympathy of man for man as a political law, the whole brood of socialistic schemes which are based on the notion of universal brotherhood. These, the immediate offspring of Rousseauism and German romanticism, are, as Nietzsche saw, the actual religion of the world to-day; and against these, and against the past as the source of these, his diatribes are really directed. His protest is against "sympathy with the lowly and the suffering as a *standard* for the *elevation of the soul.*" (p. 178)

All this is merely Nietzsche's spasmodic way of depicting the uneasiness of the age, which has been the theme of innumerable poets of the nineteenth century—of Matthew Arnold, to take an instance, in his gloomy diagnosis of the modern soul. And to a certain point the cause of this nihilism, to use Nietzsche's word, is the same for him as for Arnold. They both attribute it to the shattering of definite ideals that had so long ruled the world, and especially to the waning of religious faith. But here the two diagnosticians part company. Arnold looked for health to the establishing of new ideals and to the growth of a fresh and sounder faith in the Eternal, though he may have failed in his attempt to define this new faith. Nietzsche, on the contrary, regarded all ideals and all faith as themselves a product of decadence and the sure cause of deeper decay. "Objection, evasion, joyous distrust, and love of irony," he says, "are signs of health; everything absolute belongs to pathology." Nihilism, as the first consequence of the loss of ideals, may be a state of hideous anarchy, but it is also the necessary transition to health. If, instead of relapsing into the idealistic source of evil, the eyes of mankind are strengthened to look boldly at the facts of existence, then will take place what he calls the Transvaluation of all Values, and truth will be founded on the naked, imperishable reality. There is no eternal calm at the centre of this moving universe; "all is flux"; there is nothing real "but our world of desires and passions," and "we cannot sink or rise to any other 'reality' save just the reality of our impulses—for thinking itself is only a relation of these impulses to one another." So be it! When a man has faced this truth calmly and bravely and definitely, then the whole system of morality which has been imposed upon society by those who regarded life as subordinate to an eternal ideal outside of the flux and contrary to the stream of human desires and passions—then the whole law of good and evil which was evolved by the weak to protect themselves against those who were fitted to live masterfully in the flux, crumbles away; that man has passed Beyond Good and Evil.

Mankind is thus liberated from the herd-law, the false values have been abolished, but what new values take their place? The answer to this question Nietzsche found by going to Darwinism and raising the evolutionary struggle for existence into new significance; he would call it, not the Schopenhauerian will to live, but the Will to Power. (pp. 179-80)

This is Nietzsche's transvaluation of all values, the change from the morality of good and evil depending on supernatural rewards to the non-morality of the purely natural Will to Power. And as the former idealism resulted in the suppression of distinction and in the supremacy of the feeble, so the régime of the Will to Power must bring back into society the sharp division of those who have power and those who have it not, of the true philosophers who have the instinct to surpass and the slaves whose function it is to serve and obey. The philosopher, to use Nietzsche's famous term, is the Superman, the *Uebermensch*. He has passed beyond good and evil, and Nietzsche often describes him in language which implies the grossest immorality; but this is merely an iconoclast's way of emphasizing the contrast between his perfect man and the old ideal of the saint, and it would be unfair to take these ebullitions of temper quite literally. The image of the Superman is, in fact, left in the hazy uncertainty of the future; the only thing certain about him is his complete immersion in nature, and his office to raise the level of society by rising on the shoulders of those who do the menial work of the world. At the last analysis the Superman is merely a negation of humanitarian sympathy and of the socialistic state of indistinguished equality. (pp. 181-82)

Nietzsche regarded the self-assertive Superman as a true reaction against the prevalent man of sympathy and as a cure for the disease of the age. That much of Nietzsche's protest against the excesses of humanitarianism was sound and well directed, I for one am quite ready to admit. He saw, as few other men of our day have seen, the danger that threatens true progress in any system of education and government which makes the advantage of the ordinary rather than the distinguished man its first object. He saw with terrible clearness that much of our most admired art is not art at all in the higher sense of the word, but an appeal to morbid sentimentality. There is a humorous aspect to his quarrel with Wagner, which was at bottom caused by the clashing of two insanely jealous egotisms. Nevertheless, there is an element of truth in his condemnation of Wagner's opera as typical of certain degenerate tendencies in modern society; and many must agree with him in his statement that Wagner "found in music the means of exciting tired nerves, making it thereby sick." Not without cause did Nietzsche pronounce himself "the highest authority in the world on the question of decadence." But the cure Nietzsche proposed for these evils was itself a part of the malady. The Superman, in other words, is a product of the same naturalism which produced the disease it would counteract; it is the last and most violent expression of the egotism, or self-interest, which [David] Hume and all his followers balanced with sympathy as the two springs of human action. (pp. 183-84)

The great tragedy of Nietzsche's existence was due to the fact that, while he perceived the danger into which he had fallen, yet his struggles to escape only entangled him more desperately in the fatal mesh. His boasted transvaluation of all values was in reality a complete devaluation, if I may coin the word, leaving him more deeply immersed in the nihilism which he exposed as the prime evil of modern civilization. With Hume and the romantic naturalists he threw away both the reason and the intuition into any superrational law beyond the stream of desires and passions and impulses. He looked into his own heart and into the world of phenomena, and beheld there a ceaseless ebb and flow, without beginning, without end, and without meaning. The only law that he could discover, the only rest for the mind, was some dimly foreseen return of all things back into their primordial state, to start afresh on the same dark course of chance—the Eternal Recurrence, he called it. . . . At times he sets up the ability to look undismayed into this ever-turning wheel as the test that distinguishes the Superman from the herd. And this is all Nietzsche could give to mankind by his Will to Power and his Transvaluation of Values: the will to endure the vision of endless, purposeless mutation; the courage to stand without shame, naked in a world of chance; the strength to accomplish—absolutely nothing. At times he proclaims his creed with an effrontery of joy over those who sink by the way and cry out for help. Other times pity for so hapless a humanity wells up in his heart despite himself; and more than once he admits that the last temptation of the Superman is sympathy for a race revolving blindly in this cycle of change—"Where lie thy greatest dangers? In compassion." (pp. 187-89)

The end of it all is the clamour of romantic egotism turned into horror at its own vacuity and of romantic sympathy turned into despair. It is naturalism at war with itself and struggling to escape from its own fatality. As I leave Nietzsche I think of the ancient tragedy in which Heracles is represented as writhing in the embrace of the Nessus-shirt he has himself put on, and rending his own flesh in a vain effort to escape its poisonous web. (pp. 189-90)

Paul Elmer More, in his Nietzsche *(Copyright 1912 by Paul Elmer More. Copyright renewed 1940 by Mary Darrah Fine and Alice Dymond. Reprinted by permission of Houghton Mifflin Company), Houghton Mifflin, 1912 (and reprinted as "Nietzsche," in his* The Drift of Romanticism: Shelburne Essays, *eighth series, Houghton Mifflin, 1913, pp. 145-90).*

PAUL CARUS   (essay date 1914)

[*Though Carus finds Nietzsche a "bold thinker" and a "Titan among philosophers," he argues that his disregard for morals, for truthfulness, and for justice—if adopted—would reduce civilization to the level of "savagery." Carus concludes that Nietzsche's philosophy must be condemned "as unsound in its basis" and the "result of an immaturity of comprehension." Other critics, such as Bernard Shaw, George Santayana, and J. P. Stern, also stress the immaturity of Nietzsche's thought (see excerpts above and below).*]

Nietzsche is unquestionably a bold thinker, a Faust-like questioner, and a Titan among philosophers. He is a man who understands that the problem of all problems is the question, Is there an authority higher than myself? And having discarded belief in God, he finds no authority except pretensions.

Nietzsche apparently is only familiar with the sanctions of morality and the criterion of good and evil as they are represented in the institutions and thoughts established by history, and seeing how frequently they serve as tools in the hands of the crafty for the oppression of the unsophisticated masses of the people, he discards them as utterly worthless. Hence his truly magnificent wrath, his disgust, his contempt for underling man, for the masses, this muddy stream of present mankind.

If Nietzsche had dug deeper, he would have found that there is after all a deep significance in moral ideals, for there is an authority above the self by which the worth of the self must be measured. Truth is not a mere creature of the self, but is the comprehension of the immutable eternal laws of being which constitute the norm of existence. Our self, "that creating, willing, valuing 'I,' which (according to Nietzsche) is the measure and value of all things," is itself measured by that eternal norm of being, the existence of which Nietzsche does not recognize.

What is true of Nietzsche applies in all fundamental questions also to his predecessor, Max Stirner. It applies to individualism in any form if carried to its consistent and most extreme consequences.

Nietzsche is blind to the truth that there is a norm above the self, and that this norm is the source of duty and the object of religion; he therefore denies the very existence of duty, of conviction, of moral principles, of sympathy with the suffering, of authority in any shape, and yet he dares to condemn man in the shape of the present generation of mankind. What right has he, then, to judge the sovereign self of to-day and to announce the coming of another self in the overman? From the principles of his philosophical anarchism he has no right to denounce mankind of to-day, as an underling; for if there is no objective standard of worth, there is no sense in distinguishing between the underman of today and the overman of a nobler future.

On this point, however, Nietzsche deviates from his predecessor Stirner. The latter is more consistent as an individualist, but the former appeals strongly to the egoism of the individual.

Nietzsche is a Titan and he is truly Titanic in his rebellion against the smallness of everything that means to be an incarnation of what is great and noble and holy. But he does not protest against the smallness of the representatives of truth and right, he protests against truth and right themselves, and thus he is not merely Titanic, but a genuine Titan,—attempting to take the heavens by storm, a monster, not superhuman but inhuman in proportions, in sentiment and in spirit. Being ingenious, he is, in his way, a genius, but he is not evenly balanced; he is eccentric and, not recognizing the authority of reason and science, makes eccentricity his maxim. Thus his grandeur becomes grotesque. (pp. 128-30)

Being giant-like, the Titan Nietzsche has a sense only for things of large dimensions. He fails to understand the significance of the subtler relations of existence. He is clumsy like Gargantua; he is coarse in his reasoning; he is narrow in his comprehension; his horizon is limited. He sees only the massive effects of the great dynamical changes brought about by brute force; he is blind to the quiet and slow but more powerful workings of spiritual forces. The molecular forces that are invisible to the eye transform the world more thoroughly than hurricanes and thunderstorms; yet the strongest powers are the moral laws, the curses of wrong-doing and oppression, and the blessings of truthfulness, of justice, of good-will. Nietzsche sees them not; he ignores them. He measures the worth of the overman solely by his brute force.

If Nietzsche were right, the overman of the future who is going to take possession of the earth will not be nobler and better, wiser and juster than the present man, but more gory, more tiger-like, more relentless, more brutal.

Nietzsche has a truly noble longing for the advent of the overman, but he throws down the ladder on which man has been climbing up, and thus losing his foothold, he falls down to the place whence mankind started several millenniums ago.

We enjoy the rockets of Nietzsche's genius, we understand his Faust-like disappointment as to the unavailableness of science such as he knew it; we sympathize with the honesty with which he offered his thoughts to the world; we recognize the flashes of truth which occur in his sentences, uttered in the tone of a prophet; but we cannot help condemning his philosophy as unsound in its basis, his errors being the result of an immaturity of comprehension. (pp. 130-31)

Nietzsche calls himself an atheist; he denies the existence of God in any form, and thus carries atheism to an extreme where it breaks down in self-contradiction. We understand by God (whether personal, impersonal, or superpersonal) that something which determines the course of life; the factors that shape the world, including ourselves; the law to which we must adjust our conduct. Nietzsche enthrones the self in the place of God, but for all practical purposes his God is blunt success and survival of the fittest in the crude sense of the term; for according to his philosophy the self must heed survival in the struggle for existence alone, and that, therefore, is his God.

Nietzsche's God is power, i.e., overwhelming force, which allows the wolf to eat the lamb. He ignores the power of the still small voice, the effectiveness of law in the world which makes it possible that man, the over-brute, is not the most ferocious, the most muscular, or the strongest animal. Nietzsche regards the cosmic order, in accommodation to which ethical codes have been invented, as a mere superstition. Thus it will come to pass that Nietzsche's type of the overman, should it really make its appearance on earth, would be wiped out as surely as the lion, the king of the beasts, the proud pseudo-overbrute of the animals, will be exterminated in course of time. The lion has a chance for survival only behind the bars of the zoölogical gardens or when he allows himself to be tamed by man, that weakling among the brutes whose power has been built up by a comprehension of the sway of the invisible laws of life, physical, mental and moral. (pp. 136-37)

Paul Carus, "Individualism," in his Nietzsche and Other Exponents of Individualism *(copyright by The Open Court Publishing Company 1914), Open Court, 1914, pp. 128-41.*

GEORGE SANTAYANA (essay date 1920)

[*Santayana, an important twentieth-century philosopher, agrees with the assessments of Paul Carus and Bernard Shaw (see excerpts above) that Nietzsche's philosophy is mostly the product of "an immature, half-playful mind." However, he argues that Nietzsche remains an important figure, if not for what he said, then for "the fact that he said it."*]

Nietzsche was personally more philosophical than his philosophy. His talk about power, harshness, and superb immorality was the hobby of a harmless young scholar and constitutional invalid. He did not crave in the least either wealth or empire. What he loved was solitude, nature, music, books. But his imagination, like his judgment, was captious; it could not dwell on reality, but reacted furiously against it. Accordingly, when he speaks of the will to be powerful, power is merely an eloquent word on his lips. It symbolizes the escape from mediocrity. What power would be when attained and exercised remains entirely beyond his horizon. What meets us everywhere is the sense of impotence and a passionate rebellion against it.

That there is no God is proved by Nietzsche pragmatically, on the ground that belief in the existence of God would have made him uncomfortable. Not at all for the reason that might first occur to us: to imagine himself a lost soul has always been a point of pride with the romantic genius. The reason was that if there had been any gods he would have found it intolerable not to be a god himself. Poor Nietzsche! The laurels of the Almighty would not let him sleep.

It is hard to know if we should be more deceived in taking these sallies seriously or in not taking them so. On the one hand it all seems the swagger of an immature, half-playful mind, like a child that tells you he will cut your head off. The dreamy impulse, in its inception, is sincere enough, but there is no vestige of any understanding of what it proposes, of its conditions, or of its results. On the other hand these explosions are symptomatic; there stirs behind them unmistakably an elemental force. That an attitude is foolish, incoherent, disastrous, proves nothing against the depth of the instinct that inspires it. Who could be more intensely unintelligent than Luther or Rousseau? Yet the world followed them, not to turn back. The molecular forces of society, so to speak, had already undermined the systems which these men denounced. If the systems have survived it is only because the reformers, in their intellectual helplessness, could supply nothing to take their place. So Nietzsche, in his genial imbecility, betrays the shifting of great subterranean forces. What he said may be nothing, but the fact that he said it is all-important. Out of such wild intuitions, because the heart of the child was in them, the man of the future may have to build his philosophy. We should forgive Nietzsche his boyish blasphemies. He hated with clearness, if he did not know what to love. (pp. 212-14)

> *George Santayana, "Nietzsche," in his* Little Essays Drawn from the Writings of George Santayana, *edited by Logan Pearsall Smith, Charles Scribner's Sons, 1920, pp. 212-14.*

STEFAN ZWEIG (essay date 1925)

[*Zweig compares Nietzsche's lust for knowledge to Don Juan's lust for women—a lust which led to his eventual madness. A similar idea is also considered by James Huneker (see excerpt above).*]

[Nietzsche's] attitude towards truth was a passionate and breathless tremor, was high-strung and inquisitive, never satisfied, never appeased, never contented with achievement but precipitating itself, beyond every response, into further impatient and insatiable questionings. Having acquired the knowledge he was in search of, he was incapable of making it his own in perpetuity, of espousing it, of shaping it into a system, a doctrine. Everything allured him; nothing was able to retain his interest. So soon as a problem had lost its virginity, had lost the charm and mystery of maidenhood, he forsook it pitilessly, without jealousy, for others to enjoy if they cared to—as did Don Juan, his brother so far as the impulsive life was concerned, in the case of his "mille e tre." For just as genuine seducers are for ever seeking among womankind the one and only woman of their hearts, so did Nietzsche seek among all kinds of knowledge the unique knowledge of his choice, the knowledge doomed to everlasting unreality and eternally eluding his grasp. It was not desire for conquest and possession and sensual enjoyment which stirred him, thrilled him, and reduced him almost to despair; but invariably questionings, doubts, the pursuit of knowledge. He loved insecurity not certainty; and consequently his lusts turned for gratification to metaphysics and consisted of "amour-plaisir" in knowledge. He yearned to seduce, to lay bare, to penetrate voluptuously, and to violate every spiritual object—"to know" in the Biblical sense of the word, when a man "knows" a woman and thereby filches her secret. This everlasting relativist of values recognized that his acts of possession never knew truth to the uttermost limits, for, in the last resort, truth never gives herself wholly to anyone: "He who fancies he is in possession of truth, has no inkling of how much eludes his grasp."

Nietzsche, therefore, never set up house with knowledge so as to economize and preserve; he built no spiritual home over his head. Maybe it was a nomadic instinct which forced him into a position of never owning anything. Like a Nimrod of the mind, he ranged through the forests of the spiritual world, alone, with no roof to protect him, no wife, no child, no servant; nevertheless, he was filled with the pleasures of the chase, a hunter incarnate. As in Don Juan's case so in Nietzsche's the duration of an emotion was a matter for indifference; what held import for him was the fleeting "moments of grandeur and rapturous delight." Hazardous activities of the mind, those "dangerous maybes" which make a man glow with ardour and which goad him to the pursuit but fail to satisfy his longing when once attained, these were the only adventures that attracted Nietzsche. He did not desire the quarry but the spirit, the spur, the pleasures of the hunt for knowledge, upward and onward to the outermost stars, until in the end there was nothing left for him to hunt but the residue of all that is harmful in knowledge—"like a toper who finally comes down to drinking absinth or nitric acid."

For the Don Juan in Nietzsche was not an epicure, he was not dainty in his choice, neither could he enjoy robustly: this finical aristrocrat with his quivering nerves lacked the sleepy ease of digestion, the lazy contentment of satisfied appetite, the boastfulness which makes the common mortal parade his conquests. The woman-hunter is himself hunted by his insatiable desires: thus, likewise, the Nimrod of the mind; the unscrupulous seducer is himself seduced by consuming curiosity, he is a tempter who is everlastingly tempted to tempt women to forgo their innocence, just as Nietzsche was perpetually interrogating the universe for the mere pleasure of questioning and to gratify his inextinguishable psychological lust. For Don Juan the mystery was contained in everything and in nothing, in each woman for one night and in no woman thereafter. Thus is it also in the case of a psychologist for whom in every problem truth resides but for a moment and never permanently.

Nietzsche therefore was denied repose and calm in the realm of thought. His mental life was full of unexpected twists and turns. Other German philosophers lived in a quasi-epic tranquillity; they spun their theories quietly from day to day, sitting commodiously in an armchair, and their thought-process hardly raised their blood-pressure by a single degree. Kant never produces the impression of a mind seized by thought as by a vampire, and painfully enduring the terrible urge of creation; Schopenhauer from thirty onwards, after he had published *The World as Will and Idea*, seems to me a staid professor who has retired on a pension and has accepted the conviction that his career is finished. They have chosen a road, and calmly walk along it to the end; whereas Nietzsche was for ever tracked down and pushed towards the unknown. That is why Nietzsche's intellectual story (like Don Juan's bodily story) assumes a dramatic aspect, constitutes a chain of unforeseen episodes, a tragedy which passes unintermittently from one vicissitude to another even more perilous, until it culminates in annihilation.

Now, what renders this life unique and tragical is precisely the absence of repose in Nietzsche's searchings, his incessant urge to think, his compulsory advance. These make his life a work of art. Nietzsche was doomed to think without respite like the legendary hunter who was condemned to an everlasting chase. What was once a pleasure became for him a bugbear, an affliction, so that his style grew breathless and spasmodic like a panting beast which recognizes that it will soon have to face the hounds, at bay. Nietzsche's complaint, therefore, moves us profoundly. "One falls in love with something, and hardly has this something had time to become a deep-felt love than the tyrant within, which we should do well to name our higher self, claims our love for the sacrifice. And we yield to the dictator, though ourselves consumed in a slow fire." Don Juan natures have ever to be wrenched from love's embraces, for the daimon of dissatisfaction incessantly urges them to further exploits—the same daimon that harried Hölderlin and Kleist and harries all those who worship the infinite. (pp. 467-70)

[Nietzsche] gave himself completely, fronting danger not merely "with the antennae of cold and inquisitive thought," but with voluptuous ardour, with the whole weight of his destiny. His thoughts do not come only from on high, are not simply conjured out of his brain, but are at the same time engendered by the fever of his blood, by violently quivering nerves, by ungratified sense organs, by the consuming might of the entirety of his vital forces. Hence his ideas, like those of Pascal, tend to become "a passion-fraught history of the soul"; they are the extreme consequence of perilous, nay, almost mortal, adventures, a living drama moving us profoundly. Yet even when he was in the bitterest distress Nietzsche had no desire to change his lot for another, milder, fate; he did not wish to exchange his "dangerous life" for stability and repose of mind, would not for any consideration dam up the overflow of his feelings. Nietzsche hated such a prospect, seeing therein a diminution of vitality. (p. 471)

For the first time on the ocean of German philosophy the black flag was hoisted upon a pirate ship. Nietzsche was a man of a different species, of another race, of a novel type of heroism; his philosophy was not clad in professorial robes, but was harnessed for the fray like a knight in shining armour. . . . Just as the filibusters invaded the Spanish world towards the close of the sixteenth century—a lawless gang of desperadoes, lacking restraint, acknowledging no king, men without a flag and without a home—so Nietzsche made an irruption into the philosophical world, conquering nothing either for himself or for those who should come after; his victories were not achieved for the sake of a monarch or dedicated to the greater glory of

God, but purely for the intrinsic joy of conquest, since he did not wish to possess or to acquire or to conquer. He was a disturber of the peace, his one desire being to plunder, to destroy property relationships, to trouble the repose of his fellow-mortals. With fire and sword he went forth to awaken the minds of men, an awakening as precious to him as is a fusty sleep to the vast majority of mankind. In his wake, as in the wake of the filibusters of old, churches were desecrated, altars were overturned, feelings injured, convictions assassinated, moral sheepfolds sacked; every horizon blazed with incendiary fires, monstrous beacons of daring and violence. Never did he look back to gloat over his acquisitions or to appropriate his conquests. He strove everlastingly towards what had never been explored and conquered; his one and only pleasure was to try out his strength and to rouse up those who slumbered. He was a member of no creed, had never sworn allegiance to any country. With the black flag at his masthead and steering into the unknown, into incertitude which he felt to be the mate of his soul, he sailed forward to ever-renewed and perilous adventures. Sword in hand and powder-barrel at his feet, he left the shores of the known behind him and sang his pirate song as he went. . . . (pp. 471-73)

Stefan Zweig, "The Struggle with the Daimon: Nietzsche" (originally published under a different title in his Der Kampf mit dem Dämon: Hölderlin, Kleist, Nietzsche, Insel-Verlag, 1925), in his Master Builders: A Typology of the Spirit, *translated by Eden Paul and Cedar Paul (translation copyright © 1939, copyright renewed © 1966, by the Viking Press, Inc.; reprinted by permission of the Estate of Stefan Zweig), Viking Penguin Inc., 1939, pp. 441-532.*

GEORGE BURMAN FOSTER   (essay date 1931)

[*Foster is one of many critics who have recognized the three stages in Nietzsche's work. In the following excerpt, he traces the influence of Schopenhauer through each period, stressing the similarities between the first and third stages in Nietzsche's career. For an alternate reading of Nietzsche's development read Eric Bentley (see excerpt below).*]

When he was twenty-one, and living in Leipzig, Nietzsche happened one day to purchase in an antiquarian's shop (in fact, in the shop of Rohn, the bookseller, with whom he was lodging), a copy of Schopenhauer's *Die Welt als Wille und Vorstellung.* A single reading sufficed. Schopenhauer had made a new convert, one who, although he subsequently broke with his master, never again escaped his influence. At the first perusal he was overwhelmed by the magnificent prospects opened out to him by this book and even more so by the personality of the philosopher himself, whom he perceived behind the book. In Nietzsche's *Schopenhauer as Educator* . . . the following confession occurs:

> I am one of those readers of Schopenhauer who know for certain, after they have read a page of him, that they will read this book from the first to the last, and that they will listen with rapt attention to every word that falls from his lips. My confidence in him was instantly full and entire.
>
> (p. 16)

Such was the beginning, and in this temper of mind he wrote the books of his first, or artistic period, namely [*The Birth of Tragedy, Thoughts out of Season,* and especially *Schopenhauer as Educator*]. . . . (p. 17)

But very soon, in the second,—positivistic, intellectualistic, or scientific—period, Nietzsche had resigned his place in the school of Schopenhauer, and was writing *Human, all-too-Human* in its various parts, especially *The Wanderer and his Shadow* . . . and *The Dawn of Day*. . . . In these books we find him rejecting the ideal of the artist and accepting the life-ideal of the scientist. It is not the artistic man through his subjective constructions who enfranchises us, it is the scientific man through his objective thought who is free himself, and who makes us free. But in rejecting the artistic ideal of life. Nietzsche rejected with it its presupposition, namely, the Schopenhauerian metaphysics, along with its pessimism and nihilism. He became a sober empiricist. It is no longer Schopenhauer and Wagner, representatives of art; it is Socrates and Voltaire, representatives of intellectualism.

Then ensues Nietzsche's third period, in which he turns away from intellectualism back to Schopenhauer's voluntarism, from which he set out. But when he went back to Schopenhauer, he took with him the optimism of his second period. Henceforth, he is not a pessimistic but an optimistic Schopenhauer, *mutatis mutandis*! (p. 18)

Nietzsche accepts Schopenhauer's judgment of what the world is—godless, chaotic, meaningless, goalless—accepts Schopenhauer's premise, but denies his conclusion, pessimism, and affirms optimism. To be sure it is an unusual kind of optimism, denied to be such by not a few; but optimism it is, for all that. (p. 19)

Nietzsche's doctrine is Schopenhauerism given a positive instead of a negative turn of application. This alteration, or, if the reader will, revaluation, took place under the influence of Charles Darwin. Nietzscheanism is equal to Schopenhauerism plus Darwinism, each of the two modified by the other, and both transmuted in the alembic of Nietzsche's own original genius. (pp. 24-5)

As I have already pointed out, Nietzsche passed through several periods of development before he reached his own original doctrine. In the first period, as I have said, Nietzsche was mainly a Schopenhauerean. *The Birth of Tragedy, Thoughts out of Season,* and *Schopenhauer as Educator* prove this assertion. . . . The main features of Schopenhauer's philosophy are to be found in Schopenhauer's metaphysics of the will and in his pessimism. For Nietzsche, too, the world is will and idea! For Nietzsche, too, the insatiable and eternally unsatisfied will is the foundation of all our misery and torment. Moreover, Nietzsche, also, finds redemption from this torment of will in aesthetic idea and production, therefore in art, so that the artist is ideal for Nietzsche. This artist-ideal he sees realized in Richard Wagner; this art-ideal he sees realized in Wagner's dramatic music. The artist, through his art, frees himself and his brothers from the torment and torture of the will and of illusion. It was in this sense that Wagner named his house at Bayreuth—*Wahnfried*.

Now, the presupposition of this art enthusiasm is pessimism—pessimism which sees in the usual living and dying of men, only ever-new forms of blind, insatiable will and illusion. Art lifts man above himself and out of his pain, frees him from his self, makes him noble and good, and even holy. In this sense, art is the necessary complement of the tragic disposition, which Nietzsche, with Schopenhauer, required of men of deep thought and high endeavor, in opposition to the "incurable," "enervating" optimism of the type which, as represented in and by David Strauss, was anathematized by Nietzsche.

Even the Greeks, from whom art, and especially tragedy, were first born, were pessimists, at least the nobler Greeks, *e.g.,* Empedocles. The rationalist Socrates was an optimist, but with Socrates the decay of genuine Hellenism begins. But only the *tragic* man is the true teacher of man. Schopenhauer, therefore, was the best *educator* also. Only the tragic artist produces truly liberating art; Richard Wagner, therefore, is the best artist. (pp. 25-6)

[But] when *Parsifal* came to light, the ideal of the Wagnerian art was destroyed for Nietzsche; for, in *Parsifal,* Nietzsche saw an unworthy genuflexion of his former sovereign artist before the altar,—a humiliation, a debasement of art through church. Nietzsche was horrified at this turn of the Wagnerian course of life. Nietzsche was a worshiper of classic antiquity. He was a classic philologist from conviction. He belonged to the generation of the Renaissance, humanists who could not forgive Christianity for causing the downfall of antique *kultur*. In his very first work, *The Birth of Tragedy,* he had tried to fuse the German Nibelung music of Wagner with Greek art. But he now saw Wagner putting his wonderful art at the service of the medieval ideal in *Parsifal*. Here, then, the Nietzsche who was at home in classic antiquity, living in it and on it, proudly favoring it as a humanist in preference to Christianity and medievalism—this Nietzsche now experienced disillusion in the cruelest epoch of his life. With nausea, he turned his back upon his hitherto deified ideal, Richard Wagner. But to what did he turn? With characteristic one-sidedness and violence he now rushed into the science camp. Not art, but *science,* is ideal now. He substituted objectivity, for subjectivity, experience and exact observation for the metaphysics and pessimism and nihilism of Schopenhauer.

His slogan was: Only experience and its utilization through the understanding, excluding metaphysics on the one hand, and the unquiet, impulsive life on the other; only *empirical understanding!* Nietzsche, the passionate man, now found his satisfaction transitorily in science as in a kind of medical institution, a Karlsbad.

The Schopenhauerian metaphysics of the will was forsaken. Nietzsche was at this time a sober empiricist. He dedicated his books to the memory of Voltaire. In his first period he despised the rationalistic Socrates, who died without pathos, as Schopenhauer lived with nothing else. Now he adored Socrates—Socrates and Voltaire, *advocates of intellectualism, who saw in the victory of the intellect the victory of the good* and were, therefore, representatives of optimism. Nietzsche turned his back upon pessimism consistently with his new point of view. Pessimism passed consistently with the passing of the metaphysics of the will.

Furthermore, another change of great importance took place at this time. In his first period, under the influence of the unhistorical standpoint of Schopenhauer, he complained of the exaggeration of history in education and life. But in this second period, the historical treatment of things and their evolution became a problem of interest to him. In this connection Darwinism became for him a matter of profound study. Especially did he turn his attention to the development of moral ideas and to the problem of the progress of *kultur*.

Nietzsche's nature, however, was impulsive and passionate, and he could not tent long in his pathetic pilgrimage in the camp ground of the scientist. The golden mean was not for him. He must mount to the highest heights or descend to the deepest deeps. Science is objective, dispassionate, judicial, complacent. Not so Nietzsche, who was artist and prophet more than scientist. So, in his third period, he turned back to his old self again, but in a new form. From Schopenhauer's voluntarism he had set out on his pilgrimage; to it he now returned. As soldiers might wander over a trackless plain during the day, and return at night to the same camp fires which they had left in the morning, but return modified by the experience of their day's march, so Nietzsche returned to Schopenhauer, enriched and modified by the experiences of his second, the science period.

What was it that Nietzsche carried out of his second period into his third? Not only an interest in history, not only an interest in the historical development of morals and of *kultur* in general, but a particular optimism—the vital, joyous affirmation of the world and the will to live. He returned—this is the crucial and all-important point in the understanding of Nietzsche's philosophy—he returned to exactly Schopenhauer's world and Schopenhauer's will, that world of torture and of tears; but, whereas Schopenhauer cried *"Pessimism"* as he peered into the black abyss, Nietzsche shouted *"Optimism."* Schopenhauer with his splendid health and magnificent fortune, landed in pessimism; Nietzsche, "the crucified one," as he signed himself in his letters sometimes, in his nameless agony, landed in optimism, while facing the same Schopenhauerian facts. There is a psychological problem of the first rank.

In this third period, Nietzsche returns to Schopenhauer in so far as he accepts Schopenhauer's doctrine of the will of the world. But art no longer, as in the first period, seems to him to be the redeemer and liberator from the slavery to and torment of the blind will. Nietzsche took the optimism of the second period into the third; consequently, the will seemed to him no longer as blind, unhappy, needful of redemption, but as Will to Power, unbroken, fresh, glad of life, even though that life, like his own—not like Schopenhauer's—was one long crucifixion!

According to Nietzsche now, life is simply power and the practice of power. Life reposes on the instinct of the Will to Power, of the exercise of power; the will to life of Schopenhauer is now rebaptized as the Will to Power. To live is to widen out on all sides the sphere of power. This Will to Power is the instinctive basic impulse of all creatures. Naturally, however, these diverse Wills to Power must fall into conflict with each other. They reciprocally fight to the death with the powerful and irresistible instincts which spring out of the Will to Power. It was just in this conflict of the different will-centers that Schopenhauer had discerned the evil in the world; evil toward whose delineation he could not do enough; evil from which Schopenhauer sought redemption in art, on the one hand, and in asceticism, on the other. What does Nietzsche see in the struggle of these diverse will-centers? Just the opposite— *the principle of the development of all Kultur.* Hence his hatred now of everything that would do away with that struggle, since it is the source of the elevation of the type man. Hence, I say, his hatred of morality, socialism, democracy, feminism, intellectualism, pessimism, Christianity, as he understood them. He hated with abysmal hatred all of these, because they softened, or eliminated, or neutralized that struggle among the will-centers which, in his belief, was the *sine qua non* of overcoming the decadence of his day and of insuring that life should travel once again the ascending curve of existence. Nietzsche could say: "I am come that ye may have power, and have it more abundantly"; Schopenhauer had to say: "I

am come that ye may have weakness, and have it more despairingly." Great Nietzsche! We shall hardly see his like again. He has posed the question of fact for our generation and for all generations: Do the seven things I have enumerated—moralism, socialism, democracy, feminism, intellectualism, pessimism, Christianism—do these seven things weaken or strengthen the soul of man? That is the question of questions and the problem of problems; and it is the imperishable merit of Friedrich Nietzsche to have raised it squarely and fearlessly. Nietzsche was our modern Heraclitus: War is the father of all things; out of war and struggle arise all development. These seven foes of War are the foes of development.—"Down with them," therefore cries Nietzsche.

But there was another man who ascribed a similar, life-promoting effect to struggle: Charles Darwin. According to Darwin, the struggle for existence is the condition of all higher unfolding of organism. In the struggle for existence power increases, and the most powerful triumph. The weaker are driven to the wall and deserve to go down. Nature wills the victory to the stronger, and perfects species through that victory and the overthrow of the weaker. In dithyrambic swing, Nietzsche celebrates this natural law, whose pitilessness was to him something sublime and ennobling.

We have reached now the innermost kernel of Nietzsche's view of life, namely, the Schopenhauerian doctrine of will, given positive features under the influence of Darwin and his doctrine of the struggle of existence. (pp. 26-31)

> *George Burman Foster, in his* Friedrich Nietzsche, *edited by Curtis W. Reese (reprinted with permission of Macmillan Publishing Company; copyright 1931 and renewed 1959 by Macmillan Publishing Company), Macmillan, 1931, 250 p.*

GUSTAV BÜSCHER (essay date 1936)

> [*In the following excerpt, Büscher discusses the role Nietzsche played in the growth of National Socialism, concluding that it "is not a paradox but a fact that National Socialism misunderstands Nietzsche, and yet is right in claiming him as its prophet." For more commentary on Nietzsche's connection with National Socialism see Thomas Mann's and Albert Camus's essays excerpted below.*]

The anti-Hitler intellectuals of Germany hear with flaming indignation that National Socialism has adopted Nietzsche, the good European, as its philosopher and prophet. How can the Brown barbarians be so impudent as to claim the man who spoke so much of culture? How can those who destroyed the freedom of the Press appeal to the writer who exploited liberty of the Press to the farthest limits? How could a cosmopolitan mind feel at ease within the confines of the narrowest nationalism? His apostles, it is true, have justified, almost without exception, the philosopher's psychological penetration when he confessed of himself: "We should not allow ourselves to be burned for our convictions; we are none too sure of them." But, if the German intellectuals have experienced the pain of seeing nearly all their leaders bowing the knee to the Brown Baal, they have nevertheless retained the consolation that all the dead would have acted otherwise, and that even Nietzsche would have hurled a steadfast "No" at the blandishments of the Third Reich. Their conviction remains unshaken that National Socialism is endeavouring to drag the famous knight of the spirit on to their side, as energetically as the pacifist and democratic intellectuals are trying to drag him on to theirs.

Hitler goes on pilgrimage to the Nietzsche Archives as to a national shrine, accepts the philosopher's walking-stick from his sister, and has the great thinker's fame officially proclaimed to the people from all the German wireless stations. National Socialism declares Nietzsche's world of thought to be its own special domain, and one of its apostles, Erich Giese, has written a book to prove that the Third Reich is only the fulfilment of the poet-philosopher's dream.

Both sides are right, without knowing why, for Nietzsche's own nature was contradictory. It is true that he was a psychological genius, but he held too firmly to the principle that in psychology the reverse is also true, and therefore, more than any other thinker, he has two different opinions on every subject. . . . It is difficult to discover any subject for which Nietzsche's words do not supply at once the fullest vindication and the most brilliant refutation. "This thinker needs no one to refute him—he does it himself," cried the philosopher in one of his earliest books.

German scholarship has thus been unable to discover, after thirty years' effort, how far Nietzsche was in earnest, whether his works are the utterances of a prophet or of a literary swindler. Was the writer who "would rather be a clown than a saint" only a Harlequin dressed up as a philosopher? Or has the world been mocked by the books of a madman without realising it? At bottom he took nothing seriously, yet he was a prophet. No ingenuity has yet fathomed his purpose: his mission time has long revealed. His teaching of the Will to Power has changed the course of history more radically than any previous philosophical argument. This effect has not, of course, been produced by the special depth or scientific value of his ideas. Scientifically considered, they form the flattest freak of fancy ever hacked out by a metaphysician—aimless, meaningless tautology. Every will expresses itself in terms of strength, or, in more elevated language, as power. To speak of a will to power is a similar discovery to that of children who speak of a grinding-mill or a write-letter. But the effect produced by this idea arose not from the sense of the words, but from their sound. "Will to Power" sounded self-confident, threatening, swaggering, like the Kaiser's speeches about shining armour and the mailed fist. Thus Nietzsche supplied the theoretical basis for the Wilhelmian age and policy. The German has a dangerous penchant for what William I called "the usual German brag," and this German swagger caught fire as never before from the high-sounding words.

Before Nietzsche, the phrases Will to Power and Policy of Power were unknown. Even Bismarck, in his last great speech in the Reichstag on February 6th, 1888, uttered a warning against "a policy of prestige and power." But Nietzsche proved stronger than Bismarck, or at all events the wind of the day blew more strongly in his sails. The more popular his books became, the more the swaggering phrases rustled through the leading articles of Nationalist newspapers—"Will to Power, Policy of Power, Growth of Power, Means of Power, Position of Power, Demands of Power"—and the more it became a habit among German patriots to speak of the Germans as a "Sovereign Race." The philosopher of the Superman, who abused the Germans as "riff-raff, barbarians and oxen," nevertheless became the declared favourite of pre-war Pan-Germans, who allowed no book, no pamphlet, scarcely even a newspaper article, to appear without calling on Nietzsche as their sworn ally.

Only those German intellectuals for whom truth must always square with their own wishes can consider it coincidence and

misunderstanding that Nietzsche's philosophy has remained, through all the vicissitudes of fate, the gospel of the wildest type of nationalism. As a matter of fact, a straight line leads from Nietzsche, through the Pan-Germans and Spengler, to National Socialism. Every page of Hitler's book and speeches betrays the fact that not the weakest link of spiritual relationship connects him with Kant, Schiller or Goethe, and that on the contrary he has his spiritual home in the modern worship of Power. It is unnecessary to quote the many passages in his book in which he recognises unreservedly the policy of power and scornfully rejects consideration for the rights of other nations. It is needless to furnish proofs that National Socialism is resuscitated Pan-Germanism, which has only put on some new social drapery and shed a few of the external errors of Pan-Germanism (such as its fanatical Anglophobia), without any real change of heart. National Socialism would be obliged to recognise Nietzsche, even against its will, for no other philosopher can take his place. It is from the central idea of his philosophy, namely the Will to Power, that the Pan-German policy of power and the reign of terror of National Socialism have inevitably developed. For power can only rule through intimidation and terror. The doctrine of the Will to Power is the spiritual basis of concentration camps and mass executions. The supermen prophesied by Nietzsche, who were to rule the great masses as slaves stripped of their rights, have arrived. In Italy they wear the black shirt, in Germany the S.A. and S.S. uniform, in Russia, as followers of the Communist Party, the soviet star. They have hurled themselves upon the state like "some herd of blonde beasts of prey, a race of conquerors and rulers, which organise for war, and, through the power of organisation, plunge their terrible talons into a population which, even if enormously superior in numbers, is still utterly unorganised." Many other sayings of Nietzsche read, in the light of current events, like the prophecies of a seer.

Could it be otherwise? Actions spring from ideas; as ideas have been in the past, actions will follow in the future. Would it be possible for National Socialism to escape contact with the thoughts that have hypnotised cultured Germany to the limits of fanaticism for decades? If the Germans were not the worst psychologists in the world, it would not be necessary for anyone to tell them that Nietzsche is Hitler's spiritual grandsire. The similarity, both spiritual and physical, between them is too great. Both are of non-German descent. Their Slavonic ancestry is still visible in their faces, and can be felt in the tone and language of their writings and speeches. Both are distinguished by an hysterical ambition, which enforces suggestion by domineering gestures. Moreover, the parvenu spirit is as unmistakable in National Socialism as in Nietzsche and Wagner— that spirit which is obliged to find vent in swagger and in offering up incense to itself.

With Nietzsche's systematic duplicity of language it is, of course, easy to select quotations that are as opposed to National Socialism as fire to water; but even in this game the Hitlerites hold the trump cards. Nietzsche, it is true, wished to have nothing to do with people who took part in "the lying race-swindle"; yet the National Socialists can compile their recipes for the purification of the German race out of quotations from Nietzsche. For one of the few ideas to which he held consistently was that the highest task of culture is to breed a higher race of men. And how can this be achieved save by the selection and segregation of those who consider themselves to be that higher race? Has not he already declared that "peasant blood is the best blood in Germany," and that there is no finer race than that of the peasants? What better foundation can the National Socialists desire for their plan of breeding a new aristocracy from "blood and soil"? (pp. 589-93)

It is not a paradox but a fact that National Socialism misunderstands Nietzsche, and yet is right in claiming him as its prophet. His glorification of harshness, force and cruelty in rulers fits in perfectly with the rubbish of National Socialism. His demand for the raising of humanity by a system of Spartan severity reads like a prophecy of the Third Reich, which seeks to redeem the German nation from all defects by an equally Draconian, pedantic multiplicity of rules. Yet the real Nietzsche longs for exactly the reverse of this omnipotence of the state, namely, the break-up of all state power—anarchy. On no subject does he speak with fiercer hatred and more scathing contempt than on the State, and if such utterances failed to prove his anarchical spirit, it would be proved in abundance by his roaming life. A man who cannot endure a settled place of residence is also unable to endure state ordinances. (pp. 594-95)

It was a prophecy after his own heart when Nietzsche in his *Will to Power* foretold anarchy as the future form of life for society. His philosophy indeed is the theory of anarchy. It contains no sentence that is not contradicted, shattered by another sentence; it formulates no logical or ethical principle which the author would accept for himself as binding. "Nothing is true, everything is permissible," is the inevitable conclusion of this philosophy, whose labyrinthine paths lead straight to chaos. In a country where such a philosophy gained the mastery it was inevitable that, sooner or later, traditional authority must break down, and a new authority could only be based on the right of the strongest.

It is only an apparent paradox that Nietzsche the anarchist also comes forward as the prophet of dictatorship. It is, in truth, one more proof of the uncanny foresight of this strange being, hypersensitive and hysterical, who had the power of sensing the ultimate issue of the modern mind decades ahead. (p. 595)

> *Gustav Büscher, "Nietzsche: A Prophet of Dictatorship," in* Contemporary Review, *Vol. 149, No. 845, May, 1936, pp. 589-96.*

KARL JASPERS (essay date 1936)

[*Jaspers's* Nietzsche: An Introduction to the Understanding of His Philosophical Activity, *from which the following excerpt is taken, is considered one of the most important critical studies of Nietzsche's philosophy. In the excerpt below, Jaspers suggests that Nietzsche can only be properly understood by focusing on his complete work and life, by stressing the "temporal development" of his thoughts and their essential interrelation in a "timeless system." Jaspers's approach revolutionized Nietzsche criticism because it most nearly incorporated all the different schools of criticism, including the psychological, biographical, and mythological.*]

The literary interpretations of Nietzsche undertaken so far have, as a rule, one basic flaw: they place him within some general class, as though they unquestionably knew all the possibilities open to existence and to man. In doing so, they subsume him as a whole. Above all it was a mistake to admire Nietzsche as a poet and writer at the cost of not taking him seriously as a philosopher. Again it was a mistake to regard him as simply a philosopher like one of the earlier philosophers and to measure him by their measure. Genuine interpretation, however, does not subsume but penetrates; it does not claim to know with finality; but, while always taking cognizance of what has just been apprehended, it proceeds by a method of questioning

and answering. It thereby begins a process of assimilation, the conditions and limits of which it determines for itself. While the above-mentioned false interpretation provides the pleasurable illusion of a general survey by placing its object at a distance and viewing it *ab extra* as an exotic specimen, the true interpretation is a means to the possibility of self-involvement. (pp. 5-6)

Only by employing the sort of interpretation that proceeds toward the whole can we derive from Nietzsche himself the criterion that we need in order to place his statements in an order or rank corresponding to their import, to judge how essential each is, and to distinguish the pertinent versions from those that are extraneous and misleading. Inevitably the decisiveness of his awareness of essentials varies from time to time. Still one can arrive at standpoints from which it is possible to apply Nietzsche's own kind of criticism to the movements of his thought. Two paths must be consciously followed:

In the first place, Nietzsche's thoughts can be organized, without any regard for the order of their occurrence, in an existing *whole composed of intelligible ideas necessarily related to each other*. In the second place, since they belong to a development that occupied several decades, they are to be viewed in their *temporal form* as the whole of a life. In the first case, the idea of a *timeless systematic whole* becomes our guide as we search for the timeless position of each thought and for the architectonic of the system itself. In the second case, the *development* of his life, his knowledge, and his illness becomes the guiding principle as we seek to discover the temporal position of every thought within the totality of the process. On the one hand, each of Nietzsche's thoughts is understood to the extent to which its modifications, contradictions, and possibilities of movement are seen within an objectively related whole; on the other hand, it can be fully understood only in relation to the point in time at which it was entertained: the reader must always know just *when* everything that he reads was written.

These two ways would seem to be mutually exclusive. The demand that we envisage a systematic whole composed of interrelated parts, each apprehensible in its own extra-temporal position, contradicts the demand that we view this whole as a biographical sequence and understand everything in terms of its temporal location within the course of a life.

There are indeed certain basic thoughts of Nietzsche, thoughts of a dominant nature, which appear from early youth on and remain more or less constant in spite of radical modifications. Such thoughts, which outnumber all the others, permeate his entire life in astounding fashion. There are others which appear for the first time as the result of a sudden break in the developmental process. Then, too, there are the rare cases of thoughts which seem to be soon forgotten after a brief period in the foreground. They too are to be assimilated within the one great process which is at once systematic and biographical, for it pertains to the reality of man that the deepest and truest system of his thought must appear in temporal form. This form may be natural and congruent with its object, or it can, so to speak, be biographically obscured or ruined through causal connections which are alien to the object and distort the empirical reality of the specific individual in question. In Nietzsche's case both possibilities were realized in a manner that is profoundly stirring.

Thus *in the first place*, the study of Nietzsche's thinking (unlike that of most great philosophers) requires that we constantly remain in touch with the realities of *Nietzsche's life*. We must concern ourselves with his experiences and his conduct in various situations in order to discover the philosophic content which constitutes the indissoluble unity of his life and thought. The interrelatedness of the two can even be discovered in the external appearance of certain thoughts and images in his works. We must concern ourselves with the course of his life in order to apprehend the process within which everything that he wrote has its proper place.

On the other hand, no biographical study of Nietzsche can be meaningful so long as the events of his life are not integrated with the world of his thoughts. When the two sides are separated, either psychological curiosity is gratified by collecting the all-too-human facts of the case and by enjoying a real-life epic, or the thoughts, abstracted from the personality, are labeled as eternally valid truths—or sheer folly.

In the second place, Nietzsche's thoughts demand an investigation of their *systematic interrelations.* However, the system that derives from Nietzsche—unlike the great systems of philosophy—appears only as a phase or function within an encompassing whole that can no longer be presented in systematic fashion. Instead, interpretation, having gathered together the widely scattered variations on a given theme, must explore them in detail, together with all their contradictions, with a view to traversing all the possibilities, as though the whole were nevertheless attainable. While in the end everything does indeed belong together, it falls back into the temporal extension of a veritable skein of ways of thinking that is by no means systematic.

In the study of Nietzsche the unity of the whole, i.e., of life and thought, of temporal development and timeless system, can only be the guiding *idea,* for Nietzsche's thinking will always elude all attempts at a well-ordered presentation. It is impossible to foresee how far one will get, objectively speaking, in an attempt to obtain a definite and well-substantiated conception of the whole. As the study proceeds, one unavoidably devotes himself completely to the empirically given series of actual occurrences in Nietzsche's life. But one must in addition to this explore his thoughts at length without regard to the time in which they were first entertained. What provides the irresistibly compelling agitation in the study of Nietzsche is precisely this ever-recurring difficulty: neither of these ways makes sense when taken separately while both, taken together, cannot be brought into complete harmony. (pp. 11-13)

One cannot present Nietzsche with a view to enabling the reader to gain exhaustive knowledge of him. Because he never attains static finality, either by emerging as a concisely delineated personality or by attaining a finished philosophical system, one can lay hold only upon detached constellations of his thoughts and specific aspects of his existence. The effort to comprehend him is bound to miscarry so long as one attempts to hold him, *in toto,* to a fixed position. Because Nietzsche indirectly reveals himself only through movement, access to him is achieved, not through *perusal* of something formal and systematic, but through a *movement* on one's own part. It is not possible to learn what he really is by merely assimilating thoughts and facts; on the contrary, one can bring forth, through Nietzsche, the meaning that Nietzsche is to have for him only through his own exertions and critical questions. (p. 14)

Our task is to remain receptive to his influence by avoiding a static view that restricts him to a specific standpoint and by gaining a conception of the lofty demands which he makes. Nietzsche finally proves to be the incomprehensible exception which, without being a model for imitation, exerts an absolutely irreplaceable quickening influence upon others who are not exceptional. In the end one cannot help but ask how a man who is by no means representative can still become as overwhelmingly significant as though he spoke for humanity itself. (p. 16)

Karl Jaspers, in his Nietzsche: An Introduction to the Understanding of His Philosophical Activity, *translated by Charles F. Wallraff and Frederick J. Schmitz (translation copyright ©1965 The Board of Regents of the Universities and State College of Arizona; reprinted by permission of the University of Arizona Press, Tucson; originally published as* Nietzsche: Einführung in das Verständnis seines Philosophierens, *W. de Gruyter & Co., 1936), The University of Arizona Press, 1965, 490 p.*

GOTTFRIED BENN   (essay date 1937)

[*Among twentieth-century German authors, Benn is often grouped with those most strongly influenced by Nietzsche. He is also regarded as one of the leading exponents of nihilism in modern literature.*]

If one surveys the white nations in the course of the last five hundred years and looks for a yardstick to assess their great minds, the only one to be found is the degree of ineradicable nihilism they bore within them and spasmodically hid under the fragments of their works. It is quite obvious—all the great minds among the white nations have felt only one inner task, namely the creative camouflaging of their nihilism. . . . Nietzsche's place in their ranks is for a long time that of an idealistic Antinoüs. Even his Zarathustra—what a child of Nature, what evolutionary optimism, what shallow utopianism about the spirit and its realization! Only in the last stage, with *Ecce Homo* and the lyrical fragments, did he let that other datum rise into his consciousness, and that, one may suppose, brought about his collapse: that brown night when he stood on the bridge staring down into the abyss, beholding the abyss—late—too late for his organism and his role as a prophet. (p. 79)

Gottfried Benn, "Wolf's Tavern," translated by Ernst Kaiser and Eithne Wilkins (1937), in his Primal Vision: Selected Writings of Gottfried Benn, *edited by E. B. Ashton (all rights reserved; reprinted by permission of New Directions Publishing Corporation), New Directions, 1971, pp. 63-82.**

JACQUES BARZUN   (essay dates 1941)

[*Barzun is a prominent American social and literary critic. Many of his most important works are concerned with the influences of Romanticism.*]

No greater mistake can be made than to consider Nietzsche's break with Wagner as a personal quarrel resulting from a difference of opinion about music. It is much more than that. It is the first critical repudiation of the second half of the nineteenth century by a herald of the twentieth. It is consequently the key to the twisted cypher of the Romantic-Realist conflict, and the reflection of the chaos created by Darwinism, socialism, nationalism, and popular culture between 1875 and 1900. Caught at the junction of these rushing streams and responsive to their slightest impulses, Nietzsche's thought was heaved up like a confused crest and scattered in all directions. That is why his work, although it is made up in part of fragments and aphorisms, must be taken as a whole and not piecemeal. His "friends" the apologists of violence and his opponents the defenders of democracy err equally in taking sentences out of their context and metaphors away from their intention. No less misleading is it to sample his anti-Wagnerian polemics.

It was in 1869, only ten years after *Tristan*, that Nietzsche, under the spell of its music, came as an unknown of twenty-five to Wagner in Tribschen. A philologist by profession, Nietzsche had been attracted to the figure of the struggling artist. . . . The affection with which Wagner responded begot also in the orphaned Nietzsche a feeling akin to the discovery of a second father. But whereas the younger man's devotion was without *arrière pensée*, Wagner's contained the usual dose of self-seeking: he saw a champion sent by fate to convert the men of the rising generation. Nietzsche's ideas on the musical origins of Greek Tragedy fitted in confusedly but satisfactorily with Wagner's old notions on the subject, and lively talks together smoothed out any glaring contradictions. Wagner became a Nietzschean as quickly as Nietzsche a Wagnerian. (pp. 325-26)

It had been planned between them that as soon as *The Birth of Tragedy* was published, Nietzsche should strike out with an essay—perhaps a book—on Wagner. But the critic delayed. He wrote instead his first *Thoughts out of Season*—the famous assault on David Strauss, the representative of false culture, false science, and false spirituality. Of these unpopular "thoughts" Nietzsche wrote another, and a third. Only in his fourth and last, seven years after their first meeting, and after Wagner had established himself at Bayreuth, did Nietzsche devote a hundred short pages to his chosen master.

The pages are not only short, they are constrained and diffident. There can be little doubt . . . that Nietzsche was already aware of his main objections to Wagnerism. These are in truth implicit in the first of the four *Thoughts* and are summed up in the the term *Bildungsphilister*,—educated Philistine,—a nickname of Nietzsche's invention to stigmatize not merely Strauss but the generation to which he spoke, the Wagnerian generation. The *Bildungsphilister* is the learned enthusiast, the canting faddist, the torchbearer of civilized mediocrity. . . . (pp. 326-27)

Between the first and fourth of the "Unseasonables," Nietzsche had gone to Bayreuth and it had been for him a revelation in the wrong sense. He had seen the stage effects, beheld the symbolic menagerie in action, heard the shouting heroes and heroines, felt the musical thrills ebbing and flowing over the united sensorium of the audience, and he had seen the master magician beam with delight at the public response. Nietzsche could still feel that it was not the time to speak out. Wagner's professed aims were as good as ever: a national art akin to Greek tragedy, combining music and acting, and not seeking to make money out of the boredom of the upper classes. But all the aims might be lost through a vulgar compromise with a vulgar audience. Crude and high-priced, Bayreuth combined snobbery with sightseeing, and was steeped in sensuality and beer. Nietzsche took a sorrowful farewell of the place where the new art might have come to brith. Tears stood in his eyes as he sighed, "And that was Bayreuth!"

The break with the Wagners . . . was brought on by Nietzsche's next work, *Human, All Too Human*. It is the record of his passage through darkness, his plunge into positivism and science, which he uses against his society without remorse. Here are found the first hints of anti-Wagnerism, mixed with suspicions of all forms of faith. Antinomies in the manner of [Pierre Joseph] Proudhon combine with satire drawn from Dar-

win and the socialists and are turned against them as well. . . . [From] Wagner came the last music drama *Parsifal*. This was the end of the end. Nietzsche was revolted by its thick sanctimonious atmosphere. The notes **Contra Wagner** were accumulating, and Nietzsche was about to seek abroad a calm of spirit which neither his native land nor his professorial conscience could afford him. Yet with a delicacy which the subject of the notes would have found superhuman, Nietzsche did not publish them until five years had passed over Wagner's death. (pp. 327-28)

[Nietzsche took] Wagnerism seriously and tested it. Not conceding that what was new to the half-educated public of Europe was necessarily made so by their decision, he judged Wagnerism by its effect upon him. His intimate acquaintance with the quality of genius from Plato and Pascal to Stendhal and Schopenhauer made him feel that in Bayreuth art took a step downwards in order to reach, not the people, but the middle classes of a decadent era. Everything in Wagner was designed for them: the size and crudity of the show, the aura of technicality and religion, the figure of the author as a wonder-worker, the association of nationalism with the turgid dramas, and finally the music. The music was not separable from the rest; it was crude, pretentious, and turgid too. It lacked the two things that define and give intellectual form to inarticulate sounds: rhythm and melody. It was the opiate of the people. (pp. 328-29)

Before Wagner, music had had no need of literature to help it. Is it possible that Wagner feared his music would be too slight, too easily understood without the paraphernalia of theory and symbol? Or is it rather an answer to the demand of the musically illiterate for something to give importance to their nervous thrills? In any case, Wagner's music is decadent and for decadents. It lacks gaiety, strength, intelligence, freedom from gross material aids; above all it lacks artistic integrity: it comes out of a bag of tricks.

This is the "Wagner Case." Six months later, the debate grows wider. Wagnerism has become the symptom of the European malady which it is Nietzsche's mission to combat and, if possible, to cure. Music has become an opiate because the world of the late nineteenth century is too dreadful to be faced, and those who have made it are too stupid and cowardly to remake it. Materialism and loss of faith have generated their seeming opposite, a makeshift mysticism of the senses. In it sensation itself disappears; as in *Tristan*, sensation is for the sake of forgetting self, love is for the sake of death. All values meanwhile have become falsehoods. Morality is an indecent sham; brutality masquerades as strength; positivism is the name for a disgusted skepticism; science and education are professional make-believes sheltering the mass mind. Nowhere is anyone found saying "yea" to life, loving his fate, knowing his mind or shaping his world. It is "the Bayreuthian era of civilization." The theories of Darwin and Marx preach fatalism, chaos, and a utopia coming thereafter through nobody's fault.

These are the reasons for Nietzsche's knowledge that he is at the antipodes from Wagner, who condones all this and gives the patient a soothing drink. Nietzsche scorns most the two things Wagner stands for most—Germanism and anti-Semitism. To be a good European, an anti-German, a lover of "Mediterranean" music, an anti-pessimist, and a witness of the rebirth after decadence, one must be first an anti-Wagnerian, a wholehearted detester of the "Music Without Any Future." (pp. 329-31)

Jacques Barzun, "Nietzsche Contra Wagner," in his Darwin, Marx, Wagner: Critique of a Heritage *(copyright 1941 by Jacques Barzun; reprinted by permission of the author), Little, Brown and Company, 1941 (and reprinted by Little, Brown, 1946), pp. 325-34.*

BERTRAND RUSSELL   (essay date 1945)

[*Russell, like the earlier Max Nordau, Paul Carus, and George Santayana (see excerpts above), takes a psychological approach to Nietzsche's work and finds that his philosophy is mostly the hyperbole of a "megalomaniac."*]

It is undeniable that Nietzsche has had a great influence, not among technical philosophers, but among people of literary and artistic culture. It must also be conceded that his prophecies as to the future have, so far, proved more nearly right than those of liberals or Socialists. *If* he is a mere symptom of disease, the disease must be very wide-spread in the modern world.

Nevertheless there is a great deal in him that must be dismissed as merely megalomaniac. Speaking of Spinoza he says: "How much of personal timidity and vulnerability does this masquerade of a sickly recluse betray!" Exactly the same may be said of him, with the less reluctance since he has not hesitated to say it of Spinoza. It is obvious that in his day-dreams he is a warrior, not a professor; all the men he admires were military. His opinion of women, like every man's, is an objectification of his own emotion towards them, which is obviously one of fear. "Forget not thy whip"—but nine women out of ten would get the whip away from him, and he knew it, so he kept away from women, and soothed his wounded vanity with unkind remarks.

He condemns Christian love because he thinks it is an outcome of fear: I am afraid my neighbour may injure me, and so I assure him that I love him. If I were stronger and bolder, I should openly display the contempt for him which of course I feel. It does not occur to Nietzsche as possible that a man should genuinely feel universal love, obviously because he himself feels almost universal hatred and fear, which he would fain disguise as lordly indifference. His "noble" man—who is himself in day-dreams—is a being wholly devoid of sympathy, ruthless, cunning, cruel, concerned only with his own power. (pp. 766-67)

It never occured to Nietzsche that the lust for power, with which he endows his superman, is itself an outcome of fear. Those who do not fear their neighbours see no necessity to tyrannize over them. Men who have conquered fear have not the frantic quality of Nietzsche's "artist-tyrant" Neros, who try to enjoy music and massacre while their hearts are filled with dread of the inevitable palace revolution. I will not deny that, partly as a result of his teaching, the real world has become very like his nightmare, but that does not make it any the less horrible. (pp. 767-68)

> *Bertrand Russell, "Nietzsche," in his* A History of Western Philosophy, and Its Connection with Political and Social Circumstances from the Earliest Times to the Present Day *(copyright © 1945, 1972, by Bertrand Russell; reprinted by permission of Simon & Schuster, a Division of Gulf & Western Corporation), Simon & Schuster, 1945, pp. 760-73.*

THOMAS MANN (essay date 1947)

[*The following excerpt is drawn from Mann's* Nietzsche's Philosophy in the Light of Contemporary Events, *an important reappraisal of Nietzsche's thought following National Socialism and World War II. In it he argues that Nietzsche deliberately committed two errors in his philosophy of ethics and morals: the first being his "misrepresentation of the power relationship between instinct and intellect on earth"; the second consisting in the false relationship he established between life and morals as opposing phenomena. Mann also reaches a similar conclusion to Gustav Büscher's (see excerpt above) when he suggests that Nietzsche was perfectly suited to the designs of fascism—and that in reality it was not Nietzsche who created fascism but rather "fascism created him."*]

[Nietzsche] is a born psychologist, psychology is his archpassion: apperception and psychology, these are fundamentally one and the same passion, and it characterizes the entire inner contradictiousness of this great and suffering spirit that he, who values life far above apperception, is so completely and hopelessly caught in psychology. He is already a psychologist only on the basis of Schopenhauer's findings that not the intellect produces will, but vice versa, that not the intellect is the primary and dominating element, but the will, to which the intellect entertains a relationship of no more than servitude. The intellect as a servile tool of will: that is the font of all psychology, a psychology of casting suspicions and tearing off masks, and Nietzsche as attorney general of life, throws himself into the arms of moral psychology, he suspects all "good" urges of originating from bad ones and proclaims the "evil" ones as those which ennoble and exalt life. That is "The Revaluation of All Values." (pp. 17-18)

His life was intoxication and suffering—a highly artistic state, mythologically speaking the union of Dionysos with the Crucified. Swinging the thyrsus he ecstatically glorified the strong and beautiful, the amorally triumphant life and defended it against any stunting by intellectualism—and at the same time he paid tribute to suffering as none other. "It determines the *order of rank*," he says, "how deeply a man can suffer." Those are not the words of an anti-moralist. . . . Nietzsche's pen has not a whit of anything exuberantly able and saltatorial. Everything "choreographic" in his attitude is velleity and disagreeable in the extreme. It is much rather a bloody kind of self-mutilation, self-torment, moralism. His very concept of truth is ascetic: for to him truth is what hurts, and he would be suspicious of any truth that would cause him a pleasant sensation. "Among the forces," he says, "raised by our morals was truthfulness: the latter finally turns on morals, discovers its teleology, its *prejudiced* manner of observation." His "Immoralism" thus is the self-cancellation of morality for the sake of truthfulness. But that this in a way is exaggeration and luxuriation of morals he hints at by speaking of an inherited treasure of morality which could well afford to waste and throw out of the window a great deal without thereby becoming noticeably impoverished.

All this stands behind the atrocities and intoxicated messages of power, force, cruelty and political deception into which his thought of life as a work of art and of an unreflected civilization dominated by instinct, degenerates splendidly in his later writings. (pp. 19-20)

As far as I can see, there are two mistakes which warp Nietzsche's thinking and lead to his downfall. The first one is a complete, we must assume: a deliberate, misperception of the power relationship between instinct and intellect on earth, just as though the latter were the dangerously dominating element, and highest time it were to save instinct from its threat. If one considers how completely will, urge and interest dominate and hold down intellect, reason and the sense of justice in the great majority of people, the opinion becomes absurd that intellect must be overcome by instinct. This opinion can be explained only historically, on the strength of a momentary philosophical situation, as a correction of rationalistic satiety, and immediately it requires counter-correction. As though it were necessary to defend life against the spirit! As though there were the slightest danger that conditions on earth could ever become too spiritualized! . . . Nietzsche acts—and in so doing he has caused a great deal of trouble—as though it were our moral consciousness which, like Mephistopheles, raises an icy, satanic fist against life. As far as I am concerned, I see nothing particularly satanic in the thought (a thought long known to mystics) that one day life might be eliminated by the power of the human spirit, an achievement which is still a long, an interminably long way off. (pp. 22-3)

The second one of Nietzsche's errors is the utterly false relationship he establishes between life and morals when he treats of them as opposites. The truth is that they belong together. Ethics support life, and a man with good morals is an upright citizen of life,—perhaps a little boring, but extremely useful. The real opposites are ethics and *aesthetics*. Not morality, but beauty is linked to death, as many poets have said and sung,—and Nietzsche should not know it? "When Socrates and Plato started talking about truth and justice," he says somewhere, "they were not Greeks any longer, but Jews—or I don't know what." Well, thanks to their morality the Jews have proven themselves to be good and persevering children of life. They, together with their religion, their faith in a just God, have survived thousands of years, whereas the dissolute little nation of aesthetes and artists, the Greeks, very quickly disappeared from the stage of history.

But Nietzsche, far from any racial anti-semitism, does indeed see in Jewry the cradle of Christianity and in the latter, justly but with revulsion, the germ of democracy, the French Revolution and the hateful "modern ideas" which his shattering word brands as herd animal morals. . . . The primary reproach he throws at Christianity is the fact that it raised the individual to such importance that one could no longer *sacrifice* it. But, he says, the breed persists only through human sacrifice and Christianity is the opposing principle against natural selection. It has actually dragged down and debilitated the power, the responsibility, the high duty to sacrifice human beings and for thousands of years, until the arrival of Nietzsche, has prevented the development of that energy of greatness which "by breeding, and on the other hand by destroying millions of misfits, forms future man and does not perish from the never before existing misery he creates." Who was it that recently had the strength to take upon himself this responsibility, impudently thought himself capable of this greatness and unfalteringly fulfilled this high duty of sacrificing hecatombs of human beings? A crapule of megalomaniacal petty bourgeois, at the sight of whom Nietzsche would immediately have gone down with an extreme case of megrim and all its accompanying symptoms.

He did not live to see it. Nor did he live to see a war after the old-fashioned one of 1870 with its Chassepot and needle rifles and therefore he can, with all his hatred of the christian and democratic philanthropy of happiness, luxuriate in glorifications of war that appear to us today like the talk of an excited adolescent. That the good cause justifies war, is much too moral for him: it is the good war that justifies *any* cause. (pp. 23-4)

[In Nietzsche we] are face to face with a Hamlet-like fate, a tragic destiny of apperception unbearably deep, one that inspires reverence and compassion. "I believe," Nietzsche says somewhere, "I have correctly guessed a few elements from the soul of highest man—*it may be that everyone* who guesses him correctly, *is destroyed*." He was destroyed by it, and the atrocities of his teaching are too frequently pervaded by infinitely moving, lyrical sorrow, by profound glances of love, by sounds of melancholy yearning for the dew of love to quicken the arid, rainless land of his solitude, for scorn and revulsion to dare and emerge before such an Ecce Homo manifestation. But our reverence does find itself in something of a tight spot when that "socialism of the subjugated caste" which Nietzsche a hundred times scorned and branded as a poisonous hater of higher life, proves to us that his superman is nothing but the idealization of the fascist Fuehrer, and that he himself with all his philosophizing was a pacemaker, participating creator and prompter of ideas to European—to world fascism. Incidentally, I am inclined here to reverse cause and effect and not to believe that Nietzsche created fascism, but rather that fascism created him—that is to say: basically remote from politics and innocently spiritual, he functioned as an infinitely sensitive instrument of expression and registration, with his philosopheme of power he presaged the dawning imperialism and as a quivering floatstick indicated the fascist era of the West in which we are living and shall continue to live for a long time to come, despite the military victory over fascism. (p. 27)

We must drop the evaluation of Nietzsche as an aphorist without a central core: his philosophy as well as that of Schopenhauer is a completely organized system, developed from one single fundamental, all-pervading thought. But then of course this fundamental and initial thought is of a radical aesthetic nature, by which fact alone his perception and thinking must grow into irreconcilable opposition to all socialism. In the last analysis there are only two mental and inner attitudes: the aesthetic and the moral one, and socialism is a strictly moral way of looking at the world. Nietzsche on the other hand is the most complete and irredeemable aesthete known to the history of the human mind, and his premise containing his Dionysian pessimism: i.e., that life can be justified only as an aesthetic phenomenon, is most exactly correct of him, his life, his work as a thinker and a poet—only as an aesthetic phenomenon can it be justified, understood, venerated; consciously, down to the self-mythologization of the last moments and into insanity, this life is an artistic show, not only in its wonderful expression, but also in its innermost essence—a lyrical and tragical drama of the utmost fascination. (p. 32)

From Nietzsche's aestheticism, which is a raging abnegation of the spirit in favor of the beautiful, strong and infamous life, i.e., the self-denial of a man who suffers deeply from life, there flows into his philosophical outpourings something unreal, irresponsible, undependable and passionately playful, an element of deepest irony that must foil the understanding of the more simple reader. Not only is it art what he offers—it is an art also to read him, and nothing clumsy and straightforward is admissible, every kind of artfulness, irony, reserve is required in reading him. Who takes Nietzsche at face value, takes him literally, who believes him, is lost. (p. 33)

An aesthetic philosophy of life is fundamentally incapable of mastering the problems we are called upon to solve—no matter how much Nietzsche's genius has contributed to the creation of the new atmosphere. At one time he presumes that in the coming world of his vision, the religious forces might still be strong enough to produce an aesthetic religion a la Buddha which would glide across the differences between the denominations—and science would have nothing against a new ideal. ''But,'' he adds carefully, ''it will not be general love of man!'' And what if it would be just this?—It would not have to be the optimistic idyllic love for ''humankind'' to which the 18th century vowed gentle tears and to which, by the way, civilization owes enormous progress. When Nietzsche proclaims: ''God is dead''—a decision which for him meant the hardest of all sacrifices—in whose honor, in whose exaltation did he do so other than of man? If he was, if he was able to be, an atheist, then he was one, no matter how pastoral and sentimental the word sounds, because of his love for humankind. He must accept being called a humanist, just as he must suffer having his criticism of morals understood as a last form of the enlightenment. The superdenominational religiousness he mentions I cannot conceive of other than tied to the idea of mankind, as a religiously based and tinted humanism which, deeply experienced, would have passed through a great deal and would accept all knowledge of what is infernal and demonic into its tribute to the human mystery. (p. 36)

That philosophy is no cold abstraction, but experience, suffering and sacrificial deed for humanity, was Nietzsche's knowledge and example. In the course of it, he was driven upward into the icy wastes of grotesque error, but the future was in truth the land of his love, and for posterity, as for us, whose youth is incalculably indebted to him, he will stand, a figure full of delicate and venerable tragedy and enveloped by the flashing summer lightning that heralds the dawn of a new time. (p. 37)

> *Thomas Mann, in his* Nietzsche's Philosophy in the Light of Contemporary Events *(reprinted by permission of S. Fischer Verlag GmbH, Frankfurt am Main; originally an address delivered at the Library of Congress on April 29, 1947), The Library of Congress, 1947, 37 p.*

ALBERT CAMUS   (essay date 1951)

[*Camus considers Nietzsche the first philosopher to treat nihilism as a conscious phenomenon. In this respect, Camus sees nihilism as the basic tenet of Nietzsche's philosophical thought. This view coincides with that of Arthur C. Danto (see excerpt below), but opposes the views of Paul Elmer More and Richard Schacht (see excerpts above and below)—both of whom believe that Nietzsche sought to overcome nihilism by treating it as a prerequisite to his revaluation of values. This argument is similar to Martin Heidegger's (see excerpt below), who considers Nietzsche's nihilism as only one element in a five-point philosophy—but a necessary element in that it is interrelated and mandatory to the existence of the other four, which include the will to power, the Übermensch, the doctrine of eternal return, and the revaluation of all values*].

It is absurdity that Nietzsche meets face to face. The better to avoid it, he pushes it to extremities: morality is the final aspect of God which must be destroyed before the period of reconstruction begins. Then God no longer exists and no longer guarantees our existence; man, in order to exist, must decide to act. (p. 57)

With Nietzsche, nihilism seems to become prophetic. But we can draw no conclusions from Nietzsche, except the base and mediocre cruelty that he hated with all his strength, unless we give first place in his work—well ahead of the prophet—to the diagnostician. The provisional, methodical, strategic character

of his thought cannot be doubted for a moment. With him, nihilism becomes conscious for the first time. Diagnosticians have this in common with prophets—they think and operate in terms of the future. Nietzsche never thought except in terms of an apocalypse to come, not in order to extol it, for he guessed the sordid and calculating aspect that this apocalypse would finally assume, but in order to avoid it and to transform it into a renaissance. He recognized nihilism for what it was and examined it like a clinical fact.

He said of himself that he was the first complete nihilist of Europe. Not by choice, but by condition, and because he was too great to refuse the heritage of his time. He diagnosed in himself, and in others, the inability to believe and the disappearance of the primitive foundation of all faith—namely the belief in life. The 'Can one live as a rebel?' became with him 'Can one live, believing in nothing?' His reply is in the affirmative. Yes, if one creates a system out of absence of faith, if one accepts the final consequences of nihilism, and if, on emerging into the desert and putting one's confidence in what is going to come, one feels, with the same primitive instinct, both pain and joy.

Instead of systematic doubt, he practised systematic negation, the determined destruction of everything that still hides nihilism from itself, of the idols which camouflage God's death. . . . According to Nietzsche, he who wants to be a creator of good and of evil, must first of all destroy all values. . . . He wrote, in his own manner, the *Discours de la Méthode* of his period, without the freedom and exactitude of the seventeenth-century French he admired so much, but with the mad lucidity which characterizes the twentieth century which, according to him, is the century of rebellion.

Nietzsche's first step is to accept what he knows. Atheism for him goes without saying and is 'constructive and radical.' Nietzsche's superior vocation, so he says, is to provoke a kind of crisis and a final decision about the problem of atheism. The world continues on its course at random and there is nothing final about it. Thus God is useless, since He wants nothing in particular. If He wanted something, and here we recognize the traditional formulation of the problem of evil, we would have to assume Him responsible for 'a sum-total of pain and inconsistency which would debase the entire value of being born.' We know that Nietzsche was publicly envious of Stendhal's formula: 'the only excuse for God is that he does not exist.' Deprived of the divine will, the world is equally deprived of unity and finality. That is why it is impossible to pass judgment on the world. Any attempt to apply a standard of values to the world leads finally to a slander on life. Judgments are based on what is, with reference to what should be—the kingdom of heaven, eternal concepts, or moral imperatives. But what should be does not exist: and this world cannot be judged in the name of nothing. 'The advantages of our times; nothing is true, everything is permitted.' These magnificent or ironic formulae, which are echoed by thousands of others, at any rate suffice to demonstrate that Nietzsche accepts the entire burden of nihilism and rebellion. (pp. 57-9)

Nietzsche's philosophy, undoubtedly, revolves around the problem of rebellion. More precisely, it begins by being a rebellion. But we sense the change of position that Nietzsche makes. With him, rebellion begins at 'God is dead' which is assumed as an established fact; then rebellion hinges on everything that aims at falsely replacing the vanished deity and reflects dishonour on a world which undoubtedly has no direction but which remains the only proving-ground of the gods.

Contrary to the opinion of certain of his Christian critics, Nietzsche did not form a project to kill God. He found Him dead in the soul of his contemporaries. He was the first to understand the immense importance of the event and to decide that this rebellion among men could not lead to a renaissance unless it were controlled and directed. Any other attitude towards it, whether it were regret or complacency, must lead to the apocalypse. Thus Nietzsche did not formulate a philosophy of rebellion, but constructed a philosophy on rebellion. (pp. 59-60)

In this world rid of God and of moral idols, man is now alone and without a master. No one has been less inclined than Nietzsche (and in this way he distinguishes himself from the romantics) to allow himself to believe that such freedom would be easy. This unbridled freedom put him among the ranks of those of whom he himself said that they suffered a new form of anguish and a new form of happiness. But, at the beginning, it is only anguish which makes him cry out: 'Alas, grant me madness. . . . By being above the law, I am the most outcast of all outcasts.' (p. 62)

Because his mind was free, Nietzsche knew that freedom of the mind is not a comfort, but an achievement that one aspires to and obtains, at long last, after an exhausting struggle. He knew that there is a great risk in wanting to consider oneself above the law, of finding oneself beneath that law. That is why he understood that the mind only found its real emancipation in the acceptance of new obligations. If nothing is true, if the world is without order, the nothing is forbidden; to prohibit an action, there must, in fact, be a standard of values and an aim. But, at the same time, nothing is authorized; there must also be values and aims in order to choose another course of action. Absolute domination by the law does not represent liberty, but nor does absolute freedom of choice. Chaos is also a form of servitude. Freedom only exists in a world where what is possible is defined at the same time as what is not possible. Without law there is no freedom. If fate is not guided by superior values, if chance is king then there is nothing but the step in the dark and the appalling freedom of the blind. At the conclusion of the most complete liberation, Nietzsche therefore chooses the most complete subordination. 'If we do not make of God's death a great renunciation and a perpetual victory over ourselves, we shall have to pay for that omission.' In other words, with Nietzsche, rebellion ends in asceticism. (pp. 62-3)

It can be said that Nietzsche rushes, with a kind of frightful joy, towards the impasse into which he methodically drives his nihilism. His avowed aim is to render the situation untenable to his contemporaries. His only hope seems to be to arrive at the extremity of contradiction. Then if man does not wish to perish in the coils that strangle him, he will have to cut them at a single blow, and create his own values. The death of God accomplishes nothing and can only be lived through in terms of preparing a resurrection. 'If we fail to find grandeur in God,' says Nietzsche, 'we find it nowhere; it must be denied or created.' To deny was the task of the world around him which he saw rushing towards suicide. To create was the superhuman task for which he was willing to die. He knew in fact that creation is only possible in the extremity of solitude and that man would only commit himself to this staggering task if, in the most extreme distress of mind, he must undertake it or perish. Nietzsche cries out to man that his only truth is the world—to which he must be faithful and on which he must live and find his salvation. But, at the same time, he teaches him that to live in a lawless world is impossible because to live implies, explicitly, the law. How can one live freely and without law? To this enigma, man must find an answer, on pain of death.

Nietzsche, at least, does not flinch. He answers and his answer is bold: Damocles never danced better than beneath the sword. One must accept the unacceptable and contend the untenable. From the moment that it is admitted that the world pursues no end, Nietzsche proposes to concede its innocence, to affirm that it accepts no judgment since it cannot be judged on any intention, and consequently to replace all judgments based on values by absolute assent, a complete and exalted allegiance to this world. Thus, from absolute despair will spring infinite joy, from blind servitude freedom without obligation. To be free is, precisely, to abolish ends. The innocence of the ceaseless change of things, as soon as one consents to it, represents the maximum liberty. The free mind willingly accepts what is necessary. Nietzsche's most intimate concept is that the necessity of phenomena, if it is absolute, does not imply any kind of restraint. Total acceptance of total necessity is his paradoxical definition of freedom. The question 'Free of what?' is thus replaced by 'Free for what?' Liberty coincides with heroism. It is the asceticism of the great man: 'the bow bent to the breaking point.'

This magnificent consent, born of affluence and fullness of spirit, is the unreserved affirmation of human imperfection and suffering, of evil and murder, of all that is problematic and strange in our existence. It is born of an arrested wish to be what one is in a world which is what it is. 'To consider oneself a fatality, not to wish to be other than one is . . . ' The Nietzschean experiment, which is part of the recognition of fatality, ends in a deification of fate. The more implacable destiny is, the more it becomes worthy of adoration. A moral God, pity and love are enemies of fate to the extent that they try to make amends for it. Nietzsche wants no redemption. The joy of self-realization is the joy of annihilation. But only the individual is annihilated. The movement of rebellion, in which man claimed his own self, disappears in the individual's absolute submission to self-realization. *Amor fati* replaces what was an *odium fati*. (pp. 63-4)

Nietzsche's whole effort is directed towards demonstrating the existence of laws which govern future events and that there is an element of chance in the inevitable: 'A child is innocence and forgetfulness, a new beginning, a gamble, a wheel which spins automatically, a first step, the divine gift of consent.' The world is divine because the world is illogical. That is why art alone, by being equally illogical, is capable of grasping it. It is impossible to give a clear account of the world, but art can teach us to reproduce it—just as the world reproduces itself in the course of its eternal gyrations. The primordial sea indefatigably repeats the same words and casts up the same astonished beings on the same sea-shore. But at least he who consents to his own return and to the return of all things, who becomes an echo and an exalted echo, partcipates in the divinity of the world. (p. 65)

Nietzsche thought that to accept this earth and Dionysos was to accept his own sufferings. And to accept everything, both suffering and the supreme contradiction simultaneously, was to be king. Nietzsche agreed to pay the price for his kingdom. Only the 'sad and suffering' world is true—the world is the only divinity. Like Empedocles who threw himself down Etna to find truth in the only place where it exists, namely in the bowels of the earth, Nietzsche proposed that man should allow himself to be engulfed in the cosmos in order to rediscover his eternal divinity and to become Dionysos himself. The *Will to Power* ends, like Pascal's *Pensées* of which it so often reminds us, with a wager. Man does not yet obtain assurance but only the wish for assurance which is not at all the same thing. Nietzsche, too, hesitated on this brink: 'That is what is unforgivable in you. You have the authority and you refuse to sign.' Yet, finally, he had to sign. But the name of Dionysos only immortalized the notes to Ariadne which he wrote when he was mad. (pp. 65-6)

In Nietzsche's mind, the only problem was to see that the human spirit bowed proudly to the inevitable. We know, however, his posterity and the kind of politics that were to be authorized by the man who claimed to be the last anti-political German. He dreamed of tyrants who were artists. But tyranny comes more naturally than art to mediocre men. 'Rather Cesare Borgia than Parsifal,' he exlaimed. He begat both Caesar and Borgia, but devoid of the distinction of feeling which he attributed to the great men of the Renaissance. As a result of his insistence that the individual should bow before the eternity of the species and should submerge himself in the great cycle of time, race has been turned into a special aspect of the species and the individual has been made to bow before this sordid god. The life of which he spoke with such fear and trembling has been degraded to a sort of biology for domestic use. Finally a race of vulgar overlords, with a blundering desire for power, adopted, in his name, the 'anti-semitic deformity' on which he never ceased to pour scorn. (pp. 66-7)

In the history of intelligence, with the exception of Marx, Nietzsche's adventure has no equivalent: we shall never finish making reparation for the injustice done to him. Of course history records other philosophies that have been misconstrued and betrayed. But up to the time of Nietzsche and national socialism, it was quite without parallel that a process of thought—brilliantly illuminated by the nobility and by the sufferings of an exceptional mind—should have been demonstrated to the eyes of the world by a parade of lies and by the hideous accumulation of corpses from concentration camps. The doctrine of the superman led to the methodical creation of submen—a fact that doubtless should be denounced but which also demands interpretation. If the final result of the great movement of rebellion in the nineteenth and twentieth centuries was to be this ruthless bondage then surely rebellion should be rejected and Nietzsche's desperate cry to his contemporaries taken up: 'My conscience and yours are no longer the same conscience.' (p. 67)

> *Albert Camus, "Metaphysical Rebellion," in his* The Rebel, *translated by Anthony Bower (translation copyright © 1956 by Alfred A. Knopf, Inc.; reprinted by permission of the publisher; originally published as* L'homme révolté, Gallimard, 1951), *Knopf, 1954, pp. 29-77.**

ERIC BENTLEY (essay date 1957)

[*Bentley argues that the chronological division of Nietzsche's work into three periods, each with its own distinct philosophy, is misleading, and suggests instead that he be studied as a thinker who hid behind a number of different masks, from which he issued his one consistent idea: heroic vitalism, or his philosophy of power. Bentley believes that from 1870 onward Nietzsche constantly held to the concept of power as the basic force in the universe, and that apparent contradictions arise in his thought only because he was forced to present this philosophy from behind numerous masks—such as those of Arthur Schopenhauer, Richard Wagner, positivism, Zarathustra, the iconoclast, and so on. For*

a detailed account of the chronological approach toward Nietzsche's philosophy, see George Burman Foster's essay excerpted above.]

Outside Germany, Nietzsche has not had his due, because those who soften his teaching blunt its cutting edge and therefore defeat its purpose, while those who see nothing in Nietzsche but brutality are undone by their own indignation. The "soft" school of critics has not recognized the importance of Heroic Vitalism in the modern world. The "hard" critics, if German, are too rhapsodic; if Germanophobe, too prone to sarcasms and debating points. There are some who consider Nietzsche brilliant but erratic and, therefore, not to be taken seriously. Nietzsche is so "abnormal" and the critic is so "normal" that the latter has little difficulty in proving his own superiority. The philistine's impression that there is nothing in Nietzsche but a string of random *aperçus* is all but confirmed by the widely accepted view that Nietzsche made radical changes in his philosophy according to the books he happened to be reading at the moment; that there is no Nietzschean philosophy but only a series of Nietzschean philosophies, all intriguing and none serious. Nietzsche is now a Schopenhauerian, now a positivist, now a creative evolutionist. It is possible to spend more time dividing up Nietzsche into periods than discussing what he had to say.

There are, doubtless, many convenient ways of parceling up the works of Nietzsche, but the chronological division is one of the most misleading. Instead, two dichotomies might be proposed as aids to the understanding of his total achievement. The first is . . . the dichotomy of the masculine and the feminine, which, on the plane of philosophy, is the opposition . . . between an Heraclitean power-philosophy and a poetic mysticism. The second dichotomy is that between the published and unpublished works of Nietzsche, that is, between the works he himself prepared for the press and the notes which executors published after his death.

This second dichotomy requires some explanation. It is not factitious. The published works were campaigns in a war against the age, campaigns in which Nietzsche would use any weapon, mystical or Heroic Vitalist, in the struggle against the old ideologies, radical and reactionary. The published works were propaganda, pamphlets designed to make enemies and influence people; the most systematic of Nietzsche's published works, *The Genealogy of Morals,* is subtitled "a polemic." One of the chief devices of warfare is camouflage, and in this department Nietzsche was so far a master that the kind of people he despised are still taken in. Where the soldier speaks of erecting camouflage, Nietzsche, in artistic metaphor, speaks of a foreground (*Vordergrund*) which conceals the more significant background from vulgar eyes. Or, Nietzsche adds in *The Will to Power,* the writer may be said to wear a mask: it would never do for his face to be visible to the uninitiated. . . .

Ever ready to regard himself as a duality, Nietzsche was particularly fond of regarding himself as a face covered by a mask, as a background obscured behind a foreground. Interpretation enters into discussion as soon as one tries to say which is face and which is mask in Nietzsche's work. The implication of Germanophobe criticism is that Nietzsche's religiousness is mask, his militarism the hidden reality. The "soft" critic, on the other hand, regards Nietzsche's harsh masculinity as mask, his tender woman's heart as the hidden reality. This was the view of [his sister] Frau Foerster. . . .

Frau Foerster thinks the philosophy of Heroic Vitalism is a trick played by her brother in order that we should not be embarrassed at his holy joy. In support of this "soft" criticism, she might have urged that Nietzsche hated anti-Semites, hated the Kaiser, hated Bismarck (off and on), hated the Reich, hated patrioteering (*Vaterländerei*), hated the apotheosis of the state.

Those, however, who have agreed that in Nietzsche the masculine and feminine were in constant collision will not want to make our two dichotomies into one by calling the masculine element a mask and the feminine a face, or *vice versa*. The mask was a wholly conscious device, whereas the struggle of masculine and feminine was seldom conscious at all. It was not because his message was too soft or too hard that Nietzsche wore a mask, but because it came too early (he was one of those, he said, who are born posthumously) and because it was not intended for the vulgar. (p. 136)

Zarathustra was a simple mask for Nietzsche himself. Dionysos was not so easy a proposition: this mask was more like a shirt of Nessus. The last mask that Nietzsche tried on was that of Jesus Christ, but by this time the face behind the mask was glazed with insanity. These are only the most celebrated and most obvious of Nietzsche's masks. In truth, when, in the early campaigns, Nietzsche sheltered behind the name of Wagner, the great musician was just as much a mask as Zarathustra. Naturally Wagner soon began to feel that he was a stalking-horse, under cover of which Nietzsche was shooting very strange barbs; and since Nietzsche could never understand why Wagner should not enjoy being a stalking-horse, estrangement followed. Schopenhauer was another mask and Nietzsche's use of his name is best expressed by the note in the *Ecce Homo:* "Schopenhauer and Wagner, or—in a word—Nietzsche."

In his published works, Nietzsche wore a mask which only the discerning could pierce. It is possible to see Nietzsche without his mask only in the various collections of posthumously published notes which comprise Volumes IX to XVI of the collected German edition and of which *The Will to Power* is the only well-known extract. These notes not only provide more direct statements of Nietzsche's philosophy: they enable us to discredit the division of Nietzsche's career into three philosophies (involving two *voltefaces*) and to establish not merely continuity but consistency throughout Nietzsche's literary life. It is no praise of a man that he never changed an opinion— Nietzsche did change many opinions—but the main principles of the power-philosophy were in his mind from 1870 onwards, that is, from the very date of his alleged "Schopenhauerian phase." The year of 1871 was that of *The Birth of Tragedy,* which is the classic statement of the first of Nietzsche's supposed three philosophies. But 1870 was the year of conversion to the power-philosophy, a conversion effected by the sight of charging cavalry, and 1871 was the year of many notes . . . explicitly stating the philosophy of Heroic Vitalism.

Posthumously published notes leave no doubt that Heroic Vitalism, the philosophy of Nietzsche's masculine mind and his public destiny, was the philosophy of all his mature years from 1870 onwards. He did not vacillate or betray. The later notes (in *The Will to Power*) simply carry the investigation further and it may be said that, however much Nietzsche's eyesight improved, he looked steadfastly in the same direction. Inconsistencies arise where the mask compelled him to say something that was not consistent with his own character: that is why Nietzsche often felt a loathing for the characters he impersonated, the higher men he kept in his cave, and in solitude tried to rediscover his real self. There are things in *The Birth of Tragedy* that could scarcely be reconciled with Heroic Vitalism. Whether such behavior on Nietzsche's part amounts to decep-

tion we can scarcely say. In mitigation of the offense it might be urged that every artist contains multitudes and contradicts himself, that Nietzsche did explain the nature of his masks, and that, finally, Nietzsche had no more pretentions than Marx to "immaculate perception," having no faith in non-participant objectivity and inert analysis. He was organizing his own life and seeking to organize the life of others. He was in the realm of action, not of contemplation. Above all, he wished to create a band of destroyers, seekers, good Europeans, free spirits, higher men, and when he spoke in their name he was using them as his rallying cry, his oriflamme, his mask, without insincerity.

He wore first the mask of Wagner, but the new era did not arrive. The mask was changed for that of a Free Spirit, not because Nietzsche had changed his philosophy, but because he had chosen another group of men to work towards the new age. Like Zarathustra, he found adequacy in none of his comrades and in the end bequeathed his philosophy as a free gift to those who should come after. He wore no mask in *The Will to Power* because the notes of which it is made up were not prepared for publication. Moreover, after *The Twilight of the Idols* . . . , in which Nietzsche wore the mask of the iconoclast and the enemy of the epoch, there was no mask left that Nietzsche need wear. The masks had failed: no man heeded the rallying cry. . . .

Eric Bentley, "The Philosopher of Heroism," in his The Cult of the Superman: A Study of Heroism in Carlyle and Nietzsche, with Notes on Other Hero-Worshippers of Modern Times *(copyright 1944, 1957 by Eric Bentley; reprinted by permission of the author; originally published in his* A Century of Hero-Worship: A Study of the Idea of Heroism in Carlyle and Nietzsche, with Notes on Wagner, Spengler, Stefan George, and D. H. Lawrence, *Beacon Press, 1957), P. Smith, 1969.*

WILLIAM BARRETT   (essay date 1958)

[*A prominent American critic and educator, Barrett has written several outstanding studies of twentieth-century philosophy.*]

No adequate psychological commentary on *Thus Spake Zarathustra* has yet been written, perhaps because the materials in it are so inexhaustible. It is a unique work of self-revelation but not at all on the personal or autobiographical level, and Nietzsche himself ostensibly does not appear in it; it is self-revelation at a greater, more primordial depth, where the stream of the unconscious itself gushes forth from the rock. Perhaps no other book contains such a steady procession of images, symbols, and visions straight out of the unconscious. It was Nietzsche's poetic work and because of this he could allow the unconscious to take over in it, to break through the restraints imposed elsewhere by the philosophic intellect. For this reason it is important beyond any of his strictly philosophic books; its content is actually richer than Nietzsche's own conceptual thought, and its symbols of greater wisdom and significance than he himself was able to grasp. (p. 167)

His most lyrical book, *Zarathustra* is also the expression of the loneliest Nietzsche. It has about it the icy and arid atmosphere not merely of the symbolic mountaintop on which Zarathustra dwells, but of a real one. Reading it, one sometimes feels almost as if one were watching a film of the ascent of Mount Everest, hearing the climber's sobbing gasp for breath as he struggles slowly to higher and still higher altitudes.

Climbing a mountain is the aptest metaphor for getting above ordinary humanity, and this precisely is what Zarathustra-Nietzsche is struggling to do. One hears throughout the book, though, in the gasping breath of the climber, the lament of Nietzsche the man.

The book begins with the recognition of this human relevance as Zarathustra, about to leave his mountain solitude, declares he is going down among men "once again to be a man." The mountain is the solitude of the spirit, the lowlands represent the world of ordinary men. The same symbolic contrast appears in Zarathustra's pet animals, the eagle and the serpent: the one the creature of the upper air, the other the one that moves closest to the earth. Zarathustra, as the third element, symbolizes the union between the two animals, of high and low, heaven and earth. He is going down among men, he says, as the sun sets dipping into the darkness below the horizon. But the sun sets in order to be reborn the next morning as a young and glowing god. The book thus opens with the symbols of rebirth and resurrection, and this is in fact the real theme of *Zarathustra*: how is man to be reborn, like the phoenix, from his own ashes? How is he to become really healthy and whole? Behind this question we see the personal shadow of Nietzsche's own illness and his long struggle to regain health; Zarathustra is at once the idealized image of himself and the symbol of a victory, in the struggle for health and wholeness, that Nietzsche himself was not able to achieve in life.

Despite the intensely personal sources of his theme, Nietzsche was dealing in this work with a problem that had already become central in German culture. Schiller and Goethe had dealt with it—Schiller as early as 1795 in his remarkable *Letters on Aesthetic Education,* and Goethe in his *Faust.* . . . *Faust* and *Zarathustra* are in fact brothers among books. Both attempt to elaborate in symbols the process by which the superior individual—whole, intact, and healthy—is to be formed; and both are identically "immoral" in their content, if morality is measured in its usual conventional terms.

Placed within the German cultural context, indeed, Nietzsche's immoralism begins to look less extreme than the popular imagination has taken it to be; it is not even as extreme as he was led to make it appear in some of the bloody creations of his overheated imagination in his last work, *The Will to Power.* Goethe in *Faust* was every bit as much at odds with conventional morality as was Nietzsche, but the old diplomatic fox of Weimar was a more tactful and better-balanced man and knew how to get his point across quietly, without shrieking it from the housetops as Nietzsche did. . . . The Devil, with whom Faust has made a pact, becomes in a real sense his servitor and subordinate, just as our devil, if joined to ourselves, may become a fruitful and positive force; like Blake before him Goethe knew full well the ambiguous power contained in the traditional symbol of the Devil. Nietzsche's immoralism, though stated much more violently, consisted in not much more than the elaboration of Goethe's point: Man must incorporate his devil or, as he put it, man must become better and more evil; the tree that would grow taller must send its roots down deeper. (pp. 168-70)

But what about the individual devil within the Superman? What about Zarathustra's devil? So far as Nietzsche attempts to make the goal of this higher individual the goal of mankind, a fatal ambiguity appears within his ideal itself. Is the Superman to be the extraordinary man, or the complete and whole man? Psychological wholeness does not necessarily coincide with extraordinary powers, and the great genius may be a crippled and maimed figure, as was Nietzsche himself. . . . Will the Superman, then, be the titanically striving individual, dwelling on the mountaintop of the spirit, or will he be the man who has realized within the world his own individual capacities for wholeness? The two ideals are in contradiction—a contradiction that is unresolved in Nietzsche and within modern culture itself.

The fact is that Zarathustra-Nietzsche did not come to terms with his own devil, and this is the crucial failure of Zarathustra in the book and of Nietzsche in his life. Consequently, it is also the failure of Nietzsche as a thinker. Not that Zarathustra-Nietzsche does not see his devil; time and again the latter pokes a warning finger at Zarathustra, and like a good devil he knows how to assume many shapes and disguises. He is the clown who leaps over the ropedancer's head at the beginning of the book, he is the Ugliest Man, who has killed God, and he is the Spirit of Gravity, whom Zarathustra himself names as his devil—the spirit of heaviness which would pull his too high-soaring spirit to earth. Each time Zarathustra thrusts aside the warning finger, finding it merely a reason for climbing a higher mountain to get away from it. The most crucial revelation, however, comes in the chapter "The Vision and the Enigma" . . . , in which the warning figure becomes a dwarf sitting on Zarathustra's back as the latter climbs a lonely mountain path. Zarathustra wants to climb upward, but the dwarf wants to pull him back to earth. "O Zarathustra," the dwarf whispers to him, "thou didst throw thyself high, but every stone that is thrown must fall." . . . This is the ancient pattern of the Greek myths: the hero who soars too high crashes to earth; and Nietzsche, as a scholar of Greek tragedy, should have given more respectful ear to the dwarf's warning.

But why a dwarf? The egotism of Zarathustra-Nietzsche rates himself too high; therefore the figure in the vision, to right the balance, shows him to himself as a dwarf. The dwarf is the image of mediocrity that lurks within Zarathustra-Nietzsche, and that mediocrity was the most frightening and distasteful thing that Nietzsche was willing to see in himself. (pp. 171-72)

[The idea of the Eternal Return] has an ambiguous status in Nietzsche. He tried to base it rationally and scientifically on the premise that if time were infinite and the particles in the universe finite, then by the laws of probability all combinations must repeat themselves over and over again eternally; and that therefore everything, we ourselves included, must recur again and again down to the last detail. But to take this as a purely intellectual hypothesis does not explain why the idea of the Eternal Return had such a powerful hold upon Nietzsche's emotions. . . . The idea of the Eternal Return . . . expresses, as Unamuno has pointed out, Nietzsche's own aspirations toward eternal and immortal life. On the other hand, the notion is a frightening one for a thinker who sees the whole meaning of mankind to lie in the future, in the Superman that man is to become; for if all things repeat themselves in an endless cycle, and if man must come again in the paltry and botched form in which he now exists—then what meaning can man have? For Nietzsche the idea of the Eternal Return becomes the supreme test of courage: If Nietzsche the man must return to life again and again, with the same burden of ill health and suffering, would it not require the greatest affirmation and love of life to say Yes to this absolutely hopeless prospect?

Zarathustra glimpses some of the fearful implications in this vision, for he remarks after expounding the Eternal Return, "So I spoke, and always more softly: for I was afraid of my own thoughts, and afterthoughts.'' Thereupon, in the dream, he hears a dog howl and sees a shepherd writhing on the ground, with a heavy black reptile hanging from his mouth. ''Bite!'' cries Zarathustra, and the shepherd bites the serpent's head off and spits it far away. . . . [The shepherd] is Nietzsche himself, and both the serpent and the dwarf set for him the same task: to acknowledge ''the heaviest and the blackest in himself.'' (pp. 173-74)

There is an inner coherence in the vision of Zarathustra, in that each of its three parts—the dwarf, the Eternal Return, and the shepherd spitting out the serpent—presents an obstacle and objection to Nietzsche's utopian conception of the Superman. They prefigure his own personal catastrophe; but since he was a thinker who really lived his thought, they indicate the fatal flaw in all such utopian thought. He who would launch the Superman into interstellar space had better recognize that the dwarf goes with him. ''Human, all too human!'' Nietzsche exclaimed in disgust at mankind as it had hitherto existed. But he who would try to improve man might do well not to make him inhuman but, rather, a little more human. To be a whole man—a round man, as the Chinese say—Western man may have to learn to be less Faustian. A touch of the average, the mediocre, may be necessary ballast for human nature. The antidote to the hysterical, mad laughter of Zarathustra's vision may be a sense of humor, which is something Nietzsche, despite his brilliant intellectual wit, conspicuously lacked. (p. 175)

> *William Barrett, ''Nietzsche,'' in his* Irrational Man: A Study in Existential Philosophy *(copyright © 1958 by William Barrett; reprinted by permission of Doubleday & Company, Inc.), Doubleday, 1958, pp. 158-83.*

MARTIN HEIDEGGER   (essay date 1961)

[*Heidegger is considered one of the foremost critics on Nietzsche's thought, and one of the most important philosophers of the twentieth century. In the following excerpt—taken from his four-volume study of Nietzsche—he discusses the historical development of nihilism and the necessary role nihilism has played in Nietzsche's philosophy. For a further discussion of nihilism and its part in Nietzsche's philosophy, see the essays by Paul Elmer More, Albert Camus, Arthur C. Danto, and Richard Schacht excerpted above and below.*]

[The] word *nihilism* came into vogue through Turgeniev as a name for the notion that only what is perceptible to our senses, that is, only beings that one experiences oneself, only these and nothing else are real and have being. Therefore, anything grounded on tradition, authority, or any other definitive value is negated. Usually, however, the name *positivism* is used to designate this point of view. (p. 3)

For Nietzsche, though, the word *nihilism* means something substantially ''more.'' Nietzsche speaks about ''European nihilism.'' He does not mean the positivism that arose in the mid-nineteenth century and spread throughout Europe. ''European'' has a historical significance here, and means as much as ''Western'' in the sense of Western history. Nietzsche uses *nihilism* as the name for the historical movement that he was the first to recognize and that already governed the previous century while defining the century to come, the movement whose essential interpretation he concentrates in the terse sentence: ''God is dead.'' That is to say, the ''Christian God'' has lost His power over beings and over the determination of man. ''Christian God'' also stands for the ''transcendent'' in general in its various meanings—for ''ideals'' and ''norms,''

''principles'' and ''rules,'' ''ends'' and ''values,'' which are set ''*above*'' the being, in order to give being as a whole a purpose, an order, and—as it is succintly expressed—''meaning.'' Nihilism is that historical process whereby the dominance of the ''transcendent'' becomes null and void, so that all being loses its worth and meaning. Nihilism is the history of the being itself, through which the death of the Christian God comes slowly but inexorably to light. It may be that this God will continue to be believed in, and that His world will be taken as ''real,'' ''effectual,'' and ''determinative.'' This history resembles the process in which the light of a star that has been extinguished for millennia still gleams, but in its gleaming nonetheless remains a mere ''appearance.'' For Nietzsche, therefore, nihilism is in no way some kind of viewpoint ''put forward'' by somebody, nor is it an arbitrary historical ''given,'' among many others, that can be historically documented. Nihilism is, rather, that event of long duration in which the truth of being as a whole is essentially transformed and driven toward an end that such truth has determined.

The truth of being as a whole has long been called *metaphysics*. Every era, every human epoch, is sustained by some metaphysics and is placed thereby in a definite relation to being as a whole and also to itself. The end of metaphysics discloses itself as the collapse of the reign of the transcendent and the ''ideal'' that sprang from it. But the end of metaphysics does not mean the cessation of history. It is the *beginning* of a serious concern with that ''event'': ''God is dead.'' That beginning is already under way. Nietzsche himself understood his philosophy as an introduction to the beginning of a new age. He envisioned the coming century—that is, the current, twentieth century—as the start of an era whose upheavals could not be compared to anything previously known. Although the scenery of the world theater might remain the same for a time, the play in performance would already be a different one. The fact that earlier aims now disappear and former values are devalued is no longer experienced as sheer annihilation and deplored as wasteful and wrong, but is rather greeted as a liberation, touted as an irrevocable gain, and perceived as a *fulfillment*.

''Nihilism'' is the increasingly dominant truth that all prior aims of being have become superfluous. But with this transformation of the erstwhile relation to ruling values, nihilism has also perfected itself for the free and genuine task of a *new* valuation. Such nihilism, which is in itself perfected and is decisive for the future, may be characterized as ''classical nihilism.'' Nietzsche describes his own ''metaphysics'' with this name and conceives it to be *the* counterstroke to all preceding metaphysics. The name *nihilism* thus loses the purely nihilistic sense in which it means a destruction and annihilation of previous values, the mere negation of beings and the futility of human history.

''Nihilism,'' thought now in its classic sense, calls for freedom *from* values as freedom *for* a *revaluation* of all (such) values. Nietzsche uses the expression ''revaluation of all values hitherto'' alongside the key word *nihilism* as another *major rubric* by which he assigns his own fundamental metaphysical position its definite place within the history of Western metaphysics.

From the rubric ''revaluation of values,'' we expect that altered values will be posited in place of earlier ones. But for Nietzsche ''revaluation'' means that the very ''place'' for previous values disappears, not merely that the values themselves fall away. This implies that the nature and direction of valuation, and the definition of the essence of value are transformed. The revaluation thinks Being for the first time as value. With it, metaphysics begins to be value thinking. In accordance with this transformation, prior values do not merely succumb to devaluation but, above all, the *need* for values in their former shape and in their previous place—that is to say, their place in the transcendent—is uprooted. The uprooting of past needs most assuredly takes place by cultivating the growing ignorance of past values and by obliterating history through a revision of its basic traits. "Revaluation of prior values" is primarily the metamorphosis of all valuation heretofore and the "breeding" of a new need for values.

If such revaluation of all prior values is not only to be carried out but is also to be grounded, then it has need of a "new principle"; that is, the establishment of a basis for defining beings as a whole in a new, authoritative way. But if the interpretation of beings as a whole cannot issue from a transcendent that is posited "over" them from the outset, then the new values and their standard of measure can only be drawn from the realm of beings themselves. Thus beings themselves require a new interpretation through which their basic character may be defined in a way that will make it fit to serve as a "principle" for the inscription of a new table of values and as a standard of measure for suitably ranking such values.

If the essence of metaphysics consists in grounding the truth of being as a whole, then the revaluation of all values, as a grounding of the principle for a new valuation, is itself metaphysics. What Nietzsche perceives and posits as the basic character of being as a whole is what he calls the "will to power." That concept does not merely delimit *what* a being in its Being *is*: Nietzsche's phrase, "will to power," which has in many ways become familiar, contains his interpretation of the *essence of power*. Every power is a power only as long as it is more power; that is to say, an increase in power. Power can maintain itself in itself, that is, in its essence, only if it overtakes and overcomes the power level it has already attained—*overpowering* is the expression we use. As soon as power stalls at a certain power level, it immediately becomes powerless. "Will to power" does not mean simply the "romantic" yearning and quest for power by those who have no power; rather, "will to power" means the accruing of power by power for its own overpowering.

"Will to power" is a single name for the basic character of beings and for the essence of power. Nietzsche often substitutes "force" for "will to power" in a way that is easily misunderstood. His conception of the basic character of beings as will to power is not the contrivance or whim of a fantast who has strayed off of chase chimeras. It is the fundamental experience of a *thinker;* that is, of one of those individuals who have no choice but to find words for what a being *is* in the history of its Being. Every being, insofar as it *is*, and is *as* it is, is "will to power." The phrase names that from which all valuation proceeds and to which it returns. However, as we have said, the new valuation is not a "revaluation of all prior values" merely in that it supplants all earlier values with power, the uppermost value, but first and foremost because power and *only power* posits values, validates them, and makes decisions about the possible justifications of a valuation. If all being is will to power, then only what is fulfilled in its essence by power "has" value or "is" a value. But power is power only as enhancement of power. To the extent that it is truly power, alone determining all beings, power does not recognize the worth or value of anything outside of itself. That is why will to power as a principle for the new valuation tolerates no end outside of being as a whole. Now, because all beings as will

to power—that is, as incessant self-overpowering—must be *a continual "becoming,"* and because such "becoming" cannot move "toward an end" *outside* its own "farther and farther," but is ceaselessly caught up in the cyclical increase of power to which it reverts, then being as a whole too, as this power-conforming becoming, must itself always recur again and bring back the same.

Hence, the basic character of beings as will to power is also defined as "the eternal recurrence of the same." The latter constitutes yet another major rubric in Nietzsche's metaphysics and, moreover, implies something essential: *only* through the adequately conceived essence of will to power can it become clear why the Being of beings as a whole must be eternal recurrence of the same. The reverse holds as well: only through the essence of the eternal recurrence of the same can the innermost core of will to power and its necessity be grasped. The phrase "will to power" tells *what* beings are in their "essence" (in their constitution). The phrase "eternal recurrence of the same" tells *how* beings of such an essence must as a whole be.

It remains for us to observe what is decisive here; namely, that Nietzsche had to think the eternal recurrence of the same *before* the will to power. The most essential thought is thought first.

When Nietzsche himself insists that Being, as "life," is in essence *"becoming,"* he does not intend the roughly defined concept of "becoming" to mean either an endless, continual progression to some unknown goal, nor is he thinking about the confused turmoil and tumult of unrestrained drives. The vague and hackneyed term *becoming* signifies the overpowering of power, as the essence of power, which powerfully and continually returns to itself in its own way.

At the same time, the eternal recurrence of the same offers the keenest interpretation of "classical nihilism," which absolutely obliterates any end above and beyond beings. For such nihilism, the words "God is dead" suggest the impotence not only of the Christian God but of every transcendent element under which men might want to shelter themselves. And that impotence signifies the collapse of the old order.

With the revaluation of all past values, an unrestricted challenge has been issued to men: that unconditionally from, through, and over themselves, they raise "new standards" under which the accommodation of being as a whole to a new order must be effected. Because the "transcendent," the "beyond," and "heaven" have been abolished, only the "earth" remains. The new order must therefore be the absolute dominance of pure power over the earth through man—not through any arbitrary kind of man, and certainly not through the humanity that has heretofore lived under the old values. Through what kind of man, then?

With nihilism—that is to say, with the revaluation of all prior values among beings as will to power and in light of the eternal recurrence of the same—it becomes necessary to posit a new essence for man. But, because "God is dead," only man himself can grant man his measure and center, the *"type,"* the "model" of a certain kind of man who has assigned the task of a revaluation of all values to the individual power of his will to power and who is prepared to embark on the absolute domination of the globe. Classical nihilism, which as the revaluation of all values hitherto understands beings as will to power and can admit eternal recurrence of the same as the sole "end," must take man himself—that is, man as he has been until now—out of and "over" himself and must fashion as his measure the figure of the "Overman." (pp. 4-9)

From Nietzsche's point of view, the Overman is not meant to be a mere amplification of prior man, but the most unequivocally singular form of human existence that, as absolute will to power, is brought to power in every man to some degree and that thereby grants him his membership in being as a whole—that is, in will to power—and that shows him to be a true "being," close to reality and "life." The Overman simply leaves the man of traditional values behind, *overtakes* him, and transfers the justification for all laws and the positing of all values to the empowering of power. An act or accomplishment is valid as such only to the extent that it serves to equip, nurture, and enhance will to power.

The five main rubrics we have mentioned—"nihilism," "revaluation of all values hitherto," "will to power," "eternal recurrence of the same," and "Overman"—each portrays Nietzsche's metaphysics from just *one* perspective, although in each case it is a perspective that defines the whole. Thus Nietzsche's metaphysics is grasped only when what is named in these five headings can be thought—that is, essentially experienced—in its primordial and heretofore merely intimated conjunction. We can learn what "nihilism" in Nietzsche's sense is only if we also comprehend, in their contexts, "revaluation of all values hitherto," "will to power," "eternal recurrence of the same," and "Overman." By starting from an adequate comprehension of nihilism and working in the opposite direction, we can also acquire knowledge about the essence of revaluation, the essence of will to power, the essence of the eternal recurrence of the same, and the essence of the Overman. But to have such knowledge is to stand within the moment that the history of Being has opened up for our age. (pp. 9-10)

The necessity of having to think the essence of "nihilism" in the context of the "revaluation of all values," "will to power," "eternal recurrence of the same," and the "Overman" lets us readily surmise that the essence of nihilism is in itself manifold, multileveled, and multifarious. The word *nihilism* therefore permits many applications. It can be misused as an empty slogan or epithet that both repels and discredits and that conceals the user's own thoughtlessness from him. But we can also experience the full burden of what the name says when uttered in *Nietzsche's* sense. Here it means to think the history of Western metaphysics as the ground of our own history; that is, of future decisions. Finally, we can ponder more essentially what Nietzsche was thinking in using this word if we grasp his "classical nihilism" as *that* nihilism *whose "classicism" consists in the fact that it must unwittingly put itself on extreme guard against knowledge of its innermost essence.* Classical nihilism, then, discloses itself as the fulfillment of nihilism, whereby it considers itself exempt from the necessity of thinking about the very thing that constitutes its essence: the *nihil,* the nothing—as the veil that conceals the truth of the Being of beings. (pp. 10-11)

Martin Heidegger, in his Nietzsche: Nihilism, Vol. IV, *edited by David Farrell Krell, translated by Frank A. Capuzzi (copyright © 1982 by Harper & Row, Publishers, Inc.; reprinted by permission of Harper & Row, Publishers, Inc.; originally published as part of* Nietzsche, Zweiter Band, *Verlag Günther Neske, 1961), Harper & Row, 1982, 301 p.*

ARTHUR C. DANTO   (essay date 1965)

[*Danto contrasts Nietzsche's philosophy of nihilism with the "Nihilism of Emptiness" practiced by the Buddhists and the "Nihilism of Negativity" that flourished during the nineteenth century in Russia and Europe. Though Danto believes Nietzsche's nihilism is more negative than these, particularly in its denial of any form of truth, it nonetheless forms the basis of his philosophy—a philosophy which seeks the affirmative in life; thus Danto terms it "affirmative nihilism." For more commentary on Nietzsche and nihilism, see the essays by Paul Elmer More, Albert Camus, Martin Heidegger, and Richard Schacht excerpted above and below.*]

For [Nietzsche's] philosophy there seems, not surprisingly, to be no ready name like Idealism or Realism or even Existentialism. At times he spoke of his philosophy as *Nihilism,* a title which . . . seems almost bitterly suitable, suggesting negativity and emptiness. If, however, we may have any wish to understand him, we must divest his Nihilism of both these connotations and come to see it as a positive and, after all, a respectable philosophical teaching. (p. 22)

"Nihilism" connotes negativity and emptiness; in fact, it denotes two bodies of thought that, although distinct from Nietzsche's, nevertheless bear it some partial resemblance. The Nihilism of Emptiness is essentially that of Buddhist or Hindu teaching, both of which hold that the world we live in and seem to know has no ultimate reality, and that our attachment to it is an attachment to an illusion. Reality itself has neither name nor form, and what has name and form is but a painful dreaming from which all reasonable men would wish to escape if they knew the way and knew that their attachment was to nothingness. (p. 28)

The Nihilism of Negativity, as I shall call it, is exemplified in the movement properly known as Nihilism, which flourished in the latter decades of the nineteenth century in Europe, especially in the 1850s and 1860s in Russia, and which found its most respectable expression in Turgenev's *Fathers and Sons* (1861). Russian Nihilism was essentially a negative and destructive attitude against a body of moral, political, and religious teachings found or felt by the Nihilists to be confining and obscurantist. As against their elders, Nihilists claimed that they believed in nothing, though what this specifically meant was that they held in total discredit the beliefs, tastes, and attitudes of their elders and those in current authority. . . . In actual fact they believed, in an uncritical and wholesale manner, in a crudely materialistic interpretation of science. It was basically in the name of science that they proclaimed, as invalid, the principles they inveighed against. (p. 29)

Nietzsche was not less but more negativistic than his Nihilist contemporaries (though he was not part of that movement in any sense whatsoever), and he is celebrated, attacked, or applauded for his bitter denunciations of many of the same traditions, beliefs, and institutions which they explicitly repudiated. *His* Nihilism, nevertheless, is not an ideology but a metaphysics, and in no respect is his difference from the Nihilists more marked than in his attitude toward science. Science he regards not as a repository of truths or a method for discovering them but as a set of convenient fictions, of useful conventions, which has as much and as little basis in reality as any alleged set of fictions which might be thought to conflict with it. It, no more and no less than religion, morality, and art, was an instance of what he termed Will-to-Power, an impulse and a drive to impose upon an essentially chaotic reality a form and structure, to shape it into a world congenial to human understanding while habitable by human intelligence. But this was its *sole* justification, and any imposed form which worked to the same purpose would be equally justifiable, content counting for less than function—counting, indeed, for nothing at all. Science . . . is not true. But in the sense in which it is not true, neither is anything else; and relative to this theory of truth, which was his, Nietzsche must say that he did not, because in metaphysical honesty he could not, believe in anything. His was accordingly a deep and total Nihilism, from the vantage point of which the contest of the Russian Nihilists with their declared ideological enemies was but an instance in the struggle of wills, a struggle for power and form which, as Nietzsche saw it, characterizes human life everywhere and always and, in a sense, was the single characteristic he was prepared to ascribe to the universe at large, which he saw as an eternal strife of will with will. (pp. 30-1)

Nietzsche's unbridled claims in behalf of this extreme Nihilism are plainly in need of considerable clarification before we can so much as raise the question responsibly as to whether there is any compelling reason for endorsing them. . . . I wish only to emphasize the way in which Nietzsche's Nihilism has little to do with the ordinary political connotations of the term, and that by "Nihilism" he had in mind a thoroughly disillusioned conception of a world which is as hostile to human aspirations as he could imagine it to be. It is hostile, not because it, or anything other than us, has goals of its own, but because it is utterly indifferent to what we either believe or hope. The recognition and acceptance of this negative fact should not lead us to "a negation, a no, a will to nothingness." Rather, he felt, it is an intoxicating fact to know that the world is devoid of form and meaning, encouraging, if anything, "a Dionysian *yes* [*Ja-sagen*] to the world as it is, without exceptions, exemptions, or deductions." To be able to accept and affirm such a view he thought required considerable courage, for it meant that we must abandon hopes and expectations which had comforted men, through religions and philosophies, from the beginning. For the attitude he felt he could and we should adopt, he provided the formula of *Amor Fati*—loving one's fate, accepting, without palliative or protection, the results of a most thoroughgoing critique of philosophical and scientific ideas, seen as fictions, the products of some human need for security; and then endeavoring to live in a world impervious to these needs, to say Yes to the cosmic insignificance, not only of oneself and of human beings generally but also of life and nature as a whole. (pp. 33-4)

[This Nihilism] finds its culmination, or so he believed, in the obscure doctrine of Eternal Recurrence, a view that the world repeats itself infinitely and exactly, the same situations in which we now find ourselves having already occurred an infinite number of times. These will happen again, without end, exactly as they always have and as they are happening now. Nietzsche took an immense and not altogether readily understandable pride in having discovered this doctrine, which he considered both as a serious scientific truth and, more importantly and even less plausibly, as the only genuine alternative to the view that the world has or can have a goal or purpose or final state. If each state of the world (insofar as we may speak so of anything as structureless as he appears to claim the world to be) recurs infinitely, then no state can be a final state, and in the nature of things there can be neither progress nor regress, but always the same thing repeated. So the fate which he encourages to accept and indeed to love is made considerably more difficult through this purposeless repetitiveness of the universe *in toto*. . . . (p. 34)

Nietzsche's philosophy is a sustained attempt to work out the reasons for and the consequences of Nihilism as I have briefly sketched this doctrine here. . . . [His] critique of other phi-losophies rests upon a psychological thesis that each metaphysical system ever advanced was due, in the end, to a need to find order and security in the world, a position where the mind might "repose and recreate itself." Each system provided, accordingly, a consolatory account of things in which this might be possible. Nietzsche was persuaded that all such views were false. The problem then was to exhibit their inviability, determine why people should have thought them viable, and then go on to ask how it might be possible to go on living in the full recognition of the inviability of every possible religious and metaphysical assurance.

The picture that results from his psychological-philosophical analyses is that of human beings trying continually to impose an order and structure upon an unordered and senseless universe so as to preserve their sense of dignity and importance. It is their prejudice that, somehow and somewhere, there must be a reason for it all, and that there *cannot* be any truth in what Nietzsche advances as the correct (if one may speak of correctness here) view of things as "change, becoming, plurality, opposition, contradiction, and war." There is then no true, rational, orderly, permanent, or benign universe for us. Our entire mode of thinking, he believed, is based on the assumption that there is such a universe; it is far from simple, accordingly, to work out a form of thought adequate to the nullity of things as they are: a total revolution in logic, science, morality, and in philosophy itself would be demanded. Nietzsche sought to achieve at least the beginning of such a revolution. . . . (pp. 34-5)

> *Arthur C. Danto, in his* Nietzsche As Philosopher *(reprinted with permission of Macmillan Publishing Company; copyright © by Macmillan Publishing Company 1965), Macmillan, 1965, 250 p.*

HENRY DAVID AIKEN (essay date 1967)

[*Aiken asserts that the poetic structure of* Thus Spake Zarathustra *allowed Nietzsche a "fuller and freer projection" of his ideas, and that, therefore,* Zarathustra *is the "least inhibited of Nietzsche's works."*]

Thus Spake Zarathustra is Nietzsche's most famous book; it was also his own favorite. In his philosophical autobiography, *Ecce Homo,* he tells us how, during his walks around the Gulf of Rapallo in 1883, "All *Zarathustra,* and particularly Zarathustra himself as a type, came to me—perhaps I should rather say—invaded me." *Zarathustra,* as he says, is an "inspired" work, and if it is not as "utterly unique" as he imagined, it nonetheless stands apart from his other works. For one thing *Zarathustra* is the most imaginatively conceived and the most constructive of Nietzsche's writings. The familiar, devastating critique of existing institutions and beliefs is there of course, but it is never permitted to obscure the more positive ideals with which, henceforth, Nietzsche was increasingly preoccupied. For another thing, *Zarathustra* is written, in large part, in what Nietzsche called the language of dithyramb rather than in the hard, terse, lucid prose for which he is justly celebrated. This partly accounts for the fact that in *Zarathustra* the meaning of individual sentences and even of whole sections is sometimes obscure, although the drift of the book as a whole should be plain enough to an informed reader.

Thus Spake Zarathustra must be regarded as a philosophical poem, an obsolescent genre in which few poets and no philosophers in the modern age have attempted to write. Because of this it is difficult for the contemporary reader to approach it in the spirit intended. As a poem, it requires to be read as a work of imaginative literature, and hence with a constant awareness that Zarathustra is not Nietzsche but, as he says, a "type" whose discourses and myths and rants are therefore to be viewed as expressions of Zarathustra's own responses to the imaginary situations in which his creator places him. That they may be also expressions of Nietzsche's own attitudes and commitments is not to be denied, but they can be ascribed to him only indirectly and at a distance. In a writer whose style and thought are ordinarily so intensely personal, this is a cardinal fact which the reader must never permit himself to forget.

As a literary creation, Zarathustra thus stands between Nietzsche and the reader as an independent voice. Let the reader identify himself too closely with Zarathustra—and for angry young men this is all too easy to do—and Nietzsche becomes liable to a charge not unlike that which the Athenians brought against Socrates: corruption of the youth. On the other hand, if the reader identifies Zarathustra too closely with Nietzsche, the latter is reduced, no less unfairly, to one of his *personae.* Zarathustra, let us face it, is something of an oracle and something of a fool—although to be sure a preternaturally acute fool. At times he reminds us of a still more garrulous Polonius whose pretentiousness and bombast are impossible to take seriously. Many of his jokes and puns are—to use a Nietzschean phrase—simply "bad air," and some of his affectations—witness his views about women—are disagreeably callow, full of the very "resentment" which Nietzsche so deplored. But if Zarathustra himself is less than godly, *Thus Spake Zarathustra,* taken as a whole, is an intensely serious book, and the issues raised in it are of the utmost importance to anyone who, like Nietzsche, is disposed to undertake, at one and the same time, a radical critique of Western culture and a radical reëxamination and overhaul of himself.

As philosophy, *Zarathustra* somewhat resembles a Platonic dialogue: that is to say, its ideas are developed dialectically rather than analytically, and our primary interest lies in the dialectic itself rather than in any specific conclusions reached in the process. In short, it is the movement of the thought and the variable moods attending this movement, rather than any "doctrines" formulated along the way, that we find ultimately absorbing. Some of Nietzsche's commentators have tried to educe a kind of philosophical system from his writings. Such an effort is even more misguided in the case of *Zarathustra* than in that of his other works. We have Nietzsche's own word for it that he was radically opposed to any and all systems of philosophy. The world did not appear to him as a cosmos, ordered by an indwelling *Logos;* nor did man appear to him as essentially the rational animal, instinct from birth with a definitive final cause, whose realization it is the fate of all men in all generations to try to attain. Rationality is an achievement, not a metaphysical necessity. Each individual, like each age, is something new under the sun, and the "higher" the man the more does he become a law unto himself. The wisdom of philosophy, or at any rate any philosophy with which Nietzsche could associate himself, does not consist in any theory or creed, but in liberation from all creeds and indeed from the need of all justifying principles for the conduct of life. In one sense, *Thus Spake Zarathustra* is precisely the story of such a liberation.

In saying all this, I should perhaps emphasize that it is no part of my intention to "save" Nietzsche from Zarathustra, as some embarrassed admirers have attempted to do, or to relieve him from responsibility for Zarathustra's sayings. In his other works,

Nietzsche frequently says things in his own voice that are no less horrendous than some of those he puts into Zarathustra's mouth. My point is rather that, whatever its imperfections either as philosophy or as imaginative literature, the form in which *Thus Spake Zarathustra* was cast made possible a fuller and freer projection of, as well as release from, the tensions between Nietzsche and his "anti-self" than he could usually achieve in his more argumentative "prose" writings. In the latter works, where Nietzsche perforce speaks in the first person, he commonly presents himself to us in the stance of a doctrinaire: that is, as a writer of mere opinions or prejudices. In them, indeed, he seems at times to be so busy "making points" that the process of reflection and self-development which most concerned him is forgotten, with the result that, so far as the reader is concerned, he defeats his own purpose.

In *Zarathustra,* however, the ever-recurrent and combative *ego,* which elsewhere Nietzsche seems to be trying to impose upon the reader, is for once submerged in the creative life, or world, of the work itself. And for this very reason, by what is only an apparent paradox, Nietzsche's whole self is able to disport itself more freely and—to adopt another favorite term of Nietzsche's—more powerfully than in his more explicitly didactic works. In *Zarathustra* the phantasmagorias, the shifting moods, the contradictions, and even the gibberish all belong essentially to the "picture" which, as a whole, is more compelling, more authentic, and more trustworthy for their presence.

In the other writings we have the aphoristic distillate; we do not know entirely what ingredients went into the production of each. In *Zarathustra,* so to say, Nietzsche exposes the life from which the distillate was made. In it there is no longer mere talk about joy and the overcoming of resentment, but rather the presentations of resentment and its overcoming and of the consequent happiness and self-mastery. In the other works the spirit of Dionysius is invoked; in *Zarathustra* it actually takes possession of the writing itself, and because of this it also possesses us. For these reasons, *Thus Spake Zarathustra* strikes us immediately as the openest, least inhibited of Nietzsche's works.

What this means is that *Zarathustra* is not only the most deeply disturbing and, in one sense, dangerous of Nietzsche's books; it is also, when properly read, the most illuminating and instructive. But its instruction will be received only by those who, like Nietzsche and unlike Plato (for whom Nietzsche had only a very qualified admiration), know how to find instruction in a work of art. From this standpoint, Nietzsche's other mature writings are perhaps best viewed as preparations for or as glosses upon *Zarathustra.* They often help to light up its darker passages or to qualify impressions which a casual or unfriendly reading of *Zarathustra* may easily convey. It should be added, however, that there is also a danger in relying too heavily upon them for such purposes. For one must bear in mind that Nietzsche's thought underwent a development both before and after the writing of *Zarathustra;* and ideas which, in his earlier work, he was merely trying out or which, in his last works, he recast in quite different terms, do not always have the same meaning which they have in *Zarathustra.* (pp. v-vii)

Henry David Aiken, "Introduction" (© 1967 by The George Macy Companies, Inc.; reprinted by permission of the Literary Estate of Henry David Aiken), in Thus Spake Zarathustra *by Friedrich Nietzsche, translated by Thomas Common, The Heritage Press, 1967, pp. v-xvi.*

JORGE LUIS BORGES [Conversation with RICHARD BURGIN]
(conversation date 1969)

[*Borges's fiction, essays, and poetry are noted for their use of philosophical themes, often sharing Nietzsche's obsession with cyclical recurrences.*]

BURGIN: . . . I have the feeling that you aren't too fond of Nietzsche as a thinker.

BORGES: No. Well, I think that I am unfair to Nietzsche, because though I have read and reread many of his books, well, I think that if you omit *Thus Spoke Zarathustra*, if you omit that book—a kind of sham Bible, no?—I mean a sham biblical style—but if you omit that book you get very interesting books.

BURGIN: *Beyond Good and Evil.*

BORGES: Yes, I've read them in German. And I greatly enjoyed them. But yet, somehow, I have never felt any sympathy for him as a man, no? I mean I feel a great sympathy for Schopenhauer, or for ever so many writers, but in the case of Nietzsche I feel there is something hard and I won't say priggish, I mean as a person he has no modesty about him. The same thing happens to me with Blake. I don't like writers who are making sweeping statements all the time. Of course, you might argue that what I'm saying is a sweeping statement also, no? Well, one has to say things with a certain emphasis.

BURGIN: Don't you feel, though, in the case of Nietzsche, he might be somewhat akin to Whitman? In that the personae of their works are quite different from the actual men behind them?

BORGES: Yes, but in the case of Whitman he gives you a very attractive persona. In the case of Nietzsche he gives you a very disagreeable one, at least to me. I feel I can sympathize with Whitman, but I can hardly sympathize with Nietzsche. In fact, I don't suppose he wanted people to sympathize with him. (pp. 102-03)

> *Jorge Luis Borges, "Darwin; Nietzsche; Existentialism and Sartre: Freud; Symmetries; the Patterns of Coincidence; Tolerance and Skepticism; Perón. . . . ," in a conversation with Richard Burgin, in* Conversations with Jorge Luis Borges *by Richard Burgin (copyright © 1968, 1969 by Richard Burgin; reprinted by permission of Holt, Rinehart and Winston, Publishers), Holt, Rinehart and Winston, 1969, pp. 101-21.**

HUGH LLOYD-JONES (essay date 1972)

[*The Birth of Tragedy*] was greeted with derision by most of [Nietzsche's] professional colleagues. Soon after publication it was bitterly attacked in a pamphlet entitled *Philology of the Future*, with allusion to Wagner's "Music of the Future," by a doctor of philology four years Nietzsche's junior and like him an alumnus of Schulpforta. This was Ulrich von Wilamowitz-Möllendorff, destined to become the most celebrated Greek scholar of his time. Nietzsche was defended in an open letter to a Swiss newspaper by no less a person than Richard Wagner, and in a pamphlet no less bitter than that of Wilamowitz and bearing the unfortunately chosen title of *Afterphilologie* by his friend and contemporary Erwin Rohde, destined in the 1890s to bring out a study of Greek beliefs about the soul that is one of the landmarks in modern classical scholarship; then Wilamowitz returned to battle in a second pamphlet. (p. 7)

Considered as a work of scholarship, *The Birth of Tragedy* has many failings. As Wilamowitz saw, it contains some annoying mistakes in scholarship; and the author even leaves out several facts which might have been used to support his thesis. That thesis, that tragedy originated through a synthesis of Apollonian and Dionysian elements, is as a statement of fact to say the least unprovable; and the defectiveness of the arguments confidently asserted to prove it is rendered doubly infuriating by the over-confident and hectic tone in which it is written. Nietzsche failed entirely to control the two intellectual passions which at that period of his life had taken possession of him, the passion for Schopenhauer and the passion for Wagner. The later passion was not simply for Wagner's music, but for his critical writings, so that Nietzsche took over from his hero the notion that Wagnerian opera was in a real sense a revival of Greek tragedy. In consequence, the importance assigned to music in the emergence of tragedy is quite out of proportion. Wilamowitz rightly pointed out that the very different music of ancient Greece was always kept in strict subordination to the words. Later Nietzsche came to regret that he had ever added to the original fifteen sections of the book the ten sections about Wagner with which it concludes.

Nietzsche's Apollo and Dionysus bear an obvious resemblance to the notions of idea and will in the philosophy of Schopenhauer. Later, when Nietzsche had abandoned his Schopenhauerian dualism in favor of a monistic position, he would have operated with Dionysus only. The manner in which the two elements became interfused, and the whole functioning of the Dionysian, are described in over-heated tones not calculated to appeal to the judicious reader; and the assertion that tragedy was killed by an alliance between Euripides and Socrates, grounded as it is on a belief in a community of opinion between these two persons, which is wholly unacceptable, leaves the book wide open to attack. Its author himself later became dissatisfied with it; in 1886 he wrote that he should have done what he had to do "as an imaginative writer." Yet with all its appalling blemishes it is a work of genius, and began a new era in the understanding of Greek thought.

Through Nietzsche's writings runs a vein of criticism of the view of the Greek world taken by the old classicism, much as he preferred its attitude to antiquity to that of the new historicism. Behind the calm and dignity praised by Winckelmann, Nietzsche saw the struggle that had been needed to achieve the balance; he saw that the Greeks had not repressed, but had used for their own purposes, terrible and irrational forces. Nietzsche, and not Freud, was to invent the concept of sublimation, so important in his mature philosophy. Nietzsche saw the ancient gods as standing for the fearful realities of a universe in which mankind had no special privileges. For him what gave the tragic hero the chance to display his heroism was the certainty of annihilation; and tragedy gave its audiences comfort not by purging their emotions but by bringing them face to face with the most awful truths of human existence and by showing how those truths are what make heroism true and life worth living. In comparison with such an insight, resting on a deeper vision of the real nature of ancient religion and the great gulf that separates it from religions of other kinds, the faults of Nietzsche's book, glaring as they are, sink into insignificance. (pp. 8-9)

> *Hugh Lloyd-Jones, "Nietzsche and the Study of the Ancient World" (originally a lecture given at Wake Forest University in November, 1972), in* Studies in Nietzsche and the Classical Tradition, *James C. O'Flaherty, Timothy F. Sellner, Robert M. Helm,*

eds. (© University of North Carolina Studies in the Germanic Languages and Literatures 1976), second edition, The University of North Carolina Press, 1979, pp. 1-15.

RICHARD SCHACHT   (essay date 1973)

[*In the following excerpt, Schacht disagrees with Arthur C. Danto (see excerpt above), who considers Nietzsche a nihilist and, therefore, nihilism as the central concept of his philosophy. Instead, Schacht argues that Nietzsche is neither a nihilist in a metaphysical sense nor in an axiological sense since he posited the concept of the will to power as the essence of being and placed supreme importance on the* Übermensch *as the goal of humanity. Also on this subject, see the essays by Paul Elmer More, Albert Camus, and Martin Heidegger excerpted above.*]

Was Nietzsche a nihilist? It is widely thought that he was; and Arthur Danto, in his book *Nietzsche as Philosopher,* subscribes wholeheartedly to this view [see excerpt above]. . . . Indeed, Danto claims that "Nihilism" is "the central concept of his philosophy." . . . (p. 58)

Is Danto right? There are several ways in which one might attempt to answer this question. First, one might examine Nietzsche's own assertions about the nature of nihilism, and see whether he explicitly subscribes to it as he himself conceives it. Second, one might consider the way in which "nihilism" as a philosophical doctrine is standardly defined, and then determine whether or not the definition is applicable to Nietzsche's philosophical views. "Nihilism" in the philosophical sense of the term may be defined either as the doctrine that there is and can be no such thing as "truth" where reality is concerned, since reality is such that nothing whatsoever—except this fact—is true about it (metaphysical nihilism); or (more narrowly) as the doctrine that axiological principles have no objective basis in reality (axiological nihilism). Nietzsche might thus legitimately be termed a "nihilist" if it were the case that he subscribed to either (or both) of these doctrines. (Danto claims that he subscribes to both.)

It is my contention that, whichever way one chooses to approach the question, the answer to it is that Danto is wrong; and that Nietzsche, at least from *Zarathustra* . . . onward, was not a "deep and total" nihilist, either as he himself conceives of "nihilism" (although he embraces a highly restricted form of it, *viz.,* one which consists simply in the denial of any realm of "true being" apart from this world and of any transcendentally grounded system of values), or in either of the senses of the term mentioned above. (pp. 58-9)

[Nietzsche] could be termed a nihilist only if it were to be arbitrarily stipulated that everyone is a nihilist who is not a Platonist, a Christian, a Rationalist or an adherent of some other such traditional philosophical or religious world-view. If, on the other hand, nihilism is understood—as I believe it should be—to involve the claim that neither the world nor values are such that anything both positive and objectively true may be said about them, then Nietzsche most emphatically is *not* a nihilist. . . .

According to Danto, "if we take 'true' in [the] conventional sense of expressing what is the case," then it is Nietzsche's position that "nothing is true and everything is false." . . . He takes Nietzsche to be saying that men have not discovered "the truth" about the world, not because anything has kept them from it, but rather because "there is none to discover." . . . (p. 66)

[Far] from holding that "nothing is true," Nietzsche in fact holds that there *is* such a thing as "truth"—truth about the nature of things and about man; and not only that it *may* be discovered, but moreover that it *has* been discovered, and that he himself has discovered it. But what is it that he has discovered, which he refers to repeatedly as "the truth"?

Many things, of course; but most importantly, in his eyes, one thing in particular. In the last lines of the last section of *The Will to Power,* he states his fundamental "discovery" and his most profound metaphysical "truth" as follows: "*This world is the will to power—and nothing besides!* And you yourselves are also this will to power—and nothing besides!" . . . Nietzsche is by no means prepared to regard his conception of the world as "will to power" as merely one more world-interpretation alongside others—the Platonic, the Christian, the Kantian, the Hegelian, the mechanistic, etc.—which is no less but also no more ultimately valid than they are. On the contrary, he argues at length that each of the others is *false;* and he further argues at length that his is *true.* In *Beyond Good and Evil,* for example, it is set forth, not as a poetic vision, but rather as a serious hypothesis, the validity of which is to be determined by its explanatory power. (p. 67)

He further holds a number of other, though related, metaphysical propositions to be true. The one for which he is perhaps best known is the proposition that all events recur eternally. Even Danto is compelled to admit that Nietzsche commits himself to the truth of his doctrine of the eternal recurrence of the same events. At times, to be sure, he seems less concerned with the truth of the doctrine than with the cultivation of an affirmative attitude toward life so great that one not only could *endure* the thought of an eternal recurrence of the same series of events which has produced and is the existing world, but moreover could *desire* such a recurrence. To *will* the eternal recurrence of the same events is for Nietzsche the ultimate expression of an affirmative attitude toward life. (p. 68)

At other times, however, that with which Nietzsche is concerned is the demonstration of the *truth* of the proposition that the same series of events which has occurred must recur eternally. And that he should have both concerns is not unreasonable. After all, there is nothing self-contradictory in both maintaining the truth of a doctrine, and desiring that people should have an attitude toward life so positive that they can embrace it gladly. Indeed, once Nietzsche became convinced of the truth of the doctrine of eternal recurrence, it is only reasonable that he should have become all the more concerned with the problem of our responses to the idea of eternal recurrence, and that he should have continued to regard one's reaction to the idea as a decisive test of one's attitude toward life; for he knew, from personal experience, that the idea could appear terrible indeed. (p. 69)

That Nietzsche does hold this doctrine to be true is clear. One of the notes in *The Will to Power* consists of an outline of a projected discussion of it, which reads, in part: "*The eternal recurrence* . . .1. Presentation of the doctrine and its *theoretical* presuppositions and consequences. 2. Proof of the doctrine." . . . He never completed, let alone published, the systematic discussion which he here contemplates; but his basic line of reasoning is indicated clearly enough in a number of other notes in *The Will to Power.* (pp. 69-70)

[I] contend that these passages clearly show him to have been convinced of the truth of the doctrine of eternal recurrence and of its demonstrability; and that this provides a further illustration of the fact that, whatever the merit of the specific positions he takes may be, his philosophy cannot be considered *nihilistic* in the sense under consideration. (pp. 70-1)

The widespread view, endorsed by Danto, that Nietzsche is a "nihilist" and that his philosophy is a philosophy of "radical nihilism," is wrong. A careful analysis of his writings shows that he neither considered himself to be a nihilist, nor deserves to be considered one, either metaphysically or axiologically. Far from considering nihilism to be the last word, he actually regards it as a mere "transitional stage"—a natural consequence of the discovery of the untenability of certain traditional metaphysical and axiological views; which he himself goes beyond, and to which his own philosophy is a "countermovement." Far from holding that there are no truths about reality which may be discovered and stated, because there is no actual nature of things to discover and describe, he in fact holds the contrary, and has a good deal to say of a substantive nature in this connection. And far from denying objective validity to all value-judgments as such, he in fact maintains that a certain standard of value has an objective basis in the very nature of things. (pp. 81-2)

> *Richard Schacht, "Nietzsche and Nihilism," in* Journal of the History of Philosophy *(copyright 1973 by the* Journal of the History of Philosophy; *reprinted by permission of the Editor), Vol. XI, No. 1, January, 1973 (and reprinted in a revised form in* Nietzsche: A Collection of Critical Essays, *edited by Robert C. Solomon, Anchor Press, 1973, pp. 58-82).*

R. J. HOLLINGDALE (essay date 1973)

[*Along with Walter Kaufmann (see excerpt below), Hollingdale is one of the leading critics and translators of Nietzsche. His study* Nietzsche, *from which the following excerpt is taken, is one of the most informative and comprehensible considerations of the philosopher's complex body of works.*]

Nietzsche's philosophy is not be to found in any single book, nor in the books of any single period of his life. It is, rather, an aggregate of all his books. It is a process of development, not a body of propositions. . . .

This philosophical development does not, however, proceed in an unbroken rising curve: it appears as a series of fairly straight lines broken off and resumed higher up. Biographically, it can be viewed as a number of situations which became intolerable and whose intolerability propelled the philosopher into action; or as a career punctuated by crises precipitated by a deeply-felt sense of frustration and attended by physical and 'psychical' symptoms. (p. 43)

Ostensibly Nietzsche was playing a secondary role in his own life: he was a 'follower' of Schopenhauer and Wagner; under the surface, however, there was an intense conflict going on between these dominating influences and all those influences which resisted such domination. (p. 51)

[Schopenhauer's] direct, permanent influence on Nietzsche was limited to the propositions that the world is not the creation of an intellect, that is to say it is not a rational structure, and that the human intellect is not an autonomous entity. The rest of Schopenhauer he subsequently repudiated. To Nietzsche, will is understood, not metaphysically, but physiologically, as a complex of drives and affects which enters the consciousness as a single sensation and is thus designated by a single word: he denies the existence of will in Schopenhauer's sense of it.

He also denies Schopenhauer's ethical conclusions by asking whence Schopenhauer thinks he has acquired the moral criteria by which he condemns the world as ethically reprehensible, and then undertaking an examination and analysis of the 'moral sense', and especially of how it was evolved. His conclusions lead him to substitute for Schopenhauer's demand for a denial of the will a demand for the total affirmation of life—though here, it must be conceded, the pathos attending this demand probably owes its intensity to its being the antithesis of Schopenhauer's.

With Wagner, Nietzsche's relationship was much more intense and complicated. He became an intimate of Wagner's household, and Wagner, thirty-one years older than he, became a second and greater father. When Nietzsche turned his back on him it was a second act of parricide. He obtained from Wagner a number of aesthetic theories which he employed in *The Birth of Tragedy;* more importantly, he obtained from him a three-dimensional picture of 'the artist' upon which his subsequent psychological explanations of the artist-nature rely very heavily; most importantly, he obtained from him an idea of 'greatness', of the possibilities still open to the human spirit even in the 'late' nineteenth century. In these respects it would probably be wrong to say that Nietzsche ever 'turned away' from Wagner at all: to the very end he never had any doubt that he was the 'greatest artist' of his time. But by then Nietzsche had redefined both greatness and the nature of the time in which he and Wagner lived, so that he was able to say that Wagner was decadent without denying his greatness. (pp. 53-4)

Through personal discussion with Paul Rée, and through reading his *Psychological Observations* and later his *Origin of the Moral Sensations* (published in 1877 but discussed with Nietzsche during the course of writing), [Nietzsche] became familiar with the idea that religion and morality are subjective phenomena, and their investigation a matter for psychology.

By the summer of 1876 he was ready for a decisive change of direction. The last of the *Meditations—Richard Wagner in Bayreuth*—took him an unconscionable time to write and the final product is hardly worthy of him even in his 'early' manifestation. Within a month of the publication of this essay in July 1876 he was at work on *Human, All Too Human*: the fundamental novelty of this book, after you have noted the stylistic transformation and the sense of having come out of a closed drawing room into a cold breeze, is seen to be a drastic difference in subject matter. Metaphysics is spoken of only to be repudiated, Schopenhauer is mentioned only in order to be contradicted, and Wagner is not mentioned by name at all; 'the artist' is no longer rhapsodized over but analysed; generalization is replaced by the examination of small, sometimes minute, particular problems which are asserted to be the only problems that matter. Above all, the profuse employment of the words 'science', 'scientific method', 'scientific observation', and the like, indicates where the interest of the writer now lies. The book, when it appeared in 1878, was dedicated 'to the memory of Voltaire'.

In his account of this time in *Ecce Homo,* he says he 'perceived a total aberration of my instincts, of which the individual blunder, call it Wagner or Basel professorship, was a mere symptom. An *impatience* with myself overcame me . . . A downright burning thirst seized hold of me: thenceforward I pursued in fact nothing other than physiology, medicine and natural sciences . . .'. . . . The last phrase is a literally false statement designed to send the reader in the right direction: if you read Nietzsche from *Human, All Too Human* onwards as if he were writing about physiology, medicine and 'natural sciences' you will never really misunderstand him. (pp. 56-7)

From here onwards the *ideal* method of studying Nietzsche's development is a command of German, chronic insomnia, and a set of the collected works. The student who read straight through from the beginning of **Human, All Too Human** to the end of Book Four of **The Gay Science** (the fifth book was added later) would need no explanation of how 'scientific scepticism' broke down all the admired and valued things but how all these broken pieces were at the same time being gathered together again by the force of a unifying theory: he would need no explanation because he would see it taking place, and how it was taking place, and would participate in the experience of living through it and suffering from it—for these emotional reactions are set down too. There is no way of faking this experience: to *know* how this philosophical tendency produced 'a crisis situation' you have to enter into the situation yourself.

This situation, which we now have to try to look into from the outside, was a product of an increasing consciousness of the nihilism inherent in sceptical analysis and a somewhat desperate awareness of the need to emerge from it through some form of 'transcendence'. Coincidentally with this there was as it were an undersea current building up and gathering momentum, drawing more and more of the water along with it, until finally it broke surface and reduced the ocean to a single directed stream. This current was the idea of the drive to power as the basic drive in man, and by extension in all other creatures. The point at which it broke surface was the moment, in January 1883, at which Nietzsche realized the possibilities inherent in it, and first became fully aware that the suggestions he had been offering as to the ubiquity of the power drive and the number of 'masks' it assumes did in fact constitute a theory of universal 'will to power'.

This evolution may appear to conflict with the assertion that if you read Nietzsche as if he were writing about physiology, medicine and natural science you would never really misunderstand him; but it does not in fact do so, because to Nietzsche 'will to power' *was* a scientific conception—or, better perhaps, he was anxious to prove that it was. He knew quite well that 'will to power' as an explanation of events is teleology, and that teleology is 'not science'; he was engaged on trying to get round that difficulty when his breakdown cut short his speculations. His notes were published in **The Will to Power**: some of them come close to identifying 'power' with 'energy', and to understanding 'energy' as '*quanta* of power'. These developments are not especially well known even to those who know Nietzsche well, so it is important to give them proper emphasis. But it must also be emphasized that, when employed as an explanation of human behaviour, 'will to power' is not identified with a 'force' of any kind, and that the need for such an identification emerged only when the principle was extended beyond man to the whole world—which may suggest that this extension is ill-considered and impermissible. In any event, these developments show that in formulating a theory of will to power Nietzsche was not relapsing into metaphysics but, in intention at least, still pursuing a 'scientific' course. (pp. 57-8)

Nietzsche had a special relationship with his **Zarathustra,** and in the end—in the latter half of 1888, when he had let all inhibitions go—he came to regard it not only as *his* best book but as *the* best book. 'I have given mankind the profoundest book it possesses, my **Zarathustra,**' he wrote. . . . (p. 72)

These and similar ravings are of course a foretaste of madness, and they are the more deplorable in that **Zarathustra** is not even Nietzsche's 'best book', though certainly it is his most famous. The ideas epitomized in it are often expressed so laconically that the book has acquired the reputation of being 'difficult', which it is not to anyone who knows his other books. In point of style, too, **Zarathustra** is an acquired taste: the prophet-tone and the far-fetched, sometimes impossible imagery are not unexampled elsewhere, but here they are all-pervading; there are passages of great beauty and intensity, and many memorable 'aphorisms', but the fact remains that when one recommends Nietzsche as a master of German prose it is not **Zarathustra** one has in mind. On the other hand, it has to be conceded that a writer's most popular work does not attain that status accidentally, or because of some mistake on the part of the public, or because its author has published extravagant claims on its behalf: it does so because it possesses certain real and attractive qualities which his other works perhaps lack or do not possess to so marked a degree. **Zarathustra** is, all its faults notwithstanding, a liberating book: it can perform for the reader what its writing performed for its author. If the circumstances under which you read it are right it can make as powerful and lasting an impression on you as any book in world literature. There is something of the inspirational tract in it; and its reputation as a sort of atheists' Bible is not altogether undeserved: but there must be many thousands of people who first discovered from its pages that conventional beliefs can without any difficulty be systematically inverted—that moral and spiritual values are not 'obvious'. It contains dozens of phrases that have become familiar, many of them of the 'outrageous' or 'provocative' sort (e.g. 'War and courage have done more great things than charity'; 'Man should be trained for war and woman for the recreation of the warrior: all else is folly'; 'Are you visiting a woman? Do not forget your whip!'; 'Life is a fountain of delight; but where the rabble drinks too, all wells are poisoned'). Above all, it is for the great majority of readers the vehicle of the 'gospel of the superman'—a conception which has stepped out of its pages and gone on to live a life of its own independently of its author's intentions.

The beginning of **Zarathustra** repeats almost literally the closing section . . . of **The Gay Science** in its original form; the following work, **Beyond Good and Evil,** was intended to elucidate in other terms the ideas set down in **Zarathustra;** the **Genealogy of Morals** is described as a supplement to and clarification of **Beyond Good and Evil;** and the short books of 1888 are a summation: the whole series from **Human, All Too Human** onwards is now consciously intended as a single evolving work. **Zarathustra** introduces the will to power, the superman, and the eternal recurrence of the same events. **Beyond Good and Evil** surveys the entire field of Nietzsche's philosophical and cultural interests, and introduces 'master morality and slave morality'. **On the Genealogy of Morals** is an inquiry into the origins of morality, elaborates the concept of sublimation, and introduces the psychology of '*ressentiment*'. At the same time the sceptical analysis of current values is not abandoned, but pursued with, if anything, greater vigour and subtlety: yet there is no longer any feeling of conflict between this nihilism and a desire to go beyond it, for Nietzsche is now convinced of the inevitability of nihilism and that it is only out of this state that a new transcendence can arise. (pp. 73-4)

[Nietzsche] invites elucidation in *psychological* terms, and the invitation has been accepted by many commentators from Lou Salomé onwards: the ideas in it are explained as a product of neurotic tensions within the author, and the exegetical principle thus established is employed to account for the existence of his entire work. The main effect of such a procedure, it goes without saying, is to devalue the work: it is reduced to a psychiatric case history. The fault in this approach is not that its findings are wrong—for it does seem evident, indeed almost palpably evident, that many of Nietzsche's 'intuitions' are a product of neurotic tensions—but that the premise from which it starts is wrong. That it should occur to anyone to undertake a posthumous psychiatric examination of Nietzsche is already and in itself proof that his works are not reducible to a psychiatric case history: for if they were really no more than that, nobody would ever have heard of him. It is the independent existence of his 'ideas' as ideas, the interest they have aroused, and the influence they have exercised, which really constitutes 'Nietzsche' as a cultural phenomenon: the human being struggling with neurotic tension is 'Nietzsche' only in a very narrow sense. To employ an analogy: if someone undertook to show that the compositions of Verdi were in some sense a product of neurotic tension he would have plenty of evidence to draw on and his investigations would be interesting: but if he concluded that *Il Trovatore* was no more than an item in a psychiatric case history he would be no longer interesting but wrong. *Il Trovatore* is a cultural fact of the first order: and in relation to it 'Verdi' is in the last resort no more than a postulate necessitated by the fact that works of art do not produce themselves. To assess the quality of *Il Trovatore* by assessing the quality of Verdi is (obviously in this case) to stand the matter on its head: but the same is true in the case of Nietzsche. The false premise of the psychologizing approach is that the phenomenon to be explained and assessed is Professor Dr Nietzsche: but he is of interest only because he was, one understands, the author of *Beyond Good and Evil* and the other 'works of Nietzsche'—he derives his interest, importance and quality from them, and *they* are the phenomena to be assessed. The psychiatric approach is from the wrong direction. It says: 'The author of these ideas was neurotic: it is in this light that we should judge them.' It should say: 'These ideas are a cultural fact of the first order: it is in this light that we should judge their author.' (p. 86)

Nietzsche's importance for the present day resides wholly in his philosophical thinking and in the attitude he represents—or even embodies—towards the concept 'a philosopher'. His productions and activities other than philosophical are of secondary interest, although some knowledge of them is of course necessary for a picture of the complete man.

Just as Wagner's earliest reputation was that of the opera composer who wrote his own libretti, so Nietzsche's was that of the philosopher who wrote poetry: in both cases it was the combination in one man of capacities not usually found together which occasioned wonderment, and in both cases also the wonderment subsequently decreased when it became clear that one of these capacities was a good deal inferior to the other.

Nietzsche's quality as a poet is, in my judgment, to be correctly assessed by reversing the cliché that poetry is language 'heightened' and made more intense: in his case, poetry is a relaxation from the intensity of his normal prose medium, and whenever he breaks into verse the temperature at once goes down. 'Verse', indeed, rather than poetry, is what he had a talent for: and not merely verse, but *light verse*. He never attempted, and clearly never felt any desire to attempt, the larger forms; and although he experimented with eccentric metres and, from the time of *Zarathustra* onwards, with a kind of *vers libre*, his usual con-

ception of 'a poem' was of something embodying strong regular rhythm and clear powerful rhyme—and of something, moreover, which says what it has to say without gravity, lightly, quickly. . . . (p. 203)

The period *Human, All Too Human* to *The Gay Science* was also the period of his finest verse: a consequence probably of the same 'break-through' which transformed his prose and, indeed, his thinking as such. (p. 207)

In *Zarathustra,* in addition to the 'prose poetry', we are offered a number of free verse poems, to which others were later added to form the *Dionysos-Dithyramben,* a collection made at the very end of 1888. I have no wish to denegrate these poems as such, for many people have clearly enjoyed them, but they are certainly not 'dithyrambic': on the contrary, their immobility is nearly incredible coming from the author of '**To the Mistral**'. They contain some telling images, and if they are read as prose they can make a powerful impression as distraught monologues: but you have only to compare them with '**Ecce Homo**' to feel their inferiority as works of art. The *heavy* hand has come down again: the *Dithyrambs of Dionysus* recall '**To the Unknown God**'.

Nietzsche's best-known poem, set by Mahler and Delius, is '**O Mensch! Gib acht!**' from *Zarathustra;* his most beautiful is a free-verse lyric sometimes called '**Venice**', sometimes '**Gondola Song**', and published in *Ecce Homo*. . . . (pp. 208-09)

So far as I know he wrote not a single love poem. (p. 209)

R. J. Hollingdale, in his Nietzsche *(© R. J. Hollingdale 1973; reprinted by permission of Routledge & Kegan Paul Ltd), Routledge & Kegan Paul, 1973, 225 p.*

ROLLO MAY (essay date 1974)

[*May, like Thomas Mann (see excerpt above), stresses Nietzsche's importance as a psychologist, and, in particular, praises him for his contributions to the field of psychoanalysis.*]

[Nietzsche] lived and wrote at a time—the last half of the nineteenth century—when European man was psychologically and spiritually disintegrating. Outwardly, the period was still a time of stability and bourgeois conformism; but inwardly, the rotting of man (if I may take my cue from Nietzsche's own words) was visible to Nietzsche, as well as to Kierkegaard, Sartre, and Heidegger in our own day. Religious faith had been transformed into resentment, vitality into sexual repression, and a general hypocrisy marked the condition of man at that time. (p. 58)

Nietzsche predicted what we now consciously know. Man is now bare, he has no clothes for protection; he is naked before himself and his fellows. This was our state unconsciously in the last half of the nineteenth century, and consciously in the middle of the twentieth century. It accounts, among other things, for the tremendous struggle in Nietzsche for honesty and authenticity. "This is Europe's true predicament," declared Nietzsche, "together with the fear of man, we have lost the love of man, confidence in man, and indeed, the will to man."

Nietzsche's famous and oft-quoted parable about the "death of God" has its importance, not in the fact of the death of god (this is now well-known, and is preached by many lesser figures) but rather because of the disintegration that sets in after this event. . . .

Nietzsche was surely brilliantly fitted for being the physician to this disoriented man. He often speaks of himself as a "psychologist" which is very affirming to those of us in the field. At one point, for example, in the book, *Beyond Good and Evil,* he writes as follows: "that psychology should be recognized again as the queen of the sciences, for whose service and preparation the other sciences exist. For psychology is now again the path to the fundamental problems."

Nietzsche's concept of "superman" and "will to power" are endeavors to rediscover some fiber, some basis for strength in his contemporaries. This is one reason he is so radically misunderstood. (p. 59)

The first essential fact about Nietzsche's philosophy is that he uses psychological terms with an ontological meaning. He shares this characteristic with his fellow existentialists, such as Kierkegaard, Sartre, Heidegger. Despair, will, anxiety, guilt, loneliness—these normally refer to psychological conditions, but for Nietzsche they refer to states of being. Anxiety, for example, is not an "affect" that you can feel at some times and not at other times. It refers rather to a state of existence. It is not something we "have," but something we "are." . . .

The same holds for will. The term "will," in Nietzsche and his colleagues, does not refer to some impetus that you drum up to help you make resolutions on New Year's night or some Sunday morning in church. It refers to, rather, a basic feature of our existence. It is potentially present at all times; without it we would not be human beings. The acorn becomes an oak regardless of any choice, but man cannot realize his Being except as he wills it in his encounters. In animals and plants, nature and being are one, but in man, nature and being are never to be identified. . . . He adjures us that we must cease letting our lives be mere accidents. The human values are not given us by nature but are set for us as tasks to be achieved. It is clear that using these psychological terms with an ontological significance gives them a much more profound and powerful meaning. (p. 60)   .

At almost any point at which you open Nietzsche, you find psychological insights that are not only penetrating and astute in themselves, but amazingly parallel to the psychoanalytic mechanisms that Freud, and others, were to formulate a decade or more later. For example, turning to the *Genealogy of Morals* . . . we find, "All instincts that are not allowed free play turn inward. This is what I call man's interiorization." Note the curiously close prediction of the later Freudian concept of "repression." Nietzsche's eternal theme was the unmasking of self-deception, and throughout that whole essay he develops the thesis that altruism and morality in his day were the results of repressed hostility and resentment, and that when an individual's potentia are turned inward, bad conscience is the result. This could come out of any contemporary psychoanalysis.

Nietzsche gives a vivid description of the impotent people who are filled with bottled-up aggression: "Their happiness is purely passive, takes the form of drugged tranquility, stretching, yawning, peace, sabbath, and emotional slackness." Such inturned aggression breaks out in sadistic demands on others. This was a process which Freud later was to call "symptomformation." The demands then clothe themselves in the garb of morality. This is a process which Freud called "reaction formation." "In its earliest phase," Nietzsche writes, "bad conscience is nothing other than instinctive freedom forced to become latent, driven underground, and forced to vent its energy upon itself."

At other points in Nietzsche one finds a striking formulation of "sublimation" a concept which he specifically developed. Speaking of the connection between a person's artistic energy and sexuality, he says that "it may well be that the emergence of the aesthetic condition does not suspend sexuality, as Schopenhauer believed, but merely transmutes it, in such a way that it is no longer experienced as a sexual incentive."

A third important point, in which Nietzsche speaks for the leaders among contemporary depth psychology, is in his approach to the question of health. Health is not a fixed state that some lucky people arrive at. (This is a great consolation to many of us who have been ill most of our lives!) Health is a dynamic balance in the struggle to overcome disease. The artist is an artist because he gains a sensitivity out of his struggle between sickness and health. (p. 61)

This points toward Nietzsche's later idea of "power," as the artist' ability to overcome disease and suffering. We also find in Nietzsche continuous denial of the common idea that survival is the highest value of life. He heaps scorn on those who think they are Darwinians and who fail to see that man seeks not to preserve his potentiality, but rather to express it. He says, "even what is greatest will risk its life for the sake of power." (p. 62)

We come now to the question of the contribution to psychology of Nietzsche's concept of power, and specifically the "will to power." "The near-most essence of Being," Nietzsche writes, "is will to power." In academic psychology, not only is this idea of Nietzsche not recognized but the concept of power itself is completely repressed. Sometimes, to be sure, it is subsumed under "will," but "will" also has been largely ignored since the days of William James. (p. 63)

I think the general repression of power, and of the topic of power, has been lamentable in the extreme. The choice of substitute terms is tremendously revealing. Take for example, the concept of "control." Control is a substitute expression for power, which puts the accent on my right to exert power over you. (pp. 63-4)

Those who, like B. F. Skinner, talk a great deal about control are generally those who have never accepted, or analyzed their own power drives. "Control" among psychologists is an acceptable term and "power" is not. Around the country there is a vast number of psychologists who identify with Skinner and the movement that he represents in psychology, because they also, by and large, are bootlegging their own desires for power into the picture, and these are legitimicized by the concept of "control."

I do not believe that "control" is an adequate substitute chiefly because it always assumes that I am going to do the controlling, and you are going to be controlled. I think Nietzsche would have abhorred that development. Instead of self-control, he believed in "self transcendence"—self surpassing, concepts which always preserve freedom in a way quite opposite to "control" as Skinner uses it. . . .

The "will to power" is a call to man to avoid the putrescense and to affirm himself in his existence with strength and commitment. The "will to power" is built into every individual because it is inseparable from life itself. "Wherever I found life," writes Nietzsche, "there I found the will to power." Nietzsche at times even makes the mistake of identifying the two. For example, he writes, "life is merely an individual instance of the will to power. Thus, will to power becomes a new specification of the concept life.'' I think this an error also. There are many things in life that are not power, or not will to power, even though they are associated with it. But nevertheless, it is a minor mistake when we consider what a vast contribution Nietzsche has made in his emphasis on the potentially healthy characteristics of power. (p. 64)

Far from being a destructive, nihilistic thinker, Nietzsche turns out on deeper inspection, to be profoundly constructive. And he is constructive in a way that seems the only way for our day. In the degree of apathy, indeed the degree of neurotic apathy that exists in our country, and the suppression, not only of anxiety, but even more deeply of guilt, we greatly need Nietzsche's gospel. This is why Nietzsche is the therapist for the therapists in our time. (p. 66)

I find Nietzsche so important because he never winces before the tragic facts of life. His personal loneliness, it seems to me, kept these facts always vividly before his attention. In mood, he is more like Freud, in content, more like Adler. He never succumbs, moreover, to the dark and despairing facts, not, at least, until he actually became psychotic.

We must undergo a revaluation of values. ''Surpass yourself,'' is the cry I always read between the lines in Nietzsche. Man must transcend himself. . . .

We can look forward to the day when not only will psychologists recognize Nietzsche but they also will recognize how much he has to teach them. (p. 67)

Rollo May, ''Nietzsche's Contributions to Psychology,'' in Symposium, Special Issue: Friedrich Nietzsche *(copyright ©1974 by Syracuse University Press; reprinted by permission of Heldref Publications), Vol. XXVIII, No. 1, Spring, 1974, pp. 58-73.*

WALTER KAUFMANN (essay date 1974)

[*Kaufmann is one of the leading translators and critics of Nietzsche. His* Nietzsche: Philosopher, Psychologist, Antichrist—*from which the following excerpt is taken—is considered one of the most thorough investigations of Nietzsche's philosophy and work. In the portion below, Kaufmann demonstrates how Nietzsche used the ''style of decadence''—a style favoring the particular rather than the whole—in an effort to overcome decadence. Kaufmann discusses a number of important points, in particular Nietzsche's refusal to establish a system in which to express his thoughts. On this same subject see also J. P. Stern's essay excerpted below.*]

Nietzsche's books are easier to read but harder to understand than those of almost any other thinker. If we ignore for the moment the symbolism of *Zarathustra,* we find that practically every sentence and every page of his writings presents far less trouble than the involved and technical periods of Kant, Hegel, and even Schopenhauer. Not even the British Empiricists would seem to have written more lucidly. Yet grave difficulties are encountered when one tries seriously to follow Nietzsche's thought. As soon as one attempts to penetrate beyond the clever epigrams and well turned insults to grasp their consequences and to coordinate them, one is troubled. Other thinkers generally accomplish this coordination for us, and if we follow their arguments, they will show us the connection that leads from one claim to the next. Frequently we may not be convinced, or we detect loopholes or inconsistencies; yet we feel for the most part that we recognize what the author is driving at. Thus it is perhaps easier to form an opinion of the general meaning of Kant's *Critique of Pure Reason* than to grasp the precise significance of any number of sentences in that work—

while in Nietzsche's books the individual sentences seem clear enough and it is the total design that puzzles us.

The best critique of Nietzsche's style is to be found in *The Case of Wagner.* The great problem with which the book deals is decadence, and Nietzsche—always eager for a historical name that may serve to represent what he has in mind—discusses Wagner as the archdecadent. At the same time he admits that he himself is ''no less than Wagner, a child of this age, that is, a *decadent*: but I comprehended this, I resisted it.'' . . . Wagner, on the other hand, chose in the end not to fight his age; he made his peace with his contemporaries and became the high priest of decadence. This is the background of Nietzsche's sketch of the style of decadence:

> What is the mark of every *literary* decadence? That life no longer resides in the whole. The word becomes sovereign and leaps out of the sentence, the sentence reaches out and obscures the meaning of the page, and the page comes to life at the expense of the whole—the whole is no longer a whole. This, however, is the simile of every style of decadence: every time there is an anarchy of atoms. . . .
>
> (pp. 72-3)

Now it might give us pause that Nietzsche claims—not only in the preface of his polemic against Wagner, but throughout his later works and notes—that he fought and overcame his decadence. Still viewing this question with an eye to his style, we are led to wonder whether the ''anarchy of atoms,'' or the maze of aphorisms, is perhaps integrated into a large design. While the epigrams evidently come to life at the expense of the whole, we should inquire whether behind them there is a whole philosophy. Of course, we cannot hope to find an answer to this question if we adopt the line of least resistance and merely browse here and there, deliberately ignoring the sequence of Nietzsche's thought. (pp. 73-4)

In one of the best books yet written about Nietzsche, [Karl] Jaspers tells us that the true alternative to merely nipping here and there in Nietzsche's works and notes consists in nowhere being satisfied until we have ''*also* found the contradiction.'' This is decidedly not the line of least resistance; and Jaspers, believing that there are fundamental antinomies, sees a virtue in Nietzsche's bold attempt to face such contradictions squarely. This, however, should not blind us to the fact that we are urged to adopt a wholly singular approach. We are to look, as it were, at the twenty-odd volumes of Nietzsche's books and notes and compare statements picked at random: if we do that, we should always find contradictions. Our success, it would seem, depends on how far we carry this approach. If we do not hesitate to break up sentences and carve our looked-for contradictions out of parentheses, we should get far; and while it is perfectly plain that Jaspers does not mean to exhort us to any such unscrupulous procedure, it seems striking that his approach would never have been even considered for, say, the works of Kant. . . . Nietzsche's writings, however, have almost invariably been approached in some such manner. . . .

[There are a number of] reasons for this state of affairs: his sister's monopolizing of the manuscript material; her decision to withhold *Ecce Homo* while publishing some random notes as her brother's last and greatest work; and the superficial similarities between the incoherence of the notes and the style of some of the books. The main reason, however, is surely to be found in the fact that Nietzsche's style makes impossible the systematic approach which is usually adopted in the study of other thinkers.

The elusive quality of this style, which is so characteristic of Nietzsche's way of thinking and writing, might be called *monadologic* to crystallize the tendency of each aphorism to be self-sufficient while yet throwing light on almost every other aphorism. We are confronted with a "pluralistic universe" in which each aphorism is itself a microcosm. Almost as often as not, a single passage is equally relevant to ethics, aesthetics, philosophy of history, theory of value, psychology, and perhaps half a dozen other fields. (p. 75)

It is difficult to find any satisfactory alternative to the systematic approach which fails us in this case. No half systematic anthology of sundry opinions can tell us "what Nietzsche means"—either in the sense of his intentions or in the sense of his significance for us. We might as well scan a digest of the plot of *The Brothers Karamazov* to find what Dostoevsky means. To art and philosophy there is no royal road, and we cannot understand Nietzsche if we deliberately ignore the thought processes by which "he came to think as he did." The opposite attempt to view Nietzsche's ideas as merely biographical data—dissolving them existentially or trivializing them psychologically—seems based on resignation that despairs of finding any coherent body of thought. (p. 76)

We are now prepared to understand how Nietzsche employed the "style of decadence" methodically in an effort to overcome "decadence" and attain a philosophy. It is very well to say that it is a sign of the spirit of the age that single passages should be so much more memorable than the whole book in which they occur; and one may even appreciate the fact that Nietzsche, with the possible exception of *Zarathustra,* made no attempt to write in a more epic vein, as so many writers have done since, when only an occasional line in a long poem, or a sketch or idea in a bulky book, sustains the reader's attention. Nietzsche's style can be taken to represent a brutally frank admission that today hardly anyone can offer more than scattered profound insights or single beautiful sentences—and his writings abound in both.

All that, however, tells no more than half the story. Nietzsche's style is more than the "style of decadence," and his aphorisms are not only monadologic but also add up to a philosophy. Literary criticism is fruitful up to a point, but Nietzsche was more than a literary figure, and we must now ask questions of a different sort: decadence apart, for what reason or purpose did Nietzsche reject systems and prefer to write aphorisms? The answer to this question will reveal his "method."

It is evident at once that Nietzsche is far superior to Kant and Hegel as a stylist; but it also seems that as a philosopher he represents a very sharp decline—and men have not been lacking who have not considered him a philosopher at all—because he had no "system." Yet this argument is hardly cogent. Schelling and Hegel, Spinoza and Aquinas had their systems; in Kant's and Plato's case the word is far less applicable; and of the many important philosophers who very definitely did not have systems one need only mention Socrates and many of the pre-Socratics. Not only can one defend Nietzsche on this score—how many philosophers today have systems?—but one must add that he had strong philosophic reasons for not having a system. (pp. 78-9)

A system must necessarily be based on premises that by its very nature it cannot question. This was one of Nietzsche's objections, although he did not put the point this way himself.

The systematic thinker starts with a number of primary assumptions from which he draws a net of inferences and thus deduces his system; but he cannot, from within his system, establish the truth of his premises. He takes them for granted, and even if they should seem "self-evident" to him, they may not seem so to others. They are in that sense arbitrary and reducible to the subjective make-up of the thinker. A strikingly similar view is found in William James: "A philosophy is the expression of a man's intimate character." And, Nietzsche would add, of the philosopher's moral notions.

While the early Nietzsche suggests that one may "delight in such systems, even if they should be entirely mistaken," because they are after all expressions of the humanity of "great human beings" . . . , it is plain that the same point can be turned negatively—and after thinking the matter over for some years, Nietzsche gave vehement expression to the other side of the question. . . . What Nietzsche objects to is the failure to question one's own assumptions. The philosopher who boasts of a system would appear more stupid than he is, inasmuch as he refuses to think about his premises. This is one of the recurrent themes of Nietzsche's later thought, and in characteristic fashion he often formulated it in more offensive language: "the will to a system is a lack of integrity." . . . (pp. 79-80)

As Nietzsche ponders the question further, he turns the point positively once more, reconciling his early appreciation of systems with his later insight that they narrow thought artificially:

> The different philosophic systems are to be considered as *educational methods* of the spirit: they have always *developed* one particular force of the spirit best by their one-sided demand to see things just so and not otherwise. . . .
>
> (p. 80)

The development of Nietzsche's view of philosophic systems, as here suggested, is reminiscent of Hegel's dialectic. This, however, does not mean that his statements contradict each other or that he claims that reality is self-contradictory. Only unqualified judgments about reality involve us in superficial inconsistencies: thus systems are good, but also bad. The contradiction disappears as soon as we qualify such statements and specify in what respects systems are good and bad.

Systems, says Nietzsche, are good insofar as they reveal the character of a great thinker—but this goodness is independent of the truth of the system. The system is reducible to a set of premises which cannot be questioned within the framework of the system—and these basic assumptions give expression to the mental make-up of the philosopher. This affirmation of the goodness or value of systems contains, implicitly (*an sich*, as Hegel would say), a negative truth about systems—and Nietzsche proceeds to state this truth explicitly (*für sich*). The thinker who believes in the ultimate truth of his system, without questioning its presuppositions, appears more stupid than he is: he refuses to think beyond a certain point; and this is, according to Nietzsche, a subtle moral corruption. In this sense, systems are bad—but this assertion does not contradict the earlier affirmation that they are good: rather it follows from this very affirmation. They are not good in every way, and their being good in one way involves their being bad in another. . . . No one system reveals the entire truth; at best, each organizes one point of view or perspective. We must consider many perspectives, and a philosopher should not imprison his thought in one system. (pp. 80-1)

Nietzsche is, like Plato, not a system-thinker but a problem-thinker. Like every philosopher, he uses premises—but not all men employ these in the manner to which Spinoza aspired in his *Ethics*: deducing a system from a set of unquestioned assumptions. Perhaps it is the most striking characteristic of "dialectical" thinking from Socrates to Hegel and Nietzsche that it is a search for hidden presuppositions rather than a quest for solutions. The starting point of such a "dialectical" inquiry is not a set of premises but a problem situation—and Plato, of course, excelled at giving a concrete and dramatic setting to this. In the problem situation premises are involved, and some of these are made explicit in the course of the inquiry. The result is less a solution of the initial problem than a realization of its limitations: typically, the problem is not solved but "outgrown." (p. 82)

It is true that Nietzsche often gave expression to opinions he had not questioned critically. In his writings, as in those of any other encyclopaedic philosopher—whether it be Plato, Aristotle, Aquinas, Kant, or Hegel—we must distinguish between the human and the all-too-human elements. Nietzsche's writings contain many all-too-human judgments—especially about women—but these are philosophically irrelevant; and *ad hominem* arguments against any philosopher on the basis of such statements seem trivial and hardly pertinent. (p. 84)

Nietzsche's aphoristic style appears as an interesting attempt to transcend the maze of concepts and opinions in order to get at the objects themselves. The "style of decadence" is methodically employed in the service of Nietzsche's "experimentalism." The key terms that Nietzsche uses time and again are now *Experiment* and now *Versuch;* but it is well to keep in mind that *Versuch,* too, need not mean merely "attempt" but can have the characteristic scientific sense of "experiment": it is quite proper in German to speak of a scientist as making a *Versuch.*

Each aphorism or sequence of aphorisms—and in Nietzsche's later works some of these sequences are about a hundred pages long, and the aphoristic style is only superficially maintained—may be considered as a thought experiment. The discontinuity or, positively speaking, the great number of experiments, reflects the conviction that making only one experiment would be onesided. . . . Nietzsche insists that the philosopher must be willing to make ever new experiments; he must retain an open mind and be prepared, if necessary, "boldly at any time to declare himself *against* his previous opinion" . . .—just as he would expect a scientist to revise his theories in the light of new experiments.

Nietzsche, no less than Hegel, wanted philosophy to become scientific, *wissenschaftlich*—but science did not mean the same thing to both thinkers. To Hegel it meant above all the rigor of a system. This he opposed to the romantics' sentimental enthusiasm which had come into flower since the publication of Fichte's *Wissenschaftslehre.* Thus he insisted that we must elevate philosophy to a science—and this programmatic declaration in the preface of his first book holds equally for all his later works. . . . Nietzsche did not want philosophy to be less scientific than this but rather more so; only he had in mind the "gay science" of fearless experiment and the good will to accept new evidence and to abandon previous positions, if necessary.

It may be recalled that Kant, in his preface to the second edition of the *Critique of Pure Reason,* had spoken of an "experiment of pure reason"—meaning the kind of singular experiment

whose outcome may furnish the decisive confirmation of an entire world-view. That was not what Nietzsche intended. In fact, he believed that he had to break with the philosophic tradition of centuries on just this point. (pp. 85-6)

The philosophers of the future, Nietzsche thought, would have no such delusions. They would not shirk small questions but consider them on their own merits and not as corollaries of a previously conceived all-solving system. (p. 86)

After scorning the ambition of the great systematizers down to Schopenhauer, Nietzsche thus develops a pride of his own. By his fearless questioning he hopes to get to the bottom of problems. The insights which he tries to formulate in his aphorisms will have to be accounted for in any comprehensive explanatory system, just as an honest scientific experiment cannot be ignored by any comprehensive scientific system. While the systems come and go, the experiment—perhaps variously interpreted—remains. This may have been what Nietzsche had in mind when he celebrated his style in the *Götzen-Dämmerung,* using the hyperboles characteristic of his last works. . . . (p. 87)

[Nietzsche's] "existentialism" prevents his aphorisms from being no more than a glittering mosaic of independent monads. The "anarchy of atoms" is more apparent than real; and while the word frequently "becomes sovereign and leaps out of the sentence" and "the sentence reaches out and obscures the meaning of the page," we cannot say in justice that "life no longer resides in the whole." . . . Life does indeed reside in the whole of Nietzsche's thinking and writing, and there is a unity which is obscured, but not obliterated, by the apparent discontinuity in his experimentalism.

This point is perhaps best illustrated by a reference to the variety of styles that distinguishes Nietzsche's literary output. This will also afford us a welcome opportunity for correcting any impression we may have given that Nietzsche's books are all aphoristic and lacking in continuity of presentation. *The Birth of Tragedy* and the four *Untimely Meditations* represent diverse forms of the essay, more or less richly blended with polemics. In these early works Nietzsche is not yet deliberately experimental. The next three books, *Human, All-Too-Human, Dawn,* and *The Gay Science* offer various treatments of an aphoristic style, and here the experimentalism reaches its climax. Nietzsche is deliberately anti-dogmatic and accumulates his observations with an open mind. He is, as it were, performing the countless experiments on which later theories might be built. *Zarathustra* is, stylistically, an experiment in dithyrambs; philosophically, certain significant conclusions are drawn, often in veiled allegories, from the empirical data of the previous three books. *Beyond Good and Evil* shows Nietzsche turning away from his previous aphoristic style: now most of the aphorisms are quite long and clearly anchored in their context. The *Genealogy of Morals* is aphoristic in appearance, but actually consists of three sustained and continuous inquiries—and the third of these represents a new experiment: the "exegesis" of a single aphorism in about eighty pages. . . . *The Case of Wagner* displays a new form of polemics, and *Götzen-Dämmerung, Antichrist,* and *Ecce Homo,* though returning to the length of the earlier *"Meditations,"* are each *sui generis.*

Philosophically, the works after *Zarathustra* do not any longer contain series of small experiments but the hypotheses that Nietzsche would base on his earlier works. As such, they may seem less tentative, and the tone is frequently impassioned: but Nietzsche still considers them *Versuche* and offers them with an open mind. (pp. 91-2)

Nietzsche's ceaseless experimenting with different styles seems to conform to the *Zeitgeist* which was generally marked by a growing dissatisfaction with traditional modes of expression. Wagner, the Impressionists and the Expressionists, Picasso and the Surrealists, Joyce, Pound, and Eliot all show a similar tendency. Nietzsche's experiments, however, are remarkable for the lack of any deliberateness even in the face of their extreme diversity. Thus Ludwig Klages, the characterologist who began his literary career as a George disciple, can speak of "the almost peerless uniformity of Nietzsche's style." What is perhaps really peerless is the concomitance of uniformity and diversity. Nietzsche is not trying now this and now that style, but each experiment is so essentially Nietzschean in its strengths and weaknesses that the characterologist experiences no trouble in recognizing the author anywhere. Involuntarily almost, Nietzsche is driven from style to style in his ceaseless striving for an adequate medium of expression. Each style is characteristically his own, but soon found inadequate, and then drives him on to another newer one. Yet all the experiments cohere because they are not capricious. Their unity one might call "existential." (pp. 92-3)

Although lacking any thorough training in mathematical or logical theory, Nietzsche realized that the coherence of a finite system could never be a guarantee of its truth. His experimentalism seems sound as a reaction against "the time when Hegel and Schelling seduced the minds" of German youth . . . , to use Nietzsche's own provocative phrase. The "gay science" which he opposed to the Idealists' conception of philosophy seems fruitful and deserves attention. Nietzsche, however, overlooked the possibility that systematization might be one of the most useful tools of the experimentalism he envisaged.

In the first place, systematization reveals errors. Previously unnoticed inconsistencies become apparent when one attempts to integrate a host of insights into a coherent system. And internal consistency, while admittedly not a sufficient condition of the truth of a system, is surely a necessary condition. The discovery of inconsistencies should prompt not automatic compromise but further inquiry and eventual revision. The same consideration applies to external inconsistencies: the ultimate test of the truth of an observation is consistency with the rest of our experience—and thus systematization of wider and wider areas of knowledge may raise ever new questions. Again, the new insight should not be sacrificed unscrupulously to entrenched prejudice—the great danger of systematizing; rather traditional beliefs should be subjected to ever new questioning in the light of new experiences and ideas. In this sense, a new insight is not exploited sufficiently, and the experiment is stopped prematurely if systematization is not eventually attempted in the very service of the "gay science."

This last point may be restated separately: while offering many fruitful hypotheses, Nietzsche failed to see that only a systematic attempt to substantiate them could establish an impressive probability in their favor. Hence his experiments are often needlessly inconclusive. Though a system may be false in spite of its internal coherence, an unsystematic collection of sundry observations can hardly lay any greater claim to truth.

Nietzsche, unlike Aristotle, Aquinas, or Hegel, did not mark the culmination and conclusion of a long development—as it were, a great harvest. Rather he marks the beginning of a new period, and he was acutely aware of this. Many of his most promising insights were developed after his death by other writers. . . . Yet it would be false were one to conclude that

Nietzsche was a mere aphorist and a sower of seeds, and not a philosopher in his own right. While he did not follow up *all* his suggestions, he succeeded in fashioning a coherent and noteworthy philosophy that may well surpass the systems of his successors in breadth, depth, and originality. (pp. 93-4)

Walter Kaufmann, in his Nietzsche: Philosopher, Psychologist, Antichrist *(copyright 1950, © 1968, 1974 by Princeton University Press; excerpts reprinted by permission of Princeton University Press), fourth edition, Princeton University Press, 1974, 532 p.*

J. P. STERN   (essay date 1979)

[*Like Walter Kaufmann (see excerpt above), Stern focuses on Nietzsche's desire for the particular rather than the whole, as demonstrated by his aphoristic style of writing. But whereas Kaufmann believes that Nietzsche used this so-called "style of decadence" to overcome decadence, Stern argues that he greatly limited the effectiveness of his thought by refusing to "stabilize" or integrate his concepts. Stern calls this Nietzsche's rejection of "the sphere of association."*]

[Nietzsche's] theoretical view of language, like his view of literature, is essentially atomistic: if meaning and value are to be found anywhere (he argues), it is in the single discrete elements, in metaphors and individual moments of truth. Just as the architectonic is the weakest aspect of his own books, so his observations on other men's books (after *The Birth of Tragedy*) tend to be confined to brilliant *aperçus* and single impressions. The category of the single and individual prevails in every argument, even where it seems irrelevant. . . . Nietzsche's consistent preference is clear: he is always for the single man against the herd, for genius against justice, for grace against deserts; he favors inspiration against the rule of rules and professional competence, and the heroic in every form against all that is 'human, all too human'. The catastrophic—nongradual—perception, the unpremeditated insight and sudden conviction, the flash-like inspiration—these, for Nietzsche, are the authentic modes of knowledge-and-experience. And even though, in the 'positivist' period of *The Joyful Science* . . . , he praises knowledge which matures slowly and convictions which are deeply considered, the very form in which he does it shows that this is not the way *he* works. The method he favours (though he does not always follow it) is to proceed *via* 'single little questions and experiments' . . . , for these alone (he is convinced) satisfy the exacting demands of the modern scientific era. He attacks historians (in the third and fourth of *Thoughts Out of Season*) for burying great men under a welter of facts, for replacing genuine insights with endless continuities, and for denying that there is genius which does not develop as they develop—slowly, gradually, tediously. 'My way of reporting historical facts,' he writes in a note of 1879, 'is really to tell the story of my own experiences *á propos* of past ages and men. Nothing coherent: some things became clear to me, others did not. Our literary historians are boring because they force themselves to talk about and pass judgement on everything, even where they have experienced nothing". . . . The single experience—'Erlebnis'—is all.

There is no end of such observations, and they all point to a pervasive limitation of Nietzsche's thinking: it is his consistent neglect of the world 'where two or three are gathered together', his indiscriminate bias against what I shall call *the sphere of association*. And to ignore this sphere, as Nietzsche ignores it, is to offer a misleading account of an important part of our world.

By this I mean that in all his philosophizing he has nothing really positive to say about, and is deeply suspicious of, all those human endeavours—in society, art and religion, in morality, even in the natural sciences—in which single discrete insights and experiences and encounters—single situations—are stabilized and made reliable by means of rules and laws and institutions—by structures—leading to new associations or combinations, which in turn bring about new situations. (pp. 126-28)

[Nietzsche] believes—the belief informs his choice of reflection and aphorism as his favourite literary media—that the part is greater, or at least truer, less misleading, than the whole.

It sometimes seems as if he regarded all entailment and continuity, which are germane to the associative process, as disconnected from specifically *human* existence, indifferent to the dictates of man's will, and therefore as something inhuman. We cannot be sure. What we do know is that he sees man's search for stability almost always as an arrest of living experience, an inauthentic pursuit, a fear of the rigours of solitude, a failure of independence and courage—as a defection from the heroism of singularity.

Tradition, dogma, formulation itself amount for him to a second order of experience, a spurious, reach-me-down reality. Institutionalization as man's only protection against arbitrariness means little to him. Nowhere is this more patent than in his wholesale rejection of the Christian Church in the world, as though the word of Jesus (which he does not reject wholesale) could get around without 'two or three gathering together in his name'. And if, in traditional Romantic fashion, Nietzsche occasionally vilifies 'the State' and glorifies 'the Nation' . . . , he does so for the simple and predictable reason that he regards the former as the coldest of cold institutional monsters, while in the latter he sees a 'natural' extension of the private self. To enlist him, on the strength of such opinions, either on behalf of the nationalists or of political liberals is equally absurd. (pp. 128-29)

'All human error is impatience, a premature breaking-off of method': this aphorism of Franz Kafka's could have been written with Nietzsche in mind, and Nietzsche would have acknowledged the verdict it implies. For what it comes to, in the last resort is that he—Nietzsche—does not believe in his own beliefs enough to be circumspect about the conditions in which they might one day be realized. Yet in voicing this criticism one is hardly doing more than applying what he teaches.

In the dialectic which lies at the core of all human experience Nietzsche always favours the unique against repetition and genius against justice. We may leave to one side for the moment the question whether this is a practicable point of view: what undermines his advocacy and limits his perception is that he hardly admits the presence of a genuine dialectic, of an inescapable human problem. Yet although it is inescapable, the problem is of course not insoluble—indeed, all civilized life depends on its on-going solutions; but then, Nietzsche often writes as though this were enough to make civilization itself suspect and by definition decadent. (p. 129)

The signs of Nietzsche's refusal to come to terms with this mode of human experience are everywhere. He writes splendidly on Goethe and shows a more intimate understanding than many literary historians of the nature of Goethe's poetic genius

and generous humanity. For Goethe's love of custom and habit, however, for that part of the poet's genius which hallows the everyday and thereby gives it lasting value, Nietzsche seems to have no spontaneous understanding at all. . . . [There] never was a philosopher who had so little of the habit of patience with things or people. He writes as one who fervently believes he ought to 'learn to love', but whose will is at odds with his intentions. (p. 130)

Nietzsche's disregard of the 'associative' mode does not, as we have seen, prevent him from launching into huge and occasionally questionable generalizations. They are conceived as multiplications of individual instances, not on the level of abstract concepts. Sometimes they are the signs of his impatience, but at other times they seem to spring from his innermost trust that the single case *he* knows, cites and generalizes is the exemplary one—a sort of epistemological *amor fati*. The fact that he is not really intent on conceptualizing his insights is one of his attractions for other writers and artists, and one of the sources of his influence as a 'philosopher of life'. But it also limits the range of his criticism when faced with conceptual problems. (p. 131)

His consistent rejection of the sphere of association forms undoubtedly the most important limitation of his philosophical thinking. It is also the most disturbing of his limitations, because it is breached by no dialectic of questions and hypothetical answers, by no speculative experiments. Moreover, in this attitude he is in no way original, in no way 'the unique event and exception' in the culture of his country. Here he belongs to a dominant German tradition which goes back to Martin Luther and perhaps beyond.

Whenever social considerations may legitimately be translated into considerations of personal value and dignity, Nietzsche's full critical understanding is brought into play. . . . But there are aspects of social life (such as the law, or politics, or economic exchange) which have a dialectic of their own and to which, therefore, immediate personal value judgements are irrelevant. Nietzsche's reflections on these topics show up the bad discontinuity of his thought; here his influence is at its most retrograde. One's criticism is not that he fails to provide what he never attempted—a systematic sociology—but that the view of society *and* of the individual entailed by his reflections on social morality issue in an almost absolute individualism which does not provide an account of the way things are in the world.

Characteristically, almost the only form of government that interests him is rule through a leader's or an oligarchy's absolute exercise of power. But because he does not explore the ways in which even autocratically governed societies are formed and sustained by custom and convention—does not ask how much of the old is bound to survive into the new—he cannot explain rule by command except with the aid of catastrophic 'natural' factors. And since for him, in this context, the 'natural' is an irreducible category . . . , the conception of society that emerges from his observations is not that of a self-contained functional system, but a system that works by virtue of its relationship to something outside itself. . . . Sometimes this outside force is nature, sometimes it is fate, sometimes it is a present god, or again a *deus absconditus*—yet what Nietzsche intends is the opposite, is a self-contained system of rule. His explicit aim, especially in **Zarathustra,** is to make men self-reliant and self-determining, content with their earthly lot and free from all need of gods, yet the arrangements of social and political life that would be required to institute such an autonomous humanity do not interest him. The 'will to power', conceived as the dominant force at work in such a system, is hypostatized into a natural force which encroaches on human society from outside.

Historical change as Nietzsche sees it is brought about by great men who impose their will on the birth-florescence-decay cycles of whole cultures, and these cycles are conceived on the analogy of plant life. Between the two poles of individual psychology and cosmic or millennial speculation—between the Superman and the doctrine of 'the eternal recurrence of the same'—there seems to be a void; or rather, not a void, but the curiously unreal picture of a society which is both rigid and provisional, and which must be totally transcended. (pp. 131-33)

It is Nietzsche's readiness to follow the fashion of 'social Darwinism' and resort to its explanations of all social change as the result of a life-and-death struggle . . . which leads to his conception of society as a thing rigid and unadaptable to gradual change. What makes the picture so unreal is that societies seem to move from complete stability (which he always identifies with oppressive inertia) through sudden catastrophe or authoritarian command to total re-formation: but this, we know, is not how societies change. (p. 133)

In addressing the heroic individual man as though such a man stood wholly outside the social nexus, Nietzsche ignores some of the most important insights of social thought in his age. Early sociologists, among them Marx and Durkheim, but also Max Weber, have shown at length that the individual self, in any living sense, *even as a self* is already implicated in a system of social and moral conventions; that it is nothing ('the merest vapourings of Idealism', Marx calls it) without having some relationship to this system. . . . He does not quarrel with the central insight of his age: he does not seem to be aware of it. What he attacks as an aspect of the decadence of his world we cannot but regard as an essential part of the human condition itself. (p. 134)

This, then, is Nietzsche's horizon, the limit of one mode of his consciousness. Why can he not think and experiment outside it? Why does he ignore the 'associative' part of our world? The question seems to have a ready answer: because, in a peculiarly radical, German way, he is preoccupied with attacking those currents of contemporary culture and social thought which render his ideal for humanity impossible. At this point the different aspects of the sphere of association fall apart. Nietzsche is reacting against the political ideas of the French Revolution, the societal ideas of Rousseau *and* of the English political economists, the nascent international socialist movement and its belief in progress, at the same time as he is reacting against Schopenhauer's and Hegel's expatiations on single themes and against Kant's idealism, which he 'unmasks' as a systematic undermining of man's faith in his senses and in the earth, their object.

However, an answer of this kind is not just obvious, it is also inadequate. His philosophizing and its limitations cannot be explained in terms of his 'reactions'. Its true and irreducible ground is his image of man, 'unhouseled, disappointed, unaneled' and for these reasons heroic, held out into the void of the circle of endless repetitions. He does not love the world—he loves the earth, but does not want it to last. His deepest and most consistent concern is not with social values of any kind, neither with the swaggering gilded fuss of the leader nor with the blood-and-iron ideology of the man of will, nor with

any of our prudentialisms. The value that is left at the end of his moral arguments is the opposite of any conceivable utopia. It is the heroism of deprivation: a strange 'value', we may think, yet part of the discontinuous, catastrophic experience which dominates his outlook and writings. (pp. 137-38)

> *J. P. Stern, in his* A Study of Nietzsche *(© Cambridge University Press 1979), Cambridge University Press, 1979, 220 p.*

MICHAEL HINDEN (essay date 1981)

> [*Hinden discusses Nietzsche's harsh judgement of Euripides as the poet who sacrificed the tragic experience in art. He suggests that Nietzsche's argument with Euripides might have been motivated by an "agonizing kinship" the philosopher felt toward the early Greek.*]

There are three contending schools regarding Nietzsche's [*The Birth of Tragedy*], each defined by its attitude toward the relation of the work to Nietzsche's subsequent production. *The Birth of Tragedy* . . . is Nietzsche's first completed book, and it differs significantly in form and substance from his later writing. Generally speaking, it rhapsodizes in the vatic voice, it pronounces authoritatively on the nature of reality, it denigrates Socratic thought, it traces an historical progression in a romantic key, and it opposes tragic truth to optimistic illusion without mocking the idea of truth itself. His later work, given occasionally to passionate ejaculations, is generally more subtle, dichotomous, ironic, witty, dialectical, self-conscious—its effort to dissect constantly undermining its impulse to expatiate. How to account for this discrepancy?

One can assume, first, that Nietzsche's style underwent a transformation in the course of his development and that *The Birth of Tragedy,* despite its oddities, may be placed in the context of his *oeuvre* without apology. From this perspective, which in the main I have adopted, Nietzsche's argument can be taken as straightforward and debated on its merits. However, Walter Kaufmann, whose interest is to fortify Nietzsche's reputation as a systematic, rational philosopher, is much troubled by *The Birth of Tragedy.* For Kaufmann this is Nietzsche's least appealing book, and he argues that it must be read between the lines. Kaufmann stresses the book's atypicality, contending that the philosopher did not actually oppose himself to Socrates and that his remarks on Euripides are uncharacteristic of the later Nietzsche and, moreover, unconvincing. The purpose of his reading is to denigrate the importance of *The Birth of Tragedy,* but although Kaufmann's scholarship commands respect, his dismissal of offending passages seems wishful and overly selective.

A third approach is that of Paul de Man [(see excerpt above)]. An admirer of the "New Nietzsche," that is to say, the ironical Nietzsche for whom parodic play and "deconstruction" of assertive modes are paramount, de Man finds that *The Birth of Tragedy* poses a unique embarrassment. He brilliantly "deconstructs" the text in order to show that Nietzsche's early work is of the same cloth as his later writing. . . . (pp. 246-47)

Now, certainly there are interfaces in *The Birth of Tragedy* as well as alternating voices, one leading to euphoria, the other to Silenus' black mood. But while it may be claimed (in part, by reference to the philosopher's unpublished notes) that Nietzsche undermined his own epistemological authority while he was writing *The Birth of Tragedy,* the book as published does remain on the whole "pan-tragic" and declaratory. Nietzsche's later self-criticism of the work tends to substantiate this impression. Like Kaufmann, de Man is desirous of "saving" this early text for honorable inclusion in the Nietzsche canon, but this operation may be unnecessary. It is not mandatory to deconstruct *The Birth of Tragedy* in order to respect its vision. (p. 248)

In neither of these readings do we learn why Nietzsche should have militated so vehemently against Euripides. One answer is suggested by Nietzsche's attraction to the Dionysian rites, a subject to which he was drawn by his training as a classical philologist. *The Birth of Tragedy* reflects his fondness for the pre-Socratics as well as Hegel, Schopenhauer and Wagner, and expresses throughout—not always with irony—an admiration for Greek nature worship. Here it is important to underscore Nietzsche's assertion that a mysterious datum is perceptible through the appearance of endless conflict: an image of primordial unity. Of course, the view that reality may appear both as unity *and* conflict constitutes a paradox. In *The Birth of Tragedy* Nietzsche implies that this paradox can be understood by recourse to early Greek religion—specifically, the Dionysian mysteries with their themes of dismemberment and reunification—but not by later analytical reasoning, or "the Socratic spirit." Dionysus is a multi-faceted god, at one with nature and the perpetual cycle of his own destruction and return. The Apollonian, by contrast, is the principle by which the cycle takes individuated form, the principle by which it *appears;* but the Dionysian paradox itself remains at the very heart of things.

Nietzsche proposes that the suffering of the tragic hero, mediated by the satyr chorus, is symbolic of the Dionysian paradox, that in fact until Euripides "the only stage hero was Dionysus himself." The hero, and through him the spectator, is compelled to experience the true nature of the cosmos, which is terrible yet joyful: will, blind energy, everything in flux but at bottom indestructible. Here at the precipice of this insight man trembles; he is in danger of being petrified by the vision of primordial conflict. But the formal qualities of art (Apollonian appearance) can vouchsafe the vision, the glimpse into the abyss, and provide the spectator with the sensation of "metaphysical comfort." (pp. 248-49)

Nietzsche charges that Euripides attended to the thinker in him, not the poet. In his writing, cool, paradoxical thoughts replaced Apollonian contemplation, epic suspense and dialectic replaced the former sweep of lyric scenes, rhetorical sophistry replaced pity and fear, the *deus ex machina* replaced true "metaphysical comfort," and fiery affects replaced the Dionysian ecstasies. Euripides, Nietzsche seems to imply, suffered from what T. S. Eliot might describe as a "dissociation of sensibility.". . . Chiefly, Euripides banished the unconscious from his poetry, following Socrates, the opponent of Dionysus, whose dictum was that "to be beautiful everything must be intelligible.". . . Under the influence of this pernicious doctrine of "aesthetic Socratism" Euripides abolished myth and in its place (with a delight in "a unique, almost anatomical preparation") offered us instead a clinical refinement in the psychological representation of character. Nietzsche bemoans in this the victory of the phenomenon over the universal, observing that, "we are already in the atmosphere of a theoretical world, where scientific knowledge is valued more highly than the artistic reflection of a universal law.". . . Most importantly, perhaps, Euripides abandoned Dionysus and the intuitive symbolism of Greek religion for a moral, critical view of nature that prompted him to ask whether the Dionysian was entitled to exist at all

and whether it should not be forcibly uprooted from Hellenic soil—if only that were possible. ¦ . . . Thus is Euripides held accountable for the demise of Attic tragedy. (pp. 251-52)

Let us grant that with Euripides a striking shift in sensibility can be detected in Greek drama. Even so, whether tragedy was subverted as a result of this new attitude toward Dionysus constitutes a separate question. On this subject some have rejected Nietzsche's theory as outlandish, but in the broadest outline his position is compelling. Nietzsche grasped that the appeal of Dionysiac religion was its view of man's essential continuity with the cosmic order—in contrast to the disjunction between man and nature posed by the theoretical world view that supplanted it (a vision Nietzsche called "Alexandrian"). The implications of such a shift in philosophical perspective may well have had an impact on the fate of tragedy in Greece. If the justification of suffering in archaic times stems from man's perception of his participation in a drama of eternal repetition, subject to a cyclical pattern manifest in nature, human life, and the divine, then man is at home in the world and his poeticizing of experience naturally gives rise to ritual and the tragic vision. But if, on the other hand, the circle linking nature, gods and man is ruptured, then death is not an imitation but a penalty, and myth and ritual give way to theory and the rise of science. Looking back, the pattern seems inexorable. Man first tries to participate in nature; then to recover it; then to control it. By then we are already speaking of an absence. However, with his characteristic boldness. Nietzsche has traced this declension to Euripides. Can any credence be given to Nietzsche's claim that the decisive shift of consciousness in Western culture coincided with the practice of the dramatist? (pp. 257-58)

Ultimately, we cannot solve the puzzle of the death of tragedy, but we can speculate additionally as to Nietzsche's fascination with the Dionysian mysteries. . . . At least one biographer theorizes that for Nietzsche *The Birth of Tragedy* was a rebellion and a psychological release. The declamatory tone of the text does suggest that during the period in which he wrote it, Nietzsche's longing for a kind of pagan ecstasy was profound. This is not to say that he misconceived the nature of the rites, or that his insight differed fundamentally from the Greek, but whereas Neitzsche may have sought the strange emotion that his studies of ancient Greece discovered to him, the Greeks themselves held the experience in dread. Such, we may conclude, was the attitude of Euripides' predecessors toward the god. In *The Bacchae*, his greatest play, Euripides too entered imaginatively into the emotions of the Bacchanals, and yet at the same time maintained his distance with disapproving, rational control. On these grounds Nietzsche argued: "the deity that spoke through him was neither Dionysus nor Apollo, but an altogether newborn demon, called Socrates.". . . (pp. 259-69)

However, in the end we must remember that the voice which spoke most loudly in Euripides was not a god or critic's but a playwright's voice, contentious and irascible. When we do remember this, we are struck again by Nietzsche's motive in unleashing so much bitterness against the poet. After all, why choose to quarrel with the dead unless the present bears a threatening analogy? With this question we return to our starting point. Underneath his ire (which indeed was a rhetorical pose), Nietzsche may have felt an agonizing kinship with Euripides. At least, it seems unlikely that the parallel escaped him. Euripides the passionate doubter, the ironic tragedian, was to his models Sophocles and Aeschylus what Nietzsche was to Schopenhauer, Hegel, Kant, his mentors in philosophy. Another age was drawing to an end. For a short while Wagner could be hailed as the reborn Sophocles: out of the spirit of music, tragedy again. But a recantation would soon follow; much of the book would "smell offensively Hegelian." The quarrel, then, was partly an internal one. In this respect de Man is right when he suggests two narrators for *The Birth of Tragedy*. We are left to wonder whether Nietzsche, railing at Euripides, had caught a glimpse of something growing in himself: an enormous doubt eating with irony not only mysticism but everything in its path. (p. 260)

> *Michael Hinden, "Nietzsche's Quarrel with Euripides," in* Criticism *(reprinted by permission of the Wayne State University Press; copyright 1981, Wayne State University Press), Vol. XXIII, No. 3 (Summer, 1981), pp. 246-60.*

ADDITIONAL BIBLIOGRAPHY

Abraham, Gerald. *Nietzsche*. New York: The Macmillan Co., 1933, 144 p.
> Biography. Abraham presents a detailed account of Nietzsche's life, in particular his student days at Leipzig.

Bennett, Benjamin. "Nietzsche's Idea of Myth: *The Birth of Tragedy* from the Spirit of Eighteenth-Century Aesthetics." *PMLA* 94, No. 3 (May 1979): 420-33.
> Interpretive study. Bennett argues that Nietzsche's conception of myth, as seen in *The Birth of Tragedy*, "belongs not to the history of anthropology but rather to the history of aesthetics, as a direct development of eighteenth-century thinking on the phenomenon of artistic illusion."

Blackham, H. J. "Friedrich Nietzsche." In his *Six Existentialist Thinkers*, pp. 23-42. New York: Harper & Row, 1952.
> Comparative study. Blackham examines a number of concerns in Nietzsche's work—such as religion, morality, and individualism—and compares Nietzsche to other existentialists, in particular Kierkegaard.

Brinton, Crane. *Nietzsche*. Cambridge: Harvard University Press, 1941, 266 p.
> Biocritical study of Nietzsche as a politician and moralist. Brinton assesses the philosopher's work in light of contemporary events.

Conroy, Mark. "The Artist-Philosopher in Nietzsche's *Jenseits von Gut und Böse*." *MLN* 96, No. 3 (April 1981): 615-28.
> Interpretive study. Conroy undertakes a deconstructionist reading of *Beyond Good and Evil*, focusing on Nietzsche's theme of the artist-philosopher.

Copleston, Frederick. *Friedrich Nietzsche: Philosopher of Culture*. New York: Barnes & Noble Books, 1975, 273 p.
> Biocritical study from a Christian perspective. Copleston focuses on the ideal of the "ascending culture" as the major leitmotif which runs through all of Nietzsche's work.

de Man, Paul. "Genesis and Genealogy (Nietzsche)." In his *Allegories of Reading: Figural Language in Rousseau, Nietzsche, Rilke, and Proust*, pp. 79-102. New Haven, Conn.: Yale University Press, 1979.
> Deconstructionist examination of *The Birth of Tragedy*. De Man argues that in *The Birth of Tragedy* Nietzsche's major concern was with the relationship between music and language.

Faletti, Heidi E. "An Aesthetic Perspective of Gide and Nietzsche: The Problem of Decadence for Creative Effort." *Revue de Litterature Comparée* 52, No. 1 (January-March 1978): 39-59.*
> Comparative study of the aesthetics of Gide and Nietzsche.

Forster-Nietzsche, Elizabeth. *The Life of Friedrich Nietzsche*. 2 vols. New York: Sturgis and Walton Co., 1912-1915.

Biography by the philosopher's sister.

Foster, John Burt, Jr. *Heirs to Dionysus: A Nietzschean Current in Literary Modernism*. Princeton: Princeton University Press, 1981, 474 p.
> Comparative study. Foster discusses the influence and transformation of many of Nietzsche's ideas in such writers as Thomas Mann, D. H. Lawrence, Gide, and others.

Halévy, Daniel. *The Life of Friedrich Nietzsche*. New York: The Macmillan Co., 1911, 368 p.
> Important biography of Nietzsche, much of which is based on the biography of Elizabeth Forster-Nietzsche.

Hanna, Thomas. "Friedrich Nietzsche: The Courageous Pessimism." In his *The Lyrical Existentialists*, pp. 103-83. New York: Atheneum, 1962.
> Comparative study. Hanna summarizes the religious and moral import of Nietzsche's philosophy in relation to the philosophies of two other existentialists, Camus and Kierkegaard.

Hayman, Ronald. *Nietzsche: A Critical Life*. New York: Oxford University Press, 1980, 424 p.
> In-depth biocritical study of Nietzsche's personal and philosophical evolution. Hayman attempts to determine the motivation behind Nietzsche's work and to reveal the essential continuity beneath the discontinuities and apparent self-contradictions.

Hoy, David Couzens. "Philosophy As Rigorous Philology? Nietzsche and Poststructuralism." In *Fragments: Incompletion & Discontinuity*, edited by Lawrence D. Kritzman, pp. 171-85. New York: New York Literary Forum, 1981.
> Discussion of the different poststructuralist methods adopted by such critics as Jacques Derrida, Maurice Blanchot, and Michel Foucault in interpreting Nietzsche's work.

Hubben, William. "Friedrich Nietzsche" and "Nietzsche and Dostoevsky." In his *Four Prophets of Our Destiny: Kierkegaard, Dostoevsky, Nietzsche, Kafka*, pp. 81-116, pp. 117-26. New York: The Macmillan Co., 1952.
> Criticism and comparative study. In one chapter Hubben reconstructs the major points in Nietzsche's thought and in the other he discusses Nietzsche's similarities to Dostoevsky.

Lavrin, Janko. *Nietzsche: An Approach*. London: Methuen & Co., 1948, 146 p.
> Biocritical study. Lavrin stresses the bond between Nietzsche's personal fate "on the one hand, and the trend of his thought on the other—as far as possible against the background of the crisis typical of contemporary mankind in general."

Lea, F. A. *The Tragic Philosopher: A Study of Friedrich Nietzsche*. London: Methuen & Co., 1957, 354 p.
> Biocritical study tracing the development of Nietzsche's thought from 1865 to 1888, as demonstrated in his works, letters, and speeches.

Ludovici, Anthony M. *Nietzsche: His Life and Words*. London: Constable & Co., 1916, 100 p.
> Discusses the major aspects of Nietzsche's thought, in particular his views on morality, religion, society, and evolution.

Magnus, Bernd. *Nietzsche's Existential Imperative*. Bloomington, London: Indiana University Press, 1978, 231 p.
> Interpretive study. Magnus argues two points in his discussion of Nietzsche's philosophy: first, that the doctrine of eternal recurrence "is a visual and conceptual representation" of the ascending life; second, that this "enigmatic doctrine of eternal recurrence takes the form of an eternalistic countermyth."

The Malahat Review: Friedrich Nietzsche Issue, No. 24 (October 1972): 182 p.
> Contains articles on Nietzsche by Franz Liszt, Karl Schlechta, David S. Thatcher, and others.

Manthey-Zorn, Otto. *Dionysus: The Tragedy of Nietzsche*. Westport, Conn.: Greenwood Press, 1975, 210 p.

Biocritical study. Manthey-Zorn discusses Nietzsche's work in chronological order, focusing on the Dionysian view and its expanding role in the "analysis and synthesis of all human culture."

Mencken, Henry L. *The Philosophy of Friedrich Nietzsche.* Boston: Luce and Co., 1908, 325 p.
    Biocritical study. Mencken elucidates the major points of Nietzsche's philosophy and attempts to "show the growth of his system, from its beginning in mute consciousness to its maturity in clear and unmistakable propositions."

Morgan, George Allen. *What Nietzsche Means.* New York, London: Harper & Row, 1965, 400 p.
    Interpretive study. Morgan discusses each aspect of Nietzsche's thought in an attempt to explain his philosophy as an entity outside the influence of historical or psychological circumstances.

Shapiro, Gary. "The Rhetoric of Nietzsche's *Zarathustra.*" *Boundary 2* VIII, No. 2 (Winter 1980): 165-89.
    Stylistic study of Nietzsche's epistemology and the rhetorical devices he utilized in *Thus Spoke Zarathustra.*

Symposium: Friedrich Nietzsche Issue XXVIII, No. 1 (Spring 1974): 93 p.
    Contains articles on Nietzsche by Walter Kaufmann, Elliott Zuckerman, Paul de Man, and others.

Wolfe, Peter. "Image and Meaning in *Also sprach Zarathustra.*" *MLN* 79, No. 5 (December 1964): 546-52.
    Stylistic study. Wolfe argues that a study of the imagery in Nietzsche's *Zarathustra* offers "the most reliable approach" to an understanding of the work.

Charles (Pierre) Péguy

1873-1914

(Also wrote under pseudonyms of Marcel Baudouin, Pierre Baudouin, and Pierre Deloire) French poet, essayist, dramatist, and editor.

Péguy's religious poetry and polemical essays pertain as much, if not more, to the sphere of French Catholicism and radical politics as they do to French literature. His lifelong inspiration was Joan of Arc, and it is through his dramatizations of this saint's spiritual ordeals that Péguy best expressed his own religious crises and development. In his prose works, Péguy usually attacked the modern world, which he despised, while he expounded his fervent convictions as a socially committed Christian.

Born in Orléans to a poor provincial family, Péguy was raised by his widowed mother and grandmother. Proud of his humble origins, Péguy paid tribute to the peasantry throughout his work. Scholarships allowed him to receive an advanced education at the École Normale Supérieure in Paris. There he was greatly influenced by the lectures of Henri Bergson, and he became one of Bergson's most celebrated disciples. In 1897 Péguy privately published his first drama, the trilogy *Jeanne d'Arc*. Though it received little attention, the drama is important as an early statement of Péguy's strong antipathy to human suffering, as well as an illustration of his deep aversion to the Catholic doctrine of eternal damnation. Although focusing on religious themes, *Jeanne d'Arc* was dedicated to the establishment of "the universal socialist republic," for by this time Péguy had become an ardent socialist disillusioned with the social and political policies of the Church. Among his early writings, Péguy also published several socialist essays, including "Marcel, premier dialogue de la cité harmonieuse," an extensive description of a socialist utopia.

Of major importance in Péguy's life was the controversial Dreyfus Affair. It not only inspired him to actively crusade against the injustice suffered by the Jewish captain falsely accused of treason, but also represented a prime example of what Péguy considered the *"mystique"* of social, political, and religious ideals degenerating into the *"politique"* of political opportunism. The essence of Péguy's life and works is often viewed as an attempt to preserve this *mystique*, or purity of ideals, while opposing the *politique*, or corruption of ideals. Péguy's proposal that "*mystique* ends with *politique*" was best explained ten years after the Dreyfus case in his well-known essay "Notre jeunesse," an examination of his generation's involvement in the Affair. During the period of political dissidence occasioned by the Dreyfus Affair, Péguy broke with the Socialist party over their refusal to publish his uncensored works and expressed disappointment with the party's reluctance to wholeheartedly support Dreyfus. The break resulted in the formation of his *Les cahiers de la quinzaine*, a publication which presented the uncensored philosophical and political thought of a diversity of French writers.

Péguy's works in his "journal of truth," as he called the *Cahiers*, mirrored his ideological views as they shifted between socialism and nationalism, and between atheism and Catholicism. Péguy's polemical essays published in the *Cahiers* were

usually protests against the bourgeois values of the modern world, often bitterly attacking the government, officials of the Catholic Church, the academic community, and the Socialist party. However, one of his most acclaimed essays, "Notre patrie," is a patriotic appreciation of the culture and heritage of France.

In 1908 Péguy returned to the Catholic faith of his youth. Though he remained outside the sacraments of the Church because of his secular marriage, his spiritual reconciliation with Catholic doctrine provided a new source of literary inspiration. Thus, thirteen years after he wrote the dramatic *Jeanne d'Arc*, Péguy returned to and expanded the story of Joan in a religious dramatic poem, *Le mystère de la charité de Jeanne d'Arc (The Mystery of the Charity of Joan of Arc)*. In the earlier "Joan" play, Péguy questioned God's role in a world of suffering, whereas in the later work he expressed faith in God to overcome universal evil and spiritual damnation. His other two dramatic poems, *Le porche du mystère de la deuxieme vertu (The Portico of the Mystery of the Second Virtue)* and *Le mystère des saints innocents (The Mystery of the Holy Innocents)*, celebrate hope, over faith and charity, as the greatest of the three virtues.

In *The Portico of the Mystery of the Second Virtue*, Péguy embraces the innocence of childhood as the solution to his quandary over the nature of spiritual salvation. For Péguy, children symbolize hope for the future because "children are not yet defeated by life." This theme is restated in *The Mystery of the Holy Innocents*, where he again finds hope for potential rebirth in future generations. Both mysteries utilize Biblical parables to reinforce their theme. Another religious work, *La tapisserie de Notre Dame*, is for the most part a record of the poet's spiritual experiences on a pilgrimage to Chartres. Péguy compared one of his last poetic works, *Les tapisseries Ève*, to Dante's *Divine Comedy*. Similar in proportion and style to an epic, it is comprised of almost ten thousand alexandrines and recounts the history of the world from the first woman to the Incarnation of Jesus. "Note sur M. Bergson et la philosophie bergsonienne," Péguy's last essay before his death in World War I, is a defense and appraisal of Bergson's philosophy of time and reality. Péguy was particularly attuned to his former teacher's metaphysics, which attempts to account for a creative pulse in all living organisms, and to his belief that intuition is the only means of knowing the "ultimate reality."

Most critics find that Péguy's literary works exist outside the mainstream of modern French literature. Although many critics praise Péguy's poetic use of simple, conversational language, his style is often criticized for its tedious repetitions. Others contend that the reiteration of certain words and phrases enables the reader to extract all possible nuances of meaning in a tightly controlled style. In the past thirty years, criticism has focused on Péguy's religious works. Maxwell Adereth echoes the critical consensus when he explains that Péguy's relevance to today's world rests on an approach to life "dominated by the acute understanding that there is no future for man if he dissociates the spiritual from the temporal, the eternal from the topical."

(See also *Contemporary Authors*, Vol. 107.)

PRINCIPAL WORKS

Jeanne d'Arc [as Marcel and Pierre Baudouin] [first publication] (drama) 1897
*Marcel, premier dialogue de la cité harmonieuse [as Pierre Baudouin] (essay) 1898
*De Jean Coste (essay) 1902
*Notre patrie (essay) 1905
*Situations (essays) 1906-07
*Le mystère de la charité de Jeanne d'Arc (poetry) 1910
  [*The Mystery of the Charity of Joan of Arc*, 1950]
*Notre jeunesse (essay) 1910
*Le porche du mystère de la deuxieme vertu (poetry) 1911
  [*The Portico of the Mystery of the Second Virtue*, 1970]
*Clio II (essay) 1912
*Le mystère des saints innocents (poetry) 1912
  [*The Mystery of the Holy Innocents*, 1956]
*La tapisserie de sainte Geneviève et Jeanne d'Arc (poetry) 1912
*La tapisserie de Notre Dame (poetry) 1913
*Les tapisseries Ève (poetry) 1913
*Note sur M. Bergson et la philosophie bergsonienne (essay) 1914
Oeuvres complètes. 20 vols. (poetry, essays, and dramas) 1917-55
Basic Verities (essays and poetry) 1943
Men and Saints (essays and poetry) 1944
God Speaks (poetry) 1945
**Clio I (essay) 1952

Temporal and Eternal (essays) 1958

*These works were published in the journal *Les cahiers de la quinzaine.*

**This work was written in 1909.

ANDRÉ GIDE (essay date 1910)

[*Gide was one of the few contemporary critics of Péguy to seriously review his* Le mystère de la charité de Jeanne d'Arc. *In the following excerpt, he praises Péguy's reiterative style and use of language.*]

Péguy's style is like that of very ancient litanies. It is like Arab chants, like the monotonous chants of heath and moor; it is comparable to the desert; a desert of esparto, a desert of sand, a desert of stone. . . . Péguy's style is like the pebbles of the desert which follow and resemble each other so closely, one so much like the other, but yet a tiny bit different; and with a difference which corrects itself, recovers possession of itself, repeats itself, seems to repeat itself, stresses itself, and always more clearly; and one goes ahead. What do I need with more variety! with these loquacious lands which, in the space of a single look and without my needing to turn my head, offer my attention more things than my life can hearken to. I no longer wish to love anything but deserts and gardens; very well-kept gardens and monotonous deserts where the same flower, or one that is almost similar, will repeat almost the same perfume for miles; and the same pebble, the same color and yet each time a tiny bit different; as the Arab flute pipes the same phrase, almost the same, during almost a whole concert; as the believer prays the same prayer during the whole space of orison, or at least, almost the same prayer, with only a trifling difference in the intonation, almost without his being aware of it and almost in spite of himself, beginning all over again. Words! I will not leave you, same words, and I will not hold you quit so long as you still have something to say. 'We will not let Thee go, Lord, except Thou bless us.' (p. 8)

> *André Gide, in his excerpt from "Appreciations" (originally published in its entirety in* Nouvelle revue française, *March, 1910), in* Basic Verities: Prose and Poetry *by Charles Péguy, translated by Ann Green and Julian Green (translation copyright 1943 by Pantheon Books Inc.; reprinted by permission of Pantheon Books, a Division of Random House, Inc.), Pantheon Books, 1943, pp. 7-12.*

CHARLES PÉGUY (essay date 1910)

[*The following is excerpted from an abridged translation of Péguy's defense of the Dreyfusards,* Notre Jeunesse, *which was first published in* Les cahiers de la quinzaine *in 1910. This essay was a response to Daniel Halévy, whose* Apology for Our Past, *also published in the* Cahiers, *took a critical view of those who supported Dreyfus. Later, Halévy detailed the background to this conflict of ideologies in* Péguy and "Les cahiers de la quinzaine" *(see additional bibliography).*]

Halévy is inclined to think, and I should be ready to agree with him, that the Republic was founded, preserved and saved and is still sustained by a small number of loyal families. Do they still preserve it in the same way? As they did for a century or more, in a sense almost since the second half of the eighteenth century? I am ready to agree with him, that a small number of families, of dynastic, hereditary loyalties, preserved the tradition, the *mystique* and what Halévy very rightly calls *"republican conservation"*. But where I should not, perhaps, follow him, is that I think that we are literally the last representatives, and, unless our children take on the task, almost the last, posthumous survivals.

In any case, the last *witnesses.*

I mean precisely this: we do not yet know whether our children will reunite the threads of tradition, of the republican *mystique.* It has become completely foreign to the intermediary generation—and that makes twenty years. . . .

We are extremely badly placed. Chronologically. In the succession of generations. We are the rearguard, in very poor touch, out of touch with the main body, the generations of the past. We are the last generation with a republican *mystique.* And our Dreyfus Affair will have been the last operation of the republican *mystique.* (p. 22)

The *de-republicanisation* of France is essentially the same movement as the *de-christianisation* of France. Both together are one and the same movement, a profound *de-mystification.* It is one and the same movement which makes people no longer believe in the Republic and no longer believe in God, no longer want to lead a republican life, and no longer want to lead a Christian life, they have had enough of it, and one might almost say that they no longer believe in idols, and that they no longer want to believe in idols, and that they no longer want to believe in the true God. (p. 23)

We therefore turn towards the young, we turn to another side, and we can only say: "Take care. You treat us as old fogies. That's quite all right. But take care. When you talk airily, when you treat the Republic lightly, you do not only risk being unjust (which is not perhaps very important, at least so you say, in your system, but risk what in your system *is* serious), you risk something much worse, you risk being stupid. You forget, you fail to recognise that there is a republican *mystique.* . . . (p. 29)

"Everything begins as a *mystique* and ends as a *politique.* Everything begins with *la mystique,* in mysticism, with its own *mystique,* and everything ends in politics, in *la politique,* in a policy. The important point is not that such and such a *politique* should triumph over another such, and that one should succeed. The whole point (what matters), the essential thing, is that *in each order, in each system,* THE MYSTIQUE SHOULD NOT BE DEVOURED BY THE POLITIQUE TO WHICH IT GAVE BIRTH." (p. 31)

And so we have in the Dreyfus Affair a unique example, a model almost, of what is meant by the degradation of a human action; but not only that, a précis of the degradation of a *mystique* into a *politique.*

There was a singular virtue in the Affair, perhaps an eternal virtue. I mean a singular power. And we can see this clearly to-day now that it is all over. It was not an illusion of our youth. First of all, it should be noted that it possessed a very singular virtue. In two senses. A singular power of virtue, as long as it remained a *mystique.* A singular power of malice as soon as it entered the field of politics. . . . (p. 43)

[The] Dreyfus Affair is one of the "chosen" events of history. It was a crisis in three histories, each of them outstanding. It was a crisis in the history of Israel. A crisis, obviously, in the

history of France. And above all, it was a supreme crisis, as appears more and more distinctly, in the history of Christianity. And perhaps in several others. And thus, by a unique election, it was a triple crisis. Of triple eminence. A culmination. (p. 44)

As for me, if I finish an infinitely more serious work and reach the age of *confessions,* which as everyone knows is at fifty years old and at nine o'clock in the morning, that is what I should most certainly propose to describe. Taking up again and concluding my old study of "the decomposition of Dreyfusism in France", I should try to give, not so much an idea, as a picture of that immortal Affair and of what it was like in reality. It was like all self-respecting affairs, essentially mystical. It lived by its *mystique.* It died of its *politique.* Such is the rule; such is the law. Such is the level of life. All parties live by their *mystique* and die by their *politique.* That is what I should try to depict. I admit I am beginning to think that it would not be entirely useless. I suspect that there are any number of misunderstandings about the Affair. And I must confess that I cannot recognise myself at all in the *portrait* Halévy traced of the Dreyfusist in these very pages [in *Apology for Our Past*]. I don't in the least feel like a whipped cur. I will agree to being victor; and I will agree (and this is my opinion) to having been vanquished (it all depends upon one's point of view). I don't admit for a moment to having been beaten. I admit to having been ruined (in the temporal, and greatly endangered in the eternal, order); I agree to having been deceived, and to having been fooled. I do not admit I was a wash-out. I don't in the least feel like a drowned rat. I do not recognise myself in that portrait. We were on the contrary proud, carrying our heads high, filled to overflowing with *military* virtue. We had, and we preserved, a very different tone, another air; we carried our heads differently, and we spoke, openly and of very different things. My mood is not at all penitential. I loathe a penitence which is not Christian, a sort of civic, lay penitence, a penitence laicised, secularised, temporalised, an imitation, a counterfeit, of penitence—a "disaffected" penitence. I loathe the humiliation, the humility that is not Christian, humility but a sort of civil, civic humility, a mock humility. In civil and civic matters, in the lay or profane sphere, I prefer to be stiff with pride. And so we were. With every right. We not only had nothing to regret. There was nothing, we had done nothing that we could not pride ourselves upon. (pp. 44-5)

There is no doubt whatsoever, as far as we are concerned, the Dreyfusist *mystique* was not only a particular instance of the Christian *mystique,* but an outstanding example, an acceleration, a crisis, a temporal crisis, a sort of transition, which I should describe as necessary. Why deny it, now that we are twelve or fifteen years distant from our youth, and that we at last see clear in our hearts? Our Dreyfusism was a religion; I use the word in the most exact and literal sense, a religious impulse, a religious crisis, and I should even advise anyone who wanted to consider, study and know a religious movement in modern times, to take that unique example, so clearly defined, so full of character. I would add that for us, that religious movement was essentially Christian, Christian in origin, growing from a Christian stem, deriving from an ancient source. (p. 50)

One might even say that the Dreyfus Affair was a *perfect example* of a religious movement, of the beginning or origin of a religion, a rare case and perhaps a unique one.

In fact, the Dreyfusist *mystique* was, for us, essentially a crisis in the French *mystique.* For us, and through us, the Affair was very definitely in the direct French line. Just as for us and through us, it was in the Christian line. We ourselves were situated very exactly in the French line, just as we had been in the Christian line. We were in it in our character as Frenchmen, just as we were in it in our character as Christians. (pp. 51-2)

Not only were we heroes, but the Dreyfus Affair can only be explained by the need for heroism which periodically seizes this people, this race, by that need for heroism which then seizes a whole generation of us. (p. 78)

We were great. We were very great. (p. 79)

In reality the true position of those opposed to us was not of saying or thinking Dreyfus guilty, but of thinking and saying that whether he was innocent or guilty, one did not disturb, overthrow, or compromise, that one did not risk, for one man's sake, the life and salvation of a whole people. Meaning of course: the *temporal* salvation, *salut temporel.* Now our Christian *mystique* was merged so perfectly, so exactly with our patriotic *mystique,* that what must be recognised, and what I shall say, what I shall put into my confessions, is that *the point of view we adopted was none other than The Eternal Salvation of France.* What, in fact, did we say? Everything was against us, wisdom and law, human wisdom that is, and human law. What we did was in the order of madness and the order of sanctity, which have so many things in common, so many secret understandings, with human wisdom and the human eye. We went against wisdom, against the law. (pp. 80-1)

What does all this mean, unless one doesn't know a word of French, except that our adversaries were speaking the language of the *raison d'état,* which is not only the language of political and parliamentary reason, of contemptible political and parliamentary interests, but the very respectable language of continuity, of the temporal continuity of the race, *of the temporal salvation of the people and the race?* They aimed at nothing less. And we, by a profoundly Christian movement, a profoundly revolutionary and traditionally Christian impulse and effort, following one of the deepest Christian traditions, one of the most vital and central, and in line with the axis of Christianity, at its very heart, we aimed at no less than raising ourselves, I do not say to the conception, but to the passion, to the care of the eternal salvation, *le salut éternel,* of this people; we achieved an existence full of care and preoccupation, full of mortal anguish and anxiety for the eternal salvation of our race. Deep down within us, we were the men of eternal salvation, and our adversaries were the men of temporal salvation. That was the real division in the Dreyfus Affair. Deep down within us we were determined that France should not fall into a state of mortal sin. Christian doctrine, alone in the whole world, in the modern world, in any world, deliberately counts death at nought, at zero, in terms of the price of eternal death, and the risk of temporal death as nothing compared with the price of sin, mortal sin, eternal death. (p. 82)

> *Charles Peguy, in his* Notre jeunesse *(copyright © 1932 and 1933 Librarie Gallimard; reprinted by permission of Editions Gallimard; in Canada by William Collins Sons & Co Ltd), third edition, Gallimard, 1933 (translated by Alexander Dru and reprinted in an adapted form as "Memories of Youth," in* Temporal and Eternal *by Charles Peguy, Harvill Press, 1958, pp. 16-87).*

ROBERT VALLERY-RADOT (essay date 1914)

In Charles Péguy's books we get the same Catholic vision [as Frances Jammes's *Géorgique Chrétiennes*], still infinite love,

the God of the Catechism loved in the heart of each man, felt and tasted in every one of His creatures. Of small importance are all the objections which may be raised in detail about the misuse of repetitions, a rather artificial and, indeed, puerile practice which the author could justify in many places. Those brusque repetitions, that obstinate, awkward insistence, that greedy dwelling upon words, all contribute to impart an impression of homespun roughness to the charm of which, I must admit, I am not insensible. But let us pass over these questions of literary taste and stick to the intimate strength of the work, its singular power in a sceptical and emasculated age, a power that seems to spring straight from the Middle Ages—from the soul of some Villon inspired with a Dantesque vision to reveal to us the invisible worlds in the simple, everyday language of a child playing hop-scotch, or a servant-girl sweeping out her kitchen, or a shepherdess spinning, the lowly language of old time cottages where the pot steamed, where duty was always apparent, tangible, imperious, in the mean, repellent, monotonous, truly heroic task. (p. 399)

It seems to me that we shall have to thank Claudel, Jammes and Péguy for curing our sensibilities of their feverish disorder, for they alone, reawakening our innermost energies, the most secret recess of our being, our very substance engendered by God, and by thus binding together again the great Catholic tradition of the Middle Ages, have known how to give back to us something beyond all the pantheistic efflorescence—the reality of Being and of that providential order which is traced here below and realized beyond this life in the integrity of all substance. (p. 400)

> *Robert Vallery-Radot, "The Renascence of Catholic Lyricism," in* The Constructive Quarterly *(copyright, 1914, by George H. Doran Company), Vol. 2, March-December, 1914, pp. 384-402.**

MARY DUCLAUX (essay date 1919)

Péguy is a great prose writer, a wonderful wielder of image and trope, a master juggler with all the intricacies of French syntax. And the nation which produced Agrippa d'Aubigné, Pascal, Voltaire, has always loved the prose of a brisk polemic. The prose works of Péguy are due to polemics. And he lays into his enemy with a dexterity, a surety, a variety of attack unrivalled—here a shower of swift and sudden blows, there a slow and paralysing envelopment of the adversary. Péguy is an incomparable wrestler.

For the rest, shall we say that Péguy was the Walt Whitman of France? Shall we translate him into English under the name of Carlyle—or even W. E. Henley? There was something of all of them in the irascible, quizzical, and lovable idealist whose life was one long struggle against conventional standards and a conventional style; against middle-class prosperity, modern commodities (generally 'tout le confort moderne'); against the preferences of a well-to-do democracy; against also, and no less, Parliamentary ideals; documentary historical methods and culture; and, compendiously and inclusively, all that is political as opposed to mystical, all that is temporal as opposed to spiritual, all that is matter as opposed to soul, all that is personal as opposed to general, and, one may add by extension, all that is rich as opposed to all that is honourably, contentedly, and modestly poor. (pp. 140-41)

The interminable poem of *Eve* (as long—but not as beautiful! as the *Iliad* and the *Odyssey* united) fulminates against the Intellectuals of France in an outburst of rhetoric which too often degenerates into mere violence. Péguy is more really poetic in his prose. The description of rural life on the banks of the Loire, in *Victor-Marie, Comte Hugo;* the death of Bernard Lazare in *Notre Jeunesse;* above all, the long but the inspired elevations and prayers of Jeannette—especially the conversation with her little fourteen-year-old friend Hanorette (which we keep in our remembrance along with the dialogue of Antigone and Ismene, and with the scene in the Gospel of Martha and Mary, as a perfect characterisation of the two great types of Charity and Piety)—are to our thinking far more interpretative of Péguy's true genius than the mighty jog-trot of his later muse. Still there is a power and an eloquence in that. So far as the meaning goes, all his voluminous outpourings have the same. There is but one thing needful, and that is to be a hero or a saint. Preferably, perhaps, a hero! (pp. 147-48)

> Mary Duclaux, "Charles Péguy," in her Twentieth Century French Writers (Reviews and Reminiscences) *(copyright 1919; reprinted by permission of William Collins Sons & Co. Ltd.),* Collins, 1919, pp. 135-54.

WILLIAM A. DRAKE   (essay date 1928)

It is difficult, in estimating the contribution of Charles Péguy to French literature and to the French spirit, to escape the temptation to overemphasis which has caused most of his contemporaries to invest this lovable and significant figure with the same sort of monumental halo which adorns the metaphorical brow of his compatriot of Orléans, Jeanne d'Arc. It is equally difficult to avoid making anew the perfectly obvious critical discovery that neither the extent nor the quality of Péguy's published writings in any way justifies the ample proportions of his reputation.

The case of Péguy is, precisely, neither purely literary nor purely political. It is the problem of a situation of the spirit, and, in view of Péguy's instinctively social attitude, it appears as an individual problem with a broad national application. For Péguy, perhaps more completely than any other man, typifies the transitional generation with which he reached maturity—the generation of national rediscovery, of Tolstoyan idealism, of Dreyfusian liberalism, and of the Neo-Catholic revival. A modest and impoverished bookseller, the son of a good old woman who mended the rush chairs of the Cathedral of Orléans for her scanty livelihood, he became the center of an important group and, for a time, its immediate means of expression. A writer of eccentric and ambiguous talent, filled with lofty but queerly twisted ideas which poured forth in his prose and verse in an unruly torrent of impossible and unheard-of constructions, yet shot through with facets of pure genius, his pronunciamentos lent a constant direction to this whole activity. His late return to Catholicism, the singular manner of his conformity, and finally, his death in action as a "champion of peace," on the Marne, on the 5th of September 1914, complete the cycle of forces which has fixed Charles Péguy in the popular mind as a symbolical archetype and a national saint.

This mantle of greatness was not of Péguy's weaving, nor of the Norns'. It came to him as the shroud prepared, in part, by patriotic hysteria for the French Rupert Brooke, and in part, by the tenderness of the hero's friends for their adored leader. It was an unsubstantial greatness, which Péguy did not ask of life, which he did not deserve, and which has already faded. (pp. 252-53)

Péguy's energies, his genius, his life, were poured unstintingly into his *Cahiers.* In the various numbers, we find his own commentary-at-large on the political life of France and that of such men as Hubert Lagardelle, Georges Sorel, Jean Jaurès, and Georges Clemenceau. We find the first verses of René Salomé and poems by François Porché; the providential first publication of Romain Rolland's *Jean-Christophe* and the early work of the brothers Tharaud, and contributions by Anatole France, Pierre Quillard, Daniel Halévy, Joseph Bédier, Pierre Mille, Pierre Hamp, André Spire, Julien Benda, Edmond Fleg, and many others, then little known or quite obscure, whom time has brought into their own. The catalogue of *Les Cahiers de la Quinzaine,* considering the poverty of the enterprise and the comparative obscurity of the editor, is one of the most amazing records in the history of modern journalism.

There is so much that is utterly worthless in Péguy's voluminous writings, that it requires a considerable hardihood to penetrate the dreary deserts of his eccentric prose and his tortured philosophical verse in search of the occasional oases of clairvoyant thought and expression which they contain. Yet, in the repetitious circumlocutions of *Notre Jeunesse, Victor Marie Comte Hugo, L'Argent, Note sur Monsieur Bergson,* and the posthumous *Clio,* an altogether exceptional prose style is disclosed, which follows the very germination of the thought which it contains. "I am not at all the intellectual who descends and condescends to the people," he writes; "I am the people." And in the verbose mazes of the verse which Péguy wrote during the last four years of his life, notably **"Eve," "La Mystère de la Charité," "Tapisserie de Sainte Geneviève,"** and **"Prière pour Nous Autres Charnels,"** there are passages of essential poetry. For Péguy, albeit he possessed the faculty of being more exhausting than any other writer of his time, concealed beneath his eccentricity a flame of the purest inspiration.

Despite the profound disorder, the extravagance, and the spasmodic and violent character of his political thought, Péguy was truly great in his moral uprightness. For politics, he had nothing but distaste; and the uncontaminated fairness of his viewpoint, his untemporizing honesty, and his candor, caused him to withdraw from the Socialist party at the moment when he detected Jaurès, his one-time idol and friend, in an act of compromise. His whole political attitude is summed up in one of his remarks on the Dreyfus appeal: "A single illegality, a single crime, if it be universally, legally, nationally, conveniently accepted, is sufficient to dishonor an entire nation. It is the fleck of gangrene which corrupts the entire body." A philosophical anarchist, his ideals for the State were impossibly high, and he fought for them valiantly, if impractically. He possessed an exceptional gift for controversy, and kept it in constant employment. "Grumble, and keep on marching," was his motto; and he did both, to the day of his death.

Yet Péguy was hardly a constructive idealist, for he was incapable of systematic thought or action: and if he had produced a system, he would himself have been the first to depart from it: for Péguy was, above all, an instinctive nonconformist. . . . He suited no fixed scheme, created none, and pursued his erratic path alone, uttering testy oracles and living up to each only until he had uttered another. He seems to have created little and to have written almost nothing which can be read without anguish. In some aspects, he appears as one of the most brilliant and predestined failures in modern France.

How, then, is one to account for Péguy's extraordinary, although already diminishing, reputation? By a bullet in the brain at the Battle of the Marne, so far as the general public is concerned. But, much as popular emotionalism has added to the luster of Péguy's name, the only substantial explanation of the veneration with which his memory is regarded by those who keep it green, is to be found in the hearts of the few but excellent men who came directly within the influence of his astounding personality. Superficially, Péguy is important as a Bergsonian political idealist, as one of the active forerunners of the recent French renaissance, and as a great editor. But others were all of this, and more so, and much more besides. Péguy's greatness was not a greatness of thought, of action, of expression, of any material accomplishment. It resided in some compelling but inexplicable spiritual energy which emanated from the depth and sincerity of his convictions and, communicating itself to those around him, inspired them to a type of action and expression which Péguy himself could never have achieved. It was this quality which gave Charles Péguy the complete devotion, almost the adoration, of men whose apparent talents are so conspicuously superior to his own. He lived as the sort of free influence which stirs men to great deeds without confining them by marking a path; and it is as such that he is gratefully remembered by those whom he helped, without himself surmising the true magnitude of his service. (pp. 256-59)

> *William A. Drake, "Charles Péguy," in his* Contemporary European Writers *(copyright, 1927, by William A. Drake), The John Day Company, 1928, pp. 252-59.*

DANIEL SARGENT   (essay date 1935)

[Some of Péguy's critics] explain that he was simply a provincial Frenchman living out of place in Paris. Others say he was a man of the fifteenth century born out of time in the nineteenth, who could not keep pace with his times. Still others say that he was a peasant associating with city-dwellers with whom he could not possibly get along. Finally there are those, more hostile, who intimate that he was out of step because he had established a sect which nobody else could join, for its one worshipper was Péguy, and its object of worship was also Péguy. These satirists called the sect "Péguyisme," and its one member, that is Charles Péguy, a "Péguyiste." . . . (p. 4)

[Péguy was] so proud of his own intellect that he fell in love with his own theories, and fancied himself for what he was not: a great philosopher. Péguy did not set his philosophy higher than his faith, but he did look on it as the best apologetic for the Christian faith that man had discovered and he was not going to throw it away. God needed it. God needed him. If the Church was not aware of it, it was because the Church had not yet turned enough attention to it. Péguy became very near to being a 'Péguyiste.'

There was only one domain in which Péguy never for an instant strutted as a Péguyiste. That was in poetry. In poetry he was humble. It is curious how the discipline of writing poetry cures a man of his pride as a private philosopher. There have, and will be, philosophical poets, but I am not the first to point out that when a poet not only invents his metaphors and images, but also his system of philosophy, his poetry becomes poor poetry. A poet has to take his philosophy as something accepted, not as something he is racking his logical faculties to defend. Péguy stepped away from the side of Bergson when he wrote his poetry. (p. 40)

The three years 1911, 1912, 1913, were those in which Péguy wrote his great series of marching chants, all of them with their prosaic, unsentimental names: *Le Mystère de la Charité de Jeanne d'Arc, Le Porche du Mystère de la Deuxième Vertu, Le Mystère des Saints Innocents, La Tapisserie de Sainte Geneviève et de Jeanne d'Arc, La Tapisserie de Notre Dame,* and finally the interminable *Ève.* The mere writing of these verses on paper must have been a prodigious effort; they covered twelve hundred pages. But they also represented intense meditation, for they were not the mere account of outward wants, which can always be found in unending quantity: they were the loving cogitations of his heart concerning the truths of the catechism which he had learned as a child. Such cogitations bore evidence of long interior concentration. When we remember that these three years were also busy with controversy, and interrupted by a crying need for money, we can readily believe that they were written, as Péguy said, in that utter abandonment induced by fatigue, which, he added, was what he needed to make him write.

One thing did make this task less impossible than it might have been: Pèguy never corrected. What he had written he had written. There was probably no other way in which his impetuosity could write. When he thought second thoughts he became a 'Pèguyiste,' not a Péguy, and ceased to be a poet. If he had corrected his poems he would have spoiled them. But also he found this manner of writing defended by his Bergsonian philosophy. What had leaped up in him as from a fountain was sacred. It was spontaneous, young, hopeful, living.

To be sure, he was not the stupid man who has found what he has written adequate. Quite the contrary. He found no single phrase satisfactory. Therefore in the next line he said it differently. His attitude was this: the truth is inexpressible, but it can be indicated, and indicated only by trying to say it a thousand ways. It was as if he said to his readers, "I am shooting at a bull's-eye. No shot has hit it, but if you look in the centre of the scattering shots you will know where the bull's-eye is." Stanza repeats stanza. More than that, poem repeats poem. With slight exaggeration it was charged that he had but one subject, Jeanne d'Arc. He acknowledged the truth of the charge. How many "Jeanne d'Arcs" was he going to write? Twenty-four was his answer.

Fortunately the repetitions were not absolutely repetitions. There is a progress to the stanzas, and a progress to the poems, an unfolding. Péguy began by meditating on charity, then on hope. Two of his long poems are about hope, hope that is youthfulness: *Le Porche du Mystère de la Deuxième Vertu,* and *Le Mystère des Saints Innocents.* Then he meditated on how and when God summoned his saints to sanctity, on God's power to call men to Him. He presented the whole world to God. Finally he meditated on the wonderful relation between this world and Heaven, and on the intertwining of nature and grace, all of which God Himself made a picture of in his Christmas infancy: Omnipotence turned a child, lying before the sagacious solemnity of his rustic courtiers, the ox and the ass.

There was a change too in the rhythms his verses marched to. Péguy had begun to write his poems in versicles of varying length, somewhat like the psalms, Biblical—a style which he came very near to in his prose, even in his controversial prose. Before he was half through, his words began to fall into measured quatrains, which sometimes he rhymed alternately, sometimes otherwise. The constant repetition of certain phrases, the re-echoing of certain thoughts gave a unity to the endless digressive stanzas, but the lines themselves were also closely knit together by the rhyme. He used rhyme well, to give a manly trimness to his poetry and to bring out the sense by surprise. (pp. 41-4)

But although there is a slight variation in style and a slight variation in subject, all these poems of Péguy are but one poem. There is but one pattern of things which Péguy tries to celebrate, and the pattern does not change. Each separate poem is but a fragment of one poem, which is entirely theological in subject, though not inspired by the latest learned book on theology, nor by the careful and calm discriminations of St. Thomas Aquinas, but simply by Péguy's Catholic instructions as a child, through reciting his catechism, joining in the litanies, and listening to the heroic stories of his grandmother. (p. 45)

> *Daniel Sargent, "Charles Péguy," in his* Four Independents *(copyright 1935 by Sheed & Ward Inc.; copyright 1962 Daniel Sargent; reprinted with permission from Andrews and McMeel, Inc.),* Sheed and Ward, Inc. 1935 *(and reprinted by Books for Libraries Press, 1968; distributed by Arno Press, Inc.), pp. 3-71.*

JULIAN GREEN (essay date 1944)

[Green and his sister, Anne Green, have provided the majority of English translations for Péguy's poetry and prose.]

It is not easy to state in a few sentences what Charles Péguy's poetry consists of or, indeed, why it is poetry. Its language is made up of every day words, words which might sometimes appear almost worn out for having been used so often; yet those are the words which Péguy seems to prefer to all others, those he handles with greatest care, one might almost say: with piety, as if age and hard work had made them more venerable than the rarer words used by the educated. In Péguy's mind, a word is all the more beautiful if it is used by his charwoman, or by the 'bus conductor, or by the man who sweeps the streets of Paris with a large broom that makes a noise like a storm as it drives the dead leaves into the gutter. Péguy himself talks like those people, and he makes God the Father talk like them too. Neither is his thought lowered by such a process. What happens is that the simple language he uses is incredibly exalted and takes on a majesty which can only remind one of the Scriptures.

Such is the medium he uses: plain language so plain that in some unaccountable way it puts so-called literary styles to shame. With these every day words, what kind of poetry does he write? To begin with, his poetry, on the printed page, looks like poetry, blank verse, modern in its irregularity. But if we read it aloud, it will seem to us that it is really prose cut up into lines of different lengths and that if these lines were to be put together again, we should have excellent prose. However, if we read it again and listen to the sound of it, and stop ever so little at the end of each line, we will catch a rhythm, not exactly the rhythm of speech, but what might be termed the rhythm of thought. And there, I believe, lies the essence of Péguy's poetry.

When his characters are allowed to speak, they make the most of their opportunity. Their conversation is an exchange of monologues. They go into a monologue as one goes into a trance and whatever remains outside of their monologue ceases to exist. Nor do they ever speak as if they expected an interruption or wished to argue their point. They are constantly making a profession of faith, and just as some people think aloud, they believe aloud. Their real audience is the sun and the moon and the stars, earth, man in general and finally the person with

whom they may happen to be at the time. However there is nothing vague about these monologues; they are not the ravings of a dreamer; on the contrary, they come from as logical a brain as France ever produced.

Here we have another element in Péguy's poetry, an element which might be called the beauty of his reasoning. Péguy's reasoning goes from the particular to the general with a magnificent sweep which carries one along as only logic can do when it is enlivened by imagination. Its scope is apparently boundless. Like a true poet, Péguy instinctively, and logically, sees "a world in a grain of sand," but—and here your true 'Normalien' comes out—he is ever ready to patiently trace all the steps from the grain of sand to its cosmic fulfilment, and he enjoys the trip immensely. No poet ever had a keener sense of the poetry of logic. This passionate love of reasoning, which he shares with his race, is probably one of the strongest intellectual links between France and ancient Greece, which France so often resembles, and we can well imagine the pleasure a platonic philosopher would have found in listening to God the Father's monologue on leprosy and mortal sin, surely as serious a monologue as was ever spoken, yet spoken with occasional smiles and sallies and, in one place at least, with an unmistakable wink.

Another characteristic of Péguy's logic is its beautiful emotional quality. It is strong but not unbending, and it has a way of suddenly moving us almost to tears. The heart has its reasons of which reason knows nothing, wrote Pascal, and in Péguy it is not only the head but the heart that reasons, a hard head and a big, generous, human heart. When the French peasant who is hewing wood in the forest stops to think of the time when he will no longer be among the living, he thoroughly examines the question and by slow degrees comes to the conclusion that his own existence is bound to the very existence of France, that he as an individual is merged into the greater individuality of his country, and that although he may cease to exist, France must and will go on. This he sees as a peasant can see it, a French peasant of the XVth century, as Joan of Arc's father might have seen it, but he sees it in such a way that, in 1944, we are more than ever struck by the inevitability of such a reasoning, we are listening to France herself telling us that she will not die, but live.

Turning to the contents of those mammoth poems which Péguy called **Mysteries,** it seems to me that of all the characters involved, God the Father is the most real if, for want of a better term, the word character can be applied to the first person of the Trinity. He is more real than Joan of Arc, because in a way he is more Joan of Arc than she could ever be herself, that is, all the qualities that are in her, he has to a supereminent degree. We sometimes smile when we listen to him, but we are awed. He is never pompous, he never has to remember to be majestic, being majesty itself. He makes us feel like children and somehow he makes us feel a little better, a little more hopeful. He has a way of making clear what seemed irreparably involved in our spiritual life and with one word unties many knots. At the same time he lowers us somewhat in our self-esteem, he makes us a little ashamed, he makes us look a little foolish in our own eyes, but he does so in such a way that we are happier in consequence; he is eminently "le bon Dieu," the good Lord.

When God the Father enlarges on the subject of his universe, in the Mystery of the Second Virtue and in the Mystery of the Holy Innocents, he does so with poise and tremendous authority. He is certainly not lyrical. He blends the simplicity and wisdom of an old French peasant with the knowledge and shrewdness of a Church father. There is something almost overwhelming about his simplicity, because it is the simplicity of truth and the simplicity of real wisdom. When he speaks of the stars, his stars, of the saints, his own saints, of Faith, of Charity, and of his "little Hope," he does so quietly, in fact so very quietly that our breath is taken away. It is not enough to say that he is great; he is great beyond any conception that we may have of greatness, he is the Lord, and because he is the Lord he can speak of creation not only with the authority of the creator, but at the same time with the humor and the matter of fact tone of the farmer who talks about his crops. He is immensely good and immensely forgiving; he grieves to punish the wicked; he is for justice with a strong leaning toward mercy; he loves all his children, particularly the French, for reasons which he explains at length.

Whatever this conception of God the Father may be worth theologically, it bears the stamp of genius and has its origin in the depths of a truly religious heart. The mere attempt to make God the Father deliver long speeches shows courage, and genius is a form of intellectual courage, the courage it takes to allow inspiration to carry one as far as possible, sometimes too far in the eyes of many. In literature as in other fields, the man who is afraid of going too far will never be among the great, and Péguy, with his firm, steady tread and that logical head of his, and his obstinate common sense, Péguy obviously went too far according to the world's method of reckoning distances, that is, he walked straight into the kingdom of Heaven. (pp. 9-13)

> *Julian Green, in his introduction to* Men and Saints: Prose and Poetry *by Charles Péguy, translated by Anne Green and Julian Green (copyright 1944 by Pantheon Books Inc.; reprinted by permission of the publisher), Pantheon Books, 1944, pp. 9-20.*

HARRY LEVIN   (essay date 1945)

[Charles Péguy] upsets all preconceptions of a French writer. That generic figure, posing upon some pedestal in our minds, remains the academic precisian, the cynical rationalist. Péguy, while not less important or typical than many who live up to the textbook requirements, is their very antithesis. Hence his reputation has been strengthened by the reversals that have overtaken the Third Republic. Martyred by the first World War, he has been canonized by the second. Frenchmen, both at home and abroad, have taken their solace from his writing, which has been equally—though differently—cited to support the contending slogans of *Famille, Travail, Patrie* and *Liberté, Egalité, Fraternité.* Happily, a saint is not to be blamed for the sins of those that pray to him. (p. 486)

From his earliest catechisms and schoolbooks, Péguy tells us, he always took everyone seriously, always believed everything he was told. It was this high seriousness that helped him, no doubt, to escape from conventional frivolity; but, in escaping what may be a French weakness, he abandoned one of the prime sources of French strength. His will to believe, accordingly, was untempered by critical judgment. Catholic in the broadest sense, his beliefs were so all-embracing that they strained the credulity of his followers. To his utopia, *la cité harmonieuse,* fraternity was more essential than equality. His distrust of the middle classes was based on a respect for labor and a sense of craftsmanship. His reiterated plaint, "The modern world debases," was a plea for cultural tradition in all its phases—biblical, classical, medieval. It has been all too easy,

with the positive and constructive force of his personality no longer behind them, to turn these affirmations into denials. Though the values he championed stand in ever-increasing jeopardy, he has provided their contemporary exponents with no criterion for distinguishing between progress and reaction, resistance and collaboration, allies and enemies. Though he left a rich testament, he left it so encumbered and entangled that his heirs may not be speaking to each other for still another generation. (p. 487)

Doubts and dilemmas were resolved, however, by the staunch independence and wholehearted vigor of the man himself. His Catholicism was unorthodox and his socialism was not doctrinaire. He overrated the *dreyfusard* Bernard-Lazare and underrated the pacifist Jaurès because he judged others as a comrade-in-arms. So must he be judged. It is the personal inflection that integrates his ideas and lends form to his writing. The same style is broad enough to encompass poetry and prose, intimate journals and journalistic polemics, the speech of the Orléans peasantry and the jargon of the École Normale. Puns, proverbs, and prayers, counterpointing his exhortations, reassert the coherence of the French language, as well as the continuity of French culture. He attains with ease the note that Whitman forces. Our best analogy is Emerson's well-seasoned mixture of pith and eloquence, homely idioms and dazzling generalizations. (p. 488)

Here, championing as always the spirit against the letter, is where Péguy joins the Emersons, the Carlyles, the Nietzsches, and the minor prophets who have cried in the wilderness of modernity. Few of them, significantly, have been French. If this justifies Péguy's unique position, it also explains why—despite his generous and heartening qualities—we have never needed him. For ours is an affirmative tradition, too rarely questioned or interrupted, an everlasting yea. The spirit that denies, the critical temper, the traditional virtues of the major French writers—we stand in greater need of these. Today more than ever, when every publicist is touting his own inflated version of faith, we need reason. Péguy is still enough of a Frenchman to remind us that the honest man must be a perpetual renegade, his life a perpetual infidelity. (pp. 488-89)

> *Harry Levin, "A Serious Frenchman," in* The Sewanee Review *(reprinted by permission of the editor; © 1945, copyright renewed © 1973, by The University of the South), Vol. LIII, No. 3, Summer, 1945, pp. 486-89.*

HANS SCHMITT   (essay date 1953)

[*Schmitt disagrees with critics who maintain Péguy's spiritual evolution occurred in three phases. He contends that Péguy's first major work,* Jeanne d'Arc *represents the formulation of all his spiritual ideas, and that subsequent works were an elaboration on these pre-existing thoughts.*]

[*Jeanne d'Arc,* the] first and only play of Péguy's, has yet to be performed in its entirety, and its significance as the basis and essence of his doctrines has never been sufficiently recognized. As a native of Orleans, Peguy had, since childhood, felt a deep attachment for the maid who had freed his city. He had grown up surrounded by her memory, and his play revealed to what extent he had come to identify his life with hers. Peguy's Jeanne—like her creator—was incessantly probing into the causes of suffering, both physical and spiritual, and searching for modes of salvation. What must be done to assure the salvation of all mankind: Who must be saved? How must we save?'' That was the basic problem of the play. There were other motifs. Salvation was discussed not only as a social and spiritual goal, but also in the context of national survival. Joan, though commenting in moving terms on the horrors of war, would not countenance peace until liberation of her land was complete. Nor would she accept foreign aid. France must be saved by the French. Finally, the events leading to the execution of his heroine symbolized to Peguy the eternal struggle between good and evil, between ''mystique'' and ''politique,'' between the ideal and the expedient; a struggle in which he saw evil forever triumphant. ''Men are what they are,'' he concluded, adding, however, defiantly: ''We must give thought to what they should be.'' It is this sentence which in a lightning flash illuminates Peguy's true vocation. His life was to be devoted not to the making of scholars but to the making of good men.

The many biographers of Peguy are unanimous in the view that his spiritual development can be divided into three parts: First, his socialist period, ending about 1903; next his conversion to nationalism and finally, in 1908, his return to the Catholic fold. Such an interpretation rests on either ignorance or misunderstanding of the contents of *Jeanne d'Arc.* As early as 1897 Peguy was preoccupied not only with social misery, but also with the quest for the salvation of his soul. Guilt and sin play an important role in the thinking of his Joan of Arc. Furthermore he had her insist that France be freed by Frenchmen and well before the turn of the century he attacked France's alliance with Russia as a sign of fatal weakness. Finally, Peguy's distinction between the expedient (politique) and the ideal (mystique) which has been ascribed to his disillusionment over the Dreyfus Affair, was already well developed when he wrote *Jeanne d'Arc* in the middle '90's. This trilogy is without a doubt a miniature reproduction of his world of ideas. Everything that followed was elaboration and development. His basic message had been formulated.

That Peguy's interest in socialism was of paramount importance during the '90's can, of course, not be denied. (pp. 26-7)

But Peguy's early essays reveal his continuous grappling with problems that far transcend the social world. An illness brought him face to face with death and the dictatorship of the proletariat became inconsequential in the presence of eternity. Added to this personal issue were growing differences with socialist doctrine as such. In his *De Jean Coste,* for instance, the editor of the *Cahiers* pointed out that the greatest physical enemy of man was not poverty, but misery. The poor, he maintained, have roofs over their heads and a bowl of soup and a crust of bread on their table. They have all that is needed for existence. The miserable, on the other hand, are face to face with starvation and perdition. They have nothing except the everlasting companionship of sickness and death. The socialists, Peguy claimed, instead of addressing themselves to the salvation of this lowest layer of society, preferred to cater to the poor through parades, rallies and manifestos. They offered not bread to the miserable, but games to the poor. (pp. 28-9)

In 1898 [Peguy] had written a tract entitled *De la Cite Harmonieuse* in which he had outlined his vision of a Socialist society in the image of Fourier rather than of Marx. Men were to pool their resources in terms of labor and of goods for the benefit of all. This precluded any kind of competition and, so Peguy was at pains to point out in the *Cahiers,* it excluded the notion of the class struggle. The conflict between the classes, he explained, was based on competition and competition was

a fixture of the capitalist world. It had no place in a truly socialist society. (p. 29)

In 1904 [Peguy] published his essay *Zangwill* which initiated a ferocious assault on the lay state and its academic institutions. Peguy, the passionate ''Dreyfusard'' was becoming increasingly indignant over the persecution of the Church which preceded and accompanied the enactment of the Separation Laws. He noted grimly that the State and the Church had become separated, but that in the place of old clerical superstitions there was now arising a metaphysical cult of the state which was equally nefarious. While there were frequent desecrations of churches, there were equally conspicuous consecrations of shrines to such apostles of laicism as Taine and Ranan. The intellectual heritage of these two men in particular, Peguy felt, was having an effect that was fully as stultifying as that of a conservative clerical tradition. He attacked their memory not only because he blamed them for the rise of a new secular tyranny. He also deplored the intellectual sterility which he claimed they had bequeathed to subsequent generations of scholars. In *Zangwill* as well as in a striking essay in literary criticism—*Les Suppliants parallels*—Peguy very effectively singled out the historical approach to literary study as one such instance and made a strong case for the ''new criticism'' in its stead.

Peguy's dissatisfaction with the anti-clerical regime reached new heights when, in 1905, France was forced to back down in the face of a German show of force at Tangier. In *Notre Patrie,* a strange reflective essay, employing a mode of writing reminiscent of later stream-of-consciousness techniques, Peguy recalled the events and the Parisian atmosphere of the days of the First Moroccan Crisis. ''Like everyone else,'' he wrote, ''I had come to Paris at nine o'clock in the morning'' of June 6th, the day of Delcasse's resignation. ''Like everyone else I knew at 11:30 that within the space of two hours and a half a new period had begun in the history of my own life, in the history of my country and assuredly in the history of the world.'' The next day, Peguy and his wife went shopping for any supplies he might need in case of mobilization. For the remainder of his life he was in a state of perpetual readiness, warning his countrymen against the siren-song of Jaures, who advertised the presumable solidarity of French and German Socialists as the one effective safeguard against war. Like a latter-day Cato he incessantly conjured up the image of the invader and dreamt that he might be granted—as indeed he was—a part of the foiling of the unfolding plot. (pp. 29-30)

[*Le mystere de la Charite de Jeanne d'Arc*], with which the thirty-seven year old playwright, critic, editor and polemicist emerged as a poet as well, was his first great public success. (p. 31)

However, Peguy and success did not mix for long. The ink was hardly dry on the nationalist paeans of praise for the *Mystere de la Charite de Jeanne d'Arc* when there appeared one of his finest effusions in prose, entitled *Notre Jeunesse.* Written in reply to Daniel Halevy's anti-Dreyfusard *Apologie pour notre passe,* it was an affirmation of Peguy's loyalty to the past. While he admitted that the ideal for which he and his friends had fought had been defiled by the politicians, he insisted on remaining true to it. The Dreyfusards, he maintained, had been heroes who had nothing to regret and nothing to be ashamed of. Such sentiments created understandable consternation on the Right, but even an editorial in Charles Maurras' *Action Francaise* which asked Peguy to abandon his republican ''mystique'' for a nationalist and monarchist ''politique,'' fell on deaf ears. He was not interested in making friends by abandoning principle.

Even more imprudent and aggressive was Peguy's attack on certain enlightened Catholic journalists who criticized his wholly unhistoric and mystic approach to Joan of Arc. In a blistering diatribe of more than three hundred pages he hurled his personal excommunication against such men, asserting at the same time that he, Peguy, was the guardian of the faith and the spearhead of a religious revival. Considering that he was at the time the father of three children, none of whom had been baptized, the husband of a free-thinking wife with whom he had been united in a purely secular ceremony, and—finally—himself unwilling to enter a Church that would not accept or sanction these relationships, it will hardly surprise that the self-appointed apostle was cold-shouldered by the Catholic hierarchy. With some notable exceptions Catholics did not accept Peguy until he was safely in his mass-grave near the banks of the Marne. (pp. 31-2)

One might perhaps say that Peguy though neglected as a writer, was already at the time of his death in the process of becoming a religious and political symbol. This trend was accentuated and accelerated by the war. His death at Villeroy-LaBaste was front page news. Maurice Barres phrase: "He died like a hero, facing the enemy," was to some the quintessence of Peguy's achievement. The poet was considered but little, the ideologist and thinker was overlooked, while the patriot began to assume superhuman proportions. At the same time, as events confirmed the rapprochement between Church and State in France, the hero of the Republic was gradually restored to good standing in the community of the faithful. (pp. 33-4)

> *Hans Schmitt, "Charles Peguy: The Man and the Legend, 1873-1953," in* Chicago Review *(reprinted by permission of* Chicago Review; *copyright © 1953, copyright renewed © 1981, by* Chicago Review), *Vol. VII, No. 1, Winter, 1953, pp. 24-37.*

WALLACE FOWLIE   (essay date 1957)

[Fowlie is one of the leading critics writing on modern French literature.]

The vast amount of critical writing in France and outside of France during the past thirty years which has been concerned with assessing and explaining modern French poetry has given no place of importance to Charles Péguy. In fact, it has hardly even mentioned his name. The work of Valéry, for example, who was born two years before Péguy, has elicited a large number of critical and exegetical studies and his place is firmly established in the tradition of modern French poetry founded by Baudelaire. Péguy's poetry has nothing to do with that central tradition. It cannot be approached in the same way because it presents no linguistic and no metaphorical difficulties, and any other approach to a serious study of Péguy as poet has been heretofore somewhat impeded or discouraged by the tenacious and picturesque legends of his life. . . .

The easier task of defining Péguy's position as prose writer has been more or less accomplished. What he represents as a patriot and a Christian and a revolutionary is fairly well known. But his accomplishment as poet has not only been questioned, it has been almost totally neglected. . . .

Péguy's ultimate reputation as a poet will doubtless rest on *Eve* and his three *Mysteries* (on *The Charity of Joan of Arc,* on *The Porch of the Mystery of the Second Virtue,* and *The Mystery of*

the Holy Innocents). [Albert] Béguin's book, which is brief, opens up the way to an understanding of *Eve,* but so far there are no studies on the art of the *Mystères.* Prior to Béguin's study of *Eve,* the critics had looked upon the ten thousand alexandrines comprising the work as a return to the traditional line of French poetry—and had pointed out the excessive monotony and repetition of the Péguy alexandrine. Although it was generally acknowledged that Péguy had fashioned an alexandrine that was peculiarly and recognizably his own, he was accused at the same time of having exaggerated its monotony.

In September 1908, Péguy confided to his friend Joseph Lotte that he was becoming a Catholic again. A year previously he had said the same thing to Jacques Maritain but had pleaded for secrecy. On one level, *Eve* is Péguy's literary expression of his return to the Church. It is a kind of vision of human history as well as a poetics. Béguin's book, *L'Eve de Péguy,* treats the work as one of the most important in the tradition of French poetry. He sees in it a structure which no critic had surmised before him. To the objection, made many times, that Péguy himself had forgotten his themes and confused the antecedents of his pronouns: *je, nous, il,* Béguin replies that if several characters seem to speak in succession, there is only one real character, the figure of Christ who is present in all men.

Eve should not be looked upon as a poem about Christianity and its history. It is the poem of Christianity with a circular composition moving from the Incarnation to the Redemption. Béguin discovered that all the other themes center around these two, which appear as a long dialogue carried on between the flesh (Incarnation) and the soul (Redemption), between the Fall, associated with Eve, and the Redemption, associated with Christ. (p. 594)

The recent posthumous publication of some of Péguy's writings (*Par ce demi-clair matin*) in which very familiar themes are continued, has confirmed some readers in their belief that Péguy endlessly repeats himself. This is not the case. What is called repetition is actually a deepening of understanding, a widening of theme and perception. Péguy is always moving ahead in his writing, attentive to the demands of his spirit and his mind. After finishing the "cahier" *L'Argent,* he wrote *L'Argent suite.* Whatever theme Péguy chooses to write on, he amplifies to such a degree that all themes are finally incorporated in it.

As soon as Péguy begins writing, he moves instinctively into a domain which he himself has called *temporellement éternel.* This is why André Rousseaux, one of the most penetrating critics and interpreters of Péguy, calls him the "poet of the Incarnation" in his volume *Le Prophète Péguy,* published in 1942. It is not totally surprising that the posthumous publication adds to themes firmly associated with his name, such as a brilliant meditation on the subject of genius during which he refers to Corneille and Pascal, and offers a portrait of the "man of the people," which may in time be looked upon as a self-portrait of Péguy himself. . . .

Only the mere beginnings of Péguy's justification as poet have been written. If there is to be a future exegete to continue the analysis of Béguin's study of *Eve,* he will have to be a combination of aesthetician, fully aware of the ambitions and achievements of modern poetry, and theologian, able to discover how poetry was the instrument given to Péguy to reach the love of God. His poetry will have to be studied, I think, as the act itself of conversion rather than as a testimonial to his conversion. The exceptional length of his poems will be understood and accepted only when we are able to follow the slow analysis of Péguy's feelings concerning the unity of all things created, the unity of each human being, and the presence of God everywhere. (p. 595)

Wallace Fowlie, "Péguy As Poet," in Commonweal (copyright © 1957 Commonweal Publishing Co., Inc.; reprinted by permission of Commonweal Publishing Co., Inc.), Vol. LXVI, No. 24, September 13, 1957, pp. 594-95.

N[ELLY] JUSSEM-WILSON (essay date 1965)

[*Jussem-Wilson's* Charles Péguy *is a comprehensive introductory study of the author and his works.*]

Péguy's first *Joan of Arc,* a dramatic trilogy in prose with lyrical verse monologues, is often called the *Socialist* Joan in order to distinguish her from the *Christian* Joan of 1910. But the two Joans are not as unlike each other as this might suggest. The crux of the religious debate is the same, and it concerns the doctrine of Hell and the meaning of the Redemption. In the long 1897 drama, however, this is not the only debate.

In the opening scene of *Domrémy,* the first play of the trilogy, the thirteen-year-old Joan is in conversation with her friend Hauviette. This earthy peasant child lives through war and the peace of defeat with that unheroic and serene lucidity which sees things as they are, accepts them without asking too many questions, and gets on with the formidable business of simple living. In war, Hauviette looks upon the ever-recurring cycle of the seasons as proof of God's intention that life should go on. (p. 15)

Hauviette is not meant to be a contemptible character. Far from it. She is probably very like the peasants and craftsmen Péguy knew at home. But she is no match for Joan, for whom mere repetitive duration proves nothing. Joan is consumed by an embittered anguish, haunted by the vision of the hungry and the damned, and rebelling against the concept of Hell. In her endless questioning she goes from the immediate to the fundamental, and it is with the latter that she is really concerned. The real problem, for instance, is not the presence of the English army, but the existence of war. The problem is not to stop two starving children from yelling, 'I am hungry.' What is infinitely more painful is to see them throw themselves on a piece of bread like beasts and to think that there are whole legions like them. (pp. 15-16)

To a large extent Joan is of course Péguy. This is most obvious in her angry rejection of the concept of Hell, her compassion for the poor, her revolt against injustice, human and divine. Like Péguy, she will face the problem of means and end, thought and action. Like Péguy, she bids a sad farewell to her home. She is also proud, intransigent, capable of a rigorous self-discipline, but a rebel against authority imposed by tradition, social position or material wealth. In her complex attitude to war and peace she also acts as mirror image to the young Péguy. A certain 'spirit of revenge' had been an important ingredient of his primary education. If his early writings show no trace of the sabre-rattling patriotism à la Paul Déroulède so fashionable at the time, he was none the less secretly ashamed of the peace of defeat concluded by his elders in 1870. (p. 17)

Domrémy is historically largely unauthentic—little is known about Joan's childhood—and rich in personal invention. Psychologically and spiritually, it is the most intense and perhaps the most moving of the three plays. It is also the most lyrical and the least dramatic. Joan's farewell to the Meuse, possibly inspired by a similar farewell in Schiller's *Die Jungfrau von Orléans,* is certainly among the purest lyrical poetry Péguy has ever written. Echoes of Hugo and Ronsard mingle with what is already a characteristic *Péguy* style: the beginning of the famous repetitions, the forcefulness of popular speech, the spontaneity of the spoken language.

This language is free both from picturesque archaisms and modern slang. Unlike Anouilh's Joan, for example, who expresses herself in modern and sophisticated slang, Péguy's heroine is linguistically earthy and her language could be the popular language of any age, but she is never *slangy* and quite unsophisticated.

Linguistic simplicity, however, does not limit the range of her thoughts and vision. Dealing with complex and abstract concepts in a concrete and nonintellectualised idiom will be a feature of Péguy's writing.

From the second play, *Les Batailles,* all the spectacular episodes recalled by history and usually treated by dramatists have been eliminated: the interview with Baudricourt, her arrival at court, the test recognition of Charles, coronation at Reims, etc., etc. Instead, Péguy lets soldiers, craftsmen, merchants, servants, a student, a housewife, governors, politicians and theologians hold the stage and talk about themselves and about Joan. And within this lively tableau of an age, the central drama unfolds swiftly and sadly. Attention is concentrated on three significant stages in Joan's brief, active life: her success at Orléans, the failure to liberate Paris and the last desperate campaign planned from her retreat on the Loire. Joan, now plunged into the world of action, encounters all the complexities and impurities she had not known in the innocent world of Domrémy: treachery, cruelty, violence, hatred, rape, greed, ambition and the peace of defeat at its source: political manoeuvring. On setting out on her mission, she had feared the brutality of soldiers. She is now progressively disillusioned by humanity. Man, whether friend or foe, thinks, speaks and commits evil. And her voices offer neither consolation nor guidance. (pp. 17-19)

The mounting atmosphere of suspicion and accusation form an integral part of the drama of the second play, a drama all the more poignant because Joan is unaware of its full implications. It reaches its climax in the scene at the abbey of Saint-Denis . . . where a group of theologians meet to discuss the 'case of Madame Jeanne'.

In this invented scene, as in the largely historical trial scene of the last play, Péguy gives free reign to his contempt for the Schoolman who mechanically proves and disproves, who obscures issues with quotations from learned texts which are interpreted and re-interpreted *ad infinitum.* (p. 20)

For the interrogation, central episode of *Rouen,* the last play, Péguy has closely followed historical sources, textually transcribing some of the well-known questions and replies. But there are eloquent omissions and stresses. His Joan was not to be condemned by politicians, fanatics or neurotics. Not even by the Church. But by the doctors of the Church. And among the forty learned assessors perplexed, as Péguy later remarked, by 'a form of sanctity which was not labelled, catalogued; no index card to correspond to her [Joan's] case', two Sorbonne theologians play a prominent part. Thomas de Courcelles is made into the chief interrogator. He does not harass the unusual candidate, he simply confounds her with the greatest of calm and elegance. Maitre Guillaume Evrard, 'a man of prodigious eloquence', pronounces the inspired and terrible damnation speech in the chamber of tortures, an invented scene, at which Joan breaks down.

This is the height of her despair. From despair at the ways of God in *Domrémy* and helpless inaction, she plunges into the world of action in *Les Batailles* and despairs at the ways of Man. And, finally, total despair as all her aspirations are condemned by the doctors of *Rouen* who send her into Hell. Before her lies eternal damnation with no prospect of saving anyone. Joan now doubts everything and everybody. Above all, she doubts herself to the point of self-denigration. Before going to the stake in the very last scene, she has regained a certain calm. She re-affirms her faith in her voices and her mission, but the problem of evil and the problem of damnation remain. (pp. 21-2)

'A new period had begun in the history of my own life, in the history of this country, and surely in the history of the world,' Péguy writes almost calmly at the end of *Notre Patrie*. At the beginning he stresses that 'the event' was 'a revelation', 'a shock', and then goes from *digression* to *digression* until, on the last two pages, he describes the event itself in a few terse words and the shock and revelation are briefly suggested rather than explained.

Stylistically, *Notre Patrie* is one of the best examples of Péguy's explorations round a central theme or event, but here a greater impression of linearity is created because the *digressions* can be seen to converge on the final, key pages. (p. 39)

Notre Patrie can be read on many levels. It relies greatly on the power of suggestion, on gentle taps to open mental doors. And the taps are as deceivingly casual as the tone of all but the Hugo *digression* is light-hearted.

Thus, underlying the off-hand comments on internal strife, is the serious situation of Frenchman detesting Frenchman and the tragic memory of Civil War. Had not Frenchman slaughtered Frenchman under the benevolent smile of Bismarck 35 years ago, on the occasion of another invasion?

The sprightly stroll through Paris is a secret plea for unity through a common past and heritage. The monuments, and they are carefully chosen for that purpose—hence the special place of the Panthéon—are there to remind us that régimes and governments come and go but France remains. There is mortality and immortality at every step in this stroll through Paris. There is, too, the anguished thought, fully developed in sombre sequels to *Notre Patrie,* that a whole nation, a whole people, can perish in modern war. (p. 41)

Paul Valéry's famous words of 1918, 'We civilisations now know that we are mortal', sum up the mood of *Par ce demi-clair matin* and the *Suppliants Parallèles,* both written in the same eventful year of 1905 when the one time dreamer of Harmonious Cities went to a big department store to 'equip himself with everything one needs on the day of mobilisation'. (p. 44)

Behind the call to arms of *Par ce demi-clair matin* lies what henceforth will be another obsession: 'entire civilisations have died, in the old and the new worlds. Absolutely, entirely and totally died.'

The extraordinary *Suppliants Parallèles* in which everything seems a digression and to which this obsession lends a profound unity, develops a rather unexpected comparison between the petition of the people of Thebes presented to Oedipus and the petition of the workers of Saint-Petersburg presented to the Czar on the 'bloody Sunday' of January 1905. Both were supplications for survival, for the right to live and to continue life. But the real purpose of the comparison is to show how, in spite of many similarities, the spirit has profoundly changed. Oedipus sacrificed himself. The Czar had his supplicants shot.

Péguy's refusal to bestow any grandeur on the Russian supplicants seems unusually harsh, and in the context of the work as a whole rather contradictory. On the one hand, he insists on the tragic nobility of the figure of the supplicant: the sacred victim bearing misfortunes for some mysterious purpose. On the other hand, he reproaches the Russian supplicants for not having behaved like revolutionaries. The whole uprising is dismissed as a mere revolt. It does not possess the heroic grandeur of a revolution. But supplicants, after all, cannot be at one and the same time supplicants and revolutionaries.

The truth is that the crisis of 1905 had complicated such issues as heroism and self-sacrifice, war and peace, life and death, being a victim ennobled by defeat and a victim crushed by defeat. Because the Russian supplicants symbolised for him all the oppressed nations of the modern world, including France, prostrating themselves before their different Czars and Kaisers, he could not bring himself to sing the praise of men who pleaded and died.

It does not come as a surprise that in the following *cahier, Louis de Gonzague* (December 1905), he should turn to the Jewish people for lessons in racial survival and to Christianity for its belief in eternal life.

Henceforth, life and death and, above all, time, will become constant preoccupations. And not only on the scale of nations and civilisations, but also in a very personal sense. For Péguy seems suddenly to have aged. Soon he will be thinking of founding a party for the men of forty and over, men who know that it is vain to look forward and who begin to look backward. In the *Suppliants Parallèles* he goes in search of time lost, transcribing long passages in Greek script in an attempt to recapture the excitement of his first Greek lessons.

To the Bergsonian Péguy, however, the look backward was a forbidden look. Just as the leap forward into the future was an abstraction and the peace of eternity timelessness. Henceforth, in certain moods, all three will be temptations, but they are usually followed by an effort to live in the real time of the present. This effort is the story of *Louis de Gonzague.* Asked what he would do if the end of the world were shortly to come, the young saint looked up from his game and said: continue to play ball. (pp. 44-6)

On the surface [Péguy's] Dreyfusard *youth* [*Notre Jeunesse*] is a reply to the melancholy apology for Dreyfusism offered from the *Cahiers* themselves by Daniel Halévy in *Apologie pour Notre Passé* (April 1910). The latter's tone of regret and remorse no doubt angered the impenitent Dreyfusard Péguy, proudly proclaiming 'we were heroes'. (p. 58)

In *Notre Jeunesse* [Péguy] reflects on the singular destiny, role and position of the Jewish people, people who brought time, absolutes and justice; a restless people, living in modern times with their ancient heritage, dispersed all over the world and yet most united. In his subsequent concern with such questions as the relation between the Old and New Testaments, Catholic liturgy, the question of guilt; in the embarrassment of the poet of the Incarnation *vis-à-vis* 'obstinate' Israel, and in his search for unity and understanding, Péguy strikes us as a singularly modern Christian in dialogue. (p. 61)

If one were to look for a common denominator to the many and very diverse problems which Péguy deepened, and at the end of which he found Christianity, one would not go very far wrong with the denominator of time. He had felt the shiver of time in many ways. Through history; through the mystery of birth and presences: to be born and not to be born at a certain moment of time, to come too soon or too late, at the right moment or the wrong moment. Most frequently he approached it from its tragic end because in one form or another he had come up against the inevitable descent down the slope of time in all fields of human activity from politics to man's psychic and moral life. In time, the child loses its purity and innocence; in time, the youthful spirit of adventure degenerates into balancing risks against security; the young man's sense of freedom becomes imprisoned in the old man's sense of systems; in time, everything becomes a habit; in time, absolute ideals turn into relative interests, mystique ends in politique. The greatest civilisations have had their peaks and their decadence, and the greatest civilisations have died, in time. This ageing and dying was Péguy's despair. 1905 is an important milestone on his Christian journey not because he discovered Christ among the monuments of Paris, but because he could not resign himself to their mortality and began to look towards Christianity which speaks of eternal life and salvation. Christianity, however, also speaks of Hell and damnation. It is significant that this is the subject of his first Christian work, almost as if he had to exorcise an old nightmare before he could concentrate on the now much more important question of time. After the first *Mystery of Joan of Arc* Hell and damnation will not appear again. But time, transferred to a Christian plane and discussed in a Christian context, will remain a constant problem, a problem which Christianity, even if it relieved Péguy by removing the absurdity of mortality, could not altogether solve for him. In various forms, the problem of time already appears in the *Joan Mystery* and already there we see Péguy oscillating between two opposing poles: the Bergsonian and the Pascalian. (pp. 76-7)

In the *Porch of the Mystery of the Second Virtue* and the *Mystery of the Holy Innocents* the main debate is time, in one form or another, and the speaker is God, a kindly paterfamilias with a sense of humour. He is well acquainted with Bergsonian philosophy but he has also read Pascal. (p. 86)

[But] the deity is not at all a consoling father encouraging in man idle dreams. He is a very exacting Bergsonian à la Péguy asking of man a difficult act of confidence in God and in time.

This is the Bergsonian pole of Péguy's Christianity. It is neither optimistic nor facile, but it is confident and militant. A universe not subject to laws of gravity and weight but ruled by the light and young hand of grace and hope. Time here is not an inevitable de-creation; there is no ageing and hardening, but a creative evolution in which man affirms his being through acts of being.

At the other pole, in the world of the Recluse of *Port Royal*, Péguy found an odd physical repose and an immense spiritual anguish. In the Pascalian universe, duration, active and demanding, was meaningless because time on earth was vanity, and gravity and the Fall were inexorable laws. Evil and suffering loomed large.

Suffering, Péguy depicts most frequently through the physical suffering endured by Christ-man. Ultimately he seems to have been more haunted by the Crucifixion than by Hell. Cross and calvary scenes abound in his poetry. Was this a religious nightmare? Or some sort of 'psychological' fascination with physical suffering? Whatever the reason, Péguy could not rest until, in *Eve,* he found his own special way of ridding humanity of the burden of the Cross.

Evil is closely associated with the fall down the slope of time, of which the child's loss of purity and innocence was proof. Hence the importance of childhood in his Christian poetry and the return to childhood. Hence, too, the more unusual glorification of young death, those who die before the earth has marked them.

For all the hope and advice that an affectionate deity offers to his creature man at the beginning of the *Holy Innocents,* there is something tragic about his final glorification of the Jewish children massacred by Herod's soldiers . . . who only left their mothers' breasts to enter the kingdom of Heaven. Of all his saints and martyrs Péguy's God loves best those white milky children, the only Innocents. (pp. 86-7)

[*Eve,* the] monumental poem of nearly 8000 unbroken Alexandrines—excluding the posthumously published fragments—was composed in six months, from June to December 1913.

From what he said and wrote about it to friends it is quite clear that Péguy envisaged it on the scale of an epic, a Christian *Iliad,* more precisely a new *Divine Comedy* with this capital difference, however, that the poet would not be a 'tourist' but a participant.

The hero of the epic is Christ and he evokes for Eve the different 'climates' of the spiritual history of humanity. Climates is Péguy's own description and it is an aptly chosen term which throws light on the manner in which this history has been conceived and composed.

A climate, unlike a series of events, is not subject to any strict time sequence. It is too supple and too dense, too flowing. The succession of climates too is different from the succession of events. Between one event and the next are analysable transitions and graduations. But between climates there is a constant tension and fusion and this tension and fusion can only be grasped once we are in the heart of a particular climate itself, that is to say from within and not from without. (p. 89)

Throughout the poem we are constantly moving on two planes: the abstract and the concrete, the spiritual and the physical, the idea and its incarnation in the image. The Resurrection climate affords a striking example of Péguy's thought process and imagination. He is probably unique among modern French writers in combining a capacity for abstract thought with an immense need for its incarnation. The poet here joins the polemicist. Both were obviously capable of dealing with abstract concepts but naturally and almost instinctively visualised them in physical shapes and forms. Here for example the difficult concept of the resurrection of the dead does not frighten Péguy; but the concept is immediately made concrete by giving the souls names—King Louis, the people of Paris and Orléans, etc.—and bodies. And since Péguy is incapable of visualising perfectly shaped bodies suddenly arising at the call of the trumpet, we have the realistic and very tender depiction of bodies hastily and clumsily reassembled, bewildered at their nakedness, ill at ease in the physical shell. Shaky on their legs and dazzled by the unaccustomed light, they 'grope with their hands along the walls [as] they look for the way'. When Christ turns to Eve to ask whether she has any light to offer to her groping descendants, we have evidently crossed once more into the other, the spiritual plane.

In the second climate of the Fall, humanity is busy counting: calculating interest, balancing risks against securities, weighing chances before placing its bet, bargaining with God. Man has forgotten what everyone before the Fall knew, namely that 'only God gives a hundred for one'. In this Stock Exchange passage of figures and finances it is not difficult to recognise Péguy's objection to the 'buying of future security'. In a work which strives to reintegrate the physical in the spiritual, man's immorality consists in banking on 'winning his soul with his body', in making sure of eternity by sacrificing the temporal and the carnal. To Péguy's Christ this is a denial of his very Incarnation.

In the central and best-known part of the epic, Christ insists on the unity, through him, of the carnal with the spiritual. They are two trees with their roots plunged deeply in the same soil and so thoroughly intertwined that they are of the same essence. They have become one. This image of the tree—suggested perhaps by the Biblical story—is the heart of the poem. There is no duality in which the physical and spiritual orders, forced to co-exist, are perpetually opposing each other and provoking in man a constant dramatic conflict. Hugo, as we know, built a whole dramatic theory on this conception. As far as Péguy is concerned, such a conflict only arises if man introduces an unnatural split into his oneness; more profoundly, if he denies his physical being. With God the Father who will judge man, with Eve, man's carnal mother who will intercede for him, Christ pleads to remember that men are carnal. (pp. 93-4)

[The *Mystery of Joan of Arc* ends] on a note of temporal triumph. Joan, who has never left her village, looks *forward* in time to the victory at Orléans. In *Eve* we have an extraordinary time inversion which allows the poet to end human history on a note of triumph. He places the Crucifixion *before* the Nativity. No Cross to follow the cradle. (p. 102)

In the Christian 'Creative Evolution' of *Eve,* where a time of birth, a never ending Christmas, acts as an inexhaustible vital impulse, the poet offers to the glory of God, in the simplest language of the earth, an immense glorification of the terrestrial city from which no one has been excluded. (p. 103)

> N[elly] Jussem-Wilson, in her Charles Péguy (re-
> printed by permission of Humanities Press, Inc., At-
> lantic Highlands, NJ 07716), Hillary House Pub-
> lishers Ltd, 1965, 111 p.

M. ADERETH (essay date 1967)

How did Péguy react to the situation of his country and the influences of his childhood? He reacted as a *poet*. Alexander Dru is quite right when he says that "the key to Péguy is the poetry, and it alone supplies the point of view for everything he said and did". This does not mean that his prose works are unimportant, but rather that his approach to life is always poetic. The word "poet" is used here to describe a man endowed with two essential qualities, a powerful imagination, capable of going beyond what is immediately accessible (hence the prophetic character of much of Péguy's message), and the ability to grasp a whole situation or a whole problem in a *condensed form* and to communicate this vision adequately. The two qualities are naturally closely connected, and they

manifest themselves through poetic imagery, images being the special way in which the poet sees the world as well as his most vivid way of condensing reality. To these qualities, one might perhaps, add a striving for the absolute in all things, what Aragon calls "le goût de l'absolu", which is the hallmark of a great poet. Péguy was such a man. His commitment was the devotion of a poet to an ideal for which it is worth living—and dying. (p. 58)

It was at the Ecole Normale that Péguy first discovered what he later denounced as a typically modern evil, "intellectualism". French university thought in those days was dominated by a barren and uninspiring positivism. In philosophy and in literature, facts alone seemed to matter, whilst the spirit of a thinker or the beauty of a work of art lay hidden beneath an impressive mass of so-called objective scholarship. Péguy was horrified, and his hatred for the Sorbonne, the first of many lasting hatreds which he developed, dates from this early experience. From then onwards, the "intellectuals" became the special target of his attack and his abuse. Although one may find that some of his later remarks on the subject are marred by passion, it should be admitted that, as a young man, eager to commune with the living thoughts of the great masters, he must have found the meticulous dissecting of artistic masterpieces fruitless and irksome and the whole intellectual atmosphere quite stifling. He was also profoundly disturbed by the system of state grants which were awarded on the basis of competitive examinations. To achieve success at these examinations, one did not need talent or an original mind, but an infinite capacity for memorizing as many facts as possible. Thus did the bourgeoisie deprive those who had a lively enquiring mind from the benefits of a higher education, whilst at the same time preserving a pretence of democracy through a system which claimed that university places were given to those who "deserved them". This led to the formation of an intellectual "aristocracy" and to a divorce between culture and the common people. Péguy immediately associated this aspect with the previous one and believed that the false scientific façade of modern culture stemmed from the fact that it was the culture of a privileged minority, that the so-called devotion to facts and nothing but facts betrayed a passive acceptance of the status quo. He suggested that the remedy lay in the intellectual's commitment, for this would bring him into contact with the living needs of the people and would turn him away from the goal of specialization, whose aim was not culture for its own sake, but the securing of comfortable sinecures in "the temporal world". He had no time for those who made a living out of the cause they were supposed to serve, be they university professors or professional politicians. When he later founded his own review *Les Cahiers de la Quinzaine* (Fortnightly Notebooks) he thought little of financial rewards, but was mainly concerned with the value of a regular periodical dedicated to Truth. It was in this spirit that Péguy turned to socialism. The poverty of his childhood and his hatred of injustice had already convinced him that something must be done in the economic and social sphere; now, his recent intellectual experience suggested to him that a radical change was also needed in order to bring about a "harmonious society" in which art and culture might blossom. (pp. 59-60)

The year 1897 marks the beginning of Péguy's literary career. He published five articles in the *Revue Socialiste,* of which the most important was *De la cité socialiste,* a kind of blueprint of the future socialist state in which he predicted that the "administration of things" would replace the "government of men" (a formula borrowed from Saint-Simon, the nineteenth-century thinker) and where the means of production would become collective property, "that is to say, returned to the city, to all citizens". This was followed a year later by *Marcel, premier dialogue de la Cité Harmonieuse (Marcel—First Dialogue of the Harmonious City),* in which Péguy stressed that the purpose of a "harmonious" organization of material life was to ensure the full and free development of spiritual life. The latter, he said, must be quite free, and no man, not even the "Cité" itself (the socialist state) could give orders in this essentially individual province. The poet was already fighting for the freedom of poetry. (pp. 60-1)

Some of Péguy's most important works appeared in the *Cahiers.* They fill many volumes of his *Complete Works,* and it is of course impossible to mention them all. Attention should, however, be drawn to a few significant ones in his earlier period, such as *De la grippe* (1901) *(About Influenza),* in which he ridicules the antics of parliamentary politicians; *Pour moi* (1901) *(For Me),* in which he defends the right of minorities to express themselves, voices his fears about the "contamination" of "revolutionary socialism by its political army, just as the French nation was contaminated by its military army", and defines propaganda as "the communication pure and simple of the truth one knows"; *Personnalités* (1902), in which he refuses to support the anti-clerical laws of Radical Socialists on the grounds that deprivation of freedom is a bourgeois vice; the 1903 *Cahier* in which he criticizes socialist deputies for demanding a state monopoly for alcohol instead of opposing alcoholism as such and showing its links with capitalist profits; the 1904 *Cahier* in which he states his refusal to sacrifice his "socialist ideal" in favour of the "distortions of Radical-Socialism", or "the inalienable rights of personal conscience before the altar of reasons of state"; the 1905 *Cahier* in which he asserts that nothing is more immoral than what is "artificial and against nature"; the *Suppliants parallèles* (1905), written after the Russian Revolution, a *Cahier* in which he compares the Russian peasants with the supplicants of ancient times, saying that both were morally greater than the rulers to whom they addressed their petitions, and in which he defines a revolution, not as a "destructive operation" but as "an act of founding"; *Louis de Gonzague* (December 1905), in which he asserts the importance of culture for a free nation; and the various *Cahiers* (1906-7), in which he published parts of a doctorate thesis which he never completed and in which he goes to battle against intellectualism and the modern world. In 1908, he wrote an essay against "historicism" which he called after the Muse of History, *Clio,* but it appeared posthumously.

Péguy's devotion to the *Cahiers* reveals his faith in the power of literature. He seldom envisaged that any other action was possible, except perhaps for street fights when they were needed, as in the days of the Dreyfus Affair. In particular, he rejected the class struggle and pinned his hopes on the written word. This, needless to say, further alienated him from the Socialist Party. Modern socialism, inasmuch as it draws its inspiration from Marx, considers that it is not the logical brilliance of socialist ideas alone which will "convert" the world, but the concrete activity of the working class, for whom a new social system is a vital necessity.

Few works constitute a better illustration of Péguy's poetic reaction to the "shock" of events than his 1905 *Cahier, Notre Patrie (Our Motherland).* It represents an important landmark in his spiritual evolution because it expresses his newly found patriotism. The event itself was the coming of the Spanish king to Paris, with its usual accompaniment of visits to historical monuments and military parades. It produced in Péguy a "startling shock" ("un saisissement") because it made him realize more vividly than ever the powerful national traditions embodied in Parisian monuments, and the function of the Army as an instrument which can safeguard these traditions. He had been aware, like everyone else, of the German threat, but he needed this concrete experience in order to appreciate the value of what was at stake. The poet in him had to visualize "an abstract concept in physical shape and form". He saw the monuments not only as artistic masterpieces but as an expression of the faith and greatness of his people. Such a great and cultured people, he felt, must remain free, and in the face of a possible attack from a powerful neighbour, it had to strengthen its military defences. This led Péguy to praise the Army, an unusual step for an old Dreyfusard, but he was quick to draw a distinction between the Army as an indispensable institution and a reactionary General Staff. From then onwards, until his tragic death on the battlefield, he became increasingly convinced of the need to resist Germany by making France militarily powerful. But the whole issue had been suggested to him as a result of a concrete experience, a visual experience: he had seen the monuments, he had seen the parade, and immediately his poetic imagination had gone beyond sensory experience to divine the spiritual truth of patriotism.

In order to appreciate the shock that this discovery represented both for Péguy and for his contemporaries, it is necessary to remember that at the beginning of this century, patriotism (or what passed as such) seemed to be the prerogative of right-wing politicians. Socialists had the reputation of being more concerned with class realities than with national realities, so that the sight of a socialist coming down heavily in favour of "the motherland" and drawing the practical consequence that militarism had its uses was startling and unexpected. For Péguy, however, there was no contradiction. Was not socialism the highest expression of one's love for one's countrymen, and did it not require a land in which it could be built? "Our antipatriots," he wrote a few years later, "will learn the value which a little bit of earth can have as a basis for a Revolution."

Péguy's patriotism, which was a very genuine sentiment, and not a narrow nationalism, did, however, affect his political judgement in a negative way. It led him in the end to support the most chauvinistic and military-minded politicians of his day. He was so obsessed with the thought that 1871 must not happen all over again that he lost his sense of proportion and was prepared to give his unqualified approval to any policy which did not appear to be defeatist. It made him particularly unfair to [Socialist leader Jean Jaurès], whose internationalism he interpreted as cowardly pacifism and nothing short of treason. The truth is that Jaurès was not taken in by the patriotic pretence of his own government; he saw war as the way of resolving the economic rivalry between two capitalist states and he counted on the alliance of the working classes in both France and Germany as a means of averting war and of defeating the reactionary rulers of both countries. But Péguy never saw the economic interests behind war. As one of his admirers said, although he could discern the harmful role of money in the internal life of France, he seemed strangely unaware of the part it plays in the preparation of armed conflicts. For his wars were always crusades undertaken to defend Honour and high principles, and it is sad to recall that he fell for the lying propaganda that the 1914 war was a war in defence of civilization. It is equally sad to remember that, a few months before Jaurès was assassinated by a right-wing brute, Péguy had actually demanded that the great leader's voice should be silenced, and had claimed that this was necessary for "national defence". The sincerity of his patriotism cannot excuse this open incitement to murder. (pp. 65-8)

[*Notre Jeunesse*], which is probably the finest of Péguy's prose works, was an answer to an earlier *Cahier* in which Daniel Halévy, dealing with the same theme [a retrospective view of the Dreyfus Case], had adopted what Péguy considered to be an unwarranted apologetic tone. It is a difficult book to read because, superficially, it looks like a collection of disjointed remarks and rambling thoughts on a great variety of topics. In fact, it is solidly constructed around a central idea from which everything else stems. This central idea is the poetic vision of the significance of the Dreyfus Case. Everything converges on the Affair. Péguy begins with the background, not the sordid story of forgeries and lies, but the kind of world in which the Affair was born. He calls this world "modern" because it is the first time in history that former cultures have not been given up in favour of a new one, but have been replaced by the universal worship of money and by selfishness. In such a debased world, ideals are bound to lose their purity (this is the famous distinction between "mystique" and "politique" to which we shall return). The condemnation of an innocent man was not only a crime of right-wing military leaders, it was in the logic of "modern" worldly wisdom which puts the temporal interests of the state before the rights of the individual. In this, Péguy remarks, the "modern world" had invented nothing, for it was merely following the wisdom of Ancient Times, a *temporal wisdom*. Those who refused such a shameful theory were animated by a *spiritual* ideal, and Péguy sees the Affair as the meeting-point of three such ideals, that of Israel, which was the continuation of the prophetic thirst for justice and righteousness, that of Christianity, which was the belief that eternal salvation mattered more than temporal salvation, and that of France, which was the tradition of Saint Louis, Joan of Arc and the early Revolutionaries who had all put honour before everything else. And to show how little prepared he was to join with the anti-Semites, among whom most of the Church's supporters were found, Péguy went out of his way to describe in glowing terms the role of his Jewish friend Bernard Lazare, "that atheist who was brimming over with the word of God", and to defend the Jews against the slanders of their enemies. The argument is then taken one step further in order to show the connection between Dreyfusism, an essentially French and Christian ideal, and socialism. Péguy's socialism was neither anti-Christian, because it was based on charity, nor anti-French, because in his view a nation which took the socialist road would become stronger than all the others, economically, politically, militarily and spiritually. The book concludes with the assertion that the defence of Dreyfus was a fight for the eternal salvation of France. (pp. 70-1)

The main weakness of *Notre Jeunesse*, in my opinion, even if one accepts the author's philosophy, is that it does not really give an accurate picture of the Dreyfus Case itself, but rather a special interpretation of it which ignores two important aspects. Péguy, in his effort to emphasize the "mystique" of Dreyfusists, simply forgets that many supporters of Dreyfus, no less sincere than he, did not see the Affair as an issue involving the "eternal salvation" of France, but as a straightforward case of a reactionary clique trying to impose its will on the country; and they fought that clique because they considered it highly dangerous as a political force. One can certainly speak of a "mystique" in this context, in the sense that no selfish interests were pursued, but it was a "mystique" which was very much concerned with the temporal. What is

more serious is that Péguy, looking back on the event, tends to whitewash the enemies of Dreyfus. When he describes them as being inspired by the "very legitimate" and "highly respectable" ideals of national interest, he really ought to make a distinction between the mass of honest supporters of the General Staff (many of whom may have sincerely held the view that the Army was incapable of a crime and that probing too deeply into the case would be a threat to France's security), and the high-ranking officers who deliberately sent a man to Devil's Island in the full knowledge of his innocence. (pp. 72-3)

Of Péguy's last prose works, four deserve to be singled out—a 1910 *Cahier* entitled **Victor-Marie Comte Hugo,** in which he clearly shows his predilection for a literature of ideas, *Un Nouveau Théologien* (1911), in which he re-states against the "bien pensants" that his Christianity is not opposed to socialism, and the two *Notes* of 1914, which are largely devoted to Bergson, although one is called *Note sur Monsieur Bergson et la philosophie bergsonienne* whilst the other is *Note conjointe sur Monsieur Descartes et la philosophie cartésienne*. Péguy was an early admirer of Bergson, and in the first of the two *Notes* he hails his philosophy as a spiritual liberation, because it delivers us from habit and routine, and as an inspiration for action, because it emphasizes the importance of the present. Whether Bergson himself fully realized the militant way in which his disciple interpreted his thought is an open question, but what is certain is that few other disciples used the philosophy of the master as a theoretical justification for commitment. Péguy's enthusiastic acceptance of the Bergsonian "present", which he describes, "not as the morrow of yesterday", but as "the eve of tomorrow", i.e. as a challenge to action, serves as a reminder that his denunciation of the "modern" world does not imply a romantic longing for the past. Certainly, he was fond of the ancient virtues of honour and fidelity, but he wanted them to become inspiring ideals for the men of his time. His interest in the past was the interest of the man of action who refuses to give up his responsibility to his contemporaries.

The Note conjointe is Péguy's last work, but he did not have time to complete it before his death. As it stands, it contains nearly all the themes he developed throughout his career. . . . His hatred of habit, of intellectualism, of the power of money, of an unjust peace, as well as his committed message that "nothing is ever acquired eternally" and that one must "always start afresh" are stressed once again, and for the last time. It is the moving spiritual testament of a man who, having committed himself to the truth as he saw it, is fighting for this truth with his last breath. This last book shows that commitment is difficult but irresistible, demanding but stimulating. Although written in prose, it is the work of a poet whose imaginative vision and loving heart both led him to take the road of "littèrature engagée". (pp. 78-9)

M. Adereth, "Péguy," in his Commitment in Modern French Literature: A Brief Study of "Littérature engagée" in the Works of Péguy, Aragon, and Sartre *(© M. Adereth 1967; reprinted by permission of the author), Victor Gollancz Ltd, 1967, pp. 55-80.*

CONRAD AIKEN (essay date 1968)

[Like the German poet Stefan George,] Péguy, who died in action in the Battle of the Marne—*"Heureux ceux qui sont morts dans les grandes batailles"*—left to his country a handful of great poetry, and a name which has seemed steadily to grow in importance, and yet has had to wait thirty years for his first adequate appearance in English.

Perhaps in neither case was the delay wholly accidental; and in neither case, one ventures to think, will the transplantation be very successful. For the two poets, dissimilar as they are in most respects—if not indeed in all—are both primarily poets of the *word,* poets of the genius of language itself; and of all poetry this "pure" poetry is the most difficult to translate, the most unrewarding; the luster disappears, and with it, somehow, the very life-blood of the meaning; it seems to require of the translator a genius comparable to that of the poet himself. The luster *is* the poetry. And where, as in the intensely religious and Catholic poems of Péguy, the language is reduced to an almost monosyllabic simplicity, and a vernacular simplicity at that, with endless ingenuities of liturgical repetition, there are no "right" English equivalents to be found. "Blessed are they that died in great battles"—is this the same thing at all? No, it would have to be reinvented by an English or American poet who felt profoundly the beauty of Péguy's diction and the oldness and purity of the French rhythm, worn, smooth, with its deceptive clarity, its limpid ambiguities, and always the little quarreling overtones and undertones, like ghosts, of Latin and the Catholic Church.

This is where the French *song* is, its individual magic, and of this Péguy was a master, and it is this, primarily, that makes him a poet, and not his Catholicism or his socialism. His passionate belief, after his conversion, and his extraordinary love of his fellow man, the poor, the sick—*"Et qui les aime tant les ayant connus"*—gave him the same singleness and saintliness that we see in Van Gogh: his poems, like Van Gogh's paintings, always say simply, "I love this." . . . The **"Vision de Prière"** is surely one of the greatest of religious poems—if not so profound or rich as Thompson's "Anthem of Earth" nor so spectacular as *The Hound of Heaven,* it is tenderer than either, homelier, sweeter. And **"L'Innocence et l'Expérience"** and **"La Passion de Notre Dame"** are very nearly as fine. (pp. 318-19)

> Conrad Aiken, "Charles Péguy" (originally pub-
> lished in a different version as "The Untranslatable
> Message," in The New Republic, Vol. 108, No. 24,
> June 14, 1943), in his Collected Criticism (copyright
> © 1935, 1939, 1940, 1942, 1951, 1958 by Conrad
> Aiken; reprinted by permission of Brandt & Brandt
> Literary Agents, Inc.), Oxford University Press, New
> York, 1968, pp. 318-20.

WILLIAM R. KEYLOR (essay date 1976)

Maurice Barrès once remarked that Péguy's own writings on Jeanne d'Arc constituted a masterly effort to re-experience a historical reality of which the surviving documents were merely indirect reflections. Péguy's conception of historical knowledge coincided with Barrès's own notion of the invisible bond that stretches across the ages to link successive generations in a common consciousness of their heritage. "We have a secret memory of our history," he declared, which can be reactivated only by a process of sympathetic imagination. The individual best suited to appreciate the historical significance of the maid of Orléans was not some erudite scholar steeped in the latest methods of paleography and armed with a myriad of manuscripts, but rather an inhabitant of her native province who personally shared the peasant mentality of his subject.

The rather unorthodox treatment accorded this important historical figure by Péguy in his *Mystère de la charité de Jeanne d'Arc* may have satisfied Barrès, but it prompted harsh criticism from observers less inclined to the mystical view of things. One critic, in what he described as an attempt to "introduce the scientific process and method to the Péguy school," accused Péguy of confusing history with legend by presenting a simplistic portrait of the holy heroine which was familiar to every schoolchild but anathema to serious scholars. Péguy's defense of his work emphasized that his objective had been to intuit the inner experience of the saint, while historians customarily address only her external, historical significance. He remained convinced that the deeper realities of the past, whose essence could never be recorded in historical manuscripts, were accessible only to the intuitive grasp of a sympathetic mind, regardless of previous scholarly training. He frequently hailed the untutored capabilities of his grandmother as a storyteller, always adding that she was incapable of reading a newspaper, let alone an archival manuscript. He described his own method as that of "never writing anything except that which we experience ourselves," and later defined the ideal historian as "a man who remembers."

This unconventional conception of historical understanding had been formed not in the scholarly seminars of the Ecole Normale or the Sorbonne, but rather in the spacious amphitheatre of the Collège de France, where Péguy went each Friday afternoon to receive his philosophical edification from Henri Bergson. Péguy came to believe that the inability of Clio, the Muse of Scientific History, to grasp the profound realities of the past which lay beneath their superficial, transient manifestations necessitated the intervention of her half-sister Minerva. It was from Bergson that he appropriated the philosophical scaffolding for his methodological critique of the putative "science" of professional history.

Péguy learned from Bergson that the chronological approach to human history was a misguided attempt to apply temporal categories to a subject which properly belonged to the realm of eternal duration. He maintained that the scholar was too often led astray by his relentless effort to record the events of the past without understanding their underlying, eternal significance. He charged that most modern historians erroneously viewed history as a linear, chronological progression of events to be classified as curiosity pieces. Whereas his own Muse, Clio, striving to embrace the fluid reality of the living past, announces that "I, history, temporality, time, transcience itself, have my source deep in eternity," the scientific Clio of the academic historians declares that she is "not a Bergsonian" but rather, "a woman who notes things down. All I need is a little *guichet* and some pidgeon holes. I am the chief clerk of all those employed in cataloguing, filing, and registration. Movement and reality are not my business." The eternal significance of past events eludes this queen of the temporal world. When her scribes approach her throne for instructions, she does not demand of them a direct, intuitive reconstruction of the past, but inquires instead: "Where are your documents, your monuments, your proofs, your testimonies?" "Do you have your papers?" she asks, warning them that she recognizes only scholars who possess "those papers that fill the archives." These masters of erudition were, in Péguy's eyes, nothing but the "trustees and guardians" of historical evidence.

Péguy saw in the contemporary attitude toward the Dreyfus Affair the confirmation of his suspicion that the historical record inevitably reduces the living drama of the past to dry-as-dust commentary. He was deeply discouraged by the disparity he observed between his personal recollection of the Affair from the vantage point of an active participant and the recorded history of the event. This discrepancy was so blatant as to move him to predict that the Affair's essential meaning would never be understood by the future historian who had access only to the written record. He seemed to be implying that the eternal meaning of a historical event can survive only in the form of a perpetually revived memory. The historian who equated the Dreyfus Affair with the collection of contemporary newspaper clippings, official documents and personal testimonies that recorded it was committing a grave error of omission. For the documentary evidence presented merely a single perspective on past reality, and was destined to be incomplete even if it embraced all the relevant facts. Péguy never forgave Daniel Halévy, his former comrade in the Dreyfusard cause, for what he regarded as the insufficiently reverential tone of the brief history of the Affair that Péguy had persuaded him to write for the *Cahiers*. Halévy subsequently explained that he could no longer see anything sacred about the Affair, remarking that while he approached the events as a historian, Péguy approached them as a poet.

Bergsonian philosophy had taught Péguy that a documentary reconstruction of the past produces only discontinuous, fragmentary traces of a few memorable dates, names and events which have little to do with the real existence of past peoples. He noted that the term "history" had always had a double meaning, denoting both "the past" and "the written record of the past," and argued that the modern historian's preoccupation with producing the second had progressively separated him from the first. Historical reality enjoys an independent existence apart from its residual manifestations, which represent nothing more than what is commemorated. The historical observer must seize historical reality directly in order to achieve a direct communion with the past, instead of "always touching it lightly with those circumlocutory glances" which characterize the scholarly method.

Péguy's mordant criticism of the *methods* employed by the academic historians was accompanied by an equally vociferous attack on their historical *interpretations*. These, he believed, dissolved the traditional certainties which had inspired respect for France's heritage among successive generations of Frenchmen. He repeatedly insisted that a people can remain optimistic about its nation's future only if it retains reverence for its past. It is a serious matter when a society begins to "cut itself off from its ancient roots," because these latent historical connections preserve the sense of continuity that represents the lifeblood of a healthy civilization. Péguy accused the university historians of jeopardizing this fragile link to the past. He denounced their irreverent treatment of those historical institutions which they judged incompatible with the political ideology of Radical Republicanism they had embraced during the Dreyfus Affair. (pp. 200-03)

Péguy's indictment of the methods, doctrines and professional orientation of French academic history expressed the mounting resentments of those amateur, freelance writers of history among the non-academic literary intelligentsia, the successors of Lamartine, Tocqueville and Thiers, who had seen their traditional function usurped and monopolized by the prophets of scientific history in the centers of higher learning. By raising the standard of the Republic of Letters against the encroachments of the Republic of Professors, he was embracing a cause for which many members of the French intellectual élite were prepared to do battle. (p. 208)

William R. Keylor, "Clio on Trial: Charles Péguy As Historical Critic" (copyright © 1976 by Harper & Row, Publishers, Inc.; reprinted by permission of the author), in From Parnassus: Essays in Honor of Jacques Barzun, *edited by Dora B. Weiner and William R. Keylor, Harper & Row, 1976, pp. 195-208.*

ANGELO P. BERTOCCI   (essay date 1979)

A major thrust of the offensive against the modern world of Charles Péguy aimed at recapturing a "pureté" lost, and reestablishing an order of personal and social life which he called "classique." His term bears some relation, of course, to what literary history calls "classicism," and even to the "classiques" of the *grand siècle,* whose principal exemplar was for Péguy the Corneille of *Polyeucte.* It encompasses not only Greek and Roman antiquity but Christianity in all periods, and even the Hebraic. All four are presented not so much as cultures influencing one another, but as participants in the excellently normal, in the essential "rhythm" of creation. Since around 1880, however, a debased and debasing rhythm, ever present in civilization, has become dominant. *Voilà l'ennemi!*

"Classique" is the head of a family of terms such as "exactitude," "dureté," "probité" and "pureté," the last of these coming closest to its essence. All of them bathe in the aura of the "sacré." To come to a relatively exact sense of "pureté"—and this is our enterprise—is to encompass an "aesthetic" as a total response to life in which philosophy of literature becomes involved with philosophy proper, ethical and social thought, and religion, all under pressure of a sense of crisis in culture.

If one of the stigmas of modern man is the search for something unconditioned at least in the self, Péguy in his effort to rediscover and promote such "pureté," was modern. His permutations and combinations of ideas and motives could not bring a solution because he had, as of old in humanity, "two men" in him and more, each with a voice so persuasive that, hearing it, he could forget the other, and tempts us to do the same. In other words, he was a poet; but he thought himself a philosopher, a critic of literature and of society, a man of action, and perhaps a prophet. (p. 193)

[According to Péguy, Henri Bergson was the philosopher who] had freed men from the chains of a scientific determinism and whose philosophy could inspire the will to climb upstream toward man's pure source of creative freedom. He uses the new master against another favorite, Pascal, whose idea that antiquity is to the modern age as the child to the adult had been exploited by positivism and a deterministic evolutionism in order to diminish the role of Greek culture in the curriculum of French higher education. In this latest version in France of the battle between the "anciens" and the "modernes," Péguy argues that civilization does not progress in a linear fashion. Yet the mode of its renewal is also not linear; it is achieved only through "résonance," getting back to the well-spring of the life-giving rhythm in a "ressourcement." The past is recaptured not in imitation but in a fresh identification with the original creative *élan.* The "classique," then, for Péguy, is not an ideal state once and for all perfected to serve as a model. It is a primordial and life-giving rhythm. In every return to the source there is a free and creative beginning, a sacred "tremblement" known to God Himself in the act of creating a "nouveau irreversible."

Such cogitations on the "classique" and on "pureté" of the period 1905-1909, we should emphasize, were to be confirmed in Péguy's polemics and in his commentary, at the very end of his life, on the epic poem *Eve* of 1913. . . . In the intoxication of this dithyramb, Péguy knows no bounds. He affirms that he has surpassed Dante in his poem; the latter has "inventé" while he has "trouvé." . . . (pp. 196-97)

The progressive weakening of education in the classics Péguy saw as a threat to a basic human experience of the ideal possibilities of human life given to us in childhood. It diminishes our view of an innate portrait, the "portrait de la vie que nous avons tous au coeur avant de vivre," and which life never fulfills. He had glimpsed it in children, and in his own childhood. This self-styled "classique" could respond to what Wordsworth sensed as the intimations of immortality in childhood and even to the "volupté pure" of Baudelaire's more exotic "paradise of childhood." A *ressourcement* of the child in us, a getting into step with the rhythm of the sacred childhood of the Greeks, could only come from a study of the classics. Therefore even to diminish such study was a blasphemous subversion of human life.

The danger was magnified by Péguy's tendency to darken Bergson's doctrine of the irreversible nature of time into the irretrievable loss of the good. What is, he thought, need not have been, and what we lose we lose for good. Beware of disturbing a point of perfection once attained! (p. 198)

In the *Deuxième Elégie XXX* of 1908, he had mourned his losses in a Ronsardian version of "Woodsman, spare those trees!" The worst barbarism derives from an intellectualist ossification, a new byzantinism in which the Bergsonian sets up, side by side, scholasticism and sociology! On the other hand, "justice—justesse" suggests the link which he sees between his "socialism" and his "classicism." Neo-Scholasticism, an Aristotelian philosophy revived by Maritain in opposition to Bergson, and the social "science" of a Durkheim really go together. For the *Parti intellectuel*, the historians and their apes, sociologists like Durkheim and Mauss, though affecting to be above metaphysics, are actually engaged in a metaphysics of a rationalist kind called Positivism. . . . True history as a living process achieves concretions of meaning through "events," happenings characterized by particularity and freedom and whose meaning can be seized only directly by what Bergson, though not liking the term, called "intuition."

Péguy's "classique" and his belief in the peculiar power of literature to apprehend "truth" thus rest squarely on his version of Bergson's intuition. The common foe of Péguy and of Bergson's French enemies was a methodology which in the name of science seemed to postpone reform of the right or of the left indefinitely. The heart of Péguy's "socialism" had been from the beginning the reformer's indignation against an evil that is evident now and must be remedied. The man of action in him and the early historian of Jeanne d'Arc had identified themselves with the poet, and his religious impulse was emerging as prophetism. Péguy's Jeanne d'Arc had been impatient even with prayer and waiting for God's will to be done. One must make war to "kill" war brought on by injustice. While in the meantime *la misère*, a state far worse than a respected poverty, was damning human beings in an *inferno* on earth, who can abide in prayer until "all the facts are in"? Man's freedom to act is radical and metaphysically basic. (pp. 198-99)

To the real knowledge of human motives and actions and their outcomes there is a way more direct than the modern historian's

external and exhausting description. A great *chroniqueur* showed what was possible in his witness to the life of Saint Louis. In dealing with Jeanne d'Arc the right dramatist might also find the way. He might come from Orléans, share in her cult, be "peuple" like her, like her hold fast to the ancestral Catholicism "de la paroisse," devote himself to "le peuple," and finally commit himself without stint like her to save France from the enemy both internal and external. . . . Why not Péguy! Could not such a man, such a genius, with an affinity for Jeanne, come to know directly the inner life of the Maid of Orléans? Could there be insight even in the interpretation of documents without such affinity, such commitment! Péguy was moving steadily from history even of Michelet's kind toward the theory of a special literary insight. Already in the [*Marcel, premier dialogue de la cité harmonieuse*] he had been less than clear in the distinction between history and philosophy; now, as we shall see, he will deal with philosophical cognition in such a way as to blur distinction from literature. (p. 199)

[According] to Péguy, even if philosophy alone, not science, can give direct knowledge "littéralement," poetry, though by means of a certain indirection, can also offer an immediate apprehension, a *saisie directe* of the real. Péguy's movement from history to literature without abandonment of the "truth" he always believed a proper history could give, is presented by Clio, dialoguing with herself about the restrictions imposed on her by the latest historical method, but not on the poet. . . .

Clio, then, is ready for a conflation of history and poetry in the most inclusive sense of the term. Such a conflation Péguy called a *chronique*, of which Michelet was the modern master. The notion of a *chronique* was the bridge over which Péguy passed, with a not too critical awareness, from the "truth" which the older history at its best had been presumed to give to the same kind of truth for which poetry offers special facilities.

His idea of the approach to reality made possible by poetry, which achieved revelation in depth, sudden illumination, and certitude through an interplay of modes of expression going from foreshortening to allusion and analogy, sets up a "jeu" as hand-to-hand conflict between the "I" and the "thou," and nourishes the mind in a deep and personal understanding. Poetry makes known a reality not to be confirmed factually and quantitatively. . . .

But if a literary work fully "classique" enables a *saisie directe* of reality, how is a work of art in prose or a poem distinguished from those philosophies which admit such "intuition," especially Bergson's? Péguy sensed a distinction, after all, and labored over it. In the end, like some of our contemporaries, he satisfied himself by taking away from philosophy in the traditional sense what he gave to poetry, or better, he smudged the line between their modes of operation. (p. 200)

[According] to Péguy, whoever would speak of the intelligible world in its relation to the world of the sense, of ideal reality in contrast to the passing show, of dialectic in its ascent, and of mythical symbolization, of the gods and of temporal beauty, of wisdom and sound health, of harmony and of divine intelligence, of fatality or of the earthly *cité*, must use to all eternity the language of Plato, Plotinus and Hellas.

On the other hand, he who would speak of the fall and of redemption, of judgment and eternal salvation, of God made man and of man made in the image of God, of one God in a trinity of persons, infinitely the Creator, infinitely powerful, just, and good, or of the eternal communion of the saints, the eternal city, and of charity, also eternal, must use to all eternity the language of the Christian people. (pp. 202-03)

Thus in 1907 Péguy seeks a language, in writing of philosophy, that will express what belongs to the eternal and yet also to the temporal, to a *logos* and also to direct vision. He seeks to fuse what belongs in the domain of public knowledge and what is heard and overheard—perhaps only by a happy few—in the tone and rhythm of the unique. His language, as well as his theory of philosophy, approaches the dramatistic and the poetic. As a matter of fact, though he calls it a "méthode," his description of philosophic procedure makes of it an approach, as in his **"Note sur la philosophie bergsonienne"** of 1914. Philosophy achieves no coverage of reality but lights up permanently here and there in a creative language certain promising approaches into the mystery of things. A great philosophy does not impose its judgments upon us, but serves us even as it requires something of us. It installs no definitive truth but "introduit une inquiétude, qui ouvre un ébranlement" ["introduces an uncertainty which disturbs"]. Yet this stirring of the depths of us in a sense of something demanded of us, this challenge, as with Descartes, to do battle in uncertainty, Péguy does not allow to get out of hand in the mere subjectivity of emotional and imaginative creation. It is characteristic of Péguy to want both sufficient "inquiétude" ["uncertainty"] and sufficient certainty. He recoups his seeming indifference to objectivity with a: "Parlezmoi surtout d'une fidélité à la réalité, que je mets au-dessus de tout" ["Speak to me above all with a faithfulness to reality, which I put before everything else"].

Péguy's efforts to revise the traditional conception of philosophy will have a special appeal for those in our time who have reduced philosophies to a series of "visions" and poetry itself to "vision" where the term can mean anything from authentic insight to a vague panorama, philosophical or religious, or even political, with the element of illusion quite indeterminate. But we must never forget that Péguy never sought anything but *le réel* and, feeling increasingly the pressure of the divine afflatus, was struggling to work out some fusion of philosophy and poetry as bearers within their own linguistic organisms (and organicisms) of a "truth" somehow *in* them and yet at the same time *beyond* them. (pp. 204-05)

The *réel* must be there eternally in order to be "real," and as such can only be discovered. Yet nothing can be more real than time, which means irreducible novelty and creation. How can one be made to see the "insertion" of the eternal into time, indeed its demands upon time if time is to be kept fresh and new? In other moments time is, for Péguy, the disaster. "Le temps passe et tout est dit" [Time passes and all is said"]. Unless, indeed, time can be revitalized. Thus he inserts himself into the process of time in order to discover in his day the eternal and unconditional and to preserve it, for time's sake, from the perils of time. There is no creation without full commitment and its risk. A man must be ready in his lifetime to "mettre tout en cause" ["put everything into a cause"] not once but several times. Perhaps he is the "creator" of what he "finds" if it would have been lost irretrievably for mankind had he not stepped into the breach. Sometimes Péguy uses the language of a Platonic eternalism when, it seems, he would have been better off to work with Bergson. For we must remember that even to capture the "pureté" of the "classique" is not to reinstate an established model but to get into step with a life-giving rhythm.

On every level, then, Péguy spun out of his own nature what he called the "classique." What he called "classique" was

an attitude, a world-view, an aesthetics of discovery and creation in which creativity, burning into ordinary reality, purified it into the intensity of *le réel* being born. Hence that stress on the literal humanity of Jesus which shocked fellow Catholics but which he seemed to have no difficulty in reconciling with an orthodox Christology. The "insertion" of the "eternal" into the "temporal," this was the *mysterium tremendum et fascinans* on which Péguy brooded endlessly in the *Eve*. And in the *Eve* he considered himself most "classique," as one who "found," whereas Dante had merely "invented." (p. 206)

Angelo P. Bertocci, "Charles Péguy and the Aesthetics of 'Pureté'," in Philological Quarterly *(copyright 1979 by The University of Iowa), Vol. 58, No. 1, Winter, 1979, pp. 193-217.*

ADDITIONAL BIBLIOGRAPHY

Dru, Alexander. *Péguy*. London: The Havill Press, 1956, 121 p.
　　Perceptive biocritical study.

Gallie, W. B. "Péguy the Moralist." *French Studies* II, No. 1 (January 1948): 68-82.
　　Considers Péguy's moral outlook during his atheistic period.

Gilmary, Elizabeth. "Péguy's Madonna." *Renascence* VI, No. 2 (Spring 1954): 112-16.
　　Briefly examines Péguy's peasant concept of the Blessed Virgin in his poem "The Passion of Our Lady."

Green, Julian. Introduction to *Basic Verities: Prose and Poetry*, by Charles Péguy, translated by Ann Green and Julian Green, pp. 13-41. New York: Pantheon Books, 1943.
　　Biographical sketch which characterizes Péguy as a Catholic and a patriot.

Guy, Basil. "Notes on Péguy and Antiquity." In *The Persistent Voice: Essays on Hellenism in French Literature since the Eighteenth-Century in Honor of Professor Henri M. Peyre*, edited by Walter G. Langlois, pp. 93-110. New York: New York University Press, 1971.
　　Describes Péguy as a "classicist" and a "classic" in terms of Greco-Roman tradition in his work.

Halévy, Daniel. *Péguy and "Les cahiers de la quinzaine"*. Translated by Ruth Bethell. New York: Longmans, Green and Co., 1947, 304 p.
　　Biocritical account of Péguy and his journal. Within this book, Halévy recounts how his friendship with Péguy was affected after the publication of *Notre Jeunesse* (see excerpt above), a bitter attack on Halévy's *Apologie pour notre passé (Apology for Our Past)*. Each was a retrospective look at the Dreyfus Affair from opposing viewpoints.

Humes, Joy Nachod. *Two against Time: A Study of the Very Present Worlds of Paul Claudel and Charles Peguy*. Chapel Hill: North Carolina Studies in the Romance Languages and Literatures, 1978, 171 p.*
　　Comparative study of Claudel and Péguy. Humes maintains that the two French poets are similar in their rejection of the modern world and that each transcends time in their works by recreating their own world, thus offering a doctrine of hope.

Jones, Grahame C. "Graham Greene and the Legend of Péguy." *Comparative Literature* XXI, No. 2 (Spring 1969): 138-45.*
　　Study of Péguy's influence on Greene's work.

Jussem-Wilson, Nelly. "Present State of Péguy Studies." *Journal of European Studies* 3, No. 1 (March 1973): 45-58.
　　Focuses on the current activities and publications of the literary society *Amitié Charles Péguy*.

MacDonough, Richard B. "A Thematic Study of Péguy's Tapisseries." *Claudel Studies* I, No. 4 (1974): 60-70.

Examines themes of "Woman," "Incarnation," "Salvation," and "Alienation" in *La tapisserie de Sainte Geneviève et de Jeanne d'Arc, La tapisseries de Notre Dame,* and *Eve.*

O'Donnell, Donat. "The Temple of Memory: Péguy." *The Hudson Review* III, No. 4 (Winter 1951): 548-74.
    Analysis of Péguy's use of language in his religious poetry. O'Donnell states that Péguy used repetition and enumerations so that the inexactitude of words would not diminish his written thoughts.

Pfleger, Karl. "Péguy: The Good Sinner." In his *Wrestlers with Christ,* translated by E. I. Watkin, pp. 73-120. London: Sheed & Ward, 1936.
    Discusses Péguy's struggle to return to Catholicism. Pfleger describes Péguy as an "extraordinary but nevertheless typical chapter in the history of the Christian soul."

Pilkington, A. E. "Charles Péguy." In his *Bergson and His Influence: A Reassessment,* pp. 27-98. Cambridge: Cambridge University Press, 1976.
    Thorough examination regarding Péguy's philosophical adaptations of Bergsonian philosophy.

St. Aubyn, F. C. *Charles Péguy.* Boston: Twayne, 1977, 175 p.

Valuable introduction to Péguy and his works.

Schmitt, Hans A. *Charles Péguy: The Decline of an Idealist.* Baton Rouge: Louisiana State University Press, 1967, 211 p.
    Contends Péguy's work reflects a "process of moral decline." Schmitt disagrees with many critics who portray Péguy as "morally flawless."

Turquet-Milnes, G. "Charles Péguy." In his *Some Modern French Writers: A Study in Bergsonianism,* pp. 212-41. New York: Robert M. McBride & Co., 1921.
    Examines philosopher Henri Bergson's influence on Peguy's life and work. Peguy, who often attended Bergson's lectures, was attuned to the Bergsonian philosophy of *élan vital.*

Villiers, Marjorie. *Charles Péguy: A Study in Integrity.* London: Collins, 1965, 412 p.
    First English language biography of Péguy.

Wilson, Nelly. "A Contribution to the Study of Péguy's Anti-Intellectualism: Early Revolt Against the Spirit of the Sorbonne." *Symposium* XX, No. 1 (Spring 1966): 63-78.
    Study of Péguy's rejection of intellectualism. Wilson contends Péguy's bitterness toward "the spirit of the Sorbonne" was inspired much earlier than the Dreyfus Affair.

Damon Runyon

1880-1946

(Born Alfred Damon Runyan) American short story writer, journalist, dramatist, essayist, and poet.

Runyon was one of America's most popular newspaper columnists and sports writers from the time of the Jazz Age through World War II. He is best known as a humorist who popularized a colorful first-person idiom called "Runyonese" in his short stories of life on Broadway. Consisting largely of urban colloquialisms, Runyonese is the common dialect of an array of comical lower-class gangland characters. Although Runyon based many of his fictional characters on such figures as journalist Walter Winchell and mobster Al Capone, his short stories offered readers a highly romanticized version of their world. In their day, Runyon's stories were quite popular in the United States and Great Britain, and theater audiences still enjoy the hoodlum heroics of *Guys and Dolls*, the popular musical comedy based on Runyon's fiction.

Runyon was raised in Pueblo, Colorado, where he lived with his widowed father, an itinerant newspaper printer and editor. Runyon quit school in the sixth grade and went to work as an errand boy on a local newspaper—by the age of fifteen he was a full-time reporter. After a short stint in the Philippines during the Spanish-American War, Runyon returned to Colorado, where he held a series of jobs for several newspapers. In 1911, he was hired as a sports writer for the Hearst-owned *New York American*. Runyon's move to the East marked a lucrative turning point in his journalistic career. His sharp eye for detail and vigorous writing style landed him top reporting assignments, and he was versatile enough to give equally vivid accounts of everything from baseball games to murder trials. His flamboyant style made everything he covered, no matter how seemingly inconsequential, an event.

Early in his career Runyon experimented with several short-story forms. Most of the tales were simple, local color stories drawn from his childhood memories of frontier towns. A few of these early works were published in national magazines, but received little attention. In 1929, Runyon wrote the first of his Broadway stories, "Romance in the Roaring Forties." The "guys and dolls" of his Broadway beat fascinated readers, and demand for his short stories grew. As his popularity increased, several of his stories were made into motion pictures: *Lady for a Day*, adapted from "Madame La Gimp," was very successful, and *Little Miss Marker* launched the career of Shirley Temple. In addition to his many collections of stories, such as *Guys and Dolls*, *Blue Plate Special*, and *Money from Home*, Runyon published selections of his best-liked newspaper columns in *Short Takes* and in *My Old Man*, which contained both authentic and fictional sketches of his father. *Short Takes* prompted a famous self-deprecating review of his own book, in which he said: "It contains enough gummed-up syntax to patch hell a mile." Other favorite columns, featuring the humorous domestic tribulations of Ethel and Joe Turp, were collected as *My Wife Ethel*. Many of Joe's and Ethel's amusing conversations dealt with contemporary political and social issues. These three collections of Runyon's newspaper work represent only a small part of his prolific journalistic career; by

his own estimation, Runyon wrote over eighty million words. He continued writing until his death from cancer in 1946.

Runyon's most enduring literary contributions are his Broadway stories. Though narrow in scope and often repetitive, these stories depict an American subculture similar in appeal to that of the American cowboy. Throughout his career, he portrayed members of the gangster community as unlikely heroes and heroines living on the periphery of mainstream society. Much of the satirical humor of Runyon's stories is provided by this juxtaposition of underworld characters with the rest of society. According to some critics, these tales contain subtle social commentary that often reveals the pretensions and hypocrisy of "respectable" people. All of Runyon's Broadway fiction is told from the point of view of an unnamed narrator who, by happenstance, becomes involved with thugs, touts, gamblers, and various petty criminals. Fred T. Marsh finds that Runyon's narrator "emerges as not only the most interesting guy in the book, but as an unforgettable mug in the rogues' gallery of American fiction." Critics suggest that Runyon's consistent use of the present tense in the Broadway stories reflected the speech patterns of the hobo and underworld subcultures. The present tense narration diminishes the importance of time, thus expediting the action of the story. Runyon's underworld idiom, Runyonese, is the most prominent element of his style, and is based on the slang of actual gangsters with whom he was acquainted. "Monkey business," "fuzz," "shoo-in," and "shiv" are but a few of the gangland terms he popularized in his fiction, as well as several of his own invention, such as "hotsy totsy" and "phonus balonus."

Throughout his career, Runyon was primarily reviewed in terms of his journalistic prowess and versatility, and his short stories were frequently dismissed as popular entertainment for the semiliterate. Although he was never considered a serious fiction writer during his lifetime, critics today find Runyon to be a natural story teller, similar to O. Henry and Mark Twain. Jean Wagner has demonstrated that many critics have failed to see the satirical social comments artfully hidden beneath the lighthearted gangland antics of his stories. Biographer Tom Clark has attributed Runyon's lack of scholarly acceptance to his unusual role-reversal that placed "criminals and 'legitimate people' on unfamiliar sides of the sympathy meter."

Runyon was consistently praised by his colleagues for his unique writing style, and respected Hearst editor Arthur Brisbane called him "America's greatest reporter." As a journalist, Runyon reported some of the most exciting news events of the early twentieth century, such as the Lindbergh kidnapping and the Sacco and Vanzetti trial. In his fiction he portrayed the complexity of human nature, using his keen reporter's eye to humorously chronicle a lost American subculture.

(See also *Contemporary Authors*, Vol. 107 and *Dictionary of Literary Biography*, Vol. 11: *American Humorists, 1800-1950*.)

PRINCIPAL WORKS

The Tents of Trouble   (poetry)   1911
*Guys and Dolls   (short stories)   1931
*Blue Plate Special   (short stories)   1934
*Money from Home   (short stories)   1935
**More than Somewhat   (short stories)   1937
The Best of Runyon   (short stories)   1938
**Furthermore   (short stories)   1938
**Take It Easy   (short stories)   1938
My Old Man   (sketches)   1939
My Wife Ethel   (fictional letters and short stories)   1939;
    also published as *The Turps*, 1951
In Our Town   (sketches)   1946
Short Takes   (sketches)   1946
Trials and Other Tribulations   (sketches)   1948
Runyon First and Last   (short stories)   1949; also
    published as *All This and That*, 1950
More Guys and Dolls   (short stories)   1951
The Bloodhounds of Broadway and Other Stories   (short
    stories)   1981

*These works were published as *The Damon Runyon Omnibus* in 1939.

**These works were published as *Runyon on Broadway* in 1950.

MURRAY GODWIN   (essay date 1931)

[*Godwin ventures into Runyonese in a negative review of* Guys and Dolls.]

I am not trying to say why it is, but it seems sure that unless Mr. Damon Runyon is giving one and all the phonus bolonus,

the citizens along Broadway have a very quaint way of talking indeed. I do not think it is so much that their pick of words is different from that of the rest of us, for if you will ask me I will say that there is no line of Mr. Damon Runyon's [*Guys and Dolls*], which will give a moment's pain to anyone, even if he never makes it a point to keep watch of the wellsprings of the American slanguage. In fact, I will go so far as to say that personally I will talk more slanguage in ten minutes as a usual thing than you will be able to find in Mr. Damon Runyon's book. No, what is very noticeable about the talk along Mr. Damon Runyon's Broadway is the way in which the citizens one and all limit themselves to the use of two tenses, namely the present and the future, no matter if they are talking of the far past, the near past, the present, the future, or what I will call the hypothetical past, present or future. And also I cannot help noticing that the citizens one and all seem to have a great yen for advancing their various narratives in a manner which will remind you of the style of a good First Reader, providing you go to grammar school about the time that I do, personally, and I am not such an old bird at that.

Yet that is not saying that you will find it slow going when you set out to read Mr. Damon Runyon's book. In fact, I will say that personally I find his tales move along with the best of them, and that what I will call the slow stretches are very few and far between indeed. Now if you will ask me what is the rating of his thirteen tales if they are put on the line against those of Mr. Anton Chekhov or Mr. Guy de Maupassant, I will have to say that personally I will not lay a penalty bet of Bohemian Club gin that they will not occasionally lose by a nose. And I will also say that personally I find a few of them that are very rich with Cinderella flavoring and one thing and another. Yet even these are not hard reading, at that. It does not seem to me personally that a great deal of character comes out in Mr. Damon Runyon's tales, because when you try to see these people he talks about in the round, you will find they have about as much round as a slice of toast has. But I think this is all to the good, at that, for if you will ask me I will tell you that personally I think of all these guys and dolls like the citizen who does Mr. Damon Runyon's talking for him thinks of The Brain, when he claims that if there is one thing The Brain never has it is a conscience. I mean I will say that if there is one thing these characters never have it is a character, and I think I will be right, at that.

> *Murray Godwin, "Broadway in Two Tenses," in* The New Republic *(reprinted by permission of* The New Republic; © *1931 The New Republic, Inc.),* Vol. 68, No. 880, October 14, 1931, p. 240.

HEYWOOD BROUN   (essay date 1931)

[*A fellow newspaperman and New Yorker, Broun cites the veracity of the characters and speech patterns in his friend's fiction.*]

The mantle of O. Henry has been distributed by many who did not own it to several who did not deserve it. Accordingly, there will be no suggestion here that Damon Runyon, in **"Guys and Dolls,"** has fallen heir to the glory and dignity of another author who wrote short stories about the life of New York.

As a matter of fact, there is no similarity in method and point of view. Mr. Runyon has not taken over the technique of the deeply compressed plot and the whiplash ending. Nevertheless, it is hardly possible to neglect the fact that since the death of an author who shall hereafter be nameless, Damon Runyon is one of the first fiction writers who fastened his attention intently upon the byways of this particular great city.

His concentration is more limited than that of the master because Runyon has chosen a single segment out of New York. He has followed Broadway—not even all of Broadway. Every one of his stories can be located as having its principal routes somewhere between Times Square and Columbus Circle.

I think this is a healthy development in the business of fiction. I don't like authors who cover too much territory. It has always been my theory that any writing man can find a score of plots right in his own backyard, or not further away than just around the corner.

To me the most impressive thing in **"Guys and Dolls"** is the sensitivity of the ear of Damon Runyon. He has caught with a high degree of insight the actual tone and phrase of the gangsters and racketeers of the town. Their talk is put down almost literally. Of course, like any artist, Damon Runyon has exercised the privilege of selectivity. But he has not heightened or burlesqued the speech of the people who come alive in his short stories.

It would be presumptuous for a mere newspaperman like myself to pass any judgment on the plot and construction of these stories. That may be left more properly to the reader. All I can say is that the happenings excite me and sometimes move me. And this is so because I recognize the various characters concerned as actual people who are at this moment living and loving, fighting and scuttling no more than a quarter of a mile from the place in which I live. (pp. 3-4)

> *Heywood Broun, in his introduction to* Guys and Dolls *by Damon Runyon (copyright 1929, 1930, 1931 by Damon Runyon; copyright renewed © 1958 by Damon Runyon, Jr. and Mary Runyon McCann; reprinted by permission of Raoul L. Felder, Esq. and American Play Co., Inc. of New York, NY), Frederick A. Stokes, 1931 (and reprinted by J. B. Lippincott, 1950?, pp. 3-4).*

WALTER WINCHELL (essay date 1934)

[*Fellow journalists and friends, Winchell and Runyon shared the experiences of the Broadway scene in their work and lives. Winchell pays tribute to his friend in this essay.*]

Ask any of us who jot down notes for the various gazettes in New York our idea of a big-time, first-rate, Grade-A reporter—and eleven times out of ten, the retort will be "Damon Runyon!"

Because, among other things, Runyon is the most exciting and spellbinding of historians—whether his assignment is the Kentucky Derby, the Madison Square Garden farces, the current murder mystery, the sitchee-ay-shun in the Orient, the Dillinger matter, or Ted Lewis' battered old hat. . . .

He was content, until recently, it appears, to rest on his laurels as a sports chronicler for the more widely read journals throughout the country. (p. 343)

Then suddenly like an old Dempsey left hook—he startled his best critics and severest friends with magazine articles. The sort that not only were read and enjoyed, but the sort that tilted circulation. From these delightfully comical stories about Broadway, the prize ring and the banditti—embroidered in a language rich with style—came a book by Damon called **"Guys and Dolls."**

Stop reading this foreword and phone for a copy of it—and then thank Walter. Particularly, **"Romance in the Roaring Forties,"** which is in it, and then choke from laughing—but loud! I say—send for **"Guys and Dolls"** now—because after you've ached all over reading it—you will be better prepared to take the laugh convulsions in [*Blue Plate Special*], his newest hit.

Yet—with all the grand pieces Damon has done for the editors—I suspect he will never be forgotten for his thrilling document on Sande, the jockey of his time. The one line in it that always "got" me was "Gimme a handy guy like Sande bootin' those winners home!" It has the tempo of the winner in the race. But so has everything he paragraphs. (pp. 343-44)

The outlaws on both coasts, who respect his opinions on sports, also respect his articles on crime. The lethal sock he packs in his pillars of pithy patter for the paper—has driven mobsters out of New York faster than an extra girl in Hollywood says "Yes."

His initial screen achievement was an incessantly robust laugh-provoker named "Lady for a Day." But this is the lustiest of the laughs about that grand flicker. An Academy in Hollywood awards prizes annually for the best this and that. "Lady for a Day" copped three of them. One prize went to the director—another to the adapters—and the third to the star. Damon Runyon, the author, didn't rate a nod! Haw!!!!!

Then came his **"Little Miss Marker"** which the critics acclaimed. Don't tell anybody you missed it. Because you'll be listed among the clunks. (p. 344)

> *Walter Winchell, in his foreword to* Damon Runyon's Blue Plate Special *by Damon Runyon (copyright, 1931, 1932, 1933, 1934, by Damon Runyon; copyright renewed © 1961 by Damon Runyon, Jr. and Mary Runyon McCann; reprinted by permission of Raoul L. Felder, Esq. and American Play Co., Inc. of New York, NY), Frederick A. Stokes Company, 1934 (and reprinted in* Guys and Dolls *by Damon Runyon, J. B. Lippincott Company, 1950, pp. 343-44).*

E. C. BENTLEY (essay date 1937)

[*Bentley's selection of Runyon stories in* More than Somewhat *and* Furthermore *helped popularize Runyon's work in Great Britain. The British were enthralled with the tales of the American underworld as depicted by Runyon. In this excerpt from his introduction to* More than Somewhat, *Bentley dismisses any comparison between Runyon and O. Henry, stating that each dealt with a different era of New York life, a different class of characters, and, most importantly, each had his own distinct style.*]

Before Damon Runyon began writing his stories of the bandits of Broadway, he had made himself a national reputation in America as a newspaper-man; a descriptive reporter who could deal with any event in the day's doings, from a horserace at Miami to an electrocution at Ossining, in a manner that put him in a class by himself. In particular, he wrote of sporting matters with a style and a fund of expert knowledge that were enjoyed from ocean to ocean. But this was not, by its nature, the sort of work that endures. He broke into literature, quite suddenly, with a hilarious short story of the gangsters and crooks infesting a certain section of Broadway, the main artery of New York's life—the Hardened Artery, as Walter Winchell has called it. He followed it up with many others of the same sort; all of them, in fact, told by the same imaginary narrator, and told in a tone and a language that make up one of the richest contributions to comic literature in our time. (p. 3)

I have made this selection of Damon Runyon's stories with the idea of showing as many aspects as possible of his narrative genius, ranging as they do from the most uproarious farce to such sadness as goes to the depths of the heart. The note of pathos is not often touched, it is true: when it is, it gains force from the contrast with its setting of quaint, unemotional, unconscious cynicism. If, after reading *The Lily of St. Pierre* in this book you do not agree with that judgment, then—as Runyon's narrator would say—you must be such a guy as will never be moved by anything short of an earthquake.

In the little world inhabited by Runyon's people every male human being is a guy, every female a doll. There are in that world other names for dolls, it is true, such as broads, or pancakes, or tomatoes; but the narrator prefers not to use such terms, which he claims are not respectful. Do not ask me if there really is such a world. I only know that it is a world, and a very lively world, at that. But it is certainly founded on fact, if you like things founded on fact. We have been hearing of guys like Dave the Dude, and Benny South Street, and Germany Schwartz, and Franky Ferocious (whose square monicker is Ferroccio), and Milk Ear Willie, and Izzy Cheesecake, for many years past; ever since gangsters and racketeers began to be news: also of dolls like Rosa Midnight, and Miss Cleghorn, the Arabian Acrobatic dancer, and Miss Muriel O'Neill, who works in the Half Moon night club, and the doll named Silk, who associates so much more with guys than she does with other dolls that she finally gets so she thinks like a guy, and has a guy's slant on things in general. We have heard of them all before; but Damon Runyon puts life into them as no other writer has done yet, and I do not expect any other in the future to make crime, and violence, and dissipation, and predatory worthlessness, together with occasional off-hand decency where you would least expect it, as keenly interesting and as frantically funny as Damon Runyon does. (pp. 3-4)

[The style of these stories] is exclusively a conversational style. They are all talk; the talk of the guy who is telling them, or of other guys as reported by him. For English readers, I suppose, the most curious thing about that guy's talk will be his resolute avoidance of the past tense; the remarkable things he does with the historic present. (pp. 5-6)

Very interesting, to my mind, is the personality of the guy who tells these stories. He does not give himself a name at any time, but it will do no harm to call him X. In some ways X is a strange guy to be mobbed up with such characters as he tells about. He is a nervous guy, for one thing; and even more remarkable, in the circumstances, than his nervousness, is his passion for respectability. He is "greatly opposed to guys who violate the law," as he insists again and again; and he can think of a million things he will rather do than be seen in the company of such guys. But as he is, on his own showing, practically never in any other kind of society, he must spend a harassing time. The truth is, X is very far from being one of the high shots, but is simply known to one and all as a guy who is just around. In fact, they figure him as harmless as a bag of marsh-mallows. Just the same, X is well known to every wrong gee on Broadway; and if one of them sees him and gives him a huge hello, what can X do? (p. 7)

The most renowned short-story-teller of New York life in the past was O. Henry, whose work has long been the delight of a multitude of readers in this country. The question of a com-

parison between O. Henry and Damon Runyon is therefore bound to arise; and it can be easily answered. The two have hardly anything in common, apart from the faculty of invention. To begin with, O. Henry wrote of the New York life of thirty to forty years ago, which is a long time in the history of that metropolis. Also, while he knew its rich and its poor, its clerks and its shopgirls, its politicians and its sportsmen and its loafers, there is no sign—despite one or two romantic efforts of the Jimmy Valentine sort—that he had much acquaintance with the habitual criminal class. Again, if he had known it as it was in his day, he would have known a class very different from the one to which most of Runyon's characters belong, children as they are of a new age of crime, equipped with all the technical resources of the twentieth century; freed at the same time, by the advance of a brutish materialism, from the last rags of scruple and compassion; and to a great extent financed as crime never was financed before, first, by the enormous profits of a generally tolerated, not to say welcomed, smuggling trade, and then by the even easier money from organized extortion on a grand scale. O. Henry did not live to see national Prohibition, and never heard of racketeering.

His style and method, too, were wholly different from Damon Runyon's. All of the Runyon stories, as I have said, are told with the mouth and in the distinctive speech of one of the characters, who is a very real person indeed. O. Henry seldom resorted to this way of story-telling; and when he did—as in *The Gentle Grafter*—both the imaginary narrator and his talk were obviously not intended to be like life; they were meant merely for the producing of burlesque effect.

One English reader of these stories made the remark—so I am told—that a glossary would help you to understand them. I do not suppose he really meant this: if he did, I cannot imagine a more abject confession of dullness. Let us take it that he was paying an indirect compliment to the freshness and pungency of this variety of American speech. The truth is, X is particularly easy to understand. It is the greatest of the many merits of his style. Even if a term or a phrase is unfamiliar the context tells you instantly what it means. It may be news to you that to cool a guy off means to kill him; or that a doll taking a run-out powder on her husband means her deserting him; or that playing the duck for a guy means trying to avoid him: but if when you read these things in a Runyon story you do not understand what they mean, then you must be such a guy as will never understand much of anything in this world. (pp. 11-13)

E. C. Bentley, in his introduction to More than Somewhat *by Damon Runyon, edited by E. C. Bentley (reprinted by permission of Raoul L. Felder, Esq. and American Play Co., Inc. of New York, NY; in Canada by Constable Publishers), Constable, 1937 (and reprinted in* Runyon on Broadway: Omnibus Volume Containing All the Stories from More than Somewhat, Furthermore, Take It Easy *by Damon Runyon, Constable, 1950, pp. 3-13).*

FRED T. MARSH   (essay date 1938)

[In this critique of The Best of Runyon, *Marsh maintains that Runyon's style compares favorably with that of O. Henry. This is in sharp disagreement with E. C. Bentley, who states "the two have hardly anything in common" (see excerpt above).]*

Contrasting Runyon with O. Henry, [E. C. Bentley] seems to feel that while O. Henry, in his "Gentle Grafters" stories, was a mere burlesquer for passing amusement, Runyon represents the last word in naturalism on that subject so fascinating to Englishmen—the American underworld.

Well, Runyon is more like O. Henry than he is like the still starker and tougher naturalists of the latest school. Compared to a book like "I Can Get It for You Wholesale," Runyon's stories read very much like O. Henry's, allowing for changes of time and circumstances. They are plotted; most of the plots are incredible; as in "The Gentle Grafters" they are told by a funny man; they are skits that illuminate a real world by creating a fictitious one of comedy. Runyon's underworld is more brutal than O. Henry's. Compared to his wise guys, O. Henry's racketeers were truly gentle grafters. But the methods are much the same. . . .

"The Bloodhounds of Broadway" is an O. Henry farce. "The Lily of St. Pierre" is in the authentic O. Henry sentimental tradition—the story of a tough guy who gets sentimental about a little doll only to find some much tougher guy getting in ahead of him. "Gentlemen, the King" is O. Henry burlesque—the story of three mobsters hired to bump off the king of a small European country like Zenda or Moravia.

But the important thing about these tales is that they are so readable, so true to the spirit of the times and conditions they represent, that you can't lay the book down and wish there were more. These are not naturalistic stories. But in their details they are probably extraordinarily sound realism. Runyon shares the gift with O. Henry of telling the tall tale (in the old American tradition) and at the same time making his characters and his language thoroughly credible, very real.

All the stories are told by a narrator whose name is not given but who emerges as not only the most interesting guy in the book, but as an unforgettable mug in the rogues' gallery of American fiction. He is a wit, a storyteller, an ironist; a wise guy looking to keep out of trouble; a small-timer hanging on the fringes of big-shot life, tolerated because he's a humorist and a tower of strength, with his fine baritone in impromptu harmonizing after the shooting (he always ducks) is over. As he says himself, he's known to one and all as a guy who is just around. He's got a pawky way of telling a story, using understatement all along the line to make his incredible tales sound convincing. I think he makes half of them up out of his own head and embellishes the rest. But there's no mistaking him. He's a character. He's the archtype of a hundred others. Always prudent, he wouldn't miss a day of his life in spite of its strains and stresses. It's the guy from around the edges who makes the best historian.

"The Best of Runyon" is just about the best of its kind and time and place and peculiar condition of servitude.

> *Fred T. Marsh, "'The Best of Runyon' and Other Recent Works of Fiction," in* The New York Times Book Review *(©1938 by The New York Times Company; reprinted by permission), March 13, 1938, p. 6.**

DAMON RUNYON (essay date 1946)

[*Runyon's revealing critical review of his collected columns,* Short Takes, *is partially reprinted.*]

I do not commend [*Short Takes*] for its literary qualities. It contains enough gummed-up syntax to patch hell a mile. But as a study in the art of carrying water on both shoulders, of sophistry, of writing with tongue-in-cheek, and of intellectual dishonesty, I think it has no superior since the beginning of time. . . .

Damon Runyon in a simulation of humor often manages to say things which, if said in a serious tone might be erased because he is not supposed to say things like that. By saying something with a half-boob air . . . he gets ideas out of his system on the wrongs of this world which indicate that he must have been a great rebel at heart but lacking moral courage. . . . The newspapers of today are full of high-wire walkers like the Runyon of *Short Takes* . . . he is a hired Hessian of the typewriter . . . a disguised defeatist. . . .

He has one not easily acquired trick which is conveying a thought by indirection. He makes it appear that he is not personally responsible for the thought, but there it is. . . . I tell you Runyon has subtlety but it is the considered opinion of this reviewer that it is a great pity the guy did not remain a rebel out-and-out, even at the cost of a good position at the feed trough. (pp. 70, 72)

> *Damon Runyon, "Runyon with the Half-Boob Air," in* Time *(copyright 1946, copyright renewed © 1973, Time Inc.; all rights reserved; reprinted by permission from* Time*), Vol. 48, No. 25, June 24, 1946, pp. 70, 72.*

SVEND RIEMER (essay date 1947)

[*Riemer was one of the first critics to recognize in Runyon's work all the proponents of "urbanism." In this perceptive analysis, he states that if we understand urbanism to mean "human helplessness in a complex and artificial environment" then Runyon makes use of "the central theme of our present civilization."*]

The trend toward literary regionalism is unmistakable on the bookmarket of recent years. (p. 402)

Overwhelmed by this flood of premeditated environmental exploration which dissects the 48 states of the nation and probes them for literary exploitation, which adds historical "period"-literature and, thus, peruses the dimension of time as well as that of space, our attention has been diverted from fiction in which background and plot are molded so well into each other that the purpose of sociological penetration becomes less conspicuous. Nobody, to be sure, has been daring enough to affiliate a writer like Damon Runyon with the proponents of literary regionalism. Yet, in plot and language and sentence structure, in mood and descriptive intention, he arrives at the symbolic presentation of new and pertinent mass experiences. In some such manner, it appears, Damon Runyon has achieved the crystallization of attitudes which we are accustomed to associate with urbanism.

His effects are not premeditated. As a sportswriter and roving reporter, he gives attention to the task at hand and prides himself on having "never turned down an assignment." With his short stories, however, he falls into a pattern which transcends the immediate intention of popular entertainment. Yet, his success is based upon unreflected enjoyment. He is gathering fans, not followers. There is something evasively suggestive about his form of expression. The manner of speech with which he endows his "characters" leaves an imprint upon the mind of the reader who finds coined phrases and slang and a stereotyped sentence structure sneak into his own language. He finds himself in debt to Damon Runyon for a peculiarly detached sense of humor.

The most devoted fans are by no means found among the "characters of Broadway." They are more frequent in the "smart-set" than among those more solidly barricaded behind set values. But we do find fans of his in London as well as in the Far West of this country. We find them among the rich as well as the poor. His humor appears cosmopolitan, bohemian, smart-aleckey or whatever other expression we want to use to indicate the rootlessness of the city dweller.

The peculiar fascination of Damon Runyon's short stories does not derive from the exploration of a quaint and bizarre social environment as such. Harry the Horse and Isidor Cheesecake stand for a wider set of experiences than those shared in the small hours on Broadway. Mindy's restaurant is the meeting place of a larger congregation than that assembled on the spot.

Damon Runyon breathes the atmosphere of city life. It shapes his rendition and it carries the story. It molds his characters and it constitutes his sense of humor. To be sure, Damon Runyon does not plunge descriptively into the stage-setting of an "urban environment" with all paraphernalia provided. The roaring of the subway and the clanking of the trolley underneath the elevated, the lack of plumbing and the stink of unsatisfactory garbage collection are not mentioned.

There is none of that. Or not more than necessary to literally support Runyon's guys and dolls while they drink, gamble or make love; or necessary to convey them from one place of action to another. Yet, the atmosphere of the big city is right there, more intensely than in WeeGee's photographic explorations.

If "urbanism" means a cosmopolitan attitude rather than a pattern of real estate development, if urbanism is associated with human helplessness in a complex and artificial environment—made by man and yet not mastered—if urbanism suggests the paradox of solitude in milling crowds and that of sentimental yearning in a highly rationalized machine culture—then, indeed, Damon Runyon in his short stories has laid his finger on the very core of a phenomenon which reporters and novelists, historians, sociologists, and scribes, concerned with city life in past, present, and future, are apt to consider the central theme of our present civilization.

Let's see how it works. One of the most characteristic features of Damon Runyon's jargon is the persistent and exclusive use of the present tense. If some sort of time perspective is needed, it is provided bluntly by the use of a special adverb or conjunction, or an explicit statement of time relationship. "*Two days before* she *looks* at me for the last time. . . .'' and so on and so forth. Time is essentially unstructured. It is congealed into an everlasting present. Events occur, and neither narrator nor listener is concerned with chronological sequence for other than the immediate purposes of the story. Historical perspective is meaningless where fortuitous happenings rather than cause-and-effect relationships, anchored in the characters of the agents of the plot, carry the progress of the story. We stand confronted with kaleidoscopic change, a jumble of bizarre events that strike from the outside and provide new thrills in an existence that is real only for the short span of the immediate moment.

This form of literary expression stands as a symbol for a way of life that is dependent upon luck and good fortune rather than systematic effort. There is no relation between reward and endeavor, and the individual drifts along, bewildered by the overpowering robot of a social machinery that is too complex to be mastered or even understood by stray individuals. Good fortune or bad, It is "here today and gone tomorrow." There

is no conceivable connection in time and thus this dimension disappears as a framework for purposeful action.

Similarly, the sentence structure of Damon Runyon presents a dimorphous and atomized appearance. Short sequences of noun and verb are attached to each other by means of simple addition. There are neither hierarchy nor intricate relationships. The flow of language is characterized by a "primitivism" far too purposeful to be explained by the lack of mastery of the English language on the part of urban immigrant groups. Notion is added to notion by the use of simple "and" and "as" and "but" and "so" and "even." There might as well be a period every five words or so. But the stream of words flows on, uninterrupted and with a minimum of cohesion, until it finally comes to an end by the narrator's elementary physical need of having to take a deep breath before plunging into further verbiage. (pp. 402-03)

Dialogue and spoken language are introduced without subtlety. ". . . yelling as follows: 'Hold to it.''' Or, ". . . says nevermind." Or "He says like this" . . . follow the most trivial statements such as "hello" or "thank you," etc. There is emphasis upon the colon. Language is compounded with utmost simplicity. An element of humor derives from the poster-like announcement and the let down of subsequent routine expressions. It sounds like pidgin English. Elementary phrases are crudely put together, reminding of a child's play with blocks from which a primitive structure is erected.

Yet the appearance is deceptive. Such "primitivism" serves the piecemeal accounting of events "as they occur." The accent is upon the momentary, the immediate communication. Neither paragraphs, nor sentences, nor parts of sentences "shade over into each other." Literary form gives symbolic expression to a peculiarly dissociated human environment.

But Runyon offers more than "Basic English." A playful sophistication shines through a rather cultivated naivité. His style, although in some respects reminiscent of, does not actually represent the language of children or the helpless phrasing of recent immigrants. The language of the metropolis is facile rather than undeveloped. Its structure, however, is smashed into particles. It has lost coherence and is aimed at an infinitesimal interest span.

It would be a mistake to interpret this negatively as a disintegration of linguistic power. The creative effort, however, is transferred to the coining of pert phrases, to the use of striking similes, and to the development of lazy habits of speech which, in the hustle and bustle of the large city, serve as sufficient signals of wasteless communication. There is, as a matter of fact, a scintillating firework of innovations that satisfies the zest for new thrills in a routine burdened atmosphere. (p. 403)

The use of descriptive adverbs and adjectives is replaced by an astounding array of similes, attached to stereotyped notions that are easily recognized in their connotations. A story is "chick soup for the newspapers." Skillful and efficient behavior is "entitled to a medal." There is the "high class liar" and the man with a "lot of big cigars sticking out." If you act quickly, you do things "before she can say hellow sucker," and she replies "before you can say scat." We all "hang around" and "go tearing up the stairs" possibly "with quite a delegation following." But in Damon Runyon's world events are at all times described in this manner, and an unending mosaic of imaginative tidbits are crowded into the lines of his short stories. There is a lot of "illegality going on" while people are "popping into" or "poking out of" the Broadway "hop joints." Things are "hotter than mustard" and the dolls are wearing "no more clothes than will make a pad for a crutch."

A great variety of techniques is applied in making language colorful. There are childlike simplifications side by side with sophisticated allusions to the complicated institutional environment of our cities. Some of these lines will stick, and others will soon be forgotten. This is true even within the sequence of Damon Runyon's short stories, as they are published. Some stereotyped phrases return persistently, others are dropped, and new permutations, we may say, see the light of day. Such plugging and fading out, however, is congenial to the milling crowds in the downtown area where contacts are rapid but temporary, where individuals reach quick understanding because they are handling a linguistic material and ideas that are readily accessible. A continuous playful discussion is going on in which originality is asserted by surprising permutations of a common stock of experiences and verbiage taken from radio, newspaper, and the language of the popular magazines. There is unceasing tension between a forced effort of wanting to be different and the tendency of succumbing to a stereotyped pattern of expression.

Runyon's genius—on however limited scale—derives from a natural fusion of form and content. His style is in close affinity to the mood that predominates in his narrative, and the plot of his stories furthermore underlines the sociopsychological attitude that he wants to get across, or, better, in the attitude which he exploits and upon which he elaborates.

His humor is that of the "dead pan." There is a minimum of emotional reaction to extreme situations. His skepticism is near-cynical. People are shot, children freeze and starve to death in a condition of utter neglect, true love is befooled by prostitution and gold digging, wealth dwindles away and is piled up again haphazardly, while the narrator confines himself to statement of brutal fact.

One of Runyon's favorite expressions is the ". . . at that," attached with predilection to pale and colorless statements. He achieves, in this manner, a peculiar effect which emphasizes a mood of skepticism and astonished surprise. The most prominent humorous device is that of over- and understatement. Combined with the affectation of a complete lack of emotional concern, combined with cosmopolitan indifference that takes things for granted as they occur in the melting pot of widely heterogeneous customs, manners and mannerisms, these under- and overstatements provide an inexhaustible foundation for contrasts that shock us into a grin, a chuckle, or a belly laugh. (p. 404)

The reader is challenged, when groggy by repeated shocks, to revaluate a pattern of life which, so far, he has taken for granted. The gangland of Broadway is amorphous so far as the private lives of these drifting individuals is concerned. They are not married, and the "ever-loving wife" is considered at the fringes of their personal experiences only. Children are absent in this scene. If they make an occasional appearance they find themselves in the center of events as elements of contrast which throw into relief the casual and disorganized and unproductive relations between the two sexes. We are dealing with a Bohemian environment which is highly individualized and which, in fortuitous changes between good fortune and bad luck, does not permit for life plans of sufficient duration to allow for family and offspring.

It would be unfair, however, to see in Runyon a cynic, and nothing but. . . . As a strange flower of romantic embellishment and emotional revival, there arises in slum and tavern, in degeneration and moral depravity, a rather consistent pattern of very elementary values draped around a notion of basic human decency. There is generosity and kindness, there is solidarity and compassion. There are tender feelings and strong bonds of loyalty. Yet, what impedes a more permanent and a more conventional cohesion of these peculiar people is the completely haphazard and unreliable manner in which these constructive motivations appear and vanish. Friend turns into foe at a moment's notice, and cynical indifference changes into dripping sentimentality as you turn the page.

Not only the downtown crowd, but each single individual is the battleground of conflicting ethics and etiquette. By and large, sincere emotional attachments have to be repressed where stray individuals lose themselves in an assembly of anonymous humanity, where everybody looks out for himself and where there is no guarantee for reciprocity of commitments. Thus, the urge for personal intimacy, for "true love" and protective tenderness is eruptive and unreliable. It is a freak occurrence which, however, belongs in this world as an outburst of ever-present yearning, as a reaction to the bloodless carrousel of casual contacts.

As a matter of fact, it is the continuous reassertion of human nature in a highly artificial and inhuman environment that is the eternal theme of the Runyon short story. We always find this contrast at the core of the plot. No wonder Damon Runyon had to admit that he confined himself to variations upon the theme of Cinderella. We are touched to tears, while we rock with laughter, at true sentiment that is glorified by a particular halo because we are able to observe how it melts the heart of the toughest guy. There is friendship and mother love, there is lifelong devotion to a member of the opposite sex, and there is attachment to children that deserves the more hallowed frame of a fairy tale. The gangster plays Santa Claus to a poor old woman, or he takes care as best he can, of a stray orphan. The gambler carries his dough—in the form of emeralds that happen to strike her fancy—to the woman he adores, or he protects the innocent girl from the fate of becoming a prostitute.

This melodrama is bearable only because it is diluted by tough and hard humor which moves the author's message into realistic perspective. The guys and dolls know how to take as well as they know how to dish it out if the spirit moves them. The story has no moral, because the lives of Broadway are seen in a fair equilibrium. There are recompenses to want and deprivation.

Runyon, the journalist, does not moralize. He accepts the assignment and gives an adequate account. He achieves a striking adaptation of form and content. He selects the proper medium of expression for the story that he wants to tell. In every line that he writes, Runyon oozes urbanism as an extreme type of human experience. He can scarcely be surpassed in the genre that he has made so uniquely his own. (p. 405)

Svend Riemer, "Damon Runyon—Philosopher of City Life," in Social Forces (*copyright © 1947, Social Forces*), *Vol. 25, No. 4, May, 1947, pp. 402-05.*

JOHN LARDNER   (essay date 1949)

[*In this critique of* Runyon First and Last, *Lardner surveys Runyon's literary development from his little-known early works to the popular Broadway stories.*]

["**Runyon First and Last**"], compiled by Clark Kinnaird, consists entirely of pieces never previously published in book form, including several stories written before 1911, the year Runyon left Colorado for New York. . . . The first stories are crude and boyish. Runyon had certainly become a more competent technician by the time he struck the Broadway vein, the mother lode. Just the same, "**Runyon First and Last**" is to me far and away the most interesting of all the Runyon collections made to date. Mr. Kinnaird has begun by providing a good short biography of the author. Then, by adding two recent stories of the guy-and-doll category to the rough early fiction and including a quantity of middle-period stuff, which combines Western subject matter with the guy-and-doll manner, he has drawn a clear chart of Runyon's professional course. That course was spectacularly direct and single-minded, as such things go in the world of letters. The Kinnaird collection deserves to be kept on file as a textbook after its entertainment value has been tapped. Few writers in America or elsewhere have submerged their native talents, their deepest experiences in early life, as deliberately and expertly as Runyon submerged his in favor of the box office. The effect is made more vivid by the fact that the first stories show Runyon to have had better-than-average native talents and a richer-than-average early experience. As he went along, he learned to exchange straight writing for oblique writing, ideas for pictures of ideas, and heard speech for manufactured speech. It is an old trick of professional artists to travel a street approximately parallel with reality but three or four blocks removed from it, where the going is smoother and one-way. The special thing about Runyon was the purposeful speed with which he mastered such dodges. He was a truly precocious pro. The first stories he wrote had no plots to speak of—at least their plots were not important—but in the very next ones he wrote he went in for plots per se, as did O. Henry and, when he had nothing better to do, Mark Twain. Mr. Kinnaird and others have accounted for this by describing Runyon as a natural, or "innate," storyteller. The fact is, though, that he would use the same kind of plot for a piece with a boyhood setting at the Water Wheel Hole, up the "Arkansaw" River, as he would for one about two Manhattan horseplayers in love with the same doll. The idea in both cases would be: the doll had seen to it beforehand that neither guy's gun was loaded.

After a time, when he had whipped his last, most successful style into shape, Runyon took the logical step of becoming his own imitator. In imitating Runyon, he had lots of company, not only among the Broadway characters who ostensibly inspired him, and who found that they preferred Runyon's version of their speech to the real thing, but among other writers. It's an important point of commercial ethics that a man who invents a style has a better right to imitate it than anyone else has. Runyon did not like to be aped in print by strangers. "The guy who said imitation is the sincerest form of flattery," he observed, "was probably trying to alibi some idea larceny of his own." However, as soon as he had begun, for sound business reasons, to repeat and exploit himself and the synthesis he had created, his stories took on a queer, mixed flavor. They were sustained pretending by someone with a private aversion to pretense. They were fairy tales written by a practicing cynic, Cinderella dreams composed by a man with an obvious grasp of the betting odds against Cinderella, a man who produced romance at so many coconuts a word. Runyon the author is incongruous in the same way as is one of his standard creations—the bookmaker or hairy-armed gunsel committed to the care and feeding of a small girl-child or an innocent old lady. (pp. 58, 61)

"One thing . . . imitators never appeared to comprehend," writes the compiler of "**Runyon First and Last**," "was that 'Runyonese' wasn't pure invention. In all his work, there's evidence his ears were ever constantly attuned to authentic American speech and habits of thought." Runyon's ears were attuned, all right, but he deliberately refused to repeat what he heard as he heard it. Runyonese is a successful commercial alloy. American habits of thought were something Runyon understood pretty well, but he did not care to rub them into the public for which he wrote fiction. If Runyon imitators failed to match him, it was simply because they had less ability to write Runyonese, or anything else, than he had.

In the beginning, as "**Runyon First and Last**" demonstrates, Runyon wrote straight. By that I mean that he set down one idea after another with no pauses for effect, and that he was more interested in what he had to say than in how he said it. Two of the early stories in particular—"**Two Men Named Collins**" and "**The Informal Execution of Soupbone Pew**"—are fresh and vigorous in a way that nothing he wrote afterward is. He had a thorough first-hand knowledge of Army life and of hobo life. He had been raised in—or, rather, left by his father to run wild in—the sort of Western town, half frontier, half industrial, about which very little has been written, and he knew its local color well. . . . Pretty soon, however, astonishingly soon, he stopped describing things that had actually happened, or might conceivably have happened, in such surroundings and began to paste regional words and place names onto standard plots, the kinds of plot that serve equally well, or equally badly, for stories laid in the Far West, on Broadway, or in Spanish Morocco. "**Runyon First and Last**" contains a section of pieces about "young squirts" in Runyon's home town of Pueblo. In a small way, these pieces resemble "Tom Sawyer;" they are full of good local touches but synthetically plotted and written. Runyon's work shows clear signs that the author was influenced by his reading of Mark Twain, O. Henry, Kipling, and Dickens, among others. For his own purposes, he naturally preferred the Mark Twain of "Tom Sawyer" to the Mark Twain of "Huckleberry Finn." (pp. 62-3)

> John Lardner, "*The Secret Past of a Popular Author*," in The New Yorker (© 1949, copyright renewed © 1976, by The New Yorker Magazine, Inc.), Vol. XXV, No. 27, August 27, 1949, pp. 58, 61-3.

CLARK KINNAIRD   (essay date 1951)

[*Kinnaird compiled* Runyon First and Last, *a collection of Runyon's early works and some of his more popular later stories. In the following tribute, written as an introduction to* More Guys and Dolls, *Kinnaird concludes, as did Fred T. Marsh (see excerpt above), that Runyon's unnamed narrator is one of the author's most interesting characters.*]

It has been suggested repeatedly that Runyon "glorified" the murderers, dope-dealers, rum-runners, thieves, kidnapers, bookmakers, horse-players and parasitical hangers-on who comprised most of the principal protagonists in his Broadway stories. The impression may be due to too hasty or unperceptive reading, or lack of understanding of the background of the stories. When Runyon began his satiric Broadway saga, a new phenomenon was making itself felt in the American press. This was the Broadway columnist who sought all his news, or what passed for it, in speakeasies, and came to see gunmen, smugglers, and white-slavers in the likenesses of Rolands, Robin Hoods and Galahads. Runyon began by making gay with the Broadway columnists. He delineated the type as a "hundred per cent sucker,'' a two-timer, a craven. He went on to poke fun at the outlaws and bums about whom the columnists wrote with such awed or reverent hyperbole. As J. C. Furnas observed, Runyon made ''a hard-boiled enemy of society behave like St. Francis of Assisi, demonstrating for all and sundry that the softest hearts beat beneath the latest fashions in bullet-proof vests.'' It was not a new device, for Western outlaws had been treated in similar fashion by Alfred Henry Lewis and other humorists, but Runyon used it skillfully and distinctively. The result was that he captivated readers of *Cosmopolitan, Saturday Evening Post,* and *Collier's* (and the subsequent collections of the stories in book form) with his humor, his realistic reporting of human nature, and his argot.

Runyon had no illusions concerning the stuff of which his Broadway characters were made. In one of his own newspaper columns of the time he remarked, ''There are only three men in the night life of Broadway whose word is worth a nickel.'' Similar realistic views of the habitués of Broadway and the sporting fraternity run through the verse of which he produced a large quantity in the Thirties, verse in which he evidenced the gift for metaphor which Aristotle defined as the supreme power of the poet. **''Just a Good Man,'' ''The Three Cheers Boys,'' ''Ghosts of the Great White Way,'' ''The Manly Art,'' ''The Old Horse Player,''** are among Runyon poems that leave us without doubts about his feelings. From the last-named came that tag-line that became the title of one of the stories in [*More Guys and Dolls*], **''All Horse Players Die Broke.''**

The proof that Joe and Ethel Turp, whom we meet in these pages in **''Nothing Happens in Brooklyn''** and **''A Call on the President,''** were his favorite characters in his later years, is that he made them the principals in a long series of his daily columns and in his weekly contributions to *Pictorial Review,* in which he had complete freedom in choice of subjects. He wrote several dozen stories of the Turps after **''Blonde Mink''** and **''Big Boy Blues,''** which were the end of his Broadway saga. The Turps he delineates are basic Americans with all the homely and broad virtues, and without anything in common with the persons of the narrow world of Broadway. In several stories in which he has the Turps visit that small world, he makes them feel out of place and glad to get away from it. He endows them with the traits of which he wrote with sentiment in his earliest fiction. They obviously were folks he cherished, as he did My Old Man, the most frequently recurring character in the earlier fiction.

Understanding this, we may enjoy the gargantuan humor of the *comédie humaine* he lays in Broadway, without any after-feeling of shame for having laughed at the crimes, violence, dissipation and predatory worthlessness of most of his Broadway people. We may begin to appreciate the quality of his craftsmanship. As W. Somerset Maugham is quoted (by Leonard Lyons) as saying, there is another good way to memorialize Runyon. It is to buy Runyon's books and give full recognition to his talents as a writer.

Runyon had pride in and appreciation of his craftsmanship. Once he called my attention to the fact that he was represented in more anthologies with more different stories than any other writer of the time. But he lacked confidence in his ability to produce longer works. He did not believe he could write a novel. He rejected proposals that he work on one, as he passed off suggestions that he give up his daily newspaper work to concentrate on fiction. Yet he maintained interest in a single character through hundreds of thousands of words, more than the average novel contains.

I submit that one of the most artfully delineated and fascinating characters in modern American literature is this character, who tells us, ''names make no difference to me, especially on Broadway, because no matter what name a man has, it is not his square moniker,'' and offers us no square moniker, or any shape moniker at all, for himself. Namely, and nameless, the narrator of most of the stories in [*More Guys and Dolls*] and the other Broadway tales of Runyon. (pp. vii-ix)

> *Clark Kinnaird, ''Introduction'' (copyright, 1951, by J. B. Lippincott Company; copyright renewed © 1979 by Clark Kinnaird; reprinted by permission of Clark Kinnaird), in* More Guys and Dolls *by Damon Runyon, J. B. Lippincott, 1951, pp. vii-ix.*

DAMON RUNYON, JR.   (essay date 1954)

[*In this excerpt from* Father's Footsteps, *Damon Runyon, Jr. offers insights into his father's use of real-life characters and language in his fiction. He also discusses the compromises and restrictions imposed upon his father's columns by his public persona and by editors.*]

The Runyon guys and dolls tales of Broadway, I believe, will gain more respect with time, and some day may be foisted on students as homework for study in English IV, for in them the short story form was brought to perfection.

There is some argument as to who invented the short story with the neat plot and twist ending. Some will go back to de Maupassant, or Aesop, while others plug Poe and still others will swear by O. Henry. No matter who started the form, I think careful study will show the doctors of learning that in the Runyon stories the form was rounded out to where nothing could be added nor removed. Since so few writers could match the standard of this type it was dropped almost universally.

I am not beating any drum but pointing out something that, as far as I know, has escaped the high minds of literature. It is possible the time-pent ''guys and dolls'' of the Prohibition era led the professors to overlook the perfection of the frame in which the characters cavorted. I leave the rest to writers of dust-catchers to explore. I add only a few points of light where I can.

A controversy grew over whether Runyon characters were fictional or had real counterparts. Columnists Louis Sobol and Dorothy Kilgallen of the *New York Journal-American* argued they were fictions while columnist Walter Winchell of the *New York Mirror* and all the ships at sea took the opposite view to claim they were real. Well, to quote Professor H. L. Mencken, the eminent Baltimore boob-bumper, ''you may be right.''

Take **''All Horse Players Die Broke.''** This short story involved a once successful handicapper, Unser Fritz, who lost even his title to the rank of handicapper and ''is spoken of as a bum.'' The story opens with the tale teller (always unidentified) standing under the elms in front of the Grand Union Hotel in Saratoga when who comes along but Unser Fritz.

This actually happened, give or take a few details. We were walking under the elms along Broadway in Saratoga when who comes along but—I spare his name, for he was indeed real. He was in fact a once wealthy handicapper who had become a bum. He was ''maybe seventy-five,'' greasy, and threw a scent three yards. We stood to windward while my father pressed him with questions and scribbled notes.

Standing there he told his story in low tone and with such a thick German accent we had difficulty with his text. The rough essentials are in the story, even to a doll he showered with jewels until she held her chin so high she wouldn't ride in the same elevator with him "because I am not always tidy enough to suit her." The fictional doll is named Emerald Em, but I understood the real doll was the original Diamond Lil. (pp. 108-10)

In all the Runyon stories the same background could be noted about the characters. In **"The Brain Goes Home,"** about a big gambler with an accumulation of dolls around and about who bar their doors when he shows up well-stabbed, anyone who knew the Prohibition era will recognize Arnold Rothstein, a fellow customer at Lindy's restaurant.

But Rothstein gets shot, not stabbed, and he does not stagger around to a lot of dolls' houses, but comes out of a hotel service entrance to the street and is rushed to Polyclinic Hospital where he dies neat in a surgical bed. The Brain may resemble Rothstein but what happens to him is strictly Runyon.

In **"Romance in the Roaring Forties"** it would not be hard to pin down the original inspiration for Waldo Winchester of *The Morning Item* who "writes about the goings-on in night clubs, such as fights, and one thing or another, and also about who is running around with who, including guys and dolls." But I leave it to a realist like Walter Winchell to say whether what happens to the character is true.

Another controversy stewed over whether the real Broadwayites talk in the present tense slanguage used by the fictional Runyon guys and dolls. The controversy was taken seriously in England where the Runyon stories were as popular as they were here. Do guys and dolls really talk like that?

Unser Fritz' English was mangled like a shirt in a same-day laundry, yet in **"All Horse Players Die Broke"** he speaks pure Broadwayese, or more correctly, Runyonese. What escapes most who claim Runyon reported what he had heard is that in his stories an anonymous "I" tells the tales. It is he who speaks in the present tense even when he is quoting someone like Unser Fritz. The anonymous "I," of course, is Runyon.

It is true that some Broadwayites, especially in the Lindy's set, fall into the present tense in their gabble. (pp. 111-12)

However, even those to whom the present tense comes naturally usually mix in the past tense, too. In the Runyon stories this present tense was pure, carried out to every word, and it was laborious writing to make it read smoothly. If anyone talks like that along the Big Street they come after the fact, or rather fiction. (pp. 112-13)

My father did not approve of law-breaking despite the whimsical viewpoint in his stories but he was a western realist. In theory the republic was against dice and drink, but in fact was shaking both behind the door. The gambler and gangster were merchants who supplied the demand. (p. 113)

His column, like the short stories, usually was peopled by the uncommon characters of sports and Broadway or dealt with their ideas. He once tried the heavy think routine but gave it up to entertain the readers. **"The Brighter Side,"** as the column finally was called, was more a stage than a platform. (pp. 113-14)

My father never liked writing a column for the simple reason that he could not say what he wanted to say. Even columnists have reins on them. My father was supposed to stick to **"The Brighter Side"** and the most optimistic would admit that was a strict limitation especially in wartime.

He was forced to devise gimmicks for the rare occasions when he wanted to sneak over the limits. One of these was to make it appear he wasn't responsible for what he wrote, as in the columns featuring **"My Old Man,"** whose views were cynical, caustic and cutting. I have seen these picked up and used literally as "quotes" from my father's father, my grandfather, but of course they were from my old man.

My father suppressed himself and ground out **"The Brighter Side"** even when life was darkest, as when Death came calling, because somewhere along the line he had come to the choice all writers face—whether to work for love or money. He wrote what he wrote because that was what he got paid the most for, not because it was what he wanted to say.

He was, as he himself put it, a "hired Hessian." (p. 120)

Damon Runyon, Jr., in his Father's Footsteps *(copyright 1953 by Curtis Publishing Co.; 1954 by Damon Runyon, Jr.; reprinted by permission of Random House, Inc.), Random House, 1954, 180 p.*

JEAN WAGNER (essay date 1965)

[*Wagner was one of the first critics to seriously study the technical aspects of Runyon's short stories. In this important critical evaluation he discusses rebellion as a "shaping force" behind Runyon's fiction, and indicates that "Runyonese" not only refers to an idiom but represents Runyon's own rebellious social philosophy cloaked in humor.*]

To look at the Broadway stories [of Runyon] as telling nothing more than the adventures of safe-crackers, gamblers and other such characters of New York would be very much like seeing the Houyhnhnms and overlooking the Yahoos in the last part of *Gulliver's Travels*. Whoever is willing to subscribe to this narrow view of Runyon's universe must be prepared to miss half the story and many other things besides. With his underworld characters alone his stories could never have come to life. Just as an electric spark cannot very well spring from only one pole, humor cannot proceed from one set of things or characters alone. In addition to his underworld characters, Runyon avails himself of another set from the legitimate world, and there is hardly any case indeed where he does not go to the greatest of pains to arrange some way of bringing them together and setting them off against each other. It is his clever juxtaposition of these two worlds, each with its own culture, manners, etiquette, code of honor and outlook on life that provides the fundament of his art, from which practically all his other devices are more or less directly derived. But especially do these two conflicting halves of society afford him an ideal setting for the expression of what, for want of an apter phrase, may be termed his philosophy of life, and more particularly of life in the social environment of urban America in the second quarter of the twentieth century. (p 21)

An important clue to Runyon's own involvement with his twinsided subject matter may be discovered in his review of *Short Takes* [see excerpt above], a collection of his own articles published shortly before his death in 1946. This is a strangely gripping document indeed, exceptionally pregnant with meaning for our understanding of the writer's mind. (p. 22)

One comes to wonder, then, if there did not at heart exist some secret affinity between his own stray impulses toward rebellion and the spirit of those other rebels from the underworld whom he made into the heroes of his stories and often painted with such likable colors. (p. 23)

Rebellion in many forms perceptibly runs throughout his fiction, and may be considered as one of the principal shaping forces behind it. As has been suggested, it was more than mere coincidence if Runyon selected for his typical characters a set of "guys and dolls" who, in his own often-recurring phrase, are "a great knock to the community generally", and whose way of life openly bids defiance to the respectable world of law and order with its accepted institutions and scale of values. But the writer's own rebellion, as well as his unmistakable originality, is more especially illustrated in his peculiar portrayal of these obnoxious characters, which is in itself something of a defiance to and a questioning of the conventions of genteel society. Between the latter and the underworld, the distances are shrunk or completely abolished. Sometimes they are even wilfully reversed, so that the strain of gentility in the underworld characters is italicized while respectability is gently, but effectively disrobed of its aureole and luster. Thus, Runyonese gradually emerges as a specific vision of the world founded primarily on a deliberate disruption of the relations and proportions conventionally admitted to exist between men and things. It implies a denial of the established categories, classifications and yardsticks which we have devised as convenient instruments to apprehend what we call reality. It deflates the myth of their absoluteness and invites us to reappraise them in the light of the writer's personal scale of values and measures, in which we can readily recognize, not a disorderly jumbling, but a methodical and purposeful rearrangement of our own.

This message is conveyed and forcibly driven home through Runyon's self-created idiom, which only a careless observer could dismiss as "illiterate, imaginative slang". Here again, as has been observed in connection with his underworld characters, many readers seem to have been struck only by the grosser aspects of the writer's materials, completely overlooking the significant subtleties in his elaborate treatment of them. In fact, Runyonese as an idiom is nothing less than a closely-fitting correlative of Runyonese as a philosophy of life,—a resonance box not merely for the action and characters, but for the writer's mind itself. To his idiom, slang contributes the same basic connotations of rebellion and defiance that the underworld characters contribute to his subject matter. It should be stressed, however, that Runyon does not rest content with the straight forms and structures of slang any more than he could be satisfied with a straight portrayal of the underworld. Within the terms and system of reference congenial to general slang, he conjures up a new language entirely his own as a result of the quaint and eminently personal angle of his vision of men and things. The unexpectedness of his metaphors, which wrest fresh and vivid meanings from familiar-looking old words, the singularities of his tense pattern, in which the validity of our traditional conceptions of time is questioned, as well as his typical structures of sentence and paragraph, with their absolute statements immediately followed by counter-statements just as absolute, their sheer irrelevancies offered as rational explanations, or their tongue-in-cheek suggestions of actually non-existent relations between people, things and events,—every detail and device in the intricate fabric which is Runyon's typical idiom concurs to inspire us with his own acute sense of relativity and opens up strikingly original avenues for our apprehension of the nature of reality.

To portray Runyon as an outright iconoclast would, however, be overdrawing the picture considerably. Though it is impossible not to recognize, beyond the more obvious levels of his fiction, a definite alertness to the self-critical attitudes which emerged as major trends of American literature in the first half of the twentieth century, it is equally clear that in many respects he is still holding fast to the old ideals. His over-all optimism is certainly founded on a belief in the ideal values of an earlier age, and it is at best tempered, but never destroyed, by his skepticism and irony, which are leveled, not at those ideal values, but rather at the actual depreciated values by which success was measured in the America of his age. On the whole, he strikes an even and wholesome balance between rebellion and conformity, which explains that he never was in any danger of becoming infected with the bitterness and despair that all but overwhelmed his friend Ring Lardner when the latter found out that he "was also occupying the throne that he was disestablishing" and that "he himself was the image he was breaking". Runyon knew better than to go sawing off the branch on which he was sitting or playing the rebel to the limit of jeopardizing his "position at the feed trough". Therefore, though Lardner and Runyon both experienced the high point in their popularity in the period following the stock-market crash of 1929, it certainly was for quite different reasons. While Lardner's fiction could quite easily appeal to a society eager to find out about the social conditions that had led up to the disaster, Runyon's more genial tone was better suited to gratify those,—and they were probably the majority both in America and abroad,—who refused to believe that no way out could be found and that everything could not end well after all.

If Runyon's short-story formula proved so successful, it was no doubt because the patient apprenticeship which he had served on the staffs of numerous newspapers throughout the United States had taught him effectively how to handle the types of emotions by which his reading public could be swayed. Whenever he ventured to deliver a message, he was careful to tone it down, never offering it in the raw, but always wrapping it up with a generous dose of genuine, good-natured humor.

As we know, it is never a far cry from the philosopher to the humorist, and the difference between the two is one of tone and manner rather than of nature and viewpoint. Runyon, then, lest his philosophy should have blinded us to his humor, is most decidedly an addict of the latter, and as such, he is capable of playing the most unusual tricks, focusing our attention on some characters and diverting it from others more important, affecting to believe one thing while actually convinced of the contrary, distorting some events while allowing us a straight view of others, so that we must always be on the lookout for fear of being taken in and becoming ourselves his laughing-stock even while we are busy deriding him and his characters. We should not quarrel with him if a number of things—and characters, too—are occasionally knocked out of shape, not even when he knocks out of shape the King's English. All this is just as it should be when a humorist really starts plying the tools around his workshop: humor and irony, satire, parody, and distortion through overstatement or understatement. (pp. 24-7)

[The] egocentristic organization of Runyon's short stories is perhaps nowhere better apparent than in the particular story-telling technique for which he showed such consistent fondness. Though Henry James called the first-person narrative the most "barbarous" of all techniques, we cannot fail to recognize into what an effective instrument Runyon turned it in time and how well it served his purpose in story after story. There is hardly anything artificial in the way he handles it; on the contrary, one gathers the impression that no other medium could have been better suited to the writer's natural temperament, to his particular subject matter and to his very personal treatment of it. That he had at any rate a special affinity to this method of expression can be ascertained from a comparison between his Broadway stories and his newspaper columns as exemplified in the *Short Takes* selection, in both of which the same basic manner and the same highly personal type of language will be found to prevail. (p. 32)

If the story-teller had so little difficulty in taking up the cue from the columnist, it was for the simple reason that, from the beginning, Runyon never worked like a straight reporter. He was not the type of newspaper man who would strive to give his readers an objective, impersonal, matter-of-fact account of the events he had witnessed. To be sure, he did eventually manage to get the facts across to his audience, but at the same time he could not help putting forward his personal angle, giving his own feelings and opinions at least as much prominence as he gave the facts themselves, so that no column of his,—and no short story either, for that matter,—ever reached the printed page that did not also include a liberal dose of his personal philosophy, characteristically dispensed in the first person. (p. 33)

Nobody would seriously claim that Runyon gives us anything but a very biased report of people and events, but it would be just as hard to claim that a positive effect is not achieved on the way. It is indeed this particular bias of the writer's, this extremely personal angle from which he views reality, that brings his philosophy to light and finally accounts for the special flavor which no one ever exposed to a Runyon story can fail to recognize as the essence of Runyonese.

However, though he assumes the role of the demiurge in his universe, he cannot be said to force his own slant of mind upon the reader; what he claims for it is that it is not more slanted than other people's, and this he significantly suggests by allowing his own first-person report to be confronted on an equal footing with those of the other characters. Between these equally biased, and therefore often contradictory versions of reality, the reader is ultimately left to sift out the truth for himself,—an essential task this, since he could not otherwise have been treated to the rare pleasure of discovering to their full extent the subtleties and far-reaching implications of the writer's humor. The first-person technique, which Runyon uses with such consummate mastery in story after story, may therefore be considered as the basic instrument by means of which we are made conscious of his keen sense of relativity. (p. 34)

Runyon's settings are certainly of a kind that deserves our attention for reasons beyond their mere picturesqueness. As far as orthodox geography is concerned, the Broadway stories are, of course, inaccurately termed, neither do they warrant the legend that has somehow taken root over the years to the effect that their setting "invariably was Lindy's restaurant on Broadway".

Actually, many of the stories concerned have no connection whatever with the famous New York thoroughfare beyond the fact that their ever-present first-person narrator is evidently a prominent Broadway character. Even such a genuinely Runyonesque story as **"Butch Minds the Baby"** is not, strictly speaking, a Broadway story. Though the story-teller, artificially enough, starts it off in Mindy's, Big Butch, in whose home the initial bargaining with Harry the Horse, Little Isadore and Spanish John takes place, lives on West Forty-Ninth Street

near Tenth Avenue, which is at least two blocks west of Broadway, while the actual safe-cracking job is performed by Butch in West Eighteenth Street, between Seventh and Eighth Avenues, which is again two or three blocks removed from Broadway. But in well over half the stories, the action moves out of New York City altogether toward a variety of settings most often related to the world of sports, entertainment, gambling or crime. (p. 37)

Essential developments of over half a dozen so-called Broadway stories really take place abroad. **"Earthquake"** ends in Nicaragua, where Johnny Brannigan, the policeman of the New York gunman squad, finally catches up with the obnoxious character for whom the story is named. Although **"The Lily of St. Pierre"** winds up just off Broadway in Good Time Charley Bernstein's little joint in Forty-Eighth Street, a major phase of the story is set in the French island of St. Pierre, off Newfoundland, as well as in Canada. **"Gentlemen, the King!"** tells of a killing expedition to some unnamed country in Europe, where Izzy Cheesecake and Kitty Quick from Philadelphia, together with Jo-Jo from Chicago, have been commissioned to murder the boy-king. . . . **"A Light in France"** relates Blond Maury's adventures in "a sleepy little town on the seacoast" of France under the German occupation, whereas **"The Lacework Kid"** is set in a POW camp in Germany where Lace is a prisoner and outgambles the German commanding officer.

Runyon does not always take his reader quite so far afield, but underlying all of his stories is an unmistakable inclination to move his characters around and about the map a good deal. The examples just quoted should be sufficient to make it clear that, a die-hard legend to the contrary notwithstanding, Broadway is neither the only nor even the most common locale of Runyon's stories, so that whatever unity they may possess could not very well derive from a unity of place which they appear to lack.

And yet, in spite of their almost endless geographical diversity, there is a certain sameness to all of Runyon's settings. Even though they may be as widely distant as France is from Nicaragua or Mindy's restaurant from a battlefield in Spain, most of them have this in common that they are expressly chosen to make both possible and plausible either actual contacts, or at least an implicit parallel between characters representative of social strata otherwise far apart. A Runyon locale is generally one where high meets low and where social distances are abolished as a matter of course because they are instinctively perceived as fundamentally and utterly irrelevant. Night clubs, speakeasies, restaurants, football fields, race tracks or even battlefields are places where people from every walk of life are brought together for a specific purpose independent of their normal individual status,—where they are stripped, as it were, of their conventional identity and reduced to the common denominator of naked human nature. For a time at least, they cease to be kings or crooks, actors or newspapermen, policemen or criminals, rich or poor, to become mere human beings, just "guys and dolls", eaters and drinkers, lovers and haters, pleasure seekers and money getters. (pp. 38-9)

It is doubtful, therefore, whether Runyon can be explained away merely as a writer of picturesque local color stories. It seems, on the contrary, that this aspect of his fiction has already been widely overstressed, and the fact that some of his readers or critics have found his colorful portrayals of unusual environments so arresting *per se* may go a long way to explain why they were so easily induced to let it go at that, without thinking it worth their while to find out that which local color was only meant to help convey. Rather than to achieve typical characterizations of either East or West, his settings are designed to drive home the idea that human nature is basically identical all around the globe and, more specifically, that it works the same way in every category of human society. (p. 42)

Swift and Runyon have at least this in common, that their fiction can be read on two different levels, not even speaking of the entertainment which may be derived from it as from stories well told. For one thing, the Broadway stories have to a very large extent the value of authentic documents about Gangland. As such, they afford a number of good pieces of reporting about a social category whose sub-culture and practices Runyon knew particularly well. But the Broadway stories hardly ever present the underworld for its own sake, not more at any rate than Swift presents Lilliput or Brobdingnag independently from the country and culture of which Gulliver is the representative. The two antagonistic social elements of the community are not only closely linked up, but consistently portrayed or parodied in terms of each other, thus inviting us to reassess our valuations and to correct the stereotyped or prejudiced views which we may hold concerning ourselves and our social equals as compared with those whom we consider as socially inferior. . . . [The] major themes of Runyon's social criticism proceed in fact from a comparative view of Gangland and respectability. (p. 47)

One of the most original devices that account for the special flavor of Runyonese is undoubtedly the queer tense pattern adopted by the author in most of his My Old Home Town stories and in practically all of his Broadway stories, in which this technique was brought to its highest point of perfection. Because of the extensive use made of it, this stylistic device of the writer's deserves to be attentively examined. First of all, it is important to define the rules which, as far as one can judge from his general usage, Runyon seems to have laid down for himself with respect to tense value and meaning, though it should be kept in mind that in Runyonese as in any other language there are not only a number of exceptions to the rules, but also certain areas of laxity where optional solutions wide of the basic pattern become available. (p. 113)

Runyon's tense scheme, on the contrary, may be said to rest fundamentally on the systematic avoidance not only of the tenses signifying the past, but also of any tenses or moods built with verb forms standing in the past, whatever their meaning as to the time of the action. (p. 114)

Runyon has often been credited, and probably rightly so, with having a very good ear for recording the particular types of languages spoken around him. Knowing this makes it the harder to believe that these present-tense forms were sprinkled at random, out of mere carelessness or without any definite purpose, over a narrative basically kept in the preterit. The most likely explanation is that such present forms had struck Runyon's ear as typical of the speech of certain sub-groups with which he had come into contact, and that it was in an attempt to reproduce this type of speech with some degree of faithfulness that he introduced them into several of his short stories. (p. 120)

Moreover, there may have been yet another influence at work that helped considerably in giving his tense pattern its final shape. It is a well-known fact that Runyon always felt greatly attracted by motion pictures, and his interest in them was probably as old as the movies themselves. As early as 1933, at any rate, his story **"Madame La Gimp"** was filmed in Hollywood, later followed by many other stories, until he eventually be-

came a film producer himself. Now, there can be no doubt that his story-telling technique in very extensive portions of his short fiction directly suggests the technique of the motion picture. . . . This accent upon the momentary, fleeting images of the present is an unquestionable point of likeness between Runyonese and the language of the motion picture, for neither in the Broadway stories nor on the screen does the past seem to have any existence worth considering. And yet, in both cases, this present is so transitory and so changeable that it becomes ever again pregnant with the expectancy of the future. "What will happen next?" is the spectator's perpetual, though unworded query as he keeps his eyes riveted on the screen. "If the gangster *sees* the men of the police squad who are trailing him, he *will fire* at them". Thus, the present and the future stand out as the two specific poles on which the universe is hinged both in Runyonese and in Hollywood parlance,—a kinship which may go a long way to explain the success of the Broadway stories with a public whom the movies had well prepared to appreciate Runyon's device. (pp. 121-22)

That Runyon's methodically sustained use of his self-concocted tense pattern contributes an essential share to the humorous atmosphere of his short stories is a fact that hardly needs to be stressed. In the first place, it is a deliberate deviation from the norm of general speech habits, and as such it is bound to be one of the first elements in Runyonese to strike the reader. But at the same time its effect is magnified by the skill with which the artist brings it to bear on the general economy of his story. Far from being a casually superimposed piece of apparel, it represents an essential component in a carefully blended whole. In a way, it may be considered as a protracted, masterly pun on time, which is permanently viewed with tongue in cheek. The present may mean the present, though it may also mean the past, but even then it does so only by virtue of what is to be regarded as a real tense metaphor, implying that what is known as present reality can validly be approached from both ends. (pp. 123-24)

Moreover, his wilful distortions of the values of time, which is one of the fundamental dimensions of human existence, run parallel not only to his distortions of respectable speech . . . , but also to those which situation, plot and characterization wreak on the accepted scale of social and moral values, and thus they tend to emphasize the author's personal philosophy concerning the nature of reality. Just as his secret iconoclasm achieves a sort of leveling by gently, but firmly taking down the socially prominent from the pedestals which they have erected for themselves and which public opinion in the dominant culture seems to condone, even so does his tense pattern rise in defiance to the hypocritical attitudes of a society which professes an idealistic reverence for the past when its actual endeavors are chiefly employed to wrest whatever it can from the present.

This goes to show how little is said about the deeper implications of his technique when Runyon is called "a devotee of the historical present". His carefully constructed tense pattern cannot easily be dismissed as a cheaper sort of mechanical contraption designed for mere public entertainment. It must, on the contrary, be appraised as a remarkably efficient instrument patiently devised by the writer to serve the expression of his own point of view concerning the realities of life in the America of his age. (p. 124)

Jean Wagner, in his Runyonese: The Mind and Craft of Damon Runyon *(copyright 1965 by Jean Wagner; reprinted by permission of the author), Stechert-Hafner, Inc., Paris, 1965, 173 p.*

BENNY GREEN (essay date 1975)

[*Runyon's use of the historic present tense in his short stories is praised by Green in the following excerpt. In his comparison of Runyon to O. Henry, Green, like E. C. Bentley (see excerpt above), finds that the two utilized totally different styles of writing. Green credits Runyon with inventing his own style.*]

[Links] between Runyon's world and the real thing have cost him dear, critically speaking, and there are still some people who imagine that he wrote the stories in some bar while chatting with friends, or knocked the tales off in a spare moment between assignments. Seventy two short stories knocked off in a spare moment? I doubt if there was any American writer of his period who pursued the techniques of fiction with more conscious devotion, or who pursued his own criteria of literary excellence more doggedly. The use of the historic-present tense, the inspired phrase-making, the admirable structural economy, were nothing like a photographic representation of life in the streets and speakeasies. That was where the fables began; they ended inside Runyon's head, with twenty or thirty rewrites, each word an agony, each paragraph a military operation. It was Runyon, and not Hemingway or Scott Fitzgerald or the Algonquin clowns who made the wisest remark of the period: "The words will not put themselves down on paper in dreams or in conversation."

Of course the stories are uneven. Sometimes they are not really narratives at all, but descriptive essays masquerading as narratives. **'The Bloodhounds of Broadway'**, for instance, is really an elegiac description of incongruity, with the two pooches, straight out of a Holmes story, dashing around the New York joints with such a nose for skullduggery that the policemen who are running with them are embarrassed to be so consistently confronted by their own crook-clients. "Why," says one copper, "these mutts are nothing but stool pigeons," which is a line worth manufacturing an entire story round. At other times the long arm of coincidence chokes off our credulity, as in **'The Brakeman's Daughter'**, where the hero just happens to go to the one house in the whole town, etc, etc. The other blemish on Runyon's work is the sentimentality which keeps breaking through. **'The Old Doll's House'** is the archetype of that sort of tale, where the twist in the plot depends on the maudlin elements of the characterisation.

But in the best tales, in those stories where style balances successfully on the knife-edge of events, Runyon achieves the dizziest heights. Nobody ever wrote a more ironic pearl than **'Blood Pressure'**, and not even Maupassant worked out a better last line than the one with which Runyon ends **'Breach of Promise'**. As for incongruity of the kind which dominates **'The Bloodhounds of Broadway'**, Runyon was its consummate master. I had forgotten the extent of the callous farce which constitutes **'Butch Minds the Baby'**, an extraordinary piece based on the idea that when a hoodlum has to look after a small child, business matters sometimes intervene. Butch saves his own skin by keeping cool in a crisis:

> 'I dast not run', he says, 'because if any coppers see me running they will start popping at me and maybe hit John Ignatius Junior, and besides will joggle the milk up in him and make him sick. My old lady always warns me never to joggle John Ignatius Junior when he is full of milk!'

The extract will serve as well as any other to make a point about Runyon's style which can easily be overlooked. Run-

yon's most daring ploy was his use of the historic present. Not simply in narration; most self-respecting writers could do the same. But Runyon constructed an entire world built on the historic present. It is not just the "I" who tells the tales who uses it, but everyone in every story. Notice how Butch, as well as the narrator, is aware of only one tense, and has mastered the art of achieving coherence while using only it and no other kind of time-scale. It was an extraordinary convention for Runyon to have adopted, and an even more extraordinary one for him to have justified so brilliantly so many times.

And yet for all his careful rewriting, for all his painstaking and his midnight oil, Runyon managed to inject the breath of life into his dialogue. Although there are no real people who have the poetic gift of Good Time Charlie Bernstein or Frankie Ferocious, the lines read as though you might go out on the streets and hear their echo. Runyon once wondered aloud whether his track record, sixteen short stories adapted for the cinema, was a world record. Whether it was or not, one writer who could never have challenged it was O. Henry, with whom Runyon is often bracketed. Apart from the fact that they were both small-town hicks in love with the Big City, and that they both mastered the trick ending, they seem to have been diametric opposites. . . . O. Henry used a kind of overripe mandarin style picked up in books; Runyon invented his own. The most striking thing of all about those seventy-two short stories is that Runyon would still have written them in exactly the same way if Europe had never existed. In the entire oeuvre I have only ever come across a single example of Runyon borrowing from what might loosely be called the bank of English Literature. The incident occurs in a story called **'The Melancholy Dane'**, in which the dramatic critic Ambrose Hammer blatantly plagiarises W. S. Gilbert. . . . The duplicity is doubly incongruous because Hammer, when he is not burglarising the classics, has a wonderful Runyonesque turn of phrase of his own, which inspires him to describe the cast as "a bunch of plumbers". And in the end, it is the turn of phrase, even more than the plot construction, which endears the reader to the Runyon stories, which mirror a world where horizontal heavyweights can't punch their way out of a paper bag, and the guy who gets slugged on the beezer folds up like an accordion. Furthermore. . . . (pp. 693-94)

Benny Green, "Benny Green on Guys, Dolls and Real People," in The Spectator *(© 1975 by* The Spectator; *reprinted by permission of* The Spectator*), Vol. 235, No. 7692, November 29, 1975, pp. 693-94.*

TOM CLARK (essay date 1981)

[*In this excerpt, Clark, the author of a comprehensive biography of Runyon (see additional bibliography), discusses the irony of Runyon's popularity in relation to his inability to provoke serious literary criticism.*]

Damon Runyon's Broadway tales are ironic mini-comedies based on the American outlaw code. It is the old Code of the West, transposed to Manhattan and the twentieth century. To live outside the law you must be honest, the saying used to go. Runyon rearranges it to read: To live outside the law you must be an interesting character, and anyway, no one is more honest than he has to be. (p. v)

The gangsters of Runyon's tales are patterned on the great outlaw-individualists of his era—the Buffalo Bills and Billy the Kids of the Jazz Age. (p. xiv)

For an earlier generation of readers, Runyon was an everyday experience. His newspaper columns and stories and his fictional tales were enjoyed by millions. One negative spin-off of this immense popularity was that it became a barrier to the acceptance of Runyon's fiction in "serious" literary circles, where in many cases the sheer success of a writer's work may be cited as an excuse for discriminating against it. At any rate, it would be no more fair to dismiss Runyon as a "popular writer" than it would be so to dismiss, say, Ring Lardner, who held an approximately equal position with Runyon in the public esteem, and who was an equally gifted writer. . . . That's always been half of Runyon's problem in academic circles.

The other half, I think, relates to the trick of "indirection," or the "half-boob air," which Runyon said he used to conceal the fact that he was always "a rebel at heart." The irony in the Broadway tales continues to waft like smoke over the heads of many of his academic readers. Runyon's trick of role-reversal, placing criminals and "legitimate" people on unfamiliar sides of the sympathy-meter in his stories, seems to bother many professors. (pp. xvi-xvii)

His reputation as a pioneering reporter is solid. His old columns can still be read for pleasure today. The *Dictionary of Slang* will tell you that Runyon, in his Broadway tales, nudged into the great common pool of spoken American a whole boatload of underworld expressions—the patois of Broadway. These expressions, to give only a token list, include such popular favorites as "cheaters" (for glasses), "cock-eyed" (for unconscious), "croak" (for die), "dukes" (for fists), "equalizer" (for gun), "hot spot" (for predicament), "kisser" (for mouth), "knock" (for criticism), "shill" (for pitch), "shiv" (for knife), "shoo-in" (for easy winner), "the shorts" (for lack of funds), and "monkey business" and "drop dead," which need no translation. (p. xviii)

> *Tom Clark, in his introduction to* The Bloodhounds of Broadway and Other Stories *by Damon Runyon (copyright © 1981 by American Play Company, Inc.; reprinted by permission of Raoul L. Felder, Esq. and American Play Co., Inc. of New York, NY), William Morrow and Company, Inc., 1981, pp. v-xviii.*

PATRICIA WARD D'ITRI (essay date 1982)

[*D'Itri's* Damon Runyon, *from which the following is excerpted, provides a valuable critical study of all of Runyon's work.*]

For the audience who read his short stories in popular magazines and anthologies, Damon Runyon was and still is identified with a small section of Broadway. . . .

Contrary to the popular myth fostered by Walter Winchell and other friends, however, the famous Runyonese format by no means sprang forth in its mature form with the first Broadway story. Rather, it culminated a long apprenticeship in the fiction-writing craft that began with the early short stories published in major magazines. . . . (p. 23)

[Clark Kinnaird's collection, ***Runyon First and Last***,] includes several of these short stories. They show an uneven quality and style, an experimental approach wherein Runyon tested various narrative formats, points of view, and devices for creating tone, humor, and dialect. The tales seem quite stilted, especially when told by an omniscient narrator. Without the famous Runyonese slang, tag expressions, and present tense, only occasional flashes of humor are reminiscent of the Broadway stories. Runyon adopted some stock literary characters

and plots as well as drawing from his own western culture, particularly the former pioneers, Denver politics, current news, and his experiences in the military and among hoboes. The best of these early stories reflect the western frontier humor of the tall tales. (pp. 23-4)

Runyon's humor was generally derived from circumstances of plot or linguistic contrasts, sometimes understatement, elevated language, or localisms and grammatical errors. Although his ear was more tuned to the prospect of getting a laugh than conveying an accurate representation of character and situation, in the early stories Runyon often exhibits a more accurate ear for regional dialect than he does in the Broadway stories. He did not use the tags of highly stylized speech such as "no little and quite some" that attracted the popular audience and repelled critics in later years. Runyon did incorporate slang and regional expressions although without the familiar "which is a way of saying" that often defined terms in the later stories. Instead, he simply inserted the meanings of words between dashes, as in these examples from **"The Informal Execution of Soupbone Pew."** "We had jungled up—camped—. . . and was boiling our soup—nitroglycerine—from Dynamite."

More loosely plotted than the Broadway tales, the stories have a natural if rambling evolution without the carefully forced twist at the end that later reminded critics of O. Henry. The plots are sufficiently structured to be fairly predictable, however; and Runyon very early tended to repeat any formula that would sell, as evidenced by the similar plots of **"As Between Friends"** and **"The Breeze Kid's Big Tear-Off."** (pp. 27-8)

Three groups of anecdotes and character sketches—Grandpap and Grandmaw, My Old Home Town, and Young Squirts—were also included in ***Runyon First and Last***. They were written after Runyon had developed a reputation as a humorist and had advanced from sports reporter to columnist on the *New York American*. First introduced as a correspondent to the column in 1916, A. Mugg later became the narrator through whose viewpoint Runyon commented on current news and sporting events, frequently by comparison with an event recalled from my old hometown out West. Between 1916 and 1926 Runyon often expressed an opinion on the editorial page and then developed the same idea in a more anecdotal recounting through the perspective of My Old Man or A. Mugg. Complete with plot and dialogue, these vignettes foreshadow Runyon's later Broadway stories more than the earlier short stories did because of their cynical attitude and mode of achieving humor as well as the use of the present tense, slang, and some of the tag expressions that later became famous Runyonese trademarks. The short vignettes often had twists at the end and a format that was extended into the more involved plots of the later Broadway tales. Thus, they reveal a significant stylistic shift away from the early stories. (pp. 31-2)

My Old Man is one of the most frequently depicted characters in Runyon's newspaper columns. The nostalgic and mild-mannered homespun philosopher with just a touch of larceny and malice is the central character in the collected edition of columns entitled ***My Old Man***. This culminated the fictional representations that began with **"My Father,"** a short story about the old pioneers that was published in 1911, the year Runyon's father died. This fictional character is more rebellious, resembling Grandpap Mugg, who is also a former pioneer trying to reclaim the western frontier spirit. Like Mark Twain's characters, My Old Man has "an almost preternatural shrewdness thinly veiled under the assumption of simplicity." (pp. 42-3)

The somewhat bland My Old Man columns probably would not have been collected in 1939, much less republished as part of *Short Takes* in 1946, but for Runyon's well-established reputation as a newspaper columnist and writer of short fiction. Whereas many of the uncollected columns are frolicsome vignettes in the same style as the Broadway short stories, at the height of its popularity Runyon sacrificed this writing style in the collected edition. Instead, the dialogue of the *My Old Man* collection is generally in the past tense. The sense of immediacy is lost and the prose is deadened by the seemingly endless repetition of "my old man said." Nonetheless, a few flashes of Runyon's cynicism enliven the vignettes. They sometimes end with a twist that reinforces a point set forth at the beginning or on a related but less significant matter. While some of the slang expressions are included, the linguistic color is more often provided by local western expressions or clichés. (pp. 43-4)

Whereas the *My Old Man* columns generally express a moderate, even tolerant outlook on his own and other people's foibles, the *In Our Town* vignettes often have a bitter outlook and enough cynicism to suit the audience attracted to Runyon's darker Broadway tales. They most graphically demonstrate Runyon's increasing alienation from the American society both because of the starkness of the negative behavior and its preponderance. (pp. 46-7)

Whereas My Old Man derides pretension and exposes hypocrisy with a sham *mea culpa* attitude that the narrator occasionally exposes, in *In Our Town* he makes no attempt to excuse or explain the violence, greed, and hypocrisy that are only occasionally interspersed with acts of kindness, generosity, or courage. The conflicts are usually between intimates, often husbands and wives whose social training in morals and ethics is overcome as they succumb to baser impulses. "Our best citizens" have few redeeming virtues and often reflect due cause for Runyon's alienation. (pp. 47-8)

In Runyon's character sketches the antisocial attitude is quite graphic as the Puritan ethic is frequently reversed. Then the lazy, evil, or incompetent are rewarded. Widely held beliefs are often also refuted, such as the idea that money corrupts and goodness and virtue must win out over evil. Instead, good fortune is as likely to be showered upon the undeserving citizens profiled in *In Our Town* as on those to whom respectability would give a greater claim. (p. 50)

Many of [Runyon's] news stories followed the now traditional format, presenting the major facts first and then a detailed exposition in decreasing order of importance. Like all good writers, however, Runyon allowed himself substantial latitude for different approaches. He was especially adept at describing small details and angles that were often overlooked by other reporters. Runyon probably adapted easily to writing fiction because many of his news stories often did not follow a traditional reporting style anyway. Three volumes of columns demonstrate his skill and versatility as a news reporter and columnist: *Short Takes, Trials and Other Tribulations,* and *My Wife Ethel.* . . .

[*Short Takes*] received one remarkable review, the one written by Runyon himself [see excerpt above]. (p. 56)

[He contended] that he was more of a social critic than people generally realized. Saying things with a half-boob air, he was able to get ideas out of his system on the wrongs of the world, although his ability to convey thoughts by indirection made it appear that he was not personally responsible for what he said,

thus undercutting its significance. In his own defense Runyon said that his social comments were allowed if passed off as humor whereas they would have been erased if said in a more serious tone. (pp. 56-7)

Unlike the *My Old Man, In Our Town,* and *My Wife Ethel* collections, *Short Takes* does not maintain a single point of view, theme, or format. Each section includes Runyon's columns on a particular topic, such as autobiographical notes, sports, Broadway and Hollywood characters, animals, domestic issues, his illness, and even some fairy tales. The diversity of writing styles, formats, and opinions in this collection effectively demonstrates Runyon's versatility. (p. 57)

[For *Trials and Tribulations,* Runyon] chose and edited daily columns of five trials and one Senate hearing that related some clear morals or comments on the American social system. One distinctive theme is the humorous contempt with which Runyon views the upper echelons of society when their hypocrisy is exposed in trials for murder or separate maintenance. In contrast, Runyon was more respectful in references to the dead gambler Arnold Rothstein when George C. McManus was on trial for his murder. And his account of Al Capone's trial for income tax evasion is especially conservative. This is notable in comparison with the accounts of an investigation by a subcommittee of the Senate Committee on Banking and Currency into allegations that J. P. Morgan, the financier, paid no taxes during the years that Capone was accused of paying too little. These two final segments of *Trials and Other Tribulations* in themselves reflect some of Runyon's most cynical views on the American social structure.

The facts of these trials are presented so that good and evil have less relevance than the arbitrary distinctions of social status, especially when reinforced by "a lot of potatoes." Moreover, wealth stolen within the law warrants more respect than the ill-gotten gains by members of the underworld, the same code of ethics often expressed in recollections of my old hometown out West. (p. 63)

[Runyon] understood the prejudices, fears, and interests of the audience for whom he wrote. They wanted to know about such external badges of status as the participants' clothing and automobiles. His careful eye for detail and his subjective reactions pander to the readers' interest in sensationalism. Runyon served as Everyman's eyewitness in the courtroom. The old sports reporter also was very crowd conscious. He bitingly portrays the hordes of people who scrambled for the few spectator seats in the crowded courtroom so they could watch the sordid revelations unfold firsthand. At one point, Runyon recalled the works of a British artist as he remarked that "it seems a pity that old man Hogarth isn't living to depict the crowd scene in the courtroom yesterday." (pp. 63-4)

In the 1930s Runyon hit upon one of his most successful vehicles for expressing his views on mundane daily matters ranging from domestic wars to local politics. In this format, something like Ring Lardner's *You Know Me, Al,* a citizen of Brooklyn named Joe Turp writes to the columnist to describe wife Ethel's witticisms and methods of manipulating her husband, something in the manner of the George Burns and Gracie Allen comedy team. Runyon spoke through the Turps on social and political issues to the end of his life. In addition, two short stories about the Turps were also published, **"A Call on the President"** in 1937 and **"Nothing Happens in Brooklyn"** in 1938. They demonstrate Runyon's transition from feature column to short story as the same characters and style are woven into a more complicated plot. (pp. 71-2)

The daily columns in the form of Joe's letters are briefer and have less elaborate plots than the short stories. They could serve as a kind of Everyman's history of the late 1930s and early 1940s as well as a diary of domestic life. Joe and Ethel discuss everything from shaving cream to why Joe Kennedy would not wear short pants to meet the King of England and who might get the lead in the movie version of "Gone With the Wind." (p. 73)

All of these columns [collected in *My Wife Ethel*] turn on a small incident, a bit of homespun advice, or an opinion. They add humor and insight regarding ordinary domestic life. As Runyon himself went from boy outcast to man celebrity, the Turps reflect his ability to describe a large subgroup of the American society with which he was never directly affiliated, the working class. (p. 74)

Runyon usually is not given credit for writing what is assumed to be folk poetry with a more distant heritage. Like Thayer's "Casey at the Bat," however, some of Runyon's poems have passed into national folklore. Among those particularly are **"Pool Shootin' Roy"** and **"The Old Horse Player."** Others like **"Left"** and **"What the Shell Says"** also have been widely and usually anonymously quoted although Runyon's authorship is still generally acknowledged for his most famous poem, **"A Handy Guy Like Sande."**

Runyon must have recognized that his poems were not likely to enhance his literary reputation because he later claimed that he did not even keep copies of them. What is certain is that he did not list the two earliest books of poetry, [*The Tents of Trouble* and *Rhymes of the Firing Line*] . . . , among his collected works in later years. They were again acknowledged, however, when *Poems for Men* was published in 1947. (pp. 78-9)

[In his poetry,] Runyon drew graphic portraits that touch a humorous or sentimental vein among readers who like the vernacular and the common touch. Reviewer Leo Kennedy noted his "brilliant and thrifty character drawing" and contended that Runyon's poetic forebears were Robert Service, from whom he learned his favorite ballad forms, and Rudyard Kipling, from whom he learned dramatic lyricism. But the overriding factor is that Runyon's poems were written in much the same popular format that was and still is common in magazines and newspapers. Limericks, rhymed couplets, word puns, and verse vignettes made household words of names like Edgar Guest and Richard Armour as well as Robert Service and numerous colleagues of Runyon's. . . . (p. 79)

Horse racing inspired Runyon's most famous poem, **"A Handy Guy Like Sande,"** which was revised and reprinted several times between 1922 and 1940. The first version celebrated Earl Sande's ability to win. When an injury sustained in a fall from a horse at Saratoga Springs prompted Sande's retirement in 1924, Runyon added a touch of sentimentality that was enhanced fourteen years later when Sande came out of retirement to win the Kentucky Derby. "Say, but I'm young agin', Watchin' that handy / Guy named Sande, / Bootin' a winner in!"

The gambler's greed and ultimate debacle are affirmed in Runyon's second most famous poem, **"All Hawse Players *Must* Die Broke!"** The refrain, "The sucker is a terrible institution!"

is a theme that underlies most of the poems about gambling. (p. 88)

[Despite] their frequently irregular form and awkward rhyme schemes, the substance of these poems maintains a kind of universal appeal because again Runyon speaks as Everyman. He was not a poet but a rhymester whose verses convey some of the hopes, fears, and regrets that his readers readily understand. The selections included in *Poems for Men* are particularly likely to have an optimistic note or cynicism qualified by humor. Those republished from earlier editions are not always the best, but they more accurately reflect Runyon's reputation as a colorful commentator on sports, gambling, war, and the ordinary conditions of life. Notable among these are: loneliness, failure, and disappointment, whether in the big city, military service, or athletics. (pp. 88-9)

> *Patricia Ward D'Itri, in her* Damon Runyon *(copyright © 1982 by Twayne Publishers, Inc.; reprinted with the permission of Twayne Publishers, a Division of G. K. Hall & Co., Boston), Twayne, 1982, 168 p.*

ADDITIONAL BIBLIOGRAPHY

Bentley, E. C. "Furthermore." *The Spectator* 159, No. 5203 (15 October 1937): 636-37.
    Letter to the editor in reply to J.F.L. (see entry below). Bentley's letter, written in Runyonese, is a tongue-in-cheek defense of his introduction to *More than Somewhat*.

Brown, Calvin S. "The Luck of Little Miss Marker." *The Western Humanities Review* XI, No. 4 (1957): 341-45.*
    Traces remarkable similarities in the lives and works of Runyon and Bret Harte.

Clark, Tom. *The World of Damon Runyon*. New York: Harper & Row, 1958, 303 p.
    Fresh biography, with many anecdotal references to Runyon's contemporaries.

Du Bose, La Rocque. "Damon Runyon's Underworld Lingo." *Texas University Studies in English* XXVII (1953): 123-32.
    Examines words of nonliterary origin in Runyon's short stories.

Hoyt, Edwin P. *A Gentleman of Broadway*. Boston: Little, Brown and Co., 1964, 369 p.
    Comprehensive biography.

Iddon, Don. "Memoir of the Author." In *Runyon on Broadway*, rev. ed., by Damon Runyon, pp. xi-xviii. London: Constable, 1954.
    Reminiscences of Runyon's newspaper days.

J.F.L. "More Late than Somewhat." *The Spectator* 159, No. 5702 (8 October 1937): 589.
    Letter to the editor regarding E. C. Bentley's introduction to *More than Somewhat*. J.F.L. uses Runyonese in this humorous reproval of the English critics who hailed Bentley for introducing Runyon's stories to Great Britain. There had been, in fact, previous British publication of Runyon's work.

Kinnaird, Clark. Foreword to *Runyon First and Last*, by Damon Runyon, pp. 7-29. Philadelphia: J. B. Lippincott Co., 1949.
    Perceptive biographical essay.

Weiner, Ed. *The Damon Runyon Story*. New York, London: Longmans, Green and Co., 1948, 258 p.
    Early biography, written with conversational scenes "to give the book interest and continuity."

Tess Slesinger

1905-1945

American novelist, short story writer, and screenwriter.

During her short career, Slesinger was famous as a satirist and working-class activist. Her novel *The Unpossessed*, an insider's sardonic portrait of life among New York's radical intellectuals, attracted wide, enthusiastic critical attention. Slesinger was an acknowledged master of the short story, and her work in the genre has often been compared to that of Dorothy Parker, Virginia Woolf, and Katherine Mansfield. Among her screenplays, Slesinger's adaptations of Pearl S. Buck's *The Good Earth* and Betty Smith's *A Tree Grows in Brooklyn* are particularly accomplished.

Slesinger was born in New York of immigrant Hungarian and Russian parents. As a child, she was high-spirited, faddish, and a remarkable liar, who once presented her parents with a copy of *Pinocchio* and claimed that she was the author. "I was born with the curse of intelligent parents, a happy childhood and nothing valid to rebel against," she later explained. "So I rebelled against telling the truth." Slesinger wrote stories as part of her youthful revolt, and later pursued her literary interests at Swarthmore College and the Columbia School of Journalism. Graduating from Columbia in 1925, she held a number of odd jobs over the next several years, working for a short time at the *New York Evening Post Literary Review*. She married Herbert Solow in 1928 and was immediately brought among his circle of associates, a group of leftist Jewish intellectuals that included Lionel Trilling, Elliot Cohen, Philip Rahv, and Clifton Fadiman. Solow was himself the assistant editor of the *Menorah Journal*, a periodical which served as an organ for the "New York Intellectuals," as the group was called, and which first published Slesinger's short fiction. During her four years of marriage to Solow, Slesinger published several short stories that reflected the increasing unhappiness caused by her association with a self-styled elite who, in her opinion, were possessed by little but vanity, ennui, and inertia. The most powerful and well known of all her stories, "Missis Flinders," was published soon after Slesinger's divorce from Solow; it is a semiautobiographical story of a woman denied understanding, love, and children by a radical, Byronic husband who cannot be bothered by such restrictions on his all-important work. "Missis Flinders" later served as the final chapter of Slesinger's novel *The Unpossessed*, in which she introduced, and then skewered, a group of intellectuals similar to the group she had known.

The Unpossessed was an immediate critical and commercial success. According to Clifton Fadiman, the novel marked "one of the first times in which a group of people were portrayed who were, as we say now, looking for their identities. They were unpossessed people who wanted to be possessed by something, by a sense of career or a sense of love, by something, and weren't." Encouraged by the success of the book, Slesinger wrote and published in quick order the stories that were collected in *Time: The Present* in 1935. Written in the depths of the Great Depression, the stories express her concern for the unemployed, her sadness at life's many unfulfilled expectations, and her perceptions of the personal effects of sudden economic success. *Time: The Present* was critically praised for

its well-drawn characters, sensitivity, and satiric wit, for which the author was frequently compared to Dorothy Parker (a comparison Slesinger hated). Soon after this success, Slesinger was offered steady employment as a motion-picture screenwriter, and in mid-1935 she moved to Hollywood. There she met and married her second husband, Frank Davis, and the two worked for Metro-Goldwyn-Mayer and RKO Studios—often in collaboration—until Slesinger's death. While in Hollywood, Slesinger became known as an outspoken member of the fledgling Screen Writer's Guild and the Anti-Nazi League. Accustomed to New York's timid radicalism, which had stifled her own Stalinist leanings, Slesinger enjoyed her role as an activist as well as her newfound career. Although her treatment of such works as *The Good Earth*; *Dance, Girl, Dance*; and *A Tree Grows in Brooklyn* has been praised, Slesinger wrote very little original material after moving to Hollywood. Shortly after completing work on *A Tree Grows in Brooklyn*, she died of cancer.

Early reviews of Slesinger's books were highly favorable. Since the 1930s, much of the critical discussion of her work has centered on *The Unpossessed*, with the author's intent becoming a common point of departure for critical conjecture. Murray Kempton has described the novel as a document which presents portraits of actual figures from among the New York Intellectuals, a position rebutted by Alan Wald, who perceives

The Unpossessed as a satire written less out of malice than for instructive illumination. In recent years, with reprints of both of Slesinger's books, the author has been interpreted as a feminist who artfully melded women's concerns with socio-economic thought. Her technical skill, in particular, is highly praised. George Stevens wrote that Slesinger's "observation is acute, her style is alive, and her timing is as perfect as O. Henry's"—an appraisal which has often been reaffirmed. Although Slesinger's work is not well known today, she is important, according to Wald, for creating in *The Unpossessed* "a prototype of the Jewish/intellectual writings of Saul Bellow, and the social/satirical stories and novels of Mary McCarthy."

(See also *Contemporary Authors*, Vol. 107.)

PRINCIPAL WORKS

The Unpossessed (novel) 1934
Time: The Present (short stories) 1935; also published as *On Being Told That Her Second Husband Has Taken His First Lover, and Other Stories* [enlarged edition], 1971
*The Good Earth (screenplay) 1937
Dance, Girl, Dance [with Frank Davis] (screenplay) 1940
**A Tree Grows in Brooklyn [with Frank Davis] (screenplay) 1945
A Hollywood Gallery (sketches) 1979; published in journal *Michigan Quarterly Review*

*This screenplay is an adaptation of the novel *The Good Earth*, by Pearl S. Buck.

**This screenplay is an adaptation of the novel *A Tree Grows in Brooklyn*, by Betty Smith.

JOHN CHAMBERLAIN (essay date 1934)

[*Chamberlain provides an approving and enthusiastic review of* The Unpossessed.]

Tess Slesinger's **"The Unpossessed"** . . . is, quite simply and dogmatically, the best novel of contemporary New York City that we have read. It has a ferocious drive, a wild and unfaltering rhythm, a quality of wit that is lightly blended of malice and understanding, a complete grasp of most of the characters concerned in the plot, a terrifically effective denouement, a contemporaneity that is as absolutely of 1934 as that of Floyd Dell's "Janet March" was of 1923 or "This Side of Paradise" of 1919, and construction that is impeccable. Its clever intellectuals are not merely described as clever; they are exhibited making clever remarks, observations and speeches. The book will wreak havoc among many of its readers; it should teach a generation to know itself, and to do something about itself. But perhaps that is too wild a hope.

Any one who has been to a New York literary party and caught phrases about the "revolution" through the clink of ice will immediately recognize the cousins and the brothers and even the uncles and the aunts of his friends in Miss Slesinger's "uniquely disinherited class" of intellectuals.

Are the characters of **"The Unpossessed"** a hothouse group, to be found only in New York? Probably, but they are as valid a part of the American present, and as necessary to an understanding of the present, as Turgeniev's nihilists were to a full understanding of pre-revolutionary Russia. **"The Unpossessed"** constantly recalls to us those Russian novels of impotence and despair, novels in which the semi-westernized intellectuals sit around country houses talking of the end of "Holy Russia," hearing the crunch of the axes in the cherry trees, and expressing their wills to action by drinking more tea. Only, in Miss Slesinger's story, they talk of founding a magazine, of "boring from within," of the "role of the intellectual in the class struggle," of the "individualism," now outmoded, of the Nineteen Twenties. As Miss Slesinger says, they "play at making revolutions for a band of workers we've never even seen," and "our meetings are masterpieces of postponement."

This sounds like very feminine and very snooty satire. But it isn't. A merely satirical book, born of contempt for the human animal who can never match promise with performance, would never leave the reader quivering with pity and quaking with terror as **"The Unpossessed"** succeeds in doing. Miles Flinders, the eternal Calvinist, the eternal New Englander, is too close to home to be passed off lightly as the object of an extended sneer. The Black Sheep, Columbia undergraduates who object to overemphasizing football, have all appeared in the news; in Miss Slesinger's book they go to Washington with the hunger marchers; in actual life, their counterparts went to Harlan County, Ky. Their professor and mentor, the bitter Jewish intellectual, Bruno Leonard, whose contempt for himself is constantly exploding in speeches that are masterpieces of combined invective and self-pity, has been heard on a hundred rostrums. The particular speech that disrupts Miss Slesinger's group, delivered at a drunken party, might be thought too clever for actuality—but Ben Hecht has made equally brilliant speeches at the moon on 3 o'clock of a morning in a Chicago street. . . .

The plot of **"The Unpossessed"** is brilliantly cockeyed. The components of an old college triumvirate—Miss Flinders, eternal New Englander; Jeffrey Blake (the only unconvincing character in the story), who is a wandering Don Juan, and Bruno, the bitter, compassionate, rueful, self-loathing Bruno—have long plotted the Perfect Magazine, the only real Open Forum in the Western World, an organ for the expression of any one's revolt, provided that revolt be sincere. The complications turn on the friendship of a young undergraduate, Emmett Middleton, for Bruno. . . .

Miss Slesinger is an adept, a psychic adept, at picking things out of the air. All of the characters in the drawings of The New Yorker are adumbrated in **"The Unpossessed."** Even a hint of Thurber's preposterous "The War Between Men and Women" is here. But Miss Slesinger is not oblique; the case of Margaret against Miles is that Miles won't bring a child into this world, this lousy world (where have we heard this speech before?), and she is left—to smoke cigarettes, to stare at the blooms in geranium pots on Charles Street and to lament (below the surface of her consciousness) her lack of the normal interests of her species. Miles and Margaret are symbolic of a class come to nothingness.

> John Chamberlain, "Books of the Times: 'The Unpossessed'," in The New York Times (© 1934 by The New York Times Company; reprinted by permission), May 9, 1934, p. 18.

PHILIP RAHV (essay date 1934)

[*One of the founding editors of* The Partisan Review *and a central figure among the "New York Intellectuals," Rahv was a fervent*

Marxist at the time he wrote this essay. His review of The Unpossessed, *a novel which pillories figures similar to his own
colleagues, is alternately favorable and derisive.*]

Generally speaking, [the characters in ***The Unpossessed***] are
"neither fish nor flesh nor good red herring, just lousy intellectuals." There is Bruno Leonard, a professor, a top-notch
sophisticate inundating page after page with his brilliant rhetoric of futility; his cousin Elizabeth ("she gave him the glad
eye, the mad eye, the sad eye"); . . . and Al, the cynical
business man who swings a sinuous wisecrack into the wretched
crew. On the positive side we find the Black Sheep, a little
band of class-conscious students as charming in their own way—
in the purely esthetic sense—as Proust's frieze of young girls
on the shore of Balbec. On the whole an orchestra of first
violins out of tune.

And the plot. The chorus sings and sobs: *Why Can't We Have
a Magazine?* while Margaret fills in with her tremulous solo:
Why Can't I Have a Baby? in the long intervals between stimulus and fumbled action there are domestic scenes, discussions
on the Magazine and the Revolution, the Plight of the Intellectuals, Elizabeth's sex-express that fails to stop at Bruno's
station, and the machinations of "Comrade" Fisher, who is
kneaded out of the same mud-pile as those insufferably clever
young men, veterans of the Zionist salvation army, who are
now writing articles for liberal weeklies on the strategy and
tactics of the world revolution and the villainy of Stalin. Finally
we hit the climax—the combined Hunger March and Magazine
Party, which is a real Walpurgis night of intellectual and emotional decomposition.

It is hard to formulate an attitude to this book. It is undoubtedly
a significant work, if only because it points sharply to the
ideological cul-de-sac in which the esthete-modernists of the
twenties now find themselves. It shows that sophistication,
with the consequent isolation of its victims from the mainland
of revolutionary struggle, is simply a different facet of the
Babbittism that it aimed to undermine. It shows that sophistication is dying, and Miss Slesinger is lending a hand in erecting its tombstone. To do this, however, is relatively easy and
is not enough. Her novel fails to give a disciplined orientation
to the intellectual whose need for it she makes so palpable.
The intellectual's relation to the revolutionary movement is the
focus of the book, yet the author's own attitude to the movement is ambiguous. More than once we become unpleasantly
aware of a certain psychological spite in her. Her knife slashes
indiscriminately, and we get the impression that the hand that
wields it is in frenzy. Hence we are justified in asking Miss
Slesinger where she is in all this turmoil. Has Dr. Bruno Leonard absconded with her, or is she really wise to him?

The very title of the novel, ***The Unpossessed,*** is in itself confusing. The intellectuals are only superficially a unique social
grouping; basically they belong to the middle class, sharing all
its vacillations and alliances. It is only the fact that in art and
literature they at times operate at an oblique angle from their
class that deceives writers like Miss Slesinger, leading them
to the conception of the intellectuals as a socially independent
group. One must also protest against the author's assumption
that the characters she draws are truly representative of the
intellectuals. Her people are merely a special little sub-group-
ing of hyper-sophisticates. And it is this assumption which
results in largely ignoring the thousands of related individuals—within the category of her subject as a whole—who have
ceased straddling the fence.

This book proves Miss Slesinger to be a highly conscious
literary technician. She has put to good use a variety of methods
that only the best of modern writers have used effectively. But
her writing suffers somewhat from a lack of economy. Too
often her ideas and perceptions are dissolved in the flow of
verbal excitement. (pp. 26-7)

> *Philip Rahv, "Storm over the Intellectuals," in* New
> Masses *(copyright, 1934, The New Masses, Inc.),
> Vol. XI, No. 9, May 29, 1934, pp. 26-7.*

TESS SLESINGER   (letter date 1934)

[*Slesinger recalls the beginning of her career, then discusses her
intent and characters in* The Unpossessed.]

I was born with the curse of intelligent parents, a happy childhood and nothing valid to rebel against. So I rebelled against
telling the truth. I told whoppers at three, tall stories at four,
and home-runs at five. From six to sixteen I wrote them in a
diary. Instead of being spanked I was dressed up one day for
a visit to a psychoanalyst; he listened while I lied for an hour
and agreed that I might as well settle down to writing my lies
for a career. My further equipment for writing is an insatiable
memory for unimportant details, and (still more uninteresting)
the fact that unlike most of my writing friends I get a kick out
of writing.

Altho the background of my novel is New York, the idea in
my head is intellectuals anywhere (but Russia) in the twentieth
century. I discovered when traveling abroad that national barriers were nothing compared to class barriers, and similarly
that class bonds were stronger than any bond I could have,
even in Budapest, with a New Yorker who hadn't read Proust.
Whether we like it or not I think intellectuals are a class by
themselves, belonging rather less than any other class to society
as it functions today; which is why I called the novel ***The
Unpossessed.*** I can't attempt any dogmatic definitions because
many intellectuals seem unintelligent; but let's say the doubt-
ers, the worriers, the weighers of the world; the class interested
in things not essentially economically remunerative. I picture
them—us, my contemporaries, my fraternity brothers— on board
the fast twentieth century express, the twentieth century unlimited, hell-bent for nowhere' on which one of my characters
very consciously pictures herself. I do not mean at any point
to treat my characters lightly or view their quandaries with
nasty amusement. Neither do I wish to portray them as singularly tragic. But I have attempted to catch them at the vital
point in their lives, both individually and collectively, the point
from which they split off and save themselves or acknowledge
and face their defeat. If they seem unusually hard-hit and too
self-knowing, it is because I have tried to picture them on the
level in their consciousness where they are forced to tell themselves the truth.

> *Tess Slesinger, in a letter to her publishers, in the*
> Wilson Bulletin for Librarians, *Vol. 9, No. 4, No-
> vember 1934, p. 170.*

EDITH H. WALTON   (essay date 1935)

[*Walton discusses the stories in* Time: The Present *and compares
Slesinger's writings to those of Dorothy Parker.*]

Miss Slesinger would appear to be standing in line for Dorothy
Parker's shoes. The differences between them—and they are
many—can largely be explained in terms of the gulf between

the late Nineteen Twenties and the middle Nineteen Thirties. If Miss Slesinger's work has soberer implications, if she shows marked evidences of social consciousness, if her manner is less flippant and personal—all this can be traced to the prevalent temper of the day. Since Miss Slesinger is alertly contemporary, it is natural that her tone should differ from Mrs. Parker's. Both, however, have the same type of wit, the same extremely feminine sensitiveness, the same ability to reflect their age.

"Time: The Present" is a book of short stories, through which runs the identical note of rueful satire which distinguished **"The Unpossessed."** Miss Slesinger's young intellectuals are not nearly so pleased with themselves as were their counterparts in the giddy Nineteen Twenties. Faced with social choices, rootless, fettered by a code of modernity which has come to seem irksome, they are inclined to wish that their emotions were less tortuous and complex. **"Missis Flinders,"** having agreed to an abortion, is resentful against her husband for encouraging her to shrink from life. The woman whose husband has been unfaithful rebels against the need to accept his defection gallantly. All of them are conscious of being sterile, empty, and divided in their allegiances.

By no means all the stories, to be sure, have a sophisticated background. Probably the best tale in the book is the much-discussed **"Missis Flinders"**—which formed the final chapter of **"The Unpossessed"**—but close to it comes **"White on Black,"** a restrained and very effective commentary on racial discrimination. A Negro brother and sister have an astonishing early success at a "liberal" private school in New York. They are good athletes, born leaders, young gods to their white classmates. As the children grow older, however, and prejudice creeps in, the Negroes are slowly and inevitably thrust beyond the pale. Humbly they take the place which is to be theirs for the rest of their lives.

As further evidence of Miss Slesinger's versatility there is **"Jobs in the Sky,"** a stinging cross-section of the Christmas rush at a department store, and **"The Friedmans' Annie,"** which concerns a German servant girl, lately and proudly emerged from her greenhorn state, who is torn between loyalty to her fiancé and to the family which so selfishly exploits her. Both of these are well done, but because she is less sure of her ground Miss Slesinger's acid does not bite so deep as in **"After the Party"**—a devastating burlesque of a literary tea and of a professional hostess who has turned to entertaining as an anodyne for pampered neuroticism. This story is as malicious as the wickedest parts of **"The Unpossessed."**

Not so consciously clever, and therefore superior, are **"Mother to Dinner,"** the story of a girl whose love is distractedly divided between her mother and her husband, and **"The Answer on the Magnolia Tree,"** a shrewd study of the cross-currents and atmosphere of a fashionable girls' school. Both these tales are very delicately and sensitively done and lack the meretriciousness of such unconvincing yarns as **"Relax Is All"** or **"The Times Unsettled Are."** Even at her worst, as in these stories, Miss Slesinger is always glib and entertaining, but her polish conceals a kind of easy sentimentality which she would do well to suppress.

Aside from her personal brilliance there is no doubt that Miss Slesinger synthesizes the mood and the gestures of a large group as Dorothy Parker and others have done before her. Her intellectuals are as up to date as the country club wastrels of John O'Hara; her views on love, marriage and the social order are such as the best young minds can cheerfully sponsor. What

her future will be is still doubtful. There is an element of trickiness and caricature in her writing, more glitter than real feeling in spite of her frequent moments of tenderness. It is always dangerous to be quite so ardently contemporary and to constitute one's self a spokesman for ephemeral fashions of thought.

At the moment, however, Miss Slesinger is as witty and exhilirating a storyteller as one can find anywhere. Her very modernity is naturally appealing—an asset in the short run whatever it may be hereafter. There is not a single dull story in **"Time: the Present,"** nor one that is not written with a kind of crackling zest. To return to the original parallel, she has chosen worthier material for satire than Dorothy Parker and her eye for human weaknesses is almost as piercing and uncanny.

> *Edith H. Walton, "The Satirical Stories of Tess Slesinger," in* The New York Times Book Review *(© 1935 by The New York Times Company; reprinted by permission), May 26, 1935, p. 7.*

ROBERT M. ADAMS   (essay date 1966)

[Slesinger's vision is compared with that of Émile Zola and Fyodor Dostoyevsky.]

As a novelist of social protest, Miss Slesinger was altogether in the respectable tradition of Zola when she depicted the proletarian sufferer as sexually deprived and exploited—an owned but not possessed—woman. Like Zola, too, she hesitated over making her mystique of woman (natural, vital, instinctual woman) a black or a white religion. There is, to be sure, no figure of diabolic proportions in [*The Unpossessed*], whether witch or warlock; but several of the women in the book serve, no less effectually than the men, as agents of muddle and impotence. Indeed, Miss Slesinger's characters are just as much "possessed" as those in the Dostoevsky novel which, evidently, she had steadily in mind as she wrote. They are all pretty much dominated by phantoms, to the point sometimes of caricature and burlesque; if one of the four major females is allowed to suggest, for a pathetic moment, the possible goodness and richness of life, that scarcely gives the sex as a whole redemptive powers or functions. There isn't really more than a token center of positive value in the book; it is one of the most anti-political revolutionary novels of an age which often thought ideology an imposed but unfortunate necessity.

A perspective on its happy peculiarities can be had by reading *The Unpossessed* alongside Miss Slesinger's book of short stories, *Time: the Present* . . . ; the novel, it seems, succeeded in getting out of its author's ideological control, as too few of these contrived and limited stories ever did. . . . But *The Unpossessed* is more complicated, because at least in its tone of false romantic despair it is authentic. Bruno Leonard's catastrophic speech at the climactic party for the Hunger Marchers corresponds to a similar disastrous venture toward articulation by Stepan Trofimovitch at the literary fete which climaxes Dostoevsky's novel; and both speeches are haunted by a sort of buffoonish sincerity. The total collapse of rhetoric is supposed to provide evidence of insights reaching beyond rhetoric; intellectual contrivance and artifice go down the drain in a swirl of destructive language. If anyone attains transcendent insight in *The Unpossessed* that insight is entirely bleak and negative. No harm to this, quite the contrary; whatever its technical deficiencies, *The Unpossessed* is not work done to a formula. But perhaps it supplies in itself a reason why Miss

Slesinger, in the last decade of her sadly foreshortened life, did not write another novel, or carry further, in any literary direction, the talent so apparent in this book. (p. 32)

Robert M. Adams, "Restorations," in The New York Review of Books *(reprinted with permission from* The New York Review of Books; *copyright © 1966 Nyrev, Inc.), Vol. VII, No. 6, October 20, 1966, pp. 31-3.**

ANNIE GOTTLIEB (essay date 1974)

[*Gottlieb examines feminist elements in Slesinger's work.*]

[Reviewing Tess Slesinger] gives me a particular sense of futility because in her writing she is so very much alive.

But there's no futility in recommending her to readers, and perhaps especially to women. I don't mean to be parochial, or to imply that she is; there is so much in Tess Slesinger's writing to interest anyone; her shrewd observation of social class behavior, her acid and self-ironic version of left-leaning 1930's idealism (hers may be the first devastating portrait of the liberal), her striking ability to penetrate *both* sides of a man-woman relationship, especially in her novel, where she has more room to maneuver. Like all good writers she is ultimately an androgyne and knows it; the protagonist of . . . **"A Life in the Day of a Writer,"** is male, but listen as the author records the drunken, Dionysian possession of the writer by his tale:

> "Listen, non-writers, this is *passion*. I am trembling, I am weak, I am strong, pardon me a moment while I go and make love to the world, it may be indecent, it may be mad—but as I stalk about the room now I *am not* a man and I am not a woman. . . ."

Yet there are qualities about Tess Slesinger that are immutably female; and it is a mark of progress that this may now be regarded, not as a handicap but as a definite advantage. Women writers may well feel like stout Cortez silent upon a peak in Darien: their own living experience is largely unexplored territory—one field, at least, in which everything has *not* been said. And in this respect Tess Slesinger was, and still is, a pioneer.

One must remember the times she lived in (one can rarely forget them—yet they never make a barrier between her work and us). And I think the most important point to remember about those times, from the point of view of Tess Slesinger's writing as a woman, is that marriage in the 1930's was still an established institution, something that young people—and of course especially women—entered into with the fervent expectation of making a life of it. This curiously abstract yet passionate commitment to marriage, and the ambivalent and often terrifying reality underlying it, gave Tess Slesinger something to probe: what it means and what it does to a woman to try to live for a man; the pride and terror of becoming Mrs. So-and-So; playing grownup, imitating Mother's rituals of marketing and making dinner; living with a stranger, and being so hyper-aware of his wishes, so bound to his word and glance (in **"The Unpossessed,"** she writes of Margaret Flinders's husband Miles "who made his wishes felt not by a bell in her ears but by a constant frightened consciousness in the very lining of her being" . . .). (p. 31)

Experiences that are *still* familiar, but that no woman could write about now in so pure a laboratory of situation, or so free

of analytical commentary; the germ of "consciousness" has invaded not only our thoughts but our lives, and it is merciful, but it means we are often in too much of a hurry to cast off significant experiences, too appalled by them to examine them unless to explain them away. Tess Slesinger examines them for us in a calm and curious way without value judgments. In **"Mother to Dinner,"** one of her best stories, she shows the young wife of 11 months utterly torn—in a way that is really ancient, archetypal—between the cradling matriarchal continuity of her relationship with her mother and the new, intellectually superior, sexually compelling, but frightening and lonely commitment to that stranger, her husband. (There is one brief critical moment in the story when she says: *"Why couldn't they both leave her alone?"* You see, Tess Slesinger *is* "conscious," but it is the consciousness of an artist, not an ideologue.) In the title story, we see a very bright young woman using every ounce of wit and energy in her overactive brain to fend off her own hurt and put on an insouciant act at learning, once again, of a husband's infidelity.

The more total involvement of women in love and marriage, and their consequent vulnerability, is not by far Tess Slesinger's only theme—there are working women braving their bosses, writing women (the delightful self-parody Regina Sawyer, author of "The Undecided," in **"After the Party"**), a spinster in triumphant sexual awakening (**"Relax Is All"**), an immigrant maid conned by her employer into betraying her own class and kind (**"The Friedmans' Annie"**). But marriage is one of her best subjects, and it is, I'd venture to guess, what she would have written about if she had lived into her forties. In her novel, she perceptively explores the other side of the story—the man's dread that the woman will drown him in love and shameful safety—and suggests that, while women's horizons may be narrowed by their immersion in love, men's lives may be impoverished and constricted by their fear of it.

Which brings us to the other thing that is female about Tess Slesinger—her sense of life as a burgeoning, sensual force that wants to express itself in sex and childbearing, and which, if denied, if not taken at the full, leaves people sterile in every sense of the word. It's strange, but in writing about sexuality as the expression of life, Miss Slesinger is peculiarly advantaged by the conventions of her time. Whether she's writing about an old maid at a dude ranch or young prep-school girls on the verge of life (**"The Answer on the Magnolia Tree"**), she can be frank where we are forced to be explicit. She can write about *forces* where so many of us—women included—feel compelled to write about *organs*. Since women's experience of sexuality *is* arguably one of being swept and mastered by natural forces—I think the horseback-riding metaphor in **"Relax Is All"** is a particularly female one—we are faced here with an ironic time reversal, in which a rediscovered writer from the 1930's presents us with a resource that seems new and refreshing: the art and pleasure of suggestion. (pp. 31, 34)

Annie Gottlieb, "A Woman Writer before Women Writers," in The New York Times Book Review (© *1974 by The New York Times Company; reprinted by permission), October 13, 1974, pp. 31, 34.*

ALAN M. WALD (essay date 1976)

[*Wald examines* The Unpossessed *as a satirical work written in the tradition of other American books by and about radical intellectuals, notably, Max Eastman's* Venture *and Edmund Wilson's* I Thought of Daisy. *From this premise, Wald disagrees* with Murray Kempton's interpretation of The Unpossessed *(see additional bibliography).*]

The Unpossessed is an outstanding book—a prototype of the Jewish/intellectual writings of Saul Bellow, and the social/satirical stories and novels of Mary McCarthy. Technically, *The Unpossessed* is grounded in the Modernist mode (using certain formal methods inspired by Joyce, Proust, the early Hemingway), and thematically it is informed by a strongly feminine perspective (suggestive of Dorothy Parker and Katherine Mansfield). Yet the novel also remains in the stream of earlier American books by and about radical intellectuals—particularly Max Eastman's *Venture* and Edmund Wilson's *I Thought of Daisy.* As in these two, personal and political themes run together in *The Unpossessed,* overlapping, intertwined, often infused with an intentional ambiguity.

In *The Unpossessed,* the conception and ultimate abortion of Margaret Flinders's baby and Bruno Leonard's magazine run parallel. And, as in *Venture* and *I Thought of Daisy,* the "problem" of the novel is that of a radicalized intellectual, disaffected from capitalist society, striving for a bond with common people and a more natural existence. What Eastman's Jo Hancock finds in the woods with his Russian proletarian beauty, and Edmund Wilson's narrator seeks in the chorus girl of *I Thought of Daisy,* Margaret Flinders hopes to locate through motherhood. In each of these novels the unifying character is derived largely from the author's own personality and experiences. The novels are expressions of the unabashed and frankly honest self-consciousness and self-scrutiny particularly characteristic of the Bohemian-radical intellectuals whose basic intellectual formation occurred prior to the 1930s domination of the literary movement by the Communists.

Furthermore, like its predecessors, Tess Slesinger's novel is rooted in the actuality of the historic moment: *Venture* is thematically locked in the "Golden Age" of pre-World War I radicalism; *I Thought of Daisy* expresses the discomfort of the twenties; and *The Unpossessed* transmits the disorientation of the early Depression. Slesinger's work communicates the pain and contradictions of the intellectuals trained and instructed by the special environment of the twenties, as they now struggle to relate to the new realities and demands of the thirties.

Venture, I Thought of Daisy, and *The Unpossessed* are all *romans à clef:* but Slesinger's book is closer to Wilson's in that it is a study of the precise milieu which produced and was led by distinct character types. Such a study indicates how certain radical intellectuals have employed the novel as a tool in the search for truth and the moral meaning of the lives and actions of their associates. That they could afford to satirize themselves and their group before the public (including their enemies), demonstrates a high degree of independence and self-reliance, personal qualities which in the 1930s tended to clash with the mainstream of the Communist-led literary current.

At least one attempt has been made to equate each major figure in *The Unpossessed* with its original from the *Menorah Journal* group. In *Part of Our Time,* Murray Kempton identifies Bruno Leonard with Elliot Cohen, Miles Flinders with Herbert Solow, and Jeffrey Blake (incorrectly) with Lionel Trilling [see excerpt above]. Yet *The Unpossessed* cannot be fully understood in terms of such analogues. Edmund Wilson's Hugo Bamman, for example, is close to a literary portrait of John Dos Passos in every detail; but the characters of *The Unpossessed* are more accurately composites designed to capture a variety of themes and currents from the milieu.

Herbert Solow, assistant editor of the *Menorah Journal,* was hardly the New England Calvinist that Miles Flinders is; yet that one aspect of the fictionalized persona is an effective vehicle for capturing the gloomy disposition and intense, almost monomaniacal, search for high principles which has been associated with Solow's personality in memoirs by his contemporaries. (pp. 313-14)

The important characteristic assigned to the intellectuals as a group in *The Unpossessed* is that they are sterile. They are sterile not by nature, but because of the social patterns, values, and lifestyles they have established for themselves. The major manifestation of the sterility is suggested by Slesinger's title: Dostoevski's *The Possessed* is reversed to *The Unpossessed,* to suggest "uncommitted." This is a group whose often-spouted convictions are more rhetorical than real. (p. 315)

[Dependent upon Bruno Leonard] is Emmett Merle, sheltered and miserable son of a wealthy family, whose relation to Bruno permits the author to probe homosexual aspects of Bruno's personality and role as a teacher. In scenes between Bruno and Emmett, Slesinger examines the psychological dynamics of male-male interaction and dependency.

The Unpossessed, with its narrative structured around aspects of marriage, friendship, adultery, is above all a study of group dynamics. Weaving in and around the story of Bruno and his students is a subplot of the failing marriage of Margaret and Miles Flinders. Slesinger employs the relationship to suggest an eternal, almost mystical dialectic of male and female interrelations. It is suggested that a man and a woman, as ideal lovers, create a third entity. Yet Miles cannot give himself wholly to this synthesis the way Margaret can. He fears drowning if he relinquishes himself totally and feels that he must retain a certain part of himself, his restlessness, as private and secretive. Women, Slesinger concludes, are perceived by men as rivals to the world.

Miles resents Margaret's desire for complacent happiness, her belief that lovers can achieve sufficiency through "each other." He associates her talk of happiness with his stern Calvinistic Uncle Daniel's remark that "pigs are happy." Miles is opposed to Margaret's having a baby which, as Lionel Trilling points out, was a common attitude of radical intellectuals of the time. Miles sees childbirth as a capitulation to bourgeois society, an acceptance of it and a sell-out incompatible with his own higher principles. Deeply pessimistic, he resents Margaret's hopefulness about the future, which he characterizes as "balmy."

Margaret, on the other hand, embodies a variety of feminine themes. She is oppressed in her subservience to Miles and by her own feelings of guilt because she cannot satisfy him. (All she can offer is comfort, which only seems to irritate him.) She and Norah Blake also seem possessed of a feminine mystical quality—they seem more natural and less self-contrived than the male characters, or even Bruno's cousin Elizabeth who lives "like a man."

Desiring to realize herself in a less artificial world, especially through the act of childbirth, Margaret especially resents the ersatz culture of the group, she notes particularly the way they surround themselves with German newspapers and Russian movies when in fact, she herself has hardly even stepped outside her own city. Margaret aspires to be one of the ordinary people, the simplicity of which is represented in minor characters such as Mr. Papenmeyer (with his children and his *Verstandt*) and Arturo Tresca (a musician full of love for his wife and children).

Norah, as others have pointed out, is a kind of Lawrentian ideal of a woman: raised in the country, she has maintained the simplicity of childhood (which Margaret has lost in her urban upbringing); she has become the open, comfortable port to which the womanizing Jeffrey returns safely after each of his numerous voyages. Feminine themes in *The Unpossessed* are of far greater importance than in either *Venture* or *I Thought of Daisy*, where they constitute merely one distinct component.

The molding of character by social environment was a common theme of 1930s literature. In *The Unpossessed* the atmosphere of the twenties and the small intellectual clique conditioned the Leonard group so that its members could not relate effectively to concerns of ordinary people or even fulfill their own aspirations. The group members are political only in drawing rooms and at parties, and have only a parasitic relation to the class struggle.

The formative years of several characters—Miles, Margaret, Bruno, Elizabeth, and Norah—are analyzed as well. (pp. 315-16)

Thus we have in imaginative literature an attempted portrayal of the *Menorah* group with its clique and cult and insular features, its combination of witty rhetoric (provided by Bruno) and bottled-up fanaticism (offered by Miles), both leading nowhere. Yet, as Lionel Trilling emphasized in a critical response to Murray Kempton's too literal interpretation of the book, the essentially apolitical nature of Slesinger's fictional group divests the portrait of its verisimilitude. (p. 317)

In this respect, then, the novel contains more invention than fact, and Kempton erred in presenting it, as he did in *Part of Our Time*, as the bitter reality. Tess Slesinger, like any satirist, depended upon exaggeration of certain tendencies in the satiric objects, and this had to be done at the expense of a truly rounded picture of the *Menorah* group. Slesinger did communicate some penetrating insights into the social relations of the group, especially their attitudes toward marriage, children, sex, and how the various personalities coped with the Depression's radical movement; but the resulting novel was predominantly psychological. Its realism is mixed: the atmosphere of the Depression, the conformist rebellion of the Black Sheep, the contradictions and pretensions of Bruno's group, are all captured through little incidents, scenes, scenarios. Yet there is no sense at all of the *Menorah* group as a highly politicized, dynamic entity whose members would ever go anywhere or do anything. One would not know from reading *The Unpossessed* that this was a group which would carry the stamp of its unique politicization along with it over decades and ultimately leave its impress upon the cultural establishment of New York. (pp. 317-18)

The failure of *The Unpossessed* to portray the political essence of the group cannot be divorced from the fact that Tess Slesinger herself chose to follow a very different course from that of her earlier associates. She followed the road to Hollywood and then to liberal acceptance of Stalinism during the Popular Front, of course, only after the success of *The Unpossessed*. But this was nevertheless a course frowned upon by the leaders of the quondam *Menorah Journal* group. (p. 318)

The characters in *The Unpossessed* suffer from an affliction which prevents them from acting out their convictions. The source of Bruno's affliction is a compulsion to travel endlessly and narcissistically into the recesses of his own mind; Jeffrey's stems from personal opportunism; and Miles's results from the transference of his Puritan temperament to politics. In Slesinger's portrait they are all victims of emotional diseases asso-

ciated with their intellects, and are hardly diabolical counter-revolutionaries. (p. 319)

To label *The Unpossessed* a "document" of this group in the early thirties, as Murray Kempton did, is far from accurate. An important stream of literature in the 1930s was, in fact, documentary, and many novels used documentary techniques. But Tess Slesinger's *The Unpossessed* is not a documentary; like the radical-Bohemian novels of Max Eastman and Edmund Wilson, it is not even a political tract, but rather a satire of the present and an inquiry of sorts into the dialectic of human emotions and human thought, and into the character of the intellectuals' relation to conflicts and issues of the time. (p. 320)

Alan M. Wald, "The Menorah Group Moves Left," in Jewish Social Studies *(copyright © 1976 by the Editors of* Jewish Social Studies*), Vol. XXXVIII, Nos. 3 & 4, Summer-Fall, 1976, pp. 289-320.**

SHIRLEY BIAGI   (essay date 1977)

[*Biagi surveys Slesinger's career.*]

[When Tess Slesinger] died in 1945 at age thirty-nine, she had written twenty-one short stories, one novel, and eight screenplays. She became associated with literary notables Clifton Fadiman, Max Eastman, Dorothy Parker, Lionel Trilling, and movie producer Irving Thalberg. During the thirties, she was often called Dorothy Parker's heir-apparent, though she disliked the comparison. Reviewers praised her "quality of wit . . . lightly blended with malice and understanding" and her "penetrating character portrayal." Yet in the current flurry of rediscovery of gifted women writers, she has been overlooked. (p. 224)

[Tess Slesinger] graduated in 1925 from Columbia with a degree in literature, and worked for the *New York Post* writing book reviews. Three years later, she married Columbia classmate Herbert Solow. . . .

[Solow] was bright, learned in the social sciences, and a member of a group which pridefully called themselves intellectuals, a group which included Lionel Trilling and Clifton Fadiman. (p. 225)

Tess joined her husband's literary circle and began writing fiction regularly. For many years she had kept a diary, and she began to transform her observations into stories. In March 1930, less than two years after her marriage, her first published story appeared in the [*Menorah*] *Journal*. "**Mother to Dinner**" details the competition for a daughter's devotion between the girl's mother and her husband. This story set the pattern for most of Tess's stories—they are embellished versions of her own experience.

In the next two years, she published four stories—in the *American Mercury*, the *Menorah Journal*, *This Quarter*, and *Pagany*. The last two involved increasing bitterness between a married man and woman. In fact, the Slesinger-Solow marriage was slipping.

Tess divorced Solow in Reno in the winter of 1932, and she also abandoned the intense dogmatic left-wing loyalty that characterized her former husband. (p. 226)

During this year after her divorce, Tess wrote "**Missis Flinders,**" considered later her finest story, which appeared in December 1932 in the very popular *Story* magazine. It is the first example of a uniquely evolving Slesinger style, which one reviewer called "stream of rationalization." **"Missis Flinders"** would become the last chapter of Tess's novel, *The Unpossessed,* finished two years later.

In the story, Missis Margaret Flinders is recently married to Miles Flinders, clearly modeled on Herbert Solow. Both Miles and Margaret are members of the intellectual excitement of the thirties which Tess knew so well.

"Missis Flinders" begins with Margaret standing on the steps outside Greenway Maternity Home, waiting for her husband to hail her a taxi. But instead of having had a baby, Margaret has just had an abortion, "giving up a baby for economic freedom which meant that two of them would work in offices instead of one." . . .

"Missis Flinders" showed the quality of Slesinger's maturing talent, the beginning of healthy anger, and the denial of the self-centered intellectualism Herbert Solow seemed to represent. **"Missis Flinders"** also made Tess somewhat notable, certainly controversial, among thirties intellectuals following and seeking literary direction. She seemed anxious to challenge conventional mores, delighting in the shock value of her topics.

Clearly now in the salad days of her literary career, Tess moved to New York's Briarcliff Manor, a private girls' school, where she was hired to teach writing. . . . (p. 227)

At Briarcliff, Tess worked on the project she had begun while still married, *The Unpossessed,* a fictional re-creation of her years with Herbert Solow. She mailed the first fifty pages to her friend Clifton Fadiman, who was now a promising young editor at Simon and Schuster. According to Fadiman, *The Unpossessed* "was, if not the first time, then one of the first times in which a group of people were portrayed who were, as we say now, looking for their identities. They were unpossessed people who wanted to be possessed by something, by a sense of career or a sense of love, by something, and weren't." . . .

To create *The Unpossessed,* Tess took Miles and Margaret Flinders, the characters in the story **"Missis Flinders,"** and added Bruno and Elizabeth Leonard and Jeffrey and Norah Blake. *The Unpossessed* described the machinations motivating a group of young leftists determined to start a new magazine. The editor is Bruno Leonard, a Jewish professor, witty and wry, much like Elliot Cohen [editor of the *Menorah Journal*]. Assistant editor Jeffrey Blake pursues women with the same ardor as Max Eastman. And, of course, Miles Flinders, who is to be a writer for the magazine, shares many characteristics with Herbert Solow. (p. 228)

"Those who knew Tess Slesinger when she wrote *The Unpossessed,*" wrote Lionel Trilling later (in an afterword to a 1966 reprint of the novel), "were aware that the book was not only a literary enterprise but also a personal act. It passed judgment upon certain people; in effect it announced the author's separation from them and from the kind of life they made." . . .

[Encouraged] by her achievement and with a public awaiting her writing, Tess wrote thirteen stories, of which four are of special note.

In October 1934 *Vanity Fair* published **"The Old Lady Counts Her Injuries."** Here the old lady is very much like the mother in **"Mother to Dinner,"** though the author's view is more sympathetic. The old lady is dominating, dependable, loving,

yet reflectively lonesome, clearly modeled after Tess's mother, now sixty-one. (p. 229)

Slesinger expressed her socialist instincts and captured the vulnerability of the working class in **"Jobs in the Sky,"** published in *Scribner's* in March 1935. In this story it is the last shopping day before Christmas at the M & J Department Store. Tess, who had worked in such a store, captures best the two characters who, anxiously scurrying all day to keep their jobs, will (unknown to them) be dropped at the end of the day, after being carefully monitored by the story's pecuniary master, Mr. Marvell. (p. 230)

The subject of Slesinger's 1935 *Story* magazine contribution, **"On Being Told That Her Second Husband Has Taken His First Lover,"** is self-explanatory. . . . Whit Burnett, *Story's* editor, remarked of Tess Slesinger's characters that they "have been around, they see themselves as a little foolish, a little like actors, even when their hearts are almost breaking."

The fourth notable story, **"Mr. Palmer's Party,"** *The New Yorker* published in April 1935. In about fifteen hundred words, Tess, who was attending frequent literary parties, creates a very self-conscious party host, Mr. Palmer, who "had wondered guiltily just which were the interesting people and which the guests who had just been asked to meet the interesting people."

One year after *The Unpossessed,* Simon and Schuster collected Tess's published stories and some new ones in *Time: The Present.* The collection maintained her reputation, perhaps bettered it. (pp. 230-31)

Tess's witty style was one generation too late for the Algonquin Round Table but in mid-July 1935, she joined more than 150 Eastern writers gobbled up by Hollywood to write movies, a group that included the Round Table's Robert Benchley, Donald Ogden Stewart, and Dorothy Parker. (p. 231)

M-G-M's studio was run by "the little genius," Irving Thalberg, an enigmatic perfectionist. . . .

Tess was shortly assigned by Thalberg to write the first script for Pearl S. Buck's *The Good Earth,* the story of a Chinese peasant named Wang who becomes a large landowner and almost destroys himself with his own greed. (p. 232)

The movie's most memorable, and ironically prophetic, line belonged to Tess. Withered from illness on her deathbed, the passive, devoted slave bride O-Lan (portrayed by Luise Rainer) asks of her husband Wang (Paul Muni), "Forgive me," [for dying]. The line, as well as the greater part of the screenplay written by Tess, survived all of Thalberg's subsequent revisions. (pp. 232-33)

[In] 1944, Twentieth-Century Fox asked [Slesinger and her second husband, Frank Davis,] to write the screenplay for *A Tree Grows in Brooklyn,* based on a story about a poor family living in a Brooklyn tenement, sprinkled with a socialist message about the downtrodden. When the movie opened at New York's Roxy Theatre on 1 March 1945, the *New York Times* called it a "pictorial demonstration of emotion that is sublimely eloquent." . . .

Tess Slesinger was clearly a woman of the first half of the twentieth century—as an important intellectual chronicler of leftist thought, as a screenwriter projecting the images Hollywood wanted us to believe, yet remaining an individualist who challenged Hollywood's single-minded politics. Most pointedly, she would probably like to be remembered as a writer. In her last major story, **"A Life in the Day of a Writer,"** the writer is male, but it is as if Tess Slesinger had described herself:

> I am a writer if I never write another line, I am alive if I never step out of this room again; Christ, oh, Christ, the problem is not to stretch a feeling, it is to reduce a feeling, *all* feeling, all thought, all ecstasy, tangled and tumbled in the empty crowded head of a writer, to one clear sentence, one clear form, and still preserve the hugeness, the hurtfulness, the enormity, the unbearable all-at-onceness, of being alive and knowing it too. . . .
>
> (p. 236)

Shirley Biagi, "Forgive Me for Dying," in The Antioch Review *(copyright © 1977 by the Antioch Review Inc.; reprinted by permission of the Editors), Vol. 35, Nos. 2 & 3, Spring-Summer, 1977, pp. 224-36.*

JANET SHARISTANIAN (essay date 1979)

[Sharistanian examines Slesinger's career as a screenwriter and discusses three sketches: "The Old Man," "The Old Man's Wife," and "Brick," which were recently reprinted together as A Hollywood Gallery.*]*

Slesinger went to Hollywood in July, 1935 to work on the screenplay of *The Good Earth,* which was being produced by Irving Thalberg at M-G-M, the leading studio in one of the few industries to prosper during the Depression. Slesinger knew little about films; her characters, often urban sophisticates articulate to the point of nervous verbosity, were the opposite of Pearl Buck's peasants (Luise Rainer, playing the female lead in the film, had fewer than a dozen lines of dialogue). Nevertheless she quickly became fascinated by the craft of screenwriting and the manufacture of movies, learning, for instance, to make skillful use of camera angles and silences in her script. . . .

Between 1935 and 1945 when she died, at thirty-nine, of cancer, Slesinger wrote the scripts for seven films which were produced and another eight which were, in Hollywood parlance, "shelved." (p. 430)

Hollywood gave Slesinger material for what would have been her next novel. *A Tree Grows in Brooklyn* (released after her death) was to be her last film, after which she would return to the novel for which she had been preparing not only by living and working in the Hollywood *milieu,* but also by systematically studying the various departments in the studio in a deliberate attempt to learn about the people in the industry and the work that they did there.

Though Slesinger's novel remained incomplete at her death, the approximately 150-page manuscript, divided into sections labeled Notes, Characters and Beginning (of which there are several versions), is comprehensive enough to reveal her general intentions. Moreover, Slesinger discussed her plans for the book with her husband. Judging from both these sources, Slesinger's aim was to write about Hollywood not from the viewpoint of its elite, as Fitzgerald did in *The Last Tycoon,* nor from the viewpoint of its thrill-seeking aspirants and fans, as Nathanael West did in *Day of the Locust.* Instead, she meant to write something more comprehensive, a novel about Hollywood written from the perspective of the ordinary talented

workers of the film industry in their personal, professional and political interactions. (pp. 432-33)

[The character] sketches comprise a broad spectrum of workers in the movies and related areas, with those at the bottom end of the social and salary scale—such as the secretaries, script clerks and set boys—seen from their own perspective as well as externally, from that of their superiors. Often in sketches of industry "types" Slesinger pays special attention to the characters' professional motivations, which run the gamut from greed and social ambition to the pleasures of power to delight in specialized skills to romantic idealism. Chief among them, however, at least in the broad middle of movie occupations, is the pragmatic ambition to do a job well in order to live decently—a little better, if possible, this year than last. Implicit in these sketches is Slesinger's adherence to a typical 1930's theme, that of earning a living as one of the basic human experiences. (p. 434)

Two of the sketches . . . , "The Old Man" and "The Old Man's Wife," are based upon producer Irving Thalberg and his wife, actress Norma Shearer. The sketches deviate from Thalberg and Shearer's biographies in several respects. Norma Shearer's success was not solely the result of her husband's guidance. In fact, when they married in 1927 he suggested that she retire, but her response was instead to demand (and receive) better roles. She made forty films at M-G-M between 1923 and her self-imposed retirement in 1942, and is described in studies of the film industry as a professional determined to overcome her limitations in order to achieve success. (p. 435)

These two sketches may seem to be about exceptions to the common run of film-industry workers. However, like most of the sketches—as well as the sections marked "Beginning"—they show the interaction between character and *milieu,* the ways in which place and profession impinge upon personality. The capaciousness of Slesinger's vision, evident in *The Unpossessed* and in such short stories as "After the Party," "Jobs in the Sky," "The Mouse-Trap" and "The Answer on the Magnolia Tree," would have found ample scope in the extremely productive and highly politicized Hollywood of the 30's for dealing with individuals in groups and organizations whose rules or expectations are constantly modifying behavior. For this reason, if for no other, it is easy to see why Slesinger, rather than looking down on film work as a divergence from her literary calling, found in it a means to the end of writing, a source of material particularly suited to her talents.

Another example of the interaction between personality and environment is evident in the third sketch, "Brick," also based upon a figure with whom Slesinger was acquainted. In this case, however, the interaction is doubly complicated, with the sketch turning upon the question of who, literally and psychically, this man is, who has adapted himself so thoroughly to the contradictory demands of Party-line politics and Hollywood luxury that all signs of a purely private self have been obliterated. "Brick" is seen from without in this sketch, but from his own perspective in the narrative segment which may have been Slesinger's choice for a beginning for the novel. (p. 436)

Given the incompleteness of Slesinger's manuscript, and the fact that she was generally a prodigious re-writer, it is impossible to predict with any certainty what the finished novel would have been. . . .

[Yet,] it is clear from the tenor of almost every entry in the manuscript that the relationship between the facts of life in the movie industry and the fictions that it produces would have been central to Slesinger's novel. (p. 437)

> *Janet Sharistanian, "Tess Slesinger's Hollywood Sketches," in* Michigan Quarterly Review *(copyright © The University of Michigan, 1979), Vol. XVIII, No. 3, Summer, 1979, pp. 429-38.*

ADDITIONAL BIBLIOGRAPHY

Benét, William Rose. "Observation of the Human Spectacle." *The Saturday Review of Literature* XII, No. 4 (25 May 1935): 5.
Finds *Time: The Present* "convincing as a transcript of life." Benét praises Slesinger's brevity in including discomforting details for the purpose of added realism.

Brickell, Herschel. "Books on Our Table." *New York Post* (12 May 1934): 11.*
Review of *The Unpossessed* which deals very briefly with the critical controversy surrounding the book.

Burnett, Whit. "The People of the Present: Clever, Sad, Tragic, Comic." *New York Herald Tribune Books* (26 May 1935): 7.
A favorable review of *Time: The Present* and a discussion of Slesinger's art, by the editor of *Story* magazine.

Gregory, Horace. "These Neurotic Young Folks." *New York Herald Tribune Books* (13 May 1934): 2.

An enthusiastic review of *The Unpossessed*. Gregory writes that "Miss Slesinger proves in her first book that she is a writer of unquestionable ability, that she can sustain a point of view with somewhat of the same tenacity and skill that has characterized the work of Dorothy Parker."

Kempton Murray. "The Social Muse." In his *Part of Our Time: Some Ruins and Monuments of the Thirties*, pp. 105-50. New York: Simon & Schuster, 1955.*
Reads *The Unpossessed* as a document drawn directly from the lives of specific persons. Kempton identifies Miles Flinders with Herbert Solow ("an editor of *Fortune*"), Jeffrey Blake with Lionel Trilling ("a critic of notable powers"), and Bruno Leonard with Elliot Cohen ("the editor of a monthly magazine").

Kempton, Murray. "From the Depths of the Thirties." *The New Republic* 155, No. 19 (5 November 1966): 25-8.
Discusses the American radical community of the 1930s, Slesinger's relationship to it, and Lionel Trilling's thoughts on Slesinger's novel as revealed in his afterword to the Avon edition of *The Unpossessed*.

Nuhn, Ferner. "The Lost Generation and the New Morality." *The Nation* CXXXVIII, No. 3594 (23 May 1934): 597-98.
Favorably reviews *The Unpossessed* while mentioning some weaknesses.

Trilling, Lionel. "Young in the Thirties." *Commentary* 41, No. 5 (May 1966): 43-51.
A discussion of life among the New York Jewish intelligentsia during the 1930s and of Slesinger's aim and technique in *The Unpossessed*. This essay was reprinted as the afterword to the Avon edition of *The Unpossessed*.

(Philip) Edward Thomas

1878-1917

(Also wrote under pseudonym of Edward Eastaway) English poet, essayist, critic, novelist, biographer, autobiographer, and editor.

Thomas is the most prominent twentieth-century representative of the tradition of nature poetry in English literature. Despite affinities with the Georgian movement of the early twentieth century, Thomas's verse consistently defies classification. Like the work of his Georgian contemporaries, his verse displays a profound love of natural beauty and, at times, an archaic use of diction. However, Thomas's personalized voice and intensity of vision give his poetry an artistic force which the Georgians never approached.

Thomas was born of Welsh parents in London. His father was a railway clerk who neglected his six sons in favor of politics and intellectual pursuits. Temperamentally, he was the opposite of his son, and the two disagreed on nearly all matters, including Thomas's desire for a literary career. Much later Thomas was to portray this adversarial relationship with his father in the poem "P.H.T." In 1894, while attending St. Paul's School, Thomas met the successful literary journalist James Ashcroft Noble, who encouraged Thomas in his literary ambitions and was instrumental in getting his first book, *The Woodland Life,* accepted for publication. Shortly thereafter, while still a student at Lincoln College in Oxford, Thomas married Noble's daughter, Helen. Faced with the necessity of supporting a growing family, Thomas began accepting assignments of all sorts from London publishers. Much of the work he received was uncongenial hack-work, but Thomas wrote steadily, sometimes producing as many as three books a year. His work included essays, natural history, criticism, biographies, reviews, fiction, introductions, and topographical descriptions. Thomas wrote his first poems in 1914 at the urging of the American poet Robert Frost. Two years later his first book of verse, *Six Poems,* was published. Due to Thomas's fear that it would be unfairly dismissed by the critics if it were published under his own name, this collection was published under the pseudonym of Edward Eastaway. These six were the only poems that Thomas lived to see in print: in 1915 he enlisted in the infantry and was killed two years later in the Battle of Arras, while the first edition of his *Poems* was being prepared for press.

Thomas's many reviews and critical studies—such as *Richard Jefferies, Walter Pater,* and *The Feminine Influence on the Poets*—represent the best of his prose work. Much of Thomas's prose was written according to the demands and deadlines of his publishers. Many critics believe that Thomas wasted his talents on hack work, and the author himself felt that his artistic potential was being destroyed under the strain of constant production. In spite of these circumstances, Thomas developed into a respected critic, and his reviews for various newspapers and journals were widely quoted. All of Thomas's criticism has been praised for its lucid style, precision of speech, and intelligent observations. Vernon Scannell has said that Thomas's "verse criticism shows not merely an intuitive awareness of what poetry should be about, but an intelligent

familiarity with refinements of technique and a fine sense of the historical continuity of English literature."

While an accomplished prose writer, Thomas is of far more interest for the poetry which he began to write relatively late in his career. From his first poems, Thomas demonstrated, according to John Lehmann, an "intensity of vision" which set him apart from his contemporaries. His earliest poems bear the influence of Frost in their treatment of nature and in their simple style. However, Frost's influence was to decrease as Thomas discovered his own personal voice. Numerous critics, including Jeremy Hooker and J. P. Ward, have stressed the two principal themes in Thomas's verse: one, the presence of war and its effect on the individual; the other, the poet's profound sense of solitude. Though he wrote only one war poem per se—"This Is No Case of Petty Right or Wrong"—throughout his poetry Thomas subtly portrays the influence of war on the natural order. Thomas's sense of solitude has led Ward to consider him an early existentialist. Though this might be an isolated point of view, most critics agree that Thomas remains appealing to the modern reader—while many of his contemporaries have fallen out of favor—because his poetry expresses an awareness of individual alienation commonly associated with existentialism.

Such prominent critics and authors as Walter de la Mare and Aldous Huxley have called Thomas one of England's most

important poets. In recent years much serious consideration has been given to Thomas's work. Most critics would agree with Andrew Motion, who states that Thomas occupies "a crucial place in the development of twentieth-century poetry" for introducing a modern sensibility, later found in the work of such poets as W. H. Auden and Ted Hughes, to the poetic subjects of Victorian and Georgian poetry.

(See also *Contemporary Authors*, Vol. 106.)

PRINCIPAL WORKS

The Woodland Life (essays and diary) 1897
Horae Solitariae (essays) 1902
Oxford (prose) 1903
Beautiful Wales (essays) 1905
The Heart of England (essays) 1906
Richard Jefferies (criticism) 1909
The South Country (essays) 1909
Feminine Influence on the Poets (criticism) 1910
Rest and Unrest (essays) 1910
Light and Twilight (essays) 1911
Maurice Maeterlinck (criticism) 1911
Algernon Charles Swinburne (criticism) 1912
George Borrow (criticism) 1912
Lafcadio Hearn (criticism) 1912
The Happy-Go-Lucky Morgans (novel) 1913
The Icknield Way (prose) 1913
Walter Pater (criticism) 1913
In Pursuit of Spring (prose) 1914
Four-and-Twenty Blackbirds (fairy tales) 1915
The Life of the Duke of Marlborough (biography) 1915
Six Poems [as Edward Eastaway] (poetry) 1916
A Literary Pilgrim in England (criticism) 1917
Poems (poetry) 1917
Last Poems (poetry) 1918
Collected Poems (poetry) 1920
The Last Sheaf (essays) 1928
The Childhood of Edward Thomas (autobiography) 1938

***THE BOOKMAN*, London (essay date 1907)**

The highest expression of the intellectual life of our day is probably to be found in the small group of essayists and miscellaneous writers of whom Mr. Thomas is one. He has had, it is true, no popular success to balance Mr. Belloc's "Bad Child's Book of Beasts," or Mr. Chesterton's entertaining skit on Browning, and is consequently not so widely known; his work has not the wide virility of Mr. Cunninghame Graham, nor the champagne sparkle of Mr. Beerbohm, nor the Lamb-like felicity of Mr. Lucas, nor the energy of Mr. Belloc, nor the happy tavern enthusiasm of Mr. Chesterton; but he expresses something in the modern attitude that not one of them attempts to express, and that some of them, perhaps a little indignantly, would refuse to understand. He is different from all of them, and included in none of them, so that his place among them is assured.

He has written six books of essays, . . . [including] **"Oxford,"** **"Wales,"** and **"The Heart of England."** . . . He has edited Dyer's Poems, and Borrow's "Bible in Spain." He is shortly to publish an anthology of country songs, and is the editor of a large volume of nature study. . . .

There is a kind of fireside essayist who is always sure of an effect because he chooses subjects and affects sentiments that convention has already made delightful. . . . Mr. Thomas is not that kind of man. He expresses a new, an individual attitude that has not been expressed before, and consequently his work finds a less ready welcome than stuff for whose enjoyment long custom has prepared a host of readers. Mr. Thomas's readers are readers worth having.

He was influenced by Pater and Richard Jefferies; by Pater in his precision of speech, by Jefferies in his accuracy of observation. These two characteristics mark his criticism as clearly as they distinguish his original essays. His reviews, which carry weight in more than one of the least degraded of the newspapers, demand always these two things, and, of these things, the last first. To have seen with his own eyes, and to have expressed with his own choice of words, are Mr. Thomas's wishes for himself, and he judges other men's books by the same standard. . . .

In his own writing Mr. Thomas is a zealous observer first, and an accurate workman afterwards. His writing is always the result of his observation, never *vice versa*. . . . On this point, of the preference of observation over writing, he is very sensitive, as he has often been accused of preciosity. Mr. Thomas's writing certainly has with it such an air of elaboration and revision that it is difficult not to believe that he writes as Pater or the Goncourts wrote, altering his words and their order, until they seem as near perfection as he chooses to expect. It is not so. Mr. Thomas writes fast. He does not hack his work out in the rough, and then cut and polish it into its final form. For him, writing as he has almost always had to write, in a race with time, such a method would be impossible. Indeed, accustomed to write at speed, he finds himself unable to do better by writing slowly, and even his favourite essays are not more laboriously tinkered than his reviews. Any writing that is not mere manufactured stuff takes its character from its author's mind, and Mr. Thomas is a careful-minded man. However fast he may have to write, his work never has the appearance of haste. His sentences are ready in his head before he sits down to write them. He hardly corrects them at all, so that if his writings have the atmosphere of an individual and precise style, it is his good fortune, and not, as some would have it, his fault. (p. 244)

[Thomas] has made no wild exuberant pilgrimage from point of view to point of view. His first book, written when the lead weight of suburban life was still heavy on him, when brief holidays in Wiltshire, and such breaths of country air as may be snatched by a town boy in a Saturday afternoon, were all the opportunities he had had, was a book of woodland studies. His last volume is a collection of essays on the heart of English country.

It was, however, his second book, written, we think, before he was twenty-one, that contained the first prophecy of his later work. The author of **"The Woodland Life"** might have turned out a naturalist. The author of **"Horae Solitariae"** could only have been Edward Thomas. **"Horae Solitariae"** is the book of a young scholar, able to quote Latin with enthusiasm; it is made more than that, by an earnest feeling for form and colour, by passionately sincere studies in landscape and still life. The same passionate sincerity, in writing of the same things, characterises the broader and more human work he does to-day. But he has developed, simply and directly. His studies of landscape are now revelations of a grown man's temperament, no longer of the more shallow enthusiasms of a youth. In his studies of still life he has come to see behind the things themselves, and to give them a deeper, a more pertinent vitality. (pp. 244-45)

We have heard people lament that Mr. Thomas has had to waste so much of his time on reviewing. It is true that much of his best work has whistled down the wind in old literary pages; but it is also true that the doing of it made him write more than he would otherwise have written, and read much that he would otherwise not have read. Mr. Thomas has so consistent a mind that he owes his development to his perpetual business, that kept him writing, and at the same time compelled him to realise a world outside his own. . . . If he had not written so much, we are convinced he would not have written so admirably. If he had not been kept so busy we doubt if he would have broadened as he has. As it is, he has become one of the best critics and most delightful country essayists we possess. (p. 245)

> "Mr. Edward Thomas," in The Bookman, London, Vol. XXXI, No. 186, March, 1907, pp. 244-45.

JOHN FREEMAN (essay date 1917)

[Freeman was one of the first critics to emphasize Thomas's preoccupation with self-discovery in his poetry. This point is taken up by most of Thomas's later critics, particularly C. Day Lewis and Vernon Scannell (see excerpts below).]

The poems of Edward Thomas present an unusual case. During twenty years he wrote the many books—itineraries, descriptive pieces, critical essays, sharp prose-etchings . . . , some dealing with the south country which he loved, and some with English poetry which he loved no less. Then, quite suddenly, after a long, unrepining abandonment, he turned to poetry again, not a day passing without its lyric, scarce a poem begun and not finished, scarce a line written which the musing jealousy of friends might have wished mended or removed. The reader of [Poems by Edward Thomas] who happens to be familiar with a few of the prose writings will probably agree that fine as the best of these books may be—and few contemporary authors wrote with so natural an ease and conscience—Edward Thomas did not find his full utterance until the first poem sang on his lips. . . . Is it, then, because the self-discovery came so late and startlingly that there is a personal eagerness almost painful to witness in much of his poetry? He has written so much of others and for others that now he will write only for himself and out of love for something more dear to him than self. Every poet begins with an autobiography of his emotional life, but it is seldom indeed that this tyrannously sweet possession dictates to so mature a hand. . . . All but unparalleled is the frankness with which he speaks of himself, of his hopes and moods, speaking indeed so closely as to persuade you that nobody but yourself can be meant to hear. . . . Now and then the sense of self-revelation is so sharp that you think the poet's consciousness of his own personality has become morbid, as in Gone, Gone Again. . . . Every reader will see that the final clarification of the personal has not yet been reached, the immediate human anxiousness not yet transcended. Poem after poem shows the author in the course of "finding himself" through and in his poetry, and the preoccupation is profound as well as simple.

Apart from this immediate and half-painful "interest" there are two significant things to be spoken of; and one of these, to take the lesser first, is the individual and masterful manner of speech. Rhythm is treated like fire—as a good servant but a bad master. There is the rhythm of poetry everywhere, but often it is to be felt in the whole poem more than in the line; so that it is only when the whole poem echoes in your head, as so many of the lyrics do, that you notice how naturally the license, the abruptness, the irregularity of the line falls into and forms part of the rhythm of the poem. Such verse as, "And I should not have sat here. Everything would have been different. For it would have been another world"—owes a little more than verse should to the printer's craft; but yet it holds its place in the natural, easy rhythm of As the Team's Head-Brass. This way of speaking has a double origin; it comes from a somewhat determined effort to be quite exact, not less and certainly not more than truthful, since poetry is the finest truth; and it comes also from an impatience of discipline, a revolt against bonds, to which he has earned his right by submission to discipline. Hence in very many of these poems you are aware at once of the submission and the revolt, the very form, the unrest of the poet's style, showing so beautifully the conflict of his mind. The style is the man. Few poets gain so much from the most literal simplicity of phrase, because with few is that simplicity so faithfully expressive. . . . And hence, too, he may seem to some a little wilful in his avoidance of mere prettification; as when he ends the clear, romantic beauty of Cock-Crow with, "The milkers lace their boots up at the farms." . . . The beautiful success of Thaw is repeated again and again, because he is speaking of what he loves—of the country, the birds, the songs, houses, places, human beings, trees, names and all that he loves. This is the second of the significant things which cannot be overlooked. No other book of English verse, published within my own time, shows the same vivid spirit of love, the same saturation with English country life and tradition. There is no suggestion of indoors even when the subject is a house, nothing of airless or precious; but everywhere a sense of the generations of men who lived freely and boldly when "this England, Old already, was called Merry"; when men hunted the badger, "That most ancient Briton of English beasts." . . . Half the poems in this book are lanes in an old, blessed country, and as your thought travels these lanes you become aware, with growing sharpness of delight, of the fruitfulness of the land, of its richness in beauty and strength, in humanity and history. Of Edward Thomas it is right to say, in his own phrase, "He is English as this gate, these flowers, this mire"; and the comparisons reveal his own mind. He loves concrete things and shuns abstractions—shunning them sometimes as just possible pitfalls and not always for instinctive distaste. (pp. 133-34)

If nothing hitherto has been said to show that Edward Thomas's poetry has beauty, it is only because even a single line will speak for itself, and because the beauty may almost be taken for granted with such subjects and such passions as have been mentioned. . . . As if to show that he too could touch the sweet stops of English verbal beauty, he writes a whole poem echoing with a half-earthy, half-watery music—The Mill Pond. . . . [And] The Bridge, in which the music is simply the music of ordinary human speech. . . . But the beauty of this poetry is not a thing of lines and stanzas, not a match struck here and there, but a fire burning bright and smelling green in the wide "wood of thoughts."

That warring reserve and eagerness which marked much of the prose work of Edward Thomas with sharp and significant lines linger here in his poetry, but the reserve is weakened and in the best of the poems is gone; only the simplicity of clear sight remains and the eagerness of frank speech. To himself the writing of poetry brought a great unloosening, a very real discovery—sign and effect of a spiritual change. He discovered himself, and then something else was discovered to him. . . .

What was this second discovery? The last stanza [of *Lights Out*] answers:

> The tall forest towers;
> Its cloudy foliage lowers
> Ahead, shelf above shelf;
> Its silence I hear and obey
> That I may lose my way
> And myself.

To find himself only to lose himself, that was the difficult thing, the last thing that life taught him—the priceless discovery, impossible to forget. It was even before he lost his life in France, "in a moment of victory," that he lost himself. What our loss was when he died these poems cannot do more than suggest. (p. 134)

> *John Freeman, "Edward Thomas," in* New States-
> *man (©1917 The Statesman Publishing Co. Ltd.),*
> *Vol. X, No. 240, November 10, 1917, pp. 133-34.*

J. MIDDLETON MURRY (essay date 1920)

Year by year the universe grows vaster, and man, by virtue of the growing brightness of his little lamp, sees himself more and more as a child born in the midst of a dark forest, and finds himself less able to claim the obeisance of the all. Yet if he would be a poet, and not a harper of threadbare tunes, he must at each step in the downward passing from his sovereignty, recognise what is and celebrate it as what must be. Thus he regains, by another path, the supremacy which he has forsaken.

Edward Thomas's poetry has the virtue of this recognition. It may be said that his universe was not vaster but smaller than the universe of the past, for its bounds were largely those of his own self. It is, even in material fact, but half true. None more closely than he regarded the living things of earth in all their quarters. '**After Rain**' is, for instance, a very catalogue of the texture of nature's visible garment, freshly put on, down to the little ash-leaves. . . . But it is true that these objects of vision were but the occasion of the more profound discoveries within the region of his own soul. There he discovered vastness and illimitable vistas; found himself to be an eddy in the universal flux, driven whence and whither he knew not, conscious of perpetual instability, the meeting place of mighty impacts of which only the farthest ripple agitates the steady moonbeam of the waking mind. In a sense he did no more than to state what he found, sometimes in the more familiar language of beauties lost, mourned for lost, and irrecoverable. . . . That search lies nearer to the norm of poetry. We might register its wistfulness, praise the appealing nakedness of its diction and pass on. If that were indeed the culmination of Edward Thomas's poetical quest, he would stand securely enough with others of his time. But he reaches further. In the verses on his 'home' . . . he passes beyond these limits. He has still more to tell of the experience of the soul fronting its own infinity. . . . [In his poems there] speaks a deep desire born only of deep knowledge. Only those who have been struck to the heart by a sudden awareness of the incessant not-being which

is all we hold of being, know the longing to arrest the movement even at the price of the perpetuation of their pain. So it was that the moments which seemed to come to him free from the infirmity of becoming haunted and held him most. . . . Sometimes he looked within himself for the monition which men have felt as the voice of the eternal memory; sometimes, like Keats, but with none of the intoxication of Keats's sense of a sharing in victory, he grasped at the recurrence of natural things. . . . (pp. 33-6)

But he could not rest even there. There was, indeed, no anchorage in the enduring to be found by one so keenly aware of the flux within the soul itself. The most powerful, the most austerely imagined poem in [his *Last Poems*] is that entitled '**The Other**,' which, apart from its intrinsic appeal, shows that Edward Thomas had something at least of the power to create the myth which is the poet's essential means of triangulating the unknown of his emotion. Had he lived to perfect himself in the use of this instrument, he might have been a great poet indeed. (p. 37)

No; not a great poet, will be the final sentence, when the palimpsest is read with the calm and undivided attention that is its due, but one who had many (and among them the chief) of the qualities of a great poet. Edward Thomas was like a musician who noted down themes that summon up forgotten expectations. Whether the genius to work them out to the limits of their scope and implication was in him we do not know. The life of literature was a hard master to him; and perhaps the opportunity he would eagerly have grasped was denied him by circumstance. But, if his compositions do not, his themes will never fail—of so much we are sure—to awaken unsuspected echoes even in unsuspecting minds. (pp. 37-8)

> *J. Middleton Murry, "The Poetry of Edward*
> *Thomas," in his* Aspects of Literature *(reprinted by*
> *permission of The Society of Authors as the literary*
> *representative of the Estate of John Middleton Murry),*
> *W. Collins Sons & Co. Ltd., 1920, pp. 29-38.*

WALTER DE LA MARE (essay date 1920)

[De la Mare, who called Thomas's poetry "a mirror of England," was the poet's intimate friend and one of the first to urge him to write verse.]

All that Edward Thomas was as a friend lies only half-concealed in his poems. He wrote many books. A few of them—'**Light and Twilight**', '**The Happy-Go-Lucky Morgans**', '**Richard Jefferies**', for instance—were of his own choice and after his own heart. Many of the others were in the nature of obligations thrust upon him. . . .

His complete freedom of mind, his fine sense of literature, his love of truth, his delicate yet vigorous intuition are never absent even in his merest journey-work. But there cannot but be a vital difference between this and what is done for pure love of it. (p. 5)

Nevertheless his rarer qualities were obviously not such as can please a wide public; nor was he possessed of some of the admirable faculties that can and do. He was not a *born* story-teller; nor that chameleonic creature, a dramatist. He had less invention than fantasy. He detested mere cleverness; and compromise was alien to his nature. He could delight in 'a poor man of any sort down to a king'; but the range intended here is obviously exclusive and graduated. He was not therefore possessed of that happy and dangerous facility of being all things to *all* men. Faithful and solitary lover of 'the lovely that is not beloved'—not by most of us at much expense, he could not, then, as have other men of genius simultaneously woo fame and win fortune. His chief desire was to express himself and his own truth—and therefore life and humanity; and compared with a true artist's conscience, Tamerlane is tenderhearted. (pp. 5-6)

Late in his life, when he seemed to have given up hope of it, there came to him this sudden creative impulse, the incentive of a new form into which he could pour his thoughts, feelings and memories with ease and freedom and delight. Utterly unforeseen also may have been the discovery that he was born to live and die a soldier. Yet in those last years, however desperate at times the distaste and disquiet, however sharp the sacrifice, he found an unusual serenity and satisfaction. His comradeship, his humour blossomed over. He plunged back from books into life, and wrote only for sheer joy in writing. To read **'The Trumpet', 'Tears',** or **'This is no Case of Petty Right or Wrong'** is to realise the brave spirit that compelled him to fling away the safety which without the least loss of honour he might have accepted, and to go back to his men, and his guns, and death. These poems reveal, too, that he was doubly homesick, for this and for another world, no less clearly than they show how intense a happiness to him was the fruition of his lifelong hope and desire to prove himself a poet. (pp. 6-7)

[His] impassioned, almost trancelike delight in things natural, simple, 'short-lived and happy-seeming', 'lovely of motion, shape and hue', is expressed—even when the clouds of melancholy and of self-distrust lour darkest—on every page of [his *Collected Poems*]. A light shines in it, like that of 'cowslips wet with the dew of their birth'. If one word could tell of his all, that word would be England. **'The Manor Farm', 'The Mill-Water', 'Adlestrop', 'Roads', 'The Gallows', 'Lob', 'If I should ever by Chance', 'The Mountain Chapel', 'An Old Song'** —it is foolish to catalogue—but *their* word is England; and if music and natural magic are not the very essence of such poems as **'The Unknown Bird', 'The Child on the Cliffs', 'The Word', 'Beauty', 'Snow', 'The Brook', 'Out in the Dark',** then I have never even guessed the meaning of the phrase.

When, indeed, Edward Thomas was killed in Flanders, a mirror of England was shattered of so pure and true a crystal that a clearer and tenderer reflection of it can be found no other where than in these poems. . . . England's roads and heaths and woods, its secret haunts and solitudes, its houses, its people—themselves resembling its thorns and juniper—its very flints and dust, were his freedom and his peace. He pierced to their being, not through dreams, or rhapsodies, not by the strange light of fantasy, rarely with the vision that makes of them a transient veil of the unseen. They were to him 'Lovelier than any mysteries'. 'To say "God bless it", was all that I could do.'

There is nothing precious, elaborate, brilliant, esoteric, obscure in his work. The feeling is never 'fine', the thought never curious, or the word farfetched. Loose-woven, monotonous, unrelieved, the verse, as verse, may appear to a careless reader accustomed to the customary. It must be read slowly, as naturally as if it were talk, without much emphasis; it will then surrender himself, his beautiful world, his compassionate and suffering heart, his fine, lucid, grave and sensitive mind. This is not a poetry that will drug or intoxicate, civicise or edify— in the usual meaning of the word, though it rebuilds reality. It ennobles by simplification. Above all, it will reveal what a friend this man was to the friendless and to them of small

report, though not always his own serenest friend—to the greening stoat on the gamekeeper's shed, the weed by the wayside, the wanderer, 'soldiers and poor unable to rejoice'. 'If we could see all, all might seem good.'

These poems, moreover, differ from most poems, not only because they usually share so quiet a self-communion. They tell also, not so much of rare, exalted, chosen moments, of fleeting inexplicable intuitions, but of Thomas's daily and, one might say, common experience. They proceed from a saturation, like that of Gideon's fleece; from contemplation rather than from sheer energy of insight. They are not drops of attar in a crystal vase, inestimably precious though such drops and vessels may be. Long-looking, long-desiring, long-loving— these win at last to the inmost being of a thing. So it was with Edward Thomas. Like every other individual writer, he had unlearned all literary influences. The anxious and long-suffering labourer was worthy of his belated hire, and this volume is a crockful of the purest waters of his life. (pp. 9-11)

[When] it is considered how long and diligently, and at what expense of spirit, Edward Thomas worked as a man of letters; how many books he wrote; how much of his best writing is practically lost in the newspapers that so swiftly seduce the dead past into burying its dead; then it is little less than tragic to think how comparatively unheeded in any public sense was his coming and going. Nevertheless, it is a pious duty to have confidence in the children of this and of succeeding generations. Thomas has true lovers to-day; but when the noise of the present is silenced—and the drums and tramplings of the war in which he died—his voice will be heard far more clearly; the words of a heart and mind devoted throughout his life to all that can make the world a decent and natural home for the meek and the lovely, the true, the rare, the patient, the independent and the oppressed. (pp. 14-15)

> *Walter de la Mare, "Foreword" (reprinted by permission of The Literary Trustees of Walter de la Mare and The Society of Authors as their representatives),* Collected Poems *by Edward Thomas, Selwyn & Blount, 1920 (and reprinted by Faber and Faber Limited, 1936, pp. 5-15).*

ROBERT FROST (letter date 1921)

[The excerpt below is a portion of a letter from Frost to Grace Walcott Conkling. In it Frost makes his often-quoted statement concerning his possible influence on Thomas: "Anything we may be thought to have in common we had before we met."]

I am grateful that you should have thought to link Edward Thomas' name with mine in one of your lectures. You will be careful, I know, not to say anything to exalt either of us at the expense of the other. There's a story going round that might lead you to exaggerate our debt to each other. Anything we may be thought to have in common we had before we met. When Hodgson introduced us at a coffee house in London in 1913 I had written two and a half of my three books[,] he had written all but two or three of his thirty. The most our congeniality could do was confirm us both in what we were. There was never a moment's thought about who may have been influencing whom. The least rivalry of that kind would have taken something from our friendship. We were greater friends than almost any two ever were practising the same art. I don't mean that we did nothing for each other. As I have said we encouraged each other in our adventurous ways. Beyond that anything we did was very practical. He gave me standing as a poet—he more than anyone else, though of course I have to thank Abercrombie, Hueffer, Pound and some others for help too. I dragged him out from under the heap of his own work in prose he was buried alive under. He was throwing to his big perfunctory histories of Marlborough and the like written to order such poetry as would make him a name if he were but given credit for it. I made him see that he owed it to himself and the poetry to have it out by itself in poetic form where it must suffer itself to be admired. It took me some time. I bantered, teased and bullied all the summer we were together at Ledington and Ryton. All he had to do was put his poetry in a form that declared itself. The theme must be the same, the accent exactly the same. He saw it and he was tempted. It was plain that he had wanted to be a poet all the years he had been writing about poets not worth his little finger. But he was afeared (though a soldier). His timidity was funny and fascinating. I had about given him up, he had turned his thoughts to enlistment and I mine to sailing for home when he wrote his first poem. The decision he made in going into the army helped him make the other decision to be a poet in form. And a very fine poet. And a poet all in his own right. The accent is absolutely his own. You can hear it everywhere in his prose, where if he had left it, however, it would have been lost. (pp. 22-3)

The point is that what we had in common we had from before we were born. Make as much of that as you will but don't tell anyone we gave each other anything but a boost. (p. 23)

> *Robert Frost, in his letter to Grace Walcott Conkling on June 28, 1921 (reprinted by permission of the University of Virginia Library and the Literary Estate of Robert Frost), from the* Robert Frost Collection, *No. 6261c, Clifton Waller Barrett Library at the University of Virginia (and reprinted in* Poetry Wales, Special Issue: Edward Thomas, *Vol. 13, No. 4, Spring, 1978, pp. 22-3).*

ALDOUS HUXLEY   (essay date 1923)

[*In the excerpt below, Huxley considers Thomas one of England's purest nature poets and praises him for his ability to express the difficult emotions "induced by a contact with nature." This assessment is also reached by such later critics as John Lehmann and W. J. Keith (see excerpts below).*]

The poetry of Edward Thomas affects one morally as well as æsthetically and intellectually. We have grown rather shy, in these days of pure æstheticism, of speaking of those consoling or strengthening qualities of poetry on which critics of another generation took pleasure in dwelling. Thomas's poetry is strengthening and consoling, not because it justifies God's ways to man or whispers of reunions beyond the grave, not because it presents great moral truths in memorable numbers, but in a more subtle and very much more effective way. Walking through the streets on these September nights, one notices, wherever there are trees along the street and lamps close beside the trees, a curious and beautiful phenomenon. The light of the street lamps striking up into the trees has power to make the grimed, shabby, and tattered foliage of the all-but autumn seem brilliantly and transparently green. Within the magic circle of the light the tree seems to be at that crowning moment of the spring when the leaves are fully grown, but still luminous with youth and seemingly almost immaterial in their lightness. Thomas's poetry is to the mind what that transfiguring lamplight is to the tired trees. On minds grown weary in the midst of the

intolerable turmoil and aridity of daily wage-earning existence, it falls with a touch of momentary rejuvenation.

The secret of Thomas's influence lies in the fact that he is genuinely what so many others of our time quite unjustifiably claim to be, a nature poet. To be a nature poet it is not enough to affirm vaguely that God made the country and man made the town, it is not enough to talk sympathetically about familiar rural objects, it is not enough to be sonorously poetical about mountains and trees; it is not even enough to speak of these things with the precision of real knowledge and love. To be a nature poet a man must have felt profoundly and intimately those peculiar emotions which nature can inspire, and must be able to express them in such a way that his reader feels them. The real difficulty that confronts the would-be poet of nature is that these emotions are of all emotions the most difficult to pin down and analyze, and the hardest of all to convey. In **"October"** Thomas describes what is surely the characteristic emotion induced by a contact with nature—a kind of exultant melancholy which is the nearest approach to quiet unpassionate happiness that the soul can know. Happiness of whatever sort is extraordinarily hard to analyze and describe. . . . But quiet happiness, which is at the same time a kind of melancholy— there you have an emotion which is inexpressible except by a mind gifted with a diversity of rarely combined qualities. The poet who would sing of this happiness must combine a rare penetration with a rare candour and honesty of mind. A man who feels an emotion that is very difficult to express is often tempted to describe it in terms of something entirely different. Platonist poets feel a powerful emotion when confronted by beauty, and, finding it a matter of the greatest difficulty to say precisely what that emotion is in itself, proceed to describe it in terms of theology which has nothing whatever to do with the matter in point. (pp. 143-45)

Thomas's limpid honesty of mind saves him from the temptation to which so many others succumb, the temptation to express one thing, because it is with difficulty describable, in terms of something else. He never philosophizes the emotions which he feels in the presence of nature and beauty, but presents them as they stand, transmitting them directly to his readers without the interposition of any obscuring medium. Rather than attempt to explain the emotion, to rationalize it into something that it is not, he will present it for what it is, a problem of which he does not know the solution. In **"Tears"** we have an example of this candid confession of ignorance. . . . The emotion is nameless and indescribable, but the poet has intensely felt it and transmitted it to us who read his poem, so that we, too, feel it with the same intensity. Different aspects of this same nameless emotion of quiet happiness shot with melancholy are the theme of almost all Thomas's poems. They bring to us precisely that consolation and strength which the country and solitude and leisure bring to the spirits of those long pent in populous cities, but essentialized and distilled in the form of art. They are the light that makes young again the tattered leaves.

Of the purely æsthetic qualities of Thomas's poetry it is unnecessary to say much. He devised a curiously bare and candid verse to express with all possible simplicity and clarity his clear sensations and emotions. . . . "This is not," as Mr. de la Mare says in his foreword to Thomas's **Collected Poems,** "this is not a poetry that will drug or intoxicate. . . . It must be read slowly, as naturally as if it were prose, without emphasis" [see excerpt above]. With this bare verse, devoid of any affectation, whether of cleverness or a too great simplicity,

Thomas could do all that he wanted. . . . The same bare precision served him well for describing the interplay of emotions, as in **"After you Speak"** or **"Like the Touch of Rain."** And with this verse of his he could also chant the praises of his English countryside and the character of its people, as typified in Lob-lie-by-the-fire:

> He has been in England as long as dove and daw,
> Calling the wild cherry tree the merry tree,
> The rose campion Bridget-in-her-bravery;
> And in a tender mood he, as I guess,
> Christened one flower Love-in-idleness. . . .
>
>   (pp. 146-49)

> *Aldous Huxley, "Edward Thomas," in his* On the Margin: Notes and Essays *(copyright 1923, 1951 by Aldous Huxley; reprinted by permission of Harper & Row, Publishers, Inc.; in Canada by Mrs. Laura Huxley and Chatto and Windus Ltd.), George H. Doran, 1923, pp. 143-49.*

F. R. LEAVIS   (essay date 1932)

[*Leavis was one of the first critics to allude to Thomas's "modern sensibility"—his sense of the "disintegration" of the modern individual. For this reason Leavis separated Thomas from his contemporary Georgians. This point is further developed by J. P. Ward and W. J. Keith (see excerpts below).*]

[Thomas] was a very original poet who devoted great technical subtlety to the expression of a distinctively modern sensibility. His art offers an extreme contrast with Mr. [Edmund] Blunden's. Mr. Blunden's poems are frankly 'composed,' but Edward Thomas's seem to happen. It is only when the complete effect has been registered in the reader's mind that the inevitability and the exquisite economy become apparent. A characteristic poem of his has the air of being a random jotting down of chance impressions and sensations, the record of a moment of relaxed and undirected consciousness. The diction and movement are those of quiet, ruminative speech. But the unobtrusive signs accumulate, and finally one is aware that the outward scene is accessory to an inner theatre. Edward Thomas is concerned with the finer texture of living, the here and now, the ordinary moments, in which for him the 'meaning' (if any) resides. It is as if he were trying to catch some shy intuition on the edge of consciousness that would disappear if looked at directly. Hence, too, the quietness of the movement, the absence of any strong accent or gesture. (p. 69)

October illustrates the method; but to see how subtly Thomas can use it (it is a method of exploration at the same time as one of expression) one must go to such a poem as *Old Man*. It starts with a quiet meditation upon 'Lad's-love or Old Man,' the 'hoar-green feathery herb almost a tree.' . . . A phrase in the last passage—'listening, lying in wait for what I should, yet never can, remember'—describes admirably Thomas's characteristic manner. The intimations that come, as here, are not of immortality. And it would be difficult to set off Hardy's Victorian solidity better than by contrast with this poem. A far larger proportion of Thomas's work is good than of Hardy's (indeed, the greater part of the collected poems is good), but, on the other hand, one cannot say 'great' confidently of anything of Thomas's, as one can of Hardy's best. The very fidelity with which Thomas records the modern disintegration, the sense of directionlessness

> —How dreary-swift, with naught to travel to,
> Is Time—

implies limitations. But Thomas's negativeness has nothing in common with the vacuity of the Georgians. He was exquisitely sincere and sensitive, and he succeeded in expressing in poetry a representative modern sensibility. It was an achievement of a very rare order, and he has not yet had the recognition he deserves. (pp. 70-2)

> *F. R. Leavis, "The Situation at the End of the War," in his* New Bearings in English Poetry: A Study of the Contemporary Situation *(reprinted by permission of Chatto & Windus Ltd and the Literary Estate of F. R. Leavis), Chatto & Windus, 1932 (and reprinted by AMS Press, 1978), pp. 27-74.**

CORNELIUS WEYGANDT   (essay date 1937)

His discovery of himself as poet must have come to Thomas as a great surprise and delight. It was Frost who did most to help him to that discovery. It was a happy meeting, that of these two men, the one English and the other American, both of them so "well-versed in country things." Frost not only encouraged Thomas in his verse-writing, but he was, in a sense, his master. **"The Sign-Post," "The Manor Farm," "The Path," "Up in the Wind," "Wind and Mist," "After Rain,"** and **"The New Year"** show in one way and another the influence of Frost. It is now in a fall of words you note it, now in a way of presentation, now in the tone, now in the atmosphere. Each is distinctively of his own countryside, the one of New England, the other of Old England. Thomas had Welsh blood in his veins, but I can find little "Celtic" in his writing. He had tramped over Wales, but he knew it less well than Southern England, and its landscape does not color his verse as does that of Hampshire and Wiltshire. There is testimony from all who knew him that no other writing man of his time had walked so much about the countries south of the Thames, hill-paths, sheep-tracks, old Roman roads, byways as well as highways.

A large part of his verse is a record of these wanderings, his moods brought up by people he met, vistas that opened before him, places that he happened on, chalk-pits, copses, ploughlands. There are not many narratives among these verses, almost all being meditative lyrics, but one of the best of them is partly narrative. I mean **"Up in the Wind."** There is here a presentation of a wild and unfrequented place, an old publichouse and blacksmith's forge back from the roads. In old years its neighborhood was a district of charcoal-burners, but now there are "eleven houseless miles" on one road that runs near it. A girl who is lonely here, but wedded to the place, tells its story to the poet. **"Up in the Wind"** is a poem of a sort that had he lived he had doubtless done more of. It is the tendency of middle years to be interested in other forms of poetry than the purely lyric. This place of **"Up in the Wind"** and the girl its narrator stand as samples of many such out-of-the-way corners and people he had stumbled on in his wanderings.

"Lob" is another poem partly narrative. It is concerned with that figure of folklore that appears under so many disguises, as Robin Goodfellow and Puck more often perhaps than as Lob. Thomas is interested in him because he is so definitely a symbol of the time when "This England, Old already, was called Merry."

It is their fidelity to what the poet has seen and felt, their discovery of beauty of landscape and feeling, that is best in these verses of Thomas. (pp. 359-61)

Certain lines in Thomas you mark, so that you may return to them and savor them. Such a one is that describing a farmhouse as "So velvet hushed and cool under the warm tiles." Another gives you the very quality of a particular farm by telling you, "The flint is the one crop that never failed." A third is, "When Gods were young This wind was old." And a fourth, perhaps the most haunting he has written, is "The past is the only dead thing that smells sweet." (p. 361)

For all his greyness of landscape and for all his many variations on the greyness of life Thomas has moments of exaltation. These moments are expressed so restrainedly, so reticently, so quietly, that sometimes you miss the feeling that underlies the expression. Even his Englishman's front of indifference cannot, however, repress the joy in beauty that cries out in:

> Forget, men, everything
> On this earth newborn,
> Except that it is lovelier
> Than any mysteries.

Thomas had never left the England that was his share of the earth that was "lovelier Than any mysteries" until he went to the War in France. England would undoubtedly have been dearer than ever to him had he survived to come back to it in peace. One miracle having happened in the late flowering of poetry in the hardened prose-writer that Thomas was, it could hardly be hoped that the further miracle of the deepening and broadening of his poetic power would have followed. And yet we cannot tell. It happened in Hardy. The verses of his youth count for little. He was old when he mastered the new medium. From Thomas we had only two volumes; [*Poems* and *Last Poems*]. . . . Their rhythms are often the rhythms of prose, though their material is always the material of poetry. Only now and then, in **"Two Pewits," "Swedes," "If I Should ever by Chance," "Melancholy," "Adlestrop,"** and **"Cock-Crow"** are material and rhythm completely at one.

Other sets of verses, many of them, despite strained rhymes and awkwardnesses of expression of one kind and another, are so poetical in feeling that they make their intended effects. The force and directness and utter sincerity of the man, his gift of caring greatly for all things English great or small, compensate in a measure for the shortcomings of his art of poetry. (pp. 361-62)

> Cornelius Weygandt, "Realists of the Countryside," in his The Time of Yeats: English Poetry of To-Day Against an American Background (© 1937, renewed 1965; reprinted by permission of Prentice-Hall, Inc., Englewood Cliffs, New Jersey 07632), D. Appleton-Century Company, Inc., 1937 (and reprinted by Russell & Russell, 1969), pp. 336-62.*

JOHN LEHMANN (essay date 1952)

[*In the excerpt below, Lehmann considers Thomas one of the most "intimate" of nature poets. He also believes that it is Thomas's "profound melancholy" and "intensity of vision" which separates his verse from "the great mass of pleasing nature poetry which has been produced since Wordsworth." For differing views on the effect of Thomas's melancholy on his poetry read Aldous Huxley, Jeremy Hooker, and J. P. Ward (see excerpts above and below).*]

I suppose I had met Edward Thomas in the anthologies, and admired the pieces anthologies always choose, such as *Out in the Dark* and *Lights Out,* some time before he began to speak to me with a voice that seemed to respond more and more subtly to my own feelings about *things*—old houses, hidden streams, woods under rain, bonfires in gardens and twisting country lanes—than that of any other poet I had read. . . .

There are nature poets in our literature who have made one particular landscape of England their own special raw material; the East Anglican coast found its poetic transmuter supremely in [George] Crabbe, the Lakes in Wordsworth; the southern counties, the England of the Thames Valley, the Icknield Way and the Pilgrims' Way, the Cotswolds, the Chilterns and the South Downs, with their mildness of climate, their lush sweetness of nature, their gentle variety of contour, and their so unsensational antiquity of habitation and cultivation have been celebrated by more poets than one can count, but by none—so I have felt now for almost two decades—with more intimate and understanding love than by Edward Thomas. (p. 77)

There was also something else about Thomas's nature poetry that drew me strongly towards it: an intensity of feeling, entirely different from the happy hiker's appreciation of green fields and birds twittering in the copses, something that suggested that he found in nature a spiritual revelation so important that the world might be meaningless if it were to disappear. And at the same time this intensity was expressed with the utmost simplicity and transparency, and absence of rhetorical flourishes and ingenious elaboration that enormously heightened the conviction it carried. . . . (p. 78)

I did not at that time know how much the long friendship with Robert Frost, which began just before the 1914 war, helped Thomas to find himself in this style and perfect it; nor did I altogether realize the truth that, if the unemphatic, almost conversational tone was the most powerful method Thomas could have found to express his deepest feelings, such a tone would mean nothing at another level without the passionate intensity, would, in fact, be more tedious and unmemorable than conventional couplets and quatrains. But the discovery of such poems as *The Brook, October,* and *Over the Hill* set me in a distrust of the elaborately wrought and euphuistic manner which has found so many practitioners since Thomas's day (though I willingly admit the great beauty of some notable exceptions), and created a decisive ferment in my imagination at a time when I was looking for my own style in poetry and the solution of problems of approach that every generation has to face afresh—but seemed then peculiarly difficult to me.

The mastery which Thomas displayed in this kind of writing, the skill with which he chose words for their precise appropriateness without ever neglecting their overtones, the melody and harmonious texture of the whole, had been prepared by his long wearisome years of work to order and against the clock in prose. . . . He was in his late thirties before he began to write poetry; the remarkable absence of any fumbling at the start, even though his mastery increased in the two or three years that remained of his life, can be directly attributed to the experience in self-expression that his prose works—sometimes three, four and even five in a year—had given him; and a poet who could write *Two Houses, The Dark Forest* or *Roads* after such exhausting labours cannot be accused of having lost his ear or wasted his intuitive powers. It is an astonishing phenomenon, and proves that Thomas was a man of exceptional creative force; but one should also remember that most of the prose that he was obliged to write for a living was, except in such rare cases as his study of Swinburne where he seemed totally unmatched with his theme, on subjects that were naturally sympathetic to him: the countryside and the people who lived in it, and writers like Richard Jefferies who had loved the countryside as he did himself. There are even a number of extremely interesting parallels between the prose and the poetry, where the later poet-Thomas re-works in verse themes and moods which the essayist-Thomas had expressed in prose many years before: it is as if, in the last years of his life, under the stress of war and the desperate sense of urgency it gives to the creative artist who is threatened with annihilation by it, he had recovered the whole range of his inspiration over twenty years, so that he could resume and concentrate it in the new medium, the medium that was to give him immortality. (pp. 79-80)

[Precisely] because Thomas's poetry keeps so close to the natural prose order of words in modern English, with the rhymes, assonances and internal rhymes happening as if by fortunate accident, and because the rhythms of the poetry are based on the rhythms of intimate conversation and letter-writing, there may seem at first very little to choose between them to anyone who responds to Thomas's feeling about the world: the man is whole, and what you love of his work in one medium, you will find to love in the other. Equally, however, Thomas's case defines more clearly than almost any other in our modern literature the superiority of poetry as the medium for the kind of thing that Thomas wanted to convey, which was not scientific analysis or rational argument or narration of fact, but emotion and intuition, the world of the senses' apprehension transformed by the light of imagination. It is the poetry that haunts the memory and burns itself into the deeper layers of our consciousness, by the incalculable power that basic poetic forms and the counterpointing of one rhythm against another in that concentrated field endow it with; and in making that judgement I am thinking of the best of the prose, not the passages in the early work which are marred by a rather whimsically mannered note, the fashion perhaps of their time.

The war years led me, as I believe they led a great many other people, to read Edward Thomas's poetry with a new attention, and to discover that it was standing up to the sorting of time and new circumstance quite extraordinarily well. Thomas only wrote one poem about the issues of the 1914 war. *This is No Case of Petty Right and Wrong* was not the kind of patriotic poem to please the mood of the early years of that war, nor was it a poem that voiced the bitter disillusionment that followed; it was a statement of cool, tolerant judgement and absolutely clear faith in the England he knew; a poem, in fact, that any young man of unmilitaristic sentiments without a political axe to grind could find sympathetic in 1939. It stands by itself, however, and the real reason for the power he seemed to radiate at that time lies in deeper and more general causes. In all his writing Thomas expressed the most profound melancholy; and the intensity of vision of which I spoke earlier, and which sets his poetry apart from the great mass of pleasing nature poetry which has been produced since Wordsworth, is also an intensity of suffering. Again and again he speaks of his delight in a landscape, the song of a bird, an old farm, or a mill stream, being crossed with pain, of scarcely knowing where the one emotion ends and the other begins. His melancholy is not that of languor or sensuousness, it comes from caring deeply about living things that meet misfortune or are destroyed before fulfilment, and it is haunted by their unhappiness even when the past in which he imagines them is a past still to come in the future. . . . (pp. 82-3)

If Thomas had written poetry at the beginning of his career I think one might well have found melancholy in it, because he had a temperamental propensity towards it; but not the melancholy of the actual poems he left us, which is a tragic mel-

ancholy, that is an awareness not only of the beauty and the possibility of success and happiness in our lives, but also of the inherent imperfection of the world that brings disaster in a new shape just when we have vanquished it in another, and makes our idealism the breeding-ground of our evil. (p. 83)

But Thomas does not merely tell one poetically that grief always has been and will be again; he goes one step further. He is, as it goes almost without saying, one of those writers who are only likely to emerge in an epoch when new knowledge and new possibilities in life cannot be fitted into the patterns established by the old religions and the conventional, time-hallowed systems of thought. Like Wordsworth, Thomas found in nature what other men in other ages found in religion; but there is, in his poetry, even less attempt than in Wordsworth's to construct a philosophical apology for this faith in nature. His aim is always the maximum of self-effacement: nature is to speak for herself as far as the medium of words can make it possible, and the imaginative experience is to be conveyed by that other dimension of poetry which resides in imagery, music and rhythm. So far, as a general rule, is he from attempting to rationalize or systematize his faith, that he is continually reaching towards an apprehension beyond words; he wants to think 'only with scents', he wants to use 'a language not to be betrayed' like birds and trees, and seizes his illumination in a chance appearance or word uttered by someone else, as in *The Brook*. . . . (pp. 83-4)

Thomas's writing is steeped in the 'majestic sentiment of our oneness with the future and the past', in a 'sense of oneness with all forms of life', and that 'he had nature to rest upon' is perhaps the most perfectly appropriate epitaph one could imagine for the poet himself. And yet those phrases of his own are almost too magniloquent when applied to him. (p. 85)

[One] can feel in his poetry a continual aspiration towards a lucidity and naturalness so complete that one would forget to be aware of it, an impulse to strip away all rhetoric and the slightest nuance of pretended emotion. In his pursuit of absolute naturalness and transparency he quickly found, with the example and encouragement of Robert Frost beside him, an individual style that creates the appropriate rhythmic shape for what he has to say. It is amazing to reflect that a man whose whole career in poetry only lasted from 1914 to 1917 was writing before his death poems such as *Words, Two Houses*, and *Out in the Dark*, which show a subjection of the medium to the imaginative ferment so complete that they are altogether new events in English poetry. It is equally amazing to remember that he had so much difficulty in placing them with editors at the outset; poems which are precious to us today, not for any deep intellectual probings or speculations, not for any brilliant dramatization of the predicament of our century, nor for even a single line consciously written in the grand manner, but for the passionate faith that underlies them in the elemental things from which our civilization—with a kind of implacable yet helpless momentum—is exiling us: in nature, in the rhythm of the seasons and birth and death, in the mystery of love and human personality, and that tragic sense of the past within the present. . . . (pp. 85-6)

> *John Lehmann, "Edward Thomas," in his* The Open Night *(reprinted by permission of David Higham Associates Limited, as literary agents for John Lehmann)*, Longmans, Green and Co., *1952, pp. 77-86.*

C. DAY LEWIS (essay date 1954)

[*Lewis, like John Freeman and Vernon Scannell (see excerpts above and below), stresses the confessional aspect of Thomas's verse. He also discusses the stylistic similarities between Thomas and Frost. For a further discussion of the Thomas-Frost relationship read R. George Thomas and C. H. Sisson (see excerpts below).]*

Thomas was in the Georgian movement, as a critic, rather than of it. He did not begin to write verse till he was over thirty-five years old. 'If I am consciously doing anything', he wrote then, 'I am trying to get rid of the last rags of rhetoric and formality which left my prose so often with a dead rhythm'. The Georgians, too, were in revolt against the rhetorical, the hectic, the grandiose, the bardic. Too often, though, this revolt produced a flat, trivial kind of poetry no more distinguished than that which they set out to supplant. What separates Edward Thomas from the ruck of his contemporaries is not so much his keen observation and familiar knowledge of nature as his attitude towards it—an attitude which expresses itself in a certain tone of voice and justifies itself by the hard core we feel in his poems. (pp. 75-6)

This poetry, when at last it got written, turned out to be an extraordinarily honest kind of poetry. It has both the awkwardness and the irresistibleness of absolute sincerity. It is very much in character; for Thomas was a shy, reticent man, with great personal charm and an honesty that could at times be ruthless. In his poetry he made a virtue—you could almost say a virtuosity—of this reticence and diffidence. It is what we call personal poetry; yet we find no emotionalism in it, and little laying bare of the writer's soul—only a hint here and there of that incubus of melancholy which had so oppressed him since he was an undergraduate at Oxford. Mr. de la Mare has recorded what style there was in Edward Thomas's talk: and equally there was talk in his style; his poetic language is based on the idioms and cadences of the voice talking—a technique he developed, as we shall see, from Robert Frost's. Reviewing Frost's first book of poems, Thomas said, 'He has trusted his conviction that a man will not easily write better than he speaks when some matter has touched him deeply.' It seems a variant of the old Wordsworthian fallacy; but Thomas, like Robert Frost, had the courage of this conviction and the skill to justify it. (pp. 76-7)

To Edward Thomas, Frost's poems came as revelation of his own latent genius: he wrote of them, 'These poems are revolutionary because they lack the exaggeration of rhetoric, and even at first sight appear to lack the intensity of which rhetoric is an imitation. . . . Many, if not most, of the separate lines and separate sentences are plain and in themselves nothing. But they are bound together and made elements of beauty by a calm eagerness of emotion.' That phrase, 'a calm eagerness of emotion', fits Edward Thomas's verse almost equally well.

[It] is no disparagement of his verse to point out its affinities with Frost's. Sometimes there are close verbal echoes: in Thomas's **'The Manor Farm'** we have 'up and down the roof white pigeons nestled. There was never a sound but one': Frost's 'Mowing' begins, 'There was never a sound beside the wood but one'. The resemblances, however, go deeper than such verbal echoes: they spring from a special tone of voice—musing, tentative, often faintly ironic—and from a certain leisurely deployment of the material. . . . [There is a] stylistic affinity between Frost and Thomas: a manner without rhetoric, without poetic gestures; a conversational rather than a lyrical manner. Their style has a twinkle behind its gravity: at any moment fancifulness may bubble up, but it is saved nearly always from archness by the dry tone, by a touch of irony. 'What to make of a diminished thing': de la Mare said of

Thomas's poems, 'They tell us . . . not so much of rare, exalted, chosen moments, of fleeting inexplicable intuitions, but of Thomas's daily and, one might say, common experience' [see excerpt above]. That is equally true of Frost's poetry. One may say that the dialectic in it is more highly organized than in Edward Thomas. But it is the same kind of dialectic—a poetic argument formed deep within the experience and articulating it; a good bony structure. Both poets make frequent use of parenthesis, modification, double negatives; the syntax of their verse is often elaborate, more like that of prose, with much variety and complexity of phrasing. Rhythmically, Thomas is the more interesting of the two: he takes greater liberties with the five-stress line, produces more variation of tempo from it; and he was learning—de la Mare influenced him here, I imagine—how to give a delicate and subtle movement to shorter-lined poems: we can hear it in **'Snow'**, for instance, and **'The Hollow Wood'** and **'Out in the Dark'**.

With Thomas, as with Frost, we are aware of pattern. This pattern, I have suggested, is created by a dialectic—a dialectic, if you like, of the commonplace, never imposed upon the theme but worked out in consultation with it. They are both honest craftsmen, who allow the grain of an experience to have a say in the shape of the final product. They take advice from their material. This act of submission, which means closely following the outline of an experience, diligently studying its surface, also helps to produce the hard core we feel in their best poems. There is nearly always—we can hardly call it a 'moral'—let us say a moral truth at the centre of them. Every good poem has a truth in it, no doubt: but Frost's and Thomas's poems give most singularly the impression of not having searched for truth—of having hit upon it, rather, as a mower might light upon a rare orchis while wholeheartedly engaged with the common grass. (pp. 78-80)

Edward Thomas in his verse seldom lost touch with the countryman's attitude to nature as a series of facts—often very hard facts. These facts he may seem to be allowing to speak for themselves. But it is not as simple as that: his poems are not purely descriptive—if indeed there can be such a thing as a purely descriptive poem. He asks nature a question, or some fact of nature puts a question to him; and a sort of chain-reaction is set up which, though it does not get out of control, extends far wider than the original fact might have appeared to warrant. (p. 80)

Edward Thomas, lacking religious belief, could not direct this search toward its traditional objective: he can only accept, stoically and resignedly, the gulf between things as they are and things as they might be. . . .

But his poetry, for all its sombre cast and its reticence, for all the qualifications it puts even upon human love, is life-enhancing: it does not reject life, even though death be the only thing that 'cannot disappoint'. It takes comfort wherever it can, and sometimes in unexpected ways. . . . (p. 90)

Even in the countrysides he most loved, we do not feel him to be quite at home—not all of him all the time. Part of him is chafing to be off, somewhere else: but where? (pp. 90-1)

It is clear at last what he was chafing at—the limitations of life itself; and it was this chafing which prevented him from putting roots down permanently anywhere, from committing himself absolutely to any one place, or any one person. Nothing less than God, we might say, could have given that kind of peace to that kind of man; but with God he did not feel himself in touch. So, for him, it was a matter of 'what to make of a diminished thing'. Just now and then, as often as most poets, he found the answer and communicates to us—those of us who will listen to his shy, intimate, simple yet almost secretive language—the sense of a discovery made, a fulfilment reached. (pp. 91-2)

> C. Day Lewis, *"The Poetry of Edward Thomas"* (reprinted by permission of A D Peters & Co Ltd; originally a lecture read before the Royal Society of Literature on July 1, 1954), in Essays by Divers Hands: Being the Transactions of the Royal Society of Literature, n.s. Vol. XXVIII, Oxford University Press, London, 1956, pp. 75-92.

H. COOMBES (essay date 1956)

[*Coombes's* Edward Thomas, *from which the following study of his prose is taken, is an important survey of Thomas's entire career as an essayist, critic, travel writer, and poet.*]

[One] of the most interesting things about [Thomas's] prose is the way in which it shows something of the writer's struggle through an accumulation of themes, thoughts, attitudes, stylistic devices, towards sincerity, the sincerity of vision and expression that the artist has to win. Thomas was a long time reaching that; he didn't necessarily reach it by discarding showiness and artifice and coming to the more direct writing, good as it is, of much of (say) *The Last Sheaf, The Happy-Go-Lucky Morgans, The Childhood of Edward Thomas,* or the biographical and critical books. Though that greater directness and simplicity do in this instance indicate an advance. (pp. 19-20)

Sometimes Thomas's prose is little more than the effect of a self-conscious literariness. But even in this, the derivative and the overwritten, there are elements that are present consistently enough to suggest something of the Thomas we know from the poetry, of his interests, themes, feelings, moods, sympathies, and antipathies. From a reading of this section of his prose a man of character and unusual gifts emerges. But what we have is ultimately quite unlike the 'vision' expressed with economy in the poetry. One of the chief impressions we are likely to carry away from this prose is that of a man with something to say but impeded from satisfying utterance by a strong inclination towards a style of managed effects. Thomas came to be highly skilled in this management, and the effects may come together to make a real beauty of sound and cadence. (pp. 22-3)

The poorest of the essays—on the whole they are the earliest—are irritating in their typical essay-like manner and approach, showing palpably the effects of reading Lamb, Wilde, Pater, and others. They have affected archaisms of the 'I have been fain' kind; there are several 'amber fervid evenings'. French and Latin quotations and classical names are plentifully strewn about, as are references to English writers and writings. Sometimes the descriptions are in the main a composite of literary memories and echoes, as . . . of Tennyson, Wilde, Shelley, Keats. . . . (p. 23)

In this overwriting there is a surface impressiveness [and a] . . . tendency to lose the actual in large abstractions—'old dreads and formless awes', and so on. Yet beneath the relatively inflated manner one feels a certain reality, the reality of an uncommon way of apprehending. Moreover, the writing is in its way thoughtful; the musical rhetoric contains several quite deliberately stated thoughts. (p. 26)

[Tennyson's] *Morte d'Arthur* was one of those books—another was *The Compleat Angler* ('the sweetness and antiquity of England')—which for a long time were to Thomas a kind of symbol or picture of a perfection and a beauty beyond that of the actual present. We could readily collect thirty romantic essays from his work, romantic in their preoccupation with the desire for lost Edens, and extending over a period of some fifteen years; he was still writing them when he was past thirty. But his romanticism was not that of the best-seller in prose or poetry, which passes off falsification of fact and actuality as truth, whether through self-deception or by design. it is true that his 'dream' often attracts him powerfully, and that he indulges in feelings and attitudes which, as he himself is likely to point out, can't reasonably be justified. But a certain self-awareness is almost always evident. . . . (p. 28)

Thomas has many tales and incidents where the pathos is very thin and which, if it were not for the touches of fresh perception scattered through them, we could well consign to the stock Victorian-pathetic. The little girl who is drowned while gathering flowers; Alice Lacking, the young woman growing into middle age with memories of past happiness, and after an illness deciding to adopt a child no one wants; a group of down-and-outs sitting on seats in a London park: these and similar subjects gave Thomas opportunities for an indulgence which, though we cannot say the opportunities were eagerly and excitedly grasped and though the indulgence was rarely gross, could have done nothing towards enlarging and deepening his experience. To say, as many have, that **'The Flower Gatherer'**, **'The First of Spring'**, **'A Group of Statuary'**, are 'beautifully written' is to indicate nothing, for the writing is of the accomplished kind that overlays the feeling which was its ostensible inspiration, and the final effect has too much of manufacture about it to be pathetic. (pp. 33-4)

[Thomas's] most interesting pages, especially to those who have some knowledge of Thomas the poet, are those for which the best word (for the moment) is 'impressionistic'. And the impressionism is romantic in that it has to do with themes that are normally so called and with moods that are usually of simple regret and simple yearning. There are waste lands where snow drifts down for ever; castles at the sea's edge or in the mountains, so old that they are indistinguishable from the crags on which they are built; princesses dying young, and men on quests; islands that appear and disappear through the mists; all this, and never far away the people of the *Morte d'Arthur,* and Tennyson's gloomy shores, and Swinburne's cliff-ledge gardens. Yet it isn't altogether a matter of emotional simplicities and literary derivativeness; something more than an effete and melodramatic romanticism is conveyed. . . . (p. 34)

There is much humour scattered about the prose. Thomas can smile at many things, not least at himself and with various shades and intentions. (p. 39)

Four and Twenty Blackbirds, which tells twenty-four stories as the source of the same number of proverbs, is pervaded by a humour which comes from the union of delightful inventiveness with a quiet factual tone. The book was written for children, and here and there the humour seems to be rather too subtle and sophisticated. (p. 40)

The tone of the humour in *Oxford* is often uncertain, the attitude sometimes superior—it was the Oxford of the turn of the century—but on the whole the humour is happy and pleasant. A youthful facetiousness comes out at times, particularly when he adopts the manner of the seventeenth-century character writers; it seems clear that Thomas was over-impressed by their clever terseness. But his sketches of University types are amusing, and a close perusal of them would show a Thomas who, despite all the smart writing, is exercising a certain shrewdness of observation and finding a pleasure in recording it. (p. 41)

[In] addition to his possessing certain extraordinary qualities of vision, in a more than visual sense, and of sensuous perceptiveness, Thomas was a man who thought much about life. And though this thought is nowhere embodied in great prose, over and over he expresses ideas and incorporates values which enhance both our sense of his fineness and our own sense of life. When he ponders on the effects of what he rather affectedly calls 'the rash burial of rural divinities', on the nature of an old countrywoman's Christianity, on narrowness of living, and frustration, on industry, suburbanism, puritanism, and much more, he is interesting by the quality of his thought as well as by his attitudes. Moreover, out of the observing and the pondering there emerges much of the man who is the author of the poems. It is interesting to see how the meaning, for the Thomas of the prose, of a phrase like 'the annihilating sea and night' is taken up and transformed in the more subtle experience of the poetry. . . . (pp. 46-7)

I do not think there is any prose work of Edward Thomas of which we can say that the quality is sustained. Inside the covers of a book by him we are likely to get different intentions, approaches, styles. Even a nature book with a definite theme is likely to be a mixture of plain reporting, live description, verbose description, strong or delicate feeling, 'literary' feeling, and so on, with uneasy transitions from mood to mood, from subject to subject, from the actual to the 'dream' and back again. But many pages, and many essays, have the interest and the beauty of individual writing: **'The Stile'**, **'The Moon'**, **'Mike'**, **'Insomnia'**, **'In the Crowd at Goodwood'**, **'This England'**, **'London Miniatures'**, **'Glamorgan'**, are among the best single essays. Another is **'A Third-class Carriage'** (from *The Last Sheaf*, in which most of the above are to be found).

This essay is not only interesting because it shows the attitude and feeling, the values, that we associate with Thomas; it is also in itself clear in intention, forceful, unrepetitive, and vivid. It is not, of course, force and immediacy of the order of Lawrence's or Conrad's that we are dealing with; nevertheless, the writing is firm and clear enough to give the incident something of the force of a metaphor. (pp. 47-8)

When it is suggested that Thomas's essay has something of the force of a metaphor, the implication is that we are aware of a significance below the narrative, the descriptions, and the dialogue. . . . One would not wish to labour this point: we are not dealing with a tale by Lawrence or Henry James. But Thomas does neatly and firmly communicate his sense of the indifference and insentience that develop in convention-ridden lives. . . . 'Horror' is a strong word, but so long as we do not reserve it for *Macbeth* and *Heart of Darkness* I think we shall be doing no more than justice to Edward Thomas to say that he experienced it when he contemplated some aspects of the civilization he lived in. Such a contemplation was not, as most readers will know, his main subject. But it helped strongly to form his mature consciousness. (pp. 50-1)

H. Coombes, in his Edward Thomas *(reprinted by permission of Chatto & Windus Ltd and The Literary Estate of H. Coombes), Chatto & Windus, 1956, 256 p.*

VERNON SCANNELL (essay date 1963)

[*In Scannell's* Edward Thomas, *from which the following excerpt is taken, the critic takes a unique approach to Thomas's work, suggesting that much of his prose and poetry can be seen as elaborate metaphors of a "search for an imperfectly envisaged lost happiness which will never again be found." This kind of interpretation of Thomas's work has been attacked by W. J. Keith (see excerpt below).*]

The figure of the traveller, the lonely seeker, and the motif of the questing journey, the search for an imperfectly envisaged lost happiness which will never again be found, can be seen occurring again and again in [Thomas's] prose and in his poetry; but in the poems, which are so much more sharply focused than the prose meditations, it becomes clear that there is another, more personal preoccupation symbolized by his image of the Search: the lonely quest is no longer a dramatization of romantic despair, it is a psychological reality, a search for his own identity, for the reconciliation of the divided self, and his Nirvana becomes the healing peace which such a reconciliation would effect. Of course, one of the most familiar ways for the romantic poet to resolve his struggle with the problems of love and death is to direct the first against the second, to make of death his true love and to find ultimate peace only in consummation. As . . . in the poem **'Rain'**, Thomas was led towards just this resolution, yet, in other poems, although the shadow of death is rarely absent, a healthy relish of the good gifts of nature and rueful sense of irony prevent its domination. (p. 23)

The images of the search for the unattainable are scattered through the poems, and often Thomas writes a simple description of some remembered scene such as **'The Path'** which can be enjoyed for its exact observation of detail whether or not one realizes that it is also an unemphatic symbol of the poet's obsessive and always abortive quest. (p. 24)

One of the most interesting of the quest poems (and in many ways one of the most interesting works in the *Collected Poems*) is **'The Other'**, in which the inner conflict which was central to Thomas's doubting, lonely personality is objectivized quite unequivocally. The poem is a narrative allegory told in skilfully controlled ten line stanzas: the narrator is travelling through the countryside when he comes to an inn where he is asked if he had not been there on the previous day. He realizes that, moving just ahead of him is **'The Other'**, a man so like himself that strangers cannot distinguish between them. He feels a nameless fear, but he is determined to pursue his other self, though he is uncertain as to what he will do if he catches his quarry. (p. 25)

The poem is a searching allegory, and it never slips into fantasy because of the poet's seriousness and because the imagery is rooted firmly in the earth and is relayed accurately through the senses. (p. 26)

[The] poet has learned that the knowing self and the Other which challenges him must not meet face to face, for each is eternally hostile to the other and the judgements which each would pass on the other would be intolerable to both because they would be without charity, without love. This, I believe, is the main theme of the poem. Through the poem, Thomas understood or he reached towards an understanding of his condition. His self-contempt, his inner struggle, his inability to love were the consequences of his being unable to love himself, to extend charity towards himself. 'I am also other than what I imagine myself to be. To know this is forgiveness', wrote Simone Weil, the Christian mystic. Edward Thomas seemed to be moving towards this truth towards the end of his life. (pp. 27-8)

Vernon Scannell, in his Edward Thomas *(© Profile Books Ltd. 1963), British Council, 1963, 36 p.*

JEREMY HOOKER   (essay date 1970)

[*Hooker, more than any other critic, has stressed the effect of the war on Thomas's verse. In the following excerpt, he discusses the two predominant themes in Thomas's poetry: one, the effect of war on the individual; the other, the poet's sense of solitude. For differing treatments of these themes read John Lehmann, J. P. Ward, and W. J. Keith (see excerpts above and below).*]

To read and re-read the **Collected Poems** of Edward Thomas is to become aware of two principal themes, which are indeed . . . not so much themes as mental and emotional experiences that have coloured the poet's mind so thoroughly that they dye almost all his utterances. First, one realizes that these poems, written in the shadow of an annihilating war, have some of the darkness of that shadow in them. Reference to the war is explicit in a few, but in many the shadow is palpable. Its cold touch makes more urgent the poet's self-questioning; it provokes by its constant mementoes of a real human predicament the struggle of his mind from self-consciousness to the self-awareness which is also, inevitably, his awareness of others, and leads him to express with increasing directness his fears, his loves, and his failures in love and the achievement of wholeness. One feels, too, that the death this war has made him foresee, not as dream but as dung, has compelled him to write, thus acknowledging himself to be the poet he has always been too modest, too proud and too afraid to acknowledge before. To the influence of Robert Frost in making Thomas know himself a poet must be added the war's influence in actualizing the ever-present sense of death that is, too often in his prose, more literary than real. As if to acknowledge the debt, as Keats does in his Odes, death is frequently a presence in these poems. . . . Secondly, and . . . by no means divorced from the companionship of death, we are made aware of Thomas's 'solitude'—less poetically, his loneliness—which is much more than the sense of solitude common to most lyrical poems and demanded by the medium. In part this is because, although he writes three poems called **'Home,'** he has no real home— and we must take the force of the word's metaphorical sense. He is homeless literally; in a way, I believe, partly because of his Welsh ancestry and his consequent pain at exile from a tradition which, though he loves it, he cannot be absorbed by wholeheartedly; and he is also homeless for other reasons which I shall try to define: in the broadest but most pressing sense he feels himself to have no place in human society. (pp. 20-1)

What Thomas represents spiritually is the writer banished by his trade from Eden. Yearning for the wholeness of the relationship with nature of the man who follows the plough, he finds himself, pen in hand, divided by his work and selfconsciousness from that at-one-ness. (p. 22)

A brief examination of **'The Owl'** should help to clarify the perspective I am trying to establish. In the first place one notes that the poet in the poem figures as a traveller, as he often does in Thomas's work—in **'Lob',** for example, where he travels 'in search of something chance would never bring'. His travels are presented as actual journeys and also as symbolic quests for wholeness, so that the image of the hiking Georgian is neutralized by the unearnest seriousness, the lack of posture, in Edward Thomas. And the actual journey is freed from the

hackneyed formula of Journey-Quest by its particularity and thus achieves translation into metaphor simply because it does not flourish its symbolic significance. In **'The Owl'** the poet-traveller is, as usual, alone. Significantly, the feelings stirred in him by the owl's cry are of sympathy for his fellows from whom he is cut off by his own charmed solitude. His heart goes out to 'soldiers and poor', victims of a society to which he is peripheral and from which they too, though abused by it, are isolated. But the full significance of the poem is conveyed by Thomas's use of one telling word. At the inn

> All of the night was quite barred out except
> An owl's cry, a most melancholy cry
> Shaken out long and clear upon the hill,
> No merry note, nor cause of merriment.

These lines, principally in the use of 'merry', deliberately echo Shakespeare's 'Winter' ('When icicles hang by the wall') at the end of *Love's Labours Lost;* but in echoing it Thomas reverses the meaning—the whole order of thought and feeling—of Shakespeare's poem. For Edward Thomas, on this occasion, the owl's cry is 'no merry note, nor cause of merriment'. But in 'Winter' Tom, Dick, Joan, and Marian, though the tracks are foul and their blood is 'nipp'd', have their individual roles to fulfil in the natural order from which they receive their identity; and one notes how Shakespeare in evoking them assigns to each an occupation essential to the general good. For them—and the beautiful poem as a whole bears this feeling—the owl's cry is a seal, as it were, upon their security in relation to each other and to nature. . . . [It] is this sense which Thomas evokes, in order to reverse it. The soldiers and poor of **'The Owl'** testify to the essential inhumanity of the society which exploits them. The natural order of the world of Shakespeare's poem has become a society of isolated classes and isolated individuals, which is, therefore, diffuse but also rigid. Thomas's conscious use of 'merry', then, evoking its Shakespearian context, as well as the potent image of 'Merry England' (in 1915-16!), brings into the poem an historical perspective which places critically the desolating nature of modern society. The poet has been made to feel the loneliness of his fellows, and their isolation is his, too. It is not, of course, simply the loneliness courted by a melancholy temperament— which we poeticize by calling solitude—or the loneliness of a remote inn; it is a state fundamental to the poet's society and it expresses itself as his deprivation of a role within that society, and society's imposition—in its own basic fear—of a negative role upon its soldiers and poor. In my view, one feels in this poem, though it is only alluded to, the presence of the war by which the poet's mind is coloured; it is there in almost all the poems. . . . Again, it may seem a pity to thrust upon a beautiful lyric the suggestion of such a weighty metaphysic, but it is there, nevertheless, in the poet's selection of words.

In a sense the England loved by Edward Thomas had begun to die between two and three hundred years before his birth, but remnants of it survived (and still survive) to provoke in him a painful love. Indeed, in **'The Manor Farm',** the other England, so different from its industrial successor, is seen to exist still, but its continuation can be expressed only as a state of timelessness, as a dream that lives on in the stones of a village, undisturbed by the gross temporal fact of change. There the poet sees it; he is nourished by it, but he is not part of it, nor is it reflected in a social order. . . . As we have seen Thomas can use 'merry', with its deep historical potency, to show its sad irrelevance to his own society, and also to show implicitly, I think, its bitterly ironic critique of a civilization deep in the mud of a hideous war. But he can also use it lovingly, of an England he can still perceive and of a continuity whose image is far removed from the object of Lucky Jim's shallow jibes. Indeed, the idea of continuity, and Edward Thomas's ambivalent attitude towards it, is a theme central to these war-darkened poems and sharpened in its poignancy precisely because the shadow of war does fall upon them. In **'Haymaking',** for example, he sees the presence in the fields of an age-old tradition of beauty in the harmony of man and nature, and of the fulfilling labour of men on earth. . . . (pp. 23-5)

'Haymaking' celebrates a rural life untouched by the war which all but completed its destruction. But it is by no means typical of Edward Thomas's attitude: the love it expresses is only one serene moment among poems which, while expressing no less love, regard the object of their emotion darkened by shadows. Only rarely, when he is betrayed into rhetoric, does Thomas see the future as the perpetuation of an England that he knows in his heart is already dying. (p. 25)

One of the best poems in Thomas's meditative, conversational mode, **'As the Team's Head-Brass',** embodies much of what I have said about his relationship to the countryside, the shadow of war, his prescience of death, and the posthumous life which . . . many of his poems shows him to have been leading in wartime England. The conversation in this poem, between the poet and the ploughman, is, in marked contrast to the monologues in a poem roughly contemporary with it, Eliot's 'Portrait of a Lady', a true dialogue wherein the men are responsive to one another. Meeting casually, they are at once in touch, while the ploughman reveals in his speech the deliberation—a rhythm of thought related to the slow rhythms of nature—and the unassuming wisdom of some of Hardy's folk. The men are so easy in each other's company that this may be thought to damage my contention that Thomas was isolated. Indeed, a number of occasions comes to mind in which Thomas shows himself to be perfectly happy among country people. He was; but the isolation I refer to was also a basic condition of his life since it stemmed from his severance from the natural order: the breakdown in himself and within rural society itself of the natural order that stands behind Wordsworth's 'Nature' and is reflected in it. Wordsworth's vision is sustained from without by the existence of a culture—a world of thought, feeling and belief whose foundation is the land. But it is a feature of the modern world that it begins in the death of Wordsworth's vision. Looking deep into nature Edward Thomas may perceive images of his own anguish, images, too, of Wordsworth's vision and Shakespeare's world, but the latter are fleeting and they are of what is dying. Thus for him the love of nature becomes in itself an affair with isolation.

The talk, in **'As the Team's Head-Brass',** is of the war, and this poem, more than any other of the period, reveals the effect upon England of the war. Indeed, its priority as the subject of conversation in such a rural fastness shows what I have said repeatedly, that the war is constantly in Thomas's mind as the background of all his thoughts and experiences. The poem brings the war home to England in a very simple and, in afterthought, obvious way: by showing the land empty of men who once tilled it, and implicit in its imagery is the recognition that the land can never again be free of their loss—and of the Pandora's box opened by what such loss in such circumstances means for the values by which the earth has been tended. Lovers pass by them at the beginning and end of the poem, forming as it were a frame for its desolation: like Hardy's rural scene

these will go on 'though dynasties pass'. The procreative principle of life goes on—that at least was not menaced then—but life's form is undergoing a change so radical that it might be described as an image of the Fall (Thomas's imagery is of falling) in which the essential innocence, the naturalness, of the rural order is giving way to a life which the poet fears, but which, in his prescience, he knows he will not live to see established. . . . [On] a close reading of the poem in which the poet's tone is considered and, in particular, the way in which he sees what he is describing, it becomes clear that the naturalistic surface demands to be interpreted as metaphor. So 'for the last time' is recognized as valedictory, the poet is saying goodbye to a way of life he loves, for he, too, like the ploughman's mate before him, is bound for a war he does not expect to survive; but it is also his valediction to a way of life the war will help to end. The horses, too, are going from the land. Then, in the final images, we are shown the poet's premonition of a whole order on the verge of collapse. It is not only the clods which 'crumble and topple over', and the horses which 'stumble', but the civilization of which they have been the foundation. Nowhere else does Thomas express as movingly as in this poem his knowledge that he and what he loves are dying together.

It should be clear from the foregoing argument that where Edward Thomas differs from a poet like, say, John Drinkwater—a Georgian's Georgian—quite apart from the difference between dead and living use of language, is in his understanding that the countryside, in terms of whose imagery he expresses his inner experience, is also, primarily, the foundation of a civilization, a 'cultural landscape'. There, as in the old mill, 'once men had a work-place and a home', and they do so still though both it and they are becoming derelict. Like our major 'nature' poets Edward Thomas knows that Nature is not picturesque, not a pastoral tapestry the poet can unpick to adorn his own fancy, or only a neutral source of imagery, but first and foremost the 'maternal stone' of a civilization, and the home of the society which tends it. This knowledge is a shaping influence on his poetry. (pp. 28-30)

When we examine that inner life, from poem to poem, we find that it represents the quest for wholeness—the relationship of a whole man to human society and its home on earth—that will always be urgent, whether tractors or cart-horses plough the land, and whether trees or pylons ride over it. And in this quest he achieves one positive stage where his love of earth is embodied in clear, strong outlines, rising sharply from the haze which disfigured his prose style at its worst. (p. 31)

Jeremy Hooker, "Edward Thomas: The Sad Passion" (originally published in a slightly different form as "The Writings of Edward Thomas: II," in Anglo-Welsh Review, *Vol. 19, No. 43, Autumn, 1970), in his* Poetry of Place: Essays and Reviews 1970-1981 *(© copyright 1982 by Jeremy Hooker; reprinted by permission), Carcanet Press, 1982, pp. 20-31.**

J. P. WARD   (essay date 1978)

[*Ward advances perhaps the most interesting interpretation of Thomas's work when he considers the poet an early-day existentialist. This is the most extreme development of the ideas of such earlier critics as F. R. Leavis, John Lehmann, Vernon Scannell, and Jeremy Hooker (see excerpts above), concerning Thomas's "modern sensibility" and "solitude."*]

If one throws off the spectacles that still reveal to some Thomas the 'Georgian', the 'nature poet', we see that at the most cursory level he had the attributes of a twentieth-century existentialist. He is privatized, inner and alienated; he is colloquial; he is concerned with poetry's and language's difficulty; he is secular (in religious terms he is neither believer, atheist or agnostic). Most important, he seems free of the burden of reverence of the individual word of vast, historical, 'poetic', elevating associations. He does not use a wide vocabulary at all. He is wholly uninterested . . . in resurrecting ancient words, or present words' ancient meanings. His attention is not on single words and their associations, their 'richness'. In this respect . . . he seems surprisingly close to the modes of Kafka and Beckett, and even Wittgensteinian philosophy. He uses the skeleton of language not its flesh, the wires and strings rather than what they join. It is as though at least one strand of modern urban sensibility does not need, perhaps cannot bear, the weight of too heavy a verbal heritage, and when the diminished—many would say impoverished—language is resultingly used it is often in fatigued or whimsical tone or even, as in [Harold] Pinter, a sort of dumb expression of nothing, an utterance arrested. That is as may be. But it does seem that in our century the new self-consciousness toward words can go two ways. As with Thomas and the existentialists the word may slip away and go self-effacing, elided and thin, whereas with the symbolists and imagists the word, precisely through our decreasing sense of its everyday value, may all the more be detachable from human intercourse and thus usable as objective medium for art, for artifice. The way to the *parole-langue* distinction opens. Which of these two responses any poet took to the crisis of the world depended presumably on his sense of language at the moment of first poetic decision. What Thomas had to express necessitated for him the first of these two ways, a contention we can perhaps support by considering some of the ways in which he used it and their implications.

By trusting very directly the cadence of his own mind as it occurs in words on each occasion, Thomas was first able to produce lines of extraordinarily subtle and rippling cadence themselves. In this he was incidentally able to obey [T. E.] Hulme's dictum to capture 'the exact curve of the thing' differently on each occasion in a way not envisaged by Hulme himself. (He also gave if not a heave, perhaps a small nudge, to the pentameter). . . . [His] poetry is reflexive. It curls back on itself and the voice makes this possible. . . . [His] lines, detached from context, scarcely seem to have been part of poems at all; their success therefore lies in their cumulative orchestration within whole poems and indeed within the entire body of Thomas' very homogeneous work; their incessant restriking, in fact, of the solitary note. That they are successful is confirmed by the experience they give us in reading, their integrity contrasting furthermore with the occasional lapse as in *The Other* where the line 'I quite forgot I could forget' sounds merely like a verbal trick and empty jingle. His cadences are seldom such jingles.

These cadences can work so single-mindedly, though still tentatively, precisely because they are not tied to a firm body of vocabulary representative of any objective, solid 'content' about which Thomas writes and which would amount to a duality of focus by distracting our attention from the voice itself. Certainly Thomas writes about 'nature', in a special way, but this is merged with the compulsion by which many lines direct their rhythm to something not finally said, to something half-verbalized and elusive. This has of course been repeatedly noticed about Thomas; it is inescapable. . . . But his willingness to leave the elusive entity as it is does not arise, it seems, from some congenital inability to pursue the ineffable to its finish. On the contrary, such straining after what he 'seeks' is at times the only justification for what might otherwise be merely cloying. Thus in *Melancholy*—almost the prototype Thomas poem—his reference to that mood as 'sweet' and 'soft as dulcimers' can work only because it is not an inert pair of poeticizing opposites but a contradiction left where it is, in order to capture, not so much some particular elusive thing, but his very feeling ('sweet melancholy') in the face of elusiveness itself. Furthermore there are contrasting strong lines in Thomas' poetry which in their clinching of the position he is left with are direct and often monosyllabic. . . . (pp. 76-8)

[Thomas'] repeats express the finitude of a man's reaching and accepting the bounds of his own thinking, in a way analogous to repeat-phrases like 'a sociology of sociology' and 'the meaning of meaning' in more explicit disciplines. A barrier in intellectual penetration is reached so that, with nothing further to add, we start using the same words over, as though a man were to bump into an invisible perspex frame and begin to notice the doubling-up of his own footprints. Not that Thomas was on such an overt intellectual quest. Rather in more rounded human way he trusts his copulative and skeletal language to find its own boundaries, to stop pushing outwards when the mind's rhythm ceases naturally to ask for it. He trusts the connection between language and mind, language and emotions. . . . Thomas' cadences, ripples, monosyllabic irreducible lines, his drop-aways (so often, and surely rarely in poetry, to that word 'it'), his returning, recycling repetitions—all these . . . seem to mean a concern not to find *what* is elusive but rather to leave it so and therefore to capture the quality and feeling of elusiveness itself. Certainly he pursues, hesitates, and is sad, but this is not fear of the elusive itself. Rather, to find the unknown at the edge of the known and normal is itself wholly normal; the elusiveness is normal as is the melancholy it brings. To the austerely enquiring mind this is tame and tedious. As Pound said, the poet must learn to use his tools as sharply and exactly as he can: 'a term must mean one particular thing . . . (otherwise) all metaphysical thought descends into soup. A soft terminology is merely an endless series of indefinable middles'. That is wholly legitimate, and was arguably indeed the main challenge to poets at the start of this century. But if the very quality of the indefinable, of indefinableness itself, is what compels the poet's attention then the twentieth-century poet will be thrown back not on language's treasure-chest but its action and structure, its inseparability from his mood and mind themselves. Thomas is nearer to Wittgenstein's precept, that 'Whereof one cannot speak, thereof one must be silent'. The difference with Thomas is that he would almost try to express that very silence; in his own term . . . , to whisper. (pp. 80-1)

[It is], oddly enough, the rooted community—the community, but as rooted in nature—which Thomas writes in and assumes. Here he parts company with Kafka and Beckett; though 'tired, angry and ill at ease' he inhabits a sane natural world rather than one of lunar impossibility or mere nightmare, and it is the tension between this and the necessarily solitariness of the expression of it that seems Thomas' creative source. . . . Yet finally, despite the emphasis on the bared, existential language, Thomas is a nature poet, sad and wistful. His nature is very immediate indeed, he is down in it rather than astride mountains and contemplating huge landscapes; he writes of tall nettles and jam-jars set to catch wasps, and his answer, 'literally, for this' (when asked what he was fighting for in World War I) was accompanied not by a sweeping manual gesture to include wide plains and counties, but by taking a handful of soil at his feet. Thus his roll-calls of names, often noted by critics as some object of attention, seem to me themselves to be part of his articulation. His lists of lowers, his 'Codham, Cockridden and Childerditch', his recounting of the stages of Lob through English rural history, seem to present the names themselves, their sounds, as constitutive of the country of which and in which he is talking. I confess to finding it too pious an interpretation of *Lob* to see in it a deliberate injunction to us to respect or adhere to some particular traditional value. That may result in the reader but not through that kind of persuasion. That is perhaps why so much of the poem *Lob* is itself talk, itself the articulation of the trusted language. If simply trusting the language can produce so solitary a note as this poetry seems to—'solitary' not only in the loneliness which so sadly tenses against the sociality implied by the voiced language, but solitary also in the singleness of voice of the result, then we can see in what sense even normally so analytical a critic as Leavis is content to leave it that Thomas' poems 'seem to happen' [see excerpt above]. (pp. 82-4)

J. P. Ward, "The Solitary Note: Edward Thomas and Modernism" (reprinted by permission of the author), in Poetry Wales, *Special Issue: Edward Thomas, Vol. 13, No. 4, Spring, 1978, pp. 71-84 (revised by the author for this publication).*

R. GEORGE THOMAS   (essay date 1978)

At the still centre of [Thomas's] best prose and verse writing, spread over twenty years, lies a compulsive desire to speak directly and without equivocation to someone else. . . . Instinctively—in self-defence—he sought solitude, but he returned inevitably from it to share the still small voice with others, like the rustle of the aspen leaves or the man who always returned for tea. Rigorously self-exactly as a professional writer, his ideal was to be at once fixed and free. (pp. 34-5)

His poems, like the numerous insets in his enormous prose output, are concerned with many things he could not explain; not least, the twists and turns of his own temperament and the mysterious sources of healing joy that he had treasured so highly in his life out-of-doors and had recorded frequently in his notebooks since the age of fourteen. The unsatisfactory nature of his prose as a suitable medium for the precise expression of such visitations may lie behind his often repeated statement to his friends that he lacked the power of intellectual formulation. Rarely can any writer have misunderstood with such harsh candour and misleading precision, one of the principal sources of his strength.

A brief statement of the recurrent concerns that characterise the poetry provides a necessary bridge-passage between Thomas's eighteen years as a 'prose-master' and his twenty-five months as a poet. Between the two activities was a bridge and not a chasm: the one developed naturally, if hesitantly, out of the other. . . . From late adolescence he was primarily attracted by the changing face, yet unalterable structure, of the countryside as refuge, work-place, and repository of promptings from the mysterious past. To its interpretation he brought the skills of a naturalist, an historian, and an ecologist. Behind any present moment of joy or despair, he detected, and sought to bring to the surface, survivals of antiquity that merged imperceptibly into his acute awareness of the deeply hidden origins of these evanescent moods. Many lines in numerous poems set a scene before the reader, but such landscapes are never offered merely as vividly recalled 'stills' as in a film. They are in-

evitably peopled with chance vagrants, country workmen, animals, scents, verbal encounters, and the movement of birds. Especially with birds whose songs often suggest the half-realised evocation of past moments that lay 'spiritualized' in the 'perpetual yesterday' that, as his notebooks show, he never ceased to attempt to record with the aid of his finely developed gifts of vivid verbal and visual recall. (pp. 36-7)

The much needed confidence that Frost transmitted to his friend was undoubtedly a vital impulse towards Thomas's early experiments with verse—and Thomas claimed Frost as the 'onlie begetter' of his verse—but it was only a necessary first push.

For in 1914 Edward Thomas was much more than an introspective, irresolute writer: he was a highly respected critic of contemporary poetry whose quality was much appreciated by the leading writers of the day. When his poetry merged with his decision to enlist, the verse took on an inward-looking, illuminative quality. . . . I think it can be shown that, as Thomas's confidence in his own poetic craft developed, he was able to move beyond the Frostian injunction to convert chunks of his best prose into conversational verse. He gained the necessary confidence to uncover his own nature more fully and less obliquely. . . . (pp. 38-9)

The following poems suggest the exactitude with which Thomas followed Frost's suggestion that he should transmogrify into verse many passages from his prose that were essentially embryonic poems: **'Up in the Wind', 'The Signpost', 'The Mountain Chapel', 'The Manor Farm', 'The Combe', 'A Private', 'Adlestrop', 'Swedes', 'Man and Dog', 'The Gypsy', 'House and Man', 'May 23', 'The Path', 'Wind and Mist', 'A Gentleman'.** Some rely on already published prose, others are still among his unpublished prose. They all seem to answer Thomas's early wish that his own poems should in some way resemble Frost's poems in *North of Boston*. They are records of rural encounters, chance observations, or overheard remarks that had found their way into the hundred or more notebooks Thomas had kept with scrupulous care throughout his life, frequently interspersed with rapid pen and ink sketches, and always dated with the place of observation. But among the sixty poems Thomas wrote in his first five months as a verse-writer, there are many others that are lyrical in mood, personal and introspective in substance, and in no sense resembling the 'North of Boston' style. I refer especially to **'Old Man', 'The Other', 'An Old Song' (I), 'Tears', 'The Unknown Bird', 'Beauty', 'Ambition', 'Parting', 'Two Pewits', 'Lob',** and **'Health'.** All of these can be traced directly to moods, observations or themes which are recorded in notebooks or inserted into his books and reviews, and which antedate his first meetings with Frost by many years. He quickly seized on Frost's example as one way of fusing his long-frustrated desire to tell a tale while retaining at its centre a careful imprint of his most cherished moments of luminous, extra-sensory perception, but he quickly tired of the boundaries imposed upon him even by the flexible, Frost-like, blank verse. Thomas sensed that such precious moments of recall were best expressed in a more varied verse-form. (pp. 39-42)

The Frostian element became rarer in his poems after May 1915, although it still exists in a few poems like **'The Huxter', 'Fifty Faggots', 'Under the Wood', 'Digging' II, 'As the team's head-brass',** and **'Bob's Lane'.** But these are a mere handful compared to the remainder of his poetry composed after he had decided to enlist (in July 1915).

The key to this changed attitude as to what poetry meant for Edward Thomas is provided for me in the ten poems composed between '**I built myself a house of glass**' and '**A Prayer**' ('**For these**'), his last pre-enlistment poem. Four of them ('**Words**', '**Haymaking**', '**Aspens**' and '**A Prayer**') would amply repay extended scrutiny of the kind often termed 'Explication'. . . . (p. 43)

'**Words**'—the seventy-seventh of his 144 poems—sums up the joy and exhilaration the poet had discovered for himself in verse-making. . . . The poem's structure (like that of another 'ecstatic' poem, '**Roads**')—based on long sentences, balancing an initial question by statements supported by colons or asides; swiftly moving because of the urgent thrust of the syntax, yet held at key points by monosyllabic short lines, or by echoic rhymes that neither impede the statement nor draw attention to themselves—is a direct exemplification of what Thomas meant by the necessary union between the spoken language and the practice of rhetoric. The conclusion . . . is confident in tone yet unassertive in a manner that is so different from the rhetorical last lines of the most finished lyrics of Yeats or Dylan Thomas. The poem has free movement containing moments of stillness: it is both fixed and free.

A week later, he wrote '**Haymaking**' for inclusion in his anthology. *This England,* under the pseudonym of 'Edward Eastaway'. The poem is in the free-running heroic couplets he had already used in '**Lob**' two months earlier. Beginning with a limpid description of a perfect summer day, reminiscent of some pre-Hellenic, Earthly Paradise world, it leads the reader by sight, sound, and smell to the central point of a hay-field lunchtime when all is at rest around a point of stillness. . . . It conveys the mood of 'Ode on a Grecian Urn' but centred around a workaday world: within it, movement and quietude, work and restful pleasure collaborate. For this poet, in all his writings, never forgets the customs of use in rural England; close to this Constable-like scenery is a farm-house that is a home. The poem—itself an elaborate construction of movement and description—shows that, slowly but continuously, Edward Thomas had found his way towards an acceptable manner of recording, without the obtrusion of himself as narrator, what was permanent, complex, and healing in his past life as an observer of nature, a writer, a lover of books and of man. Like the long experience of writing prose and judging verse that preceded it, this poem is itself an accumulative act. It sheds introspection based on compulsive observation and substitutes symbolic images which, as in this poem, re-interpret older prose themes that hint at a new determination to respond directly to the promptings of the poet's former 'character'. The Thomas who refused to join Frost in America and led inevitably to his enlistment and the quite different poetry that characterised his last year as a writer, 1916. [The year of the Somme.]

'**Aspens**', written in quatrains three days later, exploits the basic religious symbol of a tree at the cross-roads of a village close to a smithy and an inn. The poem enshrines a moment of moonlit recollection of the War in France that turns "the cross-roads to a ghostly room". . . . According to Helen Thomas, '**Aspens**' was one of her husband's favourite poems. And one can see why. It reconciles the deep sense of uncertainty that he had often experienced in dealing with other people with his equally strong conviction that he had something worthwhile to say, if he could but find the right audience. In this poem he at last accepts that indifference to others which is a necessary, though not a sufficient, condition for artistic creation.

'**For these**' (which he himself entitled '**A Prayer**'), composed immediately before he went to London for his medical examination prior to enlisting in the Artists' Rifles, is his final,

oblique rejection of an escapist plan to join Robert Frost on a farm in New Hampshire. The poem combines a mood of rejection of much that had conditioned his past life as a writer (''The lovely visible earth and sky and sea'') with a stolid, stoical anticipation of his future life as a soldier. Written in a quatrain form quite distinct from '**Aspens**', it flows—like '**Words**' and '**Roads**'—along a long sentence structure, interspersed with clauses marked off meticulously by colons, that seem to emphasise the cautious reflective nature of his prayer, almost like a poem of George Herbert. . . . (pp. 43-5)

Almost exactly twelve months after he wrote '**Words**', Edward Thomas began to write his last seventeen poems which testify, without any need of explication here from me, to the progress he had made in understanding himself and the War more completely. Six of these poems (namely, '**Green Roads**', '**The Gallows**', '**Blenheim Oranges**' [i.e. '**Gone, gone again**'], '**The Trumpet**', '**Lights Out**', '**Out in the Dark**') seem to me to provide the most tangible evidence we can possibly have—apart from his *War Diary*—of the manner in which his poetry would have developed. Certainly I find them alive, vivid, and (blessed vogue-word!) even 'relevant' to the reader today. They reflect a mood and a tone with which anyone can face, as most people must do at some time, an uncertain future. They commend themselves to our accident-prone Western democratic attempts to infuse meaning and comfort into a way of life that seems to have foundered on the fitful comprehension in theory, and half-realisation in practice, of how little the exaggerated hopes of the 18th Century Enlightenment, and of the scientific and technical revolution of the 19th and 20th centuries, can really offer to the modern reader of poetry. Edward Thomas's *War Diary* shows that the mood and the concept of life which underpin his most mature poetry were adequate to sustain the extreme demands made upon his sensitive nature by the front-line war in France. Experience, thoroughly sifted, and poetry, achieved through a rigorous discarding of verbal excess, came together. His penultimate poem, '**Out in the Dark**', with its four stanzas each of five lines linked together by a single rhyme, is a magnificent virtuoso performance that combines a particular occasion with a life-time of experience and moves at times swiftly between poised moments of stillness. On the surface it can be read as a hesitant, almost pessimistic acceptance of his inevitable death in France. But the final stanza is an affirmation of the joy to be found in the simple, primitive things of ordinary experience, a courageous invitation to go forward without fear; sustained by clear truth and not by false hope. . . . (pp. 47-8)

> *R. George Thomas, "Edward Thomas's Poetry Now," in* Anglo-Welsh Review, *Vol. 27, No. 62, 1978, pp. 32-49.*

ANDREW MOTION   (essay date 1980)

[*The following discussion of Thomas's relation to such Georgians as Thomas Hardy and such modernists as T. S. Eliot is taken from Motion's* The Poetry of Edward Thomas, *an important bio-critical study of the author's life and works.*]

Many Georgian attempts to escape the constraints of the nineteenth century appear at best half-hearted and at worst futile. But [criticism of the Georgian poets] has had unfortunate side effects. While accurately identifying weaknesses in the Georgians themselves, it has risked misrepresenting those who were only loosely connected with them. And among the casualties of this general condemnation, Thomas is pre-eminent. Either he is found guilty by association or—more usually—separated from them altogether on the grounds that no one who sympathised with their aims could write with his distinction. As a result, the proper context of his work has been denied, and its various debts and allegiances overlooked. . . . [He wrote] slightly to the left of centre—drawing much from the Georgians but also anticipating the Modernists in several important respects. It is a position which allowed him, like Thomas Hardy and Robert Frost, to effect 'a "quiet" and unaggressive poetic revolution as important as the more publicised *coup d'état* of Pound and Eliot'. (p. 2)

[The] Imagists' juxtaposition of miniature fragments, and the Modernists generous use of collage and montage, both find their discreet counterpart in [Thomas's] poems. 'The long small room' is typical of the way in which he refers to a variety of objects with such quick clarity that orthodox pictorial and narrative techniques are replaced by what one of his earliest reviewers called 'disconnected impressions'. (p. 3)

But Thomas's 'intolerable wrestle / With words and meanings' is more reticent than Eliot's. Instead of toying with incoherence in order to reflect a bafflingly complex and fragmented society, he prefers to record individual moods and intuitions hovering at the limit of articulation. **'Old Man'** shows him doing so at length, and in a number of other poems his fascination with what is evasive takes a more local form. As he struggles to bring himself as close as possible in language to the very grain and texture of experience, he is aware that the words he employs establish a difference between themselves and their object. (p. 4)

[Various] kinds of disruption affect the form as well as the content of Thomas's poems. . . . [His] persistent modifications of the regular iambic pentameter anticipate Eliot's bolder experiments. (Seventy-six of his 142 poems show this in operation.) Both poets arouse traditional expectations only to disappoint them, with the result that attention is drawn to the autonomy of the artefact at the same time as its subject becomes apparent. One consequence of this is that 'reality' is denied an absolute identity, and is seen instead to be conditioned by the temperament, mood and circumstances of the person observing it. Prufrock, for example, acknowledges that his view of the universe is highly individual, and thereby insists on the plurality of experience. And when Eliot introduces phrases from foreign languages and other poets—as he frequently does in *The Waste Land*—this emphasis is still more strongly felt. Every inclusion shows the concern with relativism which stands at the heart of the Modernist movement. . . . (p. 5)

Thomas's borrowings . . . always create a specifically English rather than an international context. References to folk-songs and ballads are particularly common, and although they have gone almost unnoticed, Bottomley's observations that 'his memory for them was extraordinary, his repertoire unfathomable' is amply justified by numerous outbursts of enthusiasm in [his] prose. (pp. 5-6)

All these borrowings, and the characteristics they summarise, testify to a number of important distinctions between Thomas's aims and those of his avant-garde contemporaries. Where he gives only 'disconnected impressions', they provide a series of fragments; where he subtly upsets conventional forms and modes of depiction, they radically reshape them; and where he establishes a national context for his work, they create a cosmopolitan one. No matter how much one insists on the similarity in intent, the differences in degree are significant.

But while they make it impossible to call him a covert Modernist, they are not absolute enough to brand him as a pure and simple Georgian either. He built his poems in the same wide gap between the two camps that he had occupied in a theoretical sense during his years as a reviewer. From 1900 to 1912 he chronicled the rise of Georgian poetry and commended many of its aspects—particularly its appearance of being 'English yet not aggressively imperialist.' But he also criticised its defects with such vigour that he may be said to have taken the role of mentor to an entire poetic generation. Close friendship with many of its members—notably Bottomley, W. H. Davies and Walter de la Mare—strengthened his association: it did not prevent him from asserting [his independence]. (pp. 7-8)

As well as defining his poetic theories in relation to the Georgians and early Modernists, Thomas also acknowledged the influence of two other contemporaries who resist categorisation: Robert Frost and Thomas Hardy. He called Frost's *North of Boston* (1914) 'one of the most revolutionary books of modern times' and, in his reviews, outlined his own aesthetic. . . . Hardy's example was equally supportive. Like Frost, he encouraged Thomas to cultivate an understating and colloquial diction, and shared his dislike of the bardic and mythological modes used by the avant-garde. Hardy's folk-songs, and his presentations of rural scenes and characters also show strong resemblances to Thomas's, and there are a number of moments at which these become specific. In **'Lob',** for instance, Thomas uses the blackbird's song ('Pretty dear') from Hardy's poem 'The Spring Call' as an expression of stable Englishness. But such similarities should not conceal the fact that, in at least two respects, the poetic temperaments which inform them are substantially different. Where Hardy's irony is cosmic, Thomas's is provisional; and where Hardy usually trusts the past as a means of illuminating the present, Thomas is less sanguine about the chance and value of recall. As **'Over the Hills'** indicates, he has no difficulty in relating 'now' to 'then', but habitually does so only to find the connections imperfect and the comfort unreliable. . . . (pp. 9-10)

For all its singularity, Thomas's 'distinctively modern sensibility' was formed by profound familiarity with writers who were, to use his own words in **'Lob',** 'English as this gate, these flowers, this mire'. It is this quality which he believed that Hardy and (in theory more than practice) a few Georgians exemplified. By manifesting it himself he came to occupy a crucial place in the development of twentieth-century poetry. Although frequently passed over by critics—Donald Davie, for instance, does not mention him once in *Thomas Hardy and British Poetry*—he was one of the first, and most subtle, colonisers of the fruitful middle ground on which many subsequent poets have established themselves. W. H. Auden, R. S. Thomas, Philip Larkin and Ted Hughes have all recorded their debts to him. In doing so, they have made clear the good effect of his originality, and justified his evolutionary rather than revolutionary aims. (p. 11)

Andrew Motion, in his introduction to The Poetry of Edward Thomas *by Edward Thomas (© Andrew Motion 1980), Routledge & Kegan Paul, 1980, pp. 1-11.*

W. J. KEITH (essay date 1980)

[*Keith's study comes closest to encompassing all of the major trends and approaches undertaken in an attempt to evaluate Thomas's prose and poetry: his relation to the Georgians and Mod-*

ernists, his profound sense of solitude, his use of nature as symbol or metaphor, and his indebtedness to Frost. Keith's determination that Thomas was both a Georgian and a Modernist—because of his attraction to the natural world, on the one hand, and his sense of individual isolation, on the other—seems to suggest a new consensus in Thomas criticism.]

Thomas is essentially a poet of southern England, of Wiltshire and Hampshire in particular, a countryside of low rolling hills with villages tucked away in sheltered coombes off main roads, of thick hedgerows and overgrown pathways. He is not a poet of wild ranges and rocky crags; his nature is less dramatic and on a smaller scale. Himself a lover of the gentle beauty of the unnoticed (he hated recognized 'beauty-spots'), chronicler of the tall nettles in the corners of neglected farmyards, of sedge-warblers rather than the more publicized skylarks and nightingales, Thomas was closer to Hardy's 'man who used to notice such things' than to the Wordsworth who sought the more sublime scenery of the Alps, Snowdon, or the Lake District, but who, according to his own testimony, took thirty years to notice the beauty of the lesser celandine.

Perhaps because Thomas did not begin to write poetry seriously until he had attained literary maturity, he had no need to go through an apprenticeship of influences. Even the influence of Frost is more apparent than real. The story of Frost's releasing of Thomas's poetic gifts by encouraging him to recast some of his prose-descriptions in the form of verse is well known. Less often noted are various earlier references suggesting that Thomas was himself thinking along these lines. That he had dabbled in verse as an undergraduate may not be particularly significant, but, when writing to Gordon Bottomley in 1906, he referred to much of the contents of *The Heart of England* as 'spurred lyric,' and although this is said in criticism it suggests an awareness of poetic possibilities. Indeed, Thomas is frequently on the brink of verse in this book—even to the extent of producing an iambic-pentameter line, 'The high white halcyons of summer skies,' set off, verbless and unconnected, as a separate paragraph as if it were an imagistic poem. Others, including Bottomley and Walter de la Mare, had advised him to turn his attention to poetry before Frost. Moreover, Thomas seems actually to have initiated the discussion that led to Frost's specific suggestion. 'I wonder whether you can imagine me taking to verse,' he wrote to the American in May 1914. Sufficient evidence exists to indicate that Thomas was impelled towards poetic expression long before the outbreak of the First World War. This in no way lessens the importance of Frost's role in drawing a reluctant poet into being; it merely insists on the fact that Thomas's verse was the last stage in a continuous development, not an unprecedented new start. (pp. 144-45)

Although Thomas's poetry presents a remarkable evenness of texture, three individual strands can be recognized within it. The first, a concern to present simple rural experience in a direct and unpretentious manner, links him to his contemporary Georgians; the second, an interest in the poetic tensions possible within dialogue poems, can be traced to the friendship with Frost; the third, an impulse to isolate his own individual response to the natural world, produces his most important and characteristic verse, though this is stimulated by his sense of a continuing if threatened rural culture derived from the earlier writers. . . . (pp. 145-46)

As a prolific, astute, and conscientious reviewer, Thomas brought to the writing of his own poetry an intimate and sensitive knowledge of the verse that was being written in his own time. This verse has come to be labelled 'Georgian' and assigned

the doubtful designation of a 'Movement.' Ever since the so-called Georgians . . . fell into poetic disrepute, admirers of Thomas have generally insisted that he cannot properly be considered in their company, stressing the fact that his verse was continually rejected by editors during his lifetime and that it never appeared in Edward Marsh's famous *Georgian Poetry* anthologies. That Thomas's verse shares some of the qualities of Georgianism seems to me undeniable; on the other hand, his unique viewpoint and independent practice inevitably set him apart. Anyone who knows his work at all intimately must grant that his interests, circumstances, and (particularly) his temperament all prevented him from becoming closely associated with any tightly knit movement or clique. Like Frost, Joseph Conrad, and W. H. Hudson (all his friends, probably because they were all, at heart, solitaries), Thomas went his own way. In that sense the Georgian label (or any other, for that matter) has no meaning. At the same time, Thomas, however independent, was a man of his age and shared many of the attitudes of his fellow-poets. If we see the essential characteristics of Georgian poetry as a loving concern for the minutiae of rural life, a distrust of the sublime and an avoidance of high-flown 'poetic' rhetoric, then Thomas's poetry becomes not so much an honorable exception as an impressive centre. His work differs from that of the acknowledged Georgians in profundity and quality rather than in any basic response to life and letters. If we define 'Georgian' in purely historical terms as the generation of poets—good, bad, or indifferent—who began to come to prominence at the time of the accession of George V in 1910 (and this seems to me the only practical definition), then Thomas need not be seen in isolation but rather as representative, the hesitant, scrupulous, but none the less individual mouthpiece of a confused and puzzled age.

If we wish to examine the kind of poetry that Thomas shares with his Georgian contemporaries, **'Thaw'** is a convenient example. . . . The thought which the poem embodies is simple and unremarkable, but its expression is sufficiently accomplished to render it of more than passing interest. 'Freckled' and 'speculating' are challenging words within the context; not only are they unexpected so that we are forced to linger over them and thus come to acknowledge their clear-cut appropriateness, but the hint of an internal rhyme between them, repeated in 'cawed' and 'saw' a few words later, indicates that Thomas is a dexterous manipulator of words with noteworthy technical resources at his command. The rhythmical felicity of 'delicate,' startling after the aptly harsh sounds used to imitate the cawing rooks, similarly jolts us into appreciating Thomas's control of perspective. Part of the symmetry of the poem, indeed, lies in the juxtaposition of the rooks' perspective with our own. Whereas we can look up and see the delicacy of the elm-tops which the rooks, perched on them, miss, so they can watch the passing of Winter which eludes us.

I have said enough, perhaps, to show that the poem is considerably more complex than a cursory reading might indicate. It may be, in a limiting sense, 'Georgian' but it exemplifies what a skilled poet can achieve within the Georgian mode. At the same time, though not out of place in his work, **'Thaw'** can hardly be considered typical of Thomas at his best. In sheer artistry, in formal conception and poetic control, it is beyond the capacity of many of Thomas's contemporaries (W. H. Davies's name springs to mind), though it could, I think, have been written by Andrew Young. . . . But for Thomas it represents no more than a minor success; the subject gives him no challenge to stretch his poetic abilities to their fullest extent. (pp. 146-47)

A number of Thomas's poems, including '**The Cherry Trees,**' '**April,**' '**Snow**' and even '**Cock-Crow,**' would not have seemed out of place in one of the *Georgian Poetry* volumes. In other poems, such as '**Head and Bottle**' and the well-known '**Tall Nettles,**' we can see Thomas in the process of transcending the Georgian norm. Here the development of a distinctive individual voice proves a crucial factor, and the simultaneous presence of colloquial rhythms and conventional poeticisms in '**Adlestrop**' is indicative of Thomas's uncertain progress towards full artistic mastery. Forms like ''Tis' and ''Twas,' self-conscious inversions of customary word order and elevated words that depend upon a stock response too often suggest a preciosity alien to Thomas's true self. Even some of his most effective poems are marred (though generally the blemish is only slight and temporary) by an awkward unevenness of diction. Frost had already learned to purge his style of archaisms and poetic clichés. He once remarked that he had taken out 'a poetic license' to use the word 'beauty' no more than three times in his verse, and at the time of the conversation claimed not to have used it once; one sometimes wishes that Thomas had done the same. As it is, we can never say with confidence of Thomas, as Thomas himself had said of Frost, that he 'refused the "glory of words" which is the modern poet's embarrassing heritage.' But Frost had taken twenty years to lay the foundations of his art, and to refine his language with the radical but effective assistance of the waste-paper basket. Thomas had neither the time nor the leisure to follow Frost's example; most of his poems were produced under less than ideal conditions—some, indeed, in army camps—and he had no opportunity to collect his work together and either suppress or (in any extended sense) revise in the light of subsequent experience. None the less, his search for 'a language not to be betrayed' ('**I Never Saw That Land Before**') was constant and unswerving. In his best poems, whether dialogues or interior meditations, this quest was achieved. (pp. 148-49)

Although not conspicuously so, Thomas's poems are among the most personal in rural poetry. . . . If we discount three untypical and not really successful experiments in dramatic monologue ('**The Cuckoo,**' '**The Child on the Cliffs,**' '**The Child in the Orchard**'), the first person in Thomas's poetry is always himself, and moreover it is an 'I' who, despite occasional variations of mood, never changes in essentials. It is not the generalized 'I' we often find in Frost, whom the reader can take over and assume as himself, and only rarely the selective 'I' favoured by Wordsworth, in which particular aspects of the self are emphasized or suppressed in the interests of the individual poem. (The exceptions in Thomas are a few of the later poems written in the army, in which the 'I' may be said to represent any thinking soldier.) The speaking voice in the poems, then, is that of a wanderer and outsider, countrylover rather than countryman, hesitant, self-questioning, yet doggedly independent, for whom happiness and melancholy are inseparably connected, a man always in search but not always sure what he is looking for. None the less (and this distinguishes the 'I' of the poetry from the weaker, less attractive first person in the prose) Thomas is not immersed in his own consciousness. In the shorter introspective poems the 'I' can be subjective and personal (though not in the high romantic sense) yet at the same time aloof, capable of seeing himself and the world as related objects. Out of this tension comes a subtle, deceptively straightforward, but inimitable poetry.

John Burrow has pointed out that the phrase which Thomas used to describe Keats's 1817 volume, 'an intimate poetic journal,' is readily applicable to his own verse. This is especially true of the considerable number of quietly introspective poems written in blank verse or rhymed couplets or employing an irregular and inconspicuous rhyme-scheme that are to be found scattered throughout the *Collected Poems*. These may be regarded as the central core of Thomas's verse. While they can legitimately qualify as nature poetry, since the occasion of the poem is almost invariably a rural experience, the emphasis is firmly on the self, a self that is always alone, brooding on its responses, and continually preoccupied with the condition of being 'born into this solitude' ('**Rain**'). Thomas rarely offers us descriptive poetry for its own sake, and the effect differs from that of his earlier prose because here he concentrates on understanding the self rather than expressing or even flaunting it.

These poems are about time and change and what does not change, whether in the outer landscape of the natural world or in the inner landscape of Thomas's psyche. Often, indeed, they are carefully isolated 'spots of time,' though they differ from Wordsworth's in *The Prelude* because, far from demonstrating a progressive stage in the growth of a poet's mind, they bear witness to the painful slowness and uncertainty of comprehending the significance of any experience. Wordsworth's rhythms reflect his attitude by being generally confident and assertive; Thomas's (at least, in these poems) are hesitant, tentative. Wordsworth addresses us; we feel we are overhearing Thomas. What distinguishes his poems more than anything else is a tone in which quiet assertiveness never becomes languid, in which troubled sensitivity, though tremulously poised at times, never falls into weakness or self-pity. (pp. 156-57)

[The] greatest and most unfortunate temptation is to allegorize Thomas. More than anything else, his discreet use of speech that verges on the symbolic but never insists on a universalizing dimension has proved a stumbling-block. Twentieth-century critics, whatever the theorists may say, have shown themselves notoriously heavy-handed when treating symbolic reference, and the delicacy with which Thomas makes possible a more than literal reading without ever losing contact with the specific object, itself and incomparable, is all too often destroyed by extended, abstract interpretation. It is tempting but fundamentally misguided to invoke, for example, Dante's *selva oscura* whenever Thomas alludes to woods or forests, or to turn every road, path, or way into the starting-point for an allegorical journey. While I am by no means denying that possible associations of this kind exist on the periphery of Thomas's meaning, he is not a poet whose work responds to an overlay of erudite and forced exegesis. (pp. 164-65)

Frost is closest to Thomas in consciously skirting the symbolic possibilities ('After Apple-Picking' is a supreme example), but never unequivocally committing either the reader or himself to a meaning that extends beyond the literal. Thomas's phrase 'naturally symbolical' in discussing 'The Road Not Taken' brilliantly epitomizes this process. In Thomas himself, however, the attainment of an effect poised between literalness and metaphor is recurrent and even pervasive. It may well be that twentieth-century experience is particularly fitted for this kind of treatment, that a scrupulous compromise between specificity of facts and openness of interpretation is best conveyed by this method. If so, it is yet another indication that Thomas is closer to the mainstream of modern literature than a judgment based on his relatively narrow subject-matter and quiet, undemonstrative tone would suggest.

Modern or not, he took the path less travelled by. The speaker in Frost's poem may well have been modelled on Thomas . . . , but in any case the identification is appropriate. The image is itself comparable to Thomas's literal statements that simultaneously suggest and evade broader connotations. In this way, Thomas is able to mediate the enduring qualities of traditional nature poetry to our own more skeptical age. When he associates himself with natural or rural objects, he does so with a defensive irony acceptable to the modern sensibility. With the aspen in the wind, for instance, he 'ceaselessly, unreasonably grieves, / Or so men think who like a different tree' (**'Aspens'**). Is Thomas writing personally or presenting himself as emblem of all neglected poets? We cannot be sure. In another poem, an elm overhanging a dilapidated barn is 'old / But good, not like the barn and me' (**'The Barn'**). The elm is about to be felled; the barn is spared because ''Twould not pay to pull down.' Left 'as I shall be left, maybe,' the barn will soon collapse in decay, but it represents tradition and connection with the past. Again, possible larger meanings are left unstated, but the association of man and barn has been firmly but quietly established. Thomas may write of subjects no longer considered 'modern,' but his personal voice is congenial and we are inclined to trust him, even when he celebrates 'the triumph of earth' (**'The Source'**). Like all good poets, Thomas eludes the rigid categories. I would submit, however, that he is best considered as an independent associate of those who explore human consciousness as it defines itself against the ever-varying background and challenge of the natural world. (pp. 165-66)

> *W. J. Keith, "Edward Thomas," in his The Poetry of Nature: Rural Perspectives in Poetry from Wordsworth to the Present (© University of Toronto Press 1980), University of Toronto Press, 1980, pp. 141-66.*

C. H. SISSON (essay date 1981)

Thomas has been one of the most accessible of twentieth-century poets, with readers of all kinds—people who take a book in their pockets and might be going anywhere except to a seminar. One hopes he still is, but with younger generations he has come also to academic exposition and judgment, a fate he would, perhaps, have regarded ruefully.

In a letter of 1908 to Gordon Bottomley, Thomas says that "if it were not for the blank necessity of keeping a house and household going" he would "have nothing to do with books." The cry was uttered under the pressure of excessive reviewing, and no doubt the sentiment is exaggerated, but any reader of Thomas can see that he was a man who hankered for the sensible world. . . . The drive to strip his mind of words which stood between him and reality found its resolution at last in discarding prose altogether. That Thomas understood that this is what he had to do, six or seven years before he succeeded in doing it, is clear from his saying to Bottomley: "Poetry in verse is at one with the tides and pulse; prose is chaos cut up into beds & borders and fountains and rusticwork like a garden." It is tempting to believe that, had the pressure of hackwork been less, Thomas would have started to write poetry sooner than he did. . . .

The poems as we have them are those of a man who did not have tranquillity, and who had come to take "hardship" for granted. The poet of 1915 and 1916 was a grown-up who could say, writing from France: "One gets—I mean I get—along moderately well, or even more, with all sorts of uncongenial people".

The width of Thomas's sympathy is the counterpart of his profound realism, and this sympathy extended to past and future as well as to the present. . . .

The accidents which brought it about that Thomas's career as a poet fell wholly within the period of the war and was practically co-extensive with his life as a soldier certainly affected the nature of his utterance, but they can have done no more than give a slight twist to the matter and the manner which had been formed by the thirty-six years before he started to write the poems. . . . The sobriety and integrity with which he carried out [his early prose] work is something rarely matched in his time or in any time, and without it the quality of his verse would not have been what it is. Thomas came to verse as a man thoroughly and meticulously trained in the use of language and utterly free from showing-off. Moreover, through those early years he had—what the excessive encouragement of verse in our day does not encourage—an almost religious regard for poetic talent and a sense of the unlikelihood of being able to do anything in that line himself.

The question of the part played by Robert Frost in the loosening of his poetic tongue has come to occupy an important place in discussion of Thomas's work. . . . Thomas's encounter with the American poet, at the precise moment when he did encounter him, was a piece of singular good fortune. While he was still tongue-tied, there he was face to face with a poet only a few years older than himself with whom he felt himself profoundly in sympathy, and who had made use of technical liberties of a kind suited to his own cast of mind. Frost's statement that "anything we may be thought to have in common we had before we met" [see excerpt above] is no doubt correct, and indeed things could hardly have been otherwise with two men on the wrong side of thirty-five. . . .

[Thomas] did not attempt to come to poetry by a deliberate act, but waited till the moment came to him. . . . There is no doubt that Thomas had thought hard about metrical practice before he came to write verse himself. . . . [But] it is a long way from theory to practice, and the impact of Frost's performance must have been very great, and no doubt helped to shake Thomas into writing verse himself. . . .

It was F. R. Leavis, in *New Bearings in English Poetry,* who first gave academic respectability to Thomas's work [see excerpt above]. The subject must have been a recalcitrant one, for that was in 1932, and it has taken nearly fifty years to produce [Andrew Motion's] "first full length study to devote itself entirely" to Thomas's poetry. If one has oneself come to Thomas's work, as indeed to other poetry, through inspection of the work itself, through a recommendation, or at most an enthusiastic essay, one cannot be entirely convinced of the necessity for so much expatiation. . . .

[In Thomas's case, the] moral would seem to be not to waste too much time on the critics but have a look at the work they criticize. And the truth is that Thomas has survived well enough among the mere readers, many of whom did not know that he was supposed to be a casualty.

> *C. H. Sisson, "Provisional Conclusions," in The Times Literary Supplement (© Times Newspapers Ltd. (London) 1981; reproduced from The Times Literary Supplement by permission), No. 4060, January 23, 1981, p. 80.*

ROBERT RICHMAN (essay date 1982)

When we look back on the period in English poetry that stretches from 1910 to the early 1920s, Edward Thomas looks more and more to be its most significant poet. . . .

[Thomas's] verse reflected the best qualities of his prose in distilled form: brilliant clarity devoid of all rhetoric and presumption. Thomas himself characterized something of its quality when he spoke, in a review of Frost's first book of poems, of "an absolute fidelity to the postures the voice assumes in the most expressive intimate speech." (p. 1)

[Thomas believed that poems should be] centered around the phrase rather than the foot (making the rhythms of speech dominate meter). . . . [He] believed, in a word, that poetry should be colloquial, "more colloquial," said Thomas, "and idiomatic than the ordinary man dares to use even in a letter." (p. 2)

The search for Edward Thomas's quality as a poet is made all the more difficult because the whole Georgian movement is now so totally misunderstood. The Georgian poets are regarded today, if they are regarded at all, as one of the casualties of modernism. Yet at the time they did cause something of a stir in the literary world. Their earnest pastoralism and deep love of little things was the latest, and probably most significant, challenge to the prevailing orthodoxy of the day—Victorian scientific materialism—that dominated the world of their youth. Represented best by Tennyson, this orthodoxy displayed, in the eyes of the Georgians, a love of nature divorced from a true belief in it—and a poetry that had an unhealthy coldness, or at least a vagueness, of emotion. The Georgians also rebelled against the (by then) numerous other currents Victorianism had spawned—"art for art's sake," for example. They sidestepped other intellectual temptations of the time, too—the "universal" theories of Ruskin and William Morris, and Swinburne's theory (and practice) of vice and debauchery. In the end, poetry seemed to them even further separated from the everyday experiences of the real world. In place of these imagined essences of life, the Georgians chose what they felt was life itself, in all its unpretentious, mundane glory. (p. 3)

But the avant-garde not only succeeded in making the Georgians seem superannuated by contrast; it also made them the butt of its jokes. Who, it was asked, could in his right mind, after an event of such cosmic proportion as the war (an event that, as more than one writer put it, separated one age from another much the same way the Middle Ages was separated from the Renaissance), write a poem about "Goldfish"? . . . To the postwar literary generation, the fact that Harold Monro, a Georgian poet, and a very good one, could write such a poem (he also wrote one admonishing a man for taking his furniture and kitchen utensils too lightly) seemed the height of absurdity. (p. 4)

What all this means as far as Thomas's reputation is concerned can be gleaned by examining the curious fate meted out to him in the standard anthologies. . . . [The] tiny place (usually one poem) Thomas is given in collections such as Yeat's *Oxford Book of Modern Verse, 1892-1935* and Quiller-Couch's *The Oxford Book of English Verse, 1250-1918* (1939) is occupied by second-rate poems supposed to represent his "bucolic" Georgian spirit. . . .

Misrepresented and excluded as a "Georgian," Thomas has also often been left out of the company of war poets by critics and editors, who all seem agreed about what constitutes a war poem and what does not. There is an especially cruel irony in this. Thomas was, in many ways, the archetypal Georgian poet. But he was also the period's preeminent war poet, and this is very much the result of his having brought the best aspects of the Georgian sensibility to his response to the war. Indeed, his

Georgianism allowed him to understand war in a deeper way than such less-talented, but better-known, war poets as Siegfried Sassoon and Wilfred Owen. . . .

Thomas's confused status as a war poet is evident in the latest anthology of war poetry, *The Penguin Book of First World War Poetry* (second edition), edited by Jon Silkin. While Silkin hardly mentions the Georgian movement in his introduction (which takes up nearly one quarter of the entire book), he does manage to say, in a variety of imaginative ways, that poetry which "doesn't try and do away with, or limit, the war that causes the suffering [is] indulgent." . . . [Silkin] can only muster up one rather uninspired paragraph about Thomas—though, it must be admitted, his representation of Thomas in the book is not as bad as his prescriptions would seem to require.

If by "about" war we mean rehashing battles, lamentations for the dead, or depictions of blood- and sorrow-drenched fields, Thomas's poems certainly do not qualify. The one or two poems that do expressly discuss the war reveal only a tempered patriotism. One such poem is called **"This is no case of petty right or wrong."** (p. 5)

[Thomas's] patriotism lacks the rhetoric of patriotism one finds traces of in Brooke's "1914" sonnets. Both **"Tears"** and **"This is no case . . ."** are accounts of moods; they never seem to express one sentiment exclusively. Similarly, Thomas frames the story in **"As the team's head brass"** (which involves a farmer complaining that he has "lost many" to the war) with a pair of lovers who appear at the beginning and end of the poem: agents of fertility and growth in the midst of war. (Even the stumbling horses seem to be reacting to the chaos war has brought. In another poem, **"Roads,"** Thomas begins with a Wordsworthian invocation to nature in his own pared-down, plain-spoken style. . . . But in stanza fourteen one reads:

> Now all roads lead to France
> And heavy is the tread
> Of the living; but the dead
> Returning lightly dance:
>
> Whatever the road bring
> To me or take from me,
> They keep me company
> With their pattering. . . .

Thomas feels immense pain for the dead, but refuses to grieve for them. Instead, he brings them back into his life as ever-present companions who might alleviate his worldly pain. Thomas's shifting rhythms underscore his various moods and emotions, his reliance on suggestion rather than statement. A reviewer of the first edition of Thomas's collected poems, writing in the *Times Literary Supplement* in 1920, spoke of his habit of placing crucial words after line-endings, creating "a certain suspension of emotion that is itself emotional." Likewise, the poems themselves are suspensions of war that are all about war. Emphasizing, as he himself would have explained it, phrases rather than feet, Thomas effects a tension between the established meter and the patterns of speech—a perfect arrangement for poetry that seeks to bring together opposing feelings: confidence and insecurity, love and fear, nature and war.

"The outward scene," wrote F. R. Leavis (in one of the first intelligent and serious discussions of Thomas's poetry), "is accessory to an inner theatre" [see excerpt above]: hence Thomas's half-articulations of the "inner" psychological scene, which in turn illuminates the many sides or "moods" of reality. Thomas's imaginative interaction with the scene pushes his language beyond denotation to connotation—for him, just as valuable a way of writing about war as any catalogue of death and destruction.

What is the nature of the "inner theatre" Thomas brings to his war poems? For the man who contemplated suicide more than once before the war, it was the certainty of his own imminent death in the war. . . . Such poems hardly conform to facile notions of the pastoral, the nostalgic, the rural, or the sentimental.

In "**Blenheim Oranges**," Thomas goes further with death. (pp. 6-7)

Thomas mentions war only once in this poem, but war is its overriding subject nevertheless. The regenerative image of dung . . . expresses, along with the rivers, harvest rain, and "grubby" Blenheim oranges, the comforting knowledge that all things, including war, must pass. But again Thomas's melancholy colors this perception with a very "modern" doubt: even the naming of months, an emotional effort to assure himself of time's potential healing, does not seem to work. (One feels the poet would like to touch them, if he could.) The "old house" no doubt represents England, but Thomas extends the metaphor to stand for himself, too: "still breathing and interested" though no longer able to "reflect the sun" (do the work of representing nature in poems) for the "schoolboys" (is he referring to the younger generation of blood-and-gore poets, or the modernists?) have delegitimized the task. **Blenheim Oranges**" conveys, then, four threats Thomas felt closely: the death of the countryside, of England, of Edward Thomas the man, and of Edward Thomas the poet. This is surely one of the consummate poems of the First World War. (p. 8)

It still seems so odd that poetry of this quality was overlooked while writers of smaller gifts achieved such notoriety. Is it too much to suggest that the answer to this paradox lies beyond a mere appreciation of poetry? The poetry of the celebrated war poets is more explicitly "about" war than Thomas's, but to say this is hardly to make a judgment about poetic merit. In this regard, it might be worthwhile to consider the work of two of the "accepted" war poets, Siegfried Sassoon and Wilfred Owen. The poetry of Sassoon and Owen is similar, but it is from an order of experience entirely different from Thomas's. Indeed, one can scarcely believe that these three men were at times, no doubt, very close to each other along the front line. . . .

Sassoon's traditionally metered verse (usually rhymed decasyllables) clashes with grotesque detail and a tone of venomous sarcasm. (p. 9)

Owen is certainly a better poet than Sassoon. He handles his more or less traditional meters with greater skill than Sassoon, and his para- or half-rhymes (shell/shall) are bolder experimentally than anything Sassoon ever tried. (p. 10)

Yet Owen too hoped to affect public opinion, and even went a step further than Sassoon by actually carrying photographs of war casualties with him, which, "at the appropriate moment of civilian obtuseness" (as Silkin elsewhere pointed out), he would bring forth for the desired effect. (p. 11)

Unlike Thomas's active imagination, where "inner theater" constantly controls the outward scene, the photographic imaginations of Sassoon and Owen passively duplicate the horror of war. These static poems—which are just as often passive in their verbal construction as well—reflect Owen's stated view

of action in the human world: "Passivity at any price! . . . Suffer dishonor and disgrace, but never resort to arms. Be bullied, be outraged, be killed; but do not kill."

It was precisely this celebration of passivity that so offended Yeats, when, as editor of the *Oxford Book of Modern Verse, 1892-1935*, he refused, against the insistence of many, to include any of the war poets. . . . He felt that "man's soul is active" and that the best creative work arises when the imagination actively interacts with the world's plastic material, rather than simply records a fortuitous scene or thought, where, according to Yeats, "no great event becomes luminous in the poet's mind." (p. 12)

What photographic poetry clearly lacks is the poem's embodiment of its own creative unfolding. It is the process that transforms (slowly, through the accretion of words and images) the poem's merely documentary details into a vibrant account of a reality much more profoundly complex than a photograph could capture. This process of self-discovery—in which each word in the poem is revised, embellished, and shot through with meaning by the next—is what makes poems what they are rather than fortuitous photographs. . . . Exploratory poems such as these also avoid the tacked-on moral. "Anything more than the truth would seem too weak," said Frost, pinpointing the problem with Sassoon and Owen. Also, poems that depend on metaphors—as Thomas's do, and Sassoon's and Owen's do not—give the reader the actual degree of correspondences among a verbal image, what it purports to describe in nature, and the abstract statement behind both. Such an exercise—Frost called it a poetical education, or an education by metaphor—allows the reader to determine for himself how close a particular utterance (and not just one in poetry) is to both experience and emotion. The politically "activist" or photographic poetry of Sassoon and Owen, with its arrogant (and false) presumption of an exact correspondence between image and reality (a fault of the passive eye that does not metaphorically "work" on the material it sees), fittingly called propagandistic, promotes precisely the kind of automatic acceptance of that correspondence between image and world that it is the first job of poetry to question. (pp. 12-13)

Thomas's "language not to be betrayed," however, only cautiously attempts to represent the reality these other poets seem scarcely to do justice to poetically. Thomas's "inner theater," by fashioning the metaphors, rhythms, and tones that endlessly scrape against reality, reminds one of the crucial difference and distance between reality and its representation in language. It is precisely this remove that allows Thomas to be a war poet and a nature poet simultaneously. This inherent two-sidedness, or contradictoriness, which Thomas takes advantage of in his poems, is the crux of the poetic act—the source of its ability to educate by metaphor. The poetry of Sassoon and Owen betrays this essential aspect of poetry. . . . (pp. 13-14)

[The] immensely disturbing poem [*The Green Roads*] was written on June 28, 1916, when Thomas was only a few months away from embarkation to France. It contains all the traditional Romantic images: goose-feathers, a cottage, an old man, a child, the month of June, and a thrush. But, in an ironic reversal, the poet has them all lead down "the green road" to death (represented by the forest). But in an even more significant reversal, Thomas replaces the equally traditional figure of the embattled young soldier with the death-bound man and child. This is indeed ironic, but its net effect is wholly unironical. Thomas's chosen figures convey a deeper, more significant grief—for all England, and, by extension, all Europe—

than the narrower images of Sassoon and Owen (like that of many earlier war poets) convey for the fate of a particular class, generation, and sex. Thomas's version of war is at once more humane and more terrifying than that of Sassoon and Owen because it understands the war as a tragedy of wider dimension, something that threatens not only the nation's people but the "memories" (line fourteen) of its entire history and culture too. It would seem, then, that **"The Green Roads"** is scarcely evidence of the remark of one critic that Thomas is "utterly at home in the world of nature."

The next to last poem Thomas wrote, called **"Out in the Dark"** (which sounds strikingly like Frost), makes an even more compelling connection between the poet's physical death in war and the imminent loss of the ability to write *his* particular kind of war poetry. (pp. 14-15)

The crisis of civilization that the war embodies endangers nothing less than an *entire way of seeing*. But, says Thomas, given the chance, its "weak and little" light might perhaps someday become, once again, a powerful "universe of sight."

The passive eye Yeats observed in the war poets in 1936 has become a common affliction today. To him, the trenches must have been the twentieth century's ghastly enactment of the Victorian mechanistic universe—where, fighting against an unseen and unpredictable enemy, poets like Sassoon and Owen thought they were creating a truly *engagé* poetry. Unfortunately, poetry such as theirs is only *engagé* in the world of politics and propaganda. In the world of poetry it is its opposite.

Another development, the result, at least partially, of the homoeroticism of Owen and Sassoon, is, as [Paul] Fussell points out, a contemporary literature in which truth can very often only be divined through obscenity. . . . In Thomas's poems, and the tradition of "disinterested" lyrics of which he is a part, the sexual self is never the poet's primary subject, as it is in Sassoon and Owen's work. Thomas's subdued eroticism, directed at the people and places of England, never explodes into the raw sexuality Silkin and Fussell think is necessary for the literary interpretation of war.

Finally, the long legacy of irony and sarcasm that the war made the standard vocabulary for artistic communication in the twentieth century has, among other things, obscured the real achievement of the Georgians and Thomas especially. War poems such as **"Out in the Dark,"** **"Blenheim Oranges,"** and **"The Green Roads"** cannot be appreciated as long as the Georgians are not given their due as artists and interpreters of the First World War; and that won't happen, it seems, as long as irony and sarcasm are perceived as the war's most ideal literary mode.

Thomas is sooner or later going to emerge as the central poet of the Georgian period, properly defined. It is now a question of time—the poems must be read and reflected upon, and that takes time—but also a question of how powerfully these non-literary prejudices will continue to postpone our appreciation of his importance. Unfortunately, much seems to stand in the way, for today the sentimentality of patriotism that he (and Brooke) was accused of showing has been replaced by a sentimentality of cynicism and "opposition"; for a sentimentality of politics we have exchanged, it would seem, an aspect of our creative will.

Thomas did not have Frost's combative spirit—something necessary for such poets in this century. This is the central reason his reputation has suffered so much over the years. One wonders how long it will take for us to come to terms with a man who, as Leavis said, was incapable of insincerity, or where we can find a place for a poet who, as W. H. Hudson remarked, was "one of the most loveable human beings I have ever known." . . . Thomas refused the glibness the war called forth from so many of its "poets," which is one reason, no doubt, that we know so little—and misunderstand the little we know—about this complex, inscrutable man. But his outward reticence should not blind readers today (as it clearly has in the past) to his haunting and deeply expressive poetry about the century's first significant crisis. (pp. 15-16)

Robert Richman, "In Search of Edward Thomas," in The New Criterion *(copyright © 1982 by The Foundation for Cultural Review), Vol. I, No. 4, December, 1982, pp. 1-16.*

ADDITIONAL BIBLIOGRAPHY

Adcock, A. St. John. "Lieutenant Edward Thomas, Royal Garrison Artillery." In his *For Remembrance: Some Soldier Poets Who Have Fallen in the War*, pp. 96-111. London, New York, and Toronto: Hodder and Stoughton, 1918.
  Brief, eulogistic portrait of Thomas. Adcock's sketch contains little critical information.

Bullough, Geoffrey. "Georgian Poetry." In his *The Trends of Modern Poetry*, pp. 44-63. Edinburgh and London: Oliver and Boyd, 1934.*
  Mentions Thomas in a short essay concerning the merits of Georgian poetry. Bullough praises Thomas's technical versatility.

Cooke, William. *Edward Thomas: A Critical Biography, 1878-1917*. London: Faber and Faber, 1970, 292 p.
  Survey of Thomas's life and work. Citing examples from Thomas's prose, Cooke argues convincingly that Thomas had independently arrived at many of the poetic theories he discussed with Robert Frost long before he met the American poet.

Coxe, Louis. "Edward Thomas and the Real World." In his *Enabling Acts: Selected Essays in Criticism*, pp. 88-95. Columbia: University of Missouri Press, 1976.
  Critical study focusing on Thomas's use of metaphor. Coxe discusses the manner in which Thomas uses the phenomena of the objective world to depict his inner states. He then draws a contrast between Thomas's technique and that of the Imagists and Symbolists whose verse is equally introspective, but non-objective.

Cubeta, Paul M. "Robert Frost and Edward Thomas: Two Soldier Poets." *The New England Quarterly* LII, No. 2 (June 1979): 147-76.*
  Provocative article on Thomas's relationship with Frost. Cubeta presents an interesting argument concerning Frost's influence on Thomas which runs contrary to the opinion held by most contemporary critics.

Davie, Donald. "Lessons in Honesty." *The Times Literary Supplement*, No. 4001 (23 November 1979): 21-2.
  Discusses the merits of Thomas's poetry. Davie praises Thomas's technical abilities, but he maintains that Thomas's poetry is flawed because he lacked a modern poet's vocabulary and erudition. He feels that Thomas should properly be classed among the Georgians.

Eckert, Robert P. *Edward Thomas: A Biography and a Bibliography*. New York: E. P. Dutton and Co., 1937, 328 p.
  Biography emphasizing Thomas's literary friendships. The bibliography provides a complete publication history for each of Thomas's works.

Fairchild, Hoxie Neale. "More Mavericks." In his *Religious Trends in Modern English Poetry, 1880-1920: Gods of a Changing Poetry, Vol. V,* pp. 296-346. New York: Columbia University Press, 1962.*
> Discussion of the humanitarian aspects of Thomas's poetry. The mystical role that nature plays in Thomas's poetry is also examined.

Kirkham, Michael. "The Desert Places in Edward Thomas's Poetry." *The University of Toronto Quarterly* XLVIII, No. 4 (Summer 1979): 283-301.
> Examines the way in which Thomas's poetry recreates the sense of "impregnable isolation" that led to his attacks of depression and melancholia.

Marsh, Jan. *Edward Thomas: A Poet for His Country.* New York: Barnes & Noble, 1978, 225 p.
> Biocritical study. Marsh attempts to define where Thomas's work belongs in the English literary tradition and discusses at length why she feels Thomas is closest in spirit to Thomas Hardy.

Moore, T. Sturge. "Edward Thomas." In his *Some Soldier Poets,* pp. 77-85. London: Grant Richards, 1919.
> Praises Thomas's poetry for the "complex and subtle" moods it evokes, but finds fault with the poet for what Moore describes as "a greater preoccupation with manner than with matter."

Thomas, Helen. *World without End.* New York and London: Harper and Brothers, 1931, 218 p.
> Semifictional account of Helen and Edward Thomas's love affair and subsequent marriage. Referring to Edward Thomas as "David," Helen Thomas describes her husband's struggles with depression and the detrimental effect his emotional illness had on their marriage.

Whicher, George F. "Edward Thomas." *The Yale Review* IX (1920): 556-67.
> Analytical study. Whicher discusses the author's mystical insight, the naturalness of his style, and the uniquely English quality of his verse.

Ernst Toller

1893-1939

German dramatist, poet, essayist, and autobiographer.

Toller is considered one of the most significant writers of the German Expressionist movement. His plays—in particular *Masse Mensch* (*Masses and Man*) and *Die Maschinenstürmer* (*The Machine-Wreckers*)—dominated the German stage during the early 1920s. Toller's dramas are among the most characteristic works of Expressionism, and nearly all his plays develop themes peculiar to that movement: the quest for a "new" humanity, the regenerative power of love, the diabolical effects of war and industrialization, and, especially, the need for a peaceful overthrow of the existing social order. These concerns appealed greatly to a German audience seeking solutions to the turmoil of postwar Europe. Because of this commitment to social change, Toller has earned the admiration of numerous critics.

Toller was born to Jewish parents in the Prussian province of Posen. After graduating from the Bromber Realgymnasium in 1912, he traveled to Denmark and France and spent a brief period studying law at the University of Grenoble. He was in Lyons when he heard of the outbreak of the First World War. Eager to demonstrate his nationalistic fervor, he returned to Germany and immediately enlisted in the infantry. After thirteen months at the front he was discharged, possibly due to mental exhaustion, though the exact reasons remain ambiguous. By this time Toller was convinced of the senseless horror of war, and he soon began organizing students and workers in pacifist demonstrations. In 1918 he was briefly imprisoned for his attempt to organize a strike of munition laborers in Munich. During his incarceration he wrote his first play, *Die Wandlung* (*Transfiguration*), based largely on his own experiences in the war. Upon release, Toller returned to his revolutionary activities. In 1919 he was arrested again for participating as an elected official of the short-lived Bavarian Soviet Republic. Toller spent the next five years in prison, and it was during this period that he wrote his first poems, collected in two volumes—*Gedichte der Gefangenen* and *Das Schwalbenbuch* (*The Swallow-Book*)—and his most famous plays, including *Masses and Man*, *The Machine-Wreckers*, and *Der Deutsche Hinkemann (Brokenbrow)*. After his release from prison, Toller had a difficult time adjusting to life in Germany. He became more and more disillusioned with world affairs, especially the events in Spain during the Spanish civil war. In 1932, with the advent of Nazism, he fled Germany and eventually settled in the United States. His final years were spent struggling against impending poverty and diminishing popularity. At the age of forty-five, shortly after the publication of the play *Pastor Hall*, he committed suicide in his New York hotel room.

In the broadest sense, Toller's work demonstrates the essential conflict between the world of thought and the world of action, and nowhere is this more apparent than in his first three plays—*Transfiguration, Masses and Man*, and *The Machine-Wreckers. Transfiguration*, perhaps the model play of the Expressionist theater, follows the progress of a sensitive patriot as he leaves his dull life and middle-class family to fight in the First World War. The work is broken into a series of stages—

or "stationen"—and each scene alternates between portraying external events and displaying the protagonist's subconscious mind. The horrors of war transform the hero from a patriotic volunteer into a revolutionary fighter for humanity. Toller's other best-known dramas, *Masses and Man* and *The Machine-Wreckers*, express the disillusionment of the frustrated revolutionary. In *Masses and Man* Toller examined the personal conflict of a revolutionary who seeks to realize the highest ideals of peace and brotherhood during a time of war and nationalistic fervor. *The Machine-Wreckers*, a more realistic play than *Masses and Man*, is based on the 1815 Luddite labor disturbances in England in which a village of workers attempted to halt local industrialization. Both plays depict an idealistic leader destroyed by the hatred and ignorance of the masses. More importantly, these works pose the fundamental dilemma in Toller's art: how to achieve revolutionary ends without violence or bloodshed. In his later plays—such as *Hinkemann* and *Hoppla, wir Leben!* (*Hoppla! Such Is Life!*)—Toller moved away from avant-garde and abstract characterization to present a more realistic picture of life. For this reason, Pierre Loving has called *Hinkemann* "the finest tragedy of the post-war years." However, many critics believe that these later works are marred by the author's growing pessimism and lack of constructive vision. It is not until his final play, *Pastor Hall*, that we find a character who is able to maintain a positive vision of humanity. Based on the true story of a clergyman in Nazi Germany, *Pastor Hall* demonstrates Toller's belief in the power of faith and ideological commitment, even in a world of persecution and fear.

Toller had a profound effect on German literature, and also influenced the work of such playwrights as Sean O'Casey and Eugene O'Neill. However, all of his plays suffer from such typical excesses of Expressionism as crude characterization, melodramatic action, and disconnected presentation of dramatic incidents. Numerous critics, among them Desmond MacCarthy and Raymond Williams, have criticized Toller for consistently reducing his work to a conflict of ideas rather than presenting a struggle between fully realized, flesh-and-blood personalities. He has also been called a propagandist who could not distinguish between the stage and the political platform. Nevertheless, Toller is often praised for introducing new forms of expression to the theater, for the integrity of his humanist vision, and for his deep concern with ageless social and political conflicts. So intense was Toller's social commitment in his art that Herman George Scheffauer has called him "the most dominant and flagrant genius hatched by the German Revolution."

(See also *Contemporary Authors*, Vol. 107.)

PRINCIPAL WORKS

Die Wandlung   (drama)   1919
  [*Transfiguration* published in *Seven Plays*, 1935]
Masse Mensch   (drama)   1920
  [*Masses and Man*, 1923; also published as *Man and the
    Masses*, 1924]
Gedichte der Gefangenen   (poetry)   1921
Die Maschinenstürmer   (drama)   1922
  [*The Machine-Wreckers*, 1923]
Der Deutsche Hinkemann   (drama)   1923
  [*Brokenbrow*, 1926; also published as *Hinkemann* in *Seven
    Plays*, 1935]
Das Schwalbenbuch   (poetry)   1924
  [*The Swallow-Book*, 1924]
*Vormorgen   (poetry)   1924
Der entfesselte Wotan   (drama)   1925
Hoppla, wir Leben!   (drama)   1927
  [*Hoppla!*, 1928; also published as *Hoppla! Such Is Life!*
    in *Seven Plays*, 1935]
Feuer aus den Kesseln   (drama)   1930
  [*Draw the Fires*, 1935]
Quer Durch   (essays and history)   1930
  [*Which World—Which Way?* (partial translation), 1931]
Die blinde Göttin [first publication]   (drama)   1933
  [*The Blind Goddess*, 1934]
Eine jugend in Deutschland   (autobiography)   1933
  [*I Was a German*, 1934]
Mary Baker Eddy; oder, Wunder in Amerika [with Hermann
    Kesten]   (drama)   1934
  [*Mary Baker Eddy* published in *Seven Plays*, 1935]
Briefe aus dem Gefangnis   (letters and reminiscences)
    1935
  **[*Letters from Prison: Including Poems and a New
    Version of "The Swallow-Book,"* 1936]
Seven Plays   (dramas)   1935
***Blind Man's Buff* [with Denis Johnston]   (drama)   1936
Nie wieder Friede [first publication]   (drama)   1936
  [*No More Peace!*, 1937]
Pastor Hall [first publication]   (drama)   1939

*This work is a revision of the earlier *Gedichte der Gefangenen*.

**This work includes a revision of the earlier *The Swallow-Book*.

***This work is a revision of the earlier *Die blinde Göttin*.

HERMAN GEORGE SCHEFFAUER   (essay date 1922)

[*Scheffauer was one of the first critics outside Germany to recognize Toller as a leading dramatist of the post-war generation.*]

[Ernst Toller is a] student, proletarian poet and dramatist—the most dominant and flagrant genius hatched by the German Revolution. (p. 230)

Toller's first play was called "**Wandlung**" ("**Transformation**"), in six stations of the *via crucis* of war. He was himself the hero, and led us into the external and internal hells and horrors he underwent from the first day of the red overture of war to his own "transmogrification." Scenes never before risked upon a stage were presented as matters of course in this torrential play. Thus in the *Vorspiel*, foreplay, so to speak, the War Death (in steel helmet and military gear) and the Civilian Death (in top hat and gaiters) meet on a vast field of graves—to strike a balance in their business. The War Death calls his victims, officers and men, out of their graves and commands a parade—a scene of immense *macabre* power. (pp. 230-31)

This play paved the way (with crosses, graves, prison stones, fragments of the social order) for his greater work "**Masse Mensch.**" This strange drama seizes and shakes and harrows up its audiences somewhere in Germany night after night. The play, "A visionary show," as Toller calls it, was the product of a kind of spiritual eruption. The student-poet flung it upon paper in October, 1919, in two days and a half, hiding himself in his cell like an animal, refusing food, refusing to have the cell cleaned, refusing to talk with comrades. But he spent a whole year in giving it higher form and finish.

Ernst Toller is more than a proletariat party dramatist, sinking art in theory and political polemics. He offers his fire and brimstone in vessels shaped by art. The artist in him rejects all compromises with his aesthetic conscience. The dramatist in him sees always both sides of both sides. His passion is Humanity and he is a truculent protagonist for the rights of the Masses, but his championship is never blind; he preserves the balance necessary to create true drama. He sees the eternal human-all-too-human wrecking the very cause of humanity.

"**Masse Mensch**"—the title translates but lamely and baldly into "Mass Mankind" or "Man in the Mass" or "Herd Mankind"—is a dramatic conflict between the abstract state and the spirit of the masses. The play is divided into "pictures" and these again into "real" and "dream" pictures. The characters are nameless—Workmen, Workwomen, the Nameless One, Officer, Priest, Man, Bankers, Prisoners, Guards, Shadows. Only the heroine, Sonia Irene L., a woman of the caste of officials who makes common cause with the workers, is given a name—significantly Russian. She is the Blue Woman embodying Love doomed to crucifixion, relentless loyalty to Truth—herself the human sacrifice.

The scenes are intensely visionary, the language lyrical, yet the dramatic seizure never loosens, but knots up the loose structure of the play into a glowing chain. This chain, like some great transmission cable, keeps racing forward, bearing the scenery and characters over profounds that seem dramatic impossibilities. Some of the scenes are merely projections of the dreams and visions of the heroine Sonia—events that enact themselves upon the stage of her own soul.

The "Mass Man" is incorporated in the "Nameless One," who appears first in this scene, then in that, revealing the face of the Mass, now as Might, now as Madness, now as God, now as Destiny, now as Guilt. The human relationship between the revolutionary Sonia and her orthodox husband, faithful to his post and to the State, is brought to bear poignantly at times. But it is secondary to the real theme and the real forces of the play. These may be summed up as Man against Man, the Mass against its confines, the Will-to-Power of the Multitude flattering itself with a formula of Release. (pp. 231-34)

[At] the close of this flaming drama two forces confront each other as before—the State is Moloch—the Mass is Moloch. But even in the symbolism of the last action in the last act, Property and the Rights of Property utter their immemorial *noli me tangere*—touch me not! (p. 243)

> *Herman George Scheffauer, "The Drama on Fire" (originally published in* The Double Dealer, *Vol. IV, No. 21, September, 1922), in his* The New Vision in the German Arts *(copyright, 1924, by B. W. Huebsch, Inc.), Huebsch, 1924, pp. 228-43.*

ASHLEY DUKES   (essay date 1923)

[European] history must be understood if the passion and pity of [Toller's] dramas are to be comprehended. They are documents of his time and our own, written in our common blood. The thought of literature is remote from this poet's mind; his inspiration is the beat of the living pulse. Such a creative mind is not to be regarded with the observer's eye trained in the calm assimilation of the headline, or with the half-humorous pharisaic spirit of the victorious islander who thanks God daily that he is not as other Europeans are. They are our dead who rise up in fantasy on Toller's stage, they are our poor who cry in the streets and our maimed who hug the secret of their impotence. If there be an epic of war and peace fit to embrace all the happenings of these years—the wrestling of nation with nation and man with man and body with spirit, the stirring of the soul beneath the vast encumbrance of mechanical fate, the light of meaning illuminating depths of horror—it must be sought in these dramas that come glowing from the anvil of suffering, and are at once phantasmagoric in semblance and ardent in reality. (pp. 165-66)

Here is an imagination that ennobles not only common things, but common conceptions. With Toller there are no *clichés*, no hackneyed phrases, no worn and weary metaphors. Passion transfigures them . . . , and dead words rise up again to do battle for the living thought.

Masse-Mensch (*Masses and Man*), "a play of the social revolution in the twentieth century," is a work that defies summary in outward form. A workman's strike and a rattle of machine-guns; a Bourse crowded with noisy jobbers and brokers gambling on the fortunes of war; a woman labour leader who is far-sighted and masses who grope for passion in the dark; a prison cell, warders and prisoners, a farewell, and a salvo in the yard; how can these outward semblances represent the drama? The action lies deep in the mind, where image calls to image and word echoes word with a gaunt and passionate will to utterance. The appearance of action is thrown up, as it were,

by burning thought; it is volcanic, luminous, unearthly, terrible. But the mind is swept by winds that sow beauty; it is warmed by the radiance that blisters and scorches the world of unreality. (pp. 167-68)

Here the key-words of expressionism ring out: "Masses are trampled cornfields, masses are buried men." The thought moves swiftly to a goal. An image rises of a man able to match his own inward strength against the assault of Fate; to stand and withstand, alone and in the mass. A drama rises behind the appearance of action that has held the stage, the drama of the individual and the mass, the drama indeed of our century.

In *Die Maschinenstürmer* (*The Machine-Wreckers*), Toller's play of the English Luddites, the symbols of historical drama are made to represent the realities of our own day. It is the legacy of European war, as well as the introduction of steam-driven machinery, that reduces the weavers of Nottingham to starvation and despair. (pp. 168-69)

In [these] historical symbols, and in the intermingling of prose with verse to meet emotional necessity, we recognise dramatic forms handed down by long tradition and abandoned by modern playwrights only under the stress of emotional barrenness. Also in the closing scenes of the play, with their swift movement to the climax of the idealist's martyrdom by his fellow-workmen, we are aware of a tragic sense that may be called classical. In the ecstatic figure of the Engineer who seeks to plead with the destroying mob, in the partly mistaken figure of the Old Reaper who seeks God, in the engine, and in the mass-effect of weavers and their womenfolk chanting their demands in unison, the other aspect of Toller's drama appears. The spirit of man wrestles with mechanical civilisation, with war and the engines of war, with material darkness and the powers of ignorance. (pp. 170-71)

> *Ashley Dukes, "Poets and Historians," in his* The Youngest Drama: Studies of Fifty Dramatists *(reprinted by permission of the Literary Estate of Ashley Dukes), Ernest Benn, Limited, 1923, pp. 141-80.**

LUDWIG LEWISOHN   (essay date 1924)

We have heard a good deal about plays that deal with ideas. But these plays have hitherto always been plays in which the human characters were interested in ideas and flung these ideas back and forth and discussed them and, at times, tried to live by them. In "**Masse Mensch**" the idea itself steps forth—terrible, gigantic, overwhelming. And the idea is dramatic, because it holds at its core one of the rooted antinomies of which the universe is built. The idea is dramatic because, rightly thought upon, the universe is so. Think far enough in any direction and you come upon a hopeless contradiction, a conflict that is from the beginning and nature of things. Hegel built up his whole dialectic to harmonize these contradictions. The average man says "God" and thinks that he has driven conflict out of the universe. Alas, it is at home there.

This fact has been known to thinkers since the days of Job. It has been known to dramatists, too. But their knowledge of it, except in the cases of Hebbel and Shaw, was always an instinctive one and did not rise into the operative artistic consciousness. It rose into Toller's consciousness because he lived the idea which he has here dramatically projected. It is well known that he took part in the Munich Communist revolution under Kurt Eisner and is still in prison. He is no less a Communist today because he has transcended Communism, no less an impassioned friend of mankind because he sees most clearly today the hopelessness of its struggle—the hopelessness which arises from this fact: If you use force, you incur guilt; if you do not use force you are destroyed by those who use it. That is the dramatic idea of **"Masse Mensch"**; it is the most dramatic of all ideas, the most catastrophic for the entire race.

The play shows a White Terror in full operation: war, hunger, industrial slavery. The masses rise, tempted to institute a Red Terror, partly as revenge but more largely to make the revolution prevail. But that is only exchanging murder for murder, oppression for oppression, guilt for guilt. The voice of the Woman who *is* the tragic conflict within the idea rises in great accents of compassion, of despair, of accusation of the Eternal who has cursed man with force and therefore with guilt. The masters, of course, try to turn the antinomy that is at the root of things to their advantage and try to differentiate their guilt from that of the rising masses. The Woman, though she goes to her death rather than be liberated by force and rejoin the revolutionaries, is not to be corrupted. Though guilt cannot rectify guilt nor murder atone for murder the masters are the more responsible. They taught the masses war and slavery. (pp. 512-13)

> Ludwig Lewisohn, *"Drama: Conflict," in* The Nation *(copyright 1924 The Nation magazine, The Nation Associates, Inc.), Vol. 118, No. 3069, April 30, 1924, pp. 512-13.*

DESMOND MacCARTHY   (essay date 1924)

[*MacCarthy's comments reflect the negative attitude adopted by some critics toward Expressionism in general, and Toller's work in particular. In a discussion of* Masses and Men, *he asserts that Expressionism "cannot triumph" because it fails to treat individual cases. For further commentary on the perceived shortcomings of the Expressionist theater see Harry Slochower and Raymond Williams excerpted below.*]

[Toller's **Masses and Men**] is something new. It is, I believe, considered a masterpiece of the Expressionist movement, of which, though its vogue is already nearly over on the Continent, the effects are likely to remain. (p. 191)

The Expressionist Theatre seems to be a device for treating a subject epically on the stage; I believe it cannot succeed. We can learn from it, but it cannot triumph, for the point of view of art is that of human feeling, and human feeling is roused by particular cases, and is hardly increased by the knowledge that each case is one of countless many. In the great epics it is our interest in individuals that makes them significant. The slaughter in the *Iliad* would be uninteresting if it were not for Hector, Hecuba and the grief of Achilles. To reduce human beings, even in an epic, to X, Y, and Z is fatal. Yet how hard to design dramatically a story of an individual life so that it shall contain on the stage the essence of a whole movement, or a great upheaval! Herr Toller has given it up. He aims directly at his theme, presenting the German post-war revolution in a series of nightmare pictures, through which we are intended to divine the forces behind. I do not think highly of the result as a work of art. Interesting it is, and interesting, too, as showing how the stage can enlarge its methods to include new effects. I did not think highly of **Masses and Men** as a work of art, because I did not really believe in his "masses," I did not really believe in his "financiers," and though I did believe in his "Woman," she was not critically enough presented. The dramatist's diagnosis is at once grandiose, sum-

mary and superficial. It claims to be the result of visionary insight. In an interesting letter from the author to the German producer, he describes his state of mind while writing the play. It was written in prison in feverish haste. He says that when he saw two women pass the window of his cell he did not see them for a moment as "realistic human beings." "It was a dance of death, one old maid and her mirrored death that stared me in the face." For the phrase, "realistic human beings" read simply "human beings," and you lay your finger on the weakness of his play. For tragedies can only happen to *human beings.* Generalised miseries, generalised desires and impulses can be symbolised and made to caper and dance either to our horror or our delight, but such bloodless ballets cannot reach the pitch of tragedy.

"Bourgeois Society," he continues, "and the art which reflects it, sees only idle wrangling about abstractions in a theme which, to the working-classes, represents most tragic and shattering conflicts. The proletarian, on the other hand, is quite unmoved by the 'profound' and significant expression of the spiritual experiences of the middle-classes." The conflict between them is represented in the opposition of the two principal figures, "The Nameless One" and the "Woman." "The Woman" is a Shelleyan idealist who has led the revolution to find that it leads to battle and murder. The power slips from her hands into those of "The Nameless One" who is ruthless, and though beaten now, sure of his end—the destruction of society as it is. Here is a real emotional conflict; but how much more moving it would have been had it been a conflict between human beings, instead of a grinning phantasm and an abstract type!

I am, myself, one of the most bourgeois people I ever met, satisfied with happiness, kindness, knowledge, health, affection. Any bourgeois with imagination can credit those who are oppressed with hatred and desperation; but you are never going to persuade him that a mysticism of violence is anything but a foolish "rationalisation," totally without philosophic truth, of very natural passions, or prevent him from believing that the proletarians, too, really desire the same solid goods, and are prepared for anything, simply because they lack them. (p. 192)

> Desmond MacCarthy, *"Drama: 'Masses and Men'," in* New Statesman *(© 1924 The Statesman Publishing Co. Ltd.), Vol. 23, No. 579, May 24, 1924, pp. 191-92.*

PIERRE LOVING   (essay date 1929)

[*Loving's essay is typical of much of the critical response toward Toller's work. Loving criticizes the dramatist for his "lack of range," his didacticism, and his dependence on unusual stage effects. At the same time, he praises Toller for his poetic sensibility.*]

In Ernst Toller's plays there is one conspicuous flaw, and this has nothing to do with the feeling that animates them; the plays have body, they have social passion, they are timely; but there is in almost all of them too great a strictness in the manipulation of the theme. And it is this, I believe, that gives them the effect of a lack of range. The plays do not merely put certain significant questions, questions which intimately concern every one of us to-day, but they set out to answer them, and chiefly in one way. (p. 205)

Ernst Toller has up to the present given us a continuum of but a single play. He narrows himself to one disturbing question and is not abashed to represent himself in nearly every one of his plays as the one who asks it. While the protagonist is now querulous and now strong, he never loses his title of protagonist; he is at bottom a fighter, a dissident, an active nonconformist. Sometimes he is a poet. Toller is at his best, indeed, when he portrays the poet's fine sensibilities at odds with the mechanical drift and coarseness of the modern world.

If he were not so good a dramatist, the *tendenz* speeches of his minor characters, even granting their appositeness, would be unimaginably irksome; but Toller is careful to restrain himself in this, as though he acknowledged his native weakness. He still over-points; he has not yet learnt spareness and suggestion; but his crimes on this score are not so heinous as they used to be. Mr O'Neill surpasses him in this, and both Toller and O'Neill, one imagines, would profit a good deal by studying the dialogue method of Mr Hemingway. Crispness, parsimony in the use of words, a sense of impendingness which life has for us at certain moments—these are some of the qualities which when added to a grasp of form, confer upon a man a brevet in this art. Thus far Toller's plays have been loosely built, episodic; but he compensates for this in a measure by his strength in bringing off individual scenes, into which he can pack the profoundest emotion without having recourse to maudlin tricks. There is a certain dignity about his plays; and this is due, curiously enough, to their seeming lack of form. They do not, however, genuinely lack form, just as a memorable or immediately telling lyric by Shelley lacks form; it is simply that we are so carried away by the *effect* that we have no time to reason about the *cause*. What we remember chiefly of the plays of Toller are precisely these lyric effects, these trenchant individual scenes that seem to be constructed without effort and make us forget the looseness of the rest of the piece. As in *Hinkemann*, in *The Transformation*, in certain scenes in *Mass Man*, he is at his happiest when he puts two people on the stage and lets them talk—not as they talk in their daily give-and-take, but as they might conceivably talk before the Maker of their Consciences. (pp. 206-07)

The strictness of Toller's dramatic method is clearly visible in his four important plays: *Masse Mensch, Die Maschinenstürmer, Hinkemann,* and *Hopla, Wir Leben.* In so far as the people motivated before our eyes unburden themselves without *arrière-pensée*, we feel that they are just and uncoloured by the political bias of the author; no one, of course, objects to the subtle presence of coloured lenses, concealed from the eyes of the spectator, in the air that surrounds his characters and the action: this also is dramatic, *un effet de plus.* It is another matter when the lenses, like the cinema machine in the production of *Hopla*, become obstreperously visible; it is then that the true poet is buried under the social or theatrical reformer. (p. 207)

In the four plays cited above a social protest is voiced against the *materia mechanica* of our lives. The hero may be a man or a crowd, but what is mainly objectified in the course of the action is something quite different; it is, in a word, the hurt sensibilities of the poet. The effect is not less but more impressive when we perceive that the dramatist has invested his subsidiary characters (so poignantly alive are they to him!) with this human magic of poetic sensibility. Instead of seeing life through their eyes—the usual method of the realistic writer—Toller by main force makes them participate in his own passion, his wayward unrest, his personal Calvary. On the plane of the emotions this technique operates without strain; on the plane of ideas, however, the characters incline to the conventional. And especially is this true when the author bluntly turns himself

into a mouthpiece for his own generation, as he has done, notably, in *The Transformation* and in *Hopla.* But in *Hinkemann*, dealing with a character which could by no stretch of the imagination be identified with himself, he managed to evade this jeremiad obsession of his own mind and gave us the finest tragedy of the post-war years.

In several particulars *Hopla* bears a resemblance to *Hinkemann;* but whereas a burly workman maimed by the war is the hero of the latter play, Toller himself is beyond doubt the hero of *Hopla.* After eight years of withdrawal from the world, spent in prison and in an insane asylum, Karl Thomas returns to what we would call normal life and finds the world topsy-turvy, mad; he is quite unable to cope with the radical changes that have taken place in modern life. And this is not due to a sense of sterility; on the contrary, he teems with unspent impulses which have been kept pure in solitude, he aches to become an effective unit, a creative unit. The world, however, will have nothing of him; he is *unmechanized*, unregimented, but the dominating values are barren, deaf and blind automata and they rule all life. (pp. 207-08)

In this play, as in his others, Toller claims the right for men to revolt, but I do not think that he expects the entrenched powers to give ear to his doctrine. Manifestly, the entrenched powers would not for long retain themselves in the saddle if they grew suddenly tolerant. Toller does not anticipate that the poet will be less lonely; or the revolutionist less of a pariah in any of the forms proposed for modern society. His plays are not less dramatic because they challenge our smugness or ask embarrassing questions that cannot be answered. If his doctrine were to be summed up it would be, I imagine, something like Thoreau's. "The remembrance of the baseness of politicians," said the author of Walden in 1854, "spoils my walks. My thoughts are murder to the state; I endeavor in vain to observe nature; my thoughts involuntarily go plotting against the state. I trust all just men will conspire." (pp. 209-10)

> *Pierre Loving, "A Note on Ernst Toller," in* The Dial *(copyright, 1929, by The Dial Publishing Company, Inc.), Vol. LXXXVI, No. 3, March, 1929, pp. 205-10.*

THE SATURDAY REVIEW OF LITERATURE (essay date 1931)

Although, as he admits in an autobiographical chapter of his **"Quer Durch,"** expressionism in Germany has now given way before the "Neue Sachlichkeit," the "New Realism," the passionate sincerity, the really dramatic gifts, and the excellent adaptation of expressionist technique to revolutionary subjects shown in his best plays are sufficient to give Toller a permanent place in German literature as the finest literary expression of German post-war revolutionary history. (p. 780)

[Toller] is a strong opponent of what he calls the "Banal-Optimismus" of some Socialists; he is under no illusion that a mere alleviation of material injustice and want will bring about a Paradise on earth. He is also a thorough-going pacifist—and the extreme Left movement now is not at all inclined that way; in fact, as he tells us, the pacifism of his **"Masse-Mensch"** brought him much criticism from the political circles to which he belonged. At bottom, it is clear enough, Toller is no politician; he is an acute observer, with generous principles and a large heart, an idealist with little patience with what falls short of his utopia. His impulses are the mainspring of his dramatic power; they disqualify him for effective political leadership, or even impartial political observation. This is interestingly illustrated in some of the chapters of **"Quer Durch."**

The greater part of the book is taken up with Toller's account of his experiences in the United States and in Soviet Russia. Given Toller's sympathies, his experiences with "authority"—even up to his short detention on Ellis Island—it should be easy enough to predict his verdict. And in fact, of course, we do find the superficial, erotic, mechanized side of American life emphasized out of all due proportion; on getting to Russia, we also find, of course, the idealism, the noble striving for a new order of society, the Communist endeavor to obtain a fair deal for the worker at the expense of the so-called "exploiter," which Toller discovered in Russia, extolled to the almost complete disregard of other factors in Soviet policy. But Toller, even in Moscow, did not close his eyes; in fact, his account of the mechanized administration of a Soviet factory, where the admitted aim is to turn the worker into an efficient machine (at wages which Toller confesses to be low), is, almost in spite of himself, as bitter a criticism as his account of the Ford factory. He also, with the years of his own prison experience in his mind, finds cause for complaint in the Soviet prisons. We seem to be justified in concluding that Toller, the pure idealist, is disappointed at finding that the Utopia of his dreams has not been realized even in Russia.

And yet, further on, Toller again surprises us by criticizing—gently but unmistakably—the absolute doctrinaire policy of the Soviets, the purely external compliance with an arbitrary code of "proletarian" social customs. "The demands of ideology," he says, "must some time capitulate before the elemental power of the individual and collective soul." Thus an artist speaks, a man of the imagination, and it is as both that Toller will be long remembered, when his day-to-day political activities, his speeches, for example, which he reprints in **"Quer Durch,"** are forgotten amid the outworn formulas produced by an abnormal state of society and of mind. (pp. 780-81)

> *"A Revolutionary Writer," in* The Saturday Review of Literature *(© 1931 Saturday Review Magazine Co.), Vol. VII, No. 40, April 25, 1931, pp. 780-81.*

DAVID GASCOYNE (essay date 1934)

[Toller's **"I Was a German"**] is something more than an autobiographical account of the political situation in Germany immediately after the War—it is an impassioned cry of the utmost sincerity and a very fine and moving piece of writing. Coming amid a welter of books of varying merit on the problem of modern Germany, this book, more than any other I have read, helps one to understand the psychological causes underlying the phenomena of German Fascism. Toller's descriptions of the White Terror in Munich bear a more than superficial resemblance to the tales of Nazi atrocities in our daily press. That Ernst Toller, persecuted for his beliefs by his countrymen all his life, should be enormously prejudiced against such a form of government as Hitler's is only too grimly obvious, but the sensibility and the humanity evident in all his writings could not allow any conscious distortion of facts.

From these pages emerge the figure of a poet and a study in suffering. **"The Swallow Book"** is practically the only verse that Toller has written, but his nature is a poet's with all its vulnerability. The opening chapter contains his memories of his childhood; they are not happy memories. Somehow, in spite of the difference in style, they remind one of certain parts of Rilke's **"Notebooks."** (pp. 508-09)

It seems incredible that a man of Toller's greatness and sensitivity should have been made to suffer the torments of mind and body that are described in **"I Was a German."** It is in every way a terrible book and one to make you think and think again. "Beneath the yoke of barbarism one must not keep silence; one must fight. Whoever is silent at such a time is a traitor to humanity," writes the author in his introduction. And these words are dated: *"The day my books were burnt in Germany."* (p. 509)

> *David Gascoyne, "The Bookman's Table: 'I Was a German'" (reprinted by permission of the author), in* The Bookman, *London, Vol. 85, No. 510, March, 1934, pp. 508-09.*

R. ELLIS ROBERTS (essay date 1936)

[*In his preface to Toller's* Letters from Prison, *Roberts argues against the assumption that Toller was "primarily a party man," suggesting instead that he was a poet who sought truth and cultivated a devotion to men and women.*]

I think that most readers will agree that Ernst Toller did rightly when he decided to publish [**Letters from Prison**]. He had doubts about it, as any man of forty would have when he reads what he wrote in his twenties, and wrote in circumstances of such strain and anguish that at times cool judgment was extremely difficult. Publication will make it easier to kill the legend that Ernst Toller was ever a doctrinaire, or primarily a party man. He is that much rarer and more valuable person—a poet with principles. I have never understood how the legend of the doctrinaire Toller ever existed—even in Germany where the desire to classify has so often been too strong for the need to see. How could anyone read the early plays and fail to know that Ernst Toller was a poet with two passions—a passion for truth and a devotion to men and women? I do not add a passion for freedom since this is an integral part of the other two passions. Toller is, it is true, a good left-wing Socialist; but, as a poet, he must know that no man can hold any party doctrine fruitfully, beneficially, unless he realizes that there is good in men of other parties. Not in their systems; there is no need to hold that, but in the men and women. . . . Toller did, it is obvious, occasionally wander a little way along that path of political idealism which would accept one formula, one doctrine as absolutely true. He used—though never, I think, with a whole-hearted acceptance—those convenient words "proletariat" and "bourgeois," as if class was a matter of eternal determination, and as if in one class certain ideas were foreordained and unalterable. The creative poet in him soon relieves him of that illusion. There are moments . . . when the race of man seems to him a box of marionettes, scattered, in lunatic caprice, over a disordered meaningless world. Then, in contact with his comrades, he sees, as the dramatist must see, not masks and shadows but men and women, individual, willfull, breaking, in heroism, in kindness, in brutality, in stupidity, through the neat patterns woven by pedants and doctrinaires. (pp. vii-viii)

[Toller] is a truly civilized human being; and knows that the unexamined life is not a life worthy of man. It is his misfortune, both as man of affairs and artist, to be claimed by different schools: that is always annoying to one who wishes to remain free, and regards all forms as means, not in themselves sacred or inviolable. For Ernst Toller forms are but an expression of the human spirit; they may be essential in a society, just as clothes are and manners, but they are not an integral part of a man's mind or soul.

One result of the tradition that would class Ernst Toller as a good party-man in literature, as an Expressionist or modernist or what-not, has been that his own very individual style has been insufficiently recognized. . . . Even in the letters he writes as in his poems—the style is a style of direct speech, swift in transition, the thought catching up the emotion. . . . Occasionally the style in its direct, abrupt, emotional force, may remind an English reader of D. H. Lawrence, an author from whose general attitude Toller is remote enough, except in his keen eye for nature, and his sense of unity with the animal world. (p. ix)

Ernst Toller's letters seem to me to have a character which should put them among the most remarkable prison literature. They are noteworthy for the mixture of personal and public interest. They are the work of a man insatiably eager for knowledge of his fellows, of an idealist who never wearies of seeking a solution for the misery that is still the lot of so many, of a dramatist who is quick to seize on the clash of temperament, of a poet whose heart is weary at mankind's needless anguish and finds the acutest pleasure in the slightest sign of natural beauty. The peculiar quality of his passion for social righteousness is shown by the fact that it is not incompatible in him, as in so many prophets of revolution and reform, with a passionate sympathy for the sufferings of Hans and Gretchen as individuals. That sympathy often occludes his sense of his own suffering and he nowhere suggests that those five years in prison were harder for him than for most men; that they were so is a fact which the reader of the letters must find out for himself. (p. x)

> *R. Ellis Roberts, in his preface to* Letters from Prison: Including Poems and a New Version of ''The Swallow-Book'' *by Ernst Toller, translated by R. Ellis Roberts, John Lane/The Bodley Head, 1936, pp. vii-x.*

ERNST TOLLER   (essay date 1939?)

[*In the following excerpt, Toller discusses a number of his plays and attempts to clarify his attitudes toward Expressionism, the proletariat, and the role of modern drama. He also replies to those critics who consider him simply a proletarian dramatist.*]

Transfiguration I wrote in the middle of the war. I made copies of the scenes in the military hospital, and handed them out to women during the strike in the beginning of 1918. At that time only one thing mattered to me in my writing: to work for freedom. The play is called Expressionistic. ''Reality scenes'' and ''dream scenes'' alternate with each other. Today many people smile at Expressionism; at that time it was a necessary artistic form. It took a stand against that kind of art which was satisfied with lining up impressions side by side, asking no questions about the essence, the responsibility, the idea. The Expressionist wanted to do more than take photographs. Realizing that the artist's environment, as it were, penetrates him and is reflected in the mirror of his soul, he wanted to re-create this environment in its very essence. For it was the intention of Expressionism to influence this environment; it was to be changed, to be given a juster, a brighter face. Reality was to be caught in the bright beam of the idea.

Everything that happened resolved itself into an outer and an inner happening, both being equally important, as equally strong motive forces. The style of Expressionism—I only speak about good style—was terse, almost like a telegram, avoiding minor issues, always penetrating to the center of things. In the Expressionist drama, man was no incidental private person. He was a type, applying to many by leaving out their superficial features. By skinning the human being one hoped to find his soul under the skin. (pp. 219-20)

Every author wants to crowd into his first work all he knows, all he has ever experienced. I did the same. And thus it is not surprising that the private, the lyrical element is more prominent than dramatic structure may permit.

In ***Masses and Man,*** the form is purer. It was very strange: after the play had been performed, one group said it was counterrevolutionary because it condemns any form of violence; others said that it was Bolshevistic because the representative of non-violence is destroyed, and the masses, in spite of suffering defeat for the time being, remain victorious in the long run. Only a few recognized that the battle between individual and masses did not take place merely on the outside, that everyone is intrinsically individual and ''mass'' at the same time. As an individual he acts in accordance with the moral idea that is considered right. He wants to live by it, even if the world goes to ruin. As a part of the mass, he is driven by social impulses and situations; he wants to reach the goal, even if he has to give up the moral idea. Even today this paradox is insoluble for the politically active man, and I wanted to demonstrate this very insolubility. (pp. 220-21)

In periods of violent social battles, the theatre will reflect these battles. The proletarian who appears in drama today is no longer the proletarian of the nineteenth century. The stagnating, hopeless air of [Maxim Gorky's] *The Lower Depths*, though deeply moving, is not his air any more. The proletarian of the nineteenth century suffered gloomily under the burden of his fate, under want, exploitation, excessive work, little pay. The proletarian of the twentieth century became a conscious fighter, the defender of an idea. He does not only criticize, he creates pictures of new realities that he wants to build. His language, influenced by the leading article of his party newspaper, is poorer in strong images, richer in dialectic strength. It could not surprise anyone, then, that on the stage too he repels those who attack him in real life.

In ***The Machine-Wreckers*** I tried to show the rise of this new proletarian type.

I consciously reject the tendency to worship the proletarian, to carry on an inverted Byzantine cult in his honor. He is the historic bearer of a great new idea; that is what matters. It is possible that the central figure in a poetic work is a bourgeois with a ''pure heart,'' the ideal, ''good'' human being. In spite of this, he confutes the system of society in which he lives because of the divergency between his own personal actions and the actions of the ruling forces, thus producing an effect upon the audience that we might call spiritually revolutionizing. (p. 222)

Political literature merely elaborates upon the daily editorials of the party, it is occasioned by the demands of the idea.

All the dramas which I wrote in prison suffer from ''too much.'' The artist who is ''free'' can experience this or that excitement, this or that resentment, this or that thought in some form unconnected with his art. My mouth was closed, and my pen was bound by the strict censorship of the fortress. The only place where I could to a certain extent let off steam was in a work of art. There the censorship was not as strict as with letters.

Thus I crowded into my dramas all suppressed thoughts and feelings, even those that did not necessarily belong to the individual work. When my dramas are staged again today, I always shorten them and try to cut sentences which arose from an accidental situation.

Hoppla, Such Is Life! is the title of the first work that I wrote "in liberty." Again it dealt with the clash of the man who wants to realize the absolute completely, this very day, with the forces of the era and with his contemporaries who either give up that wish through weakness, treachery, cowardice, or else prepare for a later realization of the wish through force, loyalty, courage. Karl Thomas does not understand either group, he equates their motives and actions, and is destroyed. Having been alienated from true art by the American "happy end," many critics and members of the audience today demand of the dramatist something that is not his task at all: to send them home at the end of the play with those silly little verses for the home which our parents had painted on Chesterfield cushions, plates, picture posters for utility purposes. . . . Officials of the proletarian cult and critics in the entertainment column of capitalistic newspapers, having a bad conscience and craving to saunter through newspaper columns as eternal happy wanderers, became more aggressively revolutionary than those who worked actively for the revolution, called the outcome of this drama which has been repeated and will be repeated many times, not "revolutionary" because it did not send them home with little moral treatises and the cry: "Long live political trend number 73."

Today I am sorry that, influenced by the fashion of the day, I destroyed the architecture of the original work in favor of the architecture of the directing. Its intended form was stronger than the one that was shown on the stage. I alone am responsible for this but I have learned something, and today I prefer a director to get too little out of a work rather than put too much into it. By the way, Piscator in . . . *The Political Theatre* [see excerpt below] has really no reason to complain about me and my style.

While working at it I took into consideration three conclusions, but never the one of "voluntary return to prison" which has been unhesitatingly forced on me in the above-mentioned book. In my first draft, Thomas, who did not understand the world of 1927, runs into the asylum to the psychoanalyst, realizes in his conversation with the physician that there are two types of dangerous madmen: those who are kept in isolated cells, and those who rage against humanity as politicians and military men. At this point he understands the old comrades who carry on the idea in dogged daily work, he wants to leave the asylum but, as he has comprehended, as he has reached the mature human being's sense of reality, the psychiatric official will not let him out any more. Only now, the latter claims, has he become "dangerous to the state," not before when he had been an inconvenient dreamer.

A few more words about a new play *Draw the Fires!* It deals with the battle in the Skagerrak, the German navy revolt, and the lawsuit against Köbis, Reichpietsch, Beckers, Sachse, Weber. I call this play a historical drama. I have changed places of action, shifted the time of events, invented characters, because I think that a dramatist should create that picture of an era out of his experience of it without photographing each historical detail. Artistic truth may coincide with historical truth, but the two are not necessarily identical in every detail. (pp. 223-26)

When I am working I am possessed by work, but I know that again decisions may be taken in which personal efforts are more important than art. (p. 227)

> *Ernst Toller, "My Works," translated by Marketa Goetz (1939?), in* The Tulane Drama Review *(reprinted by permission of* The Drama Review*), Vol. III, No. 3, March, 1959 (and reprinted as "Ernst Toller," in* Playwrights on Playwriting: The Meaning and Making of Modern Drama from Ibsen to Ionesco, *edited by Toby Cole, Hill and Wang, 1960, pp. 218-27).*

WILLIAM ANTHONY WILLIBRAND (essay date 1945)

[*Willibrand is considered one of the foremost experts on the life and works of Ernst Toller. His* Ernst Toller and His Ideology, *from which the following excerpt is taken, is an important survey of the dramatist's work and an analysis of his ideological development.*]

Ernst Toller was one of the most successful and most widely translated German dramatists of the epoch immediately following the First World War. He was also in all probability the most misunderstood. He fought demagoguery but was constantly regarded as a dangerous agitator. In the quarrel over *Masse-Mensch*, his enemies of the left regarded him as a counterrevolutionary, while those of the right suspected him of communism. Moscow frowned upon him for a time, and so did the United States immigration service. On the one hand, he was accused of harboring "the absolute pessimism of Thomas Hardy," and, on the other hand, credited with an optimistic faith in a better world of the future. (p. 5)

From his earliest wartime verse to his last drama, Toller was a steadfast champion of world peace. To this ideal he devotes two dramas, *Die Wandlung* and *No More Peace!*, a number of poems, and a few other scattered passages in his writings. (p. 31)

War is stripped of all its traditional patriotism in the poems of Toller's youth, the *"Verse vom Friedhof,"* which constitute the first division of the collection, *Vormorgen*. There is not a single poem on the military enthusiasm which he had felt in the summer of 1914. On the contrary, there is a silent, fatalistic gloom. Toller expresses it in his *"Marschlied,"* which has just the opposite of the joyous spontaneity usually associated with this type of song. Very traditional in its form, it is reminiscent of a funeral dirge rather than of a marching rhythm. . . . *Wandlung* is a representative document of its time. It stood for a triumph over the dominant nineteenth-century fatalism of heredity and environment. Any education, any religion worthy of the name must mean a "Wandlung," a rebirth of the individual. The tragedy of Toller's life lies partly in the fact that he abandoned the faith in this central necessity. A little more than three years after the drama was completed, we find him saying in a letter that he no longer believes in this kind of transformation. At that time, in 1921, he was already thoroughly disappointed with the political and social behavior of his fellow mortals. That disappointment continued to grow. In 1936, it found expression in a comedy, *No More Peace!*, which is far removed from the idealistic Utopia to which *Die Wandlung* looked forward in 1918. (pp. 41-2)

[*No More Peace!*] is a satire on the chaos of human madness and human stupidity. It is full of satirical musical-comedy features and manifests a corresponding disregard for the normally probable. Christian doctrine mingles with Greek mythology, a streamlined Olympus becomes a mixture of monotheism and polytheism. The spirit has fled from the maddened world of mortals, where reason passes for lunacy, falsehood becomes the officially stamped "truth," "law" and "justice" serve as the agencies of dictatorship. Both peace and war are materialistically inspired and celebrated by the same people. Peace is a lie; so is war; so are all the banalities expressed on behalf of either. The saving—though not entirely convincing—idealistic feature is that the Olympian St. Francis of Assisi is still able to regard the human mess from the standpoint of eternal verities. (p. 42)

This optimistic note on which the play ends is certainly not justified by the attitudes and actions of the mundane characters. The society that Toller presents is essentially shallow and totally incapable of meditating upon the deeper implications of peace. This society is one thing, and the idea to which he clings in spite of all disillusionment is quite another. He saw the cruelty and the barrenness of life to the very end, but, as in *Pastor Hall,* he recognized the redeeming influence of spiritual leadership. Instead of the peace of oratory, treaties, and international legislation, he posited a return to fundamentals through deep meditation. . . .

But any "deep meditation" upon the subject of peace is essentially religious. By using a Christian Saint to represent the cause of truth, love, and human brotherhood, Toller expresses a reaffirmed faith in spiritual regeneration. Negatively, he shows a tendency in the same direction by satirizing racial and economic materialism and by linking this up with shallowness, hostility to reason, and stupidity. Also he deals a couple of blows to the materialistic interpretation of science as represented by the popular notion of Darwinism. (p. 47)

But all of this is rather mild compared with the satire directed against National Socialist theory and practice. This is too obvious to require much comment. Finance capitalism setting up a dictatorship and then losing to it all power in the affairs of state; the mystery and the popular idealization of the dictator himself; the diversion of the masses through banners, music, speeches, and parades; the substitution of myths for reason and truth; the exaltation of blood, soil, and nationalism; the political use of propaganda, intimidation, and distrust of one's neighbor; the reversal of moral and institutional values; the insistence upon heroism and militarism—all of these elements are associated with the National Socialist regime. From Toller's point of view, they succeed because of the low order of mass idealism and thus become hindrances to world peace. But the chief object of satire is, of course, the peace movement itself, with its unstable foundation, its superficiality, and its insincerity. Toller's idea of peace certainly must mean, among other things, that man must break radically with his primitive pugnacious instincts. Only a higher order of humanity would be capable of meditating efficaciously upon the nature of peace as the St. Francis of the play would have it. The types caricatured in this play and the proletarians that Toller presents in other dramas lack the moral and spiritual qualities necessary for the establishment of a new social order. (pp. 47-8)

[The] soul-crushing effect of the machine [in *Die Maschinenstürmer*] had previously appeared in *Die Wandlung* and in *Masse-Mensch*. But already in *Masse-Mensch* this pessimistic outlook concerning the machine was opposed by the noble conception of the machine as the servant of a worthy life. This attitude is carried over into *Die Maschinenstürmer* with redoubled force. The weavers of the machine age should unite, and their spirit should dominate the machine. Like Friedrich in *Die Wandlung*

and the woman in *Masse-Mensch,* Jimmy affirms the inward revolution. By implication, all of these characters oppose the basic Marxian thesis that the economy determines the mental life of man. To blame the economy for all trials and tribulations is to shift the culpability from spiritual degeneracy, where it belongs, to a material instrument which man has the power to control. All he needs to do is to turn from the ego to brotherhood, from *Masse* to *Volk*. Labor will then cease to be a dismally inadequate economic activity and become soulful—*beseelt* is the word Toller uses in this connection. He does not pause to ask himself whether or not this is "realistic thinking." (p. 62)

The dialectic of the machine as a social problem appears again in Toller's next drama, *Hinkemann.* (p. 63)

But *Hinkemann* is primarily concerned with something quite different. While repeating his opposition to the Marxist idealization of the proletariat, Toller now takes the next consistent step by attacking the unreserved idealization of the future communist society and by at least suggesting a spiritual need which the materialistic philosophy of Communism cannot supply. (pp. 63-4)

One critic has maintained that Hinkemann is a character that can in no way be identified with Toller himself [see Loving excerpt above]. Just the opposite is true. Eugen Hinkemann is Ernst Toller. To be sure, the author escaped the physical fate of his hero, but emasculation is only a symbol of the profound change of outlook Toller experienced as a result of the war. The things which Hinkemann and Toller have in common are fundamental: both are socialists whose experience prevents them from accepting the Utopian claims of Marxist orators; both realize that the ultimate questions of human destiny cannot be answered by dialectical materialism; both are deeply affected by all forms of human cruelty and all the suffering it causes in man and beast; both want a better world, but they almost despair of achieving it because of the hopeless stupidity of human beings themselves; and, finally, both are bewildered by the coarse and noisy display of everything that tends to crush the finer aspirations of civilized humanity. These aspirations have their source in religion, a domain of human experience which Toller-Hinkemann saw but never entered because he was himself enmeshed in the materialism which he hated but from which he did not have the strength to escape.

One might call this tragedy Toller's *Kritik des reinen Sozialismus,* to borrow from the title of Kant's most celebrated work. For the author is not only moved by the dominant sins of the age; he also sees the tragic limitations of socialism, which a considerable part of the intellectual leadership of the age regards as a panacea. That *Hinkemann* is intended as a critique of socialism is apparent in a letter which Toller wrote to Stefan Zweig. But the drama is not only a critique of the limitations of socialism but, at least by implication, of secularism generally, just as Hinkemann is a symbol of all humanly unconquerable suffering. (pp. 66-7)

Hinkemann has been called Toller's masterpiece. The present writer finds the last act too unconvincing to share this view. There is too much intellectual manipulation. A minor improbability is that of the worker-hero buying a statue of an ancient pagan god and dragging his grief-stricken wife into its presence. That becomes a major improbability when this hero has been consistently portrayed as a model of kindness. More serious is the lack of motivation for the final catastrophe. Hinkemann was not the kind of person to drive his wife to suicide, especially after he discovered that she never ridiculed his emasculation. But the power of the work stands out in spite of its shortcomings. As a symbol of those human tragedies with which no society can deal adequately, the hero will long be remembered. . . .

The poignancy of Toller's disillusionment with humanity comes to the surface in *Hinkemann*. It is even more apparent in *Hoppla, wir leben!*, a play he wrote in 1927, three years after his release from prison, when he had had time to observe the postwar decade at first hand. The title takes its name from a new song hit, which is announced over the radio in Act III, Scene 2, the song title serving the author as a symbol of the age of jazz and of moral disintegration. (p. 68)

Hoppla, wir leben! is another play in which Toller did not resist the temptation of drawing too heavily upon his inventions, observations, and experiences. The simplicity of the theme is spoiled by an unusual amount of scene shifting and stage carpentry. Wearisome trivialities are crowded into the action at vital points. There is, for instance, Herr Pickel, a timid, simple-minded provincial, who comes to see the minister of the Interior, blunders in where he is not wanted, and bores everybody with his own petty concerns. He is unable to get anywhere with his lengthy explanations and is always cut off by people who are too busy to listen to him. . . . Toller is not a successful humorist. His satirical scenes are often mere caricature. (p. 72)

[In 1923 Toller] wrote the last of his prison plays, *Der entfesselte Wotan*, which Gabriele Reuter aptly calls "a blunt, farcical derision of the mischief that can be wrought by patriotic phrases in the mouths of the stupid and the vicious." Toller's own purpose in writing this satiric comedy was to contribute towards helping Germany out of the *"Taumel der Dumpfheit"* which, he felt, had been brought on by the nationalist elements. (p. 77)

For once Toller wrote a stage play which is entirely outside of his own personal experience and which is therefore not overcrowded with too many scenes and too much action.

A mere glance at the list of characters foreshadows Toller's ideological purpose: The hero is a barber, Wilhelm Dietrich Wotan. His lowly trade connects him with the people, and his pompous name suggests a combination of reaction, Germanic hero legends, and ancient Teutonic religion. Then there are people who are out of jobs: a couple of army officers, von Wolfblitz and von Stahlfaust; an ex-salesman by the name of Schleim; a countess and a royal *"Heldendarsteller."* . . . [There are also] a young worker, a policeman, and a waiter—all of them representative of elements that contributed to the success of the Nazi Revolution. (pp. 77-8)

It is futile to judge *Wotan* according to the ordinary canons of the drama, as some critics have done. The play was not intended to be anything else but plainspoken roughhewn propaganda to influence the masses, who were listening to equally unartistic propaganda from nationalist sources. Toller seems to have been incapable of subtle humor, but such a gift would have availed him little in the present instance. Subtle badinage never had a place in postwar German political discussion. (pp. 79-80)

The play of course satirizes the modern revival of old Germanic mythology, but it does far more than that. From the beginning to the end its shafts are directed against Nazi doctrine. Thus Wotan's anti-Semitism is very similar to that of Hitler. . . . Outside of Jews and Marxists, he promises everything to everybody, making his appeal like Nazism primarily to the vast majority of conservative Germans. Brazil seems to be the sym-

bol of that era when the bourgeoisie, the nobility, the bureaucrats, investors, and militarists will get everything they want—a symbol of the Third Reich as pictured by its champions before 1933. (p. 80)

During his own political experience Toller learned how easy it was to sway the postwar masses. He was taken off the political arena in pre-Nazi days but in the prison of Niederschönenfeld he saw clearly—and sometimes prophetically—the dangerous implications of the National Socialist movement. In *Wotan* he sounded a warning which Germany and the rest of the world would have done well to heed. (p. 81)

[Toller] felt very deeply the agony of all unjust punishment regardless of who the victims might be. In 1932 he wrote a play entitled *The Blind Goddess*, in which the problem is dealt with in a strictly bourgeois milieu. A self-centered, cruel, and utterly unlikable weakling is falsely accused of the murder of his wife. (p. 94)

[It is] a weakness of the play that the attorney for the defense does not point out all the good qualities of his client. Dr. Färber is deliberately portrayed as such an unappealing character that it would be impossible to impress the jury with his virtues in the same degree that the prosecution has been able to impress it with his vices. The point is that the machinery of criminal procedure should be sound enough for even such a character to receive a just trial. . . . [Anna Gerst and Dr. Färber] are ultimately the victims of circumstantial evidence and Toller's play is a warning against the unsupported admission of this kind of testimony.

The Blind Goddess also presents other instances of legal injustice. The president of the court urges the accused to make a public confession and makes other remarks which tend to influence the jury against them. The accused is helpless in the hands of a clever lawyer, who distorts the truth and harrows his victim. Public officials regard the conviction of the prisoners as a step towards promotion. . . . On the whole, the play is a drab and one-sided portrayal of criminal procedure in Republican Germany.

The play is marred by a piling up of somewhat unusual things. A rural physician keeping a mistress in his home along with his wife and young daughter; a licentious village official flaunting his immoral relationships with local women in the face of even a deceived husband; the doctor's wife lecturing him in front of his patients; a prejudiced witness called to the stand and having no evidence to offer except what he read in the newspapers; the president of a criminal court obviously influencing the jury against the accused—these are a few of the salient crudities which the reader cannot believe as likely to happen in pre-Nazi Germany.

It is little wonder, then, that Toller was obviously not satisfied with the play. He and Denis Johnston rewrote it and published the new version, *Blind Man's Buff* in the volume *Pastor Hall* in the spring of 1939. In workmanship, psychology, and theatrical concentration *Blind Man's Buff* is far superior to *The Blind Goddess*. (pp. 95-7)

[With *Blind Man's Buff*] the crudities and the improbabilities of the earlier version have been eliminated. Even the cocksure scientist is now a convincing egoist who fears for his own reputation but not for the integrity of science because of his mistake. The doctor is no longer a domestic tyrant who insists on keeping a mistress in the family circle. The long prison scenes and the amours of the reprobate village official drop out entirely, and the emphasis is on good drama rather than on a one-sided criticism of judicial procedure. The new play is more coherent, and it manifests a more subtle psychology and a more convincing familiarity with the work of legal practitioners. Drabness and crudity have vanished entirely, and in their stead we have a sense of humor, which is too often lacking in Toller's plays. (pp. 97-8)

Mary Baker Eddy is the title of a five-act play on which Toller collaborated with Hermann Kesten. It paints a very unflattering picture of the founder of Christian Science and her entourage. . . . The authors reveal considerable familiarity with the facts of the heroine's actual life, but they deal with them in a crude, episodic manner. They invent freely, they twist and manipulate unduly the chronology of biographical events, and they fail to present a heroine who becomes convincing as the successful founder of a widespread movement. On the whole, the play is a cheap presentation of a challenging force in modern religious history. (pp. 102-03)

We turn now to Toller's last play, *Pastor Hall,* in which the expression of religious sympathies is clear and unmistakable. By 1939 the author had realized that orthodox Christianity was by no means ready to betray itself in the interest of the German totalitarian state. He had seen all the forces once opposed to National Socialism go the way of cowed submission and of State coördination—except the leaders of Catholicism and of orthodox Protestantism. These also publicly opposed the antireligious, antihumanitarian aspects of National Socialism, and they persevered in the brave fight of which Pastor Hall becomes a symbol. (p. 110)

From the viewpoint of plot continuity and stage economy this is Toller's best play. For that reason it can be easily summarized. From the beginning to the end the central conflict is always present. There is no padding, no crowding in of unnecessary material. *Pastor Hall* lacks the expressionistic eloquence and power of *Die Wandlung* and *Masse-Mensch,* but its simplicity and sincerity will appeal to an epoch that is struggling with the fundamental issues of civilized society.

Like the heroine of *Masse-Mensch,* but in a deeper spirit of Christian humility, Pastor Hall feels that, though his body will be destroyed, his spirit will live forever. Even before the crisis, he looks upon himself and his family as symbols of resistance to National Socialism in so far as it conflicts with his religious and moral convictions.

In his earlier days Toller, in Marxist fashion, had made his proletarian characters reject Christianity as the agency of the exploiting classes. Now they are represented as its most faithful followers, while "enlightened" Marxists bow to the courage of Pastor Hall, who is on the point of being whipped for fearlessly expressing his convictions to the commandant of the concentration camp.

Finally, attention must be called to the recurrence of a mystical tendency which had previously drawn Toller's attention to Angelus Silesius, a seventeenth-century Catholic mystic. Some two years before *Pastor Hall,* he wrote this mystical characterization of art:

> There are indeed timeless elements in art, the formation of man's relation with the cosmos, with the whole, with death. This relation is timeless. Always there is consciousness of that last-of-all which Angelus Silesius called the "Unio Mystica," the union with the whole.

In *Pastor Hall* this "union with the whole" is called the "Brotherhood of God" and is interpreted as a practical, yet orthodox Christian way of living. . . . (pp. 111-12)

The religious element makes Toller's last play more optimistic than any he wrote after *Die Wandlung.* His final message seems to be that the courage born of unwavering religious faith alone triumphs over human iniquity and human frailty. (p. 113)

> *William Anthony Willibrand, in his* Ernst Toller and His Ideology *(a condensation of a dissertation submitted to the State University of Iowa in August, 1940), The University, Iowa City, Iowa, 1945, 123 p.*

HARRY SLOCHOWER (essay date 1945)

[*Slochower is one of the foremost scholars of German literature. In the excerpt below, he discusses what he considers Toller's central dilemma: the problem of mass control "thwarting the individual ethos." Like Desmond MacCarthy and Raymond Williams (see excerpts above and below), Slochower also points out a number of the philosophical and literary failings inherent in the Expressionist method. For a further discussion of Toller's theme of the individual versus the masses, see W. H. Sokel excerpt below.*]

As happened to many middle-class intellectuals, the War of 1914 acted as a socializing momentum to Toller. He was abroad, disporting himself in bohemian revels. Toller eagerly grasped the opportunity to coöperate at home. He insisted on joining the infantry rather than the artillery in eagerness to come to corporeal, immediate grips with his object. And his individualistic temper became apparent when he asked to be changed to the air force, "not from any heroic motive, or for love of adventure, but simply to get away from the mass, from mass living and mass dying." Here we see the seeds of Toller's dilemma. He had plunged into the war out of a social conscience. But in it the individual lost "the very sense of identity." Moreover, he soon realized that this was an anti-social war. Following the murder of Kurt Eisner, Toller, a mere youth, with only his boundless enthusiasm and fervent idealism to recommend him, was placed in charge of an army battling for a socialist Bavaria. His record in that dramatic event reveals the deadlock which he never resolved: how to bring about a coöperative sociality without the shedding of blood; how to support parties without submerging individual values; how to follow collectivistic lines while maintaining critical awareness. (p. 82)

Man and the Masses and the expressionistic lyrics of *The Swallow Book,* written in prison, sum up the conflict he felt throughout between man as an individual and man as part of a group. To be sure, Toller had advanced beyond the problem of the machine against man, raised in *The Machinewreckers.* But the issue of technics returns in the form of organizational mass control thwarting the individual ethos. Yet Sonia (the only character bearing a *name,* that is, possessing individuality, in *Man and the Masses*) admits her guilt to the Nameless in refusing to sanction the hard means necessary to liberate her: "You . . . are . . . the Masses. You . . . are . . . right." It is this indecision which leads to her death—a kind of suicide. And Toller confesses: "The problem seemed to me insoluble. I had come up against it in my own life, and I sought in vain to solve it."

In this irresolution, Toller summed up the problem central to the expressionistic movements. The expressionists reversed the naturalistic homage to time, space and causality, presenting characters and situations freed from determining coördinates. But their universal types were as much testimony to the loss of personal identity as to their representation of the classless "Man." Their timeless essences were as much a surrender as a challenge to historic forces. They hid a despairing impatience with actuality, a helplessness in dealing with existing factors. Their "Man," free in the universal ether, was as bound to his "freedom" as Hauptmann's weavers had been to their hand-looms, and his ecstatic stammering was as inarticulate as the broken dialect of the naturalistic characters. In repudiating their heritage, the expressionists were extreme Nietzscheans. Their rebellion against the past was "thorough," as though they had come into the world through self-generation. Nietzsche stated: "As my own father, I am already dead, as my own mother, I still live and grow old." (p. 83)

To be sure, Toller went beyond his expressionistic colleagues who regarded technics as the whole of man's problem and who continued to cry for some vague universal Man to be born in prayer. Yet even as Toller moved toward the Marxist perspective, he emphasized its directive of *humanizing the individual*. . . . His socialism was, already in this pioneer stage, of an aristocratic tenor. "Men who are politically, socially, culturally able, will form an aristocracy, not of birth but of the mind, an aristocracy of duty, not of 'material privilege.'" At the same time, *Toller realized the limits of individuation*. Thus, his individualism tended to move toward the collective pattern, and his ethical persuasion admitted the sometime necessity of hard compulsion. (p. 84)

[While in prison, Toller] was a celebrated martyr for humanity, was allowed unrestricted communion with his spirit and for a time the company of his "free" swallows. In his last year in prison, he actually "dreaded the duties and responsibilities" which would call him. With his release, there entered into his life a distracted, nervous will-lessness, broken spasmodically by explosive calls for militance. His verse stammered and cried in a feverish staccato. It was as if his fire lacked material for its objectification, as if it were feeding on itself. His works became quick precipitates, revealing restlessness of form, impatience with concrete situation and characters. They are, like most of the expressionistic dramas, youthful stormings, nervous short cuts toward the great consummation. Toller's Hinkemann, a physical giant emasculated by the war, asks his socialist comrade: "But look here, supposing a man had something the matter with him inside—or outside, for that matter—that could never get better—would it make him happy, if there were to be sensible social conditions?" The tragedy of the Hinkemanns is their physical inability to produce. It is the theme of post-war impotence, dwelt upon by writers from Lawrence and Eliot to Wassermann and Thomas Mann. (pp. 84-5)

Toller's reaction to the victory of Hitlerism was spectacularly forceful. In his open letter to Goebbels he wrote that Nazism taught him the moral necessity of militance: "We are not guiltless. . . . We have made many mistakes, the greatest of which was our patience. We will, thanks to what you have taught us, correct our mistakes. And that is your contribution." In *No More Peace*, written in [the United States], Toller's earlier creed of love and peace is modified. St. Francis is converted to the belief that the wise must act and quotes the line written by "a rebel" to the effect that our task is not merely to explain the world but to change it.

Yet despite its playful humor, *No More Peace* is "dangerous" comedy. It presents the masses as easily swayed by mob psy-chology, directed by clever ministries of propaganda. "The people themselves," Toller writes in his autobiography, "not their opponents, are their own greatest enemy." This indicates that Toller still lacked confidence in mass reaction, even while he hoped for a fusion of love and power. Fascism seemed to have still further undermined his faith in the people. (pp. 85-6)

It is significant that his post-Hitlerite autobiography closes with the revolution in Bavaria. Did he feel that this had been his last significant deed? Was his suicide a confession that the individual, lonely way leads nowhere on earth? Was the only militance his sensitive nerves could organize, militance against his own person? Toller's suicide was his final effort to break through the suffocating network of things, to show that here at least man can act out his will.

Throughout his work, as in that of the expressionists, the gas metaphor predominates. It was the cry for air on the part of a generation which felt itself choked by the collectivistic pressure of monopoly technics. Toller could not breathe in a world of hypocritical appeasements, of bureaucratic walls, of diplomatic sphinxes. Together with Wassermann, Ossietsky, Muehsam and Carel Čapek, Toller was a victim of the post-war mind in exile, for which Hitlerism has provided the most brutal contingency. There are suicides which are acts of murder.

But Toller's last gesture has its positive note. We know that Toller labored with burning moral fervor for a democratic order. His death was a summons toward the restoration of a home for the exiles, of *their* home, now occupied by the brown robots: a summons to work for a world in which the Ernst Tollers might be able to live. (pp. 86-7)

> *Harry Slochower, "Uncertainty As a Principle: The Negation of Substance," in his* No Voice Is Wholly Lost . . . *Writers and Thinkers in War and Peace (reprinted by permission of Farrar, Straus and Giroux, Inc.; copyright © 1945, 1972 by Harry Slochower), Creative Age Press, 1945 (and reprinted by Octagon Books, 1975), pp. 41-126.**

RAYMOND WILLIAMS   (essay date 1952)

A play like *Hoppla!* requires considerable discrimination in judgment. A common reaction is to call Toller's political views extremist, and so dismiss the play. This is inadequate on two grounds. First, one cannot be sure that the so-called extremism does not in fact present a more accurate picture of certain phases of public life than do many so-called moderate views. Second, and more to the critical point, one cannot dismiss a play because one dislikes the views on which it is based; any such judgment is a grave limitation of the enjoyment of literature. And yet *Hoppla!*, and Toller's other plays, leave one essentially dissatisfied. The expressionist devices of spectacle are striking, but they come to seem essentially external, the visual elements particularly so. The panorama unrolls, but increasingly one has the impression that it *shows* nothing. It ought, according to Toller's intention, to show the social background, but the substance of the devices has so much the element of *cliché*, and the techniques involved—the newspaper headline, the wireless announcement, the newsreel—are in themselves so much the embodiment of simplification, that one comes to feel that the whole expression is commonplace and superficial. But here again one must be careful of one's terms. There is a place in literature—a place which includes work of very high value—for the expression of the commonplace, and for work which is deliberately superficial, of the surface, in intention. The condition of success in such work, however, is not only power of expression, but also consistency of treatment. Once a different order of experience is touched upon the convention tends to disintegrate. As to consistency, Toller is frequently successful, but there is at the root of his art a profound doubt:

> In my political capacity, I proceed upon the assumption that units, groups, representatives of social forces, various economic functions have a real existence; that certain relations between human beings are objective realities. As an artist, I recognise that the validity of these "facts" is highly questionable.
>
> (pp. 182-83)

The recognition is important; and it puts Toller, as a man, in a very different category from the usual "social realists." But one cannot feel that he ever resolved the tension which the recognition implies, or expressed its irresolution, in his art. The intelligent doubt, the personal reservation, remains in the social plays, not as an element of communication, but as an almost sardonic disintegrator. The simplification which the social view involves seems at times, in *Hoppla!* in *Hinkemann,* in *Transfiguration,* a deliberate, virtually hysterical attempt to repress the profounder consciousness. The very real hysterical element in Toller does not reside in the violence and clarity of his political views, but rather in this attempt to repress a part of the pattern of his experience, which has too much vitality to be simply and easily neglected.

The power of *Hoppla!* and of the other plays is primarily a spectacular power. The language is as deliberately general and unspecific as the visual panorama. Its method is essentially that of the slogan; it very rarely has any power to surprise or, in its own right, to convey emotion. It is a slogan summary of experience, and too many of the slogans are too familiar even to interest. This is especially so in his deliberately expressionist episodes, such as those in the hotel; it is true also of his longer single scenes, where he writes in an explicit kind of naturalism. . . .

When expressionist drama is set against poetic drama, or against the very best of the naturalists—Ibsen, Chekhov, Synge—it is true that it must be judged inferior. But when it is set against the cosy, standardised naturalism which still occupies so many of our stages, it is seen as a real attempt at vitality and seriousness. The trouble was—and it is here that expressionism may be seen as an integral part of the development of modern drama—that it served to confirm the impoverishment of dramatic *language,* and sought its reforms in the substitute devices of spectacle. (p. 184)

> Raymond Williams, "Two Social Plays," in his Drama: From Ibsen to Eliot, *Chatto & Windus, 1952, pp. 175-84.**

WALTER H. SOKEL (essay date 1959)

[*In the following excerpt, Sokel states that the conflict between the individual and the masses in Toller's work is in reality an extension of the Expressionist artist's isolation in the modern world. Other critics, such as Harry Slochower, have also focused on Toller's treatment of this conflict (see excerpt above).*]

Ernst Toller suffered the shock of collision between revolutionary dream and reality perhaps more acutely than other Expressionists, because he fought to make the dream come true.

His "Soviet democracy" in Bavaria was to be the republic of love and universal brotherhood which Expressionist dramas, poems, and manifestoes had so often prophesied. But immediately arose the problem of force. How could the new state assert itself against those who were preparing to destroy it by force, without resorting to force in turn?

The Expressionist belief that man could be persuaded to goodness and reason did not pass the test of reality, and as soon as that initial assumption collapsed the activist Expressionist had to end tragically, no matter what course he followed. If he tried to live up to his ideal of nonviolence, he had to allow his experiment to be wiped out; if he decided to protect it, he had to use force and thus betray his ideal. . . . In assuming leadership of a "Red army," in order to bring about a society of peace and fraternity, Toller knew that he betrayed the essence of *his* revolution. Yet he saw no alternative. (p. 196)

These disheartening experiences formed the autobiographical basis of Toller's play *Masse-Mensch.* The heroine is modeled on the wife of a university professor who hanged herself in prison, but her experiences with the Revolution are Toller's own, projected onto a symbolic and universal plane. *"Man and the Masses* was liberation from emotional anguish, after experiences whose impact a man can perhaps bear only once without breaking."

In this drama, the conflict between the Woman and the Nameless One, as the Bolshevik is called, is the conflict between the Expressionist intellectual and the proletarian masses, who are not yet ripe for his vision. (p. 197)

The unbridgeable gulf that opens between the intellectual and the masses distinguishes the basic mood of *Man and the Masses* from that of Toller's *Wandlung.* Friedrich, in *Die Wandlung,* influences and converts the people without difficulty; the Woman in *Man and the Masses* fails to sway them and finds herself completely alone. Thus, the original isolation of the Expressionist comes to the fore again. He is a leader without a following. Cut off from the *bourgeoisie,* he has not been accepted by the proletariat. Once more he stands in the vacuum from which he sought to escape. (p. 198)

By her decision to die rather than take the life of another human being, the Woman has attained her second *Wandlung.* The first made her leave marriage, class, comfort, and prestige to join the revolutionary movement against war. The second *Wandlung* actually crowns the first by making nonviolence an absolute principle of conduct, even for the revolution that is to end all violence. But the high-pitched optimism of the first *Wandlung* has been toned down. The Woman still believes that the ideal community will come into being some day, when the violent bitterness of mass man will have given way to sympathy and love, but that day has been moved into a vague and distant future. It will not be here tomorrow. Infinite patience is necessary. Man as he is, mass man, is not ripe for the building of a new world. (p. 199)

Thus, the Woman remains an optimist. True, experience has defeated the axiom "Man is good"; but it can be said that he *tries to be good.* . . . As though to confirm her unflinching optimism in the face of failure, her execution in the prison courtyard transforms the two new occupants of her cell into better human beings. The regenerating mission of the activist heroine continues in her death.

In Toller's poetry and correspondence, however, despair frequently erupts and breaks the thin crust of activist optimism. . . . Toller recognizes that the needs of intellectuals and masses are not the same, and that the glorious joy of 1918, when they seemed to merge, has proven a cruel delusion. The poet who loves mankind must always be an unhappy lover, because in reality he and mankind have nothing in common. (pp. 200-01)

Toller maintains only a shell of his humanist faith; beneath it there lurks the old frightful isolation of the Expressionist *poeta dolorosus*, which now, after the collapse of his activist hope, he diagnoses as universal and irremediable. . . . The isolated poet-intellectual realizes that there is no remedy and no escape for him. No matter what detours he may take, he "becomes what he is." Yet Toller always checks this pessimism by his tempered, long-range belief in socialism. The tension and counterplay between this belief and his pessimism result in his acceptance of the tragic as the basis of existence; even in the most perfect society there will always be an element of ineradicable tragedy. (p. 201)

> Walter H. Sokel, "The Recoil," in his The Writer in Extremis: Expressionism in Twentieth-Century German Literature *(with the permission of the publishers, Stanford University Press;* © *1959 by the Board of Trustees of the Leland Stanford Junior University), Stanford University Press, 1959, pp. 192-226.**

RICHARD BECKLEY (essay date 1964)

[*The excerpt below is drawn from Beckley's survey of Toller's major works. In it he discusses many of the Expressionist themes and techniques adapted by Toller for his own drama. For other discussions of the Expressionist method read Desmond Mac-Carthy, Harry Slochower, and Raymond Williams (see excerpts above).*]

In the history of modern German literature Ernst Toller stands out not only on account of his achievements as a creative writer—considerable though these may be—but also by virtue of the fact that his life and work are typical to a remarkable degree of that of so many dramatists of the Expressionist generation. The disastrous course of the First World War with its senseless waste of life and subsequent loss of human values, and the social and economic chaos which followed upon it in Germany as perhaps nowhere else in Europe, are events which find their reflection, direct or indirect, in the work of most Expressionist writers; but for Toller they became the central experience which dictated the course of his life, shaped his attitude to it, and virtually determined its end, while in his creative work he was almost exclusively concerned with the conflicts this experience presented. (p. 85)

In attempting to understand Toller's work as a whole, therefore, and to assess its value as a contribution to literature in the twentieth century, the conditions attending its origins and the public recognition which promoted it are considerations of particular importance. No less important is the question of the extent to which the experience his plays reflect is still significant for us, though this depends not only on whether a succeeding generation produces a writer interested in developing his themes and making them part of the literary tradition, but also on the modifications our own apprehension of life undergoes. (pp. 85-6)

Toller's first play, *Die Wandlung,* covers his experiences from the outbreak of war up to [his first imprisonment]. He seems to have begun work on it soon after his release from the army,

and it would be interesting to know how far he had progressed with it before he himself had lived through the incidents it reflects. *Die Wandlung* is a play of the type which had already become to be known as the *Stationendrama*. As a specific genre it was the creation of the Expressionist generation, who used it to present in a series of stages or tableaux the spiritual progress or conversion of a man to a new ideal type symbolising their aspirations in a society that was felt to have become spiritually sterile and decadent. The great danger for many playwrights attempting this kind of drama lay not only in the frequent vagueness of their ideals but also in the difficulty of conveying visually and in terms of action an essentially inner process. The task demanded the mastery of a new technique which employed the newly-discovered technical resources of the stage, such as spotlighting and the revolving platform, to present the rapidly changing dreamlike quality of inner reality.

In one respect Toller was fortunate. Other dramatists had already experimented with this technique and discovered some of its limitations and possibilities. Toller learnt from their mistakes, and though he must have read more than he actually saw in the theatre his vivid imagination and innate dramatic sense helped him to distinguish the good from the bad.

There is a sureness of conception and an inevitability of dramatic sequence in *Die Wandlung* which is striking even in this period, when dramatists' first plays were frequently their most memorable. (pp. 87-8)

[Toller] presents a series of scenes alternating between nightmare-like exposures of the monstrous reality behind the patriotic façade of war and Friedrich's frantic attempts to maintain his belief in his country's cause as a means of fulfilling his need to belong. On the troop train he meets the ordinary soldiers who see the war in its true colours—a mean struggle for selfish ends. Service at the front reveals to him its degrading brutality, and later on in the military hospital he sees how it perverts men's minds. The doctors rejoice in the opportunities it affords for perfecting artificial limbs for the maimed and mutilated, and a Red Cross nurse, a "Sister of Mercy" is elated at the news that 10,000 of the enemy have been killed in a single battle.

The crisis brought about in Friedrich's mind by the clash between his idealism and the reality of the situation occurs when, invalided out of the army, he tries to express in artistic terms the justification for so much human suffering by sculpting a statue which symbolises the "victory of the fatherland". He is interrupted in his work by two beggars, a crippled ex-soldier and his wife who is riddled with venereal disease contracted from the invading army. The plight of these two figures represents the true extent of the victory of the fatherland in human terms. By presenting a married couple Toller shows how war strikes at the most fundamental and positive expression of man's social instincts. Friedrich sees that the dividing force of war is greater than its uniting force, through which he had hoped to attain his own personal salvation. Overwhelmed with horror he destroys his statue, symbol of his earlier ideal, and goes off in search of a new orientation. (pp. 88-9)

One of the charges most frequently brought against the Expressionist dramatists was that their situations had no foundation in reality and that their solutions were incapable of practical application. A certain abuse of the Expressionist style and technique, which had to resort to some very bold effects to gain attention in a world of confused and warring ideas, tended to show up any deficiencies in inner content. The dramatists themselves were conscious of these problems, and this consciousness affected their work. Writers like Werfel insisted on presenting the inner regeneration of man uncomplicated by the social and political issues of the day on which Germans were so passionately divided, while Toller was classed with the opposing group of Activists, who saw spiritual reform as primarily a matter of social and political change.

In *Die Wandlung,* however, Toller presents these two elements as inseparably connected. Both are necessary, and neither is possible without the other. From his experience of the social and political situation he distils the conception of a spiritual conflict which is valid both as art and as a comment on the particular problems of the age. (pp. 89-90)

Masse Mensch made Toller famous and brought him to the notice of the general public. It presented events in which the whole nation had in some measure been concerned; its theme was highly controversial; and certain scenes, such as that in which the capitalists do a fox-trot round the desks of the stock exchange to celebrate the profits they make out of war, scored a theatrical success which made their attack all the more effective. Moreover, Sonia's proud rejection of the belief in man's need for divine grace accorded with the general revolutionary tone of the play. Its ending was more satisfactory and convincing than that of *Die Wandlung,* where a certain contradiction between mood and message had not been resolved. (p. 94)

[Toller's next play, *Die Maschinenstürmer,*] deals with the Luddite riots in Nottingham in the year 1815. Toller's leading figure is a young man called Jimmy Cobbett. Like the figure of Jäger in Gerhart Hauptmann's Naturalist drama *Die Weber,* with which Toller's play has not a little in common, he is a man "from the outside", who has travelled and can see the problem of the weavers with an objectivity which the conditions of their upbringing and environment have denied to them. He has absorbed the ideals and the bitter lessons of the French Revolution. (p. 95)

In *Die Maschinenstürmer* Toller seems to have set out to illustrate once and for all the practical application of his ideals. Socially as well as spiritually, man cannot stand divided against his fellow man. The use of violence is not only immoral: it positively hinders the process of social emancipation. We must not only believe in the essential goodness of man, but, as one of the characters says at the end of the play, we must *be* good and help each other.

The social scene itself is presented with a harsh realism produced by stark contrasts, yet the historical setting gives to the resulting oversimplification and tendentiousness something of the dimensions of a myth. Byron, the poet-champion of the oppressed, and Castlereagh, the aristocratic ogre, are like the personified forces of good and evil in some primeval conflict. The other characters are grouped on these two sides, and between them and the mass of the weavers stands the mysterious machine, with its potentialities for good or evil, depending on what man can make of them. Toller's treatment of the external world in *Die Maschinenstürmer* might be considered the poetic counterpart to his treatment of the inner world in *Die Wandlung.*

Toller did not produce anything so impressive as *Die Maschinenstürmer* again. It represents the peak of what he was able to work out of his own particular vein, though a later attempt at revolutionary drama which dealt with mutiny in the German Navy at Kiel during the First World War, and to which he gave

the title *Feuer aus den Kesseln,* is not without considerable merits as a documentary play.

His last work to be written in prison betrays perhaps not so much the limitations of his art as the dire effects which the tensions produced by his unnatural confinement had on his artistic judgment. Toller was a man with an excess of nervous energy and a feverishly alert mind. He needed both physical liberty and frequent contact and communion with other human beings to maintain his emotional equilibrium and develop his talents. Denied this relief, he was bound at some stage to be turned in on himself and to become absorbed in his private misfortunes. (pp. 96-7)

This strain shows through the painful incidents of his play, *Hinkemann,* in which a soldier returns home from war with his genitals shot away, and tries to compensate his faithful wife for the pleasures missing from the marriage bed by providing her with material comforts. These can only be obtained by his taking employment which pays a high salary. The only job available is one of a peculiarly revolting nature: he must bite open the throats of live rats and drink their blood before a fairground audience lusting for new sensations! Hinkemann accepts, and reconciles himself to the situation by interpreting it as his chance for an act of self-sacrifice which will reward his wife for her faithfulness. She unfortunately succumbs under the increasing pressure of her husband's self-pity and her own desires to the brutal advances of a seducer, but commits suicide in horror at her own treachery when she learns the secret of her husband's employment and his motives for taking it. (p. 97)

[The] unsatisfactory impression which *Hinkemann* makes may not only lie in a choice of subject-matter unsuited to Toller's talents or the stresses under which it was written. The overcharged action and inflated dialogue could be partly attributed to the fact that the action of the play derives to a considerable extent from [Georg] Büchner's *Woyzeck,* which had recently been revived in the theatre with great success. In some respects the mood of this play was too near to Toller's own mood. It encouraged tendencies which when given free rein developed into faults. . . .

A comparison of *Woyzeck* and *Hinkemann* suggests however that Toller was not unconscious of the risks he ran in the choice of such a subject. Whereas in Büchner our sympathy is concentrated mainly on the figure of Woyzeck, whose mental torment causes him to murder the unfaithful woman he loves, Toller transfers much of this sympathy to Hinkemann's wife, whose suicide throws a critical light on her wounded husband's self-pity. Hinkemann recognises at the end of the play that his wife's misfortunes were equal to his own and that he had failed in his duty as a member of the stronger sex. (p. 98)

The place which Toller's main work occupies in the chronological development of modern German drama is not difficult to define. Growing out of the first phase of Expressionism, which is characterised by a forward-looking youthful idealism and a delight in formal experiment resulting in the creation of the *Stationendrama,* it leads over to the disillusion of the postwar years and the preference for a more regularly constructed type of play better suited to the presentation—in historical guise, for reasons of safety—of the realities of the contemporary political and social scene, with which dramatists were becoming increasingly concerned. (p. 101)

Richard Beckley, "Ernst Toller," in German Men of Letters: Twelve Literary Essays, *Vol. III, edited* by Alex Natan (© 1964 Oswald Wolff (Publishers) Limited), Wolff, 1964, pp. 85-104.]

ERWIN PISCATOR   (essay date 1968)

[*Piscator was one of the most prominent directors in modern theater. His commentary on the dramas he directed was first published in 1929 in* The Political Theatre, *a revised edition appearing in 1963. Excerpted below are Piscator's comments on* Hoppla! Such Is Life!, *which he staged in 1927.*]

The basic idea [of Toller's *Hoppla, Such Is Life!*] was to take a revolutionary who has been in a lunatic asylum for eight years and confront him with the world of 1927.

This was another idea which afforded the possibility of giving a social and political outline of a whole epoch. But the documentary material was overlaid with poetic lyricism, as was always the case in Toller's work. All our efforts in the subsequent course of the work were directed towards providing the play with a realistic substructure. You cannot prove a single point against the bourgeois world order if your evidence is inaccurate, and it is always inaccurate when the emotions play a decisive role. Even at the very first reading in my old house in Oranienstrasse, the figure of the "hero," Karl Thomas, came under heated attack. His character was accused of being too passive and ill-defined. Toller tends to impose the burden of his own feelings on such characters, and these are subject to the restless fluctuations which are typical of artists, particularly if they have been through as much and suffered as much as Toller. This is only natural. (p. 207)

Our analysis of Toller's hero had inevitably produced the conclusion that we incorporated in the staged version. (Toller himself later repudiated this conclusion; and remember, Schiller constantly altered the endings of his plays.) But with the play as it stood, I fail to see to this day what other ending we could have used. The decision was taken only after long debates and interminable suggestions.

The hero of Toller's play, Karl Thomas, was a postwar revolutionary who was condemned to death after the Revolution had been put down. In 1919, shortly before the hour at which he was to be executed—along with his friend Kilmann, who had also been condemned to death—he was pardoned. Karl Thomas goes out of his mind, is committed to a lunatic asylum and drops out of sight for eight years until 1927, when he returns to an entirely new world. His friend Kilmann has made his peace with the new regime and has been made a government minister; his former girlfriend has become a political agitator. When he reappears on the scene, she takes him in for a while but eventually turns him out onto the street. Karl Thomas becomes a waiter. In his desperation at the times, he conceives a plan to shoot Kilmann, who is now a reactionary. A right-wing radical student beats him to it, but Karl Thomas comes under suspicion and is arrested and put back in the lunatic asylum; he hangs himself at the moment at which his innocence is established. . . . The defeatism of this conclusion later came in for some criticism from both the radical and bourgeois camps, and at this point I can offer the following explanation.

Thomas is anything but a class-conscious proletarian. He finds it no easier to make contact with the bourgeois world than with the world of the proletariat. The theme does not plot the course of an erratic adherent of the Revolution; if it did, his suicide would be utterly misguided. Thomas is, in fact, an anarchist of the sentimental variety and his breakdown is perfectly log-

ical. He constitutes a proof from the converse. What his case demonstrates is the insanity of the bourgeois world order. (pp. 207-09)

His counterparts, who represent the positive side of the Revolution, are Eva, Mother Meller, and above all Kroll, who represents the one hundred percent party man.

In giving the leading role to Alexander Granach, I committed a deliberate casting "error" which effectively turned that role into a proletarian type. This was my way of avoiding the standard "hero" who recurs in each of Toller's works; but at the same time I wanted to show that the petit bourgeois attitude of mind is not the exclusive privilege of the "intellectuals."

Toller's language proved to be a serious handicap in dealing with a subject which I would have preferred to analyze soberly, clearly and unambiguously in the play.

Example:

(During the last sentences two policemen appear. They both go up to Thomas and grab him by the wrists.)

First Policeman: Well, young man, I suppose you just found that revolver?

(A calm, factual question from which a situation can develop, because it causes a certain tension. What reply does Toller give him?)

Karl Thomas: How do I know? How do you know? Even the gunman's revolver turns against him, and the barrel spouts laughter.

(This is supposed to mean: Thomas, who intended to shoot Kilmann, the minister, himself, but was beaten to it by a Nazi student, does not yet grasp the sequence of events and feels mocked by his own revolver.)

Toller himself can see that this reply is impossible, but it does not occur to him to cut it. Instead he tries to save it with the next line:

Second Policeman: We'll have a little more respect from you, right?

His formative years lay within the period of Expressionism. I myself am well aware of how difficult it is to shake this off. And nothing is further from my mind than a repudiation of linguistic concentration. But the process of formulation must not become an end in itself. It must always be functional, it must always carry the dramatic action forward and increase the mental tension; it must never simply passively reflect itself. (pp. 209-10)

Erwin Piscator, "Confrontation with the Times" (originally published in a somewhat different form under a different title in his Das Politische Theater, *revised edition, Rowohlt Verlag, 1963), in his* The Political Theatre, *translated by Hugh Rorrison (copyright © by Rowohlt Verlag Publishing Co., Reinbek bei Hamburg, 1963; reprinted by permission of Avon Books, New York), Avon Books, 1968, pp. 206-21.*

BERNARD F. DUKORE and DANIEL C. GEROULD   (essay date 1969)

Ernst Toller's famous play [*Man and the Masses*] dramatizes the relationship between man, the state, and the masses—a major theme in much of the avant-garde drama of [the 1920s]—in the abstract style of expressionism, blending dream and revolution, inward and outward explosions. *Man and the Masses* presents a stage of social upheaval following that depicted in [Stanislaw Ignacy Witkiewicz's] *The Water Hen.* Whereas Witkiewicz's "spherical tragedy" deals primarily with the crumbling of the old regime, showing the eruption of revolution only at the last moment from the viewpoint of dreamers stumbling through a nightmare-like life, *Man and the Masses* takes as its entire subject the process of revolutionary uprising caused by war and capitalist oppression. Curiously, however, the revolution is still dramatized in the form of a dream. But Toller's expressionist dream offers hope as well as terror, aspiration as well as destruction, and conveys powerful emotions and messianic fervor. (p. 7)

Man and the Masses is the journey of the heroine's soul through real and dream experiences of social upheaval during a revolutionary strike called to end an imperialist war. But this revolt is at the same time a subjective rebellion for the heroine, since she leaves her place in society and breaks with her husband, an authoritarian figure who represents both the state and the masculine principle of dominance to which she has been bound physically and psychologically. Her personal redemption blends with the transformation of society. In the experience of revolution, in which all former habits, conventions, and certainties are destroyed, the real seems dream-like and the dream-like real. The audience participates in the spiritual history of the heroine's soul, freed from the normal bonds of time and space, as she strives toward a salvation that can be accomplished only through the affirmation of love over the institutions of the industrial state and the triumph of man over the concept of the masses.

Sonia Irene L., the central figure of *Man and the Masses,* is the only character who has a name—and it is Russian. The characters of expressionist drama are almost always generic figures. Representatives of classes, defined and identified by their social functions and outer appearances, the other characters in *Man and the Masses* are not individuals but abstract, universal types. The masses themselves become a generalized chorus, oppressed and enslaved by capitalistic, militaristic, and bureaucratic institutions which have depersonalized them and drained them of individuality. Man's inner life is denied by the external reality in which he lives, and Death-in-Life (an abstraction from Toller's first play, *Transfiguration*) proves more deadly than actual death on the battlefield or before the firing squad. From the rupture between man and his social environment come the non-realistic techniques of expressionism, polarized toward dream consciousness on the one hand and the mechanical gestures and movements of masses on the other.

Telescoping and exaggeration, the shorthand of psychic reality, portray the distorted world of expressionism, in which the entire drama is seen through the subjective consciousness of the hero. All the principal voices and figures may be fragments of his own mind and extensions of his own inner conflicts. The hero's identity is subject to change; objects and characters undergo multiple transformations and incarnations. . . . The heroine's husband in the first scene of *Man and the Masses* becomes the clerk in the dream sequence at the stock exchange in Scene Two; he is the Man, symbol of allegiance to the system. In the dream vision in scene Four, the face of the prisoner changes into the face of the guard, for victim and victimizer are interchangeable as long as force rules. The

Nameless One appears in many different guises: demagogue, revolutionist, vengeance, fate. If *Man and the Masses* is viewed as the inner struggle of the heroine, then the Man (her husband) and the Nameless One are projections of her own psyche and conflicting viewpoints within her own nature: her ties to her own past versus her passionate feeling of the need for social change at all costs. (pp. 8-9)

A great success in its own time, *Man and the Masses* fell from prominence with the demise of expressionism and what seemed to be the end of revolutionary politics. Until recently, Toller's play appeared to have only historical interest. However, once again *Man and the Masses* has immediate impact for a world in which major cities are racked by riots and revolutionary strikes. Taking as his subject the contemporary ethical problem of the use of violence in bringing about social justice and urgent changes in society, Toller dramatizes the dilemma of the intellectual: are revolutionary means justified by revolutionary ends? This drama is enacted in the mind of the Woman as her emotions drive her toward and against revolution. Can violence, abhorred as a weapon of the warfare state, be used against the state to destroy violence and create pressing social changes? In *Man and the Masses,* Toller analyzes the crisis of the bourgeois liberal who recognizes the need for change but draws back before the consequences when conscience becomes translated into action. (p. 9)

> *Bernard F. Dukore and Daniel C. Gerould, "Explosions and Implosions: Avant-Garde Drama between World Wars" (copyright ©1969 by Bernard F. Dukore and Daniel C. Gerould), in Educational Theatre Journal, Vol. XXI, No. 1, March, 1969, pp. 1-16.* *

MALCOLM PITTOCK (essay date 1979)

[*The following excerpt—an in-depth analysis of Toller's poetry—is taken from Pittock's* Ernst Toller, *an important biocritical survey which treats in detail all of Toller's major works.*]

Toller wrote a good deal of verse, which is unequal in quality. His first volume *Gedichte der Gefangenen: Ein Sonnetenkreis,* (The Prisoners' poems-a sonnet cycle) consisting for the most part of poems written during imprisonment, was published in 1921 at about the same time as two poems especially written for choral recitation: *Tag des Proletariats* (Day of the Proletariat) and *Requiem den gemordeten Brüdern* (Requiem for the murdered Brothers). In 1924 appeared *Das Schwalbenbuch* (The Swallowbook) and *Vormorgen* (Tomorrow), a revised edition of *Gedichte der Gefangenen,* to which an early group of poems, now collected for the first time and entitled *Verse vom Friedhof,* (Verses from the Graveyard), had been added. After 1924 Toller wrote little verse; only another piece for choral recitation, *Weltliche Passion* (Secular Passion) an elegiac celebration of Karl Liebknecht and Rosa Luxemburg, and *Die Feuer-Kantate* (The Fire-Cantata), a propagandist poem on the burning of the Reichstag, which was set to music by Hanns Eisler. Neither was republished in book form.

These poems are the least interesting. The last two, *Weltliche Passion* and *Die Feuer-Kantate,* even more clearly than the plays of the last period, evince a willed simplification of experience; and the mode of retrospective elegiac celebration in *Weltliche Passion* is reminiscent of that in *Feuer aus den Kesseln!* (Draw the Fires!).

Even *Die Feuer-Kantate,* however, shows skill in getting its simple point across effectively by a deliberate exploitation of the antinomies, Helios (sun) and hell, latent in the concept, fire. Through their use of the swastika the Nazis identified themselves (falsely of course) with regenerative fire and by burning down the Reichstag tried to associate the Communists with destructive fire. But the poet predicts that their stratagem will rebound on themselves and the Reichstag fire will become a symbol of the fire of regeneration which is to destroy them.

Weltliche Passion, however, is a much more accomplished work and might be genuinely impressive in performance, though there is no evidence that it was performed. (pp. 148-49)

As with *Die Feuer-Kantate,* Toller constructs his poem out of simple antinomies. Successful revolution is associated with natural growth, harvest, and purposeful work. By contrast, capitalist war is regarded as a perversion of meaningful human activity. (p. 149)

In *Weltliche Passion* an allusion is made through an adapted quotation to the second poem in the diptych for the Sprechchöre *Tag des Proletariats* and *Requiem den gemordeten Brüdern:*

> Senkt die Fahnen
> Fahnen des Kampfes
> Fahnen der Freiheit
> Senkt sie zur Erde
> Zum Schoss der Mutter.

> (Haul the flags down, the flags of struggle,
> the flags of freedom; haul them to the
> ground, to the mother's womb.)

Of Toller's propaganda poems these two are the most interesting, for though they are simplifications of, they are related to, Toller's deeper experience. As pieces intended for public performance they are more elaborate than *Weltliche Passion,* the first particularly so. In *Tag des Proletariats* not only are parts taken by a full choir and various of its subdivisions and several soloists, but there are musical interludes for orchestra or organ.

Tag des Proletariats, unlike *Weltliche Passion* written in regular rhyming verse, opens with a call by the full choir for centuries of oppression to end, a process that is associated with struggle: "Erkämpft! Erkämpft, Erkämpft euch den Tag!'' . . . (Win, win, win the day for yourselves). But, as in *Die Wandlung,* the struggle is not envisaged at all. By some mysterious process "Fesseln zerfallen / Gebändigter Wucht'' (mastered, the fetters' burden collapses into fragments). It is just a matter of holding up the Red Flag and "Der Tag bricht an! Die Fackel loht'' (The day dawns: the torch blazes).

But the meanings of *Tag des Proletariats* are deliberately qualified by those of *Requiem den gemordeten Brüdern.* And this poem, because of its somber nature, has none of the musical accompaniment of the first and is mostly in unrhymed verse. *Requiem den gemordeten Brüdern* begins with the chorus, quoted in a slightly adapted version in *Weltliche Passion,* which is repeated twice, each time with an accession of meaning, once during and once at the end of the poem. The failure of the revolution is admitted at the start, and this colors what follows, while it alters the meaning of *Tag des Proletariats,* the achievement celebrated there now appearing premature or perhaps merely an anticipatory triumph of the imagination. (pp. 150-51)

Verse vom Friedhof (Verses from the Graveyard), the first section of *Vormorgen* (Tomorrow), is an impressive cycle of poems. By what must have been careful arrangement, Toller

has given to these poems, written between 1912 and 1918, the effect of a sequence. There are weak poems in *Verse vom Friedhof,* but these cannot be isolated from the context, which by juxtaposition and implicit allusion qualifies that weakness, so that they emerge as records of a state of feeling whose limitations are known to the author.

The sequence begins with *Der Ringende* ('The Striver'), which is about the adolescent's struggle to achieve self-sufficient manhood by transcending both alienation from and lingering dependence on the mother. The stages in Toller's experience of and attitude to the war are then systematically embodied. First in *Marschlied* ('Marching Song'), which denies the self-fulfillment glimpsed in *Der Ringende:* for the young there is only a common fate; a perversion of childhood brought about by a Germany which is symbolized as an unfulfilled mother. The next five poems *Morgen; Geschützwache* ('On Duty by the Cannon'); *Gang zum Schützengraben* ('On the Way to the Trenches'); *Gang zur Ruhestellung* ('On the Way to Rest Quarters'); and *Stellungskrieg* ('War of Attrition') evoke different but typical aspects of the war, in consonance with the consciousness expressed in *Marschlied,* in a bare imagistic manner. Then with *Konzert,* written almost certainly out of an experience Toller had when on leave, there is a countermovement of feeling, a vision of a fundamental change of consciousness wrought by music, which though temporary, is an earnest of what human life could be. The note of explicit rhetorical protest against the war is heard first in *Leichen in Priesterwald* ('Corpses in Bois le Prêtre') and is continued and extended in *Alp* ('Nightmare'), an exercise in the symbolic grotesque which can be related to *Die Wandlung.* The mode is used again, but with a more explicit didacticism, in *Menschen,* which attacks the society back home. Then follow three weak poems of political protest against the war: *An die Dichter* ('To the Writers'), *Den Müttern* ('To the Mothers'), and *Ich habe euch umarmt* ('I have embraced you'). In the first two poems there is an embarrassingly emotional stridency and in the last, which is about Toller's contact with the workers, an equally embarrassing emotionalism. But the last two poems in the collection *Über meiner Zelle* ('Over my Cell') and *Deutschland,* written clearly when Toller was in a military prison for his political agitation against the war, in their somber but wistful acceptance of defeat, imply a criticism of the simple stridencies of the poems that have immediately preceded them.

The finest poems in the collection are undoubtedly *Morgen* ('Morning'), *Geschützwache* ('On Duty by the Cannon'), *Gang zum Schützengraben* ('On the way to the Trenches'), *Gang zur Ruhestellung* ('On the way to Rest Quarters'), and *Stellungskrieg* ('War of Attrition'). Their poetic method is unlike that used in any other of Toller's poems. They are economical; direct and rhetorically heightened statements of feeling are usually absent; and their meanings develop largely by implication. They are examples of expressive form; their indirect method notates the partial anaesthesia of feeling consequent on an attempt to believe that what is happening is inevitable. The imagic collocations and implications, however, exhibit the subterranean workings of a sensitive and humane feeling. (pp. 152-53)

The poems that Toller wrote in prison, with the exception of the concluding poems in *Verse vom Friedhof,* (Verses from the Graveyard) can be found in the *Lieder der Gefangenen* (The Prisoners' Songs) section of *Vormorgen* (Tomorrow) and *Das Schwalbenbuch* (The Swallowbook). On the whole, the first of these covers the earlier period of his imprisonment, *Das Schwalbenbuch* the later.

Like *Verse vom Friedhof, Lieder der Gefangenen* is intended as a sequence: its subtitle, when published earlier and separately as *Gedichte des Gefangenen,* was *ein Sonettenkreis* (a sonnet cycle). . . . The theme of the collection is indicated in the first prison poem proper (**'An alle Gefangenen') ('To All Prisoners')** with its key line "Wer kann vom sich sagen, er sei nicht gefangenen" ("Who can say of himself that he is not imprisoned?").

But as a sequence, *Lieder der Gefangenen* is not successful. In the body of the work we fail to note the dramatic progress discoverable in *Verse vom Friedhof,* while the framing poems mentioned above exhibit the simplifying histrionicism of Toller's public manner. The poems in the body of the volume reflect various aspects of the strain of prolonged imprisonment, which are vividly evoked in Toller's prose works, *Eine Jugend in Deutschland* (**Growing up in Germany**) and *Briefe aus dem Gefängnis* (**Letters from Prison**). The extreme strain meant that Toller's emotions were frequently feverish. In particular, the perpetual struggle to adjust himself to his situation and his inability to do so for very long together led to emotional oscillations. To communicate feelings in an extreme situation to those who have not experienced it is always difficult, of course, but a heightened emotionalism acts as a further barrier to empathy and too frequently leads to a detached, patronizing pity in the reader: "poor chap, he must have been in a state to write like that." Moreover, Toller is constantly attempting, through a projected generalization of his own emotions, to articulate what he thinks is a common feeling among his fellow prisoners. No doubt there were correspondences, but Toller does not seem to have allowed for differences.

Nonetheless, there is a handful of impressive poems: **'Nächte' ('Nights'), 'Gefangener und Tod' ('Prisoner and Death'), 'Verweilen um Mitternacht' ('Watch at Midnight'), 'Gefangener reicht dem Tod die Hand' ('A prisoner shakes hands with Death').** (pp. 155-56)

Without doubt *Das Schwalbenbuch* (**The Swallowbook**) is Toller's most celebrated collection of poems. More explicitly than either *Verse vom Friedhof* (**Verses from the Graveyard**) or *Lieder der Gefangenen* (**The Prisoners' Songs**) it is a poetic cycle, though even the finest poems are inferior to the best in these earlier collections. Moreover, *Das Schwalbenbuch* contains poems that, isolated from their context, would be too frail and vague to be considered poems at all.

But the observation of nonhuman creatures gives Toller, on the whole, a discipline of feeling too often absent from *Lieder der Gefangenen.* Just because the swallows are fundamentally different from himself he cannot use them as easily as he can other human beings as pegs on which to hang his own emotions. Nonetheless, an occasional archness of tone indicates a lapse into anthropomorphism, and sometimes Toller forces his feelings or becomes crudely didactic. Moreover, the cycle is in free verse, which because it is not a disciplined form—and some of the less successful pieces not surprisingly move toward prose—offers a strong temptation to emotional indulgence, even though at the same time it enables Toller to cultivate a fuller tonal range in poetry than ever before. But whatever the faults of the cycle, they are held in sufficient check to ensure its success as a whole.

Toller responds to the swallows in three ways; as creatures different from men with ways of their own from which men can learn; as creatures whose behavior is analogous in certain respects to human behavior; and as repositories of symbolic meaning—or, to put it more technically, as vehicles for new tenors. The flexibility of method enables Toller to notate the trajectory of his own feelings with spontaneity and naturalness as they change from despair to something akin to joy and finally to a quiet stoical strength. . . . And this inner change is accompanied by, indeed depends upon, the wider meanings learned from the swallows. This involves a renewed commitment to revolution, whose significance the poet becomes more fully aware of through the swallows. . . . The natural, spontaneous, creative fulfillment of being characteristic of the swallows, an implied concept which has all the authority of close observation behind it, painstakingly and lovingly built up in the cycle, is the goal for men, too. (pp. 157-59)

[The] swallows provide a paradigm of revolutionary activity. [Toller] describes how, in the prison yard, he saw a crowd of swallows attack a sparrow hawk, making it disgorge its prey. . . . The application is obvious.

There follow a number of poems describing the hatching of the swallows' eggs and the nurture and growth of the nestlings. What is implicitly stressed is an ideal of parenthood and family life naturally realized by the birds. . . . However the swallows are subject to the primeval curse; they must destroy other creatures to live ("Weh uns! Was lebt mordet"—Alas, any being that lives murders) . . . , an insight relatable to the recognition in *Hinkemann* of a residuum of unavoidable suffering.

Through the swallows Toller learns to cultivate a joy of the spirit that will make his imprisonment more endurable and to rejoice in the phenomenal world, seeing it with the eyes of the fledgling making its first flight. . . . Lastly, the way in which the swallows face unavoidable tragedy is both an implicit criticism of the way human beings behave under such circumstances and an example; the loving care with which the parent birds sustain each other after frost has killed off their second brood is that which men should display but do not. . . . (pp. 160-61)

Malcolm Pittock, "Poetry," in his Ernst Toller *(copyright © 1979 by Twayne Publishers, Inc.; reprinted with the permission of Twayne Publishers, a Division of G. K. Hall & Co., Boston), Twayne, 1979, pp. 148-61.*

MICHAEL OSSAR (essay date 1980)

It has been claimed that, from an ideological point of view, *Die Maschinenstürmer* adds very little to the problems which are the focus of *Masse Mensch.* In a sense, this is true. Both plays involve enlightened leaders, redeemer-figures, who point the way to a new society. This new society is recognizably the same in both plays and is compared to two extreme alternatives, both of which are rejected by the author but not by the masses. The extremes are incorporated in two figures in each play who compete for the favor of the masses. The problem of violence is central to both plays. And finally, each play ends with the apparent defeat of the redeemer and what he stands for, but also with the ambivalent indication that this defeat may not prove final, that his example may eventually inspire future generations to follow him.

But there are also important differences between the plays. Whereas in *Masse Mensch* the Woman compromises herself and then must atone for this failing, Jimmy in *Die Maschinenstürmer* remains throughout the pure revolutionary whose fate appears on that account all the more inexorable and existentially necessary, and thus tragic. Jimmy's martyrdom is for this reason even more impressive than the Woman's, and we shall see that it too has its effect on his comrades. And yet, whereas in *Masse Mensch* we feel perhaps a definite though realistically skeptical hope for future regeneration, in *Die Maschinenstürmer* that hope is very much attenuated. . . .

[The] Nameless One in *Masse Mensch* is the pure authoritarian revolutionary who exists only to the extent that he embodies a particular ideological position antagonistic to the Woman's, and who has no other, personal, motives for opposing her. John Wible [in *Die Maschinenstürmer*] on the other hand is a humanly interesting and highly complex character in a psychological sense. It is obvious that Toller took some pains to develop his personality and motivations. He is in fact proof that Toller is capable of transcending mere black-and-white characterization. (p. 98)

Egoism is at the focus of his character, and ultimately motivates both his longing for luxury and a better life for himself at the expense of both his comrades and his wife (who is in consequence reduced to prostitution), and his more significant betrayal of Jimmy, and thus of the future. His injured self-esteem, his longing for power, are distilled into an urge for revenge at all costs when he sees himself replaced by Jimmy as leader of the workers. Wible's commitment to his fellows proves weaker than his egoism. This fact is interesting because it shows Toller's insight, gained during his years in prison, into the pettiness and selfishness of his fellow revolutionaries. It vividly brings home to us the inertia against which the new order must fight. But most important, it underscores how drastic a transformation is necessary to bring about the birth of the "new man," a kind of *coincidentia oppositorum*, for he must be at once an individual who retains his moral freedom and a communal being who voluntarily submits his will to the service of the community. (pp. 99-100)

[In] *Die Maschinenstürmer* Toller emphasizes for the first time not the metaphysical nature of the transformation in the redeemer himself, the "epiphany" of *Die Wandlung*, not the philosophical context, the crystal-hard choice that the redeemer must make, as in *Masse Mensch*, but instead the economic reality which forms the background of his choice. We are shown the pernicious effects of international competition, of the introduction of machinery, of strikebreakers, of economic exploitation and dislocations of all kinds, very much as Gerhart Hauptmann portrayed the same kind of impoverishment (to use Marx's term) in *Die Weber*, set nearly thirty years later. To do so, it was necessary for Toller to abandon the abstract austerity of *Masse Mensch* in favor of a more traditional five-act tragedy with a large cast of characters who are named, and behind whose names more or less fully developed personalities stand. (p. 100)

This is the only one of Toller's plays set in the distant past, and one of three plays based on historical themes (the others being *Feuer aus den Kesseln* and *Wunder in Amerika*) and we know from Toller's own remarks and from the researches of [N. A.] Furness and [Hans] Marnette that he actually used Engels' *Lage der arbeitenden Klasse in England (Situation of the Working Class in England)* and Marx's *Das Kapital* in its composition.

In his use of historical data and psychological realism, Toller was attempting to present a broad panorama of the economic conditions and imperatives with which the "new" proletariat had to contend. To do so, he needed people, not abstractions or embodiments of ideologies, and they had to be people about whom we care. (p. 102)

[Toller] gives the fully-developed characters certain ideological burdens to carry in addition to their functions as living, breathing representatives of various traits of bourgeois and proletarian social groups. Ure is a real person, a wealthy man struggling with his conscience and inventing the same sort of self-delusions and justifications as Gerhart Hauptmann's realistically-drawn Dreissiger [in *Die Weber*]. But at the same time he represents on a more abstract level ruthless capitalism quite unconcerned with the effect of its actions on human beings. . . . (p. 103)

[In *Die Maschinenstürmer*] some figures achieve a degree of psychological three-dimensionality, while others serve either abstract or symbolic roles. Among the former, certain relationships realize their full significance only when their connections with each other are emphasized. Thus, for example, Ure and Jimmy form two extremes on one level, for each is completely convinced of the harmony of his own ideology with the laws that govern the universe—Jimmy believes completely in brotherhood, whereas Ure believes that his actions are justified by such maxims as the survival of the fittest.

Another level is inhabited by Wible on the one hand and Henry Cobbett on the other. Each of these is too weak to conquer the selfish impulses which drive him to hypocritical opportunism. (p. 105)

There are three important ideological confrontations in *Die Maschinenstürmer*. The first occurs in the prologue, and, like the "Prologue in Heaven" of *Faust*, it sets the cosmic framework for what is to follow and anticipates the economic philosophies at the root of the more specific debate to come. The function of the state as handmaiden to the economic interests of the bourgeoisie, its "executive committee," is underscored by the fact that Ure appears in the mask of Castlereagh, just as Jimmy in the mask of Byron represents the Expressionist poet's mission to cry out the demands of humanity. . . .

The defeat of the poet Byron in the prologue anticipates Jimmy's rejection by the children in the first scene—a scene which in turn foreshadows the brutal ending of the play. Jimmy tries to awaken the children's perceptions with a tale of social injustice, and they react by quarreling over a scrap of bread. (p. 106)

Just as Jimmy's rejection by the children at the beginning of the first act points to his betrayal by their parents in the last, so Jimmy's rejection by his mother and brother at the beginning of the second act anticipates the collapse of his hope for a true community, a family of all mankind. This hope, which achieves its most eloquent expression in Jimmy's encounter with Ure, is first expressed in the second important confrontation, his speech to the workers at the end of Act II. . . . (p. 107)

[The third confrontation is] that of Act IV between Jimmy and the industrialist Ure. In a scene which can be compared to the meeting of the Marquis Posa and Phillip II in Friedrich Schiller's play, *Don Carlos* (1787), Jimmy pleads the cause of the workers and begins by describing their misery and exploitation. In doing so, he does not aim, as Gerhart Hauptmann did in *Die Weber*, at primarily awakening a sense of sympathy in the spectator, a sense of conscience and a desire to mitigate the weavers' want. In Hauptmann one feels that the entrepreneur Dreissiger, for all his callousness and cruelty is neither a depraved nor an evil man, but simply one who like Ibsen's heroes is too weak to do good. In his dealings with the tutor and theology student, Weinhold, we observe quite clearly that he is intelligent enough to have to delude himself in order to live with his conscience. But the situation seems to be one that calls for feeling rather than willful ignorance, Christian charity rather than callousness. The structure of society itself is not called into question.

In *Die Maschinenstürmer,* however, Jimmy's description of the workers' misery does not aim primarily at awakening sympathy—either in Ure or in the spectator. Instead he delivers a ringing indictment of the system itself, an attack which is nothing less than a call (to Ure, who is in Jimmy's eyes its victim as much as the least of his employees!) for revolution. . . . (p. 108)

Die Maschinenstürmer begins with the arrival of Jimmy in Nottingham. His appearance serves two functions. The episode with the children referred to above anticipates Jimmy's betrayal later on, and Jimmy's questions to Ned Lud provide an occasion for exposition. Jimmy, like the outsider in Ibsen and like Moritz Jäger in Gerhart Hauptmann's *Die Weber,* serves as catalyst whose presence decisively alters the course of events, though he cannot control them. Unlike Jäger, however, Jimmy, with the insight of a higher level of consciousness, is prompted to preach restraint—to place spiritual strength and humility above physical retribution and more conventional worldly dignity. . . . There are a great many more or less superficial similarities between the two plays: the women who are more zealous than their husbands, the entrepreneur who is physically confronted with starving and exploited children, the alliance of Church, State and bourgeoisie, the moral depravities of the workers in which they find their only solace, the former worker become parvenu who is more brutal than the manufacturers themselves, the pious old worker, the workers who stand in almost religious awe before the God-machine that they had been bent on destroying. Many of these elements, which we may call "clichés of the genre," are common to works such as *Germinal* (1885), *L'Assommoir* (1877), *Gas* (1919) and even *Hard Times* (1854), all of which depict the impact of the industrial revolution on human relationships. But where works like *Germinal* are ultimately defeatist (as the Marxists claim), Toller for all his pessimism adumbrates the possibility of a solution, the conviction that a solution is conceivable, if not realizable by man in his present state of consciousness. This solution lies in Jimmy's anarchistic vision, a vision which revolves around the concept of the true community of men. (pp. 115-16)

> Michael Ossar, "'Die Maschinenstürmer': Anarchism and Social Darwinsim," in his Anarchism in the Dramas of Ernst Toller: The Realm of Necessity and the Realm of Freedom (reprinted by permission of the State University of New York Press; © 1980 State University of New York), State University of New York Press, 1980, pp. 97-122.

ADDITIONAL BIBLIOGRAPHY

Bell, Clair Hayden. "Toller's *Die Maschinenstürmer*." *Monatshefte* XXX, No. 2 (February 1938): 59-70.
　　　Historical study. Bell presents an analysis of the historical background of *The Machine-Wreckers*. In particular, he compares certain elements in the play with those found in Gerhart Hauptmann's *Die Weber* and Georg Kaiser's *Gas* trilogy.

Chandler, Frank W. "Expressionism at Its Best: Kaiser, Toller, Werfel." In his *Modern Continental Playwrights*, pp. 407-37. New York: Harper & Brothers, 1931.*
　　　Brief critical examination. Chandler discusses the plots and themes to Toller's major plays—including *Masses and Man, The Machine-Wreckers, Hinkemann,* and *Hoppla!*

Durzak, Manfred. "From Tragedy to Farce: Toller's Comedy of Revolution, *Wotan Unchained*." *Review of National Literature* 9 (1978): 86-100.
　　　Biocritical study. Durzak examines Toller's *Wotan Unchained* and discusses the historical events which led the dramatist to shift his artistic perspective from "revolutionary tragedy to revolutionary farce."

Fishman, Sterling. "Ernst Toller and the Drama of Nonviolence." *The Midwest Quarterly* VII, No. 1 (October 1965): 29-41.
　　　Biocritical study. Fishman focuses on Toller's reaction to violence and the role it plays in his work, in particular the question of whether violence ought to be used as a means of freeing humanity from an oppressive social system.

Furness, N.A. "Toller: *Die Maschinenstürmer*—The English Dimension." *German Life & Letters* n.s. XXXIII, No. 2 (January 1980): 147-57.
　　　Discusses the facts surrounding the London production of *The Machine-Wreckers*. In particular, Furness focuses on the individual personalities behind the English production of the play in 1923.

Isherwood, Christopher. "People: The Head of a Leader." In his *Exhumations*, pp. 125-32. New York: Simon and Schuster, 1966.
　　　Personal reminiscences. Isherwood reconstructs the final meetings he had with Toller before the playwright's suicide.

Mann, Klaus. "Ernst Toller." *The New Republic* LXXXXIX, No. 1279 (7 June 1939): 140-41.
　　　Biographical essay. Mann speculates on the reasons behind Toller's suicide, suggesting that one answer could be found in the devastating effect world events—such as the growth of Nazism and the Spanish Civil War—had on his essentially idealistic personality.

Pinthus, Kurt. "Life and Death of Ernst Toller." *Books Abroad* 14, No. 1 (Winter 1939-1940): 3-8.
　　　Personal reminiscences. Pinthus, a close friend of Toller's for many years, discusses the playwright's political ideology and the events which led to his eventual suicide.

Spalek, John M. "Ernst Toller: The Need for a New Estimate." *The German Quarterly* XXXIX, No. 4 (November 1966): 581-98.
　　　Critical history. Spalek reconstructs the different approaches critics have taken in an attempt to evaluate Toller's work and influence. Spalek considers Toller "the most controversial and misunderstood playwright" of the Expressionist movement.

Untermeyer, Louis. "Another Europe." In his *From Another World*, pp. 362-76. New York: Harcourt, Brace and Co., 1939.*
　　　Personal reminiscences. Untermeyer attempts to draw a picture of Toller's personality while discussing the depth of his social vision.

West, Rebecca. "Toller." In her *Ending in Earnest: A Literary Log*, pp. 59-65. Garden City, N.Y.: Doubleday, Doran & Co., 1931.
　　　Personal reminiscences. West reconstructs her meeting with Toller in London during the production of *Hoppla! wir Leben!* She ends by calling him "a sensitive talent" who was "obviously helped by his friendly relationship to his own times."

Juan Valera (y Acalá-Galiano)

1824-1905

(Also wrote under pseudonyms of Eleutorio Filogyno and Currita Albornoz.) Spanish novelist, critic, poet, essayist, short story writer, dramatist, and translator.

Valera is best known for his novel *Pepita Jiménez,* which is considered a graceful model of modern Spanish prose. This novel also has a reputation as a rare work of art in which subtle human impulses are analyzed in a manner both psychologically and artistically refined. Valera regarded the pursuit of formal beauty as the only legitimate purpose of literature. This forms the method and motive of his fiction and the subject of much of his critical writing. His works, however, are also appreciated for their insightful character portraits, philosophical subjects, and regional descriptions of Andalusia, as well as for their stylistic artistry.

Valera was born in Cabra, Cordoba, to a wealthy aristocratic family. After receiving a degree in law from the University of Madrid, he began a long career in the Spanish diplomatic corps. His first position was attaché on the staff of the Duke of Rivas, Spanish ambassador at Naples. Valera's stay in Italy deepened his emotional affinity for classical art and literature, and helped form the neoclassic sensibility that became a central trait of his literary works. His later diplomatic posts throughout the world—including North and South America, Europe, and Russia—provided Valera with the opportunity to cultivate the urbane, cosmopolitan temperament that is conveyed in his writings. Because literature was for Valera an avocation and not a source of income, he had no need to please a public and was uncompromised in his literary techniques and attitudes. Valera's diplomatic background also enabled him to write intelligently on political and historical subjects in addition to his strictly literary interests. He entered Parliament in 1858 and became a life senator in 1881. From this time until 1895 Valera served in various diplomatic positions. A victim of progressive blindness in his later years, he continued to write by dictating his works to his secretary.

Valera holds a relatively isolated position among his contemporaries. While many Spanish authors and critics in the nineteenth century allied themselves with the current movements of Naturalism or Romanticism, Valera advocated a pure aestheticism in negation of the Naturalist literary school and practiced an analytical classicism alien to the Romantic. In critical works such as *Del la naturaleza y carácter de le novela,* and in prefaces to his novels, Valera repeated the artistic dictum that character and realistic details are irrelevant to a novel's value, which is only to be found in its artistic organization. As a critic of other authors' works, Valera's chief shortcoming was a tendency to be as reluctant in attacking inferior works as he was unrestrained in his praise of those that pleased him. Often Valera's critical essays are the occasion for an informal mingling of wit and stylistic ingenuity. But although numerous commentators view Valera's critical writings as more elegant than intellectually serious, some find his aesthetics based at its deepest level on profound ethical and philosophical beliefs, and critics often read his novels as insightful documents of psychological or social analysis.

In his novels Valera put into practice his critical principles. The theories of literary Naturalism, which held the novel to be a social and psychological document more than an artistic form, were strongly contradicted by Valera's conception of the novel as an exhibition of narrative and linguistic strategies. Displaying a polished classical style, rather than the romantic grandiloquence common to the literature of his time, Valera's novels also achieve the best effects of more humanistic fiction. *Pepita Jiménez,* Valera's most popular and artistically successful work, is often considered a psychological tour-de-force. Concerning this tale of the romance of a young seminarian, Gerald Brenan comments that "the gradual awakening of the young man's love, the sophistries he uses for concealing it from himself and the opposition it finally encounters in his religious scruples are conveyed with a fine truth and subtlety." However, some critics contend that *Pepita Jiménez* is flawed by Valera's literary precepts, which focus on artistic form at the expense of creating complex and realistic characters. In the manner of *Pepita Jiménez,* the novel *Doña Luz* portrays the love between a married woman and a priest. Although not a wholly acceptable subject for its time, the style of this, as well as most of Valera's works, is acclaimed by critics as a high point of Spanish prose. This work also develops the "Valeran woman" found in many of his novels, a female character who embodies a number of diverse qualities—sensuality and mysticism, simplicity and sophistication—combined within a person of great physical and spiritual charm. One of Valera's most successful creations of this kind is found in his last major novel, *Juanita la larga*.

Valera chose not to write for the popular taste or be classified in any literary school. His works were a natural outgrowth of his love for learning and literature, promoting no other interests than their author's personal expression. "I worshipped form, but it was the internal and spiritual form," Valera explained. "I was a fervid believer in the mysteries of style, in that simplicity and purity by which style realizes ideas and feelings, and embodies in language of indestructable charm an author's whole mind and heart." Throughout his prolific writings Valera consistently pursued, with sometimes remarkable success, this artistic and personal ideal.

PRINCIPAL WORKS

Ensayos poéticas (poetry) 1844
Cartas de un pretendiente (novel) 1849
Del romanticismo en España y de espronceda (criticism) 1854
Sobre los cuentos de Leopardi e del romanticismo en España (criticism) 1854
Del la naturaleza y carácter de la novela (criticism) 1860
El pájaro verde (short story) 1860
Parsondes (short story) 1860
Mariquita y Antonio (unfinished novel) 1861
Estudios críticos sobre literatura, politica y costumbres de nuestros días. 2 vols. (essays) 1864
Sobre el Quijote y sobre las differentes maneras de commentarle y juzgarle (criticism) 1864
Pepita Jiménez (novel) 1874
   [*Pepita Jiménez*, 1886]
Las ilusiones del Doctor Faustino (novel) 1875
El comendador Mendoza (novel) 1877
   [*Commander Mendoza*, 1893]
Asclepigenia (dialogues) 1878
Pasarse de listo (novel) 1878
   [*Don Bravlio*, 1892]
Doña Luz (novel) 1879
   [*Doña Luz*, 1891]
Cuentos y diálogos (short stories and dialogues) 1882
Apuntes sobre nuevo arte de escribir novelas (criticism) 1886-87
Cuentos, dialogos y fantasias (short stories and dialogues) 1887
Cartas americanas (criticism) 1889-90
Estudios críticos sobre filosofía y religión (essays) 1889
Nuevas cartas americanas (criticism) 1890
Juanita la larga (novel) 1895
Genio y figura (novel) 1897
Morsamor (novel) 1899
Obras completas. 52 vols. (novels, short stories, dramas, poetry, criticism, essays, dialogues, and letters) 1905-35

JUAN VALERA (essay date 1886)

[*In his preface written especially for the American edition of* Pepita Jiménez, *Valera discusses aspects of his writings which later became the focal points of criticism on his works: his emphasis on style, art for art's sake doctrine, subtle psychological analysis of characters, and good-natured irony.*]

"**Pepita Jiménez**" has enjoyed a wide celebrity, not only in Spain, but in every other Spanish-speaking country. I am very far from thinking that we Spaniards of the present day are either more easily satisfied, less cultured than, or possessed of an inferior literary taste to, the inhabitants of any other region of the globe; but this does not suffice to dispel my misgivings that my novel may be received with indifference or with censure by a public somewhat prejudiced against Spain by fanciful and injurious preconceptions.

My novel, both in essence and form, is distinctively national and classic. Its merits—supposing it to have such—consist in the language and the style, and not in the incidents, which are of the most commonplace, or in the plot, which, if it can be said to have any, is of the simplest.

The characters are not wanting, as I think, in individuality, or in such truth to human nature as makes them seem like living beings; but, the action being so slight, this is brought out and made manifest by means of a subtle analysis, and by the language chosen to express the emotions, both of which may in the translation be lost. There is, besides, in my novel a certain irony, good-humored and frank, and a certain humor, resembling rather the humor of the English than the *esprit* of the French, which qualities, although happily they do not depend upon puns, or a play upon words, but are in the subject itself, require, in order that they may appear in the translation, that this should be made with extreme care. (p. 12)

I am an advocate of art for art's sake. I think it is very bad taste, always impertinent, and often pedantic, to attempt to prove theses by writing stories. For such a purpose disserations or books purely and severely didactic should be written. The object of a novel should be to charm, through a faithful representation of human actions and human passions, and to create by this fidelity to nature a beautiful work. The object of art is the creation of the beautiful, and whoever applies it to any other end, of however great utility this end may be, debases it. But it may chance, through a conjunction of favorable circumstances, by a happy inspiration—because in a given moment everything is disposed as by enchantment, or by supernatural influences—that an author's soul may become like a clear and magic mirror wherein are reflected all the ideas and all the sentiments that animate the eclectic spirit of his country, and in which these ideas and these sentiments lose their discordance, and group and combine themselves in pleasing agreement and harmony.

Herein is the explanation of the interest of "**Pepita Jiménez**." It was written when Spain was agitated to its centre, and everything was thrown out of its regular course by a radical revolution that at the same time shook to their foundations the throne and religious unity. It was written when everything in fusion, like molten metal, might readily amalgamate, and be molded into new forms. It was written when the strife raged fiercest between ancient and modern ideals; and, finally, it was written in all the plenitude of my powers, when my soul was sanest and most joyful in the possession of an enviable optimism and an all-embracing love and sympathy for humanity that, to my misfortune, can never again find place within my breast.

If I had endeavored by dialectics and by reasoning to conciliate opinions and beliefs, the disapprobation would have been general; but, as the conciliating and syncretic spirit manifested itself naturally in a diverting story, every one accepted and approved it, each one drawing from my book the conclusions that best suited himself. Thus it was that, from the most orthodox Jesuit father down to the most rabid revolutionist, and from the ultra-Catholic who cherishes the dream of restoring the Inquisition, to the rationalist who is the irreconcilable enemy of every religion, all were pleased with **"Pepita Jiménez."**

It would be curious, and not inopportune, to explain here how it came about that I succeeded in pleasing every one without intending it, without knowing it, and, as it were, by chance.

There was in Spain, some years ago, a conservative minister who had sent a godson of his to study philosophy in Germany. By rare good fortune this godson, who was called Julian Sanz del Rio, was a man of clear and profound intelligence, of unwearied application, and endowed with all the qualities necessary to make of him a sort of apostle. He studied, he formulated his system, he obtained the chair of metaphysics in the University of Madrid, and he founded a school, from which has since issued a brilliant pleiad of philosophers and statesmen, and of men illustrious for their learning, their eloquence, and their virtues. Chief among them are Nicolas Salmeron, Francisco Giner, Gumersindo Azcarate, Frederico de Castro, and Urbano Gonzalez Serrano.

The clerical party soon began to stir up strife against the master, the scholars, and the doctrines taught by them. They accused them of mystical pantheism.

I, who had ridiculed, at times, the confused terms, the pomp of words, and the method which the new philosophers made use of, regarded these philosophers, nevertheless, with admiration, and took up their defense—an almost solitary champion—in periodicals and reviews.

I had already maintained, before this, that our great dogmatic theologians, and especially the celebrated Domingo de Soto, were more liberal than the liberal rationalists of the present day, affirming, as they do, the sovereignty of the people by divine right; for if, as St. Paul declares, all authority proceeds from God, it does so through the medium of the people whom God inspires to found it; and because the only authority that proceeds directly from God is that of the Church.

I then set myself to demonstrate that, if Sanz del Rio and his followers were pantheists, our mystical theologians of the sixteenth and seventeenth centuries were pantheists also; and that, if the former had for predecessors Fichte, Schelling, Hegel, and Krause, St. Theresa, St. John de la Cruz, and the inspired and ecstatic Father Miguel de la Fuente followed, as their model, Tauler and others of the Germans. In saying this, however, it was not my intention to deny the claims of any of these mystical writers as founders of their school in Spain, but only to recognize, in this unbroken transmission of doctrine, the progressive continuity of European civilization.

For the purpose of carrying forward my undertaking, I read and studied with ardor every Spanish book on devotion, asceticism, and mysticism that fell into my hands, growing every day more charmed with the richness of our literature in such works; with the treasures of poetry contained in them; with the boldness and independence of their authors; with the profound and delicate observation, in which they excel the Scottish school, that they display in examining the faculties of the soul; and with their power of entering into themselves, of penetrating to the very centre of the mind, in order there to behold God, and to unite themselves with God, not therefore losing their own

personality, or their capacity for an active life, but issuing from the ecstasies and ravishments of divine love more apt than before for every work that can benefit the human species, as the steel is more finely tempered, polished, and bright after it has burned in the fires of the forge.

Of all this, on its most poetic and easily understood side, I wished to give a specimen to the Spanish public of to-day, who had forgotten it; but, as I was a man of my epoch, a layman, not very exemplary as regards penitential practises, and had the reputation of a freethinker, I did not venture to undertake doing this in my own name, and I created a theological student who should do it in his. I then fancied that I could paint with more vividness the ideas and the feelings of this student by contrasting them with an earthly love; and this was the origin of **"Pepita Jiménez."** Thus, when it was farthest from my thoughts, did I become a novelist. My novel had, therefore, the freshness and the spontaneity of the unpremeditated.

The novels I wrote afterward, with premeditation, are inferior to this one.

"Pepita Jiménez" pleased the public, also, as I have said, by its transcendentalism.

The rationalists supposed that I had rejected the old ideals, as my hero casts off the clerical garb. And the believers, with greater unanimity and truth, compared me with the false prophet who went forth to curse the people of Israel, and without intending it exalted and blessed them. What is certain is that, if it be allowable to draw any conclusion from a story, the inference that may be deduced from mine is, that faith in an all-seeing and personal God, and in the love of this God, who is present in the depths of the soul, even when we refuse to follow the higher vocation to which He would persuade and solicit us—even were we carried away by the violence of mundane passions to commit, like Don Luis, almost all the capital sins in a single day—elevates the soul, purifies the other emotions, sustains human dignity, and lends poetry, nobility, and holiness to the commonest state, condition, and manner of life. (pp. 13-16)

Juan Valera, "Author's Preface to the First American Edition," in his Pepita Jiménez *(copyright, 1886, D. Appleton and Company), Appleton, 1886 (and reprinted in* Pepita Jimenez *by Juan Valera;* A Happy Boy *by Bjornsterne Bjornson;* Skipper Worse *by Alexander L. Kielland, P. F. Collier & Son Company, 1917, pp. 11-17).*

THE CRITIC   (essay date 1891)

What we really have in **'Doña Luz'** is a simple story and a most extraordinarily delicate and pure style. One gets an impression of diffusiveness, here and there, and does not wholly wonder at the excisions made by Valera's French translators on the ground that his stories contained 'trop de théologie.' Some life-like touches show that modern Spanish politics is not so different from the article we are familiar with, in point of local 'bosses' and their intrigues. The heroine's character is one of gracious strength, and throughout she is an attractive figure. If the book has none of those vigorous strokes that characterize the leading contemporary novelists of Spain, it is certainly saved from the grossness into which they too often fall. Its main charm is its style, and that cannot be wholly preserved in a translation. . . . Valera's chief literary significance is as a critic, a stylist; that a writer who is only incidentally a novelist could have produced **'Pepita Jiménez,' 'Doña Luz,'** and **'El Comendador Mendoza,'** is at once a proof of his versatility, and a hint at the fecundity and power of the men who are the Spanish novelists *par excellence.*

> *"Valera's 'Doña Luz,"* in The Critic (© The Critic 1891), Vol. 18, No. 379, April 4, 1891, p. 178.

WILLIAM DEAN HOWELLS (essay date 1891)

[*A pioneer and leading advocate of realism in American literature, Howells admired Valera as a psychological realist though concluding that* Pepita Jiménez *falls short of being true to human experience.*]

[A] Spanish novelist of our day, whose books have given me great pleasure, . . . boldly declares himself, in the preface to his *Pepita Ximenez* [see excerpt above], "an advocate of art for art's sake." I heartily agree with him that it is "in very bad taste, always impertinent and often pedantic, to attempt to prove theses by writing stories," and yet I fancy that no reader whom Señor Valera would care to please could read his *Pepita Ximenez* without finding himself in possession of a great deal of serious thinking on a very serious subject, which is none the less serious because it is couched in terms of delicate irony. If it is true that "the object of a novel should be to charm through a faithful representation of human actions and human passions, and to create by this fidelity to nature a beautiful work," and if "the creation of the beautiful" is solely "the object of art," it never was and never can be solely its effect as long as men are men and women are women. If ever the race is resolved into abstract qualities, perhaps this may happen; but till then the finest effect of the "beautiful" will be ethical and not aesthetic merely. . . . What is it that delights us in this very *Pepita Ximenez,* this exquisite masterpiece of Señor Valera's? Not merely that a certain Luis de Vargas, dedicated to the priesthood, finds a certain Pepita Ximenez lovelier than the priesthood, and abandons all his sacerdotal hopes and ambitions, all his poetic dreams of renunciation and devotion, to marry her. That is very pretty and very true, and it pleases; but what chiefly appeals to the heart is the assertion, however delicately and adroitly implied, that their right to each other through their love was far above his vocation. In spite of himself, without trying, and therefore without impertinence and without pedantry, Señor Valera has proved a thesis in his story. They of the Church will acquiesce with the reservation of Don Luis's uncle the Dean that his marriage was better than his vocation, because his vocation was a sentimental and fancied one; we of the Church-in-error will accept the result without any reservation whatever; and I think we shall have the greater enjoyment of the delicate irony, the fine humor, the amusing and unfailing subtlety, with which the argument is enforced. In recognizing these, however, in praising the story for the graphic skill with which Southern characters and passions are portrayed in the gay light of an Andalusian sky, for the charm with which a fresh and unhackneyed life is presented, and the fidelity with which novel conditions are sketched, I must not fail to add that the book is one for those who have come to the knowledge of good and evil, and to confess my regret that it fails of the remoter truth, "the eternal amenities" which only the avowed advocates of "art for art's sake" seem to forget. It leaves the reader to believe that Vargas can be happy with a woman who wins him in Pepita's way; and that is where it is false both to life and to art. For the moment, it is charming to have the story end happily, as it does, but after one has lived a certain number of years, and read a certain

number of novels, it is not the prosperous or adverse fortune of the characters that affects one, but the good or bad faith of the novelist in dealing with them. Will he play us false or will he be true in the operation of this or that principle involved? I cannot hold him to less account than this: he must be true to what life has taught me is the truth, and after that he may let any fate betide his people; the novel ends well that ends faithfully. (pp. 82-6)

> *William Dean Howells, in a chapter in his* Criticism and Fiction, *Harper and Brothers, 1891, pp. 82-91.**

GEORGE SAINTSBURY (essay date 1892)

[*Saintsbury's opening statement in his review of the English edition of* Pepita Jiménez *is disputed and qualified by a critic writing in* The Westminster Review *(see excerpt below).*]

There is no doubt at all that [*Pepita Jiménez*] is one of the best stories that have appeared in any country of Europe for the last twenty years. The excellence of the manners-painting may perhaps strike one "more than [critical] reason" because it is somewhat unfamiliar; there can be no such disturbing influence in judging the characters. The skill with which the hero and his not in the least *niais* innocence are drawn is prodigious, and the slighter but not less characteristic and rather unexpected figure of his father deserves hardly less commendation. Nor, though the heroine can hardly be said to appear directly at all save in the central scene, is she less ingeniously presented to the reader. There is no mistake about this book. (p. 120)

> *George Saintsbury, "Literature and the Drama: Literature," in* The New Review (© TNR Publications, Ltd., London), Vol. VI, No. 33, January, 1892, pp. 112-22.*

THE WESTMINSTER REVIEW (essay date 1892)

There is no book-critic whose opinion has more weight with us than Mr. Saintsbury's; but in this case his eulogy seems to us to be somewhat extravagant. We willingly admit that *Pepita Jimenez* is a good novel . . . but between that and being one of the best in Europe during the last twenty years there is a wide margin. . . . To begin with, a young *séminariste* is not, to us, a *persona grata* as the hero of a love story. There is something sickly and uncomfortable (if we may be allowed such a homely word) in a hero who has to be wooed like a modest maiden, and won by sap and mine. Then the tale is told by means of letters—always an unsatisfactory method—and here the letters are from the young shaveling himself (he has received the tonsure) to his uncle, who is also his spiritual director, and head of the seminary where he has received his education and the minor Orders. Thus the tone of the letters has a painfully sacerdotal ring—*ça sent la sacristie.* On the other side of the account, it must be admitted that "Don Luis" is by nature a fine, spirited, lad; his instincts are brave and manly, though warped by his training. His self-revelations, in his letters and journals, are wonderfully natural; the struggle between the promptings of his fiery Spanish temperament, and the quietism superinduced by the revered teachings of a lifetime, is most skilfully depicted, and the gradual triumph, of healthy human feeling over the monkish mysticism in which he has been steeped, is wonderfully set forth. The book, too, gains a certain glamour from the unfamiliar atmosphere of provincial Spanish manners which pervades it.

As for "Pepita" herself, she is *entrevue,* rather than actually put on the stage. Her simplicity, her goodness, her retired habits, and her winning, dazzling, beauty, are in everybody's mouth, but her outlines are a little vague; she is surrounded by a sort of mysterious halo, and the reader cannot quite make up his mind what manner of woman she really is, till, in the great scene which brings about the *dénouement*—is, in truth, itself the *dénouement*—she reveals herself, and stands confessed, a loving, passionate, woman. This scene will, we fear, lose her in the estimation of many English readers, and condemn the book into the bargain. But it must be pleaded, in extenuation of poor Pepita's frailty, that she was forced to the employment of *les grands moyens;* nothing less would have overcome the holy scruples and the blushing chastity of her timid adorer. The father of Don Luis is a most successful bit of characterisation. His light *insouciance* towards all moral and religious questions, his *bonhomie* and thorough manliness, make him not only a pleasant, amusing, personage in himself, but a capital foil for his son. Though we cannot rate this clever sketch of contemporary Spanish manners as a thing apart— one of the great masterpieces of the age—. . . we are not insensible to its merits. (pp. 221-22)

> *"Belles lettres: 'Pepita Jimenez',"* in The West-minster Review, *Vol. 137, No. 2, February, 1892, pp. 221-22.*

COVENTRY PATMORE   (essay date 1892)

[*The themes of love and religion, which this English Catholic poet makes the focus of his remarks on* Pepita Jiménez, *are prominent concerns in his own works. One of Patmore's best-known collections,* The Angel in the House, *is a four-volume celebration of love in marriage.*]

[The] very same distinguishing vein which makes such plays as Calderon's *Life is a Dream,* and *The Wonder-working Magician* the astonishment and delight of every reader who comes upon them for the first time—an astonishment and delight almost like that of the acquisition of a new sense—this very same vein sparkles through and vivifies the modern novel *Pepita Jiménez.* Alike in Calderon and in this work of Juan Valera we find that complete synthesis of gravity of matter and gaiety of manner which is the glittering crown of art, and which out of Spanish literature is to be found only in Shakespeare, and even in him in a far less obvious degree. It is only in Spanish literature, with the one exception of Dante, that religion and art are discovered to be not necessarily hostile powers; and it is in Spanish literature only, and without any exception, that gaiety of life is made to appear as being not only compatible with, but the very flower of that root which in the best works of other literatures hides itself in the earth, and only sends its concealed sap through stem and leaf of human duty and desire. The reason of this great and admirable singularity seems mainly to have been the singular aspect of most of the best Spanish minds towards religion. With them, religion has been, as it was meant to be, a human passion. . . . (pp. 91-2)

Pepita Jiménez is essentially a "religious novel," none the less so because it represents the failure of a good young aspirant to the priesthood to attain a degree of sanctity to which he was not called, and depicts the working in his aspirations of a pride so subtle as to be very venial, though, in some degree, disastrous. . . . One of the many points in which Catholic philosophy shows itself superior to the philosophy of Protestant religionists in the knowledge of the human mind is its distinct

recognition of the fact that there are as many degrees of human capacity for holiness as for any other kind of eminence, and that for most men a very moderate degree of spirituality is the utmost for which they are entitled to hope. (p. 92)

That disgusting abortion, the English "religious novel," would have made the enthusiastic young deacon relapse into despair and profligacy, instead of letting him marry the pretty girl who had turned him from his supposed "vocation," and caused him to live an exemplary, conscientious, and religious life as a country gentleman and farmer of his own land. . . .

A most important consequence of the human character of Spanish faith, a character manifest alike in the religious philosophy of the times of Calderon and of those of Juan Valera, is the utter absence of the deadly Manicheism which is the source of modern "nicety" in that portion of literature and art which does not profess, like French, and, in great part, American literature and art, to have abandoned all faith and real decency. (p. 93)

In consequence of the characteristics I have endeavoured to indicate, this novel, though expressly "religious" in its main theme and most of its details, is as "natural," concrete, and wholesomely human and humanly interesting as one of Sir Walter Scott's. There is in it no sense of dislocation or incompatibility between the natural and the spiritual. From the dainty, naive, innocently coquettish, and passionate Pepita, who is enraged by her lover's pretensions to a piety which, though she is devoted to her beautifully adorned "Infant Jesus," she cannot understand, and in which she sees only an obstacle to the fulfilment of her love for him, to the saintly ecclesiastic, who, almost from the first, sees the incapacity of his pupil, Don Luis, for the celibate heights to which he aspires, but who understands life in all its grades too well to look upon his strivings and his "fall," as Don Luis at first esteems it, with other than a good-humoured smile, all is upon one easy ascending plane and has an intelligible unity. Valera has taken no less care with and interest in the subordinate characters than the principals in the story. They are all true and vivid and unique in their several ways, and we have the most complete picture of a very foreign world without the slightest drawback of strangeness or want of verisimilitude. (p. 94)

> Coventry Patmore, *"A Spanish Novelette,"* in The Fortnightly Review, *Vol. LII, No. CCCVII, July 1, 1892, pp. 91-4.*

JAMES FITZMAURICE-KELLY   (essay date 1908)

Valera is a bland and disinterested spectator, to whom life is a brilliant, diverting comedy. He had lived much, reflected long, and seen through most people and most things before committing himself to the delineation of character. To the end of his life he never learned the trick of construction, but he was a born master of style and had an unsurpassed power of ingratiation. . . . Though he has no prejudices to embarrass him, he has a rare dramatic sympathy with every mental attitude, and this keen, intelligent comprehension lends to all his creative work a savour of universality which makes him—of all modern Spanish novelists—the most acceptable abroad. Yet, despite his sceptical cosmopolitanism, which is by no means Spanish, Valera is an authentic Spaniard of the best age in his fusion of urbanity and authoritative insight. This politely incredulous man of the world is profoundly interested in mysticism, and still more in its practical manifestations. Nothing human is alien to him, and nothing is too transcendental to escape criticism. (pp. 243-44)

Patmore praises *Pepita Jiménez* as an example of 'that complete synthesis of gravity of matter and gaiety of manner which is the glittering crown of art, and which, out of Spanish literature, is to be found only in Shakespeare, and even in him in a far less obvious degree' [see excerpt above]. Patmore has almost always something striking to say, and even his critical paradoxes are interesting. We have no means of knowing how far his Spanish studies went, but we may guess that his acquaintance with Spanish literature was perhaps not very wide, and not very deep. As regards *Pepita Jiménez* his verdict is conspicuously right: it is conspicuously wrong with respect to Spanish literature as a whole. The perfect blending of which he speaks is as rare in Spain as elsewhere. In Valera it is the result of deliberate artistic method; his gravity is a necessity of the situation; his gaiety is rooted in his sceptical politeness. . . . [In] his novels Valera strikes no attitude of impertinent or sublime condescension. He analyses his characters with a subtle and admirably patient delicacy.

A hostile critic might perhaps urge that Valera's novels are too much alike; that *Doña Luz* is cast in the same mould as *Pepita Jiménez*, that Enrique is a double of Luis, and so forth. There is some truth in this. Valera does repeat the situations which interest him most, but so does every novelist; his treatment differs in each case, and is logically consistent with each character. There is more force in the objection that he overcharges his books with episodical arabesques which, though masterly *tours de force*, retard the development of the story. Now that we have them, we should be sorry to lose the brilliant passages in which the quintessence of the great Spanish mystics is distilled; but it is plainly an error of judgment to assign them to Pepita. However, this objection applies less to *Doña Luz* than to *Pepita Jiménez*, and it applies not at all to *El Comendador Mendoza*—doubtless a transfigured piece of autobiography, both poignant and gracious in its evocation of a far-off passion. And in his shorter stories Valera often attains a magical effect of disquieting irony. Most authors write far too much, either from necessity or from vanity; and Valera, who was too acute to be vain, wasted his energies in too many directions and on too many subjects. Still he has improvised comparatively little in the shape of fiction, and, even in extreme old age, when the calamity of blindness had overtaken him, he surprised and enchanted his admirers with more than one arresting volume. Speaking broadly, the characteristics of the best Spanish art are force and truth, and in these respects Valera holds his own. Yet he is more complicated and elaborate than Spaniards are wont to be. His work is penetrated with subtleties and reticences; his force is scrupulously measured, and his truth is conveyed by implication and innuendo, never by emphasis nor crude insistency. Compared with his exquisite adjustment of word to thought, the methods of other writers seem coarse and brutal. You may refuse to recognise him as a great novelist, if you choose; but it is impossible to deny that he was a consummate literary artist. (pp. 244-46)

> *James Fitzmaurice-Kelly, "Modern Spanish Novelists" (originally a lecture delivered in a somewhat different form at University of Columbia in 1907), in his* Chapters on Spanish Literature, *Archibald Constable and Company Ltd., 1908, pp. 231-51.**

HAVELOCK ELLIS (essay date 1908)

[*In his collection of essays on Spanish life and culture,* The Soul of Spain, *Ellis provides a survey of Valera's major works.*]

If we ask why it is that Valera yet meets with so little recognition, I do not think the answer is far to find. He always stood outside the literary currents of his time. He was never a disciple in any school; he was never a master in any school. There were many literary fashions during his long life: romanticism, naturalism, decadentism, symbolism. All these currents successively carried away a large part of literary Spain. Zola and the naturalistic current, more especially, disturbed the literary equilibrium of Spain. . . . But from the first Valera remained serenely unaffected by this as by every other fashionable stream of tendency. "Human documents," he said, "were out of place in novels; their proper place was the hospital report or the asylum bulletin." Baudelaire, again, seemed to Valera perverse and incompletely human, while for Carducci, on the other hand, even when chanting the praise of Satan, he felt strong admiration because Carducci represents a vehement faith in human life and human destiny. In an article on **"La Moral en el Arte,"** written in old age, Valera attempted, not for the first time, to set forth his attitude in this matter. Perfect poetry, he argues,—using poetry in its widest sense, to cover all forms of creative literary art,—must exist for its own sake; it has no duty save to be sincere and to avoid affectation; it must never pretend to teach science; it must never attempt to inculcate morality. Yet at the same time he asserted with equal emphasis—careless whether or not there lay here any contradiction—that great art is always true and always moral. There is no discrepancy between morals and aesthetics, between the good and the beautiful. "Wisdom, beauty, and truth, when they attain perfection, coincide and mingle." (pp. 245-47)

It is easy to see how a writer who, in the practice of his art, as well as in theory, consistently maintained this attitude was little likely to win either the applause of the multitude or the admiration of the literary coteries. (p. 247)

He was not "academical," but there was another epithet sometimes applied to him which, rightly understood, may be accepted as fitting, and was by himself accepted. He was not "classical" in the narrow sense, though undoubtedly he experienced a vivid and sympathetic delight in Greek literature, nor was his serene optimism in the face of life that superficial cheerfulness which, by some curious misunderstanding, is commonly supposed to mark the paganism of antiquity. Valera's Hellenism, it is true, was less that of Pindar and Thucydides than the later Alexandrian and cosmopolitan type of Hellenism, that of Theocritus and the *Daphnis and Chloe* which he translated into Spanish. But he was none the less genuinely classical, and even in a double sense. He possessed by nature the simple strength and breadth, the love of fine surface and clear depth, the delicate taste and sense of measure, the tendency to combine the real and ideal harmoniously in presentation—instead of setting them in violently picturesque contrast—which marked ancient literature, and which therefore always seems to us classic, in opposition to romantic. He was, further, classic in a more narrow and national sense. He represented, more finely and more truly than any of his contemporaries, the best ancient traditions of Spanish literature. He was a genuine descendant of Cervantes. (pp. 248-49)

Valera's verse [in the collection *Poesías*] is of a deliberate and somewhat learned order, revealing the influence of the Greeks and also of the Italians. Leopardi is the poet whom he more especially recalls, and it has been said that he wrote like Leopardi even before he knew his work and became a passionate admirer of it. In this volume was fully revealed that Platonism which subtly penetrated the whole of his work. "Erotic Platonism,'' said Menendez y Pelayo, ''is the soul of Valera's amatory verses'': love is to him a continuous progress from beautiful bodies to beautiful souls, and thence to the idea of beauty itself, while he also hovers over the Platonic doctrine of reminiscence and Plotinus's notion of nature as the mirror of the formula of beauty. Such Platonic suggestions occur again and again throughout his novels even in the unlikeliest places. In the Dedication of *Doña Luz* he seeks a moral for his story—notwithstanding his dislike of stories with morals—in a Platonic passage from Bembo, and in *Genio y Figura* he represents Rafaela la Generosa, after her bath, kissing her image in the mirror, and explaining the act in the spirit of a Platonism which would scarcely have presented itself to the courtesan of Cadiz.

It could not be expected that the public would be interested in the restrained and aristocratic art of the *Poesias.* Valera now turned to criticism for self-expression, but he always cherished a love for poetry, and regarded himself as a poet even in his novels, while to the last, also, he was very susceptible to any praise of his verse. In the Preface which he wrote at Washington in 1885 for the collected edition of his *Romances, Canciones y Poesias,* he affirmed: ''The principal reason for writing is poetry. Writings become famous and immortal by their beauty and not by the truth they teach. The pretension of those who believe that it is possible to teach by writing is nearly always vain. The great masters of humanity write nothing, neither Christ, nor Sakyamuni, nor Pythagoras, nor Socrates.'' (pp. 252-54)

It was at this period of life, when he had reached full maturity, that Valera became, almost, it would seem, by accident, though his ambition had long pointed in this direction, a novelist. His earlier literary occupations, the whole course of his life, were admirably fitted to prepare him for the literary work which more than all others demands a wide and mature experience of the world. It seems to have been out of the sympathetic interest which the poet and artist in Valera felt towards mysticism, and in the inspiration which his style received from reading the old mystics, Luis de Granada and Saint Theresa, that *Pepita Jimenez* was slowly developed, although the sceptic and the cosmopolitan in Valera saved him from any undue insistence on this mystic interest. . . . The fine quality of the novel lies very largely in the delicate skill with which Valera has avoided the pitfalls which beset such a story, harmonising all the conflicting interests and impulses involved, and infusing the whole with the temper of his own mingled gaiety and dignity. (pp. 254-56)

In Pepita herself, who may almost be called the hero of the story, we meet at the outset one of the most typical of Valera's women. They are not generally in their first youth, but they retain the qualities of virginal youthfulness combined with the energy and experience of maturity. They belong to the country or to small country towns, sometimes to the country aristocracy, sometimes to the poorest elements of the population, not seldom they are illegitimate children, combining an aristocratic distinction with plebeian vigour; in any case they are represented as the finest flower of country life. Their skill and discretion is always emphasised as well as their physical energy. . . . [Valera] has chosen carefully selected types, occurring under special yet peculiarly Spanish conditions out of the beaten track. According to his method, he mingled the real and the ideal, certainly utilising—in *Juanita la Larga,* his most detailed portrait of a woman, very fully and precisely—his own observation and early reminiscence. The essential qualities of Valera's women correspond to the qualities we may see or

divine in the ordinary working-class women of Spain to-day, and the fundamental veracity of the types he presents is sufficiently evidenced by the likeness they reveal to the heroines of Cervantes and Tirso de Molina, of all Spanish writers those who have most faithfully presented the genuine Spaniard. (pp. 256-58)

Pepita Jimenez was quickly followed by *Doña Luz.* Here, indeed, though he writes in a less impersonal manner than in the earlier novel, [Valera] clings a little timidly to the same subject—the conflict between religion and love. . . . It is not a story which lends itself to the dramatic and effective situations of *Pepita Jimenez,* but it is developed with the same delicacy and skill,—indeed, perhaps in an even greater degree,—and takes high rank among Valera's books.

Las Ilusiones del Doctor Faustino marks a further progress along the path of freedom in narrative, and in Valera's tendency to give a more and more personal character to his books. This was not entirely a sound tendency, for it sometimes led to the introduction of a waywardly fantastic element as well as to many scarcely relevant digressions. *Doctor Faustino* is lengthier than usual; it is a series of loosely connected episodes, some of which for the first time show a love of incidents lying on the border of the mysterious, which in some later books, especially *Morsamor,* becomes pronounced and is associated with the weakest elements in his work. There is, however, a seriously symbolic idea running through *Las Ilusiones del Doctor Faustino.* The hero, a miniature Faust without supernatural accompaniments, represents the Spaniard of the contemporary generation, ''a man of noble and generous nature, though vitiated by a perverse education and by the environment in which he has lived.'' He combines the three defects most apt to afflict the educated middle-class Spaniard: pedantic philosophy, uncombined with energy for the tasks of life, political ambition with failure to distinguish true liberty from tumult and disorder, the mania of noble descent united with complete lack of aptitude for practical affairs. Apart from the charm of certain figures and episodes in it, the book thus has a serious interest as Valera's chief contribution to the criticism of contemporary Spanish conditions.

Valera's personality as an artist, as a master of the novel, was now firmly established, and in a number of shorter stories, at times *contes* somewhat in the manner of Voltaire, as well as in a constant succession of delightful essays, in which usually some new book or topic of the moment is made the excuse for discussing the most various subjects, his philosophy and moral personality now began to be clearly visible. As a literary critic of modern writers it can scarcely be said that Valera is at his best. A very courteous and considerate gentleman, who occupies a high social and intellectual position and knows everybody, is not likely to be an epoch-making critic. . . . [He] usually confined himself to the sometimes rather extravagant eulogy of minor writers, or else to classic books where he was at his best as a critic. Once, indeed, he had a famous controversy on poetry and metaphysics with the distinguished poet Campoamor, but, as Valera was careful to point out, their polemics were of a purely playful kind and revealed no violent difference of opinion. Campoamor defends the utility of poetry and metaphysics; Valera, in accordance with the principles he always maintained, affirms their inutility, and denies even to the drama the right of presenting moral lessons. As to metaphysics, Valera declares that he has read many metaphysical systems: they enchant him; he marvels at them; but they do not convince him that metaphysics is anything more than a science of pure luxury. Valera carried something of the same spirit of genial scepticism into all spheres of thought. We may perhaps say of him as he says of his heroine Calitea in **La Buena Fama,** "sometimes she doubted about everything, sometimes she believed a little, sometimes she believed nothing." He might have added that sometimes she believed everything, for Valera's attitude was inconsistent with contempt or indifference for any genuine human belief. He objected to call anything "fabulous," because, he said, "so bold and offensive a qualification can to-day be applied to hardly anything. There are no limits to the possible." So it was that when, in 1899, the hour of Spain's dejection in the war with the United States, Valera turned back to the days when Spain was great and wrote his **Morsamor,** the story of a Franciscan monk in Seville in the early sixteenth century, he introduced Mahatmas and the paraphernalia of occultism, which latterly acquired a peculiar fascination for him.

Valera, it has been said, was of the school of Montaigne and of Goethe; it might be added that both in thought and in morals his attitude was even closer to that of Renan. His scepticism was always tolerant, even when it could not be sympathetic, and always allied to the optimistic temper. "The Muse that has inspired me," he remarks in the prologue to his tales **De Varios Colores,** "is neither melancholy nor tragic, but joyous and cheerful, as is fitting to console me for my real griefs, and not to increase their weight by imaginary troubles." Valera remained a child of Spain, where, if the sinners have sometimes been grave, even the saints have often been gay, as they felt that it befitted them to be.

Valera's practical moral attitude towards his fellow-men, what he himself called his Panphilism, is well illustrated by the *conte,* somewhat in the manner of Voltaire, called **"Parsondes,"** published in the volume of *Cuentos, Dialogos y Fantasias.* . . . This delightful *conte moral,* in which Valera playfully set forth the moral temper which all his work reveals, may perhaps recall *L'Abbesse de Jouarre,* in which Renan, also in old age, pointed a not dissimilar moral, while we may remember how Goethe, even in youth, had been impressed by the saying of the humane and yet austere Thraseas: *Qui vitia odit homines odit,* He who hates vices hates mankind. (pp. 258-65)

Two novels—*Juanita la Larga* and *Genio y Figura*—which belong to the most mature period of Valera's art deserve special mention, because they stand in the first rank of his work. *Juanita la Larga,* the history of a young country girl who by her own sterling personal qualities surmounts all the difficulties in her path, is a minute and delightful picture of rural Andalusian life, avowedly founded on reminiscences of a childhood and youth spent in the province of Cordova. In the preface Valera remarks, indeed, that he scarcely knows whether the book is or is not a novel, for he is here a historian rather than an inventive novelist. *Juanita la Larga* differs from nearly all Valera's books by presenting almost exclusively the lives of simple and uncultivated persons, presenting them indeed graciously, harmoniously, humorously, without any of the crudity which was constitutionally alien to Valera's temperament, but yet with a realism which proves that, whatever his dislike of the French naturalistic novel, he was still true to the traditions of the Spanish novel. For in the fundamental sense the Spanish novelists, with Cervantes at their head, have always been realists, in the same way in which in England Fielding and Defoe were realists.

The same realism, combined with the same wholesome and joyous vision of human life in a more difficult situation, meet

us in *Genio y Figura,* the last in date of Valera's great novels, the most mature, the most daring, perhaps the finest. It is the story of a woman who, like Juanita, and with similar high qualities of intelligence and character, though not the same ideals of conventional morality, springs from nothing and slowly living down social disapprobation wins general esteem and respect. . . . [*Genio y Figura* is] a novel in which Valera has put the most personal and mature spirit of his wisdom and humanity, a novel in which realism and poetry are wrought together with an art and a charm that may well entitle it to rank as a masterpiece. (pp. 266-69)

It has already been necessary to point out that Valera stood a little aloof and alien from the most popular men and movements of his time. He was not a partizan, he was too wise and clearsighted to be a fanatic even on behalf of the causes he believed in. Galdos, his contemporary as a novelist, though much younger in years, has again and again aroused the enthusiasm of the more progressive Spanish public who, except when *Pepita Jimenez* was published, have always been unresponsive to the wisdom of Valera. Blasco Ibáñez, the Valencian, the latest of the really significant novelists of Spain, is still farther away from the spirit of Valera. Rough, vigorous, not always even grammatical, sometimes crudely naturalistic, sometimes breaking out into impassioned lyricism, always an uncompromising revolutionist, aggressive and combative, ardently concerned with social problems, and a faithful painter of the common people whose life he knows so well, Blasco Ibáñez is a great force in literature, but he is far indeed from the sunny and serene Greek temper of Valera.

"I have always been inspired," Valera once wrote, "by the pure love of beauty." In a certain sense his novels have the quality of poetry, and it is not surprising that many authoritative Spanish critics of to-day are inclined to deny to him any high place as a novelist. He is too cold and correct, they say; his characters speak as he would himself speak; he is more concerned with expressing himself than with creating original types, or objectively describing the real people of the real world around him. . . . There is a certain amount of truth in these criticisms. Yet Valera is in little need of apology; his books are their own sufficient justification; they constitute an achievement in Spanish literature. The Spanish genius, though never gross and sensual, is sometimes sombre and violent. But if it burns smokily in its lower ranges, in its higher reaches it bursts into gay and lucent flame. It is so in Velazquez; it is so in Cervantes. Valera is not indeed with these men; his fine superficies and breadth are not accompanied by the passion and intensity needed for self-realisation in the highest original achievement. But he has the temperament of these supreme men, their vision, their clarity, their serenity, their humanity. His best works are a fine and permanent manifestation of the Spanish spirit, and the personality that produced them is even finer than the works. (pp. 270-72)

Havelock Ellis, "Juan Valera," in his The Soul of Spain *(reprinted by permission of Francois Lafitte), Archibald Constable & Co., 1908, pp. 244-72.*

L. A. WARREN (essay date 1929)

Moderation and harmony dominate in Valera. These qualities are supreme in Italian and Greek art and Valera is the most classical of Spanish writers. His novel **Doña Luz** deals with the same religious question as **Pepita Jiminez:** the love of a priest for a woman. Valera treats this matter partly because when these books were written in the 'seventies the liberal revolution had brought the social side of religious matters into discussion, and partly because with his mystical feeling and with the blending of divine and sensuous love in his own character he was eminently suited to handle the subject.

What makes this novel readable and enjoyable? Is it readable and enjoyable? To the general public I should say not, for it is an acquired taste. A few with classic feeling and a liking for literature will have the taste for Valera's novels but the general public will not. There is nothing violent or stimulating about a Valera novel. Neither in *Pepita* nor *Doña Luz* is the plot brought to a crisis; in *Pepita* the hero had not definitely entered orders and was not definitely committed; in *Doña Luz* the hero is a priest, but the two disengage from each other in time without any direct love-making. There are no strong situations, no jagged edges, everything is smoothly rounded off in gentle curves and softened by his mellow style; it is like a layer of snow concealing and covering up harshnesses and angularities. And so the book flows on gently with smooth gracefulness. It is like being put to bed on soft cushions and lulled with sweet music and the scent of flowers. There is nothing unwholesome or tainted in this novel, but there is voluptuousness; the tone lacks virility and energy. The work is idealistic, not realistic; there are no descriptions of scenery, houses, furniture, dresses; we are concerned only with the states of mind of ideal people—of two people, for the accessory figures are not important. The priest is not a living man, but a personified argument in Valera's mind between human and divine love.

There is but one character left, Doña Luz; she is the famous Valera woman who has given celebrity to his novels. It is said that she is not a real type, that no Spanish women are like her. This is so; her outward graces and charms are, of course, transferred to her from the outward graces and charms of Andalucian women. But her soul is constructed out of Valera's personality. She is endowed with the sensuous, the voluptuous, the religious and mystical feelings of his nature, and his classic sense for proportion, harmony, grace and elegance. She is not given his more masculine qualities such as his intellectual powers and his delicious irony. And as she was created out of a Spaniard and an Andalucian, she *is* Spanish and Andaluz. The Valera woman, however, gives the impression of being more Italian than Spanish. Valera is a mystic and the division in his mind between celestial and terrestrial love is not very evident. The priest's conception of Doña Luz is of a Raphael Madonna. The religious feeling, as in Italian painting, is very close to sensuousness and the voluptuous. In general, Spanish religious feeling is ascetic and Italian sensuous. Compare Raphael with El Greco. But although Valera is sensuous and not ascetic, yet the Italian is concrete and practical and could not have the mystic sense of the love of God. Valera's mystic love of God, in the passages not reproduced in the French translation as being uninteresting, is almost Moslem. . . . (pp. 105-06)

With *Las ilusiones del doctor Faustino* Valera undertook a wider and more ambitious enterprise. (p. 107)

Valera constructs his typical nineteenth-century man externally from the men all round him, but his thoughts and feelings are his own. The hero is a poor, aristocratic, country hidalgo, who lives in an Andalucian village.

Valera's descriptions and accounts of life in the Andalucian country are always attractive and delightful. The country undergoes a certain transformation in his writing into something cheerful, bright and sunny; or else into something dreamy and idyllic. The small narrow society—the hidalgo, the priest, the indiano, the usurer, the chemist—figures agreeably. The boredom, the dullness, the intense petty rivalries and jealousies are not brought forward with their squalid ugliness as in Baroja, or to make tragic ruin of people and country, as in Picavea; this side of things is indicated and is mixed up in the picture which, on the whole, gives the impression of a quiet, leisurely, old-fashioned country life of health and happiness.

The hero has romantic ambitions of going forth and conquering the world; but he is a hidalgo and expects the world to fall at his feet. He has in him the spirit of unrest and adventure which made Don Quixote and the Conquistadores. The Conquistadores reached power, fame and glory by great deeds of arms. . . . But this hero—largely made up out of Valera himself—is an intellectual, reflective man who dreams his time away with problems of philosophy and religion—spirit and matter, the natural and the supernatural, the finite and the infinite. (p. 108)

But religious and philosophical problems are among the hero's main interests; his ambition and career form another; his love affairs the third. These different interests are connected and intermingled. He has three love affairs. Valera is quite at his best when he deals with love. He has a great admiration for women and an intuitional grasp of their mentality. He has himself made love often, and over love-scenes especially can he throw the charm and glamour that he casts upon everything he writes. (p. 109)

Valera is not a great novelist, and his most ambitious effort is not one of the great novels of his country. Like most southerners, he is unimaginative. He has no sense of the grotesque; he lacks power; his plots are poor. His characters, men and women, are all variants of himself; they further lose in individuality and the whole novel in objectivity by everybody talking in Valera's rich, artificial language. This perfect artificiality of the dialogues at once removes his novels from absolute reality to an ideal fancy land. There is not sufficient incident; the narrative is often held up by his discursiveness; his ideas, his religion, his reflectiveness and his supernatural ideal often impede the story. To such an extent is this so that large parts of his fiction are scarcely distinguishable from his essays. Valera, nevertheless, has written one first-rate novel, *El Comendador Mendoza*. He was inspired by a real story. The characters stand out and are individualized; the story holds one's attention; the narrative goes straight with directness and increasing speed from start to finish; there is scarcely an interruption, no meandering or digressions; incidents and situations follow quickly one after another. The whole is rapid, picturesque, full of liveliness, feeling and colour. It has some slight resemblance to *El sombrero de tres picos*.

Valera's lack of intensity is sufficient to distinguish him from the genuine Spanish mystics. He is platonic; but love of comfort and good things prevent him from being a pure Platonist and Hellenist. He is pagan and Andalucian in love of gay material life; Hellenist and Platonist in love of harmony, of beauty, of the ideal. These two tendencies combined make him a highly civilized hedonist and give to his writings a quality of their own unique in European literature. (pp. 110-11)

L. A. Warren, "The Realists," in his Modern Spanish Literature: A Comprehensive Survey of the Novelists, Poets, Dramatists and Essayists from the Eighteenth Century to the Present Day, Vol. I, *Brentano's Ltd, 1929, pp. 94-151.**

EDITH FISHTINE [later EDITH F. HELMAN] (essay date 1933)

A critic who was at once a humanist, a classicist, and an impressionist was indeed a rarity in Spain and most of Valera's contemporaries were aware of his superiority. Unanimously they declared him Spain's greatest prose writer since Cervantes. (p. 100)

The most valuable and lasting elements in his work seem rather to be his elevated conception of art, and his firm and stable esthetic principles stressing the significance of form and the importance of such qualities as symmetry, restraint and good taste. Firmly grounded on these clear and unchanging principles, Valera consistently opposed the excesses and enthusiasms of three successive generations of writers: in the Romantics their unbridled imagination and exaggerated individualism; in the realists, their servility to science, their limitation of art to representational accuracy, their depressing portrayal of life; in the modernists, their too close dependence on French models, and their worship of novelty for its own sake. In a period of experimentation and shifting values in art, of obscure symbolism, of excessive freedom in expression, Valera's sound doctrine of lucidity and purity, of tradition and balance, may prove extremely useful. (p. 105)

His novels are simple stories, delightfully told; but Valera was too self-absorbed to be able to create characters. For criticism he was more highly endowed, but even here he was only an amateur, hampered by his insufficient will, his exquisite urbanity, and his ironic inconclusiveness.

But criticism was Valera's surest calling. Not that he wielded the critic's scalpel with great force; his manner was always suave, but he alone among his contemporaries wrote criticism that was purely literary, for he was convinced that it was not incumbent upon the critic to examine or refute the doctrine of a work, be it religious, social or political. . . . But perhaps Valera'a detachment is merely the result of his lack of interest in the causes espoused, issues discussed, and doctrines expounded in the works of his more earnest contemporaries. Valera alone was moderate in almost all his censure and praise; with all his tepid praise, to only few did he grant warrants of immortality, of the moderns only to Leopardi, and possibly Quintana and Rivas. . . . Valera could hardly wax enthusiastic over the prosaic verse of Campoamor or the mediocre plays of López de Ayala; and from a just estimate of the most important literary form of the period, the novel, he was kept by his petty prejudice against the disagreeable or depressing in a work of fiction. He never did penetrate Galdós' art of impregnating the most humble and lowly character with imperishable beauty, or *Clarín's* power of outlining with a few forceful strokes an unforgettable individual; Valera's sensibility was not attuned to realistic art; to the originality of both these novelists Valera would have preferred an elegant amenity. And Valera, finally, had precise esthetic principles upon which his opinions were based. But if these principles helped him to tell infallibly the good from the bad, they also restricted his artistic appreciation to one kind of art, that of classical Greece and of the Renaissance; to the beauty of primitive, medieval and modern art he remained forever refractory. (pp. 107-08)

A typical essay of Valera's is without plan or order; its theme is a tenuous thread, often lost sight of, which holds together numerous sensations, perceptions, opinions and ideas. A review consists of an analysis of the work at hand, occasionally some interpretation, but rarely any incisive judgment. The main thing is the untiring display of ingenuity, extensive information—Valera, though questioning the validity of the new, nevertheless closely followed every literary and philosophic current—, all that he had gleaned from his wide reading, glints of humor, sense and nonsense intimately united, savory language and polished style. The method of some of his essays might be indicated graphically by a spiral, the subject being the axis, and the course of the essay receding from and approaching to that point. Any pretext may take him far afield, and he weaves a most elaborate network, a magic web, in which the reader feels hopelessly entangled, but from which Valera blithely emerges with incredible facility. The reader is delighted with this intellectual game, until he tries to separate the serious from the jocular, until he attempts to reduce to a system the scattered impressions and opinions, rereading the same essay many times, fearing that the seductive manner has made him overlook the substance, only to conclude upon the last reading that the substance is extremely frothy, be it ever so delicious. And the reader is not exhilarated as he might be by the creative energy of a great mind; he is entertained, charmed, and perhaps cheered by Valera's unfailing optimism. . . . Or, again, the reader first attracted by Valera's perspicuous and subtle reasoning, may be disconcerted, even irritated in the end, by his interminable qualifications and reservations, and he may conclude that Valera is perhaps only a delightful trifler, and nothing more.

Valera's letters and articles reveal above all his incapacity to concentrate, to sustain interest in any subject long enough to gain an intimate knowledge of it. He never overcame his native indolence and inconstancy; his rigorous esthetic does indeed stand in striking contrast to his general indecision and wavering. He made no pretense to serious scholarship; extensive documentation, dry profundities in an article would be a crime of *lèse-critique,* since the important thing was to divert oneself and one's reader. His essays, like his poems, stories, dialogues and novels, are just variations on the main theme—Valera. From his earliest prose writings, and ever thereafter, he is the egotist, the intellectual epicure and dilettante, whose sole occupation is the amusing play of his mind with ideas and sensations. There is no logic in his critical essays; logic is dull. There is no passion; passion is vulgar. There is no enthusiasm; enthusiasm is only for the naive and unenlightened. There *are* convictions: no culture has come up to that of the Hellenes, there has been no greater philosopher than Plato, no greater poet than Homer. Valera never lost interest in his Greek: late in life he planned to translate with Menéndez y Pelayo *The Persians* and the *Prometheus* of Aeschylus, but Menéndez had finished his share before Valera had even begun. He did translate *Daphnis and Chloe,* and in spirit he was indeed far closer to the graceful romances of Heliodorus and Longus, and to the pastoral poetry of Theocritus, than to the austere genius of Greek tragedy. The scene of *Asclepigenia,* Valera's masterpiece, is Alexandria of the fifth century A.D., although not a few of its allusions are to the Krausists of Madrid in the middle of the last century. . . . (pp. 108-10)

Some of Valera's other convictions are that epic poems can be written only among primitive peoples; didactic poems can be written only early in the history of a nation, while science, philosophy and poetry are still one; human intelligence has been substantially the same through the ages, and the more elaborate material surroundings of modern times have made man neither wiser nor happier; finally, the artist is concerned only with the creation of beauty, and the beauty of art is higher and has a greater validity than that of nature. Beauty resides in the mind, which elicits supra-sensible beauty from sensuous or earthly objects, and gives universality to what is most individual or particular. The artist must have native talent, but must as well be self-critical and technically skilful. Good taste becomes a shibboleth, and by good taste is meant discrimination in the choice of subject matter, and restrained and polished expression.

Around these basic convictions Valera wrote numerous articles, always in the same manner, ironical and frivolous. But his frivolity and cheerfulness are particularly gratifying in a period in which the somber elements predominated; and so are his lightness, dexterity, love of knowledge and art, in a period devoid of fancy, grace, poetry and taste. His independent liberalism stands in singular contrast to the rabid absolutism and democratic demagogy of the times, his tranquil pyrrhonic attitude of mind to the passion of the neo-Catholics on the one hand and to the gloomy doubt of the positivists on the other; his literary idealism to the uncompromising realism of Pereda and *Clarín* (in his novels), and to the half understood naturalism of Pardo Bazán, and his volatile grace, lambent charm, simple naturalness to the heaviness and fustian of his contemporaries. Of the ideal triad, ingenuity, grace and force, Valera had ingenuity and grace, but lacked force; a deficiency which he shared with his contemporaries, and which caused him to say with the most weary and sullen of them, when Spain lost Cuba: "It is a pity, but nothing can be done about it; Spain is exhausted and must rest."

It is this lack of energy which kept Valera from becoming a really effective critic. His greatest service as a critic lies perhaps in having brought some intellectual light into a dense darkness, some pregnant facts into a dismal ignorance, some comeliness to literary expression; in having opened attractively new vistas to the public at large: European, South American, contemporary Spanish, literature and thought; in having encouraged young writers and scholars; in having insisted always on the prime importance of form, giving himself, in all that he wrote, a perfect example of classical language that is not archaic or affected, of beautiful style, natural, simple and flowing; and finally, in having recorded for posterity the rich and delightful experience of his mind with the books of many ages. (pp. 110-11)

> *Edith Fishtine [later Edith F. Helman], in her* Don Juan Valera, the Critic *(copyright 1933 by Edith Fishtine; reprinted by permission of the author), Bryn Mawr, 1933, 120 p.*

SHERMAN EOFF (essay date 1938)

[*In contrast with most criticism treating Valera as an author of essentially realistic narratives, Eoff discusses the romantic, exotic, and fantastic aspects of Valera's short stories.*]

In virtually every phase of Valera's writing the Orient receives an appreciable amount of attention. The number of writings is such that one is led to ask what attracted the author to this field of interest. A natural inference is that the Orient represents simply one of the many spheres of knowledge with which Valera casually concerned himself. In a way, this is true. . . . There was in Valera also, in addition to his curiosity, a patriotic desire to keep his country abreast of the times. He was aware of the Oriental renaissance which had taken place in Europe in the eighteenth and nineteenth centuries and wanted his own people to know the kind of literature that such writers as Voltaire and Gautier had given to France. He himself would serve as leader in encouraging the Oriental story in Spain. The question thus arises as to whether Valera used the Oriental story

as an instrument for the expression of ideas or whether he was interested in it purely for imaginative purposes. It has been intimated that the former is true, for Valera is commonly spoken of as a writer of tales after the manner of Voltaire, and some of his Oriental stories are cited as examples although no point is made of the Oriental tale as such. But an examination of Valera's writing shows that in turning to the Orient he followed an aesthetic and imaginative impulse greater than his curiosity or his desire to emulate other writers and far greater than a desire to express philosophic ideas. The remoteness of the East and the limited knowledge of its past offered him an opportunity to give free rein to his imagination and provided an outlet for a romantic vein which to a large extent has been either overlooked or ignored by students of Valera. (pp. 193-94)

Some of [Valera's] compositions indicate little more than a casual interest in the Orient although they do show a liking for exotic literature. Such are the translations, the two episodes from the *Mahabharata*, and the Japanese tales. Further, the fairy tale in verse (*Romance*) and *El pájaro verde* may be said to have only an incidental connection with the Orient, for though probably Oriental in origin, they were doubtless taken by Valera from local folk-lore and are significant for their fantastic element rather than for their Oriental appearance. The majority of the works, however, when taken together point to manifest generalizations. For one thing, most of them are either legends or historical tales with a mixture of fantasy and legend. For another, the most conspicuous theme is ideal beauty and ideal love. A favorite literary theme of Valera is thus found in the romantic background of the *leyenda*.

Throughout his life Valera manifested a liking for the legendary, the historical, and the fantastic. The prose short story more than any other kind of writing gave expression to this liking, although in his youth the author tried the story in verse. (pp. 194-95)

Not all Valera's tales are Oriental but he seems to enter with most enthusiasm into his story when under the influence of the East, and his best short stories are *Parsondes, El pájaro verde, Garuda o la cigüeña blanca*, and *Morsamor*, if the latter be considered a *cuento* instead of a novel. What attracted Valera to the Orient was its vague and legendary past, which had for him a strong poetic appeal. . . . Consequently, when the author directed his attention to the historical narrative, he found Oriental history more interesting than European. He was concerned with history solely for suggestive purposes and his imagination turned to what is unknown rather than to what is known about figures of the past. In reality he was more interested in legends and prehistory than in history itself. He affirmed that he lacked the patience for the documentation of historical novels, and this was probably true, although the vast reading evident from his discussion in "**Leyendas del antiguo Oriente**" indicates that it was more a question of interest than of patience. Valera did not attempt a historical novel based on careful investigation because he preferred a free hand in building up the historical characters of the past. The Orient gave him an excellent opportunity for this, while he felt that so much was known about European history that little was left for the imagination.

It was under such a historical inspiration that *Parsondes, Zarina*, and *Lulú* were written. *Parsondes* is the leading example offered to show Valera's resemblance to Voltaire in the short story. (pp. 195-96)

It is worthwhile to consider the source of this story. The somewhat discredited Greek historian Ctesias of Cnidus relates in his *Persica* a story of Parsondas and Nanarus which unmistakably furnished the framework for Valera's *Parsondes*. . . . (p. 197)

The essential change of Valera was to make a saintly and religious man of Parsondas and to point out a moral which is only suggested in the original: the futility of pride in one's own virtue as compared to the virtue of one's neighbor. What he did, then, was little more than embellish his source, using a language and style befitting the Orient and the remoteness of his subject. The main justification for a comparison of his story to the tales of Voltaire lies in its expression of antipathy to self-satisfied piety and the fact that it is possible to call the tale a *cuento filosófico*. . . . In any event, one can only believe that the author was more interested in telling an entertaining story than he was in the philosophic accompaniment. The fragment of history had appealed to his imagination and he simply dressed it up and passed it on to his readers.

A further recourse to ancient Iranian history is found in *Zarina,* whose title and heroine were in all probability also suggested by the fragments of the *Persica,* although the historical introduction obviously proceeds from various sources. Diodorus of Sicily in his *Bibliotheca Historica* repeats briefly Ctesias' account of Zarina, beautiful and daring ruler of the Scyths at the time that Astibaras was king of the Medes. There is another story in Ctesias, about Stryangaeus and Zarinaea. The three names Zarina, Astibaras, and Estrianges appear in Valera's *Zarina,* and the woman of whom the reader is given but a brief glimpse in the unfinished story, might easily have been inspired by the Scythian Zarina. *Lulú,* which has Scythia as a setting, was obviously written under the same inspiration as *Zarina.* Like several other stories of Valera it shows how the author proceeds from a scant historical basis to the realm of the imaginative, thus producing stories which more resemble legends than historical novels.

Morsamor is also referred to as a story in which Valera followed Voltaire. Describing as it does the travels and meditations of its hero, it is closer to Voltaire than is *Parsondes*. But *Morsamor* recalls several writings, particularly Goethe's *Faust,* and even *Don Quijote* and the romances of chivalry. . . . But more than anything else it is a tale of adventure and romance. . . . (pp. 197-98)

The author is obviously anxious that [*Morsamor*] entertain on the strength of its narrative alone. Seemingly he writes with most enthusiasm when under the spell of the Orient. . . . But nowhere is the satire of Voltaire in evidence, and the philosophic character of the story along with the attention given to occultism is purely secondary.

Gopa, more than the preceding examples, reminds one of Voltaire, because it serves for little more than to express the author's estimate of certain current philosophies. . . . Similarly, *Asclepigenia* serves as a vehicle for a philosophic presentation. But *Gopa* and *Asclepigenia* are philosophic dialogues rather than philosophic stories.

The influence of Voltaire upon Valera as a story-teller, therefore, should be minimized. The tendency to compare the two writers no doubt is due in part to the air of skepticism and humor frequently found in Valera. Valera himself recognized that he was likened to Voltaire on the basis of his habit of speaking in the same breath of the serious and the comic but considered the comparison as groundless. Certainly he was right as regards his stories. The statement of Pardo Bazán that Voltaire was Valera's master in the short story is a serious

mistake. It would be more accurate to say that Valera is like Théophile Gautier. Both writers are drawn to the nebulous past, both delight in resurrecting historical personages, often Oriental, and both write of ideal and phantom beauties. But Valera is much more moderate than Gautier both in style and his taste for exoticism. Further individual comparisons would probably be fruitless, but it is appropriate to remark that in the legendary and historical tale Valera showed his liking for a type of story that was characteristic of the Romantic period and very popular in Spain throughout the nineteenth century after the outbreak of Romanticism.

By means of the legend and tale Valera sets in a romantic frame what might be called his most cherished theme. His guiding literary principle is beauty. The sentiment expressed in his early poems to the effect that man is brought into the closest possible understanding of the universe through the contemplation and enjoyment of beauty may be said to attend the major part of Valera's creative writing. His characters are constantly longing for the realization of perfect beauty. To the men characters the supreme manifestation of beauty is woman; to the women, it is the enjoyment of an ideal love. While not always an obvious theme, the thought of ideal beauty and ideal love does find expression in Valera's novels. It is repeatedly dwelt upon in *Las ilusiones del doctor Faustino;* the most notable characteristic of Rafaela, in *Genio y figura,* is her inextinguishable yearning for an infinite love, which she hopes to find in death, having failed in life; and the poetic climax perhaps of *Doña Luz* is the monologue in which Padre Enrique laments the fact that God has allowed him to become enamoured of beauty in an individual and physical form instead of keeping his mind centered on the universal and divine beauty of the realm of ideas.

It is not necessary here to discuss the Platonism or neo-Platonism of Valera's conception of love and beauty, but it is interesting to note that the novelist pursues in some of his legends and tales the theme of ideal beauty together with an occasional reference to reminiscence which also brings Plato to mind. The theme is treated purely in the realm of fantasy, and it happens that in nearly every case the stories are Oriental. (pp. 199-201)

The best example of the theme of ideal love in Valera's legends is *Garuda o la cigüeña blanca*. . . . (p. 201)

This story is a mixture of the legendary, anecdotal, and novelistic. Although the last part is a modern tale, which the author may have heard in Austria, the first part and by far the best is undoubtedly Oriental in inspiration. Poldy, while thinking of the manner in which she has received the message of love, speaks of the swan of Leda, but the author probably has in mind the story of Nala and Damayanti, of which he was very fond, to judge from his frequent references to it. . . . Poldy further mentions a story from the *Arabian Nights* in which two genies meeting in the air agree to bring together a princess and a prince whom they just left in widely separated countries. These romantic stories in which two lovers living in widely separated lands eventually find in each other the realization of their dreams are common in Oriental literature. They appealed to Valera because they gave him an opportunity to dwell upon the subject of ideal love in a background of poetic fancy.

Closely associated with the idea of reminiscence is the author's speculation on the transmigration of souls, an idea with which he plays in a romantic and spiritualistic mood in *Las ilusiones del doctor Faustino.* (pp. 202-03)

From the standpoint of aesthetics, it matters little whether or not Valera believed in Platonic reminiscence or the transmigration of souls. The essential thing is that the ideas appealed to him as poetic possibilities because of the unknown spirit world which they suggest. . . . To a very important degree, Valera identifies beauty with mystery, vagueness, and remoteness. Thus it is that spiritualism, reminiscence, mysticism, occultism all serve a distinctly aesthetic purpose in his writings.

It seems clear then, in way of summary, that Valera's interest in the Orient proceeds primarily from his love for poetic and imaginative literature, particularly in narrative form. In some instances the story-teller resorts to specific Oriental sources: the Persian history of Ctesias as it is preserved in fragmentary form, the story of Nala and Damayanti from the *Mahabharata,* and the *Arabian Nights.* At other times the spell of the Orient is apparent and allusions to Oriental literature are frequent, notable among them, references to the *Ramayana* and Firdusi's *Shāh-Nāma.* The writings which the author produces under this inspiration show certain definite aspects of Romantic literature: love of mystery, vagueness, magic, supernaturalism and the world of spirits; dream beauties and the longing for ideal love; and a general liking for fantastic, legendary, and historical tales. Valera's occasional inclination toward romantic episodes in his novels is an acknowledged fact. Consider in this connection the mystery surrounding the birth of Doña Luz; a similar circumstance in *Mariquita y Antonio;* the liking for combats manifest in *Pepita Jiménez, Genio y figura,* and *Mariquita y Antonio;* various episodes of mystery and adventure in *Las ilusiones del Doctor Faustino.* On more than one occasion in the latter novel the author writes as though he were telling an outright ghost story, and neither his eventual explanation of the supernatural as being an illusion, nor his willingness for the novel to be considered philosophic and semicomic conceal the pleasure which he derives from romantic situations. One can readily believe that the spectres of Romanticism which he speaks of as clashing in his youth with his classic studies were never entirely expelled from his mind. The romantic tendency in his most famous novels, however, is at the most spasmodic and relatively unimportant. But it reaches a much fuller expression in his short compositions: to a certain extent in his narrative poems but chiefly in his prose stories. Whereas he thinks that the novel should restrict itself to the happenings of real life, he feels that the *cuento* may relate impossible and even absurd events as long as it is skillfully and artistically told. Hence he enters into the short story without the responsibility of realistic narration, and in the legend and tale finds outlet for a love of the fantastic and imaginative, which was strong in him throughout his life. He finds the Orient a most suitable background for his romantic writing, as is shown both by the number of his Oriental compositions and the frequency with which he clothes the theme of ideal love and ideal beauty in Oriental dress. It must be admitted that the romanticism of Valera is a mild type in keeping with his aversion for the extravagances of Romantic literature and his love for classic tranquility. It is often found also in combination with an atmosphere of erudition and intellectualism. But when a novelist can write with such evident pleasure and charm as Valera does in some of his tales and particularly in the episode of Morsamor and Urbási, the romantic side of his personality should not go unnoticed. (pp. 203-05)

> Sherman Eoff, "Juan Valera's Interest in the Orient," in Hispanic Review, *Vol. VI, No. 3, July, 1938, pp. 193-205.*

ROBERT E. LOTT   (essay date 1962)

[Lott is one of the principal critics writing on Valera's works.]

It is apparent that the strictly formal structure, in the sense of the sequential arrangement of events, of *Pepita Jiménez* is essentially different from that of *Don Quixote.* The *Quixote* is primarily based on the epistemological riddle of the Don Quixote-Sancho Panza antithesis: idealism versus materialism, humanistic learning versus the common sense of a peasant, monomania versus sanity. The contrast is greatly complicated by the multiple interactions of the two characters, and, although some critics now disagree with Salvador de Madariaga's theory of the sanchification of Don Quixote and the quixotification of Sancho, there is undoubtedly some harmonization of the antithesis. But in *Pepita Jiménez* there is no Sancho; the contrast between illusion and reality is primarily psychological and usually occurs within the protagonist's mind. The *Quixote* is episodic, with many subplots and by-stories, and gives a vast panorama of Spanish society. In its symphonic structure, interwoven leitmotifs and themes, almost infinitely amplified or modified, suggest the complexity of life itself. In each part there is a focal setting—the inn in the first part, the ducal palace in the second—, and the action, represented by the sallies of Don Quixote and Sancho, is offset by the counteraction, the return to the village. The structure of *Pepita Jiménez* is dramatic, since space and settings are secondary to the progressive development of the plot and the evolution of Luis de Vargas' character. Formally, the first half of the novel is one side of an exchange of letters between Don Luis and his uncle, the Dean. This one-sided epistolary form contributes greatly to the psychological validity of the protagonist (it necessitates much reading between the lines and probing into the motives behind the protagonist's thought processes), to the pleasing ambiguity of the novel (many initial concepts formed by the reader must be modified later), and to the subtle pastiche of ascetical-mystical and general *Siglo de Oro* language (it permits the direct representation of the parodied, stilted speech of the seminarian). The second part is regular third person narrative, supposedly written by the Dean, and there is a brief ironical epilogue, which, we are told, consists of extracts from Don Pedro's letters.

Yet, in thematic structure and basic purpose, Valera's novel is much closer to the *Quixote* than these differences might indicate. What Valera learned from Cervantes, broadly speaking, were techniques of parody and irony, and of the representation of the reality problem as it appears in the quixotic mind of Luis—all assimilated and toned down to match his more restrained and sophisticated style. Valera could not go to extremes in his parody of the seminarian without disrupting the carefully arranged balance between sincerity and irony. Valera avoided Cervantes' more drastic parodistic measures because he wanted to achieve greater subtlety and penetration and to depict, not a monomaniac, but a self-deceiver and false mystic. With his characteristic classical restraint, he refused to fall into a facile, peripheral imitation of Cervantes by interspersing his novel with obviously Cervantine phrases, as other Spanish novelists of the nineteenth century sometimes did. What we see in *Pepita Jiménez,* rather than a direct imitation, is a thoroughly assimilated utilization of Cervantine resources and techniques.

The major common purposes of Cervantes in *Don Quixote* and Valera in *Pepita Jiménez* may be reduced to those of parody and the treatment of the reality problem. In both novels literature is extremely significant, and both protagonists are profoundly affected by their readings. Don Quixote, from having read novels of chivalry, imitates them anachronistically in word and deed. Luis, from his reading of mystical and spiritual writings, imitates the mystics (although he lacks the proper ascetical preparation) and mimics their speech (*habla*), as well as that of preachers and theologians, while also reflecting his general knowledge of literature. Thus both protagonists are characterized by stilted speech—Don Quixote, markedly; Luis, subtly—and both often interpret reality, especially when placed in new situations, according to their readings. Each author exemplified in one man what he considered a common folly of his age, thus universalizing the implied criticism.

But, from the outset, there are essential differences in the two parodies. Cervantes' is of the obviously untrue novel of chivalry and even, as Ramiro de Maeztu has remarked, of the chivalric and adventurous spirit. And (although this is a much debated matter), it is still, I think, in the Catholic tradition. Valera's parody is undoubtedly anticlerical and anti-Catholic (though not bitterly so), for it is of the selection and training of candidates for the priesthood, and even of mysticism in general, since the false mystic, in a basically comic context, is allowed to parody the true Spanish mystics, for whom Valera, on other occasions, often expressed admiration. Even so, there is perhaps in each writer a common note of regret, of reluctant admiration for a world of lost beauty and ideals, and, what is of greater importance, each is carried far beyond the original parodistic purpose of his novel: Cervantes to ''. . . the modern genre of the critical novel, . . . a new integration of the critical and the imaginative, . . .''; Valera to a new synthesis of *Siglo de Oro* expression forms and traditions, refined by nineteenth-century sophistication and critical empathy, in his formulation of one of the earliest novels of modern adolescent psychology. Finally, the parody in each case is mitigated by the author's humanitarian sympathy for the protagonist and his appreciation of the positive values of what is parodied. (pp. 395-96)

The correct evaluation of the parody, reality problem, and ambiguity of each of the two novels is largely dependent upon the recognition of the author's irony, which in each case permeates the whole and provides unity. Cervantes' irony is an outgrowth of his sound humor and is, I believe, essentially constructive. But since Valera's irony is at least partly directed against the established order, it is basically of the destructive type, although softened by his humor and empathy. Among the ironical devices used by both Cervantes and Valera are the following: the use of concessive clauses and other qualifying remarks in characterizations, erudite periphrases, extended litotes, the juxtaposition of abstract and concrete or learned and popular phrases for humor, and the ironization of erudition in the pseudo-humanistic device (that someone else wrote the novel which the author is merely editing). (p. 399)

In addition to the ironical devices listed above, one finds in *Pepita Jiménez* other style features, allusions, and situations reminiscent of *Don Quixote*. These tend to corroborate the basic comparisons and contrasts between the two novels as I have tried to show them: the subtle parody, the ironical treatment of the reality problem, and the thematic structure of *Pepita Jiménez* compared with the more drastic and obvious parody and the structure of the *Quixote*, in which the reality problem, though having far greater philosophical significance, is perhaps of less psychological complexity, at least in the characterization of the protagonist. All these well-assimilated adaptations, however, are subjected to Valera's careful avoidance of affectation,

true classical restraint, and ironical-critical purposes within his parody of Luis as a false mystic and misguided seminarian. (p. 400)

Robert E. Lott, '' 'Pepita Jiménez' and 'Don Quixote': A Structural Comparison,'' in Hispania (© 1962 The American Association of Teachers of Spanish and Portuguese, Inc.), Vol. XLV, No. 3, September, 1962, pp. 395-401.**

CYRUS DeCOSTER   (essay date 1974)

[*DeCoster's* Juan Valera *provides a comprehensive examination of the author's works in each of the literary genres in which he wrote, as well as examining Valera's life, his aesthetic theories, and his philosophical values. In the concluding section of his study, excerpted below, DeCoster reviews his appraisal of Valera's writings.*]

If we disregard the unfinished works, as the fragments are brief and in most cases were not published during his lifetime, Valera's novels fall into two widely-spaced periods: the series of five novels beginning with *Pepita Jiménez* in 1874 and ending with *Doña Luz* in 1879, and the final three, *Juanita la larga*, *Genio y figura*, and *Morsamor*, between 1895 and 1899. Special mention should also be made of *Mariquita y Antonio*, for Valera did complete an appreciable part of it, and it is significant for its early date, 1861. Qualitatively, the novels might be ranked in the following order: *Pepita Jiménez, Juanita la larga, El Comendador Mendoza, Doña Luz, Las ilusiones del doctor Faustino, Morsamor*, with the other two, *Genio y figura* and *Pasarse de listo*, bringing up the rear. *Pepita Jiménez* is a nearly perfect work of its kind, a minor masterpiece. *Juanita la larga* has a charming freshness to it, although it lacks the psychological depth of *Pepita Jiménez*. The next three novels do not quite come up to these two. The plot of *El Comendador Mendoza* is somewhat static, while *Doña Luz* and *Las ilusiones del doctor Faustino*, with their melodramatic episodes, are uneven works. *Morsamor*, as a historical novel, is a work sui generis and difficult to judge for that reason, while *Pasarse de listo* and *Genio y figura*, though flawed works, are of interest because of the characterization of their protagonists.

In his novels Valera drew upon his personal experiences for his settings, themes, and for many of his characters. The locale, at least in the contemporary novels, is invariably based on places familiar to him, usually his native Andalusia, although he never insists on the topography. . . . It is significant that, of his seven novels dealing with contemporary life, five of them, including the best ones, are laid in a small area in the province of Cordova near his birthplace.

Valera put something of himself in many of his protagonists. Antonio is the youthful, precocious Valera, yearning for love, but at the same time self-centered. Luis in *Pepita Jiménez* has less in common with the author, but the nostalgic appreciation for the Andalusian landscape he expresses is similar to that found in Valera's letters written during his visits to Cabra. The liberal, skeptical Comendador Mendoza reflects that part of Valera which is derived from the *philosophes* of the eighteenth century. Still another aspect of Valera is found in Faustino and to a lesser degree in Braulio and Morsamor. Faustino was ambitious and was not without talent, but he lacked willpower and accomplished nothing. The youthful Valera likewise procrastinated, trying to decide what career to follow. He did not feel that he had attained a position commensurate with his

TWENTIETH-CENTURY LITERARY CRITICISM, Vol. 10

talents until well into middle age, with the publication of his first novels.

Many of Valera's other characters are based on people he had known. Doña Ana (in *Faustino*) has similarities to Valera's own mother. A Juanita *la larga* once lived in Doña Mencía, and he borrowed the nicknames of various local citizens, *El maestro Cencias,* Respetilla, Don Juan Fresco, the *Civiles,* Father Piñón, altering their characters to suit his purpose. Although he drew heavily on his personal reminiscences, his novels were not copied directly from life. Such slavish imitation was diametrically opposed to his aesthetic principles. Art, for Valera, must be based on the real, but it must be idealized to accord with the artist's concept of beauty. He took characters he had known, incidents he had witnessed, and arranged them as he saw fit.

Several times in his critical essays Valera stated that a novel should have one central action. Such works as *Don Quijote* and the picaresque novels, by their very nature, consist of a series of largely unrelated incidents, but the conventional novel should adhere to the Classical ideal of unity of action. Valera's best novels do have a concentrated quality to them. *Pepita Jiménez* has a simple theme—the conflict in Luis between his love for Pepita and his vows to enter the priesthood. There are no digressions or subsidiary actions. The story proceeds directly to the climax, the seduction scene, with love winning out. The action of most of Valera's novels, *Mariquita y Antonio, Pepita Jiménez, El Comendador Mendoza, Pasarse de listo,* and *Doña Luz,* takes place in a few weeks or, at the most, a few months. *Juanita la larga* spans a period of three years, but it still has a simple, unified plot. *Las ilusiones del doctor Faustino* and *Genio y figura,* in which the action is spread over many years, lack the concision of the other novels, and partly for that reason, they are less successful. Maintaining that the action of the novel should be interior, Valera condemned chance happenings on the grounds that, although possible, they are less interesting. Yet, occasionally, apparently at a loss as to how to resolve a situation, he himself had recourse to fortuitous incidents. The abductions of Mariquita and Faustino fall into this category, and the whole conclusion of *Doña Luz* is melodramatic. Still, in his best novels the conflict does spring from the characters. (pp. 157-59)

As in most nineteenth-century Spanish novels, the clergy plays an important role, even in the works of a skeptic like Valera. Only Father Piñón (*Faustino*), with his good-humored common sense and humanity, and the liberal Father Jacinto (*El Comendador*) come off well. The Vicar (*Pepita*) and Miguel (*Doña Luz*) are portrayed as good-hearted but simpleminded country priests, but only the narrowly intolerant Father Anselmo (*Juanita*) is frankly unsympathetic. (p. 160)

A surprising number of Valera's characters were born out of wedlock. Luis in *Pepita Jiménez* is the only male; the others are all women. Luis and Doña Luz are ashamed of their illegitimate birth, and their pride causes them to react so as to atone for it. It largely explains Luis's decision to enter the priesthood and Luz's early resolution to remain a spinster. Rafaela (*Genio y figura*), mortified at her sordid life, tries to keep knowledge of it from her daughter, Lucía. She sets her on a pedestal and wants her to live a blameless life. But both Lucía and Irene, Faustino's daughter, renounce this world and enter a convent. They cannot forget their mothers' transgressions. In *El Comendador Mendoza,* Valera studies the problem as it affects the mother, not the daughter. Clara never finds out that she is the Comendador's daughter and ends up marrying

the man she loves, but Blanca dies of remorse. Only Juanita rises above the stigma of her illegitimate birth. After her early indiscretion of flaunting her elegant attire in church, she behaves circumspectly and eventually marries Paco.

Several of Valera's characters reappear in later novels, occasionally in a major role, more often in a minor one. This technique gives an added depth to the novels, although, compared to Galdós, Valera uses it to a very limited extent. When the reader meets an old friend from a previous novel, he immediately recalls associations; the character already has an identity. Juan Fresco appears in *Las ilusiones del doctor Faustino, El Comendador Mendoza,* and *Doña Luz,* as well as in several of the unfinished novels and short stories, usually as the narrator. Faustino himself, the great-nephew of the Comendador, is mentioned again briefly in *Doña Luz.* Rosita, Faustino's vindictive paramour, reappears as a *cursi* society matron in *Pasarse de listo.* (p. 161)

The themes found in Valera's contemporary novels are repeated in the historical ones. The settings are, of course, completely different, and there is also a marked difference in tone. In the contemporary novels, Valera portrays an idealized but still recognizable view of life in nineteenth-century Spain. In the historical ones, with the exception of the first part of *Morsamor,* he makes no attempt to recapture the quality of the life of a past age. He deliberately chooses exotic settings, and the fantastic also plays an important role in these novels. The adventures are developed at length at the expense of incisive character study. It is perhaps understandable that of the five historical novels he began, he finished only one. His talent did not really lie there, and he must have realized it.

Valera cultivated all the genres, but for the present-day reader, as for his contemporaries, he is primarily a novelist. His poetry, neo-Classic in its inspiration, is of significance today largely for what it tells us about the author, who was something of an anomaly in the nineteenth century. Its intrinsic appeal is slight. Of his theatrical efforts, only the philosophical dialogue, *Asclepigenia,* which is more essay than drama, holds up today. His short stories are more significant. **"Parsondes"** and **"El pájaro verde"** are delightful works of their kind, but the longer tales, even the best ones, **"La buena fama,"** **"El bermejino prehistórico,"** and **"Garuda,"** similar in tone and techniques to his historical novels, are overshadowed by *Morsamor.*

As a critic, Valera's position is more secure. He is one of the important Spanish critics of the nineteenth century. In the fifties and sixties he stood almost alone. In the seventies Revilla and Clarín appeared on the scene, and later in the century, Gómez de Baquero. There is also, of course, Menéndez y Pelayo, who is more of a scholar than a critic. Yet, our interest in Valera's criticism is largely historical today. Good as his essays on Cervantes, the Duke of Rivas, and Espronceda are, when we want to read something about these writers, we generally turn to more recent studies. We read his essays, rather, to learn about him and what he thought. (pp. 162-63)

Valera's position has remained steady. Today we would rank him behind Galdós and Clarín, but ahead of Pardo Bazán and certainly of Pereda. His novels stand somewhat apart from those of his contemporaries; but his ironically idealized portrayal of nineteenth-century Andalusian life continues to appeal to contemporary readers. (pp. 163-64)

Cyrus DeCoster, in his Juan Valera *(copyright ©*
1974 by Twayne Publishers, Inc.; reprinted with the

permission of Twayne Publishers, a Division of G. K. Hall & Co., Boston), Twayne, 1974, 186 p.

ROXANNE B. MARCUS (essay date 1979)

[*Marcus bases her analysis of one of Valera's most complex characters, Doña Inés in* Juanita la larga, *on Carl Gustave Jung's theory of archetypal divisions in individual psychology, focusing on his concepts of persona, animus/anima, and shadow.*]

Toward the conclusion of *Juanita la larga,* Juan Valera states that Doña Inés was a figure of such a complex and involved nature that he often regretted having included her as one of the heroines because of the difficulty he found in describing her and in clarifying, for his readers, the concept of her that he had already formulated for himself. . . . Although Inés' intriguing personality and behavior pattern invite psychological speculation and analysis, she remains one of the least studied major characters in the critical bibliography of Valera's fiction. . . . Valera does not attempt to explore the interior motives and psychological effects in relation to the three contradictory *energías* or forces that together constitute Inés' uniqueness or personality. It is the aim of this study to demonstrate that psychological insights suggested by Jung's theory of archetypes, principally *persona, animus/anima,* and *shadow,* prove to be highly illuminating in providing an explanation for the motives of Inés' passions and actions. In light of these insights, the change in Inés' attitude and behavior toward Juanita, hitherto viewed as necessary to the story but seemingly out of character and difficult to accept, proves to be plausible and does not destroy the impression of unity in Valera's portrayal of this character.

When Valera introduces Inés, in the second chapter of the novel, he clearly establishes her *persona:* "the public image or mask behind which she has chosen to live". The conventional role that she has assumed as the "first lady" of the village of Villalegre imposes on her the obligation of adopting the characteristics of that position and, consequently, she strives to give the appearance of being a noble aristocrat and an exemplary Christian in the varied social roles that she plays as wife, mother, daughter, friend, neighbor. We are told that she indeed occupies a position of social respect, prominence, and power as the daughter of Don Paco, the right-hand man of the *cacique,* Don Andrés, as the "venerada esposa" of Don Álvaro, and as the close friend and admired associate of Andrés and of the village priest, *padre* Anselmo. These two men are, in fact, her closest associates, her constant companions at her *tertulias,* and the three of them together constitute the ruling triumvirate of Villalegre. The novel bears out that Andrés, the only one, we are told in Chapter 2, who really understands her, serves well the function of novelistic elaboration of Inés' personality through his involvement (explicit and suggested) with her on the level of external action and that he represents, by virtue of their similar natures, another avenue of clarification in the investigation of Inés' personality, especially, as we shall see, in terms of her *shadow.* Anselmo, in expressing his admiration for Inés, emerges as a voice within the novel that defines the characteristics of the *persona* that Inés has chosen and affirms that she has succeeded in playing her part well. . . . It is also in the second chapter, however, that Valera initiates the process of undermining the notion that Inés' public image or *persona* is synonymous with her real or complete personality. Accordingly, she is described not only as elegant, attractive, and discreet, but also as the most conceited (*empingorotada*) woman in the village. True, she is married to the most illustrious *caballero* of the village, but he is, in reality, dissolute, ignoble, a gambler and woman chaser; in short, the antithesis of aristocratic distinction, dignity, nobility, and Christian virtue, who, it is rumored, gambles beyond his means and whose penchant for the hunt and for extra-marital affairs keeps him away from home more than half the time. It becomes evident that Inés married him not for love, but for his social position and for the power that it would bring to her. Her social pretentiousness is revealed by the fact that she has few, if any, female friends, since she considered herself superior to the rest of the women (*hidalguitas* and *labradoras*) in the town. Finally, Valera sows the seeds of suspicion with the intimation, which continues throughout the novel, of an affair between Andrés and Inés.

Through a skillful interplay of irony and ambiguity Valera establishes as fact or strongly suggests that there exists a series of discrepancies, if not outright contradictions, between the characteristic traits of the *persona* that Inés has chosen and the less socially acceptable or desirable emotions, attitudes, and actions that are also facets of her personality and that express themselves either consciously or unconsciously. Recalling that it is Anselmo who defines, in terms of the social reality, the *persona* of Inés, it is also to be noted that he is described initially as an excommunicated Dominican friar, and Valera proceeds to depict him satirically, in the course of the narration, as a shallow, narrow-minded figure, typical in outlook, according to Valera, of the neo-Catholic mentality, seeing only what he wants to see and incapable of penetrating beneath the surface reality. Accordingly, we are told in chapter XVI that Anselmo is totally blind to Inés' sins and personal defects which, we are aware, are known to others, especially to Paco and Juanita. In terms of the psychological analysis of Inés, Anselmo's blindness can be viewed as a reflection of Inés' repression or pushing into the unconscious of her defects. . . . By the conclusion of this chapter, then, Valera has made it abundantly clear, with the economy and fun characteristic of his art of suggestion and ironic wit, that there is a substantial gap between Inés' *persona* and other aspects of her personality. (pp. 259-62)

Valera does not pursue a systematic psychological investigation of the whys and wherefores of the paradoxical personality traits of Inés, nor does he ponder through letters, dialogue, or monologue how she copes with the gap between appearance and reality. His repeated suggestions of contradictions in her life between theory and practice do indicate, however, that she is caught up in a web of hypocrisy and deceit, a predicament common to those, according to Jung, who attempt to live as better or nobler people than they really are and who fall into the category of the overvirtuous—those whose ideals are too high or are based on an illusion. The resulting conflict between their *persona* and their *shadow* manifests itself very often through irritability and intolerance, symptoms that are borne out by example in the novel as attributable to Inés. These traits, associated with Inés from the start, take on special meaning within the context of the conflict between Paco and Juanita on the one hand, and Inés, on the other, in light of the projection by Inés of her *shadow* onto Juanita.

Considering Inés specifically in terms of her *shadow,* that aspect of personality associated with the primitive, uncontrolled, and animal part of one's nature, we find that a striking parallel can be drawn between Jung's theoretical generalizations about the influence exerted by this archetype on the individual and Inés' behavior pattern. Jung maintained that everyone has a *shadow*, must live with it, and that if one comes to know and recognize aspects of one's *shadow* (facing thus the shame and guilt involved), one is then able to live more comfortably with it, has grown psychologically, and taken a step toward greater personality integration. Each sex has a *shadow*, but Jung stipulates that "a man's shadow is personified by another man, a woman's shadow by another woman." "The shadow appears in dreams, personified as an inferior or very primitive person, someone with unpleasant qualities or someone we dislike." Rather than face her defects as revealed by her *shadow*, a woman often, according to Jung, projects her defects onto another woman through such means as malicious gossip or public condemnation.

Valera's portrayal of Inés accurately reflects the psychological process of projection within the context of the action that revolves around the conflict between her and Paco and Juanita. This conflict becomes intensified as Paco publicly courts, regales, and wishes to marry Juanita, this illegitimate daughter of a domestic, thus making Juanita the step-mother of the "illustrious" Doña Inés de Roldán. On the conscious level, Inés despises Juanita because of her illegitimate birth and her inferior social position, and she opposes the marriage, therefore, in the name of safeguarding the dignity of the existing social hierarchy. . . . (pp. 262-63)

Inés is thus thrust into a psychological crisis when confronted with the possible marriage, and her inability or unwillingness to meet the crisis by facing up to her own weaknesses and personal defects—egotism, narcissism, vanity, greed, *cursi* pretentiousness, and possibly an affair with Andrés—can be interpreted as the underlying cause at the heart of her negative attitude and destructive criticism of Juanita that culminate in the brutal, emotional scene that occurs in church one Sunday. . . . The proposed marriage thus becomes the catalytic agent of conflict on the external level of action, and this conflict is best understood in light of the motives of inner struggle existing within Inés and their psychological effects.

Linked to the effect of projection is the arousing of the negative-destructive voice of Inés' *animus*, an unconscious result that is dramatically highlighted by Anselmo's delivery of his Sunday sermon in chapter XVI. . . . The sermon demonstrates how religion was used by ultra-conservatives to justify attacks on personal enemies and was brought to bear on social and political matters; but it holds far greater significance for this study on account of the fact that Anselmo can be viewed as the personification of the negative function of Inés' *animus* voice and he can be seen, for the second time in the light of the psychological analysis of Inés, as considerably more than a *costumbrista* figure who merely contributes to local atmosphere, reflects Valera's controlled satirical wit, and facilitates plot movement. The *animus* carries spiritual values and is the seat of unconscious assumptions and critical judgment. While the *anima* of a man is personified as one woman, the *animus* is usually expressed as a group of men, and it can appear in dreams or is often heard simply as a voice. In the novel, then, as in dreams, the personified *animus* provides an opportunity to comprehend what has been unconscious and thus to understand, with new insight, Inés' dogmatic stand against the marriage. This voice thus allows the reader to hear, via Anselmo, the inner voice of Inés' *animus*, intensely aroused in negative activity.

The destructive potential of Inés' *animus* is discernible from the outset. . . . Relying on Anselmo as a symbolic authoritative body, the Church, Inés manipulates him into preaching "hidden sacred convictions" of her *animus* and, in doing so, a brutal, emotional scene is created in the church, a scene which Valera refers to as a "formidable tempestad" and "inmerecida afrenta" that causes both Juana and Juanita great anguish and that arouses their anger.

In the course of his sermon Anselmo makes references to Satan and such references can be interpreted, in light of Jungian theory, as a collective expression of the *shadow*. When Inés decides to lash out via Anselmo, she confidently counts on public reaction to sustain and intensify the effects of her attack on Juanita. On the collective level, the reaction of the *pueblo* to Juanita is tantamount to an echo of Anselmo's voice and, by extension, can be associated with Inés' *animus* which we could reasonably expect to embody sacred convictions. Such an association is reinforced by the fact that Valera links the *pueblo*'s agreement with the views preached and its sanctioning of the attack on Juanita to a collective popular expression of a people's sacred convictions, namely proverbs. (pp. 263-66)

Determined to avenge the public indignity and condemnation that she and her mother have suffered, Juanita embarks on a clever and well-calculated scheme to win Inés' favor, to disprove the accusations of moral indecency and lack of integrity, and to have her dignity publicly affirmed. As determined and calculating a female as Inés, Juanita works her way into Inés' home as the latter's seamstress, after having spent more than a year firmly establishing a convincing public image of herself as a repentant Mary Magdalene. . . . The trajectory of this relationship can be traced from suspicious acceptance by Inés of Juanita, to love and respect for Juanita as a model of virtue and piety who should enter a convent, and finally to Inés' enthusiastically accepting Juanita's decision not to become a nun and thus approving Juanita as her step-mother and as a respected, admired friend whom Inés knows will no longer be dominated by her. One of the aims of this study is to demonstrate that the gradual about-face in Inés' behavior and attitude toward Juanita is not difficult to accept when it is understood as indicative of a degree of psychological growth on Inés' part as she comes to face up to her personal failings as revealed by her *shadow* and learns to live with it more comfortably, thus bringing into greater harmony the disparate elements that define her personality. As the gradual acceptance of her *shadow* progresses, the projection onto Juanita diminishes and finally ceases, as it should according to Jung, at the moment when it becomes conscious. (p. 266)

Juanita carefully plots her eventual liberation, but delays it until the right moment presents itself and, in the meantime, cleverly creates situations in the course of her daily conversations with Inés in which she disagrees just enough to allow Inés to believe that she is finally imposing her view and for Juanita's benefit. (p. 267)

At this juncture in Inés' relationship with Juanita, Inés appears to have succumbed to the influence of the "great mother image" which coexerts influence on her together with the positive voice of her *animus*. This dual influence has the effect of greatly obscuring Inés' perception of Juanita who decides to take advantage of this situation in order to strengthen their friendship. Therefore, Juanita is determined to restrain herself from opposing the plan for her entrance into a convent, while maintaining Inés' friendship and respect, until the moment is ripe for her to liberate herself from the "gloriosa servidumbre" imposed by her demanding and domineering friend who, in turn, views herself as Juanita's protector.

By having Juanita not oppose Inés' plan until the proper moment, Valera creates the setting for the next crucial episode in the psychological drama of Inés, an episode in which she faces up to her *shadow* and in which the projection of it onto Juanita ceases. . . . Inés has in effect given evidence of moral resolution by admitting her shame and guilt, and has thus brought into greater harmony the conflicting exigencies of her *persona*, the sacred convictions of her *animus*, and aspects of her *shadow*. The very nature of the self-admission satisfies the continuing need to protect her public image and this in itself emphasizes that a degree of moral courage on her part was necessary to face up to her *shadow*. (pp. 267-68)

By allowing herself to be dominated by Juanita, Inés is, in effect, signalling the moment in the story for which Juanita has planned and waited—the moment in which Juanita frees herself from "gloriosa servidumbre" and is fully recognized as an individual. As well, this moment represents, in terms of Inés' psychic life, the point at which her "great mother" image and her *animus* voice in its negative activity can no longer exert their dominating influence on the life of Juanita. Inés' acceptance on the conscious level of this change in her relationship with Juanita can be taken as further evidence of Inés' facing up to unpleasant truths about herself. . . . Dramatic proof of the psychological growth experienced by Inés is furnished by none other than Andrés, the character who best understands Inés at the beginning of the story. Expecting her to react negatively to Juanita's final act of liberation and to the proposed marriage, he believes it very likely that Inés will explode like a bomb. . . . In not doing so, Inés is not acting out of character once we see her gradual, total reversal in attitude and behavior toward Juanita as evidence of her bringing into greater harmony the paradoxes that define her personality. (pp. 268-69)

This study reinforces the literary relevance of generalizations formulated by Jung that we have applied in the elucidation of the "móviles de sus actos y pasiones" with respect to Inés. Although Valera judged his own efforts to clarify her personality to be inadequate, we have found in his presentation of Inés intuitive illustration of several of Jung's major formulations. The application of Jung's theory of the principal archetypes and their influence on personality also greatly enhances the quality and significance of the characterization of Inés perhaps beyond Valera's own appreciation of the acumen of his

insights into this enigmatic figure. Certainly from the standpoint of Jungian psychology, Inés emerges as a far more engaging, complex, and plausible literary creation than hitherto thought. In effect, she is no less convincing or plausible with respect to the verisimilitude of psychological motives and effects than are the other characters in Valera's novels whose inner lives he pursued as his central point of interest. (p. 270)

> *Roxanne B. Marcus, "An Application of Jungian Theory to the Interpretation of Doña Inés in Valera's 'Juanita la larga'" (reprinted by permission of Carleton University and the Author), in* Revista Canadiense de Estudios Hispanicos, *Vol. III, No. 3, Spring, 1979, pp. 259-74.*

ADDITIONAL BIBLIOGRAPHY

Chandler, Richard E., and Schwartz, Kessel. "Spanish Prose Fiction" and "Nonfiction Prose." In their *A New History of Spanish Literature*, pp. 155-266, pp. 412-594. Baton Rouge: Louisiana State University Press, 1961.*
  General appraisal of Valera's major works.

DeCoster, Cyrus C. "Valera and Andalusia." *Hispanic Review* XXIX, No. 3 (July 1961): 200-16.
  Examines Valera's use of Andalusia, his native region, as background material for his writing.

Eoff, Sherman H. "The Spanish Novel of 'Ideas': Critical Opinion (1836-1880)." *PMLA* LV, No. 2 (June 1940): 531-58.*
  Discussion of the philosophical basis of the Spanish novel. Valera is considered a proponent of "art for art's sake" as opposed to didacticism.

Lott, Robert. *Language and Psychology in "Pepita Jiménez."* Urbana: University of Illinois Press, 1970, 284 p.
  Divided into two major sections: the first a linguistic analysis and study of rhetorical devices, the second an examination of character psychology. The introduction to this study is a survey of critical reaction to Valera and *Pepita Jiménez*.

Marcus, Roxanne B. "Contemporary Life and Manners in the Novels of Juan Valera." *Hispania* 58, No. 3 (September 1975): 454-66.
  Examines Valera's attitude toward fictional use of details and modes of behavior patterned after contemporary life.

Olguín, Manuel. "Valera's Philosophical Arguments against Naturalism." *Modern Language Quarterly* 11, No. 2 (June 1950): 164-68.
  Advanced philosophical discourse on Valera's literary principles.

Booker T(aliaferro) Washington

1856-1915

American autobiographer, essayist, lecturer, and biographer.

Washington's *Up from Slavery* is a classic American autobiography that has served as an inspiration for both black and white readers from the time of its first publication in 1901 to the present day. A respected educator and founder of the Tuskegee Institute, Washington was one of the most important social thinkers of the early twentieth century. His 1895 speech before a racially mixed audience at the Atlanta Cotton States and International Exposition won him national recognition when he stated his basic philosophy: "In all things that are purely social we can be as separate as the fingers, yet one as the hand in all things essential to mutual progress." This accommodating racial policy appeased northern and southern whites during the discordant post-Reconstruction era and helped motivate many black Americans toward economic independence. However, Washington was often criticized by other prominent black intellectuals, most notably W.E.B. Du Bois, for social policies which emphasized industrial education for black students while repudiating black political agitation. Today Washington is viewed by critics as a complex man whose "accommodation" policies were used in conjunction with covert political activities for improving the social and economic conditions of his race.

Washington was born on a small Virginia plantation. He spent the first nine years of his life in slavery, but shortly after the end of the Civil War he and his family moved to West Virginia. There, Washington worked with his step-father in the salt mines. When a school for black children was started, Washington was allowed to attend after work and at night. He later worked as a household servant for the wife of the mine owner, Lewis Ruffner. It was Mrs. Ruffner who encouraged Washington to study and helped fulfill his ambition to attend the Hampton Institute, a vocational school for black students, from which he graduated in 1875. His experiences at Hampton formed the educational philosophy that would guide his own Tuskegee Institute: the belief that social and economic independence for black Americans could only be achieved through diligent work in an industrial trade. The founding of Tuskegee in 1881 marked the beginning of Washington's endless work and fund raising for the school. As he toured the country on behalf of the Institute, his reputation as a public speaker on educational and social problems grew. His prominence gained him access to American presidents, as well as to some of the country's wealthiest philanthropists, an exceptional accomplishment for a former slave. Eventually Washington filled the gap left by the death of Frederick Douglass as the most visible spokesman for black Americans.

At the height of his popularity, Washington was urged by publishers to write his life story, for it was felt that tracing the rise of a black hero would offer an appealing twist to the Horatio Alger success story. With the assistance of Edgar Webber, a ghostwriter, Washington produced *The Story of My Life and Work*, a brief, poorly written account of his childhood that was padded with reprints of his addresses and speeches. Washington was dissatisfied with the book and immediately

began work on *Up from Slavery*, a new version of his autobiography, written with the aid of a new ghostwriter, Max Bennett Thrasher, and with closer attention to detail by Washington. The second book was an overwhelming success.

Up from Slavery is an emotionally arousing account of Washington's life from slave to renowned educator. Often referred to by critics as a minor classic, its style is simple, direct, and reminiscent of biblical writing. Similar to Washington's numerous essays and speeches, *Up from Slavery* promulgates the tenets of his racial philosophy. As in his speeches, Washington repeatedly used anecdotes throughout his autobiography to illustrate important points. The book's optimistic tone suggested to turn-of-the-century black readers that they could succeed economically and socially through practical self-improvement. Although some critics contend that *Up from Slavery* assumes a conciliatory stance which ignores many of the brutalities experienced by black Americans, others maintain that Washington's autobiography was a justification for black pride and provided his race with a successful role-model. Washington's other two autobiographical works, *Working with the Hands* and *My Larger Education*, examined in detail his life as an educator while again reiterating his racial doctrines. Neither of these books was as successful as *Up from Slavery*.

Throughout his career Washington's racial policies drew diverse critical reactions. He was often harshly criticized by black intellectuals for his "separate but equal" concept, as well as for his seeming acceptance of disfranchisement. According to critic August Meier, however, those who accepted his accommodating doctrines "understood that through tact and indirection he hoped to secure the good will of the white man and the eventual recognition of the constitutional rights of American Negroes." The contents of Washington's recently released private papers have led many critics to reinterpret his role as a spokesman for accommodation. They have found many examples of his behind-the-scenes manipulation of prominent black and white Americans (including President Theodore Roosevelt), and now agree that the social prominence gained by his placating demeanor enabled him to work surreptitiously against segregation and disfranchisement, and to win political appointments that helped advance the cause of racial equality.

PRINCIPAL WORKS

Black-Belt Diamonds: Gems from the Speeches, Addresses, and Talks to Students of Booker T. Washington (speeches) 1898
The Future of the American Negro (essays and speeches) 1899
The Story of My Life and Work [with Edgar Webber] (autobiography) 1900
Character Building (essays) 1901
Up from Slavery [with Max Bennett Thrasher] (autobiography) 1901
Working with the Hands: Being a Sequel to "Up from Slavery" Covering the Author's Experiences in Industrial Training at Tuskegee (autobiography) 1904
Putting the Most into Life (essays) 1906
Frederick Douglass [with S. Laing Williams] (biography) 1907
My Larger Education: Being Chapters from My Experience [with Robert E. Park and Emmett J. Scott] (autobiography) 1911
Selected Speeches of Booker T. Washington (speeches) 1932
The Booker T. Washington Papers. 9 vols. (autobiography, essays, interviews, letters, and speeches) 1972-80

BOOKER T. WASHINGTON (lecture date 1895)

[*This summation of Washington's views on the role of black people in American society was delivered to a predominantly white audience at the Atlanta Exposition of 1895. It is often referred to as the* Atlanta Address.]

"Mr. President, Gentlemen of the Board of Directors and Citizens: One-third of the population of the South is of the negro race. No enterprise seeking the material, civil, or moral welfare of this section can disregard this element of our population and reach the highest success. I but convey to you, Mr. President and Directors, the sentiment of the masses of my race, when I say that in no way have the value and manhood of the American negro been more fittingly and generously recognized than by the managers of this magnificent exposition at every stage of its progress. It is a recognition that will do more to cement

the friendship of the two races than any occurrence since the dawn of our freedom.

"Not only this, but the opportunity here afforded will awaken among us a new era of industrial progress. Ignorant and inexperienced, it is not strange that in the first years of our new life we began at the top instead of at the bottom; that a seat in Congress or the state legislature was more sought than real estate or industrial skill; that the political convention or stump speaking had more attractions than starting a dairy farm or truck garden. . . .

"To those of my race who depend on bettering their condition in a foreign land or who underestimate the importance of cultivating friendly relations with the southern white man, who is their next-door neighbour, I would say cast down your bucket where you are, cast it down in making friends in every manly way of the people of all races by whom we are surrounded. Cast it down in agriculture, mechanics, in commerce, in domestic service, and in the professions. And in this connection it is well to bear in mind that whatever other sins the south may be called to bear, when it comes to business, pure and simple, it is in the south that the negro is given a man's chance in the commercial world, and in nothing is this exposition more eloquent than in emphasizing this chance. Our greatest danger is, that in the great leap from slavery to freedom we may overlook the fact that the masses of us are to live by the productions of our hands, and fail to keep in mind that we shall prosper in proportion as we learn to dignify and glorify common labour and put brains and skill into the common occupations of life; shall prosper in proportion as we learn to draw the line between the superficial and the substantial, the ornamental gewgaws of life and the useful. No race can prosper till it learns that there is as much dignity in tilling a field as in writing a poem. It is at the bottom of life we must begin, and not at the top. Nor should we permit our grievances to overshadow our opportunities.

"To those of the white race who look to the incoming of those of foreign birth and strange tongue and habits for the prosperity of the south, were I permitted I would repeat what I say to my own race: 'Cast down your bucket where you are.' Cast it down among the 8,000,000 Negroes whose habits you know, whose loyalty and love you have tested in days when to have proved treacherous meant the ruin of your firesides. Cast down your bucket among these people who have, without strikes and labour wars, tilled your fields, cleared your forests, builded your railroads and cities, and brought forth treasures from the bowels of the earth, and helped make possible this magnificent representation of the progress of the South. Casting down your bucket among my people, helping and encouraging them as you are doing on these grounds, and to education of head, hand, and heart, you will find that they will buy your surplus land, make blossom the waste places in your fields and run your factories. While doing this, you can be sure in the future, as in the past, that you and your families will be surrounded by the most patient, faithful, law-abiding, and unresentful people that the world has seen. As we have proved our loyalty to you in the past, in nursing your children, watching by the sick-bed of your mothers and fathers, and often following them with tear-dimmed eyes to their graves, so in the future, in our humble way we shall stand by you with a devotion that no foreigner can approach, ready to lay down our lives, if need be, in defense of yours, interlacing our industrial, commercial, civil, and religious life with yours in a way that shall make the interests of both races one. In all things that are purely social we can be as separate as the fingers, yet one as the hand in all things essential to mutual progress. . . .

"Nearly sixteen millions of hands will aid you in pulling the load upward or they will pull against you the load downward. We shall constitute one-third and much more of the ignorance and crime of the south, or one-third its intelligence and progress; we shall contribute one-third to the business and industrial prosperity of the south, or we shall prove a veritable body of death, stagnating, depressing, retarding every effort to advance the body politic.

"Gentlemen of the Exposition: As we present to you our humble effort at an exhibition of our progress, you must not expect overmuch; starting thirty years ago with ownership here and there in a few quilts and pumpkins and chickens (gathered from miscellaneous sources), remember the path that has led us from these to the inventions and production of agricultural implements, buggies, steam-engines, newspapers, books, statuary, carving, paintings, the management of drug stores and banks, has not been trodden without contact with thorns and thistles. While we take just pride in what we exhibit as a result of our independent efforts, we do not for a moment forget that our part in this exhibition would fall far short of your expectations but for the constant help that has come to our educational life not only from the southern states, but especially from northern philanthropists, who have made their gifts a constant stream of blessing and encouragement.

"The wisest among my race understand that the agitation of questions of social equality is the extremest folly, and that progress in the enjoyment of all the privileges that will come to us must be the result of severe and constant struggle, rather than of artificial forcing. No race that has anything to contribute to the markets of the world is long in any degree ostracized. It is important and right that all privileges of the law be ours, but it is vastly more important that we be prepared for the exercise of these privileges. The opportunity to earn a dollar in a factory just now is worth infinitely more than the opportunity to spend a dollar in an opera-house.

"In conclusion, may I repeat that nothing in thirty years has given us more hope and encouragement, and nothing has drawn us so near to you of the white race, as this opportunity offered by this exposition; and here bending, as it were, over the altar that represents the results of the struggles of your race and mine, both starting practically empty handed three decades ago, I pledge that in your effort to work out the great and intricate problem which God has laid at the doors of the south, you shall have at all times the patient, sympathetic help of my race; only let this be constantly in mind—that while from representations in these buildings of the product of field, of forest, of mine, of factory, letters, and art, much good will come, yet far above and beyond material benefits will be that higher good, that, let us pray God, will come, in a blotting out of sectional differences and racial animosities and suspicions, and in a determination, even in the remotest corner, to administer absolute justice, in a willing obedience among all classes to the mandates of law and a spirit that will tolerate nothing but the highest equity in the enforcement of law. This, coupled with our material prosperity, will bring into our beloved south a new heaven and a new earth."

> *Booker T. Washington, "A Plea for His Race" (originally an address delivered in Atlanta on September 18, 1895), in* The Constitution, *Atlanta, September 19, 1895, p. 4.*

JAMES CREELMAN   (essay date 1895)

[*Written the day of the* Atlanta Address, *Creelman's article describes the emotional impact the speech had on both black and white members of the audience.*]

When Prof. Booker T. Washington, principal of an industrial school for colored people in Tuskegee, Ala., stood on the platform of the Auditorium, with the sun shining over the heads of his hearers into his eyes and his whole face lit up with the fire of prophecy, Clark Howell, the successor of Henry W. Grady, said to me: "That man's speech is the beginning of a moral revolution in America."

It is the first time that a negro has made a speech in the South on any important occasion before an audience composed of white men and women. It electrified the audience, and the response was as if it had come from the throat of a whirlwind. (p. 3)

There was a remarkable figure, tall, bony, straight as a Sioux chief, high forehead, straight nose, heavy jaws and strong, determined mouth, with big white teeth, piercing eyes and a commanding manner. The sinews stood out on his bronzed neck, and his muscular right arm swung high in the air with a lead pencil grasped in the clenched brown fist. His big feet were planted squarely, with the heels together and the toes turned out. His voice rang out clear and true, and he paused impressively as he made each point. Within ten minutes the multitude was in an uproar of enthusiasm, handkerchiefs were waved, canes were flourished, hats were tossed in the air. The fairest women of Georgia stood up and cheered. It was as if the orator had bewitched them. (p. 9)

I have heard the great orators of many countries, but not even Gladstone himself could have pleaded a cause with more consummate power than did this angular negro standing in a nimbus of sunshine surrounded by the men who once fought to keep his race in bondage. The roar might swell ever so high, but the expression of his earnest face never changed.

A ragged ebony giant, squatted on the floor in one of the aisles, watched the orator with burning eyes and tremulous face until the supreme burst of applause came and then the tears ran down his face. Most of the negroes in the audience were crying, perhaps without knowing just why. (pp. 9-10)

> *James Creelman, in his article (originally published in* New York World, *September 18, 1895), in* The Booker T. Washington Papers: 1895-98, Vol. 4, *edited by Louis R. Harlan & others (© 1975 by the Board of Trustees of the University of Illinois), University of Illinois Press, 1975, pp. 3-15.*

GEORGE N. SMITH   (letter date 1895)

[*The following letter is one of the first expressions of opposition to Washington's* Atlanta Address *by black Americans.*]

The Negro is made, indeed, of queer stuff. To compare Mr. Booker T. Washington with Frederick Douglass is as unseemly as comparing a pigmy to a giant—a mountain brook leaping over a boulder, to great, only Niagara. It seems that Mr. Washington, himself, and his friends would blush at the use of the name of the great Douglass in this connection. Mr. Washington has done a good work. So have hundreds of other young colored men in the south. He has attained some prominence as a collector of funds—simply this, nothing more. He has been more a creature of combinations and circumstances than a man who has wrung success, usefulness and fame from the clouds of adversity. (p. 345)

Leaving out "chickens from miscellaneous sources," the speech which Mr. Washington made at Atlanta has been repeated a hundred times by him. . . . His charge of theft against the Negro must make every race-lover hang his head with shame. It was unworthy of the occasion and a stab at his race. Was this like great Douglass? No, but the "old man eloquent" must have turned over in his grave, ashamed of the speaker.

The spirit of Douglass wept, 'but some people applauded'! No, no, Mr. Washington did not make a great speech. But the combinations and circumstances of the hour made it prominent. It was simply 'pushed' by cold business men, seeking the money success of the [Atlanta] exposition, to serve their ends. Mr. Washington was simply an instrument. Was this like the great Douglass? Was he ever an instrument in the hands of an organization seeking money gain? Money, money, money, is the sole purpose of the exposition. We will not deny that it has given the Negro a chance to 'show off' while the white man 'goes off' with the money bags, as usual.

Then did you ever stop to think that the press, loudest in praise of Mr. Washington, was most bitter in denouncing the great Douglass? Have you not seen in the same article in the last few weeks the praise of Washington and the curse of Douglass? 'And the Negroes applauded it.' Where is the blush of shame? Are we, indeed, a race of sycophants and time-serving scullions? (pp. 345-46)

Where is the memory of the immortal Daniel Alexander Payne, J. C. Price, Robert Brown Elliott and others? Did they say nothing? Did they do nothing? Where are Bishop Turner, B. K. Bruce, N. W. Cuney, Peter H. Clark, James Hill, of Mississippi, Fortune and others, whose manly, noble utterances and well-fought battles paved the way for Mr. Washington? These men have made the very heavens ring with their eloquence, while the old earth trembled beneath the tread of the hosts which they led up out of the Egypt of ignorance and oppression. Did you ever stop to think that the men who are exalting Mr. Washington see no good in these noble men? Did you ever stop to think that the newspapers which laud Mr. Washington curse these men?

It is supreme folly to speak of Mr. Washington as the Moses of the race. If we are where Mr. Washington's Atlanta speech place us, what need have we of a Moses? Who brought us from Egypt, through the wilderness to these happy conditions? The men mentioned above. Let us pray that the race will never have a leader, but leaders. Who is the leader of the white race in the United States? It has no leader, but leaders. So with us.

Yes, Mr. Washington's Atlanta popularity is simply cat's paw. His speech was simply ordinary, cannot stand the test of fair criticism in cool moments, and will pass away with the excitement of the hour.

It is a sad mistake on the part of Mr. Washington's friends to undertake to boost him as the "Moses," "the Frederick Douglass," "the leader of the race," or to place his Atlanta speech among the "classics." (pp. 346-47)

> *George N. Smith, in his letter of November 16, 1895 (originally published in* Voice of Missions, *December, 1895), in* The Journal of Negro History *(reprinted by permission of The Association for the Study of Afro-American Life and History, Inc. (ASALH), Vol. LV, No. 4, October, 1970, pp. 344-47.*

JOHN HOPE   (lecture date 1896)

[Atlanta University president, John Hope, attacks the propositions Washington set forth in his Atlanta Address *in this important piece of early criticism.]*

If we are not striving for equality, in heaven's name for what are we living? I regard it as cowardly and dishonest for any of our colored men to tell white people or colored people that we are not struggling for equality. If money, education, and honesty will not bring to me as much privilege, as much equality as they bring to any American citizen, then they are to me a curse, and not a blessing. God forbid that we should get the implements with which to fashion our freedom, and then be too lazy or pusillanimous to fashion it. Let us not fool ourselves nor be fooled by others. If we cannot do what other freemen do, then we are not free. Yes, my friends, I want equality. Nothing less. I want all that my God-given powers will enable me to get, then why not equality? Now, catch your breath, for I am going to use an adjective: I am going to say we demand social equality. In this Republic we shall be less than freemen, if we have a whit less than that which thrift, education, and honor afford other freemen. If equality, political, economic, and social, is the boon of other men in this great country of ours, then equality, political, economic, and social, is what we demand. Why build a wall to keep me out? I am no wild beast, nor am I an unclean thing.

Rise, Brothers! Come let us possess this land. Never say: "Let well enough alone." Cease to console yourselves with adages that numb the moral sense. Be discontented. Be dissatisfied. "Sweat and grunt" under present conditions. Be as restless as the tempestuous billows on the boundless sea. Let your discontent break mountain-high against the wall of prejudice, and swamp it to the very foundation. Then we shall not have to plead for justice nor on bended knee crave mercy; for we shall be men. Then and not until then will liberty in its highest sense be the boast of our Republic.

> *John Hope, in his speech delivered before the Nashville Negro Debating Society on February 22, 1896, in* The Story of John Hope *by Ridgely Torrence (reprinted with permission of Macmillan Publishing Company), Macmillan, 1948 (and reprinted in* A Documentary History of the Negro People in the United States: From the Reconstruction Era to 1910, Vol. II, *edited by Herbert Aptheker, fourth edition, The Citadel Press, 1968, p. 758).*

CHARLES W. CHESNUTT   (essay date 1900)

[In addition to his review of The Future of the American Negro, *Chesnutt, a black author, offers a realistic assessment of Washington's role as a racial leader.]*

Mr. Booker T. Washington has secured so strong a hold upon the public attention and confidence that anything he has to say in his chosen field is sure to command the attention of all who are interested in the future of the American negro. This volume [**The Future of the American Negro**], which is Mr. Washington's first extended utterance in book form, cannot fail to enhance his reputation for ability, wisdom, and patriotism. It is devoted to a somewhat wide consideration of the race problem, avoiding some of its delicate features, perhaps, but emphasizing certain of its more obvious phases. The author has practically nothing to say about caste prejudice, the admixture of the races, or the remote future of the negro, but simply takes up the palpable problem of ignorance and poverty as he finds it in the South, and looking neither to the right nor the left, and only far enough behind to fix the responsibility for present conditions, seeks to bring about such immediate improvement in the condition of the negro, and such a harmonious adjustment of race relations, as will lay the foundation for a hopeful and progressive future for the colored people. The practical philosophy of the book is eminently characteristic; it fairly bristles with the author's individuality.

As might be expected, much of the volume is devoted to discussing the importance of industrial education for the negro, of which the author is the most conspicuous advocate. . . . The argument for industrial education is not based upon any theory of the inferiority of the negro, which is beside the question, but upon the manifest conditions under which he must seek his livelihood. . . . It is to the building up of a substantial middle-class, so to speak, that industrial education and the lessons of industry and thrift inculcated by Mr. Washington are directed. He insists, somewhat rigidly, on the rational order of development, and is pained by such spectacles as a rosewood piano in a log schoolhouse, and a negro lad studying a French grammar in a one-room cabin. It is hardly likely that Mr. Washington has suffered very often from such incongruities, and some allowance should be made for the personal equation of even a negro lad in the Black Belt. (pp. 114-15)

Mr. Washington is a pioneer in another field. He has set out to gain for his race in the South, in the effort to improve their condition, the active sympathy and assistance of the white people in that section. This is perhaps a necessary corollary to his system of education, for it is in the South that he advises the negroes to stay, and it is among their white neighbors that they must live and practise the arts they acquire. If Mr. Washington succeeds in this effort, he will have solved the whole problem. But he has undertaken no small task. . . . The student of history and current events can scarcely escape the impression that it is the firm and unwavering determination of the Southern whites to keep the negro in a permanent state of vassalage and subordination. . . .

It is to be hoped that Mr. Washington may convince the South that the policy of Federal non-interference, which seems to be the attitude of the present and several past administrations, places a sacred trust upon the South to be just to the negro. . . .

There will undoubtedly be a race problem in the United States, with all its attendant evils, until we cease to regard our colored population as negroes and consider them simply as citizens. . . . In the meantime, if the work led by Mr. Washington shall succeed in promoting better conditions, either by smoothing over asperities; by appealing to the dormant love of justice which has been the crowning glory of the English race—a trait which selfishness and greed have never entirely obscured; or by convincing the whites that injustice is vastly more dangerous to them than any possible loss of race prestige, Mr. Washington will deserve, and will doubtless receive, the thanks of the people of this whole nation. (pp. 115-16)

Charles W. Chesnutt, in his extract from "The Negro World Looks at Washington" (originally published in an expanded form as "A Plea for the American Negro," in The Critic, *Vol. XXXVI, No. 2, February, 1900), in* Booker T. Washington, *edited by Emma*

Lou Thornbrough (copyright © 1969 by Prentice-Hall, Inc.), Prentice-Hall, 1969, pp. 114-16.

W. D. HOWELLS   (essay date 1901)

[*Howells, the foremost American literary critic at the turn-of-the-century, wrote this laudatory appraisal of Washington upon the publication of* Up from Slavery.]

Except for the race ignominy and social outlawry to which he was born, the story of Booker T. Washington does not differ so very widely from that of many another eminent American. His origin was not much more obscure, his circumstances not much more squalid, than Abraham Lincoln's, and his impulses and incentives to the making of himself were of much the same source and quality. . . . There is nothing more touching in his book [*Up From Slavery*] than the passages which record [his mother's] devotion and her constant endeavor to help him find the way so dark to her. There is nothing more beautiful and uplifting in literature than the tender reverence, the devout honor with which he repays her affection. His birth was a part of slavery, and she was, in his eyes, as blameless for its conditions as if it had all the sanctions. The patience, the fearless frankness, with which he accepts and owns the facts, are not less than noble; and it is not to their white fathers, but to their black mothers, that such men as Frederick Douglass and Booker Washington justly ascribe what is best in their natures.

The story of his struggle for an education is the story of Booker Washington's life, which I am not going to spoil for the reader by trying to tell it. He has himself told it so simply and charmingly that one could not add to or take from it without marring it. The part of the autobiography which follows the account of his learning to read and write, in the scanty leisure of his hard work in the West Virginia coal mines, and of his desperate adventure in finding his way into Hampton Institute, is, perhaps, more important and more significant, but it has not the fascination of his singularly pleasing personality. It concerns the great problem, which no man has done more than he to solve, of the future of his race, and its reconciliation with the white race, upon conditions which it can master only through at least provisional submission; but it has not the appeal to the less philosophized sympathies which go out to struggle and achievement. It is not such interesting reading, and yet it is all very interesting; and if the prosperity of the author is not so picturesque as his adversity, still it is prosperity well merited, and it is never selfish prosperity. (pp. 281-82)

The dominant of Mr. Washington's register is *business;* first, last and all the time, the burden of his song is the Tuskegee Industrial Institute. There is other music in him, and no one who reads his story can fail to know its sweetness; but to Tuskegee his heart and soul are unselfishly devoted, and he does not suffer his readers long to forget it. He feels with his whole strength that the hope of his race is in its industrial advancement, and that its education must, above all, tend to that. His people must know how to read and write in order to be better workmen; but good workmen they must be, and they must lead decent, sober, honest lives to the same end. It was the inspiration of this philosophy and experience which enabled him, in his famous speech at the opening of the Atlanta Exposition [see excerpt above], to bring the white race into kindlier and wiser relations with the black than they had known before. Social equality he does not ask for or apparently care for; but industrial and economic equality his energies are bent upon achieving, in the common interest of both races. Of all slights and wrongs he is patient, so they do not hinder the negro from working or learning how to work in the best way. (p. 283)

White men rise from squalor almost as great as that which has left no taint upon the mind and soul of the born thrall, Booker T. Washington. But it must be remembered to his honor, and to his greater glory as a fighter against fate, that they rise in the face of no such odds as he has had to encounter. No prejudice baser than the despite for poverty bars their way. But the negro who makes himself in our conditions, works with limbs manacled and fettered by manifold cruel prepossessions. These prepossessions yield at certain points to amiability, to mildness, to persistent submissiveness, but at other points they yield to nothing.

In spite of them, though never in defiance of them, Booker T. Washington has made himself a public man, second to no other American in importance. He seems to hold in his strong grasp the key to the situation; for if his notion of reconciling the Anglo-American to the Afro-American, by a civilization which shall not seem to threaten the Anglo-American supremacy, is not the key, what is? He imagines for his race a civilization industrial and economical, hoping for the virtues which spring from endeavor and responsibility; and apparently his imagination goes no farther. But a less deeply interested observer might justify himself in hoping for it, from the things it has already accomplished in art and literature, a civilization of high aesthetic qualities.

As for the man himself, whose winning yet manly personality and whose ideal of self-devotion must endear him to every reader of his book, something remains to be said, which may set him in a true perspective and a true relation to another great Afro-American, whose name could not well be kept out of the consideration. Neither by temperament nor by condition had Frederick Douglass the charm which we feel when Booker T. Washington writes or speaks. The time was against him. In that time of storm and stress, the negro leader was, perforce, a fighter. The sea of slavery, from which he had escaped with his bare life, weltered over half the land, and threatened all the new bounds of the Republic. By means of the Fugitive Slave Law, it had, in fact, made itself national, and the bondman was nowhere on American soil safe from recapture and return to his master. Frederick Douglass had to be bought, and his price had to be paid in dollars by those who felt his priceless value to humanity, before he could be to it all that he was destined to become.

It would have been impossible that the iron which had entered into the man's soul should not show itself in his speech. Yet, his words were strangely free from violence; the violence was in the hatred which the mere thought of a negro defying slavery aroused in its friends. If you read now what he said, you will be surprised at his reasonableness, his moderation. He was not gentle; his life had been ungentle; the logic of his convictions was written in the ineffaceable scars of the whip on his back. Of such a man, you do not expect the smiling good humor with which Booker T. Washington puts the question of his early deprivations and struggles by. The life of Douglass was a far more wonderful life, and when it finds its rightful place in our national history, its greater dynamic importance will be felt.

Each of these two remarkable men wrought and is working fitly and wisely in his time and place. It is not well to forget slavery, and the memory of Frederick Douglass will always serve to remind us of it and of the fight against it. But it is not well to forget that slavery is gone, and that the subjection of the negro race which has followed it does not imply its horrors. The situation which Booker T. Washington deals with so wisely is wholly different from the situation which Douglass confronted, and it is slowly but surely modifying itself. The mild might of his adroit, his subtle statesmanship (in the highest sense it is not less than statesmanship, and involves a more than Philippine problem in our midst), is the only agency to which it can yield. Without affirming his intellectual equality with Douglass, we may doubt whether Douglass would have been able to cope so successfully with the actual conditions, and we may safely recognize in Booker T. Washington an Afro-American of unsurpassed usefulness, and an exemplary citizen. (pp. 287-88)

> *W. D. Howells, "An Exemplary Citizen," in The North American Review, Vol. CLXXIII, No. 537, August, 1901, pp. 280-88.*

WILLIAM MONROE TROTTER   (essay date 1903)

[*Editor of the black owned newspaper, the Boston* Guardian, *Trotter vehemently opposed Washington's social policies and voiced his disagreement in editorials such as the following. Trotter was also responsible for one of the first public demonstrations against Washington. During Washington's speaking engagement in a Boston church, Trotter began shouting questions that incited a well-publicized riot (see Henry M. Turner excerpt below).*]

From Booker T. Washington's speech before the Twentieth Century Club at the Colonial Theatre last Saturday we have clipped some excerpts which, we feel, can properly be classed as "Tuskegee gems." . . .

Here is a gem of real value:

"Those are most truly free who have passed through the greatest discipline."

Then slavery was the best condition of society, for all admit it was the severest discipline yet experienced by man. Was it not wrong in Lincoln to deprive our race thus of the highest freedom?

Here are two more gems:

"My request to the white men of the north is that they bring more coolness, more calmness, more deliberation and more sense of justice to the Negro question."

"As soon as our race gets property in the form of real estate, of intelligence, of high Christian character, it will find that it is going to receive the recognition which it has not thus far received."

The coolness is needed in the South, not in the North; this section needs to warm up a little in the interest of its former ideals.

As to the question of wealth and character, etc., winning one recognition, we see quite the contrary in the South. These things are damned there in Negroes. For proofs see the efforts made there to keep all Negroes from places of preferment. . . .

Gem No. 4 says:

"We have never disturbed the country by riots, strikes or lock-outs; ours has been a peaceful, faithful, humble service."

Now, it is a doubtful compliment to have this said about us; for the reason that strikes and lockouts are sometimes necessary conditions in society, and people who brag that they do not resort to these necessities are not always to be commended. In fact, the Negro in any and all professions and callings is safest in doing just the same, and no different from his white brother.

Gem No. 5:

"One farm bought, one house built, one home sweetly and intelligently kept, one man who is the largest taxpayer or who has the largest banking account, one school or church maintained, one factory running successfully, one garden profitably cultivated, one patient cured by a Negro doctor, one sermon well preached, one life cleanly lived, will tell more in our favor than all the abstract eloquence that can be summoned to plead our cause."

All of this last is mere claptrap. All the wealth, skill and intelligence acquired and accumulated by Negroes before '61 did not do half so much toward freeing the slave as did the abstract eloquence of [Frederick Douglass, Samuel Ringgold Ward, William Lloyd Garrison and Wendell Phillips]. . . . This habit of always belittling agitation on the part of Washington, that very thing which made him free, and by which he lives and prospers is one of his great faults if a man with such a blundering can have any degrees in stupidity. (pp. 28-30)

> *William Monroe Trotter, "Some Real Tuskegee Gems" (originally published in* The Guardian, *Boston, April 4, 1903), in* Negro Protest Thought in the Twentieth Century, *edited by Francis L. Broderick and August Meier (copyright © 1965 by The Bobbs-Merrill Company, Inc.), Bobbs-Merrill, 1966, pp. 28-30.*

HENRY M. TURNER   (essay date 1903)

[*Turner was a prominent black American who advocated the emigration of blacks to Africa after the Civil War. The following attack on Washington came after a riot at a Boston church in which Washington was to speak.*]

The newspapers bring tidings that since our last issue quite a riot was created in A.M.E.Z. church, where Professor Washington was to address a very large assembly of people, colored and white. It appears that hisses, cat squalls, groans, with the cry, "Take him out!" and many kinds of interruptions were indulged in till many got up and left the hall. Police were called for, arrests were made and a general confusion ensued, and perfect order was never restored while strenuous and vehement efforts were put forth to establish harmony. It seems from the papers, that Prof. Washington had used terms, phrases and sentences that were countenancing or excusing, or palliating disfranchisement of our race in Alabama, South Carolina and other states. And from the trend of his discourses, he was educating the white people of the nation to regard the Negro as a simple laborer and scullion, and that he was not fitted or qualified by nature to pursue professions, callings and studies of the higher kind.

We will neither commend or condemn Washington or the Boston rioters or mass meeting disturbers, as neither party meets our idea. Washington's policy is not worth a cent. It accomplishes no racial good, except as it helps about a thousand students at Tuskegee, and while we endorse the manhood of the race and agree with our Boston friends in spitting upon everything that would appear to underrate the value of the Negro in every particular, they are doing no more ultimate

good than Washington, as we see. They are all timberheads together, fussing and calling each other fools. Nothing less than a nation owned and controlled by the Negro, will amount to a hill of beans. We are individually friendly with Dr. Washington, and he would do anything he could, we believe, to favor us and we know we are on friendly terms with everybody in Boston. We have spoken in different churches and in Tremont Temple, and we have never seen larger meetings than have come to hear us in Boston. But neither the policy of Washington or of our Boston friends is worth a pinch of snuff. Anything less than separation and the black man relying upon himself is absolutely nonsense. Negro nationality is the only remedy, and time will show it.

> *Henry M. Turner, "Two Editorials: Booker T. Washington and Boston" (originally published as "Booker T. Washington and Boston," in* Voice of the People, *September, 1903), in* Booker T. Washington and His Critics: Black Leadership in Crisis, *edited by Hugh Hawkins (copyright 1962 by D. C. Heath and Company; copyright © 1974 by D. C. Heath and Company), second edition, Heath, 1974, p. 100.*

H. G. WELLS   (essay date 1906)

[*On an American sojourn, the well-known English author H. G. Wells had the opportunity to meet with Washington and discuss American racism. That meeting is recounted in the following excerpt.*]

I have attempted time after time to get some answer from the Americans I have met, the answer to what is to me the most obvious of questions. "Your grandchildren and the grandchildren of these people [Negroes] will have to live in this country side by side; do you propose, do you believe it possible, that they shall be living then in just the same relations that you and these people are living now; if you do not, then what relations do you propose shall exist between them?"

It is not too much to say that I have never once had the beginnings of an answer to this question. . . . (p. 102)

I certainly did not begin to realize one most important aspect of this question until I reached America. I thought of those eight millions as of men, black as ink. But when I met Mr. Booker T. Washington, for example, I met a man certainly as white in appearance as our Admiral Fisher, who is, as a matter of fact, quite white. A very large proportion of these colored people is more than half white. One hears a good deal about the high social origins of the Southern planters, very many derive undisputably from the first families of England. It is the same blood flows in these mixed colored peoples veins. [*Sic*] Just think of the sublime absurdity, therefore, of the ban. There are gentlemen of education and refinement, qualified doctors and lawyers, whose ancestors assisted in the Norman Conquest, and they dare not enter a car marked white and intrude upon the dignity of the rising loan-monger from Esthonia. . . .

But whatever aspect I recall of this great taboo that shows no signs of lifting, of this great problem of the future . . . there presently comes to my mind the browned face of Mr. Booker T. Washington, as he talked to me over our lunch in Boston. (p. 103)

He answered my questions meditatively. I wanted to know with an active pertinacity. What struck me most was the way in which his sense of the overpowering forces of race prejudice weighs upon him. It is a thing he accepts; in our time and condition it is not to be fought about. He makes one feel with an exaggerated intensity (though I could not even draw him to admit) its monstrous injustice. He makes no accusations. He is for taking it as a part of the present fate of his "people," and for doing all that can be done for them within the limit that it sets.

Therein he differs from Du Bois, the other great spokesman color has found in our time. Du Bois is more of the artist, less of the statesman; he conceals his passionate resentment all too thinly. He batters himself into rhetoric against these walls. He will not repudiate the clear right of the black man to every educational facility, to equal citizenship, and to equal respect. But Mr. Washington has statecraft. He looks before and after, and plans and keeps his counsel with the scope and range of a statesman. I use "statesman" in its highest sense; his is a mind that can grasp the situation and destinies of a people. . . .

I argued strongly against the view he seems to hold that black and white might live without mingling and without injustice, side by side. That I do not believe. Racial differences seem to me always to exasperate intercourse unless people have been trained to ignore them. . . . "You must repudiate separation," I said. "No peoples have ever yet endured the tension of intermingled distinctness."

"May we not become a peculiar people—like the Jews?" he suggested. "Isn't that possible?"

But there I could not agree with him. . . . The colored people . . . are not a community at all in the Jewish sense, but outcasts from a community. They are the victims of a prejudice that has to be destroyed. These things I urged, but it was, I think, empty speech to my hearer. (pp. 103-04)

"I wish you would tell me," I said abruptly, "just what you think of the attitude of white America towards you. Do you think it is generous?"

He regarded me for a moment. "No end of people help us," he said.

"Yes," I said; "but the ordinary man. Is he fair?"

"Some things are not fair," he said, leaving the general question alone. "It isn't fair to refuse a colored man a berth on a sleeping-car. I? I happen to be a privileged person, they make an exception for me; but the ordinary educated colored man isn't admitted to a sleeping-car at all. If he has to go a long journey, he has to sit up all night. His white competitor sleeps. Then in some places, in the hotels and restaurants—it's all right here in Boston—but southwardly he can't get proper refreshments. All that's a handicap. . . .

"The remedy lies in education," he said; "ours—*and theirs*.

"The real thing," he told me, "isn't to be done by talking and agitation. It's a matter of lives. The only answer to it all is for colored men to be patient, to make themselves competent, to do good work, to live well, to give no occasion against us. We feel that. In a way it's an inspiration." (pp. 104-05)

Whatever America has to show in heroic living today, I doubt if she can show anything finer than the quality of the resolve, the steadfast efforts hundreds of black and colored men are making today to live blamelessly, honorably and patiently, getting for themselves what scraps of refinement, learning and beauty they may, keeping their hold on a civilization they are grudged and denied. . . .

But the patience the negro needs!

No, I can't help idealizing the dark submissive figure of the negro in the spectacle of America. He, too, seems to me to sit waiting—and waiting with a marvelous and simple-minded patience—for finer understandings and a nobler time. (p. 105)

> *H. G. Wells, in his extract from "The White World Looks at Washington: Two British Opinions" (originally published as "The Tragedy of Color," in* Harper's Weekly, *Vol. L, No. 2595, September 15, 1906), in* Booker T. Washington, *edited by Emma Lou Thornbrough (copyright © 1969 by Prentice-Hall, Inc.), Prentice-Hall, 1969, pp. 102-05.*

BOOKER T. WASHINGTON   (essay date 1915)

[*In this posthumously published essay, Washington gives his assurance that segregation laws are unnecessary because black Americans have no intention of mixing socially with white Americans. This essay is considered a harsher assessment of the white South by Washington after several years of discouraging setbacks in race relations.*]

In all of my experience I have never yet found a case where the masses of the people of any given city were interested in the matter of the segregation of white and colored people; that is, there has been no spontaneous demand for segregation ordinances. In certain cities politicians have taken the leadership in introducing such segregation ordinances into city councils, and after making an appeal to racial prejudices have succeeded in securing a backing for ordinances which would segregate the negro people from their white fellow citizens. After such ordinances have been introduced it is always difficult, in the present state of public opinion in the South, to have any considerable body of white people oppose them, because their attitude is likely to be misrepresented as favoring negroes against white people. They are, in the main, afraid of the stigma, "negro-lover." . . .

Personally I have little faith in the doctrine that it is necessary to segregate the whites from the blacks to prevent race mixture. The whites are the dominant race in the South, they control the courts, the industries and the government in all of the cities, counties and states except in those few communities where the negroes, seeking some form of self-government, have established a number of experimental towns or communities.

I have never viewed except with amusement the sentiment that white people who live next to negro populations suffer physically, mentally and morally because of their proximity to colored people. Southern white people who have been brought up in this proximity are not inferior to other white people. The President of the United States was born and reared in the South in close contact with black people. Five members of the present Cabinet were born in the South; and many of them, I am sure, had black "mammies." . . .

It is true that the negro opposes these attempts to restrain him from residing in certain sections of a city or community. He does this not because he wants to mix with the white man socially, but because he feels that such laws are unnecessary. The negro objects to being segregated because it usually means that he will receive inferior accommodations in return for the taxes he pays. If the negro is segregated, it will probably mean that the sewerage in his part of the city will be inferior; that the streets and sidewalks will be neglected, that the street lighting will be poor; that his section of the city will not be kept in order by the police and other authorities, and that the "undesirables" of other races will be placed near him, thereby making it difficult for him to rear his family in decency. It should always be kept in mind that while the negro may not be directly a large taxpayer, he does pay large taxes indirectly. (p. 113)

White people who argue for the segregation of the masses of black people forget the tremendous power of objective teaching. To hedge any set of people off in a corner and sally among them now and then with a lecture or a sermon is merely to add misery to degradation. But put the black man where day by day he sees how the white man keeps his lawns, his windows; how he treats his wife and children, and you will do more real helpful teaching than a whole library of lectures and sermons. Moreover, this will help the white man. If he knows that his life is to be taken as a model, that his hours, dress, manners, are all to be patterns for someone less fortunate, he will deport himself better than he would otherwise. Practically all the real moral uplift the black people have got from the whites—and this has been great indeed—has come from this observation of the white man's conduct. The South to-day is still full of the type of negro with gentle manners. Where did he get them? From some master or mistress of the same type. . . .

Finally, as I have said in another place, as white and black learn daily to adjust, in a spirit of justice and fair play, those interests which are individual and racial, and to see and feel the importance of those fundamental interests which are common, so will both races grow and prosper. In the long run no individual and no race can succeed which sets itself at war against the common good; for "in the gain or loss of one race, all the rest have equal claim." (p. 114)

> Booker T. Washington, "My View of Segregation Laws," in The New Republic (© 1915 The New Republic, Inc.), Vol. 5, No. 57, December 4, 1915, pp. 113-14.

W. E. BURGHARDT Du BOIS   (essay date 1915)

[*A prominent black intellectual, Du Bois publicly opposed Washington's educational and social doctrines, stating that their submissive attitudes relegated blacks to an inferior social position. The following is an important piece of criticism in understanding the Washington-DuBois controversy.*]

Booker T. Washington arose as essentially the leader not of one race but of two,—a compromiser between the South, the North, and the Negro. Naturally the Negroes resented, at first bitterly, signs of compromise which surrendered their civil and political rights, even though this was to be exchanged for larger chances of economic development. The rich and dominating North, however, was not only weary of the race problem, but was investing largely in Southern enterprises, and welcomed any method of peaceful cooperation. Thus, by national opinion, the Negroes began to recognize Mr. Washington's leadership; and the voice of criticism was hushed.

Mr. Washington represents in Negro thought the old attitude of adjustment and submission; but adjustment at such a peculiar time as to make his programme unique. This is an age of unusual economic development, and Mr. Washington's programme naturally takes an economic cast, becoming a gospel of Work and Money to such an extent as apparently almost completely to overshadow the higher aims of life. Moreover, this is an age when the more advanced races are coming in closer contact with the less developed races, and the race-feeling is therefore intensified; and Mr. Washington's programme practically accepts the alleged inferiority of the Negro races. Again, in our own land, the reaction from the sentiment of war time has given impetus to race-prejudice against Negroes, and Mr. Washington withdraws many of the high demands of Negroes as men and American citizens. In other periods of intensified prejudice all the Negro's tendency to self-assertion has been called forth; at this period a policy of submission is advocated. In the history of nearly all other races and peoples the doctrine preached at such crises has been that manly self-respect is worth more than lands and houses, and that a people who voluntarily surrender such respect, or cease striving for it, are not worth civilizing.

In answer to this, it has been claimed that the Negro can survive only through submission. Mr. Washington distinctly asks that black people give up, at least for the present, three things,—

First, political power,

Second, insistence on civil rights,

Third, higher education of Negro youth,—

and concentrate all their energies on industrial education, the accumulation of wealth, and the conciliation of the South. This policy has been courageously and insistently advocated for over fifteen years, and has been triumphant for perhaps ten years. As a result of this tender of the palm-branch, what has been the return? In these years there have occurred:

1. The disfranchisement of the Negro.

2. The legal creation of a distinct status of civil inferiority for the Negro.

3. The steady withdrawal of aid from institutions for the higher training of the Negro.

These movements are not, to be sure, direct results of Mr. Washington's teachings; but his propaganda has, without a shadow of doubt, helped their speedier accomplishment. The question then comes: Is it possible, and probable, that nine millions of men can make effective progress in economic lines if they are deprived of political rights, made a servile caste, and allowed only the most meagre chance for developing their exceptional men? If history and reason give any distinct answer to these questions, it is an emphatic *No*. And Mr. Washington thus faces the triple paradox of his career:

1. He is striving nobly to make Negro artisans business men and property-owners; but it is utterly impossible, under modern competitive methods, for workingmen and property-owners to defend their rights and exist without the right of suffrage.

2. He insists on thrift and self-respect, but at the same time counsels a silent submission to civic inferiority such as is bound to sap the manhood of any race in the long run.

3. He advocates common-school and industrial training, and depreciates institutions of higher learning; but neither the Negro common-schools, nor Tuskegee itself, could remain open a day were it not for teachers trained in Negro colleges, or trained by their graduates.

This triple paradox in Mr. Washington's position is the object of criticism by two classes of colored Americans. One class is spiritually descended from Toussaint the Savior, through Gabriel, Vesey, and Turner, and they represent the attitude of revolt and revenge; they hate the white South blindly and distrust the white race generally, and so far as they agree on definite action, think that the Negro's only hope lies in emigration beyond the borders of the United States. And yet, by the irony of fate, nothing has more effectually made this programme seem hopeless than the recent course of the United States toward weaker and darker peoples in the West Indies, Hawaii, and the Philippines,—for where in the world may we go and be safe from lying and brute force?

The other class of Negroes who cannot agree with Mr. Washington has hitherto said little aloud. They deprecate the sight of scattered counsels, of internal disagreement; and especially they dislike making their just criticism of a useful and earnest man an excuse for a general discharge of venom from small-minded opponents. Nevertheless, the questions involved are so fundamental and serious that it is difficult to see how . . . representatives of this group, can much longer be silent. Such men feel in conscience bound to ask of this nation three things:

1. The right to vote.

2. Civil equality.

3. The education of youth according to ability.

They acknowledge Mr. Washington's invaluable service in counselling patience and courtesy in such demands; they do not ask that ignorant black men vote when ignorant whites are debarred, or that any reasonable restrictions in the suffrage should not be applied; they know that the low social level of the mass of the race is responsible for much discrimination against it, but they also know, and the nation knows, that relentless color-prejudice is more often a cause than a result of the Negro's degradation; they seek the abatement of this relic of barbarism, and not its systematic encouragement and pampering by all agencies of social power from the Associated Press to the Church of Christ. They advocate, with Mr. Washington, a broad system of Negro common schools supplemented by thorough industrial training; but they are surprised that a man of Mr. Washington's insight cannot see that no such educational system ever has rested or can rest on any other basis than that of the well-equipped college and university, and they insist that there is a demand for a few such institutions throughout the South to train the best of the Negro youth as teachers, professional men, and leaders.

This group of men honor Mr. Washington for his attitude of conciliation toward the white South; they accept the "Atlanta Compromise" in its broadest interpretation; they recognize, with him, many signs of promise, many men of high purpose and fair judgment, in this section; they know that no easy task has been laid upon a region already tottering under heavy burdens. But, nevertheless, they insist that the way to truth and right lies in straightforward honesty, not in indiscriminate flattery; in praising those of the South who do well and criticising uncompromisingly those who do ill; in taking advantage of the opportunities at hand and urging their fellows to do the same, but at the same time in remembering that only a firm adherence to their higher ideals and aspirations will ever keep those ideals within the realm of possibility. (pp. 49-54)

In failing thus to state plainly and unequivocally the legitimate demands of their people, even at the cost of opposing an honored leader, the thinking classes of American Negroes would shirk a heavy responsibility. . . . The growing spirit of kindliness and reconciliation between the North and South after the frightful differences of a generation ago ought to be a source of deep congratulation to all, and especially to those whose mistreatment caused the war; but if that reconciliation is to be marked by the industrial slavery and civic death of those same black men, with permanent legislation into a position of inferiority, then those black men, if they are really men, are called upon by every consideration of patriotism and loyalty to oppose such a course by all civilized methods, even though such opposition involves disagreement with Mr. Booker T. Washington. We have no right to sit silently by while the inevitable seeds are sown for a harvest of disaster to our children, black and white. (pp. 55-6)

It would be unjust to Mr. Washington not to acknowledge that in several instances he has opposed movements in the South which were unjust to the Negro; he sent memorials to the Louisiana and Alabama constitutional conventions, he has spoken against lynching, and in other ways has openly or silently set his influence against sinister schemes and unfortunate happenings. Notwithstanding this, it is equally true to assert that on the whole the distinct impression left by Mr. Washington's propaganda is, first, that the South is justified in its present attitude toward the Negro because of the Negro's degradation; secondly, that the prime cause of the Negro's failure to rise more quickly is his wrong education in the past; and, thirdly, that his future rise depends primarily on his own efforts. Each of these propositions is a dangerous half-truth. The supplementary truths must never be lost sight of: first, slavery and race-prejudice are potent if not sufficient causes of the Negro's position; second, industrial and common-school training were necessarily slow in planting because they had to await the black teachers trained by higher institutions,—it being extremely doubtful if any essentially different development was possible, and certainly a Tuskegee was unthinkable before 1880; and, third, while it is a great truth to say that the Negro must strive and strive mightily to help himself, it is equally true that unless his striving be not simply seconded, but rather aroused and encouraged, by the initiative of the richer and wiser environing group, he cannot hope for great success.

In his failure to realize and impress this last point, Mr. Washington is especially to be criticised. His doctrine has tended to make the whites, North and South, shift the burden of the Negro problem to the Negro's shoulders and stand aside as critical and rather pessimistic spectators; when in fact the burden belongs to the nation, and the hands of none of us are clean if we bend not our energies to righting these great wrongs.

The South ought to be led, by candid and honest criticism, to assert her better self and do her full duty to the race she has cruelly wronged and is still wronging. The North—her co-partner in guilt—cannot salve her conscience by plastering it with gold. We cannot settle this problem by diplomacy and suaveness, by "policy" alone. If worse come to worst, can the moral fibre of this country survive the slow throttling and murder of nine millions of men?

The black men of America have a duty to perform, a duty stern and delicate,—a forward movement to oppose a part of the work of their greatest leader. So far as Mr. Washington preaches Thrift, Patience, and Industrial Training for the masses, we must hold up his hands and strive with him, rejoicing in his honors and glorying in the strength of this Joshua called of God and of man to lead the headless host. But so far as Mr. Washington apologizes for injustice, North or South, does not rightly value the privilege and duty of voting, belittles the emasculating effects of caste distinctions, and opposes the higher training and ambition of our brighter minds,—so far as he, the

South, or the Nation, does this,—we must unceasingly and firmly oppose them. (pp. 57-9)

W. E. Burghardt Du Bois, "Of Mr. Booker T. Washington and Others," in his The Souls of Black Folk: Essays and Sketches (copyright A. C. McClurg & Co.), tenth edition, McClurg, 1915, pp. 41-59.*

LYMAN ABBOTT (essay date 1921)

[*Abbott was the editor of* The Outlook *magazine, in which* Up from Slavery *first appeared serially. He also advised Washington on the organization and style of the autobiography before its publication.*]

Booker T. Washington was a great statesman because he understood the meaning of his age and gave himself a willing and intelligent instrument to the beneficent solution of his nation's problem. The Civil War had established the authority of the National Government, but it still remained to unite North and South by a common spirit and a common purpose; it had set free the slave, but it still remained to establish new relations of mutual friendliness and respect between the races; it had abolished the old system of compulsory labour, but it still remained to create a new system of free labour; it had stricken the shackles from the limbs of the slave, but it still remained to strike the shackles from his mind and to teach him and his neighbour the rights, the duties, and the responsibilities of freedom. To this task Booker Washington devoted his life with singleness of purpose, clearness of vision, and patience of endeavour.

He has told the story of his life very simply and very modestly in his autobiography: **"Up from Slavery"**; a book which is a valuable addition both to American history and to American literature. It is preëminently a book for American boys and girls and ought to be in every school library in the country. Out of this book the thoughtful reader can easily get some impression of the spirit that animated Mr. Washington and the principles that governed him during his extraordinary career. (pp. 260-61)

[Washington] interpreted the North to the South and the South to the North, for he never modified his opinions in order to adapt them to the current opinion of the geographical section in which he was speaking.

He interpreted the Negroes to the whites and the whites to the Negroes; drew sharply the distinction between social equality and industrial equality; never demanded more for the Negro than an opportunity for self-development and useful service, and never conceded that anything less than this would be justice.

He spent no time in discussing dead issues; but he unhesitatingly condemned slavery when he spoke of it at all, pointed out the evils it wrought upon the white race as upon the black race, and urged his own people to justify emancipation by demonstrating the superior value of free labour.

He made no demands upon the white race to respect the Negro; but he pointed out to the Negroes how they could earn that respect, and this he did not only by his words, but by his life of unselfish and devoted labour.

He saw no hope for the Negro in conferring upon him political power until he had the capacity to use it intelligently. Looking back upon the past he declared his belief that it would have

been better to make the possession of a certain amount of education or property, or both, a test for the exercise of the franchise, but that test should be made to apply honestly to both the white and the black races. In other words, while seldom discussing the political question, he made it clear that he believed taking part in the government of others is a responsibility to be earned, not a natural right nor a privilege to be universally granted. (pp. 278-80)

In building the Tuskegee Institute Mr. Washington built his own monument. Greater educators there may have been; but it would not be easy to find in the history of any race the story of a life more Christ-like in its patient devotion to an unselfish cause than was his. This monument is a witness to the possibilities of the Afro-American. For the possibilities of a race are to be always measured, not by their averages but by their leaders, and Doctor Washington is a conclusive answer to the ignorant assertion that the Negro is incapable of great things. Nor is Tuskegee less a monument to the white people of the South. It was called into existence by them; received its first appropriation from a Southern legislature; and so hearty and unanimous has been the support awarded to it by the community in which it is situated that Doctor Washington was able to say that he had never asked anything of his white neighbours which they did not cordially grant to him if it was in their power so to do. Finally, Tuskegee affords conclusive demonstration that it is possible to unite both races in a common effort to promote the common welfare. (pp. 280-81)

Lyman Abbott, "Booker T. Washington, Statesman," in his Silhouettes of My Contemporaries (copyright 1921 by Doubleday & Company, Inc.; reprinted by permission of the publisher), Doubleday, 1921, pp. 258-81.

MARCUS GARVEY (essay date 1923)

[*A well-known proponent of African nationalism, Garvey at one time was influenced by Washington's philosophy. In this excerpt, Garvey speaks of a new black spirit that transcends Washington's policies.*]

The world held up the great Sage of Tuskegee—Booker T. Washington—as the only leader for the race. They looked forward to him and his teachings as the leadership for all times, not calculating that the industrially educated Negro would himself evolve a new ideal, after having been trained by the Sage of Tuskegee.

The world satisfied itself to believe that succeeding Negro leaders would follow absolutely the teachings of Washington. Unfortunately the world is having a rude awakening, in that we are evolving a new ideal. The new ideal includes the program of Booker T. Washington and has gone much further.

Things have changed wonderfully since Washington came on the scene. His vision was industrial opportunity for the Negro, but the Sage of Tuskegee has passed off the stage of life and left behind a new problem—a problem that must be solved, not by the industrial leader only, but by the political and military leaders as well.

If Washington had lived he would have had to change his program. No leader can successfully lead this race of ours without giving an interpretation of the awakened spirit of the New Negro, who does not seek industrial opportunity alone, but a political voice. The world is amazed at the desire of the

New Negro, for with his strong voice he is demanding a place in the affairs of men.

> Marcus Garvey, *"Booker T. Washington's Program" (1923), in his* Philosophy and Opinions of Marcus Garvey; or, Africa for the Africans, *edited by Amy Jacques Garvey, second edition, Frank Cass & Co. Ltd., 1967, p. 41.*

MERLE CURTI (essay date 1935)

[*Curti's Pulitzer Prize-winning* The Growth of American Thought *was the first successful attempt to relate all the aspects of American thought to the American social setting. In the following excerpt from his* The Social Ideas of American Education, *Curti maintains that Washington's social philosophy mirrored the values held by middle-class white Americans as a realistic way in which to "fit into the existing system."*]

Washington's emphasis on a practical education for the Negro is explained by his belief that, in order to break down racial prejudice and to achieve real progress for the black, the Southern white must be convinced that the education of the former slaves was in the true interest of the South—in the interest, in short, of the Southern white himself. Far from appealing to disinterested motives, this black leader believed in the efficacy of appealing to the self-interest of the dominant whites. In their hands lay the granting or withholding of funds for Negro schools. In their hands, moreover, lay the administration of court justice and the alternative device of the rope and faggot—the year after Washington arrived at Tuskegee forty-nine black men were lynched, and in 1892, ten years later, the number was 155. In the hands of the ruling race, too, lay a thousand other matters which vitally affected the blacks. It was clear to Washington that the alliance with Northern whites during Reconstruction had failed to effect any permanent guarantees to his race; and it was equally clear that the more militant and aggressive behavior of the post-war days had provoked reaction and the violence of the Ku Klux Klan. Where aggressiveness and militancy had failed, an appeal to the self-interest of the dominant whites might succeed. The founder of Tuskegee faced the facts and acted according to his light.

In his effort to enlist the sympathy and co-operation of the white community in Tuskegee Washington was surprisingly successful. His warning that white men, by holding blacks in the gutter, would have to stay there with them, was a compelling argument when it became clear that the whole community actually did profit by what was being done for the Negro. . . . When he insisted that the great majority of his race did not expect or desire social equality, he still further disarmed the whites.

The astute Negro leader also did much to dispel the bugbear of black political domination. At first he said very little about the constitutional right of the Negro to vote. Only very cautiously and gradually did he come to advocate the desirability of permitting educated and property-owning blacks to exercise the right of suffrage. . . .

Subsequent lectures, articles, and books consolidated the position thus won. In view of the bids that the South was making for Northern capital, it was not without significance that the Negro educator declared in the Atlanta speech, as he had done before and continued to do, that his people had never engaged in strikes or given any labor trouble. . . .

Regardless of the extent to which Washington succeeded in convincing Northern financial groups that industrial education of the Negro promised a skilled, docile, and cheap labor supply, and that racial friction would diminish, he certainly found it, after his reassuring speeches, less of a struggle to obtain endowment for his institution. (pp. 136-37)

Convinced that the Negro was at his best in the country and that he showed up worst in the city, Washington made every effort to persuade his people to acquire the farms on which they lived. Yet, as the years passed, he came more and more to sympathize with the Negro business man and to reverence the business ideal of life. . . .

If the Negro business man was successful, Washington felt that then prejudice and color could not long shut the race out from a share in any of the responsibilities of the community in which they lived, or in any opportunity or position that a self-respecting people would desire to possess. . . . He sponsored the National Negro Business League and in refutation of the charge that the race was lacking in thrift, executive talent, and organizing ability, cited with pride the success of colored men in business.

The black leader was merely accepting the dominant business philosophy of his day. Like most Americans, he did not ask how fortunes were made, nor question the ethics of the captains of industry and finance. Accepting the tenet that whenever the Negro failed to find steady employment, it was due to his shiftlessness, his unreliability, and his easy-going ways, he begged his people, in heart to heart talks, to cultivate the business virtues. . . .

Believing that if the blacks knew something of the burdens borne by the masses of Europe they would realize that their own position was by no means unique or hopeless, as many had supposed, Booker T. Washington went to Europe in 1910 to study the "man farthest down." He came back with an optimistic message for his people. . . .

Although Washington found much evidence that the masses in Europe were getting ahead, he doubted whether trade unions, strikes, Socialism, and revolution could improve their lot. Wherever the governing classes had made concessions, wherever remedial measures and reforms had been granted, the spirit of revolution had subsided. While he admitted that he did not very clearly understand Socialism, he expressed doubt whether, human nature being what it was, the Socialist program could be realized in the way its adherents believed. It was the American individualist of the middle class, not the Negro, who spoke when he declared that as human capacities differed, so opportunities and rewards must also differ. As a Southerner he paid tribute to the *laissez-faire* theory that the best government was that which governed least; and as an American, he repudiated reform by revolution and by political machinery which directed and controlled the individual from the outside. Neither his own race nor the substantial friends of Tuskegee could doubt where he stood. Possibly, however, there was something of an ironical warning in his statement that the dominant class in Europe had patriotically striven to strengthen the existing order by freeing it from the defects that endangered its existence. . . .

Washington's social philosophy was, in fine, more typical of middle-class white Americans, whom he wanted his people to be like, than it was of the Negro as such. It is true that in appealing to former slaves and their offspring to eschew militancy and conflict with the whites in the effort to improve the status of the race, he capitalized the black man's way of getting along by laughing, dancing, and singing. But little was said about the qualities of gayety, humor, and wistful whimsicality, virtues and gifts which some thought might enrich and soften the driving, efficient, and machinelike ways of the American whites. On the contrary, Washington made simplicity, earnestness, frugality, and industry the great desiderata. One searches his writings in vain for any appreciation of the aesthetic and cultural values of the African background, of the "spirituals," or of the generally pleasant, easy-going ways of the black man. Although very occasionally he made a bow to the need of cultivating the beautiful, he resembled Franklin in paying much greater deference to whatever was useful and practical.

In other ways Washington was like the average American. His insistence on looking at the bright side of things, his devotion to getting ahead by self-help, his conviction that every one had his future in his own hands, that success came to him who was worthy of it, and that the greater the obstacles, the greater the victory over them—all this characterized the thought and feeling of most Americans. Equally typical of the dominant psychology of the middle and upper classes was his denial of any conflict or cleavage of interest between worker and employer, white and black. His was the gospel of class co-operation. . . . His patriotic belief that, however bad conditions were for his race at home, the masses of Europe were even worse off, was likewise good American doctrine. . . .

Washington's position is better understood when it is remembered that he began his work when race hatred was at its height and when emotions were strained and tense. . . .

Education of the hands helped in fact to bridge the gap between slavery and freedom; it taught thousands of Southern whites to accept Negro education, not merely as a necessary evil, but as a possible social benefit. The good will that Washington won was at least partly responsible for increasing public support to Negro colleges and schools. . . .

The industrial school was . . . realistic and not without victories in its practical object of aiding the black man to find a place in American life in which he could make a decent living as the foundation of culture. . . .

Yet . . . industrial training did not keep the Negro farm population from decreasing; it did not enable the Negro artisan to gain proportionately in industry; it did not establish Negro business on a sound footing. Leaders of the movement ignored the fact that at the very time when the crusade for industrial training was being launched, the technological basis of industry was rapidly shifting from that of the skilled artisan to machine production. (pp. 137-39)

In view of the hostility of organized labor to the black and the general ineffectiveness of Socialism on the one hand, and the friendliness of men of great wealth on the other, it was, of course, entirely natural for Washington to take the stand he did. Moreover, there was much justification for his emphasis on the immediate amelioration of his race within the system that actually existed. Until collaboration with the dominant class among the whites had been proved to be ineffective as an instrument for elevating the race, it was natural to pin great faith to it. . . .

If the Negro were to fit into the existing system—and what could seem more natural and desirable to a former slave?—

Washington offered a realistic approach to the problem. . . . The limitations of his social thinking were not, primarily, those of a Negro—they were those of the class which, on the whole, determined American values and governed American life. (pp. 139-40)

> *Merle Curti, "The Black Man's Place: Booker T. Washington 1856?-1915," in his* The Social Ideas of American Education *(copyright © 1935 by Charles Scribner's Sons; renewal copyright © 1963; reprinted by permission of Charles Scribner's Sons), Charles Scribner's Sons, 1935 (and reprinted as "Booker T. Washington in History: Merle Curti," in* Booker T. Washington, *edited by Emma Lou Thornbrough, Prentice-Hall, Inc., 1969, pp. 136-40).*

W. EDWARD FARRISON   (essay date 1942)

[*In a balanced discussion of Washington's educational principles, Farrison contends that Washington's theory of industrial education was a failure because he did not recognize the need for political power as a means to gain economic stability for black Americans. However, since Farrison wrote this essay, it has been discovered that Washington had strong political influence in the Roosevelt and Taft administrations, which he exerted to aid the careers of many black political appointees and leaders (see August Meier essay excerpted below).*]

Although Mr. Washington is often accredited with developing a new theory of education, the lessons which he endeavored to teach were not new. His doctrine concerning work was essentially the same as the "gospel of labor" which Thomas Carlyle—whom he probably had not read extensively—had preached in spluttering and cryptic exclamations earlier in the nineteenth century. The lessons of economy and thrift, as everyone knows, had been promulgated in colonial America more than a hundred years before by that apostle of material comfort and progress, Benjamin Franklin—whom Mr. Washington, doubtless, had read. Moreover, Mr. Washington's teachings were of the very form and pressure of his time. Mr. Washington came forth at the time when a great many other Americans whose beginnings were unpromising, but whose opportunities were greater than his, were working diligently and shrewdly—if not always honestly—to make themselves gods of the very comfort and well-being and respectability for which Mr. Washington taught Negroes to strive. Incidentally, it may be noted that in a large measure Tuskegee was built and has thrived on the blessings of the gods of ease who during the Gilded Age enshrined themselves in temples of wealth and power.

It should also be noted that the idea of inculcating in Negroes lessons of industry, thrift, and economy by means of a school devoted to industrial education was not original with either Mr. Washington or General [Samuel C.] Armstrong. As Mr. Washington himself knew, the idea was much older than the Emancipation Proclamation; and as he also knew, his basic arguments in favor of industrial training for free Negroes had been set forth by Frederick Douglass in his proposal for the establishment of an industrial college for Negroes long before the Civil War. But in advising Negroes in the South to work to regain by an industrial efficiency suggestive of that advocated by Milton's Mammon what they lost by disfranchisement, Mr. Washington veered altogether away from Douglass's point of view.

In a half-dozen books, several articles, and numerous speeches Mr. Washington reiterated his views, frequently using the same phraseology and the same examples. Here and there he pointed to individual Negroes who had succeeded by means of industrial training, thrift, and tact. What these had done, he said, Negroes as a group could do. But he seemed to overlook the fact that these isolated instances were more often the exception than the rule and, therefore, proved little or nothing about the group, hampered as it was, and still is, by crushing circumstances which individuals now and then succeed in surmounting.

Almost fifty years have passed since Mr. Washington came into prominence as an educator and leader. In spite of notable industrial progress and economic advancement, and the make-believe of the over-optimistic, the masses of Negroes, especially in the South, are still living in poverty and ignorance. During the last fifty years but few of the blessings envisioned by Mr. Washington have come; and the economic and social, as well as the political, problems of the masses of Negroes still remain to be solved. If time has thus belied Mr. Washington's views, it is probably due less to chance than to their inherent weaknesses.

Granted that there is moral value as well as dignity in manual labor, and that economic independence may be achieved by industrial skill—though the depression of the 1930's leads one to wonder whether any amount or kind of education or training can guarantee economic security—how can the Negro secure to himself the benefits of his labor unless he has some influence in the determination of his value to his community as a worker? And how can he have this while, because of a lack of influence and power in the body politic, he can still work only at such jobs as are *given* to him? Obviously, one who is powerless to choose his job is equally as powerless to demand full reward for his labor. The very respectability and influence which Mr. Washington said Negroes could expect to have conferred upon them as rewards for industry and thrift are indeed the only desiderata by which Negroes can ever achieve economic independence. Thus it appears that in Mr. Washington's argument ends and means were confused, and Negroes were urged to lift themselves by their own bootstraps.

As a result of the promulgation of Mr. Washington's views industrial training of a kind became a feature of Negro education in the South and has remained thus ever since. Numerous private and public institutions devoted wholly or partly to industrial training were established, and some schools already existing were tempted to add industrial departments. In ***Working with the Hands*** . . . , the principal work in which he tried to explain his program of education, Mr. Washington mentioned sixteen schools of this kind that grew out of Tuskegee.

Despite the increase in the number of industrial schools, however, industrial training has remained principally a verbal feature of Negro education—for reasons which one needs no philosopher's lantern to see. First, with but one or two exceptions the private schools have never been adequately equipped to offer thorough industrial training to anybody, and the one or two exceptions could accommodate only a negligible minority of those who might have profited by such training. Second, until recently, after industrial training was transformed into "mechanical arts" and "technical education," probably nowhere in the South was it given anything approaching adequate support out of public funds. The fact is, the sham industrial education provided for Negroes at public expense would have been altogether farcical if it had not had so many tragic aspects.

There have been, of course, considerable improvements in recent years; but when one considers the changes which have been constantly taking place in organized industry, he becomes woefully conscious that public industrial education for Negroes in the South is still far from adequate. And as to equitableness, except in a few places there has hardly been any pretension to that. Witness the rapidity and aplomb with which vocational education on the secondary school level—the school level of the masses—was recently being provided for everybody except Negroes, until national defense became urgent.

Why have matters developed thus? Not because everybody has been naïve enough to believe that everything has been lovely, but because Negroes as a group have not been sufficiently influential and powerful politically to demand better consideration from those in control of public funds and public policies. The fact that the very kind of education advocated by Mr. Washington for the masses of Negroes and verbally supported by others has never really been made available demonstrates graphically one of the most palpable weaknesses in his argument. The very means—namely, industrial education—by which he taught the masses of the Negroes to achieve civil and political independence is itself a part of a larger end—namely, equal educational opportunities—towards which civil and political independence is the only sure means.

A belief held by many, especially by those who have never taken the trouble to read Mr. Washington carefully, is that he advocated industrial training for Negroes to the exclusion of liberal education. There are in his writings, to be sure, querulous criticisms of liberal education and its advocates, as in the latter half of the fifth chapter in ***Up from Slavery*** . . . and in the chapter "The Intellectuals and the Boston Mob" in ***My Larger Education***. . . . But in spite of such criticisms this belief is erroneous. He believed profoundly in industrial education for the masses, but he also believed in liberal and professional education for some. In both his speeches and his published writings Mr. Washington repeatedly disclaimed the advocacy of any one kind of education to the exclusion of *all* other kinds, and there seems to be no reason to doubt his sincerity. In ***Working with the Hands*** he asserted: "While insisting upon thorough and high-grade industrial education for a large proportion of my race, I have always had the greatest sympathy with first-class college training and have recognized the fact that the Negro race, like other races, must have thoroughly trained college men and women. There is a place and a work for such, just as there is a place and a work for those thoroughly trained with their hands."

This statement was ably supported by Mr. Washington's practice. As is well known, in developing his program at Tuskegee he found places and work for many who had been educated in the best liberal-arts traditions in Negro colleges as well as in famous Northern universities. However theoretical arguments might go, this was an actual step toward conjoining the two kinds of education for the betterment of the masses of Negroes.

Mr. Washington's frequent ridicule of the study of French, instrumental music, and foreign geography in dirty cabins was not an argument against liberal education. Plainly, it was not intended to be such. Rather, it was an argument against any kind of learning that did not meet the immediate needs of the learner. Unfortunately, it reminds one of the spurious "Mandy, is you done your Greek yet?" argument; but in substance and force it was one with the now familiar and generally accepted argument against teaching fudgemaking and embroidering as home economics where more practical matters of homemaking need to be emphasized. As an argument it was concrete, simple, familiar, and slightly humorous; and because of this very fact it was subject to easy overemphasis on the part of both Mr. Washington and his critics.

As it has been with many other pleaders for particular causes, so it was with Mr. Washington. His belief in industrial education became a faith which he defended short of discrediting all other faiths. In the light of his molding experiences his emphasis on industrial training, even though possibly out of proportion to its value, is understandable, if it was not altogether justifiable—which is also true of his early critics' attitudes towards him in the light of their backgrounds and experiences. He himself probably was not confused, but there was the danger that those who would follow him might be misled into putting too much emphasis on merely making a living and too little on living. Had Mr. Washington lived twenty years longer, he could hardly have missed seeing that no one kind of education is sufficient even for the masses of Negroes—unless the Negro is to remain some special kind of American and something less than an American citizen. Seeing this, great American that he was, Mr. Washington, doubtless, would have changed his philosophy of education and also his views as a "leader of the Negro people." Otherwise the ascription of greatness to him would have been a mistake. (pp. 314-19)

W. Edward Farrison, "Booker T. Washington: A Study in Educational Leadership," in South Atlantic Quarterly (copyright © 1942 by Duke University Press, Durham, North Carolina), Vol. XLI, No. 3, July, 1942, pp. 313-19.

OLIVER C. COX   (lecture date 1950)

[*Cox offers a Marxian analysis of the nature of Washington's leadership, referring to him as a collaborator who promoted restraints on black social power favored by white society and who "could never again be imposed upon the race because even the rural Negroes of the South are conditioned to respond negatively to him." Cox's view is disputed by Alfred Young (see excerpt below).*]

On the pre-Civil War plantation talented black men tended to become principally either discontented bondsmen with ideas of escape and revolt, or trusted slaves. Washington's slavery experience seems to have conditioned him to the latter type of personality. He had no insurrectionary tradition in his family, and nothing at all like the kind of contempt for the institution which obsessed Frederick Douglass. As a slave he would most likely have been a capital danger to such exploits as those of Harriet Tubman. Kelly Miller makes the observation that "but for Lincoln's proclamation, Washington would probably have arisen to esteem and favor in the eyes of his master as a good and faithful servant." The favorite slave was frequently very firm in dealing with the rank-and-file of his class for being remiss in their duties. Indeed one feels constantly that Washington never fully lost the attitude of the favorite slave.

In freedom, however, he was very ambitious. His fervid aspiration to build an educational institution comparable to that of his alma mater presented him with certain material necessities which only persons of wealth could satisfy. Thus the financing of his project and the arrangement of a financially secure life for himself provided the essential *quid pro quo* in his collaboration. The material achievements of the collaborator must necessarily be small relative to the vital interests of the people which he serves to obscure and vitiate.

Washington's leadership, therefore, should be thought of as spurious. He was not a leader of the masses in the Garvian sense; his function was rather that of controlling the masses. He deflated and abandoned their common cause. He demanded less for the Negro people than that which the ruling class had already conceded. And because he was in reality sent with a mission to subdue the spirit of protest in the masses instead of his arising among them as a champion of their cause, he was frequently insulting and "harsh" toward them. (p. 95)

It has been commonly averred that Washington's leadership may be "justified" if his "times" are taken into consideration. By a like assumption, however, the manner of action of virtually all persons and all things may be explained away. To describe, for example, the social situation, the "times," which made the rise of Savonarola possible is not necessarily to demonstrate that his leadership was inevitable. During slavery there was in the same locus a social opportunity for both the insurrectionist and the traitor. The meaningful procedure seems rather to be that of typifying the social roles and of indicating the nature of their consistency with the interests and movements of social groups. Time here is a common factor.

Although Washington functioned as a restraint upon the Negroes' democratic progress, he still embodied some residual value. The propaganda which exalted him, his friendship with powerful members of the ruling class, and the honor which it frequently conferred upon him became a heartening symbol to the Negro people. Many influential southern whites, principally those schooled in the old plantation ethics, envied even his derived prestige and railed against fraternization with the Negro. On this issue of color prejudice even protest leaders, with reservations, sprang to his defense. Thus arose a collateral problem centered about Washington as a symbol. His high social status, freely conceded for a purpose, tended to animate a large section of the Negro people.

There is a certain very simple but to many persons quite pertinent question as to whether the Negro people would have been "better off" without Washington. It may be possible to weigh this question. In the first place the Negro people never really followed Washington, for he did not lead but rather sought to divert them. The common cause of the Negro before, during, and after Washington's ascent remains the acquisition of full civil rights. This cause was seriously obscured by the pressures of the larger interests which brought Washington himself into use. (pp. 95-6)

[Let us repeat] Washington's position on the crucial issue in the Negro's cause: "The wisest among my race understand that the agitation of questions of social equality is the extremest folly . . ." This is, in fact, the sensitive core of the Negro's problem; and Washington couches it in the exact terminology of the most determined detractors of the Negro people. (p. 96)

Leaders of Washington's type are exceedingly serviceable to the southern ruling class. They are vastly more effective than white spokesmen in controverting the movement for democracy among Negroes. Against white workers to the latter end they are an almost complete answer, for it is assumed that no white liberal could be more interested in the Negro's welfare than the Negro himself. It should be remembered, moreover, that the effective white leadership of the South had already put a transcendent value on the maintenance of its side of the cause. That the Negro shall not vote in the South, [Henry] Grady affirms, is a truth that "has abided forever in the marrow of our bones and shall run forever with the blood that feeds Anglo-

Saxon hearts.'' The value of Washington as an impediment to the efforts of both white and Negro pleaders for civil rights is related directly to his financial success and power over Negro affairs.

The social opportunity for the collaborating leader is still available, and his devices remain identical with those perfected by Washington. The reason, evidently, why such a leader cannot again rise to Washington's stature is that the relatively feeble reaction of the Negro people, which Washington greatly feared but which he was able to overawe, has now grown to such formidable proportions that he is effectively localized. Recently one of Washington's institutional successors publicly voiced the opinion that "the South is capable of solving its problems without outside assistance." He was given immediate and wide publicity in the dominant press of the South as "a recognized leader of his race," but the tactic also readily aroused the indignation of the Negroes of the community. Negroes apparently will no longer permit such views among responsible persons to go unrebuked even though they be manifest material expedients. Probably a collaborator of Washington's magnitude could never again be imposed upon the race because even the rural Negroes of the South are conditioned to respond negatively to him. (pp. 96-7)

> *Oliver C. Cox, "The Leadership of Booker T. Washington" (originally a speech read before the Association of Social Science Teachers on May 5-6, 1950), in* Social Forces *(copyright © 1951, Social Forces; copyright renewed © 1979 by The University of North Carolina Press), Vol. 30, No. 1, October, 1951, pp. 91-7.*

AUGUST MEIER (essay date 1957)

[*For this important essay, Meier examined Washington's unpublished papers and revealed his widespread political involvement, proving that Washington worked more actively for political and social rights than many of his critics maintained.*]

Washington was associated with a policy of compromise and conciliation toward the white South that is not in keeping with the trend of our times. Yet Washington's own correspondence reveals such extensive efforts against segregation and disfranchisement that a re-evaluation of his philosophy and activities is in order.

Undoubtedly in reading Washington's books, articles, and speeches, one is most strongly impressed with the accommodating tone he adopted toward the white South. He minimized the extent of race prejudice and discrimination, criticized the airing of Negro grievances, opposed "social equality," accepted segregation and the "separate but equal" doctrine, depreciated political activity, favored property and educational qualifications for the franchise (fairly applied to both races), largely blamed Negroes themselves for their unfortunate condition, and counselled economic accumulation and the cultivation of Christian character as the best ways to advance the status of Negroes in American society. His ultimate ends were stated so vaguely and ambiguously that Southern whites mistook his short-range objectives for his long-range goals, although his Negro supporters understood that through tact and indirection he hoped to secure the good will of the white man and the eventual recognition of the constitutional rights of American Negroes.

Now, although overtly Washington minimized the importance of political and civil rights, covertly he was deeply involved in political affairs and in efforts to prevent disfranchisement and other forms of discrimination. For example, Washington lobbied against the Hardwick disfranchising bill in Georgia in 1899. While he permitted whites to think that he accepted disfranchisement, he tried to keep Negroes believing otherwise. In 1903 when Atlanta editor Clark Howell implied that Washington opposed Negro officeholding, the Tuskegeean did not openly contradict him, but asked T. Thomas Fortune of the leading Negro weekly, the New York *Age,* to editorialize, "We are quite sure that the Hon. Howell has no ground . . . for his attempt to place Mr. Washington in such a position, as it is well understood that he, while from the first deprecating the Negro's making political agitation and office-holding the most prominent and fundamental part of his career, has not gone any farther."

Again, while Washington seemed to approve of the disfranchisement amendments when he said that "every revised constitution throughout the Southern States has put a premium upon intelligence, ownership of property, thrift and character," he was nevertheless secretly engaged in attacking them by legal action. As early as 1900 he was asking certain philanthropists for money to fight the electoral provisions of the Louisiana constitution. Subsequently he worked secretly through the financial secretary of the Afro-American Council's legal bureau, personally spending a great deal of money and energy fighting the Louisiana test case. (pp. 220-21)

Although he always discreetly denied any interest in active politics, he was engaged in patronage distribution under Roosevelt and Taft, in fighting the lily-white Republicans, and in getting out the Negro vote for the Republicans at national elections. He might say, "I never liked the atmosphere of Washington. I early saw that it was impossible to build up a race of which their leaders were spending most of their time, thought, and energy in trying to get into office, or in trying to stay there after they were in," but under Roosevelt he became the arbiter of Negro appointments to federal office.

Roosevelt started consulting Washington almost as soon as he took office. The Tuskegeean's role in the appointment of Gold Democrat Thomas G. Jones to a federal judgeship in Alabama was widely publicized. Numerous letters reveal that politicians old and new were soon writing to Tuskegee for favors. Ex-congressman George H. White unsuccessfully appealed to Washington after the White House indicated that "a letter from you would greatly strengthen my chances." [His secretary, Emmett J.] Scott reported that the President's assertion to one office-seeker that he would consider him only with Washington's "endorsement" had "scared these old fellows as they never have been scared before." Some of the established politicians played along and were helped along. Thus P.B.S. Pinchback, at one time acting governor of Louisiana, was favored throughout the Roosevelt and Taft administrations. In the case of J. C. Napier, Nashville lawyer and banker, Washington first turned him down as recorder of deeds for the District of Columbia and minister to Liberia, then named him as one of two possibilities for consul at Bahia, later offered him the Liberian post which Napier now refused, and finally secured for him the office of register of the Treasury. Examples of Washington's influence could be multiplied indefinitely, for a number of port collectorships and of internal revenue, receiverships of public monies in the land office, and several diplomatic posts, as well as the positions of auditor for the

Navy, register of the Treasury, and recorder of deeds were at his disposal. Among his outstanding appointments were Robert H. Terrell, judge of municipal court in Washington; William H. Lewis, assistant attorney-general under Taft; and Charles W. Anderson, collector of internal revenue in New York.

Furthermore, Roosevelt sought Washington's advice on presidential messages to Congress and consulted him on most matters concerning the Negro. Every four years, also, Washington took charge of the Negro end of the Republican presidential campaign, he and his circle, especially Charles Anderson, recommending (and blackballing) campaign workers and newspaper subsidies, handling the Negro press, advising on how to deal with racial issues, and influencing prominent Negroes.

If Washington reaped the rewards of politics, he also experienced its vicissitudes. From the start he was fighting a desperate and losing battle against the lily-white Republicans in the South. His correspondence teems with material on the struggle, especially in Louisiana and Alabama, and in other states as well. As he wrote to Walter L. Cohen, chairman of the Republican state central committee of Louisiana and register of the land office in New Orleans, on October 5, 1905: "What I have attempted in Louisiana I have attempted to do in nearly every one of the Southern States, as you and others are in a position to know, and but for my action, as feeble as it was, the colored people would have been completely overthrown and the Lily Whites would have been in complete control in nearly every Southern State."

Troubles came thick and fast after Taft's inauguration. The new President did not consult Washington as much as Roosevelt had done, and Washington exercised somewhat less control over appointments. . . . Not until 1911, after persistent efforts to convince the administration of the need for some decent plums in order to retain the Negro vote, were a few significant appointments finally arranged. The most notable was that of W. H. Lewis as assistant attorney-general—the highest position held by a Negro in the federal government up to that time.

In areas other than politics Washington also played an active behind-the-scenes role. On the Seth Carter (Texas) and Dan Rogers (Alabama) cases involving discrimination against Negroes in the matter of representation on jury panels, Washington helped with money and worked closely with lawyer Wilford Smith until their successful conclusion before the United States Supreme Court. He was interested in protecting Negro tenants, who had accidentally or in ignorance violated their contracts, from being sentenced to the chain gang. He was concerned in the Alonzo Bailey peonage case, and when the Supreme Court declared peonage illegal, confided to friends that "some of us here have been working at this case for over two years," securing the free services of "some of the best lawyers in Montgomery" and the assistance of other eminent Alabama whites.

In view of Washington's public acceptance of separate but equal transportation accommodations, his efforts against railroad segregation are of special interest. When Tennessee in effect prohibited Pullman space for Negroes by requiring that such facilities be segregated, he stepped into the breach. He worked closely with Napier in Nashville, and enlisted the aid of Atlanta leaders like W.E.B. DuBois. This group did not succeed in discussing the matter with Robert Todd Lincoln, president of the Pullman company, in spite of the intercession of another railroad leader, William H. Baldwin, Jr. And, though Washington was anxious to start a suit, the Nashville people

failed to act. In 1906, employing Howard University professor Kelly Miller and Boston lawyer Archibald Grimké as intermediaries, Washington discreetly supplied funds to pay ex-senator Henry W. Blair of New Hampshire to lobby against the Warner-Foraker amendment to the Hepburn Railway Rate Bill. This amendment, by requiring equality of accommodations in interstate travel, would have impliedly condoned segregation throughout the country, under the separate but equal doctrine. The amendment was defeated, but whether owing to Blair's lobbying or to the protests of Negro organizations is hard to say.

It is clear, then, that in spite of his placatory tone and his outward emphasis upon economic development as the solution to the race problem, Washington was surreptitiously engaged in undermining the American race system by a direct attack upon disfranchisement and segregation; that in spite of his strictures against political activity, he was a powerful politician in his own right. The picture that emerges from Washington's own correspondence is distinctly at variance with the ingratiating mask he presented to the world. (pp. 222-27)

> *August Meier, "Toward a Reinterpretation of Booker T. Washington," in* The Journal of Southern History *(copyright © 1957 by the Southern Historical Association), Vol. XXIII, No. 2, May, 1957, pp. 220-27.*

DONALD J. CALISTA   (essay date 1964)

[Calista believes, as does August Meier (see excerpt above), that Washington wore a "mask of compromise" in order to achieve his long-range goals.]

[By the mid-1890's, someone] had to meet the shattered hopes of the socially and economically demoralized Negro, and to soothe his open political wounds. Someone was needed, in short, who could be all things to all men. Such a man was Booker Taliaferro Washington. (pp. 245-46)

Washington's triumph with Negroes resulted from a number of reasons. . . . First, and foremost, was the timing: the Atlanta speech in the fall of 1895, came at the peak of the Negro's troubles. By the mid-1890's the forces working against the Negro abruptly and painfully erupted: depression raged on, government deserted him, friends disappeared, disfranchisement picked up steam, lynching ran rampant, and then Douglass died; a year later Populism collapsed. The ray of hope lit by Washington at Atlanta immediately burst into a bonfire of salvation—Negroes cried as he spoke. Whatever subsequent value picked up on his views, given these conditions, it would take another revolution in Negro (and white) thought to unleash the sway that Washington held over it. This kept DuBois as an underdog challenger, even after Washington's death. Then there were Washington's methods and personality. He sought to heal bleeding wounds while DuBois actually sought to pour salt on them. Washington also possessed the rare capacity of saying just the right thing at the right time. While Washington fancied himself a tactician, DuBois possessed a trait of tactlessness. Next, DuBois remained an outsider to the mass of Negroes. He learned of the institution of slavery through books and perhaps understood abstractly what kind of toll it took on the Negro personality. No one need tell Washington of its dehumanizing effects; he lived with it before and after 1865. DuBois even held the masses of Negroes in contempt. Finally, Washington tried to work within the confining circumstances of the 1890's. So his immediate goals often appeared accommodating, while his ultimate aims were purposefully rarely mentioned. Political and economic salvation would develop simultaneously, he felt. DuBois disagreed; he believed as other Progressives that political rights were a must. DuBois's panacea remained the ballot. Frequently he stated that politics and economics were bound together, but he spent little time on economic salvation, which Washington believed was sorely needed by the Negro masses in the 1890's. If Washington was the pragmatist from the school of hard knocks, DuBois was the aloof New England idealist from Harvard Square. In addition, the accident of birth helped frame their views: as Washington groped for a working solution to the complete abandonment of the Southern Negro in the 1890's, DuBois escaped to Europe to drink deeply from the cup of culture. (pp. 248-49)

Even if Washington's public image became associated with an economic doctrine of self-help and politically with compromise, this should not hide what went unheard or unknown to his contemporaries. Behind his facade of serenity lived a man harboring horrible memories of his youth—born into slavery and freed into abject poverty, his first memories of a bed were a bundle of dirty rags. As an adult, both he and Tuskegee were fed and clothed by philanthropic whites. Plagued by the distressing conditions of the 1890's, he knew the worst thing to do would be to alienate anyone, especially white Southerners. Life itself seemed to prepare him to wear this mask of compromise. But what went on behind this mask? One thing seems certain—beneath his ingratiating manner boiled a man filled with contempt for the injustices done to his race by whites. Even his rival, DuBois, remarked, "actually Washington had no more faith in the white man than I do." (pp. 250-51)

Washington's allusions about social equality also had special significance for Negroes. He gave the alienated Negro a chance to build up a positive sense of race pride. Since Washington emphasized the separateness of Negroes he may even be thought of as a supporter of militant Negro nationalism. In his writings he maintained that when the Negro developed a strong phalanx of internal solidarity his rights would then become undeniable. The trouble was that in 1890 the Negro had too many white friends, but by 1900 his only friends endowed segregated schools. Washington felt Negro energies had dissipated because Negroes supported any white who baited them—from Alliances, to Populists, to Republicans and so on. Now was the time, he believed, to make Negroes less dependent upon whites. In fact, Washington's major concern was directed towards lifting the Negro personality out of its demoralized state by fighting to make the Negro more independent and self-reliant. So as the Tuskegee philosopher played his tune to the tempo of Southern temperament he carefully laid the foundation for the destruction of social inequality for Negroes.

Yet in spite of the stinging past attacks heaped on Washington the Atlanta Compromise had additional positive results. It provided a vehicle for Negroes to maintain their basic faith in American democracy—this was the most "remarkable" thing of all in the Age of Booker T. Washington. The Compromise also had some psychological value for Negroes: if the man farthest down in America, all around, could even boast privately that he was *in* a bargaining position with the white world in the 1890's, that boast said a lot. Many Negroes must have been comforted knowing that the South would consider compromise with a Negro. Washington was. Through the Atlanta Compromise Washington tried to own up to the Negro's plight. Faced with overwhelming pressures, Negroes were virtually forced to give up public agitation for reform and equality. Expression in their new and eerie environment found a voice through the slower process of change publicly advocated by Booker T. Washington. His soothing ideas gripped both Negroes and whites tenaciously. Yet only when the Negro's plight of the 1890's changed drastically could Washington as an historical figure ever hope to be viewed with any degree of objectivity—and not as offering a continuing panacea to the race issue. (pp. 253-54)

Perhaps in the last analysis Washington does not need to wait for someone with "our present outlook" for reassessment. He may have written his own. In an article published posthumously in the *New Republic* [see excerpt above], the name of Booker T. Washington took a final stand against a double-dealing South. His attack was blistering. "Personally I have little faith in the doctrine that it is necessary to segregate the whites from the blacks to prevent race mixture," he charged. . . . That was Booker T. Washington in 1915. When the South viciously broke its half of a gentleman's agreement Washington tore into the region's faithlessness. (pp. 254-55)

> *Donald J. Calista, "Booker T. Washington: Another Look," in* The Journal of Negro History *(reprinted by permission of The Association for the Study of Afro-American Life and History, Inc. (ASALH), Vol. XLIX, No. 4, October, 1964, pp. 240-55.*

EUGENE D. GENOVESE   (lecture date 1966)

[*The following is an excerpt from the main paper of the 1966 Socialist Scholars Conference. Genovese states that Washington had an "enormous" influence on later black nationalists, a point sharply attacked by Herbert Aptheker in the next essay.*]

Slavery and its aftermath left the blacks in a state of acute economic and cultural backwardness, with weak family ties and the much-discussed matriarchal preponderance. They also left a tradition of accommodation to paternalistic authority on the one hand, and a tradition of nihilistic violence on the other. Not docility or infantilization, but innocence of organized effort and political consciousness plagued the black masses and kept plaguing them well into the twentieth century. As a direct result of these effects and of the virtually unchallenged hegemony of the slaveholders, the blacks had little opportunity to develop a sense of their own worth and had every opportunity to learn to despise themselves. The inability of the men during and after slavery to support their families adequately, and especially to protect their women from rape or abuse without forfeiting their own lives, has merely served as the logical end of an emasculating process.

The remarkable ascendancy of Booker T. Washington after the post-Reconstruction reaction must be understood against this background. We need especially to account for his enormous influence over the black nationalists who came after him. Washington tried to meet the legacy of slavery on its own terms. He knew that slavery had ill-prepared his people for political leadership; he therefore retreated from political demands. He knew that slavery had rendered manual labor degrading; he therefore preached the gospel of hard work. He knew that slavery had undermined the family and elementary moral standards; he therefore preached the whole gamut of middle-class virtues and manners. He knew his people had never stood on their own feet and faced the whites as equals; he therefore preached self-reliance and self-help. Unhappily, apart from other ideological sins, he saw no way to establish self-reliance and self-respect except under the financial and social hegemony of the white upper classes. Somehow he meant to destroy the effects of paternalism in the long run by strengthening paternalism in the short run. It would be easy to say that he failed because of this tactic, but there is no way to be sure that the tactic was wrong in principle. He failed for other reasons, one of which was his reliance on the paternalistic, conservative classes at a time when they were rapidly losing power in the South to racist agrarian demagogues.

Washington's rivals did not, in this respect, do much better. The leaders of the NAACP repeatedly returned to a fundamental reliance on white leadership and money. Even Du Bois, in his classic critique of Washington, argued:

> While it is a great truth to say that the Negro must strive and strive mightly to help himself, it is equally true that unless his striving be not simply seconded, but rather aroused and encouraged by the initiative of the richer and wiser environing group, he cannot hope for great success.

The differences between these militants and Washington's conservatives concerned emphases, tactics and public stance much more than ideological fundamentals. The differences were important, but their modest extent was no less so. The juxtaposition of the two tendencies reveals how little could be done even by the most militant without white encouragement and support. The wonder is that black Americans survived the ghastly years between 1890 and 1920 at all. Survival—and more impressive, growing resistance to oppression—came at the price of continuing many phases of a paternalistic tradition that had already sapped the strength of the masses.

The conflict between Washington and Du Bois recalled many earlier battles between two tendencies that are still with us. The first has accepted segregation at least temporarily, has stressed the economic development of the black community and has advocated self-help. This tendency generally prevailed during periods of retrogression in race relations until the upsurge of nationalism in our own day. Washington was its prophet; black nationalism has been its outcome. The second has demanded integration, has stressed political action and has demanded that whites recognize their primary responsibility. Frederick Douglass was its prophet; the civil rights movement has been its outcome. Yet, the lines have generally been blurred. Du Bois often sounded like a nationalist, and Washington probably would have thought Malcolm X a madman. This blurring reflects the dilemma of the black community as a whole and of its bourgeoisie in particular: How do you integrate into a nation that does not want you? How do you separate from a nation that finds you too profitable to release? (pp. 14-16)

> *Eugene D. Genovese, "The Legacy of Slavery and the Roots of Black Nationalism" (originally a paper presented at the Socialist Scholars Conference in 1966), in* Studies on the Left *(copyright 1966 by Studies on the Left, Inc.), Vol. 6, No. 6, November-December, 1966, pp. 3-26.**

HERBERT APTHEKER   (essay date 1966)

[*Commenting at the 1966 Socialist Scholars Conference, Aptheker, Communist party historian on black Americans, disagrees with Eugene D. Genovese's views on Washington's influence (see excerpt above). Harold Cruse attacks Aptheker's premise in an essay excerpted below.*]

I do not find an "enormous influence" exerted by Booker T. Washington upon black nationalists. And Genovese's acceptance of Mr. Washington's own public rationalizations for his program of acquiescence is extraordinary [see excerpt above]. Thus, Washington justified his insistence that Negroes avoid political activity on the grounds that they were not experienced in such activity; but this was not why he put forth the program of acquiescence. He put forth that program because of the insistence of Baldwin of the Southern Railroad, and Carnegie and Rockefeller who subsidized the Tuskegee machine. And they insisted on that program for obvious reasons.

The differences between Du Bois and Washington were basic and not simply tactical, and no single quotation from a 1903 essay will change that. Du Bois rejected subordination; Washington accepted it. Du Bois rejected colonialism; Washington assumed its continuance. Du Bois was intensely critical of capitalism, long before World War I; Washington worshiped it.

Genovese asks: How do you integrate into a nation that does not want you? This is not and has not been the point. The point is that through integration one transforms. The effort is not simply to integrate *into* the nation; the demand is to transform a racist nation into an egalitarian one. Hence to battle for integration is to battle for basic transformation. (pp. 33-4)

> *Herbert Aptheker, in his commentary given at the Socialist Scholars Conference in 1966, in* Studies on the Left *(copyright 1966 by Studies on the Left, Inc.), Vol. 6, No. 6, November-December, 1966, pp. 27-35.**

MARTIN LUTHER KING, JR.   (essay date 1967)

[*A renowned civil rights leader of the 1960s, King advocated racial equality through nonviolent methods as did Washington. However, in the following excerpt, King points out a basic flaw in Washington's approach to racism.*]

We must get rid of the false notion that there is some miraculous quality in the flow of time that inevitably heals all evils. There is only one thing certain about time, and that is that it waits for no one. If it is not used constructively, it passes you by. (p. 128)

Equally fallacious is the notion that ethical appeals and persuasion alone will bring about justice. This does not mean that ethical appeals must not be made. It simply means that those appeals must be undergirded by some form of constructive coercive power. If the Negro does not add persistent pressure to his patient plea, he will end up empty-handed. In a not too distant yesterday, Booker T. Washington tried this path of patient persuasion. I do not share the notion that he was an Uncle Tom who compromised for the sake of keeping the peace. Washington sincerely believed that if the South was not pushed too hard, that if the South was not forced to do something that it did not for the moment want to do, it would voluntarily rally in the end to the Negro's cause. Washington's error was that he underestimated the structures of evil; as a consequence his philosophy of pressureless persuasion only served as a springboard for racist Southerners to dive into deeper and more ruthless oppression of the Negro. (pp. 128-29)

> *Martin Luther King, Jr., "The Dilemma of Negro Americans," in his* Where Do We Go from Here: Chaos or Community? *(copyright © 1967 by Martin*

Luther King, Jr.; reprinted by permission of Harper & Row, Publishers, Inc.), Harper & Row, 1967, pp. 102-34.*

HAROLD CRUSE (essay date 1968)

[*Cruse contends that the civil rights movement of the 1960s basically echoed Washington's separatist philosophy. In addition, he disagrees with Herbert Aptheker's thesis that Washington had little influence on black nationalists (see excerpt above).*]

What really lies behind all of the varied and conflicting reactions to the slogan of Black Power? Strange to conclude, there happens to be a certain validity in nearly all these reactions. For any slogan that has not been adequately defined, there will be reasons for doubt as well as for strong support. Bayard Rustin has put his finger on something very crucial about the Black Power slogan. *Black Power is nothing but the economic and political philosophy of Booker T. Washington given a 1960s militant shot in the arm and brought up to date.* The curious fact about it is that the very last people to admit that Black Power is militant Booker T-ism are the Black Power theorists themselves. A Roy Inniss and a Ben-Jochannan, for example, will characterize Booker T. Washington as a historical conservative (if not an Uncle Tom) and refuse to recognize him as a part of their black nationalist tradition. Both of them will, of course, uphold Marcus Garvey with much nationalist fervor—completely overlooking the fact that Garvey was a disciple of Booker T. Washington. When Garvey came to the United States in 1916, he came to see Booker T. Washington, who had died in 1915. Both Garvey and his wife Amy-Jacques Garvey thought: "Since the death of Booker T. Washington, there was no one with a positive and practical uplift program for the masses—North or South." But the NAACP "radicals" of the time, especially the Du Bois tendency, were staunchly opposed to Washington's program. Later on all the Marxist Communist and Socialist tendencies combined to relegate poor old conservative Booker T. Washington to historical purgatory for having failed to conduct himself like a respectable militant or radical in Negro affairs. Dr. Herbert Aptheker, the chief Communist party historian on the Negro, for example, also became the chief castigator of Washington. The prejudice of the political left against Washington accounts in part for Bayard Rustin's denigration of Black Power in 1967, the only difference being that Rustin is perceptive enough to see that Black Power is, clearly, Booker T-ism. (pp. 177-78)

Aptheker is one of the most un-Marxist Marxists quotable these days when it comes to heaping radical mystification on the Negro movement. In native American terms, Aptheker's Marxism is European "book" Marxism; hence his approach to the Negro is totally lacking in imagination, depth, or perception. For one to see no "enormous influence" [see excerpt above] of Washington on black nationalists [see excerpt above] is like seeing no enormous influence of Hegel or the Greeks—Democritus or Heraclitus—on Karl Marx's dialectical materialism.

Aptheker does not distinguish between what Washington said (tactically) and what he *did* practically, both North and South. In 1900 he established the National Negro Business League, which still exists in Washington, D.C. Long before Du Bois's Niagara Movement (which sold itself out inside the NAACP) Washington was organizing Southern Negro farmers, sharecroppers, and small businessmen through yearly Tuskegee conferences. During the same period, it was Washington's protegés in the North, Philip A. Payton and others, who organized the

Afro-American Realty Company, which waged a most militant economic struggle against entrenched white real estate interests in order to win living space in the previously all-white Harlem of 1900. The winning of Harlem and better housing for Negroes between 1903 and World War I was a direct outgrowth of Washington's National Negro Business League, of which both Payton and Anderson were members.

Booker T. Washington built a school in Alabama, a permanent, lasting, and functional institution in the Deep South. Aptheker is rather naive about Southern life-realities in 1900 if he thinks that one built institutions in Dixie without "acquiescing" to something sacred within the status quo. . . . The point is that as a *historian* he should understand certain facts that he doesn't. Marcus Garvey had so much admiration for what Washington had done with Tuskegee that he wanted to get his advice on how such a school could be developed in Jamaica, B.W.I. . . . Now since black nationalists admire the memory of Garvey, it stands to reason historically and ideologically that Washington's influence on black nationalism was rather enormous. But Aptheker professes not to understand this phenomenon; and this is because Aptheker refuses to understand what black nationalism is all about. A historian *must* understand *all* social phenomena out of history or stop pretending to be a historian. Negro historians are not much better. Many of the young black nationalists of today are misinformed on the real meaning of Booker T. Washington's role because of the obfuscation that permeates Negro historiography and that has prevented the development of a black social theory on historical and class trends in Negro history. . . .

[The] Nation of Islam was nothing but a form of Booker T. Washington's economic self-help, black unity, bourgeois hard work, law-abiding, vocational training, stay-out-of-the-civil-rights-struggle agitation, separate-from-the-white-man, etc., etc., morality. The only difference was that Elijah Muhammad added the potent factor of the Muslim religion to a race, economic, and social philosophy of which the first prophet was none other than Booker T. Washington. Elijah also added an element of "hate Whitey" ideology which Washington, of course, would never have accepted. The reason that a Washington would have considered a Malcolm X a madman was that Washington practiced moderate accommodationist separatism while Malcolm and Elijah preached militant separatism. *But it is still the same separatism whose quality only changes from one era to another.* (pp. 180-82)

The Negro is politically compromised today because he owns nothing. He can exert little political power because he owns nothing. He has little voice in the affairs of state because he owns nothing. The fundamental reason why the Negro bourgeois-democratic revolution has been aborted is because American capitalism has prevented the development of a black class of capitalist owners of institutions and economic tools. To take one crucial example, Negro radicals today are severely hampered in their tasks of educating the black masses on political issues because Negroes do not own any of the necessary means of propaganda and communication. The Negro owns no printing presses, he has no stake in the networks of the means of communication. Inside his own communities he does not own the houses he lives in, the property he lives on, nor the wholesale and retail sources from which he buys his commodities. He does not own the edifices in which he enjoys culture and entertainment or in which he socializes. In capitalist society, an individual or group that does not own anything is powerless. In capitalist society, a group that has not experienced the many sides of capitalistic development, that has not learned the techniques of business ownership, or the intricacies of profit and loss, or the responsibilities of managing even small or medium enterprises, has not been prepared in the social disciplines required to transcend the functional limitations of the capitalistic order. Thus, to paraphrase Lenin, it is not that the Negro suffers so much from capitalism in America, but from a *lack of capitalistic development*. This is why the Black Power Conference heard so many procapitalistic resolutions, such as the old ''buy black'' slogan of Harlem's 1930s nationalist movements. Not a single one of the economic resolutions of this conference was new; they were all voiced ten, twenty, thirty, forty years ago. The followers of Washington raised them, the followers of Garvey raised them, even Du Bois raised them in his nationalistic moments. (pp. 182-83)

> *Harold Cruse, ''Behind the Black Power Slogan,'' in his* Rebellion or Revolution? *(copyright © 1968 by Harold Cruse; abridged by permission of William Morrow & Company, Inc.), Morrow, 1968 (and reprinted in extracted form in* Booker T. Washington and His Critics: Black Leadership in Crisis, *edited by Hugh Hawkins, second edition, D. C. Heath and Company, 1974, pp. 174-83).**

THEODORE L. GROSS (essay date 1971)

[*Gross finds* Up from Slavery *to be an admirable description of one man's success, but a failure as a work of literature that attempts to illuminate the soul and sensibility of black Americans in the late nineteenth century.*]

Washington's work is the most famous slave narrative in our literature. Earlier autobiographies—notably Frederick Douglass' powerful indictment of slavery, *My Bondage and My Freedom* . . .—illuminate the Negro's attitude toward white supremacy in the nineteenth century, but *Up From Slavery* comes at a moment in American history which affords Washington a special opportunity to write a public document as well as a personal memoir—*Up from Slavery* is, at all times, directed to its white audience.

''I was born a slave on a plantation in Franklin County, Virginia,'' Washington records; ''my life had its beginnings in the midst of the most miserable, desolate, and discouraging surroundings.'' With this straightforward, unpretentious opening, one is prepared for a faithful depiction of Negro life on the plantation—from the inside, as it were, and not through the benevolent, paternalistic eyes of Thomas Nelson Page or Joel Chandler Harris; one is prepared for an iconoclastic autobiography of real historic, if not aesthetic, value. But except for several descriptions of the impoverished condition of Washington's family, the early pages of *Up From Slavery* presents a picture of slavery no different essentially—no more human, or inhuman, as the case may warrant—from that of Page or Harris, and, moreover, one that is continually conditioned by Washington's optimism and religious faith. . . . (pp. 127-28)

The title of Washington's narrative suggests his inexorable optimism: he is interested in the Negro's movement away from slavery, up rather than through, a movement that in Washington's own case was effected by his ''struggle for an education.'' He based his personal confrontation with white America, although at times it scarcely seems to be a confrontation, on the belief that ''every persecuted individual and race should get much consolation out of the great human law, which is universal and eternal, that merit, no matter under what skin found,

is in the long run, recognized and rewarded''; and the tension that exists in *Up From Slavery* is between Washington's unwavering self-belief, his tenacious self-reliance and idealism, and the society that excluded him. By accepting without question *laissez-faire* capitalism and by adopting those puritanic virtues—hard work, cleanliness, earnestness, and thrift—of the American culture which had suppressed the development of his race, he knew that he must succeed.

And from all practical points of view he did succeed. His life story is a lesson for persecuted people, a kind of primer on how to succeed in spite of your background. ''As I now look back over my life,'' he reminds us, ''I do not recall that I ever became discouraged over anything that I set out to accomplish.'' This unwillingness to be dismayed is reflected in his comments upon racial conditions in America: conditions are improving, movement is upward and away from slavery, the Negro simply has to improve himself to improve his situation. . . . Improvement is the keynote that is struck in *Up From Slavery*, an improvement that results from honest labor—''nothing ever comes to one, that is worth having, except as a result of hard work''—and Washington presents his simple lesson simply, earnestly, entirely unconscious of what seem to us platitudes, employing a bare, unpretentious, utilitarian prose that suits his practical ideas. His autobiography is characterized by the sentimental idealism of a good man—particularly of a good American—whose every line is poised deliberately between teaching and preaching.

One reads *Up From Slavery* as one reads a moral tract and not a work of literature, for it is infused with how life could be if only one were as virtuous, as selfless, as determined, as self-confident as Booker T. Washington himself. The book lies heavily in one's hands, for it lacks the essential ingredient of literature—the ingredient that Richard Wright's *Black Boy*, with all its obvious blemishes, possesses—that is necessary for enduring autobiography: the complexity of the inner life. Toward the end of his autobiography, Washington confesses that ''fiction I care little for. Frequently I have to almost force myself to read a novel that is on every one's lips. The kind of reading that I have the greatest fondness for is biography. I like to be sure that I am reading about a real man or a real thing.'' Although this is the natural bias of that kind of American who traditionally has considered fiction frivolous, it nevertheless suggests the imaginative dimension that is lacking in *Up From Slavery;* and one concludes that Washington succeeded in life, if not in literature, precisely because he did not permit himself to explore the complex results of slavery on the Negro's sensibility in the late nineteenth century. (pp. 128-30)

> *Theodore L. Gross, ''The Black Hero,'' in his* The Heroic Ideal in American Literature *(reprinted with permission of Macmillan Publishing Company; copyright © 1971 by Theodore L. Gross),* The Free Press, *1971, pp. 125-92.**

LOUIS R. HARLAN (essay date 1972)

[*Harlan is the author of the definitive biography of Washington, from which the following excerpt is taken, and editor of the* Booker T. Washington Papers. *This excerpt deals with the impact* Up from Slavery *had upon its publication.*]

[*Up from Slavery*,] conceived and guided by some of the country's leading editors and publishers, was deliberately designed to enhance Washington's image among the general reading public as the spokesman of his race. It promoted his school, his social philosophy, and his career. Employing a better ghost-writer [than the one he had used for *The Story of My Life and Work*], writing more of the book himself, and having a clearer sense of purpose than in the earlier book, he produced a minor classic, read all over the world, widely translated, and continuously in print for successive generations. Its principal fault was also a cause of its popularity, that it presented Washington's experience mythically rather than with candor, and thus gave an overly sunny view of black life in America. (p. 245)

Up from Slavery was a *succès d'estime*. Reviewers uniformly commended the simplicity, directness, and eloquence of Washington's style. He presented himself to the world in a most pleasing image, and many reviewers compared Washington's autobiography with that of Benjamin Franklin. (p. 249)

A more significant measure of the success of a book was its impact on the lives of its readers. Black people particularly identified themselves with the protagonist and lived vicariously through his hardships, struggles, and success. A black attorney of Nashville wrote to Washington: "My early experience was very similar to your early ones. I only wish the similarity were kept up to this day." The book provided for many blacks a success model. If Washington could successfully transcend not only poverty but prejudice, any other black man could believe that he too could rise above his lowly beginnings. And despite his occasional humorous jibes at the "old-time" Negroes, Washington's account of his life exuded black pride and individual self-confidence.

Whites also found inspiration in the book. This was partly because the story appealed to certain universal qualities of human nature and the taste for a good narrative, but also because it was so full of goodwill toward whites. Many whites who felt twinges of guilt about their long history of oppression of Negroes derived warm comfort from this evidence that a representative Negro did not hate them. (pp. 252-53)

As an elaborate exposition of Washington's racial philosophy, *Up from Slavery* completed the work of the Atlanta Compromise speech. It clothed Washington's message of accommodation and self-help in the classic success story, the Horatio Alger myth in black. From slavery there was no other direction than up, and Washington saw the hardships of his early life as a challenge to be up and doing, not as a deterrent. He presented himself simply but without false modesty as possessing all the virtues extolled by Cotton Mather, Poor Richard, and Ralph Waldo Emerson, and his life as a string of anecdotes illustrating these virtues. To him as to his readers, his life seemed evidence of the capacity and future of his race and of mankind. Washington was the hero of his own life. His life promised black men as well as white men that they could find "acres of diamonds" in their own back yards—if they had any. Together, but for different reasons, white and black Americans welcomed Washington's faith that not through social conflict but through upward striving, white benevolence, and a benign Providence, his race could overcome, as he had overcome, the obstacles of the color line. (p. 253)

Louis R. Harlan, *"The Self-Made Image,"* in his Booker T. Washington: The Making of a Black Leader, 1856-1901 *(copyright © 1972 by Louis R. Harlan; reprinted by permission of Oxford University Press, Inc.), Oxford University Press, New York, 1972, pp. 229-53.*

HOUSTON A. BAKER, JR.   (essay date 1972)

[Baker examines the "institutional frame of mind" manifested throughout Up from Slavery, *which he considers a major work in the black literary tradition.]*

Washington felt that he had formed a social and educational philosophy that was compatible with the times; through his educational labors and his public pronouncements, he attempted to show that the educated black American could be a "useful" citizen, an improver of the community, a clean and well-mannered manual laborer of high moral character. Moreover, such a black man, he insisted, would not trouble himself with social equality. . . . The president, southern governors, and a host of politicians were grateful, enthusiastic, overwhelmed; while America went its imperialistic way in the Philippines, and white William Sumner and other race theorizers poured forth their doctrines, there was a black leader at home to keep the masses at peace. It must truly have seemed that God was in an American heaven and all was right with the Yankee world.

Even today, both revolutionaries and scholars who should know better take Washington's hand-and-finger metaphor ("In all things that are purely social we can be as separate as the fingers, yet one as the hand in all things essential to mutual progress.") as the whole of his teaching, and write off one of the most famous black Americans as a traitor on the basis of his 1895 address to the Atlanta Cotton States and International Exposition, which catapulted him to a position of national leadership. When we turn to *Up from Slavery,* however, we are forced to take another view, for Washington's autobiography is far more than an ameliorative treatise on race relations. The book is first of all a representative work in a major genre in the black literary tradition. Originally published in 1900 as *The Story of My Life and Work, Up from Slavery* . . . was one of the last slave narratives published in America.

The first chapter rings a familiar note—it seems almost an imitation of Douglass's *Narrative*. The straightforwardness of the opening is the same ("I was born a slave on a plantation in Franklin County, Virginia"), the setting is again agrarian, and we see the familiar ironic equation of the status of slaves with that of the farm animals: "My mother, I suppose, attracted the attention of a purchaser who was afterward my owner and hers. Her addition to the slave family attracted about as much attention as the purchase of a new horse or cow." . . . Finally, Washington assumes the "tragic mulatto" posture at the outset: "Of my father I know even less than of my mother. I do not even know his name. I have heard reports to the effect that he was a white man who lived on one of the near-by plantations." . . . (pp. 86-7)

The similarities between Douglass and Washington are not surprising when we consider that Washington wrote one of the earliest biographies of Douglass and was familiar with his writing; nevertheless, we have similarity with a difference. Washington's view of slavery is quite unlike that of Douglass. The perspective in the first chapter of *Up from Slavery* is almost antebellum, considering the narrator's forgiving nature, his view of the positive good derived from slavery, and his discussion of the sadness felt by both master and slave when freedom arrived and parted their ways. . . . Heightening his antebellum tone, Washington speaks of the slave's fidelity, his willingness to lay down his life for his master, his sadness (his tears mingled with those of the master) when freedom came, and his desire, in some cases, to stay on the plantation after emancipation.

This is not to say, however, that Washington totally ignores the oppression and violence of slavery; he too talks of men reduced to brutes and treated as such, but in a tone which is, at best, compromising. More important though, is the institutional frame of mind that manifests itself throughout *Up from Slavery*. Slavery itself, as we have seen above, is designated as an "institution" and a "school," and at other points a "system" or a "net." Washington's book, therefore, like all slave narratives, begins with the "peculiar institution" of slavery, to which Washington juxtaposes another institution, the schoolhouse. . . . (pp. 87-8)

According to Washington, the institution was a failure; unhinged gates, broken window panes, unkempt gardens, lack of refinement in diet, and general waste were the evidence of its inefficiency. The basis of Washington's condemnation is the inability of slavery to produce useful men, efficient operations, or social refinement. Ignorance, the absence of self-help, and the low value placed on self-reliance nurtured an unproductive institution. Surely the writer had imbibed his Benjamin Franklin, Ralph Waldo Emerson and Samuel Smiles, either by reading, or simply by breathing in the spirit of his age.

The dichotomy between the "peculiar" institution and the educational institution continues into the second chapter of *Up from Slavery*—"Boyhood Days." While we see that the work situation could encompass educational opportunities (Washington, like Douglass, learned his letters while doing manual labor), we also see the narrator assuming the role of trickster in order to escape work and get to school on time. Moreover, Washington philosophizes on education in this chapter and tells us of his own struggle for literacy. The motivation behind his struggle is obvious; education produces merit, and "Every persecuted individual and race should get much consolation out of the great human law, which is universal and eternal, that merit, no matter under what skin found, is in the long run recognized and rewarded." . . . Washington's subscription to the maxim (which seems to contain but little truth) is understandable in the light of his age: when proscription is so severe that a group's chances of upward mobility seem almost nil and when its merit is studiously ignored, one alternative to despair or revolt is to predict that "in the long run" things will be better. Washington's movement, therefore, is toward "merit" and its corresponding recognition and reward. At one pole of his thought stands slavery, the opprobrious institution, and at the other stands Harvard, one of America's oldest and most renowned universities, from which he received an honorary degree in 1896. Institutions thus mark the depth and height of his perspective.

In the intermediate sections of *Up from Slavery* it is still the institution that delineates stages of development. In chapters two and three, for example, the salt and coal mining industries are accorded terse descriptions and negative comments. Mrs. Ruffner's home, however, where Washington worked as a "servant," receives a positive evaluation, because here he learned habits of cleanliness and was allowed to continue his education while working. The major feature of the Ruffner home, in fact, was its role as an educational institution: "the lessons that I learned in the home of Mrs. Ruffner were as valuable to me as any education I have ever gotten anywhere since." . . . The truth of this statement is driven home when the narrator tells us of his cleaning the recitation room at Hamp-

ton: "It occurred to me at once that here was my chance. Never did I receive an order with more delight. I knew that I could sweep, for Mrs. Ruffner had thoroughly taught me how to do that when I lived with her." . . . The significance of his accomplishment is expressed in institutional terms: "The sweeping of that room was my college examination, and never did any youth pass an examination for entrance into Harvard or Yale that gave him more genuine satisfaction." . . . (pp. 89-90)

From the time of his entry into college until he goes off to found a school of his own, one institution dominates the narrative. Hampton Institute and its educational concerns are always in the forefront in chapters three through six, and we are told what Washington learned about helping others, recognizing the dignity of labor, and aiding in the preparation of students (both black and red) for study at Hampton. It is in chapter seven, "Early Days at Tuskegee," however, that we witness the start of an interesting coalescence—the merger of a man and an institution. Washington and Tuskegee become almost inseparable for the remainder of *Up from Slavery*.

The growth of Tuskegee parallels the progress of its founder. Still a young and inexperienced man when he went to Alabama, Washington slowly achieved recognition as his institution grew in size and merit. We have almost a new beginning of the narrative at chapter seven, "Teaching School in a Stable and a Hen-house," since Tuskegee starts as a relatively loose-knit organization in agrarian quarters and a rural setting. As the work proceeds, however, it moves (with the school) toward greater urbanity and sophistication: the initial plantation setting becomes a "Southern Campus"; the original enrollment of thirty rural pupils becomes a body of students from twenty-seven states and territories of America and several foreign countries; the initial limited curriculum broadens to include thirty industrial departments; and the stable and henhouse become sixty-six buildings, "counting large and small." In a sense, Tuskegee almost seems to assume a life of its own; it is fed money, which is collected by Washington and his wives, and it grows into something beautiful and healthy. . . . While the school is growing, its founder is given recognition and reward, and he likewise grows in stature. The man and the institution complemented each other, but it was only through a multitude of men that Washington and Tuskegee were able to survive.

In one respect, *Up from Slavery* resembles the *Autobiography* of John Stuart Mill. Mill said at the outset of his work that he not only wished to record the important events of his life, but also to acknowledge the debts he owed to the great men of his age. Washington's autobiography is filled with acknowledgements to such men: General Samuel Armstrong, A. H. Porter, President McKinley, Andrew Carnegie, President Cleveland, and Charles Eliot are only a few. If at times these names read like a patron's list for a cultural event, they do indicate the degree of recognition the author received during his life, and they represent the sources of the nourishment of Tuskegee Institute as well as the great men of Washington's acquaintance.

As the institute grew, the behavioral patterns that it encompassed were perpetuated, expounded, and affirmed by the founder before large audiences. The result, of course, is that Tuskegee came, as all institutions must, to stand for a particular behavioral pattern that was of value to the community as a whole. Those connected with, enrolled in, or responsible for the institution were considered affirmers of this pattern, and when we see some of the greatest names of Washington's time associated with Tuskegee, we can logically deduce that the school expressed, to a great extent, the values of its age. (pp. 90-2)

In light of his traditional American point of view, it is not difficult to see why, writing in the early twentieth century, Washington chose the progression from institution to institution as a means of developing his autobiography. America itself was making exemplary institutional leaps throughout the nineteenth century, and the educational institution was particularly important. The school constitutes not only a "behavioral pattern" itself, but also an organization inculcating behavioral patterns. And Washington was able to found an institution that instilled an "American way of life" into black Americans.

Washington received perhaps his most fitting reward when his labors were recognized by one of the oldest institutions in America. The narrator seems aware of the appropriateness and momentousness of his honorary degree from Harvard, for he even arranges his autobiography so that the 1896 Harvard commencement is described, climactically, in the last chapter, while the 1899 trip to Europe is presented in the chapter before. The founder of an educational institution that perpetuated the "American way" standing before the representatives of the oldest and one of the most renowned universities in the country to receive meet homage—this is indeed a celestial position when it is juxtaposed against that peculiar institution with which *Up from Slavery* begins. And the upward path is paved by educational institutions and the men who breathed life (money and labor) into them.

Washington thus shared the American frame of mind in regard to institution-building, and as a champion of American virtues he received fitting reward for his labors. Yet it is not difficult to discover the sources of the vociferous condemnations of the Tuskegeean. The most significant charge concerns Washington's narrowness of scope; life is reduced, particularly in the later chapters of *Up from Slavery*, to a chronicling of grants, a recording of newspaper comments on the founder's speeches and awards, and a listing of famous men met and impressed. Moreover, there is a narrowness in the very behavioral pattern that Washington endorsed, a contraction of perspective indigenous to Tuskegee Institute and its founder, a narrowness revealed in the four characteristics that mark the ideal Tuskegee graduate, the ideal Washingtonian man—skill, high moral character, a sense of expediency, and a belief in the dignity of labor. . . . In *Up from Slavery* there is no orientation toward the future; no cherishing of the aesthetic, the abstract, or the spiritual; there is little belief in the value of institutions beyond educational (and philanthropic) ones. More significantly, there is no social idealism looking toward a day of complete liberation, when all men shall possess their freedom as equals. In *Up from Slavery* "spirit" is translated into dollar signs, idealism into manual labor, and the desire for "freedom now" into useful work.

One hates to think what D. H. Lawrence would have made of Booker T. Washington had he turned an eye upon him in *Studies in Classic American Literature*. Washington appears even more culpable than the Benjamin Franklin who emerges from Lawrence's essays, for he had not only a Puritan ethical monomania, but also a condemnatory zeal. He championed all the American values, but also condemned those institutions that attempted to deal with aspects of the human condition that Tuskegee did not encompass or encourage. The church, labor unions, political structures, idealistic educational enterprises,

and creative writing are all belittled directly or by implication in Washington's autobiography. (pp. 92-4)

In a final analysis, however, we cannot write off as a myopic organization man the former slave who served as America's "black leader" for twenty years, built a thriving educational institution in the heart of a racist South, and aided thousands in the struggle for dignity. Washington's achievements would be considered great in any age or in any country, and in late nineteenth-century America they were just short of miraculous. Moreover, social scientists and historians such as Gunnar Myrdal, August Meier, and Louis Harlan have demonstrated that Washington was more complex than would appear from "the ingratiating mask" he presented to the world. (p. 94)

Further research is likely to modify our overall evaluation of the man, but new information cannot alter *Up from Slavery*. The social philosophy set forth in this autobiography and the manner in which it is presented indicate that the author was not as fine a champion of black American rights as he might have been. At a time when the broadest possible perspective and the greatest aid were needed in the black man's struggle for freedom and equality, Washington failed in one of the primary roles of the leader. He opened too few of the doors toward his followers' most sought-after goal; in fact, he closed the doors and barred the shutters on all that lay beyond the ultimate welfare and informing philosophy of his own autonomous, somewhat mechanized institution. By championing the value of education, however, and by producing a sort of Horatio Alger handbook of how to acquire an education and how to set up an educational institution, Washington was following in the path of men such as [David] Walker and Douglass, and anticipating Du Bois. In any meaningful examination of black literature and culture it is impossible to ignore *Up from Slavery*, the book that presents the man Washington and the institution Tuskegee. (p. 95)

Houston A. Baker, Jr., "Men and Institutions: Booker T. Washington's 'Up from Slavery'," in his Long Black Song: Essays in Black American Literature and Culture *(copyright © 1972 by the Rector and Visitors of the University of Virginia), The University Press of Virginia, 1972, pp. 84-95.*

LAWRENCE J. FRIEDMAN (essay date 1974)

[Friedman disagrees with such revisionist critics as August Meier, Donald J. Calista, and Louis R. Harlan (see excerpts above) as to the actual race relation gains made by Washington's overt or covert activities.]

Although failure characterized the efforts of many leading blacks, particularly in the South, Booker T. Washington seemed to have been eminently successful. . . . Influential white Northerners from the President of the Long Island Railroad to Theodore Roosevelt, President of the United States, consulted regularly with Washington. If American race relations at the turn of the century could be characterized by white conquest and black defeat, the Tuskegeean was an important exception—or so it seemed.

"I always make it a rule to make especial preparation for each separate address." Washington once noted, "No two audiences are exactly alike. It is my aim to reach and talk to the heart of each individual audience, taking it into my confidence very much as I would a person." This practice was crucial to Washington's success in the Age of Jim Crow. Year after year, he took special precautions to adapt his words explicitly to his audience—to appeal to its peculiar biases and interests. He "was neither a black Christ nor an Uncle Tom but a cunning Brer Rabbit, 'born and bred in the brier patch' of tangled American race relations," Louis R. Harlan contends. Piecing together Washington's rhetoric, one finds no coherent ideology but a veritable maze of apparent conflicts and contradictions. Pleasing different audiences with different messages, he had few enemies and a wide variety of admirers. (pp. 339-40)

[Many] examples may be cited to demonstrate this pattern of conflicting and equivocating rhetoric that characterized Booker T. Washington's active years. According to the Tuskegeean's brilliant contemporary, Kelly Miller, Washington's "carefully studied deliverances upon disputed issues often possess the equivocalness of a Delphic oracle." Within the recent past, scholars like August Meier, Louis R. Harlan, Emma Lou Thornbrough, and Donald J. Calista [see excerpts above], have begun to analyze these seeming contradictions and ambiguities and have offered clear explanations for the pattern. To garner substantial funds and resist racism in the Age of Jim Crow, they insist that Washington had to say different things to different people. Shrewd and expedient, he would not press racist whites to give blacks greater justice but urged blacks and white liberals to combat racist barriers. Thus, Washington has not been characterized by these revisionist historians as an Uncle Tom but rather as a hardnosed realist who made limited but significant gains for his race while militant black leaders achieved less.

The most obvious problem with this revisionist approach is the imprecise nature of a racial gain. Although some of Washington's more covert words and deeds may have eased the segregation or disfranchisement process, for example, we must also consider the negative impact upon white and black of public pronouncements like the 1895 Atlanta Exposition speech. In totaling his gains, we must calculate the confusion that a speech like that must have caused among blacks (even among those blacks who detected hidden pleas for civil rights within that speech or who noted Washington's pleas in certain black publications). We must also calculate the white racist stereotypes a message like that fortified. More explicitly, it is incumbent upon revisionists to systematically define racial "gain" and to correlate Washington's covert and overt activities with specific gains and losses in diverse local communities. A quantitative study of the economic effects of certain of Washington's words and deeds upon specific black populations and occupation groups would represent a good beginning. An analysis of more nebulous results of his activities could follow. By thus systematizing the issue of racial gain, we may find that the material gains Washington achieved through covert tactics have been exaggerated. Indeed, material gains may have dwarfed against the psychic gains he could have rendered blacks had he been openly defiant and patently courageous. The problem of racial gain is exceedingly complex and cannot be circumvented by hasty, ambiguous revisionist phraseology. (pp. 343-44)

> Lawrence J. Friedman, "Life 'In the Lion's Mouth': Another Look at Booker T. Washington," in The Journal of Negro History (reprinted by permission of The Association for the Study of Afro-American Life and History, Inc. (ASALH), Vol. LIX, No. 1, October, 1974, pp. 337-51.

ALFRED YOUNG (essay date 1976)

[Young believes Washington's philosophy of education reflected a "'black perspective of education' and that it functioned as a liberating force for the ubiquitous Afro-American." Also stating that most Washington critics have "failed to understand the complexities of their subject." Young disagrees with the conclusions of Washington drawn by Merle Curti and Oliver Cox (see excerpts above).]

I believe that most of Washington's interpreters failed to understand the complexities of their subject. Washington's educational philosophy must be seen as an attempt by an individual, representing a group of the powerless, to redirect as much as possible of the nation's resources from the white to the black segment of the nation, by guile and infiltration.

A review of the literature on Washington points out the scholarly preoccupation with two themes: the Booker T. Washington—W.E.B. DuBois controversy, and the shortcomings of Washington as a "race leader." Similarly scholars have failed to discern any distinctions between Washington's philosophy of education and that of his white counterparts. For example, in *The Social Ideas of American Educators* (1935), Merle Curti, an historian, concluded: "Washington's social philosophy was, in fine, more typical of middle-class white Americans, whom he wanted his people to be like, than it was of the Negro as such" [see excerpt above]. By this statement Curti is totally rejecting the implications of Washington's "black experience" for his social philosophy and is assuming that the expression of similar ideas must suggest similar motives. (p. 226)

Throughout his life Washington emphasized industrial education and economic self-sufficiency as the basis necessary for black liberation. The idealistic Washington envisioned a society where human solidarity and the recognition of man by man would prevail. Yet, American history during his lifetime seemed to suggest the opposite. (p. 229)

In order to prevent total black reenslavement, Washington promoted the idea that Negroes must learn to "love labor, not alone for its financial value, but for labor's own sake." Through a process of industrial education, Negroes would become independent and self-reliant. They would, then, be rewarded for doing something the world wants.

In his first major address, delivered before the National Education Association in 1884, Washington enunciated the mission of industrial education—"kills two birds with one stone," "viz.: secures the cooperation of the whites, and does the best possible thing for the black man." He confirmed Southern approval of his educational proposal by citing the Alabama state legislature's apportionment of $2,000 annually to pay Tuskegee teachers' salaries and shrewdly stated, "From the opening of the school to the present, the white citizens of Tuskegee have been among its warmest friends." The tone of this speech suggests that Washington was appealing to his Northern audience to assist the South, in general, and Negroes, in particular.

In contrast, Washington's "Presidents' Annual Address" delivered at the Alabama State Teachers' Association in 1888, outlined the requisites for realizing his educational philosophy. He saw education extending beyond the teaching of reading, writing, and arithmetic and the ability to master and converse in a foreign language. . . . The end Washington was seeking through education, as expressed in this address, was an interlinking of the total human experience—mind, body, and soul which would produce a moral man and a society where all men would be considered men. . . . Washington was criticized for his blind faith in mankind. Nevertheless, his views exemplified a pronounced "spiritual orientation" which evolved out of his experience in an oppressive situation.

The variations in tone and emphasis in the two speeches reflected Washington's ability as an orator to judge his audience and adapt his remarks to fit the specific conditions. In all of his speeches before black audiences, "his concern for his race seems as consistent as his attention to what he considered primary issues."

The theme of "concern for race," exemplified in Washington's speeches to black audiences, constituted a "black perspective" which combined his identification with love for his people with a spiritual commitment to human well-being.

In an extensive analysis of Washington's speeches, Willis Norman Pitts found that Washington stressed: (1) the need of his people for education, (2) industrial education as a means to an end; (3) the value of practicing goodwill between the races; (4) the South as the best place for blacks to live; and (5) the duty of both sections (North and South) in building up the citizenship potential of his race. These points often built the case which then allowed him to focus in on Tuskegee Institute as a prime example of industrial achievement.

In 1895, Booker Taliaferro Washington was asked to deliver what became his most famous and controversial address at the Atlanta Cotton Exposition. Much of what he said reflected ideas he had espoused on other occasions. He seemingly accepted the dominant view that blacks should remain separate in society and relegated to a second-class status. But, to others, this speech "was one of the most effective pieces of political oratory in the history of the United States." (pp. 230-31)

[Oliver Cox] regarded Washington's speech as similar to one of Henry W. Grady's which relegated the black population to a racial caste position [see excerpt above]. Cox, paraphrasing parts of the "Atlanta Address" wrote: "Negroes and whites should remain separate and should never agitate for 'socially equality,'" and quoted Washington to support this view, "In all things that are purely social we can be separate as the fingers . . . The wisest among my race understand that the agitation of questions of social equality is the extremest folly . . .'"

This author would challenge Cox's methodological approach to the question of Washington's leadership. Writing from a Marxian perspective, Cox conceived "talented black men" in slavery as destined to become either "discontented bondsmen with ideas of escape and revolt, or trusted slaves." He concluded that, "Washington's slavery experience seems to have conditioned him to the latter type of personality."

The Marxian analysis is based upon the dialectical process which assumes a "class struggle" between the owners of the means of production (bourgeoisie) and the workers who sell their labor (proletariat). Through an increase of exploitation and alienation of the proletariat by the bourgeoisie, there evolves a political and class consciousness which leads to the inevitable social revolution.

Applying this analysis to the lives of individuals who lived under the "peculiar institution," Cox failed to understand the dynamics of the slave situation. As a consequence, his analysis precludes the "day to day" resistance activities of the large multitude of "not so talented black men." It did not take into account the importance of the slave family as a "survival mechanism," and the significant role religion, folktales, and legends played in the resistance activities in the slave community. Cox

has fallen into the familiar trap of using only slave revolts as a measurement of opposition to slavery.

When Washington stated, "In all things that are purely social we can be separate as the fingers," he was merely painting the picture of race relations in the South as it was or as he hoped it would be if whites would share his social and religious vision. The perceptive Washington realized the necessity of "black integration" before blacks could integrate into the larger society. Through a combination of industrial education and economic self-sufficiency, blacks could consolidate their wealth. . . . Washington took advantage of the imposed segregation of blacks in order to promote black hegemony through economic interdependence.

Cox refused to accept the assertion that "Washington's leadership may be 'justified' if his times are taken into consideration." He argues that "such an assumption allows us to explain away all behaviors of all persons." Nevertheless, when viewed in the context of his time, Washington was a master "of techniques of manipulating white public opinion"—of infiltration. He placated Southern whites while laying the foundation for black liberation. When he told the white South in his "Atlanta Address," "Cast down your bucket among my people . . . and . . . you will find that they will buy your surplus land, make blossom the waste places in your fields, and run your factories," he was appealing for assistance for his brethren who were three decades removed from slavery— illiterate, disfranchised, and without an economic base.

When he told his black listeners, "Cast down your bucket where you are," "cast it down in making friends in every manly way of the people of all races by whom we are surrounded," he was employing the words of a pragmatist. Here was a man who was cognizant of the conditions of his people and thoroughly familiar with the racial peculiarities of the South.

For blacks to throw off the yoke of economic repression, he urged them to cast down their buckets—"down in agriculture, mechanics, in commerce, in domestic service, and in the professions." This was a practical solution necessitated by their slave experience and the prevailing economic circumstances. Blacks have been "jacks of all trades but masters of none" during slavery. Thus, Washington emphasized the need of industrial training.

It was this emphasis on industrial education which has been interpreted as Washington's rejection of liberal arts training. But his conception of an ideal education was not that limited. (pp. 231-33)

Washington's success as an educator was interwoven with his ability to relate his proposal for industrial education to the prevailing social, economic and political mood of the times. He decided to implement industrial training at a time when the majority of the white population believed that blacks should be given a limited standard of education to condition them for their racial caste position in society. (p. 233)

The juxtaposition of Washington's industrial education ideas and his alleged acquiescence on questions concerning political and social rights with that of the dominant view of a "special education" for Afro-Americans has led to the conclusion that Washington's philosophy of education simply reflected dominant educational trends. It is true that Washington's determination to effect transformation in American society through the educative process of interlinking "learning and doing, theory and practice, culture and vocation" closely parallels the characteristics of ''progressive'' education. But the question remains, was there any difference between Washington's perspective of education and that of his white contemporaries? It is the view of this author that there was: a qualitive difference. (p. 234)

Overall, there were similarities between Washington's philosophy of education and that of his white counterparts, yet there remained a qualitative difference. Like his white counterparts, Washington emphasized the interlinking between theory and practice. But his interest derived from a different set of experiences. Washington approached education as a survival mechanism rather than another approach to pedagogical theory.

Washington's philosophy of education represented an attempt to liberate the black masses. In this attempt, he did not reject liberal education. In fact, his view of industrial education included the inculcation of values and attitudes that were generally associated with liberal education. Washington's industrial education was designed not only to teach skills, but also to transform attitudes toward work at a time when the Afro-Americans could not afford the luxury of rejecting ''common but honest labor.''

Washington stressed the importance of interlinking the mind, body, and soul in all human experiences. He emphasized the love of labor for labor's sake rather than for its financial value. He believed that education should be directly related to life and life problems. In such ways, Washington attempted to liberate the black population economically, through tapping its deep reservoir of spiritual strength. (pp. 234-35)

> *Alfred Young, ''The Educational Philosophy of Booker T. Washington,'' in* PHYLON: The Atlanta University Review of Race and Culture, *37 (copyright, 1976, by Atlanta University; reprinted by permission of* PHYLON), *Vol. XXXVII, No. 3 (September, 1976), pp. 224-35.*

JAMES M. COX (essay date 1977)

[*Cox discusses* Up from Slavery *as both a personal document and a work of literary art which must be ranked with Benjamin Franklin's* Autobiography *and Henry Adams's* The Education of Henry Adams.]

Up from Slavery is a resistant text. The autobiography of a prominent public figure, it almost affronts the literary critic with the bleak inertia of its prose. Its content is equally resistant—its didacticism, its self-gratulation, its facts, and its policies are all but in front of its form. Thus cultural historians will see it as representative of a time which they hope history has transcended; black militants will see it as the record of an Uncle Tom who made his way at the expense of his people; white liberals will see it in a light much the same but weaker. Representatives of all these constituencies would inevitably choose W.E.B. Dubois's *Souls of Black Folk* (1903) as a stronger piece of writing. . . . Yet the cultural fact to remember is that Dubois knew how powerful Booker T. Washington was, and in powerfully risking a counterview to Washington's life and vision he initiated a dialectic upon the racial question which has no more been settled than the racial question itself has been settled. More important for my immediate purposes than the actual controversy between two black views of the racial question is the resistance which Washington's text raises against my own reflections on autobiography. It is not, first of all, Washington's only autobiography. A year before he published

it, he had published *The Story of My Life and Work*. . . . It is not uncommon for an autobiographer to write two versions of his life. Dubois was to write at least three in his long life; so did Sherwood Anderson; so did Frederick Douglass. . . . Though such strategies allow the writer a chance for revision, each succeeding effort throws more and more into doubt his capacity for any secure point of view. The insecurity may keep him alive, but it diminishes the finality of each life that he writes.

Even here Washington is different. He wrote neither of his lives alone. Instead he supervised them, something in the manner of an overseer. *The Story of My Life and Work* was, as Louis Harlan points out in his biography of Washington, actually written by Edgar Webber, a black journalist whom Washington brought to Tuskegee in 1897 largely for the purpose of assisting him in his life story. But Washington was so busy and so exhausted that he took his first vacation, a trip to Europe, and did not oversee the final chapters of the manuscript. Webber on his part proved inadequate to the task, making many errors and resorting to the short-cut methods of padding the book with schedules, letters, and copies of speeches, which are in reality substitutions for the text rather than fulfillments or extensions of it. (pp. 246-47)

Even before Webber had finished the book, Washington was, according to Harlan, already planning another book, this time for the regular rather than the subscription trade; and this time he got a white journalist, Max Thrasher from St. Johnsbury, Vermont, to help him with the project. This time, too, Washington supervised the work every inch of the way, leaving Thrasher practically no freedom. He dictated to Thrasher on trains, took Thrasher's notes and in turn wrote his own draft of the autobiography, letting Thrasher check the manuscript. I have on occasion heard scholars of black studies point gloatingly to Thrasher's presence in the project as evidence of Washington's having been a captive to the white mind. It would actually be difficult to imagine a more reduced role than Thrasher was forced to play; even to call him a ghost, as Harlan does, is to use the term loosely. He seems much more like a slave to Washington's narrative. That fact, concealed from the text, provides both a starting point and index for scrutinizing the life story which Washington ordered for himself.

That story is, as everyone knows, one of the great success-stories of American history. Washington tells in the simplest, most straightforward terms of his rise from slavery to a position as leader of his people. . . . By dint of hard work, ceaseless diplomacy with the white population of Macon County, and unremitting perseverance in the face of ignorance, poverty, inertia, and doubt, he builds Tuskegee from nothing but dilapidated outbuildings of a ruined plantation into Tuskegee Normal and Industrial Institute. Money for the school comes primarily from white northern philanthropists; students come from the black population of the United States, though largely from the South; survival comes from Washington's carefully orchestrated interdependence between Tuskegee and the dominant southern whites. The climax of Washington's career, as he narrates it, is his speech at the Atlanta Exposition in 1895. That speech not only represents the achievement of an ex-slave addressing a largely white southern audience; it also marks Booker T. Washington's emergence as a national leader of his people.

That is the barest outline of Washington's story—or the story he chooses to tell. The way he tells it is simple and unadorned. His prose is reduced to an almost impoverished simplicity; metaphor is sparse; eloquence is all but absent; there is neither richness of texture nor complication of consciousness; even the simplicity never condenses into the energy of compression but retains an air of immobility being put into slow and steady motion. Although Washington was a successful public speaker and although the Atlanta speech (which he quotes in full in his text) shows oratorical flourish and declamatory urgency, the narrative throughout is characterized by what can best be called almost pure inertia.

In calling Washington's style purely inertial, I mean that he writes as if language were matter rather than energy. The words are things which, added one to another, do not record so much as they build the narrative life upon the line that the structure of his life has taken. Thus the events which Washington recounts are not so much dramatized as deadened into matter with which to make the narrative. They are being set steadily in place by the narrator, as if he were constructing the model of his life. The pain, fear, anguish, self-doubt, and anxiety which attended Washington's life are there, of course; but they are muted into the very matter of the narrative. This tendency to treat language as material causes Washington's narrative consciousness to seem literally housed in his narrative. If Washington is moving the blocks of his life into position, they seem to rest in place by their own weight.

That solid stability is one aspect of Washington's inertial style; but there is also motion—for Washington is moving his material into place. Yet here again he seems to be following the course of his life rather than directing it. The relatively strict chronology of autobiographical convention to which he adheres provides the form that draws him along. If he drove himself to make his actual life—and he explicitly indicates that he did—his belief in the existence of that life gives him the powerful illusion that it has created him as the narrator of it. This combination of conventional form and self-belief conveys the strong sense that Washington is pursuing the slow and steady motion of his life.

His use of chronological convention to order his life is but a reflection of his capacity to use time to make his life into a book just as he had used it to make his life as a man. His belief in the weight of his life puts all his language into a rhetorical rather than a dramatic or imaginary relation to that life. The solid reality to which his language refers now exists for language to use. If it was the result of desire, ambition, and fierce determination, it now becomes the matter from which Washington will read higher laws. Here again Washington's book is conventional, embracing as it does the moral and exemplary fatalities of autobiography. The exemplary autobiography is the secularized version of the Christian confessional form. The confessional form (with the exception of the revolutionary Rousseau!) denigrates the man by relating his conversion into God; the exemplary form converts godlike achievement into a model for man to follow. The one portrays the fallen child attaining to the spirit of the Father; the other becomes the model father to provide principles for the children. The one seeks goodness as truth, the other goodness as conduct. [Benjamin] Franklin's *Autobiography* is a classic example of the exemplary convention, and Washington is clearly Franklin's descendant. Having achieved success, he publishes his life as an example of the virtues he believes that he practiced in gaining the high ground from which he writes.

If Franklin is almost disarmingly simple in his exemplary narrative, Washington is dismayingly simple in his. Franklin enunciates principles with sufficient ease to disclose the possibility that he lacks principle altogether; he can thus reveal an implicit

amusement in his life of himself. Washington clings almost desperately to his virtues. What for Franklin is policy becomes gospel for Washington. Keeping his life under much stricter control than that of Franklin, Washington is constrained to reiterate his smaller number of principles—the principle of constant work, the principle of helping others to help themselves, and the principle of building a life from the ground up. Thus where Franklin takes pleasure in the disclosure of his principles—he even writes the autobiography in moments of leisure—Washington's principles are themselves his only pleasure. He hardly knows how to play. If Franklin's very model of himself is a gift that he easily bequeaths to posterity, Washington's life is all but asking for the reader's charity—as if he were waiting in the parlor for one more contribution.

Then one must confront Washington's idea of education. It is as single-minded as his adherence to the Protestant work ethic—and as unpopular to critics of his life and work. Believing that education for people on the bottom of society has to begin at the bottom, Washington wants the body and hands cleaned and disciplined before he cultivates the head. Foreign languages and even books themselves have little benefit in his eyes unless students are able to command a trade. He championed industrial education, and particularly he champions it in his autobiography, as a means of teaching his people how to work. This philosophy of education, reiterated throughout the book, galled blacks in Washington's own time, and it galls them all the more in our time when they can see, just as white readers can see, that this was a means of placating whites. Washington was assuring them, in effect, that Tuskegee graduates would know how to work more than they would know how to think.

These aspects of Washington's narrative make it singularly unprepossessing for both the literary and the cultural critic. They are there, and I could not wish them away even if I would. Yet a reader willing to encounter the book and give it a degree of consciousness—Washington's book, like his life philosophy, is going to ask for something—has a chance for revelations in Washington's inertial narrative.

First of all, there is the fact that Washington was born in *Franklin* County, Virginia. That inertial fact reveals its energy once we think of the book in relation to Franklin's autobiography. He was born a slave, but does not know his father, who is said to be a white man. Thus he has white blood from an unknown father. When he goes to Malden he has no name—but names himself Booker Washington, in a schoolroom. For all his matter-of-factness Washington does note that one of the advantages of having been a slave was his freedom to name himself. He even mentions other slaves taking names such as John S. Lincoln. But he chose Washington; at the time he did it he was no doubt attempting to follow a pattern he saw others pursuing. Yet in light of all that he was to do, the early act is charged with significance—a significance which Washington never stresses because he does not need to. George Washington was, after all, a Virginian who owned slaves yet was the father of his country. Booker Washington is also a Virginian who has been a slave and has an unknown white father. In naming himself he lays claim to the white blood in him and relates himself to the father of his country. He himself clearly sees his original naming of himself as a promise of being a father to his people.

As for Washington's actual call to his vocation, here is what he says about it:

> One day, while working in the coal mine, I
> happened to overhear two miners talking about

a great school for coloured people somewhere in Virginia. That was the first time I had ever heard anything about any kind of school or college that was more pretentious than the little coloured school in our town. . . .

As they were describing the school, it seemed to me that it must be the greatest place on earth, and not even Heaven presented more attractions for me at that time than did the Hampton Normal and Agricultural Institute in Virginia, about which these two men were talking. I resolved at once to go to that school, although I had no idea where it was, or how I was going to reach it. I remembered only that I was on fire constantly with one ambition, and that was to go to Hampton.

That quotation stands out in my context much more than it does in Washington's text. I have seen students read right through it, numbed by the patient plod of Washington's inertial style. Yet it is Washington's *calling,* as he makes unmistakably clear. The whole episode may be a fiction; certainly there would be no way to prove its actual existence, since the two men conversing were unaware of Washington's secret presence. In any event here is a *black boy in a coal mine* hearing his life's direction named, and any wish to call it a fiction seems to me merely a weak theoretical formulation in the face of Washington's capacity, from the established ground he has come to hold, to *make the facts of his life.* If his identity as ex-slave gave him the freedom to name himself and make that name a fact, his achievement as founder of Tuskegee gives him the freedom to make the fact of his call. He even shows that he is creating the fact when he intrudes the full name of Hampton, which the two men could hardly have named. When we consider that it is a coal mine, that he is black, that both he and the coal possess the implicit or inertial energy, we begin to see both the act and style of *Up from Slavery.* The inertia of the style produces the effect of an indeterminate consciousness on the part of Washington, the autobiographer. If I say that he intended the significance that I see, both the style and the skeptical readers reading it almost smile in my face, implicitly accusing me of trying to make a "symbol" of that passage. And of course the accusation is to a large extent right. That is why I am willing to leave it as a made or earned fact—inertial in its existence until it is put into relation to a consciousness prepared to invest it with dynamic energy.

Such a consciousness, once attracted to that inertia, feels the whole possibility of Washington's life about to come to life; relationships start up like rabbits from a blackberry patch. It was Henry Adams, after all, who in his dynamic *Education* determined to measure the line of force of American history in terms of coal production. And it is coal which to this very moment holds the inertial energy of all the weight of geological ages pressing down upon it to create the potential fire of civilization. Set against Henry Adams's autobiography of a failed education, Washington's calling to a successful education strikes sparks. Yet the very critic who would write a book on Henry Adams's art would likely smile indulgently at the comparison.

But let that go. The point is that coal is in the earth. It is the earth into which Booker T. Washington's life is driven and out of which it stands. In his slave cabin, which had no wooden floors, he tells us, there had been a hole where sweet potatoes were kept. When he comes up out of the coal mine to go to Hampton Institute, he makes his way to Richmond where,

without enough money to get a meal or a room, he sleeps under a board sidewalk on the ground. Though beneath the pedestrians, he is yet on the earth. And when he ultimately goes to Tuskegee, the first thing he does is to acquire land on which to build his school from the ground up. He helps clear the fields of this farm—it is actually a ruined plantation—which his school is to occupy. The first building takes the place of the burned-down ruin of the original plantation house; he and his students "dig out the earth" where the foundations are to be laid. Washington is proud that the cornerstone is grounded in the great "black belt" of the South; he knows, and says, that the black belt refers both to the dark soil of the deep South and to the dark people who live there. All this is the ground of Washington's world—the ground where slavery had existed and the ground in which he is determined to found his school. Both his act of life and his vision of education are rooted in this land. (pp. 248-55)

All this is not to praise Washington's vision of education but to see that vision. His discipline is the measure of the rudimentary struggle to gain the ground on which education can be founded. That ground is in the South, under the political sway of whites who, having been dispossessed of their slave world, have nonetheless ridden out reconstruction to regain their damaged dominion. Washington is placating them. He has to; to do otherwise would be to abandon his school or go north to relocate it. His whole theory of education can justifiably be viewed as a promise to southern whites that Tuskegee graduates will not have big ideas; but it cannot justifiably be seen as simply that. The desperate order of the skilled hand, the toothbrush, the clean body, and the clean school is a great hope rooted in a great fear.

We might want to say that the hope represses the fear, but that simply isn't true. Fear is everywhere present in Washington's narrative. When he was a slave boy bringing food home late from the mill he feared that he would be caught in the dark and have his ears cut off by deserting soldiers. On the way to West Virginia with his mother and brothers, the family spent the night in an abandoned house, only to be frightened away by a blacksnake. Even when he names himself, he is in anxiety at not having a name as the teacher begins to call the roll. There is fear present in being "called" in the coal mine; thus he noiselessly creeps to hear the two men talking. He is glad to be called to be a teacher—partly out of fear of being called to be a preacher. He is afraid of the whites around Tuskegee and afraid of the whites in the North from whom he has to beg money, but most of all he is afraid of the psychological space he occupies between the two hostile camps. The space and the fear are almost one and the same thing. (pp. 256-57)

This fear never diminishes with Washington's success; if anything, it increases—not in intensity, since the inertial style precludes emotional crescendo, but in presence. For as Washington gains recognition, he is more and more exposed. Beyond fearing lack of money for Tuskegee from the North or resistance to the school from the South, he has to fear how his action as a public figure will be interpreted by his conflicting constituencies. In preparing to speak at Atlanta, he faces fear on every hand—fear of what southern whites may say, fear of whether he will hurt his school, fear of the visiting northern whites, and fear of the speaking act itself. That fear is, to be sure, a rhetorical background for the success of the speech, but it is also one of the great facts in Washington's book. He discusses his profound fear of public speaking—the fear that some single member of the audience may walk out, the performer's fear of going on stage, the gnawing anxiety of eating a multicourse dinner with the knowledge of having to give an after-dinner speech. When he at last takes his first vacation—the trip to Europe—he fears the luxuries, the dinners, the society, and the possible misunderstandings the Tuskegee community may have about his absence. As he ends the book he is very much on the defensive. He knows that Dubois and hundreds of northern blacks are raising their voices in criticism; he knows that the Tuskegee teachers and students are restive; and it seems to me that he profoundly knows that his own success is being accompanied by mounting victories of anti-negro legislation; for all his success and all his placation he knows about lynching and raises one last plea against it. He ends his book with an account of his triumphant welcome in Richmond, the capital of his native state, yet anyone sensitive to the narrative will feel Washington's anxious wonder whether he may have been as secure under the sidewalk as he is on top of it.

In citing this fear in the book, I am once again forced to distort the nature of its presence. The inertial style cannot and does not express it dramatically but contains it constantly. That, it seems to me, is the mastery of the inertial style. To speak of Washington's mastery may again provoke a smile. But my point in using the word is that Washington is a master. His whole book is devoted to coming up *from* slavery, not up against it. Slavery is the deep ground of his experience; to reject it totally would remove all possibility of becoming a master of the self—and self-mastery is what much of Washington's book is about. It is the iron discipline that he pursues, and it is the basis on which he builds a school and is its master. He becomes the master speaker who aspires to total control of his audience; the description of that control he leaves to white reporters, whose description of his galvanizing presence he almost self-servingly enters in the text.

It would be easy to misconstrue the figure of Washington as master. By converting it into a metaphor, I could jump on the bandwagon with Washington's innumerable critics and say that Washington is playing the role of white master on the old plantation, getting along with the white society of former masters, and making his students the same old black laborers on the new Tuskegee plantation. I have heard it said and I cannot quite unsay it. For Washington is deeply related to the old white world. He is a slave son of an unknown white father from that world; and even George Washington, the white father of freedom whom Washington "adopts" once he is free, did own slaves—a paradox which Henry Adams contemplated with almost paralyzed dismay.

The fact remains, however, that Booker Taliaferro Washington, if not all black, defines himself as black, not white. He determines to remain in a society which will aggressively see him as black. If the name he takes is white and the civilization which he is set on acquiring for himself and for his people is white, these are to be acquisitions, not being; they are property, not identity. They constitute a self to be moved and built, both in Washington's life and in his book. If it is possible to say that this model self is white, I think it equally possible to say that the white model self is Washington's very slave. It is simple, fiercely reduced in its outlines, kept rigidly in line, and controlled with an iron discipline. It has enormous dynamic energy which can only be implicitly seen.

The inertial style makes Washington seem like an old man, rather than a relatively young man. He was at most forty-five when it was published; he was only twenty-five when he went

to Tuskegee. It is hard to believe, this youth so given over to age, this drive which moves so slowly. Yet it is just this slow and steady movement which is the black being of Washington—the being that he retained for himself, yet represents for his people. He does not create the motion; it has been created by the force which ended slavery. It is slow, but it is relentless: it is both a force and a fact—the emotion of identity and the motion of history—which cannot be stopped. Since it is everywhere present it cannot be revealed.

To have said so much may not prove that *Up from Slavery* is literature. I certainly cannot prove it so to anyone disposed to exclude it from the shelf of our "major" works of art. I do believe that it is a wonderful parallel text to Henry Adams's *Education*, just as I believe that it is a remarkable counterpart to Dubois's *The Souls of Black Folk*. (pp. 257-60)

James M. Cox, "Autobiography and Washington,"
in The Sewanee Review *(reprinted by permission of*
the editor; © *1977 by The University of the South),*
*Vol. LXXXV, No. 2, Spring, 1977, pp. 235-61.**

ROGER J. BRESNAHAN (essay date 1980)

[*In his essay, Bresnahan posits that Washington's two autobiographies,* The Story of My Life and Work *and* Up from Slavery, *were carefully crafted to favorably relate to two distinct readerships—poor black, and affluent white, Americans.*]

When *The Story of My Life and Work* was published in 1900 by an obscure Chicago publishing house, Booker T. Washington and his collaborators had for some time been at work on a second autobiography which would narrate many of the same events, though with a substantially different emphasis. Louis R. Harlan, the editor of Washington's papers, makes a powerful case on external evidence for two distinct sets of readers. The reference to "Lincoln and his armies" at the beginning of *Up From Slavery* and its absence from *The Story of My Life and Work* offers an early internal clue to what Washington himself called two "wholly separate" kinds of readers. . . .

Northern white readers could be expected to be flattered by the knowledge that Washington was mindful of the role they or their forefathers had played in emancipating the slaves. It may be that the reference to Lincoln was added to the core story because Washington had noted how it pleased such audiences on his Northern speaking tours. Such a reference would, however, have been out of place in a book designed for the black masses, who would not have liked to think that Washington's mother placed all her hopes in Lincoln. Indeed, he may well have considered such an allusion to Lincoln in *The Story of My Life and Work* a dangerous political reference at a time when Kelly Miller was advising Blacks to abandon the Republican Party as it had abandoned them.

Black readers of *The Story of My Life and Work* were more likely to be enamored of Washington's picture of his mother as a survivor. The plantation cook, she stealthily procured eggs and roasted chickens for her family. The same core story is related in *Up From Slavery,* but the generalizations offered are strikingly different. There, the chiefly white readers were reminded that "she was simply a victim of the system of slavery." . . . In the earlier work, ever mindful of his role as preceptor, Washington draws a careful distinction between such acts in slavery and in freedom. Reminding his black readers that "some people blame the Negro for not being more honest, as judged by the Anglo-Saxon's standard of honesty," he asserts that his mother's act was not stealing but survival. Capping off the brief moral lesson, he returns once more to his mother, declaring that "after our freedom no one was stricter . . . in teaching and observing the highest rules of integrity." . . . (p. 15)

Similar differences in emphasis are found throughout the two autobiographies. Washington's reference to his own paternity in *The Story of My Life and Work* comprises a stark, two-sentence paragraph: "Who my father was, or is, I have never been able to learn with any degree of certainty. I only know that he was a white man." . . . He asserts his identification with his black readership when he describes the poverty of his family, the cruelty of slavery even under a master who resorted to the whip only "in a few cases," the ignorance in which his early life was spent, and the exploitation of black women by white men.

In *Up From Slavery*, however, Washington wishes to place enough distance between himself and his readers that they will be conscious that they are in unfamiliar territory and will accept him as a guide. As he identified himself with the masses of Southern black people in *The Story of My Life and Work*, so he uses the same core story to differentiate himself from his white readers in *Up From Slavery*, playing on their collective guilt or their sentiment for justice and thus softening them up to accomplish his objectives later in the book. (pp. 15-16)

Washington's purpose in writing the two very different autobiographies was not simply to appeal to different audiences. Internal mechanisms are designed to lead black readers of *The Story of My Life and Work* to conclude that adherence to the Tuskegee model will bring about lasting progress because that model was fashioned by one who had himself risen from poverty to power. Similar mechanisms would lead white readers of *Up From Slavery* to the ineluctable conclusion that they must cooperate with Washington to bring about gradual progress which would not threaten white economic and political hegemony. Affluent white readers would be led to contribute, and contribute heavily, to the cause.

These two works, composed and published in the same period, present a clear picture of the bifurcated readership Washington anticipated. Contemporary reader-centered esthetics, although it tends to focus mainly on the actions of readers of novels, is especially useful in illuminating Washington's skillful manipulation of his readers. Because Washington intends to frustrate the reader's expectation of "an 'authentic' image of the man 'who held the pen,'" he portrays himself as a novelist portrays a character. . . . The identity of the persona in Washington's autobiographies is articulated through the engagement of the anticipated reader. The characteristics of that reader, the changes Washington expected to bring about in that reader's attitudes, and, finally, the behavior he expected to induce modify the identity of the author as persona. In short, Washington neither fabricates a new identity nor liberates his own existing one; rather, he guides the reader to liberate an identity for the persona from the reader's own consciousness. The Booker T. Washington whom the reader is permitted to see originates in the behavior Washington expects the reader to exhibit after reading the book.

The act of autobiography demands that the writer should have previously come to grips with the fact of self and that he work out the recovery of a lost identity. But it is a mistake to assume that the role of the reader will be merely to follow this process. Washington's autobiographies do guide the reader to reconquer a lost image of the writer's identity. At all times during the act of reading, however, it is the reader's reconquest of his own surrendered concept of Washington's identity. It is Washington's intention to create a reader who is convinced that he knows the real Booker T. Washington and thereby to gain the reader's trust. From this will follow the cognitive orientation the reader is to manifest. Leaving little to chance, Washington will approvingly suggest forms of behavior the reader may also manifest.

The question in such autobiography, where the object is to elicit specific responses in the reader, is not the discovery of the identity of the author so much as it is the revelation to the reader of his own identity vis-à-vis the carefully articulated image of the writer. It is significant that *Up From Slavery* is not intended for all white readers; it is directed only to those persons of some affluence who would be likely to subscribe to the conservative journal in which it was first serialized or to purchase it in a bookstore. The anticipated reader is the one who can help Washington in his work, either the influential Southerner who will publicly exhibit good will or the Northern Republican who will donate money. (p. 16)

Washington's method in the autobiographies is to tap the reader's own identity and then to modify it. . . . Washington as writer is not probing his own identity but rather the identity of the reader. That the image of himself which he seems to present is that of a simple man engaged in an uncomplicated task for which he needs only money and trust is the most creative component of the autobiographical process. . . . Throughout *Up From Slavery* he seeks to arouse the reader's resistance to forms of racial progress which might encroach on the economic and political hegemony enjoyed by Whites. The same principle operates in *The Story of My Life and Work*, in which Washington stresses the function of the Tuskegee Negro Conference as a forum for black farmers to discuss their problems. He recalls his refusal "to allow those people who were far above them in education and surroundings to take up the time merely giving advice to these representatives of the masses." . . . The appeal for confidence is based on the mutuality of their experiences. (pp. 16-17)

For those Northern white readers of *Up From Slavery* who may have admired the educational work of the Freedmen's Bureau, Washington makes frequent allusion to General Samuel C. Armstrong, founder of Hampton Institute, and to "that Christ-like body of men and women who went into the Negro schools at the close of the war by the hundreds to assist in lifting up my race." . . . A deplorable past is being redeemed at Tuskegee by trusty, black hands; readers will be allowed to assist so that an honorable future may be secured to black people within an economic and social scheme which will remain comfortable to these Armstrongites. For Southern aristocrats reading *Up From Slavery*, Washington disavows bitterness, saying less than he might have about slavery. Their future is secure within Washington's scheme because black people will be trained as farm laborers, tenant farmers, and domestic servants. Like their Northern counterparts, these aristocrats of the class that formerly held slaves are reinforced in their own positive self-images. Blacks of the rural South witness the significance of their past affirmed in *The Story of My Life and Work*. They see a man like themselves who wields immense power in the white world. Their own experiential knowledge—that Blacks are safest when Whites are not around—is confirmed negatively in the Atlanta Compromise and positively in Washington's practice at Tuskegee where the Hampton education is applied by an almost totally black faculty. (pp. 17-18)

The reader of *Up From Slavery* or of *The Story of My Life and Work* is meant to believe he is following Washington's course of development and witnessing his confrontation with self—both legitimate expectations of readers of autobiographies. But Washington's reader will everywhere find a narrative detachment which deflects interest from the author and serves to entangle the reader with the events of the story itself rather than with the persona. The narration of the events of Washington's life effects the reader's entanglement with the story on unfamiliar ground; he has no choice but to place his confidence in Washington as his guide. (p. 18)

The Story of My Life and Work recounts the hardships endured in the early days of Tuskegee. Much of this information, though new to the readers, would have a ring of familiarity. Thrusting in the direction of the unfamiliar, however, is the effect of Tuskegee on the world beyond. The school had been visited by the Secretary of Agriculture and even by President McKinley. The chapter relating the President's visit, like the one recounting the campaign to secure a permanent endowment, juxtaposes the familiar and the unfamiliar. The reader must accept Washington's version of these events because the known is entangled in so much of the unfamiliar. One chapter, for example, refers to at least a hundred wealthy or influential persons by name and reproduces a letter from Grover Cleveland. From the reader's point of view, Washington's importance is magnified by his association with so many known and unknown persons. Similarly, Washington's importance grows when, in the chapter purporting to describe the educational work of Tuskegee, he enumerates the value of the land and its capital improvements, the physical facilities, and the qualifications of the faculty.

Up From Slavery relies heavily on a strategy of negation to win support for the Tuskegee model. With not a little buffoonery, Washington parades the image of the Negro dandy who had gone to school so that he can wear fine clothing. This canard is trotted out again in the chapter on Reconstruction. In the District of Columbia, Washington found a class of people dependent upon the federal government and bent upon a life of material pleasure far above their station. "How many times I wished then, and have often wished since, that by some power of magic I might remove the great bulk of these people into the country districts and plant them upon the soil, upon the solid and never deceptive foundation of Mother Nature, where all nations and races that have ever succeeded have gotten their start . . .". . . . He reminds the reader of what is known—that Tuskegee and Hampton have long been engaged in such a program. And he underscores what is feared—that the problem still exists. (p. 19)

As he had done at Atlanta in 1895, Washington reassures the reader of *Up From Slavery* that the Tuskegee model is predicated on an economic gradualism that would keep black labor toiling at menial tasks in the rural South for many years to come. It is interesting that in *The Story of My Life and Work* the chapter on the Atlanta Compromise speech is immediately followed by one on Washington's efforts to preserve the electoral franchise in South Carolina. This material is not omitted from *Up From Slavery*, but it occupies a much less prominent place. *The Story of My Life and Work* frankly, though briefly, acknowledges the abuse which the black press heaped on Washington after the Atlanta Compromise speech, but he appeals to his readers' trust in his good judgment, explaining how conscious he was that it would have been "very easy . . . to have uttered a single sentence which would have thrown a wet blanket over . . . the harmonious relations of the races." . . . As a final appeal for trust, he relates that this criticism subsided after his speech before the Bethel Literary Association in Washington, D.C., where he explained his Atlanta address, "but of course went into more detail." The implication that he had somehow put something over on the Southern Whites at Atlanta is not borne out by the extracts from the Bethel speech printed in his collected papers, but his is a clever strategem since most of his readers would never see the text of the speech. . . . (pp. 19-20)

Political and financial support is the reader-response sought in *Up From Slavery*. Washington's narration of his own life up to his entrance into Hampton delineates the problem. The chapters on Hampton show his development as a man espousing values dear to his readers. And the five chapters devoted to Tuskegee demonstrate Washington's ability to transmit the Hampton values in a black setting; now, through reflecting on Washington's professed gratitude for the political and financial help he has received from Whites, the reader is permitted to determine what role he can play in the work of uplift. By exploiting the preconceived and often racist notions held by readers of *Up From Slavery*, Washington performed an ultimate disservice to achieve a short-term goal. But there is nothing in his life, work, or writings to suggest that he sought any form of interracial cooperation other than what he suggested as appropriate responses for white readers of *Up From Slavery*, namely political influence and money. The growing concentration of power in what came to be known as the Tuskegee Machine bears this out.

Washington's two autobiographies are susceptible to the sort of criticism usually practiced with works of narrative fiction because they are less concerned with the personal development of the author, even the author as main character, than with the response of the reader. Unlike narrative fiction, however, autobiography must be an open-ended form. . . .

In both *Up From Slavery* and *The Story of My Life and Work* the ending is embedded in the continuing narrative. The final chapter of *The Story of My Life and Work* relates some of the joys and hardships of soliciting funds, as well as the furor created by Washington's uncomplimentary remarks on the Negro ministry in the South printed in *The Outlook* in 1892. Only on the last page does he come to the point—that good things come from hard work, from "being willing to toil while others are resting, being willing to work while others are sleeping, being willing to put forth the severest effort when there is no one to see or applaud." . . . Similarly, the final chapter of *Up From Slavery* relates the last visit of the dying General Armstrong to Tuskegee, the Harvard honorary degree, and the elaborate preparations made for the visit of President McKinley, before concluding with the apparently sober observation, made at a time that Rayford Logan accurately labels the nadir of race relations in America, that "despite superficial and temporary signs" to the contrary, "there never was a time when I felt more hopeful for the race than I do at the present." . . .

Relying on his experience as a skillful platform orator, Washington leaves sympathetic readers of *The Story of My Life and Work* prepared to accept the conclusion that they must toil on, creating their own opportunities within the Tuskegee model. Relying on the same skills which had produced in the North more than a million dollars in gifts for Tuskegee, he leaves readers of *Up From Slavery* prepared to acknowledge that in a single generation great progress had been made with meagre resources. It would be up to them to decide how they might bring the story to an ending. (p. 20)

Roger J. Bresnahan, "The Implied Readers of Booker T. Washington's Autobiographies" (© Indiana State University 1980; reprinted with the permission of the author and Indiana State University), in Black American Literature Forum, Vol. 14, No. 1, Spring, 1980, pp. 15-20.

DEBORAH CANNON PARTRIDGE WOLFE (essay date 1981)

[*Wolfe maintains that Washington's practical educational theories are still valid today.*]

Perhaps less generally recognized than his leadership skills are the important contributions that Washington made to the theory and practice of education—contributions that transcend their time and remain relevant today.

Washington put his ideas about education into practice at Tuskegee Normal and Industrial Institute, which he founded in 1881 in Tuskegee, Alabama. Today, as Tuskegee Institute looks back on its first 100 years, it seems appropriate to re-examine the ideas that made Washington an educator who was ahead of his time.

The mission of Tuskegee Institute has always been to produce educated individuals. Washington defined an educated person as one possessing 1) both cognitive and problem-solving skills, 2) self-discipline, 3) moral standards, and 4) a sense of service.

His recognition that true learning is more than memorization was unusual in his day. Only in the 20th century have we begun to define cognitive learning as the acquisition of knowledge *and* of those thinking skills that enable us to use knowledge to solve problems. . . . Washington's writings are replete with evidence of his concern for real understanding, not mere book learning. . . .

If Washington emphasized both cognitive and problem-solving skills as essential educational goals, he believed self-discipline to be of equal importance. "[T]hat race is greatest that has learned to exhibit the greatest self-control, the greatest forbearance," he wrote.

The requirement that every Tuskegee student do some manual labor was intended as much to develop self-discipline as to develop healthy respect for honest labor. In his emphasis on learning by doing, Washington foreshadowed John Dewey and the Progressive education movement by nearly two decades. . . .

Washington also believed that he could not develop a truly educated person without stressing moral development. "That education . . . that gives one physical courage to stand in front of a cannon and fails to give him moral courage to stand up in defense of right and justice is a failure," he wrote. (p. 205)

[What] does Washington's concept of the educated person suggest for education in the Eighties and beyond? As the 20th century draws to a close, we are confronted by problems of greater magnitude and complexity than we have ever met before. Rapid change is a fact of life. Thus we are challenged to prepare youngsters for a world we can only dimly foresee. More than ever, we must be committed to producing truly educated individuals—selfless, self-confident, flexible young people who are able to learn, to solve problems, to make moral and humane choices. The words of Booker T. Washington,

written a century ago, continue to define the mission of education today:

> There never was a time in the history of the country when those interested in education should more earnestly consider to what extent the mere acquiring of the ability to create and write, the mere acquisition of a knowledge of literature and science, makes men producers, lovers of labour, independent, honest, unselfish, and above all good. Call education by what name you please, if it fails to bring about these results among the masses, it falls short of its highest end.

(p. 222)

Deborah Cannon Partridge Wolfe, "Booker T. Washington: An Educator for all Ages," in Phi Delta Kappan (copyright 1981 by Phi Delta Kappa, Inc.), Vol. 63, No. 3, November, 1981, pp. 205, 222.

ADDITIONAL BIBLIOGRAPHY

Amann, Clarence A. "Three Negro Classics: An Estimate." *Negro American Literature Forum* 4, No. 4 (Winter 1970): 113-19.*
    Comparative study of three autobiographies by black writers: *Up from Slavery*, *The Souls of Black Folk* by W.E.B. Du Bois, and *The Autobiography of an Ex-Colored Man* by James Weldon Johnson. Amann states that *Up from Slavery* is limited in scope and outranked by Du Bois's *The Souls of Black Folk*.

Brawley, Benjamin. "The Maturing of Negro Literature." In his *The Negro Genius: A New Appraisal of the Achievement of the American Negro in Literature and the Fine Arts*, pp. 143-70. New York: Dodd, Mead, & Co., 1937.*
    Discusses Washington's eloquence as a speaker.

Dillard, James Hardy. "A Christian Philosopher: Booker T. Washington." *Southern Workman* LIX, No. 5 (May 1925): 209-14.
    Views Washington's Christian faith as the motivating force behind his ideas and methods of change.

Eddy, Sherwood, and Page, Kirby. "Freedom from Ignorance: Booker T. Washington." In their *Makers of Freedom: Biographical Sketches in Social Progress*, pp. 32-62. New York: George H. Doran Co., 1926.
    Discusses the political and economic climate during Washington's era and examines his accomplishments in relation to the beliefs of the time.

Gottschalk, Jane. "The Rhetorical Strategy of Booker T. Washington." *Phylon* XXVII, No. 4 (Winter 1966): 388-95.
    Examines Washington's weekly talks at the Tuskegee Institute.

Harlan, Louis R. "Booker T. Washington and the *Voice of the Negro*." *The Journal of Southern History* XLV, No. 1 (February 1979): 45-62.
    Discusses Washington's attempts to gain editorial control of the black journal *Voice of the Negro*.

Johnston, Harry. "The Education of the Negro: Tuskegee." In his *The Negro in the New World*, pp. 398-420. 1910. Reprint. New York, London: Johnson Reprint Corp., 1969.
    Personal observations on Washington, Tuskegee Institute, and the Afro-American from an English viewpoint.

Meier, August. "Booker T. Washington and the Negro Press: With Special Reference to the *Colored American Magazine*." *The Journal of Negro History* XXXVIII, No. 1 (January 1953): 67-91.
    Discusses Washington's involvement with the black journals of the time, especially the *Colored American Magazine*.

Morris, Charles. "Booker T. Washington, the Pioneer of Negro Progress." In his *Heroes of Progress in America*. 2d rev. ed., pp. 335-44. Philadelphia, London: J. B. Lippincott Co., 1919.
    Biographical sketch of Washington.

Roosevelt, Theodore. Preface to *Booker T. Washington: Builder of a Civilization,* by Emmett J. Scott and Lyman Beecher Stowe, pp. ix-xv. New York: Doubleday, Page & Co., 1916.
    Laudatory evaluation of Washington's social and political contribution based on President Roosevelt's high regard for Washington.

Spencer, Samuel R., Jr. *Booker T. Washington and the Negro's Place in American Life*. Boston: Little, Brown and Co., 1955, 212 p.
    Biography that emphasizes Washington's personality and his social contributions.

Stepto, Robert B. "Lost in a Cause: Booker T. Washington's *Up from Slavery*." In his *From Behind the Veil: A Study of Afro-American Narrative,* pp. 32-51. Chicago: University of Illinois Press, 1979.

Detailed analysis of *Up from Slavery* as an Afro-American classic.

Thornbrough, Emma L. "Booker T. Washington As Seen by His White Contemporaries." *Journal of Negro History* LIII, No. 2 (April 1968): 161-82.
    Excellent critical account of Washington from the point of view of his white contemporaries.

Whitfield, Stephen J. "Three Masters of Impression Management: Benjamin Franklin, Booker T. Washington, and Malcolm X As Autobiographers." *The South Atlantic Quarterly* 77, No. 4 (Autumn 1978): 399-417.*
    Comparative study of Franklin, Washington, and Malcolm X as men whose autobiographies were artfully crafted to create specific impressions of their authors.

Woodward, C. Vann. "Booker T. Washington in History." In *Booker T. Washington,* edited by Emma Lou Thornbrough, pp. 130-73. Englewood Cliffs, N.J.: Prentice-Hall, 1969.*
    Explains the influence and effects of Washington's policies from an historical perspective.

Appendix

THE EXCERPTS IN TCLC, VOLUME 10, WERE REPRINTED FROM THE FOLLOWING PERIODICALS:

The Academy
The American Catholic Quarterly Review
The American Fabian
The American Scandinavian Review
Anglo-Welsh Review
The Antioch Review
Ariel
Arizona Quarterly
The Athenaeum
The Atlantic Monthly
Blackwood's Magazine
The Bookman (London)
The Bookman (New York)
Les cahiers de la quinzaine
Chicago Evening Post
Chicago Review
The Church Review
Commentary
Commonweal
The Constitution (Atlanta)
The Constructive Quarterly
Contemporary Review
The Critic
Criticism
The Dallas Morning News
The Denver Quarterly
The Dial
The Double Dealer
The Dublin Magazine
Educational Theatre Journal
The Enemy
Essays in Criticism
Ex Libris
The Explicator
The Fortnightly Review
Forum
Forum and Century
The French Review
The Guardian (Boston)
Harper's Weekly
Hispania
Hispanic Review
History Today
Housman Society Journal

The International Fiction Review
International Journal of Slavic Linguistics
   and Poetics
Jewish Social Studies
Journal of European Studies
The Journal of Negro History
The Journal of Southern History
Journal of the History of Ideas
Journal of the History of Philosophy
The Kenyon Review
Lacerba
The Literary Review
The Little Review
London Evening Standard
The Malahat Review
Meanjin
Michigan Quarterly Review
The Midwest Quarterly
Modern Fiction Studies
Modern Philology
Monumenta Nipponica
The Nation
The Nation and the Athenaeum
The New Age
The New Criterion
New Orleans Time-Democrat
The New Republic
The New Review
New Statesman
The New Yorker
New York Evening Post
The New York Herald
New York Herald Tribune Books
The New York Review of Books
New York Times
The New York Times Book Review
New York World
The Nineteenth Century
The North American Review
Nouvelle revue française
Les Nouvelles Littéraires
Phi Delta Kappan
Philological Quarterly
PHYLON

Pioneer
PMLA
Poet Lore
Poetry
Poetry Wales
The Princeton University Library Chronicle
The Quarterly Review
Renasence
Revista Canadiense de Estudios Hispanicos
Riverside Quarterly
Russian Review
St. Louis Republic
The Saturday Review (London)
The Saturday Review of Literature
Scribner's Magazine
Seven Arts
The Sewanee Review
Slavic and East European Journal
Social Forces
South Atlantic Quarterly
The Southern Review
The Spectator
Story
Studies in American Fiction
Studies in Short Fiction
Studies on the Left
Symposium
Time
The Times Literary Supplement
Transactions of the Royal Society of
   Literature
The Tulane Drama Review
Twice a Year
The University Review
Vanity Fair
Virginia Quarterly Review
Voice of Missions
Voice of the People
Westminster Review
Wilson Bulletin for Librarians
World Union
Writer's Digest
The Yale Review
Zagadnienia Rodzajów Literackich

THE EXCERPTS IN TCLC, VOLUME 10, WERE REPRINTED FROM THE FOLLOWING BOOKS:

Abbott, Lyman. Silhouettes of My Contemporaries. *Doubleday, 1921.*

Adams, J. Donald. The Shape of Books to Come. *Viking, 1944.*

Adereth, M. Commitment in Modern French Literature: A Brief Study of 'Litterature engagee' in the Works of Péguy, Aragon, and Sartre. *Gollancz, 1967.*

Aiken, Conrad. Collected Criticism. *Oxford University Press, 1968.*

Aiken, Henry David. Introduction to Thus Spake Zarathustra, *by Friedrich Nietzsche. Translated by Thomas Common. Heritage, 1967.*

Aldiss, Brian W. Billion Year Spree: The True History of Science Fiction. *Doubleday, 1973, Schocken, 1974.*

Allen, D. C., ed. The Moment of Poetry. *Johns Hopkins University Press, 1962.*

Alvarez, A. Afterword to Jude the Obscure, *by Thomas Hardy. New American Library, 1961.*

Alvarez, A. Beyond All This Fiddle: Essays 1955-1967. *Random House, 1969.*

Anderson, David D., ed. Critical Essays on Sherwood Anderson. *G. K. Hall, 1981.*

Anderson, Sherwood. Introduction to Free, and Other Stories, *by Theodore Dreiser. Boni & Liveright, 1918, Scholarly Press, 1971.*

Apollonio, Umbro, ed. Futurist Manifestos. *Translated by Robert Brain & others. Viking, 1973.*

Aptheker, Herbert, ed. A Documentary History of the Negro People in the United States: From the Reconstruction Era to 1910, Vol. II. *4th ed. Citadel, 1968.*

Archer, William. Poets of the Younger Generation. *John Lane, 1902, Scholarly Press, 1969.*

Atheling, William, Jr. The Issue at Hand: Studies in Contemporary Magazine Science Fiction. *Edited by James Blish. Advent, 1964.*

Auchincloss, Louis. Reflections of a Jacobite. *Houghton Mifflin, 1961.*

Baker, Houston A., Jr. Long Black Song: Essays in Black American Literature and Culture. *University Press of Virginia, 1972.*

Balakian, Anna. The Symbolist Movement: A Critical Appraisal. *Random House, 1967.*

Barrett, William. Irrational Man: A Study in Existential Philosophy. *Doubleday, 1958.*

Barricelli, Jean-Pierre, ed. Chekhov's Great Plays: A Critical Anthology. *New York University Press, 1981.*

Barzun, Jacques. Darwin, Marx, Wagner: Critique of a Heritage. *Little, Brown, 1941.*

Beach, Joseph Warren. The Twentieth Century Novel: Studies in Technique. *Appleton-Century-Crofts, 1932.*

Beaumont, E. M. & others, eds. Order and Adventure in Post-Romantic French Poetry. *Barnes & Noble, 1973.*

Bellman, Samuel I. Constance M. Rourke. *Twayne, 1981.*

Benn, Gottfried. Primal Vision: Selected Writings of Gottfried Benn. *Edited by E. B. Ashton. New Directions, 1971.*

Bennett, Arnold. The Savour of Life: Essays in Gusto. *Doubleday, 1928.*

Bentley, E. C. Introduction to More than Somewhat, *by Damon Runyon. Edited by E. C. Bentley. Constable, 1937.*

Bentley, Eric. A Century of Hero-Worship: A Study of the Idea of Heroism in Carlyle and Nietzsche, with Notes on Wagner, Spengler, Stefan George, and D. H. Lawrence. *Beacon Press, 1957.*

Bentley, Eric. The Cult of the Superman: A Study of Heroism in Carlyle and Nietzsche, with Notes on Other Hero-Worshippers of Modern Times. *P. Smith, 1969.*

Beyer, Harald. Masterpieces of the Modern Scandinavian Theatre. *Edited by Robert W. Corrigan. Collier, 1967.*

Bishop, John Peale. The Collected Essays of John Peale Bishop. *Edited by Edmund Wilson. Charles Scribner's Sons, 1948.*

Bluestein, Gene. The Voice of the Folk: Folklore and American Literary Theory. *University of Massachusetts Press, 1972.*

Boyd, Ernest. Literary Blasphemies. *Harper & Brothers, 1927.*

Boyesen, Hjalmar Hjorth. Essays on Scandinavian Literature. *Charles Scribner's Sons, 1895.*

Bradbury, Malcolm, and McFarlane, James, eds. Modernism: 1890-1930. *Penguin, 1976.*

Bradbury, Ray. Preface to The Best of Henry Kuttner, *by Henry Kuttner. Doubleday, 1975.*

Brandes, Georg. Reminiscences of My Childhood and Youth. *Duffield, 1906.*

Brandes, Georg. Friedrich Nietzsche. *Translated by A. G. Chater. Heineman, 1909.*

Broderick, Francis L., and Meier, August, eds. Negro Protest Thought in the Twentieth Century. *Bobbs-Merrill, 1966.*

Bronowski, J. The Poet's Defence. *Cambridge University Press, 1939, Hyperion Press, 1979.*

Brooks, Van Wyck. New England: Indian Summer, 1865-1915. *Dutton, 1940.*

Brooks, Van Wyck. Preface to The Roots of American Culture and Other Essays, by Constance Rourke. *Edited by Van Wyck Brooks. Harcourt Brace Jovanovich, 1942.*

Brophy, Brigid; Levey, Michael; and Osborne, Charles. Fifty Works of English and American Literature We Could Do Without. *Stein and Day, 1968.*

Broun, Heywood. Introduction to Guys and Dolls, by Damon Runyon. *Stokes, 1931.*

Brown, John Mason. Two on the Aisle: Ten Years of the American Theatre in Performance. *Norton, 1938.*

Bruford, W. H. Anton Chekhov. *Bowes & Bowes, 1957.*

Bryusov, Valery. The Diary of Valery Bryusov (1893-1905). *Edited and translated by Joan Delaney Grossman. University of California Press, 1980.*

Burgin, Richard. Conversations with Jorge Luis Borges. *Holt, Rinehart and Winston, 1969.*

Cabell, James Branch. Some of Us: An Essay in Epitaphs. *McBride, 1930.*

Caldwell, Helen. Machado de Assis: The Brazilian Master and His Novels. *University of California Press, 1970.*

Camus, Albert. The Rebel. *Translated by Anthony Bower. Knopf, 1954.*

Carter, Lin. Imaginary Worlds: The Art of Fantasy. *Ballantine, 1973.*

Carus, Paul. Nietzsche and Other Exponents of Individualism. *Open Court, 1914.*

Chesterton, G. K. The Well and the Shallows. *Sheed and Ward, 1935.*

Churchill, Kenneth. Italy and English Literature, 1764-1930. *Macmillan, 1980.*

Clark, Tom. Introduction to The Bloodhounds of Broadway and Other Stories, *by Damon Runyon. Morrow, 1981.*

Claudel, Paul, and Gide, Andre. The Correspondence between Paul Claudel and André Gide, 1899-1926. *Translated by John Russell. Pantheon, 1952.*

Cockshut, A.O.J. Man and Woman: A Study of Love and the Novel 1740-1940. *Collins, 1977, Oxford University Press, 1978.*

Cole, Toby, ed. Playwrights on Playwriting: The Meaning and Making of Modern Drama from Ibsen to Ionesco. *Hill and Wang, 1960.*

Coombes, H. Edward Thomas. *Chatto & Windus, 1956.*

Crawford, F. Marion. The Novel: What It Is. *Macmillan, 1893, Books for Libraries Press, 1969.*

Cruse, Harold. Rebellion or Revolution? *Rev. ed. Morrow, 1968.*

Curti, Merle. The Social Ideas of American Education. *Charles Scribner's Sons, 1935.*

Danto, Arthur C. Nietzsche As Philosopher. *Macmillan, 1965.*

Davis, Robert Bernard. George William Russell ("AE"). *Twayne, 1977.*

Davison, Edward. Some Modern Poets and Other Critical Essays. *Harper & Brothers, 1928.*

DeCoster, Cyrus. Juan Valera. *Twayne, 1974.*

De la Mare, Walter. Foreword to Collected Poems, *by Edward Thomas. Selwyn & Blount, 1920, Faber and Faber, 1936.*

D'Itri, Patricia Ward. Damon Runyon. *Twayne, 1982.*

Donchin, Georgette. The Influence of French Symbolism on Russian Poetry. *Mouton, 1958.*

Douglas, Norman. Looking Back: An Autobiographical Excursion. *Harcourt Brace Jovanovich, 1933, Scholarly Press, 1971.*

Drake, William A. Contemporary European Writers. *John Day, 1928.*

Dreiser, Theodore. Letters of Theodore Dreiser: A Selection, Vol. 2. *Edited by Robert H. Elias. University of Pennsylvania Press, 1959.*

Du Bois, W. E. Burghardt. The Souls of Black Folk: Essays and Sketches. *10th ed. McClurg, 1915.*

Duclaux, Mary. Twentieth Century French Writers (Reviews and Reminiscences). *Collins, 1919.*

Dukes, Ashley. The Youngest Drama: Studies of Fifty Dramatists. *Ernest Benn, 1923.*

Eagle, Solomon. Books in General, second series. *Knopf, 1920.*

Ellis, Havelock. The Soul of Spain. *Constable, 1908.*

Ellis, Havelock. Views and Reviews: A Selection of Uncollected Articles, 1884-1932, first and second series. *D. Harmsworth, 1932, Books for Libraries Press, 1970.*

Erlich, Victor. The Double Image: Concepts of the Poet in Slavic Literatures. *Johns Hopkins University Press, 1964.*

Ervine, St. John G. Some Impressions of My Elders. *Macmillan, 1922.*

Farrell, James T. The League of Frightened Philistines and Other Papers. *Vanguard, 1945.*

Farrell, James T. Introduction to The Best Short Stories of Theodore Dreiser, *by Theodore Dreiser. World, 1956.*

Field, Norma Moore. Afterword to And Then: Natsume Sōseki's Novel "Sorekara," *by Natsume Sōseki. Translated by Norma Moore Field. Louisiana State University Press, 1978.*

Fife, Robert Herndon. Introduction to Georg Brandes in Life and Letters, *by Julius Moritzen. D. S. Colyer, 1922.*

Fishtine, Edith. Don Juan Valera, the Critic. *Bryn Mawr, 1933.*

Fitzmaurice-Kelly, James. Chapters on Spanish Literature. *Constable, 1908.*

Foster, George Burman. Friedrich Nietzsche. *Edited by Curtis W. Reese. Macmillan, 1931.*

Fowlie, Wallace. Clowns and Angels: Studies in Modern French Literature. *Sheed and Ward, 1943.*

France, Anatole. On Life and Letters, first series. *Translated by A. W. Evans. John Lane, 1911, Dodd, Mead, 1924.*

France, Anatole. On Life and Letters, third series. *Translated by D. B. Stewart. John Lane, 1922.*

Frank, Waldo. Our America. *Boni & Liveright, 1919.*

Frank, Waldo. Introduction to Dom Casmurro, by Machado de Assis. *Translated by Helen Caldwell. Noonday Press, 1953.*

Galsworthy, John. Candelabra: Selected Essays and Addresses. *Heinemann, 1932, Charles Scribner's Sons, 1933.*

Garvey, Marcus. Philosophy and Opinions of Marcus Garvey; or, Africa for the Africans. *Edited by Amy Jacques Garvey. 2d ed. Frank Cass, 1967.*

Gerber, Philip L. Theodore Dreiser. *Twayne, 1964.*

Gerould, Gordon Hall. The Patterns or English and American Fiction: A History. *Little, Brown, 1942.*

Gide, André. The Journals of André Gide: 1928-1939, Vol. III. *Translated by Justin O'Brien. Knopf, 1949, Secker & Warburg, 1949.*

Goldberg, Isaac. Brazilian Literature. *Knopf, 1922.*

Goldberg, Isaac. The Drama of Transition: Native and Exotic Playcraft. *Kidd, 1922.*

Gosse, Edmund. Books on the Table. *Charles Scribner's Sons, 1921.*

Graham, Stephen. Introduction to The Republic of the Southern Cross, and Other Stories, *by Valery Brussof. Constable, 1918.*

Green, Julian. Introduction to Men and Saints: Prose and Poetry, *by Charles Peguy. Translated by Anne Green and Julian Green, Pantheon, 1944.*

Gregory, Horace. Introduction to The Portable Sherwood Anderson, *by Sherwood Anderson. Edited by Horace Gregory. Viking Penguin, 1949.*

Gross, Theodore L. The Heroic Ideal in American Literature. *Free Press, 1971.*

Grossman, William L. Introduction to Epitaph of a Small Winner, *by Machado de Assis. Translated by William L. Grossman. Noonday Press, 1952.*

Grossman, William L. Introduction to The Psychiatrist and Other Stories, *by Machado de Assis. Translated by William L. Grossman & Helen Caldwell. University of California Press, 1963.*

Gumilev, Nikolai. Nikolai Gumilev on Russian Poetry. *Edited and translated by David Lapeza. Ardis, 1977.*

Gunn, James. Voices for the Future: Essays on Major Science Fiction Writers. *Bowling Green University Popular Press, 1976.*

Gustafson, Arik. Introduction to Scandinavian Plays of the Twentieth Century: Nordahl Grieg, Helge Krog, Kaj Munk, Kjeld Abell. 2d series. *Princeton University Press, 1944.*

Haber, Tom Burns. A. E. Housman. *Twayne, 1967.*

Hakutani, Yochinobu. Young Dreiser: A Critical Study. *Fairleigh Dickinson University Press, 1980.*

Hall, Wayne E. Shadowy Heroes: Irish Literature of the 1890s. *Syracuse University Press, 1980.*

Hardy, Evelyn. Thomas Hardy: A Critical Biography. *Hogarth Press, 1954.*

Harlan, Louis R. Booker T. Washington: The Making of a Black Leader, 1856-1901. *Oxford University Press, 1972.*

Harlan, Louis R., & others, eds. The Booker T. Washington Papers: 1895-98, Vol. 4. *University of Illinois Press, 1975.*

Harris, Frank. Latest Contemporary Portraits. *Macaulay, 1927.*

Hawkins, Hugh, ed. Booker T. Washington and His Critics: Black Leadership in Crisis. *2d ed. Heath, 1974.*

Hearn, Lafcadio. Essays in European and Oriental Literature. *Edited by Albert Mordell. Dodd, Mead, 1923.*

Heidegger, Martin. Nietzsche: Nihilism, Vol. IV. *Edited by David Farrell Krell. Translated by Frank A. Capuzzi. Harper & Row, 1982.*

Henn, Thomas Rice. Last Essays: Mainly on Anglo-Irish Literature. *Barnes & Noble, 1976.*

Hicks, Granville. The Great Tradition: An Interpretation of American Literature since the Civil War. *Rev. ed. Macmillan, 1935.*

Hollingdale, R. J. Nietzsche. *Routledge & Kegan Paul, 1973.*

Hooker, Jeremy. Poetry of Place: Essays and Reviews 1970-1981. *Carcanet Press, 1982.*

Howells, William Dean. Criticism and Fiction. *Harper and Brothers, 1891.*

Huneker, James. Overtones, a Book of Temperaments: Richard Strauss, Parsifal, Verdi, Balzac, Flaubert, Nietzsche, and Turgénieff. *Charles Scribner's Sons, 1904.*

Huneker, James. Variations. *Charles Scribner's Sons, 1921.*

Huxley, Aldous. On the Margin: Notes and Essays. *Doran, 1923.*

Hyman, Stanley Edgar. The Armed Vision: A Study in the Methods of Modern Literary Criticism. *Knopf, 1948.*

Innes, Christopher. Holy Theatre: Ritual and the Avant Garde. *Cambridge University Press, 1981.*

James, Henry. The Letters of Henry James, Vol. I. *Edited by Percy Lubbock. Charles Scribner's Sons, 1920.*

Jarrell, Randall. Kipling, Auden & Co.: Essays and Reviews 1935-1964. *Farrar, Straus and Giroux, 1980.*

Jaspers, Karl. Nietzsche: An Introduction to the Understanding of His Philosophical Activity. *Translated by Charles F. Wallraff and Frederick J. Schmitz. University of Arizona Press, 1965.*

Joll, James. Intellectuals in Politics: Three Biographical Essays. *Weidenfeld and Nicolson, 1960.*

Jussem-Wilson N. Charles Péguy. *Hillary House, 1965.*

Kaufmann, Walter. Nietzsche: Philosopher, Psychologist, Antichrist. *4th ed. Princeton University Press, 1974.*

Kazin, Alfred. On Native Grounds: An Interpretation of Modern American Prose Literature. *Reynal & Hitchcock, 1942.*

Kazin, Alfred. Introduction to An American Tragedy, *by Theodore Dreiser. Dell, 1959.*

Kazin, Alfred. Contemporaries. *Little, Brown, 1962.*

Keith, W. J. The Poetry of Nature: Rural Perspectives in Poetry from Wordsworth to the Present. *University of Toronto Press, 1980.*

King, Martin Luther, Jr. Where Do We Go from Here: Chaos or Community? *Harper & Row, 1967.*

Kinnaird, Clark. Introduction to More Guys and Dolls, *by Damon Runyon. Lippincott, 1951.*

Kirby, Michael. Futurist Performance. *Dutton, 1971.*

Klein, Holger. The First World War in Fiction: A Collection of Critical Essays. *Macmillan, 1976, Barnes & Noble, 1977.*

Knapp, Bettina L. Paul Claudel. *Ungar, 1982.*

Knight, Damon. In Search of Wonder: Essays on Modern Science Fiction. *Rev. ed. Advent, 1967.*

Krutch, Joseph Wood. "Modernism in Modern Drama: A Definition and an Estimate. *Cornell University Press, 1953.*

Laffitte, Sophie. Chekhov, 1860-1904. *Translated by Moura Budberg and Gordon Latta. Angus and Robertson, 1974.*

Lawrence, D. H. The Letters of D. H. Lawrence: June 1913-October 1916, Vol. II. *Edited by George J. Zytaruk and James T. Boulton. Cambridge University Press, 1981.*

Leavis, F. R. New Bearings in English Poetry: A Study of the Contemporary Situation. *Chatto & Windus, 1932, AMS Press, 1978.*

Leggett, B. J. Housman's Land of Lost Content: A Critical Study of "A Shropshire Lad." *University of Tennessee Press, 1970.*

Lehmann, John. The Open Night. *Longmans, Green, 1952.*

Lemaître, Jules. Preface to Cosmopolis, *by Paul Bourget. Maison Mazarin, 1905, Current Literature, 1923.*

Lewis, Wyndham. Paleface: The Philosophy of the "Melting Pot." *Chatto & Windus, 1929, Scholarly Press, 1971.*

Lovecraft, H. P. Dagon and Other Macabre Tales. *Edited by August Derleth. Arkham House, 1965.*

Ludwig, Richard M., ed. Aspects of American Poetry. *Ohio State University Press, 1962.*

Lundquist, James. Theodore Dreiser. *Ungar, 1974.*

Lydenberg, John, ed. Dreiser: A Collection of Critical Essays. *Prentice-Hall, 1971.*

Lynn, Kenneth S. The Dream of Success: A Study of the Modern American Imagination. *Little, Brown, 1955.*

Lynn, Kenneth S. Introduction to Trumpets of Jubilee, *by Constance Rourke. Harcourt Brace Jovanovich, 1963.*

Lynn, Kenneth S. Visions of America: Eleven Literary Historical Essays. *Greenwood Press, 1973.*

MacAdam, Alfred J. Modern Latin American Narratives: The Dreams of Reason. *University of Chicago Press, 1977.*

Mann, Thomas. Nietzsche's Philosophy in the Light of Contemporary Events. *The Library of Congress, 1947.*

Marlow, Norman. A. E. Housman: Scholar and Poet. *Routledge & Kegan Paul, 1958.*

Marsden, Kenneth. The Poems of Thomas Hardy: A Critical Introduction. *Athlone Press, 1969.*

Maule, Harry E., and Cane, Melville H., eds. The Man from Main Street: A Sinclair Lewis Reader; Selected Essays and Other Writings, 1904-50. *Random House, 1953.*

McClellan, Edwin. Introduction to Grass on the Wayside (Michikusa): A Novel, *by Natsume Soseki. Translated by Edwin McClellan. University of Chicago Press, 1969.*

Mencken, H. L. Introduction to An American Tragedy, *by Theodore Dreiser. World, 1946.*

Mencken, H. L. Letters of H. L. Mencken. *Edited by Guy J. Forgue. Knopf, 1961.*

Mirsky, D. S. Contemporary Russian Literature: 1881-1925. *Knopf, 1926, Routledge, 1926.*

Moran, John C. An F. Marion Crawford Companion. *Greenwood Press, 1981.*

More, Paul Elmer. Nietzsche. *Houghton Mifflin, 1912.*

More, Paul Elmer. The Drift of Romanticism: Shelburne Essays, Eighth series. *Houghton Mifflin, 1913.*

Moskowitz, Sam. Seekers of Tomorrow: Masters of Science Fiction. *World, 1966.*

Motion, Andrew. Introduction to The Poetry of Edward Thomas, *by Edward Thomas. Routledge & Kegan Paul, 1980.*

Murry, J. Middleton. Aspects of Literature. *Collins, 1920.*

Naess, Harald S. *Introduction to "Our Power and Our Glory" in* Five Modern Scandinavian Plays: Carl Erik Soya, Walentin Chorell, David Stefansson, Nordahl Grieg, Par Lagerkvist, Vol. III. *Edited by Erik J. Friis. Twayne, 1971.*

Natan, Alex, ed. German Men of Letters: Twelve Literary Essays, Vol. III. *Wolff, 1964.*

Nolin, Bertil. Georg Brandes. *Twayne, 1976.*

Nordau, Max. Degeneration. *Appleton, 1895, Howard Fertig, 1968.*

O'Flaherty, James C., & others, eds. Studies in Nietzsche and the Classical Tradition. *2d ed. The University of North Carolina Press, 1979.*

Okazaki, Yoshie, ed. Japanese Literature in the Meiji Era. *Translated by V. H. Viglielmo. Obunsha, 1955.*

Olgin, Moissaye J. A Guide to Russian Literature (1820-1917). *Harcourt Brace Jovanovich, 1920.*

Orage, A. R. Readers and Writers. *Knopf, 1922.*

Ossar, Michael. Anarchism in the Dramas of Ernst Toller: The Realm of Necessity and the Realm of Freedom. *State University of New York Press, 1980.*

Péguy, Charles. Basic Verities: Prose and Poetry. *Translated by Anne Green and Julian Green. Pantheon, 1943.*

Péguy, Charles. Temporal and Eternal. *Translated by Alexander Dru. Harper and Brothers, 1958.*

Penzoldt, Peter. The Supernatural in Fiction. *P. Nevill, 1952.*

Pilkington, John, Jr. Francis Marion Crawford. *Twayne, 1964.*

Piscator, Erwin. The Political Theatre. *Translated by Hugh Rorrison. Avon, 1968.*

Pittock, Malcolm. Ernst Toller. *Twayne, 1979.*

Poggioli, Renato. The Poets of Russia: 1890-1930. *Harvard University Press, 1960.*

Pritchett, V. S. The Myth Makers: Literary Essays. *Random House, 1979.*

Putnam, Samuel. Marvelous Journey: A Survey of Four Centuries of Brazilian Writing. *Knopf, 1948.*

Quinn, Arthur Hobson. American Fiction: An Historical and Critical Survey. *Appleton-Century-Crofts, 1936.*

Rayfield, Donald. Chekhov: The Evolution of His Art. *Barnes & Noble, 1975.*

Rexroth, Kenneth. Classics Revisited. *Quadrangle, 1968.*

Rice, Martin P. Valery Briusov and the Rise of Russian Symbolism. *Ardis, 1975.*

Ricks, Christopher, ed. A. E. Housman: A Collection of Critical Essays. *Prentice-Hall, 1968.*

Rideout, Walter B., ed. Sherwood Anderson: A Collection of Critical Essays. *Prentice-Hall, 1974.*

Rimer, J. Thomas. Modern Japanese Fiction and Its Traditions: An Introduction. *Princeton University Press, 1978.*

Robb, Nesca A. Four in Exile. *Hutchinson, 1948.*

Roberts, R. Ellis. *Preface to* Letters from Prison: Including Poems and a New Version of "The Swallow-Book," *by Ernst Toller. Translated by R. Ellis Roberts. John Lane/The Bodley Head, 1936.*

Rose, Mark. Alien Encounters: Anatomy of Science Fiction. *Harvard University Press, 1981.*

Rubin, Joan Shelley. Constance Rourke and American Culture. *University of North Carolina Press, 1980.*

Runyon, Damon, Jr. Father's Footsteps. *Random House, 1954.*

Russell, Bertrand. A History of Western Philosophy, and Its Connection with Political and Social Circumstances from the Earliest Time to the Present Day. *Simon & Schuster, 1945.*

Salzman, Jack, ed. Theodore Dreiser: The Critical Reception. *Lewis, 1972.*

Santayana, George. Little Essays Drawn from the Writings of George Santayana. *Edited by Logan Pearsall Smith. Charles Scribner's Sons, 1920.*

Sargent, Daniel. Four Independents. *Sheed and Ward, 1935, Books for Libraries Press, 1968.*

Sayers, Raymond S. The Negro in Brazilian Literature. *Hispanic Institute in the United States, 1956.*

Scannell, Vernon. Edward Thomas. *British Council, 1963.*

Scheffauer, Herman George. The New Vision in the German Arts. *Huebsch, 1924.*

Secor, Walter Todd. Paul Bourget and the Nouvelle. *King's Crown Press, 1948.*

Seidlin, Oskar. Essays in German and Comparative Literature. *The University of North Carolina Press, 1961.*

Sherman, Stuart P. On Contemporary Literature. *Holt, Rinehart and Winston, 1917.*

Sinclair, Upton. Money Writes! *A. & C. Boni, 1927, Scholarly Press, 1970.*

Singer, Armand E. Paul Bourget. *Twayne, 1976.*

Sitwell, Edith. Aspects of Modern Poetry. *Duckworth, 1934.*

Slochower, Harry. No Voice Is Wholly Lost ... Writers and Thinkers in War and Peace. *Creative Age Press, 1945, Octagon, 1975.*

Smith, Henry Nash. The Business Establishment. *Edited by Earl F. Cheit. Wiley, 1964.*

Smith, Virginia Llewellyn. Anton Chekhov and "The Lady with the Dog." *Oxford University Press, 1973.*

Sokel, Walter H. The Writer in Extremis: Expressionism in Twentieth-Century German Literature. *Stanford University Press, 1959.*

Southerington, F. R. Hardy's Vision of Man. *Barnes & Noble, 1971.*

Stanislavski, Constantin. My Life in Art. *Translated by J. J. Robbins. Little, Brown, 1924, Theatre Arts, 1948.*

Steiner, Rudolf. Friedrich Nietzsche: Fighter for Freedom. *Translated by Margaret Ingram de Ris. Steiner, 1960.*

Stephens, James. James, Seumas and Jacques. *Macmillan, 1964.*

Stern, J. P. A Study of Nietzsche. *Cambridge University Press, 1979.*

Taine, Hippolyte. Life and Letters of H. Taine, Vol. 3. *Edited and translated by E. Sparvel-Bayly. Constable, 1908.*

Thompson, Francis. The Real Robert Louis Stevenson, and Other Critical Essays. *Edited by Terence L. Connolly. University Publishers, 1959.*

Thornbrough, Emma Lou, ed. Booker T. Washington. *Prentice-Hall, 1969.*

Torrence, Ridgley. The Story of John Hope. *Macmillan, 1948.*

Twain, Mark. The Complete Essays of Mark Twain. *Edited by Charles Neider. Doubleday, 1963.*

Valera, Juan. Preface to Pepita Jiménez, *by Juan Valera. Collier, 1917.*

Van Doren, Mark. The Private Reader: Selected Articles and Reviews. *Henry Holt, 1942.*

Viglielmo, V. H. Afterword to Light and Darkness: An Unfinished Novel, *by Natsume Soseki. Translated by V. H. Viglielmo. Owen, 1971.*

Wagner, Jean. Runyonese: The Mind and Craft of Damon Runyon. *Stechert-Hafner, 1965.*

Walkley, A. B. More Prejudice. *William Heinemann, 1923.*

Warren, L. A. Modern Spanish Literature: A Comprehensive Survey of the Novelists, Poets, Dramatists and Essayists from the Eighteenth Century to the Present Day, Vol. I. *Brentano's, 1929.*

Weidlé, Wladimir. The Dilemma of the Arts. *Translated by Martin Jarrett-Kerr. SCM Press, 1948.*

Weiner, Dora B. and Keylor, William R., eds. From Parnassus: Essays in Honor of Jacques Barzun. *Harper & Row, 1976.*

Wellek, René. A History of Modern Criticism: The Late Nineteenth Century, 1750-1950. *Yale University Press, 1965.*

West, Anthony. Principles and Persuasions: The Literary Essays of Anthony West. *Harcourt, Brace, 1957.*

Weygandt, Cornelius. The Time of Yeats: English Poetry of To-Day Against an American Background. *Appleton-Century, 1937, Russell & Russell, 1969.*

Williams, Raymond. Drama: From Ibsen to Eliot. *Chatto & Windus, 1952.*

Willibrand, William Anthony. Ernst Toller and His Ideology. *The University of Iowa, 1945.*

Wilson, Edmund. The Triple Thinkers: Twelve Essays on Literary Subjects. *Rev. ed. Oxford University Press, 1948, Noonday, 1976.*

Winchell, Walter. Foreword to Damon Runyon's Blue Place Special *by Damon Runyon. Frederick A. Stokes, 1934.*

Winner, Anthony. Characters in the Twilight: Hardy, Zola, and Chekhov. *University Press of Virginia, 1981.*

Woolf, Virginia. The Common Reader. *Harcourt Brace Jovanovich, 1925.*

Yamanouchi, Hisaaki. The Search for Authenticity in Modern Japanese Literature. *Cambridge University Press, 1978.*

Yeats, W. B. Essays and Introductions. *Macmillan, 1961.*

Yu, Beongcheon. Introduction to The Wayfarer (Kojin), *by Natsume Sōseki. Translated by Beongcheon Yu. Wayne State University Press, 1967.*

Ziff, Larzer. The American 1890s: Life and Times of a Lost Generation. *Viking, 1966.*

Zweig, Stefan. Master Builders: A Typology of the Spirit. *Translated by Eden Paul and Cedar Paul. Viking Penguin, 1939.*

Cumulative Index to Authors

Cumulative Index to Nationalities

Owen, Wilfred 5
Powys, T. F. 9
Richardson, Dorothy 3
Saki 3
Sayers, Dorothy L. 2
Shiel, M. P. 8
Sinclair, May 3
Sutro, Alfred 6
Swinburne, Algernon
  Charles 8
Thomas, Edward 10
Thompson, Francis 4
Van Druten, John 2
Walpole, Hugh 5
Wells, H. G. 6
Williams, Charles 1
Woolf, Virginia 1, 5

FRENCH
Alain-Fournier 6
Apollinaire, Guillaume 3, 8
Artaud, Antonin 3
Barbusse, Henri 5
Bernanos, Georges 3
Claudel, Paul 2, 10
Colette 1, 5
Éluard, Paul 7
France, Anatole 9
Gide, André 5
Giraudoux, Jean 2, 7
Huysmans, Joris-Karl 7
Jacob, Max 6
Jarry, Alfred 2
Larbaud, Valéry 9
Péguy, Charles 10
Proust, Marcel 7
Rostand, Edmond 6
Saint-Exupéry, Antoine de 2
Teilhard de Chardin, Pierre 9
Valéry, Paul 4
Verne, Jules 6
Vian, Boris 9
Zola, Émile 1, 6

GERMAN
Benn, Gottfried 3
Borchert, Wolfgang 5
Brecht, Bertolt 1, 6
Feuchtwanger, Lion 3

George, Stefan 2
Hauptmann, Gerhart 4
Heym, Georg 9
Heyse, Paul 8
Kaiser, Georg 9
Mann, Heinrich 9
Mann, Thomas 2, 8
Morgenstern, Christian 8
Nietzsche, Friedrich 10
Rilke, Rainer Maria 1, 6
Sternheim, Carl 8
Toller, Ernst 10
Wassermann, Jakob 6
Wedekind, Frank 7

GREEK
Cafavy, C. P. 2, 7
Kazantzakis, Nikos 2, 5
Palamas, Kostes 5

INDIAN
Tagore, Rabindranath 3

IRISH
A. E. 3, 10
Cary, Joyce 1
Dunsany, Lord 2
Gregory, Lady 1
Joyce, James 3, 8
Moore, George 7
O'Grady, Standish 5
Shaw, Bernard 3, 9
Stephens, James 4
Stoker, Bram 8
Synge, J. M. 6
Tynan, Katharine 3
Wilde, Oscar 1, 8
Yeats, William Butler 1

ITALIAN
Betti, Ugo 5
D'Annunzio, Gabriel 6
Giacosa, Giuseppe 7
Marinetti, F. T. 10
Pavese, Cesare 3
Pirandello, Luigi 4
Svevo, Italo 2
Verga, Giovanni 3

JAMAICAN
Mais, Roger 8

JAPANESE
Natsume, Sōseki 2, 10
Shimazaki, Tōson 5

LEBANESE
Gibran, Kahlil 1, 9

MEXICAN
Azuela, Mariano 3

NEW ZEALAND
Mansfield, Katherine 2, 8

NICARAGUAN
Darío, Rubén 4

NORWEGIAN
Bjørnson, Bjørnstjerne 7
Grieg, Nordhal 10
Hamsun, Knut 2
Ibsen, Henrik 2, 8
Kielland, Alexander 5
Lie, Jonas 5
Undset, Sigrid 3

PERUVIAN
Vallejo, César 3

POLISH
Borowski, Tadeusz 9
Reymont, Wladyslaw
  Stanislaw 5
Schulz, Bruno 5
Sienkiewitz, Henryk 3
Witkiewicz, Stanislaw
  Ignacy 8

RUSSIAN
Andreyev, Leonid 3
Babel, Isaak 2
Bely, Andrey 7
Blok, Aleksandr 5
Bryusov, Valery 10
Bulgakov, Mikhail 2
Bunin, Ivan 6
Chekhov, Anton 3, 10

Esenin, Sergei 4
Gorky, Maxim 8
Hippius, Zinaida 9
Kuprin, Aleksandr 5
Mandelstam, Osip 2, 6
Mayakovsky, Vladimir 4
Sologub, Fyodor 9
Tolstoy, Leo 4
Tsvetaeva, Marina 7
Zamyatin, Yevgeny
  Ivanovich 8

SCOTTISH
Barrie, J. M. 2
Bridie, James 3
Gibbon, Lewis Grassic 4
MacDonald, George 9
Muir, Edwin 2

SOUTH AFRICAN
Campbell, Roy 5
Schreiner, Olive 9

SPANISH
Baroja, Pío 8
Benavente, Jacinto 3
Echegaray, José 4
García Lorca, Federico 1, 7
Jiménez, Juan Ramón 4
Machado, Antonio 3
Martínez Sierra, Gregorio 6
Miró, Gabriel 5
Ortega y Gasset, José 9
Unamuno, Miguel de 2, 9
Valera, Juan 10
Valle-Inclán, Ramón del 5

SWEDISH
Heidenstam, Verner von 5
Lagerlöf, Selma 4
Strindberg, August 1, 8

WELSH
Davies, W. H. 5
Lewis, Alun 3
Machen, Arthur 4
Thomas, Dylan 1, 8

YIDDISH
Aleichem, Sholom 1
Asch, Sholem 3

Cumulative Index to Critics

Critic Index

Corn, Alfred
  Andrey Bely 7:66

Cornford, Frances
  Rupert Brooke 7:123

Correa, Gustavo
  Federico García Lorca 7:294

Corrigan, Matthew
  Malcolm Lowry 6:244

Corrigan, Robert W.
  Bertolt Brecht 1:119
  Federico García Lorca 1:324
  Henrik Ibsen 2:239
  Gregorio Martínez Sierra and
    María Martínez Sierra 6:284

Cortissoz, Royal
  Hamlin Garland 3:190

Cosman, Max
  Joyce Cary 1:141

Costa, Richard Haver
  Malcolm Lowry 6:246

Costello, Peter
  Jules Verne 6:499

Costich, Julia F.
  Antonin Artaud 3:62

Cournos, John
  Fyodor Sologub 9:434

Coustillas, Pierre
  George Gissing 3:236

Coward, Noël
  Saki 3:373

Cowley, Malcolm
  Sherwood Anderson 1:51
  Guillaume Apollinaire 3:33
  Henri Barbusse 5:13
  A. E. Coppard 5:176
  Hart Crane 2:117
  Theodore Dreiser 10:179
  F. Scott Fitzgerald 1:238, 272;
    6:166
  Lafcadio Hearn 9:130
  Amy Lowell 1:371, 378
  Katherine Mansfield 2:445
  Arthur Schnitzler 4:392
  Virginia Woolf 1:533

Cox, C. B.
  Joseph Conrad 1:218

Cox, James M.
  Booker T. Washington 10:538

Cox, James Trammell
  Ford Madox Ford 1:286

Cox, Oliver C.
  Booker T. Washington 10:526

Coxe, Louis O.
  Edith Wharton 3:567

Coxhead, Elizabeth
  Lady Gregory 1:335

Craig, G. Dundas
  Rubén Darío 4:63

Craige, Betty Jean
  Federico García Lorca 7:297

Crane, Hart
  Sherwood Anderson 10:32
  Hart Crane 5:184

Crankshaw, Edward
  Jakob Wassermann 6:511

Crawford, F. Marion
  F. Marion Crawford 10:141

Crawford, John
  Will Rogers 8:332

Crawford, Virginia M.
  Joris-Karl Huysmans 7:407
  Edmond Rostand 6:373

Creary, Jean
  Roger Mais 8:241

Creelman, James
  Booker T. Washington 10:514

Crews, Frederick
  Joseph Conrad 1:216

Crispin, Edmund
  C. M. Kornbluth 8:217

Crites
  See also **Eliot, T. S.**
  Bernard Shaw 9:417

Croce, Arlene
  Eugene O'Neill 1:404

Croce, Benedetto
  Émile Zola 1:588

Cross, Richard K.
  Malcolm Lowry 6:253

Cross, Wilbur
  Arnold Bennett 5:33
  John Galsworthy 1:297

Crowley, Aleister
  James Branch Cabell 6:65
  Aleister Crowley 7:205, 208

Cruse, Harold
  James Weldon Johnson 3:246
  Booker T. Washington 10:531

Cuénot, Claude
  Pierre Teilhard de Chardin
    9:481

Cullen, Countee
  James Weldon Johnson 3:240

Cunliffe, John W.
  A. E. Housman 1:354

Cunningham, J. V.
  Wallace Stevens 3:454

Cuppy, Will
  Raymond Chandler 7:167

Currey, R. N.
  Alun Lewis 3:289

Curti, Merle
  Booker T. Washington 10:523

Curtis, Penelope
  Anton Chekhov 3:170

Curtius, Ernst Robert
  José Ortega y Gasset 9:339

Cushman, Keith
  Ernest Dowson 4:93

D., B.
  Kahlil Gibran 1:327

Dabney, Virginius
  Ellen Glasgow 7:337

Daemmrich, Horst S.
  Thomas Mann 2:441

Dahlberg, Edward
  Sherwood Anderson 1:56
  F. Scott Fitzgerald 1:256

Dahlie, Hallvard
  Nordahl Grieg 10:211

Daiches, David
  Willa Cather 1:157
  Joseph Conrad 1:211
  A. E. Housman 1:355
  James Joyce 3:258
  Katherine Mansfield 2:449
  Wilfred Owen 5:362
  Dylan Thomas 1:469
  Virginia Woolf 1:539
  William Butler Yeats 1:558

Daleski, H. M.
  Joseph Conrad 1:220

Dalphin, Marcia
  A. A. Milne 6:309

Damon, S. Foster
  Amy Lowell 1:374

Dane, Clemence
  Hugh Walpole 5:497

Daniel, John
  Henri Barbusse 5:16

Daniels, Jonathan
  Marjorie Kinnan Rawlings
    4:359

Danielson, Larry W.
  Selma Lagerlöf 4:242

Danto, Arthur C.
  Friedrich Nietzsche 10:382

Dario, Ruben
  F. T. Marinetti 10:310

Darrow, Clarence
  Theodore Dreiser 10:171

Darton, F. J. Harvey
  Arnold Bennett 5:25

Dathorne, Oscar R.
  Roger Mais 8:244

Dauner, Louise
  Joel Chandler Harris 2:212

Davenport, Basil
  Lewis Grassic Gibbon 4:120,
    121

Daviau, Donald G.
  Karl Kraus 5:282

Davidow, Mary C.
  Charlotte Mew 8:299

Davidson, Donald
  Joseph Conrad 6:114

Davie, Donald
  D. H. Lawrence 2:373
  Wallace Stevens 3:449

Davies, A. Emil
  Laurence Housman 7:354

Davies, Barrie
  Wilfred Campbell 9:33

Davies, J. C.
  André Gide 5:237

Davies, John
  Alun Lewis 3:289

Davies, Margaret
  Colette 5:165

Davies, Robertson
  Stephen Leacock 2:381

Davies, Ruth
  Leonid Andreyev 3:27
  Anton Chekhov 3:168

Davis, Arthur P.
  Countee Cullen 4:44
  Wallace Thurman 6:450

Davis, Beatrice
  Miles Franklin 7:267

Davis, Cynthia
  Dylan Thomas 1:475

Davis, Robert Bernard
  A. E. 10:20

Davis, Robert Murray
  F. Scott Fitzgerald 6:167
  Katherine Mansfield 8:282

Davis, Oswald H.
  Arnold Bennett 5:45

Davison, Edward
  A. E. 10:16
  Robert Bridges 1:125
  Walter de la Mare 4:74
  Alfred Noyes 7:507
  Saki 3:365

Day, Douglas
  Malcolm Lowry 6:241, 247

D'Costa, Jean
  Roger Mais 8:247

Dean, James L.
  William Dean Howells 7:394

Debicki, Andrew P.
  César Vallejo 3:530

De Bosschere, Jean
  May Sinclair 3:437

De Camp, L. Sprague
  Robert E. Howard 8:130

De Castris, A. L.
  Luigi Pirandello 4:342

Decavalles, A.
  C. P. Cavafy 7:162

Decker, Donald M.
  Machado de Assis 10:290

DeCoster, Cyrus
  Juan Valera 10:507

De Fornaro, Sofia
  Giuseppe Giacosa 7:305

Degler, Carl N.
  Charlotte Gilman 9:103

DeKoven, Marianne
  Gertrude Stein 6:415

De la Mare, Walter
  Rupert Brooke 2:53
  Edward Thomas 10:451

Delany, Paul
  Katherine Mansfield 8:286

De la Selva, Salomón
  Rubén Darío 4:55

Dell, Floyd
  Charlotte Gilman 9:100
  Olive Schreiner 9:395

Critic Index

Critic Index

Critic Index

Critic Index